BUSINESS POLICY
Text and cases

BUSINESS POLICY

Text and cases

C. ROLAND CHRISTENSEN, D.C.S.
*George Fisher Baker, Jr. Professor of
Business Administration*

KENNETH R. ANDREWS, PH.D.
*Donald Kirk David Professor of
Business Administration*

JOSEPH L. BOWER, D.B.A.
Professor of Business Administration

RICHARD G. HAMERMESH, D.B.A.
*Associate Professor of
Business Administration*

MICHAEL E. PORTER, PH.D.
Professor of Business Administration

*All of the
Graduate School of Business Administration
Harvard University*

FIFTH EDITION • 1982

RICHARD D. IRWIN, INC.
Homewood, Illinois 60430

ISBN 0-256-02626-2
Library of Congress Catalog Card No. 81–86114

Printed in the United States of America
1 2 3 4 5 6 7 8 9 0 H 9 8 7 6 5 4 3 2

To
Edmund P. Learned
For reasons he knows well

Preface

THIS FIFTH EDITION of *Business Policy: Text and Cases* provides educational concepts, text, and cases for a course in Business Policy and/or Corporate Strategy. Building on previous editions, the authors have incorporated a number of changes in both text and case material; we hope that modifications of our basic format will increase the usefulness of this edition for all concerned.

In the development of this fifth edition we have retained those cases which our users have found most helpful in accomplishing the objectives of their seminar or course. Indeed, 10 of our holdover cases are listed as all time classic "best sellers" by the Intercollegiate Case Clearing House. They provide, as some of you know, challenging and "fun" discussion vehicles for education in the policy process.

In this fifth edition, as in preceding efforts, we have emphasized four basic, educational themes. First, this material focuses on the tasks of general management in leading the overall enterprise, in contrast to the tasks of a specialist manager whose responsibilities are limited to a subdepartment of the total organization. Second, our text and cases highlight strategic management as a key function and responsibility of the line general manager, not as a staff planning activity. Third, critical to the success of any firm, is the general manager's ability to manage the *process* by which an organization both formulates and implements its strategy. These case histories encourage apprentice managers to practice vicariously the organizational process of goal definition and accomplishment. Finally, a study of this material emphasizes the importance of general management practice as a professional activity. The general manager is responsible to multiple constituencies with conflicting needs and goals. He or she must manage that organization so as to achieve both economic and social-ethical goals.

In this fifth edition we have made a number of significant changes from earlier efforts. We have increased the reader's opportunity for systematic exploration of the industry dimension of strategic analysis. The revised text material provides the reader with a practical framework for analyzing industries, and additional case histories provide opportunities to apply that framework to complex, real-life situations. We are indebted to one of our two new authors, Michael E. Porter, for this contribution to the evolution of the Business Policy field.[1]

Much of the new case material in Book Two has been developed under the supervision of our other new author, Richard G. Hamermesh with the collaboration of coauthor Joseph L. Bower. These implementation cases provide us with rich data for the practice of the general manager's critical job—"getting things to happen." Some of these cases are drawn from new industries, including service industries. Another case emphasizes the challenge to women managers as they assume senior management positions. The problems of new leadership in one of our nation's oldest industrial organizations is illustrated in depth in the International Harvester case. That case series offers all of us an opportunity to learn from this ongoing corporate drama.

We believe you will be specially interested in studying the concluding text section of this fifth edition, which gives added emphasis to the general manager's task of corporate governance. In an increasingly egalitarian world, the general manager who leads a traditional pyramidal organization faces major questions as to his or her authority and administrative practices. He or she must govern in such a way as to achieve the granted cooperation and contribution of all involved parties.

The evolution of this book has been encouraged by many individuals—both business managers and academic instructors and students—who have taken the time and effort to send us suggestions for improvements. We are in their debt. Their continuing interest has helped us to develop a policy course which can be taught effectively at the undergraduate, graduate, and executive seminar level.

All students of business policy participate in a long-term, evolving intellectual adventure. The basic administrative processes and problems with which business policy is concerned have been part of organizational life for centuries, but the history of business policy as an academic field dates back less than seven decades.

This edition builds on substantial contributions made by former and present policy colleagues; it carries their efforts further along the way to better understanding and greater applicability. The specific core idea—the concept of corporate strategy, and the organizational plan used in this book—were developed at the Harvard Business School in the early 1960s under the leadership of Kenneth R. Andrews, C. Roland Christensen, and now Professor Emeritus Edmund P. Learned. While course concepts and material have undergone steady modification, course objectives and organization have been maintained. Our teaching focus then, as today, emphasizes the determination of corporate strategy (Book One) and the implementation of corporate strategy (Book Two). This format has stood the test of time.

Opportunities for further evolution of the concept of corporate strategy, however, remain large. As coauthor Andrews notes:

---

[1] See Michael E. Porter, *Competitive Strategy* (New York: Free Press, 1980).

This concept is far from complete. But its early development shows this framework allows all other fields to be brought to bear upon the highest function of the general manager—supervision of the continuous process of determining the nature of the enterprise and setting, revising, and attempting to achieve its goals. So far the development of organizational behavior fits well into the framework of implementation. The sophisticated developments in quantitative analysis are not yet readily available to policy problems, but if all goes well, this will come.

The idea of corporate strategy constitutes a simple practitioner's theory, a kind of Everyman's conceptual scheme. It is nonetheless capable of including the most extensive combination of interrelated variables involved in the most important of all business decisions. It is a definition of the manager's central function, whether he is a staff specialist contributing in depth and detail to the identification of alternatives and to the predicted return on investment for each of these alternatives, or the senior executive who must finally make or complete the decision.[2]

In summarizing the relationship of strategy to the education of general managers, coauthor Christensen has noted:

The uniqueness of a good general manager lies in his ability to lead effectively organizations whose complexities he can never fully understand, where his capacity to control directly the human and physical forces comprising that organization are severely limited, and where he must make or review and assume ultimate responsibility for present decisions which commit concretely major resources for a fluid and unknown future.

These circumstances—lack of knowledge, lack of an ability to control directly, and a mixture of past, present, and *future* time dimensions in every decision—make the concept of strategy so important for the generalist, senior manager. For strategy gives the manager reasonably clear indications of what he should try to know and understand in order to direct his organization's efforts. It counsels him on what to decide, what to review, and what to ignore. It gives him guidelines as to what critical, central activities and processes to attempt to influence—or in rare occasions—to attempt to control. It encourages him to view every event and question from multiple time dimensions.

Chester Barnard said that the highest managerial traits are essentially intuitive "being so complex and so rapid, often approaching the instantaneous, that they could not be analyzed by the person within whose brain they take place." If Barnard is correct, and I think that he is, how do those of us interested in management education strive to contribute to the development of future general managers? We do this first by disciplined classroom drill with the concept of strategy. Drill in the formal and analytic— what is the current strategy of the firm? What are its strengths and weaknesses? Where, in the firm's perceived industry, are profit and service opportunities? And, how can those corporate capacities and industry opportunities be effectively related? This framework of questions helps to give order to the familiar chaos of complex organizations. It provides the manager with a map relating past, present and future, industry and company, and specific decisions to wider corporate strategy.

Moreover, this analytic classroom process focuses attention on a key administration skill—the process of selecting and ordering data so that

[2] Kenneth R. Andrews, "The Progress of Professional Education," in Olga Craven, Alden L. Todd, and Jesse H. Ziegler, eds., *Theological Education as Professional Education* (Dayton, Ohio: The Association of Theological Schools, 1969).

management asks the critical questions appropriate to a particular situation. Here the choice of abstraction level is key, for the question has to be stated in a way that avoids the "specific that has no meaning and the general that has no content."

We seek also, via the classroom group discussion process, to educate in the nonlogical—that mixture of feelings and sentiment, comment and commitment, certainty and uncertainty—which goes into every decision and judgment. Such directed group discussions force attention to the human dimensions through which the analytic framework is filtered in real life. It serves further to emphasize the ongoing or process nature of the general manager's world.

It is a combination of these two forces: the analytic framework of strategic planning and the process framework emphasizing human interaction, the complexities of persons, and the difficulty of communication and persuasion that make up our business policy educational fare. It is the discipline of practicing these two processes via a case discussion countless times, that helps us to contribute to education for the future generalist.[3]

The business policy subject area continues to evolve and develop. The need for professionally trained generalists—the men and women who make our organized society's critical decisions—is great; our present efforts are limited. Sir Eric Ashby has put the challenge well:

But the world needs generalists as well as specialists. Indeed you have only to read your newspaper to know that the big decisions on which the fate of nations depends are in the hands of generalists. I do not think that universities, American or British, are satisfied with the education they give to the man who is to become a generalist. Some believe he should have a rigorously specialist training in some field which he then abandons for life. Others believe he should have a synoptic acquaintance with the ways of thinking of humanists, social scientists, and natural scientists. And I suppose there are still a few antique persons who cling to the view that generalists need no higher education at all. We can with some confidence prescribe the minutiae of curriculum for doctors, physicists, and lawyers. The unpalatable fact is that we have no such confidence in prescribing curricula for men who will become presidents of industries, newspaper editors, senior civil servants, or Congressmen.[4]

We continue to believe that this challenge will be met, at least in part, by all of us who work in the policy area, both in academic and practical pursuits, throughout this country and the world. And we hope this book will be of some help in meeting that challenge.

C. ROLAND CHRISTENSEN
KENNETH R. ANDREWS
JOSEPH L. BOWER
RICHARD G. HAMERMESH
MICHAEL E. PORTER

[3] C. Roland Christensen, "Education for the General Manager," unpublished working paper, Harvard Business School.

[4] Sir Eric Ashby, Master, Clare College, Cambridge, "Centennial Convocation Address," delivered at the 100th anniversary of the granting of the charter to Cornell University, October 9, 1964.

Acknowledgments

THE HISTORY of the Business Policy course at the Harvard Business School began in 1911, when a small group of instructors first developed a course outline and materials for a pioneering venture in education for senior management. Those of us who currently teach and do research in the business policy area are in debt to those pioneers who provided the academic platform on which current efforts rest. We wish to especially recognize and thank the pioneering efforts of A. W. Shaw, the first policy professor at the Harvard Business School, and M. T. Copeland, George Albert Smith, Jr., and Edmund P. Learned, who provided almost 40 years of dedicated leadership to course ideals and development. We are in their debt, as we are to those colleagues who worked under their leadership and who assisted in past course development.

Many members of the Harvard Business School faculty have contributed to the constant development of our field. We appreciate the help of the present members of the business policy teaching group: Francis J. Aguilar, Joseph L. Badaracco, Jr., Christopher A. Bartlett, Norman A. Berg, Richard R. Ellsworth, Mark B. Fuller, Laura L. Nash, and Malcolm Salter; and we also appreciate the contributions of our associates J. Ronald Fox, Kenneth E. Goodpaster, Claudine B. Malone, John B. Matthews, Jr., Thomas K. McCraw, Bruce R. Scott, Hugo E. R. Uyterhoven, Howard H. Stevenson, Michael Y. Yoshino, and Abraham Zaleznik.

Our sincere appreciation goes to the supervisors and authors of the cases included in this edition. To the following our thanks: Robert W. Ackerman for the Xerox Corporation case; Francis J. Aguilar (assisted by Robert E. Swensk) for the Introductory Note to DAAG Europe and DAAG Europe (A); Alexander Bergmann for Air, Inc.; Robert F. Bruner for The Real Paper, Inc.(A); Ram Charan for his case, Hawaii Best Company; E. Tatum Christiansen for her cases, Mitek Corporation, PC&D, Inc., and the International Harvester series; Paul Cook, who wrote Strategy Revisited or Strategy with a Grain of Salt; Jesse B. Dougherty for the EG&G series; Linda Elmer for Charles River Breeding Laboratories and her support research for the Note on the Soft-Drink Industry in the United States; John J. Gabarro for the Robert F. Kennedy High School case; Karen D. Gordon and John P. Reed for Crown Cork & Seal Company, Inc., a revised case based on an earlier document written by James Garrison and William D. Guth; Taieb Hafsi for General Health Company; and John W. Hennessey for The Viking Air Compressor, Inc.

We are also indebted to Edmund P. Learned for his development of The Rose Company case; Leslie Levy and Cheryl Suchors for their contributions to the Note on the Soft-Drink Industry in the United States; Michael Lovdal for the Mead Corporation and Dayton Hudson cases; Susan Mayer, David Collis, James C. De Belina, Jon T. Elsasser, James J. Hornthal, and Robert G. Shearer for The Chain-Saw Industry in 1974; and John Priedeman (assisted by Robert C. K. Valtz) for Rugby Portland Cement Company Limited (A) and (B) series.

We would also like to thank Elizabeth Lyman Rachel for the BIC Pen Corporation (A) and (B) cases; Stephen J. Roth for Hospital Affiliates International, Inc., and the Hospital Management Industry material; John W. Rosenblum for Basic Industries and Industrial Products, Inc.; Howard H. Stevenson for the Head Ski Company, Inc. case; Roderick White for The Dexter Corporation case; H. Edward Wrapp (assisted by L. A. Guthart) for Texas Instruments, Incorporated cases; George S. Yip for Sweco, Inc. (A); and Abraham Zaleznik (assisted by John M. Wynne) for *The Saturday Evening Post* case.

We continue to be indebted to Kenneth R. Andrews for the text material found in this book. His capacity to articulate course concepts and principles for a practitioner is demonstrated not only in this book but in his pioneering volume, *The Concept of Corporate Strategy*.[1]

We owe special thanks to M. Liotard-Vogt, chairman of Nestlé Alimentana, and chairman of the board of trustees of IMEDE and to M. Jacques Paternot, general manager, Nestlé Alimentana, formerly a member of the Harvard Business School Visiting Committee and member of the board of trustees of IMEDE, and finally to Dean Derek F. Abell, director of IMEDE for their willingness to let us use IMEDE cases in this fifth edition. IMEDE continues as the leader in education for international and European general management. We are indebted to Dr. Ram Charan for his willingness to let us use the Hawaii Best Company (A) case, written when he was a member of the Business Policy faculty at the Northwestern Graduate School of Business Administration.

Edmund P. Learned, a "great" in the development of the business policy field of study, continues to enjoy his well-deserved retirement. We rededicate this book to him. All who have been touched by his teaching and research efforts realize his major contributions to private and public administration. He was our teacher, counselor, and friend.

Former Dean Donald K. David, the late Dean Stanley F. Teele, Dean George P. Baker, and Dean Lawrence E. Fouraker provided the steady

---

[1] Kenneth R. Andrews, *The Concept of Corporate Strategy*, rev. ed. (Homewood, Ill.: Dow Jones-Irwin, 1980).

encouragement and support which was so essential for the development of the policy area. Dean John H. McArthur and Senior Associate Dean for Educational Programs, James L. Heskett, encouraged us in the development of this edition; we appreciate their interest and assistance.

Dyanne Holdman took on the management task of producing this fifth edition of *Business Policy: Text and Cases* and carried out this assignment with efficiency and good humor. Victoria Lancaster directed the production of the accompanying Instructors' Guide. We owe them special thanks.

Professor Raymond Corey, director of the Division of Research, was most helpful in providing us with intellectual support and practical administrative assistance. We are in his debt.

We hope this book, in which the efforts of so many good people is compressed, will contribute to constructive concern for corporate purposes and accomplishments and to the continuing and effective study and practice of business policy, in private and semiprivate and public organizations.

C.R.C.
K.R.A.
J.L.B.
R.G.H.
M.E.P.

Contents

of opportunities and risks. Opportunity as a determinant of strategy. Identifying corporate competence and resources. Application to cases.

The company and its strategists: Relating corporate strategy to personal values 359

Strategy as projection of preference. The inevitability of values. Reconciling divergent values. Modification of values. Awareness of values.

The company and its responsibilities to society: Relating corporate strategy to ethical values. 448

The moral component of corporate strategy. Categories of concern: *Review of management concerns for responsibility. Impact of control systems on ethical performance. The individual and the corporation. The range of concerns.* Choice of strategic alternatives for social action. Determination of strategy.

BOOK TWO: Implementing corporate strategy

The accomplishment of purpose: Strategy and organization 541

Interdependence of formulation and implementation. Strategy and organizational structure. Subdivision of task responsibility. Coordination of divided responsibility. Effective design of information systems. Strategy as the key to simplicity.

The accomplishment of purpose: Organizational processes and behavior **636**

Establishment of standards and measurement of performance: *Fallacy of the single criterion. Need for multiple criteria. Effective evaluation of performance.* Motivation and incentive systems: *Executive compensation. Role of incentive pay. Nonmonetary incentives.* Systems of restraint and control: *Formal control. Integrating formal and social control. Enforcing ethical standards.* Recruitment and development of management: *Advanced recruitment. Continuing education. Management development and corporate purpose.*

Cases

CONCLUSION

In retrospect: Strategic management of corporate governance **827**

Strategy as a process. Managing the process. The strategic function of the board of directors.

Index of cases **837**

Introduction

Introduction

BUSINESS POLICY AS A FIELD OF STUDY

THIS BOOK is an instrument for the study of Business Policy. As a field in business administration, Policy is *the study of the functions and responsibilities of senior management,* the *crucial problems* that affect success in the total enterprise, and *the decisions* that determine the direction of the organization and shape its future. The problems of policy in business, like those of policy in public affairs, have to do with the choice of purposes, the molding of organizational identity and character, the continuous definition of what needs to be done, and the mobilization of resources for the attainment of goals in the face of competition or adverse circumstance.

The presidential point of view

In Business Policy, the problems considered and the point of view assumed in analyzing and dealing with them are those of the chief executive or general manager, whose primary responsibility is the enterprise as a whole. But while the study of Business Policy (under whatever name it may be called) is considered the capstone of professional business education, its usefulness goes far beyond the direct preparation of future general managers and chief executives for the responsibilities of office. In an age of increasing complexity and advancing specialization, and in companies where no person knows how to do what every other person does, it becomes important that the functional specialists—controller, computer scientist, financial analyst, market researcher, purchasing agent—acquire a unique nontechnical capacity. This essential qualification is the ability to recognize corporate purpose; to recommend its clarification, development, or change; and to shape their own contributions, not by the canons of specializations but by their perception of what a cost-effective purposeful organization requires of them. The special needs of individuals and the technical requirements of specialized groups and disciplines inevitably exhibit expensive points of view that ultimately come into conflict with one another and with the central purposes of the organization they serve. The specialists who are able to exercise control over this tendency in organizations and keep their loyalty to the conventions of their own specialty subordinate to the needs of their company become free to make creative contributions to its progress and growth. To be thus effective in their organization, they must have a sense of its mission, of its character, and of its importance. If they do not know the purposes they serve, they can hardly serve them well. Most users of this book will neither be nor become corporate chief executive officers. But virtually all can benefit from the detachment implicit in the impartial, functionally unbiased, results-oriented attitude we will call the presidential point of view.

Relevance of Policy to all organization members

The purposes of organized effort in business as elsewhere are usually somewhat unclear, apparently contradictory, and constantly changing. Except in abstract language they cannot be communicated once and for all to the variety of persons whose effort and commitment are demanded. It is not enough, therefore, for senior executives to issue statements of policy and for junior managers to salute and go about their business. In each subunit of an organization and in each individual, corporate purpose must become meaningful in ways that announcement cannot accomplish. It must be brought into balance with individual and departmental needs, satisfactions, and noneconomic aspirations. But if corporate purpose is to be reconciled with (rather than subordinated to) individual and departmental purposes, then there must be widespread knowledge of the considerations on which corporate policy is based and understanding of the risks by which it is threatened. In addition, the adaptation of corporate purpose to changing circumstances, to tactical countermoves by competitors, or to newly identified opportunities, is assisted if there can be *informed* participation in policy thinking by subordinate managers from different ranks and groups. This advantage, however, can be realized only if these subordinates are capable of looking beyond the narrow limits of their own professionalization. Thus the study of Policy is not as remote from the immediate concern of apprentice managers or students of business as it first appears. In fact whenever people are challenged—in business or out—by the problem of establishing goals for *themselves* that will shape productive and satisfying lives, they will find the study of the process of determining institutional purpose of central relevance. It is helpful to personal as well as to corporate decision. It permits discovery of the individual's own powers and the purposes to which they might well be devoted.

The study of Business Policy provides therefore a direct if distant preparation for performance as a general manager and a less direct but more immediate broadening of the perspective of the technician. In addition, it may be viewed as resulting in certain *knowledge, attitudes,* and *skills.* Some of these are unique to Policy studies. Others may have germinated in other activities in learning. But the latter are brought to fruition by examination of the most fundamental issues and problems that confront the professional manager in the course of a business career. It may prove useful to characterize briefly the expected outcomes.

OBJECTIVES IN KNOWLEDGE

The choice of objectives and the *formulation* of policy to guide action in the *attainment* of objectives depend upon many variables unique to a given organization and situation. It is not possible to make useful generalizations about the nature of these variables or to classify their possible combinations in all situations. Knowledge of what, *in general,* Policy is and should be is incomplete and inconclusive. The knowledge to be gained from Policy studies is therefore primarily a familiarity with an approach to the policy problems of business and public affairs which makes it possible, in conjunction with attitudes and skills to be discussed later, to combine these variables into a pattern *valid for one organization.* This pattern may then be examined against accepted criteria and tested for its quality. Policy must first be a study of situations.

Knowledge of concepts

The basic concept that students of Policy will in time come to understand is the concept of *strategy,* since the design and implementation of strategy provide the intellectual substance of this study. What is meant by *strategy* and, more important, how this concept may be usefully employed in the choice and accomplishment of purpose is the subject of the rest of this book. Strategy will be the idea unifying the discussions in which students will engage. These discussions will involve cerebral activities more important than simply acquiring information.

Knowledge of situations

An abundance of information about business practice is, nonetheless, a by-product of the study of Business Policy and other cases. In their deliberately planned variety, the cases in this book encompass many industries, companies, and business situations. Although the information contained in these cases is provided mainly to permit consideration of policy issues, the importance of this incidental knowledge should not be underestimated. Breadth of exposure to the conventions, points of view, and practices of many industries is inoculation against the assumption that all industries are basically the same or that all men and women in business share the same values and beliefs. Thus consideration of the policy problems of a number of different industries guards against distraction by the particular in seeking out the nature of the universal.

For this reason it is hoped that students—although they may be, or plan to be, engineers in a utility or vice presidents of a railroad—will not resent learning about the economics of the cement industry of England. Knowledge of the environment and problems of other industries and companies is something that students may never consciously use.

It will nevertheless widen the perspective which they bring to their own problems. It may stimulate the imagination they put to work in introducing innovation into the obsolescent practices of their own industry. It should provide a broader base for their powers of generalization.

The study of strategy as a concept will be relatively systematic. The acquisition of information about the management problems of the many firms and industries whose strategic problems are presented in this book will be less orderly. Both are important. In particular the time spent in mastering the detail of the cases will ultimately seem to be of greater value than at first appears. Graduates of a demanding Policy course feel at home in any management situation and know at once how to begin to understand it.

The literature of Policy

A considerable body of literature purporting to make general statements about policymaking and strategic management is in existence. It generally reflects either the unsystematically reported evidence of individuals or the logical projection to general management of concepts taken from engineering, economics, psychology, sociology, or mathematics. Neither suffices. What people wise in practice have to say is often instructive, but intuitive skill cannot be changed into conscious skill by exposition alone. The disciplines cited have much to do with business, but their purposes are not ours. Knowledge generated for one set of ends is not readily applicable to another. Besides reported experience and borrowed concepts, the literature of the field also includes the first fruits of independent research in Business Policy, guided by designs derived from the idea of strategy. Such research has been for some time under way and begins to make a claim on our attention. We shall often allude to the expository literature of Business Policy. The most useful literature for our purposes, however, is not that of general statements, but case studies.[1] These present, not illustrations of principle, but data from which generalizations may to a limited degree be derived and to which the idea of strategy may be usefully applied. The footnotes of the text portions of this book constitute a useful bibliography for further reading. The books referred to comprise a relevant but incidental source of knowledge. Look to these books in order to learn not information or theory but skills in using both.

OBJECTIVES IN ATTITUDES

Knowledge of either concepts or cases is less the objective of the study of Policy than certain attitudes and skills. What managers know by way of verifiable fact about management appears to us less important than

---

[1] In addition to the cases in this book, the reader is referred to such volumes as C. Roland Christensen, Norman A. Berg, and Malcolm S. Salter, *Policy Formulation and Administration*, 8th ed. (Homewood, Ill.: Richard D. Irwin, 1980); and H. E. R. Uyterhoeven, R. W. Ackerman, and J. W. Rosenblum, *Strategy and Organization: Text and Cases in General Management*, rev. ed. (Homewood, Ill.: Richard D. Irwin, 1977). Many other cases from a variety of sources are listed in the bibliographies of HBS Case Services, Soldiers Field, Boston, Mass. 02163.

the attitudes, aspirations, and values they bring to their tasks. Instructors in Policy do not have a dogma which they force upon their students, but most of them, like their students, appear to be influenced in their analysis and conclusions by characteristic assumptions. Thus indoctrination is implicit in the study of ideas and cases included in this book. This indoctrination—tempered by the authors' exhortation to students to think for themselves—is comprised of some important beliefs of which you should be aware.

The generalist orientation

The attitudes appropriate to the resolution of policy problems are several. First, the frame of mind which you will be encouraged to adopt and which will influence the outcome of your thinking is that of the *generalist* rather than the specialist. Breadth, it follows, takes precedence over depth. Since attitudes appropriate for the generalist are not always appropriate for the specialist, the two will sometimes come into conflict. Efforts to resolve this conflict in practice should help to prove that breadth which is shallow is no more satisfactory than depth which is narrow.

The practitioner orientation

A second outlook encountered in the study of Business Policy is the point of view of the *practitioner* as opposed to that of the researcher or scientist. A willingness to act in the face of incomplete information and to run the risk of being proved wrong by subsequent events will be developed in the classroom as pressure is brought to bear on students to make decisions on the problems before them and to determine what they, as the managers responsible, would do about them. Despite the explosion of knowledge and the advance of electronic data processing, it is still true that decisions affecting the business firm as a whole must almost always be made in the face of incomplete information. Uncertainty is the lot of all thoughtful leaders who must act, whether they are in government, education, or business. Acceptance of the priority of risk taking and problem resolution over completeness of information is sometimes hard for students of science and engineering to achieve. Though natural and understandable, hesitation in the face of the managerial imperative to make decisions will impede the study of Policy. At the same time, rashness, overconfidence, and the impulse to act without analysis will be discouraged.

The professional

The third set of attitudes to be developed is the orientation of the professional manager as distinct from the self-seeking contriver of deals and of the honest person rather than the artist in deception. The energetic opportunist sometimes has motives inconsistent with the approach to policy embodied in this book. This is not to say that quick response to opportunity and entrepreneurial energy are not qualities to be admired. Our assumption will be that the role of the business manager *includes but goes beyond* the entrepreneurial function. We shall examine what we acknowledge to be the obligations of the business community to the rest of society. We shall be concerned with the *quality* as well as the *clarity* of the alternative purposes we consider and of our final choice. Maximum short-run profit is not what we mean when we consider the purpose of business enterprise. At the same time it is assumed that profit is desirable and indispensable. It is one of the necessary *results* of business activity.

The innovator

A fourth set of attitudes to be evoked is one that attaches more value to creativity and innovation than to maintenance of the status quo. We have grown accustomed to innovation stemming from new inventions and advancing technology. But suiting policy to changing circumstances includes also the application of a firm's long-established strengths to unexplored segments of the market via innovations in price, service, distribution, or merchandising.

In any course of study that has as its object enabling practitioners to learn more from subsequent experience than they otherwise might, the attitudes appropriate to the professional activity being taught are as important as knowledge. It is therefore expected that students will take time to determine for themselves the particular point of view, the values, and the morality they feel are appropriate to the effective exercise of general management skills. Much more could be said about the frame of mind and qualities of temperament that are most appropriate to business leadership, but we will expect these to exhibit themselves in the discussion of case problems.

OBJECTIVES IN SKILLS

Extensive knowledge and positive attitudes, desirable as both are, come to nothing if not applied. The skills that a course in Business Policy seeks to develop and mature are at once analytical and administrative. Since even with a variety of stimulation and the use of case situations drawn from life, the reality of responsibility can only be approximated in a professional school, we may look to make most progress now in analytical power and to use it later in actual experience to develop executive ability.

Analytical ability

The study of Policy cases, unlike, for example, the effort to comprehend these expository notes, requires the students to develop and broaden the analytical ability brought to the task from other studies. The policy problems of the total enterprise are not labeled as accounting, finance, marketing, production, or human problems. Students are not forewarned of the kind of problem they can expect and of which tool kit they should have with them. They must now consider problems in relation to one another, distinguish the more from the less important, and consider the impact of their approach to one problem upon all the others. They will bring to the cases their knowledge and abilities in special fields, but they will be asked to diagnose first the total situation and to persist in seeking out central problems through all the distraction presented by manifest symptoms.

The study of Policy, besides having its own jurisdiction, has an integrative function. It asks the analyst to view a company as an organic entity comprising a system in itself, but one related also to the larger systems of its environment. In each diagnostic situation, you are asked to pull together the separate concepts learned in functional and basic discipline courses and adapt them to a less structured set of problems. The strategic analyst must be able to see and to devise patterns of information, activities, and relationships. The facts given or the problems observed, if dealt with one at a time, are soon overwhelming.

Strategic analysis

Besides extending to the company as a multifaceted whole the knowledge and analytic skills developed in less comprehensive studies, students of Policy must acquire some additional abilities. These are particularly needed to deal with the concept of strategy. Under the heading of thinking about strategy, you will be asked to examine the economic environment of the company, to determine the essential characteristics of the industry, to note its development and trends, and to estimate future opportunity and risks for firms of varying resources and competence. You will appraise the strengths and weaknesses of the particular firm you are studying when viewed against the background of its competition and its environment. You will be asked to estimate its capacity to *alter* as well as to *adapt* to the forces affecting it. Finally you will be expected to make a decision putting market opportunity and corporate capability together into a suitable entrepreneurial combination.

At this point you will realize the full measure of the new skill required. The strategic decision is the one that helps determine the nature of the business in which a company is to engage and the kind of company it is to be. It is effective for a long time. It has wide ramifications. It is the most important kind of decision to be made for the company. It requires the best judgment and analysis that can be brought to it. Practice in making this decision while still safe from most of the consequences of error is one of the most important advantages offered by an education for business.

Making analysis effective

But the analysis is not the whole of the task implied by the concept of strategy. Once the entrepreneurial decision has been determined, the resources of the organization must be mobilized to make it effective. Devising organizational relationships appropriate to the tasks to be performed, determining the specialized talents required, and assisting and providing for the development of individuals and subgroups are essential tasks of strategic management and policy implementation. These tasks, together with prescribing a system of incentives and controls appropriate to the performance required and determining the impetus that can be given to achievement by the general manager's personal style of leadership, demand that you bring to the discussion of Policy everything previously learned about administrative processes.

Administrative skills can be approached, though not captured, in the classroom. Patterns of action will be judged as consistent or inconsistent with the strategy selected according to criteria which must be developed. Students approach the study of Business Policy with skills nurtured in studies like accounting and control, personnel and human relations, financial management, manufacturing, and marketing. The balanced application of these skills to the accomplishment of chosen purpose in a unique organizational situation is the best test of their power. Any failure to see the impact on the program as a whole of a decision based on the tenets of a special discipline will be sharply called to its proponent's attention by the defenders of other points of view.

General management skills

General management skills center intellectually upon relating the firm to its environment and administratively upon coordinating departmental specialties and points of view. Some students of business and even some students of Policy believe that these skills cannot be taught. General management is indeed an art to be learned only through years of responsible experience. And even through experience it can be learned only by those with the necessary native qualities: intelligence, a sense of responsibility, and administrative ability.

But if education means anything at all, students with the requisite native qualities can learn more readily and more certainly from experience and can more readily identify the kinds of experience to seek if they have at their disposal a conceptual framework with which to comprehend the analytical and administrative skills they will require and the nature of the situations in which they will find themselves. If, in addition, they have had practice in making and debating the merits of policy decisions, they will be more likely to grow in qualification for senior management responsibility than if they are submerged in operational detail and preoccupied by intricacies of technique.

This book is not a manual for policymakers or a how-to-do-it checklist for corporate planners. In fact it virtually ignores the mechanisms of planning on the grounds that, detached from strategy, they miss their mark. The authors do not believe that the conceptual framework described here can take the place of informed judgment. All the knowledge, professional attitudes, and analytical and administrative skills in the world cannot fully replace the intuitive genius of some of the natural entrepreneurs you will encounter in this book. Native powers cannot be counterfeited by reading textbooks.

We do not propose the acquisition of knowledge in the usual sense. We plan instead to give men and women with latent imagination the opportunity to exercise it in a disciplined way under critical observation. We expect to prepare people for the assumption of responsibility by exposing them, for example, to the temptation of expediency. We plan to press for clarification of personal purposes and to challenge shoddy or ill-considered values. We expect to affect permanently analytical habits of mind in a way that will permit assimilation of all, rather than part, of experience. The ideas, attitudes, and skills here discussed are adequate for a lifetime of study of one of the most vitally important of all human activities—leadership in organizations. Education is the prelude to true learning, which often does not take place without it.

Universal need for Policy skills

The need for general management ability is far too acute to be left to chance. The ideas, attitudes, and skills that comprise this study are much in demand not only throughout our own economy but also—in this age of rapid economic development abroad—throughout the world. In addition to their utility, these ideas are their own reward. For those who wish to lead an active life, or to provide for themselves and their families the material comfort and education that make culture possible, or to make substantial contributions to human welfare, the acquisition of policy skills is essential. Not all who turn to business are called to leadership, to be sure, but all are affected by it. No one suffers from study of its place in business.

THE NATURE OF THE TEXT AND CASES

The vehicles here provided for making progress toward these objectives are the text and cases that follow. All the cases are drawn from real life; none is selected to prove a point or draw a moral. Accuracy has been attested to by the sources from which information was taken; disguise has not been allowed to alter essential issues.

The text is designed to assist in the development of an effective approach to the cases. Its content is important only if it helps students make their analyses, choose and defend their conclusions, and decide what ought to be done and how it can be accomplished.

The text is dispersed throughout the book so as to permit a step-by-step consideration of what is involved in corporate strategy and in the subactivities required for its formulation and implementation. The order of cases is only partially determined by the sequence of ideas in the text. Each case should be approached without preconceptions as to what is to come. To make conceptual progress without predetermining the students' analysis of the problem or the nature of their recommendations, the cases focus initially on problems in strategy formulation and later on problems of building the organization and leading it to the accomplishment of the tasks assigned. As the course unfolds, considerations pertinent to previous cases are included in new cases. Students should not feel constrained in their analysis by the position of the case in the book; they are free to decide that an apparent problem of strategy implementation is actually a problem of strategy choice. However, the increasing complexity of the material provided will enable most students to feel a natural and organic evolution of subject matter, in keeping with their own evolving understanding, perspective, and skill.

The text suggests only that order is possible in approaching the enormous purview of Policy. The concept of strategy is an idea that experience has shown to be useful to researchers and practitioners alike in developing a comprehension of, and an approach to, policy problems. It is not a "theory" attended in the traditional sense by elegance and rigor. It is not really a "model," for the relationships designated by the concept are not quantifiable. But in lieu of a better theory or a more precise model, it will serve as an informing idea to which we can return again and again with increasing understanding after dealing with one unique case situation after another. The idea is intended to sharpen the analytical skills developed in the process of case discussion, and to serve as the basis for identifying uniformities and generalizations that will be useful later on, in practice. Our energies should be spent not so much on perfecting the definition of the concept as on using it in preparing to discuss the cases and in coming to conclusions about their issues. Students will not really learn how to distinguish effective from ineffective recommendations and good from bad judgment by study of these words or any others, but rather by active argument with their classmates. Such discussion should always end in the clarification of their own standards and criteria. The cases, we know from experience, provide stimulating opportunity for productive differences of opinion.

The chief executive's job: Roles and responsibilities

WHAT GENERAL MANAGEMENT IS

WE POINTED OUT in the introduction to this book that Business Policy is essentially the study of the knowledge, skills, and attitudes constituting general management. *Management* we regard as leadership in the informed, planned, purposeful conduct of complex organized activity. *General* management is in its simplest form the management of a total enterprise or of an autonomous subunit. Before we examine some cases presenting the range of decision issues we will consider more thoroughly later on, we should look at the position of the general manager. The senior general manager in any organization is its chief executive officer, who for the purposes of simplicity we will often call the *president*. As we said earlier, the role of the chief executive in examining the situation of a company may be initially an uncomfortable assignment for students of some modesty who think themselves insufficiently prepared for such high responsibility. It is nonetheless the best vantage point from which to view the processes involved in (1) the conception of organization purpose, (2) the decision to commit an organization to deliberately chosen purposes, and (3) the effort required to achieve purposes decided upon.

ROLES OF THE PRESIDENT

We will therefore begin by considering the *roles* which presidents must play. We will examine the *functions* or characteristic and natural actions that they perform in the roles they assume. We will try to identify *skills* or abilities to put one's perceptions, judgment, and knowledge to effective use in executive performance. As we look at presidential *roles*, *functions*, and *skills*, we may be able to define more clearly aspects of the *point of view* which provides the most suitable perspective for high-level executive judgment.

Many attempts to characterize executive roles and functions come to very little. Henri Fayol, originator of the classical school of management theory, identified the roles of planner, organizer, coordinator, and controller, initiating the construction by others of a later vocabulary of remarkable variety. Present-day students reject these categories as vague or abstract and indicative only of the objectives of some executive activity. Henry Mintzberg, who among other researchers has observed managers at work, identifies three sets of behavior—interpersonal, informational, and decisional. The interpersonal roles he designates as *figurehead* (for ceremonial duties), *leader* (of the work of his organization or unit), and *liaison* agent (for contacts outside his unit). Information roles can be designated as *monitor* (of information), *disseminator* (internally), and *spokesman* (externally). Decisional roles are called *entrepreneur, disturbance handler, resource allocator,* and *negotiator.*[1]

Empirical studies of what managers do are corrective of theory but not necessarily instructive in educating good managers. That most unprepared managers act intuitively rather than systematically in response to unanticipated pressures does not mean that the most effective do so to the same extent. If in fact the harried, improvisatory, overworked performers of 10 roles do not really know *what* they are doing or have any priorities besides degree of urgency, then we are not likely to find out what more effective management is from categorizing their activities. On the other hand it is futile to offer unrealistic exhortations about long-range planning and organizing to real-life victims of forced expediency.

The simplification which will serve our approach to policy best will leave aside important but easily understood activities. The executive may make speeches, pick the silver pattern for the executive lunchroom, negotiate personally with important customers, and do many things human beings have to do for many reasons. Roles we may study in order to do a better job of general management can be viewed as those of *organization leader, personal leader,* and *chief architect of organization purpose.* As leader of persons grouped in a hierarchy of suborganizations, the president must be taskmaster, mediator, motivator, and organization designer. Since these roles do not have useful job descriptions saying what to do, one might better estimate the nature of the overlapping responsibility of the head of an organization than to draw theoretical distinctions between categories. The personal influence of leaders becomes evident as they play the roles of communicator or exemplar, and attract respect or affection. When we examine finally the president's role as architect of organization purpose, we may see entrepreneurial or improvisatory behavior if the organization is just being born. If the company is long since established, the part played may be more accurately designated as manager of the purpose-determining process or chief strategist.

---

[1] See Henry Mintzberg, "The Manager's Job: Folklore and Fact," *Harvard Business Review,* July–August 1975, pp. 49–61; and for more detail, *The Nature of Managerial Work* (New York: Harper & Row, 1973).

COMPLEXITY OF GENERAL MANAGEMENT TASKS

The point of this nontechnical classification of role is not its universality, exactness of definition, or inclusiveness. We seek only to establish that general managers face such an array of functions and must exercise so various a set of skills as to require a protean versatility as performing executives. When you see Howard Head invent and perfect the metal ski, set up his company, devise a merchandising and distribution program of a very special kind, you see him in a role different from his arranging for the future of his business, his maintaining year-round production in a cyclical industry in order to meet the needs of his work force, his withdrawal from supervision of the company, and his selection of a successor. We make no claim to definitiveness in distinguishing executive roles as just attempted. It is essential to note, however, that the job of the general manager demands successful action in a *variety* of roles that differ according to the nature of the problem observed or decision pending, the needs of the organization, or the personality and style of the president. The simpleminded adherence to one role—one personality-determined, for example—will leave presidents miscast much of the time as the human drama they preside over unfolds.

We are in great need of a simple way to comprehend the total responsibility of chief executives. To multiply the list of tasks they must perform and the personal qualities they would do well to have would put general management capability beyond that of reasonably well-endowed human beings. Corporate presidents are accountable for everything that goes on in their organizations. They must preside over a total enterprise made up often of the technical specialties in which they cannot possibly have personal expertness. They must know their company's markets and the ways in which they are changing. They must lead private lives as citizens in their communities and as family members, as individuals with their own needs and aspirations. Except for rare earlier experience, perhaps as general managers of a profit center in their own organizations, they have found no opportunity to practice being president before undertaking the office. Only the brief study of Policy, for which this book is intended to be the basis, has been available as the academic preparation for general management. New presidents are obliged to put behind them the specialized apparatus their education and functional experience have provided them. Engineers, for example, who continue to run their companies strictly as engineers will soon encounter financial and marketing problems, among others, that may force their removal.

This book, together with the directed series of case discussions which will bring its substance alive, is intended to provide a way for the observer to comprehend the complexity of the president's job and for the president to put past experience in a new perspective and comprehend the world of which he or she has been put in charge. We will elaborate briefly the functions, skills, and points of view which give force and substance to the major roles we have just designated. This may lay a foundation for later discussion of the performance of chief executives in the cases that follow. In due course we will have an organizing per-

16

spective to reduce to practicable order the otherwise impossible agenda of the president.

THE PRESIDENT AS ORGANIZATION LEADER

Chief executives are first and probably least pleasantly persons who are responsible for results attained in the present as designated by plans made previously. Nothing that we will say shortly about their concern for the people in their organizations or later about their responsibility to society can gainsay this immediate truth. Achieving acceptable results against expectations of increased earnings per share and return on the stockholder's investment requires the president to be continually informed and ready to intervene when results fall below what had been expected. Changing circumstances and competition produce emergencies upsetting well-laid plans. Resourcefulness in responding to crisis is a skill which most successful presidents develop early.

But the organizational consequences of the critical taskmaster role require presidents to go beyond insistence upon achievement of planned results. They must see as their second principal function the creative maintenance and development of the organized capability that makes achievement possible. This activity leads to a third principle—the integration of the specialist functions which enable their organizations to perform the technical tasks in marketing, research and development, manufacturing, finance, control, and personnel, which proliferate as technology develops and tend to lead the company in all directions.[2] If this coordination is successful in harmonizing special staff activities, presidents will probably have performed the task of getting organizations to accept and order priorities in accordance with the companies' objectives. Securing commitment to purpose is a central function of the president as organization leader.

The skills required by these functions reveal presidents not solely as taskmasters but as mediators and motivators as well. They need ability in the education and motivation of people and the evaluation of their performance, two functions which tend to work against one another. The former requires understanding of individual needs, which persist no matter what the economic purpose of the organization. The latter requires objective assessment of the technical requirements of the task assigned. The capability required here is also that required in the integration of functions and the mediation of the conflict bound to arise out of technical specialism. The integrating capacity of the chief executive extends to meshing the economic, technical, human, and moral dimensions of corporate activity and to relating the company to its immediate and more distant communities. It will show itself in the formal organization designs which are put into effect as the blueprint of the required structured cooperation.

---

[2] See P. R. Lawrence and J. W. Lorsch, *Organization and Environment: Managing Differentiation and Integration* (Boston: Harvard University Graduate School of Business Administration, 1967), for a study of the process of specialization and coordination.

The perspective demanded of successful organization leaders embraces both the primacy of organization goals and the validity of individual goals. Besides this dual appreciation, they exhibit an impartiality toward the specialized functions and have criteria enabling them to allocate organization resources against documented needs. The point of view of the leader of an organization almost by definition requires an overview of its relations not only to its internal constituencies but to the relevant institutions and forces of its external environment. We will come soon to a conceptual solution of the problems encountered in the role of organizational leader.

THE PRESIDENT AS PERSONAL LEADER

The functions, skills, and relevant point of view of chief executives hold true no matter who they are or who makes up their organizations. The functions that accompany presidential performance of their role as communicator of purpose and policy, as exemplar, and as the focal point for the respect or affection of subordinates vary much more according to personal energy, style, character, and integrity. Presidents contribute as persons to the quality of life and performance in their organizations. This is true whether they are dynamic or colorless. By example they educate junior executives to seek to emulate them or simply to learn from their behavior what they really expect. They have the opportunity to infuse organized effort with flair or distinction if they have the skill to dramatize the relationship between their own activities and the goals of corporate effort.

All persons in leadership positions have or attain power which in sophisticated organizations they invoke as humanely and reasonably as possible in order to avoid the stultifying effects of dictatorship, dominance, or even markedly superior capacity. Formally announced policy, backed by the authority of the chief executive can be made effective to some degree by clarity of direction, intensity of supervision, and the exercise of sanctions in enforcement. But in areas of judgment where policy cannot be specified without becoming absurdly overdetailed, chief executives establish in their own demeanor even more than in policy statements the moral and ethical level of performance expected. At the national level of executive behavior, even presidents reveal in their deportment their real regard for the highest levels of ethical conduct. The results are traceable in the administrations of Presidents Kennedy, Johnson, Nixon, and Carter. Failure of personal leadership in the White House leads to demoralization different only in scale and influence from corporate analogies. The behavior of President Reagan strikingly illustrates the influence of personal style—one which can outshine doubts about the clarity of his foreign policy.

Formal correctness of structure and policy is not enough to inspire an organization. Enthusiasm for meeting ethical problems head on and avoiding shoddy solutions comes not so much from a system of rewards and punishments as from the sentiments of loyalty or courage stimulated by the personal deportment of the chief executive. By the persons they are, as much as by what they say and do, presidents influence their organizations and affect the development of individuals and the level of organized performance. At this moment in the history of American business enterprise, conscious attention to the essential integrity of the chief executive becomes an important requirement if confidence in the corporate institutions of a democratic society is to be restored.

The skills of the effective personal leader are those of persuasion and articulation made possible by having something worth saying and by understanding the sentiments and points of view being addressed. Leaders cultivate and embody relationships between themselves and their subordinates appropriate to the style of leadership they have chosen or fallen into. Some of the qualities lending distinction to this leadership cannot be deliberately contrived, even by an artful schemer. The maintenance of personal poise in adversity or emergency and the capacity for development as an emotionally mature person are essential innate and developed capabilities. It is probably true that some personal preeminence in technical or social functions is either helpful or essential in demonstrating leadership related to the president's personal contribution. Credibility and cooperation depend upon demonstrated capacity of a kind more tangible and attractive, than, for example, the noiseless coordination of staff activity.

The relevant aspects of the presidential point of view brought to mind by activities in the role of personal leader are probably acknowledgment of one's personal needs and integrity as a person, and acceptance of the importance to others of their own points of view, and acceptance of the importance to others of their own points of view, behavior, and feelings. Self-awareness will acquaint leaders with their own personal strengths and weaknesses and keep them mindful of the inevitable unevenness of their own preparation for the functions of general management. These qualities may be more important in the selection of a general manager than in the study of general management. But students of the cases that follow will quickly see the personal contributions of M. Bich in BIC Pens, the values of John Connelly in Crown Cork & Seal, Sir Halford Reddish in Rugby Portland Cement, and Joseph C. Wilson of the Xerox Corporation.

Michael Maccoby, author of *The Gamesman*,[3] has conducted a provocative inquiry into executive character types. Using some terms of dubious usefulness, he designates these as the craftsman, the jungle fighter, the company man, and the gamesman. The craftsman is dedicated to quality but unable to lead changing organizations. The jungle fighter is the antihero who after rising rapidly is destroyed by those he has used. The company man is committed to corporate integrity and success but is said to lack the daring required to lead innovative organizations. The gamesman is the dominant type—able and enthusiastic, a team leader whose main goal is the exhilaration of victory. His main

---

[3] Michael Maccoby, *The Gamesman* (New York: Simon & Schuster, 1976). For a brief summary, see "The Corporate Climber Has to Find His Heart," *Fortune*, December 1975, pp. 98–108.

defect is said to be that his work has developed his intellectual but not his emotional gifts. Despite the disclaimer that each person is a combination of types, these attention-getting labels produce caricature in the effort to distinguish overlapping or coexisting traits. Similarly labels applied to roles suggest distance between them.

Despite the shortcomings of such classification, the work of psychoanalysts like Maccoby and Zaleznik brings support to the thesis developed here that such qualities as generosity, idealism, and courage should accompany the gifts of the persons devoted to their company and its objectives. If Maccoby is right in saying that the gamesman (by which he seems to mean quarterback or captain) is the representative type in leading American corporations today, then we have come a long way from the Carnegies, Rockefellers, and Astors of the 19th century. We would still have a long way to go. The route passes directly through the pages that follow.

The prototype of the chief executives we are developing is, in short, the able victory-seeking organizational leader who is making sure in what is done and the changes pioneered in purpose and practice that the game is worth playing, the victory worth seeking, and life and career worth living. If the stature of corporation presidents as professional persons is not manifest in their concern for their organizations, they will not perform effectively over time either in the role of organization or personal leader. If we concede that the gamesman should be concerned with what the game is for, we are ready to consider the role of the president in the choice of corporate objectives. That choice determines what the contest is about.

THE PRESIDENT AS ARCHITECT OF ORGANIZATION PURPOSE

To go beyond the organizational and personal roles of leadership, we enter the sphere of organization purpose, where we may find the atmosphere somewhat rare and the going less easy. We think students of the companies described in these cases will note, as they see president after president cope or fail to cope with problems of various economic, political, social, or technical elements, that the contribution presidents make to their companies goes far beyond the apparently superficial activities that clutter their days.

The attention of presidents to organization needs must extend beyond answering letters of complaint from spouses of aggrieved employees to appraisal (for example) of the impact of their companies' information, incentive, and control systems upon individual behavior. Their personal contribution to their company goes far beyond easily understood attention to key customers and speeches to the Economic Club to the more subtle influence their own probity and character have on subordinates. We must turn now to activities even further out—away from immediate every day decisions and emergencies. Some part of what a president does is oriented toward maintaining the development of a company over time and preparing for a future more distant than the time horizon appropriate to the roles and functions identified thus far.

The most difficult role—and the one we will concentrate on henceforth—of the chief executive of any organization is the one in which he serves as custodian of corporate objectives. The entrepreneurs who create a company know at the outset what they are up to. Their objectives are intensely personal, if not exclusively economic, and their passions may be patent protection and finance. If they succeed, like Howard Head, in passing successfully through the phase of personal entrepreneurship, where they or their bankers or families are likely to be the only members of the organization concerned with purpose, they find themselves in the role of planner, managing the process by which ideas for the future course of the company are conceived, evaluated, fought over, and accepted or rejected.

The presidential functions involved include establishing or presiding over the goal-setting and resource-allocation processes of the company, making or ratifying choice among strategic alternatives, and clarifying and defending the goals of the company against external attack or internal erosion. The installation of purpose in place of improvisation and the substitution of planned progress in place of drifting are probably the most demanding functions of the chief executive. Successful organization leadership requires great human skill, sensitivity, and administrative ability. Personal leadership is built upon personality and character. The capacity for determining and monitoring the adequacy of the organization's continuing purposes implies as well analytic intelligence of a high order. The president we are talking about is not a two-dimensional poster or television portrait.

The crucial skill of the president concerned with corporate purpose includes the creative generation or recognition of strategic alternatives made valid by developments in the marketplace and the capability and resources of the company. Along with this, in a combination not easily come by, runs the critical capacity to analyze the strengths and weaknesses of documented proposals. The ability to perceive with some objectivity corporate strengths and weaknesses is essential to sensible choice of goals, for the most attractive goal is not attainable without the strength to open the way to it through inertia and intense opposition, with all else that lies between.

Probably the skill most nearly unique to general management, as opposed to the management of functional or technical specialties, is the intellectual capacity to conceptualize corporate purpose and the dramatic skill to invest it with some degree of magnetism. As we will see, the skill can be exercised in industries less romantic than space, electronics, or environmental reclamation. John Connelly did it with tin cans; Sir Halford Reddish with cement. Ralph Hart of Heublein, Inc., thought he could do it with beer because he did do it with Smirnoff vodka. No sooner is a distinctive set of corporate objectives vividly delineated than the temptation to go beyond it sets in. Under some circumstances it is the president's function to defend properly focused purpose against superficially attractive diversification or corporate growth that glitters like fool's gold. Because defense of proper strategy can be interpreted as mindless conservatism, wholly appropriate defense of a still valid strategy requires courage, supported by detailed documentation.

Continuous monitoring, in any event, of the quality and continued suitability of corporate purpose is over time the most sophisticated and essential of all the functions of general management alluded to here. Because of its difficulty and vulnerability to current emergency, this function may not be present in some of the companies the student will encounter in the pages that follow. Because of its low visibility, this activity may not be noticed at first in cases where it is properly present. The perspective which sustains this function is the kind of creative discontent which prevents complacency even in good times and seeks continuous advancement of corporate and individual capacity and performance. It requires also constant attention to the future, as if the present did not offer problems and opportunities enough.

ENORMITY OF THE TASK

Even so sketchy a record of what a president is called upon to do is likely to seem an academic idealization, given the disparity between the complexity of role and function and the modest qualifications of those impressed into the office. Like the Molière character who discovered that for 40 years he had been speaking prose without knowing it, many managers have been programmed by instinct and experience to the kind of performance that we have attempted to decipher here. For the inexperienced, the catalog may seem impossibly long.

Essentially, however, we have looked at only three major roles and four sets of responsibilities. The roles deal with the requirements for organizational and personal leadership and for conscious attention to the formulation and promulgation of purpose. The four groups of functions encompass (1) securing the attainment of planned results in the present, (2) developing an organization capable of producing both technical achievement and human satisfactions, (3) making a distinctive personal contribution, and (4) planning and executing policy decisions affecting future results.

Even thus simplified, how to apply this identification of presidential role and function to the incomparably detailed confusion of a national company situation cannot possibly be made clear in the process of generalization. Students using this text will wish to develop their own overview of the general manager's task, stressing those aspects most compatible with their own insight and sense of what to do. No modifications of the deliberately nontechnical language of this summary should slight the central importance of purpose. The theory presented here begins with the assumption that the life of every organization (corporate or otherwise), every subunit of organization, and every human group and individual should be guided by an evolving set of purposes or goals which permit forward movement in a chosen direction and prevent drifting in undesired directions.

NEED FOR A CONCEPT

The complexity of the president's job and the desirability of raising intuitive competence to the level of verifiable, conscious, and systematic analysis suggest the need, as indicated earlier, for a unitary concept as useful to the generalist as the canons of technical functions are to the specialist. We will propose shortly a simple practitioner's theory which we hope will reduce the four-faceted responsibility of the company president to more reasonable proportions, make it susceptible to objective research and systematic evaluation, and bring to more well-qualified people the skills it requires. The central concept we call "corporate strategy." It will be required to embrace the entire corporation, to take shape in the terms and conditions in which its business is conducted. It will be constructed from the points of view described so far. Central to this Olympian vantage point is impartiality with respect to the value of individual specialties, including the one through which the president rose to generalist responsibilities. It will insist upon the values of the special functions in proportion to their contribution to corporate purpose and ruthlessly dispense with those not crucially related to the objectives sought. It necessarily will define the president's role in such a way as to allow delegation of much of the general management responsibility described here without loss of clarity. After students have examined and discussed the roles, functions, and skills evident or missing from the cases that immediately follow these comments, we will present the concept of corporate strategy itself. Our hope will be to make challenging but practicable the connection between the highest priority for goal setting and a durable but flexible definition of a company's goals and major company-determining policies. How to define, decide, put into effect, and defend a conscious strategy appropriate to emerging market opportunity and company capability will then take precedence over and lend order to the fourfold functions of general management here presented.

Despite a shift in emphasis toward the anatomy of a concept and the development of an analytical approach to the achievement of valid corporate strategy, we will not forget the chief executive's special role in contributing quality to purpose through standards exercised in the choice of what to do and the way in which it is to be done and through the projection of *quality* as a person. It will remain true, after we have taken apart analytically the process by which strategy is conceived, that executing it at a high professional level will depend upon the depth and durability of the president's personal values, standards of quality, and clarity of character. We will return in a final comment on the management of the strategic process to the truth that the president's function above all is to be the exemplar of a permanent human aspiration—the determination to devote one's powers to jobs worth doing. Conscious attention to corporate strategy will be wasted if it does not elevate the quality of corporate purpose and achievement.

Head Ski Company, Inc.

THE HEAD SKI COMPANY, INC., of Timonium, Maryland, was formed in 1950 to sell metal skis which had been developed by Howard Head during three years of research. In the first year six employees turned out 300 pairs of skis. By the 1954–55 skiing season, output reached 8,000 pairs, and by 1965 it passed 133,000. Growth in dollar sales and profits was equally spectacular. When Head went public in 1960, sales were just over $2 million and profits just under $59,000. By 1965 sales were up to $8.6 million and profits to $393,713. In the next two years, volume continued upward, though growth was less dramatic. In the 53 weeks ended April 30, 1966, sales were $9.1 million and profits $264,389. For a like period ending April 29, 1967, sales were $11.0 million and profits $401,482. (For financial data, see Exhibit 1.)

THE INDUSTRY

Head was an enthusiastic participant in the growing market generated by leisure-time activities, of which skiing was one of the most dynamic segments. The industry association, Ski Industries America (SIA), estimated that skiing expenditures—including clothing, equipment, footwear, accessories, lift tickets, travel, entertainment, food and lodging—rose from $280 million in 1960 to $750 million in 1966–67. Gross sales were expected to reach $1.14 billion by 1969–70. This growth was attributed to both the rising number of skiers and greater per capita expenditures. In 1947 it was estimated that there were fewer than 10,000 active skiers in the United States. SIA estimated that there were 1.6 million in 1960, 3.5 million in 1966–67 and predicted 5 million for 1970. Another industry source estimated that the number of skiers was increasing by 20 percent a year.

As of 1966–67 the $750 million retail expenditures of skiing were estimated to be divided into $200 million going for ski equipment and ski

Exhibit 1

HEAD SKI COMPANY, INC.
Consolidated Balance Sheet, 1965–1967

ASSETS

	As of April 24, 1965	As of April 30, 1966	As of April 29, 1967
Current assets:			
Cash	$ 162,646	$ 233,330	$ 263,896
Short-term commercial paper receivable	1,200,000	800,000	1,200,000
Notes and accounts receivable—less reserve	334,503	174,127	242,632
Inventories—valued at lower of cost or market	2,815,042	3,522,235	3,102,069
Prepayments and miscellaneous receivables	207,279	223,864	402,879
Total current assets	4,719,470	4,953,556	5,211,476
Fixed assets, at cost:			
Building—pledged under mortgage	1,014,738	1,012,085	1,010,149
Machinery and equipment	847,974	1,059,274	1,540,707
Other	147,336	213,692	715,089
	2,010,048	2,285,051	3,265,945
Less accumulated depreciation	822,255	892,153	1,123,203
Total fixed assets	1,187,793	1,392,898	2,142,742
Other assets:			
Unamortized bond discount and expenses	277,636	263,564	252,004
Cash surrender value of life insurance	103,117	120,589	133,568
Other	28,583	22,364	70,194
Total other assets	409,336	406,517	455,766
Total assets	$6,316,599	$6,752,971	$7,809,984

LIABILITIES AND STOCKHOLDERS' EQUITY

	As of April 24, 1965	As of April 30, 1966	As of April 29, 1967
Current liabilities:			
Accounts payable	$ 521,031	$ 299,040	$ 829,826
Current portion of long-term debt	20,600	21,000	23,100
Accrued expenses	451,062	413,865	549,720
Income taxes payable	39,102	299,452	333,514
Other	94,899	91,271	51,120
Total current liabilities	1,126,694	1,124,628	1,787,280
Long-term debt:			
Mortgage on building—5¾%, payable to 1978	396,646	376,036	331,115
Convertible subordinated debentures	2,125,000	2,125,000	2,125,000
	2,521,646	2,501,036	2,456,115
Less current portion	20,600	21,000	
Total long-term debt	2,501,046	2,480,036	2,456,115
Commitments and contingent liabilities, stockholders' equity:			
Common stock—par value 50¢ per share (authorized 2 million shares; outstanding 1966, 915,202 shares; 1965, 882,840 shares adjusted for 2-for-1 stock split-up effective September 15, 1965)	220,710	457,601	459,401
Paid-in capital	1,820,323	1,679,700	1,694,700
Retained earnings	647,826	1,011,006	1,412,488
Total stockholders' equity	2,688,859	3,148,307	3,566,589
Total liabilities and stockholders' equity	$6,316,599	$6,752,971	$7,809,984

Exhibit 1 *(continued)*

CONSOLIDATED STATEMENT OF EARNINGS

	52 weeks ended* April 25, 1964	52 weeks ended* April 24, 1965	53 weeks ended* April 30, 1966	52 weeks ended* April 29, 1967
Net sales	$6,018,779	$8,600,392	$9,080,223	$11,048,072
Cost of sales	4,033,576	5,799,868	6,357,169	7,213,188
Gross profit	1,985,203	$2,800,524	$2,723,054	$ 3,834,894
Expenses:				
Selling, administrative and general	1,169,392	1,697,659	2,029,531	2,756,939
Research and engineering	102,358	303,884	239,851	327,857
Total expenses	1,271,750	2,001,543	2,269,382	3,084,796
Income before income taxes and nonrecurring charges	713,453	798,981	453,672	750,088
Federal and state income taxes	367,542	392,515	221,034	348,606
Income before nonrecurring charges	345,911	406,466	232,638	401,482
Nonrecurring debt expense—after giving effect to income taxes	—	63,678	—	—
Net earnings	345,911	342,788	232,638	401,482
Net earnings as restated	376,788	393,713	264,389	401,482
Earnings per share before nonrecurring charges	0.40	0.51	0.26	0.44
Earnings per share after nonrecurring charges	0.40	0.43	0.26	0.44
Earnings per share as restated	0.48	0.49	0.29	0.44

Earnings per share are based on average shares outstanding of 904,237 in 1966 and 801,196 in 1965 after giving effect to the 2-for-1 stock split-up effective September 15, 1965, and the 3-for-1 stock split on July 7, 1964.

* Earnings restated April 29, 1967, to give effect to an adjustment in the lives of depreciable assets for federal income tax purposes.

	52 weeks ended April 27, 1963	52 weeks ended April 25, 1964	52 weeks ended April 24, 1965	53 weeks ended April 30, 1966	52 weeks ended April 29, 1967
Net sales	4,124,445	6,018,779	8,600,392	9,080,223	11,048,072
Net earnirns	191,511	376,788	393,713	264,389	401,482
Expenditures for plant and equipment	272,154	513,130	558,865	304,102	1,027,854
Depreciation	79,719	132,497	211,683	238,161	949,961
Working capital	654,676	1,525,015	3,542,857	3,828,928	3,424,196
Plant and equipment and other assets, net	701,875	1,187,246	1,745,839	1,799,415	2,598,508
Long-term debt	287,245	1,176,647	2,501,046	2,480,036	2,456,115
Shareholders' equity	1,069,306	1,535,614	2,787,650	3,148,307	3,566,589
Earnings per share	0.25	0.48	0.49	0.29	0.44
Average shares outstanding	777,600	777,600	801,196	904,237	916,542

Average shares outstanding reflect the 2-for-1 stock split-up effective September 15, 1965, and 3-for-1 stock split on July 7, 1964.

Statistical data for the years 1963 to 1966, inclusive, have been adjusted to reflect retroactive adjustments.

Source: Company records.

wear, and $440 million going to the 1,200 ski areas and the transportation companies carrying skiers to their destinations. Ninety-eight manufacturers belonged to the SIA. *Skiing International Yearbook* for 1967 listed 85 brands of wooden skis available in 260 models, 49 brands of metal skis in 101 models, and 53 brands of fiberglass skis in 116 models. For each model there could be as many as 15 sizes. Many manufacturers made all three types of skis and some had multiple brands, but even so the industry was divided into many competing units.

The ski business, industry observers noted, was undergoing rapid change. *Ski Business* summed up an analysis of industry trends as follows:

> Imports of low-priced adult wood skis into the United States are skidding sharply.
>
> U.S. metal skis are gaining faster than any other category.
>
> The ski equipment and apparel market is experiencing an unusually broad and pronounced price and quality uptrend.
>
> Ski specialty shop business appears to be gaining faster than that of the much publicized department stores and general sporting goods outlets.
>
> The growth in the national skier population is probably decelerating and may already have reached a plateau.[1]

Supporting these statements of trends, *Ski Business* made some other observations.

> Foreign skis clearly lost in 1966 at the gain of domestic manufacturers. (The total of imported and domestic skis sold in the United States is believed to be running at over 900,000 pairs annually.) By conservative estimate, U.S. metal ski production in 1966 (for shipment to retail shops for the 1966–67 selling season) was up by at least 40,000 pairs from 1965. . . .
>
> But far more important than the domestic American ski gain (which will continue now that American fiberglass ski makers are entering the market) is the remarkable upward price shift. Thus while 10 percent fewer foreign skis entered the United States in 1966, the dollar value of all the skis imported actually rose by more than 10 percent or $700,000. . . . Here was the real measure of growth of the ski market; it was not in numbers, but in dollars.
>
> The principal beneficiary of this remarkable upward shift in consumer preference for higher product quality is, of course, the ski specialty shop. The skier bent on purchasing $140 skis and $80 boots will tend to put his confidence in the experienced specialist retailer. The ski specialist shops themselves are almost overwhelmed by what is happening. Here's one retailer's comment: "Just two or three years ago, we were selling a complete binding for $15. Now skiers come into our shop and think nothing of spending $40 for a binding. . . ."
>
> . . . Most of the department store chains and sporting goods shops contacted by *Ski Business* were also able to report increased business in 1966–67, but somehow the exuberant, expansionist talk seems to have evaporated among nonspecialty ski dealers. Montgomery Ward, for instance, says that ski equipment sales have not come up to company expectations. Ward's has specialized in low end merchandise for beginning and intermediate skiers. . . . Significantly, department stores or sporting goods shops which

---

[1] John Fry, *Ski Business,* May–June 1967, p. 25.

reported the largest sales increases tended to be those which strive hardest to cast their image in the ski specialist mold. . . .[2]

Ski imports for 1966 served both the low-priced and high-priced market. More than half the Japanese imports of 530,000 pairs of skis were thought to be children's skis which helped to explain the low valuation of the Japanese skis. This value of $6.84 a pair was the FOB price at the door of the Japanese ski factory and does not include shipping, duty, importer's or retailer's margins.[3] *Ski Business* reported imports into the United States as follows:

1966 SKI IMPORTS INTO THE UNITED STATES
(by country of origin)

Country of origin	Number of pairs	Change: 1966 vs. 1965	Dollar value	Average dollar* value per pair 1965	Average dollar* value per pair 1966
Canada	7,091	+6,350	$ 149,961	$23	$21.14
Sweden	2,767	+1,131	22,386	9	8.09
Norway	1,125	−698	18,221	6	16.20
Finland	10,184	+5,411	98,275	9	9.65
Belgium	129	+129	6,327	—	49.05
France	5,257	+2,828	265,018	49	50.41
West Germany	44,736	+9,959	1,010,354	18	22.58
Austria	72,536	−20,872	1,511,563	21	20.84
Switzerland	2,835	+1,155	124,068	39	43.76
Italy	7,494	+351	195,723	14	26.12
Yugoslavia	22,540	+5,122	254,962	11	11.31
Japan	529,732	−89,632	3,625,639	5.54	6.84
Australia	2,307	+2,307	114,091	—	49.45
1965 total	785,746	—	6,692,451	—	8.52
1966 total	708,733	−77,013	7,396,588	8.52	10.44

* The average value per pair of skis represents an FOB plant price and does not include charges for shipping and handling, tariff, excise tax, or profit for trading company or wholesaler. Tariff on skis was 16⅔ percent.
Source: *Ski Business*, May–June 1967, p. 31.

In the high-price market segment, where skis retailed at $100 or more, the annual market was estimated by industry sources to be approximately 250,000 pairs of skis. Here estimates of the leading contenders according to these industry sources were:

Brand	Type	Estimated sales (pairs)	Price range
Head (United States)	Metal	125,000	$115.00–$175.00
Hart (United States)	Metal	44,000	$ 99.50–$175.00
Kniessl (Austria)	Epoxy	20,000	$150.00–$200.00
Yamaha (Japan)	Epoxy Wood ⎫	13,000	$ 79.00–$169.00
Fischer (Austria)	Metal ⎬ Epoxy ⎭	13,000	$112.00–$189.00

Source: *Skiing International Yearbook, 1967*, pp. 90–91. Copyright by Ziff-Davis Publishing Co.

[2] Ibid.

[3] Ibid.

Fischer was believed to have $15–$18 million sales worldwide. Kniessl was believed to be about the same size as Head worldwide, but only about one-tenth Head's size in the United States. In addition Voit, the recreational products division of AMF, was entering the market with a fiberglass ski. Voit also manufactured water skis, a wide variety of aquatic equipment, and rubber products. AMF's total 1966 sales were $357 million. Recreational equipment accounted for approximately 20 percent, not including bowling equipment which accounted for an additional 22 percent of sales.

The skier's skill level was one determining factor in his choice of skis. (For those unfamiliar with the differences among skis designed for each group, a discussion of ski construction is included as the Appendix.) Of the 3.5 million active skiers, 17,000 were regarded as racers, another 75,000 were considered to be experts, and another 100,000 were classed as sufficiently skillful to be strong recreational skiers.

THE MARKET

Skiing was considered to be a sport which attracted the moderately well-to-do and those on the way up. This conception was borne out by the following market data:

> A statistical study released early this year [1965] by the Department of Commerce disclosed that the American skier has a median age of 26.2 and a median annual income of $11,115. Moreover, it showed that about two thirds of all skiers are college graduates.
>
> How do these young, affluent and intelligent men and women spend their skiing dollars? At a typical resort, a person might spend each day $10 for accommodations, $10 for food, $5 for a lift ticket and $10 for renting everything needed to attack the slopes from pants and parka to skis, boots, poles and bindings. . . .
>
> The initial purchases of a person determined to have his or her own good equipment and to look well while skiing could easily be about $200. For this amount, a skier could buy everything from winter underwear to goggles and perhaps even have a bit left over for a rum toddy in the ski lodge the first night of his trip.
>
> For instance, ski boots cost from $20 to $150 and average $50 a pair. Skis range from $30 to $200 and poles from $5 to $35.
>
> When it comes to apparel, costs vary considerably. Snow jackets or parkas might cost as little as $20 or as much as $1,000 for those made with fur. Many jackets are available, though, at about $30.
>
> Stretch pants have an average price of about $20. Other apparel requirements for skiing include sweaters which retail from $10 to $50, winter underwear which costs about $5, and ski hats and caps which sell for $3 and up.[4]

There was an apparent fashionability to skiing. Fashion consciousnesss was apparent in the design of ski equipment, ski wear, and the

---

[4] *The New York Times,* December 12, 1965. © 1965 by The New York Times Company. Reprinted by permission.

influx of a new type of skier. Under the headline "The Nonskiers: They Flock to Ski Resorts for the Indoor Sports," *The Wall Street Journal* reported as follows:

> Want to take up a rugged, outdoor sport?
>
> Cross skiing off your list.
>
> The sport has gone soft. Ski resorts now have all the comforts of home— if your home happens to have a plush bar, a heated swimming pool, a padded chair lift, boutiques and a built-in baby sitter. . . . Skiing, in fact, has become almost an incidental activity at some ski resorts; indeed, some of the most enthusiastic patrons here at Squaw Valley and other resorts don't even know how to ski. They rarely venture outdoors.
>
> So why do they come here? "Men, M-E-N. They're here in bunches, and so am I, baby," answers slinky, sloe-eyed Betty Reames as she selects a couch strategically placed midway between the fireplace and the bar. . . .
>
> Squaw Valley houses half a dozen bars and restaurants and often has three different bands and a folksinger entertaining at the same time. Aspen, in Colorado, throws a mid-winter Mardi Gras. Sun Valley, in Idaho, has a shopping village that includes a two-floor bookstore and boutique selling miniskirts.
>
> Life has also been made softer for those skiers who ski. . . . Also some resorts are making their chair lifts more comfortable by adding foam padding. But even that isn't enough for some softies. "What? Me ride the chair lift? Are you crazy? I'd freeze to death out in the open like that," says blond Wanda Peterson as she waits to ride up the mountain in an enclosed gondola car. She doesn't stand alone. The line of the gondola is 200 strong; the nearby chair lift, meanwhile, is all but empty. . . .
>
> . . . for beginning skiers most resorts offer gentle, meticulously groomed inclines that make it almost impossible to fall. "We try to make it so that the person who has no muscle tone and little experience can't be fooled, can't make a mistake," says one resort operator. "Then we've got him. He's a new customer as well as a happy man."
>
> Once he gets the hang of it—whether he's any good or not—the happy man starts spending lots of money, and that's what the resorts love.[5]

In line with the concern for style, some manufacturers of skiwear and ski equipment developed new colors and annual model changes to inspire annual obsolescence and fad purchases.

HEAD COMPANY HISTORY

Howard Head, chairman and founder of the company bearing his name, was the man responsible for the development of the first successful metal ski. Combining the experience of an aircraft designer with dedication to a sport which he enjoyed, he spent more than three years developing a ski which would not break, turned easily, and tracked correctly without shimmying and chattering. Others had tried to produce metal skis, but Head succeeded almost five years before his nearest competitors, Hart and Harry Holmberg, introduced the Hart metal skis. *Ski Magazine* described the reason behind Howard Head's success:

---

[5] *The Wall Street Journal,* February 1967.

. . . He was obsessed, to be sure, and being relatively unencumbered by stockholders, high overhead and strong yearnings for luxurious living, he was well braced for the long haul. . . .

"I made changes only where I had to make them," he has said of the days when his skis were undergoing trial by fire. "When they broke, I made them stronger only where they broke. . . ."[6]

In 1960 Howard Head described the early years of his enterprise and the trials which surrounded it as follows:

Twelve years ago I took six pairs of handmade metal skis to Stowe, Vermont, and asked the pros there to try them out. It had taken about a year to make those six pairs of skis. The design, based on engineering principles of aircraft construction, was radically different from any ever tried before. I thought it was sound but the pros weren't a bit surprised when all six pairs promptly broke to pieces. After all, others before me had tried to make metal skis and all they had proved was what everyone knew anyway—a ski had to be made of wood.

That was in January 1948. Today about 60 percent of all high-grade skis sold in the United States are metal skis. The reasons for this revolution in ski manufacturing industry are simple. People like the way metal skis ski, they like their durability, and they like their easy maintenance. . . .

Many small refinements and changes in design have been introduced through the years because of our continued testing and development program and to meet the advances in technique and changes in skiing conditions. But the basic structural design hasn't changed, which speaks well for the original concept.[7]

Mr. Head further indicated that his personal interest in technical problems played a major part in leading him to create his business:

When I started out, I was a mechanical design engineer—the whole origin of the business was the feeling that it should be possible to build a better ski. What started as an engineering puzzle ended as a business.

I distinctly remember wondering at that time whether we would ever grow to the point where we would be making 5,000 pairs of skis a year.

Price-volume considerations exerted small influence over initial marketing policy. Mr. Head priced his first metal skis at $75 in spite of the fact that most skiers were using war surplus skis that cost $20, including bindings. Mr. Head discussed his early ideas on quality, costs, and prices as follows:

The great disadvantage of all metal skis is simply their high price. This became apparent to us when we were pioneering the original metal ski and found it was going to cost a good bit more than a wood ski. We didn't let that stop us because we believed the striking advantages of a metal ski more than compensated for its high price. As it turned out, even with a higher initial price, Head Skis proved to cost less in the long run because they are so durable. . . .

In the early days people had no way of knowing the skis would last so

---

[6] *Ski Magazine,* January 1964.

[7] "On Metal Skis" (manuscript by Howard Head, 1960).

long that they actually ended up costing less than cheaper skis. They simply liked them enough to go ahead and buy them in spite of the price.[8]

Mr. Head found a market which was quite unexpected. In spite of the high price, Head skis appealed more to the average beginner or slightly better skier than to racers. Among skiers, Heads became known as "cheaters." This designation grew out of the skis' ability to make almost anyone look good. "They practically turned themselves." Soon the black plastic top of the Head ski became a ubiquitous status symbol on the slopes.

PRODUCT POLICY

The keynote of Mr. Head's product policy was quality. His fundamental belief was that the consumer should get all he pays for and pay for all he gets. The 17-year history of the company had seen considerable upgrading of the products. Several times in the past the company had called in particular models or production runs of skis which had been found to be defective. One executive commented that this had been done without hesitation, even when the company was in precarious financial condition.

Asked what set Head apart from its competition, Mr. Head replied as follows:

> I believe that it is a tradition of attention to detail which grew out of its entrepreneurial history. In every aspect we attempt to follow through. Service, dealer relations, product quality, style, advertising are all important and must be done in the best way we know how.
>
> We stress continued emphasis on quality of product and quality of operating philosophy. We pay meticulous attention to the individual relationships with dealers and the public.
>
> I have attempted to make creativity, imagination, and standards of perfection apply across the board. This was always our desire, and we only failed to live up to it when the business got too big for the existing staff. The philosophy remained constant, and now we have the people to live up to it.
>
> We get a return on this attention to detail. The feedback from success allows us to maintain the necessary staff to insure continuation of this philosophy.
>
> We allow no sloppiness.

Head skis came in one color—black. There was no special trim to designate the model, only a modification in the color of the name "Head" embossed on the top of the ski and a change in the color of the base: red for some models, yellow or black for others. Although at one time a chrome top was considered, it was rejected because of the glare and because it was difficult to see against the snow. In addition to these factors, one executive described black as being a conservative color which would go with anything. Howard Head explained that he "did not want to complicate the consumer's choice."

---

[8] Ibid.

engineer

but it won't!

what of style?

No!!!

I deeply believe in sticking to function and letting style take care of itself. We have stuck so rigorously to our black color because it is honest and functional that it has become almost a trademark. While we constantly make minor improvements, we never make an important model change unless there is a performance reason for it. In other words, we skipped the principle of forced obsolescence, and we will continue to skip it.

This policy had been consciously chosen and maintained, in spite of competition which had introduced six or eight different colors and yearly color changes to keep up with fashion.

Apart from color and style, skis had to perform well on the slopes. There were three fundamental things which a ski had to do. It has to "track,"[9] "traverse,"[10] and "turn."[11] The need to perform these functions imposed certain constraints on ski design, and the necessity to both track and turn required some compromises in design.

Researcher interviews with ski distributors and retailers noted some of the characteristics which this "balancing" involved. These experts detailed a number of critical features of a ski's design. The ski had to be flexible, designed with a cambered or arched shape to distribute the skier's weight over the entire ski, and manufactured so as to be straight without warp or twist. The tip of the ski played an important role. It had to be pointed and turned up to permit the skier to navigate difficult terrain and soft snow without changing direction. The bottom of the ski was also critical: it had to provide a slippery surface for ease of travel and had to be perfectly flat except for a center groove which helped the skier to achieve tracking stability. The edges of the ski had to be sharp for holding and turning purposes. All of those interviewed stressed that for maximum performance, the skier had to select the proper length ski.

recreation skier

Mr. Head found a proper combination of these elements for the recreational skier in his earliest metal ski. Designated the Standard, this model underwent substantial improvement over its 17-year history. Until 1960, however, the goal of providing the best ski for experts eluded Head and other makers of metal skis. Mr. Head said of this period, "During the early years at Head Ski, we were too busy making the best ski we could for the general public to spend much time developing a competition ski."

experts left out

detail

For experts, the basic complaint against metal skis was that they were too "soft" and tended to vibrate badly at racing speeds. This problem was substantially solved in 1960, when Head introduced its Vector model, to be followed in 1962 (and later entirely replaced) by the Competition. In these skis, an imbedded layer of neoprene dampened vibrations

---

[9] Track: If you point a ski down a slope and allow it to run freely, it should hold a straight course—over bumps and through hollows and on every type of snow surface.

[10] Traverse: A ski should be able to hold a straight line while moving diagonally across a slope over obstacles and various snow conditions.

[11] Turn: When a skier releases the edges of his skis, the skis must be capable of slipping sideways, and when edged, they must bite into the snow evenly. (A skiing turn is nothing more than a slideslip carved into an arc by the controlled bite of the edges.)

and considerably improved performance. Whereas in 1960 most competitors in the Squaw Valley Olympics had stuck to their wooden skis, by the end of 1962 Head skis were in wide use, and they had carried 77 racers out of 141 to positions among the top six contenders at races conducted by the International Professional Ski Race Association in Canada and the United States. Also about half the skis used in the U.S. National Junior and Senior Championships that year were Heads.

By 1966 Head had established itself as an important factor in the ski racing world. Two Americans had set the world speed record—106.527 mph—on Head skis. In major international competition in 1966, one third of all finishers in the top 10 places at all events were on Head skis, and Head was the outstanding single manufacturer on the circuit with 18 gold medals, 15 silver medals, and 15 bronze medals.

The 1968 Head line included a ski for every type of skier from the unskilled beginner to the top professional racer. The line was described in Head's *Ski Handbook* as follows:

> . . . the most important design consideration is you—the type of skier you are and where you ski. That's why your dealer was able to offer you nine different models of Head Skis to choose from. You can be sure the model he helped you select was the optimum—for you.
>
> STANDARD—THE MOST FORGIVING SKI: For beginners of average size and athletic ability up to intermediates learning stem christies. Also for the better, occasional skier who prefers an easy-going, lively, lightweight ski that practically turns for him.
>
> The *Standard* is medium soft in flex overall for easy turning and responsiveness. Engineered side camber and relative overall width contribute to ease and slow-speed stability. Its light weight and torsional rigidity make traversing and other basic maneuvers simple. Thin taper in the tip allows the *Standard* to cut easily through the heaviest snow instead of ploughing.
>
> Standard. $115. Thirteen sizes from 140 to 215 cm. Black top, sidewalls and bottom; white engraving.
>
> MASTER—MORE OF A CHALLENGE: For the skier who has mastered the basic techniques and wants to begin driving the skis and attacking the slope. As lively as the *Standard,* this is also the ski for the heavier, more athletic beginner who wants more "beef" underfoot.
>
> The *Master* is like the *Standard* in basic shape but thicker and heavier. The tip radius is longer for extra shock absorption. Slightly stiffer flex overall acts as a heavy-duty shock absorber over bumps.
>
> Master. $135. Nine sizes from 175 through 215 cm. Black top and sidewalls; blue base and engraving.
>
> THE FABULOUS 360—THE MOST VERSATILE SKI: Finest all-around ski ever made—for the skier beginning stem christies on through the expert class. Remarkable for its ease of turning as well as its steadiness and precision, the *360* is the serious skier's ski for attack or enjoyment on the slope, under any condition of snow or terrain.
>
> With its smooth-arcing flex pattern, the *360* has the supple forebody of the other recreational skis, but is slightly stiffer at the tail. Its side camber is similar to that of the *Giant Slalom.* Narrower overall than the *Standard* or *Master.* Rubber damping in the lightweight top-skin unit makes the *360* a very responsive ski, allowing the expert to control his turns beautifully and set his edges precisely. Tip splay is designed to give easiest entrance

through snow and to provide excellent shock absorption, particularly in heavily moguled areas.

The Fabulous 360. $155. Eleven sizes from 170 to 220 cm. Black top and sidewalls; yellow base and engraving.

SLALOM—THE HOT DOG: For the expert skier who likes to stay in the fall-line, slashing through quick short-radius turns on the steepest, iciest, slopes. The *Slalom* has been totally redesigned this year to fit the special needs of the expert recreational skier, who wants the lightest, fastest-reacting, and best ice-holding ski possible.

Slalom is Head's narrowest ski overall. And, thanks to the light-weight top-skin unit and core, it is also one of Head's lightest skis. Lightness and narrowness allow for carved or pivoted turns, reflex-fast changes in direction. Special engineered side camber and relative softness at the thin waist give the ultimate in "feel" and control on ice. Neoprene rubber gives the damping and torque necessary for a top-performance ice ski.

Slalom. $160. Five sizes from 190 to 210 cm. Black top and sidewalls. Racing red base and engraving.

DOWNHILL—BOMB!: Widest and heaviest Head ski, the *Downhill* is for the advanced skier—recreational or competitor—who wants to blast straight down the slope. It offers the ultimate in high-speed performance, tracking ability, and stability over bumps and moguls.

The long tip splay and supple forebody is the secret of the *Downhill's* exceptional speed advantage. It virtually planes over the surface of the slope. With its firm midsection and tail acting like the rudder of a hydroplane, the *Downhill* affords the skier utmost control coupled with great turning ability at slower speeds. Heavy duty topskin unit and added rubber damping contribute to the stability and high-speed "quietness" of the *Downhill*. This is the elite international-class racing ski, and experts have found it an excellent powder ski as well.

Downhill. $175. Seven sizes from 195 to 225 cm. Black top and sidewalls. Yellow base and engraving.

GIANT SLALOM—GRACE PLUS SPEED: The *GS* incorporates the best features of the *Downhill* and *Slalom* models. It offers the expert skier—recreational and/or competitor—the optimum in stable all-out speed skiing, combined with precise carving and holding ability in high-speed turns. It is another favorite on the international racing circuit.

The *Giant Slalom's* stability and precision come from a unique combination of sidecut and relatively stiff flex. The *GS* is similar to the *360* in overall dimensions, but has a stiffer flex pattern than the *360,* particularly underfoot. This gives the *GS* the versatility of the *360* but with greater control at high speeds. Tip splay is designed for maximum shock absorption and easy riding.

Giant Slalom. $165. Nine sizes from 175 to 215 cm. Black top and sidewalls. Yellow base and engraving.

YOUNGSTER'S COMPETITION—JUNIOR HOT DOG: Carrying the *Giant Slalom* engraving, this ski is designed for expert youngsters who want, and can handle, a faster, more demanding ski than the small-size *Standard.* Similar in cut and performance characteristics to the *Giant Slalom,* but without the *GS's* neoprene damping, to provide the junior racer with easier turning ability.

Youngster's Competition. $120. Two sizes, 160 and 170 cm. Black top and sidewalls. Yellow bottom and engraving.

SHORTSKI—FUN WITHOUT EFFORT: Not just a sawed-off *Standard,* but a totally different ski with totally different proportions. Very wide for its length, quite stiff overall, the *Shortski* is the only ski of its kind with an engineered side camber. Ideal for quick learning of the fundamentals of skiing. Also for the older or more casual skier who enjoys being on the slopes and wants the easiest-possible tracking and turning ski ever built.

Shortski. $115. Four sizes from 150 to 190 cm. Black top, sidewalls and bottom. White engraving.

DEEP POWDER—SHEER BUOYANCY ON THE SLOPES: Super-soft flexibility and buggy-whip suppleness allow this specialized ski to float in powder, while maintaining easy turning plus full control and tracking ability on packed slopes.

The *Deep Powder* is very wide and soft overall, with a "hinge-like" effect in the forebody that enables it to glide through the deepest powder.

Deep Powder. $115. Five sizes from 195 to 215 cm. Black top, sidewalls and bottom. White engraving.

Head was constantly experimenting with new designs and introducing minor modifications to improve the performance and durability of its product. When asked about a major change in product construction, such as to the fiber-reinforced plastic type ski, Mr. Head gave the following reply:

We think that the metal sandwich construction is the best material. We do not see this situation changing in the foreseeable future. Certainly now the other exotic materials are not gaining ground. They lack the versatility of application of the metal sandwich ski. The epoxy or fiber reinforced plastic have low durability and don't have the wide performance range of our skis.

We believe that the advantage of the metal ski is that you can build in any performance characteristic which you desire. Naturally, we have a research department investigating other materials, but until a major improvement is found, we should stick to our basic material. We can always build the best ski for beginners, and we can adapt that ski to get the performance required by experts.

MARKETING POLICIES

Head's emphasis on quality extended beyond the product to the dealer and service network. The company sold through only a limited number of franchised dealers, who had satisfied management that "they know something about skis and skiing." Ten district sales managers were employed, who sold to about 900 dealers throughout the United States. Of these about 85 percent were ski specialty shops, 12 percent were large full-line sporting goods stores, and the remainder were full-line department stores (see Exhibit 2). Head skis were distributed in Europe through an exclusive distributor, Walter Haensli of Klosters, Switzerland. In 1964 he sold 19 percent of Head's output. This figure appeared to be declining gradually.

Head believed that a Head franchise was valuable to a dealer. Many

Exhibit 2

Dealer Organization, 1962–1967
(franchised dealers)

Year	Number at beginning	Newly franchised	Terminated or not renewed	Number at end
1962	390	105	41	454
1963	454	136	30	560
1964	560	167	57	670
1965	670	96	39	727
1966	727 (est.)	n.a.	n.a.	900
1967	900 (est.)	30	n.a.	—

n.a.—Not available.
Note: In addition the franchised dealers had approximately 300 branches which are not included in the above figures.
Source: Company records.

large stores had wanted to sell Heads, but had been turned down. Saks Fifth Avenue had waited eight years before it was given a franchise. Mr. Head commented on dealer selection as follows:

> Getting Saks Fifth Avenue as a dealer is consistent with our operating philosophy of expecting the same quality from our dealers as from ourselves.
>
> Once they become a dealer, however, we get to know the people involved and work closely with them. Increasingly, we are recognizing the business value of providing more assistance and leadership to our dealers in helping them to do a better job for their customers.
>
> Even a large, well-managed department store or sporting goods store may need help in the specialized area of skis. They may need help in display stock selection, or even personnel selection. We are increasingly concerned about the type of personnel who sell skis. There is a high degree of dependence on the salesman. He must be a good skier himself.
>
> We have seen instances of two department stores of essentially identical quality in the same area where one store could sell 8 pairs of skis a year and the other 300 simply because of a different degree of commitment to getting the right man to sell. Skis can only be sold by a floor salesman who can ski and who can sell from personal experience.

The company was committed to the belief that selling skis was an exacting business. The ski size had to be matched to the individual's height and body weight, flexibility had to be chosen correctly depending on use, and bindings had to be mounted properly.

Following up on the initial sale, Head offered extensive customer service. Dealers were expected to have service facilities for minor repairs and the factory had facilities for sharpening edges, rebuilding the plastic portion of the ski, and matching a single ski if the mate had been broken beyond repair. Even in the busiest part of the season, service time was kept under three weeks.

In March 1967, Mr. Harold Seigle, the newly appointed president and chief operating officer of Head, sent out a "management news bulletin" outlining Head's marketing philosophy:

Harold Seigle — March '67 :

Marketing Philosophy

1. Our current selective dealer organization is one of Head Ski Company's most valuable assets, next to the product itself.
2. Our continued sales growth will be based on a market-by-market approach aimed at increasing the effectiveness of our present dealers and by the very selective addition of new dealers wherever present dealers prove to be inadequate rather than by mass distribution and merchandising techniques.
3. Our future marketing efforts, particularly personal selling, advertising, merchandising, and sales promotion, will be geared to the specific needs of our dealers to sell all Head Ski products.
4. We want and will have the finest sales forces in the industry . . . who rely upon personal integrity, service, and hard work to do a professional selling job rather than inside deals and short cuts.
5. We feel that, next to quality products, strong personal selling at the manufacturer's level and the retail level is paramount to our continued success and tends to transcend other facets of marketing that contribute to the sale of merchandise.

Advertising was done on a selective basis. An outside source reported as follows:

> The company invests about 2 percent of gross sales in advertising, split between the skiing magazines (50 percent) and *Sports Illustrated, The New Yorker,* and *Yachting*—"the same kind of people like to sail."
> The most effective promotion, however, is probably the ski itself. Head is delighted at the growing demand for his skis in the rental market. "We sold 10,000 pairs—almost 10 percent of our business—for rental last year," he points out, "and everyone who rents those skis becomes a prospect."[12]

To aid in placing rental skis, Head gave an additional 12 percent–15 percent discount on skis which a dealer purchased for rental. Ski rental was seen as the best way to introduce a customer to the ease of skiing on Heads.

The Head Ski Company approach was a "soft sell." Unlike many sporting goods companies, Head did not rely on personal endorsements of famous skiers. According to one executive, it was impossible under American Amateur rules even to have posters featuring an amateur skier. Professional endorsements were probably ineffective anyway, since so many other sporting goods companies used them, and most of the public knew that such endorsements could be bought. Head tried to get actual news pictures of famous skiers or racers using Head skis and winning. To make certain that top skiers would use Head skis, the company did lend skis to racers for one year. Even this practice was expensive and had to be tightly controlled. A good skier might need upward of nine pairs of skis a year, which would represent an expenditure of nearly $1,000. Head did feel this type of promotion yielded a secondary benefit of product development information which could not be overlooked.

Head had received many requests for a promotional film made in

---

[12] *Sales Management,* February 5, 1965.

conjunction with United Airlines showing famous ski slopes. Head was mentioned in the title, at the end, and in a few identifiable spots in the body of the show. This film was used by ski clubs and other organizations to promote interest in the sport.

Other Head promotion came as a result of skiwear and resort advertisements. As *Sales Management* put it:

> So great is the worldwide prestige of Head skis that although Howard Head claims he makes no promotional tie-in deals, the ski buff can hardly miss seeing the familiar black skis in ads for anything from parkas to ski resorts. They're status symbols.[13]

PRODUCTION

Head skis were produced in three steps. The detail department made up the various components which were to go into the assembly, including the core, the nose piece, the tail piece, the top plastic, the top and bottom skins, the running surface, and the edges. The separate pieces were then taken to the cavity department, where they were assembled. Here, too, the various layers were laid into a mold and heated and bonded under controlled time, temperature, and pressure. At this point the skis were roughed out on a band saw. From that time on, all work was done on the skis as a pair. In the finishing department, the skis were ground to final form, buffed, polished, and engraved.

Manufacture involved a great deal of handwork, of which 70 percent was characterized as requiring a high degree of skill. The basic nature of the assembly process meant that operations did not lend themselves to mass production techniques.

In May 1967, Head completed the fifth addition to the plant since its construction in 1959. Prior to the new addition, the plant contained 105,668 square feet, of which 93,040 was devoted to manufacturing and warehouse facilities, and 12,628 to office space. Included were a cafeteria, locker rooms, and shower areas for the workers.

Howard Head commented on the difficulty of the manufacturing process and on the relationship between costs and price:

> [There are] approximately 250 different operations, involving a great number of specially developed machines, tools, and processes. None of the processes is standard. It all had to be developed more or less from scratch.
>
> Some of the special-purpose machines involved are those for routing the groove in the bottom aluminum, for attaching the steel edges, and for profiling the ski after it comes out of the presses. Also there are the bonding procedures which require an unusual degree of control of heat and pressure cycles.
>
> Supplementing all the special-purpose machines, we have learned to make rather unusual use of band saws. A good example of a demanding band-saw operation is the profiling of the plywood and plastic core elements. Since the stiffness of a ski at any point goes up as the square of the spacing between the top and bottom sheets—i.e., the core thickness— a normal band-saw tolerance of about 0.010″ would grossly affect our flexi-

---

[13] Ibid.

bility pattern and would be out of the question. However, by special adapters and guides, we are actually able to band saw these parts in high production at about 10 seconds apiece to a tolerance of plus or minus 0.002″ over the entire contour.

An example of effective but low cost equipment in our factory is the press used to laminate 3′ x 10′ sheets of plywood core material to their corresponding sheets of sidewall plastic. This operation requires a total load of some 90,000 pounds. By using a roof beam as the reaction point, the floor for a base, and three screw jacks for pressure, we are able to produce enough material for 600 pairs of skis at one shot with equipment costing a total of about $250.

It's been our policy from the start to put absolute emphasis on quality of product. We never compromise on old material, nor reject a new one on the basis of cost. In principle, if better skis could be made out of sheet platinum, I suspect we would wind up with it. In other words, it is our policy to make the best product we can regardless of cost and then price it accordingly to the trade.

Production at Head was on a three-shift basis throughout the year, with skis being made for inventory during the slow months. There were over 600 employees.

Six attempts had been made to unionize the plant, but all had been rejected, several times by three-to-one majorities. One warehouse employee with 12 years' seniority said, "It's a nice place to work. We don't need a union. If you have a problem, Mr. Head will listen to you."

All employees received automatic step raises based on seniority, as well as merit reviews and raises. In addition there was a profit-sharing trust plan which in the past had generally added 6 percent–7 percent to the employees' salaries. These funds became fully vested after three years.

Another important benefit in which exempt salaried employees participated was the year-end bonus plan. Under this plan, three groups received different bonus rates. For the lowest paid group, the rate was 3 percent if pretax profits on sales were under 2 percent, but 10 percent–11 percent if profits were 8 percent–12 percent. For the middle group, no bonus was paid if profits were 2 percent or below, but the rate was 20 percent–22 percent if profits ranged between 8 percent and 12 percent. For the top group rates were not disclosed, but it was indicated that their bonus plan was even more steeply peaked. For most of the past several years, the payoffs had been at or near the upper range.

FINANCE

The initial financing of Head Ski Company was $6,000 from Howard Head's personal funds. In 1953 Mr. Head sold 40 percent of the stock in the company for $60,000. This, together with retained earnings and normal bank debt, financed expansion until 1960 when common stock was issued. Additional financing was required to continue the rapid expansion, and in January 1965 a $3,527,500 package was sold, made up of 5½ percent convertible subordinated debentures in face amount of $2,125,000, and 42,500 shares of common stock. Until the stock issue of

1965, Howard Head had owned 42.4 percent of the common stock, and the other directors and officers had owned 46.1 percent. At no time had there been any question about the commanding role of Howard Head when important decisions were made. Full conversion of the new issue would represent 17.1 percent ownership.

Expansion was viewed by many in the company as a defensive tactic. The belief was expressed that "if you do not grow as fast as the market will allow you to, you are taking substantial risk that someone else will come in and take that market away from you." In addition, the new funds provided capital for two diversifications started in 1966: The Head Ski and Sportswear Co., and the Head plastics division.

In spite of the drop in earnings growth, the stock market continued to evaluate Head's prospects at 29 to 60 times previous years' earnings. During the period January 1966 to July 1967, its stock sold in the range from 9⅜ to 17¾. As late as January 1965, however, the stock had sold at 22¾.

ORGANIZATION

As of June 1967, the Head Ski Company was organized along functional lines. Reporting to the president were the vice president for operations, the treasurer, and the directors of marketing, quality control, and the director of personnel. This organization pattern had been introduced by Mr. Harold Seigle when he was named chief operating officer on January 16, 1967 (see Exhibit 3).

Of the 26 men shown on the organization chart, 12 had been with Head one year or less. When asked about the potential difficulties of that situation, Mr. Head responded,

> I would only say that if you are to have a lot of new people, you must have one man in command who is an experienced and gifted professional at utilizing people. My job is to support and use that man.

Mr. Head reviewed the history of the organization which had led to the current structure as follows:

> I think that this is typical of the kind of business that starts solely from an entrepreneurial product basis, with no interest or skills in management or business in the original package. Such a business never stops to plan. The consuming interest is to build something new and to get acceptance. The entrepreneur has to pick up the rudiments of finance and organizational practices as he goes along. Any thought of planning comes later. Initially he is solely concerned with the problems of surviving and building. Also, if the business is at all successful, it is so successful that there is no real motivation to stop and obtain the sophisticated planning and people-management techniques. Such a business is fantastically efficient as long as it can survive. One man can make all of the important decisions. There is no pyramidal team structure.
>
> In our case this approach worked quite successfully until about 1955 when we sold 10,000 pairs of skis and reached the $500,000 sales level. The next five years from 1955 to 1960 saw a number of disorganized attempts to acquire and use a more conventional pyramidal organizational

Exhibit 3

Organization Chart
(June 1967)

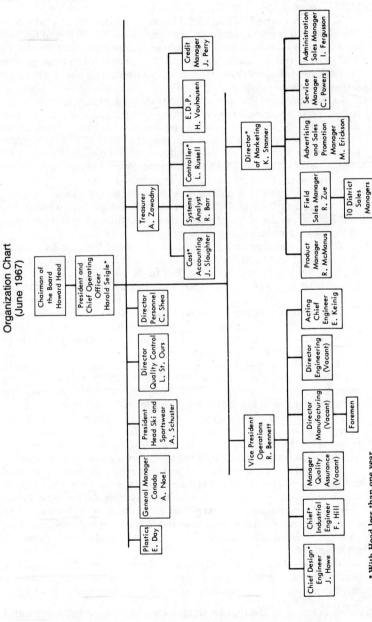

* With Head less than one year.
Source: Company records.

system. To put it succinctly, what was efficient at the $500,000 level was increasingly inefficient as we reached $1 million, then $2 million in sales. One man just couldn't handle it. I made too many mistakes. It was like trying to run an army with only a general and some sergeants. There were just no officers, to say nothing of an orderly chain of command.

In 1960 came the first successful breakthrough, where I finally developed the ability to take on a general manager who later became an executive vice president. It was hard for me to learn to operate under this framework. The most striking thing missing from this period was a concept of people-management. I spent five years gradually learning not to either over- or under-delegate.

Let me interject that the final motivation necessary to make a complete transition to an orderly company came because the company got into trouble in 1965–66. Even five years after the beginning of a team system, the company got into trouble, and this was the final prod which pushed me to go all the way. It is interesting that it took 12 years. Up until 1960 the company was totally under my direction. From 1960 to 1965 we stuttered between too much of my direction and not enough.

The chief difficulty for me was to learn to lay down a statement of the results required and then stay out of details. The weakness was in finding a formula of specifying objectives, then giving freedom as long as the objectives were met.

The appointment of Hal Seigle as president brought us a thoroughly sophisticated individual who can bring us the beginning of big business methods. On my part, this change has involved two things: first, my finally recognizing that I wanted this kind of organization; second, the selection of a man with proven professional management skills.

Unfortunately, with an entrepreneur, there are only two courses which can be taken if the company is to grow beyond a certain size. He can get the hell out, or he can really change his method of operation. I am pleased that this company has made the transition.

Now more than ever the company is using my special skills and abilities, but I am no longer interfering with an orderly and sophisticated management and planning system. We have given the company new tools to operate with, and I have not pulled the rug out from under them.

I am reserving my energies for two things. First, there is a continuation of my creative input—almost like a consultant to the company. Second, I have taken the more conventional role of chairman and chief executive officer. In this role I devote my efforts to planning and longer range strategy.

I feel that I can serve in both capacities. I can only be successful in the role of creative input if I can be solely a consultant without authority. It has to be made clear in this role that anything said is for consideration only. It has been demonstrated that this role is consultative, since some of my suggestions have been rejected. I like this role because I like the freedom. I can think freer, knowing that my suggestions will be carefully reviewed.

Of course, in areas of real importance like new product lines such as binding or boot, adding new models to the ski line, or acquisitions, etc., I must exert authority, channeled through the president.

Prior to coming to Head, Mr. Seigle had been vice president and general manager of a $50 million consumer electronics division of a $150 million company. His appointment was viewed as "contributing to a more professional company operating philosophy." He hoped to introduce more formalized methods of budget control and to "preside over the transition from a 'one-man' organization to a traditionally conceived functional pattern."

Mr. Seigle introduced a budgeting system broken down into 13 periods each year. Reports were to be prepared every four weeks comparing target with actual for each of the revenue or expense centers, such as marketing, operations, the staff functions, and the three subsidiaries. The hope was eventually to tie the bonus to performance against budget. Previously statements had been prepared every four weeks, but only to compare actual results against previous years' results.

Being new to the company, Mr. Seigle found that much of his time was being spent on operating problems. He believed, however, that as the budget system became completely accepted and operational, he would be able to devote more of his time to looking ahead and worrying about longer term projects. He said: "Ideally, I like to be working 6 to 18 months ahead of the organization. As a project gets within six months of actual operation, I will turn it over to the operating managers." He had hired a manager for corporate planning with whom he worked closely.

Under the previous organization from March 1966 until Mr. Seigle's appointment, Howard Head had presided directly over the various departments and marketing functions. There was no overall marketing director at that time. Even in the period from 1960 to 1966 when there was an executive vice president, Mr. Head indicated that he had concerned himself with the operating details of the business.

A VIEW TOWARD THE FUTURE

Head's first diversification was to ski poles. These were relatively simple to manufacture and were sold through existing channels. As with the skis, Head maintained the highest standards of quality and style. The poles were distinguished from competition by their black color and adoption of the tapered shape and extra light weight which at the time were unavailable on other high-priced, quality ski poles. Head's prices were well toward the upper end of the spectrum: $24.50, as compared with as little as $5 for some brands. Success in selling poles encouraged the company to look at other products it might add.

Two further steps taken were toward diversification in late 1966 when Head formed a plastics division and established a subsidiary, Head Ski and Sportswear Co.

The plastic division's activity centered on high molecular weight plastics. In March 1967 a press release was issued concerning this activity:

> Head Ski Co., Inc., has signed a license agreement with Phillips Petroleum Company . . . to use a new method developed by Phillips for extruding ultra-high molecular weight high density polyethylene into finished products. . . .
>
> Developmental equipment has been installed at the Head plant here and limited quantities of sheet have been extruded and tested in the run-

ning surface of Head skis with excellent results. . . . Production of ski base material is scheduled for this Spring. . . .

In addition to its own running surface material, the Head plastics division has been developing special ultra-high molecular weight high density polyethylene compound to serve a variety of industrial applications. . . .

Ultra-high molecular weight high density polyethylene is an extremely tough abrasion-resistant thermoplastic capable of replacing metal and metal alloys in many industrial areas. Compared with regular high density resins, the ultra-high molecular weight material has better stress-cracking resistance, better long-term stress life and less notch sensitivity.

The diversification into skiwear was considered by company executives to be the more important move. Howard Head talked about the logic of this new venture as follows:

Skiwear is "equipment" first and fashion second. We are satisfied that our line of skiwear is better than anything done before. It represents the same degree of attention to detail which has characterized our hardware line.

The president of the new subsidiary, Alex Schuster, said:

Many people thought that Head should stay in hardware such as poles, bindings, and wax. As I see it, however, by going into skiwear we are taking advantage of ready-made distribution and reputation. There is no reason why the good will developed through the years can't be related to our endeavor.

This new market offers a greater potential and reward than the more hardware-oriented areas. Any entry into a new market has difficulties. These can only be solved by doing things right and by measuring up to the Head standards. Having a Head label commits us to a standard of excellence.

Assuming that we live up to those standards, we shall be able to develop into a supplier in a small market but with formidable potential. We are creating a skill base for further diversification.

Our products are engineered, not designed. We are concerned with the engineered relationship among fabric, function, and fit. The engineering details are not always obvious, but they are related to functional demands. Emphasis is placed on function over fashion, yet there is definite beauty created out of concern for function. We are definitely in tune with fashion trends.

[See Exhibit 4 for examples of the new products.]

We will provide a complete skiing outfit—pants, parkas, sweaters, accessories, sox, and gloves. We will offer a total coordinated look.

Along with the design innovations, we shall offer innovations in packaging, display and promotion. We have to go beyond simply preparing the proper apparel.

Head Ski and Sportswear did both manufacturing and subcontracting. The products which had the highest engineering content were made in the Head plant. Sweaters, with less engineering, were contract-made to Head specifications by one of Europe's leading sweater manufacturers.

The collection was first shown to dealers in April 1967 and was scheduled for public release for the 1967–68 skiing season. Initial response

Exhibit 4

SAMPLES OF THE NEW HEAD SKIWEAR

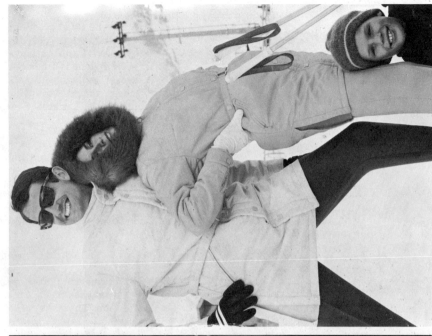

Exhibit 4 *(Continued)*

SAMPLES OF THE NEW HEAD SKIWEAR

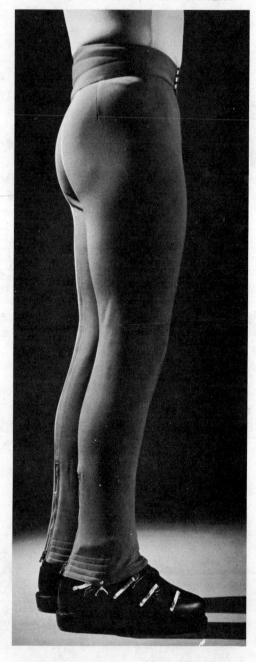

by dealers and by the fashion press had been extremely encouraging. *Ski Business* reported:

> HEAD'S UP.
>
> . . . way up, in fact 194 percent ahead of planned volume on its premier line of skiwear.
>
> Anyone who expected Howard Head's entry into the world of fashion to be presented in basic black was in for a surprise. Ironically the skiwear collection that blasted off with the hottest colors in the market is offered by a man who is totally color blind. . . .
>
> *On pants:* The $55 pant was the big surprise. It was our top seller—way beyond expectations—and the basic $45 pant came in second in sales. Another surprise was the $70 foam-waisted pant for which we only projected limited sales—it's a winner. . . .
>
> *On orders:* Way beyond expectations. Ninety percent of the orders are with ski shops and 10 percent with the department stores. Naturally we are committed to selling Head Ski dealers but it definitely is not obligatory.[14]

The sportswear subsidiary had been set up in a separate plant five miles from Head's Timonium headquarters. It was an autonomous operation with a separate sales force and profit responsibility. The initial premise was that the sportswear should be distributed through current Head dealers, although according to Mr. Seigle the marketing decisions of the sportswear division would be made independently of decisions in the ski division. Although Head dealers were offered the Head sportswear line, it was not sold on an exclusive basis. Distribution would be directly from factory salesmen to the dealer. Within the company, the necessity for a separated and different type of sales force was acknowledged. As one executive phrased it, "I can't imagine our ski salesmen trying to push soft goods. Our salesmen got into the business first and foremost because they were excellent skiers." As with skis and poles, the product line was to be maintained at the high end of the spectrum in both quality and price.

When asked about future growth potential, Mr. Seigle replied that he believed Head would continue to grow rapidly in the future. He saw the potential of doubling the ski business in the next five years. Although he characterized the sportswear business as a "good calculated risk," he believed it offered the potential of expanding to $5 to $8 million per year. Beyond that he felt that Head might go in three possible directions. First, he believed that Head should once again explore the opportunities and risks of moving into the other price segments of the ski market, either under another brand or with a nonmetallic ski. Although he believed that by selling in a lower price range Head could sell 50,000 or more pairs of skis, the risks were also high. Second, he felt that Head should explore the opportunity in other related ski products, such as boots or bindings. Third, he felt that eventually Head should expand into other specialty sporting goods, preferably of a contraseasonal nature.

---

[14] *Ski Business,* May–June 1967.

In looking to these new areas, Mr. Seigle had formulated a two-part product philosophy as follows:

> Any new product which Head will consider should:
> 1. Be consistent with the quality and prestige image of Head Skis.
> 2. Should entail one or more of the following characteristics:
>   a. High innovative content.
>   b. High engineering content.
>   c. High style appeal.
>   d. Be patentable.
>
> We will consider getting into new products through any of the normal methods such as internal product development, product acquisition, or corporate acquisition. If we are to move into a new area we definitely want to have a product edge. For example, if we were to manufacture a boot, we would want to be different. We would only seriously consider it if we had a definite product advantage such as if we were to develop a high quality plastic boot.

Howard Head, in speaking of the future, voiced the following hopes:

> I would like to see Head grow in an orderly fashion sufficient to maintain its present youth and resiliency. That would mean at least 20 percent–25 percent per year. This statement does not preclude the possibility that we might grow faster. We believe the ski business alone will grow 20 percent–25 percent per year. As our staff capabilities grow, we will probably branch into other areas.
>
> As to our objectives for the next five years, I would say that the first corporate objective is to maintain healthy growth in the basic ski business. It is the taproot of all that is good in Head. Second, we must be certain that any new activity is carefully selected for a reasonable probability of developing a good profit and an image platform consistent with the past activity of Head.

APPENDIX*

TYPES OF SKIS

ELEMENTS OF A WELL-DESIGNED SKI

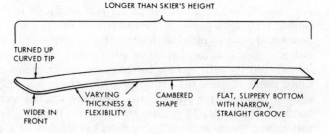

LONGER THAN SKIER'S HEIGHT

TURNED UP CURVED TIP

PHOTO IMPRESSION SHOWS HOW SKI MUST TORQUE OVER BUMPS

WIDER IN FRONT

VARYING THICKNESS & FLEXIBILITY

CAMBERED SHAPE

FLAT, SLIPPERY BOTTOM WITH NARROW, STRAIGHT GROOVE

---

*Source: *Skiing International Yearbook, 1967*, pp. 63–68. Copyright by Ziff-Davis Publishing Co.

Wood skis

If you are on a tight budget, well-designed wood skis at low prices are available from domestic and foreign manufacturers. Wood is a bundle of tubular cellulose cells bound together in an elastic medium called lignin. The internal slippage of wood skis not only lets them torque over the bumps in traverse, but damps any tendency to vibrate or chatter on hard rough surfaces. There are wood skis for any snow, any speed, and they are fun to ski on. Their only problem is a lack of durability. Wood skis are fragile. Besides, as wood skis are used, the internal slippage of the fibers increases, and they lose their life.

WOOD SKI CROSS-SECTION

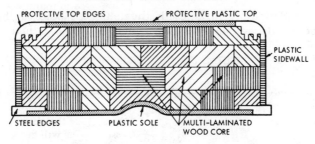

In choosing a wood ski, it is probably wise to pay more than the minimum price. Multiple laminations of hickory or ash, a soft flex pattern, interlocking edges, polyethylene base, plastic top and sidewalls, tip and tail protectors are some of the features a beginner or intermediate should look for in a better wood ski. When you get past the $40 to $70 range, your own dealer's recommendations will be your best guarantee of value.

FRP skis

A few years ago there were only a handful of "epoxy" skis on the market, and skiers were eyeing them with mixed interest and distrust. Now the available models have multiplied almost unbelievably. New companies have been formed, and many of the established manufacturers have now brought out versions of their own. The plastic skis are still new enough for most skiers to be confused about their true nature— and with good reason, since there are so many types.

The word *epoxy* is part of the confusion. The true family resemblance of all the skis that are currently being lumped under that designation is the use of glass fibers locked into a plastic medium to create layers of great strength. The plastics engineers use the term *fiber-reinforced plastic* (FRP) to designate this type of structural solution. It is very strong.

The reinforcing layers used in these new designs derive their strength from the combined strength of millions of fine glass fibers or threads locked in the plastic layer. The potential strengths of materials in this family of structural plastics can exceed those of aluminum or steel.

Unfortunately, there is no simple way to evaluate them or describe the materials actually in use. The wide variety of glass fibers, resins, and systems of molding and curing the fiber-reinforced layer produces a wide range of results. These can be evaluated only by laboratory tests or, finally, by actual in-service results.

FRP materials are being used for all sorts of sporting goods, industrial, and space-age applications. The strength-to-weight ratio is attractively high, and the possibility of creating new reinforced shapes by means of molding operations has proved to be attractive enough to encourage a great deal of experimentation. Skis seem to adapt to this structural technique.

Metal skis

In the search for more durable skis, the metal skis took over the quality market about a decade ago, and are widely accepted as ideal for both

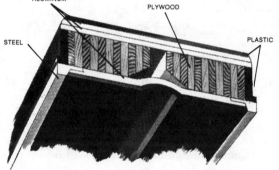

Northland Golden Jet—Cross-laminated fir plywood core with no filler in center, full-length bonded steel edge, aluminum sheets on both the top and the bottom.

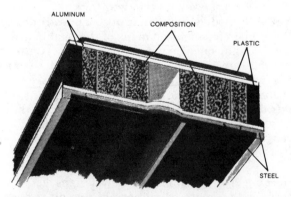

Hart Javelin—Grainless core of pressed particles, continuous full-length steel L edge welded to steel sheet, revealed aluminum top edge, phenolic plastic top.

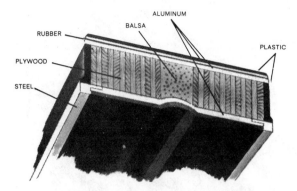

Head Competition—Cross-laminated fir plywood core, rubber damping layer on top of structure, full-length bonded steel L edge, high-density plastic base.

FRP CROSS-SECTIONS

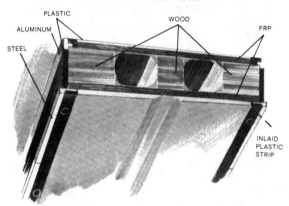

Kneissl White Star—Epoxy sandwich with interrupted wood core for lightness, sectional steel L edge screwed-in, aluminum top edge, two-color inlaid base.

A&T K2—Vestigial core of pine, full wrap-around construction, bonded full-length L edge. ABS plastic top sheet. Bonded edges have tab construction for strength.

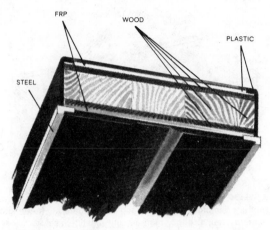

STEEL FRP WOOD PLASTIC

Yamaha Hi-Flex—FRP sandwich, hardwood core with grain running lengthwise, full-length bonded stainless steel L edges on bottom, with top edges of celluloid.

recreational skier and expert. Except for specialized racing uses, the wooden skis have been largely outmoded in the better ski market. Today, the fiber-reinforced plastic designs are the only challengers to the primacy of the metals.

Metal skis obtain their strength from aluminum sheets that are light in weight but very strong. The structure of a metal ski is somewhat like an "I" beam; when the ski is bent, the bottom sheet is stretched and the top sheet is compressed. The core material serves as the web—the vertical portion of the "I"—and must be attached to the top and bottom metal sheets securely enough to resist the shearing stress that occurs when the ski is bent.

Service potential of metal skis

The possibility of rebuilding and refinishing metal skis has been one of the key sales attractions of the metal ski in this country. So long as bonding remains intact, only the effects of wear and tear—rocks, skis banging together, rough treatment in transportation, etc.—limit the life of the skis. The possibility of having the plastic surfaces and edges, or even the structural members themselves, replaced has strong appeal for the skier investing well over $100 in his skis. The rebuilding potential also tends to keep the trade-in and used resale value of the skis higher, making it less expensive for the skier to move to higher performance or more recent models as his skiing ability—or his desire for something new—dictates. The American companies were the first to develop rebuilding techniques, but more recently European factories have been establishing service centers in the U.S.

There are three basic elements of FRP construction: the plastic material or resin; the glass fibers themselves; and the method of combining, curing, and shaping the composite reinforcing layer. Variation of any of these three elements affects the characteristics of the end product.

Service potential of FRP skis

One of the problems facing the manufacturers of fiber-reinforced plastic skis has been how to service and rebuild them—once the normal wear and tear of skiing has taken its toll. Only the metal skis, it has seemed, could be refinished and rebuilt.

Though it is true that you cannot heat up an FRP ski, melt the glue, resand, recoat, and reconstruct it quite as easily as you can a metal ski, progress has been made in this direction during the past season. Several manufacturers have set up regional service centers.

What these various service centers can accomplish is considerable. They are replacing bases and edges. They are renewing and refinishing top surfaces. In some cases, the structural fiberglass members can be separated from the wood core and replaced, producing in effect a brand-new ski. The sum of all this is real benefit to the average skier, who is unwilling to discard a pair of skis every season or so. The gap between metal and FRP skis, as far as service potential is concerned, is being narrowed. You will find that the costs range over approximately the same spread as the metal skis and that guarantee provisions are similar.

Charles River Breeding Laboratories

DESCRIBED by a competitor as the General Motors of the laboratory animal industry, the Charles River Breeding Laboratories of Wilmington, Massachusetts had achieved major corporate success both in terms of financial results as well as in technical reputation. Company sales were $25,000 in 1950 with operating net profit of $1,400; comparable 1975 fiscal year data were $15,405,100 and $1,565,600. The company's technical publication *The Charles River Digest*, unique to the industry, circulated quarterly to 13,000 members of the international research community.

Charles River specialized in the production of scientifically bred, high-quality laboratory animals for pharmaceutical and chemical companies, commercial testing laboratories, hospitals and universities. Other firms in the industry manufactured cages and scientific equipment, feed and bedding supplies, animal by-products for use in research, and operated independent testing laboratories.

Charles River's first and still primary products were laboratory rats and mice; in 1976, sales of these animals comprised over 90 percent of the company's sales revenues. The company had been the leader in the breeding and introduction of disease-free rats and mice. Beginning in 1955, Charles River commercialized a process known as COBS®, allowing the company to produce disease-free animals which enabled researchers to conduct more effective experimental research. In 1976 this process had been adopted widely by breeders throughout the world.

The executive group of Charles River had been relatively stable over the past decade with company policy being to promote from within whenever possible. Executives described Charles River as a "family firm" and took pride in the Foster family's public generosity in giving Brandeis University a bio-medical research laboratory building and the furnishing of a contemporary gallery at the Boston Museum of Fine Arts.

54

In reviewing his company's current situation, Dr. Henry L. Foster, D.V.M., president and chief executive, commented, "So far it has been great. We just do what is necessary to produce the best and the results follow. When we went public, we announced a 15 percent–20 percent per year growth goal in both sales and earnings and we are sticking to that target. Once you become a public company, you enter a race and are always out of breath.

"Observers and investors are now asking—what next? We have to deal with that question *now* since the action lead time is a long one. Of course we will continue to grow in our basic animal product lines—but that is not enough. We are going to have to expand into new areas and there are lots of opportunities.

"Where do we go now? How does a manager answer that question? And, how do I organize to get these decisions made? We want internal growth, new product additions and acquisitions. But how do we do this without getting a case of corporate indigestion? We don't want to eat *too* much but we want a good meal."

LABORATORY ANIMAL USE

Laboratory animals, primarily rats and mice, were the basis for product safety testing, drug development and human health research, especially cancer treatment research. Most pharmaceuticals, cosmetics, toiletries, and food additives were tested on animals for toxic side efects before the FDA would approve their sale. Lab animals were used to measure side effects of environmental pollutants and industrial and agricultural chemicals. Medical research on the causes and treatment of cancer, heart disease, nutritional deficiencies and birth defects also relied on experiments with laboratory animals. Studies using lab animals took place at drug companies, independent testing laboratories, universities, hospitals, and a variety of government agencies. The largest governmental users were the National Institutes of Health, the Food and Drug Administration, and the Environmental Protection Agency.

There were two important distinctions to be made about laboratory animals. One refers to the genetic makeup of the animals: whether they were inbred or outbred. The second concerns the method of raising the animals and their consequent state of health: "conventional" breeding methods versus various pathogen-free" or "disease-free" methods.

Inbred versus outbred lab animals

Although any animal may be inbred or outbred, these terms usually referred to genetic and physical characteristics of the various rodent species[1] which accounted for over 98 percent of all lab animals used in

---

[1] Laboratory animals were distinguished by *species* and *strains*. As defined by the National Academy of Sciences in *Animals for Research,* a *species* is all animals of the same kind that can (actually or potentially) mate together and produce fertile offspring. Examples of common species names are cats, dogs, mice, hamsters, etc. A *strain* is a subset of a species comprised of a group of animals of known ancestry maintained by a deliberate mating system, generally with some distinguishing characteristics.

the United States. The most common rodents were: mice, rats, guinea pigs, and hamsters.

Inbred animals were brother-sister mated for a minimum of 20 generations to produce specific heritable characteristics, such as susceptibility or immunity to a particular disease. For example, the C-3H inbred mouse strain carried a virus which can develop breast cancer in its young, while the SHR (spontaneous hypertensive) rat consistently exhibited blood pressure above 180°. These and hundreds of other inbred rodent strains were used to understand the effects of diseases and to develop drugs and other treatment methods. The largest user of inbred animals was the National Cancer Institute, but medical and drug researchers in universities, hospitals, pharmaceutical firms, and contract testing laboratories also required inbred animals. Inbred strains were more expensive than outbred because of the additional labor and record keeping required by brother x sister mating.

Breeders produced outbred animals by consistently avoiding brother-sister mating in order to produce a heterogeneous population. Heterogeneous populations were made up of animals with a variety of characteristics, much like the human population. These animals were used to test overall product safety and effectiveness. Many more outbred animals were used than inbred, and the largest consumer groups for outbreds were pharmaceutical companies and independent testing labs.

"Conventional" versus "disease-free" animals

"Conventional" methods of lab animal breeding involved putting animals in an enclosed pen or cage, and feeding, watering, and cleaning them. The breeder then waited for the animals to mate and sold the offspring as soon as they were weaned.

Until the mid-1950s, the "conventional" method was the principal way commercial breeders raised lab animals. It was a high-risk, labor-intensive business with many small-scale participants. Risk came from the frequent outbreaks of disease which could rapidly destroy a breeder's entire animal inventory. Commercial breeding businesses were small-scale operations because they were part-time endeavors and few breeders would risk the capital necessary to support larger scale breeding. Animals properly housed and cared for under small-scale conventional methods could sometimes perform as well as animals reared under the more elaborate "disease-free" methods described below. All animal species and both inbred and outbred strains could be raised in a "conventional" manner.

In 1955 Charles River introduced the first of various disease-free animal breeding methods to commercial lab rodent breeding. Disease-free breeding techniques improved animal health, reduced the risk of losing animals from disease, but required special breeding facilities and processes. By the mid-1970s almost half of all lab rodents were raised using one or more of the following "disease-free" techniques.

Specific pathogen-free (SPF) animals were free of specific parasites, and microorganisms which could impair their health, for example, salmonellosis.[2] The specific pathogens eliminated depended both on the species and on the breeder supplying the animal. The process required obtaining a healthy animal through selection or through chemotherapy to eliminate one or more specific pathogens and then following strict quarantine procedures to keep the animals from outside contamination.

Cesarean derivation was a technique which prevented diseases and parasites from being transferred from mother to her young, and resulted in healthier longer living, more vigorous animals. The process is termed a hysterectomy, because the mother's entire uterus containing the pups is removed shortly before normal birth would occur. The uterus is then introduced, using sterile techniques, into a germ-free plastic bubble where the pups are surgically removed and then nurtured by a germ-free foster mother or hand-fed sterile milk. The animals could then remain in a germ-free environment or be placed in a barrier system (see below).

Germ-free animals were cesarean-derived in a germ-free environment, as described above, and were continuously maintained in a germ-free isolator. They were completely free of all identifiable bacteria, viruses, fungi, protozoa, or other parasites (collectively called flora). The most common type of isolator was a two foot by five foot completely sealed clear plastic chamber. All water, feed, and bedding were sterilized, and researchers handled the animals through rubber gloved sleeves which protruded into the isolator. Animals could die within 12 to 24 hours if removed from their germ-free bubble. The advantage of using germ-free animals was that a researcher could be more certain that any animal abnormalities were directly related to a research procedure rather than due to an environmentally induced disease.

Cesarean-derived-barrier-reared (or barrier-sustained) animals began as germ-free pups delivered by hysterectomy. Specific flora were then associated with the animals so that they developed normal digestive and immunological systems, enabling them to survive outside of the germ-free isolators. The animals were housed in barrier buildings which were equipped with filtered air systems, temperature and humidity controls, autoclaves to sterilize feed and bedding, and controlled personnel access in order to prevent contamination.

Barrier facilities and germ-free equipment required substantial capital investment. A plastic germ-free bubble, for example, to house 50 mice cost $400 in 1976. (Prior to the development of plastic isolators in the mid-50s, a steel isolator cost $5,000–$10,000.) There were different degrees of barrier systems and each company employed a unique combination of barrier styles. The simplest method provided a number of separate rooms for animals and controlled the direction of air flow and personnel from "clean" to "dirty" areas. The most sophisticated facilities involved the construction of many small breeding rooms and corridors with extensive air conditioning and filtration systems, sterilizing facilities for equipment, feed and bedding, and elaborate personnel

---

[2] Salmonellosis, in man, is a type of "food poisoning" which can cause severe dehydration.

locks. One industry source estimated the minimum, initial investment for an acceptable small-scale barrier facility to be at least $500,000.

Scope of animal-based research and testing

The majority of laboratory animals were used in human health-related research, drug development, and drug testing. According to the National Instiues of Health (NIH), U.S. government expenditures for research and treatment development totaled $1.5 billion in 1975.[3] U.S. pharmaceutical firms spent $930 million on research and development in 1974, according to the Pharmaceutical Manufacturers' Association. Pharmaceutical companies accounted for about 50 percent of the dollar volume of animals purchased, and government-funded research purchases accounted for over 20 percent.

The cost of the compound tested, physical facilities, and salary costs for Ph.D.s, M.D.s and technicians were the major research budget expense items. One industry source estimated that, of the $930 million pharmaceutical companies spent to screen 700,000 new compounds in 1974, lab animal purchases accounted for 5 percent of the total and lab animal maintenance accounted for an additional 5 percent of R&D expenditures.

Animal usage by species

Rats and mice were the most widely used laboratory animals because they were small, readily available, and inexpensive. Hundreds of strains of mice and rats had been developed to be hosts for specific human cancer tumors or to exhibit signs of a specific disease such as arthritis. However, each species and strain had characteristics which were preferred for different types of research, and consequently there was limited substitutability among species and strains.

Dr. Joseph Mayo, director of the Animal Breeding Program at the National Cancer Institute (NCI) and a former researcher, explained why mice were widely used to evaluate cancer treatment drugs.

> First of all, through careful genetic control, mice can be bred to develop a susceptibility to a particular tumor. Secondly, mice are small and easy to handle, so the expense of housing and feeding the animals is minimized. More importantly, it means that the dosage level can be low. Vincristine, a compound we are testing now, interfered with cell division and costs $100,000 a gram.

U.S. research used 41.7 million animals each year and a comparable number, Dr. Foster estimated, were used annually in Europe. Rats and mice accounted for 96 percent of all laboratory animals used in the

---

[3] Of the total $1.5 billion NIH budget, $1.1 billion was allocated to research conducted by various agencies of the NIH itself (e.g., $30 million for the National Cancer Institute's Division of Cancer Treatment), or to researchers in universities, hospitals, and medical schools. Four hundred million dollars was allocated to contract research and testing by independent commercial testing laboratories such as Arthur D. Little or Hazelton, by universities, and by pharmaceutical firms. Much of this $400 million allocation supported animal-based research.

United States, with rabbits, guinea pigs, hamsters, dogs, cats, and monkeys also popular research subjects. Table 1 shows the number of animals used yearly for U.S. research by species. "Wild animals," a heterogeneous category of animals collected from nature, includes amoebas, frogs, marine animals, cattle, poultry, lions and elephants, most of which were used in agricultural and veterinary research.

Table 1

U.S. LABORATORY ANIMAL USAGE
BY SPECIES, 1974

Species	Number
Mice...........................	30,000,000
Rats...........................	10,000,000
Guinea pigs....................	430,400
Hamsters......................	430,800
Rabbits.......................	425,600
Dogs..........................	199,200
Cats..........................	74,000
Primates......................	51,300
Wild animals..................	81,021
Total.........................	41,692,321

Source: Mice and rats estimates by Charles River Breeding Laboratories and the Institute for Laboratory Animal Resources. Other species data from *Animal Welfare Enforcement 1974*, Report of the Secretary of Agriculture, U.S. Department of Agriculture.

Lab animal performance requirements

Lab animal users considered animal performance and availability more important than price. One industry observer noted:

> Time pressures on researchers are great. Pharmaceutical companies are under pressure to meet market introduction dates and academic research grants usually have a calendar year limit. Therefore any delay in receiving the right number of animals at the right time, or receiving animals that die before the experiment is concluded, has cost the researcher both time and money far beyond the mere cost of the animals.

Lab animal performance during an experiment depended on the animal's state of health when it arrived at the researchers' facility. Breeding the animals in a healthy environment and minimizing transportation stress were the most important determinants of animal health. A breeder's ability to supply a healthy animal depended on obtaining a clean animal to start his breeding colony and then on maintaining production processes and facilities adequate to prevent disease introduction. The division leader of Arthur D. Little's Tumor Screening Program for the National Cancer Institute, Mr. Wodinsky, discussed the importance of familiarity with a breeder's operations in ascertaining animal quality.

> Most suppliers now offer cesarean-derived animals, so the basic animals do not differ much among breeders. The difference is facilities and

production colony management that keeps the animals separate and healthy. It is the people working for them that are the critical factor in controlling contamination. I know the actual setup of all the breeders who supply us.

Dr. Henry Agersborg, associate director of research for Wyeth Laboratories, elaborated on the problem:

> A rat can lose 20% of its body weight in a day and will die of starvation in 5 to 7 days. Loss of weight during transport is a shock to the animal's system. It may regain weight rapidly, but it might be permanently weakened and break down part way into an experiment. That is why transport stress can be a potential problem and why we prefer a breeder who can guarantee same day delivery. A local breeder only has an advantage if he does not use a public carrier. REA can take three days to transport animals 12 miles.

Almost half of the animals used in laboratory research were transported by air freight. Airborne, an air freight forwarder specializing in lab animals, confirmed the problems of timely delivery and promoted its services which monitored the location and status of shipments. Product availability and reliable delivery were important to researchers in three ways. First was obtaining the specific strain and species required among the several hundred varieties raised. Second was securing enough animals of the specific age, sex, and weight required to meet the needs of several hundred to several thousand animals per program per week. Finally, delivery reliability was very important because research procedures were frequently standardized on a particular breeder's animals.

INDUSTRY TRENDS

An industry observer identified four trends which were having a major impact on the laboratory animal breeding industry in the mid-1970s. These included slower market growth, more sophisticated uses of lab animals, rising quality standards for animals and facilities, and consolidation among breeders.

Slower market growth

Between the late 1940s and early 1970s, the demand for laboratory animals had grown from a few million mice and rats to approximately 42 million animals of many species. The most rapid growth in demand had occurred between 1965 and 1970 when volume doubled. The rapid growth in the mid-60s was spurred by a large influx of funds into government-sponsored research on cancer and viral diseases in combination with stricter Food and Drug Administration test data requirements on the efficacy and safety of new drugs. In the early 70s a cutback in federal funding for health research had slowed the growth of lab animal use for basic research, but pharmaceutical and chemical company use of lab animals for testing continued to expand at a rate of 7 percent–

12 percent per year. By 1974, government-sponsored research expenditures had resumed a growth rate of 5 percent to 10 percent per year. Table 2 shows U.S. drug company research and development expenditures from 1950 to 1974.

Table 2
U.S. DRUG INDUSTRY RESEARCH AND DEVELOPMENT EXPENDITURES, 1950–1974 (in thousands)

Year	Expenditures
1950	$ 39,000
1955	91,000
1960	212,000
1965	351,000
1970	619,000
1974	930,000

Source: Pharmaceutical Manufacturers Association, *Annual Survey Report 1973–74* and *1968–69*.

More sophisticated uses of lab animals

Continuing from the late 1960s was a long-term trend toward increased use of "life-span" studies of animals in both research and drug testing. In research, long-term studies were spurred by the desire for more information about the long-term effects of environmental and industrial pollutants and by intensified study of long-term health problems such as cancer and cardiovascular diseases. In drug testing long-term studies had become more common as a result of increasingly stringent requirements by the FDA to identify and disclose long-term effects of drugs. One pharmaceutical industry spokesman stated that 1975 R&D budgets had risen to twice 1970 budgets in order to get the same number of new drugs approved by the FDA. In addition to increasingly longer studies, experiments using lab animals had become increasingly complex, frequently investigating the interactions of two or three drugs in a living organism. Both of these trends pointed to an increasing demand for well-defined,[4] healthy animals which would survive the rigors of longer experiments.

Rising quality standards

The increasing demand for healthier, well-defined animals was responsible for the growing proportion of cesarean-derived-barrier-reared (CDBR) and specific pathogen-free (SPF) animals sold by the larger commercial breeders since the mid-1960s. CDBR and SPF rodents lived longer and were more vigorous than the conventional animals breeders had traditionally raised. Although CDBR and SPF animal breeding re-

[4] The "definition" of a laboratory animal included, among other things, information about its "normal" heart rate, blood count, respiratory rate, blood chemistry, and intestinal flora.

quired a substantial capital investment in facilities and equipment, the improved facilities allowed breeders to raise more animals per square foot and to better control infectious diseases within production colonies. The larger breeders' ability to supply SPF and CDBR animals in large volume at a cost only slightly above that of conventional animals was credited with further increasing demand for these improved lab animals.

Longer term and increasingly complex research and testing procedures continued to stimulate increasing demand for higher quality animals in the mid-1970s. Dr. Albert Jonas, director of Laboratory Animal Services at the Yale Medical School, was among a growing group of users imposing higher standards. Quality control screening procedures for animals brought in from the outside involved detailed pathology tests, bacteriology tests, and veterinary exams. Quality control standards were high both to screen out substandard animals and to ensure a stable and consistent data base for experiments.

Dr. Jonas commented:

> Quality in lab animals is becoming increasingly important because of the trend toward long-term studies, especially in carcinogenesis and in long-term effects of pharmaceuticals.

Dr. Mayo agreed that users would be increasingly critical of animal quality, commenting:

> There will be big changes in animal breeding in the next five years. Users will demand more uniformity, in terms of health and, for inbred animals, in genetic control. Researchers will be saying, "My results are different from yours. What animals did you use?" Few breeders will be able to supply the higher quality animals. Few are in a financial position to make the heavy investment in buildings and equipment.

Breeder consolidation

The decade between 1955 and 1965 had brought the transfer of most laboratory animal breeding from users' in-house facilities to commercial breeders. At the same time, many new breeders entered the industry and established breeders prospered. Even "backyard breeders" who raised animals in garages or sheds were successful in the early years. With the recent increase in quality demands and attendant capital investment requirements, few new companies entered into rat and mouse production after the late 60s. Smaller companies went out of business each year or were acquired by larger breeders, and by 1975 "backyard breeders" of rats and mice had largely disappeared.

In the new environment more than financial strength was needed to be a successful laboratory animal breeder. The failure of two large corporations who attempted to enter the industry in the 1960s, Ralston-Purina and Becton, Dickinson & Company, attested to the difficulties of breeding.

Ralston-Purina, which supplied over 50 percent of the lab animal diet market, attempted to establish a breeding facility in Puerto Rico. One industry observer commented that the original product had been good but transportation to major market areas was difficult because of the remote location. In addition to its production and distribution problems, Ralston-Purina encountered marketing problems. Their animal diet sales force was not effective in selling animals since the purchasing agents who bought animal diets could not control a researcher's lab animal purchase patterns. Finally, minimum management attention was given to the endeavor because the $1.5 million facilities investment was such a small part of Ralston-Purina's overall capital budget. Dr. Foster commented that the purchase was like Ralston-Purina's buying another water cooler.

In 1964 Becton, Dickinson & Company, a large manufacturer of medical and laboratory supplies, acquired the Carworth Company, at that time the largest commercial breeder of mice in the industry. The company prospered for a few years after its acquisition, but began a downward spiral that continued until the division's sale in 1974 to Charles River. Between 1968 and 1973 Carworth's fiscal year sales declined from $3.4 million to $2.9 million and gross margins declined from 38 percent of sales to 7 percent of sales. During the same period net income after tax went from a profit of $110,000 to a loss of $471,-000.

why buy?

THE MARKET FOR LABORATORY ANIMALS

The $78.5 million market for laboratory animals was fragmented and regionalized. In addition to government agencies, pharmaceutical com-

Table 3

ESTIMATED LABORATORY
ANIMAL SALES BY SPECIES, 1975
(in thousands)

Species	Sales
Mice	$25,000
Rats	20,000
Rabbits	3,000
Hamsters	1,000
Guinea pigs	3,500
Primates	10,300
Other species*	11,500
	$74,300

* Includes dogs, cats, gerbils, sheep, poultry, and a wide variety of animals from nature such as fish and frogs.
Source: Researcher estimates.

panies and universities, food manufacturers, and cosmetic and toiletries firms were steady users of lab animals. The total number of lab animal purchasers was well over 2,000 with a multitude of departments and project groups purchasing animals at each company or institution. Most users of lab animals were located along the eastern seaboard between Washington, D.C. and Boston, or in the Great Lakes region between Chicago and Cleveland. California and Texas were the other sizable market areas.

Mice and rats were the most widely used species, accounting for 96 percent of the unit volume of sales and close to 50 percent of dollar volume. Most customers for laboratory animals used some hamsters, guinea pigs, and rabbits in addition to mice and rats. Markets for primates and animals from nature were significantly different from the market for smaller animals. Primates were used almost exclusively by the National Institutes of Health and by contract testing laboratories. Universities and government agencies were the primary users of animals from nature.

Table 4 shows the number of registered users and number of animals

Table 4
REGISTERED USERS AND NUMBER OF ANIMALS USED, BY STATE, 1974

| | Number | |
State	Users	Animals Used
California	85	156,400
Illinois	63	122,800
Indiana	20	75,500
Massachusetts	46	69,500
Michigan	13	72,500
New Jersey	42	126,100
New York	102	227,100
Ohio	69	68,800
Pennsylvania	57	69,000
Texas	31	142,700
Total	518	1,130,400
Total U.S.	867	1,692,500

Source: U.S. Department of Agriculture, Report of the Secretary of Agriculture, *Animal Welfare Enforcement 1974.*

employed in research for the United States as a whole and for the ten largest user states. Table 4 includes data only for species controlled under the Animal Welfare Enforcement Act.[5] Mice and rats were uncontrolled species, so comparable data were not available.

Laboratory animal markets outside the United States

Outside the United States, the majority of medical research and pharmaceutical testing using laboratory animals was conducted in Japan and western Europe. Most users maintained in-house breeding

[5] "The Laboratory Animal Welfare Act of 1966, as amended by the Animal Welfare Act of 1970 (referred to as the Animal Welfare Act), empowers the Secretary of Agriculture to establish standards to regulate the transportation, purchase, sale, housing, care, handling and treatment of animals intended for use for research or experimental purposes or for exhibition purposes or for use as pets." *Animal Welfare Enforcement 1974,* Report of the Secretary of Agriculture, U.S. Department of Agriculture.

facilities and commercial breeding activities were limited, although conditions varied widely among countries. Pharmaceutical and chemical companies comprised the largest user group as they did in the United States, and mice and rats were the most commonly used animals.

There was little data available on the dollar size of lab animal markets outside the United States or on the number of animals used, but Dr. Foster estimated the annual market at $60 million–$80 million, of which Europe accounted for $40 million–$60 million. The researcher estimated that of that total, $6 million was spent on laboratory animals by United States companies in their overseas facilities in 1974.[6] Table 5 presents the researcher's estimates of the market available to commer-

Table 5

ESTIMATED LAB ANIMAL SALES
(dollar equivalents)

	Sales
France	$10,000,000
England	7,500,000
Italy	3,200,000
Japan	10,000,000
Canada	7,500,000

cial breeders in France, England, Italy, Japan, and Canada based on Charles River data.

LABORATORY ANIMAL BREEDERS

The laboratory animal breeding industry was specialized and localized, with most breeders clustered around customer concentrations on the Atlantic seaboard, and in the Midwest. Although the Institute of Laboratory Animal Resources cited 113 sources of laboratory animals in 1975, 27 firms produced over 98 percent of the animals used, and only 5 firms had annual sales of $2 million or more. Some firms participated in allied industries serving the health research community, such as lab animal cage, feed and bedding supply, and the operation of commercial testing and research laboratories.

Within the laboratory animal breeding industry there were three major types of businesses, which were distinguished by the species of animals raised and by their production methods: (1) large-scale breeding of cesarean-derived-barrier-maintained and germ-free rodents; (2) small-scale breeding of conventional animals; and (3) primate importing and breeding.

Large-scale rodent breeding   — account for 50% of Sales

The five large-scale breeding businesses with annual sales over $2 million were primarily producers of mice and rats, and accounted for

[6] Based on an allocation for lab animals of 5 percent of total overseas R&D expenditures of $124.5 million in 1974, as reported by the Pharmaceutical Manufacturers Association, *Annual Survey Report 1973–74.*

approximately 50 percent of total industry rodent sales (in dollars). Most of their sales were in cesarean-derived-barrier-maintained and germ-free animals. Twenty-two small local breeders competed for the remaining 50 percent of the rodent market and raised animals in "conventional" or simple barrier facilities.

Charles River and the four other large-scale breeders carried a wide variety of rodent strains, and severeal of the firms raised additional species, such as hamsters, guinea pigs, or primates. Each company had a strong market position in its immediate geographic area as well as selling to major users across the United States. Charles River and ARS/Sprague-Dawley were the only public firms in the group, and the only firms to operate multisite facilities.

Jackson Laboratories, Bar Harbor, Maine. A nonprofit genetic research foundation, Jackson laboratories had started the large-scale production of inbred mice in the United States in the 1930s. It raised over 75 strains of mice bred for specific research needs and had a quality reputation. The company commercially marketed 50 percent of its animals, the balance of which were internally for its own research. It offered animals raised by germ-free and conventional methods.

ARS/Sprague-Dawley, Madison, Wisconsin. With approximately $3 million in annual sales, ARS/Sprague-Dawley was the second largest commercial breeder in the United States. It was a division of the Mogul Corporation (1972 sales $32 million). Sprague-Dawley was a brand name so widely recognized that it had become a generic term for laboratory rats in the same way Kleenex had for facial tissues. A significant proportion of the company's business involved raising animals under government contract.

Harlan Industries, Indianapolis, Indiana. Harlan was the second largest breeder in the Midwest and had a substantial customer base among pharmaceutical companies. The firm was relatively young and was highly respected for the quality of its animals.

Simonsen Laboratories, Gilroy, California. Simonsen was the only significant supplier of animals on the West Coast. Company products included mice and rats, and guinea pigs. No information on company sales was available.

Small-scale commercial breeding

Traditionally, the laboratory animal breeding industry had been composed of small-scale, family-operated businesses which specialized in a single species delivered to a limited number of local customers. In 1975, these small-scale breeders still accounted for approximately 55 percent of lab animals sold and close to 30 percent of industry dollar volume. They produced about half of the rats and mice available in the United States, as well as almost all hamsters, guinea pigs, rabbits, cats, and dogs. Small breeders raised animals by "conventional" methods or with simple "barrier" systems where the direction of airflow and personnel access were controlled from "clean" to "dirty" areas. Except for mice and rats, the animals were neither specific pathogen-free nor cesarean-derived.

The operations of the Murphy Breeding Laboratory, Inc., were representative of a successful small-scale breeder. The company, founded in 1968, was the largest producer of quality guinea pigs in the United States and also raised mice for the National Cancer Institute. Company revenues were approximately $300,000 in 1975. As it was for many small breeders, the National Cancer Institute contract was crucial to the company's financial stability. It was one of the few companies to successfully enter the lab animal breeding business in recent years.

Jobber, satellite, or "backyard" breeding described the method used to raise most guinea pigs and rabbits. It differed from small-scale breeding businesses in that demand for these animals was erratic and few producers engaged in the business year-round. Under a satellite breeding system, the jobber or main breeder maintained a small conventional breeding colony at his own facility and subcontracted additional production demands to part-time breeders who kept under a hundred animals in a garage or backyard pen.

Primate importing and breeding

After mice and rats, primates accounted for the largest dollar volume of sales in the United States lab animal industry: approximately $10.3 million in 1975. This represented the sale of approximately 48,000 animals, including gorillas, baboons, and a wide variety of monkeys. Another 1,500 primates were raised each year by the National Institutes of Health in their Regional Primate Centers.

Most primates available commercially in the United States were trapped abroad. Primate importers purchased animals from trappers in the host country, arranged for transportation and quarantine, and treated any obvious diseases at their U.S. holding facilities before offering the animals for sale. Two major companies engaged in primate importing: Prime Labs, and Primate Imports Corporation, which was 50 percent owned by Charles River Breeding.[7]

The market for primates was split equally between two user groups. Universities and government agencies comprised the first group and used a wide variety of primates in medical, psychological, and sociological studies. Commercial testing laboratories and pharmaceutical companies comprised the second group and used the smaller rhesus monkeys for drug screening and for testing cosmetics. About half of all primates used in research were rhesus monkeys.

The major sources of supply for primates were the Indian subcontinent (the rhesus' only natural habitat), Africa, South America, and Indonesia. Rhesus prices had almost doubled since 1973, when the government of India had declared the monkeys an endangered species and reduced exports from 50,000 to 20,000 per year. Further regulations

---

[7] In August 1973, Charles River acquired 50 percent of the stock of Primate Imports Corporation for $268,400 and an option to acquire the remaining 50 percent prior to October 1976. In early 1976 Charles River indicated its intention to exercise that option at a price not to exceed $375,000.

were imposed in subsequent years. Both the export quotas and regulations were expected to be permanent.

The researcher estimated that commercial primate breeders in the United States produced fewer than 1,500 animals a year. In addition to Charles River, only three companies engaged in domestic primate breeding, and it represented a small part of their total annual sales. Litton Bionetics was primarily a supplier of biological and scientific equipment, while Gulf South was one of the largest commercial testing laboratories and used most of the primates it raised on its own research activities. Hazelton Laboratories, a company newly organized in 1969, was a rapidly growing diversified enterprise. (See the Appendix.)

CHARLES RIVER BREEDING LABORATORIES

Company history

From a warehouse loft with a $1,200 investment in used rat cages in 1947, Henry Foster built Charles River Breeding Laboratories into the industry's dominant producer of rats and mice with 1975 sales of $15.4 million, net assets of $16.9 million, and an OTC stock whose price-earnings ratio fluctuated between 20 and 60. (See Exhibits 1 and 2 for company financial information.)

Dr. Henry Foster commented:

> In 1947 I graduated from Middlesex Veterinary School in Waltham and wanted to establish a practice near Alexandria, Virginia. I couldn't find a location I could afford, but in my search I bumped into an abandoned rat farm in Clinton, Md. They sold me their old rat cages for $1,200 and showed me their records and customer lists.
>
> I had the cages shipped to Boston and started looking for a location. It was hard to find a landlord who would take a bunch of smelly rats, but I finally got the loft of an old warehouse on Leverett Street, behind Beacon Hill near the Charles River.
>
> I really didn't have a product to sell. No other veterinarian was in the field of animal breeding. Ventilation control in the loft consisted of opening and closing the window. I didn't really know what I was doing. There was no formal training in lab animals sciences available but the one thing I had was my veterinary degree. I could create an image of professionalism, and "Dr. Foster" gave me access to researchers. I didn't get left in the waiting room with the other salesmen.

When Charles River first went public in 1968, the company was still regarded as specializing in rats and was the largest commercial breeder with sales close to $4 million. Between 1969 and 1975 Charles River sales grew 400 percent from both internal growth and acquisitions.

Still, in 1976 COBS® (cesarean-originated, barrier-sustained) rats and mice accounted for 90 percent of sales, and Henry Foster attributed much of the company's success to its pioneering commercialization of the COBS® technique for breeding *rats* in 1955. Dr. Foster described the COBS® introduction.

I was aware of a germ-free derivation technique developed at Notre Dame. Building upon this technique we developed colonies of disease-free animals that could survive experiments without succumbing to an endemic disease and would not cloud results with the side effects of those diseases. Germ-free animals were not in abundant supply because they were so expensive to maintain in a germ-free state. What we did was to develop a technology that started with clean, germ-free animals, then introduced flora which would allow them to live outside of isolators. The barrier facility we built kept them from being recontaminated by germs in the environment.

In order to build the new facility, I took out a $100,000 loan. With this we were able to construct a building with three separate units. We equipped it with the first steam and gas autoclave in New England for sterilizing feed, bedding and cages. This was far in advance of the equipment anyone else had. We also installed a mechanized feed and bedding transport system.

All that investment and innovation appeared to be an unjustifiable capital expenditure, but it gave us some life insurance. With three separate areas we'd still have animals to sell even if an entire room were wiped out. Once you started to work with an institution and they developed baseline data on your animals, they wouldn't dump you unless you fell on your face and failed to supply them with quality animals on a continuing basis.

Not everyone could have gotten into the COBS® business. Notre Dame was willing to give me three or four germ-free animals to start only because I had a veterinary degree. I put myself completely in hock with the SBA loan. At the same time that our new facilities went up, I began to publish in scientific journals about developing techniques for large-scale animal breeding. This commitment to raise cesarean-derived animals was an indication of professionalism and gave us recognition. Harvard Medical School and Smith, Kline and French discovered we could teach them something.

I started out with a handicap because the veterinary college I attended was not accredited. That made me work harder. It pushed me to do things I wouldn't have done otherwise.

The year 1955 also heralded a major shift in Charles River Breeding Laboratories' (CRBL) marketing efforts. From supplying mainly universities, medical schools, and hospitals, Dr. Foster set out to break into the large lab animal market at pharmaceutical and chemical companies. Not only did this provide a new outlet for CRBL's increased production, but it smoothed demand for animals throughout the year.

Charles River Breeding Laboratories grew steadily and profitably between 1955 and 1965. At the urging of their now substantial pharmaceutical company customers, Charles River entered into the production of cesarean-derived *mice* in 1959. New breeding facilities went up in Wilmington and new rat strains were added. In 1964 the company built its first overseas COBS® facility in Elbeuf, France. By 1965 all facilities at Wilmington were upgraded to guarantee that Charles River was the only commercial breeder all of whose rodents were cesarean-derived, barrier-sustained [COBS®]. Other breeders began to adopt similar techniques to remain competitive.

Exhibit 1

CHARLES RIVER BREEDING LABORATORIES
Consolidated Balance Sheets
October 31, 1968–1975
(in thousands)

ASSETS	1968	1969	1970	1971	1972	1973	1974	1975
Current assets:								
Cash	$ 320	$ 203	$ 340	$ 202	$ 352	$ 284	$ 373	$ 316
Certificates of deposit	105	100	100	208	200	633	492	388
Marketable securities	949	712	150	646	—	1,009	577	452
Accounts receivable	585	761	808	1,284	1,357	1,775	2,495	2,635
Inventories and supplies	256	262	366	508	657	886	1,445	1,618
Other current assets	44	132	117	91	114	140	142	134
Total current assets	$2,259	$2,170	$1,881	$2,939	$ 2,680	$ 4,727	$ 5,524	$ 5,543
Property and equipment, at cost:								
Land	173	183	262	306	626	683	1,139	1,143
Buildings and improvements	1,643	2,277	2,707	3,135	4,284	5,462	7,078	7,519
Equipment	1,217	1,559	1,908	2,387	3,427	3,870	4,843	5,851
Motor vehicles	75	121	200	248	272	325	374	454
Construction in progress	187	47	571	1,579	1,491	1,120	520	1,390
	$3,295	$4,187	$5,648	$7,655	$10,100	$11,460	$13,954	$16,357
Less—accumulated depreciation	(912)	(1,179)	(1,543)	(1,975)	(2,355)	(2,823)	(3,437)	(4,215)
	$2,383	$3,008	$4,105	$5,680	$ 7,745	$ 8,637	$10,517	$12,142
Investments and other assets:								
Investment in Primate Imports Corporation	—	—	—	—	—	284	378	535
Cost of purchased businesses in excess of net assets	—	—	—	108	104	102	97	91
Investment in Japanese joint venture, at cost	—	—	—	—	106	114	—	—
Cash surrender value of insurance on lives of officers and key employees	25	29	37	44	51	140	208	645
Other assets	44	69	63	105	266	257	211	188
	$ 69	$ 98	$ 100	$ 257	$ 527	$ 897	$ 894	$ 1,459
	$4,711	$5,276	$6,086	$8,876	$10,952	$14,261	$16,935	$19,144

LIABILITIES AND STOCKHOLDERS
INVESTMENT

	1968	1969	1970	1971	1972	1973	1974	1975
Current liabilities:								
Loans payable	$ —	$ —	$ —	$ 185	$ 322	$ 445	$ 365	$ 410
Current installments of long-term debt	268	298	163	113	121	13	154	388
Accounts payable	203	279	370	465	460	718	842	974
Accrued payroll						106	147	217
Accrued expenses and taxes	183	213	212	286	369	437	741	885
Accrued federal and foreign income taxes	254	255	228	340	147	338	321	360
Total current liabilities	$ 908	$1,045	$ 973	$1,389	$ 1,419	$ 2,057	$ 2,570	$ 3,234
Long-term debt:	1,611	1,573	1,504	1,978	3,138	723	1,771	1,893
Less—current installments included above	(268)	(298)	(163)	(113)	(122)	(12)	(154)	(388)
	$1,343	$1,275	$1,341	$1,865	$ 3,016	$ 711	$ 1,617	$ 1,505
Deferred income taxes	8	31	203	218	285	331	337	475
Stockholders' investment:								
Common stock outstanding, $1 par value	686	686	690	752	1,414	1,531	1,531	1,534
Capital in excess of par value	1,063	1,056	1,132	2,246	1,632	5,442	5,451	5,478
Retained earnings	703	1,183	1,747	2,406	3,186	4,189	5,429	6,918
	$2,452	$2,925	$3,569	$5,404	$ 6,232	$11,162	$12,411	$13,930
	$4,711	$5,276	$6,086	$8,876	$10,952	$14,261	$16,935	$19,144

Source: Charles River Breeding Laboratories, Inc., *Annual Reports 1968–1975.*

Low- and High-Bid Prices for Charles River
Common Stock Calendar Year 1975

1975	Low Bid	High Bid
First quarter	19	24½
Second quarter	22	28
Third quarter	15	25½
Fourth quarter	17	24

Source: Adams, Harkness and Hill.

Exhibit 2

CHARLES RIVER BREEDING LABORATORIES
Consolidated Statements of Income
For the Years Ended October 31, 1968–1975
(in thousands)

	1968	1969	1970	1971	1972	1973	1974	1975
Net sales	$4,243	$4,717	$5,505	$6,469	$7,993	$9,875	$12,574	$15,405
Cost and expenses:								
Cost of sales	2,535	2,678	3,185	3,791	4,781	6,091	7,768	9,921
Selling and administrative expenses	925	1,042	1,213	1,350	1,683	1,824	2,406	2,595
	$3,460	$3,720	$4,398	$5,141	$6,464	$7,915	$10,174	$12,516
Income from operations	783	997	1,107	1,328	1,529	1,960	2,400	2,889
Other income (expenses):								
Equity in net income of affiliate, less amortization of goodwill	—	—	—	—	—	16	94	157
Interest income	—	—	—	—	—	94	88	87
Interest expense	(56)	(75)	(75)	(85)	(119)	(116)	(179)	(200)
Income before income taxes	$ 727	$ 922	$1,032	$1,243	$1,410	$1,954	$ 2,403	$ 2,933
Provision for income taxes:								
Current	354	441	416	547	519	951	1,163	1,367
Deferred	—	—	52	37	111	—	—	—
	$ 354	$ 441	$ 468	$ 584	$ 630	$ 951	$ 1,163	$ 1,367
Net income	373	481	564	659	780	1,003	1,240	1,566
	$ 354	$ 441	$ 564	$ 659	$ 630	$ 951	$ 1,163	$ 1,367
Earnings per share	$ 0.59	$ 0.70	$ 0.82	$ 0.48	$ 0.55	$ 0.67	$ 0.81	$ 1.02
Average number of shares of common stock outstanding (000s)	631	686	689	1,376	1,412	1,493	1,531	1,534

Source: Charles River Breeding Laboratories, Inc., Annual Reports 1968–1975.

After going public in 1968, CRBL entered a period of rapid expansion. Between 1969 and 1971 Charles River acquired five companies including facilities in Canada, England, and Italy. It entered into a joint venture with Ajinomoto to form Charles River Japan in October 1972,[8] a 50 percent interest in Primate Imports Corporation in October 1973. More strains of rats and mice were added to the Charles River product line, as well as four new species, including hamsters, rabbits, guinea pigs, and rhesus monkeys.

Product line

Fourteen strains of COBS and germ-free mice and rats accounted for 90 percent of Charles River Breeding Laboratories fiscal 1975 sales of $15.4 million, with COBS® guinea pigs, COBS rabbits, and conventional hamsters rounding out the company's broad line of small lab animals.

Table 6

SALES BY SPECIES, FISCAL 1975
(000s)

Species	Sales
Rats	$ 8,500
Mice	3,500
Guinea pigs	200
Hamsters	500
Direct government business	2,500
Rabbits	—
Key Lois primates	—
Primate imports (income share only)	160
Other (e.g., preserved specimens)	200
Total	$15,560

Source: Researcher estimates.

A 50 percent-owned Charles River subsidiary, Primate Imports, Inc., sold a wide variety of imported primates accounting for approximately a third of all U.S. primate sales. A new Florida production facility on company-owned Key Lois Island was to sell its first domestically bred, rhesus monkeys in 1976. Table 6 shows Charles River estimates sales by species for 1975.

Charles River production facilities

Almost half of Charles River's productive capacity was located at company headquarters in Wilmington, Massachusetts, 14 miles outside of Boston, where COBS® mice, rats, guinea pigs, and rabbits were raised; all administrative and research and development facilities were also located there. Other Charles River Breeding Laboratories production facilities were located at four sites in the United States, as well as over-

---

[8] During fiscal 1974, the joint venture was converted to a percentage of sales licensing agreement which provided for the use of the Charles River name and a continuing transfer of technical know-how.

Table 7

PRODUCTION CAPACITY

Location	Products	Hour a day capacity number of animals per year*	General information
Wilmington, Mass.........	Rats, mice, rabbits, and guinea pigs	6,000,000	
Newfield, N.J.............	Hamsters (not COBS®)	400,000	
Stoneridge, N.Y..........	Rats, mice	3,000,000	
Portage, Mich.† (beginning 1976)........	Rats, mice	2,500,000	
Port Washington, N.Y.....	Primate conditioning (imports)	24,000	
Key Lois, Florida........	Primate breeding	1,500	
Elbeuf, France...........	Rats	1,000,000	
	Mice	2,000,000	
St. Constant, Quebec......	Mice	1,000,000	Also non-COBS
	Rats	520,000	rabbits and guinea pigs.
Margate, England........	Mice	600,000	Flexible space
	Rats	300,000 +	for 156,000
	Guinea pigs	20,000	rats or 488,000 mice.
Milan, Italy..............	Mice	900,000	
	Rats	300,000	
Atsugi, Japan...........	Rats and mice	1,000,000 (1976/77)	Licensing agreement only.

* Except for Stoneridge, Portage, Margate, Atsugi, and Key Lois, all facilities operated at close to 100 percent of capacity.

† Acquired as part of 1974 Carworth purchase. In 1975, $1.7 million was invested in upgrading and expanding capacity to serve the Midwest market.

Source: 1972 Annual Report and 10–K.

seas. Table 7 shows Charles River locations, products produced at each site, and production capacity.

The barrier system

The barrier rooms and their associated environmental control systems formed the core of the Wilmington production facilities and accounted for the capital intensity of Charles River's business. A barrier room was a sealed room about 40 feet by 50 feet by 10 feet high. Animals were housed in metal or plastic cages stacked in tiers five to ten cages high and arranged in neat rows. Each separate breeding area had its own feed and bedding holding tanks. Sterilized feed and bedding were delivered to the breeding areas through an extensive pneumatic pipe system. A separate vacuum system removed waste to a central silo in the Charles River compound.

Personnel "entry locks" or cubicles prevented the people caring for the animals from bringing any contaminants into the barrier. In the first cubicle, the employee undressed and left all of his or her street clothes in a locker. Then in the second lock, the employee showered and washed his hair. In the third lock, the employee put on a complete sterile surgical style uniform maintained in the unit. Even the employees' lunch containers were sterilized before being passed into the unit.

Charles River took extensive precautions to maintain contaminant-free breeding areas. All air entering the areas was filtered to exclude particles larger than 0.3 microns and each area was kept at a higher pressure than the external atmosphere in order to prevent air leaks. Room controls were checked hourly to monitor room pressures and maintain temperatures between 72° and 74° F. A IBM System 7 computer automatically regulated energy use and monitored temperature, pressure, and energy alarm systems. The company also maintained six emergency generators.

Additionally, Charles River supported its own in-house maintenance team. Bill Keough, CRBL's treasurer and financial vice president, explained why.

> We have an environmental control oriented facility that allows us to raise twice as many animals per square foot as any other breeder. Preventive maintenance on this system is high, and emergency repair is crucial. We can lose animals or a whole barrier facility if the system is down for long. Maintenance workers must be familiar with the system so that they can repair it rapidly and their work must be perfect. Our own people know how to do it, will work overtime to get it done, and respond immediately. It's our insurance policy. These people are also a good technical resource when we build or renovate purchased facilities. We're better at building and equipping facilities than anyone else in the business.

Charles River labor force

Laboratory animal breeding was a labor-intensive as well as a capital-intensive enterprise. Production employees, called animal technicians, were needed to feed, water, and clean the animals; weigh, select, and pack animals for shipment. Tasks were routine but exacting and the work pace was fast. Two hundred of Charles River's Wilmington employees were directly involved in production. Their wages and fringe benefits accounted for close to 25 percent of total costs. Three shifts of technicians worked 24 hours a day, seven days a week, operating the sterilization equipment while animal technicians worked one shift, seven days a week caring for the animals. Bud Otis, vice president of Operations and officer of the corporation, described the work force and the difficulty of managing the production operation at Charles River.

> It is crucial that the entire work force follows entry and exit procedures exactly in order to preserve the integrity of the barrier. People are the greatest source of potential contamination. Someone may have a sick cat at home.
>
> It takes about twenty minutes for a technician to pass through the three lock barriers entry system, so employees do not leave the breeding

rooms during their shift. People remain in a 40' by 50' room for 8 or 9 hours a day with only 2 or 3 other people. Personalities play a big part in maintaining morale.

This is an unskilled job. Most of the animal technicians are men and women between 18 and 24 who are just out of high school. Average tenure is about 18 months.

The real strength of our production areas is our supervisory personnel. We always promote from within and we have a good supervisory training program. Supervisors are mainly policemen, although they are also responsible for setting the pace and meeting production deadlines.

Mr. Otis, who had begun working for Charles River 13 years ago as an animal technician, showed the researcher the Wilmington facility. They stood in the spotlessly clean shipping area outside one of the 46 breeding rooms, looking in through a plate glass window. Inside the breeding room three animal technicians and a group leader were working. They were all wearing one piece white and green jumpsuits with soft boots that overlapped the jumpsuits and tied above the ankle. White surgical caps covered their hair and all wore surgical masks. Every hour a buzzer went off and they replaced their masks and prepowdered disposable surgical gloves with fresh ones. A public address system piped in popular music. One technician was rapidly weighing animals and sorting them into weight groups. Two other technicians were moving back and forth along the banks of cages replacing water bottles. The group leader was checking the sex and weights marked on the exterior of cages of animals set aside for standing orders. Three animal technicians could pack 10,000 animals in a day, but would have to handle 20,000 in order to achieve customer weight tolerances.

Marketing

Sumner Foster, CRBL's executive vice president, described to the researcher the marketing policies which he had designed and implemented. He attributed the company's 40 percent share of the East Coast rat and mouse markets to its ability to provide a reliable source of quality animals. CRBL's award winning advertising program stressed quality and reliability, while extensive customer relations activity and efficient order processing supported the company's high-quality, high-service position. Charles River animals commanded a 10 percent price premium. Dr. Foster elaborated on the meaning of quality:

We have credibility. Our animals perform well because our product is consistent and people know that our quality control is good. We bring our customers here to show them our innovative facilities and production processes. Our best sales tools are our animals and facilities wherever they are.

Sumner Foster emphasized the importance of a reputation for reliability when seeking new customers.

We are a sure source of supply and guarantee delivery on standing orders. This is something few other breeders are able to do. When we go after a new customer who is standardized on another breeder's strain, we compete on the basis of superior quality and reliability of supply. Our size is important here because we can bring in animals from our subsidiaries to cover peak periods.

Animals were sold FOB at the production facility and customers paid all freight charges. Charles River transported 60 percent of its animals in the company's climate controlled delivery vans. The remaining animals were shipped air freight.

Advertising

Charles River's advertising activities included regular paid advertisements in scientific journals, plus the publication of a quarterly newsletter, *The Charles River Digest,* and a research bibliography. Mr. Foster explained that these activities were designed to project an image of quality, reliability, and scientific innovation. No other breeder engaged in such an extensive program.

Magazine advertisements were placed in a variety of specialty scientific journals, such as the *Journal of Toxicology* and the *Journal of Endocrinology,* in order to reach the researchers who were the primary decision makers for lab animal purchases. Other breeders advertised only in the *Journal of Laboratory Animal Science,* which targeted a less specific audience. Annual advertising expenditures were approximately $200,000.

The Charles River Digest was an informational quarterly with articles of general interest to the research community which reported all major projects using Charles River animals. It was received by over 13,000 researchers and scientific libraries. Every two years, the company also published an extensive bibliography of all scholarly articles and research reports mentioning Charles River animals. Mr. Foster stated that this extensive literature on Charles River animals was one of the major reasons for their wide acceptability.

Customer relations

Mr. Foster explained that the company's focus was on personal customer contact by top management at Charles River. "Top management has to be the visible part of the company. Users want to talk to someone responsible." Charles River engaged in three customer relations activities which he said emphasized CRBL's position as the only commercial breeder with in-house laboratory support, quality control, and research ability. These activities included management attendance at trade shows associated with national scientific conferences, participation in scholarly symposia, and consultation on lab animal health.

Gil Slater, director of Marketing and operating head of Lakeview Hamster Colony, attended all regional and national scientific conferences and called directly on customers. Dr. Foster and Dr. George Pucak, director of Veterinary Services, attended and made presentations at symposia in the United States and abroad.

Since joining the company three years ago, Dr. Pucak had gradually assumed Dr. Foster's former role in consulting with customers and other researchers on lab animal health problems. Dr. Pucak spent close to

50 percent of his time with correspondence and user telephone calls in response to customer problems. He diagnosed and recommended treatments for diseases, as well as answering more general questions about research procedures and animal health problems.

Selling and order processing

Sumner Foster explained that most orders for small laboratory animals were placed over the phone for delivery in three to five days and were very specific as to strain, age, sex, and weight within tolerances of a few grams. Consequently, up-to-date inventory systems and rapid order processing were important to Charles River in meeting the wide, short-term fluctuations in demand. All U.S. order processing was centralized in Wilmington. This allowed the company to maintain a computerized order processing system which provided a daily updated stock list of animal inventories in all U.S. and overseas facilities, with data supplied by remote access terminals in all subsidiary locations. Charles River sold a high percentage of animals raised and produced at close to 100 percent of capacity. Sumner Foster commented that the effective use of the computer for order processing and customer sales analysis was one of the company's major advantages over the rest of the industry.

Pricing

According to Mr. Foster, the greatest volume of Charles River animals were outbred rats and mice sold in the lower price ranges, but there was

Table 8

Species	Price range (per animal)
Mice	$ 0.46–$ 3.30
Hamsters	1.20– 5.50
Rats	1.35– 8.75
Guinea pigs	3.90– 50.00
Rabbits	3.50– 60.00
Primates	50.00–500.00

steady demand for other species and for the more expensive inbred strains. Aged animals, pregnant and lactating females, and surgically altered animals also commanded higher prices. Table 8 shows price ranges by species for Charles River animals.

Bill Keough explained the company's position of price leadership in the industry.

> Charles River Breeding Laboratories is the industry price leader in every product. Our goal is to achieve an overall corporate margin of 10% after tax and we are usually able to achieve price levels which cover costs and meet margin goals. Others in the industry follow our prices, at a level about 5%–10% lower. However, our new COBS® rabbits, which are more expensive to produce, sell at two to three times current prices

for conventional rabbits, but we initially only want the premium quality segment on the market.

Dr. Foster explained his view of the company's pricing strategy.

We are lucky in our industry because it is price flexible, but sometimes I wonder how we operate so profitably when Charles River charges only $1.35 for a rat and competitors get as much as $1.28. Maybe a wise manager would say that you should get everything you can, but I don't want to lose credibility by being a pirate. I think there are ethics and morals and we can practice them because we deal with ethical and moral people.

Charles River customers

Mr. Foster said that Charles River Breeding Laboratories now sold to over 2,000 customers in every segment of the laboratory animal market. Its preferred customers were the large East Coast pharmaceutical companies because they regularly purchased large quantities of animals. A good customer could place orders amounting to $167,000 per year. Table 9 shows the percentage of 1974 dollar sales accounted for by each customer segment.

Table 9

Customer type	Percentage of CRBL's 1974 dollar volume
Pharmaceutical and chemical companies	54%
Governmental agencies	17
Universities	16
Commercial testing labs and hospitals	13
	100%

Dr. Foster was pleased with this customer mix:

We have a broad market base and no single customer accounts for more than 5% of sales. No one customer could dramatically cripple us or chip away at our margins if they stopped buying animals for 8 to 10 weeks. Smaller breeders are very vulnerable to interrupted purchases and something like that could put a small breeder out of business.

RESEARCH AND DEVELOPMENT

Charles River Breeding Laboratories was the only commercial breeder in the industry to maintain its own professional research staff and laboratory which was responsible for production quality control and for new product development. Sumner Foster commented that the Research Department gave Charles River a competitive advantage by providing a uniquely healthy product and an advantage in adding new species and strains.

The research staff at Charles River included Dr. George Pucak, a veterinarian who was a specialist in laboratory animal medicine; Dr. Roger Orcutt, a microbiologist specializing in intestinal flora; and a staff of ten full-time laboratory technicians. The Research Department operated from a fully equipped laboratory and animal quarantine facilities located at company headquarters in Wilmington.

Every eight weeks 25 animals were selected from each breeding colony. Tissue samples, cultures, and blood samples were taken from and tested for each animal. Technicians also inspected animals for parasites. Diagnostic technicians working in a separate necropsy, microbiological, and pathology lab examined all the animals which died in production colonies to determine cause of death. Also, randomly selected healthy animals were sacrificed for extensive testing to establish baseline data on bacteriology, serum chemistry, and tissue values which helped researchers to improve the efficiency of their experiments.

These extensive quality control procedures and in-house laboratory capability, management stated, were unique to Charles River. Dr. Foster explained the rationale behind these expenditures which amounted to $175,000 in 1974:

> We have imposed standards on ourselves by learning what kind of infections will cloud a researcher's results. We learned how to improve the environment and microbiologically define the animals. If you learn of something to give you a better product, you do it because you know it's all right, and later the benefits will be there.

New product development

New product introductions had contributed 30 percent of Charles River's growth in sales between 1970 and 1975, and were expected to contribute to the company's growth over the next five years. There were three separate new product development activities at Charles River: (1) adding new mice and rat strains, (2) developing new COBS® species, such as guinea pigs and rabbits, and (3) entering new lines of business, such as primate breeding.

The National Institutes of Health's genetic center supplied samples of newly developed strains of breeding animals to lab animal breeding companies. This has enabled Charles River to introduce two new rat strains and three mouse strains into commercial production in the last three years. Sumner Foster described the process.

> The whole process for introducing new rodent strains is rather routine because it's little different from starting foundation and breeding colonies for animals already in production. It takes about one year from the first cesarean to volume production of 10,000 to 20,000 animals per week. I can't even tell you how much it costs to start a new strain of small rodents because it is a normal part of our production activity. Any problems encountered are usually surgical and might take time, but are not expensive.

COBS® development

The development of COBS® animals in new species, such as guinea pigs and rabbits, was initiated as part of the company's growth plans after going public in 1968. Charles River saw the development of COBS® rabbit and guinea pig products as a way to enter new markets with a domestic sales potential of $4 million a year. The company would introduce a unique product which no other commercial breeder had either the R&D expertise to develop or the production economies of scale to produce competively. It would also enable Charles River to maintain its reputation for scientific innovation in commercial breeding techniques. The market risk inherent in the traditionally erratic demand patterns for these animals also made the necessary facilities investment very difficult for a less securely financed company.

Research efforts for COBS® rabbits and guinea pigs focused on developing the correct feed formulas and the correct intestinal flora to introduce to the germ-free animals so that they could be raised in barrier rooms on a large scale similar to the rat and mouse operations. Guinea pig development took six years, but by late 1975 Sumner Foster considered their 10 percent market share reasonable in light of their price level which was initially double that of conventional guinea pigs.[9] Rabbits had been a more difficult task and were just coming into production in early 1976. Sumner Foster related the problems encountered in developing the COBS® rabbit that had cost the company close to $500,000 in expenses and committed facilities during its eight-year development period.

> We started to work on a COBS® rabbit in 1968 and thought we could get it into production in a year as we did with new rodent strains. But, unlike rats and mice, nothing was known about the animal before we started and it involved a much bigger R&D effort. We had no foster mother for the germ-free young and had to hand-feed them every hour, which is very expensive. We lost a lot of animals trying to develop the correct milk formula for hand-feeding. Also the rabbit was a special problem in association from the germ-free to a COBS® state.

Primate breeding

Charles River began plans to engage in rhesus monkey breeding in 1971 with the goals of entering a growing new market and of continuing to develop its reputation for improved laboratory animals. By breeding animals under controlled conditions in the United States, the company hoped to eliminate major health problems that made rhesus difficult to use in research. Rhesus trapped in the wild had an unknown medical history and frequently carried tuberculosis, a Herpes B virus which was lethal to man, and other diseases, communicable to humans. The animals also frequently suffered from Salmonella and Shigella, bacterial diseases which could weaken or kill the animals through severe dehydration. Charles River's rhesus breeding program began with trapping the animals themselves in remote areas of northern India in order to select the healthiest animals and to bypass the usual quarantine compounds in India and the United States. The company by 1976 had developed an expertise in testing, diagnosing, and curing rhesus diseases and designed innovative feeding, trapping, and quality control procedures for production colonies.

---

[9] Due to a tight supply situation, breeders of conventional guinea pigs quickly followed with price increases of their own.

By early 1976 there were 1,500 healthy, thoroughly tested rhesus on Key Lois, which comprised a breeding stock expected to eventually produce 900 marketable animals annually. Rhesus dollar sales were expected to grow to $500,000 by 1978 from $50,000 in 1976. At the end of 1975 total development costs to date amounted to $700,000, of which the federal government had cost shared approximately $300,000 for noncapital expenditures.

Overseas operations

Charles River operations in Canada, England, France, and Italy accounted for a third of total company sales and net income in 1975. COBS® rats and mice were each division's main product, but competitive situations, product lines, profitability, and growth potential varied substantially among the divisions. Lab animals bearing the Charles River name were first produced in Japan in 1976 under a licensing and royalty agreement with the Ajinomoto Company.

Table 10

Division and product lines	Approximate 1975 sales (dollar equivalents: in millions)	Net profit after tax as a percent of sales	Estimated market share (commercial breeders only)	Additional sales potential by 1980 (in millions)
Canada				
Rats				
Mice				
Rabbits	$1.5	8%	n.a.	n.a.
Guinea pigs				
France				
Rats				
Mice	$2.5	11–16	44%+	$1.5
England				
Rats				
Mice	$1	10	25	$2
Guinea pigs				
Italy				
Rats				
Mice	$1+	10	33+	$1+

n.a.—not available.
Source: Researcher estimates.

Dr. Foster stated that his overseas expansion strategy required establishing an independent operating division in each country where a large market share was desired. Each division was managed by a national of the country where the facilities were located, although the parent corporation supplied assistance in facilities construction, production management techniques, quality control, and pricing decisions. All of Charles River's overseas divisions, except for France, had been acquired between 1969 and 1971 and substantial investments had been made in upgrading facilities and training production personnel. Serving multinational markets from a single facility was difficult due to language barriers, currency exchange problems, customs clearance, tariffs, and tax structures. Charles River was currently investigating acquisition candidates in Germany.

Charles River France was constructed in 1965 with the aid of Rhone Poulenc, S.A., one of France's largest chemical and pharmaceutical firms. Their agreement included a 15-year contract for Charles River to supply Rhone Poulenc's lab animals at a reduced price, in return for their assistance in local financing, engineering, land acquisition, and zoning problems. One eighth of Charles River France's current production was sold under contract to Rhone Poulenc. CRBL's initial cash investment was low, and as a result the French division's ROI was substantially higher than the ROI for the company as a whole.

Financial policies

Charles River's vice president of Finance, Bill Keough, characterized the company's capital structure as very conservative because of a heavy internal cash flow and a highly successful common stock issue in 1973. In that year Charles River had issued 110,000 common shares, raising close to $3.9 million, $2.3 million of which was used to retire a long-term debt. Mr. Keough described the issue as an attempt to get a more widely held stock and to take advantage of an inexpensive source of capital. He commented:

> As a result, we have no problem getting money. I could pick up the phone and borrow $2 million within the next few hours. Our total unused debt capacity is between $5 million and $6 million. Right now we're not more leveraged because we can't use it.

Since becoming public, the company had been gradually revising its performance goals. Mr. Keough explained the situation.

> We were previously getting a 10 percent ROI with a dollar of annual sales per dollar of facilities investment. Because we were willing to accept that 10 percent ROI, and because our operations were more efficient—no one else's sales margins are as good as ours—the marginal guy has gone out of business and we've discouraged others from entering. The financial community has been insisting that the return was too low, so now we're looking for 15 percent.[10]

Charles River declared its first dividend in 1975 in an attempt to broaden the company's base of stockholders[11] and to stabilize its stock price which fluctuated between 20 and 60 times earnings. The company was investigating the possibility of becoming listed on a major stock exchange during 1976, and Bill Keough described the type of investor he hoped these actions would attract:

---

[10] Part of that increase was expected to come from increased sales yield per square foot of plant and equipment costs achieved by changing male/female rodent production ratios to more closely approximate demand. This change had already contributed 1 percent to after-tax margins in fiscal 75 and was expected to produce an additional 1 percent in fiscal 76.

[11] In mid-1976 Charles River Breeding Laboratories had 1,007 shareholders. Dr. Foster, held approximately 40 percent of the company's stock and his brother, Sumner Foster, held approximately 2 percent.

We don't want to become a speculative stock, we're just trying for steady growth. We want a loyal investor who believes in us and plans to be with us for the long haul.

Planning and management systems

Formal planning and reporting systems at Charles River were kept as simple as possible in order to minimize the company's administrative overhead. All company officers reported directly to Sumner Foster as executive vice president, who in turn reported to Dr. Foster. The primary management planning document was an annual business plan and budget, reviewed monthly in conjunction with computer-produced financial statements comparing budgeted to actual results. The only other regular financial reporting documents were weekly reports of the number of animals produced and shipped and a weekly payroll and overtime report. Mr Keough commented:

> It's a conscious effort to keep things simple. The company is basically run by four people: the Fosters, Bud Otis and myself. We all wear a lot of hats so that we're not burdened with staffing and can stay flexible, adapt quickly to change. We don't want the expense of having all the answers, so we just control the key areas, labor and sales. You can't run this business with a bureaucracy.

Although Mr. Otis, Mr. Keough, Sumner Foster, and Dr. Foster held a formal meeting every Friday morning and reviewed major management control documents weekly, the main communications channels in the company were personal and informal. Executives were in and out of each other's offices several times a day. Mr. Keough kept in his office closet a large refrigerator well-stocked with beer, affectionately referred to as "Duffy's." Everybody from delivery truck drivers to Dr. Foster dropped by after five o'clock.

Dr. Pucak described the atmosphere that contributed to such a high degree of internal cooperation at Charles River.

> Everybody is involved with everything around here. The atmosphere is open and any idea you come up with, no matter how far out, is going to be discussed. We can all speak our minds. Dr. Foster creates a tremendous sense of pride. He works hard and sets the tone, yet we all feel we have contributed to the success of the company and share in its financial rewards.

Meeting strategic goals

In June of 1976, Dr. Foster spoke with the researcher about his company's future plans.

> Come on in. What do you think of our new conference table? We put it to good use every Friday when the four of us get together. Sometimes when we meet we have an agenda—specific questions; other times we just review our general situation.

Dr. Foster's office was a large, zebra-wood paneled room with a crisp, modern decor. A small marble conference table occupied one end of the room; at the other was a massive desk and chair. On the desk was an intercom system which allowed Dr. Foster to speak immediately with any of his officers or staff members. Behind the desk was a large digital clock and a hi-fi system capable of programmed output. The walls were decorated with abstract art, pictures of wife and family, replicas of the plaques honoring the Henry and Lois Foster gifts to Brandeis University and The Museum of Fine Arts, and a dozen or so framed organizational honorary awards and memberships in distinguished technical, industrial, and service (Rotary) institutions.

Dr. Foster continued:

> We have a real challenge ahead of us in meeting our growth goals of 15 percent in both sales and earnings. Because of our current dominance in the industry, we cannot acquire additional laboratory animal breeding firms. We can, however, expect continued growth from our existing lines. But that won't be enough; we will never get to a hundred million that way! We are going to have to add some new products and do some acquisitions. In five years we must be in other areas.
>
> I'm only interested in ideas related to the general area of biomedical research. There is, for example, the whole area of potential uses of invertebrates for teaching rather than research purposes, and we should get involved. There is a San Diego business that collects marine specimens, but it is 3,000 miles away and too much of a management drain for sales of $200,000 a year.
>
> What Charles River can bring to an acquired company is capital and management expertise. We need to get into a growing market with an already profitable company. We don't want any more businesses that needs a dollar of facilities investment to produce a dollar of sales, and we can't absorb losses of $100,000 to $300,000 a year like our early Japanese joint venture experience.
>
> We would want the principal to stay on for at least two or three years to provide operating expertise. We can't rebuild an organization or train a whole new team of people.

Biologicals

> A natural area of interest would be the production of biologicals.[12] We could use our retired breeders[13] and substandard animals; our entry would be essentially in the animal parts by-product business. We already have generated $100,000 in preserved organ sales as a by-product of our monkey importing business with only a couple of people working on it. One of the problems though is that the market is so unorganized, and we don't have a marketing organization that sells to one of the key markets—schools and universities.
>
> There is a possible, fine acquisition here—it's Quality Biologicals.[14] They are one of the largest in the business—I think about 20 million

---

[12] The production of biologicals was a $30 million a year business in 1975, company officers estimated. The products included monkey kidney cell cultures which were used as a growing media for producing Salk polio vaccine, rodent liver powder used as a filter in separating portions of cells, and animal organs such as rodent lungs, brains, or eyes for special experiments. This estimate did not include school sales of related products, for example, slides, models, or laboratory specimens for dissecting purposes.

[13] Retired breeders were one year or older female rodents which had produced many litters of young in the production colonies.

[14] Disguised name.

in sales, and a superior profit record. Let's look at their Dun and Brad-street!

After studying it, Dr. Foster continued. "Guess they are only 5 or 6 million in sales and about 2 million in assets. It's a private family firm and their management is getting old. They sell things such as one-celled animal slides, plastic models of specimens, and the general biologicals line to schools plus universities and wholesale suppliers in the United States and 30 different countries.

Contract testing and research

"Another area we might consider is what some people call contract testing and research—I prefer to call that type of business an industrial toxicology laboratory. Its purpose would be to help get new products through the constantly changing testing regulations required by the Food and Drug Administration before human clinical trial tests can be done. Firms in this field are growing at 10 to 20 percent per year.[15] We were offered a $20 million diversified biomedical company, which had an industrial toxicology lab, several years ago, but we couldn't swallow it at the time. We would have to enter this field through an acquisition."

People like Revlon [cosmetics], Gillette [personal health care prod-ucts] and Du Pont [paint]—all are customers, all are now doing in-dustrial toxicology work. Some of their tests are long—two years or so —and they can't do everything themselves so they subcontract. We have a natural interest in this field.

At our March meeting of the Society of Toxicology Dr. Russell Peter-son, chairman of the Council on Environmental Quality talked about the proposed Toxic Substances Act. If that is passed every drug will have to be tested for long-term cancer-inducing possibilities. That will be good for our basic business. And, since they can't do all that long-term testing work themselves, they will have to use outside firms for some of this testing work.

To enter the field it takes good physical space and environmental controls (costing in total about $80–$100 a square foot), the technical competence to maintain large animal colonies over long time periods, good management, and superior toxicology competence. We would have to hire the latter and it would have to be good. The risk would be that you have contamination when you are 18 months into a test or that your toxicologist misinterprets the data. That happened with a large midwestern drug company recently, and it really gave that com-pany a black eye. In our case that "black eye" might damage our basic business reputation and that would be serious. I worry about that.

A middle ground would be to subcontract the use of our facilities; we have some excess space in upstate New York. We could set up the colony, feed and care for the animals per their instructions, sacrifice animals per their schedule, and send the specimens to the main com-pany.

On another occasion, Sumner Foster commented on some of the drawbacks of establishing a large-scale contract testing business. "With

---

[15] The Pharmaceutical Manufacturers Association estimated that U.S. pharma-ceutical companies alone purchased $106 million worth of supplementary R&D services in 1974.

a general contract testing business, Charles River would be directly competing with some of our largest lab animal customers. Testing is very people dependent. The principals must be well known, respected in their field, and have personal contacts at the FDA. It is very easy for a principal to go off and start his own testing business."

The director of product testing for a large cosmetic and personal care products company commented on contract testing noting that, beginning in 1974, many of the firms in his industry had brought this work back "in-house." "There are few capable companies in the field. Many do tests, but they are not reliable enough to keep you out of the courts. The 'in-house testing' trend may be because of this lack of reliability and short supply of competent firms. We went in-house out of necessity. We have 30,000 very expensive square feet of facilities; the best air-handling units in the country. We don't have as extensive facilities as CRBL and we are not as automated as they are nor do we use COBS® or pathogen-free animals for our work."

Clinical testing

Dr. Foster continued, "You know we were once in the clinical testing field—that's different from contract testing. You analyze throat cultures, blood samples or human tissue for your local doctor or hospital. We built up a $0.5 million business and then quit. We were early in the game too and an innovator. But the little lab down the street would cut the price on a test a nickel or a dime and kill you. The only way to bring needed quality to this important field is to move away from human to instrumental analysis. You ought to talk with Bill on this."

Bill Keough in a later interview emphasized that much of the company's success had resulted from staying out of areas about which the company didn't know anything. He cited, as an example, Charles River's venture into the clinical testing business between 1968 and 1970. "Charles River was one of the first New England businesses in clinical testing, and now successful companies have sales of a $100 million a year. But we got out of it because it took too much management time for its profitability. The technology was changing so fast, each year you'd need a new machine, and price competition was more important than quality."

Cage manufacturing

"We were offered a chance again recently to buy a cage company in Maryland. It was a good company with a good record—there is money to be made there—but, we don't have expertise in that area," Dr. Foster said.

Charles River, the researcher learned later, had had an opportunity to enter the lab animal cage manufacturing business when the company purchased Carworth from the Becton, Dickinson & Company, but had chosen to sell Carworth's cage manufacturing division. The total market for both metal and plastic lab animal cages, company officers estimated, was between $7 million and $10 million a year. Hazelton Laboratories had recently acquired several leading metal cage producing companies, and one New Jersey Company accounted for nearly $4 million in annual sales of plastic cages. Plastic cage manufacturing was a simple technology and only required a $50,000 to $60,000 capital investment. Lab animal cages were a durable commodity product. Company officers believed there had been little recent design innovation and that patent protection was not available. The business was price competitive and relied on a substantial sales organization. Marketing costs alone were estimated to amount to 50 percent of sales.

Animal colony management and consulting services

"We are now performing lab animal colony management services for our licensee in Japan," commented Dr. Foster. "We have an administrator there who was trained here at Wilmington and who reports to us weekly by phone.

"But animal colony management for a drug firm or institution holding test animals is different from our production-oriented process at Charles River. I'm concerned about offering other expertise to our current customers. If anything went wrong, we could lose the total relationship. However, we could consult on facilities design. That's an area where we have expertise and most people are not qualified.

Making the strategic choice

"How do I choose? It's terribly difficult to get started and there is risk. What is my 'vehicle' to get involved? There are so many possibilities open to us.

"How do we go about this choice? Do I set up a prestigious scientific biomedical committee, like the committees of the Academy of Science, to discuss where we should be going, where we should be looking? They should be paid a fine honorarium, and we could meet in Bermuda.

"I have to get staff assistance to give me the time to work on this. We missed a company in Canada, and I ought to go down and see the owners of Quality Biologicals. We need to start now. But I don't really know what button to push. What is the right button?"

APPENDIX

INFORMATION ON FIRMS INVOLVED IN THE BIOMEDICAL INDUSTRY*

INTERNATIONAL RESEARCH AND DEVELOPMENT COMPANY—1972[1]

. . . let me state that International Research and Development is an independent research laboratory engaged primarily in safety evaluation of chemical compounds. . . . Much of our business is in the areas of toxicology [the study of possible harmful effects of substances] and pharmacology [the science of drugs]. Other major areas of involvement include environmental health studies, pathology and chemistry; and more specific areas such as carcinogenesis, mutagenesis, and microbiology.

* Information abstracted from latest annual report available in Charles River Breeding's files on firms involved in the biomedical industry.

[1] 1972 President's report by Dr. F. X. Wazeter, Ph.D. In 1972 company revenues were $2,134,377 with net earnings of $324,098, and 1972 revenues were $3,601,343 with net earnings of $384,391. Stockholders' equity in 1972 was $4,370,660.

In addition to this research work, we provide all clients with computerized statistical analysis; preparation of all types of material to be filed with governmental regulatory agencies; and overall counsel on research needs. In short, IRDC serves as a totally self-contained, safety evaluation research arm for big business and small . . . for private industries of all types, government and institutions . . . and for locations here and in other countries.

NATIONAL LABORATORIES, INC.[2]

The company's product

The company's products can be conveniently grouped as living cells, chemical media, animal sera, diagnostics, laboratory animals, and specialty laboratory equipment.

A changing market

. . . Cancer research and treatment has been a high priority of the health industry over the past several years with the budget for the National Cancer Institute rising sharply each year. There are signs that the general budget tightening within the National Institutes of Health is now extending to the Cancer Institute, which is an imporant source of funding for the company's services and products. Spending in research appears to be shifting away from the large "goal-oriented problems" into more modest beasic research programs. . . .

News release[3]

CAMBRIDGE, Mass.—National Laboratories, Inc. announced today that Dr. Arthur S. Sterling, Senior Vice President, has resigned effective March 1, 1976. Dr. Sterling has been with the company since 1965 and during that time has been instrumental in enabling the company to carry on a continuing cancer research program funded by contracts with the National Cancer Institute. His departure is likely to affect the company's ability to retain these contracts, the loss of which would have an adverse effect on the company's earnings.

HAZELTON LABORATORIES CORPORATION

As Hazelton Laboratories Corporation completes its sixth most successful year, it is appropriate at this time that we reflect on our past

[2] Disguised name. This material abstracted from the company's 1975 annual report. In 1975 National sales were $14,109,000 and net income was $576,000. Comparable results in 1974 were $11,763,000 and $432,000. Stockholders' equity in 1975 was $4,090,070; 1974—$3,513,796.

[3] This material contained in a company news release published November 26, 1975.

[4] Information abstracted from 1975 annual report. Hazelton revenues in 1974 were $11,306,892 with net earnings of $231,900 while revenues in 1975 were $15,961,946 with net earnings of $425,600. Contract revenue and costs were, respectively $7,709,601 and $5,987,390 in 1974, and $11,152,951 and $8,421,459 in 1975. Net stockholders equity was $3,832,232 in 1974 and $4,077,426 in 1975. Hazelton Laboratories division and Hazelton Laboratories employed approximately 600 scientific and technical personnel. Company officers stated that Hazelton was the largest independent biological contract research organization in the world.

accomplishments, present growth and future potential. Hazelton today is the result of a corporate growth program initiated in 1969. At that time it appeared that the life science industry offered unlimited growth potential. Subsequent analysis of this industry proved it to be in an embryonic state, highly fragmented in terms of specialized resources, and lacking a single company responsive to the increasingly integrated demands of the industry on a broad scale. Plans were formulated to amalgamate several of the leading companies of this industry into one large, well-financed company. This strategy was followed and the company today is the culmination of 11 acquisitions.

The businesses of Hazelton all relate to the life science industry, and as originally projected in 1969, the industry continues to grow at a rate at least double that of the overall economy. The demand for safety and efficacy testing is increasing at an accelerating rate as industry and government develop new compounds and evaluate old ones. Demand is further increased by new government regulations requiring additional evaluation of well-established and widely used compounds and products.

Services provided: Testing of products and chemical compounds; consultation on regulatory affairs; laboratory facilities design; laboratory animal colony management. *Products evaluated:* agricultural, industrial and household chemicals; drugs; food and color additives; cosmetics; medical devices. *Products manufactured:* animal housing systems; metabolism units; germ free environmental equipment; veterinarian surgical instruments and hospital equipment; intensive care oxygen units; pathological waste disposal systems. *Laboratory animal breeding:* primate colony management; canine breeding; primate breeding.

BOOK ONE

Determining corporate strategy

The concept of corporate strategy

WHEN WE were looking at the chief executive's job, we promised that a simple central concept called *corporate strategy* would be developed here. It would be offered, we said, as a means to reduce the general management function to manageable proportions and enable technical specialists to understand the proper relationship between their departmental objectives and the goals of their companies. We come now to the central idea of this course and this book. We will look at what strategy is, what form it takes in different kinds of companies, what tests of validity may be applied to it, and what it is good for. If you think back to your discussions of Head Ski and Charles River Breeding, you may already be able to see or imagine what does or can happen to this idea in living organizations and sense both its inherent difficulties and its power.

WHAT STRATEGY IS

As the outcome of the decision process we will later analyze in detail, corporate strategy is the pattern of decisions in a company that (1) determines, shapes, and reveals its objectives, purposes, or goals; (2) produces the principal policies and plans for achieving these goals; and (3) defines the business the company intends to be in, the kind of economic and human organization it intends to be, and the nature of the economic and noneconomic contribution it intends to make to its shareholders, employees, customers, and communities. In an organization of any size or diversity, corporate strategy usually applies to the whole enterprise, while business strategy, less comprehensive, defines the choice of product or service and market or individual businesses within the firm. *Business strategy*, that is, determines how a company will compete in a given business and position itself among its competitors. *Corporate strategy* defines the businesses in which a company will compete, preferably

93

in a way that focuses resources to convert distinctive competence into competitive advantage. Both are outcomes of a continuous process of *strategic management* that we will later analyze in detail.

The strategic decision contributing to this pattern is one that is effective over long periods of time, affects the company in many different ways, and focuses and commits a significant portion of its resources to expected outcomes. The pattern resulting from a series of such decisions will probably define the central character and image of a company, the individuality it has for its members and various publics, and the position it will occupy in its industry and markets. It will permit the specification of particular objectives to be attained through a timed sequence of investment and implementation decisions and will govern directly the deployment or redeployment of resources to make these decisions effective.

Some aspects of such a pattern of decision may be in an established corporation unchanging over long periods of time, like a commitment to quality, or high technology, or certain raw materials, or good labor relations. Other aspects of a strategy must change as or before the world changes, such as product line, manufacturing process, or merchandising and styling practices. The basic determinants of company character, if purposefully institutionalized, are likely to persist through and shape the nature of substantial changes in the allocation of resources and of product policy.

It would be possible to extend the definition of strategy for a given company to separate a central character and the core of its special accomplishment from the manifestations of such characteristics in changing product lines, markets, and policies designed to make activities profitable from year to year. *The New York Times,* for example, after many years of being shaped by the values of its owners and staff, is now so self-conscious and respected an institution that its nature is likely to remain unchanged, even if the services it offers are altered drastically in the direction of other outlets for its news-processing capacity.

It is important not to take the idea of strategy apart—to separate goals from the policies designed to achieve those goals, or even to overdo the difference between the formulation of strategy and its implementation. The interdependence of purposes, policies, and organized action is crucial to the particularity of an individual strategy. It is the unity, coherence, and internal consistency of a company's strategic decisions that gives the firm its identity and individuality, its power to mobilize its strengths, and its likelihood of success in the marketplace. It is the interrelationship of a set of goals and policies that crystallizes from the formless reality of a company's environment a set of problems an organization can seize upon and solve.

What you are doing, in short, is never meaningful unless you can imply what you are doing it for; the quality of administrative action and the motivation lending it power cannot be appraised without knowing its relationship to purpose. Breaking up the system of corporate goals and the character-determining major policies for attainment leads to narrow and mechanical conceptions of strategic management and endless logic chopping.

We should get on to understanding the need for strategic decision and for determining the most satisfactory pattern of goals in concrete instances. Refinement of definition can wait, for you will wish to develop definition in practice in directions useful to you.

SUMMARY STATEMENTS OF STRATEGY

Before we proceed to clarification of the strategy concept by application, we should specify the terms in which strategy is usually expressed. A summary statement of strategy will characterize the product line and services offered or planned by the company, the markets and market segments for which products and services are now or will be designed, and the channels through which these markets will be reached. The means by which the operation is to be financed will be specified, as will the profit objectives and the emphasis to be placed on the safety of capital versus level of return. Major policy in central functions, such as marketing, manufacturing, procurement, research and development, labor relations, and personnel, will be stated where they distinguish the company from others; and usually the intended size, form, and climate of the organization would be included.

In a statement of Howard Head's intuitive or consciously designed strategy for Head Ski, some of these categories would be missing (profit objectives, for example) but others stressed (for example, quality of product). Each company, if it were to construct a summary strategy from what it understands itself to be aiming at, would have a different statement with different categories of decision emphasized to indicate what it wanted to be or do.

To indicate the nature of such a statement, a student of Heublein, a famous old policy case, deduced this statement from the account of the company when it was much smaller and less diversified than it is now and was about to acquire Hamm's Brewery:[1]

> Heublein aims to market in the United States and via franchise overseas a wide variety of high-margin, high-quality consumer products concentrated in the liquor and food business, especially bottled cocktails, vodka, and other special-use and distinctive beverages and specialty convenience foods, addressed to a relatively prosperous, young-adult market and returning over 15 percent of equity after taxes. With emphasis on the techniques of consumer goods marketing [brand promotion, wide distribution, product representation in more than one price segment, and very substantial offbeat advertising directed closely to its growing audience] Heublein intends to make Smirnoff the number one liquor brand worldwide via internal growth [and franchise] or acquisitions or both. Its manufacturing policy rather than full integration is in liquor to redistill only to bring purchased spirits up to high quality standards. It aims to finance its internal growth

---

[1] The Heublein case may be found in earlier editions of this book or obtained from HBS Case Services.

through the use of debt and its considerable cash flow and to use its favorable price earnings ratio for acquisitions. Both its liquor and food distribution are intended to secure distributor support through advertising and concern for the distributor's profit.[2]

Although it might be argued that the statement was not clearly in the chief executive's mind when he contemplated purchasing Hamm's Brewery and therefore did not help him refrain from that decision, it was in his experience and in the pattern of the company's past strategic decisions—at least as reported in the case. Note also that this statement must be regarded as only a partial summary, for it omits reference to the kind of human organization Heublein means to be for its members and the responsibility its leaders feel for such strategy-related social problems as alcoholism. But even without mention of organization or social responsibility substrategies, this statement raises a multimillion dollar question about the beer business as a compatible element in the company's marketing mix.

REASONS FOR NOT ARTICULATING STRATEGY

For a number of reasons companies seldom formulate and publish as complete a statement as we have just illustrated. Conscious planning of the long-term development of companies has been until recently less common than individual executive responses to environmental pressure, competitive threat, or entrepreneurial opportunity. In the latter mode of development, the unity or coherence of corporate effort is unplanned, natural, intuitive, or even nonexistent. Incrementalism in practice sometimes gives the appearance of consciously formulated strategy, but may be the natural result of compromise among coalitions backing contrary policy proposals or skillful improvisatory adaptation to external forces.[3] Practicing managers who prefer muddling through to the strategic process at the heart of Business Policy would never commit themselves to an articulate strategy.

Other reasons for the scarcity of concrete statements of strategy include the desirability of keeping strategic plans confidential for security reasons and ambiguous to avoid internal conflict or even final decision. Skillful incrementalists may have plans in their heads which they do not reveal to avoid resistance and other trouble in their own organization. A company with a large division in an obsolescent business which it intends to drain of cash until operations are discontinued could not expect high morale and cooperation to follow publication of this intent. Finally, since in any dynamic company, strategy is continually evolving, the official statement of strategy, unless it were couched in very general terms, would be as hard to keep up to date as an organization chart. Finally, a firm that has internalized its strategy does not feel the need

---

[2] Kenneth R. Andrews, *The Concept of Corporate Strategy,* rev. ed. (Homewood, Ill.: Dow Jones-Irwin, 1980), p. 22.

[3] For an extended account of incrementalism, see David Braybrooke and Charles E. Lindblom, *A Strategy of Decision* (New York: Free Press, 1963).

to keep saying what it is, valuable as that information might be to new members.

DEDUCING STRATEGY FROM BEHAVIOR

The cases in this book enable students of Policy to do what the managements of the companies usually have not done. In the absence of explicit statements, we may deduce from decisions observed what the pattern is and what the company's goals and policies are, on the assumption that some perhaps unspoken consensus lies behind them. Careful examination of the behavior described in the cases will reveal what the strategy must be. At the same time we should not mistake apparent strategy visible in a pattern of past incremental decisions for conscious planning for the future. What will pass as the current strategy of a company may almost always be deduced from its behavior, but a strategy for a future of changed circumstance may not always be distinguishable from performance in the present. For all of Howard Head's skill in integrating a series of product development, distribution, merchandising, service, manufacturing, and research and development decisions around the metal ski, was he as well prepared as he might have been for the advent of the fiberglass ski? The essence of strategic decision is its reach into the future.

FORMULATION OF STRATEGY

Corporate strategy is an organization process, in many ways inseparable from the structure, behavior, and culture of the company in which it takes place. Nevertheless, we may abstract from the process two important aspects, interrelated in real life but separable for the purposes of analysis. The first of these we may call *formulation,* the second *implementation.* Deciding what strategy should be may be approached as a rational undertaking, even if in real life emotional attachments (as to metal skis or investigative reporting) may complicate choice among future alternatives (for ski manufacturers or alternative newspapers). The principal subactivities of strategy formulation as a logical activity include identifying opportunities and threats in the company's environment and attaching some estimate or risk to the discernible alternatives. Before a choice can be made, the company's strengths and weaknesses should be appraised together with the resources on hand and available. Its actual or potential capacity to take advantage of perceived market needs or to cope with attendant risks should be estimated as objectively as possible. The strategic alternative which results from matching opportunity and corporate capability at an acceptable level of risk is what we may call an *economic strategy.*

The process described thus far assumes that strategists are analytically objective in estimating the relative capacity of their company and the opportunity they see or anticipate in developing markets. The extent to which they wish to undertake low or high risk presumably depends on their profit objectives. The higher they set the latter, the more willing they must be to assume a correspondingly high risk that the market opportunity they see will not develop or that the corporate competence required to excel competition will not be forthcoming.

So far we have described the intellectual processes of ascertaining what a company *might do* in terms of environmental opportunity, of deciding what it *can do* in terms of ability and power, and of bringing these two considerations together in optimal equilibrium. The determination of strategy also requires consideration of what alternatives are preferred by the chief executive and perhaps by his or her immediate associates as well, quite apart from economic considerations. Personal values, aspirations, and ideals do, and in our judgment quite properly should, influence the final choice of purposes. Thus what the executives of a company *want to do* must be brought into the strategic decision.

Finally strategic choice has an ethical aspect—a fact much more dramatically illustrated in some industries than in others. Just as alternatives may be ordered in terms of the degree of risk that they entail, so may they be examined against the standards of responsiveness to the expectations of society that the strategist elects. Some alternatives may seem to the executive considering them more attractive than others when the public good or service to society is considered. What a company *should do* thus appears as a fourth element of the strategic decision.

The ability to identify the four components of strategy—(1) market opportunity, (2) corporate competence and resources, (3) personal values and aspirations, and (4) acknowledged obligations to segments of society other than stockholders—is nothing compared to the art of reconciling their implications in a final choice of purpose. Taken by itself, each consideration might lead in a different direction.

If you put the various aspirations of individuals in *The Real Paper* against this statement you will see what we mean. Even in a single mind contradictory aspirations can survive a long time before the need to calculate trade-offs and integrate divergent inclinations becomes clear. Growth opportunity attracted many companies to the computer business after World War II. The decision to diversify out of typewriters and calculators was encouraged by growth opportunity and excitement. But the financial, technical, and marketing requirements of this business exceeded the capacity of most of the competitors of IBM. The magnet of opportunity and the incentive of desire obscured the calculations of what resources and competence were required to succeed. Most crucially, where corporate capability leads, executives do not always want to go. Of all the components of strategic choice, the combination of resources and competence is most crucial to success.

THE IMPLEMENTATION OF STRATEGY

Since effective implementation can make a sound strategic decision ineffective or a debatable choice successful, it is as important to examine the processes of implementation as to weigh the advantages of available strategic alternatives. The implementation of strategy is comprised of a series of subactivities which are primarily administrative. If purpose

Figure 1

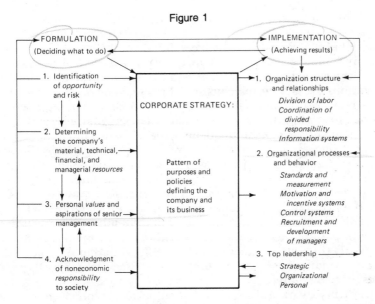

is determined, then the resources of a company can be mobilized to accomplish it. An organizational structure appropriate for the efficient performance of the required tasks must be made effective by information systems and relationships permitting coordination of subdivided activities. The organizational processes of performance measurement, compensation, management development—all of them enmeshed in systems of incentives and controls—must be directed toward the kind of behavior required by organizational purpose. The role of personal leadership is important and sometimes decisive in the accomplishment of strategy. Although we know that organization structure and processes of compensation, incentives, control, and management development influence and constrain the formulation of strategy, we should look first at the logical proposition that structure should follow strategy in order to cope with the organizational reality that strategy also follows structure. When we have examined both tendencies, we will understand and to some extent be prepared to deal with the interdependence of the formulation and implementation of corporate purpose. Figure 1 may be useful in understanding the analysis of strategy as a pattern of interrelated decisions.

KINDS OF STRATEGIES

The most important characteristic of a corporate pattern of decision that may properly be called strategic is its uniqueness. A creative reconciliation of alternatives for future development is made unique by the special characteristics of an organization, its central competence, history, financial and technical resources, and the aspirations and sense of responsibility of its leaders. The environment—market opportunity and risk—is more nearly the same for major companies operating in the same geographical regions than are the resources, values, and responsibility components of strategy. For the company unequipped to dominate the full range of opportunity, the quest for a profitable segment of, or niche in, a market is, if successful, also likely to distinguish one company from another. In fact in an industry where all companies seem to have the same strategy, we will find trouble for all but the leaders—as at various times American Motors, Chrysler, and Ford have had different degrees of difficulty following General Motors, which got where it is by *not* following the previous industry leader, Henry Ford.[4]

In seeking its position of uniqueness, there are two fundamental types of competitive advantage that a company can possess: *lower cost* and/ or *differentiation.* A lower cost position can potentially come from many sources that reflect the firm's strategy, among them larger scale, favorable raw material supplies, or proximate location. A lower cost position yields the firm higher profitability than rivals at whatever the industry price. Differentiation, or the superiority of the company in meeting special or important customer needs, yields the firm higher profitability than rivals through a premium price. Differentiation may potentially result from many aspects of the company's strategy, including its product quality, servicing ability, or delivery time.

Every truly successful strategy that outperforms competitors exploits one or both of these two sources of competitive advantage, achieved in a manner that is *sustainable* against rivals. Viewing strategies broadly, there are three possible generic strategies for doing this:

1. *Overall cost leadership.* While producing a product or service of good quality, the company strives to be the overall cost leader across its entire product line in the industry. This position is achieved through a range of supporting functional policies compatible with industry economics.

2. *Differentiation.* The company strives to be distinctive in an important aspect of most of its products or services that the customer values. Costs are kept close to those of competitors, but the strategic emphasis is on achieving and maintaining the chosen form of differentiation, quality, or style, for example, through the coordinated activities of each functional department. Again this selective superiority is attempted across the entire product line and in all its markets.

3. *Focus.* Unable to be the low-cost producer industrywide or to achieve comprehensive differentiation, the firm selects a narrower strategic target and concentrates its entire efforts at serving a distinctively defined market segment. In so doing, the firm is able to achieve lower costs, differentiation, or both in serving the chosen market even though it cannot achieve these competitive advantages industrywide or across the broadest possible product line. Possible strategic targets may include portions of the product line, particular customer segments, limited geographic areas, particular distribution channels, or some combination of these. The essential logic of the focused strategy is that the firm competing in this way can serve its target better than the competitor with

---

[4] For a basic study in strategy formulations, see Alfred P. Sloan, *My Years at General Motors* (Garden City, N.Y.: Doubleday & Co., 1964).

the divided loyalties of serving a special target along with others in a more broadly based strategy.

Usually, the firm must make a choice among these three fundamentally different approaches to achieving a competitive advantage because the functional requirements and organizational needs of each are different. Generally, for example, the firm achieving differentiation does so at the price of higher costs. In a few industries where the economics allow it, however, a firm can be both cost leader and differentiated at the same time. The enviable position is nirvana, remote from the pain and turmoil of competition.

On the way to this happy state, companies encounter other generic strategies, less universal than low-cost differentiation and focus but more common. The generation of strategic alternatives is sometimes approached with growth the dominant consideration, as follows:

Low-growth strategies:

1. *No change.* The strategy properly identified and checked out against the tests of validity outlined below can be closely monitored, fine-tuned for minor defects, managed for maximum cash flows, with low investment in forced growth. Defensive contingencies will be designed for unexpected change, and efficient implementation will be the focus of top-management attention. During recessions and since the onset of conservation and environmental protection, this strategy is more attractive than it was in the heyday of "more is better." The profit to be made from doing better what a company already knows how to do rather than investing heavily in growth is the attraction of this strategy, which can be protected by achievement of low costs. Its disadvantage is the possibility of being overtaken or displaced by new developments and the restriction of opportunity for organization members. Positions in cost advantage and differentiation may be less vulnerable if growth goals are modest.

2. *Retreat.* The possibility of liquidation is not to be sought out but may be for companies in deep trouble a better choice than continuing the struggle. Less drastic alternatives than complete liquidation include discontinuance or divestment of marginal operations or merging with a ceding of management control. This alternative may come to mind as you look at one or two of the cases in this book. It would have come up more often in earlier editions around cases from the farm equipment, typewriter, and sewing machine businesses. Consolidation may protect a market niche.

3. *Focus on limited special opportunity.* A more constructive course of contraction is concentration on a profitable specialty product or a limited but significant market niche, as if Head had elected to concentrate on high-priced, high-quality skis without diversification into ski wear and other equipment. Success in a narrow line almost always tempts a company to broaden its line, but the McIlhenny strategy (Tabasco sauce only) may not be totally

obsolete. If the proper focus is chosen, the limits may relax and growth may come in any case. Once the risk of limited life is accepted, the advantages of the no-change strategy can be sought.

Forced-growth strategies:

1. *Acquisition of competitors.* In the early stages of its development, a company with a successful strategy and proven record of successful execution can acquire small competitors in the same business to expand its market. Eventually antitrust regulation will put an end to this practice, unless the prospective acquisition is very small or on the edge of bankruptcy. Such acquisitions are usually followed by an adaptation of strategy either by the parent or acquired company to keep the total company a single business or one dominated by its original product-market specialization. Lower costs do not follow automatically from growth by acquisition.

2. *Vertical integration.* A conservative growth strategy, keeping a company close to its core competence and experience in its industry, consists of moving backward via acquisition or internal development to sources of supply and forward toward the ultimate customer. When a newspaper buys a pulp and paper mill and forest lands or news agencies for distribution, it is extending its strategy but not changing materially the nature of its business. Increasing the stages of integration provides a greater number of options to be developed or closed out as, for example, the making of fine paper and the distribution of magazines. Vertical integration serves lower costs better than it serves product differentiation.

3. *Geographical expansion.* Enlargement of territory can be accomplished by building new plants and enlarging marketing organizations or by acquisition of competitors. For a sizable company the opportunity to enlarge international operations, by export, establishments of plants and marketing activities overseas, with or without foreign partners, may protect against contraction forced by domestic competition. You could have considered the possibility of Head Ski's seeking growth overseas, where 19 percent of its sales were accomplished by a single agent about whom almost nothing is said in the case.

4. *Diversification.* The avenue to growth which presents the most difficult strategic choices is diversification. Diversification can range from minor additions to basic product line to completely unrelated businesses. It can be sought through internal research and development, the purchase of new product ideas or technology, and the acquisition of companies. It may have nothing to do with either lower costs or differentiation of product or service and distract seriously from both.

KINDS OF COMPANIES

The process of strategic decision differs in complexity depending upon the diversity of the company in question. Just as having the range of strategy from liquidation to multinational diversification in mind will stimulate the generation of strategic alternatives, so a simple way of differentiating kinds of companies will help us see why different kinds of companies have different kinds of problems in making their activities coherent and effective and in setting a course for the future.

Bruce Scott has developed a model of stages of corporate development in which each stage is characterized by the way a firm is managed and the scope of strategic choice available to it.[5] *Stage I* is a single-product (or line of products) company with little or no formal structure run by the owner who personally performs most of the managerial functions, uses subjective and unsystematic measures of performance and reward and control systems. The strategy of this firm is what the owner-manager wants it to be.

Stage II is the single-product firm grown so large that functional specialization has become imperative. A degree of integration has developed between raw materials, production processes, distribution, and sales. The search for product or process improvement is institutionalized in research and development, and performance management and control and compensation systems become systematic with the formulation of policy to guide delegation of operating decisions. The strategic choice is still under top control and centers upon the degree of integration, size of market share, and breadth of product line.

Stage III is a company with multiple-product lines and channels of distribution with an organization based on product-market relationships rather than function. Its businesses are not to a significant degree integrated; they have their own markets. Its research and development is oriented to new products rather than improvements, and its measurement and control systems are increasingly systematic and oriented to results. Strategic alternatives are phrased in terms of entry into and exit from industries and allocation of resources by industry and rate of growth.

If a company grows, it may pass from stage I to stage III, although it can be very large in stage II. Its strategic decisions will grow in complexity. The stages of development model has proved productive in relating different kinds of strategies to kinds of companies and has led other researchers into productive classification. Leonard Wrigley and Richard P. Rumelt have carried Scott's work forward to develop suggestive ways of categorizing companies and comparing their strategies.[6]

First, of course, is the *single-business* firm (stages I and II firms) with 95 percent or more of its revenues arising from a single business— an oil company or flour-milling company, for example, to say nothing of Crown Cork & Seal.

---

[5] See Bruce R. Scott, "Stages of Corporate Development, Parts I and II" (unpublished paper, Harvard Business School, 1970).

[6] Leonard Wrigley, "Division Autonomy and Diversification" (unpublished doctoral dissertation, Harvard Business School, 1970); and Richard P. Rumelt, *Strategy Structure and Economic Performance* (Division of Research, Harvard Business School, 1974). Malcolm Salter has added a refinement to stage III in "Stages of Corporate Development," *Journal of Business Policy* 1, no. 1 (1970), pp. 40–51.

2)   Second is the *dominant business* consisting of firms diversified to some extent but still obtaining most of their revenues from a single business. The diversification may arise from end products of integration, with products stemming from strengths of the firm or minor unrelated activities. A large oil company in the petrochemical and fertilizer business would fall in this category.

3)   Third is the *related business* comprising diversified firms in which the diversification has been principally accomplished by relating new activities to old—General Electric and Westinghouse, for example.

4)   Fourth is the *unrelated business.* These firms have diversified primarily without regard to relationships between new businesses and current activities. The conglomerate companies fall in this category.

Each of these categories have subdivisions devised by Rumelt which you may wish to examine at a more advanced stage of Policy studies. In the meantime it is interesting to note that Rumelt has found significantly superior performance in the related businesses, suggesting that the strategy of diversifying from the original business to a significant degree has been the most successful strategic pattern among the *Fortune 500* under conditions prevailing in recent years.

The range of strategy and the kinds of company which different growth strategies have produced suggest, in short, that the process of defining the business of a company will vary greatly depending on the degree of diversification under way in the company. The product-market choices are crystal clear in Crown Cork & Seal and a single-business oil company; they could not even be exhaustibly listed for General Electric. That top management decides product-market questions in such a company, except in such instances as entry into nuclear energy, is conceivable only as an oversimplification.

As diversification increases, the definition of the total business turns away from literal description of products and markets (which become the business of the separate product divisions) toward general statements of financial results expected and corporate principle in other areas. A conglomerate firm made up of many different businesses will have many different strategies, related or not depending upon the desire for synergy in the strategic direction of the total enterprise. The overall strategy of a highly diversified firm may be only the total of its divisional strategies. That it should be more than that is a matter for argument. To make it so puts heavy demands on the ability to conceptualize corporate purpose.

The task of identifying the coherence and unity of a conglomerate is, of course, much greater than that of even a multidivision-related business. Students should be prepared, then, to adapt the beginning definition offered here to the complexity of the business they are examining. Since the trend over time is product diversity in growing firms and evolution from stage I to stage III, it is well to have this complication in mind now.

For as Norman Berg makes clear in "Strategic Planning in Conglomerate Companies," strategic choice is not merely the function of the

conglomerates

chief executive office.[7] It is of necessity a multilevel activity, with each unit concerned with its own environment and its own objectives. The process will reflect the noneconomic goals of people at the level at which proposals are made. In a conglomerate of unrelated businesses the corporate staff is small, the divisions relatively autonomous, and the locus of strategic planning is in the divisions. This makes supervision of the strategic planning process and allocation of resources, depending upon the evaluation of strategies submitted, the strategic role of the corporate senior managers.

The differences in the application of a concept of strategy to a modest single business on the one hand and to a multinational conglomerate on the other—although important—mean that the ability to conceive of a business in strategic terms must be distributed throughout the organization in a complex company. The problems of choosing among strategic alternatives and making the choice effective over time, together with the problems of ensuring that such organization processes as performance measurement do not impede the choice, must be part of the management ability of many people besides the general managers. All those involved in the strategic process, it follows, are vitally concerned with how a strategy can be evaluated so that it may be continued, amended, or abandoned as appropriate. Operating level managers who make a strategic proposal should be able to test its validity against corporate norms if for no other reason than their own survival. Those who must approve and allocate funds to such proposals should have a criterion to evaluate their worth going beyond a general confidence (or lack of it) in the ability of the proponents.

CRITERIA FOR EVALUATION

How is the actual or proposed strategy to be judged? How are we to know that one strategy is better than another? A number of important questions can regularly be asked. As is already evident, no infallible indicators are available. With practice they will lead to reliable intuitive discriminations.

1. Is the strategy identifiable and has it been made clear either in words or practice?

The degree to which attention has been given to the strategic alternatives available to a company is likely to be basic to the soundness of its strategic decision. To cover in empty phrases ("Our policy is planned profitable growth in any market we can serve well") an absence of analysis of opportunity or actual determination of corporate strength is worse than to remain silent, for it conveys the illusion of a commitment when none has been made. The unstated strategy cannot be tested or contested and is likely therefore to be weak. If it is implicit in the intuition of a strong leader,

---

[7] Norman Berg, "Strategic Planning in Conglomerate Companies," *Harvard Business Review*, May–June 1965, pp. 79–92. See also his "What's Different about Conglomerate Management?" *Harvard Business Review*, November–December 1969.

the organization is likely to be weak and the demands the strategy makes upon it are likely to remain unmet. A strategy must be explicit to be effective and specific enough to require some action and exclude others.

2. *Does the strategy exploit fully domestic and international environmental opportunity?*

An unqualified yes answer is likely to be rare even in the instance of global giants such as General Motors. But the present and future dimensions of markets can be analyzed without forgetting the limited resources of the planning company in order to outline the requirements of balanced growth and the need for environmental information. The relation between market opportunity and organizational development is a critical one in the design of future plans. Unless growth is incompatible with the resources of an organization or the aspirations of its management, it is likely that a strategy that does not purport to make full use of market opportunity will be weak also in other aspects. Vulnerability to competition is increased by lack of interest in market share.

3. *Is the strategy consistent with corporate competence and resources, both present and projected?*

Although additional resources, both financial and managerial, are available to companies with genuine opportunity, the availability of each must be finally determined and programmed along a practicable time scale. This may be the most difficult question in this series. The key factor which is usually left out is the availability of management for effective implementation or the opportunity cost implicit in the assignment of management to any task.

4. *Are the major provisions of the strategy and the program of major policies of which it is comprised internally consistent?*

A foolish consistency, Emerson said, is the hobgoblin of little minds, and consistency of any kind is certainly not the first qualification of successful corporation presidents. Nonetheless, one advantage of making as specific a statement of strategy as is practicable is the resultant availability of a careful check on fit, unity, coherence, compatibility, and synergy—the state in which the whole of anything can be viewed as greater than the sum of its parts. For example, a manufacturer of chocolate candy who depends for two thirds of his business upon wholesalers should not follow a policy of ignoring them or of dropping all support of their activities and all attention to their complaints. Similarly, two engineers who found a new firm expressly to do development work should not follow a policy of accepting orders that, though highly profitable, in effect turn their company into a large job shop, with the result that unanticipated financial and production problems take all the time that might have gone into development. An examination of any substantial firm will reveal at least some details in which policies pursued by different departments tend to go in different directions. Where inconsistency threatens concerted effort to achieve budgeted results within a planned time period, then consistency becomes a vital rather than merely an esthetic problem.

5. *Is the chosen level of risk feasible in economic and personal terms?*

Strategies vary in the degree of risk willingly undertaken by their designers. For example, a small food company in pursuit of its marketing strategy, deliberately courted disaster in production slowdowns and in erratic behavior of cocoa futures. But the choice was made knowingly and the return was likely to be correspondingly great. The president was temperamentally able to live under this pressure and presumably had recourse if disaster struck. At the other extreme, another company had such modest growth aspirations that the junior members of its management were unhappy. They would have preferred a more aggressive and ambitious company. Although risk cannot always be known for sure, the level at which it is estimated is, within limits, optional. The riskiness of any future plan should be compatible with the economic resources of the organization and the temperament of the managers concerned.

6. *Is the strategy appropriate to the personal values and aspirations of the key managers?*

Until we consider the relationship of personal values to the choice of strategy, it is not useful to dwell long upon this criterion. But, to cite an extreme case, the deliberate falsification of warehouse receipts to conceal the absence of soybean oil from the tanks which are supposed to contain it would not be an element of competitive strategy to which most of us would like to be committed. A strong personal attraction of leisure, to cite a less extreme example, is inconsistent with a strategy requiring all-out effort from the senior members of a company. Or if, for example, a new president abhors conflict and competition, then it can be predicted that the hard-driven firm of an earlier day will have to change its strategy. Conflict between personal preferences, aspirations, and goals of the key members of an organization and the plan for its future is a sign of danger and a harbinger of mediocre performance or failure.

7. *Is the strategy appropriate to the desired level of contribution to society?*

Closely allied to the value is the ethical criterion. As the professional obligations of business are acknowledged by an increasing number of senior managers, it grows more and more appropriate to ask whether the current strategy of a firm is as socially responsible as it might be. Although it can be argued that filling any economic need contributes to the social good, it is clear that manufacturers of cigarettes might well consider diversification on grounds other than their fear of future legislation. That the strategy should not require violations of law or ethical practice to be effective became abundantly clear with the revelation in the mid-70s of widespread bribery and questionable payments, particularly in overseas activities. Honesty and integrity may seem exclusively questions of implementation, but if the strategy is not distinctive, making it effective in competition may tempt managers to unethical practice. Thus a drug manufacturer who emphasizes the production of amphetamines at a level beyond total established medical need is inevitably compelling corruption. The meeting of sales quotas at the distribution level necessitates distribution of the drug as "speed" with or without the cooperation of prescribing physicians. To the extent that the chosen economic opportunity of the firm has social costs, such as air or water pollution, a statement of intention to deal with these is desirable and prudent. Ways to ask and answer this question will be considered in the section on the company and its responsibilities to society.

8. *Does the strategy constitute a clear stimulus to organizational effort and commitment?*

For organizations which aspire not merely to survive but to lead and to generate productive performance in a climate that will encourage the development of competence and the satisfaction of individual needs, the strategy selected should be examined for its inherent attractiveness to the organization. Some undertakings are inherently more likely to gain the commitment of able men of goodwill than others. Given the variety of human preferences, it is risky to illustrate this difference briefly. But currently a company that is vigorously expanding its overseas operations finds that several of its socially conscious young people exhibit more zeal in connection with its work in developing countries than in Europe. Generally speaking, the bolder the choice of goals and the wider range of human needs they reflect, the more successfully they will appeal to the capable membership of a healthy and energetic organization.

9. *Are there early indications of the responsiveness of markets and market segments to the strategy?*

Results, no matter how long postponed by necessary preparations, are, of course, the most telling indicators of soundness, so long as they are read correctly at the proper time. A strategy may pass with flying colors all the tests so far proposed, and may be in internal consistency and uniqueness an admirable work of art. But if within a time period made reasonable by the company's resources and the original plan the strategy does not work, then it must be weak in some way that has escaped attention. Bad luck, faulty implementation, and competitive countermoves may be more to blame for unsatisfactory results than flaws in design, but the possibility of the latter should not be unduly discounted. Conceiving a strategy that will win the company a unique place in the business community, that will give it an enduring concept of itself, that will harmonize its diverse activities, and that will provide a fit between environmental opportunity and present or potential company strength is an extremely complicated task.

We cannot expect simple tests of soundness to tell the whole story. But an analytical examination of any company's strategy against the several criteria here suggested will nonetheless give anyone concerned with making, proving, or contributing to corporate planning a good deal to think about.

PROBLEMS IN EVALUATION

The evaluation of strategy is as much an act of judgment as is the original conception, and may be as subject to error. The most common source of difficulty is the misevaluation of current results. When results are unsatisfactory, as we have just pointed out, a reexamination of strategy is called for. At the same time, outstandingly good current results are not necessarily evidence that the strategy is sound. Abnormal upward surges in demand may deceive marginal producers that all is well within their current strategy, until expansion of more efficient competitors wipes out their market share. Extrapolation of present performance into the future, overoptimism and complacence, and underestimation of competitive response and of the time required to accommodate to changes in demand are often by-products of success. Unusually high profits may blind unwary managers to impending environmental change. Their concern for the future can under no circumstances be safely suspended. Conversely, a high-risk strategy that has failed was not necessarily a mistake, so long as the risk was anticipated and the consequences of failure carefully calculated. In fact, a planning problem confronting a number of diversified companies today is how to encourage their divisions to undertake projects where failure can be afforded but where success, if it comes, will be attended by high profits not available in run-of-the-mill, low-risk activities.

Although the possibility of misinterpreting results is by far the commonest obstacle to accurate evaluation of strategy, the criteria previously outlined suggest immediately some additional difficulties. It is as easy to misevaluate corporate resources and the financial requirements of a new move as to misread the environment for future opportunities. To be overresponsive to industry trends may be as dangerous as to ignore them. The correspondence of the company's strategy with current environmental developments and an overreadiness to adapt may obscure the opportunity for a larger share of a declining market or for growth in profits without a parallel growth in total sales. The decision of American Motors not to follow trends toward big cars in the middle 1950s provides us with an opportunity to examine the strategic alternatives of adapting to, or running counter to, massive current trends in demand.

The intrinsic difficulty of determining and choosing among strategic alternatives leads many companies to do what the rest of the industry is doing rather than to make an independent determination of opportunity and resources. Sometimes the companies of an industry run like sheep all in one direction. The similarity among the strategies, at least in some periods of history, of insurance companies, banks, railroads, and airplane manufacturers may lead one to wonder whether strategic decisions were based upon industry convention or upon independent analysis. Whether the similarity of timing, decision, and reaction to competition constitutes independent appraisals of each company's situation, or whether imitation took the place of independent decision is the basis of some wonder. At any rate, the similarity of one company's strategy to that of its competitors does not constitute the assurance of soundness which it might at first suggest.

A strategy may manifest an all-too-clear correspondence with the personal values of the founder, owner, or chief executive. Like a correspondence with dominant trends and the strategic decisions of competitors, this may also be deceptive and unproductive. For example, a personal preference for growth beyond all reasonable expectations may be given undue weight. It should be only one factor among several in any balanced consideration of what is involved in designing strategy. Too little attention to a corporation's actual competence for growth or diversification is the commonest error of all.

It is entirely possible that a strategy may reflect in an exaggerated fashion the values rather than the reasoned decisions of the responsible manager or managers and that imbalance may go undetected. That this may be the case is a reflection of the fact that the entire business community may be dominated by certain beliefs of which one should be wary. A critic of strategy must be at heart enough of a nonconformist to raise questions about generally accepted modes of thought and the conventional thinking which serves as a substitute for original analysis. The timid may not find it prudent to challenge publicly some of the ritual of policy formulation. But even for them it will serve the purposes of criticism to inquire privately into such sacred propositions as the one proclaiming that a company must grow or die or that national planning for energy needs is anathema.

Another canon of management that may engender questionable strategies is the idea that cash funds in excess of reasonable dividend requirements should be reinvested whether in revitalization of a company's traditional activities or in mergers and acquisitions that will diversify products and services. Successful operations, a heretic might observe, sometimes bring riches to a company which lacks the capacity to reemploy them. Yet a decision to return to the owners substantial amounts of capital which the company does not have the competence or desire to put to work is an almost unheard of development. It is therefore appropriate, particularly in the instance of very successful companies in older and stable industries, to inquire how far strategy reflects a simple desire to put all resources to work rather than a more valid appraisal of investment opportunity in relation to unique corporate strengths. We should not forget to consider an unfashionable, even if ultimately also an untenable, alternative—namely, that to keep an already large worldwide corporation within reasonable bounds, a portion of the assets might well be returned to stockholders for investment in other enterprises.

The identification of opportunity and choice of purpose are such challenging intellectual activities that we should not be surprised to find that persistent problems attend the proper evaluation of strategy. But just as the criteria for evaluation are useful, even if not precise, so the dangers of misevaluation are less menacing if they are recognized. We have noted some inexactness in the concept of strategy, the problems of making resolute determinations in the face of uncertainty, the necessity for judgment in the evaluation of soundness of strategy, and the misevaluation into which human error may lead us. None of these alters the fact that a business enterprise guided by a clear sense of purpose rationally arrived at and emotionally ratified by commitment is more likely to have a successful outcome, in terms of profit and social good, than a company whose future is left to guesswork and chance. Conscious strategy does not preclude brilliance of improvisation or the welcome consequences of good fortune. Its cost is principally thought and work for which it is hard but not impossible to find time.

APPLICATION TO CASES

As you attempt to apply the concept of strategy to the analysis of Crown Cork & Seal, BIC Pen, and later cases, try to keep in mind three questions:

1. What is the strategy of the company?
2. In the light of (a) the characteristics of its industry and developments in its environment and (b) its own strengths and weaknesses, is the strategy sound?
3. What recommendations for changed strategy might advantageously be made to the president?

Whatever other questions you may be asked or may ask yourself, you will wish constantly to order your study and structure your analysis of case information according to the need to *identify, evaluate,* and *recommend.*

By now you have an idea of strategy, which discussion of the cases will greatly clarify. You know how it is derived and some of its uses and limitations. You have been given some criteria for evaluating the strategies you identify and those you propose. And you have been properly warned about errors of judgment which await the unwary.

The cases which immediately follow will permit you to consider what contributions if any the concept of strategy (if mostly missing as a conscious formulation) would have made to these companies. What strategic alternatives can be detected in the changing circumstances affecting their fortunes? Which ones would you choose if you were responsible or asked to advise? By the time these cases have been examined, you will be ready to turn from the nature and uses of strategy to a study in sequence of its principal components—environmental opportunity, corporate capability, personal aspirations, and moral responsibility.

Crown Cork & Seal Company, Inc.

STRATEGIC POSITION, 1977

BY 1977 Crown Cork & Seal Company was the fourth-largest producer of metal cans and crowns in the United States.[1] Under the leadership of John Connelly, Crown had raised itself up from near-bankruptcy in 1957 and emerged as a major force in the metal container market both domestically and internationally. The year 1977 marked the 20th consecutive year of sales and profit growth (Exhibit 1).

Crown Cork & Seal had concentrated its efforts on basic tinplated steel cans to hold beer, soft drinks, and aerosol products. During the past 20 years this strategy had helped Crown overcome some tough challenges from large competitors and unfavorable industry trends. However, by 1977 the emergence of the ozone controversy and the trend toward legislative regulation of nonreturnable containers had struck at the heart of Crown's domestic business. Was it time for a change in Crown's formula for success or just time for a reaffirmation of Connelly's basic strategic choices?

To explore these questions, this case looks at the metal container industry, Crown's strategy and position within that industry, and the nature of the problems facing the company during mid-1977.

THE METAL CONTAINER INDUSTRY

Although the metal container industry included 100 firms and a vast number of product lines, it is possible to focus on a few basic factors which composed Crown's competitive environment. This section will describe the product segments in which Crown competes, examine the industry's competitive structure, and look at three current industrywide

---

[1] Crowns are flanged bottle caps, originally made with an insert of natural cork; hence the name Crown Cork & Seal.

Exhibit 1

CROWN CORK & SEAL COMPANY, INC.
Financial Statements, 1956–1976
($000 except where indicated otherwise)

	1976	1975	1974	1973	1972	1971	1966	1961	1956
Net sales	$909,937	$825,007	$766,158	$571,762	$488,880	$448,446	$279,830	$176,992	$115,098
Cost of products sold (excluding depreciation)	757,866	683,691	628,865	459,183	387,768	350,867	217,236	139,071	95,803
Selling and administrative expense	31,910	30,102	28,649	23,409	20,883	21,090	18,355	15,311	13,506
Percent of net sales	3.5	3.6	3.7	4.1	4.3	4.7	6.6	8.7	11.7
Interest expense	3,885	7,374	6,973	4,407	4,222	5,121	4,551	1,252	1,150
Depreciation expense	26,486	25,402	25,525	20,930	18,654	16,981	9,381	4,627	2,577
Taxes on income	43,500	34,925	33,298	26,725	24,900	24,560	12,680	7,625	105
Net income	$ 46,183	$ 41,611	$ 39,663	$ 34,288	$ 31,193	$ 28,474	$ 16,749	$ 6,653	$ 277
Percent of net sales	5.1	5.0	5.2	6.0	6.4	6.3	6.0	3.8	0.2
Earnings per share of common stock	$ 2.84	$ 2.43	$ 2.20	$ 1.81	$ 1.58	$ 1.41	$ 0.80	$ 0.28	$ (0.01)
Plant and equipment:									
Expenditures	21,568	47,047	52,517	40,392	28,261	33,099	32,729	11,819	1,931
Accumulated investment	398,377	401,657	371,297	335,047	316,266	313,214	223,153	107,258	65,196
Accumulated depreciation	149,306	143,406	129,924	116,191	105,377	101,314	68,359	45,004	31,167
Current asset/liability ratio	1.8	1.6	1.4	1.6	1.7	1.6	1.5	2.7	3.2
Long-term debt	25,886	29,679	34,413	37,922	31,234	41,680	57,890	17,654	21,400
Short-term debt	2,984	30,419	45,043	28,504	17,221	31,381	44,784	5,190	6,500
Shareholders' investment	316,684	292,681	262,650	243,916	230,366	211,847	110,841	77,540	50,299
Preferred shares	0	0	0	0	0	0	79,370	139,540	275,000
Common shares—average	16,235,040	17,137,030	18,000,792	18,894,105	19,726,799	20,211,810	20,606,835	21,594,720	24,155,800

Source: Crown Cork & Seal Company, Inc., 1976 annual report, pp. 4, 5.

trends: (1) increasing self-manufacture, (2) new material introductions, and (3) the effect of the "packaging revolution" on the competitive atmosphere.

The products

Metal containers made up almost a third of all packaging products used in the United States in 1976. Metal containers included products ranging from traditional steel and aluminum cans to foil containers and metal drums and pails of all shapes and sizes. The largest segment, however, was metal cans which in 1976 reached $7.1 billion in total value, over three fourths of all metal container shipments.

Metal cans were formed from two basic raw materials, aluminum and tinplated steel. The traditional process had been to roll a sheet of metal, solder it, cut it to the right size, and attach two ends forming a three-piece seamed can. In the late 1960s, however, a new process was introduced by the aluminum industry. This was a two-piece can, formed by pushing a flat blank of metal into a deep cup, eliminating a separate bottom and producing a seamless container. The product adopted the name "drawn-and-ironed" can from the molding procedure.

The aluminum companies who developed the process, Alcoa and Reynolds, had done so with the intention of turning the process over to can manufacturers and subsequently increasing their own raw material sales. However, when the manufacturers were reluctant to incur the large costs involved in line changeovers, the two aluminum companies began building their own two-piece lines and competing directly in the end market.

The new can had advantages in weight, labor, and materials costs and was recommended by the Food and Drug Administration, which was worried about lead migration from soldered three-piece cans. Tinplated can producers soon acknowledged the new process as the wave of the future. They quickly began to explore the possibilities for drawing and ironing steel sheets. By 1972 the technique was perfected and investment dollars had begun to pour into line changeovers and new equipment purchases. Exhibit 2 illustrates the rapid switch to the two-piece can in the beverage industry. In the beer segment alone, almost half of the total cans used in 1974 were made by the new drawn-and-ironed process.

Growth

Between 1967 and 1976 the number of metal cans shipped grew at an average of 4.3 percent annually. As shown in Table 1, the greatest gains were in the beverage segment, while motor oil, paints, and other general packaging can shipments actually declined. The 6 percent decline in total shipments in 1975 turned around as the economy picked up in all areas except basic food cans. For the future, soft-drink and beer cans were expected to continue to be the growth leaders.

Industry structure

In 1977 the U.S. metal can industry was dominated by four major manufacturers. Two giants, American Can and the Continental Can Di-

Exhibit 2

BEVERAGE CAN SHIPMENTS
(billion cans)

	1972	1973	Percent change 1972–73	1974	Percent change 1973–74
Soft-drink cans:					
Total	15,596	17,552	+ 12.5	17,980	+ 2.4
Three-piece	14,217	15,779	+ 11.0	15,589	− 1.2
Percent of total	91.2	89.9	—	86.7	—
Two-piece	1,379	1,773	+ 28.6	2,391	+ 34.9
Percent of total	8.8	10.1	—	13.3	—
Beer cans:					
Total	21,801	24,131	+ 10.7	26,077	+ 8.1
Three-piece	14,746	14,363	− 2.6	13,237	− 7.8
Percent of total	67.6	59.5	—	50.8	—
Two-piece	7,055	9,768	+ 38.5	12,840	+ 31.4
Percent of total	32.4	40.5	—	49.2	—

Source: *Metal Cans Shipments Report 1974,* Can Manufacturers Institute, p. 6.

vision of the Continental Group, together made up 35 percent of all domestic production. National Can and Crown Cork & Seal were also major forces with market shares of 8.7 percent and 8.3 percent, respectively (Exhibit 3).

Capital barriers to entry. A typical three-piece beer can line cost $750,000 to $1 million. In addition, expensive seaming, end-making, and finishing equipment was required. Since each finishing line could handle the output of three to four can-forming lines, the minimum efficient plant cost was at least $3.5 million in basic equipment. Most plants had

Table 1

METAL CAN SHIPMENTS, 1967–1976
(000 base boxes)

	1967	1972	1973	1974	1975	1976
Total metal cans	133,980	168,868	180,482	188,383	177,063	179,449
By product:						
Food cans	67,283	64,773	68,770	73,104	68,127	64,984
Beverage cans:	42,117	75,916	84,617	89,435	85,877	90,084
Soft drinks	14,580	31,660	35,631	36,499	33,284	39,488
Beer........................	27,537	44,256	48,986	52,936	52,593	50,596
Pet foods	5,797	6,694	7,121	7,083	6,057	6,121
General packaging cans:......	18,783	21,485	19,974	18,761	17,002	18,391
Motor oil	n.a.	3,095	2,756	2,533	n.a.	n.a.
Paints	n.a.	6,086	5,562	5,202	n.a.	n.a.
Aerosols....................	n.a.	5,877	6,103	5,765	4,808	5,097
All other	n.a.	6,427	5,553	5,261	n.a.	n.a.

Note: A base box is an area of 31,360 square inches.
n.a. = Not available.
Sources: Standard & Poor's Industry Survey, *Containers, Basic Analysis,* March 24, 1977, p. C123; and *Metal Can Shipments Report 1974,* p. 6.

Exhibit 3

COMPARISON OF 1976 PERFORMANCE OF MAJOR METAL CAN MANUFACTURERS
($ millions)

	Continental Group	American Can	National Can	Crown Cork & Seal
Total company performance:				
Sales	$3,458.0	$3,143.0	$917.0	$910.0
Net income	118.3	100.9	20.7	46.2
Sales growth, 1967–76	147%	107%	317%	202%
Profit growth, 1967–76	51%	33%	160%	145%
Return on equity, 5-year average	10.3%	7.1%	11.9%	15.8%
Debt-equity ratio	34.0%	35.0%	46.0%	23.0%
Metal can segments (domestic):				
Sales	$1,307.8	$1,177.6	$616.0	$575.00
Pretax income	73.0	64.9	36.4	49.00
As percent of sales	5.6%	5.4%	5%	8.5%
Market share	18.4%	16.6%	8.7%	8.3%
Number of can plants	70	48	41	26
International:*				
Sales	$1,147.2	$475.1	n.a.	$343.0
Net income (before taxes)	63.4	41.5	Small loss	39.4

n.a. = Not available.
* International sales of *all* products.
Sources: *Wall Street Transcript,* November 3, 1975, pp. 41, 864, and company 10-K Reports.

12 to 15 lines for the increased flexibility of handling more than one type of can at once. However, any more than 15 lines became unwieldy because of the need for duplication of setup crews, maintenance, and supervision.

The new two-piece lines were even more expensive. The line itself cost approximately $8.5 million, and the investment in peripheral equipment raised the per line cost to $10–$15 million. Unlike three-piece lines, there was no minimum efficient size, and plants ranged from one line to five lines.

Conversion to these two-piece lines virtually eliminated the market for new three-piece lines. No new three-piece lines had been installed in some time, and the major manufacturers were selling complete fully operational three-piece lines "as is" for $175,000 to $200,000. Many firms were shipping their old lines overseas to their foreign operations.

Pricing. The can industry was heavily price competitive. The need for high-capacity utilization and the desire to avoid costly line changeovers made long runs of standard items the most desirable business. As a result, most companies offered volume discounts to encourage large orders. From 1968 to 1975 industrywide margins shrank 44 percent, reflecting sluggish sales and increased price competition. This trend was particularly hard for the small producer who was less able to spread its fixed costs. Raising prices above industry-set norms, however, was dangerous. Continental tried it in the fall of 1963 with the announcement of a 2 percent price hike. Other manufacturers refused to follow their lead, and by mid-1964 Continental was back to industry price levels with considerably reduced market share.

Distribution. Because of the product's bulk and weight, transportation was a major factor in the canmakers' cost structure. One estimate put transportation at 7.6 percent of the price of a metal can, with raw materials playing the largest part at 64 percent and labor following at 14.4 percent. Choice of lighter raw materials and widely dispersed plant locations could then have a large impact on total costs. Most estimates put the radius of economical distribution for a plant at between 150 and 300 miles.

Suppliers and customers

Steel companies formed an oligopoly which set the price of the canmakers' raw materials. Although can companies as a whole were major steel buyers (the fourth-largest consumers of steel products), individual companies had only minimal leverage. More important was the competitive position of steel with respect to aluminum or glass containers. Threats of substitute raw materials kept down steel prices and encouraged technological cooperation between the steel and can producers.

On the customer side, over 80 percent of the metal can output was purchased by the major food and beer companies. Since the can was about 45 percent of the total costs of beverage companies, most had at least two sources of supply. This both decreased their risk and increased their leverage with the can manufacturers. For the canmakers, then, poor service and uncompetitive prices were punished by cuts in order size. As plants were often located to supply a customer, the loss of a large order in one area could greatly cut into manufacturing efficiency and company profits. As one can executive caught in the margin squeeze commented, "Sometimes I think the only way out of this is to sell out to U.S. Steel, or to buy General Foods."[2]

INDUSTRY TRENDS

Three major trends had plagued the metal container manufacturers since the early 1960s: (1) the continuing threat of self-manufacture; (2) the increasing acceptance of substitute materials such as aluminum, foil fiber, or plastic for standard tinplate packaging needs; and (3) the "packaging revolution" where expansion of the whole industry concept forced the question, Could one stay only in the tin can business and survive?

Self-manufacture

In the last six years there had been a growing trend toward self-manufacture by large can customers, particularly in the low-technology standard items. As shown in Table 2, the proportion of captive production increased from 18.2 percent to 25.8 percent between 1970 and 1976.

---

[2] *Crown Cork & Seal Company and the Metal Container Industry,* Harvard Business School case #6–373–077.

Table 2

METAL CAN PRODUCTION

	1970	1971	1972	1973	1974	1975	1976
By market:							
For sale	81.8%	80.9%	80.8%	78.2%	76.7%	73.7%	74.2%
For own use ...	18.2	19.1	19.2	21.8	23.3	26.3	25.8

These increases seemed to come from companies gradually adding their own lines at specific canning locations rather than full-scale changeovers. However, the temptation for large can users such as food and beer producers to backward integrate into can production was high. Campbell Soup Company, for instance, had long been one of the largest producers of cans in the United States. The introduction of the two-piece can was expected to dampen this trend. Since the end users did not possess the technical skills to develop their own two-piece lines, they often had to purchase these cans from outside sources.

Substitute materials

Aluminum. The greatest threat to the traditional tinplated can was the growing popularity of the new lighter weight aluminum can. The major producers of this can were the large aluminum companies led by Reynolds Metals and Aluminum Company of America (Alcoa). Some traditional tinplate can producers such as Continental and American also produced a small proportion of aluminum cans.

From 1970 to 1976 aluminum went from 11.6 percent to 27.5 percent of the total metal can market. It was expected to reach a 29 percent share in 1977 (Table 3). In absolute numbers, steel use remained fairly level while aluminum use had tripled since 1970, (Exhibit 4).

Most of the inroads were made in the beer and soft-drink markets where aluminum held 65 percent and 31 percent shares respectively in 1976. Additional gains were expected as aluminum was in general "more friendly to beer," reducing the problems of flavoring, a major concern of both the brewing and soft-drink industries.

Aluminum had several other important advantages over tinplated steel. First, its lighter weight could help reduce transportation costs. In addition, aluminum was easier to lithograph, producing a better reproduction at a lower cost. Finally, aluminum had the edge in recycling facilities and collection systems and was expected to continue to lead as recycled aluminum was far more valuable than recycled steel.

Table 3

METAL CAN PRODUCTION BY MATERIAL

	1970	1971	1972	1973	1974	1975	1976
Steel	88.4%	86.9%	82.6%	81.4%	79.0%	74.7%	72.5%
Aluminum	11.6	13.1	17.4	18.6	21.0	25.3	27.5

Exhibit 4

METAL CAN SHIPMENTS
(million base banks used in manufacturing)

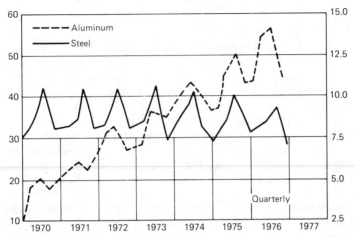

Source: Standard & Poor's Industry Survey, *Containers, Basic Analysis,* March 24, 1977, p. C123.

Aluminum's major disadvantage was in the cost area. The continuation of the trend toward greater utilization of aluminum over steel depended on expected price differentials between the two metals. In 1976 the stock to manufacture 1,000 12-ounce beverage cans cost $17.13 in steel and $20.81 in aluminum. However, steel companies were attempting to widen this gap. One account reported that "in early 1977, steel producers raised the price of tinplate by only 4.8 percent, in contrast to an increase for aluminum can stock of about 9.7 percent." They did this "in an effort to enhance the competitiveness of steel vis-à-vis aluminum and to persuade companies intending to add canning lines to go with steel."[3] Some industry observers also expected the gap to widen as the auto companies increased their usage of aluminum, thus driving up aluminum prices. The two-piece tinplate cans were also considerably stronger than their aluminum counterparts.

Other materials. Two other raw materials threatened tinplated steel as the primary product in making containers: the new paper and metal composite called fiber-foil and the growing varieties of plastics.

Fiber-foil cans were jointly developed by the R. C. Can Company and Anaconda Aluminum in 1962 for the motor oil market. They caught on immediately, and by 1977 this composite material was the primary factor in the frozen juice concentrate market as well.

Plastics represented the fastest growing sector of the packaging industry and the principal force in packaging change. The plastic bottle offered an enticing variety of advantages including weight savings, break

---

[3] Standard & Poor's Industry Survey, *Containers, Basic Analysis,* March 24, 1977, p. C123.

resistance, design versatility, and lower shelf space requirements. Although most of the competitive impact was on glass bottle makers, can companies could suffer as well if plastic successfully entered the carbonated soft-drink market.

The "packaging revolution"

Not only was the traditional package being reshaped and its materials reformulated, but the modern container also served a new purpose. From the late 1950s the package itself became increasingly important in the marketing of the product it contained. The container was an advertising vehicle whose own features were expected to contribute to the total product sales. This had serious implications for the metal can industry. Although the tin can was functional, it was not romantic. Aluminum was easier to lithograph, and plastic was more versatile. Pressure for continuing innovation meant the need for greater R&D expenditures to explore new materials, different shapes, more convenient tops, and other imaginative ideas with potential consumer appeal.

Perhaps the greatest long-term significance of the packaging revolution was that metal containers were increasingly becoming just one segment of the overall packaging industry. The implication of this trend was that the metal can companies would have to contend with the research and marketing strength of such giant integrated companies as Du Pont, Dow Chemical, Weyerhaeuser Timber, Reynolds, and Alcoa. In response to the forward integration of these major material suppliers into packaging, some metal can manufacturers began to invest in their own basic research. In 1963 American announced the start of construction on a research center at Princeton, New Jersey, which would "give major attention to basic research in such areas as solid-state physics and electrochemical phenomena, as a potential source of new products."[4]

THE COMPETITION

By the late 1960s all three of Crown Cork & Seal's major competitors had diversified into areas outside the metal container industry. However, in 1977 they still remained major factors in metal can production (Exhibit 3).

Continental Group

Because of the extent of its diversification, Continental changed its name in 1976 making Continental Can only one division of the large conglomerate. Although only 37.3 percent of the total company sales were in cans, it still held the dominant market share (18.4 percent) of the U.S. metal can market. The remainder of Continental's domestic sales were in forest products (20 percent) and other plastic and paper packaging materials (9 percent).

In 1969 Continental began refocusing its investment spending into foreign and diversified operations. In 1972 the company took a $120 mil-

---

[4] *Crown Cork & Seal Company and the Metal Container Industry,* p. 14.

lion aftertax extraordinary loss to cover the closing, realignment, and modernization of its canmaking facilities over a three-year period. Of the $120 million loss, close to 70 percent resulted from fixed asset disposals, pension fund obligations, and severance pay. By 1976 almost one third of the company's revenues came from their overseas operations which covered 133 foreign countries. Domestic investment went primarily to the paper products and the plastic bottle lines. Very little was allocated for the changeover to new two-piece steel cans.

American Can

American also reduced its dependence on domestic can manufacture and, even more than Continental, emphasized unrelated product diversification. American competed in the entire packaging area, from metal and composite containers to paper, plastic, and laminated packaging products. In 1972 American "decided to shut down, consolidate, or sell operations that had either become obsolete or marginal . . . (this) resulted in an aftertax extraordinary loss of $106 million."[5]

By 1976, 20 percent of the company's sales came from consumer products such as household tissues, Dixie paper cups, and Butterick dress patterns. American also had a large chemical subsidiary (15 percent of sales), and another 15 percent came from international sales. Return on sales for the domestic container segment of American's business remained stable at about 5 percent for the last five years, but relatively poor performance in their diversified areas gave American the lowest average return on equity (7.9 percent) of all the can manufacturers (Exhibit 3).

National Can

National's attempt to join in the trend to diversification achieved somewhat mixed results. Up until 1967 National was almost solely a can producer. Since then, acquisitions moved the company into glass containers, food canning, pet foods, bottle closures, and plastic containers. However, instead of generating future growth opportunities, the expansion into grocery products proved a drag on company earnings. Pet foods and vegetable canning fared poorly in the 1974–75 recession years, and the grocery division as a whole suffered a loss in 1976. As a result, National began a stronger overseas program to boost their earnings and investment image.

Crown Cork & Seal

While its three major competitors turned to diversification, Crown Cork & Seal had remained primarily in metal cans and closures. In 1976 the company derived almost 65 percent of its sales from tinplated cans; crowns accounted for 29 percent of total sales and 35 percent of profits. The remaining sales were in bottling and canning machinery. In fact, Crown was one of the largest manufacturers of filling equipment

---

[5] Annual report, 1972, p. 3.

Exhibit 5

ESTIMATED BREAKDOWN OF CROWN CORK & SEAL'S SALES AND PRETAX INCOME
($ millions)

	1974	1975	1976*	1974	1975	1976*
Sales						
Domestic:						
Cans:						
Beer	$180	$209	$232	23.5%	24.7%	24.6%
Soft drinks	120	128	140	15.7	15.2	14.8
Food......................	55	65	70	7.2	7.7	7.4
Other (mainly aerosols)	100	91	101	13.0	10.7	10.7
Total cans	455	493	543	59.4	58.3	57.5
Crowns	25	29	32	3.3	3.4	3.4
Machinery..................	20	24	27	2.6	2.8	2.8
Total domestic	500	546	602	65.3	64.5	63.7
International:						
Cans	46	57	73	6.0	6.7	7.7
Crowns	200	220	242	26.1	30.0	25.6
Machinery..................	20	24	28	2.6	2.8	3.0
Total international	266	301	343	34.7	35.5	36.3
Grand total sales	$766	$847	$945*	100.0%	100.0%	100.0%
Pretax income						
Domestic:						
Cans	$ 41.0	$ 43.0	$ 46.0	53.9%	52.2%	50.9%
Crowns	2.0	2.0	3.0	2.6	2.4	3.3
Machinery..................	1.5	2.0	2.0	2.0	2.4	2.2
Total domestic	44.5	47.0	51.0	58.5	57.0	56.4
International:						
Cans	4.0	6.0	8.0	5.3	7.3	8.9
Crowns	25.6	26.4	28.4	33.6	32.1	31.4
Machinery..................	2.0	3.0	3.0	2.6	3.6	3.3
Total international	31.6	35.4	39.4	41.5	43.0	43.6
Grand total pretax income	$ 76.1	$ 82.4	$ 90.4	100.0%	100.0%	100.0%
Pretax margins						
Domestic:						
Cans......................................				9.0%	8.7%	8.5%
Crowns				8.0	6.9	9.4
Machinery.................................				7.5	8.3	7.4
Total domestic :......................				8.9	8.6	8.5
International:						
Cans......................................				8.6	12.5	11.0
Crowns				13.0	12.3	11.6
Machinery.................................				10.0	12.5	10.7
Total international				11.9	11.8	11.5
Grand total pretax margins				9.9%	9.7%	9.6%

* 1976 figures are estimated and thus do not match actual numbers on other exhibits.
Source: *Wall Street Transcript,* November 3, 1975, p. 41,865.

in the world. Foreign sales, which were primarily crowns, accounted for an increasingly larger percentage of total sales (Exhibit 5).

In 1976 Crown's return on sales was almost twice that of its three larger competitors. Over the past 10 years Crown's sales growth was second only to National Can and Crown was first in profit growth. The following sections describe Crown's history and strategy.

CROWN CORK & SEAL COMPANY

In April 1957 Crown Cork & Seal lay on the verge of bankruptcy. The 1956 loss was $241,000 after preferred dividends, and 1957 looked even darker. Bankers Trust Company had called from New York to announce the withdrawal of their $2.5 million line of credit. It seemed that all that was left was to write the company's obituary. Yet by the end of 1957 Crown had "climbed out of the coffin and was sprinting." Between 1956 and 1961 sales increased from $115 to $176 million and profits soared. Since 1961 the company has shown a 15.4 percent increase in sales and 14 percent in profits on the average every year.

COMPANY HISTORY

In August 1891 a foreman in a Baltimore machine shop hit upon an idea for a better bottle cap—a round piece of tin-coated steel with a flanged edge and an insert of natural cork. This "crown cork" top became the main product of a highly successful small venture, the Crown Cork & Seal Company. Yet as the patents ran out, competition became severe. The faltering Crown Cork was bought out in 1927 by a competitor, Charles McManus, who then shook the company back to life, bursting upon the starchy firm as one old-timer recalls, "like a heathen in the temple." *Fortune,* in 1962, described the turnaround:

> Under the hunch-playing, paternalistic McManus touch, Crown prospered in the 30s, selling better than half the U.S. and world supply of bottle caps. Even in bleak 1935 the company earned better than 13 percent on sales of $14 million.
>
> Then overconfidence led to McManus's first big mistake. He extended Crown's realm into canmaking. Reasoning soundly that the beer can would catch on, he bought a small Philadelphia can company. But reasoning poorly, he plunged into building one of the world's largest can plants on Philadelphia's Erie Avenue. It grew to a million square feet and ran as many as 52 lines simultaneously. A nightmare of inefficiency, the plant suffered deepened losses because of the McManus mania for volume. He lured customers by assuming their debts to suppliers and sometimes even cutting prices below costs. The Philadelphia blunder was to haunt Crown for many years.[6]

With all his projects and passion for leadership, McManus had no time or concern for building an organization that could run without him.

---

[6] All quotes on the following pages are taken from *Fortune's* article, "The Unoriginal Ideas that Rebuilt Crown Cork," October 1962, pp. 118–64.

Neither of his two sons, Charles Jr. and Walter, was suited to command a one-man company, although both had been installed in vice presidents' offices. Crown's board was composed of company officers, some of whom were relatives of the boss. The combination of benevolent despotism and nepotism had prevented the rise of promising men in the middle ranks. When McManus died in 1946, the chairmanship and presidency passed to his private secretary, a lawyer named John J. Nagle.

In a fashion peculiar to Baltimore's family-dominated commerce, the inbred company acquired the settled air of a bank, only too willing to forget it lived by banging out bottle caps. In the muted, elegant offices on Eastern Avenue, relatives and hangers-on assumed that the remote machines would perpetually grind out handsome profits and dividends. In the postwar rush of business, the assumption seemed valid. The family left well enough alone, except to improve upon the late paternalist's largess. As a starter, Nagle's salary was raised from $35,000 to $100,000.

Officers arrived and departed in a fleet of chauffeured limousines. Some found novel ways to fill their days. A brother-in-law of the late McManus fell into the habit of making a day-long tour of the junior executives' offices, appearing at each doorway, whistling softly, and wordlessly moving on. After hours, the corporate good life continued. More than 400 dining and country club memberships were spread through the upper echelons. A would-be visitor to the St. Louis plant recalls being met at the airport, whisked to a country club for drinks, lunch, cocktails, and dinner, and then being returned to the airport with apologies and promises of a look at the plant "next time."

Into the early 1950s Crown ran on a combination of McManus momentum and the last vestiges of pride of "increasingly demoralized middle managers," both powerless to decide and unable to force decisions from above.

Dividends were maintained at the expense of investment in new plant; what investment there was, was mostly uninspired. From a lordly 50 percent in 1940, Crown's share of U.S. bottle cap sales slipped to under 33 percent. In 1952 the chaotic can division had such substantial losses that the company was finally moved to act. The board omitted a quarterly dividend. That brought the widow McManus, alarmed, to the president's office. President Nagle counseled her to be patient and leave matters to him.

Matters soon grew worse. A disastrous attempt at expansion into plastics followed a ludicrous diversification into metal bird cages. Then in 1954 a reorganization, billed to solve all problems was begun, modeled on Continental's decentralized line staff structure. The additional personnel and expense were staggering, and Crown's margins continued to dip. One observer noted, "The new suit of clothes, cut for a giant, hung on Crown like an outsized shroud." The end seemed near.

John Connelly arrives

John Connelly was the son of a Philadelphia blacksmith who after working his way up as a container salesman formed his own company to produce paper boxes. His interest in Crown began when he was rebuffed by the post-McManus regime who "refused to take a chance" on a small supplier like Connelly. *Fortune* described Connelly's takeover:

By 1955, when Crown's distress had become evident to Connelly, he asked a Wall Street friend, Robert Drummond, what he thought could be done with the company. "I wrote him a three-page letter," Drummond recalls, "and John telephoned to say he'd thrown it into the wastebasket, which I doubted. He said, 'If you can't put it into one sentence you don't understand the situation.'" Drummond tried again and boiled it down to this formula: "If you can get sales to $150 million and earn 4 percent net after taxes and all charges, meanwhile reducing the common to 1 million shares, you'll earn $6 a share and the stock will be worth $90."

That was good enough for Connelly. He began buying stock and in November 1956 was asked to be an outsider director, a desperate move for the ailing company.

The stranger found the parlour stuffy. "Those first few meetings," says Connelly, "were like something out of *Executive Suite*. I'd ask a question. There would be dead silence. I'd make a motion to discuss something. Nobody would second it, and the motion would die." It dawned on Connelly that the insiders knew even less about Crown than he did.

He toured the plants—something no major executive had done in years. At one plant a foreman was his guide. His rich bass graced the company glee club, and he insisted on singing as they walked. Connelly finally told him to shut up and sit down. The warning system silenced, Connelly went on alone and found workers playing cards and sleeping. Some were building a bar for an executive.

At another plant he sat in on a meeting of a dozen managers and executives, ostensibly called to discuss the problem posed by customers' complaints about poor quality and delivery. The fault, it seemed, lay with the customers themselves—how unreasonable they were to dispute Crown's traditional tolerance of a "fair" number of defective crowns in every shipment; how carping they were to complain about delays arising from production foul-ups, union troubles, flat tires, and other acts of God. Connelly kept silent until a pause signaled the consensus, then he confessed himself utterly amazed. He hadn't quite known what to make of Crown, he said, but now he knew it was something truly unique in his business life—a company where the customer was always wrong. "This attitude," he told the startled executives, "is the worst thing I've ever seen. No one here seems to realize this company is in business to make money."

The crisis

By April 1957 the crisis had arrived. With Bankers Trust calling in their loans and bankruptcy imminent, John Connelly took over the presidency. His rescue plan was simple; as he called it "just common sense."

His first move was to pare down the organization, or put more simply, to fire. Paternalism ended in a blizzard of pink slips. The headquarters staff was cut from 160 to 80. Included in the departures were 11 vice presidents. The company returned to a simple functional organization, and in 20 months Crown had eliminated 1,647 jobs or 24 percent of the payroll. As part of the company's reorganization, Mr. Connelly discarded divisional accounting practices at the same time he eliminated the divisional line and staff concept. Except for one accountant maintained at each plant location, all accounting and cost control was performed at the corporate level, the corporate accounting staff occupying half the space used by the headquarters group. In addition, the central research and development facility was disbanded.

The second step was to make each plant manager totally responsible for plant profitability, including any allocated costs (all company overhead, estimated at 5 percent of sales, was allocated to the plant level). Previously, plant managers were only responsible for controllable expenses at the plant level. Under the new system, the plant manager was even responsible for the profits on each product manufactured in the plant. Although the plant manager's compensation was not tied directly to profit performance, one senior executive pointed out, "he is certainly rewarded on the basis of that figure."

The next step was to slow production to a halt and liquidate $7 million in inventory. By mid-July the banks had been paid off. Planning for the future, Connelly developed control systems. He introduced sales forecasting dovetailed with new production and inventory controls. This took control back from the plant foreman who could no longer continue production to avoid layoffs and dump the products into a bottomless pit of inventory.

However, Connelly was not satisfied simply with short-term reorganizations of the existing company. By 1960 Crown Cork & Seal had adopted a strategy that it would follow for at least the next 15 years.

CROWN'S STRATEGY

Products and markets

Being a smaller producer in an industry dominated by giants, Connelly sought to develop a product line built around Crown's traditional strengths in metal forming and fabrication.[7] He chose to return to the area he knew best: tinplated steel cans and crowns and to concentrate on specialized uses and international markets.

A dramatic illustration of Connelly's commitment to this strategy occurred in the early 1960s. In 1960 Crown held over 50 percent of the market for motor oil cans. In 1962 R. C. Can and Anaconda Aluminum jointly developed fiber-foil cans for motor oil, which were approximately 20 percent lighter and 15 percent cheaper than the metal cans then in use. Crown's management decided not to continue to compete in this market and soon lost its entire market share.

In the early 1960s Connelly singled out two specific applications in the domestic market: beverage cans and the growing aerosol market. These applications were called "hard to hold" because the cans required special characteristics to either contain the product under pressure or to avoid affecting taste and to be used in high-speed filling lines. In the mid-1960s growth in demand for soft-drink and beer cans was more than triple that for traditional food cans.

Crown had an early advantage in aerosols. In 1938 McManus had

---

[7] In 1956 Crown's sales were $115 million compared to $772 million for American and $1 billion for Continental.

tooled up for a strong-walled seamless beer can which was rejected by brewers as too expensive. In 1946 it was dusted off and equipped with a valve to make the industry's first aerosol container. However, little emphasis was put on the line until Connelly spotted high-growth potential in the mid-1960s.

In addition to the specialized product line, Connelly's strategy was based on two geographic thrusts: expand to national distribution in the United States and invest heavily abroad. The domestic expansion was linked to Crown's manufacturing reorganization where plants were spread out across the country to reduce transportation costs and to be nearer the customers. Crown was unusual in that they had no plants built to service a single customer, which was characteristic of other firms in the industry. Instead, Crown concentrated on product and produced to serve a number of customers near their plants. Also, Crown developed their lines totally for the production of tinplate cans, making nothing in aluminum. In international markets Crown invested heavily in underdeveloped nations, first with crowns, and then with cans as packaged foods became more widely accepted.

Manufacturing

When Connelly took over in 1957, Crown had perhaps the most outmoded and inefficient production facilities in the industry. In the post-McManus regime, dividends had taken precedence over new investment, and old machinery combined with the cumbersome Philadelphia plant gave Crown very high production and transportation costs. Soon after he gained control, Connelly took drastic action, closing down the Philadelphia facility and investing heavily in new and geographically dispersed plants. From 1958 to 1963 the company spent almost $82 million on relocation and new facilities. By 1976 Crown had 26 plant locations domestically versus 9 in 1955. The plants were small (usually under 10 lines versus 50 in the old complex) and were located close to the customer rather than the raw material source.

Crown emphasized flexibility and quick response to customer needs. One officer claimed that the key to the can industry was "the fact that nobody stores cans" and when customers need them "they want them in a hurry and on time . . . fast answers get customers."[8] To deal with rush orders and special requests, Crown made a heavy investment in additional lines which they maintained in setup condition.

Marketing/service

Crown's sales force, although smaller than American's or Continental's, kept close ties with their customers, and they emphasized technical assistance and specific problem solving at the customer's plant. This was backed by quick manufacturing responses and Connelly's policy that, from the top down, the customer was always right. As *Fortune* described it:

---

[8] *Crown Cork & Seal Company and the Metal Container Industry*, p. 28.

At Crown, all customers' gripes go to John Connelly, who is still the company's best salesman. A visitor recalls being in his office when a complaint came through from the manager of a Florida citrus-packing plant. Connelly assured him the problem would be taken care of immediately, then casually remarked that he planned to be in Florida the next day. Would the plant manager join him for dinner? He would indeed. As Crown's president put the telephone down, his visitor said that he hadn't realized Connelly was planning to go to Florida. "Neither did I," confessed Connelly, "until I began talking."[9]

Research and development

Crown's R&D focused on enhancing the existing product line. As Connelly described it:

> We are not truly pioneers. Our philosophy is not to spend a great deal of money for basic research. However, we do have tremendous skills in die forming and metal fabrication, and we can move to adapt to the customer's needs faster than anyone else in the industry.[10]

Research teams worked closely with the sales force, often on specific customer requests. For example, a study of the most efficient plant layout for a food packer or the redesign of a dust cap for the aerosol packager were not unusual projects.

Crown tried to stay away from basic research and "all the frills of an R&D section of high-class ivory-towered scientists." Explained Mr. Luviano, the company's new president:[11]

> There is a tremendous asset inherent in being second, especially in the face of the ever-changing state of flux you find in this industry. You try to let others take the risks and make the mistakes as the big discoveries often flop initially due to something unforeseen in the original analysis. But somebody else, learning from the innovator's heartaches, prospers by the refinement.[12]

This was precisely what happened with the two-piece drawn-and-ironed can. The original concept was developed in the aluminum industry by Reynolds and Alcoa in the late 1960s. Realizing its potential, Crown, in connection with a major steel producer, refined the concept for use with tinplate. Because of its small plant manufacturing structure and Connelly's willingness to move fast, Crown was able to beat its competitors into two-piece can production. Almost $120 million in new equipment was invested from 1972 through 1975, and by 1976 Crown had 22 two-piece lines in production, far more than any competitor.[13]

In addition, in its specialized areas, Crown was credited with some important innovations. The company initiated the use of plastic as a

---

[9] *Fortune,* October 1962, p. 164.

[10] *Crown Cork & Seal Company and the Metal Container Industry,* p. 30.

[11] Mr. Luviano became president in 1976, while Connelly remained chairman and chief operating officer.

[12] *Crown Cork & Seal Company and the Metal Container Industry,* p. 29.

[13] In 1976 there were 47 two-piece tinplate and 130 two-piece aluminum lines in the United States.

substitute for cork as a crown liner, and in 1962 it introduced the first beverage filling machine that could handle both bottles and cans.

Financial

During the crisis Connelly used the first receipts from the inventory liquidation to get out from under the short-term bank obligations. Since 1956 he had steadily reduced the debt-equity ratio from 42 percent to 18.2 percent in 1976.

No dividends were paid after 1956, and in 1970 the last of the preferred stock was bought in, eliminating preferred dividends as a cash drain. Since 1970 the emphasis had been on repurchasing the common stock (Exhibit 1). Each year Connelly set ambitious earnings goals and most years he achieved them, reaching $2.84 per share in 1976. The 1976 market was a critical time for Connelly's financial ambitions. He said in the 1976 annual report:

> A long time ago we made a prediction that someday our sales would exceed $1 billion and profits of $60 per share. Since then the stock has been split 20 for 1 so this means $3 per share. These two goals are still our ambition and will remain until both have been accomplished. I am sure that one, and I hope both, will be attained this year [1977].

International

Another aspect of Crown's efforts was its continuing emphasis on international growth, particularly in underdeveloped nations (Exhibit 6). With sales of $343 million and 60 foreign plant locations, Crown was, by 1977, the largest producer of metal cans and crowns overseas.

In the early 1960s when Crown began its program of expanding internationally, the strategy was unique. At that time Connelly commented:

> Right now we are premature but this has been necessary in order for Crown to become established in these areas. . . . If we can get 20 percent to 40 percent of all new geographic areas we enter, we have a great growth potential in contrast to American and Continental. . . . In 20 years I hope whoever is running this company will look back and comment on the vision of an early decision to introduce canmaking in underdeveloped countries.[14]

In fact, 10 years later, Crown's overseas position was widely acknowledged to be its "ace in the hole."[15]

In 1976 the international divisions of Crown contributed 36 percent of total company sales and 44 percent of the profits. Growth potential overseas was greater with many countries only recently turning to convenience and packaged foods. There were few entrenched firms, and canning technology was not as well known or understood. Suppliers and customers overseas tended to be smaller than those in the United States.

Margins were particularly good for Crown, and in many cases the company received 10-year tax shelters as initial investment incentives. In addition, manufacturing costs were low as Crown used outmoded

---

[14] *Crown Cork & Seal and the Metal Container Industry,* p. 33.
[15] *Forbes,* September 1, 1967, p. 19.

Exhibit 6

LOCATIONS OF CROWN CORK & SEAL'S FACILITIES

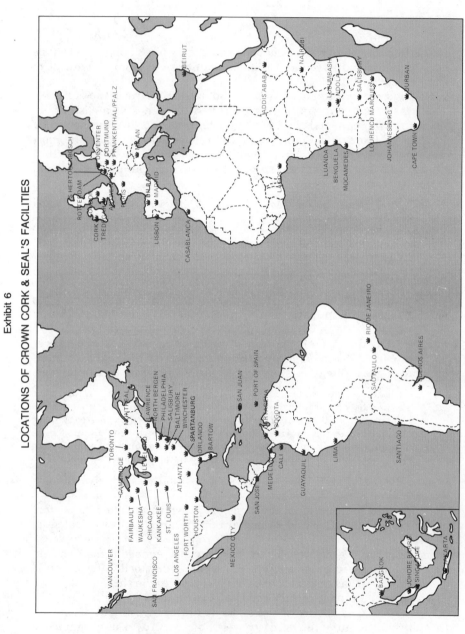

Source: Crown Cork & Seal Company, Inc., 1972 annual report

but fully depreciated equipment from its U.S. plants. For instance, when the company changed over to the drawn-and-ironed process, much of the three-piece equipment found its way into the foreign operations.

John Connelly—the person

Many claimed that John Connelly, the person, was the driving force behind Crown's dramatic turnaround, and that it was his ambition and determination that kept the company on the road to success. Connelly has been described as a strong-willed individual whose energetic leadership has convinced and inspired his organization to meet his goals.

Yet Connelly was no easy man to please. He demanded from his employees the same dedication and energy that he himself threw into his work. As one observer wrote in 1962:

> At 57 Connelly is a trim, dark-haired doer. The 7-day, 80-hour weeks of the frenetic early days is only slightly reduced now. The Saturday morning meeting is standard operating procedure. Crown's executives travel and confer only at night and on weekends. William D. Wallace, vice president for operations, travels 100,000 miles a year, often in the company plane. But Connelly sets the pace. An associate recalls driving to his home in the predawn blackness to pick him up for a flight to a distant plant. The Connelly house was dark, but he spotted a figure sitting on the curb under a street light, engrossed in a looseleaf book. Connelly's greeting, as he jumped into the car: "I want to talk to you about last month's variances."[16]

At 72, Connelly still firmly held the reins of his company.[17] "He'll never retire. He'll die with his boots on," noted one company official.[18] Although he raised John Luviano, 54 (a 25-year veteran at Crown) to the presidency, Connelly's continued presence was a concern of many who watched Crown Cork: "If Connelly wasn't around, we would question who would make those absolutely perfect strategic decisions."[19]

OUTLOOK FOR THE FUTURE

In 1977 observers of Crown Cork & Seal had a favorite question: "How long can this spectacular performance last?" Up to then, Crown's sales and profit growth had continued despite recession, devaluation, and stiff competition from the giants of the industry. However, by 1977 two additional issues had surfaced which directly affected the company's key markets. The ozone scare and the potential legislation on nonreturnable containers threatened the company's beverage and aerosol business. As a result, many wondered if government action might not pull the plug on Crown Cork.

---

[16] *Fortune,* October 1962, p. 163.

[17] Connelly reportedly owned or controlled about 18 percent of Crown's outstanding common stock.

[18] *Financial World,* November 26, 1975, p. 12.

[19] Ibid.

THE OZONE CONTROVERSY

In 1973 two University of California chemists advanced the initial theory that fluorocarbons, a gas used in refrigerators, air conditioners, and as a propellant in aerosols were damaging the earth's ozone shield. Ozone formed an atmospheric layer that prevented much of the sun's ultraviolet radiation from reaching the earth's surface. The theory was that the fluorocarbons floated up into the stratosphere where they broke up, releasing chlorine atoms. These atoms then reacted with the ozone molecules causing their destruction. The problem was compounded because after the reaction the chlorine atom was free to attack other ozone molecules causing accelerated breakup of the ozone layer. Proponents of the theory asserted that "fluorocarbons have already depleted ozone by 1 percent and will eventually deplete it by 7 percent to 13 percent perhaps within 50 to 80 years if the use of fluorocarbons continues at recent levels."[20]

The dangers

The theory argued that there was real danger in allowing the destruction of the ozone shield. Ozone filtered out most of the sun's harmful ultraviolet radiation before it could reach the earth's surface. As this shield was depleted and more radiation passed through, the number of cases of skin cancer were expected to rise alarmingly. Dr. Sherwood Rowland, one of the original proponents of the theory, predicted:

> If aerosol use were to grow at 10 percent annually (half the growth rate of the 1960s), stratospheric ozone content would fall by 10 percent by 1994. Scientists figure this would mean a 20 percent increase in ultraviolet radiation reaching the earth and cause by itself at least 60,000 new cases of skin cancer annually in the United States, roughly a 20 percent increase.[21]

Other possible dangers were crop damage, genetic mutation, and climatic change.

Although many studies were in progress, by the end of 1976 the ozone theory had not yet been conclusively proven. There were still some major questions about the types and amounts of reactions that would take place in the stratosphere. Nonetheless, most subsequent tests supported the basic thesis that fluorocarbons were in some way damaging the ozone layer.

Effects

After the ozone theory was publicized, the reaction against aerosols was severe. Aerosols provided about 60 percent of the fluorocarbons released into the air annually. In 1974 aerosol production was off almost 7 percent in reaction to the recession and the fluorocarbon problem. Only 2.6 billion aerosol containers were used, down from 2.9 billion in

---

[20] *The Wall Street Journal,* December 3, 1975, p. 27.
[21] Ibid.

1973. Action began immediately on both legislative and scientific fronts to test the ozone theory and restrict the use of fluorocarbons.

Soon a bitter battle broke out between industry spokespeople and those advocating an immediate ban: One industry spokesman, who requested anonymity, said:

> All the scientific theories against fluorocarbons are just that—theories, not facts. What we need is more research before there are any more bans or badmouthing. We don't want another false scare.[22]

A member of the Nature Resource Defense Council looked harshly upon the aerosol industry's tactics: "It's like Watergate," he said. "They want to see a smoking gun. We'll have to wait 25 years for that, and by then the irreparable damage will have been done."[23]

Despite industry protests and with the support of some additional studies, state legislators began to introduce antifluorocarbon bills. Georgia led the way in June 1975 by passing a bill banning fluorocarbon aerosols effective March 1, 1977. Effective industry lobbying kept other actions to a minimum until May 1977 when federal agencies proposed a nationwide ban. Calling fluorocarbons an "unacceptable risk to individual health and to the earth's atmosphere," the commissioner of Food and Drugs outlined a three-step phase out of fluorocarbon manufacture and use.[24] The first step in the ban was to be a halt to all manufacture of chlorofluorocarbon propellants for nonessential uses. This ban would take effect October 15, 1978. In the second step, on December 15, 1978, all companies would have to stop using existing supplies of the chemicals in making nonessential aerosol products. The third step would be to halt all interstate shipment of nonessential products containing the propellant gases. This part of the ban would go into effect April 15, 1979.[25]

The future for aerosols

Opinions differed widely as to the extent of the problems the ozone issue would cause the industry. By 1977 the latest estimates were that the fluorocarbon ban would cost container manufacturers over $132 million in lost sales from 1977 to 1980. This was much less than most of the original estimates due to the success of efforts in the last two years in finding fluorocarbon substitutes. Most of these solutions centered around finding substitute propellants or changing the aerosol valve.

New propellants. A propellant was the pressurized gas used to hold the suspended molecules of aerosol products as they were sprayed out. Up to the early 1970s the most common propellant material was fluorocarbon which was used in about half of the aerosol cans sold. By 1977 the possibility of substituting hydrocarbons was being explored for many applications. However, although they were less expensive, hydrocarbons were more flammable and thus more dangerous to mix with many per-

---

[22] *The New York Times,* June 22, 1975, p. F3.
[23] Ibid.
[24] *The New York Times,* May 12, 1977, p. 1.
[25] Ibid.

sonal care products that included alcohol. Other proposed alternatives included carbon dioxide and special pressurized cans that did not release propellants at all.

Changing the valve. In May 1977 one of the most promising ways of eliminating fluorocarbons was the new Aquasol valve. Developed by Robert Abplanalp, the inventor of the original aerosol valve, the Aquasol used a dual duct system (versus the traditional one duct) that kept the product separate from the propellant. Abplanalp claimed that fillers could get twice as much product into a can with a new valve as it did not have to be mixed with the propellant. This also meant hydrocarbons could be used more safely for many applications.

Industry recovery

By 1977 recovery had already begun in the aerosol market with shipments for 1976 up 6 percent. It seemed likely that this trend would continue because of the strong appeal aerosols had for the consumer. In a 1974 study over 59 percent of the population had heard of the ozone problem, yet about 25 percent said they would be "very disturbed to do without" aerosol products. Industry optimism was moderated, however, by the growing popularity of pump sprays and other nonaerosol products, and by the tendency of the consumer not to differentiate between fluorocarbons and aerosols using other propellants.

REGULATING NONRETURNABLE CONTAINERS

The second major threat to Crown's future was the potential legislative restrictions on the use of nonreturnable containers. In 1977 several states had already regulated the use of disposable containers. Laws requiring mandatory deposits for most beverage containers were approved in November 1976 by voter referendums in Maine and Michigan. Three other states, Oregon, Vermont, and South Dakota already had such laws while they were turned down by narrow margins in Massachusetts and Colorado. The existing laws required a five-cent deposit on all bottles and cans, refundable when the empties were brought back for recycling or reuse. Nationally, the federal Environmental Protection Agency banned throwaways from federal property—parks, federal buildings, and military posts—starting in October 1977.

The main problem was litter. Although it was estimated that only 1 percent of the American population were litterers, the extent of the damage was staggering. Unfortunately, disposable cans contributed significantly to the problem. While containers made up only 8 percent of the solid waste in the United States, they made up 54 percent to 70 percent of highway litter by volume. A second issue was the potential savings of raw materials and energy that could be obtained from reusing containers.

Economic impact

Part of the controversy centered around the potential economic impact of legislative bans on nonreturnables. Industry sources agreed that the laws would bring an increase in beer and soft-drink prices and eliminate thousands of jobs. The environmentalists countered that consumers paid 30 percent to 40 percent more for beverages in throwaway containers. "Any increased cost due to retooling would be offset by savings in the use of returnable bottles or recycled cans," claimed Mr. Washington of the Michigan United Conservation Clubs. He added that "any jobs lost in the canning or bottling industries would be offset by additional jobs in transportation and handling."[26]

Prospects for the future

Despite a powerful industry lobby, the fight against nonreturnables was gaining momentum. In July 1977 legislation was being considered by the congressional Committee on Energy and Natural Resources to require deposits on throwaways nationwide. Although the Senate had once rejected a ban on pull tops, some states, including Massachusetts, had passed such bills effective in 1978. Returnable bottles which could be used by more than one manufacturer were being encouraged under the new laws, but it seemed unlikely that cans would be totally banned. Instead, various schemes for deposits and recycling were being emphasized. Metal cans would be collected, crushed, melted, and reused to make new cans. Under the new system it was uncertain who would pay the extra transportation costs and whether or not lower raw material prices to the canmaker would result. Unfortunately for tinplate users like Crown, the new system favored aluminum cans due to the higher value of the reclaimed metal and the recycling network that already existed for aluminum products.

CROWN'S FUTURE GROWTH

Domestically Crown's usual optimistic forecasts continued into 1977. The 1976 annual report all but ignored the aerosol and bottle bill issues. The strategy stayed the same: no major basic R&D efforts, but quick attention to customer needs and leadership in new applications, such as the drawn-and-ironed process, which involved the traditional metal can. Thus, despite current problems in its markets, many observers saw no reason why the company's good record wouldn't continue:

> Even with Connelly's eventual retirement, his No. 2 man seems certain to keep Crown on its upward profits growth trend. While others—like National Can—have ventured into uncharted and at times unprofitable waters, Crown has prospered by doing what it knows best. Under that strategy, prosperity is likely to continue reigning for Crown.[27]

---

[26] *The New York Times,* October 30, 1976, p. F1.
[27] *Financial World,* November 26, 1975, p. 12.

BIC Pen Corporation (A)

DESCRIBED by an economic observer as "one of the classic success stories in American business," the BIC Pen Corporation was widely acknowledged as a leader in the mechanical writing instrument industry in 1973. "The success was dramatic," the observer had said, "because it was achieved from the residue of a deficit-ridden predecessor company, over a short period . . . , in the extremely competitive, low-price sector of the industry. 'BIC' had become a generic name for inexpensive ball-point pens."

Mr. Robert Adler, president of BIC, was extremely proud of the firm's success, which he attributed to "numerous and good management decisions based 40 percent on science and 60 percent on intuition." BIC had reported its first profit in 1964 based on net sales of $6.2 million. Over the following nine years, net sales increased at a compounded rate of 28.2 percent and the weighted average after-tax profit as a percentage of net sales was 13.2 percent. (See Exhibits 1–3 for a summary of financial data from 1964–73).

Until 1972, BIC concentrated exclusively on the design, manufacture, and distribution of a complete line of inexpensive ball-point pen products. The most successful pen was the 19-cent Crystal, which accounted for over 40 percent of BIC's unit sales in ball point pens and about 15 percent of industry unit sales in ball-point pens in 1972. That same year, BIC expanded its writing instrument product line to include a fine line porous point pen. In 1973, it added a disposable cigarette lighter.

COMPANY HISTORY

The name "Waterman" meant a writing instrument since Mr. Louis Waterman invented the first practical fountain pen in 1875. For many years, the Waterman Pen Company led the world in the manufacture of fountain pens. But in the late 1950s, when the shift to ball-point pens

Exhibit 1

FINANCIAL HIGHLIGHTS 1964–73

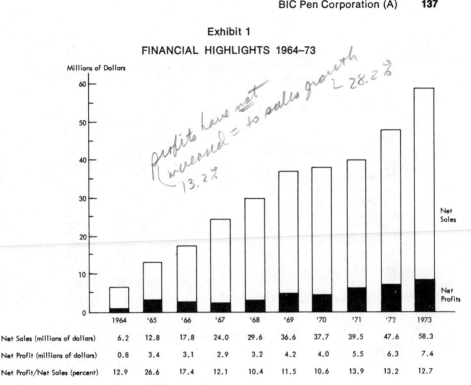

	1964	'65	'66	'67	'68	'69	'70	'71	'72	1973
Net Sales (millions of dollars)	6.2	12.8	17.8	24.0	29.6	36.6	37.7	39.5	47.6	58.3
Net Profit (millions of dollars)	0.8	3.4	3.1	2.9	3.2	4.2	4.0	5.5	6.3	7.4
Net Profit/Net Sales (percent)	12.9	26.6	17.4	12.1	10.4	11.5	10.6	13.9	13.2	12.7

Source: BIC Pen Corporation annual report, 1973.

swept the United States, the Waterman Company continued to concentrate on its fountain pen line, and its performance slipped substantially.

In 1958, M. Marcel Bich, a French businessman well established as a leading European pen maker, bought the facilities, trademark, and patent rights of the ailing Waterman Company, which then became the Waterman-BIC Pen Company. Believing strongly that the ball-point pen was the writing instrument of the future, M. Bich established the objective of becoming the leading firm in the low-price disposable ballpoint pen industry. To obtain that position, management proposed the use of forceful consumer advertising and mass distribution policies.

At the time of M. Bich's purchase of Waterman, ball-point pens constituted only 8 percent of Waterman's unit sales. By 1964, however, all fountain pen and ink products had been eliminated, and most sales came from the 19-cent stick-type ball-point pen. The conversion process was costly, as reflected in the five years of deficits (1959–63). BIC reached its turning point in 1964, marked by the national success of its Crystal pen.

From 1964 through 1973, the company expanded its ball-point pen line to include 12 models of retractable and nonretractable pens offered in varying point sizes, ink colors, and barrel colors at retail prices be-

Exhibit 2

BIC PEN CORPORATION
Consolidated Financial Statements
For the years ended December 31, 1973 and 1972
(in $1,000)

Consolidated Statement of Income

	1973	1972
Net sales	$58,326	$47,571
Cost of goods sold	26,564	19,892
Gross Profit	31,762	27,679
Selling, advertising, and general and administrative expenses	17,191	15,248
Profit from operations	14,571	12,431
Other income	589	269
Total	15,160	12,700
Other deductions	327	196
Income before income taxes	14,787	12,504
Provision for income taxes	7,357	6,240
Net income	$ 7,430	$ 6,264
Earnings per share	$ 1.15	$ 1.00

Consolidated Statement of Retained Earnings

	1973	1972
Balance—beginning of year	$11,683	$10,262
Net Income	7,430	6,264
Total	19,113	16,526
Dividends:		
Cash:		
Common shares	1,750	1,603
Preferred shares		
Total Cash	1,750	1,603
Common shares		3,240
Total Dividends	1,750	4,843
Balance—end of year	$17,363	$11,683

Source: BIC Pen Corporation annual report, 1973.

tween 19 cents and $1. A 29-cent fine line porous point pen was added in 1972 and a $1.49 disposable butane cigarette lighter in 1973. In addition to product line expansion, BIC established a 100 percent-owned operation in Canada (1967), joint ventures in Japan (1972) and Mexico (1973), and a distributor arrangement with a firm in Panama (1973).

On May 1, 1971, the company changed its name to the BIC Pen Corporation. The Waterman trademark was subsequently sold to a Zurich firm, and BIC went public with an offering of 655,000 shares of common stock listed at $25 per share on the American Stock Exchange. In 1973, BIC's parent company, Société Bic, S.A., held 62 percent of the BIC stock.

Exhibit 3

BIC PEN CORPORATION
Consolidated Financial Statement
December 31, 1973 and 1972
(in $1,000)

Consolidated Balance Sheet

	1973	*1972*
ASSETS		
Current Assets:		
Cash....................................	$ 683	$ 919
Certificates of deposit and short-term investments—at cost, which approximates market................................	8,955	10,000
Receivables—trade and other (net of allowance for doubtful accounts, 1973—$143,000, 1972—$102,000).........................	9,445	8,042
Inventories..............................	9,787	6,299
Deposits and prepaid expenses..............	644	633
Total current assets...................	29,514	25,893
Property, Plant, and Equipment—at cost (net of accumulated depreciation, 1973—$9,687,000, 1972—$7,091,000).........................	15,156	9,687
Investments and other assets.................	1,790	1,329
Total...............................	$46,460	$36,909
LIABILITIES AND SHAREHOLDERS' EQUITY		
Current Liabilities:		
Notes payable—banks.....................	21	—
Construction loan payable (due March 21, 1974)........................	560	—
Accounts payable—trade..................	3,872	$ 1,245
Mortgage payable........................	62	58
Accrued liabilities:		
Federal and state income taxes............	1,231	815
Pension plan...........................	306	265
Other.................................	488	402
Total Current Liabilities..............	6,540	2,785
Deferred liabilities..........................	361	275
Mortgage payable...........................	459	520
Minority interest*..........................	91	—
Shareholders' equity:		
Common shares..........................	6,480	6,480
Capital surplus.........................	15,166	15,166
Retained earnings.......................	17,363	11,683
Total Shareholders' Equity............	39,009	33,329
Total...........................	$46,460	$36,909

* Mexican subsidiary is 80 percent owned by BIC Pen Corporation; 20 percent by Mexican interests.
Source: BIC Pen Corporation annual report, 1973.

MEN OF INFLUENCE

M. Marcel Bich

M. Marcel Bich has been described as having done for ball-point pens what Henry Ford did for cars: produce a cheap but serviceable model.

In 1945, Bich and his friend Edouard Buffard pooled their wealth—all of $1,000—and started making ball point refills in an old factory near Paris. Soon it occurred to Bich that a disposable pen that needed no refills would be more to the point. What his country needed, as Bich saw it, was a good 10¢ pen. Today the cheapest throwaway BIC sells for close to that in France—about 7¢. In the United States the same pen retails for 19¢, and it is the biggest seller on the market. . . .

Marcel Bich is a stubborn, opinionated entrepreneur who inherited his title from his forebears in the predominantly French-speaking Val D'Aoste region of northern Italy. He abhors technocrats, computers, and borrowing money. At 58, he attributes his business successes to his refusal to listen to almost anyone's advice but his own. Bich says that his philosophy has been to "concentrate on one product, used by everyone every day." Now, however, he is moving toward diversification. A disposable BIC cigarette lighter that gives 3,000 lights is being test marketed in Sweden; if it proves out, Bich plans to sell it for less than 90¢. . . .

In the United States, Bich is best known for his fiasco in the 1970 America's Cup Race: His sloop *France,* which he captained, got lost in the fog off Newport. He speaks in aquatic terms even when describing his company: "We just try to stick close to reality, like a surfer to his board. We don't lean forward or backward too far or too fast. We ride the wave at the right moment."[1]

Société BIC, S.A., was known as a "one-man empire" which in 1972 accounted for a third of the ball-point pen sales worldwide and included full operations in 19 countries. M. Bich's personal holdings were estimated to be worth about $200 million. "The only way he could control his empire," BIC's treasurer Mr. Alexander Alexiades had said, "was to have certain rules and guidelines. All Société Bic companies were quite autonomous once they had become consistent with his philosophies."

BIC Pen Corporation had been characterized as the "jewel in M. Bich's crown." In the firm's early years, M. Bich had provided much of the machinery, production techniques, and supplies from the French parent company. By 1973, the only substantial business exchange which still remained between the two firms was in research and development. One of the few visible signs of the American company's European heritage was the Renaissance artwork which M. Bich had hung in BIC's reception and board rooms.

Mr. Robert Adler

In 1955, the day after Connecticut's Naugatuck River raged out of control and flooded the countryside, Mr. Adler reported to work at the

---

[1] "Going Bananas over BIC," *Time,* December 18, 1972, p. 93.

old Waterman Pen Company as a newly hired junior accountant fresh out of Pennsylvania's Wharton School of Finance. Instead of being shown to his desk and calculating machine, he was handed a shovel and ordered to help clean out the mud which had collected in the plant during the flood. Nine years later, at the age of 31, he became president of the Waterman-BIC Pen Corporation, which under his leadership became the largest ball-point pen manufacturer and distributor in North America.

Mr. Adler was described by a business associate as "a president who liked to be totally familiar with and completely immersed in every area of his company's operations, one who felt that he should never quash his instincts with an over-dependency on numbers and facts alone . . . a shirt-sleeved president who made it his personal concern to know intimately every facet of the BIC marketing and manufacturing process, including highly technical matters involving complex moulding equipment, advanced production techniques, merchandising, advertising, and sales . . . a do-it-yourself investigator-president who regularly made the rounds of the plant, keeping himself available at all times."

Mr. Adler had stated that he personally selected his colleagues on the basis that they demonstrated aggressiveness and an unswerving belief and conviction that they were serving a company that produced the world's finest writing instruments—products of exceptional quality and value. "A businessman is born, not made," he said, "and education can only enhance and refine what already exists." He attributed much of BIC's success to the fact that in the firm's early years he had consciously hired persons who were unfamiliar with the industry and who therefore did not question BIC's ability to succeed by selling an inexpensive ball point pen via extensive advertising. He emphasized the importance of his own role in determining BIC's performance by stating:

> A lot of decisions are easy because there is only one way to go. Sometimes you're lucky and sometimes, no matter what, you'll get the same outcome. A president gets paid to make decisions. That's his big job. What's important is once a decision is made is to make sure that it comes out right. The decision is not so important; it's the outcome. A president must say to himself: "I will now make my decision successful."

WRITING INSTRUMENT PRODUCT LINE

The BIC Pen Corporation manufactured and sold inexpensive writing instruments in a variety of shapes: stick or pocket pen; ink colors, 1–10; point sizes, medium or fine; and retail prices, $0.19–$1. All retractable pens were produced in a pocket pen shape; all nonretractables in a stick shape.

The most successful product, the Crystal, accounted for over 40 percent of all ball-point pen units sold in North America. Its sister product, the $0.25 Fine Point Pen, which differed from the Crystal only in point size, accounted for over 15 percent of all ball-point pen units sold.

In 1973, writing instruments accounted for approximately 90 percent of BIC's consolidated net sales. Nonretractable pens accounted for 80 percent of the writing instrument unit sales, retractable pens for 6 percent, fine line porous point pens for 12 percent, and refills for 2 percent. Table 1 presents the 1973 BIC writing instrument product line.

Table 1

1973 WRITING INSTRUMENT PRODUCT LINE

Product name	Ink colors	Point sizes	Retail price
Ball-Point Pens			
Nonretractable/nonrefillable:			
Crystal	4	m	$0.19
Fine point	4	f	.25
Reproduction	4	m	.25
Eraser	4	m,f	.25
Deluxe eraser	4	m,f	.29
Deluxe	4	m	.39
Accountant	4	f	.49
Retractable/refillable:			
Clic	4	m,f	0.49
2-color pen	2	m,f	.69
4-color pen	4	m,f	.98
Citation	1	m	1.00
Retractable/nonrefillable:			
Pocket pen	3	m	0.29
Fine Line Porous Point Pen			
BIC Banana	10	m,f	0.29

Source: Corporate records.

Nonretractable ball point pens

The Crystal, a nonretractable/nonrefillable ball point pen, was introduced on the market in 1959 at a retail price of $0.29. As the first product of the newly formed Waterman-BIC Corporation, the BIC Crystal was intended to become a "brand name replacement for all no-name,[2] disposable pens in a market where no dominant competitor existed." Its retail price was dropped to $0.19 in 1961. In commenting on the success of the Crystal, Mr. Jack Paige, vice president of marketing, remarked:

> We built this company on the 19¢ pen. In 1961 it was selling for 19¢, and in 1973 it is still 19¢. One-third of all retail sales are from the 19¢ stick. It's a highly profitable business. We've found ways to become more efficient and still maintain our profitability.

Between 1961 and 1968, BIC expanded its nonretractable ball-point pen line to include six other models of varying point sizes, ink colors, and usages. Nonretractables were priced from $0.19 to $0.49.

[2] No-name products were those which were not advertised and were marketed at retail prices far below the comparable, inexpensive, nationally advertised products.

Retractable ball-point pens

In 1968, BIC introduced its first retractable/refillable ball-point pen, the 49-cent Clic.[3] Management felt that the Clic would (1) improve the overall corporate profit margin, (2) enable the company to sell merchandise in multipacks (quantity selling in one package), such as for school specials, and (3) increase distribution—as some retail outlets, particularly those not dependent on BIC for their profits—had been reluctant to sell the 19-cent and 25-cent pens.

Following the Clic, four other retractable ball-point pens were added to the BIC product line. Three imported French pens: the 98-cent 4-Color Pen (1971), the 69-cent 2-Color Pen (1972), and $1 Citation Pen (1973) were introduced to "upgrade ball-point pen sales." The 29-cent Pocket Pen, the only nonrefillable pen in the retractable line, was added to "expand primary demand for ball-point pens."[4]

Fine line porous point pens

In April of 1972, BIC introduced its first nonball-point pen product, the 29 cent BIC Banana, which was a fine line porous point pen produced in a stick shape. Mr. Paige commented on the Banana decision:

> The development of the concept of entering the porous point pen market was not a sudden decision. Our philosophy was simply that as soon as we had a porous point pen that would reflect BIC quality and could be mass marketed at a popular price that anybody could afford, we would then move into that business.
>
> For openers, we were faced with a couple of major problems. First we were a late entry and the market was dominated by a 49¢ strong brand name of good quality that had a 50% market share. Maybe for some companies that stark statistic would have been enough not to enter. However, at BIC there is an aggressive attitude about marketing. That attitude manifested itself a year and one-half ago when we began plotting our sales course for the introduction of this new product. (BIC spent $3 million on advertising the BIC Banana in 1972.) We took the attitude that we weren't going to be squeezed into that remaining 50% share that the leading brand left for the rest of the field. Our plan was to expand the consumer market for this type of writing instrument—to make it grow. In a larger market, we felt we would have the opportunity to build a franchise that would give us a substantial share.

In reviewing the same product decision, Mr. Alexiades said:

> In 1966 we saw the product opportunity for the soft tip pen, but Marcel Bich owned 90% of the company, and we had a difficult time convincing him that this was the right approach. He thought that the soft tip pen was a passing thing and that it was impractical because it wouldn't write through carbon. But we're in a carbon society and

---

[3] In retractable pens, industry sales volume in dollars was concentrated in the high-priced products and in units in the no-name brands.

[4] Despite a major introductory campaign ($1.5 million spent on advertising), sales in the Pocket Pen were "disappointing," according to one company spokesman. He attributed the poor results to styling problems and a lack of room for new products in a market with a declining sales growth rate.

there's no logical explanation for the consumer. However, M. Bich's philosophy changed. Years ago, he only wanted to sell ball point pens. He's now interested in inexpensive, disposable, mass-produced items. He has the marketing know-how, the distribution, the name.

We saw that the porous point pen was not a fad so we got in, perhaps a little late, but at least we entered an expanding portion of the market. The growth rate of ball point pen sales had leveled off. If we didn't enter the porous pen market, it would have been difficult to grow since we're so dominant in the industry. We knew that the only way to grow was through product line diversification or acquisition.

Our objective is to become the largest producer of fine line porous point pens. We are in ball point pens. It might be difficult because Gillette's Flair has been there for five years. Papermate brand is not a no-name brand with no resources like those which we initially attacked in the ball point pen market.

A competitor commented on the market entry of the BIC Banana:

Many people associated BIC with the ball point pen. BIC had a difficult time because people thought that the Banana was a ball point. It's a stick shape and looks like a ball point. They don't have that problem with the lighter (1973) because it is a different looking product altogether. BIC hasn't done well with the Banana against the Flair. After all, who could enter the stick pen market now and do well against BIC? But at least BIC broke the price point (49¢) with its 29¢ point which softened the retail and commercial markets. Maybe they'll get smart and get out.

THE MARKETS

Mr. Adler's philosophy had always been "to sell BIC products wherever there was a doorknob." Consistent with that view, marketing efforts had been focused on all writing instrument markets, with special emphasis placed on the "four key sales volume opportunities": the retail, commercial, ad/specialty, and premium markets, which represented about 90 percent of the dollar sales volume in the writing instrument industry in 1973. The other three markets, government, military, and export, accounted for the remaining 10 percent. In 1973, the Writing Instrument Manufacturers Association estimated total industry sales at $353.3 million.

Retail market

The retail market, or over-the-counter market, was the largest mechanical writing instrument market, accounting for over 50 percent, or $176.6 million, of the total industry dollar sales in 1973. Of significance in the retail market was the growing trend away from indirect selling through retail distributors to independent stores towards direct selling from the manufacturers to mass merchandise outlets.

Since the national success of the 19-cent Crystal pen in 1964, BIC had completely dominated the ball point pen segment of the retail market. By the end of 1973, BIC held a 66 percent share of that segment, followed by Gillette with 15 percent and Lindy with 5 percent. In fine line porous point pens, Gillette was the front runner with a 35 percent share followed by BIC with 22 percent, Magic Marker with 8 percent, and Pentel with 5 percent.

Management attributed BIC's successful penetration of the retail market to its aggressive marketing and distribution policies, as well as to the low price and high quality of its products.

Commercial market

The commercial market, or office supply market, was the second largest mechanical writing instrument market, accounting for about 20 percent, or $70.6 million, of total industry sales in 1973. Selling in the commercial market was primarily handled through commercial distributors, who channeled products from the manufacturers to office supply dealers, who in turn sold to commercial customers. Large office supply dealers bought directly from manufacturers and used distributors to fill in inventory gaps.

At the end of 1973, management estimated that the leading market shareholders in ball-point pens in the commercial market were BIC with 50 percent, followed by Berol with 18 percent, and Gillette with 5 percent. In fine line porous point pens, it was estimated that Gillette held a 40 percent share, Berol 25 percent, Pentel 10 percent, and BIC 4.5 percent.

In commenting on BIC's 4.5 percent market share in fine line porous point pens, Mr. Adler said:

> We have had difficulty in the commercial market because that market is conditioned to something like the Flair, Pentel, or Berol porous pens which sell for 49¢ and allow good margins to the distributors. The model which BIC manufactures does not compete head on with is the Flair. Ours is a stick model; theirs is a pocket model. Because of the design of the product, it's difficult to get a certain percentage of the market. The Flair product costs twice as much to manufacture (has a clip, etc.). The 29¢ Write-Brothers also has a clip. For us, we're a long way from being Number 1. To get into the porous pen business, we had to use the stick model. Our problem is that the distributors do not want to push the Banana because they have a 49¢ market. Naturally, they make less on a 29¢ model. It will take time.

Advertising/specialty and premium markets

The ad/specialty and premium markets together accounted for approximately 20 percent or $70.6 million of the total industry dollar sales volume in 1973.

Ad/specialty sales referred to special orders made through specialized distributors for products imprinted with a slogan or organization name. Competition in the ad/specialty market was based heavily on price which accounted for the strength of the no-name brands in that market. BIC held close to a 5 percent share in the ad/specialty market in 1973.

A "premium" was defined as a free promotional item which was attached to another product in order to promote the sale of that product. Premium sales were made through distributors or direct from the manufacturer to customer. As in the ad/specialty market, competition was based upon price. Unlike in that market, it was also based upon brand recognition and included a broader base of product types, not just writing instruments. Although it was a small market, management considered BIC's participation in the premium market as important in "reinforcing the firm's dominant position in the pen business." BIC held close to a 100 percent market share among writing instrument firms in the premium market in 1973.

THE COMPETITION

In 1973, approximately 200 firms were engaged in the manufacture and sale of mechanical writing instruments in the United States. Most firms competed selectively in the industry on the basis of (1) product type: fountain pen, mechanical pencil, ball-point pen, or soft tip pen; (2) price range: high (>$1), medium ($0.50–$1.00), and low (<$0.50); and (3) market: retail, commercial, ad/specialty, premium, military, government, and export. Strong advertising programs and mass-distribution networks were considered critical for national success.

In management's view, BIC had four major writing instrument competitors: Berol, Gillette, Lindy, and Pentel.[5] The five firms competed at the following price points with similar products.

Table 2

1973 SELECTED PRODUCT LINES

			Gillette			
Product type	BIC	Berol	Paper Mate	Write- Bros.	Lindy	Pentel
Ball-Point Pens						
Retractable:						
Refillable..........	$0.49	$0.29	$0.98	$ —	$1.00	$2.98
	0.69	0.39	1.50			5.00
	0.98	0.49	1.98			7.00
	1.00	0.59	3.95			8.50
		1.49	5.00			
			5.95			
Nonrefillable.......	0.29			0.39		0.79
Nonretractable.......	0.19	0.19		0.19	0.19–	
	0.25	0.25			0.59	
		0.29			(0.20)	
		0.39				
Fine Line						
Porous point pens.....	0.29	0.29	0.49	0.29	0.59	0.29
		0.49	0.98			0.35
			1.95			0.49

Source: Corporate records.

[5] The Magic Marker Corporation was considered a strong competitor in fine line porous point pens with four models selling from $0.19–0.49 and comprising an estimated 8 percent share of the retail market. However, Magic Marker was best known for its broad tip markers (ten models, from $0.39 to $1.29). Its ball point pen products were sold strictly as no-name brands.

others are innovative

The Berol, Lindy, and Pentel corporations were well known for product innovation. In 1973, the Berol Corporation, best known for its drafting products, particularly for its Eagle brand pencils, was the second firm to introduce the rolling writer combination pen, a pen which performed like a regular fountain pen, yet could write through carbons. Lindy Pen Corporation had earned its reputation as an early entrant into new markets, yet lacked the advertising strength to back the sale of its new products. Lindy introduced a 39-cent stick pen prior to the introduction of the BIC Crystal in 1959, a fine line porous point pen in 1969, and a disposable lighter in 1970. Pentel Corporation had earned the reputation of "revolutionizing the U.S. mechanical writing instrument industry" with the introduction of the soft tip in 1964 and the rolling writer combination pen in 1969. Like Lindy, it lacked the resources to support heavy advertising and mass distribution programs.

BIC Follows Them?

Gillette

The Gillette Company was considered BIC's major competitor in all writing instrument products. The comparative performance in writing instruments for the two firms from 1968–73 is shown in Table 3.

Table 3

COMPARATIVE PERFORMANCE IN WRITING INSTRUMENTS
(consolidated statements)

	1968	1969	1970	1971	1972	1973
BIC						
Net sales ($ millions)	$29.6	$36.6	$37.7	$39.5	$47.6	$52.4
Net income ($ millions)	3.2	4.3	4.0	5.5	6.3	7.3 (est.)
Net income/sales	10.8%	11.7%	10.6%	13.9%	13.2%	14.0% (est.)
Net sales/total assets*	—	—	1.6	1.4	1.3	1.3
Total Assets/Total Equity†	—	—	1.3	1.2	1.1	1.2
Gillette (Paper Mate Division) *low earnings*						
Net sales ($ millions)	$33.2	$36.5	$47.0	$51.1	$60.9	$74.5
Net income ($ millions)	2.5	3.3	3.3	2.5	3.0	4.3
Net income/sales	4.5%	9.0%	7.0%	4.9%	4.9%	5.8%
Net sales/total assets*	1.4	1.4	1.3	1.3	1.3	1.3
Total Assets/Total Equity†	1.8	1.8	1.8	1.9	2.0	2.1

* Estimated total assets allocated to writing instruments.
† Total corporate assets and equity.
Source: Corporate 10-K reports.

In 1973, Gillette competed in the high-price market with its Paper Mate products and in the low-price market with its Write-Brothers products. The Paper Mate ball-point pens had been the mainstay of its writing instrument business since the early 1950s. In the late 1960s, management at Gillette "recognized the potential of Pentel's new soft tip pens." Backed by a large research and development capability, a well-known corporate name, and advertising and distribution strength, Gillette set out to capture that market with a fine line porous point pen

Table 4

BI-MONTHLY RETAIL MARKET SHARE PATTERNS
(units)

	JF '72	MA	MJ	JA	SO	ND	JF '73	MA	MJ	JA	SO	ND
Ball-Point Pens												
Total BIC	66%	67%	65%	65%	66%	65%	67%	66%	65%	66%	68%	66%
$0.19 Crystal	36	35	34	33	31	31	32	32	31	31	31	31
0.25 Fine Point	12	14	13	13	11	13	13	12	13	13	11	12
0.29 Pocket Pen	—	1	2	2	3	3	3	3	3	2	2	2
0.49 Accountant	8	7	7	8	9	7	8	7	7	8	10	9
0.49 Clic	8	8	7	7	9	8	8	8	8	8	9	7
Other	2	2	2	2	3	3	3	4	3	4	5	5
Total Gillette	8	8	9	13	13	13	13	15	15	14	14	15
$0.19 W-B	—	—	—	3	3	3	4	6	5	5	5	5
0.39 W-B	—	—	1	2	2	2	2	2	2	2	2	2
0.98 Retractable	4	4	4	4	4	4	4	4	4	4	4	4
Other	4	4	4	4	4	4	3	3	4	3	3	4
Lindy	7	7	8	7	6	7	6	6	6	5	5	5
Other	19	18	18	15	15	15	14	13	14	15	13	14
Total	100%	100%	100%	100%	100%	100%	100%	100%	100%	100%	100%	100%
Fine Line Porous Point Pens												
BIC	—	—	5	11	15	16	16	19	19	20	23	22
Total Gillette	49	46	45	43	43	40	39	37	36	37	35	35
$0.49 Flair	45	43	41	36	34	33	32	30	30	30	28	29
0.49 Hotliner	2	2	1	1	1	1	1	1	1	1	1	1
0.29 W-B	—	—	2	5	7	5	5	5	5	5	5	4
Other	2	1	1	1	1	1	1	1	—	1	1	1
Lindy	5	5	4	4	4	4	3	3	2	2	2	2
Magic Marker	—	—	—	—	—	—	6	6	7	8	9	8
Pentel	9	9	9	7	7	7	7	6	6	5	4	5
Other	37	40	37	35	31	33	29	29	30	28	27	28
Total	100%	100%	100%	100%	100%	100%	100%	100%	100%	100%	100%	100%

Source: Corporate records.

called "Flair," which retailed in three models from $0.40 to $1.95. In 1972 Gillette created the Write-Brothers products: a 39-cent retractable ball-point pen, a 29-cent fine line porous point pen, and a 19-cent non-retractable ball-point pen, in order "to take advantage of growth opportunities in the low-price end of the mechanical writing instrument market." The Write-Brothers name was selected to prevent confusion on the part of consumers who had associated the Paper Mate name with high-priced ball-point pen products and middle- to high-priced Flair products.

Retail market share patterns for BIC and Gillette are shown in Table 4. (The BIC Banana was introduced in May of 1972 and the Write-Brothers products in July of 1972.)

Over the five-year period 1969–73, BIC and Gillette made the following advertising expenditures on writing instruments:

Table 5

WRITING INSTRUMENT ADVERTISING BUDGET ESTIMATES
(dollars in millions)

	1969	1970	1971	1972	1973
Gillette.............	$1.9	$4.0	$6.0	$8.5	$9.0
BIC................	3.6	4.0	4.3	7.0	6.8

heavy outlay

Source: Case researcher's estimates derived from corporate records, interviews with company officials, and journal articles.

In commenting on advertising programs and the BIC/Gillette competition in general, Mr. David Furman, advertising director at BIC, said:

> Our strategy has been to emphasize profit, and therefore look for the mass market. Gillette has said: "Let's make the most money and not worry about the size of the market." Gillette had a nice profitable business with Flair. It kept Papermate alive. But they can't stay alive with one-dollar-plus pens. We expanded the market so now their unit sales are up. The philosophy of Gillette has been to spend heavily to develop the product, then let the products decay and spend on new product development. Their unit sales continue to go up but their loss of market share is considerable.

COMPANY POLICIES AND STRUCTURE

Mr. Adler had sometimes described his company as a car with four equally important wheels: sales, manufacturing, finance, and advertising, all of which had to be synchronized in order for the car to accelerate and sustain itself at high speed. That car, he claimed, had equal responsibility to its stockholders, employees, and customers. It followed, therefore, that management's attention should be focused on achieving a good return on investment, which Mr. Adler felt was derived by improving: (1) productivity (unit production per hour), (2) efficiency in production (cost savings methods), and (3) quality control standards and checks.

Finance

In the spring of 1971, BIC Pen effected a recapitalization which resulted in an aggregate number of 3.03 million outstanding common shares, 87 percent of which were owned by Société Bic, S.A., 3 percent by M. Bich, 9 percent by Mr. Adler, and 1 percent by other officers and directors (stock bonuses).[6] On September 15 of that year, 655,000 of those common shares were offered to the public at $25 per share, resulting in a new capital structure of 67 percent of the shares owned by Société Bic, S.A., 3 percent by M. Bich, 7 percent by Mr. Adler, 1 percent by other officers, and 22 percent by the public. Proceeds from the public offering after underwriting discounts and commissions amounted to $15.4 million. On July 27, 1972, M. Bich exercised his warrants for the purchase of 210,000 shares of common stock at $25 per share, totaling $5.25 million, which BIC received in cash. That same day, the company declared a 2-for-1 share split in the form of a 100 percent share dividend of 3.24 million shares, $1 par value, which resulted in the transference of $3.24 million from retained earnings to common stock. At the end of 1972, 6.48 million shares were outstanding of the 10 million shares authorized in June of 1972; none of the 1 million authorized shares of preferred stock had been issued.

Since 1967, the company paid the following cash dividends:

Table 6

BIC PEN CORPORATION DIVIDEND PAYMENT HISTORY

	1967	1968	1969	1970	1971	1972	1973
Consolidated net income (dollars in millions)	$2.862	$3.231	$4.233	$4.033	$5.546	$6.264	$7.430
Dividends (dollars in millions)	2.591	—	1.175	1.166	1.319	1.603	1.750
Adjusted net dividend/ share*	0.43	—	0.19	0.19	0.22	0.26	0.27
Stock price range*	—	—	—	—	12¼–18	16¼–37	11⅝–32½

* After giving retroactive effect to a 2-for-1 share split in 1972.
Source: BIC Pen Corporation annual report, 1973.

Regarding dividend policy, Mr. Alexiades said:

> When we were a private firm, there was no dividend policy. Dividends were only given when declared by M. Bich. In 1969 when we knew that we would be going public, we tried to establish a policy, to find the proper relationship between earnings and dividends. 20%– 25% of earnings seemed like a good target policy. Now we're having trouble increasing our dividends, due to government guidelines, although we would like to increase the payout in accordance with our rise in earnings.

[6] Four million common shares were authorized.

The purchase of the original BIC plant from the Norden Company in 1963 was financed with a 5¾ percent mortgage loan from Connecticut General, payable in monthly installments of $7,749 (principal and interest) until January 1, 1981.[7] The three plant expansions—$1 million for 110,000 square feet in 1965, $1.8 million for 100,000 square feet in 1969, and $5–6 million for 275,000 square feet in 1973—were financed through short-term loans and cash on hand. Regarding the 1973 expansion, Mr. Alexiades said: "We decided to use our own cash so that if something develops in 1974 or 1975, such as an acquisition or new product opportunity, we can always fall back on our credit rating."[8]

In keeping with BIC's informal organizational structure, management used no formalized budgets. "We use goals, not budgets. We just keep surprising ourselves with our performance," said Mr. Alexiades, "although perhaps as we mature, we will need a more structured arrangement."

BIC was known in the New Haven area for its attractive compensation plan. It was Mr. Adler's belief that good people would be attracted by good pay. Plant workers received the highest hourly rates in the area ($4.53 base rate for the average grade level of work). All employees were invited to participate in a stock purchase plan whereby up to 10 percent of their salaries could be used to purchase stock at a 10 percent discount from the market price, with BIC assuming the brokerage commission cost. Executives participated in a bonus plan which Mr. Adler described as follows:

> We have a unique bonus system which I'm sure the Harvard Business School would think is crazy. Each year I take a percentage of profits before tax and give 40% to sales, 40% to manufacturing, and 20% to the treasurer to be divided up among executives in each area. Each department head keeps some for himself and gives the rest away. We never want bonuses to be thought of as salaries because they would lose their effect. So we change the bonus day each year so that it always comes as a pleasant surprise, something to look forward to.

Manufacturing

Manufacturing had emphasized the development over the years of a totally integrated, highly automated production process capable of mass producing high-quality units at a very low cost. Except for the metal clips, rings, and plungers, all components—even the ink—were produced in the Milford plant. Société Bic had supplied the basic production technology, machinery, and research and development.[9] Some raw materials, particularly the brass, were still imported from France.

The U.S. energy crisis posed a major threat to BIC in 1973. Poly-

---

[7] The loan had not been paid off by 1973, because of its low interest rate.

[8] BIC borrowed on a seasonal basis to meet working capital needs, using bank lines of credit ($15.5 million available; maximum borrowed was $10.6 million in 1970).

[9] BIC Pen Corporation spent $30,368, $15,254, and $128,553 on R&D in 1971, 1972, and 1973, respectively.

styrene, the key raw material used in making pens, was a petroleum-derivative. Mr. Adler commented on the shortage of plastic:

> We've reached a point in our economy where it's become more difficult to produce than sell. I mean I have this big new plant out there [pointing to the new $5–$6 million addition] and I may not be able to produce any products. I have to worry about the overhead. I'm reluctant to substitute materials.
>
> I predict that in 1974 polystyrene will cost more than double what it costs in 1973, which is 15 cents per pound. It represents about 10 percent of the manufacturing cost of the ball point stick pen.

The production process consisted of three stages: (1) manufacture of parts, (2) assembly of parts, and (3) packaging. Porous pens (4 parts) were the simplest instrument to manufacture followed by ball-point pens (7 parts) and lighters (21 parts). Some parts, such as non-retractable pen barrels, were interchangeable, which built flexibility into the production process. Production rates were steady throughout the year, while inventory build-ups were seasonal. In mid-1973, BIC was producing on average about 2.5 million ball-point pen units per day and 0.5 million porous pens per day, which was close to plant capacity.

Management felt that production costs were substantially controlled by the strict enforcement of a quality control system. One fourth of the plant's employees participated in quality control checks at each stage of the production process, which was precision-oriented, involving tolerances as close as 0.0002±. Mr. Charles Matjouranis, director of manufacturing, had stated that it was his job to search for cost-savings programs which would protect profit margins on products. He said:

> We are in the automation business. Because of our large volume, one-tenth of one cent in savings turns out to be enormous. Labor and raw materials costs keep increasing, but we buy supplies in volume and manufacture products in volume. One advantage of the high volume business is that you can get the best equipment and amortize it entirely over a short period of time (four to five months). I'm always looking for new equipment. If I see a cost-savings machine, I can buy it. I'm not constrained by money.

In 1973, there were 700 persons working at BIC in Milford, of which 625 were production personnel represented by the United Rubber Workers Union under a three-year contract. Management considered its relations with employees as excellent and maintained that BIC offered the best hourly rates, fringe benefits, and work environment in the area. Weekly meetings between supervisors and factory workers were held to air grievances. Workers were treated on a first-name basis, and were encouraged to develop pride in their jobs by understanding production technicalities and participating in the quality control program and production shift competition. Most assembly-line workers were women. At least 40 percent of the factory workers had been with BIC for over ten years, and 60 percent–65 percent for over five years. Despite increased automation, very few layoffs had occurred because workers were able to be retained for other positions to compensate for the increase in pro-

duction unit volume. Over 50 percent of the workers had performed — *training*
more than one job.

Marketing and sales

In admiring his BIC ring studded with six diamonds, each representing an achieved sales goal, Mr. Ron Shaw, national sales manager, remarked:

> It's almost a dream story here. When I started with the company in 1961 as an assistant zone manager, we were selling 8 million units a year. We now sell 2.5 million units a day. Everyone said that: One, we couldn't sell 5,000 feet of writing in one unit and succeed; two, we couldn't have the biggest sales force in the writing instrument industry and make money; and three, we couldn't advertise a 19-cent pen on TV and make money. Well, we did and we're Number One!

Distribution. The BIC products were sold in the retail and commercial markets by 120 company salesmen who called on approximately 10,000 accounts. Those accounts represented large retailers, such as chains, as well as wholesale distributors. Through those 10,000 accounts, BIC achieved distribution for its products in approximately 200,000 retail outlets, of which 12,000 were commercial supply stores. In addition, the salesmen called on 20,000 independent retail accounts which were considered important in the marketplace. In the case of those accounts, the BIC salesmen merely filled orders for the distributors. A specialized BIC sales force sold ad/specialty orders to ad/specialty distributors and most premium orders directly to corporate customers.

The backbone of BIC's customer business had originally been the mom and pop stores. They had initially resisted selling BIC pens, but were later forced to trade up from the no-name products once BIC had become a popular selling brand. As product distribution patterns moved away from indirect selling toward more direct selling to large chains and discount houses, the mass merchandisers became eager to carry BIC products, which had earned a reputation for fast turnover, heavy advertising support, and brand recognition. In 1973, BIC did 60 percent of its sales volume through distributors and 40 percent through direct sales channels.

Pricing policy. BIC had never raised the original retail prices of any of its products. Management, therefore, placed a great deal of importance on retail price selection and product cost management. Advertising expenses generally ran 15 percent of the manufacturer's selling price; the combined costs of packaging and distribution approximated 20 percent–30 percent of the manufacturer's selling price. The distributor's profit margin was 15 percent off the listed retail price; the indirect retail buyer's was 40 percent; and the direct retail buyer's was 55 percent. Regarding pricing policy, Mr. Adler said:

> If I increase my price, I help my competition. The marketplace, not ourselves, dictates the price. We must see what people are willing to pay. You must sell as cheaply as possible to get the volume.

154

Customary marketing tools. In a speech made before the Dallas Athletic Club in September of 1972, Mr. Paige remarked: "We're in the *idea* business. Selling is an idea. Many people have products but we have ideas."

BIC used four basic marketing tools to sell its "ideas": (1) advertising, (2) point-of-purchase displays, (3) packaging forms, and (4) trade and consumer promotions. Management felt that the only way to enter a new market was to be innovative either by: (1) introducing a new product, (2) creating a new market segment, or (3) using unique merchandising techniques designed specifically for that market. The BIC salesmen were known to be aggressive.[10] Products were always introduced on a regional roll-out basis with the entry into each new region attempted only after market saturation had been achieved successfully in the prior region.

Advertising was considered the most important element of the BIC marketing program. Company research had shown that seven out of ten writing instruments sold were impulse purchase items. With that knowledge, management felt that widespread distribution of a generic name product line was essential for success. It was further felt that retailers and commercial stationers preferred to carry nationally advertised brands.

BIC used TV advertising, "the cheapest medium when counting heads," almost exclusively. In 1973, BIC added advertising in *T.V. Guide* and the Sunday supplements "in order to reach more women, the biggest purchasers of writing instruments."

In keeping with the belief that merchandising techniques should be designed differently for each product and market, BIC varied its TV commercials substantially, depending upon the intended product usage, time of entry into the market, and demographic interest. Each advertising message was designed to be simple and to communicate *one* idea at a time. Exhibit 4 presents examples of four different themes: (1) BIC has a lighter (BIC Butane); (2) BIC's products are durable (Crystal); (3) BIC has coloring instruments for children (Ink Crayons[11]); and (4) BIC offers a "new and fun way to write" (BIC Banana).

Another marketing tool was the *point-of-purchase display*. Mr. Paige remarked:

> Merchandise well displayed is half sold, particularly on a low consumer interest item. Displays must be designed to fit every retail requirement because, for example, what's good for Woolworth's may not be good for the corner drug store.

Packaging was considered another form of advertising. "We want to make the 19-cent pen look like a one-dollar pen," Mr. Paige had said. BIC was one of the first firms to use the concept of multipacks. Packag-

[10] On average, assistant zone managers earned $12,000 and zone managers earned $22,000 a year. Compensation consisted of a base salary plus commission.
[11] Ink Crayons consisted of multipack of BIC Banana pens in an array of ink colors.

Exhibit 4

TELEVISION ADVERTISING THEMES

BIC BUTANE	BIC CRYSTAL	BIC BANANA	BIC INK CRAYONS

"For $1.49 and thousands of lights, it's a Pretty Good Lighter. BIC Butane."

"Dear BIC . . . You're probably not going to believe this but. . . ."

"You can't write with blueberries, but you can write with a BIC Banana, the new porous tip pen."

"BIC Banana Ink Crayons. In ten bright colors. The only fruit you can draw with."

Source: BIC Pen Corporation annual report, 1972.

ing forms were changed as much as six times a year. Regarding packaging and *promotions*, Mr. Alexiades commented:

> We've created a demand for constant innovation, excitement in the marketplace. Many people say that's the reason for BIC's success. We change the manner in which we sell (blister packs,[12] multipacks, gift

[12] Blister packs were product packages which were designed to be displayed on peg boards.

packages), which makes our merchandise turn and keeps our name in front of the wholesaler and retailer all of the time. The consumer remembers us because we offer a true value. The retailer and dealer remember us because they receive special incentive offers, free merchandise, and promotional monies, plus their merchandise turns.

Exhibit 5

BIC PEN CORPORATION
1973 Internal Organizational Chart

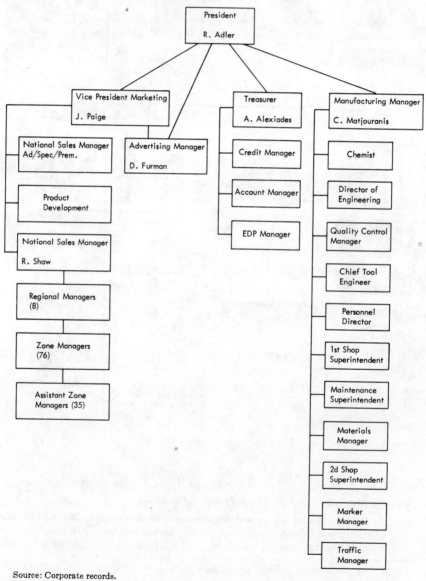

Organizational structure

Throughout its 15-year history, the BIC organizational structure had remained small and simple. (See Exhibit 5 for the 1973 organizational chart.) In 1973, the average tenure (since 1958) of the six key executive officers was 13 years. At least 40 percent of the factory workers had been at BIC for over ten years. Several of the managers commented on the BIC environment:

> We try to run this company as a family organization. We don't try to run it as a General Motors. We've been very successful with this concept. It's a closely knit management group—very informal. Decisions are made immediately. A young guy comes here. He sees that we [management] exist. We understand him. He gets his decisions immediately. We try to get him to join the family. Inside of two to three years, if he's not in the family, he won't work out.
>
> Mr. Robert Adler
> President

> Part of the success of management is our ability to communicate with one another. We're trying to remain the same. It's one of the regrets that growth has to bring in departments and department heads, but we're trying to maintain a minimum.
>
> Mr. Alexander Alexiades,
> Treasurer

> We have few managers, but the best. One real good one is better than two average.
>
> Mr. Charles Matjouranis,
> Manufacturing Director

> This company does not believe in assistants. Philosophically, we try to stay away from any bureaucracy. There are no politics involved here, no knifing, no backbiting. Part is a function of size. Everybody knows his place and area of responsibility. We don't want to break from that.
>
> Mr. David Furman,
> Advertising Director

> We promote from within. We recognize the abilities of our own people.
>
> Mr. Ron Shaw,
> National Sales Manager

THE BIC BUTANE DISPOSABLE CIGARETTE LIGHTER

The lighter decision

In March of 1973, BIC Pen Corporation introduced its first nonwriting instrument product, the BIC Butane disposable lighter, at a retail price of $1.49. Management viewed the BIC Butane as a logical extension of its current product line as it was inexpensive, disposable, of high quality, and able to be mass-produced and distributed through most writing instrument trade channels, especially retail. It differed from writing instruments in that it required 21 rather than the basic 7 assembly parts, more precise manufacturing, and was subject to strict governmental standards. Mr. Furman made the following statement regarding BIC's decision to enter the disposable lighter business:

For years we were in the high-level, profitability trap. We had had it as far as that market would go. The Banana was the first break out from the trap and now the lighter. We utilize our strengths, but we're no longer a writing instrument company. We're in the expansion stage where writing instruments are a base from which we are expanding. We're using the skills we've gained and are applying them to any kind of mass-produced product.

new strategy

Introductory campaign

The decision to sell a disposable lighter dated back to 1971 when M. Marcel Bich purchased Flaminaire, a French lighter company, with the objective of marketing a substitute for matches in Europe. Matches had never been free in Europe, and for that reason disposable lighter sales had been very successful there far before they caught on in the United States. The BIC Butane was imported from Flaminaire, but was scheduled to be produced at the Milford plant on a highly automated production line by March of 1974.

The BIC Butane was introduced first in the Southwest, where management claimed it had captured a 32 percent retail market share by year's end. Management expected its national retail market share of 16 percent to rise to 25 percent when the product reached full national distribution in February of 1974. The regional roll-out was backed with a $1 million advertising campaign. A $3 million campaign was planned for 1974. Lighter sales approximated 10 percent of BIC's consolidated net sales in 1973. An industry source estimated their pretax margin at 15 percent–21 percent.

The cigarette lighter industry

Lighters were categorized in three basic product classes: disposables, regular refillables, and electronics. Disposable lighters contained butane gas; electronic lighters contained butane gas or a battery; regular refillable lighters contained either butane gas (90 percent) or liquid fuel (10 percent). There were three basic price categories: <$2 (all disposables), $2–$12 (most regular refillables), and >$12 (all electronics and fancy regular refillables). It was estimated that 75 percent–80 percent of all cigarette lighters sold in 1972 were priced below $6.95 at retail.

trend to more disposables

Table 7

U.S. CIGARETTE LIGHTER RETAIL SALES
(dollars and units in millions)

	1969	1970	1971	1972	1973 (est.)
Total lighters ($)	$94.9	$98.1	$106.9	$115.0	153.0
Disposables ($)	n.a.	8.5	18.0	36.0	50.0
Units (no.)	—	—	13	21	40

Note: n.a. - not available.
Source: Case researcher's estimates based on trade and company interviews and unpublished figures from the *Drug Topics* magazine research group (1972).

Cigarette lighter sales in the middle price range had begun to fall off in the early 1970s. As a replacement for matches, disposable lighters had expanded the primary demand for lighters and represented the major growth opportunity in the U.S. lighter industry.

Major competitors

By 1973 many firms, particularly manufacturers of writing instruments, had entered the disposable lighter business. Most firms served as distributors of foreign-made products, many of which were reputed by trade sources to be of questionable quality. As with writing instruments, BIC's management believed that industry success was heavily dependent on the strength of a firm's advertising program and distribution network, although most firms did well initially due to the excessive demand for disposable lighters relative to the available supply.

There were three clear contenders for industry dominance in the disposable lighter business: Gillette, Garrity Industries, and BIC, with Scripto a distant fourth. Gillette's Cricket lighter was the leading market shareholder, accounting for one-third of all disposable lighter sales in 1973.

Table 8

1973 MAJOR COMPETITORS IN DISPOSABLE LIGHTERS

	BIC	*Gillette*	*Garrity*	*Scripto**
Market entry (year).......	1973	1972	1967	1972
Product.................	BIC Butane	Cricket	Dispoz-a-lite	Catch 98
Price....................	$1.49	$1.49	$1.49	$0.98
Product produced in.......	France (→'73); U.S. (after)	France (→'73); Puerto Rico (after)	France	Japan
Ad $ strategy (1973).......	Consumer	Consumer (¾) Trade (¼)	Trade	None
Distribution emphasis*.....	Mass/chains	Mass/chains	Smoke shops, hotel stands, drug stores	Independent retailers

* In 1974, Scripto planned to raise the price of the Catch 98 to $1.19, add another Japanese disposable lighter at the $1.39 price point, and produce a $1.69 disposable lighter in its Atlanta plant.

Source: Casewriter's interviews with corporate marketing managers.

In speculating on the future of the BIC Butane lighter, Mr. Paige stated:

> We think that the disposable butane will cannibalize every low-priced lighter. BIC, Dispoz-a-lite and Cricket will do 90 percent of the business in 1973. Cricket advertises extensively. BIC will compete with Cricket at the $1.49 price point. BIC and Cricket will dominate the industry in the future. The cheaper disposables of lesser quality will only sustain themselves.

BIC Pen Corporation (B)

News release: January 11, 1974

BIC Pen Corporation, which has specialized successfully in mass marketing consumer products, soon will introduce a new product which it will distribute in the $1.3 billion retail pantyhose market, Robert P. Adler, president, disclosed today.

"The sale of pantyhose is for BIC a further expansion into other mass-produced disposable consumer products," Mr. Adler said. "Because of BIC's strong reputation for value, and our ability to merchandise successfully to the consumer through more than 200,000 retail outlets, we believe our new pantyhose product will be well received in this marketplace."

THE WOMEN'S HOSIERY INDUSTRY

Hosiery had always been the most rapidly consumable apparel item in a woman's wardrobe. For years the women's hosiery industry had been stable in unit sales and repetitive in product offerings. Many low-profile brands were sold in a wide range of sizes and typical colors. The business "kicked up its heels" in the late 60s with the advent of the convenience product pantyhose and miniskirts. Hosiery became a fashion item, costing as much as $10 a pair, depending upon style, texture, color, and brand name. Prosperity did not last, however, and by 1973 the $2 billion women's hosiery business was characterized as "having to run faster to stay in the same place." The market had become plagued by an uncertainty in consumer demand, sagging profits, price battles, distribution changes, and the rising fashion trend of women's pants. Hosiery makers claimed that women had begun to go without hose or to wear ripped stockings under pants.

160

Exhibit 1

U.S. WOMEN'S HOSIERY INDUSTRY TRENDS

	1964	1965	1966	1967	1968	1969	1970	1971	1972	1973
Numbers of:										
Companies.........	645	609	576	579	574	530	502	471	457	390
Plants.............	828	782	750	746	741	734	699	665	604	521
Annual per capita consumption:										
Pantyhose........	—	—	—	—	2.3	9.0	13.3	11.0	12.7	11.7
Stockings........	1.48	15.7	17.3	19.5	18.1	12.7	6.3	4.2	3.1	2.5
Knee-highs, Anklets..........	0.1	0.1	0.1	0.1	0.1	0.1	0.1	0.3	0.6	1.2
Total Consumption	14.9	15.8	17.4	19.6	20.5	21.8	19.7	15.5	16.4	15.5

Source: National Association of Hosiery Manufacturers.

The pantyhose market

As an attempt to interject some life into the stable pantyhose market, the three big hosiery makers: Hanes Corporation, Kayser-Roth Corporation, and Burlington Industries, launched an unprecedented $33 million promotional campaign in 1973. They cast aside their established merchandising techniques and began pushing new, low-priced pantyhose in supermarkets. The firms adopted catchy brand names and used dramatic advertising campaigns centering around "trendy" packaging. Their assumption was that women would buy more pantyhose if the products were cheaper, more accessible, and more attractively displayed than before. No longer were branded products available exclusively in department or specialty stores at $3 a pair; rather they could be purchased at every corner market for 99¢ to $1.39. As a result, pantyhose sales in food outlets rose from 5 percent in 1968 to 28 percent of the industry pantyhose sales in 1973, with analysts predicting a 50 percent share by 1975. Despite the surge in supermarket buying, sales of pantyhose declined by 7 percent in 1973.

The private label business represented 50 percent of the hosiery sales in food stores in 1973, with some labels selling as low as 39 cents a pair. The supermarket invasion by known brands—"L'eggs" by Hanes, "Activ" by Burlington, and "No-Nonsense" by Kayser-Roth—resulted in a general upgrading in the quality of the private label brands, and an expansion of the branded lines to cover additional market segments, such as pantyhose in large sizes for heavier women, and pantyhose for less than $1 for price-conscious women.

In describing pantyhose purchase behavior, one industry source said:

> Generally, all women are interested in quality, price, fit, and availability, but purchasers do tend to fall into three basic categories: (1) women who think that all hosiery is the same and therefore look for the lowest price; (2) women who feel that an extremely low price implies inferior quality; and (3) women who switch off between high and low prices, depending upon their needs.

L'eggs was the largest selling brand name in 1973 with a 9 percent dollar volume share of the total hosiery market. The idea for L'eggs was born out of the recognition that no high-quality name brand dominated the highly fractionated pantyhose market; nor was one available at a reasonable price (<$2) at convenience locations (supermarkets). The L'eggs integrated marketing program centered around the theme, "Our L'eggs fit your legs," and the distinctive egg-shaped package. The L'eggs direct selling approach leaned heavily on a platoon of 1,000 young delivery women clad in hot pants and traveling their appointed routes in distinctive white vans. Their task was to restock flashy "L'eggs Boutiques" in supermarkets and drug chains. L'eggs retail sales rose from $9 million in 1970 to $110 million in 1973. Hanes spent $20 million on their promotion in 1972 and $13 million in 1973.

Activ and No-Nonsense pantyhose were priced at 99 cents a pair, in contrast with L'eggs at $1.39.[1] Both brands were backed by $10 million promotional campaigns in 1973. The "Activ Girls" competed with the "L'eggs Ladies." Similarly clad and driving red vans, they also sold products on consignment. Besides supermarkets, Activ pantyhose appeared in outlets serviced by tobacco distributors, thus supporting Burlington's motto: "Activs are everywhere." Kayser-Roth shunned the distribution system favored by the other two hosiery makers and delivered its No-Nonsense brand-name pantyhose to food brokers at supermarket warehouses. The No-Nonsense approach—without vans, hot pants, and comely delivery women—allowed the retailers a 45 percent profit margin, compared with the 35 percent return guaranteed by Hanes and Burlington.

THE PANTYHOSE DECISION

Mr. David Furman, advertising director, commented on BIC's entry into the pantyhose business:

> The hosiery industry used to be dominated by manufacturing, not marketing, companies. L'eggs was the first attempt to change that. The success of L'eggs and other industry leaders has depended on an extremely expensive direct selling distribution system which is good for large volume outlets but is not feasible for smaller stores or local advertising. BIC intends to use its usual jobbers and make it profitable for them to act as middlemen and garner the independent stores.
>
> Nearly all companies deal primarily with pantyhose as a fashion item. The market is moving away from the fashion emphasis, which cannot be successful in food stores. BIC will address the fit problem by using the slogan: "It fits there, it fits everywhere"; hence the name —Fannyhose. Ours is a utility story as it was with ball point pens.

wow !

In introducing Fannyhose to the trade, management used the theme of "taking a simple idea and making it pay off." The quality product was priced at $1.39, came in two sizes and three colors, and was packaged in a compact little can with a see-through top. The advertising

[1] Hanes introduced First-to-Last pantyhose at 99 cents a pair to counter the price competition from Activ and No-Nonsense pantyhose.

program centered around the "better fit" concept, as was illustrated in animated television commercials and Sunday supplements. Product promotions included cents-off coupons and free samples.

In contrast with its major competitors, BIC planned to act as a distributor of pantyhose, rather than as a manufacturer/distributor, and to establish a specialized sales force to sell the product direct or through distributors to its wide variety of writing instrument retail accounts. BIC's supplier was DIM, S.A., one of France's largest hosiery makers ($100 million in sales), which M. Bich bought control of in 1973. Mr. Furman called the BIC plan "a brilliant stroke around L'eggs. Theirs is a fixed system—low profits, no risk, fixed price. We add promotional profits by passing on to the trade the money we've saved by avoiding the need for our own service crews."

BIC's investors react

An article appearing in the February 4, 1974, edition of the *Wall Street Journal* described the reaction of the investment community to BIC's entry into the pantyhose business. One analyst cited several obstacles which BIC faced in its new venture, namely: (1) the limited pricing flexibility which BIC would have because of import duty costs[2]; and (2) the fact that BIC had not been particularly strong in supermarkets. Another analyst took a more positive view, citing the recent market price decline in the BIC stock to "investors' questions over the competitive nature of the pantyhose business without understanding the philosophy of BIC: to produce inexpensive disposable consumer products once there is an established market for them and to use its widespread marketing system to become a powerful force in the industry." A third analyst predicted a bright future for BIC in the pantyhose business because of its "access to materials through Société Bic, its reputation for high-quality products, its well-developed distribution system, and its commitment to marketing, rather than manufacturing, pantyhose."

---

[2] Duty fees averaged 33 percent per unit. One analyst speculated that the pre-tax margin on Fannyhose was 15 percent.

The company and its environment: Relating opportunities to resources

DETERMINATION of a suitable strategy for a company begins in identifying the opportunities and risks in its environment. This chapter is concerned with the identification of a range of strategic alternatives, the narrowing of this range by recognizing the constraints imposed by corporate capability, and the determination of one or more economic strategies at acceptable levels of risk. We shall examine the complexity and variety of the environmental forces which must be considered and the problems in accurately assessing company strengths and weaknesses. Economic strategy will be seen as *the match between qualification and opportunity that positions a firm in its environment.* We shall attempt in passing to categorize the kinds of economic strategies that can result from the combination of internal capability and external market needs, and to relate these categories to the normal course of corporate development.

THE NATURE OF THE COMPANY'S ENVIRONMENT

The environment of an organization in business, like that of any other organic entity, is the pattern of all the external conditions and influences that affect its life and development. The environmental influences relevant to strategic decision operate in a company's industry, the total business community, its city, its country, and the world. They are technological, economic, social, and political in kind. The corporate strategist is usually at least intuitively aware of these features of the current environment. But in all these categories change is taking place at varying rates—fastest in technology, less rapidly in politics. Change in the environment of business necessitates continuous monitoring of a company's definition of its business, lest it falter, blur, or become obsolete. Since by definition the formulation of strategy is performed with the future in mind, executives who take part in the strategic planning process must be aware of those aspects of their company's environment especially susceptible to the kind of change that will affect their company's future.

Technology.   From the point of view of the corporate strategist, technological developments are not only the fastest unfolding but the most far-reaching in extending or contracting opportunity for an established company. They include the discoveries of science, the impact of related product development, the less dramatic machinery and process improvements, and the progress of automation and data processing. We see in technical advance an accelerating rate of change—with new developments arriving before the implications of yesterday's changes can be assimilated. Industries hitherto protected from obsolescence by stable technologies or by the need for huge initial capital investment become more vulnerable more quickly than before to new processes or to cross-industry competition. Science gives the impetus to change not only in technology but also in all the other aspects of business activity.

Major areas of technical advance foreseen by students of the management of technology include increased mastery of energy, its conservation and more efficient use; the reorganization of transportation; technical solutions to problems of product life, safety, and serviceability; the further mechanization of logistical functions and the processing of information; alteration in the characteristics of physical and biological materials; and radical developments in controlling air, water, and noise pollution. The primary impact upon established strategies will be increased competition and more rapid obsolescence. The risks dramatized by these technical trends are offset by new business opportunities opened up for companies that are aggressive innovators or adept at technical hitchhiking. The need intensifies for any company either to engage in technical development or to maintain a technical intelligence capability enabling it to follow quickly new developments pioneered by others.

Economics.   Because business is more accustomed to monitoring economic trends than those in other spheres, it is less likely to be taken by surprise by such massive developments as the internationalization of competition, the return of China and Russia to trade with the West, the slower than projected development of the Third World countries and the resulting backlash of poverty and starvation, the increased importance of the large multinational corporations and the consequences of the host country hostility, the recurrence of recession, and the persistence of inflation in all phases of the business cycle. The consequences of world economic trends need to be monitored in more detail for an industry or company.

Society.   Social developments of which strategists keep aware include such influential forces as the quest for equality for minority groups; the demand of women for opportunity and recognition; the changing patterns of work and leisure; the effects of urbanization upon the individual, family, and neighborhood; the rise of crime; the decline of conventional morality; and the changing composition of world population.

Politics.   The political forces important to the business firm are similarly extensive and complex—the changing relations between communist and noncommunist countries (East and West) and between the prosperous and poor countries (North and South); the relation between private enterprise and government, between workers and management; the impact of national planning on corporate planning; and the rise of what George Lodge calls the communitarian ideology.[1]

Although it is not possible to know or spell out here the significance of such technical, economic, social, and political trends, and possibilities for the strategist of a given business or company, some simple things are clear. Changing values will lead to different expectations of the role business should perform. Business will be expected to perform its mission not only with economy in the use of energy but with sensitivity to the ecological environment. Organizations in all walks of life will be called upon to be more explicit about their goals and to meet the needs and aspirations (for example, for education) of their membership.

In any case, change threatens all established strategies. We know that a thriving company—itself a living system—is bound up in a variety of interrelationships with larger systems comprising its technological, economic, social, and political environment. If environmental developments are destroying and creating business opportunities, advance notice of specific instances relevant to a single company is essential to intelligent planning. Risk and opportunity in the last quarter of the 20th century require of executives a keen interest in what is going on outside their companies. More than that, a practical means of tracking developments promising good or ill, and profit or loss, needs to be devised.

TRACKING THE CHANGING ENVIRONMENT

Unfortunately the development of knowledge in a flourishing business civilization has produced no easy methodology for continuous surveillance of the trends in the environment of central importance to a firm of ordinary capabilities. Predictive theories of special disciplines such as economics, sociology, psychology, and anthropology do not produce comprehensive appraisal readily applicable to long-range corporate strategic decision. At the same time many techniques do exist to deal with parts of the problem—economic and technological forecasting, detailed demographic projections, geological estimates of raw material reserves, national and international statistics in which trends may be discerned. More information about the environment is available than is commonly used.

John D. Glover has developed an approach to the total environment of a business firm as an ecological system.[2] His framework consists of four subsystems (the immediate total community of a company, the culture in which it operates, the flow of goods and services being pro-

---

[1] George C. Lodge, *The New American Ideology* (New York: Alfred A. Knopf, 1975).

[2] Most of this work is unpublished, but Glover's approach is summarized in "Strategic Decision-Making: Planning, Manning, Organization" in John D. Glover and Gerald A. Simon, *Chief Executives' Handbook* (Homewood, Ill.: Dow Jones-Irwin, 1976), pp. 423–41.

duced or consumed, and the natural and manmade physical setting). For each of these categories an enormous amount of data is available, with projections of future movement. Schemes such as Glover's provide the means for planning staffs to reduce to rational analysis what is now practicing managers' intuitive and fragmentary vision of the developing forces offering opportunity to their firms and taking it away.

Further study of the problem of strategic information will take you to Aguilar's research in how managers in the chemical industry obtained strategic information about environmental change.[3] Aguilar found that even in this technically sensitive industry, few firms attempted any systematic means for gathering and evaluating such information. Publications provided only about 20 percent of the information from all sources, with current market and competitive information from personal sources dominating the total input of information. Internally generated information comprised only 9 percent of the total, and more information received was unsolicited than solicited. (Interestingly enough, very few people in subordinate positions felt they were getting useful strategic information from their superiors.)

Aguilar's findings were corroborated by Robert Collings's study of investment firms.[4] The obvious moral of these studies is that the process of obtaining strategic information is far from being systematic, complete, or even really informative about anything except current developments, at least in these industries. These researchers show that it is possible to organize better the gathering and integrating of environmental data through such means as bringing miscellaneous scanning activities together and communicating available information internally.

Certain large companies organize this function. General Electric has maintained for years a Business Environment Section at its corporate headquarters and prepares reports on predicted changes for use by its divisions. Consulting firms, future-oriented research organizations, and associations of planners provide guidance for looking ahead. The sense of futility experienced by executives in the face of complexity is reduced when they begin the task by defining their strategy and the most likely strategic alternatives they will be debating in the foreseeable future. Decision on direction spotlights the relevant environment. You cannot know everything, but if you are thinking of going into the furniture business in Nebraska, you will not be immoderately concerned about the rate of family formation in Japan. Clarification of present strategy and the few new alternatives it suggests narrows sharply the range of necessary information and destroys the excuse that there is too much to know.

THE COMPETITIVE ENVIRONMENT

The aspect of the environment that most tangibly affects a company is the competitive environment of the industry or industries in which

---

[3] Frank J. Aguilar, *Scanning the Business Environment* (New York: Macmillan, 1967).
[4] Robert Collings, "Scanning the Environment for Strategic Information" (unpublished doctoral thesis, Harvard Business School, 1969).

it does business. In each of its businesses, the company faces an industry structure that shapes the rules of competition it must respond to or try to influence and motivates the attempt to develop an innovatively unique strategy. It also faces a group of competitors who may attack its market position and whose behavior can thwart actions it may take to improve position. The essential task of the strategist is to find a *defensible* position for the company in its competitive environment, or one that addresses or evades the demands of industry structure and is resistant to encroachment by competitors.

INDUSTRY STRUCTURE

If we look broadly at competition in any industry, whether it produces a product or service or is domestic or international, the state of competition depends on five elemental forces which are diagrammed in Figure 2. The collective influence of rivalry among firms, the threat of new entrants, the bargaining power of customers and suppliers, and the specter of substitute products or services determines the ultimate profit potential of an industry. These pressures range from *intense* in industries like tires, metal cans, and steel, where no company earns spectacular returns on investment, to *mild* in industries like oil field services and equipment, soft drinks, and toiletries, where room remains for quite high returns.

Whatever their collective strength, the strategist's goal is to find a

Figure 2

FIVE ELEMENTAL FORCES OF COMPETITION

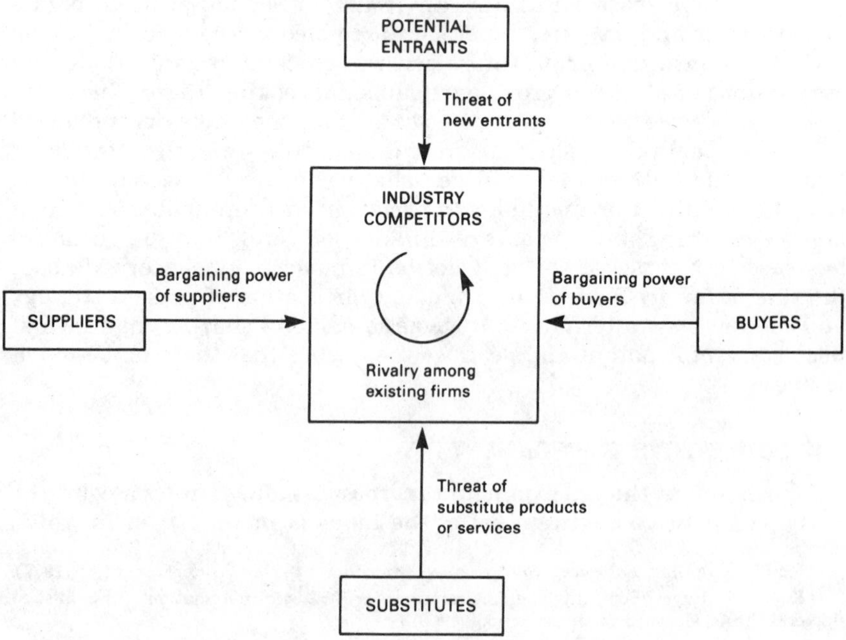

place in the industry where the company can best defend itself against these forces or can influence them in its favor. The strongest competitive force has the greatest impact on the profitability of an industry; it is usually of the greatest importance in strategy formulation. For example, even a company with a superior position in an industry unthreatened by potential entrants will earn low returns if it faces a superior or a lower cost substitute product—as the leading manufacturers of vacuum tubes and coffee perculators have learned to their sorrow. In such a situation, coping with the substitute product becomes the number one strategic priority.

Every industry has an underlying structure, or a set of fundamental economic and technical characteristics, that gives rise to these competitive currents and pressures. Determining these forces for the industry a company operates in will uncover the critical requirements for success in the industry and the areas where creative strategic readjustments will have the greatest impact on the company's profitability.

THREAT OF ENTRY

Newcomers to an industry bring new capacity, the desire to gain market share, and often substantial resources. The seriousness of the threat of entry depends on *existing barriers to entry* and on the likelihood of *strong reaction from established competitors.* If barriers to entry are high and if a newcomer can foresee sharp retaliation from the entrenched competitors, the threat of potential new entry is reduced.

There are at least seven barriers to entry:

1. Economies of scale. These economies, if present in any aspect of operation, deter entry by forcing the entrant either to come in on a large scale or to accept a cost disadvantage. Scale economies in production, research, marketing, and service are probably the key barriers to entry in the mainframe computer industry, as Xerox and General Electric once discovered.

2. Product differentiation. Product differentiation creates a barrier by forcing entrants to spend heavily to match the incumbent competitor's product features or to overcome brand loyalty. Product differentiation is perhaps the most important entry barrier in soft drinks, over-the-counter drugs, cosmetics, investment banking, and public accounting.

3. Switching costs. A barrier to entry is created by the presence of switching costs, or one-time costs incurred by the buyer in switching from one supplier's product to another's. The switching price tag may include the time and money costs of employee retraining, new ancillary equipment, testing or qualifying a new source, and technical help from the seller in engineering, product redesign, or even the psychic costs incurred in severing a long-established relationship. If these switching costs are high, then new entrants must offer a major improvement in cost or performance to persuade the buyer to switch from an incumbent.

4. Capital requirements. The need to invest large financial resources in order to compete creates a barrier to entry, particularly if the capital is required for unrecoverable expenditures in up-front advertising or R&D. Capital may be necessary not only for fixed facilities but also for customer credit, inventories, and absorbing start-up losses.

5. *Cost disadvantages independent of scale.* Existing companies may have cost advantages not available to potential rivals, no matter what their attainable economies of scale. These advantages can stem from the effects of the learning curve (and of its first cousin, the experience curve), proprietary technology, access to the best raw materials sources, long-lived assets purchased at preinflation prices, government subsidies, favorable locations, or patents.

6. *Access to distribution channels.* The new competitor must, of course, secure distribution of his product or service. A new food product, for example, must displace others from the supermarket shelf via price breaks, promotions, intense selling efforts, or some other means. Sometimes this barrier is so high that, to surmount it, a new contestant must create its own distribution channels, as Timex did in the watch industry in the 1950s.

7. *Government policy.* The government can control or even foreclose entry to industries with licensing requirements and limits on access to raw materials. Regulated industries like liquor retailing and freight forwarding are obvious examples; more subtle government restrictions operate in fields like ski-area development and coal mining. The government also can play a major indirect role by affecting entry barriers through air and water pollution standards and safety regulations.

The potential rival's estimate of the reaction of existing competitors also will influence its decision whether to enter. The potential entrant may expect strong retaliation if incumbents have previously lashed out at new entrants or if:

The incumbents possess substantial resources to fight back, including excess cash and unused borrowing power, productive capacity, or clout with distribution channels and customers.

The incumbents seem likely to cut prices because of a desire to maintain market shares or because of industrywide excess capacity.

Industry growth is slow, affecting its ability to absorb the new arrival and probably causing the financial performance of all the parties involved to decline.

Entry barriers of all kinds can and do change as industries evolve. The expiration of Polaroid's basic patents on instant photography, for instance, greatly reduced its absolute cost entry barrier built by proprietary technology. It is not surprising that Kodak plunged into the market. Product differentiation in printing has all but disappeared. Conversely, in the auto industry, economies of scale have increased with post-World War II automation and, recently, the need for enormous product development costs—virtually stopping successful new entry.

Of perhaps even more importance to the strategist is the fact that strategic decisions can have a major impact on the conditions determining the threat of entry. For example, the actions of many U.S. wine producers in the 1960s to step up product introductions, raise advertising levels, and expand distribution nationally surely strengthened the entry roadblocks by creating economies of scale and making access to distribution channels more difficult. Similarly, decisions by members of the recreational vehicle industry to integrate vertically in order to lower costs have greatly increased economies of scale and raised capital cost barriers. A company, then, can enhance the defensibility of its position through strategic actions affecting entry barriers.

POWERFUL SUPPLIERS AND BUYERS

Suppliers can exert bargaining power on participants in an industry by raising prices or reducing the quality of purchased goods and services. Powerful suppliers can thereby squeeze profitability out of an industry unable to recover cost increases in its own prices. By raising their prices, for example, soft-drink concentrate producers have contributed to the erosion of profitability of bottling companies because the bottlers, facing intense competition from powdered mixes, fruit drinks, and other beverages, have limited freedom to raise *their* prices accordingly. Buyers likewise can force down prices, demand higher quality or more service, and play competitors off against each other—all at the expense of industry profits.

The power of each important supplier or buyer group depends on a number of characteristics of its market situation and on the relative importance of its sales or purchases to the industry compared with its overall business.

A *supplier* group is powerful if:

It is dominated by a few companies and is more concentrated than the industry it sells to.

Its product is differentiated, or if it has built-in switching costs.

It does not compete with substitutes.

It poses a credible threat of integrating forward into the industry's business.

The industry is not an important customer of the supplier group.

A *buyer* group is powerful if:

It is concentrated or purchases in large volumes.

The products it purchases from the industry are undifferentiated, and there are few switching costs.

The products it purchases from the industry represent a significant fraction of its cost. Where the product sold by the industry in question is a small fraction of buyers' costs, buyers are usually much less price sensitive.

It earns low profits, which create great incentive to lower its purchasing costs. Highly profitable buyers, on the other hand, are generally less price sensitive (that is, of course, if the item does not represent a large fraction of their costs.)

The industry's product is unimportant to the quality or performance of the buyers' products or services. Where the quality of the buyers' products is very much affected by the industry's product, buyers are generally less price sensitive and willing to pay higher prices for desirable performance. Industries in which this fortunate situation exists include oil field equipment, where a malfunction can lead to large losses, and enclosures for electronic medical and test instruments, where the quality of the enclosure can influence the user's impression about the quality of the equipment inside.

The buyers pose a credible threat of integrating backward to make the industry's product. The Big Three auto producers and major buyers of metal cans have often used the threat of self-manufacture as a bargaining lever.

In view of their potential bargaining power, a company's choice of suppliers to buy from or buyer groups to sell to should be viewed as a crucial strategic decision. A company can improve its strategic posture by finding suppliers or buyers who possess the least power to influence it adversely.

As the factors creating supplier and buyer power change with time or as a result of a company's strategic decisions, naturally the power of these groups rises or falls. In the ready-to-wear clothing industry, as the buyers (department stores and clothing stores) have become more concentrated and control has passed to large chains, the industry has come under increasing pressure and suffered falling margins. The industry has been unable to differentiate its product or engender switching costs that lock in its buyers securely enough to neutralize these trends. As with entry barriers, a prime objective of the strategist is to neutralize the power of buyers or suppliers through artful strategic positioning.

SUBSTITUTE PRODUCTS

By placing a ceiling on prices, the availability of substitute products or services limits the potential of an industry. Unless it can upgrade the quality of the product or differentiate it somehow (via marketing, for example), the industry will suffer in earnings and possibly in growth.

The threat of substitutes depends on two conditions. Manifestly, the more attractive the price-performance trade-off offered by substitute products, the more firmly the lid is placed on the industry's profit potential. Sugar producers confronted with the large-scale commercialization of high fructose corn syrup, a sugar substitute, are learning this lesson currently. The threat of substitution is also modified by switching costs from the industry's product to the substitute. The switching costs of possible substitutions are analyzed in an analogous fashion to those facing buyers when switching brands.

Substitutes not only limit profits in normal times but they also reduce the bonanza an industry can mine in boom times. In 1978 the producers of fiberglass insulation enjoyed unprecedented demand as a result of high energy costs and severe winter weather. But the industry's ability to raise prices was tempered by the plethora of insulation substitutes, including cellulose, rock wool, and styrofoam. These substitutes are bound to become an even stronger force once the current round of plant additions by fiberglass insulation producers has boosted capacity enough to meet or exceed demand.

Substitute products that deserve the most attention strategically are those that (a) are subject to trends improving their price-performance trade-off with the industry's product or (b) are produced by industries earning high profits. Substitutes often come rapidly into play if some development increases competition in their industries and causes price reduction or performance improvement. A company facing substitution must either improve its product's price-performance characteristics, raise switching costs, or be prepared to harvest its position as the substitute takes a larger and larger fraction of industry demand.

RIVALRY

Rivalry among existing competitors takes the familiar form of jockeying for position—using tactics like price competition, product introduction, and advertising battles. Intense rivalry is related to the presence of a number of factors:

Competitors are numerous or are evenly balanced in size and capabilities.

Industry growth is slow, precipitating fights for market share triggered by expansion-minded members.

The product or service lacks differentiation or switching costs, which lock in buyers and insulate one competitor from raids on its customers by another.

Fixed costs are high or the product is perishable, creating strong temptation to cut prices.

Intermittent overcapacity is present due to cyclicality of large required capacity additions.

Competitors are diverse in strategies, origins, and "personalities." They have different goals and ideas about how to compete and continually run head-on into each other in the process.

Competitors perceive high stakes to succeeding in the particular industry.

Exit barriers are high. Exit barriers stem from very specialized assets, fixed costs of exits, linkages with sister business units, or management's loyalty to a particular business. Where exit barriers are high, companies remain in a business even though they may be earning low or even negative returns on investment. Excess capacity is not retired, and the profitability of the healthy competitors suffers as the sick ones hang on.

The factors affecting rivalry change as industries evolve. As an industry matures, its growth rate falls, resulting in increasing rivalry and often a shakeout. In the booming recreational vehicle industry of the early 1970s, nearly every producer did well; but slow growth since then has eliminated high returns, except for the strongest members, and wiped out weaker companies. The same profit story has been played out in industry after industry—snowmobiles, aerosol packaging, and sports equipment are just a few examples.

While a company must live with many of the determinants of rivalry—because they are built into industry economics—it may have some latitude for improving matters through strategic shifts. For example, it may try to raise buyers' switching costs or increase product differentiation. A focus of selling efforts on the fastest-growing segments of the industry or on market areas with the lowest fixed costs can reduce the impact of industry rivalry. If it is feasible, a company can try to avoid confrontation with competitors having high exit barriers and can thus sidestep involvement in bitter price cutting.

INDUSTRY STRUCTURE AND THE FORMULATION OF STRATEGY

Once the strategist has assessed the forces affecting competition in his industry and their underlying causes, he can identify his company's strengths and weaknesses. The crucial strengths and weaknesses from a strategic standpoint are the company's position vis-à-vis the underlying causes of each competitive force. Where does it stand against substitutes? Against the sources of entry barriers?

Then the strategist can devise a plan of action that may include (1) positioning the company so that its capabilities provide the best defense against the competitive forces; (2) influencing the balance of the forces through strategic moves, thereby improving the company's position; and (3) anticipating shifts in the factors underlying the forces and responding to them, with the hope of exploiting change by choosing a strategy appropriate for the new competitive balance before opponents recognize it.

The first approach takes the structure of the industry as given and matches the company's strengths and weaknesses to it. Strategy in this sense can be viewed as building defenses against the competitive forces or as finding positions in the industry where the forces are weakest. Influencing the balance is a more aggressive approach designed to do more than merely cope with the forces themselves; it is meant to alter their causes and change the competitive rules of the game. For example, innovations in marketing can raise brand identification or otherwise differentiate the product. Capital investments in large-scale facilities or vertical integration affect entry barriers. The balance of forces is partly a result of external factors and partly in the company's control.

Industry evolution is important strategically because evolution, of course, brings with it changes in the sources of competition that have been identified. In the familiar product life-cycle pattern, for example, growth rates change, product differentiation is said to decline as the business becomes more mature, and the companies tend to integrate vertically.

Technology, a particularly important driver of industry evolution, can affect every one of the five competitive forces, often in dramatic ways. Scientific discoveries can lead to entirely new products that launch whole new industries, as is happening with genetic engineering in the 1980s. Technology can accelerate the development of substitute products, alter process technology in ways that greatly change economies of scale or capital requirements, or enhance the ability of a company to differentiate its product.

Industry trends, in whatever area, are not crucially important in themselves; what is critical is whether they affect the origins of competitive pressures. Consider vertical integration. In the maturing minicomputer industry, extensive vertical integration, both in manufacturing and in software development, is taking place. This very significant trend is greatly enhancing economies of scale and increasing the amount of capital necessary to compete in the industry. This in turn is raising barriers to entry and may drive some smaller competitors out of the industry once growth levels off.

Obviously, the trends carrying the highest priority from a strategic standpoint are those that affect the most important sources of competition in the industry and those that elevate new forces to the forefront. In contract aerosol packaging, for example, the trend toward less product differentiation is now dominant. It has increased buyer's power, lowered the barriers to entry, and intensified competition.

Strategic analysis must examine present and future industry trends in order to ascertain their impact on fundamental industry structure. This is the starting point for identifying strategic changes that may have to be made. More positively, however, the strategist who can foresee structural change may well be able to turn this to the advantage of a company by repositioning it before the need is obvious to everybody.

COMPETITORS

Strategy then involves positioning a business to maximize the value of the capabilities that distinguish it from its competitors. It follows that a central aspect of strategy formulation is perceptive analysis of competitor's strategy and predictable future behavior. The objective of analysis of competitive strategy is to develop a profile of the nature and success of the changes in strategy each competitor might make, discern each competitor's probable response to the range of feasible strategic moves other firms could initiate, and forecast each competitor's probable reaction to the array of industry changes and broader environmental shifts that might occur. Sophisticated "competitor analysis" is needed to answer such questions as "Whom should we pick a fight with in the industry, and in what sequence of moves?" "What is the meaning of that competitor's strategic move and how seriously should we take it?" and "What areas should we avoid because the competitor's response will be emotional or desperate?"

It is useful to identify four components of an analysis of a competitor's strategy (see Figure 3). *Corporate strategy* with emphasis on long-term

Figure 3

THE COMPONENTS OF A COMPETITOR ANALYSIS

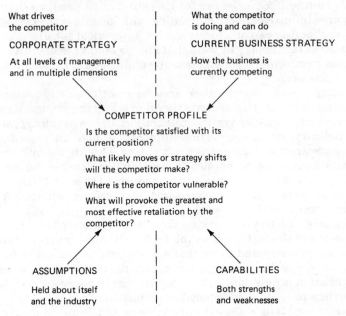

What drives
the competitor

CORPORATE STRATEGY

At all levels of management
and in multiple dimensions

What the competitor
is doing and can do

CURRENT BUSINESS STRATEGY

How the business is
currently competing

COMPETITOR PROFILE

Is the competitor satisfied with its
current position?

What likely moves or strategy shifts
will the competitor make?

Where is the competitor vulnerable?

What will provoke the greatest and
most effective retaliation by the
competitor?

ASSUMPTIONS

Held about itself
and the industry

CAPABILITIES

Both strengths
and weaknesses

goals and the interrelation of corporate and divisional goals, *current business strategy,* with emphasis on the economic strategy and operating policies of each of the competitor's businesses, *assumptions,* and *capabilities.*[5] Understanding these four components will allow an informed profile of a competitor's likely behavior, as articulated in the key questions posed in Figure 3. Most companies develop at least an intuitive sense for their competitors' current business strategies and their strengths and weaknesses (shown on the right side of Figure 3). Much less attention is usually directed at the left side, or understanding what is really driving the behavior of a competitor—its future goals and the assumptions it holds about its own situation and the nature of its industry. These underlying elements are much harder to observe than is actual competitor behavior, yet they often determine how a competitor will behave in the future.

Each component of an analysis of a competitor's strategic position will be described briefly below. The same ideas can also be turned around to provide a framework within which a company may analyze itself. The same concepts provide a company with a framework for probing its own position in its environment. And beyond this, going through such an exercise can help a company understand what conclusions its competitors are likely to draw about it.

---

[5] Although we usually treat future goals as part of strategy, it will be analytically useful to separate goals and current strategy in competitor analysis.

Future goals

By a competitor's corporate strategy we mean in this context the targets of performance it is striving for and which motivate its behavior. Although one most often thinks of financial goals, a comprehensive diagnosis of a competitor's corporate strategy will include, as we have noted before, many more qualitative factors, such as its goals in terms of market leadership, technological position, social responsibility, and the noneconomic satisfactions it offers its members. Diagnosis of strategy should be carried to all management levels. Corporatewide goals, business unit goals, and goals that can be deduced for individual functional areas and key managers can often be identified or deduced from observable behavior. Finally, any diagnosis of a competitor's goals and their place in its total corporate strategy must include an analysis of the *personal* objectives that key managers at the competitor company seem to subscribe to.

The identification of a competitor's goals (and the measures they use in recording progress against these goals), the first component of competitor analysis, is important for a variety of reasons. A knowledge of objectives will allow a prediction of the degree of satisfaction each competitor feels with its present position and financial results, and as a result, how likely that competitor is to change strategy and the vigor with which it will react to outside events (for instance, the business cycle) or to moves by other firms. For example, a firm placing a high value on stable sales growth may react very differently to a business downturn or a market share increase by another company than a firm most interested in maintaining its rate of return on investment.

Knowing the priority of a competitor's goals will also aid in predicting its reaction to strategic changes. Some strategic changes will threaten a competitor more than others, given its goals and any pressures it may face from a corporate parent. This degree of threat will affect the probability of retaliation. Finally, identification of the goal components of a competitor's strategy helps the interpretation of the initiatives the competitor takes. A strategic move by a competitor which addresses one of its central goals or seeks to restore performance against a key target is not a casual matter. Similarly, an appreciation of its objectives will help determine whether a corporate parent will seriously support an initiative taken by one of its business units or whether it will back that business unit's retaliation against moves of competitors.

Assumptions

The second crucial component in competitor analysis is identifying each competitor's apparent assumptions about *itself* and about *the industry and the other companies in it.*

Each firm acts out a set of assumptions about its own situation that may not be rooted in fact or in consciously decided strategic intentions. For example, it may see itself as a socially conscious firm, as the industry leader, as the low-cost producer, or as having the best sales force. These assumptions about its own situation will guide the way the firm behaves and the way it reacts to events. If it sees itself as the low-cost producer, for example, it may try to discipline a price cutter with price cuts of its own.

A competitor's assumptions about its own situation may or may not be accurate. Where they are not, the discrepancy provides an intriguing strategic lever. If a competitor believes it has the greatest customer loyalty in the market but it actually does not, a provocative price cut may be a good way for another company to gain position. The competitor might well refuse to match the price cut believing that it will have little impact on its share, only to find that it loses significant market position before it recognizes the error of its assumption.

Just as each competitor holds assumptions about itself, every firm also operates on asumptions about its industry and competitors. These also may or may not be correct. For example, Gerber Products is reported to have steadfastly believed that births would increase ever since the 1950s, even though the birth rate has been declining steadily and the actual upturn in births may only have just occurred in 1979. There are also many examples of firms that greatly over- or underestimated their competitors' staying power, resources, or skills.

Examining assumptions of all types can identify biases or *blind spots* that may creep into the way managers perceive their environment. Blind spots are areas where a competitor will either not see the significance of events (such as a strategic move) at all, will perceive them incorrectly, or will perceive them only very slowly. Revealing these blind spots will help the firm identify moves with a lower probability of immediate retaliation and identify moves where retaliation, once it comes, will not be effective.

Current business strategy

The third component of competitor analysis is the development of statements of the current economic or business strategy of each competitor, in just the same way as the firm identifies its own strategy as discussed earlier. Each competitor's strategy can then be probed for its implications in terms of the likely future behavior that will reinforce or support that strategy. This analysis will serve to expose likely future moves, or areas where the competitor will retaliate vigorously because an essential part of its strategy is threatened.

Capabilities

A realistic appraisal of each competitor's capabilities is the final diagnostic step in competitor analysis. A competitor's goals, assumptions, and current strategy will influence the likelihood, timing, nature, and intensity of its reactions. Its capabilities will determine its ability to initiate or react to strategic moves and to deal with environmental or industry events that occur. We will examine the identification of company competence and resources shortly.

Picking the battleground

Assuming that competitors will retaliate to the moves a firm initiates to improve its position, its strategic agenda is to select the best battleground for fighting it out with its competitors. The best battleground is the market segment or dimensions of strategy in which competitors are ill prepared, least enthusiastic, or most uncomfortable about competing as a result of the objectives in their corporate strategy, their assumptions, business strategies and capabilities. The best battleground may be competition on costs, for example, centered at the high or low end of the product line.

The ideal is to find a strategy that competitors are frozen from reacting to because of their present circumstances. The legacy of their past and current strategy may make some moves very costly for competitors to follow, while posing much less difficulty and expense for the initiating firm. For example, when Folger's Coffee invaded Maxwell House strongholds in the East with price cutting, the cost of matching these cuts was enormous for Maxwell House because of its large market share.

Realistically, competitors will not often be completely frozen or even torn by mixed motives. In this case, the analysis above should help to identify those strategic moves that will put the initiating firm in the best position to fight the competitive battle when it comes. This means taking advantage of an understanding of competitor goals and assumptions to avoid effective retaliation whenever possible and picking the battlefield where the firm's distinctive abilities represent the most formidable artillery.[6]

IDENTIFICATION OF OPPORTUNITIES AND RISKS

For the firm that has not determined what its strategy dictates it needs to know or has not embarked upon the systematic surveillance of environmental change, a few simple questions kept constantly in mind will highlight changing opportunity and risk. In examining your own company or one you are interested in, these questions should lead to an estimate of opportunity and danger in the present and predicted company setting.

1. What is the underlying structure of the industry in which the firm participates?

The company must develop an ongoing diagnosis of five competitive forces in its industry, and the underlying economic, physical, and technical characteristics that produce those competitive forces. For example, knowledge that the rigid container industry requires high fixed investment in plant, faces slow growth, enjoys little product differentiation among competitors, and faces buyers with little cost in switching suppliers suggests that competitive rivalry will be intense. Such an analysis suggests that efforts to minimize cost through low overhead and new machinery will be fruitful, as will service and technical assistance that differentiates one company's appeal and performance from others. Knowledge that the cement industry requires high investment in plant, proximity to a certain combination of raw materials, a relatively small labor force, and enormous fuel and transportation costs suggests where to look for new plant sites

---

[6] See Michael E. Porter, *Competitive Strategy: Techniques for Analyzing Industries and Competitors* (New York: Free Press, 1980), chap. 3, for a fuller statement of competitor analysis.

and what will constitute competitive advantage and disadvantage. The nature of its product may suggest for a given company the wisdom of developing efficient pipeline and truck transportation and cheap energy sources to lower its costs rather than engaging in extensive research to achieve product differentiation or aggressive price competition to increase its market share.

2. *What industry trends are apparent that might change this underlying structure?*

Industry trends with the greatest impact are those that promise to affect the five competitive forces. Changes in substitute products occurring as a result of research and development, for example, affect the substitution threat facing the industry. For example, the glass container industry's development years ago of strong, light, disposable bottles and more recently combinations of glass and plastic recouped part of the market lost by glass to the metal container. The need for the glass industry to engage in this development effort was made apparent by the observable success of the metal beer can. Similarly, the easy-opening metal container suggested the need for an easily removable bottle cap in order to cope with the substitution threat. Increased sophistication of buyers of contract aerosol packaging, coupled with increasing ease of their vertical integration into the business themselves, made buyers increasingly powerful and price sensitive and had a strong depressing effect on industry profits.

3. *How might foreseeable changes in the social, political, and macroeconomic context impact the industry or the firm?*

Broad changes in society, government policy, or macroeconomic conditions can have a dramatic impact on the industry or on the company's position in its industry. Deregulation has thrown the domestic U.S. airline and trucking industries into bitter price wars and a scramble for consolidation. Both the glass bottle and the metal container face increasingly effective attack by environmentalists, who constitute a noneconomic and nontechnical force to be reckoned with. Container industries should have begun long since, for example, to develop logistical solutions to the legislatively mandated returnable bottle and can.

4. *What are the goals, assumptions, strategies, and capabilities of the important existing and potential competitors in the industry and their likely future behavior?*

Strategy must be developed in the context of informed profiles of competitors, both existing and potential. Competitors' moves can pose a threat to the company's existing strategic position, and the company's planned strategic changes can be nullified by competitive reaction.

A realistic assessment of competitors must guide the goals a company sets for itself. A small rubber company, in an industry led by Uniroyal, Goodyear, Goodrich, and Firestone, will not, under the economic condition of overcapacity, elect to provide the automobile business with original tires for new cars. The capabilities of competitors, quite apart from the resources of the firm, may suggest that a relatively small firm should seek out a niche of relatively small attraction to the majors, and concentrate its powers on that limited segment of the market.

5. *What are the critical requirements for future success for the company?*

Industry structure, the capabilities of competitors and their expected behavior, and broader social, political, and macroeconomic trends all define the critical tasks the company must perform to insure its strategic health and survival. In the ladies' belt and handbag business, style and design are critical, but so (less obviously) are relationships with department store buyers. In the computer business, a sales force able to diagnose customer requirements for information systems, to design a suitable system, and to equip a customer to use it is more important than the circuitry of hardware given the positions of the various competitors.

Although the question of what tasks are most critical for the company may be chiefly useful as a means of identifying risks or possible causes of failure, it may also suggest opportunity. Imagination in perceiving new requirements for success under changing conditions, when production-oriented competitors have not done so, can give a company leadership position. For example, opportunity for a local radio station and the strategy it needed to follow changed sharply with the rise of television, and those who first diagnosed the new requirements paid much less for stations than was later necessary.

6. *Given the analysis of the industry, competitors, and broader context, what range of strategic alternatives is available to companies in this industry?*

The force of this question is obvious in the drug industry. The speed and direction of pharmaceutical research, the structure of the industry, the behavior of competitors, the characteristics of worldwide demand, the different and changing ideas about how adequate medical care should be made available to the world's population, the concern about price, and the nature of government regulation suggest constraints within which a range of opportunity is still vividly clear. Similarly, in a more stable industry, there is always a choice. To determine its limits, an examination of environmental characteristics and developments is essential.

OPPORTUNITY AS A DETERMINANT OF STRATEGY

Awareness of the environment and analysis of the behavior of competitors is not a special project to be undertaken only when warning of change becomes deafening; it is a continuing requirement for informed choice of purpose. Planned exploitation of changing opportunity ordinarily follows a predictable course which provides increasing awareness of areas to which a company's capabilities may be profitably extended. A useful way to perceive the normal course of development is to use Bruce Scott's stages referred to briefly in a previous discussion.

The manufacturer of a single product (stage I) sold within a clearly defined geographical area to meet a known demand finds it relatively easy to identify opportunity and risk. As an enterprise develops a degree of complexity requiring functional division of management decision, it encounters as an integrated stage II company a number of strategic alternatives in its market environments which the stage I proprietor is too hard pressed to notice and almost too overcommitted to consider. Finally, stage III companies, deployed along the full range of diversification, find even a greater number of possibilities for serving a market profitably than the resources they possess or have in sight will support. The more one finds out what might be done, the harder it is to make the final choice.

The diversified stage III company has another problem different from that of trying to make the best choice among many. If it has divisionalized its operations and strategies, as sooner or later in the course of diversification it must, then divisional opportunities come into competition with each other.

The corporate management will wish to invest profits not distributed to stockholders in those opportunities that will produce the greatest return to the corporation. If need be, corporate management will be willing to let an individual division decline if its future looks less attractive than that of others. The division on the other hand will wish to protect its own market position, ward off adverse developments, prolong its own existence, and provide for its growth. The division manager, who is not rewarded for failures, may program projects of safe but usually not dramatic prospects. The claims regarding projected return on investment, which are submitted in all honesty as the divisional estimate of future opportunity, can be assumed to be biased by the division's regard for its own interest and the manager's awareness of measurement.

The corporate management cannot be expected to be able to make independent judgments about all the proposals for growth which are submitted by all the divisions. On the other hand, all divisions cannot be given their heads, if the corporation's needs for present profit are to be met and if funds for reinvestment are limited. In any case, the greatest knowledge about the opportunities for a given technology and set of markets should be found at the divisional level.[7]

The strategic dilemma of a conglomerate world enterprise is the most complex in the full range of policy decisions. When the variety of what must be known cannot be reduced by a sharply focused strategy to the capacity of a single mind and when the range of a company's activities spans many industries and technologies, the problems of formulating a coherent strategy begin to get out of hand. Here strategy must become a managed process rather than the decision of the chief executive officer and his immediate associates. Bower and Prahalad[8] have shown in important research how the context of decision can be controlled by the top-management group and how power can be distributed through a hierarchy to influence the kind of strategic decision that will survive in the system. The process of strategic decision can, like complex operations, be organized in such a way as to provide appropriate complementary roles for decentralization and control.

To conceive of a new development in response to market information, analysis of competitive strategy, and prediction of the future is a creative act. To commit resources to it only on the basis of projected return and the estimate of probability constituting risk of failure is foolhardy. More than economic analysis of potential return is required for decision, for economic opportunity abounds, far beyond the ability to capture it. That

---

[7] See Norman Berg, "Strategic Planning in Conglomerate Companies," *Harvard Business Review*, May–June 1965.

[8] Joseph L. Bower, *Managing the Resource Allocation Process* (Boston: Division of Research, Harvard Business School, 1970); and C. K. Prahalad, "The Strategic Process in a Multinational Corporation" (unpublished doctoral thesis, Harvard Business School 1975), partially summarized in "Strategic Choices in Diversified MNCs," *Harvard Business Review*, July–August 1976, pp. 67–78.

much money might be made in a new field or growth industry does not mean that a company with abilities developed in a different field is going to make it. We turn now to the critical factors that for an individual company make one opportunity better than another.

IDENTIFYING CORPORATE COMPETENCE AND RESOURCES

The first step in validating a tentative choice among several opportunities is to determine whether the organization has the capacity to prosecute it successfully. The capability of an organization is its demonstrated and potential ability to accomplish, against the opposition of circumstance or competition, whatever it sets out to do. Every organization has actual and potential strengths and weaknesses. Since it is prudent in formulating strategy to extend or maximize the one and contain or minimize the other, it is important to try to determine what they are and to distinguish one from the other.

It is just as possible, though if anything more difficult, for a company to know its own strengths and limitations as it is to maintain a workable surveillance of its changing environment. Subjectivity, lack of confidence, and unwillingness to face reality may make it hard for organizations as well as for individuals to know themselves. But just as it is essential, though difficult, that a maturing person achieve reasonable self-awareness, so an organization can identify approximately its central strength and critical vulnerability.

Howard H. Stevenson has made the first formal study of management practice in defining corporate strengths and weaknesses as part of the strategic planning process.[9] He looked at five aspects of the process: (1) the attributes of the company which its managers examined, (2) the organizational scope of the strengths and weaknesses identified, (3) the measurement employed in the process of definition, (4) the criteria for telling a strength from a weakness, and (5) the sources of relevant information. As might be expected, the process Stevenson was looking at was imperfectly and variously practiced in the half dozen companies he studied. He found that the problems of definition of corporate strengths and weaknesses, very different from those of other planning processes, center mostly upon a general lack of agreement on suitable definition, criteria, and information. For an art that has hardly made a beginning, Stevenson offers a prescriptive model for integrating the considerations affecting definition of strength or weakness. Indicative of the primitive stage of some of our concepts for general management, Stevenson's most important conclusion is that the attempt to define strengths and weaknesses is more useful than the usual final product of the process.

Stevenson's exploratory study in no way diminishes the importance of appraising organization capability. It protects us against oversimplifi-

---

[9] Howard H. Stevenson, "Defining Corporate Strengths and Weaknesses: An Exploratory Study" (an unpublished doctoral thesis deposited in Baker Library, Harvard Business School, 1969). For a published summary article of the same title, see *Sloan Management Review*, Spring 1976.

cation. The absence of criteria and measures, the disinclination for appraising competence except in relation to specific problems, the uncertainty about what is meant by "strength" and "weakness," and the reluctance to imply criticism of individuals or organizational subunits—all these hampered his study but illuminated the problem. Much of what is intuitive in this process is yet to be identified. Both for a competitor and for one's own company, one can inquire into strengths and weaknesses in functional components like marketing, manufacturing, research and development, finance, or control; the impact that growth may have on functional capability and on the quality of management; the capacity to respond quickly to competitive moods and to adapt to the changing environment. Raising questions like these quickens the power of self-awareness, even if definitive judgments are hard to come by.

To make an effective contribution to strategic planning, the key attributes to be appraised should be identified and consistent criteria established for judging them. If attention is directed to strategies, policy commitments, and past practices in the context of discrepancy between organization goals and attainment, an outcome useful to an individual manager's strategic planning is possible. The assessment of strengths and weaknesses associated with the attainment of specific objectives becomes in Stevenson's words a "key link in a feedback loop" which allows managers to learn from the success or failures of the policies they institute.

Although this study does not find or establish a systematic way of developing or using such knowledge, members of organizations develop judgments about what the company can do particularly well—its core of competence. If consensus can be reached about this capability, no matter how subjectively arrived at, its application to identified opportunity can be estimated. Surely as much success can be achieved in developing analysis of one's own company as in preparing the competitor analysis described earlier.

Sources of capabilities. The powers of a company constituting a resource for growth and diversification accrue primarily from experience in making and marketing a product line. They inhere as well in (1) the developing strengths and weaknesses of the individuals comprising the organization, (2) the degree to which individual capability is effectively applied to the common task, and (3) the quality of coordination of individual and group effort.

The experience gained through successful execution of a strategy centered upon one goal may unexpectedly develop capabilities which could be applied to different ends. Whether they should be so applied is another question. For example, a manufacturer of salt can strengthen his competitive position by offering his customers salt-dispensing equipment. If, in the course of making engineering improvements in this equipment, a new solenoid principle is perfected that has application to many industrial switching problems, should this patentable and marketable innovation be exploited? The answer would turn not only on whether economic analysis of the opportunity shows this to be a durable and profitable possibility, but also on whether the organization can muster the financial, manufacturing, and marketing strength to exploit the discovery. The former question is likely to have a more positive answer than the latter. In this connection, it seems important to remember that individual and unsupported flashes of strength are not as dependable as the gradually accumulated product- and market-related fruits of experience.

Even where competence to exploit an opportunity is nurtured by experience in related fields, the level of that competence may be too low for any great reliance to be placed upon it. Thus a chain of children's clothing stores might well acquire the administrative, merchandising, buying, and selling skills that would permit it to add departments in women's wear. Similarly, a sales force effective in distributing typewriters may gain proficiency in selling office machinery and supplies. But even here it would be well to ask what distinctive ability these companies could bring to the retailing of soft goods or office equipment to attract customers away from a plethora of competitors.

Identifying strengths. The distinctive competence of an organization is more than what it can do; it is what it can do particularly well. To identify the less obvious or by-product strengths of an organization that may well be transferable to some more profitable new opportunity, one might well begin by examining the organization's current product line and by defining the functions it serves in its markets. Almost any important consumer product has functions which are related to others into which a qualified company might move. The typewriter, for example, is more than the simple machine for mechanizing handwriting that it once appeared to be when looked at only from the point of view of its designer and manufacturer. Closely analyzed from the point of view of the potential user, the typewriter is found to contribute to a broad range of information processing functions. Any one of these might have suggested an area to be exploited by a typewriter manufacturer. Tacitly defining a typewriter as a replacement for a fountain pen as a writing instrument rather than as an input-output device for word processing is the explanation provided by hindsight for the failure of the old-line typewriter companies to develop the electric typewriter and the computer-related input-output devices it made possible before IBM did. The definition of product which would lead to identification of transferable skills must be expressed in terms of the market needs it may fill rather than the engineering specifications to which it conforms.

Besides looking at the uses or functions to which present products contribute, the would-be diversifier might profitably identify the skills that underlie whatever success has been achieved. The qualifications of an organization efficient at performing its long-accustomed tasks come to be taken for granted and considered humdrum, like the steady provision of first-class service. The insight required to identify the essential strength justifying new ventures does not come naturally. Its cultivation can probably be helped by recognition of the need for analysis. In any case, we should look beyond the company's capacity to invent new products. Product leadership is not possible for a majority of companies, so it is fortunate that patentable new products are not the only major highway to new opportunities. Other avenues include new marketing services, new methods of distribution, new values in quality-price combinations, and creative merchandising. The effort to find or to create a competence that is truly distinctive may hold the real key to a company's success or even to its future development. For example, the ability of a cement manufacturer to run a truck fleet more effectively than its competitors may constitute one of its principal competitive strengths in selling an undifferentiated product.

Matching opportunity and competence. The way to narrow the range of alternatives, made extensive by imaginative identification of new possibilities, is to match opportunity to competence, once each has been accurately identified and its future significance estimated. It is this combination which establishes a company's economic mission and its position in its environment. The combination is designed to minimize organizational weakness and to maximize strength. In every case, risk attends it. And when opportunity seems to outrun present distinctive competence, the willingness to gamble that the latter can be built up to the required level is almost indispensable to a strategy that challenges the organization and the people in it. Figure 4 diagrams the matching of opportunity and resources that results in an economic strategy.

Before we leave the creative act of putting together a company's unique internal capability and evolving opportunity in the external world, we should note that—aside from distinctive competence—the principal resources found in any company are money and people—technical and managerial people. At this stage of economic development, money seems less a problem than technical competence, and the latter much less critical than managerial ability. In reading the cases that follow, by all means look carefully at the financial records of each company and take note of its success and its problems. Look also at the apparent managerial capacity and, without underestimating it, do not assume that it can rise to any occasion. The diversification of American industry is marked by hundreds of instances in which a company strong in one endeavor lacked the ability to manage an enterprise requiring different skills. The right to make handsome profits over a long period must be earned. Opportunism without competence is a path to fairyland.

Besides equating an appraisal of market opportunity and organizational capability, the decision to make and market a particular product or service should be accompanied by an identification of the nature of the business and the kind of company its management desires. Such a guiding concept is a product of many considerations, including the managers' personal values. As such, this concept will change more slowly than other aspects of the organization, and it will give coherence to all the variety of company activities. For example, a president who is determined to make his or her firm into a worldwide producer and fabricator of a basic metal, through policies differentiating it from the industry leader, will not be distracted by excess capacity in developed markets, low metal prices, and cutthroat competition in certain markets. Such a firm would not be sidetracked into acquiring, for example, the Pepsi-

Figure 4

SCHEMATIC DEVELOPMENT OF ECONOMIC STRATEGY

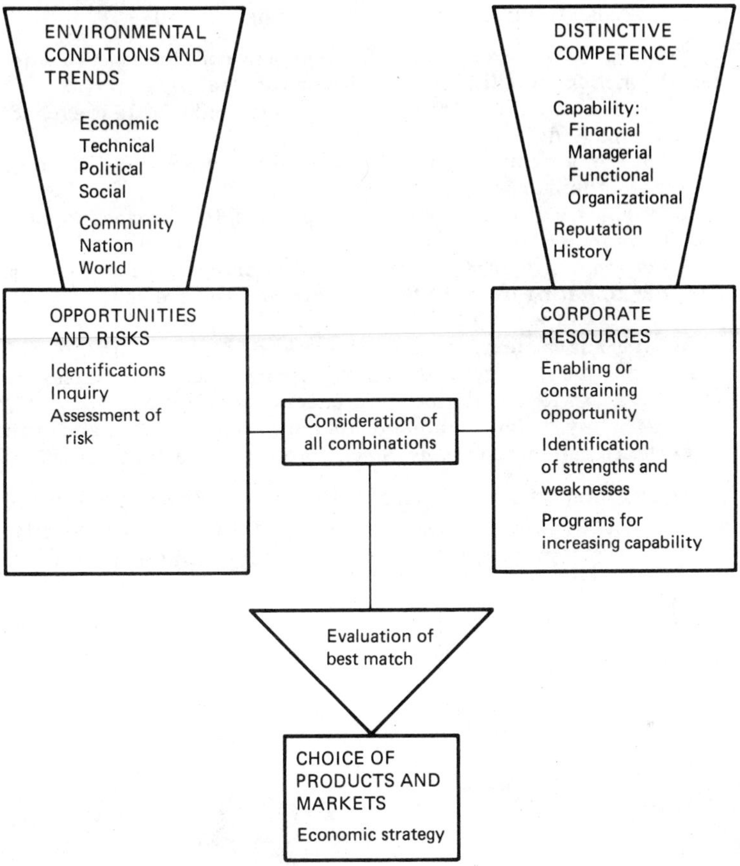

Cola franchise in Africa, even if this business promised to yield a good profit. (That such a firm should have an experimental division exploring offshoot technology is, however, entirely appropriate.)

Uniqueness of strategy.   In each company, the way in which distinctive competence, organizational resources, and organizational values are combined is or should be unique. Differences among companies are as numerous as differences among individuals. The combinations of opportunity to which distinctive competences, resources, and values may be applied are equally extensive. Generalizing about how to make an effective match is less rewarding than working at it. The effort is a highly stimulating and challenging exercise. The outcome will be unique for each case and each situation, but each achievement of a viable economic strategy will leave the student of strategy better prepared to take part in real-life strategic decisions.

APPLICATION TO CASES

Students could profitably bring to the cases they study not only the questions suggested earlier, but the following as well:

> What really is our product? What functions does it serve? To what additional functions might it be extended or adapted?
>
> What is happening to the market for our products? Is it expanding or contracting? Why?
>
> What are our company's major strengths and weaknesses? From what sources do these arise?
>
> Do we have a distinctive or core competence? If so, to what new activities can it be applied?
>
> What are our principal competitors' major strengths and weaknesses? Are they imitating us or we them? What comparative advantage over our competitors can we exploit?
>
> What is our strategy? Is the combination of product and market an optimum economic strategy? Is the central nature of our business clear enough to provide us with a criterion for product diversification?
>
> What, if any, better combinations of market opportunities and distinctive competence can our company effect, within a range of reasonable risk?

These questions will prove helpful throughout the course in the task of designing an economic strategy. However, they are never wholly sufficient, for the strategic decision is never wholly economic in character.

The chain-saw industry in 1974

AFTER A LONG PERIOD of relative stability, the U.S. chain-saw industry was experiencing rapid growth in early 1974, stimulated by increased consumer interest in chain saws as a result of the energy crisis and a trend toward back to nature and self-sufficiency. Long dominated by Homelite in the mass market and the German company Stihl in the premium segment, the industry faced other changes in the early 1970s. Two major companies in the industry had recently been acquired by large parents, and many other participants had taken a renewed interest in the industry as a result of the upsurge in growth.

THE PRODUCT

Chain saws are motorized devices for cutting wood, which are sold to a wide range of industrial, commercial, and household buyers. There are two basic types of chain saws, which differ in the nature of their power unit (power head). Gas saws are free-standing units powered by an internal combustion engine of two to over eight cubic inches of displacement. Electric saws utilize an electric motor which was fed by a cable which had to be connected to an electrical socket. Domestic U.S. sales of chain saws over the 1949–73 period were as shown in Table 1.[1]

Exhibit 1 shows a typical chain saw, identifying its major parts. Besides the basic nature of the power head, chain saws differed in two important dimensions. The horsepower of the power head varied from 1.5 to approximately 8.5. More powerful saws were designed for heavy-duty uses such as logging and construction, while less powerful saws were sufficient for the cutting of firewood and light clearing of land

---

[1] The U.S. market for chain saws was approximately as large as the rest of the world combined.

Table 1

HISTORICAL DOMESTIC CHAIN-SAW SALES
(000 units)

Year	Gas saws	Electric saws*	Total saws
1949	40	—	40
1950	60	—	60
1951	95	—	95
1952	111	—	111
1953	150	—	150
1954	220	—	220
1955	248	—	248
1956	277	—	277
1957	248	—	248
1958	321	—	321
1959	363	—	363
1960	340	—	340
1961	340	—	340
1962	375	—	375
1963	381	—	381
1964	453	—	453
1965	501	—	501
1966	515	—	515
1967	518	—	518
1968	554	—	554
1969	613	—	613
1970	633	n.a.	633+
1971	750	n.a.	750+
1972	899	175	1,064
1973	1,400	312	1,712

n.a. = Not available.
* Sales of electric saws were very small before 1970.
Source: Manufacturer interviews; for pre-1972 data, Walter J. Williams, "The United States Chain Saw Market," unpublished manuscript, Amos Tuck School, Dartmouth College.

that the homeowner was likely to require. Chain saws also differed in the length of their cutting bar (from 10 to over 24 inches), with long bar saws designed, by and large, for heavy-duty applications.

These differences translated into the availability of a wide variety of chain-saw models, with some manufacturers producing over 20 different saws. Prices for chain saws reflected this wide range of products (Table 2).

Chain saws had a useful life of approximately five years of regular use.

MARKETS

Industry participants had traditionally segmented end users of chain saws into three categories: professional, farmer, and occasional or casual user. The *professional* used a chain saw as one of the primary tools of his trade. Along with professional loggers, the pro segment included commercial and government buyers who used chain saws as an auxiliary

Exhibit 1

DIAGRAM OF A GAS CHAIN SAW

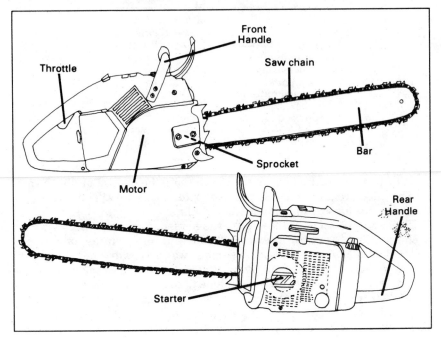

tool of their trades, such as building contractors, municipal employees, and local park district workers. Industry sources estimated that the great majority of pro users purchased saws with cubic inch displacements of 4.5 or greater.

The *farmer* used a chain saw for a variety of activities on his land, as shown in the 1972 survey (Table 3). Farmer purchased saws in the 2.7-cubic-inch to 4.5-cubic-inch displacement range, with some purchasing even larger saws.

Table 2

CHAIN-SAW RETAIL PRICE SEGMENTATION
(based on number of units in the price segment)

	1970	1971	1972
Less than $140....	12%	20%	22%
$140–170..........	12	27	26
	24	47	48
$170–300..........	} 76	49	47
$300–700..........		4	5
Total	100%	100%	100%

Source: Chain Saw Manufacturers Association and dealer and manufacturer interviews.

Table 3

FARM USES OF CHAIN SAWS

Specific farm use	Percent of survey respondents that reported use
Tree maintenance	54.1
Land clearing	49.8
Fence posts	49.4
Firewood cutting	28.8
Timber	26.2
Pulpwood	1.3

Source: *Kansas Farmer.*

Both pro and farmer users tended to make heavy use of chain saws and required regular service and repair for their saws. They were also frequent purchasers of replacement chain.

The term *casual user* referred to the homeowner or camper who used a chain saw for cutting firewood, tree trimming, pruning, or clearing storm damage. The casual-user segment was a very diverse group with a wide variety of needs, and saw usage rates within this segment varied accordingly (Table 4). Not infrequently, the casual user's need for a chain saw was very transitory, such as a one-time tree-clearing project. After this use the saw might be used very lightly if at all. Other casual users were *regular* users of saws.

Most casual-user saws were estimated to have power heads with less than 2.7-cubic-inch displacement and bar lengths of less than 16 inches. Most casual users purchased saws which cost less than $200 (Table 5).

The estimated breakdown of unit sales of chain saws by end-user segment was as shown in Table 6.

Once a purchaser of a chain saw becomes a regular user, there was a tendency to trade up to a saw with either more power or more features. Chain saws in regular use required service, repairs, and the purchase of replacement saw chain. Professional users consumed approximately 5 to 30 seven- to eight-foot loops of saw chain per year, and farmers

Table 4

SEGMENTATION OF CASUAL USERS BY TYPE OF USE

Primary type of use	Percent of casual user market
Fireplace (occasional woodcutting)	60–70
Home heating (heavy user)	10–15
Camping	10–15
Suburban acreage (light clearing work)	5–10
Nonuser (gift, etc., put immediately on the shelf)	5–10
	100

Source: Manufacturer and distributor interviews.

Table 5

	Percent of total saws sold to farm and professional users	Percent of total saws sold to casual users
Less than $100	3	23
$100–$200	7	67
$200–$250	33	8
$250 or more	57	2
	100	100

Source: Chain Saw Manufacturers Association and manufacturer interviews.

Table 6

DOMESTIC GAS CHAIN-SAW
SALES BY END-USER SEGMENT
(000 units)

	1972	1973
Professional	259	315
Farmer	210	282
Casual user	430	803
Total	899	1,400

Source: Chain Saw Manufacturers Association and manufacturer interviews.

typically used 3 to 5 four- to eight-foot loops if they were regular saw users. Pro and farm users also typically replaced the guide bar two to three times and the sprocket three to five times over the life of the saw. Usage of chain varied markedly in the casual-user segment, and there was little reliable evidence of how much chain the average casual user consumed though it was believed to be less than one four-foot loop per year. A four-foot loop of replacement chain cost approximately $10, while bars and sprockets were somewhat more expensive, though the cost varied by size and manufacturer.

While the pro and farmer segments had long been the dominant markets for chain saws and still dominated the market in terms of dollar sales because of their much higher average prices, the casual-user segment had begun to emerge as a rapidly growing segment in the chain-saw industry. Prior to 1963 gas saws were sold almost exclusively to professional woodcutters. In 1963 a leading competitor, Homelite, introduced its lightweight XL-12 saw priced under $200, soon followed by McCulloch with a similar model. The unprecedented combination of light weight and low price was cited by observers as stimulating the birth of the casual-user market. Industry sources attributed the recent spurt in casual-user sales to a number of factors, among them increased usage of fireplaces and wood-burning stoves as a result of the energy crisis, social trends emphasizing back to nature and escape from urban living, ownership of second homes, and increased leisure time, all coupled with wider availability of lower priced saws, some costing less than $100.

The casual-user market was expected to continue to grow rapidly for at least the next five years. The pro and farm segments were primarily replacement markets by 1974, though they were expected to grow at approximately 10 percent per year. Pro and farmer sales tended to be somewhat cyclical, in keeping with the cycles in their end-user industries.

DISTRIBUTION

Chain saws reached end users through a complex array of two- and three-stage distribution channels. Exhibit 2 gives a schematic diagram of chain-saw distribution, as well as indicating the most important channels of distribution for saws in 1974.

Servicing chain-saw dealers was the most important retail channel in the chain-saw market. Chain-saw dealers were full-service outlets carrying broad lines of chain saws and offering extensive customer purchasing assistance. There were some dealers who sold only chain saws, but most were lawn and garden stores or building contractor supply outlets. Chain-saw dealers were franchised to carry the brands of individual manufacturers, and approximately 25 percent of the dealers carried only one line. However, most dealers carried the product lines of more than one manufacturer, averaging approximately two such lines. Multiple-line dealers generally carried only one of the lines of the two major manufacturers, Homelite and McCulloch, and identified themselves with these firms.

Approximately 45 percent of chain-saw dealers were in rural areas, while 35 percent were in urban areas and 20 percent in suburban areas. Dealers provided service, sold replacement chain and accessories, and had an average sales volume in chain-saw and related products of $150,000–$200,000 per year. Many were owned by former gasoline engine mechanics. Sales were seasonal, at their highest levels in the summer months. Dealers advertised primarily through local newspapers and radio, and many manufacturers had cooperative advertising programs that shared advertising costs with dealers on a 50–50 basis. Dealer margins for chain saws ranged from 20 to 40 percent, with margins on service and accessories significantly higher. Margins were lowest on the lower price saws, and some dealers claimed to sell saws at or near cost and make their profit on service and accessories.

Other retail channels for chain saws were as follows:

Lumber and home centers. These outlets were both independent and chain stores catering to homeowners and contractors, and they offered a limited line of saws without service and with limited accessories. Saws were sometimes bought directly from manufacturers but usually through distributors. Chain saws were not a major item for these outlets in 1974.

Farm stores. This outlet includes both independent and chain stores supplying farmers with a wide line of farm products including feed,

Exhibit 2

DISTRIBUTION CHANNELS FOR CHAIN SAWS

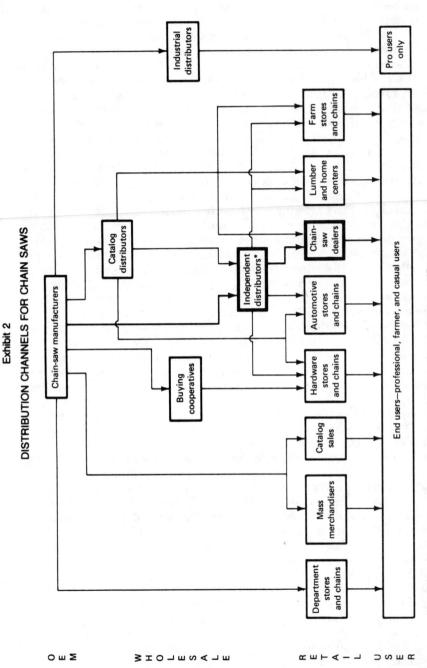

Note: The bold lines indicate the most important distribution channel for chain saws in 1974.
* Homelite had in-house distributors; it was the only manufacturer that did not use independent distributors.
Source: Manufacturer, distributor, and retailer interviews.

equipment, fertilizer, etc. Examples of farm store chains are Agway (500 stores), Tractor Supply (250 stores), and Quality Farm and Fleet (23 stores). Most farm stores carried a full line of chain saws and accessories, purchased either direct from the manufacturer or through distributors. Some of the chains handled private label as well as several lines of branded saws. Independent farm stores usually offered service on chain saws, and these outlets resembled the chain-saw dealer. Farm store chains were much less likely to offer service. Farm stores were concentrated in the west and midwest, and sold to professionals and casual users as well as primarily to farmers. Sales of chain saws in this outlet were growing, but more slowly than the market as a whole.

Department stores. This outlet includes major department stores that sell chain saws, particularly the large national chains (Sears, Montgomery Ward, and J. C. Penney). Some of the smaller department stores carried chain saws, offering relatively few models and little or no service. The three major chains were major outlets for saws, and all sold moderately full lines of saws and accessories. They did not carry expensive, high-quality saws because of the difficulty of the sales task. Sears and Ward's had their own service while Penney referred customers to the nearest manufacturer-authorized service center. All three offered credit, which was an effective marketing tool which many other channels for chain saws did not have. The three leading department store chains as well as some other department stores had significant catalog sales of chain saws as well as over-the-counter sales. The Big Three sold an estimated 20–30 percent of their saws through catalog operations.

The major department store chains sold both private label and brand name saws, purchased directly from manufacturers in large volumes. Total sales of chain saws to the top three chains was estimated at several hundred thousand units in 1973. Sears and Ward's sold only private label saws, while Penney sold brand name saws though it had sold private label saws in the past. Ward's and especially Sears required their suppliers to redesign products to give them a distinctive line.

Hardware stores. This outlet includes both local independent stores and chains that carry a full line of hardware products. Hardware stores offered moderately wide lines of saws, including products of several competing manufacturers. Many offered service and a full line of accessories for the saws, but generally service was limited in scope compared to chain-saw dealers. Hardware stores were characterized by a high level of customer purchase assistance.

While hardware stores purchased from independent chain-saw distributors, an important volume of their chain saws was purchased through wholesale hardware buying groups such as HWI, American Hardware, Ace Hardware, and Cotter & Company. Chain saws represented a minor fraction of the sales of hardware stores, and hardware stores as a group represented less than 10 percent of chain-saw sales in 1973.

Catalog sales. Aside from catalog sales through the major department stores, there were some very limited sales of chain saws through exclusively catalog firms such as Aldens. These firms typically carried models from many manufacturers, with the focus on smaller saws and related accessories. No service was offered, and customers were referred to the nearest service center.

In addition to these major channels for chain saws, there were two other kinds of outlets that had recently added chain saws to their line in some cases. A few mass merchandisers such as K mart had begun to carry very limited lines of lower priced chain saws, with limited accessories and no service. These were purchased directly from manufacturers. In addition, some of the major auto store chains such as Western Auto had begun limited sales of chain saws on essentially the same basis. These firms either bought direct or through cooperative buying groups.

The breakdown of dollar volume sold through these channels in 1973 was approximately as shown in Table 7.

Table 7

ESTIMATED CHAIN-SAW SALES BY CHANNEL

Servicing dealers	50–65%
Department stores	20–25
Farm stores	10–15
Hardware stores	5–10
Others	<10
Total	100%

Source: Manufacturer interviews.

WHOLESALE CHANNELS

There were three types of wholesale channels for chain saws. By far the most important was wholesale distributors owned by or exclusively affiliated with the chain-saw manufacturers. Most manufacturers had between 20 and 50 distributors, who sold to dealers in the various categories described above. In a few cases the distributors sold direct to large professional or industrial end users.

In addition to regular chain-saw distributors, there were catalog distributors and dealer cooperatives (or buying groups) involved in wholesaling chain saws. Catalog dealers purchased directly from manufacturers and resold saws to smaller distributors who did not specialize in chain saws. Buying groups were arrangements where a group of retailers banded together to secure favorable terms in purchasing from manufacturers. These were most important in hardware stores.

MANUFACTURING

Chain-saw manufacturing involved a complex assembly operation using a variety of fabricated parts. Parts could be divided into two major categories: those relating to the power head, and attachments (bar, chain, and sprocket). Parts fabrication included machining, die casting, forging, heat treatment, plating and metal stamping operations. Of these, die casting involved the most significant investment and degree of difficulty, and required extremely close tolerances. Exhibit 3 lists the major parts of a chain saw along with an estimate of the percentage of total costs represented by each part for a gas chain-saw model with annual production volume of 100,000 units. There were economies of scale in the production of most of the significant components of the saw. There

Exhibit 3

CHAIN-SAW MANUFACTURING COSTS*

	Percent of unit costs
Parts:	
Guide bar, saw chain, sprocket	16.1
Carburetor	6.0
Ignition	6.0
Starter	6.6
Clutch	1.1
Piston	2.1
Total purchased parts	37.9
Magnesium and aluminum die castings:	
Crankcase cover	4.5
Rear handle	1.1
Oil tank cover	1.1
Sprocket cover	0.6
Cylinder	2.7
Total die castings	10.0
Plastic parts:	
Various	3.1
Forgings:	
Crankshaft	1.5
Connecting rod	0.8
Stampings:	
Muffler, brackets, etc.	1.5
Bearings, gaskets, seals:	
Various	3.2
Miscellaneous	6.7
Total material	64.7
Labor:	
Die-cast machining	2.7
Forging machining	2.8
Heat treatment	0.1
Chrome and copper plate	2.7
Subassembly†	1.6
Final assembly†	4.0
Total labor	13.9

* Manufacturing cost of gas chain saw, assuming annual production volume of 100,000 units, and average level of vertical integration for the industry.

† May include some overhead.

Source: Testimony of Desa Industries, preliminary antitrust hearings against Black & Decker, 1972.

were also cost savings due to automation, particularly in machining and assembly. The total tooling investment required to produce all these parts (except saw chain, guide bars, and sprockets) for a chain-saw model was estimated at approximately $300,000–$500,000 in 1972.

Chain-saw manufacturers varied greatly in their level of vertical integration, with the manufacturer shown in Exhibit 3 having approximately an average level of integration. The very largest manufacturers were almost completely integrated, though they usually purchased some saw chain, bars, and other specialized parts. Saw chain and bar manufacture required significant investment, and involved quite sophisticated and often proprietary technology that had been mastered by specialist outside suppliers. Medium-sized firms purchased attachments as well as die castings and sometimes forgings, doing most of their own machining and then assembly. There were some very small manufacturers that were solely assembly operations. Industry participants believed that integration lowered unit costs if the volume of parts produced internally was large relative to volumes produced by specialist outside suppliers. Specialized suppliers existed for all the major chain-saw components, and many had been supplying the industry for decades. In carburetors, for example, there were specialized outside suppliers with such great annual and accumulated volumes that no chain-saw manufacturer produced carburetors in-house.

An approximate breakdown of costs for a typical chain-saw manufacturer was as follows:

Purchased parts and material	45–70%
Direct labor	7–10
Indirect labor and overhead	24–40
Total manufacturing costs	100%

Source: Estimates based on manufacturer and supplier interviews.

It was estimated that an efficient highly integrated chain-saw manufacturing facility with two production lines required a capital investment of in excess of $15 million for a productive capacity of 600 saws per day. A less integrated plant had a lower minimum efficient scale and capital cost.

THE ELECTRIC CHAIN-SAW MARKET

Electric chain saws had a number of characteristics which made them quite different from gas saws. The majority of electric saws sold for less than $50, and were capable of only low horsepower levels.[2] Horsepower of electric saws was inherently limited by the amperage capacity of conventional electrical wiring.

___
[2] The cost of a long heavy-duty extension cord added $10–$20 to the cost of an electric saw for a customer who did not already have one.

Electric saws were sold primarily to the construction market where the flammability of gasoline posed a safety hazard, and to casual users who had very low power requirements. The average casual purchaser of electric saws was generally believed to have some differences from the casual gas saw buyer in 1974. Electric saw purchasers were believed to be extremely price sensitive and in some cases also less "outdoorsy" and less comfortable tinkering with gasoline engines. Some observers also noted that electric saws were often purchased by women as gifts. Distribution of electric saws was primarily through contractor supply outlets, hardware chains, and home centers as part of the electric tool line. Almost no electric saws were sold through servicing dealers, who had little expertise in electric motor repair. Electric saws required little service, partly due to the reliability of electric motors and also because electric saws tended to be used less intensively than gas saws.

COMPETITION

There were approximately a dozen major manufacturers of gasoline chain saws in 1974. Some of these also produced electric saws, but the

Table 8

ESTIMATED U.S. MARKET SHARES OF GAS CHAIN SAWS*
(units)

	1970	1971	1972	1973
Homelite	35%	31%	28%	28%
McCulloch	33	33	27	27
Remington/Desa			8	12
Beaird-Poulan			8	
Stihl			7–8	6
Roper			6	
Pioneer			4	
Skil			3	
Echo (entered 1972)			1	

Very small share in the United States:
Husqvarna
Jonsereds
Partner
Solo

Note: Omitted figures were not available.
Source: Manufacturer interviews.

markets for gas and electric saws were quite distinct. There were major competitors in electric saws who did not produce gas saws and vice versa. The major firms and their estimated market position were as shown in Table 8.

Stihl and Solo were German companies; Jonsereds, Husqvarna, and Partner were based in Sweden; Echo was based in Japan; and Pioneer

Table 9

1972 MANUFACTURER SALES
IN U.S. MARKET
($ millions)

Homelite	$30
McCulloch	30
Remington/Desa	11
Beaird-Poulan	9
Roper	6
Pioneer	4
Skil	3

was based in Canada. Each was a significant producer outside the United States.[3]

European firms had been the early pioneers in the chain-saw industry, and still maintained technological leadership according to most observers. The other major competitors were U.S. firms (Pioneer was based in Canada), having grown up largely since World War II. Homelite and McCulloch sold outside the United States as well as domestically, exporting 10–20 percent of their volume to other countries, while the other U.S. companies were largely domestic competitors only. Stihl had a relatively small but stable share in the United States, and Echo had recently entered the U.S. market (1972). The other non-U.S. firms had very small shares in the U.S. markets, met exclusively through exports. Tariffs on chain saws were significant in the United States as in other countries, in the range of 5 to 15 percent.

The estimated 1972 domestic dollar sales of chain saws of the leading U.S. firms was as shown in Table 9.

A profile of each of the major competitors is given below. Exhibit 4 summarizes their product lines, Exhibit 5 their prices, Exhibit 6 their advertising spending, and Exhibit 7 their corporate financial results.

HOMELITE

Homelite was a division of Textron, Inc., having been acquired in 1955. Textron had over 30 divisions in many diverse businesses, which were overseen by a corporate staff of less than 100 people and classified into the areas shown in Table 10.

Divisions were managed autonomously, but measured and compensated based on strict annual return-on-investment criteria. A group vice president monitored division results and consulted on major decisions, but did not interfere with operations. Corporate 10-year targets were growth at an average compound rate of 8 percent, and net income growth at a compound rate of 10 percent.

Homelite had been the leader in the U.S. chain-saw industry for many

[3] In addition to the non-U.S. firms listed, a number of other producers such as Danarm, Dolmar, and Alpina exported minor volumes to the United States. None were considered significant factors in the market.

Exhibit 4

PRODUCT LINES OF MAJOR CHAIN-SAW COMPETITORS

Company	Year	Cubic inch	1.0	2.0	3.0	4.0	5.0	6.0	7.0	8.0	9.0
Homelite	1972–73	(1 electric)	X	X XX	X / X X / X	XG X / XG XX	XG	XG X			
McCulloch	1972–73	(1 electric)	X / X / X		X X / X X	XG / X	XG / X	XG / X	X		
Stihl	1972–73		X X / X X	X	XG / X / X	X / X	X	XG / X		X	
Beaird-Poulan	1972–73	(1 electric)	X	X X	X X / X / X	X X / XG	XG / X	X			
Jonsereds	1972–73			X X / X X X X	X	X		X			
Husqvarna	1972–73					DATA NOT AVAILABLE					
Remington	1972–73	(3 electric)		X X / X X / X	X / X	X X / X X	X X / X X				
Roper	1972–73	(2 electric)	X / X		X / X / X						
Skil	1972–73	(3 electrics)		X X / X X / X		X / X					
Echo	1972–73		X	X	XX	X		X			
Sears	1972–73	(3 electrics)	X / XX	X / XX	X / X / X						

Each **X** = Gas chain-saw model; Xs aligned vertically are models with the same cubic-inch engine.
XG = Gas chain saw with gear drive (for professionals).
Source: Company product literature and manufacturer and retailer interviews.

Exhibit 5

COMPARATIVE MANUFACTURER PRICES IN 1972

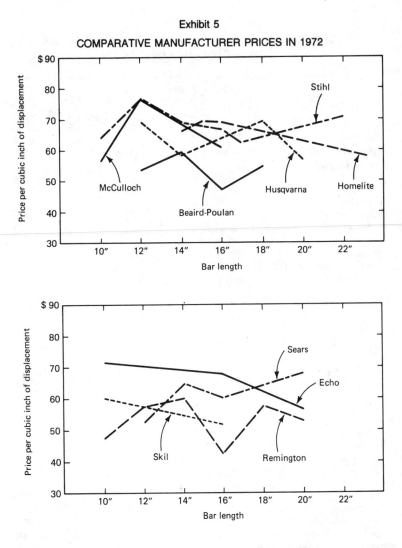

years, and had been one of Textron's most successful divisions though its market share had declined slightly in recent years. The division, classified in the consumer business segment, was one of the top Textron profit contributors. In addition to chain saws, the Homelite Division produced lawn and garden equipment, snowblowers, and some construction equipment such as pumps and generators. While chain saws were by far the largest part of division sales, Homelite's other businesses were being expanded through new product introductions.

Homelite produced a very wide product line in chain saws with a large number of models and engine sizes. It sought to produce a high-quality product which was marketed to all the major market segments through an extensive network of servicing dealers. Homelite sought to

Exhibit 6

U.S. NATIONAL CONSUMER ADVERTISING OF CHAIN SAWS BY LEADING CHAIN-SAW MANUFACTURERS, 1969–1973
($000)

	1969	1970	1971	1972	1973
*Beaird-Poulan:**					
Total	—	$ 62.2	$ 109.8	$261.9	$ 399.5
Magazines	—	59.6	76.4	166.9	121.9
Network television....	—	—	—	48.2	238.3
Spot television	—	1.3	32.4	46.0	38.6
Desa Industries (Remington):					
Total	$ 29.7	31.1	25.2	—	47.2
Magazines	29.7	30.1	24.8	—	46.0
Network television....	—	—	—	—	—
Spot television	—	—	—	—	—
Husqvarna:					
Total	—	—	—	—	—
Magazines	—	—	—	—	—
Network television....	—	—	—	—	—
Spot television	—	—	—	—	—
Jonsereds:					
Total	—	—	—	—	—
Magazines	—	—	—	—	—
Network television....	—	—	—	—	—
Spot television	—	—	—	—	—
McCulloch:†					
Total	119.5	484.2	788.1	973.3	1,340.8
Magazines	119.5	176.6	114.0	109.5	238.1
Network television....	—	—	—	456.8	743.7
Spot television	—	307.5	659.8	377.4	289.2
Roper:					
Total	—	—	—	—	0.4
Magazines	—	—	—	—	—
Network television....	—	—	—	—	—
Spot television	—	—	—	—	0.4
Stihl:					
Total	92.2	49.6	93.6	167.7	329.7
Magazines	92.2	49.6	44.7	73.1	53.4
Network television....	—	—	—	—	246.9
Spot television	—	—	48.9	93.9	29.0
Homelite (division of Textron):					
Total	825.5	864.5	1,288.2	958.7	1,025.9
Magazines	555.5	360.7	361.8	170.2	223.4
Network television....	270.0	322.1	568.7	643.9	595.4
Spot television	—	168.7	338.8	141.2	164.2

Note: Advertising figures are for advertising of chain saws only. The data omit cooperative advertising by retailers, the cost of which is shared with manufacturers. Cooperative advertising was significant in the industry and believed to be the highest as a percent of total advertising for pro-oriented firms such as Stihl. For Stihl cooperative advertising was as much as 50 percent of total advertising.

* Acquired by Emerson Electric in 1972.
† Acquired by Black & Decker Manufacturing Company in 1973.
Source: Leading National Advertisers, Inc., *National Advertising Investments,* January–December 1969, 1970, 1971, 1972, 1973.

Exhibit 7

SELECTED CORPORATE FINANCIAL INFORMATION FOR PUBLICLY HELD CHAIN-SAW MANUFACTURERS
($ millions)

	1964	1965	1966	1967	1968	1969	1970	1971	1972	1973
Black & Decker:										
Sales	$101.0	$121.5	$146.8	$168.6	$189.7	$221.8	$255.4	$286.7	$345.7	$427.0
Net income	8.8	11.0	13.0	14.3	15.4	17.6	19.5	22.0	26.6	33.3
Return on sales (ROS)	8.7	9.1	8.9	8.5	8.1	7.9	7.6	7.7	7.7	7.8
Debt/equity (percent)	—	0.1	0.2	0.4	0.4	0.3	0.3	0.2	0.1	0.1
Return on equity (ROE)	15.8	18.1	19.2	19.0	18.4	19.0	18.4	16.3	15.7	17.0
Capital expenditures	—	6.8	9.7	10.7	5.6	7.7	16.7	16.1	20.1	29.2
McCulloch Corporation (acquired by Black & Decker in 1973):										
Sales						45.4	43.2	50.6	58.9	73.1
Percent chain saws									86.0	81.6
Net income						2.7	0.4	(4.4)	(0.6)	1.1
Market value of shares paid by Black & Decker										66.7*
Emerson Electric:										
Sales	219.3	252.7	348.0	395.2	522.0	628.4	657.0	656.4	764.7	936.6
Sales of consumer products						217.8	239.7	254.1	290.0	317.9
Net income in consumer products						17.4	18.5	19.1	22.3	21.0
ROS—consumer products						8.0	7.7	7.5	7.7	6.6
Net income	15.0	17.6	26.4	30.2	39.5	49.9	54.6	56.1	63.6	75.9
ROS	6.8	7.0	7.6	7.7	7.6	7.9	8.3	8.6	8.3	8.1
Debt/equity (percent)	6.5	5.4	13.8	20.5	17.0	14.1	11.9	12.6	10.7	9.9
ROE	15.2	16.1	18.3	18.7	18.2	17.8	17.3	16.6	16.5	17.0
Capital expenditures	6.3	9.4	17.1	12.2	19.4	23.9	20.5	21.4	26.6	40.8
Roper Corporation:										
Sales	108.2	125.4	164.9	177.9	200.2	205.4	204.3	212.6	251.7	293.9
Net income	3.3	4.5	4.8	4.2	6.1	5.0	4.7	5.4	6.9	7.5
ROS	3.0	3.6	2.9	2.4	3.0	2.4	2.3	2.5	2.7	2.6
Debt/equity (percent)	19.8	28.8	56.7	58.1	85.4	81.0	90.6	84.7	98.2	132.6
ROE	10.5	13.1	10.6	8.8	11.2	8.6	7.8	8.4	9.7	9.8

* Of this purchase price, $39.4 million was represented by the value of McCulloch Oil shares acquired.

Exhibit 7 (concluded)

	1964	1965	1966	1967	1968	1969	1970	1971	1972	1973
Skil Corporation:										
Sales	33.5	39.7	48.4	51.2	63.2	68.9	61.6	74.3	94.8	106.8
Net income	2.6	3.1	3.7	2.4	3.1	3.2	.9	2.1	4.3	2.1
ROS	7.8	7.8	7.6	4.7	4.9	4.6	1.5	2.8	4.5	2.0
Debt/equity (percent)	—	18.9	31.7	77.4	97.1	99.2	120.1	116.9	63.0	122.8
ROE	15.4	16.7	17.8	11.1	13.0	12.4	3.7	7.7	12.1	5.8
Textron:										
Sales	720.2	851.0	1,132.2	1,445.0	1,704.1	1,682.2	1,611.9	1,603.7	1,678.4	1,858.4
Percent sales—consumer products					24	26	27	31		
Percent pretax net income—consumer products					37	40	40	48		
Net income after taxes	22.1	29.1	43.9	61.5	74.0	76.1	66.7	71.8	82.1	100.8
ROS (percent)	3.1	3.4	3.9	4.2	4.3	4.5	4.1	4.5	4.9	5.4
Debt/equity (percent)	34.9	25.0	25.1	18.3	31.5	27.8	36.5	28.8	37.2	33.7
ROE (percent)	13.3	16.0	18.6	16.7	16.0	15.7	13.2	13.7	14.1	15.1
Capital expenditures	19.3	22.3	38.5	41.2	47.1	48.6	41.6	36.7	42.8	64.5

Table 10

	1973		1972	
	Sales	Net income	Sales	Net income
		($ millions)		
Consumer	$614.1	$29.4	$557.4	$26.1
Aerospace	499.0	23.4	505.9	27.2
Industrial	392.6	21.1	335.9	10.3
Metal products	352.7	20.3	279.2	8.5

segment the market and offer saws aimed at all the significant customer groups. Separate marketing managers directed activities in the consumer and professional markets. Homelite had been a pioneer in producing lightweight chain saws in the 1960s, but in 1973 its products were not known as leaders in safety and comfort features.

Homelite was unique in the industry in its policy of in-house distribution. It had over 40 in-house distributors, and these distributors served over 10,000 authorized dealers. Homelite was particularly strong in hardware stores and farm stores, and sold Homelite-brand saws to J. C. Penney. Homelite did not sell through mass merchandisers nor for private label. The company spent heavily on advertising, including some consumer advertising of the Homelite brand name using television, magazine, and radio, as well as dealer-oriented advertising and advertising directed toward the farmer. Homelite also utilized occasional price promotions on selected models.

Homelite manufactured chain saws in two plants constructed in 1957 and 1959 in North and South Carolina. Homelite was not integrated into die casting but manufactured its own bars and purchased saw chain from its sister division, Townsend, which manufactured precision metal parts. Townsend had entered into saw chain manufacturing in 1971 in a South Carolina facility.

McCULLOCH CORPORATION

McCulloch had long been a highly regarded manufacturer of chain saws and other products using small, two-cycle gasoline engines, and had been a pioneer in the U.S. chain-saw industry. Until 1973 McCulloch had been privately held, and its chairman was Robert McCulloch, who was also chairman of McCulloch Oil. He had long been heavily involved in R&D, and had worked on designing products ranging from electronic ball cups for golf greens to diesel aircraft engines. Bob McCulloch had also gained some notoriety for being instrumental in moving London Bridge to Arizona, and had shifted some McCulloch chain-saw operations there to provide an employment base as well. Robert McCulloch had made several attempts in the previous decade to diversify the company into other areas. Ventures in outboard motors, snowmobile engines, and other products had proved unsuccessful, however. By 1973 McCulloch was in serious financial difficulty (due in part to some bad real estate ventures), even though its overall sales had grown from $41 million in 1963 to $75 million in 1973. Top-management attention to the chain-saw business had lagged.

McCulloch was acquired by Black & Decker in September 1973. The acquisition was immediately challenged by the Justice Department, and the matter was pending in early 1974. Black & Decker had been actively seeking entry into new markets from its strong base in power tools. Black & Decker's business was divided approximately as follows in 1974:[4]

U.S. Power Tools	35%
International Power Tools	50
McCulloch	15

The power tool market in the United States was mature, with an estimated growth rate of 5–8 percent per year. Black & Decker had approximately a 40–45 percent market share in the power tool industry, well ahead of Sears with an estimated 25 percent and Skil Corporation with an estimated 8–10 percent. Black & Decker was known for extremely strong financial controls, a cost-conscious manufacturing orientation, and a product policy which ruthlessly weeded out less profitable lines. The company was known to have used the Boston Consulting Group for strategic advice and had followed an aggressive strategy in leading the power tool industry.

McCulloch offered a wide line of chain saws sold through a large network of servicing dealers to all the major market segments. It had over 25 distributors nationwide, three of which were company owned, and approximately 8,000–10,000 dealers. McCulloch had begun selling to mass merchandisers in 1973, the only major manufacturer to do so. Its market share had been increasing until recently as a result of its leadership in introducing lighter, less expensive chain saws, though its position in the professional segment had been eroding. McCulloch had been a technological leader in manufacturing techniques for chain saws.

McCulloch had a relatively integrated manufacturing facility in Los Angeles, California, producing its own die castings and bars. The facility had been in operation for many years, and McCulloch had established a new facility in Arizona where chain-saw manufacturing operations were being gradually moved.

DESA INDUSTRIES (REMINGTON)

The chain-saw division of Desa Industries had formerly been a unit of Remington Arms until its sale in August 1969. Desa was a miniconglomerate which purchased troubled companies, and Remington had

---

[4] William P. Maloney, "An Analysis of Black & Decker Manufacturing Company," C. S. McKee & Company.

been in that category when Desa purchased them. In 1973 Desa was known to be in serious financial difficulty and short of capital.

Chain saws were sold under the Remington name. Remington had a moderately wide line of saws. A major portion of its output went to Montgomery Ward and John Deere under private label, and most of the rest was sold to other large chain accounts through a sales force of 35 manufacturers' reps (who represented other noncompeting manufacturers). Remington had little penetration of servicing dealers. It had a relatively strong position in electric chain saws.

Remington had a manufacturing facility most observers regarded as less efficient than those of the industry leaders, with a very low level of vertical integration and a low level of automation and use of special-purpose machinery.

BEAIRD-POULAN

Based in Louisiana, Beaird-Poulan had been an independent manufacturer of chain saws until its acquisition by Emerson Electric in 1972. Emerson, with 1973 sales of $937 million, had over 20 divisions producing a wide range of consumer and industrial products, classified into commercial and industrial components and systems, consumer goods (including chain saws), and government and defense products:

Table 11

	1973		1972	
	Sales	Net income	Sales	Net income
		($ millions)		
Commercial and industrial....	$610.4	$54.3	$499.0	$44.0
Consumer	317.9	21.0	290.0	22.3
Government and defense......	20.7	0.6	21.1	0.6
Intercompany sales	(11.4)		(12.2)	

Many of Emerson's products were in the electrical and electromechanical area, such as electric motors, controls, drives and heating, ventilating and air-conditioning equipment. Emerson divisions were managed with considerable autonomy, but were measured on growth and return on invested capital. Corporate targets were 15 percent growth in sales annually, with return on invested capital of at least 20 percent. Emerson placed extremely strong emphasis on planning and the setting of detailed objectives, and also emphasized cost reduction, which was termed a "way of life" at Emerson in official statements. Incentive payments based on performance could be a large part of division management compensation. Emerson had an annual cost reduction program with specific cost reduction goals at each division. The company had a stated goal of being the low-cost producer in each of its markets. Divisions that could not meet Emerson's goals were divested.

Beaird-Poulan offered a moderately wide line of chain saws which were sold primarily to the private label market and, to a lesser extent under its Poulan brand, to large accounts. Beaird-Poulan products were of acceptable but not premium quality, and were sold at low prices. There had been little emphasis on safety features or product innovation. Aside from low-price saws, Beaird-Poulan had some strength in professional saws designed for pulpwood logging which was practiced heavily in the southeast United States. Beaird-Poulan's major customers were Western Auto, Quality Farm and Fleet, John Deere, Sears and other large chains. It had recently joined Roper as a private label supplier to Sears, supplying Sears with a small 1.9-cubic-inch saw. Beaird-Poulan also had a network of servicing dealers, which accounted for less than 25 percent of sales. Poulan dealers, who numbered less than 3,000, were strongest in the South and generally smaller and less established than Homelite or McCulloch dealers.

Beaird-Poulan manufactured chain saws at a long-standing facility in Shreveport, Louisiana. It purchased most die castings, saw chain, and bars from outside suppliers.

STIHL

Stihl was the world's leading producer of chain saws in 1973. Correctly named Andreas Stihl Maschinenfabrik, Stihl was a privately controlled firm headquartered in Germany. Stihl employed over 2,000 people in 1972 and had over 60 percent of the West German market. Stihl exported 80 percent of its production to over 100 countries including approximately 70,000 units to the United States. Its worldwide corporate sales had been $56 million in 1972 and had risen to $124 million by 1974. Stihl also produced gasoline-powered industrial cutting saws. While Stihl had exported saws for sale in the United States for decades, it had also begun limited assembly of one model of saw at a U.S. facility in Virginia in the fall of 1974.

Stihl produced a very wide line of premium-quality saws for sale primarily to the pro and farmer market segments. Its products were universally acknowledged as the quality standard of the industry, and Stihl had long offered safety and comfort features just now being introduced by U.S. firms.

Stihl sold its products only through servicing dealers, a policy to which it adhered strictly. Its dealer organization was large in relation to the other non-U.S. firms, and Stihl dealers were known to be particularly knowledgeable and loyal to Stihl. Industry observers readily admitted that Stihl's dealer organization was also first in quality of servicing. Stihl promoted heavily in the trade journals and at industry trade shows, stressing its leadership in the industry and its commitment to the servicing dealer.

Stihl manufactured most of its saws in Germany, though it also had a plant in Brazil in addition to the new U.S. assembly operation. Stihl was the most fully integrated of the chain-saw manufacturers, producing all engine parts, most of its own bars and sprockets, and all of its saw chain. Stihl had also developed proprietary special machinery and processes for magnesium die casting of engine parts and for machining operations, and had its own tooling group which designed and manufactured the machinery used in Stihl production facilities. Stihl's production strategy was characterized by observers as being one of extremely high quality and relatively high cost. No sacrifices in quality were made in the interests of cost. Stihl saws were also heavier than competitor saws for any given cubic inch displacement and bar length. Stihl's new U.S. assembly facility assembled only its smallest 015 model saw, which was designed for the casual-user segment of the market.

ROPER CORPORATION

Roper Corporation had been a major supplier to Sears for over 40 years, with Sears accounting for over half of Roper's sales. Roper supplied Sears with electric ranges, gas ranges, and other hardgoods; and Roper's Outdoor Products Company supplied Sears with chain saws. Sears's employee pension fund owned 40 percent of Roper's common stock.

Until 1971 Roper had been the sole supplier of chain saws to Sears. Sears had worked with Roper over the years to develop competitive chain saws and to improve and update Roper's product line. In 1963, when Homelite introduced the XL-12 lightweight saw, Sears pressured Roper to follow. Roper had developed the new 3.7-cubic-inch engine for saws which went on the market in 1968, and had purchased the design for a 1.9-cubic-inch engine in 1969.

When Sears first bought saws from another supplier (Beaird-Poulan) in 1971, Roper began thinking about selling saws to others. Until 1973 Roper's output went exclusively to Sears, but in that year Roper began selling saws under its own brand name and to other private label accounts. Roper was making efforts to develop a servicing dealer network, though it had as yet achieved little increase in its dealer network by early 1974.

The Roper product line was limited and focused on the middle horsepower range, reflecting its heavy emphasis on Sears. Roper had little or no brand recognition. Roper products were serviced by Sears's service organization. In 1973 Roper had established a new chain-saw production facility in Nogales, Mexico, which replaced its Illinois facility and increased capacity 100 percent in the process.[5]

JONSEREDS

Jonsereds was the leading Swedish saw in terms of U.S. sales. The company was part of a large privately held Swedish holding company, about which information was scarce. Jonsereds' corporate sales were approximately $30 million in 1973, and the company produced woodworking machinery and tools and hydraulic loaders in addition to chain saws.

---

[5] Tariffs for importing chain saws into the United States from Mexico were nominal.

Jonsereds produced high-quality saws primarily for the pro and farmer market segments. It sold a relatively small number of models, though it covered a relatively wide horsepower range. Swedish loggers generally used smaller saws than loggers in the United States. Distribution for Jonsereds in the United States was handled by two companies: Tilton Equipment in the East and Scotsco in the West. Tilton was owned by two aggressive ex-Homelite salesmen and accounted for the great majority of Jonsereds' U.S. sales. It had four stocking locations. Jonsereds' saws were distributed to servicing dealers. The company had no marketing personnel of its own in the United States, and promoted exclusively through the trade press.

Jonsereds manufactured all its saws in Sweden and was not integrated into bars or saw chain. It purchased these items from Canadian and U.S. suppliers.

SKIL CORPORATION

Skil was a major producer of power tools, with 1973 sales of $107 million and an estimated market share in power tools of 8–10 percent. Skil distributed power tools through 300 distributors to 25,000 retail outlets primarily in hardware and home improvement, and through 4,000 industrial distributors to a wide variety of industrial customers. Skil had 75 factory service centers nationwide, and over 350 authorized service agents.

Skil had a small line of high-quality chain saws, both gas and electric, which were sold through its power tool distribution channels. Approximately 50 percent of its outlets carried its chain saws. The primary target market was contractors.

KIORITZ CORPORATION OF AMERICA (ECHO)

Kioritz Corporation was one of the world's largest manufacturers of two-cycle gasoline engines and had a reputation for being a high-quality engine producer. It sold its engines to OEMs and had a large share of the market for snowmobile motors. Echo also manufactured a successful line of gas-powered products such as snowblowers, power scythes, power dusters, and misters for sale worldwide. Its products were sold under the Echo name. Kioritz's sales were in the $20–$40 million range.

Kioritz entered the U.S. chain-saw market in 1972 using the Echo name. Echo's product line was initially composed of a relatively small number of models covering a wide horsepower range. Echo was aggressively seeking to build a servicing dealer network, offering high dealer margins, but it still had a very small network in early 1974. Echo was also pursuing private label sales. A major portion of Echo's sales were currently private label saws sold through John Deere's network of farm equipment stores. Echo was known to be trying to sell saws to Sears and Montgomery Ward, and had sold saws to Sears in 1973 when Beaird-Poulan could not manufacture enough 1.9-cubic-inch saws to meet demand.

Echo saws were manufactured in Japan.

HUSQVARNA

Husqvarna was a Swedish firm which exported chain saws for sale in the United States. It also produced a variety of other products including refrigerators, motorcycles, sewing machines, and lawn mowers. Chain saws represented approximately 20 percent of total worldwide revenues of approximately $140 million. Husqvarna had recently been in financial difficulty due to soaring wage and benefit costs which were prevalent in Swedish industry.

Husqvarna sold premium-quality chain saws at premium prices primarily to the pro and farmer market segments. It had a company-owned sales subsidiary located in New Jersey and sold its products through five exclusive distributors to a network of servicing dealers. Its products were known for their excellent safety features. Promotion was solely through trade publications.

Husqvarna manufactured all its saws in Sweden. It was not integrated into saw chain, bars, or engine castings.

SOLO

Solo was a German firm which manufactured a range of gasoline-powered equipment including mopeds, mist blowers, rototillers, and chain saws, with sales of approximately $25 million in 1973. Although Solo was one of the leading European manufacturers of small gasoline engines, rivaling Stihl, chain saws were not a major product for the company. Solo's chain-saw product line was quite similar in size and appearance to Stihl's, though Solo had a narrower product line than Stihl. Observers termed Solo's strategy *me-too* with regard to Stihl.

Solo had no manufacturing or marketing subsidiary in the United States, exporting a small number of saws for sale through servicing dealers. Its European production operations were not integrated into the production of saw chain or bars.

PARTNER

Partner was a Swedish firm which produced chain saws and cutting machinery with sales of approximately $17 million in 1973. It sold large powerful saws primarily for the pro and farmer segments. It had no manufacturing or marketing facilities in the United States, and exported saws for sale in the United States through a small network of servicing dealers. Partner manufactured two large saws (3.4 and 4.0 cubic inch) for Skil which were used to round out Skil's product line. Skil, in turn, manufactured smaller saws used by Partner to round out its European product line.

PIONEER

Pioneer was a Canadian firm, which was a unit of the Outboard Marine Corporation (OMC) having been acquired by OMC in 1965. OMC produced marine outboard motors, lawn mowers, and other products, and had sales of $472 million in 1973 with a return on equity of 16.3 percent. Chain saws represented 2.3 percent of OMC sales in 1973, or $10.9 million.

Pioneer offered four models of chain saws primarily directed at the farm and professional buyer. It sold exclusively through specialty chain-saw dealers. Its market position in Canada was relatively stronger than that in the United States, and it had a significant position in Europe as well with a well-developed dealer organization there.

COMPETITION IN ELECTRIC CHAIN SAWS

The market for electric saws was quite distinct from the gas-saw market. While Skil, McCulloch, Homelite, and a number of other gas-saw companies also produced electric saws, Remington, Wen, and Singer dominated the electric chain-saw market. Wen was an independent company producing a range of portable power tool products. Singer manufactured electric chain saws for Sears, along with a line of other electric tools. Neither Wen nor Singer manufactured gas saws. Remington had the Ward's account for electric saws and sold to other chains.

Note on the soft-drink industry in the United States

"THE SOFT DRINK is one of the greatest of American traditions," commented a reporter, "really far more American than apple pie (which originated in France) or hot dogs (which are of German extraction). The soft drink was born and raised in the U. S. of A., and most of us were born and raised with soft drinks—or soda pop for those of western heritage."

Some might well object to this nationalistic interpretation since naturally carbonated water was used as medicine by the ancient Greeks and soft drinks had been commercially available in Europe for years. Yet clearly the American consumer has had a long love affair with "soda pop." In 1974 total soft-drink sales were over $7.8 billion at wholesale and per person consumption was over 429 eight-ounce containers per year. And the romance has been of long duration; buoyed by population and real income growth, per capita consumption doubled from 1962 to 1973. Soft-drink case sales rose from 1,668 million to 3,772 million during that period moving from 16 percent of total beverage consumption in 1960 to almost 25 percent in 1973. This sales growth brought prosperous days to concentrate makers, bottlers, and retail organizations.

In 1974 and 1975 industry growth patterns changed, with case sales and per capita consumption remaining approximately level. Had the bloom disappeared from the rose—or should we ask, had the "fizzle disappeared and the soda pop gone flat?" Industry analysts seemed to agree that the 7 to 8 percent annual unit growth rates of the past were probably no longer possible. But what next? One analyst noted, "The industry is in a period when sales will basically plateau." Maxwell Associates, a consulting firm, predicted 3 to 4 percent sales growth in 1976. But these modestly enthusiastic future predictions by analysts did not seem to deter the competitive ambitions of the industry's leading firms. Each of the top five companies, according to Standard & Poor's *1976 Beverage Industry Reports,* had clear-cut expansion goals. "Dr Pepper expects to continue to grow at two to three times the industry rate and is confident of being number three in national sales in the not too distant future. Pepsi hopes to extend its string of 52 consecutive months of market share gain, and, nevertheless, Coke expects to continue to gain market share on a total product basis." The president of the Seven-Up Company, on another occasion, announced, "We really believe and we're seriously dedicated to the point of view that 7UP can and should be the number one selling soft drink in the United States."

In addition to this development, the industry was confronted with pressure from private environmental groups and increasing interest on the part of regulatory agencies in its operations. Private environmental groups and federal and state agencies were attempting to find ways of limiting the use of nonreturnable containers. Governmental concerns about health forced the industry to drop cyclamates as a substitute for sugar in diet drinks, and government antitrust concerns had resulted in legal action against the franchise system—regarded by many company executives as important to the industry's success.

Commenting on the overall scene, one corporate officer queried, "Where is this industry going? I'm not sure! Competition is getting worse. Nothing seems to stay pinned down—franchising, distribution, ingredients, and packaging are all 'up for grabs.' One competitive development has already started. Billboard advertising has always had a 'product message,' but now they are being directed to a 'cents per ounce' price theme. Food stores will become a battlefield." This note explores the soft-drink segment of the U.S. beverage industry; as such it gives but limited attention to the international market and to other beverages such as coffee, tea, chocolate, milk, bottled waters, juices, and alcoholic drinks. In sequence, the note will cover six areas: the product—past success and current situation, industry structure and participants, key industry functional strategies, new competitors—the intruders, the industry's critics, and future market directions—a cloudy crystal ball.

In studying this note, the reader should keep in mind the complexity of the territory being described and the simplicity of this map. He or she will note that some of these data are not comparable, that experts sometimes derive diametrically opposite conclusions from common data, and that some very useful data were simply not available. Any judgments made, by necessity, must be tentative.

PRODUCT

Soft drinks, or nonalcoholic carbonated beverages, consist of a flavoring base such as cola, a sweetener, water, and carbonation. Most soft drinks are consumed cold, and the product has a seasonal sales pattern, peaking in hot summer months.

Originating in a Philadelphia apothecary shop, soft drinks were first sold primarily through drugstore soda fountains where flavors and carbonated water would be mixed for immediate sale to an on-premise customer. This early association with apothecaries and drugstores gave soft drinks a medicinal association which still prevailed, to some degree, in the 70s. The executive vice president of Seven-Up commented, "There was a group for whom our green bottle had almost medicinal or therapeutic overtones, the thing to take when you had the flu and the doctor told you to take a lot of liquid."[1]

The development of manually operated filling and bottling machines in the mid-1800s encouraged the establishment of thousands of local bottling works. Each of these supplied carbonated beverages to its nearby market under a variety of brand names, which the researcher found fascinating: Cardinal Necter, Queer, Marrowfood, Creme Puncho, Peach Bounce, Muscadine Thrill, Wami, and Egg Soda—the latter coming in an egg-shaped bottle.[2]

In 1884 Hires Root Beer advertised in *Harper's Magazine.* The trade name Dr Pepper was copyrighted in 1885, followed by Coca-Cola in 1886. Brad's Drink, which became Pepsi-Cola, appeared in 1886. The predecessor company of Seven-Up was formed in 1906 (7UP was introduced in 1920), and the predecessor company of Royal Crown appeared in 1924 and introduced Royal Crown Cola in 1935.

In 1976 regular soft drinks came in a variety of flavors with cola accounting for 58 percent of the market. Most of these used sugar or sugar plus high fructose corn syrup as a sweetener; diet drinks (15 percent of the market) used a noncolor artificial sweetener, in 1976, usually saccharin. Diet drinks in most cases carried related brand names, for example, Diet Pepsi, Sugar Free Dr Pepper; but in some cases they were promoted under different brands, for example, Tab (Coca-Cola) and Diet-Rite Cola (Royal Crown). National brands accounted for approximately 67 percent of the U.S. market in 1975 (Exhibits 1 and 2).

The industry's past success

The soft-drink industry had enjoyed consistent and substantial growth over a period of several decades; per capita consumption had increased from 17.5 gallons in 1960 to 31.6 gallons in 1974, an increase of 65 percent. Soft drinks, a Boston physician decried, are "cradle to grave. We wean babies to Coke and serve 7UP to the geriatrics ward." A casualty in the gallonage race was water.

Four primary factors, the researchers believed, had contributed significantly to this success: the growth in disposable income, marketing innovations, packaging developments, and the industry's competitive culture (Exhibits 3, 4, and 5).

In commenting on the first factor, Emanuel Goldman of Sanford Bernstein and Company noted:

> The work that I've done clearly indicates that the industry is most sensitive to real disposable personal income . . . when real DPI was pumping along at about 3.5 to 4.0 percent growth rate in real terms, soft-drink gallonage was growing at some faster rate. . . . Similarly, during recessionary periods, 1954 and 1958, for example, the recession of '60 to '61, and the

---

[1] "Can Uncola Make Cola Cry Uncle?" *The Grocery Manufacturer,* June 1972, p. 82.

[2] Dudley Lynch, "Dr Pepper Takes on Coke," *D Magazine (Dallas/Ft. Worth),* September 1975.

Exhibit 1

MARKET SHARE BY FLAVOR

Flavors	1971	1972	1973	1974	1975	1976 (est.)
Regular cola	52.0%	51.5%	51.0%	51.0%	50.0%	50.5%
Diet cola	5.6	6.0	6.2	6.6	7.3	7.8
Total cola	57.6	57.5	57.2	57.6	58.0	58.3
Regular lemon-lime	11.4	11.3	11.4	11.3	11.0	10.9
Sugar free lemon-lime	0.6	0.7	0.8	1.2	1.7	2.0
Total lemon-lime	12.0	12.0	12.2	12.5	12.7	12.9
Regular orange	4.8	4.7	4.6	4.4	3.9	3.6
Regular root beer ..	4.4	4.4	4.0	3.9	4.1	4.2
Dr Pepper and Mr. PiBB	3.9	4.3	5.0	5.2	5.7	6.0
Diet Dr Pepper and Mr. PiBB	0.2	0.4	0.5	0.7	0.9	1.2
Total Pepper .	4.1	4.7	5.5	5.9	6.6	7.2
Ginger ale, tonic, carbonated water, and soda	4.4	4.6	4.7	4.8	4.9	5.0
All other (regular grape, Mountain Dew, chocolate, black cherry, etc.)..............	9.6	9.0	8.3	7.4	6.0	4.8
All other diet, diet orange, and root beer	2.9	3.0	3.4	3.6	3.8	4.0
Total regular drinks	90.6	89.8	89.0	87.9	86.2	85.0
Total diet drinks ...	9.4	10.2	11.0	12.1	13.8	15.0
Total	100.0%	100.0%	100.0%	100.0%	100.0%	100.0%

Source: J. C. Frazzano, Oppenheimer & Company, *Beverage World,* February 1977, p. 8.

recession of mid-'74 to mid-'75, there was a definite softness, with a decline in soft-drink volume in the mid-year to mid-year periods.[3]

Second, corporate executives stressed the importance of marketing to the industry's past accomplishments. W. W. Clements, chairman of the Dr Pepper Company, noted:

This industry has several characteristics that place it somewhere in between true service industries and purely manufacturing industries. It, in addition, does not qualify as an industry relying to any great extent on engineering development or research. The sophisticated part of the soft-drink industry is the marketing area.[4]

---

[3] "The Beverage Industry," *The Wall Street Transcript,* May 24, 1976, pp. 43, 766.
[4] Unpublished speech to Thunderbird School of International Management, June 8, 1972.

Exhibit 2

TOP 10 SOFT-DRINK BRANDS 1966–1975

1966 Brand	Percent share of market	1970 Brand	Percent share of market	1975 Brand	Percent share of market
Coke	27.6	Coke	34.8	Coke	26.2
Pepsi	16.1	Pepsi	14.2	Pepsi	17.4
7UP	6.4	7UP	5.8	7UP	6.6
Royal Crown Cola	3.8	Royal Crown	3.5	Dr Pepper	4.9
Dr Pepper	2.4	Dr Pepper	3.4	Royal Crown	3.4
Diet Pepsi	1.9	Sprite (Coke)	2.3	Sprite (Coke)	2.6
Diet-Rite Cola (Royal Crown)	1.6	Diet-Rite Cola (Royal Crown)	1.8	Tab (Coke)	2.6
Sprite	1.5	Fresca (Coke)	1.4	Diet Pepsi	1.7
Tab	1.4	Canada Dry Ginger Ale	1.1	Mountain Dew (Pepsi)	1.3
Mountain Dew (Pepsi)	1.4	Diet Pepsi	0.9	Canada Dry	1.2
	64.1	Tab (Coke)	0.9		66.7
			70.0		

Source: Maxwell, *Consumer Service Reports on the Soft Drink Industry,* February 23, 1976; used with the permission of the Dr Pepper Company.

Exhibit 3

HISTORIC PER CAPITA SOFT-DRINK CONSUMPTION AND WHOLESALE SALES LEVELS, SELECTED YEARS

Year	Wholesale sales ($ millions)	Cases (192 ounces) (millions)	Per capita (8-ounce containers)
1859	$ 1.4	2.8	2.2
1929	214	272	53.1
1950	877	1,002	158.0
1960	1,698	1,477	192.0
1970	4,800	3,097	362.8
1972	5,684	3,541	406.4
1973	6,223	3,772	429.6
1974	7,827	3,798	429.4

Source: National Soft Drink Association, 1975.

Since the 1930s, industry operations had been substantially influenced by the competitive struggle between Coke and Pepsi. Pepsi, during that era, began to challenge the industry giant with a series of marketing innovations. In 1939 Pepsi used the first singing radio commercial: "Pepsi-Cola hits the spot. Twelve full ounces that's a lot. Twice as much for a nickel too. Pepsi-Cola is the drink for you." In 1942 reporter Robert Scheer noted that a survey showed this jingle to be the best-known tune in the United States—ahead of the Star-Spangled Banner. In 1976 most soft-drink companies were heavy investors in all kinds of worldwide consumer advertising. To his dismay, Scheer found a soft-drink sign greeting visitors as they climbed the steps to the apadana to view the magnificent ruins of Persepolis in Iran.

Pepsi also began to systematically survey changing lifestyles and relate its marketing program to that moving target.

> Pepsi being a modern corporation takes its cultural contributions seriously and all of the execs . . . are quite aware that they have never been in the business of simply selling a product but rather a way of life. Throughout the years of Pepsi-Coke rivalry, the arena has always been in the packaging and sales effort and not the concentrate, which has stayed the same while the companies' fortunes have gone up and down. It was, therefore, not the taste that mattered but rather how the public was taught to perceive it. The same stuff could be "light," "sociable," a healthful tonic—it could make you "stay young and fair and debonair" and gets you into The Pepsi Generation. This magic is worked for a concentrate that is basically the same for all of the colas and the much-guarded secrets can be obtained from a flavor chemist's handbook.[5]

Industry innovations in packaging were also credited with increasing soft-drink consumption. Developments occurred on many fronts: the introduction of soft drinks in cans and nonreturnable bottles, which encouraged increased out-of-the-home consumption; the introduction of

---

[5] Robert Scheer, "The Doctrine of Multinational Sell," Esquire, April 1975, pp. 163–65.

Exhibit 4

U.S. BEVERAGE CONSUMPTION, 1960–1974

	1960 gallons per capita	1964 gallons per capita	1970 gallons per capita	1974 gallons per capita	Percent increase (decrease) 1964–74	1975 gallons per capita
Coffee	40.2	39.2	35.5	32.8	(15)	31.6
Soft drinks	17.5	19.1	27.0	31.6	65	31.4
Milk	28.0	25.9	25.0	25.9	(7)	24.5
Beer	15.4	16.0	18.5	21.3	33	21.6
Tea	6.0	6.2	6.9	7.6	23	7.4
Juices	4.0	3.2	4.8	5.7	78	6.1
Distilled spirits	1.3	1.4	1.8	2.0	43	2.0
Wine	n.a.	1.0	1.3	1.7	70	1.7
Total	112.4	112.4	125.8	126.9		126.3

Imputed water consumption: 1966, 67.3 gallons per capita; 1975, 56.7 gallons per capita.

n.a. = Not available.
Source: Maxwell *Consumer Services for 1960–1974*, used with permission of Dr Pepper Company. The 1975 data from *Advertising Age*.

Exhibit 5

DISPOSABLE INCOME AND SOFT-DRINK INDUSTRY GROWTH

Year	Disposable personal income ($ billions)	Percent increase	Constant $ D.P.I. ($ billions)	Percent increase	Soft-drink industry percent increase
1972	$795.1	6.9	$579.0	4.3	5.6
1971	744.3	8.0	544.7	4.1	8.3
1970	689.5	8.8	533.2	3.9	6.3
1969	634.0	7.3	513.6	2.9	4.9
1968	591.0	8.2	499.0	4.6	12.1
1965	473.2	8.0	435.0	6.6	8.0
1963	404.6	5.1	381.3	3.9	7.0
1961	364.4	4.1	350.7	3.1	3.2
1959	337.3	5.8	330.0	4.4	0.0

Source: Based on Bureau of the Census data, 1973.

new types of carrying containers, for example, the six-pack beverage package; and an increase in number of sizes of bottles and cans. Between 1960 and 1975, available package sizes had increased from 2 to 10 sizes ranging from 6½ to 64 ounces, plus 1- and 2-liter sizes. One executive estimated that 24 ounces and larger packages accounted for over 30 percent of all soft drinks sold for home consumption in 1975 (Exhibit 6).

Exhibit 6

SOFT-DRINK PACKAGE TYPES, 1960–1975

	1960	1965	1970	1975
Returnable bottles	94%	83%	46%	34%
Nonreturnable bottles	2	5	25	31
Cans	4	12	29	35

Source: *Soft Drink Annual Manual*, 1971–1972; *Beverage Industry*, 3/19/76; and NSDA Sales Survey, 1960.

A final factor impacting industry growth was the corporate "climate" of the leading soft-drink firms. As described by business journalists, it seemed to be a mixture of general management leadership style, a concept of business competition as a "war game" and a set of corporate values which emphasized belief in your product, volume growth, market share improvement, and by all means "beat the competition and sell that drink." The latter goal was neatly summarized by a vice president who, speaking at the prospect of the Bamboo Curtain coming down, said "There are 800 million gullets in China, and I want to see a _____ in every one of them."

Long dominated by "Mother Coke," the soft-drink industry's recent competitive posture had been substantially influenced by two men— Donald Kendall, president of Pepsi-Cola, and W. W. Clements, president of Dr Pepper. Robert Scheer characterized Mr. Kendall and Pepsi's corporate "ambience" as follows:

> In 10 years' time Don Kendall was to kick, pull, and make a bumbling, small one-product company into a modern multinational conglomerate giant. One of his first acts was to begin plans for the new world headquarters. The Purchase, New York, world headquarters of PepsiCo is on 141 acres of choice Westchester property, sullied by not a single Pepsi-Cola sign. An "elegant modern" seven-building complex designed by Edward Durrell Stone is focused on an imported-cobblestone courtyard. Five thousand new trees (38 varieties), it is said, remind Kendall of his native Washington State and, as a somewhat personal touch, there is jet d'eau in the lake which shoots up 80 feet whenever Kendall pushes a button on his desk.
>
> I asked Kendall for his opinion of John Kenneth Galbraith's theory that corporations, being large planning units, could simply plan to have lower levels of growth. I might just as well have advocated bisexual love. "No Growth! What?" It was the same disbelief that I found when I put the question to the other execs—like telling a missionary that the number of converts doesn't matter.[6]

W. W. Clements's aggressive leadership of Dr Pepper illustrated the "war game" characteristic of the industry. President of a company with profits amounting to but 1/20th of Coke's, Mr. Clements's campaign to expand Dr Pepper's sales was described in part by Dudley Lynch:

> One crisp November morning in 1969 Woodrow Wilson "Foots" Clements and his team of executives stepped into a cab outside New York's Waldorf-Astoria Hotel. Mission: To pull off what some would call the biggest coup in soft-drink history. Clements and his Dr Pepper executives, representing an easy-going beverage which had stayed home in Texas and minded its own business for 85 years, headed over to the 34th Street offices of Coca-Cola Bottling Company of New York, the world's largest distributor of soft-drink's Goliath: Coca-Cola. Objective: to convince Coca-Cola of New York to bottle Dr Pepper. Seven months later the arrangements were completed.
>
> Dr Pepper's invasion of Coke's independent bottlers didn't go unnoticed at Coke's parent company headquarters, 310 North Avenue, Atlanta. Amidst Dr Pepper's campaign to sign up Coke bottlers came the New York coup, followed two years later by Dr Pepper's signing, in Mother Coke's backyard, of Coke's independent Atlanta bottler. Now the Coca-Cola parent company would take guests through the Atlanta bottling works and find themselves walking along halls bedecked with Dr Pepper signs. That was too much. "What Dr Pepper doesn't understand," suggests an Atlanta observer, "is the insult involved. What Dr Pepper did to Coke is something you just don't do to Coca-Cola—at least that's the way Coke views things. . . ."
>
> Adding to the insult was Dr Pepper's foray two years ago into Japan, a market that in 1973 produced 19 percent of Coke's worldwide profits. Dr Pepper signed a joint venture, with yes, you guessed it, Tokyo Coca-Cola Bottling Company, to introduce Dr Pepper to Japan. . . . Jumping into Japan was like waving a red flag, says Richard McStay, formerly research director at Atlanta's Irby & Co. "To Coke, Japan is motherhood, virginity, apple pie or anything you want to call it."[7]

---

[6] "The Doctrine of Multinationals," *Esquire,* April 1975, p. 126.
[7] "Dr Pepper Takes on Coke," *D Magazine* (*Dallas/Ft. Worth*), September 1975, p. 61.

Exhibit 7

REGIONAL VARIATIONS IN THE SOFT-DRINK MARKET

	North-east	East Central	West Central	South	South-west	Western	Pacific
Diet	13%	8%	8%	9%	11%	13%	14%
Flavors:							
Cola	30	47		55	42	53	41
Lemon-lime	16	17		19	10	18	20
Package sizes:							
10 and 12 ounce	37	60		58	56	51	54
Over 24 ounces	40	16		18	16	22	20
Package type:*							
Returnable bottles	20	50		41	53	46	48
Nonreturnable bottles	38	9		25	13	10	18
Cans	33	22		24	27	30	24
Fountain	9	10		10	7	15	11
Outlets:*							
Food stores	70	54		72	60	54	73
Restaurants, bars	10	13		6	6	21	8
Service stations	5	12		10	12	10	8

* Percent of packaged volume.
Source: *Soft Drinks*, December 1974.

Exhibit 8

COLA CARBONATED DRINK CONSUMER PRICE
INDEXES (1967 = 100)

Date	CPI	Change from previous year
January 1973	129.7	1.5
January 1974	136.5	5.2
July 1974	165.6	25.9
January 1975	203.3	48.9
July 1975	197.6	19.4
January 1976 (est.)......	193.2	−4.9

Source: U.S. Bureau of Labor Statistics.

An additional industry characteristic should be noted: market characteristics for soft drinks varied substantially by region. The highest per capita consumption according to industry analysts was in the South and Southwest. The popularity of diet drinks, flavor, packaging, and retail outlet preferences also varied by region (Exhibit 7). Historically, soft-drink companies had originated in the South, and in 1976 four out of the top five firms had their headquarters in the South and Southwest.

The early 70s market

In the early 70s soft-drink sales plateaued: Per capita consumption was 31.9 gallons in 1973, 31.6 in 1974, and 31.4 gallons in 1975. Among industry analysts interviewed, there seemed to be general agreement that two critical factors at least partially explained this development: the 1974–75 decline in real disposable income and the approximately 50 percent retail price increase created by cost increases—primarily sugar (Exhibit 8). One analyst, commenting on the 1975 situation, said:

> From what I can tell, based on quarter-to-quarter changes in real income, generally soft-drink consumption varies around those changes, but more dramatically. For example, in a bottlers' survey that I completed, in the February–March period a year ago, when real income was down close to 5 percent, soft-drink consumption was off 7 or 8 percent. Generally, when real income is growing on an annual basis at 4 to 5 percent, similar to the 10 years ending in December of '73, soft-drink consumption was growing at a rate of about 7.8 percent compounded.[8]

The implications of price trends and consumer routines were viewed somewhat differently by another investigator:

> Sometime late in 1974, Andy Pearson (president of PepsiCo) made the statement that before PepsiCo's soft-drink unit volume declined, soft-drink bottling prices advanced by 54 percent. By that time, which was at the end of 1974, we did have real income starting to decline, and we had prices up 50 or 55 percent or whatever. So you did have the worst of two worlds, and I think this was one of the most important things that could happen to the soft-drink industry because they realized that they had an enormous

---

[8] *The Wall Street Transcript,* May 24, 1976, Mr. J. C. Frazzano, pp. 43, 766.

amount of pricing flexibility, and that volume was not impacted to any significant degree.[9]

INDUSTRY STRUCTURE AND PARTICIPANTS

There were four major participants involved in the soft-drink industry: concentrate producers; soft-drink bottling and distribution companies; retailers—primarily food stores, restaurants, and vending machine operators; and packaging and raw material suppliers. This industry classification system was imprecise with some firms operating in more than one category. Exhibit 9 gives the researcher's overview of the industry, with estimates, where available, as to the dollar amounts of 1974 intersector transactions.

Concentrate producers

In 1975 there were approximately 56 concentrate producing and marketing firms in the United States. Major firms sold flavoring concentrate or syrup (concentrate plus sugar) to independent, franchised bottlers. Large concentrate firms might have from 300 to 800 separate franchise operations.

The concentrate sector was dominated by the "Big Six": Coca-Cola, PepsiCo, Seven-Up, Dr Pepper, Royal Crown, and Canada Dry (Exhibit 10). Each of these firms served the U.S. markets and, in some instances, sold in international markets. Each had created a valuable consumer franchise by substantial and continuous brand, promotional, advertising, and marketing programs. Three members of the Big Six had achieved substantial diversification from their original product lines: Coca-Cola into noncola beverages and PepsiCo and Royal Crown into nonbeverage lines. Canada Dry (division of Norton-Simon), Seven-Up, and Dr Pepper had remained primarily soft-drink specialists.

The second group of concentrate producers (Exhibit 11) included smaller, independent national firms such as Dad's Root Beer (1.2 percent of 1975 market) and Squirt (0.8 percent of the market) as well as product divisions of larger companies, such as A&W Root Beer, a division of United Brands. These firms had geographically scattered representation often with smaller, less competitive bottlers. In addition, regional firms, such as Faygo in Michigan, produced a wide variety of regular and diet drinks in what the industry called flavor lines, for example, orange, strawberry, and grape. A decreasing share of market was controlled by small, local bottlers.

Two other competitive factors were the private label brands of local and national food chains and the products of the Shasta Beverage Division of the Consolidated Foods Corporation. Private labels had been on the competitive scene for many years. One trade source estimated that national brands sold in 1975 for about 2 cents per ounce (12-ounce can) while private labels sold for 1 to 1.2 cents per ounce. *Beverage Industry* in commenting about the current position of "Store Brands" noted "chain executives surveyed noted a significant decline in gross margins in pri-

---

[9] Ibid., pp. 43, 767.

Exhibit 9

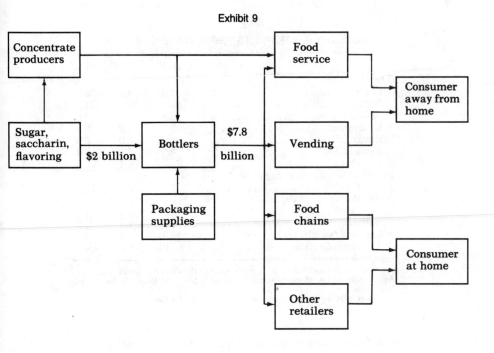

Exhibit 10

BIG SIX SALES NET PROFIT AND PRODUCT BREAKDOWN, 1975
($000)

	Sales	Net profits	Major product lines
Coca-Cola	$2,872,000	$239,304	Beverages
PepsiCo	2,300,000	104,600	Beverages, $1,035,000; food, $805,000; sporting goods, $230,000; transportation, $207,000
Royal Crown	257,451	13,294	Beverages, $159,000; citrus products, $43,000; home furnishings, $55,000
Seven-Up	213,623	20,341	Beverages and flavors
Canada Dry*	180,032	13,861	Ginger ale, mixers, and standard flavor line
Dr Pepper	138,250	11,904	Beverages

* Division of Norton-Simon; 1975 overall sales of $2,443,027.
Source: Company records.

vate label soft drinks, currently about 21–22 percent. It was high as 27 percent before current price increases. When warehouse costs (5–7 percent) are deducted from gross, the net profit is below that earned on national brands."[10] Typically, private brands were produced by nearby bottlers or contract canning companies.

[10] *Beverage Industry 1975–76 Annual Manual,* p. 38.

Exhibit 11

INDUSTRY PARTICIPANTS' PERCENTAGE OF MARKET

	1966	1972	1975
The Big Six:			
Coke	33.4	34.7	35.3
PepsiCo	20.4	19.8	21.1
Seven-Up	6.9	7.2	7.6
Dr Pepper	2.7	3.8	5.5
Royal Crown	6.9	6.0	5.4
Canada Dry	4.2	3.6	3.4
Total	74.5	75.1	78.3
Small nationals and regionals:*			
Total	7.5	11.5	11.9
Supermarket private labels:			
Total	0.2	2.4	1.1
Shasta	0.9	1.9	2.5
All others (small, local firms)	16.9	9.1	6.2
Total cases (millions)	2,910	3,675	4,460

* Includes operations such as Hires, Orange Crush, Cott's, Dad's Root Beer, Squirt, Schweppes, Moxie-Monarch, Nugrape, A&W Root Beer, No-Cal, Faygo, White Rock.
Source: Data compiled from trade sources by the Dr Pepper Company.

Shasta, a subsidiary of Consolidated Foods (1976 sales of $2,754 billion—net income, $89,453 million; soft-drink and food division, $239.3 million—pretax income of $17.2 million) produced standard flavors with diet drinks making up approximately 50 percent of overall sales. Sales were made to large purchasers, such as food stores, airlines, and government departments, with the bulk of the product being delivered directly to customer warehouses.

The Coca-Cola Company of Atlanta, Georgia, was number one among concentrate producers in terms of marketing franchise, sales, profit, share of market, and financial strength. Coke's 1975 balance sheet listed cash and marketable securities of $148 million, long-term debt of $9 million, and deferred taxes, capital stock, and surplus of $1.25 billion. Analysts estimated that Coke's international sales were growing more rapidly than domestic; the company had been the pioneer in international soft-drink operations. Originally, and for decades, a specialist in cola drinks, Coke introduced a line of flavor drinks—Fanta orange and grape; Sprite, a lemon-lime drink; Mr. PiBB, a cherry cola drink; and diet drinks—Tab and Fresca. In the 1960s Coke added Minute Maid orange juice, instant tea and coffee, and bottled spring water.

PepsiCo of Purchase, New York, was the second largest company in the industry with 1975 sales approximating 80 percent of Coca-Cola's and its net profit 44 percent of Coke's. PepsiCo was involved in four major domestic product areas plus international operations. Its principal soft drinks were regular and diet Pepsi-Cola, Mountain Dew, and a new product Pepsi Light (a semidiet, combination cola and lemon-lime drink). PepsiCo's food division was the leading snack food, for example, potato and corn-based products, producer in the United States with its own route delivery system. Two smaller divisions were involved in sporting goods and intercity truck transportation.

The 7UP brand was the third largest selling soft drink in the world; its product specialty was a lemon-lime drink sold in both regular and diet formula. Seven-Up, located in St. Louis, Missouri, dominated that flavor with an estimated 60 percent share of market, outselling the next product—Sprite—by three to one. Since 1968 the brand had grown about 7 percent annually versus an average 5½ percent for the industry. In 1970 the company began a modest acquisition program.

Dr Pepper, of Dallas, Texas, the fourth largest selling brand, shared with Seven-Up the record of having the industry's highest earnings growth rate from 1968 to 1975—18 percent. Its share of market had moved from 2.7 percent in 1966 to 5.5 percent in 1975. Company operations were concentrated in the North American market with Dr Pepper, in regular and diet formulas, comprising 99 percent of company sales. Dr Pepper, a unique fruit-based flavor, had only one direct competitor— Mr. PiBB. Company gallonage growth rates had been historically targeted by management at 15 percent, but industry analysts did not believe that objective had been reached in 1974 and in 1975 were estimating future gallonage growth of 10 percent.

Royal Crown Cola of Atlanta, Georgia, was the fifth largest selling brand (1975 market share—4.2 percent for regular and diet Royal Crown Cola plus 1.2 percent market share for associated flavor lines). Royal Crown had been a leader in the introduction of diet cola drinks, and its market share in that product segment originally equaled or exceeded Coca-Cola's. Originally a soft-drink specialist, Royal Crown began to diversify in 1969 and 1970 into home furnishings and into the processing of citrus fruits and juices. In 1976 the company announced the acquisition of Arby's, a roast beef sandwich, fast-food chain, headquartered in Youngstown, Ohio.

Soft-drink bottling and distribution companies

Franchise owners were granted, without cost, in perpetuity, the exclusive right to bottle and distribute a concentrate company's line of branded soft drinks as long as conditions of the franchise agreement were met. Key elements in the franchise involved maintaining product quality standards, bottling facilities, distribution and marketing programs within a franchise territory, not selling product to organizations that might transship to another franchised territory, and a willingness not to handle a directly competitive brand, for example, a bottler could not bottle both Coca-Cola and Royal Crown Cola.

A Pepsi-Cola franchise owner could, however, handle a noncompetitive brand such as Dr Pepper—a product type not produced by PepsiCo.[11] Also, a franchise owner might elect not to handle one of PepsiCo's secondary brands, for example, Teem, a lemon-lime drink, and instead bottle and distribute 7UP, the leading lemon-lime brand. A franchisee

---

[11] A court decision in 1962 interpreted franchise bottler agreements to allow a bottler to sell noncompeting brands.

might also take on a minor line such as Dad's Root Beer or Squirt, a citrus-flavored drink. In addition, if the territory were too small to support both a bottling and canning line, the franchisee could purchase canned products from other sources.

The franchise system was originally developed to achieve local delivery economics and to enable concentrate companies to obtain intensive market coverage at minimum capital investment. In 1975 the sector was still dominated, numerically, by family owned and operated firms despite a 42 percent decline since 1960 in the number of plants operating. Approximately 60 percent of these bottlers (1971) were located in cities with a population of 50,000 or less. An industry observer commented, "Local bottlers and the concentrate manufacturers are in a family relationship. It sounds corny, but it's true. Coke is the best example; they really try to watch out for the small bottlers. Some of them are run by the third generation of a family" (Exhibit 12).

The bottler segment of the industry could be divided into four major sectors. First were privately owned, usually small, bottlers such as Coca-Cola Bottling Company of Annapolis; it serviced 1,335 accounts and had sales of $1.1 million. Some of the larger of these franchisees, located in small metropolitan districts, had achieved substantial growth by buying up franchise operators in contiguous areas and by an aggressive policy of taking on secondary brands such as Dr Pepper or 7UP. The average sales of a bottling plant in 1973 were just over $2 million.

The second sector included large, publicly owned, multibrand firms, based in major metropolitan districts. Coca-Cola Bottling of New York, for example, bottled and distributed Coke, Dr Pepper, and minor softdrink brands and other beverages in a five-state area from multiplant sites. The company had also expanded operations into wine and the manufacture of coolers (Exhibit 13). One analyst estimated that the pretax return on assets for three large publicly owned bottlers (1968–72)

Exhibit 12

U.S. BOTTLING PLANT DISTRIBUTION BY SALES CATEGORY, 1972

Annual sales per plant	Number of plants	Change in number of plants since 1971	Percent of total bottler sales
Over $10 million	124	48%	26.6
$5–$10 million	129	50	19.4
$3–$5 million	226	13	19.2
$2–$3 million	360	56	12.2
$500,000–$1 million	539	−4	9.1
$300,000–$500,000	393	−21	3.3
$100,000–$300,000	582	−24	2.9
Under $100,000	321	−19	0.6
Unclassified	51		
Total	2,725	−4.9%	

Source: Bureau of Census data.

Exhibit 13

COMPARATIVE SALES OF SIX LARGEST PUBLICLY OWNED BOTTLERS, 1974

Bottlers	Sales ($ millions)	Bottlers	Sales ($ millions)
Coca-Cola Bottling, Los Angeles	$702	ME-1	$220
Coca-Cola Bottling, New York	645	Pep-Com	168
Associated Coca-Cola Bottlers	558	General Cinema Bottling Division	157

was 19.2 percent versus 30.3 percent for Coke, 16.4 percent for PepsiCo, and 46.8 percent for Dr Pepper.

Bottling operations of conglomerate companies such as Beatrice Foods and Borden comprised the third sector. These firms not only owned large bottling operations but in some cases minor concentrate manufacturers. Industry experts predicted that both the publicly held bottlers and the conglomerates would continue to grow in part via the acquisition of other franchise operations.

Seven of the eight largest concentrate companies owned some bottling operations. Coca-Cola owned and operated bottling facilities in Chicago, San Francisco, Seattle, Oakland, San Jose, Baltimore, and Boston. PepsiCo packaged approximately 20 percent of its domestic gallonage in company-owned plants. Senior management spokespersons for the concentrate companies unanimously supported the existing franchise system, and the presidents of Coca-Cola and Dr Pepper had taken public positions that their firms did not want to own any more bottling operations.

In surveying developments in the franchise bottling field, an industry spokesman states:

> The overall effects of the market developments since 1945 can be identified as these: (1) The increased power of retail chains strengthened the popularity of franchising through the emphasis on national brands. (2) Availability of the one-way container enabled the easy market entry of store-owned brands as well as national and regionally shipped brands, and further strengthened the retail market position of chains as soft-drink outlets. (3) Larger market spheres for many bottlers were brought about by the growth of urban centers, necessitating greater capital requirements and redefinition of territories. These needs were met by a high degree of mergers, sales, and other interindustry ownership transactions. (4) High growth rate of product volume began to attract "outside" money for the first time in the industry's history and companies not previously identified with soft drinks began entry into the industry. Availability of this new capital assisted the industry in its accommodation to newly dimensioned markets. (5) The one-way container brought substantial influence on the price of the product in the market. In 1950 the retail price was the same as it was in 1887, approximately a nickel a glass, but as a growing share

of product moved to single use packages, the cost of soft drinks has inevitably reflected the higher cost of packaging.[12]

Federal Trade Commission officials, however, took a critical view of these developments asserting they had resulted in high industry concentration levels and in the companies' ability to raise prices substantially:

> Because such large firms engage in soft-drink bottling, high-concentration levels exist in this industry. The 24 largest Coca-Cola bottlers serve nearly 61 percent of the United States population and account for approximately 24 percent of the total soft-drink sales. The 10 largest Pepsi bottlers serve 48 percent of the population and account for almost 8 percent of total soft-drink sales. The 12 largest Seven-Up franchisees, two of which are also two of the top Pepsi franchisees, serve 41 percent of the population. Approximately 40 bottlers account for more than one third of total soft-drink sales.
>
> However, the relevant measure of concentration in the soft-drink industry is the concentration in local markets. Local markets, not national markets, are the locus of competition in soft-drink bottling as territorial restrictions confine bottlers to competing in local markets. To put it simply, bottlers compete on the local level, not on the national level, and concentration of sales among local bottlers is quite high. According to the Bureau of Census, in 1963, the four largest bottlers in nine large metropolitan areas had, on the average, 68 percent of the market. This high concentration level among bottlers at the local level parallels the high concentration level of the four largest syrup manufacturers who share about 70 percent of the national market. Thus, a similar concentration level would naturally exist at the local level since bottlers' sales reflect, to a great extent, the market share of the brands they sell.
>
> One reason for the high-level concentration among bottlers is the extent to which bottlers produce products of several syrup manufacturers. For example, in New York City, both Coca-Cola and Dr Pepper products are marketed by Coca-Cola Bottling Company of New York. Certainly, there can be no real competition between these brands bottled by a common bottler as a firm is not going to engage in price competition with itself. In 1970, of the 1,654 bottlers of products of the eight largest syrup manufacturers, 738 bottled products of more than one such manufacturer. Because of the large number of bottlers who bottle more than one brand, effective competition between different brands does not exist.
>
> The high concentration among bottlers in local markets is reflected by the ease at which they have been able to increase prices in recent years. In this regard, it should be noted that for the period 1959–70, Bureau of Labor Statistics data indicates the wholesale price of cola soft drinks, which account for about 60 percent of the soft-drink industry, has increased by 65 percent. Similarly, the Consumer Price Index records a 64 percent price increase in cola soft-drink prices. This 64 percent rise in cola soft-drink prices on the Consumer Price Index is a much faster price rise than the 33 percent price rise for all food prices during the period 1959–70.[13]

---

[12] Statement of president of the National Soft Drink Association before the Subcommittee on Antitrust and Monopoly Legislation, August 8, 1972.

[13] Statement of Mr. Alan Ward, director of Bureau of Competition, Federal Trade Commission. Hearings before the Subcommittee on Antitrust and Monopoly, 92d Congress, part 1, pp 223–24.

Retailers

Industry analysts typically assigned soft drinks to three retail market segments: packaged goods sold via food stores; vending machines; and the fountain trade, the latter subdivided into two areas—restaurants and fast-food chains. A fourth category—the institutional market (e.g., hospitals and industrial plants)—was assigned in some cases to the vending section, in other statistical surveys to the fountain trade. Because of this, market share estimates varied substantially from one to another analyst's survey.

In 1975 Oppenheimer & Company, Inc., estimated food stores sales at approximately 55–60 percent, vending at 10 percent and fountain at 30–35 percent. Another analyst estimated, respectively, 50 percent, 20 percent, and 30 percent. But all agreed that food stores were still the dominant market. In 1900, 70 percent of soft drinks were consumed on the premises of the vendors and 30 percent at home. In the 50s and 60s the amount of products sold via food stores increased to 70 percent of the total market. The food store market was dominated by Pepsi-Cola and Coca-Cola with Pepsi having a modest share-of-the-market advantage. Some analysts believed Pepsi had a significant long-run strategic advantage over Coke, however, because of its major position in the snack food field.

Food stores sold $2.6 billion worth of soft drinks in 1975, making them the single largest retail outlet for soft drinks and accounting for approximately 55 percent of the cases sold that year. Case sales had increased steadily between 1960 and 1973 when industry marketing efforts had been concentrated on the take-home market segment. Food stores' share of total soft-drink sales, however, had declined from 70 percent in 1960 to 60 percent in 1970, and were expected to decline further to 50 percent by 1980. Supermarkets had been the site of most national brand, soft-drink competitive battles during the early 1970s.

Food retailers' sales of $131 billion in 1974 ranked them as one of the nation's largest businesses; supermarket chains played an important role in the industry, accounting for only 10 percent of stores but 45 percent of total sales. The three largest supermarket chains and their respective 1974 sales were Safeway, $8.19 billion; A&P, $7.03 billion; and Kroger, $4.78 billion. Many independent supermarkets were members of large cooperative buying groups or voluntary wholesaler groups which provided distribution economies of scale and staff services.

Soft drinks were of major interest to supermarkets since their 22 percent gross margin was one of the highest for any grocery items and the category achieved high turnover. In 1974 the average supermarket carried over 100 different brands and sizes of soft drinks which generated $2.3 billion in total sales and $503 million in gross margin. Product shelf space allocations by chain store management directly correlated with market share. In 1975 canned soft drinks maintained their position among the top 10 grocery product volume leaders.

The 1960s had been a period of rapid growth and prosperity for supermarkets, but the future looked less promising for the 70s and early 80s.

Predictions of things to come by supermarket executives included little growth in real per capita food expenditures and little population growth. They anticipated increasing price competition, a rapid decline in the number of supermarkets operated, and increasing pressure for operating efficiencies, including more automated warehouses and full truckload delivery systems.

Another development in food retailing was the rapid growth of convenience stores (1967 estimated sales of $6.2 billion with estimated $1.6 billion of beverage sales). These stores were relatively small, had limited stock, long operating hours patterns, and serviced a local community area. Many soft-drink bottlers viewed these expanding outlets as a prime sales opportunity. An executive of the Dr Pepper Company noted that selling to convenience stores was very different from supermarket selling. He noted, "The loss-leader approach commonly used in supermarkets was unworkable, whereas tie-in and theme promotions did seem effective. Convenience stores show a noticeable trend in selling sandwiches and other prepared-on-the-premise food items and therefore offer beverage tie-in possibilities."[14]

Vending machines, manufactured to serve a variety of containers from cans to bottles to paper cups, were employed to service the single-drink market. Costing the bottler between $800 to $1,000, these machines blanketed locations such as service stations, small stores, and sports arenas. An estimated 1.7 million machines were in operation in 1975, and some corporate executives believe this to be a mature or even potentially declining market sector. Coke was experimenting with the installation of small REFRESH office units. These units vended drinks at 10 cents a cup in private and public offices. Coke hoped to have 20,000 units in place by 1976.

Some bottlers, whose distributor salespeople originally serviced only soft-drink machines, were expanding into the full-line vending business—including foods, candy, and cigarettes. Such firms could then contract to serve a factory or a public institution where a bank of vending machines had replaced the traditional cafeteria arrangement.

The fountain trade subdivided into two segments: the traditional restaurant, specialty restaurant, and coffee shops market; and fast-food operations. Americans seemed to be in the midst of a major shift toward "eating out," and the primary beneficiary seemed to have been chain operations. An observer noted, "Many independent full-service/atmosphere restaurants have been forced to close in recent years. . . . In contrast, chain operations in the coffee shop, specialty, and fast-food areas have expanded rapidly with the greatest growth coming from multisite operations in the fast-food segment. According to the U.S. Department of Commerce and A. D. Little, total personal consumption for food and beverages spent in fast-food outlets grew from about $400 million in 1960 to over $13 billion in 1976."

Fast-food chains operated with corporate owned (one fourth) and through franchise arrangements (three fourths) with the percentage

[14] *Beverage World*, January 1977, p. 36.

of franchises gradually declining as franchisers purchased their own large franchise operation. Analysts noted further that "the top seven firms, McDonald's, Kentucky Fried Chicken, A&W Root Beer, International Dairy Queen, Tastee Freeze, Burger King, and Pizza Hut accounted for 47 percent of all fast-food units and 46 percent of sales. While fast-food chains dominate the fast-food segment they do not dominate the entire restaurant industry; the top 35 chains still accounted for only one quarter of total domestic eating and drinking industry sales. McDonald's, the largest independent, accounted for 3 percent of total food service sales (1975 sales of $2.616 billion). Burger Chef (General Foods) and Kentucky Fried Chicken (Heublein) were divisions of larger firms."

Suppliers

In 1975 the soft-drink industry purchased approximately $4 billion of raw material ingredients and packaging supplies. This included approximately $1.7 billion for sugar, $200 million for high fructose corn syrup, $5 million for saccharin, $408 million for flavorings, $1 billion for cans, over $750 million for glass containers, and $127 million for closures and cartons. The soft-drink industry accounted for 23 percent of the sugar consumed in the United States, 70 percent of the saccharin, and was one of the largest customers for companies such as Continental Can and Crown Cork & Seal.

Sugar prices were vulnerable to major short-term price fluctuations in response to small changes in demand, since 96–97 percent of world production was sold under long-term contracts. In 1974 and 1975 increasing world demand and poor crop yields pushed prices as high as 75 cents per pound, compared to 2 cents to 9 cents per pound between 1950 and 1973. Recent sugar price increases prompted the use of high fructose corn syrup (HFCS) which at 20 cents per pound was 10–15 percent less expensive than sugar for equivalent sweetening power. By 1975 most major concentrate producers, except Coca-Cola and PepsiCo, had authorized their bottlers to use a 50/50 or 75/25 sugar/HFCS mixture, but actual usage was modest due to limited high fructose production capacity. Capacity was not expected to be adequate to meet demand until 1980. Saccharin was the primary artificial sweetener used in diet soft drinks, with approximately 2 million pounds purchased in 1974 at $2.40 per pound from one domestic producer.

Glass containers accounted for a substantial percentage of all soft-drink packages used in 1974. Sales to the soft-drink industry accounted for approximately 23 percent of the $5 billion glass container market in 1976. There were two dominant glass container manufacturers: Libbey-Owens (1975 packaging material sales, $1,400 million) and Anchor Hocking (1975 sales, $411 million).

Five can companies accounted for 98 percent of the cans sold to the soft-drink industry with American Can Company (1974 sales, $2.7 billion) and Continental Can Company (1974 sales, over $3 billion) accounting for over 50 percent of the market. Crown Cork & Seal, National Can Company, and Reynolds Aluminum were the other major participants.

Packaging manufacturers, while typically dominant in one packaging technology, often engaged in the manufacture and sale of multiple types of packaging, for example, both glass and plastic. These manufacturers carried on most of the packaging research and development for the soft-drink industry. A recent improvement in the popular, large-size glass containers (all one-way packages) was a clear or semiclear plastic coating which reduced breakage and required less glass, therefore reducing package weight and distribution costs. In 1976 Owens-Illinois "Plastic-Shield" coated 33 percent of the 28- and 32-ounce bottles and 50 percent of the 48- and 64-ounce bottles which it produced.

KEY INDUSTRY FUNCTIONAL STRATEGIES

Marketing

"In this industry the key strategic function has been marketing—that includes advertising, promotion, packaging, and distribution," an analyst commented. "Finance, so far, hasn't been limiting; and with one exception, the concentrate people are in very conservative positions. Production hasn't been that critical, but changing logistics and possible changes in product technology make it increasingly important. And don't forget there are three teams playing in this game—concentrate producers, bottlers, and the government. Their interests are different, and it makes the game complicated."

Soft drinks were inexpensive, frequently purchased products often consumed on impulse by a broad spectrum of the population. According to Standard & Poor's, in 1975, 90 percent of U.S. teenagers consumed at least seven soft drinks per week, 74 percent of young adults consumed that many, and 43 percent of the population over 50 drank one soft drink a day. Efforts to increase consumer awareness, achieve extensive availability, and appeal to consumer desires for product variety and user convenience involved the joint participation of both concentrate producers and bottlers.

Large, national concentrate producers did overall market research and planning, determined advertising and promotion themes, introduced new container sizes and materials, and developed and tested products. They financed national advertising, staff and development services, and paid part of the cost of local advertising and promotion of new packages and products.

Bottlers worked with national concentrate representatives to determine the advertising media, promotion themes, product mix, package mix, and price points to most effectively meet the particular consumer preferences, distribution channels, and competitive situations of their local market area. The bottlers were responsible for day-to-day implementation of the marketing plan. They usually paid about 50 percent of the cost of local advertising and promotion, and most of the costs of new packaging and vending and dispensing equipment. Local cooperative advertising and promotion budgets were usually based on both concentrate producers and bottlers contributing a fixed amount per gallon of product sold in the territory.

Marketing strategies for local and regional companies and minor national brands generally followed a pattern of sales through food stores; few had vending machine exposure and few received much media advertising support. Local and regional firms usually concentrated on flavor lines and competed on a price basis. Minor national brands "piggybacked" on the franchise bottlers of the top six concentrate manufacturers. Schweppes and Canada Dry competed primarily as premium-priced "mixers" for use with alcoholic drinks.

An industry marketing executive commented that the seven critical ingredients for industry success were advertising, availability, promotion, packaging, pricing, personal selling, and new product introduction.

Advertising. Consumer advertising was a critical element in selling soft drinks and accounted for a large proportion of concentrate producers' annual marketing budgets. Exhibit 14 indicates amounts spent on national media alone by the largest advertisers between 1960 and 1975. Most national brand advertising was directed toward achieving or maintaining consumer "top of mind" awareness. The emergence of 7UP as an aggressively advertised soft-drink brand with its "Uncola" theme was considered to be an industry advertising success story. The initial UnCola campaign relied heavily on 60-second spots on network television. Later billboards, newspapers, radio commercials, and prime-time television spots were used. Between 1966 and 1976, 7UP case sales increased from 200 million to 340 million.

Industry executives anticipated increasing competition in the advertising arena in 1976. According to *Beverage Industry:*

> With another no-growth year just ended, the major thrust in advertising is coming from those companies who have seen their individual market shares increase at the expense of both the best known brands and the regional or private label soft drinks. Because of this, the key word for this year is product identity, and ad agencies across the country are turning out television and radio spots designed to leave the consumer with an indelible memory of their clients' product.

Availability. An ornithologist does not need a laboratory full of measuring instruments to prove that geese are migrating; rare will be the reader who has not, in the previous week, had several soft drinks, consumed in a variety of places. A researcher walking down a city street provided ample evidence of the industry's merchandising impact: soft drinks were available at 12 locations (including a funeral parlor for an undesignated clientele); men and women, young and old, black and white were observed consuming their favorite beverage; several hundred cans provided typical big city litter; and 64 soft-drink advertisements "decorated" one four-block street section.

Soft-drink availability accomplished three objectives for soft-drink marketers. It provided a safe, cold, palatable drink almost anywhere people became thirsty. Second, point-of-sale advertising in hundreds of thousands of locations contributed to brand awareness. Finally, exten-

Exhibit 14

SOFT-DRINK ADVERTISING EXPENDITURES FOR SELECTED BRANDS
($ millions)

	1960	1968	1970	1971	1972	1973	1974	1975
Coca-Cola:	$4,423							
Coke	3,837	$19,092	$20,243	$18,664	$17,965	$24,108	$22,122	$20,261
Fresca		—	3,861	4,317	2,862	2,590	2,545	2,381
Sprite		2,500	1,063	1,198	1,835	1,738	2,463	2,601
Tab		6,162	3,443	4,248	3,814	5,435	5,278	6,496
Fanta		800	470	396		392	147	74
Dr Pepper:	27							
Regular		2,950	4,098	4,945	4,082	5,363	5,402	4,872
Diet		244	24	285	687	1,208	1,759	1,548
PepsiCo:	3,148							
Pepsi		16,512	15,939	17,797	15,268	13,520	14,856	14,995
Diet Pepsi		1,465	4,034	4,593	4,254	4,321	4,139	3,673
Teem		41	22	10	—	—	—	61
Mountain Dew		796	263	148	162	350	635	2,577
Pepsi Light								918
7UP:	2,229							
Regular		8,993	11,496	13,169	12,835	10,438	10,437	10,180
Diet		2,242	576	1,481	1,725	2,398	1,967	3,255
Norton-Simon:	313							
Canada Dry		5,790	6,659	8,528	6,139	5,503	4,859	5,213
Barrelhead Root Beer						239	561	1,314
R. C. Cola:	1,003							
Regular		2,980	3,082	4,779	4,230	4,885	5,695	10,509
Diet Rite		4,961	2,303	3,095	2,472	2,351	2,131	3,497
Shasta							2,324	2,828

Source: Abstracted from *Advertising Age* and company reports.

sive availability was an important sampling device which helped to create and maintain consumer flavor preferences. Several industry sources stated that Coca-Cola dominated the cold, single-drink market. In some regions of the country, however, other brands had achieved substantial single-drink availability; Pepsi in the Midwest, for example, and Dr Pepper in the Southwest and parts of the Southeast.

In food stores and supermarkets the major national brands vied with local and regional brands and the stores' own private label soft drinks to best appeal to the consumer's varying degree of thirst (6 ounces to 64 ounces), the size of the consumer's family (single bottles, 6-ounce cartons, 8-can packs), budget, weight consciousness, desire for convenience, and ecological concern (returnable, resealable bottles, cans, non-returnable glass containers).

Sales promotion.   Recent point-of-sale promotional activity focused primarily on increasing packaged product sales through food stores. Consequently, most of the interaction took place between the bottlers, food retailers, and the consumers. Executives noted that usually the larger the size of display and shelf-space allocations and the greater the frequency of appearances in weekly food store newspaper advertising, the faster a particular soft-drink brand sold. Thus, a wide variety of programs fell under the general category of promotions in the competition for consumers' and retailers' attention. They included installing point-of-sale signs, obtaining special end-of-aisle or high-visibility display areas, providing special permanent display racks and in-store refrigerated coolers. One industry source estimated that bottlers spent as much or more money on promotions as on advertising. Another industry participant estimated that bottlers annually spent the equivalent of 2–3 percent of sales on advertising and promotion efforts, or $100–$150 million in 1975.

Packaging.   "The proliferation of packaging has led to wider availability, particularly in vendors, to greater consumer convenience, and to increased consumption," an industry analyst commented. "The explosion in larger size packages has also increased gallonage sales. The grocery store consumer usually buys the same number of bottles or cartons of soft drinks each week. The more ounces each of those bottles or cartons hold, the more ounces go home with the consumer each trip. That's why the new plastic bottles are going to give such a boost to gallonage sales. The bottles themselves are smaller and lighter, so more containers can be put in a carton at the same weight. But the big ones create shelf shortage problems too! Look at the soft-drink aisles in your supermarket; they have cases of gallon bottles stacked all over the place."

In addition to increasing total consumption of soft drinks by getting more product in the consumer's refrigerator, each new container size or material provided the opportunity to increase a brand's supermarket shelf "facings." Packaging variety also gave price choices within and among brands. Generally, soft drinks in larger size containers cost the consumer less per glass because packaging accounted for a lower proportion of total raw materials cost. The consumer also paid a lower price per ounce for beverages in returnable containers since the container cost was amortized over 10 or more fillings.

The most frequently purchased container sizes in the early 70s were 10- and 12-ounce containers with 58 percent of unit sales; followed by 16-ounce containers, 20 percent; 24 ounces and larger, 16 percent; and 6–9 ounces, 6 percent. The 10- and 12-ounce *cans* accounted for 38 percent of unit sales, one-way *bottles* accounted for 28 percent, and returnable *bottles* for 34 percent. According to one analyst:

> Packaging innovations are usually led by the companies who have the most money. This is a me-too industry—once one company brings out something new, the others aren't far behind. Coke was the first with the plastic bottle, but Pepsi was first with the 64-ounce size and 7UP with the liter bottle. Royal Crown was the first company to come out with cans, but it took Coke and Pepsi to really put that package on the map.

In 1976 one new packaging innovation was already in the market testing stage—plastic bottles. The introduction by Coca-Cola of 32-ounce plastic bottles in the Providence, Rhode Island, market had been described as "successful," capturing over 50 percent of that particular Coke bottler's entire product mix. Over the years plastics may be adding 1 percent a year to industry growth, one analyst concluded.

Plastic pouches and plastic "bags" encased in a corrugated paper box were being used in the wine and fruit juice industry. Mirolite, a plastic pouch wrapped in a paper sleeve, was manufactured by ICI in England. When European soft-drink producers first adopted the package they had to reformulate some of their high-carbonation drinks to retain their original flavor and lower carbonation level.

Can manufacturers were developing lighter, two-piece tin and aluminum cans, and nonreturnable bottle manufacturers were marketing lighter and stronger bottles. "Weight's important in this game—you are shipping water and metal around. You can't do much with the water but you sure try to cut down container weight. With the trend toward bigger bottles (64-ounce) you get difficult-to-handle products."

Pricing. Retail prices for soft drinks varied substantially by geographic region of the country, by container type, by channel of distribution, and a host of other factors such as local manufacturing costs, retailer markups, and degree of competition. For example, food retailers rarely achieved more than a 25 percent margin, while fountain retailers often achieved 65 percent to 75 percent gross margin of soft drinks. Exhibit 15 shows the range of average retail soft-drink prices by regions for 1964–72, and their steady increase over the period.

Some industry analysts believed that the market for soft drinks was relatively price inelastic. They also believed that even greater pricing flexibility existed at the concentrate producer's level because concentrate cost accounted for such a low proportion of finished product cost, 4 percent in the case of Coca-Cola, and comparable amounts for other producers' soft drinks. Seven-Up was the only concentrate producer yet to put the theory to a major test. According to one analyst, Seven-Up increased its concentrate prices 11 percent in October 1974 and 25 percent the following June. The company apparently quelled bottler resistance to the second price hike by promising to spend more money on advertising and local promotion.

Exhibit 15

RETAIL PRICING TRENDS OF FRUIT-FLAVORED SOFT DRINKS BY REGION, 1964–1972
(per 72-ounce carton)

Region	1964	1965	1966	1967	1968	1969	1970	1971	1972
Northeast	56.8¢	54.7¢	55.2¢	59.0¢	63.5¢	64.7¢	69.8¢	75.4¢	75.4¢
South	n.a.	n.a.	n.a.	n.a.	55.0	58.7	59.7	63.1	64.4
Midwest	54.7	57.6	59.5	60.4	62.8	70.2	74.9	77.2	75.6
West	63.0	64.2	63.9	64.2	69.5	72.3	81.4	83.3	84.4
All regions	53.4	53.6	54.8	57.0	60.5	63.1	69.1	72.6	72.7

n.a. = Not available.
Source: Bureau of Labor Statistics, and *Beverage Industry*, July 28, 1972. The 1972 figures as of March of that year.

Personal selling. Concentrate producers employed two types of selling organizations: bottler-oriented sales personnel and fountain salespersons. Concentrate producers' bottler sales personnel worked with franchised bottler management to tailor national brand plans to the individual requirements of the local market area. Franchised bottlers were independent business people so the persuasiveness of the concentrate producers' salesperson as marketing consultant was important. However, the salesperson did not have to rely completely on charm or intimidation: incentives such as cooperative advertising and promotion funds were available.

Some concentrate producers, including Coca-Cola, Seven-Up, and Dr Pepper, maintained their own sales organizations to sell fountain syrup directly to retailers. Pepsi-Cola and other producers relied primarily on their franchised bottlers and independent jobbers to sell to fountain outlets. Most fountain retailers carried a maximum of four different brands because standard dispensers were equipped to handle but four flavor lines. Thus, the main task of concentrate producers' fountain sales personnel was first convincing the franchise chain's home office to approve the inclusion of their brand on the list of products which the local franchisee might use. Later they might help bottlers or jobbers sell individual retailers on carrying company products. Fountain sales personnel were also responsible for placing point-of-sale advertising and implementing cooperative advertising and promotion programs. The syrup producer or supplier also provided the retailer dispenser maintenance and repair services, usually free of charge.

New product introduction. New product introductions had played a relatively minor role in the marketing of soft drinks. Companies infrequently did introduce new brands, usually for a variation in the formulation of an old standard flavor, for example, Pepsi's introduction of Teem—a lemon-lime drink. Exactly what constituted a "new" soft-drink product was difficult for industry executives to define. One type of product innovation involved introduction of a new flavor, such as Cott's diet mint; another, a new combination such as cherry-flavored chocolate drinks. One firm had recently introduced a chocolate-flavored, high-protein health drink into several foreign markets. However, 7UP, first mar-

Exhibit 16

SOFT-DRINK BOTTLERS OPERATING INCOME AND EXPENSE RATIOS AS PERCENT OF NET SALES, 1973

	Top 10 percent in net operating income	All units	Under $1,000	$1,000 to $3,000	$3,001 to $6,000	$6,001 to $10,000
Cost of sales:						
Materials	13.11	17.32	15.63	16.72	16.76	14.83
Packaging expense	10.61	12.55	4.30	9.93	17.69	15.36
Plant labor	4.14	4.83	5.89	4.85	4.87	4.36
Indirect	3.44	4.07	3.90	3.90	3.99	4.12
Total	31.30	38.77	29.72	35.40	43.31	38.67
Contract purchase (finished beverages)	26.70	24.52	32.92	28.23	19.48	25.46
Total cost of sales	58.00	63.29	62.64	63.63	62.79	64.13
Gross profit	42.00	36.71	37.36	36.37	37.21	35.87
Total other operating income	3.36	2.15	2.26	2.53	1.98	1.67
Gross operating income	45.36	38.86	39.62	38.90	39.19	37.54
Operating expenses:						
Warehousing	1.69	2.81	1.93	3.22	1.95	1.77
Selling	19.70	21.12	20.76	20.67	21.56	22.43
Administrative	5.89	7.97	12.03	7.84	7.52	7.72
Total operating expenses	27.28	31.90	34.72	31.73	31.03	31.92
Net operating income	18.08	6.96	4.90	7.17	8.16	5.62

Source: National Soft Drinks Association 1973 financial survey.

keted in 1920, and Dr Pepper, first sold in 1885, were the only flavors outside of cola which had achieved major national brand status.

Most industry observers did agree that diet beverages were a new product category. First introduced in the early 1960s, diet drinks had achieved a 15 percent market share in 1969. When the Food and Drug Administration banned cyclamates as an artificial sweetener, sales dropped precipitously to 6.7 percent of the market in 1970. By 1976 diet beverages again accounted for 15 percent of industry sales and were the fastest growing product category. One bottler characterized Coke's introduction of Fresca, its citrus-flavored diet drink, as the most successful new product introduction in which he had ever participated. "I gave Fresca away to every one of my outlets in quantities amounting to 20 percent of each outlet's monthly 12-ounce Coke sales. When Coke wants to move in—they *move in.*"

Pepsi Light, Pepsi-Cola's reduced-sugar, cola-plus-lemon was, in the view of some analysts, the major new product of the 70s. The drink used some artificial sweeteners while still containing only half the sugar (and half the calories) of regular cola. At the end of 1975, Pepsi Light was in selected markets covering about 50 percent of the U.S. population; national advertising expenditures had already reached close to a million dollars.

The Pepsi challenge.   One example of the increasing competitiveness among major national brand soft-drink producers was the major advertising campaign begun by Pepsi-Cola in April 1974, in Dallas, which declared, "Nationwide, more Coca-Cola drinkers prefer Pepsi than the taste of Coca-Cola." *The New York Times* described the genius of the campaign in an article on July 5, 1976.

> . . . research had indicated that more than half the Coke drinkers who participated in a blind test of Pepsi and Coke preferred the taste of Pepsi. . . . So Pepsi decided to launch a "challenge" campaign in a marketing area where it had been weak: Dallas and Fort Worth.

In Dallas, over nine months of heavy advertising and price promotions by both cola producers resulted in a small increase in market share for Coke, approximately 30 percent at the end of the period, and almost a doubling in market share for Pepsi, from 7 percent to 14 percent. Retail soft-drink prices had fallen to almost half their prechallenge prices, and the two colas had increased their combined market shares from 36 percent to over 44 percent at the expense of the smaller competing brands, especially Dr Pepper. The challenge, and the competitive reaction, had spread to other cities by the summer of 1976, including San Antonio, Corpus Christi, New York City, and Los Angeles. Exhibit 17 gives data on the consumption of leading soft drink brands in selected years.

Distribution

The soft-drink industry had achieved both extensive distribution of major national brands and a substantial degree of control over the distribution process itself, compared to other nonperishable food products. Exhibit 16 gives some information on distribution costs; they are in-

Exhibit 17

CONSUMPTION OF SOFT DRINKS
(selected years)

	1966		1970		1971	
	Million cases	Percent of market	Million cases	Percent of market	Million cases	Percent of market
Coca-Cola Co.:						
Coca-Cola	806.0	27.7	1,045.0	28.4	1,040.0	27.1
Sprite	43.0	1.5	65.0	1.8	71.0	1.8
Tab	42.0	1.4	49.0	1.3	66.0	1.7
Mr. PiBB	—	—	—	—	—	—
Fresca	33.0	1.1	46.0	1.3	52.0	1.3
Others	48.0	1.7	71.0	1.9	85.0	2.1
Total	972.0	33.4	1,276.0	34.7	1,344.0	34.0
PepsiCo, Inc.:						
Pepsi-Cola	470.0	16.1	625.0	17.0	687.0	17.4
Diet Pepsi	55.0	1.9	40.0	1.1	52.0	1.3
Mountain Dew ..	40.0	1.4	34.0	0.9	35.7	0.9
Teem	15.0	0.5	14.0	0.4	14.0	0.4
Pepsi Light	—	—	—	—	—	—
Others	15.0	0.5	15.0	0.4	15.0	0.4
Total	595.0	20.4	728.0	19.8	803.7	20.4
Seven-Up Co.:						
7UP	185.0	6.4	257.6	7.0	271.4	6.9
Sugar Free 7UP .	13.0	0.4	6.5	0.1	8.4	0.2
Howdy flavors ..	2.0	0.1	3.0	0.1	2.3	—
Total	200.0	6.9	267.1	7.2	282.1	7.1
Royal Crown Cola Co.:						
Royal Crown	110.0	3.8	142.0	3.8	153.0	3.9
Diet Rite Cola ..	48.0	1.6	36.0	1.0	42.0	1.0
Nehi and others	43.0	1.5	45.0	1.2	46.0	1.2
Total	201.0	6.9	223.0	6.0	241.0	6.1
Dr Pepper: Regular Dr Pepper	79.0	2.4	135.2	3.7	147.7	3.7
Sugar Free Dr Pepper	8.0	0.2	5.0	0.1	7.2	0.2
Total	87.0	2.6	140.2	3.8	154.9	3.9

Source: *Beverage World*, April 2, 1976, p. 28; based on data supplied by John R. Maxwell, Jr., Wheat, First Securities, Inc.

cluded in the category—selling. A key element in the distribution process, especially for food stores and vending machines, was the franchised bottler's sales force.

The franchised bottler's sales force comprised driver salespeople who combined both delivery and sales functions. Each morning route salespeople left the plant with trucks full of the soft-drink assortment they expected customers to buy that day. The route salespeople stocked the customers' shelves directly from their mobile inventory, often handling billing and collections on the spot. They were usually compensated with

1972		1973		1974		1975		1974–75
Million cases	*Percent of market*	*Million cases*	*Percent of market*	*Million cases*	*Percent of market*	*Million cases*	*Percent of market*	*Percent change*
1,125.0	26.8	1,190.0	26.7	1,180.0	26.5	1,170.0	26.2	−0.8
81.0	1.9	95.0	2.1	105.0	2.4	115.3	2.6	+9.8
85.0	2.0	97.0	2.2	100.0	2.2	115.0	2.6	+15.0
5.0	0.1	15.0	0.3	23.0	0.5	37.5	0.8	+63.0
48.0	1.2	44.0	1.0	38.0	0.9	35.0	0.8	−7.9
95.0	2.3	100.0	2.3	100.0	2.2	100.0	2.3	—
1,439.0	34.3	1,541.0	34.6	1,546.0	34.7	1,572.8	35.3	+1.7
735.0	17.5	777.4	17.4	780.0	17.5	778.0	17.4	−0.3
58.0	1.4	60.3	1.4	68.0	1.5	75.0	1.7	+10.3
35.0	0.8	42.0	0.9	47.0	1.0	56.0	1.3	+19.1
14.0	0.3	14.8	0.3	14.0	0.3	13.5	0.3	−3.6
—	—	—	—	—	—	2.0	0.1	—
15.0	0.4	16.0	0.4	15.8	0.4	15.0	0.3	−5.1
857.0	20.4	910.0	20.4	924.8	20.7	939.5	21.1	+1.6
289.6	6.9	317.7	7.1	311.3	7.0	295.5	6.6	−5.1
10.1	0.2	12.7	0.3	27.3	0.6	43.6	1.0	+59.7
1.8	0.1	1.4	—	1.5	—	1.4	—	−6.6
301.5	7.2	331.8	7.4	340.1	7.6	340.5	7.6	+0.1
165.0	3.9	165.0	3.9	150.0	3.4	153.0	3.4	+2.0
44.0	1.0	42.0	0.9	34.0	0.8	36.0	0.8	+5.9
49.0	1.2	53.0	1.2	56.0	1.2	51.0	1.2	−8.9
258.0	6.1	268.0	6.0	240.0	5.4	240.0	5.4	—
180.0	4.3	208.7	4.7	216.0	4.8	217.0	4.9	+.005
11.0	0.3	14.8	0.3	18.0	0.4	28.0	0.6	+55.0
101.0	4.6	223.5	5.0	234.0	5.2	245.0	5.5	+4.7

a percentage of sales commission, and their check sometimes came directly from the concentrate producer rather than the bottler.

In recent years, however, some bottlers had begun to use "presold, bulk delivery" techniques with large supermarket accounts. An advance salesperson called on the store and took orders and the product was delivered the next day, via large vans holding up to 2,000 cases. Large carts, each holding up to 40 to 70 cases, were wheeled into the store's warehouse area. The next day the bottler's merchandising staff arrived and personally stocked the store's shelves. Supermarket owners approved of the system because it improved the store's receiving and stocking efficiency; bottlers estimated they saved about 10 cents per case delivery cost.

In-store merchandising, whether carried out by a route salesperson or a separate merchandising force, was considered crucial to maintaining high sales levels. An executive of the New York Coca-Cola Bottling Company explained:

> Unlike other businesses where the product comes through a warehouse and is at the mercy of whatever the supplier may want to do with it, or even comes through a food broker who does not have the kind of service dedication that exists in the soft-drink business, the soft-drink business is service dependent. So the man who goes in there (a) rotates the stock, (b) is in a constant battle for shelf space, both in terms of quality and quantity; he is trying to get it on the shelf in the best possible place, (c) in terms of helping the dealer, (d) in terms of pricing, we believe even if our price is on the high side, it is important to have it marked, clearly marked, (e) in terms of promotion or special display that needs to be built, to be sure that it is properly in place.[15]

The efficient management of this route delivery system was a major determinant of bottler profitability and required efficient routing and skill in matching inventory load to customer demand. Five to ten percent of a bottler's accounts represented 20 percent to 45 percent of their total volume. Many of the smaller accounts, particularly those under five cases per stop, were marginally profitable at best and were serviced as a form of advertising through product availability and as an aid in keeping total plant volume above the break-even level. To support this extensive route delivery system, the industry supported the nation's largest private trucking fleet, second only to the U.S. Post Office.

Changing marketing and distribution patterns

The researchers noted several industry trends which they believed would influence concentrate company-bottler relationships and which would impact local bottler marketing and distribution patterns.

First, new cooperative relationships would be needed to handle sales to the expanding fast-food market. Food stores' share of market had been decreasing while sales to fast-food chains had increased from 20 percent (1960) to 25 percent (1970) to 30–35 percent (1975). Of the restaurant and food service market, sales to the fountain/fast-foods market, in contrast to food stores, required different sales and promotional techniques and organizational arrangements.

Second, local bottlers increasingly were dealing with chains which served market areas larger than an individual bottler's territory. A chain promotional campaign might necessitate the coordination of several franchise bottlers, a concentrate company's advertising manager, and the chain buying staff.

---

[15] Kuhn Loeb summary of *Federal Trade Commission Hearings in the Matter of Coca-Cola et al.*, May 19–23, 1975, p. 50.

Third, during the 1950s, bottlers typically handled only one concentrate company's product line. Beginning in the early 60s and spurred by Dr Pepper's aggressive campaign to sign up Coke and Pepsi bottlers, bottlers were increasingly managing multibrand operations. A Pepsi bottler might, for example, handle 7UP and Dr Pepper.

Finally, there appeared to be basic changes evolving in local bottler profit economics. Bottling executives testified that profit margins had been declining as a consequence of packaging proliferation and increased ingredient and operating costs and that their business was becoming more capital intensive as larger plants, larger sales volume, and larger market areas were needed to achieve cost economies. Smaller bottlers often lacked the capital to buy a bottling line ($250,000) or lacked a market large enough to break even on a canning-type operation ($2 million in sales). Some bottlers, to deal with this situation, had developed cooperative canning and distribution facilities with nearby bottlers holding similar franchises. A Dr Pepper executive commented that Coca-Cola and PepsiCo had been urging their franchised bottlers to cooperate among themselves for the last 8 to 10 years, while this was a relatively new policy at Dr Pepper. The most extreme illustration of this trend so far had occurred in Charlotte, North Carolina, where a dozen Coke bottlers had closed down their separate production facilities and opened a central plant ringed by a number of distribution centers. Warehousing and order filling took place at the distribution center from which bottlers served their traditional territories.

Production

Production operations in the soft-drink industry were divided between concentrate producers and bottlers. Quality control was one area where branded concentrate producers exercised influence over bottlers' and canners' production activities. Quality control required meeting plant, equipment, and process sanitation standards, as well as standards for product composition. Product composition standards covered the proportion of flavoring, sugar, and water in the drink, degree of carbonation, taste, and appearance. Quality control violations were one of the few grounds on which concentrate companies could revoke a bottler's franchise rights.

Concentrate and syrup production were simple processes involving little investment in plant or equipment and a low labor component. One analyst estimated that the Coca-Cola Company could double its syrup-producing capacity with a $200,000 capital investment. The concentrate process itself involved mixing fruit extracts and other liquefied natural and artificial flavorings with water and sugar in large vats. The resulting concentrate was shipped to bottlers and canners. Concentrate contained only a small proportion of the sugar needed in the finished drink and was more economical to ship; consequently, one or two concentrate factories might efficiently serve bottlers all over the United States.

Franchise companies which produced concentrate shifted the bulk of sugar purchasing requirements onto their franchised bottlers. Coke was the only major company to produce and ship syrup rather than concentrates. Coke maintained 22 regional syrup production centers to minimize the high costs of shipping. It partially handled the problem of sugar purchasing risks by charging its bottlers a syrup price which fluctuated depending on average quarterly sugar prices.

Soft-drink bottling was also a simple, nonlabor-intensive, manufacturing process, although it was more capital intensive than concentrate production. One source estimated that bottlers' total investment in plant, equipment, supplies, and distribution vehicles was close to $2 billion in 1975. The researcher estimated that approximately 30 percent of that $2 billion represented investment in plant (manufacturing and warehousing space) and 10 percent was in machinery and equipment.

Depending on its age, filling equipment currently in use in the industry ranged in capacity from 100 to 1,000 bottles per minute. Bottle washing, filling, and packing equipment had limited flexibility in terms of the range of container sizes and materials it could handle. Consequently, a bottler producing the full-size range of 6 to 64 ounces might require two or three lines.

Much of the industry's canned product was produced by large bottlers, by contract canners, and by concentrate company-owned canning lines because of the scale of capital investment required. Cans were lighter and easier to handle than bottles of comparable capacity, so canning production could be more easily centralized than bottling. The Coca-Cola Company was, in terms of capital investment, the most forward-integrated producer. Its canning operations were carried out by a wholly owned subsidiary called Canner for Coca-Cola Bottlers, Inc. (CCCB). CCCB put the bottling companies' syrup in cans for a fee at six different locations. The company's depreciated investment in canning plant was $21 million in 1975. CCCB accounted for approximately 1 percent of Coke's pretax profits in 1974, and 42 percent of its output went to company-owned bottling plants serving 14 percent of the U.S. population, and 38 percent went to independent franchised bottlers.[16]

NEW COMPETITORS—THE INTRUDERS

"Concentrate production is a license to steal," an industry analyst remarked. "The industry is bound to attract competitive interest." While other industry observers did not agree with the "extremity" of this judgment, they did agree that the industry was most profitable. They noted that compound earnings growth among the industry leaders ranged from 10.5 percent to 16.8 percent and ROI capital ranged from 12.3 percent to 25.4 percent for the five-year period ending in 1974.

In 1976 old players were experimenting with new games and new players were joining the battle. Cash-and-carry chains were making their appearance in the United States and Canada. Shasta Beverages, with a different concept of distribution, was moving from a regional to a national basis; beverage powders were expanding in sales volume;

---

[16] Mr. Ogden, Coca-Cola Company, quoted in summary of and excerpts from the *Hearing before the Federal Trade Commission.* Kuhn Loeb summary, May 5–9, 1975, p. 1E.

and rumors of significant new technological developments were "bubbling," in trade circles.

Cash-and-carry franchise outlets

The original cash-and-carry concept combined soft-drink bottling and retailing functions in a single company. Independent bottlers, whose proprietary brands were being pushed out of supermarkets by national brands, sold their beverages at reduced markups from their own plant or at a separate retail store. While data were difficult to obtain, some industry observers estimated that cash-and-carry sales accounted for between 2 percent and 10 percent of packaged soft-drink sales, depending on the region in the United States, and a higher percentage in Canada.

In the early 1970s, local bottlers' interest in cash-and-carry operations accelerated as two firms—Towne Club and Pop Shoppes—developed a franchise system of operations for that market. Towne Club, formerly an independent bottler, owned and operated 40 sales outlets in the metropolitan Detroit area, supplying these operations from a central bottling facility. In addition, Towne Club had franchises in six other metropolitan areas in five states with over 100 outlets.

Pop Shoppes, a Canadian operation, opened its first stateside operation in Phoenix, Arizona, in 1972. In 1976 the company had 24 factory plants in the United States and 25 in Canada supplying approximately 400 retail outlets. Both firms planned major further expansion; and in 1975, Pop Shoppes' major Canadian competitor, Pick-A-Pop, sold a 50 percent interest to Moxie Industries, an Atlanta-based concentrate producer. That firm immediately began franchising operations in the western United States.

Pop Shoppes, for example, provided a franchised store owner with site selection tips, marketing plans, advertising and co-op promotion plans, and training programs. Typically, the independent bottler would open a sales outlet at the bottling plant and expand to other retail sites later. Sales strategy was based on low prices (approximately 50 percent of supermarket prices), only returnable bottles, limited numbers of bottle sizes, a complete flavor range (25–32) from colas to fruit flavors, and fast, quick service. All sales were in case lots, and one of the two persons operating the shop managed the cash register while the other stocked floor displays and helped customers load their cars.

Shasta beverages

Shasta soft drinks were produced and distributed by the Shasta Beverage Division of Consolidated Foods, located in Chicago, Illinois. Consolidated operated in a number of food-related areas: sugar refining, meat packing, convenience food stores, institutional and volume feeding operations, and restaurants; some of its well-known brand names included Sara Lee frozen foods and Popsicles.

Shasta's competitive posture differed substantially from other industry participants. Its soft drinks were not sold via franchised bottlers but were sold directly by the company to buyers who operated their own warehouse facilities. Shasta produced 20 standard flavors, in both diet and conventional formulations, primarily in steel cans (80 percent), but also in 28-ounce and 64-ounce nonreturnable bottles. Product was manufactured in 21 plants, each of which also had warehouse distribution facilities; and in some cases was distributed in Shasta's own trucks, in truckload lots, to large-volume customers.

A 250–300 persons sales force worked with large chain store personnel assisting them with product display, pricing, and promotion. The company gave discounts off list price to chains with the view that the chains would pass that lowered price on to the consumer. More than 80 percent of Shasta's business was to food stores; the company did not attempt to sell the single-service market. Shasta did not impose a geographic limit on its wholesale purchasers. They could resell Shasta products in whatever area they liked. Retail prices were established locally; Shasta beverages were generally sold at higher prices than private labels, but lower than national brand prices.

Since 1960 Shasta (sales $6 million) had gone from regional to national distribution and had achieved a 2.5 percent share of the U.S. market with estimated 1976 sales of over $200 million. The company's 1976 annual report reported that Shasta had initiated price reductions and had increased promotional expenditure. Pretax income increased 13 percent in fiscal 1976.

"POWDERS—A $600 million stir in the soft-drink market"

So headlined the lead article in *Beverage World,* reporting that "mix-it-yourself" drinks were enjoying extraordinary sales success with a 50 percent sales gain in 1974, another 50 percent sales gain in 1975, and predictions for 1976 being similarly optimistic.

> Beverage powders, for years dismissed as "kid stuff" and virtually ignored by most beverage manufacturers, are fast making their presence felt in the market. There are no specific figures indicating that powdered beverages are cutting drastically into carbonated soft-drink volume, but their tremendous sales growth, sparked by consumer resistance to higher priced carbonated drinks . . . clearly shows that powder manufacturers are capturing a share of the carbonated soft-drink market.[17]

In 1976 finished beverage powder gallonage was estimated to be 1.2 billion, about 20 percent of the approximately 6.3 billion gallons of soft drinks expected to be purchased that year.

Beverage syrups and powders had been on the market for almost 50 years. Originally sold as fruit drinks, they offered the homemaker the advantages of low price and carrying convenience. And, in addition, they provided the fountain and institutional market a colorful visual advertising display—a large, glass container with a jet spray of constantly moving, brightly colored juice. In recent years, bottle syrups for home use had declined in sales importance and, therefore, in amount of supermarket shelf space. Beverage mixes came in five basic flavors,

---

[17] John D. Stacey, *Beverage World,* March 1976, p. 30.

and trade sources estimated consumer preferences as (1) lemonade, (2) grape, (3) orange, (4) strawberry, and (5) cherry. Mixes came with sugar, without sugar, and in Pillsbury's new entry "Squoze" a sugar-plus-artificial-sweetener formula that contained half the regular calories, and they were packaged in compact containers with lower per ounce prices for the consumer. Mixes were also available in envelopes or packets (60 percent of market), ranging from 1 to 3 ounces to 12 ounces (retail price 99 cents) and the kitchen-type canisters (40 percent of the market) from 24 to 45 ounces ($3.19 retail).

A random series of interviews with housewives in Boston supermarkets could be summarized by the following:

> I've quit buying the bottled stuff. These mixes are cheaper, they allow me to regulate the amount of sugar the kids get, they don't break my back carrying them to the kitchen from the car, and it cuts down the trip to the dump. My daughter says they are ecologically superior.

Three major food marketing companies dominated the grocery trade mix business in 1976: General Foods' Kool-Aid (40 percent of the market), Borden's Wyler's (40 percent), and Pillsbury's Funny Face and Squoze (10 percent). Each of these firms had substantial marketing skill and distributive capacity. Most employed broad-scale couponing, free premiums, special price offers, and display assistance to the supermarket. All of the companies allocated significant advertising dollar support to these products; Kool-Aid spent $7.6 million in 1974, while Wyler's allocated $1.9 million. One industry source noted that the companies spent $17 million in 1974 and estimated they would spend $30 million in 1975 on beverage powder advertising.

In April 1976, RJR Foods (a division of the former Reynolds Tobacco Company) announced its entry into the field with a powdered mix version of its single-strength, canned, Hawaiian Punch drink. The company allocated $6 million in advertising funds for the first-year introduction. "The consumer shifted away from single-strength fruit juices for economy reasons," a company spokesperson said. "What kept them from totally switching back again as sugar prices came back down was that they discovered manufacturers had vastly improved the quality since they had last tried it as kids."[18]

By 1976 other companies were testing the mix market. A&P and Kroger were leaders in introducing their own private label mixes. This decision had been spurred by the major success of "canister" packaging which gave the retailer a bigger "ticket-price" item to promote. Coca-Cola Foods Division had been test marketing fruit-flavored powders under its Hi-C (a canned single-strength juice line) for almost a year in Florida and Michigan.

There seemed to be some consensus in the trade that the boom in powders had been permanently influenced by what sales executives referred to as "product repositioning." Promotion had moved from selling "kids' " to a "family" drink. Advertising was changed to highlight *soft-*

---

[18] "The Mix-It-Yourself Boom," *Business Week*, May 17, 1976, p. 56.

drink mixes as opposed to fruit drink syrup and powders and shifted from a seasonal to a year-round promotional program. Attractive new display racks were installed next to, or near, the soft-drink shelf space in food stores. Natural flavors were substituted for artificial flavors, and powder packages were supplied to the consumers in an increased number of sizes. In predicting the future, an industry expert noted:

> Beverages powders by their nature probably will accelerate the thrust toward fruit and citrus flavors and possibly affect carbonated soft-drink flavor favorites. In view of the popularity of fruit flavors with young consumers, it poses the question of how much this might change future adult soft-drink flavor preferences.[19]

In addition to a $400 million, 1976 consumer market, the trade sold an estimated $250 million to the food service and institutional feeding market. Of the over 100 companies operating in this field, General Foods led with 15 percent of the volume, followed by Nestle (11 percent), Wyler's (10 percent), and Standard Brands (7 percent).

> This market is both huge and unseen. . . . While public eating places offer opportunities for promoting beverage brands, the institutional market (plants, hospitals, etc.) is often controlled by dieticians. Many such institutions do not serve carbonated beverages, preferring to serve beverages made from powders or syrups. In these outlets, powders compete with syrups . . . buyers frequently switch to the cheapest one.[20]

Product technology

In the course of interviews with industry executives, the researchers heard infrequent references to possible, upcoming technological changes. It was difficult, however, to obtain any definitive information about the specifics of these possible developments or their future impact on the industry. In some overseas markets, an old product—the siphon bottle—was again being pushed as a way of manufacturing carbonated drinks in the home. Another source noted that one firm was experimenting with the sale of packages of carbonated ice cubes and syrup.

A number of references were made to the possible entrance of General Foods and Procter & Gamble into the field. The alleged P&G entry basis would be a self-carbonating product—probably a coating on the bottom of a cup—which would effervesce with the addition of water and syrup. Some observers believed P&G already had patents on such a product. Procter & Gamble's interest, they stated further, was the fact that soft drinks commanded an average of 120 linear feet of chain store shelf space versus 100 for detergents and 45 for coffee; also that soft-drink sales per square foot of shelf space were almost twice that of coffee or detergents.

THE INDUSTRY'S CRITICS

"We are under attack on a number of fronts," an industry executive stated, "but our critical concerns are health issues, the bottle and can

---

[19] John D. Stacey, *Beverage World,* March 1976, p. 35.
[20] Ibid., p. 35.

disposal problems, and antitrust action to break up the franchise system. In some ways the first area is the most difficult with which to deal. Our critics range from government agencies to consumer, health-oriented, private pressure groups, to individual technical critics with strong interest in the safety of specific drugs or the nutritional value of certain ingredients. And the impact of government edict can be disastrous. Do you recall the 1969 cyclamate ban; it almost liquidated Royal Crown— they had specialized in diet drinks with sugar substitutes."

Questions as to the public health record of the industry centered on two key-related issues: first, the more general question as to the nutritional contribution—or danger—of soft drinks on American eating patterns; and, second, on the safety or hazards posed by product ingredients, for example, sugar, caffeine, and chemical additives.

A dietician in a veteran's hospital commented:

> World War I vets are strictly meat and potatoes men. World War II and Korean vets like a more balanced, varied diet. But Vietnam veterans don't eat meals at all. They don't eat breakfast . . . and in the morning they start getting hungry and begin munching hamburgers, hot dogs, French fries, and soft drinks. They'd probably eat every meal at McDonald's if they could.[21]

Nutritional experts engage in lengthy public debates about the dietary wisdom of these "fast-food" eating habits and of possible dangers in the consumption of large quantities of soft drinks.

With per capita soft-drink consumption substantially over 400 8-ounce containers, some nutrition experts questioned the wisdom of ingesting high quantities of sugar into the human body. Dr. Jean Mayer, president of Tufts University, was a strong proponent of this point of view. In a June 20, 1976, *New York Times Magazine* article entitled "The Bitter Truth about Sugar," he stated that "purveyors of health foods and natural foods are unanimous in their statements that white sugar is toxic and . . . there is a strong suspicion that a large sugar intake may be causally related to diabetes." An equally well-respected expert, Dr. Frederick J. Stare, chairman of the Department of Nutrition at Harvard University, took a diametrically opposite position: "There are hazards in foods but they don't come from sugar or additives; they come from eating (and drinking) too much and lack of elementary principles of sanitation."[22]

The Food and Drug Administration in 1969 had banned the use of cyclamates as a sugar substitute in diet soft drinks, alleging that research evidence indicated that it would cause bladder cancer in rats. In 1976 the FDA again ruled against the use of cyclamates, noting that there were "unresolved questions about the product's potential for causing cancer, its effects on growth and reproduction, and the possibility that it might damage chromosomes, the basic genetic apparatus."

In October 1976 Senator Gaylord Nelson, a consistent critic of the Food and Drug Administration, charged that a report by the General Accounting Office "shows that the FDA actually violated the law by

---

[21] *Prevention Magazine,* November 1971, p. 30.
[22] *New York Times Magazine,* Letters section, July 18, 1976.

allowing continued use of saccharin without making final determination of safety."[23] The FDA allowed the use of saccharin for more than four years on a "temporary basis." Saccharin was believed to be the industry's only practical alternative to cyclamates. The most serious circumstance would be if both sweeteners were banned. Drink reformulation would be possible if an approved, noncaloric sweetener could be developed. The risk was that the consumer might or might not like the new taste. The introduction and major success of Diet Dr Pepper and Diet 7UP had occurred during the time saccharin took the place of cyclamates.

In 1976, as a part of its review of several hundred food additives—the so-called GRAS list (Generally Recognized as Safe)—the FDA was reviewing the safety status of caffeine. A "split" report, released by the department, indicated that some members believed it was "prudent to assume" there might be a potential health hazard, particularly for children because cola drinks might expose them to daily caffeine in their period of brain growth and development. A 12-ounce cola drink contains two thirds the caffeine found in a cup of coffee.

The 1970s had witnessed a steady acceleration in criticism of the industry for its part in "trash pollution." Senators Hatfield, Javits, McGovern, Packwood, and Stafford introduced a bill in February of 1975 "to prohibit the introduction into interstate commerce of nonreturnable beverage containers." While this bill failed to pass, beginning in September 1975, "throwaways" were banned from federal installations and national parks by administrative order.

On the state level, a ban on throwaways was in force in Vermont and Oregon where proponents stated it had reduced can and bottle litter along the roads by 75 percent. Industry spokespersons disagreed with this finding. In the November 1976 elections, four states—Colorado, Massachusetts, Maine and Michigan—had proposals for mandatory deposits on bottles and cans for voter consideration. The Maine plan called for a 5-cent deposit on bottles used by several firms, a 10-cent deposit on bottles used by one firm only; deposits were also required on beverage cans. In addition, efforts were being made to ban the use of pull-top lids for beverage cans. The editor of the industry's leading trade magazine commented:

> The beverage industries and the United States of America still survive this kind of misdirected, simplistic, well-intentioned, but really dumb legislation. It is not what mandatory deposit bills will do to individual bottlers that matters so much as the potentially disruptive effect they could have on the over-all market picture. Such legislation, for example, might go a long way toward helping the food processing industry in its current effort to position various packs and sizes of powders, concentrates, fruit juices, and fruit flavored drinks as *soft drinks* in both the consumer's mind and in the supermarket. This will have a lot more impact than the development of franchise cash-and-carry soft-drink chains, which are in place and ready to reap the benefits of mandatory deposit legislation in many key states. Most soft-drink bottlers are in no position to either fight or join such a

---

[23] *The New York Times,* Wednesday, October 26, 1976, p. 40.

shift in products, packaging, sales, and marketing. And there is no evidence so far that the parent companies are going to respond directly to the threat. Everyone knows that a 4-ounce pouch is no match for a 64-ounce bottle. Right?[24]

Industry executives generally believed that the major costs of a nonreturnable ban, if such legislation were to be widely enacted, would fall on the franchised bottler. One New England–area Dr Pepper bottler commented:

> Excluding the construction of new plant and warehouse space, I would need over $1 million to convert back to returnable bottles. I would need new filling and handling equipment, more delivery trucks and route people to handle the double volume, and money to convert vending machines. The working capital invested in bottle float alone would be tremendous: each 6½ ounce bottle costs 12 cents, and I sell 3 million 24-bottle cases per year.

As an alternative to forced deposit systems and nonreturnable bans, the industry supported a group called the National Center for Resource Recovery, Inc. The group was a cooperative effort involving the federal government and packaging manufacturers whose objective would be to fund profit-making ventures to reclaim all of a municipality's solid waste, 6 percent of which would be reclaimable as energy. Pilot projects were already under way in St. Louis, New Orleans, and Macon, Georgia. Should the project expand to the national level, its initial funding might come from a tax on packaging manufacturers.

A third major regulatory uncertainty concerned Federal Trade Commission action to substantially modify the industry's franchise bottler system. In 1971 the FTC cited the eight major concentrate producers, charging their exclusive territorial agreements were anticompetitive. In what some observers described as a "counterattack," the beverage industry pressed Congress for legislative approval of the exclusive territorial franchise system. The industry's bill came close to passing in 1972, but failed. Industry efforts to gain congressional support of their position continued in 1976. In 1975 FTC Administrative Law Judge J. P. Dufresne ruled that territorial provisions in franchise agreements did not unreasonably restrain trade but resulted in greater rather than lessened competition. The FTC appealed this decision and hearings continued into 1976.

The franchise controversy was covered in the business press, was a popular topic area in industry and company publications, and was investigated by the Senate Subcommittee on Antitrust and Monopoly in the summer and fall of 1972. Thousands of pages of data resulted. The researcher has attempted to summarize the critical arguments for both government and industry; chances for error or omission, however, are substantial.

The franchise system, pioneered by Coca-Cola, authorizes a bottler to manufacture, distribute, price, and sell a soft drink only in a desig-

---

[24] "The Editor's Notebook," *Beverage World,* July 1976, p. 8.

nated territory. In summary, the FTC alleged that this exclusive franchise territory system kept soft-drink prices artificially high and prevented intrabrand price competition. The specific charge stated:

> Respondent's contracts, agreements, acts, practices, and method of competition aforesaid have had, and may continue to have, the effect of lessening competition in the advertising, merchandising, offering for sale, and sale of premix and postmix syrups and soft-drink products, deprive, and may continue to deprive, the public of the benefits of competition . . . in methods of competition and unfair acts or practices, in commerce, in violation of Section 5 of the Federal Trade Commission Act.'

The complaint ordered franchise companies to "cease and desist" from entering into agreements which prevented bottlers from selling products to any type of customer in any location, from restricting the location of the bottler's place of business, and from refusing to sell concentrate to or otherwise penalizing a bottler for selling outside his territory or selling to central warehousing customers. In the words of one industry executive, "The FTC was gung-ho to sink us, and it was frightening."

In a more philosophical vein, the counsel to the Senate subcommittee stated that committee's interest in the question:

> Isn't it inevitable that in this industry there is going to be change from the status quo in order to accommodate modern technology and modes of distribution trends, and if there is, shouldn't the shift in business be determined by the marketplace without having erected artificial restraints which in large part permit the parent company to determine who is going to stay in business and who is not going to stay in business?

At the hearings, a number of witnesses, many of whom operated small bottling operations, testified in opposition to the FTC complaint. They argued that breaking down the franchise system would (1) drive many small bottlers, particularly those near large metropolitan areas, out of business; (2) would reduce product availability because large bottlers wouldn't want to service small customers; (3) would reduce local advertising and promotion funds; (4) would increase the power of chain stores to push their own private labels; (5) the era of returnable bottles would end since chain stores would not want to handle them and door-to-door delivery and pickup would diminish; and (6) soft-drink prices would not drop.

Ms. Alice Brady, of Kuhn Loeb & Company, summarized the FTC charges and the industry's rebuttal as follows:

> The marketing structure of the soft-drink industry, as described by the Coca-Cola bottlers who have testified to date, has remained practically unchanged for almost 70 years. This structure has depended on substantial capital investment by individual entrepreneurs, whose willingness to invest in the industry was closely tied to the contractual promise of territorial exclusivity. Under the umbrella thus provided, the individual bottling organizations have been encouraged to develop their markets to the fullest extent possible, serving all potential customers in each area at a uniform price, regardless of account size . . . territorial protection has enabled (in

fact, forced) the small bottler to place his products in virtually every conceivable outlet, thereby achieving a total fluid volume that would be otherwise unattainable . . . removal of the territorial umbrella would probably cause industry-wide contraction in the number of bottling companies, package and brand varieties, and accounts served. In addition, a multi-tiered pricing structure would be the likely result, with the probability of higher average unit price. Ineluctably tied to the foregoing would be a decline in total consumption of soft-drink gallonage.[25]

The Federal Trade Commission views were summarized by Alan S. Ward, director of the Bureau of Competition, before the Senate committee. He stressed three points:

In summary, territorial restrictions in the soft-drink industry have actually contributed to the decline in the number of bottlers. Small bottlers have been denied the opportunity of expanding their sales and growing to efficient size, and, thereby, to continue to do business in this industry. Consequently, they have been induced to leave the industry. If the territorial restrictions are removed, small bottlers will be given an opportunity to expand their operations to the point at which they can support an efficient plant.

Ending territorial restrictions will neither cause the end of service to small customers nor force them to pay higher prices. Many small soft-drink buyers currently purchase other food products from wholesalers who operate warehouses. Such wholesalers will provide soft drinks to small stores along with other food products. Indeed, it may be cheaper for these small stores to depend on one source for all their food product needs rather than having to split their business as currently must be done.

The end of territorial restrictions will not have the drastic effect on ecology predicted by some bottlers. First, more and more consumers are demanding nonreusable containers and this trend would be expected to continue regardless of whether territorial restrictions are eliminated or maintained. Second, chain grocers handle the products demanded by consumers and handle returnables if consumers wish these products.[26]

An industry analyst agreed with some of Mr. Ward's conclusions, stating:

Warehouse distribution is coming. A "drop" to a vending outlet or Mom or Pop store costs 45 cents. The average delivery cost per case is 35 cents, but the cost for the warehouse delivery is but 15 cents. Major concentrate producers and the consumer would benefit from warehouse deliveries via a reduction in national brand prices. The current franchised bottler system is the main deterrent to warehouse delivery, and this is because of the relatively small size of a franchise territory. Franchise territories were originally defined when there was a single 6½-ounce returnable package, and small territories were very efficient for handling this type of distribution. Now, with package and flavor proliferation and the big increase in one-way bottles, traditional franchise territories are inefficient. Smaller territories were also advantageous to the concentrate companies because

---

[25] Summary of and excerpts from the *Hearing before the Federal Trade Commission in the matter of Coca-Cola Company et al.*, May 19–23, 1975, pp. 1792–2468.

[26] *Hearings before the Subcommittee on Antitrust and Monopoly*, 92d Congress, part I, p. 225.

they could increase consumption with total availability and pushed their bottlers to service vending machines and small outlets. Now, with the increase in transportation costs, bottlers realize they're losing money on those small stops, but they need them for volume.

Not all franchise owners were in sympathy with the "industry" position taken at the Subcommittee hearings. A critical view of the franchise system was outlined by Mr. John M. Alden, president of the Royal Crown Bottling Corporation of Denver, Colorado, in 10 pages of committee testimony. Excerpts from his testimony follow:

> What protections do territorial restrictions provide, then, if there is not sufficient business in a franchise area to support a costly, modern, and efficient plant? The concentrate houses know this. They have had game plans and programs, which they are implementing . . . they definitely plan to concentrate the industry with major production centers and major distribution centers.
>
> This concept in itself, put to work, eliminates a lot of small bottlers. At best, it permits that little bottler to become a distributor, and just a distributor. What does that have to do with territorial restrictions?
>
> We think it is only a matter of time before supermarket purchases of soft drinks will have to be totally serviced at the central warehouse. We are also convinced that every major concentrate house, in the confines of their own offices, agrees. The strategy question is, what the hell do we do about it?
>
> At the moment concentrate houses are frozen with a lot of franchise agreements. If all the franchise contracts could be washed out tomorrow, I believe the major concentrate companies would happily go ahead and operate unburdened, free of small bottlers. But, at this hour, the courts are honoring the validity of the bottlers' trademark licensing agreements.
>
> They may say, "This man has paid for this franchise. You just can't throw him out the window. He has some equity in it." And if you add it up, and laminated all these sums of money, this involves sums of money too big for even the largest concentrate houses in the country to pay off on. Therefore, another strategy and alternate must be developed.
>
> Every major concentrate house has already set targets and time schedules for the consolidation of production and distribution of their major brands concentrated in major trading areas where the food-store warehouses are located. The clue is in the hurried efforts during the past year to structure production centers and distribution enclaves in major marketing areas, and the emphasis there is on the warehouse profile rather than the old geographical county lines on which franchise areas were crudely structured. In other words, the concentrate houses are "getting on the ball" so territorial restrictions can be ignored if they are still in effect. To me, it looks like an adaptation of the cartel system used by European corporate giants to divide the world market among themselves. I think we now have in this country a version of the cartel method of allocating market areas, which will end up being shared by not more than 100 or 200 major bottler-canner companies, at most, and any remaining bottlers, still alive, will be doing yeoman's work as distributors for the key bottler and canning operations in the hands of a few giants.
>
> As one of the few voices in the soft-drink industry to speak up for elimination of territorial restrictions, I do so fully aware of continued harassment

and possible additional reprisal actions and economic sanctions that may be initiated against my operation by concentrate house interests.[27]

Senior officers of the concentrate firms unanimously and publicly backed the franchise system. W. W. Clements, president of the Dr Pepper Company, testified to the same committee about the dangers in the government's suit, noting:

> The small independent bottler would be a thing of the past. Dr Pepper would be forced into owning and operating a great number of bottling plants throughout the United States. . . . This would happen in varying degrees to other brands. However, the larger companies with greater resources would have a tremendous advantage. The industry would end up with a very few large bottling companies, and they would all be owned by large companies, such as franchise companies, public-owned companies, and food chains.

Predictions of the future varied by market segment. With regard to diet drinks an analyst stated:

> There is real potential to create new markets and increase consumption in diet beverages. Company advertising and promotional activities are very effective in increasing soft-drink consumption, but advertising expenditures for diet drinks have been disproportionately low. Most companies are one-product companies, even Coke. They never needed diet-drink sales or secondary flavors before, and were never very successful with them. Coke grew at 6.5 percent per year on sales of regular Coke alone. No company except Seven-Up has been very aggressive with their diet brands, especially the colas. They've been scared stiff to heavily promote diet brands because they thought they would lose brand loyalty and brand identity for their main products. Now the major companies can't meet their growth objectives with their flagship brands.

A number of analysts were optimistic about the fountain market; one made the following comments:

> Fountain, or on-premise sales in food service outlets, is the only growth area left in the domestic soft-drink industry, and it belongs to Coke. The growth of fast-food chains has been responsible for the rapid growth of sales in this area, and the chains' continued rapid growth will continue at 6–8 percent per year for the next five to seven years.
>
> The fountain business is very different. The retailer buys syrup from an independent jobber or directly from the concentrate manufacturer. Most bottlers did not sell fountain syrup. The syrup is mixed with carbonated water by a dispenser at the point of purchase. There are 5–6,000 independent jobbers who have no territorial limitations on their sales areas. For most jobbers, soft drinks are loss leaders, for example, Martin Brauer distributes Coke syrup to McDonald's at only pennies per gallon.
>
> Coke dominates the fountain market. Seventeen percent of its total domestic gallonage is sold through fast-food chains, and an additional 16 percent is sold through other types of food service outlets, such as restaurants and ice cream shops. Pepsi was late in entering the fountain sales part of the business and has a very convoluted distribution structure. Fran-

---

[27] Ibid., pp. 370–80.

chised Pepsi bottlers formulate syrup or purchase it from the company, then sell it to jobbers who, in turn, sell to retail outlets. Consequently, only 15 percent of Pepsi's total gallonage is from on-premise sales, and the proportion will probably diminish in the future. The only major chain to carry Pepsi is Burger King.

Another analyst commenting on Coke's competitive position stated:

> Intensified brand and price competition in the 1977–80 period would be unlikely to dent Coca-Cola's dominant position in the fountain or vending markets. About one-half of Coke's domestic fountain installations are owned by the Coca-Cola Company, and major restaurant chains are unlikely to switch allegiance. A longer term concern, albeit premature, is the possibility of backward integration into soft drinks by a restaurant chain to develop an additional and significant profit center. McDonald's Corporation currently accounts for an estimated 10 percent of Coca-Cola's fountain volume or 3 percent of Coke's domestic syrup gallonage, has a captive and expanding customer base, and has become increasingly new-product oriented.[28]

Other analysts estimated Coke's share of the fountain market as close to 80 percent, but they expected competition to increase as Dr Pepper and Seven-Up made increased fountain sales a major objective of growth strategies. "The picture spells competition, challenge, and, bluntly, we must also gain share from the competition to meet our new sales objectives," a Seven-Up executive remarked to a *Beverage World* editor in April 1976. Two analysts commented on the future of the vending machine market:

> In the past, the percent of sales through vending was higher, but the energy shortage hit vending hard. Also, prices in vendors only change in fixed increments, for example, 5 cents or 10 cents and price changes are slow to catch up with rising distribution costs. In the last year or so, vending has become more profitable due to price increases, and all the concentrate companies are trying to increase their participation in the vending market.
>
> Bottle, can, and cup vending account for approximately 20 percent of soft-drink sales in the United States today, but it's a declining area. For independent soft-drink bottlers, the vending part of their business just keeps the public aware of their products. But now, distribution costs are rising so fast that I see zero or a net decrease of 1.5 percent in industry sales through vending outlets.

A prediction as to the future of the third major market segment— food stores—was made by another analyst:

> In the last few years, the total number of food stores has been declining, and there has been a net contraction of shelf space for soft drinks. Sales growth through the industry's most important outlet will be at most 1 or 2 percent per year.

FUTURE MARKET DIRECTIONS—A CLOUDY CRYSTAL BALL

> Where is this industry going in the next decade? I wish I knew the answer. Just skim the trade press and you get a feel for the jet pace of

---

[28] Paine Webber Jackson and Curtis, "Soft Drink and Beer—Midyear, 1976 Review."

this game. Coke is test marketing a health drink called Samson! Implications? Washington is in on every issue. If franchising breaks down, this industry may go the way beer has—just a dozen major firms. Two more good-sized franchise operations have just been purchased by conglomerates.

Did you see that West German health officials have removed cyclamates and saccharin from the cancer-producing agents list, and they are both available for use in soft drinks? Our FDA won't release cyclamates! And the international market's fascinating: Schweppes is moving into the USSR and Shasta into Canada. We are even getting new products—Nestle and Lipton are pushing canned tea. They are big internationally, too, and already are in fruit drinks abroad.

OK, Professor, what's *your* answer? What's coming up, when, and what does it mean for me?

Hospital Affiliates International, Inc., and the hospital management industry

HOSPITAL AFFILIATES INTERNATIONAL, INC. (HAI), was one of the largest companies in the emerging hospital management industry in the United States, and the leader in the management contract segment of the industry with one third of the total market in 1976. HAI owned 25 hospitals in several states, and managed 50 other hospitals under contract. Founded only in 1968, HAI had grown from $20.1 million in sales and $859,000 in profits in 1969 to $137 million in sales and $5.3 million in profits by 1976, for an annual compound growth rate of 32 percent and 30 percent, respectively. Exhibits 1 and 2 present a financial summary of HAI.

Mr. Jack R. Anderson, president and chief executive officer of HAI, anticipated continued vigorous growth for HAI, especially in the contract management segment of the market:

> I am confident that over the next 5 to 10 years contract management will become one of the standard alternatives a hospital's board of directors investigates before reaching a decision about the type of management that is best for its institution. When this happens, a market of 2,000 hospitals will be created, and I would hope that HAI could keep 25 percent of that market. I would also imagine that HAI will be in businesses that we haven't even thought of yet, maybe ones that don't even exist yet. Hospital management is one of the few remaining cottage industries. The opportunities for a firm that can help promote and manage the change are very great indeed.

However, the contract management market had attracted a number of large and aggressive competitors, such as American Medical International and National Medical Enterprises, resulting in an increased frequency of multiple bids for contracts. In addition, the question of contract renewal was becoming increasingly important as the initial contracts reached maturity. The appropriate responses to these changes were among the issues facing HAI as it looked toward the future.

Exhibit 1

HOSPITAL AFFILIATES INTERNATIONAL, INC., AND THE HOSPITAL MANAGEMENT INDUSTRY

Summary of Income Statements
($ millions)

	1976	1975	1974	1973	1972	1971
Net revenues	$137.8	$105.9	$68.2	$54.8	$50.3	$38.3
Operating expenses	116.2	89.5	55.4	44.1	40.7	31.3
Depreciation and amortization	5.1	3.6	2.3	1.7	1.6	1.2
Interest expenses	6.1	5.4	3.7	3.0	2.6	1.9
Cost of new facilities	—	(0.2)	(0.5)	(0.6)	(0.4)	(0.2)
Total expenses	127.4	98.3	60.9	48.2	44.5	34.2
Profit before taxes	10.4	7.6	7.3	6.6	5.8	4.1
Income taxes	5.0	3.4	3.4	3.0	2.6	2.0
Net earnings	$ 5.3	$ 4.2	$ 3.9	$ 3.6	$ 3.2	$ 2.1
Average shares outstanding (000)	2,454	2,348	2,749	2,950	2,967	2,599
Earnings per share (fully diluted)	$1.95	$1.57	$1.34	$1.14	$0.99	$0.78

Note: Numbers may not add due to rounding.
Source: Form 10-K and annual reports.

Exhibit 2

HOSPITAL AFFILIATES INTERNATIONAL, INC., AND THE HOSPITAL MANAGEMENT INDUSTRY
Summary of Balance Sheets
($ millions)

Assets	1976	1975	1974	1973	1972	1971
Current assets:						
Cash	$ 7.2	$ 6.9	$ 6.6	$ 6.1	$ 4.8	$ 5.2
Accounts receivable (net)	28.8	25.4	20.9	12.7	10.5	8.8
Supplies, at cost	3.6	3.1	2.4	1.6	1.5	1.5
Prepaid expenses	1.2	0.7	0.4	0.3	0.5	0.6
Total current assets	40.8	36.1	30.3	20.7	17.3	16.1
Construction funds		0.1	0.6	3.2	4.9	—
Long-term accounts receivable	10.4	9.7	8.1	6.7	2.7	—
Total construction funds and long-term accounts receivable	10.4	9.8	8.7	9.9	7.6	—
Property and equipment:						
Land	7.5	7.2	6.8	7.3	8.7	8.5
Buildings	38.6	32.7	32.1	28.3	32.6	25.1
Leasehold rights	6.8	6.9	7.2	1.0	0.8	0.4
Equipment	30.1	26.9	16.1	9.3	8.1	6.2
Construction in progress	0.3	0.5	1.1	7.3	1.4	1.5
Total property and equipment	83.2	74.2	63.3	53.2	51.6	21.7
Accumulated depreciation and amortization	(13.4)	(9.9)	(7.2)	(6.6)	(5.6)	(4.2)
Net property and equipment	69.8	64.3	56.1	46.6	46.0	37.5
Other assets	20.6	21.0	17.6	17.1	17.5	19.4
Total assets	$141.7	$131.2	$112.7	$94.3	$88.4	$73.0

Liabilities

Current liabilities:						
Accounts payable	$ 8.8	$ 8.0	$ 7.4	$ 3.1	$ 4.9	$ 3.0
Accrued expenses	4.9	3.5	2.3	1.9	1.4	4.4
Income taxes	3.9	4.4	5.6	4.1	2.0	1.7
Current portion of long-term debt	3.6	3.2	3.1	3.0	2.3	2.2
Total current liabilities	21.2	19.1	18.4	12.1	10.6	11.3
Long-term debt	59.9	54.4	43.9	37.2	35.6	21.8
Deferred income taxes	6.2	5.8	2.7	1.7	1.0	0.6
Deferred income	—	1.0	1.0	1.1	—	—
Convertible and subordinated debentures	15.2	16.8	16.9	11.0	12.5	14.1
Total stockholders' equity	39.3	34.1	29.8	31.2	28.7	25.2
Total liabilities	$141.7	$131.2	112.7	$94.3	$88.4	$73.0

Note: Numbers may not add due to rounding.
Source: Form 10-K and annual reports.

THE HOSPITAL MANAGEMENT INDUSTRY

The $56 billion U.S. hospital industry was undergoing change in 1977, spurred on in large part by a new force in the industry—the hospital management company. Investor-owned hospitals, or for-profit hospitals owned by investing groups, accounted for a rapidly growing proportion of hospitals. Of the 7,100 hospitals in the United States in 1976, 1,000 were investor owned, up from 852 in 1966. Large-scale hospital management companies owned 378 of these, and the number was growing. In addition to owning hospitals, hospital management companies managed both investor-owned and voluntary not-for-profit hospitals under contract. A total of approximately 165 hospitals were under management contract in 1976, up from zero in 1970.

The 31 hospital management companies in 1976 owned from 3 to as many as 70 hospitals and managed as many as 50 hospitals. The largest management company, Hospital Corporation of America (HCA), had revenues of $392 million in 1975, and revenues for the six largest hospital chains totaled $1.1 billion in 1975. Profit growth in the hospital management industry had been at a rate of 25 percent per year since the industry was created in 1968 (health-care spending had grown at an 11.4 percent rate from 1971 to 1976), and one leading source predicted that hospital management company revenues would grow at 22 percent per year for the next decade. By 1985, therefore, hospital management could be a $20 billion industry, making the industry comparable in size to the defense segment of the aircraft industry today.

HISTORY OF THE HOSPITAL INDUSTRY

In 1873 the U.S. Bureau of Education reported 178 hospitals of all types in the United States. By 1909, according to the American Medical Association, there were 4,359 hospitals. During this period the development of surgical procedures, radiology, and the consequent need for antiseptic conditions and specialized equipment made the hospital indispensable to physicians. Previously, medical care had been administered in private homes and doctors' offices.

The rapid growth in the need for hospitals resulted in construction of a large number of investor-owned facilities. But as growth in demand for hospital beds moderated in the 1930s, investor-owned hospitals began to decline as voluntary not-for-profit hospitals without any profitability constraints were built. By 1940 the proportion of investor-owned hospitals had dropped to 25 percent. These trends were accelerated by the passage of the Hill-Burton Act in 1946, which enabled communities to obtain federal matching funds for construction of their own nonprofit hospitals. The older independent investor-owned hospitals found themselves short of capital and at a competitive disadvantage and many either closed down or sold out to their communities. By 1968 only 11 percent of all hospitals were investor owned.

During the late 1960s, however, the investor-owned segment of the hospital industry revived. Passage of the medicare and medicaid legislation in 1965 created renewed investor interest in hospitals and nursing homes. Most important in sparking this was the creation of a large potential government-paid demand, and provisions in the legislation allowing investor-owned hospitals a reasonable return on equity on government-reimbursed services (the figure was currently about 11 percent pretax). Most of the investor-owned hospitals were owned by small groups of physicians or entrepreneurs, and were not in a position to capitalize on the new boom. Many were short of capital, inefficiently operated, unable to control the inflationary increases in expenses that occurred during the period, and incapable of dealing effectively with increasingly complex government regulations.

This situation created an opportunity for new firms to enter the industry, and in the next five years over 30 hospital management companies were organized. The fledgling companies built some new hospitals themselves, but nearly all of their growth came from acquisitions. By 1970 hospital management firms had acquired 246 investor-owned hospitals with 25,135 beds, representing 24 percent and 39 percent of the investor-owned hospitals and beds, respectively. The chains purchased financially troubled but fundamentally sound hospitals, as well as some very profitable hospitals for higher prices. The buoyant stock market of the late 1960s and early 1970s resulted in hospital management company price-earnings multiples of 30–40, which permitted acquisitions of hospitals for stock and frequent public equity sales.

Hospital management company stock prices collapsed in the general economic recession in 1972, making the acquisition route for growth more difficult. Most hospital management companies shifted their emphasis in two directions. First, they moved increasingly toward construction activities (both of new hospitals and upgrading and expanding existing facilities), which were financed with internal cash flow and unused debt capacity. From 1970 to 1974, for example, HCA constructed an average of six hospitals per year, while Humana, Inc., built 21 hospitals between 1973 and 1975. By 1975, however, industry debt ratios had risen as high as 75 percent of capitalization and construction activity had slowed in the industry. Even if stock prices were to recover, industry observers saw few remaining acquisition opportunities left in the industry with most of the attractive candidates having already been acquired. Also, according to David Jones, president of Humana (a leading hospital management firm):

> Now we can only replace hospitals rather than build them because we have creamed the fast-growing parts of the country where the need for new hospitals existed. There is an untapped market, but it won't be tappable until hundreds of inefficient nonprofit hospitals being kept alive by government subsidy are allowed to die.[1]

The second major thrust of the management companies was into hospital management contracts, particularly in recent years as financial constraints led firms to seek less capital-intensive ways than ownership

---

[1] "Humana's Hopes," *Forbes*, September 1, 1977.

of achieving growth. While most of the chains, as well as some outside firms, had signed management contracts starting as early as 1971, Hospital Affiliates International (HAI) had been the industry leader in management contracts from the beginning. HAI managed 50 hospitals in early 1977 representing approximately one third of the management contracts then in force.

PROFILE OF THE HOSPITAL INDUSTRY

Hospitals could be characterized in a number of different ways, including ownership, type of patient treated, and whether they were teaching or nonteaching. Community hospitals (5,977 in 1975) represented the competitive reference group for the hospital management companies. Community hospitals were acute-care general hospitals not owned by the federal government. According to American Hospital Association, 57 percent of all community hospitals (and 70 percent of the beds) were nonprofit "voluntary" hospitals in 1975. A number of these were owned or operated by religious groups. Thirty percent of all community hospitals (22 percent of the beds) were controlled by state and local government, and 13 percent of the hospitals (8 percent of the beds) were investor owned in 1975 (Exhibit 3).

Geographic concentration of investor-owned hospitals varied considerably. Seventy-two percent of investor-owned hospitals were located in South Atlantic, West South Central, and Pacific regions. California, Texas, Louisiana, and New York accounted for 59 percent of the total, while 29 states had five or fewer investor-owned hospitals. In addition to regional differences in the concentration of investor-owned hospitals there were urban-rural differences. Fifty-six percent of investor-owned hospitals were in metropolitan areas (with 50,000 people or greater), compared to 42 percent of nonprofit hospitals.

Industry observers generally agreed that the nation's aggregate supply of beds exceeded the demand for hospital services by as much as 20 percent in 1977. However, in rapidly expanding metropolitan areas such as Houston and Phoenix, shortages of hospital facilities did exist.

THE ENVIRONMENT FOR HOSPITALS

Hospitals operated in a very complex decision-making environment relative to that of most manufacturing companies (Exhibit 4). Spending for hospital care had increased 14 percent per year between 1965 and 1975, from $13 to $56 billion. The primary stimulus for the rapid growth had been inflation and the passage of medicare and medicaid legislation. These federally sponsored health insurance plans enfranchised some 12 million people who previously had not been part of the health-care system. In addition, more comprehensive Blue Cross/Blue Shield and private insurance programs plus rising personal income were cited by industry observers as factors encouraging growth.

In 1976 nearly 90 percent of all hospital costs and charges were paid for by so-called third-party payors, with the federal government, Blue

Exhibit 3

CLASSIFICATION OF U.S. HOSPITALS IN 1975

	Number of hospitals	Number of beds (000)	Number of beds per hospital	Total assets ($ millions)
Nongovernment, not-for-profit hospitals	3,391	650	192	$31,482
State and local government hospitals	1,821	211	116	8,070
Investor-owned hospitals	775	70	90	2,288
Total "community" hospitals	5,987	931	156	41,840
Federal government hospitals.......	387	136	351	5,528
Nonfederal psychiatric hospitals......	543	383	701	4,776
Nonfederal tuberculosis hospitals.....	46	8	174	166
Nonfederal long-term general hospitals	221	54	244	1,396
Total other (federal government and long term)	1,197	581	486	11,866
Total all U.S. hospitals	7,184	1,512	211	$53,706

Source: American Hospital Association, *Hospital Statistics*, 1975 ed., and casewriter computations.

Exhibit 4

SCHEMATIC CHART OF HEALTH-CARE DELIVERY SYSTEM
(figures for 1971)

SECTORS OF THE HEALTH SYSTEM

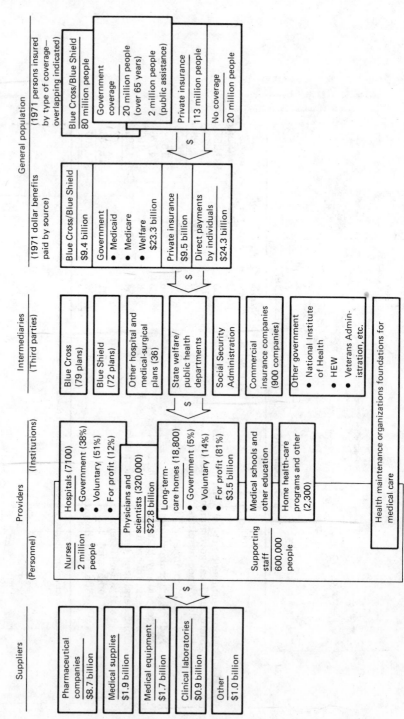

Source: J. B. Silvers and C. K. Prahalad, *Financial Management of Health-Care Industries* (Flushing, N.Y.: Spectrum Publications, 1974), p. 272.

Cross/Blue Shield, and private insurance companies providing the majority of such payments. The federal government's share of total hospital expenditures climbed sharply after the advent of medicare and medicaid, rising from 37 percent in 1965 to 55 percent in 1975. Since government at all levels and particularly the federal government was financing an increasing percentage of the national hospital-care bill, there was increasing regulation of the hospital industry. *Beware*

future

Third-party payors

Medicare was a federal program that provided persons age 65 and over, and certain disabled persons under 65, with hospital and medical insurance benefits. In 1974 medicare accounted for $8 billion (20 percent) of all hospital expenditures. These benefits included reimbursement for the costs of hospitalization for up to 90 days per incident of illness. In 1976 the medicare patient paid only the first $104 of hospital costs, and $26 per day after the 60th day of hospitalization. Hospitals were reimbursed by the government under a formula by which the government paid all "reasonable" direct and indirect costs of the hospital services that were furnished, including depreciation and interest, in addition to a fixed 11 percent pretax return on equity. Reimbursements were subject to examination and adjustments by federal auditors.   *future*

Medicaid was a cooperative federal and state medical assistance program, administered by the states, whereby hospital benefits were available to the medically indigent. In 1974 medicaid accounted for $9 billion (22.5 percent) of all hospital expenditures. While there was only one medicare program there were 50 distinct state medicaid programs, and the rules, regulations, reporting requirements, and reimbursable costs varied from state to state. Most states paid the hospital a fixed per diem rate based on its reimbursable medicaid costs as determined by that state program's individual reimbursement formula, rather than at the hospital's standard billing rate. In order to qualify for medicaid (and medicare) a hospital had to be licensed under applicable state or local laws and comply on a continuing basis with a number of standards related to safety and the quality of patient care. Other government programs administered by the Defense Department for active service personnel and veterans accounted for $4.6 billion (11 percent) of hospital-care expenditure in 1974.   *future*   *!*   *future*

Blue Cross and Blue Shield were private insurance programs that provided subscribers with hospital benefits (Blue Cross) and doctors' services (Blue Shield). In 1974 Blue Cross and Blue Shield accounted for $7.4 billion (18 percent) of hospital expenditures. The program was managed by a network of independent Blue Cross/Blue Shield organizations that varied in their geographic coverage from New York City to multistate regions. Hospitals were paid a negotiated daily (per diem) rate based on their costs as allowable by Blue Cross. The costs allowable by Blue Cross were different from those of medicare and medicaid, and differed from one regional Blue Cross plan to another. The reimbursement formula most widely used was referred to as "retrospective." In the retrospective formula, a hospital's per diem rate for the upcoming   *wow* year was based on its most recent fully audited costs. Therefore, the rate for 1977, which was negotiated in late 1976, was based on 1975 costs plus an inflation factor. The inflation factor also varied between regional Blue Cross plans. Blue Shield made payments directly to physicians on a fixed "fee for service" basis.

The final major category of third-party payors, commercial insurance companies, such as Metropolitan Life, Prudential, and Travelers, provided health insurance directly to individuals and through group insurance plans of employers. Reimbursement was generally based on the hospital's posted fees. In 1974 commercial insurance companies accounted for $6.3 billion (16 percent) of all hospital expenditures.

Trends in hospital utilization

From 1970 to 1975 total admissions to community hospitals had risen about 1.2 percent per year while inpatient days grew at 3 percent due to a rise in the average length of a hospital visit. This was caused primarily by the influx of older and medically indigent patients who often suffered from more serious illnesses, and to the medicare and medicaid regulations which paid for certain services only if such services were rendered in a hospital. Reimbursement and admission procedures under medicare and medicaid had been modified recently in an attempt to reduce the length of stay per admission.

Government regulation of hospitals

A hospital's operations were subject to myriad local, state, and federal government regulations. Hospitals were inspected periodically by state licensing agencies to determine whether the standards of medical care, equipment, and cleanliness necessary for continued licensing were being met. Hospital construction and expansion were also subject to local zoning and building codes. In most areas construction required the additional approval of local hospital planning authorities, which considered the need for additional facilities as well as the suitability of sites in decisions to approve new hospital construction. The piecemeal regulation of hospitals had become so extensive that in 1974 at least 16 federal agencies exercised some control over a hospital.

Late in 1974 the U.S. Congress enacted the Social Security Amendments of 1972 which contained numerous provisions that affected the scope of medicare coverage and the basis for reimbursement of medicare providers. One critical impact of the legislation was the strengthening of areawide health planning agencies called Health Systems Agencies (HSAs). The geographic scope of an areawide health planning agency varied considerably from single cities to multiple state regions. In general, such planning agencies were established to include areas that, from the government's perspective, should share or at least coordinate health care and hospital services.

Under the law, medicare reimbursement could be denied for such costs as depreciation, interest, other expenses, and return on equity for capital expenditures which had not received prior approval by a designated state health planning agency, if such expenditures exceeded

$100,000, altered bed capacity, or substantially changed the services of a hospital. In response to this provision, an increasing number of states had enacted legislation requiring "certificates of need" as a prior condition to hospital construction, expansion, or introduction of major new services. The Social Security Amendments of 1972 also stipulated that acquisitions of hospitals would require prior approval by the local area-wide health planning agencies. The leading investor-owned hospital companies had stated that no adverse effects had been experienced or were anticipated from this provision, but HSAs were becoming increasingly activist in denying planned expansions and promoting lower cost walk-in clinics and home health care.[2]

An additional feature of the Social Security Amendments of 1972 was an important section providing that admissions of medicare and medicaid patients had to be reviewed by an approved Professional Standards Review Organization (PSRO) within one working day following a patient's admission to the hospital, to determine if the admission was necessary. PSROs were also to commence reviewing patient utilization of hospital facilities by July 1, 1978. These provisions were designed to prevent unnecessarily long hospital stays. Though opposition from the medical profession had delayed establishment of the PSROs, industry observers expected implementation of PSROs of 1980.

A second major piece of health-care legislation, the National Health Planning and Resources Development Act, was enacted in 1975. While the full effect of the law was still uncertain, it would increase the role of the federal government in such areas as long-range planning of new hospital and clinic construction, control of discretionary hospital expenditures for such items as consultants and new diagnostic equipment, and prior review of any additions or modifications to existing health-care facilities.

HOSPITAL OPERATIONS

A hospital was in the business of providing acute medical services, such as surgery, and the diagnostic and therapeutic services necessary to support the needs of the acute-care patient.[3] The routine hospital services included room, board, housekeeping, and regular nursing care. Additional services were referred to as "ancillary" and included respiratory therapy, clinical laboratory testing, electrocardiography, ambulance, and emergency room. A hospital's patients were usually divided into inpatient and outpatient categories.

Inpatients

Inpatients were persons who had been admitted to the hospital by a physician and were resident in one of the hospital's beds. The hospital's

---

[2] "Agencies Act to Lower Health Bills by Saying No to Bigger Hospitals," *The Wall Street Journal,* May 5, 1977.

[3] There were also long-term facilities, such as mental institutions and tuberculosis hospitals. These are not discussed in this case, though their operations were basically similar.

ability to service inpatients was limited by its total number of beds and by the division of its beds between different service groups such as pediatric, obstetrics and gynecology, medical-surgical, and intensive care. A hospital was not permitted to place a medical-surgical patient in a bed certified for another area of the hospital. Consequently, it was not unusual to find one area operating at peak capacity while another was virtually unused. The process of modifying the bed composition was cumbersome, bureaucratic, and lengthy. For example, obstetrics had once been a fully utilized service, but the recent slowing of the birth rate had resulted in an oversupply of obstetric beds. However, some community planning agencies were unwilling to allow the hospital to reduce the number of obstetric beds, perpetuating the oversupply condition.

Hospital charges for inpatients were typically divided into a daily room and board fee, and a fixed fee each time an ancillary service was used by the patient. The significance of a hospital's inpatient fee structure for its financial performance was directly related to its mix of patients. If a large percentage of inpatients was covered under any of the cost-based reimbursement programs (Blue Cross, medicare, or medicaid), the fee set by the hospital had little impact on its revenue-generating ability. This was the situation many large urban hospitals found themselves in. If a hospital's patient base was primarily self-paying or privately insured, on the other hand, adjustments to the rate structure could produce meaningful changes in revenues and profits. Hospitals were forced to continually raise their posted fees because of a quirk in the Blue Cross reimbursement formula, which in most plans reimbursed the lesser of audited costs or posted charges.

The daily room and board fee included none of the ancillary services and very little of the cost of drugs (usually only aspirin) but did include meals, regular nursing care, and housekeeping services. Daily room and board charges varied substantially from hospital to hospital and even among hospitals within a community. The hospital then charged the patient for every drug dosage, ancillary service, or other hospital services (such as telephone, television, and admission paperwork) used while in the hospital. The federal and state governments required the hospital to show physical proof that all services charged for had actually been performed in order to qualify for reimbursement, even if reimbursement was on a set fee per diem basis. This meant a separate charge slip for each discrete item in the hospital.

In an attempt to streamline the billing process, many hospitals had adopted the unit packaging concept. All services provided by the hospitals were individually packaged (e.g., every penicillin pill was packaged separately) and charged for. One result of this and reimbursement regulations generally was a virtual explosion of paper flow within the hospital. Industry observers estimated that a hospital processed about 20 unique charges per day per patient. The increased volume of paperwork and the need for more complex and detailed reports to third-party payors had resulted in the rapid growth of computerization in hospitals.

Hospitals often used certain profitable services to offset relatively less profitable ones. For example, an ancillary service such as inhalation therapy was typically quite profitable because the procedure was easily administered by a technician, the required equipment was inexpensive to buy and had a high patient capacity per day, the therapy required frequent repeat visits by the patient, and the third-party payors allowed a fee of $30 per visit. An ancillary service such as this would be used to offset an unprofitable obstetrics ward operating at only 30 percent occupancy, or an open-heart surgery unit used once a month.

Outpatients

Outpatients were persons who used the ancillary services of the hospital without having been admitted. Such patients were usually former inpatients who required additional follow-up treatment in rehabilitation, speech or physical therapy, or patients referred by their private physicians to have laboratory or diagnostic tests performed. The emergency room was also a major source of outpatient visits. Outpatients tended to be more profitable for the hospital than inpatients because third-party payors reimbursed the hospital for outpatient services on a "fee-for-service" rather than a cost basis.

Organization structure

Hospitals were usually organized into two separate units divided along functional lines. The *administrator* managed the hospital and performed the scheduling and billing functions, while the *chief of medicine* was responsible for the actual health care delivered by the hospital. At the top of both organizations was the board of directors. Reporting to the administrator was a department head in charge of each ancillary service, with an assistant administrator sometimes adding a third layer of management. However, in most cases the administrator, assistant administrator, controller, and director of nursing were the key administrative officers in the hospital.

The medical organization was composed entirely of physicians, with a physician responsible for each medical service (e.g., cardiology, radiology) provided by the hospital. Physicians also served on the hospital's medical utilization review committee, which was responsible for ensuring that physicians affiliated with the hospital and permitted to admit patients met certain minimum standards of medical practice.[4] The medical side of the hospital was not as structured as the administrative functions because of the operating style of physicians who typically viewed themselves as professionally equal. The chief of medicine was the top physician in the hospital and represented the interests of the medical staff to the administrator and board. While the administrator had more direct control over subordinates, the chief of medicine often had more prestige in the hospital's community and had more influence over the board of directors. The dual organization structure in hospitals

---

[4] Industry critics argued that these standards were ineffectively low and enforcement very sporadic.

frequently resulted in internal conflicts that had to be resolved by the board over issues such as the quality of care versus the cost of care.

Hospitals' boards of directors were typically composed of prominent members of the community such as business people, educators, religious leaders, and civic-minded individuals. Board positions were unpaid and usually one of many outside commitments its members had in addition to their primary occupation. Board members generally knew little about the day-to-day operations of the hospital and the extent of their managerial sophistication varied a great deal by hospital, with larger urban hospitals generally directed by more experienced board members. Board members were more concerned with establishing and maintaining a high-quality image in the community than with the details of hospital operations, and were sensitive to the quality of care delivered by the hospital and complaints by the patients that the hospital was not responsive to their needs.

Personnel and services

The largest portion of any hospital's budget was employee salaries and related expenses. Personnel costs represented approximately 50 percent of a hospital's operating budget, with nursing services alone accounting for 35 percent of the total. The remainder of the costs were for supplies, interest, taxes, and maintenance. A typical hospital carried over 20,000 separate items in its inventory of supplies (including drugs).

Most hospitals did not act in concert with other hospitals when buying supplies or contracting for such services as laundry and equipment maintenance. However, some independent hospitals had begun to pool their resources to achieve economies in purchasing and shared services. In a few instances, independent hospitals had formed nonprofit hospital holding companies to permit significant purchasing cost reductions to be realized, and shared services on the local level were beginning to grow in 1975. Although the process was proceeding slowly, according to the American Hospital Association two thirds of all hospitals were sharing at least one service in 1976 and government pressure to increase shared services was building.[5]

HOSPITAL MANAGEMENT CONTRACTS

Management contracts were a vehicle through which hospital management companies made their cost-saving, revenue-producing, and purchasing expertise available to independent hospitals. Under the terms of such a contract made with a hospital's board of directors, the management company assumed total responsibility for the hospital's daily operations in exchange for a management fee based on a percent of gross revenues plus an incentive. Most competitors in the industry offered their full range of services only as a single package.

---

[5] Hospitals currently shared such services as laundry, food processing, expensive laboratory and diagnostic equipment, and certain medical services, such as obstetrics and gynecology.

When a management company signed a contract to manage a hospital, it *did not* utilize its own personnel to staff the entire hospital, but rather installed from one to a few key managers. While all hospital management firms installed their own administrator to manage the hospital, some firms also brought in their own director of nursing and a financial officer.

The first four to eight months of a management contract represented a turnaround situation where the management company improved the financial condition of the hospital, reviewed the operations of all the major departments, established quality standards where necessary, and generally streamlined the hospital's operations. These tasks were accomplished either by teams of staff specialists who spent full time consulting with client hospitals or by task forces assembled from the staffs of the management company's owned hospitals. For example, where the task force approach was used, the management company would borrow an administrator from one of its owned hospitals, a director of nursing from another, a financial executive from a third, and an expert in the management of ancillary services from a fourth.

Completely restructuring a hospital's departments and training its personnel could take over a year of intensive effort. As a result, management contracts typically broke even on the fees charged during the first year. Thereafter, industry observers estimated that, in 1976, as much as one half to two thirds of the annual fee was profit. At the end of the term of the contract, the management company faced the requirement that the contract be renewed by the hospital's board.

In addition to installing an administrator and providing the services of staff specialists, a hospital signing a management contract became part of the management company's group purchasing program, often resulting in substantial savings. Since 1971, HAI, HCA, American Medical International (AMI), and Hyatt Medical Management Services Division (a $30 million hospital management subsidiary of Hyatt Corporation), among others, had signed over 165 contracts, with an estimated 100 additional contracts under negotiation in 1977. The market for management contracts included investor-owned, voluntary, local, and state hospitals, many of which were beset with rapidly rising costs and confusing government regulations. Industry sources defined the primary potential market for management contracts to encompass all community hospitals with more than 100 beds, which included some 2,000 institutions.

As of 1977, hospital management companies had signed contracts primarily with that segment of these hospitals that were financially troubled, which consisted of approximately 200–300 hospitals according to industry participants. Hospital financial problems were generally the result of a combination of factors, including poor business procedures in screening patients and billing, poor physician relations, ill-informed trustees, and heavy debt service expenses resulting from past expansion.

The term of a management contract was usually three to five years before renewal, though there was no standard contract in the industry. Fees were generally calculated using a customized formula which took into consideration such factors as the financial results of the managed hospital, improvements in the quality of care delivered, and specific targets for improvements in the operation of the hospital. Average fees ranged from 4 percent to 8 percent of the annual gross revenues of the hospital, with the percentage falling as the hospital's size increased. More and more contracts were being negotiated as flat fees agreed upon in advance, rather than as percentages of revenue. A typical management contract fee could be calculated by multiplying the fee times the hospital's revenues per occupied bed day. For example, with a percentage rate of 4 percent, the revenue per patient day of $150 in a 135-bed hospital that was 70 percent occupied, the annual management fee would be approximately $200,000 per year.

A management firm could achieve some economies in servicing contracts through the clustering of client hospitals in one geographic area, allowing more efficient use of regional management and staff specialist time.

COMPETITION IN THE HOSPITAL MANAGEMENT INDUSTRY

At the end of 1975 there were 31 hospital management companies, owning or leasing a total of 378 hospitals, representing 51,230 beds. The six leading hospital management firms owned 255 hospitals and managed 79 others for a total of 47,805 beds (Exhibit 5). From 1971 to 1975 the number of beds controlled by these six companies had risen by 24 percent per year, compared to a 2.2 percent growth rate for nongovernment community hospital beds in general.

Competitors in the management contract segment of the industry were becoming more numerous. Competitors for management contracts included not only hospital management companies but hotel management companies (for housekeeping and food management services), consulting firms and certified public accounting firms (who became involved in hospital turnarounds), specialized data processing organizations (who offered payroll and accounts receivable systems), and insurance companies (who sold paperwork management systems, computer systems for billing and accounting, and assistance in maximizing third-party reimbursement). In addition, some former hospital administrators had entered the business by establishing small offices to manage one or a few hospitals. A number of these classes of competition had entered the industry recently, though others had been offering services to hospitals for many years. A final category of competitors were nonprofit groups such as the Lutheran Society and Homes Society which provided expertise to groups of hospitals who shared the costs.

Bidding for contracts among the hospital management chains was now commonplace, and fees were beginning to fall. Renewals posed a major uncertainty. According to HCA's vice president and treasurer Sam A. Brooks, Jr.:

> The whole problem of management contracts is that it usually isn't hard to turn a hospital around, and once you do, it is easy to run. Then

Exhibit 5

PROFILE OF LEADING HOSPITAL MANAGEMENT COMPANIES

	1976	1975	1974	1973	1972	1971
Hospital Corporation of America:						
Hospitals owned	68	62	56	53	46	38
Beds owned	14,000	9,946	8,405	7,764	6,834	4,788
Hospitals managed......	17	10	6	4	2	2
Beds managed	2,357	1,702	875	743	470	470
Total beds controlled	16,357	11,648	10,155	9,250	7,774	5,728
National Medical Enterprises:						
Hospitals owned	19	18	17	19	18	14
Beds owned	2,549	2,257	2,195	2,337		
Hospitals managed......	17	11	8	3	—	
Beds managed	1,481	1,481	848	283	—	—
Total beds controlled	4,030	3,738	3,043	2,620	2,342	1,952
American Medical International:						
Hospitals owned	43*	43	44	44	44	20
Beds owned	5,500	5,428	4,977	4,930	4,638	2,222
Hospitals managed......	7	6	5	—	—	—
Beds managed	936	645	599	—	—	—
Total beds controlled	6,436	6,073	5,576	4,930	4,638	2,222
American Medicorp:						
Hospitals owned	35	36	34	33	30	38
Beds owned	7,224	7,314	6,996	6,538	5,544	5,091
Hospitals managed......	15	8	1	1	—	—
Beds managed	1,964	1,089	193	73	—	—
Total beds controlled	9,188	8,403	7,189	6,611	5,544	5,091
Humana:						
Hospitals owned	63	60	54	47	45	37
Beds owned	8,696	7,796	5,940	4,691	4,168	3,090
Hospitals managed......	—	—	—	—	—	—
Beds managed	—	—	—	—	—	—
Total beds controlled	8,696	7,796	5,940	4,691	4,168	3,090
Hospital Affiliates International:						
Hospitals owned	25*	26	27	23	27	27
Beds owned	3,624	3,445	2,833	1,819	2,102	1,973
Hospitals managed......	50	40	26	16	7	2
Beds managed	6,093	5,000	3,120	2,441	571	199
Total beds controlled	9,717	8,445	5,958	4,260	2,673	2,172

* Where a company both acquires and sells hospitals in the same year, the number of beds may change while the number of hospitals remains the same.
Source: Annual reports, Form 10-Ks and Vince De Paulo "Status of Proprietary Chains," *Modern Healthcare,* February 1977, p. 38.

you have to hustle to prove to the hospital that you can do something for them.

One particularly attractive type of management contract was for development, construction, and then management of a hospital for a foreign country. In 1975 HCA was awarded a seven-year $70 million con-

future in other countries?

tract to build and manage Saudi Arabia's new 250-bed King Faisal Specialist Hospital. This was the largest management contract so far awarded.

Competitive strategies of the leading firms

Among the six leading hospital management companies, a variety of competitive strategies had been adopted (financial and operating statistics for the leading firms are shown in Exhibits 5 and 6).

Hospital Corporation of America (HCA). HCA, located in Nashville, Tennessee, was the largest hospital management company in the world. In 1976 HCA owned or leased 68 hospitals containing 14,000 beds. HCA began in 1960 as a single hospital in Nashville, but did not begin to expand until 1968 when Jack Massey, founder of the Kentucky Fried Chicken chain, assumed the position of president. From 1968 to 1970 HCA acquired 21 hospitals for common stock, the remaining 49 hospitals being built by the company from 1968–76. Approximately 50 percent of HCA's hospitals were located in the southeastern United States, especially Florida, Tennessee, Texas, and Virginia.

HCA was known in the industry for its special expertise in the design and construction of new hospitals. The 36 hospitals constructed since 1970 at a cost of $280 million had been standardized in their design and equipment specifications. This had led to shorter construction times, lower construction costs and interest charges, and a reduction in the time required for a new facility to achieve profitability from one year to five months. HCA attempted to build its hospitals in clusters, with a large central facility surrounded by smaller satellite hospitals (usually within a radius of 50 miles). Recently, HCA had begun to concentrate on building new hospitals and replacing older out-of-date hospitals with modern ones. Corporate goals were to add six new owned hospitals (900–1,000 new beds) per year over the next five years. The active building program meant that there were a large number of newer hospitals in the HCA system.

Until recently HCA had used management contracts as a means of achieving ownership of a hospital. Typically, HCA would agree to an interim management arrangement while purchase negotiations were being finalized. Therefore, HCA had only 10 hospital management contracts at the end of 1975. However, in 1976 HCA had announced the establishment of a separate management contract subsidiary under an HCA vice president who had previously been responsible for the marketing of management contracts. In the last few months of 1976 HCA had announced seven new management contracts, and its targeted goal was to have 80 management contracts bringing in $15 million in fees by 1983.

HCA still made use of personnel borrowed from its owned hospitals to staff new management contracts. According to industry observers, however, HCA was actively looking to hire its own group of staff specialists dedicated to management contract operations. HCA's initial management contract marketing activities had met with mixed success, but corporate goals were to add up to 10 new contracts per year over the next several years.

Recently HCA had become the first hospital management company to successfully raise long-term debt in the public market. The company sold $33 million of A-rated 15-year first-mortgage bonds in 1975 and $22 million of common stock in March of 1976.

2. *National Medical Enterprises (NME)*. NME was the smallest of the six leading competitors with 19 owned or leased hospitals, 80 percent located in California which was the company's home base. NME also managed 15 hospitals under contract in 1976, all of its management contracts having been signed in the previous three years. NME had focused its management contract marketing efforts on nonprofit hospitals, and its goals were to add 10 new contracts per year over the next three to five years. NME, the only firm reporting operating income on contracts, reported an operating loss of $818,000 on contract revenues of $3,505,000 in 1976.[6] Despite this, NME claimed it could achieve profit margins of 30–55 percent in the contract management business and expected the recently reorganized division to make a "significant contribution to earnings" in the future.

NME had been active in the management of county hospitals in suburban California communities. Recently, the company had begun to develop a team of staff specialists and shift its marketing focus east from its California base. NME typically installed several company employees in a managed hospital.

In addition to hospital ownership and management, NME offered services in hospital design and construction, and undertook turnkey hospital development projects. NME also managed respiratory therapy departments for 24 hospitals and sold hospital test equipment, hospital supplies, ancillary health services, and industrial and medical gasses. These businesses contributed 8 percent of sales and a 3 percent loss after taxes in 1975.

3. *American Medical International (AMI)*. AMI was the first hospital management company. Founded in California by a bioanalyst in 1956 as a clinical testing laboratory for hospitals, the company purchased two financially troubled customer hospitals. By 1975 AMI owned 43 hospitals after an aggressive facilities expansion and modernization program, the majority in California and Texas, and had been the first hospital management company to expand internationally, owning hospitals in England and Switzerland. AMI had only seven hospitals under management contracts at the end of 1976, but its corporate goals included "rapid expansion" in that market. The company also considered the international market a significant source of future expansion for its contract business. AMI did *not* have a pool of staff specialists but utilized personnel borrowed from its owned hospitals.

---

[6] The contract division contained an undisclosed amount of revenues and expenses due to a medical education subsidiary, operating medical buildings, and international development activities. International development costs were $626,000 in 1976 while losses on the medical education subsidiary were reported as $271,000 (annual report).

Exhibit 6

FINANCIAL PROFILE OF LEADING COMPETITORS

($ millions)

	1976	1975	1974	1973	1972	1971
Hospital Corporation of America:						
Sales	$506.5	$392.9	$297.7	$223.1	$172.7	$138.2
Profits	27.3	20.9	15.8	12.3	10.4	8.5
Assets	600.0	506.2	415.8	319.7	274.0	207.8
Equity	187.9	143.2	122.3	108.1	91.3	75.7
Return on sales (percent)	5	5	5	6	6	6
Return on assets (percent)	5	4	4	4	4	4
Return on equity (percent)	15	15	13	11	11	11
Current ratio	1.46	1.51	1.51	1.43	1.32	1.83
Long-term debt/stockholders' equity	1.64	2.02	1.78	1.53	1.50	1.37
Average annual price-earnings ratio	8.9	8.8	6.2	12.7	35.0	34.7
National Medical Enterprises:						
Sales	116.1	95.2	74.9	56.7	32.4	26.1
Profits	5.4	4.1	3.5	3.3	2.2	1.8
Assets	183.0	147.8	124.3	115.8	84.5	52.5
Equity	46.6	40.8	37.0	34.4	31.3	28.4
Return on sales (percent)	5	4	5	6	7	7
Return on assets (percent)	3	3	3	3	3	3
Return on equity (percent)	12	10	9	10	7	6
Current ratio	1.65	1.61	1.59	2.13	1.11	1.05
Long-term debt/stockholders' equity	2.11	1.97	1.81	1.89	1.27	0.5
Average annual price-earnings ratio	4.1	3.0	5.2	13.3	22.0	18.0
American Medical International:						
Sales	250.3	219.3	170.1	146.9	134.4	113.9
Profits	8.7	5.2	5.2	7.5	7.5	4.8
Assets	311.1	288.5	258.5	207.5	162.1	129.2

Equity	93.0	83.4	79.5	75.7	71.4	61.1
Return on sales (percent)	3	2	3	5	6	5
Return on assets (percent)	3	2	2	4	5	4
Return on equity (percent)	9	6	7	10	11	9
Current ratio	1.82	1.77	1.90	1.83	1.74	1.65
Long-term debt/stockholders' equity	1.66	1.85	1.68	1.30	0.89	0.48
Average annual price-earnings ratio	5.3	5.4	6.9	21.2	34.3	28.0
American Medicorp:						
Sales	335.0	331.8	274.7	213.6	182.2	151.2
Profits	15.8	13.0	8.5	3.7	9.9	8.6
Assets	420.0	412.5	390.4	358.1	323.9	283.8
Equity	173.2	166.2	153.3	152.5	148.8	133.1
Return on sales (percent)	5	4	3	2	5	6
Return on assets (percent)	4	3	2	1	3	3
Return on equity (percent)	9	8	6	2	7	6
Current ratio	1.56	1.46	1.61	1.63	1.46	1.12
Long-term debt/stockholders' equity	0.98	1.03	1.14	1.04	0.89	0.80
Average annual price-earnings ratio	4.4	3.8	3.0	15.0	17.8	19.8
Humana:						
Sales	260.7	195.4	134.7	106.7	83.6	64.6
Profits	8.9	6.8	6.1	5.5	4.9	1.9
Assets	340.2	310.9	264.5	199.1	167.3	150.8
Equity	73.8	66.2	59.3	54.2	48.9	39.9
Return on sales (percent)	3	3	5	5	6	3
Return on assets (percent)	3	2	2	3	3	1
Return on equity (percent)	12	10	10	10	10	5
Current ratio	1.41	1.36	1.57	1.78	2.29	1.57
Long-term debt/stockholders' equity	2.77	2.94	2.76	2.18	1.92	2.20
Average annual price-earnings ratio	7.2	5.5	5.5	11.5	23.0	35.9

Source: Form 10-Ks, annual reports.

AMI provided other health-care services such as inhalation therapy, production and marketing of health education films, medical personnel placement, turnkey development projects, and management of medical laboratories. AMI also offered computerized medical record services for 100 hospitals, and had launched a program to offer separate hospital management information systems to investor-owned and nonprofit hospitals. These business activities accounted for 6 percent of AMI's revenues and 24 percent of income before taxes in 1975.

American Medicorp (AMC). AMC was founded in Philadelphia in 1968 by a young new York investment banker and a Philadelphia lawyer, both of whom had specialized in securing long-term financing for hospitals. Within two years, AMC had acquired 27 hospitals and nursing homes in California, Florida, and Texas. Seven new hospitals were built between 1970 and 1975. One of the company's hospitals, Sunrise Hospital in Las Vegas, had 486 beds and accounted for more than 10 percent of AMC's pretax income in 1974.

AMC's rapid expansion in the 1968–72 period led to cost control difficulties. Since then the company had terminated several unprofitable operations including some hospitals and nursing homes, and reduced its capital expansion budget by 20 percent. AMC had $110 million in goodwill on its balance sheet as of December 1975 and was involved in several legal disputes as to whether a return was to be allowed on that portion of its capital base by third-party payors.

AMC signed seven management contracts in 1975 covering 1,089 beds, and seven more in 1976. According to its annual report, AMC hoped to use the management contract market as a vehicle for future revenue and profit growth. It planned five new management contracts in 1977. AMC was in the process of developing a staff specialist group and implementing an enlarged selling and advertising campaign, and industry observers characterized AMC as an aggressive marketer relative to others in the industry.

Humana. Founded in California in 1964 as Extendicare, Inc., Humana initially owned and operated extended nursing-care facilities for the elderly. The company had grown into the largest extended-care provider in the United States by 1967, primarily through acquisition. Humana had also expanded into mobile home parks during this period. In 1969 Extendicare shifted strategic emphasis and began investing its resources in hospital construction. By 1974 the company had 54 hospitals and had sold off all of its nonhospital operations (including the extended nursing-care facilities and mobile home parks) and changed its name to Humana. By the end of 1976, Humana owned 63 hospitals located primarily in Texas, Florida, Alabama, and Tennessee.

Humana's future plans were to concentrate on building new hospitals and expanding existing ones to the extent that funds were available. Humana was the only one of the six leading hospital management companies not active in the contract management business. Mr. David Jones, Humana's chairman of the board, commented on the management contract business in a 1975 interview: "It's like Wall Street—when everybody thinks it's a good idea, it's time to get out."

Everyone is after contract area for growth!

One industry observer believed that Humana had built the capacity of its owned hospitals in anticipation of demand, which provided ample near-term growth opportunity without new construction. As a result, Humana had only 55 percent occupancy in 1977, compared to a national hospital average of 75 percent.

All the major hospital management companies had made significant additions to senior management depth in the 1972–76 period. This included phasing out of original founders from active management, expanded boards, and increased corporate staffs.

← increased cost

The second tier of competitors

The second tier of management companies included Hyatt Corporation, Medenco, A. E. Brim & Assoc., Charter Medical, General Health Services, AID, and R. H. Medical. While all the second-tier companies had relatively few owned hospitals, Hyatt, Medenco, and A. E. Brim were quite active companies in management contracts. Exhibit 7 shows the number of owned and managed hospitals for the second-tier firms at the end of 1976. Second-tier firms were aggressive bidders and were sometimes willing to reduce the price and length of an initial management contract in order to gain access to a hospital. They did not have teams of staff specialists as of 1976.

Hyatt was considered by many industry observers to be a dangerous competitor because of its affiliation with a large, well-known parent organization, which lent credibility to Hyatt's marketing efforts. Hyatt

Exhibit 7

OWNED AND MANAGED HOSPITALS OF SECOND-TIER
FIRMS AS OF
DECEMBER 31, 1976

	Owned hospitals	Managed hospitals
Hyatt	4	22
	(444)*	(2,286)
Medenco	13	11
	(1,573)	(1,207)
A. E. Brim	4	19
	(208)	(1,118)
Charter Medical	14	7
	(1,462)	(1,333)
General Health Services	7	1
	(1,271)	(117)
AID	16	—
	(2,583)	
R. H. Medical	4	3
	(661)	(450)
Total		63

* Number of beds.
Source: Numbers of owned and managed hospitals at the end of 1976 for second-tier companies and their goals for 1977 are taken from a survey conducted by *Modern Healthcare* and reported in the February 1977 issue.

had been willing to accept one-year trial contracts and to lend money to financially troubled hospitals to facilitate winning contracts. Hyatt was credited with an excellent marketing information network, and it seemed to be able to learn first about many potential management contract situations.

Hyatt, Medenco, and A. E. Brim were all planning stepped-up efforts in management contracts in 1977. Hyatt had made no public projections, but was known to be seeking to increase its management contract business. Medenco predicted that it would double its management contract services in 1977, adding up to 12 new managed hospitals. A. E. Brim forecasted a doubling of its management contract services within 18 months.

FUTURE OUTLOOK FOR THE HOSPITAL INDUSTRY

A number of important factors promised to affect the shape of the hospital industry in the years ahead.

National Health Insurance

Although National Health Insurance (NHI) probably would not be enacted by Congress in 1977, industry observers unanimously expected it to become a reality in the next three to five years. The major uncertainty for the investor-owned hospital industry was what form the legislation would take. Although NHI would put hospital purchasing power in the hands of people who were not presently in the health-care system, would eliminate bad debts, and would expand the use of currently profitable outpatient facilities, certain versions of the bill would extend the current medicare reimbursement formula (with its 11 percent before-tax return on equity) to all hospital revenues. That rate of return would hurt the investor-owned hospitals by reducing their ability to borrow in the public market. Another possibility was that all hospitals could be forced to provide the public with more unprofitable services such as emergency centers and maternity and pediatric wards. Finally, if reimbursement rates were negotiated based on industry averages, well-managed concerns could benefit while marginal competitors might be hurt. However, if rate negotiation became a cumbersome, bureaucratic, and political process the entire hospital industry could be reduced to public utility status.

At the other end of the spectrum, Georgia Senator Herman Talmadge had recently introduced a bill in the Senate that would allow investor-owned hospitals a return twice as great as nonprofit hospitals, and would penalize high-cost operators and call for more involvement of the private insurance carriers to administer the NHI program. The investor-owned hospital industry was naturally in favor of such legislation.

Industry observers believed that the exact shape the final legislation would take would be a compromise between these extreme points of view. In addition, public opinion would influence the attitude federal legislation took toward the investor-owned hospitals. Historically, the public had viewed profit making in the hospital sector with mistrust.

An April 1977 initiative by President Jimmy Carter represented a new wrinkle in dealing with the health-care problem. The Carter proposal was to limit allowable increases in hospital charges to 9 percent per year, and also establish a national dollar limit on new capital expenditures, to stem the tide of cost increases which had plagued the industry. The proposal had drawn outright opposition from the hospital industry.

Expanded health planning

Industry observers predicted that either under government pressure or by overt legal mandate, hospitals would have to increase the level of coordination among themselves and with all elements of the health-care delivery system. Shared services, joint undertakings, consolidations, and satellite hospitals were some of the forms this coordination was expected to take. Hospital management companies were enthusiastic about the idea of developing "medical complexes" for communities.

Unionization

In 1974 Congress amended the National Labor Relations Act to permit unionization of all hospital employees. The amendment had resulted in increased union activity in the health-care field, but the number of covered employees was still relatively small.

Health Maintenance Organization (HMO)

Industry observers predicted that group purchasers of health services, such as corporations and employee unions, would play an increasing role in structuring the health-care industry. Group purchasers had typically paid premiums to insurance companies, who then negotiated with the hospital and physicians. To date, insurance companies had been relatively ineffective in their attempts to control the cost and quality of health care. However, the future could see competitive bidding and standardization of contracts if the group purchasers decided to establish their own health-care plans and contract directly with hospital management companies and other health-care delivery organizations to provide the desired level of medical services.

The term *HMO* referred to a variety of prepaid health plans by which a group practice of doctors or a hospital contracted with a given patient population to provide a certain level of health care for a fixed monthly fee. This differed from conventional health insurance in that doctors were paid a flat rate rather than a fee for each procedure performed. The basic concept was to shift the burden of cost control for health services from the patient to an organization which maximized profits by keeping people well and reducing the need for expensive services.

HMOs appeared to hold promise for hospital management companies because they could contract directly with corporations rather than dealing with intermediaries such as Blue Cross or Blue Shield. With government sponsorship and encouragement, the number of HMOs was expected to increase. One prediction was that there could be 10,000 HMOs in the United States by 1985. However, such a prediction was highly speculative because government support had been erratic and many of the early HMOs had failed.

(5) Technology changes

The level of technological sophistication had been increasing at a very rapid rate in the health-care industry over the previous decade. Industry observers predicted that the rate of change could continue to accelerate through the late 1980s as an increased demand for the highest quality health care and government money to absorb the increased costs encouraged private enterprise to focus additional research and development resources on the health-care industry. A prominent hospital consultant described the situation as follows:

> Five years ago an expensive piece of diagnostic equipment, costing perhaps $500,000, was expected to last at least five and, hopefully, seven years. Today the same type of equipment costs $1,500,000 and will be useful for at most three years. The pressure for change is a combination of the hospital wanting to provide the highest quality care and the physicians being afraid not to. Doctors are very sensitive about their malpractice exposure if they do not have access to the very latest, most advanced, diagnostic and therapeutic equipment.

The federal government required, by 1974, that hospitals secure the approval of local planning agencies before buying equipment that cost more than $100,000.

HOSPITAL AFFILIATES INTERNATIONAL, INC.

HISTORY

HAI was founded in 1968 by two physicians and two businessmen, Dr. Herbert J. Schulman, Dr. Irwin B. Eskind, his brother Richard J. Eskind, and Baron Coleman. The founders believed that the health-care industry was seriously lacking the modern management techniques required to meet the nation's increased demand for high-quality, reasonable-cost health care. Guaranteeing $2 million of their own capital, they began to build an organization to meet this need. Jack Anderson assumed the position of president soon thereafter, having held high-level financial positions in several large companies before joining HAI.

The original focus of HAI was to acquire or build its own hospitals in rapidly growing regions of the country that needed additional health-care facilities. However, in 1971 a unique opportunity propelled HAI seriously into the contract management business. Tulane University's Medical School had performed a financial feasibility study prior to the construction of its new 300-bed teaching hospital and was most disturbed by what it found. The study showed that similar teaching institutions suffered an average operating loss of $2 million per year that Tulane's administration was not prepared to subsidize. Tulane decided to try to interest professional hospital management companies in bidding on a contract to manage its new facility. While visiting the headquarters of the Hospital Corporation of America (the largest hospital management company, and also based in Nashville), the Tulane representative decided to see HAI as well. HAI had already entered the management contract business with two contracts. After almost seven months of negotiations, Tulane awarded the management contract to HAI in early 1972. Mr. Lanson Hyde, assistant vice president, described the significance of the Tulane agreement:

> When a prestigious, well-respected institution such as Tulane decided to use an outside company to manage its medical center, the entire concept of contract management became legitimized. Tulane was the first nationally known hospital affiliated with a medical school to use an outside management company. The industry awareness HAI gained by this is what established our reputation in the contract business.

During the next four years, HAI added about nine new hospital management contracts per year, temporarily discontinuing the construction of its owned hospitals in 1974. HAI attempted to turn over management of its owned hospitals to another hospital management company, American Medicorp, in November of 1975, to reduce the degree of leverage in the company and concentrate its efforts in the hospital management contract business. However, the agreement was never completed due to tax difficulties; and as a result, HAI decided to remain in the owned-hospital business and to expand its profile in that market by gradually building additional hospitals.

HAI's management contract business achieved another milestone for the industry in 1975 when its first significant number of hospital management agreements (five) came due for renewal. During the year the five agreements were all renewed for a longer period of time than the terms of the original contracts. While no contracts had come up for renewal in 1976, HAI had lost five contracts as a result of terminations. The terminations were the result of several unique situations which HAI did not believe were representative of its client relationships. The causes of the terminations will be described below.

On March 15, 1976, HAI entered into an agreement to manage the Flower and Fifth Avenue Hospital, the teaching hospital for the well-known New York Medical College and, with more than 400 beds, one of the largest hospitals to become associated with a hospital management company. The contract was the first hospital management contract in New York State. In late December 1976, the St. Louis County Hospital awarded a management contract to HAI. St. Louis County Hospital was a 200-bed teaching institution which functioned as a part of the county's Department of Community Health and Medical Care. The contract was HAI's 16th of 1976 and its 50th overall. In early 1977 HAI was the only hospital management company holding contracts with medical teaching hospitals, St. Louis County and Flower and Fifth being third and fourth in a group including Tulane and Texas Tech.

CONTRACT MANAGEMENT

HAI was engaged in two business areas, the management of hospitals it owned and the management of other hospitals under contract. HAI provided four basic types of services to hospitals managed under con-

contract services

specialists

tract. HAI installed a professionally trained hospital administrator who was usually the sole full-time HAI employee at the hospital. In larger hospitals the controller was sometimes an HAI employee as well. In addition, HAI provided the contract hospital with the services of a group of staff management specialists, access to a group purchasing plan, and the ability to utilize a shared hospital management information system.

The administrator was the most visible employee of HAI in contact with the hospital's board. The administrator was responsible for achieving specific health-care quality and financial goals agreed to between HAI and the contracting hospital's board of directors and acting as HAI's spokesperson to the community served by the hospital. Most administrators were financially oriented, with master's degrees in hospital administration or MBAs.

It was HAI's policy to move an administrator no more than was absolutely necessary, to maintain what management referred to as "administrative continuity" between HAI and the managed hospital. Typically, an administrator would stay at a hospital for two to three years before being promoted to a larger facility, which could be either an owned or managed hospital. The administrator was augmented by a regional manager, a group vice president, and a senior vice president, who all remained in periodic contact with the contract hospital.

Staff specialists

To help the administrator accomplish the goals of the contract, HAI maintained a group of staff specialists. Exhibit 8 lists the areas in which

Exhibit 8

STAFF SPECIALISTS

Accounting	Inhalation therapy
Accreditation	Insurance
Admitting procedures	Labor relations
Ambulatory care	Laboratory operations
Ancillary services	Long-range planning
Budgeting and finance	Maintenance
Bylaws	Management engineering
Capital financing	Medical records
Cash flow	Medical staff relations
Certificate of need	Nursing services
Community relations	Personnel
Construction	Pharmacy operations
Credit and collections	Physical therapy
Data processing	Physician recruitment
Dietary services	Purchasing
Education	Quality assurance
Environmental control	Radiology operations
Equipment	Staffing
Financial feasibility	Systems and procedures
Functional programming	Third-party reimbursement

HAI had staff specialists, representing the widest range of any hospital management company. Mr. Ray Stevenson, senior vice president in charge of HAI's Hospital Management Services Division (HMSD), was particularly proud of the quality of HAI's professional staff, a view shared by the other senior managers at HAI.

> Our people are all experienced hospital managers who have risen as high within the traditional hospital management structure as they possibly could. Betty West (vice president in charge of nursing services) had been a director of nursing and an assistant hospital administrator before we found her. HAI has given these people an opportunity to continue to grow professionally that they probably would not have been able to find anywhere else.

The on-site administrator had use of HAI's staff specialists on a regular basis during the initial "intensive-care" stage of a management contract and then on a periodic basis throughout the contract's life. Each managed hospital sent a copy of its monthly reports to HAI's headquarters where they were reviewed and analyzed by the staff specialists. If a specialist identified a potential problem area, then a phone call would be made to the hospital administrator and, if necessary, a site visit would be made. One HAI executive stated, however, that administrators were sometimes reluctant to call Nashville for help because the expense was charged to their budgets, and because of the negative connotation they believed it carried for their abilities as administrators.

Two of HAI's key staff specialists groups are described below, and were representative of the operations of the staff specialist organization.

Nursing services.   Betty West, vice president, and four staff specialists (all with previous experience as directors of nursing) comprised what she referred to as an "essential" part of HAI's marketing and contract management efforts. The cost control portion of the nursing specialists' task was usually a straightforward application of proven industrial engineering and manpower planning techniques HAI had developed in the hospitals it owned. In addition, HAI worked with the hospital to develop a patient classification system which permitted a more efficient allocation of nursing services.

In nursing, as with several other areas of hospital operations, HAI implemented a quality assurance program which consisted of a peer review program, questionnaires given to both physicians and patients concerned with how the quality of nursing could be improved (the results of the survey were used to establish new goals for the nursing staff) and the linking of administrators' bonuses to the achievement of cost and quality standards. Ms. West commented:

> This is what makes us different from our competition. HAI knows how to measure quality and set quality standards in hospitals. A small hospital could never afford the resources and skills needed to do this, nor have the ability to make comparisons among 75 hospitals.

Professional relations.   HAI had a staff specialist department with expertise in physician recruiting and planning, under the direction of Mr. James Smith. Jim Smith was, as he put it, "one of the largest finders and placers of physicians in the world." Mr. Smith reflected on his job:

This is really a pretty basic business. If you don't have enough doctors to admit patients to your hospital, then you operate below capacity and lose money. My job is to make certain that we will have enough physicians to justify building or operating a hospital. It would cost a hospital about $25,000 per physician to duplicate the kind of service we provide.

Professional relations specialists were assigned regionally, and each could handle 20–30 physician requests from client hospitals in a year. Smith believed that the size and service capabilities of his group gave HAI a competitive advantage over other firms in the industry.

Dr. Jae Hill, director of staff services, was the individual directly responsible for the scheduling and management of the staff specialists. Hill described some of the difficulties he faced:

> This is very much like running many professional services organizations. Our people seem to have a two-year life span before their productivity decreases and they begin to make a conscious effort to find work outside of their assigned specialty.
>
> To put our situation in perspective, we have had a significant turnover within the specialist group in the last four years. Some have left the company while others have taken different positions within HAI. Replacing these people is not an easy affair. We have to find a hybrid individual— one who possesses both a high degree of professional expertise and industry visibility and a keen business acumen. Being a staff specialist is not like running your area department.

However, HAI preferred not to refer to its staff specialists as consultants. The staff specialist organization had grown substantially since HAI's initial management contracts, both in breadth and depth (Table 1).

Group purchasing

In addition to gaining the assistance of HAI's purchasing and inventory control staff specialists, a hospital managed under contract became part of HAI's national purchasing program, which encompassed all of HAI's owned and managed hospitals and included most of the items a hospital purchased. The prices offered by a particular supplier were based upon the cumulative purchasing power of the group rather than the individual hospital. Mr. Anderson estimated that the purchasing savings, between 15–20 percent of what the hospital had been paying, were equal to up to one third of HAI's management fees. The group purchasing arrangement required no change in the hospital's purchas-

Table 1

NUMBERS OF STAFF SPECIALISTS IN SELECTED AREAS

	1971	1972	1973	1974	1975	1976	1977
Nursing services	0	1	1	2*	2	4*	4†
Professional relations ..	0	1	1	2	4	4	5

* One nursing specialist was added late in the year.
† Two additional positions were budgeted in 1977.
Source: Casewriter compilations.

ing operations. The hospital ordered items in exactly the same manner that they did before joining HAI, and the items were shipped directly to the hospital by the supplier with the discount reflected in the bill.

Computerized information system

HAI offered, through McDonnell Douglas national computer service network, access to a complete hospital billing, accounting, and management information system. The computer package cost a managed hospital 15–20 percent less than the normal price because of HAI's group purchasing power. HAI's staff specialists assumed responsibility for training the hospital staff in the proper use of the system's reports.

THE MANAGEMENT CONTRACT CYCLE

Management contracts progressed through a series of stages including the initial contact, management audit, formal bid, early "intensive-care" period of turnaround efforts, a "stabilized" period and finally, renewal negotiations.

1) *Initial contact.* The marketing of new management contracts had been more of an art than a science. One senior executive expressed the belief that when HAI first started in the business advertising and promotion spending would not have done any good because the market was not ready for it. Therefore, HAI had limited the primary thrust of its marketing program to bidding on contracts once a hospital had made its intentions public. Mr. Anderson described some of the constraints on HAI's marketing effort:

> You must bear in mind the sensitivity of the hospital's current managers to our being called in to review their operation, and the board's reluctance to bring its problems into the open. Even after they have admitted they need help it takes several months to get a contract signed because the board is afraid it's going to relinquish control of the hospital to outsiders. Every sale tends to be unique.

Steven Geringer, the vice president most directly involved in marketing, described HAI's marketing efforts to date:

> About 75 percent of our leads are generated "internally" from our administrators in the field, what we gather from public sources and our reputation as the industry leader. The remaining 25 percent of our leads result from external market development work on our part. However, the administrators in the field are the key to new leads. They have an amazing information network about which hospitals are in financial trouble or might be looking to change administrators.

HAI also received referrals from influential members of its client hospitals' boards. In addition to actively pursuing leads, HAI participated in seminars, industry conferences, conventions, and public forums at which management contracts as an alternative to traditional hospital management procedures were discussed. Many of HAI's competitors also participated in such activities. The company also did some very limited advertising in professional journals.

2. **Management audit.** After the initial contact had been made and the hospital's interest in exploring a management contract confirmed, HAI's staff specialists performed a management audit of the prospective client. The audit, which HAI had pioneered, permitted it to gain a thorough understanding of exactly how many person-days of staff specialist time would be needed to complete the requirements of the contract. In addition, the audit became a selling tool. Mr. Stevenson commented on the role of the management audit:

> Of the 50 hospitals presently under contract, only a relatively small percentage were healthy when they signed with us. The rest came to us out of serious need for improved management in their hospital. When we documented, department by department, what could be done by HAI and its bottom line impact, we often hit the hospitals right on the head. I'd say that the audit is a major influence on the hospital board's decision. In addition, it's a way for us to determine if the hospital can possibly pay our fees.

Often the audit revealed truly glaring defects in administration, as described by Mr. Stevenson:

> In one hospital the accounts receivable staff had been told to monitor accounts alphabetically starting at A on the first of each month. Since the staff never made it past the Ls, the last half of the alphabet never got billed. We also often see the hospital with an aging group of physicians. It is not uncommon to see the number of admissions decline as the physician approaches his late 50s or early 60s and, therefore, the revenue base of the hospital declines simultaneously.

3. **The formal bid.** The contract negotiations between HAI and the hospital focused on such issues as scope of services to be provided, the price of the contract and the contract's length. Although some of HAI's competitors were willing to accept one-year contracts, HAI sought to secure a three-year agreement. HAI's "standard" contract typically received extensive customization which made each one unique. In 1976 HAI was typically one of three companies bidding for the hospital's business whereas it had frequently been the only bidder in 1972.

HAI offered a single contract management product that provided a complete package of management services to the hospital. HAI did not offer its individual services separately. HAI charged a premium price which was typically 15–35 percent above that of its closest competitor, because of its staff specialists and experience in the contract management business. Management believed that HAI could demand a premium price because it currently offered the best service available in the marketplace. HAI sought to maintain the industry price levels by purposely not trying to meet the competition. HAI's fee was generally an annual percentage of revenues or some other measure of hospital activity and was sometimes deferred if the client was in financial difficulty.

4. **"Intensive care."** The "intensive-care" phase of the business was the period during which the HAI administrator and staff specialists sought to work a new client into shape, usually in the three to six months imme-

diately following the signing of a new hospital management contract. Mr. Ray Stevenson described the role of his staff in the intensive care phase as follows:

> Usually the hospitals that come to us are in pretty bad shape. We try to balance the need to show the client's board of directors early positive results with our desire to use the situation to begin building a more effective management team in the hospital.

During intensive care, teams of staff specialists worked closely with the administrator and the existing department managers to implement changes in the hospital's operations. During this phase the staff specialists made frequent visits to the hospital. It was also during this period that HAI's group purchasing and computerized management systems were introduced.

Stabilization. After the most serious operating problems had been resolved, cash flow and profits improved, and the hospital's organization modified, the hospital was classified as being stabilized. The hospital administrator's attention shifted toward developing the managers of the hospital's departments, gradually improving cash flow and profits and expanding the hospital's profile in the community. Staff specialists tended to visit stabilized hospitals less frequently, with the bulk of their attention directed toward newly signed contracts.

Contract renewal. A typical management contract had a life of two to five years, and the topic of renewal was of great interest to HAI and the industry as a whole. There was general agreement among industry observers that while a hospital would agree to almost anything to avoid the prospect of going bankrupt, the percentage of hospitals that would elect to continue their management contracts was still an unknown. The industry was only five years old and most of the existing contracts had been signed during the previous two to three years.

To date, HAI had a renewal rate of between 75 percent and 85 percent, which was in line with the renewal rate for the industry as a whole. HAI's management projected that the renewal rate would decline somewhat as competition increased in the industry. Mr. Geringer, the executive who was closest to the renewal situation, viewed the issue this way:

> At one time we had over 50 percent of the contract management market. Our share has fallen to about 33 percent, and we believe it will stabilize at 25–30 percent. Our biggest problems have been the five terminations we suffered this year, the confusion caused by the America Medicorp deal and the fact that we have not been able to institutionalize the sales success of a few key individuals like Ed Stolman.

The five terminations HAI experienced in 1976 had resulted from a combination of people-related problems and events out of HAI's control. In one instance a hospital was sold to another management company after HAI decided not to purchase the hospital itself. In another case, the hospital wanted HAI to put in more of its own money; and in a third case, the hospital could not be saved and closed down. In the two other cases HAI had filed suit in U.S. district court seeking damages from contracts that the company claimed were "wrongfully terminated."

In one of these suits HAI's on-site administrator had decided to try to go into business for himself.

HAI was trying to improve the quality of its client base by being more selective in the type of hospital it agreed to manage. Mr. Geringer believed that HAI's competitors were still concerned with the number of contracts they signed rather than their quality.

Stolman viewed HAI's relationship with the hospitals as being long term in nature:

> Once you are in the hospital and doing your job well, which means providing high-quality patient care at a reasonable cost and helping to make the board more important in the community, then I believe you have an excellent chance of becoming a fixture at the hospital. For example, we have just had our second renewal at Jiles County Hospital.

COMPETITION FOR MANAGEMENT CONTRACTS

According to Ray Stevenson and other executives, of all the firms in the management contract business, only HAI had really "paid its dues." Stevenson commented:

> Our competition has not made the kind of investment in its staff specialists that we have. When we bid for a contract we have a team of experts on hand to satisfy the needs of the client. Our competitors often have to take people from its owned hospitals and assign them to an engagement.

However, Stevenson conceded that contracts had become harder to obtain recently, and that competition had forced HAI to reduce its fees by as much as 10 percent over the past two years, though it remained the high bidder. One problem in the contract business was that the hospital boards of directors were not always capable of discerning the difference in quality between HAI and its competitors. However, Stevenson estimated that in 50 percent of the cases it was not the lowest bid that was accepted by the hospital.

Mr. Anderson was actively monitoring the status of HAI's competition:

> There are perhaps three dozen potential competitors in the industry. This number does not include the former hospital administrator who decides to go into business for himself, gets one contract, hires a secretary and says he is in the hospital management business. About 12 of the firms are active competitors and 5 are listed on the NYSE. The competition will be able to catch up to us technologically, given enough time and resources. However, we are still the most technologically competent firm in the business. Despite the fact that HCA is not actively involved in the business now, we view them as potentially a very serious competitor.

In late 1976 HAI had added two full-time marketing persons to its staff. The move was prompted in part by the actions of two of the company's more active competitors, Hyatt Corporation with 15–20 management contracts and American Medicorp with 15. These firms were characterized by HAI's management as being very aggressive marketing companies with business development staffs larger than HAI's.

Recently, American Medical International (AMI) had begun to offer

split it out

pieces of its total service to hospitals rather than sell the complete package. Mr. Geringer commented on AMI's action:

> When AMI split its product line, they hurt the industry. We are not planning to unbundle our basic package and wind up selling nursing services to one client and computer services to another.

↳ But could mine take advantage of it then?

future !

INTERNATIONAL OPERATIONS

HAI was presently examining the international market as a source of expansion for its management contract business. The company had one contract in Paris which it was planning to use as a base for increasing its European operations. HAI was cautious about its business exposure in foreign countries. It planned, for the present, to act as a subcontractor to large U.S.-based multinational corporations such as Abbott Labs.

OWNED HOSPITALS

HAI's 25 owned hospitals were located primarily in the southern half of the United States, especially Texas (13) and Tennessee (7). While HAI had been in negotiations with American Medicorp, no new hospital construction had been undertaken by the company. After negotiations had been terminated, however, continued expansion of its owned-hospital base was begun. Mr. Anderson expressed the policy of the company:

> In the future we will continue to be in both businesses. There are obviously very big differences between owned and managing hospitals. We believe it is important to have a strong position in both.

While new construction projects would be limited by the number of communities that had a real need for new health-care facilities, expansion was possible through acquiring existing hospitals. However, any expansion of owned hospitals would take place only in states with reasonable reimbursement formulas. States such as New York were considered to have poor plans and would be avoided, while Texas and Tennessee would continue to be primary expansion areas.

The role of competition in owned hospitals was different than in managed ones. Mr. Buncher, in charge of owned hospitals, viewed his client in the following manner:

> Our customer is the physicians; the patient largely follows. Of course, we must ensure that the needs of the patient are efficiently and properly provided for at all times, but the main competition is for doctors. It is the physicians who admit patients, and it is the patients who generate revenue.

To attract physicians, HAI either built or assisted in the construction of a medical office building adjacent to the hospitals. HAI also tried to have the latest diagnostic and therapeutic equipment available for the physician to use, ensure that all tests were completed and entered in the patient's medical chart on a timely basis, and provide a "more pleasant working environment" for the physician than other hospitals in the service area.

Mr. Buncher believed HAI had an edge in motivating health-care professionals because it provided an orderly career path for the administrators, controllers, and nurses who worked for HAI. HAI tried to equal the market salaries for administrators and offer the promise of additional compensation, in the form of a bonus, if the individual's performance exceeded budget. HAI estimated that bonuses could range from an average of 20 percent to a maximum of 50 percent of salary. In addition, administrators were eligible to receive stock options.

GOVERNMENT RELATIONS

HAI viewed the role of government with caution. HAI itself did little lobbying, and no one individual was assigned the task of coordinating the company's lobbying efforts. Lobbying activities included writing letters to representatives and senators in the states where HAI owned or managed hospitals, appearing before legislative committees, and participating in the activities of the Federation of American Hospitals. In certain instances, such as malpractice legislation, HAI lobbied more to prevent bad bills from passing than getting its own views on malpractice reform translated into law.

Within HAI's organization the attitude toward government regulation was a function of the business area the manager was involved in. Previous legislation had been a stimulus for new business in the contract management area. Geringer commented on HAI's experiences:

> I think that regardless of what form a new law takes, it will certainly increase the basic complexity of the hospital administrator's and the board's task. Anything that makes this task more difficult will increase the demand for the services of our staff specialists.

The managers in the owned-hospital business did not foresee any specific benefits from new legislation, but they did not perceive it as a threat either. Mr. Buncher expressed his opinion:

> We are managed better than the average hospital in the country. As long as we stay better than average we are OK, since I expect the law to be targeted to the average hospital's costs. Some people seem a bit frightened by the public utility concept of health care, but certain utilities do very well for their stockholders. Only overt nationalization of hospitals would be a direct threat to us.

Mr. Hilton, vice president/treasurer, and other executives viewed the specter of National Health Insurance as one of the fundamental factors influencing HAI's stock price. Pharmaceutical and hospital supply companies sold at multiples of 15 and 25 times earnings, while the hospital management business sold at 5–9 times 1976 earnings.

ORGANIZATION

HAI's organization reflected the two different business areas the company competed in. The two basic line operating groups were the Hospital

Management Services Division (HMSD), which managed the hospitals under contract, and the Hospital Operations Department (HOD), which managed the owned hospitals. The staff specialists and management contract marketing group were part of the Hospital Management Corporation (HMC), a wholly owned subsidiary of HAI.

Compensation for HAI's managers, which had historically been above average for the industry, was primarily in the form of salary and bonus. HAI did not provide benefits such as cars, comprehensive insurance programs, and retirement programs which some of its competitors had recently added to their compensation packages. HAI's salary and bonus levels were currently about average for the industry.

adds to turnover?

FINANCE AND CONTROL

The finance and control functions were divided between Bob Hilton, treasurer, and Thomas Chaney, controller. HAI's overall corporate financial goals were the reduction of debt in the capital structure, improved control over costs in owned and managed hospitals, and a general improvement in the balance sheet by stressing growth in the management contract portion of the company. Mr. Hilton viewed the latter goals as being somewhat contradictory:

> People are sometimes more expensive than bricks and mortar. We have a $5 million annual payroll that I look at as an interest payment on a bond issue. People are an expensive fixed cost.

Mr. Hilton was responsible for establishing and maintaining HAI's liaison with the financial community. He commented on HAI's financial situation:

> We are a highly leveraged firm in a highly leveraged industry which makes certain lending institutions nervous. I believe that such leverage is appropriate because we are in a very stable business where declines in revenue, if they occur, are gradual and most of our costs are reimbursed by third-party payors. In addition, we have excellent liquidity and high depreciation.

Much of Mr. Hilton's time was spent on educating Wall Street and institutions about the hospital management industry and HAI as a company.

Mr. Hilton believed that the availability of future sources of funds would be affected by the industry's ability to convince the banking and investment community that the concept of investor-owned hospitals was sound. In October 1976 HAI sold $12 million of 10 percent senior debentures. This was shortly after Hospital Corporation of America had sold the first issue of straight long-term debt in the industry.

HAI had no formal long-range strategic planning system, although profit forecasting was performed on a regular basis by the firm's senior management.

No Planning!

Malpractice insurance

The problems that all hospitals faced with respect to purchasing adequate malpractice insurance at reasonable rates was a very hot issue in the industry. The rise in both the frequency of medical malpractice suits and size of the dollar awards had resulted in a dramatic increase in malpractice insurance premiums. The hospitals that were hit hardest by the price increases were the large downtown metropolitan hospitals. These institutions typically had the largest percentage of patients subject to cost-based reimbursement and offered many high-risk (from an insurance viewpoint) outpatient and emergency room services. In certain instances when faced with a five- to tenfold increase in the size of malpractice premiums some of these hospitals had decided to operate with no insurance coverage at all.

HAI had pioneered an industry reinsurance program involving several of the leading hospital management companies that would work to keep premiums down by absorbing a certain portion of the risk within the group. The reinsurance program, started in late 1975, had been most successful thus far and had received wide publicity in trade journals. HAI did not plan to market the medical malpractice program as part of their package of management services because of the different nature of the insurance operation. In the words of one HAI executive, "We are in the hospital, not the insurance, business."

FUTURE PLANS

HAI was committed to remaining in both the owned and managed segments of the hospital industry. However, Mr. Anderson had set different growth targets for the two businesses:

> I hope and expect that our management contract business will grow by about 15 hospitals per year while we plan to add only two to three new owned hospitals per year. In five years the hospital management business should be 50 percent of profits. It should also account for a substantial portion of our earnings growth because it's starting from a smaller base

The decision to remain in both businesses caused what management termed an "ongoing organizational problem" concerning what type of management structure HAI should adopt. Mr. Anderson expressed his views on the subject:

> The two businesses have very basic differences and require a different skills mix to be managed successfully. For example, we have got to be visible in the contract business while we would prefer to maintain a low profile in the hospitals we own. We could split the two divisions completely, but then we would have to add staff specialists to service our own hospitals. As it is, we now have a hybrid organizational structure which has been partially regionalized.

While HAI was not planning to offer individual services for the medium- and large-sized hospitals, it was investigating the possibility of selling a less intensive management program as a method of penetrating the small hospital market. The institutions had between 25 and 50 beds and usually were located in rural communities. Mr. Geringer described HAI's thinking on the matter:

We would like to sell the small hospital one day per month of line management time for about $20,000–$50,000 per year of fees. The arrangement could give the small hospital access to the resources at HAI's command. That is something that has been simply out of the question for a hospital that size. We estimate that one line manager could supervise about 10–12 accounts in a given service area.

HAI was also considering becoming more active in contracts to develop and manage hospitals. Stolman commented:

In the next several years many hospitals will have to replace their existing facilities. Helping them carry out the development work provides a toehold for a management contract later. However, we plan to limit this to one or two new contracts per year.

Diversification

HAI was examining related new business areas that could offer opportunities for growth in sales and earnings. A list of about 50 businesses was maintained by Mr. Anderson, Mr. Stolman, and other senior HAI executives, containing such businesses as housekeeping services, data processing and pure financing businesses such as equipment leasing. Potential new businesses were reviewed periodically with special attention given to identifying acquisition candidates in the most promising areas. Each potential diversification move possessed some degree of vertical integration for HAI. Mr. Anderson described the type of business HAI was interested in entering:

I look for an industry that has definite barriers to entry. The barriers can be either technological or financial or some combination of both. It should also provide above-average sales and profit potential on a long-term basis.

HAI was not planning any immediate acquisition moves. Anderson stated the company's goal as wanting to move into one or two new businesses over the next five years:

We plan to postpone any vertical integration or diversification decision until the contract market begins to slow down and the role of the government in the health care system has been more clearly defined. However, you must bear in mind that acquisitions are a matter of timing, need, and who is available at what price.

Sweco, Inc. (A)

> Well, we've done it. You and I know the process works and the equipment works, but it won't be easy to convince the old-timers who have drilled all their lives without it. That includes the people in my own company.

With these words in November 1972 Dr. Peter Hamilton of the production research department of a leading international oil company encouraged Les Hansen of Sweco, Inc., to enter the oil field equipment industry with a new piece of oil well drilling equipment that Sweco had developed, partly at the former's instigation. Sweco called the new product a "sand separator," though it was known in the industry as a "mud cleaner."

SWECO, INC.

Sweco was founded in 1917 as the Southwestern Engineering Corporation. During the 1930s Southwestern went bankrupt. The Miller family, owners of some of the stock, assumed management control of the company to protect their position. Under new leadership, Sweco began to concentrate its efforts on the manufacture of heat exchangers and the engineering and construction of refineries and other process plants. This proved to be a highly competitive, and therefore not very profitable, field.

In 1947 an event occurred that would completely change the nature of Sweco's business, an event described by Howard Wright, Jr., Sweco's president, as the most important event in the history of the company. This was the acquisition of the so-called Meinzer Motion patent, a technique for inducing vibration of process equipment in three dimensions rather than two. This patent provided the basis for Sweco to enter into the production of vibratory machines for use in industrial screening, finishing, and grinding processes. In 1972 nearly all of Sweco's business

came from the manufacture of vibratory equipment based on the Meinzer Motion principle. Sweco had sold off its last nonvibratory business
in 1969, a sale that had reduced the company to one third of its previous
size. However, looking back, all Sweco executives thought that sale had
been an excellent decision.

Business areas

In 1972 Sweco's revenues of just under $15 million came from three
divisions: process equipment, finishing equipment, and environmental
systems. Foreign sales accounted for approximately 15 percent of total
sales.

Process equipment division. The process equipment division accounted for over 50 percent of revenues and was the oldest division. It
had two major product lines. The first and most important was the vibro-
energy separator. This performed the function of screening solid particles from liquids or other solid particles. Sweco supplied separators to
firms in many different industries throughout the world. More than
15,000 Sweco separators were in use in 1972 in such industries as chemicals, food, ceramics, pulp and paper, and other major process industries.
Some of the materials screened included cereals, detergents, sugar, clay,
fertilizer, sand and gravel, salts, plastic pellets, wood chips, soybeans,
paint, and apple juice.

Sweco separators were vibratory screening devices with from one
to four decks (layers) of screens of various mesh. The material to be
screened was fed to the top layer. As vibratory motion forced the material
to the periphery of the screen, the smaller particles or liquids passed
through the screen. The larger particles were funneled off from the
periphery. Further passes through lower, finer screens served to remove
increasingly smaller particles.

A vibratory separation machine consisted of a large metal cylinder
with layers of screen cloth inside and spouts for inflow and outflow of
materials. Units ranged up to six feet in diameter and were built with
a variety of special configurations and custom features. In addition to
selling separators, Sweco also sold replacement screens and spare parts.
These areas were a continuing and profitable source of follow-on business. In 1972 Sweco separators ranged in price from $1,000 to $10,000,
while replacement screens sold for between $50 and $400 apiece.

The second product line in the process equipment division was the
vibro-energy grinding mill, used for reducing the size of wet or dry
particles. A grinding mill was loaded with the material to be ground,
together with a special grinding medium (e.g., cyclindrical aluminum
pellets). The combination was vibrated at a high frequency producing
a grinding action. Applications of the grinding mill included the processing of ceramics, pharmaceuticals, cosmetics, paints, foods, electronic
memory cores, powdered metals, and pesticides.

Finishing equipment division. This division manufactured vibro-
energy finishing mills, which deburred or polished metal parts by vibrating them together with an abrasive compound. Customers for this equipment were many diverse metalworking industries.

Environmental systems division. This division manufactured a centrifugal wastewater concentrator that used a fine-mesh centrifugal screening process to purify liquids. The concentrator was used in municipal applications for removing a high percentage of the floatable, settleable, and suspended solids from raw sewage. It was also used in industrial processing plants, such as in paper, textiles, meat packing, food canning, or poultry, where the concentrator could recover large amounts of usable material while cleaning up plant effluent.

Product technology

Nearly all of Sweco's major product lines depended on vibration. The vibratory products were based on the Meinzer Motion process, which used three-dimensional vibration rather than side-to-side vibration. Many benefits flowed from the added dimension of movement in the Meinzer process. It added more ways in which the materials undergoing separation could be shaken and allowed great force to be exerted on particles. This greatly improved the control of the separation process, its capabilities for discriminating among different particles, and the rate of throughput. Second, the three-dimensional vibrating movement allowed the use of round rather than rectangular screens. This led to two advantages. A round screen allowed the use of an entire screening surface without having to worry about material becoming trapped in corners. Also, the efficient mounting of the screens was vastly improved. A key feature of an efficient screen was that it be as taut and even as possible to guard against materials concentrating at uneven spots. Rectangular screens had the problem that the mounting points on the framing rim exerted uneven pressures on the screen cloth. In contrast, the mounting points for a round screen exerted exactly even pressures. The greater resulting tautness and freedom from irregularities increased both the screening efficiency and the life of a round screen.

Sweco had also developed a patented self-cleaning device for its screens. A major problem in screening was that after operating for a while, parts of a screen would clog up with materials, an effect known as "blinding." Sweco's self-cleaning device minimized this problem.

Sweco separators combined three-dimensional motion, round screens, and the self-cleaning device to produce a machine with great advantages over competitors using rectangular screens. For example, three square feet of a Sweco screen were more efficient than six square feet of rectangular screen.

Sweco operated only in the "fine" segment of the screening business, and was not usually cost-effective in screening particles larger than ½ inch. Most of Sweco's production was of screens with 80 mesh or finer. An 80-mesh screen had 80 openings per linear inch (6,400 openings per square inch). Large-screen (coarse mesh) separators were based on a totally different applications technology than were small screens. The larger screens were also incorporated in relatively low value-added equipment, and there were many qualified competitors in this market.

There were about a dozen other fine-screen manufacturers in competition with Sweco. Because of Sweco's many technological advantages, these competitors tended to supply separators and screens for less demanding uses. Sweco had maintained its technological lead despite the fact that the Meinzer Motion patent had expired in 1959. To do so Sweco spent heavily on research and development, with an annual product development budget of about 2 percent of sales. Spending was even heavier on applications engineering to find new uses for its equipment.

Sweco estimated that in 1972 it held a 50 percent share of the U.S. market for fine screens. Its three major competitors, all small independent companies (Kason, Inc., Midwestern, Inc., and Derrick, Inc.), had combined 1972 sales of $6 million to $7 million. Kason and Midwestern had been started by ex-Sweco sales representatives and also used round screens. Sweco did not consider their equipment to be as high quality. Derrick competed with a special rectangular fine-screen design. There were also about 10 minor competitors, whose influence was primarily in the highly profitable replacement screen business where they competed with low-cost, regional strategies.

Roughly one third of Sweco's revenues came from the sale of complete units (separators, finishing mills, etc.). Total unit sales in 1972 were approximately 1,000 units, at an average price of $5,000 each. The balance of revenues came from replacement parts and screens.

Operations

In 1972 Sweco had about 325 employees, the majority located at City of Commerce, California, near Los Angeles. Most of Sweco's manufacturing was done at the Los Angeles plant, which had 100,000 square feet of space and an average daily output of three units. Production was essentially a batch process. Sweco also had assembly plants in Toledo, Ohio; Marietta, Georgia; Little Ferry, New Jersey; Cincinnati, Ohio; Toronto, Canada; and Nivelles, Belgium. In addition, Sweco had subsidiaries in Germany and Italy, and was in the process of setting up others in Spain and Mexico. The company was also constructing an 80,000-square-foot plant in Florence, Kentucky. Manufacturing employees totaled about 200.

Manufacture of a separator unit comprised the following major stages: steel-sheet, light-plate, structured shapes, and bars were cut, rolled, shaped, and welded into equipment components. Metal components were joined with manual and automatic feed welding, conventional metal arc welding, and specialized submerged arc welding. Parts for specialized motors were machined from castings, and the motors were assembled. Screen cloth was stretched and bonded to rings via spot welding or special epoxy bonding techniques. Completed units were assembled from these components as required.

Manufacturing costs were divided approximately as follows:

Materials	57%
Direct labor	13
Manufacturing overhead	30
	100%

Sweco manufactured virtually all fabricated steel components, electric drive systems, and cast polyurethane components in-house. It purchased woven wire cloth, nuts and bolts items, raw steel sheet and plate, motor bearings, rubber parts, and castings. Most of these purchases were made through local suppliers (although the woven wire cloth came from West Germany or Switzerland). Few volume discounts were available from suppliers.

Manufacturing overhead consisted of plant management, production control, scheduling and administrative personnel, plant costs such as rent, power, supplies, etc., depreciation on equipment, and special tooling.

The divisions existed for marketing and administrative purposes, while manufacturing, engineering, and accounting remained independent functions. The divisions and head office together had 40 marketing and sales employees, 35 management and general administrative employees, 25 engineering employees, and 25 accounting employees.

The compensation system consisted of hourly pay for direct labor employees, salary for most other employees. Management also received a profit-based bonus, and there was a discretionary bonus for other employees. Salesmen received both salary and commission. There was also a profit-sharing retirement fund for all salaried employees.

The chairman of the board was Robert P. Miller, Jr., 54 years old, a member of the Miller family, which owned a major portion of the company. Miller had recently been appointed chairman and had previously been vice president of the vibro-equipment division. Miller had joined Sweco six years before, after running a graphite mining business of his own. Howard W. Wright, Jr., 50 years of age, had joined the company in 1956, as vice president of the separator division, and had been Sweco's president since 1963. Howard Wright was Robert P. Miller, Sr.'s son-in-law. Zack Mouradian, 47 years of age, had recently been appointed group vice president, coordinating the marketing activities of Sweco's three operating divisions. Mouradian, who joined the company in 1957, had previously headed the separator division for seven years.

THE SAND SEPARATOR/MUD CLEANER

Background

Early in 1971 Zack Mouradian, the group vice president, received a phone call from Dr. Peter Hamilton of the production research unit of a leading international oil company. Hamilton told Mouradian that the oil company had been experimenting with conventional fine screens in the separation of sand from the drilling fluid (mud) used in the drilling of oil and gas wells. The oil company now wished to conduct additional experiments and had contacted Sweco because of its reputation as the leading industrial fine-screen separator manufacturer.

Sweco had made two abortive attempts to enter the oil field service business, with a Sweco industrial separator to be substituted for a shale shaker.[1] Both attempts, in the late 1940s and in the late 1960s, had failed. In retrospect, Sweco thought that it had made two fundamental errors. It had thought that it could just sell the equipment without providing service and maintenance. Also, the equipment had been too light duty for oil field conditions and could not handle the high flow rates encountered in drilling.

Mouradian decided to assign Les Hansen to work with Dr. Hamilton on this recent effort. Hansen had joined Sweco in 1970 in the development engineering laboratory. Hansen was 27 years of age, and his previous business experience was limited to his year with Sweco as an applications engineer and process troubleshooter. Hansen's education included some engineering training and a degree in economics. He was also attending law school on a part-time basis at the time.

Solids control equipment

In drilling for oil and gas, a slurry (called drilling mud) of liquid, solids, and chemicals was pumped through the drill pipe in order to wash away the cuttings created by the drill bit and to bring them to the surface. Depending on the depth of the hole and other factors, the liquid used would be water or oil. Generally, the deeper the hole the greater was the required density of the drilling fluid. Hence at depths of about 10,000 feet or greater, a high-density material called barite (barium sulphate) was added to the drilling mud. Barite's specific gravity was 4.2 compared to only 2.6 for typical rock formation solids.

The drilling mud coming out of a well needed to be cleaned to remove the cuttings or "drill solids" before it could be recirculated downward into the well. While no process could eliminate all the drill solids from a mud system, maximum removal was highly desirable. Reduced drill solids content of muds improved bit life and minimized drilling problems such as pipe sticking. At their worst, mud problems could stop drilling altogether.

Unfortunately, existing processes for removing fine drill solids in 1972 also removed the barite. Barite was so expensive that the cost of weighted mud often represented 10 percent to 15 percent of drilling costs. Conventional approaches for handling drill solids included chemical treatment, dilution, settling pits, and mechanical removal techniques. The suitability of particular techniques depended largely on the weight of the mud. The oil company that had contacted Sweco was working on the problem of solids control in heavier muds.

Three types of mechanical devices for removing drill solids were currently used in oil fields: shale shakers, hydrocyclones, and centrifuges. A shale shaker was similar in principle to industrial separators, with materials separated through a vibratory screening process. Generally a standard shale shaker could remove solid particles larger than

---

[1] A shale shaker was a standard type of mud cleaning equipment, to be described below.

500 to 1,000 microns.[2] More efficient fine-screen shakers could remove particles as small as 177 microns, using an 80-mesh screen.

Hydrocyclones (also called desanders and desilters) removed smaller particles in the 10–60 microns range using a different principle—centrifugal force. Hydrocyclones rotated the mud at high speeds in a cone-shaped container. Lighter, cleaned drilling mud would exit from the top of the cone, while the heavier solids gravitated to the bottom of the cone where the rotation speed was the highest. However, unlike the shale shaker, desanders and desilters[3] could deal only with unweighted muds. For muds above about 10 pounds per gallon (i.e., weighted with barite), an excessive amount of the barite was discharged and lost in the cleaning process because small, heavy barite particles would discharge from hydrocyclones as fast as smaller, lighter fine drill solids. A desilter operating on mud weighted with barite would have discarded $7 worth of barite a minute on a continuous basis.

Centrifuges used a similar principle to hydrocyclones, but for smaller volumes and using higher G-forces. Centrifuges could remove very small particles in the 3–5 microns range and could be used with very heavily weighted muds (those above 13 pounds per gallon), but they could not remove solids in the larger size range.

Thus, there was a gap in fine solids removal between the capabilities of shale shakers and of centrifuges. The problem, on which Dr. Hamilton of the oil company was working, was how to remove drilled solids from weighted mud in the 74–177 microns range. Particles this size were out of reach of shale shakers or centrifuges, but impractical for hydrocyclones.

The solution

In mid-1971 Hamilton came to Sweco's laboratory in Los Angeles and, working with Les Hansen, began to experiment with techniques to remove drill solids in the size range of the 74–177 microns gap while retaining barite. The arrangement was that the oil company and Sweco would each bear its own costs in these experiments. The oil company hoped to stimulate development of a product that would reduce drilling costs.

The process selected was one which combined a shale shaker, hydrocyclone, and Sweco fine-screen separator in three stages. First, the mud flowed through a shale shaker which removed large-sized solids. The mud then passed through second-stage hydrocyclones which separated the mud into low-density and high-density materials. The low-density material returned to the mud system. Third, the high-density material containing barite and fine drill solids flowed through another smaller screen, which passed the fine barite but rejected the drill solids larger than about 74 microns.

The first-stage shale shaker was a conventional unit of the type already in use in oil fields, and was not a Sweco product but was rented

---

[2] 25 microns = 0.001 inch.

[3] Desanders and desilters handled progressively finer particles.

or purchased by the operator from any of a number of suppliers. The (second) hydrocyclone stage was performed by a desilter, also a standard product though built into the Sweco unit. Sweco purchased desilters from Pioneer Centrifuge Company, Inc., a small manufacturer of solids control equipment. The third stage was provided by a specialized variant of Sweco's industrial separator, which was a higher technology unit than separators currently in use in oil field applications. A bank of the Pioneer hydrocyclones was combined with a Sweco fine-screen separator into one unit, referred to as the "sand separator" (Exhibits 4 to 7).

Sweco ran several field trials, with a number of progressively improved prototype machines at a number of drilling sites over a 12-month period in conjunction with Hamilton's company. These experiments showed that the fine-screen separator had to run 50 percent faster than the speeds of Sweco's industrial separators, which meant that the vibration-induced stresses were about five times greater than normal. The oil field unit also had to be more rugged than Sweco's industrial products because of its treatment by the oil field workers—or roughnecks. A Sweco machine installed in a food processing plant, for example, was well maintained and treated with care; in the oil field trials, Sweco sand separators were sometimes unloaded from the delivery truck by tying a chain around the unit, attaching the chain to the drilling rig, and driving the truck out from under the separator.

By the fall of 1972 data from the field tests had been compiled from several drilling sites. In one controlled test in a deep well in Louisiana, round-the-clock operating data proved that the separator was able to remove drill solids while saving barite. In addition, its use had prevented downtime from stuck drill pipe, common on such wells, by providing superior solids removal. Hamilton's oil company estimated that there were combined savings of over $100,000 on the well from using the mud cleaner. The oil company was now satisfied with the technique and suggested Sweco should market the mud cleaners on a commercial basis. By this time Sweco had spent approximately $100,000 in the development effort.

Sweco calculated that each sand separator unit would cost about $5,000 to manufacture in regular, large-scale production, broken down as follows:

	Materials	Labor	Other	Total
Vibrating screen	$1,000	$400	$ 800	$2,200
Skid	200	100	300	600
Motor starter	400	—	—	400
Hydrocyclones	1,800	—	—	1,800
Total	$3,400	$500	$1,100	$5,000

Sweco thought that the sand separator could be rented at the same daily rate as a centrifuge, $100.

In addition, each unit would also require an electric- or diesel-powered pump. Sweco could assemble these from purchased components for $3,000 and $6,000, respectively. Similar units were used by many drilling contractors to drive other pieces of solids control equipment, and typically rented for about $30 and $40 a day, respectively.

In operation, the sand separator wore out its fine screen every 10 days or so. Sweco sold replacement screens of a similar nature for between $100 and $200 to its existing industrial customers.

THE OIL FIELD SERVICE INDUSTRY

In 1972 a major boom in the oil and gas industry was underway, and was expected to continue over the next several years. In 1971 almost 26,000 oil and gas wells were drilled in the United States, both onshore and offshore. This number was expected to increase to 27,000 in 1972, and by at least an additional 1,000 wells per year over the next five years. The average depth of these wells was 5,000 feet with an average drilling cost of $19 per foot, increases of 17 percent and 48 percent respectively over a 10-year period. Drilling costs varied with the geographic location of the well, the type of formations penetrated, and the depth. In 1972 drilling costs ranged from $15 for shallow wells to $45 per foot for wells drilled up to 15,000 feet in depth, in the United States. Average depths were expected to continue to increase as part of the process of increasing exploitation of more "difficult" locations of oil and gas.

Drilling activity in the United States was geographically concentrated, with six states accounting for the bulk (Table 1). Almost 80 percent of world drilling activity took place in the United States, and only 1 percent in the Middle East. U.S. wells were much deeper on average than wells in other parts of the world, and therefore made much greater use of weighted drilling fluids and solids control equipment.

In the United States most wells were drilled by drilling contractors under contract to the operator (oil company).[4] There were many hundreds of drilling contractors, most very small businesses. Approximately 90 percent owned five drilling rigs or less. The drilling contractor was responsible for putting together a basic package of the necessary equipment to drill a well. It was standard practice in 1972 for the contractor to be paid a flat day rate by the operator. The operator then paid for the rental of special equipment and services, such as drilling mud and solids control equipment. Standard practice was for the contractor to own some of such equipment, and for the operator to rent additional equipment. Thus contractors did not rent, and operators did not buy.

The key piece of equipment was the drilling rig itself. There were about 1,100 active rigs in the United States in 1971, and these were generally expected to increase in number by about 100 per year over the next few years. While the drilling contractor owned the rig, suppliers provided specialized pieces of purchased or rented ancillary equipment, as well as many other services used in drilling. These suppliers constituted the oil field service industry, with revenues of about $3 billion in 1972.[5]

---

[4] The term *operator* applies to the oil company owning the hole. Actual drilling operations were carried out by the drilling contractor.

[5] The total U.S. oil and gas production industry had expenditures of over $10 billion in 1972, split about evenly among exploration, development, and production.

Table 1

State	Number of wells in 1971*
Texas	7,315
Louisiana	3,806
Oklahoma	2,490
Kansas	2,413
California	2,157
Ohio	1,157
	19,338
Other	6,513
Total	25,851

* Exploratory and development wells, both on-shore and offshore.

Source: American Petroleum Institute and the American Association of Geologists, published in *Basic Petroleum Data Book: Petroleum Industry Statistics,* 1978.

Oil field services included:

Well logging—the measurement of drilling parameters such as depth, weight on the drilling bit, torque, pump pressure, pump rate, and geological statistics.

Drill bits.

Cementing of holes after drilling, to prepare for regular production of oil or gas from the holes.

Down-hole tools, such as stabilizers and directional tools.

Drilling mud.

Rental equipment, including solids control equipment. Rental equipment included maintenance on a 24-hour on-call basis as a major part of the service.

Drilling mud

Barite-weighted drilling mud was used in most deep holes, and solids control equipment was needed to keep this mud clean of drill solids. Deep holes were those over 10,000 feet, and about 1,500 such holes had been drilled in the United States in 1971. In 1971 about 900 of the 1,100 active drilling rigs were capable of drilling more than 10,000 feet and were distributed as follows:

Texas	280
Louisiana	240
California	50
Alaska	10
All other	320
Total	900

Of these 900 rigs only about 400 were significant users of solids control equipment, because of the characteristics of the areas in which they were drilling: high drilling mud costs, soft sand formations, high waste disposal costs, high logistics costs, and deep holes. The major suppliers of drilling mud were the Magcobar division of Dresser Industries, the Baroid division of NL Industries, and the IMCO services division of the Halliburton Company. Precise estimates of market size were difficult to obtain, but the annual market for drilling mud was approximately $500 million in the United States and $150 million overseas in 1972.

Marketing of drilling mud was primarily through the use of a sales force that called on drilling contractors and oil companies. The oil drilling industry was well known for being a tight-knit community. Business in the oil field service market was typically sold on a per-hole basis. Advance knowledge from personal contacts of when and where holes would be drilled was crucial. It was necessary to sell to both the head office and local office of the oil company owning a hole, and to the contractor drilling the hole. Personal contacts and relationships were crucial in the selling process.

As part of the drilling mud service, all the companies also provided "mud engineers" who were responsible for maintaining the mud in a suitable condition during drilling operations. These mud engineers spent a great deal of time on site and were virtually members of the drilling contractor's team.

Solids control equipment

The market for solids control equipment was approximately $40 million domestically and perhaps $10 million overseas in 1972. About 85 percent of the domestic market for equipment was rental, with the remainder new equipment or aftermarket sales. The major items of equipment were:

	Percent of rental market (rental revenues)
Shale shaker	24
Desander (hydrocyclone)	7
Desilter (hydrocyclone)	13
Centrifuge	17
Power unit	38
Total	100

The power unit was the motor and pump that fed the desander and the desilter. A closely related piece of mud control equipment was the degasser which separated unwanted gases from the mud. Degasser revenues were equivalent to about one third of total solids control revenues. Of the U.S. rig population in 1972 of about 1,200 active rigs, perhaps 85 percent used shale shakers, 50 percent degassers, 25 percent desanders, 60 percent desilters, and 10 percent centrifuges. Daily rental rates were of the order of $40 for all units except the centrifuge, which had a rental rate of about $100 per day.

The effectiveness of solids control equipment was very difficult to judge precisely. The benefits of the equipment were:

Reducing mud costs.

Reducing drilling time.

Reducing downtime from pipe sticking.

Improving drill bit life.

Saving wear and tear on pumps (owned by the contractor).

However, none of these benefits could be readily quantified because the amount of barite used, drill bit life, and downtime were all subject to many factors besides solids control. Thus drilling contractors and operators tended to rely on the reputation of the supplier in purchasing solids control equipment. Also, the performance of solids control equipment was generally similar among existing suppliers, since the technology was well known. What was more crucial was the level of service. Each hour of downtime cost the operator hundreds of dollars onshore, and thousands offshore. Contractors were not directly motivated to avoid downtime because they were paid a flat daily fee. They were, however, motivated to minimize their load of activities and equipment, since they were responsible for its operation. Thus contractors tended not to be receptive to new types of equipment unless the associated benefits were fairly obvious.

Problems with oil field equipment were frequent because of the nature of the drilling process, the typically adverse operating conditions, and rough treatment in the hands of roughnecks. Suppliers of equipment had to provide 24-hour on-call service over a very wide area. Sunday morning at 3 A.M. seemed the most frequent time for breakdowns! Despite the importance of minimizing downtime, drilling contractors did not place solids control equipment high on their list of priorities because of the innumerable other problems they faced.

Solids control equipment was generally rented rather than sold because there were significant variations in the type of equipment needed for each particular well. The service component generally accounted for more than one third of the rental fee.

Solids control equipment suppliers maintained service networks consisting of a number of service centers, located near drilling areas. A prime area might have up to 100 rigs requiring solids control equipment. A minimum-size service center might service an area of approximately 200 miles in radius and be staffed by five people: a service center manager and four service reps. Such a center cost about $150,000 to maintain annually in 1972, excluding the cost of the rental equipment, with half of that cost being salaries. Such a service center could support $500,000 in rental revenues a year, based on a 50 percent utilization of its rental equipment. An average rental period per hole was about six weeks, although there was great variation in the period from hole to hole.

Suppliers depreciated their equipment over about a seven-year period. Over this period there would be extensive refurbishment of the equipment. Perhaps as much as 7–10 percent of rental revenues would be ploughed back as refurbishment.

COMPETITION

The solids control equipment business was led by the Sweco division of Dresser Industries, the Baroid division of NL Industries, and a number of other firms, including Baker Industries, Brandt, and Pioneer.

Dresser Industries

Dresser Industries had revenues of $905 million and pretax earnings of $66 million in the year ending October 1972. The breakdown by business segment was as shown in Table 2.

Petroleum group. The petroleum group provided a wide range of products and services to the exploration, drilling, production, and marketing segments of the oil and gas industries, as well as to mining and other industries. The principal products and services of the group included drilling mud additives, well logging and completion services, drill bits, down-hole tools, and other oil field equipment. The group also manufactured gasoline pumps and allied equipment for gasoline service stations.

Drilling mud and solids control equipment accounted for about $100 million, or one third of this group's revenues, of which drilling mud represented approximately $90 million. Drilling muds and related services were marketed under the Magcobar trademark. The services included Magcobar engineers who provided on-site, round-the-clock analysis and advice.

The Sweco division manufactured equipment for use in drilling, including shale shakers, desilters, and degassers. Although Sweco and Magcobar were organizationally separate, they shared the same sales force. Sweco had the largest market share in the solids control equipment market (which excluded degassers), about 30 percent. Sweco had very high visibility among operators and contractors and was widely recognized as the market leader. Sweco had about 25 to 30 oil field service locations in 1972.

Machinery group. This group produced compressors, blowers, pumps, and engines for municipal water systems and for the oil, gas, chemical, refining, paper, water pollution control, and other industries. Other activities included air pollution control and materials handling.

Table 2

	Percent revenues				Percent pretax earnings			
	1969	1970	1971	1972	1969	1970	1971	1972
Petroleum group	36	37	40	35	33	30	32	32
Machinery group	26	26	24	26	16	13	15	13
Refractories and minerals group	21	20	18	16	28	34	23	18
Industrial specialties group	17	17	18	23	23	23	30	37

Refractories and minerals group. This group mined and processed barite, bentonite, and lignite and supplied these to the petroleum group for use as drilling mud. The group also mined industrial sand, kaolin, and metallic sulfide ore. The other major activity was the mining, manufacturing, and marketing of refractories, which were nonmetallic mineral products used chiefly to line industrial high-temperature vessels.

Industrial specialties group. This group manufactured a broad line of pneumatic tools for various industrial uses and hand tools for light service trades and home use. The group also manufactured abrasives, grinding wheels, coated abrasive cloth, and related equipment. Other products included gauges, thermometers, switches, and valves for instrumentation or control of proce ses in the refining, chemical, petrochemical, electric power generation, and fire protection industries.

NL Industries

NL Industries (formerly National Lead) had revenues of $1,014 million in 1972, with pretax earnings of $62 million. These were divided as shown in Table 3.

Table 3

	Percent revenues				*Percent pretax earnings*			
	1969	*1970*	*1971*	*1972*	*1969*	*1970*	*1971*	*1972*
Chemicals group	17	19	19	20	19	27	35	32
Metals group	29	30	27	29	12	15	7	8
Pigments group	23	23	23	21	33	27	9	24
Fabricated products group	23	20	21	21	29	25	39	30
Industrial specialties group	3	3	3	3	4	3	1	3
Other activities	5	5	7	6	3	3	9	3

Chemicals group. This group supplied the petroleum industry with drilling mud additives, and specialized water-treating and corrosion-inhibiting chemicals for the petroleum industries. It also furnished extensive engineering services and equipment for well logging and testing.

The Baroid division represented about 55 percent of 1972 revenues of the chemicals group, and had supplied drilling mud for almost 50 years. It had entered the solids control equipment business in the 1950s. The same sales force sold both drilling mud and mud control equipment. Approximately 80 percent of Baroid's revenues came from selling mud, 10 percent from solids control equipment, and 10 percent from other oil field service activities. Baroid maintained oil field locations, service reps, and mud engineers worldwide. Baroid purchased a great deal of its solids control equipment from other manufacturers. For example, desilters were purchased from Demco, screens were purchased from Simco, and centrifuges were purchased from Bird.[6]

---

[6] These companies were all manufacturers of process equipment for a variety of industries.

The other major activity of the chemicals group was the production and sale of anticorrosive pigments, stabilizers, flame retardants, extender pigments, castor oil derivatives and chemical specialties for use by the plastics, paint, ink and adhesives industries, and of gellants for paint, grease, pharmaceutical, and cosmetics producers.

Industrial specialties group. This group produced zirconium and titanium chemicals for the ceramic and electronic industries, and made process alloys for the aerospace industry. It also produced and distributed radio-pharmaceuticals to hospitals and doctors for use in nuclear diagnostic medicine. NL was also the contract-operator for one of the U.S. Atomic Energy Commission's feed materials production centers. The group also sold Dutch Boy paints.

Others. The metals group produced lead products, precious metals products, and zinc and aluminum products. Its customers included the electronic, jewelry, photographic, aerospace, and railroad industries. The pigments group was a leading producer of titanium pigments used principally by the paint, paper, plastics, and rubber industries. The fabricated products group manufactured custon die castings for use as components in the production of automobiles, trucks, electrical appliances, office machinery, hand tools, and hardware.

The Brandt Company

Brandt was believed to be the third largest supplier of solids control equipment, with an approximately 7 percent market share. Brandt's total revenues in 1971 were less than $3 million. Brandt sold shale shakers only, and had been in business for less than five years. Brandt emphasized the ruggedness and simplicity of its equipment, and had a much smaller service operation than other suppliers. Brandt sold its equipment directly to drilling contractors and was not in the rental business. Thus Brandt did not maintain any service centers.

Baker Oil Tools, Inc.

Baker Oil Tools had revenues of $151 million and pretax earnings of $10 million in 1972. International operations accounted for just under 40 percent of revenues. Baker's revenues came from the segments shown in Table 4.

Drilling products. In 1971 Baker had acquired Milchem, Inc., for $12 million, thereby entering the drilling fluid business. Milchem sold both drilling mud and solids control equipment, with the revenue from mud approximately 95 percent of sales. Other components of Baker's drilling products group manufactured and marketed hole expanders, drill pipe controls, and well logging equipment. Milchem's products and services, along with other Baker petroleum products and services, were distributed primarily through Baker's 140 oil field service locations.

Other products. Baker also manufactured products used in lining holes to convert them from exploratory to production wells, and products used to restore maximum production to mature or aging wells. Baker had recently developed computer-controlled automated systems for controlling oil or gas production processes. Baker also marketed to petro-

Table 4

	Percent revenues			
	1969	1970	1971	1972
Petroleum industry				
Drilling	7	7	13	35
Completion and production	67	59	55	40
Remedial work and stimulation (of existing wells)	22	18	15	11
Other	1	3	4	4
Total petroleum	97	87	87	90
Mining industry	—	7	8	7
Other industries	3	6	5	3
	100	100	100	100

leum refineries a line of precision instruments and a line of process control instruments. Through its Galigher division, Baker manufactured processing equipment used in the mechanical and chemical extraction of metals from mined ores. Baker had also adapted for other industries some products originally designed for the petroleum industry. These other industries included cryogenics, paper pulp, chemicals, and food processing.

Pioneer Centrifuging Company

Pioneer was a small privately held company specializing in solids control equipment: centrifuges and hydrocyclones (desanders and desilters). Its revenues in 1972 were estimated at between $2 million and $3 million. Pioneer had a reputation for high-quality products, and Sweco had used Pioneer hydrocyclones as part of its experimental mud cleaners. Pioneer maintained three service centers.

Halliburton Company

Although it did not supply solids control equipment, Halliburton was a leading supplier of drilling mud through its IMCO services division, and was a leading oil field service company via IMCO and other divisions.

Halliburton had revenues of $1,422 million in 1972, with pretax earnings of $108 million. These revenues and earnings did not include $93 million of premiums and $6 million of net income from an unconsolidated fire and casualty insurance subsidiary. The breakdown by business segment of Halliburton's businesses was as shown in Table 5.

Oil field services and products. Halliburton performed a wide range of specialized services relating to drilling and production of oil and gas wells both onshore and offshore. Services included: pumping services offered in conjunction with cementing wells, hydraulic fracturing and chemical treatments, testing, logging and perforating services, specialized remedial services for high-pressure producing wells, and the supply of cement, drilling muds, fracturing sands and other bulk materials,

Table 5

	Percent revenues				Percent pretax earnings			
	1969	1970	1971	1972	1969	1970	1971	1972
Oil field services and products	27	26	23	28	46	58	56	61
Engineering and construction services	66	69	73	68	48	37	41	37
Specialty services and products to general industry ..	7	5	4	4	6	5	3	2

both for new and existing wells. In addition, Halliburton manufactured and sold a broad line of subsurface equipment, tools and controls, used in oil and gas production.

The IMCO services division was one of six Halliburton operating units providing oil field services and products. The IMCO services division had been formed from IMC Drilling Mud, Inc., whose acquisition by Halliburton had been completed in January 1972. Halliburton had paid $4 million for the remaining 50 percent interest belonging to International Minerals & Chemical Corporation. IMCO sold drilling mud and related chemicals via distribution facilities in the United States, Canada, and the North Sea area. Its 1972 revenues were estimated at between $20 million and $40 million.

Engineering and construction services. These included industrial construction (principally refineries, petrochemical and petroleum facilities, pulp and paper mills, and power plants) and marine construction (principally the fabrication of offshore drilling and production platforms and the laying of submarine pipelines). Engineering and other construction consisted primarily of project management, maintenance services, and engineering and civil construction.

Specialty services and products to general industry. Many of these involved industrial applications of techniques first developed for the oil and gas industry. These services included cleaning of petroleum refining and other industrial plants. Halliburton also manufactured specialty products including hydraulic cushioning devices for railway cars, pneumatic handling systems, pipeline testing devices, solid state relays, and a digital pressure monitoring system for oil field production automation.

THE DECISION

In November 1972 Sweco had to decide what to do about the sand separator. Should it enter the oil field service business and, if so, how? Les Hansen and the other Sweco executives could see many factors against their success. The problems of entering the oil field service business seemed enormous. Les Hansen had estimated that a full-scale effort by Sweco would require revenues from at least two service centers to support the overhead costs of setting up an oil field service division. Also Sweco had found that the mud cleaner process was not patentable nor could Dr. Hamilton guarantee that his company would rent any units.

In addition they wondered how Sweco could overcome these problems if they followed Dr. Hamilton's advice not to promote the sand separator. He had said to Howard Wright:

> If you go ahead, be careful. Don't promote it. Let the machine sell itself. If someone calls you up to ask about it, say that you don't know if it will work. Tell them to ask me. Bite your tongue if they ask you whether it will work.

Exhibit 1

SWECO, INC. (A)
Consolidated Statement of Earnings

	1972	1971	1970
Sales	$14,843,096	$11,889,643	$13,664,527
Cost of sales	7,964,294	6,391,671	8,237,809
Gross operating profit	6,878,802	5,497,972	5,426,718
Selling, administrative, and general expenses	5,647,004	5,064,099	5,043,605
Operating income	1,231,798	433,873	383,113
Other income:			
Gain on the translation of foreign currencies	—	25,887	—
Earnings from unconsolidated corporate joint venture	11,188	20,877	—
Total income	1,242,986	480,637	383,113
Interest expense, net	10,357	48,051	146,107
Earnings before income taxes	1,232,629	432,586	237,006
Income taxes	594,720	197,157	98,500
Net earnings	$ 637,909	$ 235,429	$ 138,506
Earnings per common share	$ 9.96	$ 3.63	$ 2.14

Source: Annual reports.

Exhibit 2

SWECO, INC. (A)
Consolidated Balance Sheet

	1972	1971
Assets		
Current assets:		
Cash	$ 855,608	$ 591,014
Receivables	2,897,518	2,623,654
Inventories	3,467,034	2,989,192
Prepaid expenses	169,316	169,385
Total current assets	7,389,476	6,373,245
Investments	52,685	92,497
Long-term receivables	17,494	36,312
Property, plant and equipment:		
Land	20,723	20,723
Buildings	264,976	246,957
Equipment	2,030,016	1,698,099
Leasehold improvements	367,006	332,430
Total property, plant, and equipment	2,682,721	2,298,209
Less accumulated depreciation and amortization	1,402,886	1,162,130
Net property, plant, and equipment	1,279,835	1,136,079
Patents	1,618	26,589
Deferred charges	2,581	14,295
Total assets	$8,743,689	$7,679,017
Liabilities and Stockholders' Equity		
Current liabilities:		
Notes payable to banks	350,371	594,231
Long-term lease obligation, amounts due within one year	10,114	19,932
Accounts payable	1,236,656	883,908
Accrued expenses	891,828	608,407
Income taxes	331,146	146,824
Total current liabilities	2,820,115	2,253,302
Long-term lease obligation	182,546	191,446
Unrealized gain on translation of foreign currencies	30,187	24,019
Stockholders' equity:		
Common stock	259,208	259,208
Additional paid-in capital	41,137	41,137
Retained earnings	5,445,371	4,909,905
	5,745,716	5,210,250
Less treasury stock	34,875	—
Total stockholders' equity	5,710,841	5,210,250
Total liabilities and stockholders' equity	$8,743,689	$7,676,017

Source: Annual reports.

Exhibit 3

ORGANIZATION CHART

```
                    Robert P. Miller, Jr.
                    Chairman of the Board
                              |
                    Howard W. Wright, Jr.
                         President
                              |
    ┌──────────┬────────────┬─────────────────┬──────────┬─────────────┐
Manufacturing  Administration  Zack E. Mouradian   Finance   Engineering
                             Group Vice President
                                  Marketing
                                     |
          ┌────────────┬─────────────┬──────────────────────┐
       Process      Finishing    Environmental    Les Hansen, Manager
      Equipment     Equipment       Systems       Sand Separator Project
       Division      Division       Division
```

Exhibit 4

DIAGRAM OF SWECO SAND SEPARATOR/MUD CLEANER

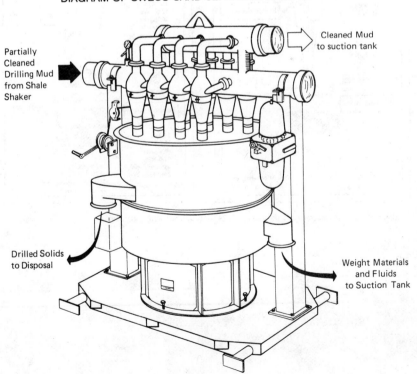

Cleaned Mud
to suction tank

Partially
Cleaned
Drilling Mud
from Shale
Shaker

Drilled Solids
to Disposal

Weight Materials
and Fluids
to Suction Tank

Exhibit 5

SAND SEPARATOR/MUD CLEANER SPECIFICATIONS

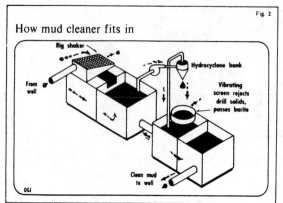

Fig. 2

How mud cleaner fits in

Table 2

Sweco sand-separator specs

Overall weight	2,600 lb
Overall dimensions	7'-5" high, 6'-0" long, 4'-0" wide
Construction	Epoxy-coated carbon steel
Hydrocyclones	
Size	4-in.
Number	8
Manifold	6-in.
Vibrating screen	
Screen diameter	48 in.
Screen mesh	150 mesh, or 200 mesh or finer for special applications
Motor	Explosionproof, 2½-hp, 230/460-v, 60-cycle

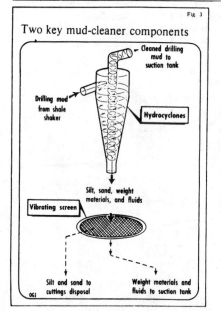

Fig. 3

Two key mud-cleaner components

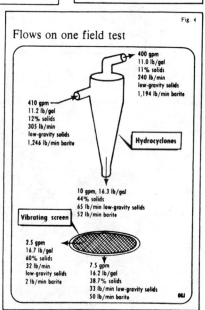

Fig. 4

Flows on one field test

Source: *Oil and Gas Journal,* January 7, 1974. Reproduced with permission.

Exhibit 6

DIAGRAM OF SELF-CLEANING SCREEN USED IN SWECO SEPARATORS

Self-cleaning screen

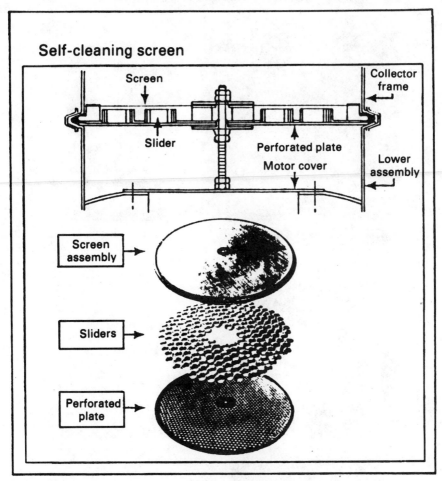

Source: *Oil and Gas Journal,* January 7, 1974. Reproduced with permission.

Exhibit 7

THE SAND SEPARATOR/MUD CLEANER ON SITE

EG&G, Inc. (A), Condensed

In 1974 EG&G was enjoying success as the manufacturer and marketer of a wide variety of technically oriented products. EG&G's operations were international in scope, and the financial community had recently sized up EG&G's performance very favorably.

> EG&G has reported successively higher quarterly sales and earnings comparisons with year-earlier results throughout the current economic recession. We believe that its energy technology related activities, successful acquisition, and strong financial management capabilities are chiefly responsible for its excellent earnings performance. . . . EG&G is uniquely associated with energy research and development and has a reputation for providing the highest quality products and services in its specialized field. (Merrill Lynch, *Institutional Report.*)

Exhibits 1 and 2 give EG&G's financial history and recent balance sheets and income statements.

BACKGROUND

During the course of America's development of nuclear energy, one of the more formidable problem-solving groups around was a trio of MIT professors named Edgerton, Germeshausen, and Grier. The three worked so well together that in 1947 they decided to form a company, whose name bore their initials, which would serve as a prime contractor to the Atomic Energy Commission and other government agencies in furnishing a variety of scientific and technical services in the electronic and nucleonic fields. From the beginning the company was technically oriented, putting the emphasis on invention and entrepreneurship. During the 1950s revenue came primarily from government contracts. However, under the impetus of Bernard O'Keefe, one of the original employees, it was at this time that EG&G took its first tentative steps toward

Exhibit 1

FINANCIAL HIGHLIGHTS
(as reported)

	Sales as reported ($000)	Net income (loss) ($000)	Income (loss) per share	Assets ($000)	Shareowners' equity ($000)	Common shares outstanding
1965	$ 51,441	$ 1,542	0.51	$12,884	$ 8,176	3,008,552
1966	64,655	2,012	0.59	16,331	10,148	3,439,978
1967	88,728	2,948	0.71	35,173	16,448	4,190,136
1968	111,628	3,619	0.78	50,327	24,800	4,554,364
1969	119,989	(2,175)	(0.49)	57,542	22,536	4,612,569
1970	112,925	1,009	0.20	52,546	23,084	5,717,712
1971	111,745	2,437	0.51	52,914	25,113	5,746,773
1972	125,387	3,393	0.65	64,580	32,063	5,765,551
1973	137,841	4,519	0.81	69,943	37,516	5,776,044
1974	162,949	5,716	0.97	77,084	44,079	5,781,898

Source: Annual reports.

Exhibit 2

EG&G INC. (A), CONDENSED
Balance Sheets
(recast)

	1974	1973
Assets		
Current assets:		
Cash......................................	$ 1,656,000	$ 2,277,000
Short-term investments, at cost which approximates market	8,362,000	8,170,000
Accounts receivable........................	24,733,000	22,089,000
Contracts in process	1,863,000	1,619,000
Inventories	20,316,000	14,340,000
Prepaid federal income taxes	—	803,000
Other current assets	800,000	474,000
Total current assets	57,730,000	49,772,000
Property, plant, and equipment:		
Land	964,000	776,000
Buildings and leasehold improvements......	12,318,000	11,332,000
Machinery and equipment	22,723,000	22,002,000
Total property, plant, and equipment....	36,005,000	34,110,000
Less: Accumulated depreciation	20,817,000	19,873,000
Net property, plant, and equipment	15,188,000	14,237,000
Investments	3,134,000	4,637,000
Other assets	1,032,000	1,144,000
Total assets	$ 77,084,000	$ 69,790,000
Liabilities		
Current liabilities:		
Notes payable and current maturities of long-term debt	$ 1,108,000	$ 1,606,000
Accounts payable	8,311,000	7,591,000
Accrued expenses..........................	8,118,000	7,906,000
Accrued taxes	5,138,000	4,003,000
Total current liabilities	22,675,000	21,106,000
Long-term debt:		
3½ percent convertible, subordinated debentures..............................	6,241,000	6,241,000
Other, less current maturities	3,395,000	3,113,000
Total long-term debt	9,636,000	9,354,000
Deferred federal income taxes	694,000	323,000
Shareowners' investment:		
Preferred stock	22,000	22,000
Common stock	5,792,000	5,783,000
Capital in excess of par value..............	6,469,000	6,399,000
Retained earnings	31,836,000	26,827,000
Total shareowners' investment	44,119,000	39,031,000
Less: Cost of shares held in treasury ..	40,000	24,000
Total shareowners' investment	44,079,000	39,007,000
Total liabilities	$ 77,084,000	$ 69,790,000

Exhibit 2 (*concluded*)

Consolidated Statements of Income

	1974	1973
Net sales and contract revenues	$162,949,000	$143,997,000
Costs and expenses:		
Cost of sales	126,336,000	113,125,000
Selling, general, and administrative expenses.................................	25,675,000	23,136,000
	152,011,000	136,261,000
	10,938,000	7,736,000
Net fee from operating contract..............	1,233,000	1,176,000
Income from operations	12,171,000	8,912,000
Equity in income of investments	310,000	319,000
Interest expense	(796,000)	(778,000)
Other income (expense), net	(267,000)	(227,000)
Income before income taxes	11,418,000	8,680,000
Provision for federal and foreign income taxes	5,702,000	3,846,000
Net income.................................	$ 5,716,000	$ 4,834,000
Earnings per share	$0.97	$0.82

diversification into the commercial market, attempting at the same time to become more "hardware" than purely service oriented.

The 1960s was a period of success for high-technology firms, and the government continued its heavy demand for EG&G's services. EG&G went public in the early 60s and enjoyed a great reception, with P/Es as high as 100. In 1965 Bernard O'Keefe was made president. At about the same time, the environment in which the company operated also began to change. Technology for technology's sake was becoming less sacrosanct, and the federal government began to shift its support from space programs into Viet Nam. O'Keefe decided it was time to take major diversification steps with the equity money then available in order to broaden the still relatively narrow focus of the firm's business. About 20 technically oriented companies were acquired during this period, which more than doubled the business areas in which EG&G was involved. During this period, the management systems used throughout EG&G were financial accounting procedures, which sometimes lacked consistency between business areas, and a periodic companywide forecast of sales and profits. Some of the more commercially oriented division were using an early planning system. Until 1969 EG&G returned outstanding financial results, with consistent earnings per share growth of 15+ percent and return on stockholders' equity of 15+ percent.

The year 1969 brought a number of traumas to EG&G. For the first and only time during its existence the company lost money (Exhibit 1) due to large cost overruns on a fixed price government contract. In addition, the stock market was no longer enamoured of high-technology companies, and thus EG&G's stock price, not to mention the value of senior management's accumulated equity holdings, took a nose dive. Several managers referred to this experience as their first realization that EG&G could make mistakes.

Following this experience, which one senior manager referred to as "an identity crisis," control became a popular goal at EG&G. Bernard O'Keefe, in particular, put great stress on planning and the ability to predict problems. He believed that management needed access to information on which to base decisions about which business units to keep in the company and which ones to spin off. The company began to pay attention to limiting the amount of resources tied up in accounts receivable and inventory. EG&G, which had always valued the innovative engineer, began to demand increased management skill as well.

O'Keefe also saw the need for planning throughout the company. The early long-range planning system which had been developed internally over the preceding eight years and used primarily in commercially oriented divisions was modified in order to make it uniform and applicable to all divisions. O'Keefe hired an outsider, Dean Freed, experienced in the use of planning, to take over the operational management of the business. At the same time he hired outside consultants, Arthur D. Little and some academics from the Boston area, to evaluate the company's planning system. Having been reassured that the system was a valid and consistent one, he encouraged operating managers to cooperate with the head of planning, George Gage, implementing the system throughout the company.

During the next two to three years, Freed and Gage worked with the operating managers to implement the system. George Gage said:

> When the planning system was being developed, much of my time was spent working on the system itself. Subsequently, as the system began to mature and stabilize, my time was increasingly spent on selling and applying the system throughout the company. Our experience indicates that about two years are required from the time a system is first introduced in an organization to the time when that organization is producing good plans.

EG&G in 1974

Although EG&G did sell off some of the acquisitions it had made in the 60s after the loss in 1969, it still produced a wide variety of products and services. By 1974 EG&G provided scientific and technically oriented products, custom equipment, systems and related or specialized services to government and industrial customers. Its products and services were classified into six business areas: components for industrial equipment, scientific instruments, environmental testing systems and services, biomedical services, high-technology systems and services for the federal government, and Energy Research and Development Administration support.

Corporate goals were explicitly stated by top management in the *Planning Manual* developed by George Gage:

> EG&G is a company dedicated to develop and prosper from the commercial, industrial, and government application of technological products and services. Since technological progress and its market acceptance are not always predictable, the company strategy is to diversify its resources into a number of market areas, a variety of products and services, and a judicious blend of mature and emerging industries. Organizationally this translates

into a number of self-sufficient divisional profit centers, grouped by market compatibility, with corporate emphasis on performance measurement, planning, and resource allocation. The corporation is thus uniquely qualified to identify and exploit opportunities in products and services for a variety of markets from mature as well as emerging technologies. . . .

The long-term growth goal we have chosen is an appreciation in earnings per share of 15 percent per year while maintaining a minimum annual return of 15 percent on our stockholders' equity. These goals will require performance considerably above average, but are reasonable and achievable with above-average effort.

EG&G tried to meet these goals by participating in a large number of high-technology industrial and government markets. Typically EG&G was, or was striving to be, a leader in its market segments.

The company milieu

EG&G's corporate headquarters was in an industrial development in Bedford, Massachusetts, near Route 128. The area contained a great number of other technical firms, and at any given lunch hour a visitor would see groups of employees jogging around the buildings or playing frisbee. EG&G's head office, built in the 1960s, had simple decorations which attempted to alleviate the cinder-block walls.

The company's senior management were located in Bedford (see Exhibit 3 for an organization chart). The president, Bernard J. "Barney" O'Keefe, was a jovial extroverted man involved in many projects outside the company, such as organizing private business in Massachusetts to fund a Chicago consulting firm's study of the management of the Commonwealth of Massachusetts. He was on the board of directors of 11 companies.

Dean Freed, executive vice president in charge of directing all of the corporation's operating divisions and subsidiaries, had an office next to O'Keefe. He had a direct, efficient manner which quickly revealed a very thorough grasp of all that went on in the company. He had joined EG&G in 1970, after having worked as a vice president responsible for three divisions at Bunker Ramo and holding executive management positions at TRW, Inc., in manufacturing and marketing. He had received a B.S. in mechanical engineering from Swarthmore College and an M.S. from Purdue University. His office was decorated with aerial photographs, and two large battered briefcases were always kept nearby. In describing Freed a colleague said:

> Dean is really a superior manager. He's like a teacher. He knows how to improve an inventory system or marketing program. When he's dealing with other managers he is completely straightforward. He likes people to argue back at him and never bears a grudge against them the next day if they do.

George Gage was vice president in charge of planning at EG&G and also had an office among the top executives at Bedford. He had joined EG&G in 1962 with the mission "to develop and implement a meaningful planning system to support long-term goals," and had recently been made a vice president. When Dean Freed joined the firm, Gage switched

Exhibit 3

ORGANIZATION CHART

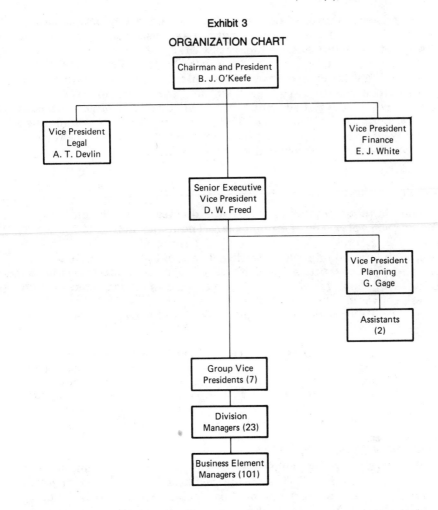

from reporting to O'Keefe to reporting directly to Freed. Gage had two assistants. Otherwise, Freed and Gage had no staff support.

Many of EG&G's managers were rarely at Bedford since the company's businesses were so geographically dispersed. The company had operations in 20 states and 16 foreign countries. The majority of employees at EG&G had similar backgrounds. When asked about the type of person who worked at EG&G, George Gage said, "Oh, of course, we're all engineers."

Critical to the management process of EG&G was the monthly management meeting. It was held at corporate headquarters in Bedford. The meeting was chaired by O'Keefe and consisted of Freed, the seven group vice presidents, and senior staff. There was a prescribed agenda which typically consisted of announcements, operations review, investments, acquisitions, and general discussion. O'Keefe used the announcement segment to inform the committee of new ideas he had gained in his travels around the country. A participant described the meeting as the "chief communication vehicle at EG&G."

A major committee within EG&G was the business development committee, which was composed of O'Keefe, Mr. Germeshausen (the retired chairman), Mr. White (vice president and treasurer), Mr. Wallace (a group vice president), Gage, and Freed. Mr. O'Keefe and Mr. Germeshausen did not attend all meetings. The major function of this committee was to review the five-year plans of the company's divisions. The reviews took place once a year at the divisional headquarters.

THE PLANNING PROCESS

The planning process at EG&G was divided into two major parts: the five-year plan and the profit plan. The major activities related to the two segments took place at different times of the year. The five-year plan focused on strategy setting. The profit plan was a financially oriented plan covering a 12-month period. Both were described in the EG&G *Planning Manual* which was provided to all managers in both a desk copy and a portable form.

In reflecting on his impression of the planning system, Dean Freed said:

> It is a great advantage for divisions managers to be given a framework of analysis, a way to test ideas. Basically, we want planning to test whether the things which a division manager wants to do with his assets are *consistent* with the strategy and competitive position of that particular division. In fact, I'd say going through our planning process and getting to fully understand all its implications is a magnificent business school.

Corporate structure and the planning process

The lowest level at which EG&G required strategic planning was the "business element." This was defined as a "business system which involves a single product line or a particular service capability being supplied to satisfy the needs of a single market segment." George Gage brought the idea of business elements to EG&G when he joined the company in 1962. During the intervening years the idea grew from use only in the commercial products divisions to corporatewide acceptance.

Top management believed that good definition of business elements was important because business elements were homogeneous products or services in a single market segment, and thereby particularly well suited for analysis and forecasting. As one manager put it:

> In many of our businesses EG&G has concentrated on specialized segments which business element managers are able to totally understand. The key is to describe the right battlefield; define the right business element.

EG&G had 101 separate business elements with total sales of $163 million, each the responsibility of a business element manager. These ranged in size from $5 million plus in sales for the largest business element to 23 business elements with less than $500,000 annual sales. In the last two years, EG&G had added 25 new business elements (16 through acquisition and 9 through internal development), divested 4, and discontinued 4 others.

Above the business element level were 27 divisions, each directed by a division manager. The division manager had responsibility for the delineation of business elements in the division and for their profit and loss and return on investment. Division managers were also responsible for developing strategies for their divisions as a whole, as well as being expected to be intimately involved in the development of the strategies of each individual business element within the division.

Divisions were grouped under seven group vice presidents. These individuals were responsible for the performance of a number of divisions or one particularly large division. They also were part of the corporate administration. One group vice president described his job as "an extension of Dean Freed." Therefore, the group vice presidents were both closely involved in the development of strategy while at the same time were responsible for aiding top management in evaluating strategic plans.

In 1974 top management published the *Planning Manual* in a permanent form. Previously, a new planning manual and directions had been prepared every year incorporating the changes which had taken place. Management now felt that the system was sufficiently mature and did not expect any large changes in the future.

The five-year planning procedure

The first half of each year was dedicated to developing the company's five-year plan. Exhibit 4 presents a graphic representation of the system as well as a timetable for the different steps involved. Basically, the business development committee provided the group vice presidents with planning guidelines which they in turn modified and cascaded down through division managers to the business elements. Then the business element and division and group managers created their own detailed five-year plans. There was a review by the business development committee of the plans. Finally, the consolidated corporate plan was reviewed by the board of directors.

1. Planning guidelines. The first step of the five-year planning process took place in January of each year. After reviewing the previous five-year plans, George Gage wrote a preliminary draft of planning guidelines for the group vice presidents. This draft was submitted to the members of the business development committee who modified it. In Gage's opinion it was Freed who had the major input into the final contents of the planning guidelines. These guidelines were on one-page forms and contained both quantitative and qualitative goals for the groups.

Once the guidelines were received, the group vice presidents began the cascading process which would eventually create guidelines for each business element based on the corporate guidelines modified by intervening levels of management. Top management expected to have its planning guidelines modified, and Gage described the procedure as "an

Exhibit 4

FIVE-YEAR PLANNING PROCESS

January   Vice president planning and executive vice president review past performance and write new planning guidelines. Send to group vice presidents.

February   Group vice presidents assess and modify guidelines and set guidelines for divisions.

March   Division managers receive planning guidelines which they amend and send on to business element managers.

Business element managers complete financial forms which result from Form K strategies.

April   Division managers work with the business element managers to perfect their plans.

Group vice presidents work with their divisions on their plans.

May   Final review meetings are held at division headquarters.

June   Corporate consolidation of all results.

Presentation to the board of directors.

opportunity to get all the ground rules and assumptions sorted out before the managers began the five-year plan."

Soon after the planning guidelines were received, the business development committee sent out a notice of the date on which each division would be reviewed. Accompanying this notice were any modifications in the planning procedure for that year and occasionally instructions to aid the uniformity of calculation such as foreign currency exchange rates.

The corporate planning staff did not provide the business element managers with any forecasts or environmental assumptions. Freed was skeptical about long-range economic forecasts. "After about one year's time I'd just as soon use astrology." Business element managers were expected to do their own environmental assessments appropriate for their units. "After all," said George Gage, "inflation is good for some of our businesses and bad for others. We don't want to provide our managers with pronouncements which will keep them from analyzing their own situations."

2. Five-year plan—the business elements.   After receiving the division manager's planning guidelines, business element managers set to work developing the information for Form K, the "Long-Range Plan, Business Element Summary" (Exhibit 5). This was the only form which was devoted to strategy itself. The *Planning Manual* described Form K as follows:

> The purpose of Form K is to provide a convenient one-page summary of its major strategic factors, a succinct statement of the business strategy, and a forecast of performance expected. The use of Form K greatly facilitates communication and discussion regarding the business element.

Once a business element manager was satisfied with the overall strategy of the element, there were several other forms to be completed in order to express the strategy in financial terms. The first was Form L which is "The Business Element Operating Statement" (Exhibit 6). This was an income statement which isolated certain expense items; the form also required actual results for previous years to be compared with those forecasted. Investment also had its own forms with which the business element manager had to contend. Form C, the "Investment Data" form (Exhibit 7), focused attention on the balance sheet and cash ratios.

3. Five-year plan—the division.   Division managers were also responsible for a strategic five-year plan. First, they worked with their business element managers in order to perfect the individual plans. After the division managers were satisfied with these individual plans, they were required to develop five-year plans for their divisions as a whole. Each consisted of (I) divisional goals, (II) divisional strategy, and (III) divisional summaries.

Divisional strategy was to discuss the direction and emphasis for the division as a whole, and provide a summary statement of the Form K for each existing business element and a summary statement of the strategy for any new business development and/or acquisition. The divi-

Exhibit 5

LONG-RANGE PLAN: BUSINESS ELEMENT SUMMARY (Form K)

Long-range plan: Business element summary

1. Product and/or service	2. Customers	3. End use

4. Direct competitors Sales this market last year (CY) Market share	5. Competitive advantages	6. Competitive disadvantages
Total direct market $ _____ K ___ 100%		

7. Market alternatives (competing techniques)	9. Summary of strategy	TYPE	Build
			Hold
			Harvest
			Withdraw
			Explore
8. Factors affecting future market growth		DIRECTION	Base
			Market seg.
			Output diff.
			Market devel.
			Output devel.
		POSTURE	Leader
			Me-too
			Performance

10. History/forecast												POSTURE	Value
Market													Price
Share of market, percent													Economy
Sales													Prestige
Operating profit, percent to sales													Quality

Date _____ _____ _____ _____
Form K (Rev. 1)   (Subelement)   (Business element)   (Division)

sional summaries were provided on forms similar to the ones completed by the business elements.

4. Five-year plan—groups. Once the business elements and divisions completed their plans, the group vice presidents consolidated them. Their job, more than the other two levels, consisted mainly of summing the results of their subordinates. They needed to verify consistency and worked with any of their managers whose plans did not meet expectations. Also, if the overall financial results were inadequate when compared to the expectations of the planning guidelines previously negoti-

Exhibit 6

BUSINESS ELEMENT OPERATING STATEMENT (Form L)

BUSINESS ELEMENT OPERATION STATEMENT

Operating statement	$000	CY*					
Market							
Share of market, percent							
Bookings							
Sales							
Cost of sales							
Gross margin							
Gross margin, percent to sales							
R&D							
Selling expense							
Local G&A expense							
Group G&A expense							
Corporate G&A expense							
Operating profit							
Operating profit, percent to sales							

SALES DETAIL

	CY sales mix	By type of contract		By geography		By source of funds	
		Cost plus fee	$ ———— 000	U.S.A.	$ ———— 000	Defense	$ ———— 000
		Fixed price standard	$ ———— 000	W. Europe	$ ———— 000	Other gov't	$ ———— 000
		Standard price	$ ———— 000	Rest of world	$ ———— 000	Nongov't	$ ———— 000
		TOTAL	$ ———— 000	TOTAL	$ ———— 000	SUBTOTAL	$ ———— 000

Date ————

Form L

_____ (Business element)

_____ (Division)

*CY = Calendar year.

Exhibit 7

INVESTMENT DATA (Form C)

INVESTMENT DATA												
Investment detail $000	CY*											
1. Accounts receivable												
2. Contracts-in-process												
3. Inventories												
4.												
5. Accounts payable												
6. Accrued (prepaid) expenses												
7. Operating capital (1+2+3−5−6)												
8. Assigned fixed assets at cost												
9. Accum. depreciation, assigned assets												
10. Assigned net fixed assets (8−9)												
11. Allocated fixed assets at cost												
12. Accum. depreciation, allocated assets												
13. Allocated net fixed assets (11−12)												
14. Net other assets (liabilities)												
15. Net investment (7+10+13+14)												
16. Long-term lease commitments												
17. Total investment (15+16)												
CASH FLOW												
18. 0.5 × Operating profit (when negative, use as 1.0 × Operating profit)												
19. Depreciation and amortization												
20. Other sources (uses)												
21. Increase (decrease) in operating capital												
22. Capital additions												
23. Net cash flow (18+19+20−21−22)												
SUMMARY												
24. Sales												
25. RONI												
26. ROTI												
27. Operating profit, percent to sales												
28. Operating capital, percent to sales												
29. Net investment, percent to sales												
30. Accounts receivable, DSO												
31. Inventory turnover												

Date ──────────

(Business element)   (Division)

Form C

*CY = Calendar year.

ated, the group vice president would work on improvements both in terms of existing operations and in developing new business ideas. At times group vice presidents became aware of a weak plan among their elements. Although they would do their best to improve that plan they might well inform the business development committee about the problem in advance of the reviews.

5. Corporate review. Prior to the corporate review, the business development committee received and reviewed copies of the five-year plan as submitted. The reviews themselves took place at the divisions' own headquarters. Each review considered all the business elements for which the division manager was responsible. Each division was represented by four or five people consisting of the division manager, his principal managers (including the controller), and possibly a divisional staff assistant. Depending on the preferences of the division manager involved and the need to explain a recent change which might be affecting a particular market, there was sometimes a brief presentation. One division manager said he used this presentation as an opportunity to give some visibility to an impressive manager in his division.

The question and answer period which followed was the heart of the review, however. Heated arguments could and often did take place during these. As one group vice president said:

> The business development committee is sometimes wrong, and specifically, sometimes Dean Freed is wrong. His strength is his ability to comprehend the masses of details which make up the operations of this company. But he tends to get fixated on one little point which doesn't fit or bothers him in some way.

Another perspective on Freed at review meetings was:

> He's a very involved manager. He likes to understand all the facts of the businesses. And sometimes the operating managers know better than he does. I guess if you had to fault him, it would be that he overmanages. Of course, that's easy to say about anyone until something goes wrong . . . and that doesn't happen very often around here.

The result of the question and answer period was either approval of the plan as presented or a consensus to do the plan again along the lines suggested by the business development committee. Every year there were three or four significant revisions of the 27 divisional plans presented.

The five-year plan was not directly linked with a manager's compensation. It did come into consideration when a manager was being considered for advancement. Although EG&G had a personnel department, it was Dean Freed and the group vice presidents who made decisions about managers advancing to the division level.

A couple of division managers had been removed for not being able to come to grips with the planning expectations at EG&G. Dean Freed reflected on the seriousness with which the inability to plan strategically was viewed:

> It is a serious problem if a division manager has one business element whose five-year plan is not rigorous and consistent. If succeeding five-year

plans exhibited the same problems, that division manager's career is in trouble. After all, if it's easy for me to see the fallacy of the strategy in the time I spend studying the plan, why didn't the manager?

When the committee was at a location evaluating a plan, they started by trying to understand the market involved, as described in Form K. From an understanding of the market, the committee then tried to evaluate whether the strategy was consistent with that market. Freed said, "If a business element has had 5 percent of a market and forecasted that it would have 30 percent of the market in five years, they need a more creative strategy than 'trying harder'." Once the business development committee approved a business element and division plan, the division and business element managers were finished with the formal preparation of the five-year plan for that year.

Although the planning process involved a great deal of time and effort on the part of EG&G managers, they seemed to appreciate the information it provided. One division manager said:

> It really takes a lot of work to complete the requirements, but once you learn the system with the aid of George Gage it becomes an extremely useful management aid. All the other managers have the same frame of reference so it makes communication easier. It's important to be forced to take a long look at what you're trying to do rather than constantly dealing with the day-to-day problems. Without the requirement I know I would postpone it in favor of the operating problems at hand. Beyond that, it is a great reference during the year with which to judge your progress.

6. Consolidation and presentation to the board. After careful review of the divisional five-year plans, Gage and Freed were chiefly responsible for producing the forecasts of sales and earnings on which corporate-wide planning was based. Bernard O'Keefe used these forecasts as part of his presentation to the board of directors of the consolidated five-year plans. Top management expected financial results to vary from forecast due to unforeseen and uncontrollable events, but EG&G had an excellent record in forecasting the performance of its ongoing businesses. The board had never rejected a corporate five-year plan but did offer suggestions, such as an adjustment in the procedure for treating inflation, which were used in planning the following year.

The profit plan (the one-year plan)

The annual profit plan was prepared in the fall of the year in the context of the five-year plan. Business element managers, division managers, and group vice presidents were all required to prepare yearly profit plans. It was the ability of the managers to meet the yearly profit plan which was tied directly to a manager's compensation. If managers met their profit plans, they received a bonus. If they did better than their plan, they received a higher bonus, but one which was lower than if they had accurately forecasted the superior performance. At the division level approximately 10–20 percent of a manager's salary was variable depending on performance versus plan. Just how the allocation was made varied among divisions depending on the nature of the risk involved and the amount of flexibility available to the manager.

The profit plan was the basis for operations management and control of the business in the next 12-month period. Like the five-year plan, the one-year plan was reviewed by a group of senior corporate executives. In this case it consisted of Freed, Gage, Jack Dolan (the corporate controller), and the applicable group executive. The coordination of business strategy and financial control was achieved through these meetings and the one-year plan.

The monthly management meeting

Each month at the management meeting, group vice presidents had to present their division's monthly financial reports which consisted of bookings, sales, operating profit, and operating capital. Each group vice president had the opportunity to fill in the narrative behind the cold financial results, and acquisitions and future acquisition candidates were also discussed as well as any new business ideas. Participants felt that the informality of this meeting led to a high degree of candor.

At approximately the same time as the management meetings were held, Dean Freed met individually with each group vice president in order to review the financial results of the divisions. During the meeting the two discussed anything of interest which was happening in the divisions. Freed said:

> During these meetings I insist on discussing strategic issues. I am just not interested in the operating problems of the divisions. They can solve them better than I can. What I want to hear about is new ideas, staffing requirements, and potential problems.

Divisions and groups prepared monthly financial results which they were able to use in judging their performances. Although the division managers had complete discretion in the management of their divisions, many of them employed a monthly meeting format, analogous to the corporate one, in order to meet with their business element managers and discuss problems or new ideas in light of the data contained in the financial results.

Planning and innovative strategy for the corporation

George Gage commented on the interaction of planning and innovation:

> Our planning system does an effective job of controlling and measuring our base operations. It even provides our managers with uniform methods of evaluating new business development. However, eliciting bright new ideas is beyond the scope of our system. Naturally in a firm like ours innovation and new business development are vital. At the very least, I hope the planning system doesn't stifle new ideas.

The compilation of element and division five-year plans identified needs of the corporation relative to its goals but did not generate innovative ideas. Many ideas for new business directions came from the business element level. There seemed to be a corporatewide belief in the ability of all managers to provide a creative input. For example, the divisional five-year plan asked for new business development ideas as the third section of its "strategy" requirement. One senior manager said, "There aren't many cases where the headquarters has been the source of creativity in terms of new products."

Top management, particularly Bernard O'Keefe and Dean Freed, did address the problem of corporatewide strategy. They held meetings from time to time specifically addressing the overall strategy of the company. In years past, EG&G had held retreat meetings in hopes that a new physical surrounding might elicit new perspectives. They were abandoned as not useful. Dean Freed felt that EG&G had less of a problem than some single-product, single-market companies in maintaining an unbiased perspective on the corporation's future. He said, "Heterogeneity is a great aid in avoiding irrational, emotional attachments to a particular strategy."

While recognizing the benefits of planning, not the least of which was a comparable basis for defending requests for capital, several managers expressed concern about continuing innovation. One group vice president said, "Really good ideas are thought of in unorthodox ways, and planning imposes an orthodox system." He went on to speculate about the possible disincentives imposed on creativity by such an exhaustive planning system. "Innovative ideas can be successfully subjected to planning, but there's always a risk of their being stifled."

EG&G, INC. (B)

In May 1974 Dean Freed, executive vice president of EG&G, wondered what he would do at the review meeting for the electro-mechanical division (EMD), scheduled for the following week. The division's previous year's results were disappointing, but division management expressed in their recently submitted 1974 five-year plan the belief that the situation could be turned around.

BACKGROUND

In the 1960s EG&G developed a new technology involving ceramic to metal seals. Management felt there was a good opportunity to exploit the new technology in connectors for electric cables. When two types of cables needed to be joined, connectors were clamped onto each end and these were fastened using mechanisms of varying complexity. The higher the frequency or voltage to be transferred, the more complex was the required connector. Depending on their complexity, connectors could cost from 5 cents to $5 or more. Higher technology, higher priced connectors were manufactured in the United States, while low-cost connectors were increasingly being manufactured abroad.

EG&G had a specific application for their new connector in the defense work they were then doing for the U.S. government's Sandia missile program. The high-technology connector was able to eliminate radio interference which affected the guidance of missiles in enemy territory. In order to be able to take advantage of the expected demand in the Sandia missile program, EG&G began to look for the best way to gain knowledge of the market and to develop the manufacturing capability necessary to produce this new connector.

The Strode Company, a small firm located in Franklin, Massachusetts, was brought to their attention. Strode was a manufacturer of standard technology connectors, had not been particularly successful, and was known to be available for sale. EG&G's management felt that the fixed costs of Strode's operation could be supported by EG&G's proprietary defense business. To this base EG&G's management hoped to enter other specialty markets in which their technological advantage could be exploited. In this way, EG&G planned to avoid Strode's competitive disadvantages in competing head to head with commodity producers who could manufacture connectors at lower costs because they produced and sold much greater standard volumes. However, the addition of specialty work to Strode's line would require the hiring of more engineers to do the designing and more highly skilled workers to produce the more varied products. EG&G acquired Strode in 1969, and it became the electromechanical division with all operations continuing in its existing facilities.

Strode's base businesses consisted of miniature, coaxial cable connectors for microwave applications and radio frequency (RF) applications. Coaxial cables were composed of a tube of electrically conducting material surrounding a central conductor held in place by insulators. They were used to transmit signals of high frequency. About one half of Strode's sales was in standardized connectors, the other half was in connectors for specialty applications.

The manufacturing process was straightforward and required only general-purpose machinery, though highly skilled machinists were necessary for some operations. Even experienced machinists, who were themselves in short supply, required about three months of training before they were competent to produce the new EG&G connector.

EMD was at a great cost disadvantage in the sale of standardized parts in comparison with its chief competitor, Amphenol Corporation, which controlled 25+ percent of the market. Strode's specialized work had greater profit potential, but this had not yet been realized because of problems with cost control and a small potential market. In an attempt to cover fixed costs, Strode produced standardized connectors in order to keep manufacturing at capacity despite the very low margins on these standardized items.

Freed remembered how Jim Sheets, the division manager, had been a driving force behind acquiring EMD. Sheets had been with EG&G for 15 years, and had had an outstanding record of achievement. As the manager of a highly successful business element, he had brought in a remarkable 10 percent of the corporation's profit in one year. Therefore, when Sheets began promoting the idea of a new division to exploit the ceramic to metal seal technology, Freed felt he had to be taken seriously. Sheets was familiar with the technology since it had been developed in his previous division. He had proven himself as a business element manager, and had earned, by part-time study, his MBA in 1968. There had been a general consensus among management that promoting Jim Sheets to division manager was a fitting reward for one of the company's outstanding young executives. EMD was placed in the technical products group under the direction of group VP Joe Giuffrida. The group consisted of six other divisions and 37 other business elements.

It was not long after its founding that EMD ran into its first problems.

By early 1970 it became clear to the management of the EMD that the defense market for connectors which EG&G had planned on would not develop due to defense budget cuts. The business development committee, group management, and the management of the EMD jointly searched for other markets in which their new technology might be applicable and profitable. It was decided to explore the possibility of selling the high-quality connector as a component to the cable television industry.

CABLE TELEVISION

Cable television was a system for carrying television signals by wire rather than transmitting them through the air. It produced better reception and, in some cases, more channels. The wire used was a coaxial cable that could carry many different channels simultaneously. A typical cable system consisted of a television antenna placed in a location with good reception such as a high hill. The signal was then fed by cable to a "headend" which amplified the signal for the system's distribution cables which consisted of "trunk" cables which extended from the "headend," "feeder" cables which were along individual streets, and "drop" cables which went into subscribers' homes (Exhibit 1). EMD

Exhibit 1

DIAGRAM OF CABLE SYSTEM

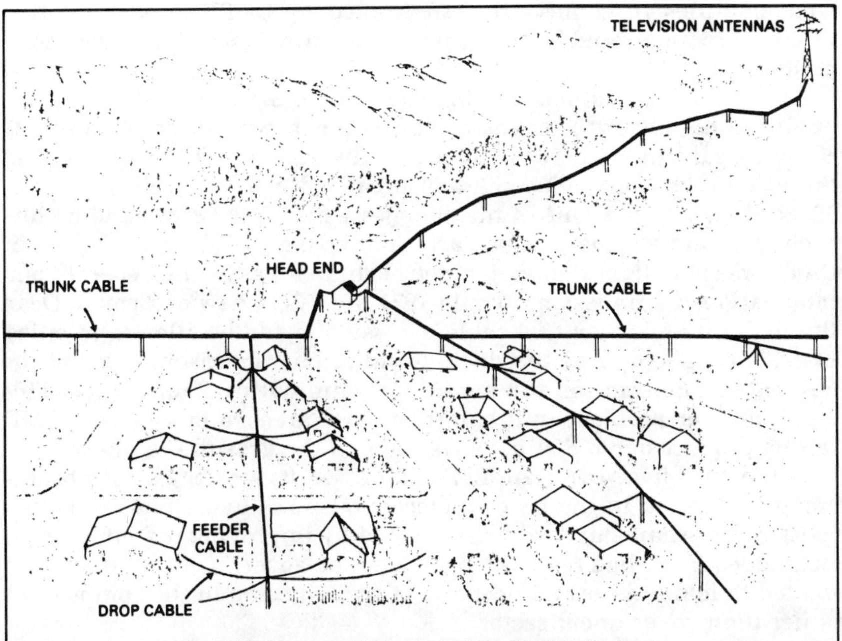

TELEVISION ANTENNAS

TRUNK CABLE

HEAD END

TRUNK CABLE

FEEDER CABLE

DROP CABLE

Conventional one-way cable system serving residential subscribers

Source: The Rand Corporation.

proposed to capitalize on the growth in this market by providing connectors between trunk and feed line distribution cables. The connector market was primarily a new rather than replacement market. Each connector was designed to have a longer life than the system in which it was placed.

Jim Sheets realized that there was no one in EG&G who was knowledgeable enough about the cable television industry to manage such a business element. Therefore, in a departure from usual EG&G procedure of advancement from within, an outside talent search was made in order to find a suitable business element manager. The search produced Mike Killion, who had a considerable track record as a marketer in the cable television industry having worked in sales for Jerrold, the leading cable television equipment producer. Killion was no longer with Jerrold and was working in sales at an electronics firm in Lawrence, Massachusetts. Killion expressed an interest in returning to the CATV business. He was impressed with EG&G's product and its prospects in the industry, and was able to communicate his enthusiasm and experience to Sheets and Giuffrida who decided to hire him after a joint interview.

Having hired Killion, EMD management looked forward with excitement to its participation in the CATV industry. In the past 15 years cable television had grown at a compound annual rate of over 20 percent. By 1970 cable television reached 7 percent of American households, and the industry had grown to a total of $500 million in annual revenue. Killion conducted extensive surveys and research in order to discover what qualities in connectors were valued by CATV builders so that EG&G's product would have distinctive features separating it from competitors.

The Rand Corporation, in a 1971 study of the cable television industry, predicted high growth for cable over the next two decades (Exhibit 2). *Barron's* said in 1971, "past success is dwarfed by future potential in the cable television industry," and predicted a total CATV market of $2.4 billion by 1980. One of the changes which led *Barron's* to predict such high growth was particularly interesting to EG&G. Before 1972, CATV was not allowed in major metropolitan areas by the Federal Communications Commission. By mid-1971 the FCC's new chairman, Dean Burch, let it be known that cable television would be allowed in cities. EG&G's connector had the distinguishing characteristic of being the best cable connector on the market for eliminating interference. This was a greater problem in urban than rural areas, and therefore EMD felt its product had a distinct advantage in the growth era ahead.

In the 1972 five-year plan, EMD expressed its strategy as one of improving margins in the base connector business by emphasizing specialty rather than standard products and by improving manufacturing techniques. EMD had reduced dependence on government contracts and wanted to maintain over 50 percent of their income in the commercial rather than government sector.

The 1972 plan went on to be more specific about the EMD's strategy for commercial business:

Exhibit 2

GROWTH OF CABLE TELEVISION

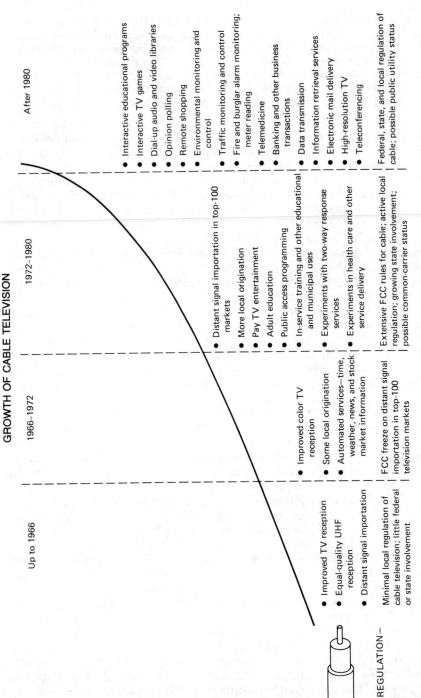

Up to 1966	1966–1972	1972–1980	After 1980
• Improved TV reception • Equal-quality UHF reception • Distant signal importation	• Improved color TV reception • Some local origination • Automated services—time, weather, news, and stock market information	• Distant signal importation in top-100 markets • More local origination • Pay TV entertainment • Adult education • Public access programming • In-service training and other educational and municipal uses • Experiments with two-way response services • Experiments in health care and other service delivery	• Interactive educational programs • Interactive TV games • Dial-up audio and video libraries • Opinion polling • Remote shopping • Environmental monitoring and control • Traffic monitoring and control • Fire and burglar alarm monitoring; meter reading • Telemedicine • Banking and other business transactions • Data transmission • Information retrieval services • Electronic mail delivery • High-resolution TV • Teleconferencing

REGULATION—

| Minimal local regulation of cable television; little federal or state involvement | FCC freeze on distant signal importation in top-100 television markets | Extensive FCC rules for cable; active local regulation; growing state involvement; possible common-carrier status | Federal, state, and local regulation of cable; possible public utility status |

—Potential growth of cable television services

Source: The Rand Corporation.

The commercial business segment of the division business will include some share of the nonmilitary communications and instrument microwave markets. The major emphasis, however, will be directed at specific and concerted entry into the newly energized CATV connector market. The business in two facets, equipment manufacturers and cable distribution operators, has the proper size and growth potential to limit competition in number and size, but still be an attractive opportunity for the division.

Freed recalled that the move into CATV was seen as an entrance into a young, dynamic market with important future growth potential. See Exhibit 3 for the unusually detailed strategy statement which EMD submitted in the 1972 five-year plan. Freed also reviewed the planning forms which EMD had completed in 1972. Two of these which were of particular interest to him are included in Exhibit 4: the business element strategy (Form K) for the CATV element and the division operating statement (Form B).

He also reviewed the Form Ks for the two other business elements in the division, "special seal and microwave devices" and "the RF connectors," both of which showed serious problems in 1972. The special seal and microwave devices were being sold mainly to Sandia as a method of eliminating radio interference. However, this limited the business element to one customer, the federal government, whose funds for and interest in such technology were being curtailed. The "summary of strategy" emphasized the need for "new product or new market activity." The RF connector also had serious problems. EG&G had a small market share, 7 percent, and ranked seventh in the market. Although EG&G had the advantage of a reputation for quality in the field, there was not enough demand for that quality to cover the fixed costs of the operation. EG&G was at a cost disadvantage to the larger producers when it came to standardized parts. EMD's "summary of strategy" discussed the need to develop better "linear programming techniques for production control, regulate operation, and business mix to optimize profit margin and growth." Sales to government contractors made up 94 percent of the RF connectors' sales.

At the first review session of a five-year plan for the new CATV business element, Freed recalled that Mike Killion had put on an impressive performance. He demonstrated a full grasp of the relationships among main actors within the cable television industry. He explained how the critical factor in selling connectors was the manufacturer's relationship with the distributors. CATV system installers were usually independent local contractors. They purchased their supplies from distributors who were organized in a number of layers. A key success factor for a producer of CATV equipment was to establish a good relationship with a national distributor who in turn had contacts in all regions. Killion had conducted conversations with a number of major distributors and had reported that they all perceived the unique advantages of EG&G's connector and looked forward to selling it. Killion developed sales forecasts for the connector, designed a sales brochure, established sales representatives around the country, and helped work on engineering problems. In fact, Killion's performance was so impressive that the business development

Exhibit 3

EMD STRATEGY FOR ENTRY INTO THE CATV CONNECTOR INDUSTRY—APRIL 1972

CATV connector

Strategic role

The strategic role of the CATV connector business element is to provide (1) divisional growth; (2) better balance between government and commercial funding sources in the electro-mechanical division marketing mix, and (3) entrance into a young, dynamic market with important future growth potential.

Strategy

It is a major division goal to establish a significant (30 percent) and ultimately leading market position in the specific area of outdoor connectors for aluminum sheath trunk and feed line distribution cable, capitalizing on the impending new growth predicted for the purely commercial CATV market. It will not be practical to establish the degree (percent) nor the timing for success until we are two or three years into the program. The necessary market penetration will be obtained by (1) exploiting an existing, unstable management situation of the present industry leader (Gilbert Electronics, a Transitron subsidiary); (2) exploiting existing EG&G-Startronics expertise in connector design and high-volume, reproducible manufacture; (3) concentration of prime sales efforts among the top 50 multiconstruction contractors; and (4) taking advantage of 17 years of personal contact and sales experience with many of the key principals among the largest MSO's and equipment manufacturers.

Market

Newly revised (March 31, 1972) FCC regulations governing the reuse, through cable distribution, of television signals in high-density population areas (top 100 markets) have motivated a formerly dormant cable television equipment and construction industry to substantially increased activity. The resulting market for outdoor connectors estimated at $4 million level in 1971 is expected to reach the $8 million level by 1976. The new FCC regulations for the high-density markets require two-way capability. Because of these factors, in addition to the pure entertainment facet of cable distribution networks, the potential for use as a special purpose two-way communication link between subscribers and vendor/ service organizations should realize a sustained high rate of new construction for the industry well beyond the time period of this business plan. Indeed, the industry which originally called itself Community Antenna Television, outgrew that small town image of itself and became Cable Television and now, with the local program organization and the exciting new two-way facilities, considers itself in the broadband communications business. At present only about 8 percent of the 60 million TV homes in the United States are connected to a CATV system.

Customer groups

The cable television customer groups can be viewed in the following segments: (1) multiple-systems operators (TelePrompTer), (2) equipment manufacturers (Jerrold), (3) construction contractors (Burnup & Sims), (4) single-system operators, and (5) distributors (Anixter-Pruzan). The current business plan is to concentrate on the 50 largest multiple system operator (MSO), 12 largest equipment manufacturer (OEM), and 20 construction contractor organizations for new/replacement business as appropriate. In the initial stages, all sales effort will be from the business element manager.

Exhibit 3 (*concluded*)

Competition

The weatherproof, radiationproof aluminum connectors used in overhead and underground CATV distribution services are within the current technical and production capabilities of the electro-mechanical division. Current suppliers are Gilbert-Transitron (58 percent of the market) and a number of smaller firms with comparably smaller market shares. These include Craftsman-Magnavox (11 percent), LRC (11 percent), Communication Dynamics (9 percent), ITT Gremar Canada (6 percent), and others (5 percent).

The Gilbert-Transitron relationship is strained and unstable. The founder, Gilbert, who until recently directly controlled the operations of the company is no longer on the scene. Transitron is not noted for management prowess nor stability. Magnavox Craftsman and Communication Dynamics are not solely dedicated to the outdoor connector market as this is only a portion of their overall business. ITT Gremar (Canada) is hampered in the U.S. market by duties and customs-clearance problems resulting in slower response. LRC is a very small company in a remote location with limited expertise and resources.

The timing for immediate market entry seems particularly appropriate. A line of five types in each of four cable sizes is adequate.

Source: Company records.

committee selected the CATV connector business element as one of its top five growth prospects for the 1972–77 period.

In the 1973 plan, the division once again submitted its optimistic projections about the opportunities for CATV:

> The electro-mechanical division strategy relates to a vigorous "build" role with special emphasis on the commercial business opportunity which is now posed by accelerated growth in the cable television industry. The market situation seems unique in terms of timing, demand, relative competitive weakness and close relation of expertise and facilities necessary to produce connectors for CATV and the microwave business.

The division also returned improved financial results in 1972 (Exhibit 5).

Due to its poor financial performance, the business development committee at EG&G studied the RF connector business of the electro-mechanical division in February 1973. The committee, with the assent of EMD management, decided that the RF connectors had to be phased out, since the product seemed to lack any real profit potential. It was felt that the CATV business would take up the slack. The business development committee stated in its 1973 planning guidelines, "The RF connector business element should go to 'Harvest' strategy, phasing down as CATV builds."

There were encouraging signs as 1973 proceeded. One of the objectives which the CATV element planned to achieve was to give the Gilbert Company, the number one supplier of connectors to the CATV market, some strong competition. Mike Killion was very optimistic about EG&G's ability to gain on Gilbert. Gilbert was having difficulty getting proper

Exhibit 4

1972 FORM K—CATV BUSINESS ELEMENT

LONG-RANGE PLAN: BUSINESS ELEMENT SUMMARY		
1. Product and/or service CATV weather proof connectors for outdoor service in overhead and underground distribution installations	**2. Customers** Multiple-system operators (50 largest) Distribution equipment mfrs. (12–16 largest) Construction contractors (20 major)	**3. End use** CATV distribution cable interconnection devices for entertainment and broadband communications

4.	*Direct competitors*	*CY71 sales this market*	*Market share*	**5. Competitive advantages** Connector manufacturing expertise Management stability Dominant competitor in management difficulty Other suppliers (small/distant) Financial and technical resources for potential expansion	**6. Competitive disadvantages** Lack of image and tangible experience in CATV market segments Significant portion of components supplied in-house by equipment OEMs
	Gilbert (Transitron)	$2,500	58%		
	Craftsman (Magnavox)	500	11		
	LRC	500	11		
	ITT Gremar (Canada)	250	6		
	Communications Dynamics	400	9		
	Others	150	5		
	Note: Figures refer to noncaptive market. Jerrold & Vikoa (OEM's) make selected types for system use.				
	Total direct market	**$4,300,000**	**100%**		

7. Factors affecting future market growth Freedom from FCC restraints for entertainment rebroadcast Deployment and utilization of two way, multichannel cable networks for nonentertainment uses Average market growth rate, next 5 years: 15% per year	**8. Competing techniques** Microwave relay links (Theta Comm) for municipal areas Satellite communications	**8. CY71 sales mix by** AEC & DOD ____ % CPFF ____ % Other gov't ____ % Fixed price ____ % Commercial _100_ % Std. prod. _100_ % Foreign ____ % Std. serv. ____ % Total _100_ % Total _100_ %

10. Summary of strategy—Establish a significant market position in the CATV connector business; exploiting the following aspects:
  1. New market growth for CATV as a result of FCC revision of rebroadcast regulations.
  2. Unstable management position of industry leader, Gilbert, as part of Transitron and in the absence of the founder.
  3. EG&G expertise in connector design and reproducible manufacture.

Date May 1972 Form K(72)	CATV Connector Business Element Electro-Mechanical Division

Note: Form K varied slightly in its format from 1972 to 1974.

Exhibit 4 (concluded)

EMD FORM B—OPERATING STATEMENT, 1972

CY 1972-1976 PLAN: OPERATING STATEMENT

OPERATING STATEMENT $000	Actual						Forecast			
	CY67	CY68	CY69	CY70	CY71	CY72	CY73	CY74	CY75	CY76
Sales	70	252	2,340	1,710	1,765	2,000	2,625	3,200	3,900	4,800
Cost of sales	66	240	2,111	1,652	1,523	1,549	1,957	2,263	2,738	3,362
Gross margin	4	12	229	58	242	451	668	937	1,162	1,438
Gross margin, percent to sales	6	5	10	3	14	23	25	29	30	30
R&D	—	—	—		—	—	15	40	60	60
Selling expense	*	—	142	143	127	150	208	268	325	452
G&A (Noncorporate) expense	*	*	*	*	103	109	143	170	228	270
Other income (expense)				*	(6)	(17)	(23)	(28)	(35)	(45)
Corporate G&A expense	*	*	*	*	45	50	74	91	114	136
Operating profit, before taxes	4	12	87	(85)	(39)	125	205	340	400	475
Operating profit, percent to sales	6	5	4			6	8	11	10	10
SALES/OPERATING PROFIT BEFORE TAXES, BY BUSINESS ELEMENT						(*included in cost of sales)				
Sp. seal and microwave devices	70/4	252/12	328/21	392/17	416/42	350/32	375/42	400/53	435/58	475/66
RF connector			2,012/66	1,318/(102)	1,349/(81)	1,650/93	1,900/113	2,000/130	2,000/162	2,000/167
CATV connector						—/—	350/50	800/157	1,465/180	2,325/242
Total sales/operating profit	70/4	252/12	2,340/87	1,710/(85)	1,765/(39)	2,000/125	2,625/205	3,200/340	3,900/400	4,800/475

Date   May 1972

Form B(72)

Electro-Mechanical
(Division)

Exhibit 5

EMD FORM B—OPERATING STATEMENT, 1973

CY1973-1977 PLAN: OPERATING STATEMENT

OPERATING STATEMENT $000	Actual				Forecast				
	CY69	CY70	CY71	CY72	CY73	CY74	CY75	CY76	CY77
Sales	2,340	1,710	1,765	1,887	2,480	3,150	4,000	5,100	6,050
Cost of sales	2,111	1,652	1,523	1,471	1,840	2,310	2,870	3,720	4,420
Gross margin	229	58	242	416	640	840	1,130	1,380	1,630
Gross margin, percent to sales	10	3	14	22	26	27	28	27	27
R&D	—	—	—	—	—	—	—	—	—
Selling expense	142	143	127	135	219	300	430	520	585
G&A (Noncorporate)	*	*	103	106	117	155	182	210	265
Other income (expense)	—	—	(6)	10	36	25	40	50	60
Corporate G&A	*	*	45	40	68	80	98	115	145
Operating profit, before taxes	87	(85)	(39)	125	205	280	380	485	575
Operating profit, percent to sales	4	(5)	(2)	7	8	9	10	10	10

SALES/OPERATING PROFIT BEFORE TAXES, BY BUSINESS ELEMENT

	CY69	CY70	CY71	CY72	CY73	CY74	CY75	CY76	CY77
CATV connector	—/—	—/—	—/—	—/—	600/100	1,200/150	2,000/300	2,800/300	3,600/375
RF connector	2,012/21	1,318/(102)	1,349/(81)	1,508/72	1,600/65	1,750/100	1,900/135	2,150/160	2,300/175
Sp. seal and microwave devices	328/21	392/17	416/42	379/53	280/40	200/20	100/20	150/25	150/25
Total sales/operating profit	2,340/87	1,710/(85)	1,765/(39)	1,887/125	2,480/205	3,150/280	4,000/380	5,100/485	6,050/575

Electro-Mechanical Division

Date   April 1973

Form B(73)

financing from its parent company, and Gilbert's main strength, its relationships with its distributors, also seemed to be deteriorating. When Killion was able to establish an exclusive distribution arrangement with Anixter/Pruzan, who had previously been the distributor for Gilbert, the division felt it was advancing according to plan. Anixter/Pruzan's initial order was for $300,000 worth of connectors at a time when EMD was carrying no inventory and EMD's previous orders had been about one tenth of that size. Also, improvements in manufacturing were enhancing the quality of the product.

Some of the interim financial results returned in 1973 were disappointing, however. Freed noticed that the CATV element was not making the sales or returning the profit that had been expected. Freed had also read that urban installation of cable systems was turning out to be more costly than expected but was not sure what impact this would have on the connector business. Financing was becoming increasingly hard to come by and expensive, and a recession had slowed economic growth. This squeeze caused those involved in CATV construction who had limited access to capital to buy their equipment from low-cost suppliers. Price cutting began to take place among suppliers of CATV components. Freed knew EMD could not compete for long on price, but he felt it was difficult to judge the danger of price cutting since EG&G's other high-quality products had tended to be immune to price cutting. When questioned about the financial results, Jim Sheets showed concern over them but insisted that headquarters was acting impatiently. Mike Killion continued to be extremely optimistic about the future of EG&G in the CATV connector market. He said at the profit plan review in 1973:

> All the clients I talk to say we have the best connector in the industry. After all, we just signed on with Anixter/Pruzan. Give us a chance to get that operation going. Gilbert is crumbling, and we are going to be the ones to take up the slack. We are now suffering from a cyclical problem of distribution, but it should be straightened out in nine months to a year. The quality which we build into our connector is very desirable in this business, but at times the higher price will temporarily cut into our sales volume.

Joe Giuffrida, the group vice president, was sympathetic to the arguments of his two managers and felt they should be given more time to be allowed to prove themselves.

It was in this context that Freed received the results of 1973 and the next five-year plan from EMD. The financial results for 1973 were disappointing (Exhibit 6). Instead of making $100,000 in the CATV market, the division lost $98,000 in 1973.

When Freed reviewed the Form Ks for the two government-oriented connector business elements, he saw a deteriorating situation. The Form K for the "special hardware" connector forecasted a decrease in its already small sales and listed no market alternatives. It had the disadvantage of being more expensive than competitors' products, and thus saw little hope of expanding out of the specialty market, which while being profitable was just too small. The RF connector had slipped from 7 percent of the market to 3 percent and now was ranked 10th in terms of

Exhibit 6

EMD FORM B—OPERATING STATEMENT, 1974

CY 1974-1978 PLAN: OPERATING STATEMENT

	Actual results				Forecasts				
OPERATING STATEMENT $000	CY 70*	CY71	CY72	CY73	CY74	CY75	CY76	CY77	CY78
Bookings		441	2,025	1,769	2,300	2,800	3,225	4,000	4,800
Backlogs			579	491	541	641	746	911	1,061
Sales	1,710	1,765	1,887	1,857	2,250	2,700	3,120	3,835	4,650
Cost of sales	1,652	1,523	1,471	1,646	1,750	2,050	2,340	2,850	3,455
Gross margin	58	242	416	211	500	650	780	935	1,195
Gross margin, percent of sales	3	14	22	11	22	24	25	26	26
R&D	—	—	—	—	—	—	—	—	—
Selling expense	143	127	135	192	210	255	285	340	400
G&A (Noncorporate)		103	106	105	115	130	140	165	190
Corporate G&A expense		45	40	52	55	70	80	100	120
Other (income) expense Under(over) applied overhead	(85)	(6)	(10)	(18)	(20)	(20)	(25)	(35)	(40)
Operating profit, before taxes	(85)	(39)	125	(156)	100	175	250	345	445
Operating profit, percent of sales	—	—	7	—	4	7	8	9	10
SALES./OPERATING PROFIT BEFORE TAXES, BY BUSINESS ELEMENT									
RF	1,318/(102)	1,349/(81)	1,508/72	1,240/(85)	1,650/88	1,800/110	2,100/160	2,500/200	2,900/255
Special	392/17	416/42	379/53	259/27	250/22	150/15	120/10	135/15	150/15
CATV				358/(98)	350/(10)	750/50	900/80	1,200/130	1,600/175
Total sales/operating profit	1,710/(85)	1,765/(39)	1,887/125	1,857/(156)	2,250/100	2,700/175	3,120/250	3,835/345	4,650/445

CY73 Sales Mix			U.S.A. Sales Only	
AEC Cont.	$ 000	U.S.A. $1,857,000	AEC	$ 000
Other CPFF	200,000	W. Europe $ 000	DOD	$1,499,000
Fixed price	59,000	Rest of world $ 000	Other gov't.	$ 000
Std. price	1,598,000	Total $1,857,000	Nongov't.	$ 358,000
Total	$1,857,000		Subtotal	$1,857,000

CY73   Intercorporate Sales = $ 000

Electro-Mechanical (Division)

Date April 1974
Form B (Rev 1)

*CY = Calendar year.

market share among the competitors. Freed also noted that lack of modern equipment was still a problem and that manufacturing costs in RF connectors were high relative to competitors. He was encouraged by the element's forecasted growth in sales and slight improvement in forecasted earnings, although he was not sure if the strategy summary for RF connectors could support such optimism:

> Continue responsive effort to build selective share of near standard connector business. Expand scope of coverage to increase marketing emphasis on individual OEM accounts served by the largest of the small competitors, nationwide. Concentrate on profitable near standard business opportunities and new client conversion list—exploiting long-term former customer relationships and organizational flexibility to provide responsive customer service and cost effective product. (Form K, 1974.)

However, CATV was the business element from which future growth was planned, and Freed wanted to review their Form K (Exhibit 7) at length. He also reviewed Form C (Exhibit 8) which highlighted the investment EG&G had in the entire EMD.

Freed tried to order his thoughts about the upcoming meeting with the EMD. EMD was not performing up to the level of EG&G's goals, and he knew Giuffrida made it a policy to distribute the financial results of all his business elements at the monthly meetings held by his group. On the other hand, Sheets and Killion had warned from the beginning that the CATV connector would take a number of years to become established. In the past, EG&G had financed promising products, such as a component for the Xerox copier, for six years before they became profitable.

Exhibit 7

1974 FORM K—CATV BUSINESS ELEMENT

LONG-RANGE PLAN: BUSINESS ELEMENT SUMMARY

1. Product and/or service CATV aluminum sheath cable connectors and adaptors	**2. Customers** Cable television manufacturers and service organizations Distributors 24% OEM 17 Multiple-system operators 42 Small-system operators 17	**3. End use** Cable network distribution connectors —Cable-to-cable splice —Amplifier or tap to cable —Terminators —Adaptors

4. Direct competitors

Direct competitors	Sales CY 73	Market share
Gilbert	1,525	36%
LRC	1,000	24
EG&G	360	9
Coral	300	7
Cambridge	250	6
Tidal	250	6
ITT	200	5
Pyramid	50	1
Others	250	5
Total direct market	$4,185,000	100%

5. Competitive advantages

—Superior product for areas and applications sensitive to radio frequency interference
—Dominant competitor (Gilbert) unstable

6. Competitive disadvantages

—Premium price
—Emerging competitor (LRC) with cost effective product
—Anixter-Pruzan distributor liaison temporarily ineffective

7. Market alternatives (competing techniques)

Conventional television reception

8. Factors affecting future market growth

—MSO access to investment funds   2
—Federal regulatory rulings
—State and local franchise practices
—Inflation-related subscriber rate hikes
—Potential for two-way consumer services

9. Summary of strategy

—Explore short-term viability of CATV business
—Appraise Anixter-Pruzan distributor potential
—Expand and improve distributor sales network selectively in key geographic areas of the United States
—Continue to cultivate OEM liaisons through direct sales effort
—Expand product line to provide adequate but lower price product for more general use in non-RFI and turnkey applications

10. History/forecast	CY72	CY73	CY74	CY75	CY76	CY77	CY78
Market compound growth 24% per year		4185	4500	5400	7000	9200	12100
Share of market		9	8	14	13	13	13
Sales		358	350	750	900	1200	1600
Operating profit, percent to sales		(3)	(3)	7	9	11	11

Date: April 1974   CATV   ELECTRO-MECHANICAL
Form K (74)   (Business element)   (Division)

Exhibit 8

EMD FORM C—1974 INVESTMENT INFORMATION

INVESTMENT DETAIL $000	Actual					Forecast				
	CY70	CY71	CY72	CY73	CY74 Estim.	CY75	CY76	CY77	CY78
1. Accounts receivable		396	424	518	525	580	640	780	950
2. Contracts-in-process			6	19	10	5	5	5	5
3. Inventories		542	493	709	5	700	755	830	900
4. Other		2	2	3	630	5	5	5	5
5. Accounts payable		73	117	247	120	140	160	190	230
6. Accrued (prepaid) expenses		75	165	137	140	170	195	210	260
7. Operating capital (1+2+3−5−6)		792	643	865	910	980	1,050	1,220	1,370
8. Assigned fixed assets at cost		678	715	712	742	782	832	832	942
9. Accum. depreciation		342	428	430	480	530	585	645	710
10. Assigned net fixed assets (8−9)		336	287	282	262	252	247	237	232
11. Allocated fixed assets at cost									
12. Accum. depreciation									
13. Allocated net fixed assets (11−12)									
14. Net other assets			7	2	—				
15. Net investment (7+13+18+14)		1,128	937	1,149	1,174	1,232	1,297	1,457	1,602
16. Long-term lease commitments									
17. Total Investment (15+19)		1,128	937	1,149	1,174	1,232	1,297	1,457	1,602

The company and its strategists: Relating corporate strategy to personal values

Up to this point we have argued that a concept of purpose and a sense of direction strengthen a company's ability to survive in changing circumstances. We have seen, to be sure, the difficulties of understanding clearly both a company's circumstances and its strengths and weaknesses. The action implied by these difficulties has been an objective and alert surveillance of the environment for threats and opportunities and a detached appraisal of organizational characteristics in order to identify distinctive competence. We have considered the suitable combination of a company's strengths and its opportunities to be a logical exercise characterized by perhaps not precise but reasoned, well-informed choices of alternatives assuring the highest possible profit. We have been examining the changing relationship of company and environment almost as if a purely economic strategy, uncontaminated by the personality or goals of the decision maker, were possible.

STRATEGY AS PROJECTION OF PREFERENCE

We must acknowledge at this point that there is no way to divorce the decision determining the most sensible economic strategy for a company from the personal values of those who make the choice. Executives in charge of company destinies do not look exclusively at what a company might do and can do. In apparent disregard of the second of these considerations, they sometimes seem heavily influenced by what they personally *want* to do.

We are ourselves not aware of how much desire affects our own choice of alternatives, but we can see it in others. Note, for example, George Romney's dramatic promotion of economic sensible transportation and the small car in the early days of American Motors and his subsequent repayment of all debt, in place of investment through research in the development of variations in the small car which might have retained leadership in an important segment of the market. Almost certainly we see reflected here the higher value Romney placed on economy than on consumer preferences, on liquidity over debt, and other values derived more from his character and upbringing than from an objective monitoring of the best course for American Motors to follow.

Frank Farwell came from IBM to the presidency of Underwood in 1955, it has been said, saying that he would be damned if he would spend his life peddling adding machines and typewriters. This aversion may explain why Underwood plunged into the computer business without the technical, financial, or marketing resources necessary to succeed in it. Similarly, when Adriano Olivetti purchased control of Underwood after three days of hurried negotiations, he may well have been moved by his childhood memory of visiting Hartford and by the respect for the world's once leading manufacturer of typewriters that led his father to erect in Ivrea a replica of the red-brick, five-story Hartford plant.[1] That he wanted to purchase Underwood so badly may explain why he and his associates did not find out how dangerously it had decayed and how near bankruptcy it had been brought.

The three presidents of J. I. Case in the years 1953 to 1963 seem to have been displaying their own temperaments as they wracked the company with alternatives of expansionism and contraction far beyond the needs of response to a cyclical industry environment.[2] In all these cases, the actions taken can be rationalized so as not to seem quite so personal as I have suggested they are.

THE INEVITABILITY OF VALUES

We will be able to understand the strategic decision better if we admit rather than resist the dimension of preference. If we think back over the discussions of earlier cases in this book, the strategies we recommended for the companies probably reflected what *we* would have wanted to do had we been in charge of those companies. We told ourselves or assumed that our personal inclinations harmonized with the optimum combination of economic opportunity and company capability. The professional manager in a large company, drilled in analytical technique and the use of staff trained to subordinate value-laden assumptions to tables of numbers, may often prefer the optimal economic strategy because of its very suitability. Certain entrepreneurs, whose energy and personal drives far outweigh their formal training and self-awareness, set their course in directions not necessarily supported by logical appraisal. Such disparity appears most frequently in small privately held concerns, or in companies built by successful and self-confident owner-

---

[1] See "Underwood-Olivetti (AR)," Edmund P. Learned, C. Roland Christensen, Kenneth R. Andrews, and William D. Guth, *Business Policy: Text and Cases,* original edition (Homewood, Ill.: Richard D. Irwin, 1965), p. 212. This case is also in the Intercollegiate Case Clearing House, No. 9–312–017.

[2] "J. I. Case Company," Learned et al., *Business Policy,* pp. 82–102, and HBS Case Services #9–309–270.

managers. The phenomenon we are discussing, however, may appear in any company, especially if it is large, in its divisions.

Our problem now can be very simply stated. In examining the alternatives available to a company, we must henceforth take into consideration the preferences of the chief executive. Furthermore, we must also be concerned with the values of other key managers who must either contribute to or assent to the strategy if it is to be effective. We therefore have two kinds of reconciliation to consider—first, the divergence between the chief executive's preference and the strategic choice which seems most economically defensible and, second, the conflict among several sets of managerial personal values which must be reconciled not only with an economic strategy but with each other.

Thus, when Mr. Edgar Villchur, inventor of the acoustic suspension loudspeaker, founded Acoustic Research, Inc.,[3] in 1954, he institutionalized a desire to bring high-fidelity sound to the mass market at the lowest possible cost. He licensed his competitors freely and finally gave up his original patent rights altogether. He kept not only his prices but his dealer margins low, maintained for a considerable time a primitive production facility and an organization of friends rather than managers, and went to great lengths to make the company a good place to work, sharing with employees the company's success. The company was dominated by Mr. Villchur's desire to have a small organization characterized by academic, scientific, and intellectual rather than "commercial" values. Product development was driven by some of these values away from the acoustical technology which Mr. Villchur's personal competence would have suggested into development of record players, amplifiers, and tuners which were to offer less in superiority over competitive products than did his speakers. Again, these were priced far below what might have been possible.

Mr. Abraham Hoffman, for years vice president and treasurer, had the task of trying to overcome his superior's reluctance to advertise, to admit the validity of the marketing function, and of maintaining the business as a profitable enterprise. That the company had succeeded in at long last developing and producing a music system of great value in relation to its cost and in winning the respect of the high-fidelity listener market does not alter the fact that the first determination of strategy came more from Mr. Villchur's antibusiness values than from an analytical balancing of opportunity and distinctive competence. The latter would have led, with perhaps much greater growth and profitability, into acoustical systems, public-address equipment, long-distance communications, hearing aids, noise suppression, and the like—all areas in which technical improvement in the quality of available sound is much needed.

We must remember, however, that it is out of Mr. Villchur's determination and goals that his company came into being in the first place. The extraordinary accomplishments of an antimarketing company in

---

[3] "Acoustic Research, Inc.," Learned et al., *Business Policy,* pp. 466–519, and HBS Case Services #9–312–020.

the marketplace are directly traceable to the determination to innovate in quality and price. The reconciliation between Mr. Villchur's values and Mr. Hoffman's more business-oriented determination to manage the company's growth more objectively occurred only when the company was sold to Teledyne, Mr. Villchur retired to his laboratory, and Mr. Hoffman became president. The quality achievements of this firm have been rewarded, but the economic potential of its strategy was for years unrealized.

We should in all realism admit that the personal desires, aspirations, and needs of the senior managers of a company actually *do* play an influential role in the determination of strategy. Against those who are offended by this idea either for its departure from the stereotype of single-minded economic man or for its implicit violation of responsibilities to the shareholder, we would argue that we must accept not only the inevitability but the desirability of this intervention. If we begin by saying that all strategic decisions must fall within the very broad limits of the manager's fiduciary responsibility to the owners of the business and perhaps to others in the management group, then we may proceed legitimately to the idea that what a manager wants to do is not out of order. The conflict which often arises between what general managers want to do and what the dictates of economic strategy suggest they ought to do is best not denied or condemned. It should be accepted as a matter of course. In the study of organization behavior, we have long since concluded that the personal needs of the hourly worker must be taken seriously and at least partially satisfied as a means of securing the productive effort for which wages are paid. It should, then, come as no surprise to us that the president of the corporation also arrives at his work with his own needs and values, to say nothing of his relatively greater power to see that they are taken into account.

RECONCILING DIVERGENT VALUES

If we accept the inevitability of personal values in the strategic decision governing the character and course of a corporation, then we must turn to the skills required to reconcile the optimal economic strategy with the personal preferences of the executives of the company. There is no reason why a better balance could not have been struck in Acoustic Research without sacrifice to the genius of the founder or the quality of life in his company. It is first necessary to penetrate conventional rationalization and reticence to determine what these preferences are. For without this revelation, strategic proposals stemming from different unstated values come into conflict. This conflict cannot be reconciled by talking in terms of environmental data and corporate resources. The hidden agenda of corporate policy debates makes them endless and explains why so many companies do not have explicit, forthright, and usefully focused strategies.

To many caught up in the unresolved strategic questions in their own organizations, it seems futile even to attempt to reconcile a strategic alternative dictated by personal preference with other alternatives oriented toward capitalizing on opportunity to the greatest possible extent. In actuality, however, this additional complication poses fewer difficulties than at first appear. The analysis of opportunity and the appraisal of resources themselves often lead in different directions. To compose three, rather than two, divergent sets of considerations into a single pattern may increase the complexity of the task, but the integrating process is still the same. We can look for the dominant consideration and treat the others as constraints; we can probe the elements in conflict for the possibilities of reinterpretation or adjustment. We are not building a wall of irregular stone so much as balancing a mobile of elements, the motion of which is adjustable to the motion of the entire mobile.

As we have seen, external developments can be affected by company action and company resources, and internal competence can be developed. If worst comes to worst, it is better for a person to separate from a management whose values he or she does not share than to pretend agreement or to wonder why others think as they do. Howard Head, whose passionate dedication to the metal ski not only produced a most successful business but delayed unnecessarily its entry into plastic skis has realistically retired from his now diversified business and has sold his holdings. It is not necessary, however, for all members of management to think alike or to have the same personal values, so long as strategic decision is not delayed or rendered ineffective by these known and accepted differences. Large gains are possible simply by raising the strategic issues for discussion by top management, by admitting the legitimacy of different preferences, and by explaining how superficial or fundamental the differences are.

MODIFICATION OF VALUES

The question whether values can actually be changed during the reconciliation process is somewhat less clear. A value is a view of life and a judgment of what is desirable that is very much a part of a person's personality and a group's morale. From parents, teachers, and peers, we are told by psychologists, we acquire basic values, which change somewhat with acquired knowledge, analytical ability, and self-awareness, but remain a stable feature of personality.[4] Nonetheless the preference attached to goals in concrete circumstances is not beyond influence. The physicist who leaves the university to work in a profit-making company because of a combined fondness for his work and material comfort, may ask to continue to do pure rather than applied research, but he presumably does not want his company to go bankrupt. The conflict in values is to some degree negotiable, once the reluctance to expose hidden agendas is overcome. Retaining the value orientation of the scientist, the ambivalent physicist might assent to a strategic alternative stressing product development rather than original investigation, at

---

[4] See, for example, W. D. Guth and Renato Tagiuri, "Personal Values and Corporate Strategy," *Harvard Business Review*, September–October 1965, pp. 123–32.

least for a specified time until the attainment of adequate profit made longer range research feasible.

AWARENESS OF VALUES

Our interest in the role of personal values in strategic formulations should not be confined to assessing the influence of other people's values. Despite the well-known problems of introspection, we can probably do more to understand the relation of our own values to our choice of purpose than we can to change the values of others. Awareness that our own preference for an alternative opposed by another stems from values as much as from rational estimates of economic opportunity may have important consequences. First, it may make us more tolerant and less indignant when we perceive this relationship between recommendations and values in the formulations of others. Second, it will force us to consider how important it really is to us to maintain a particular value in making a particular decision. Third, it may give us insight with which to identify our biases and thus pave the way for a more objective assessment of all the strategic alternatives that are available. These consequences of self-examination will not end conflict but they will at least prevent its unnecessary prolongation.

The object of this self-examination is not necessarily to endow us with the ability to persuade others to accept the strategic recommendations we consider best; it is to acquire insight into the problems of determining purpose and skill in the process of resolving them. Individuals inquiring into their own values for the purpose of understanding their own positions in policy debates can continue to assess their own personal opportunities, strengths and weaknesses, and basic values by means of the procedures outlined here. For a personal strategy, analytically considered and consciously developed, may be as useful to an individual as a corporate strategy is to a business institution. The effort, conducted by each individual, to formulate personal purpose might well accompany his or her contributions to organizational purpose. If the encounter leads to a clarification of the purposes one seeks, the values one holds, and the alternatives available, the attempt to make personal use of the concept of strategy will prove extremely worthwhile.

Introducing personal preference forces us to deal with the possibility that the strategic decision we prefer (identified after the most nearly objective analysis of opportunity and resources we are capable of) is not acceptable to other executives with different values. Their acceptance of the strategy is necessary to its successful implementation. In diagnosing this conflict, we try to identify the values implicit in our own choice. As we look at the gap between the strategy which follows from our own values and that which would be appropriate to the values of our associates, we look to see whether the difference is fundamental or superficial. Then we look to see how the strategy we believe best matches opportunity and resources can be adapted to accommodate the values of those who will implement it. Reconciliation of the three principal determinants of strategy which we have so far considered is often made possible by adjustment of any or all of the determinants.

The role of self-examination in coming to terms with a conflict in values over an important strategic determination is not to turn all strategic decisions into outcomes of consensus. Some organizations—you can see them in this book—are run by persons who are leaders in the sense that they have power and are not afraid to use it. It is true that business leaders, in Zaleznik's words, "commit themselves to a career in which they have to work on themselves as a condition for effective working with other people."[5] At the same time, a leader must recognize that "the essence of leadership is choice, a singularly individualistic act in which a [person] assumes responsibility for a commitment to direct an organization along a particular path. . . . As much as a leader wishes to trust others, he has to judge the soundness and validity of his subordinates' positions. Otherwise, the leader may become a prisoner of the emotional commitments of his subordinates, frequently at the expense of making correct judgments about policies and strategies."[6]

When a management group is locked in disagreement, the presence of power and the need for its exercise conditions the dialogue. There are circumstances when the exercise of leadership must transcend disagreement that cannot be resolved by discussion. Subordinates, making the best of the inevitable, must accept a follower role. When leadership becomes irresponsible and dominates subordinate participation without reason, it is usually ineffective or is deposed. Participants in strategic disagreements must not only know their own needs and power but those of the chief executive. Strategic planning, in the sense that power attached to values plays a role in it, is a political process.[7]

You should not warp your recommended strategy to the detriment of the company's future in order to adjust it to the personal values you hold or observe. On the other hand, you should not expect to be able to impose without risk and without expectation of eventual vindication and agreement, an unwelcome pattern of purposes and policies on the people in charge of a corporation or responsible for achieving results. Strategy is a human construction; it must in the long run be responsive to human needs. It must ultimately inspire commitment. It must stir an organization to successful striving against competition. Some people have to have their hearts in it.

---

[5] Abraham Zaleznik and Manfred F. R. Kets de Vries, *Power and the Corporate Mind* (Boston: Houghton Mifflin, 1975), p. 207.

[6] Ibid., p. 209.

[7] See Abraham Zaleznik: "Managers and Leaders: Are They Different?" *Harvard Business Review*, May–June 1977, pp. 67–78.

The Saturday Evening Post (R)

> The real history is going to have to be written by a psychiatrist.[1]
> —Cary Bok, grandson of the founder of Curtis Publishing Company.

ON THE AFTERNOON of January 9, 1969, standing before the glaring television lights at the Overseas Press Club in New York City, Martin Ackerman, Curtis Publishing Company's fourth president in six years, calmly read, "This is one of the saddest days of my life, a sad one for me, for our employees, officers, and directors; indeed, it is sad for the American public. Apparently there is just not the need for our product in today's scheme of living."[2] With Ackerman's announcement, Curtis officially ceased publication of *The Saturday Evening Post*.

The *Post*, which had been suffering from increasing costs and decreasing revenues for the past decade, had once been the most profitable magazine in the United States, considered both the pulse and maker of American opinion. The death of the *Post* had been predicted by denizens of Wall Street and Madison Avenue since its first financial troubles in the early 1960s. It is impossible, though, to isolate the plight of the *Post* from the plight of Curtis, a company whose assets included not only such national magazines as the *Post, Ladies' Home Journal,* and *Holiday,* but also paper mills in Pennsylvania, a sprawling printing plant outside Philadelphia (where every copy of every Curtis publication was printed), a circulation company, and extensive timberlands. During the years 1960–1969 inclusive, Curtis' operating revenues (net of commissions) declined from $192.8 million to $32.0 million, and the company sustained a cumulative loss of $67.6 million (Exhibit 1).

---

[1] Joseph Goulden, *The Curtis Caper* (New York: G. P. Putnam's Sons, 1965), p. 11.

[2] Otto Friedrich, *Decline and Fall* (New York: Harper and Row, 1970), p. 449.

HISTORY: 1897–1962

In 1897, Cyrus Curtis, the founder of Curtis Publishing Company, purchased a struggling journal put together for ten dollars a week by a newspaper man in his spare time. The journal, which Curtis bought for $1,000, consisted of a mailing list of 2,231 names, a wagon-load of battered type fonts, and a name, *The Saturday Evening Post*. At the time, Curtis was the publisher of the leading women's magazine in the nation, the *Ladies' Home Journal,* which he and his wife had built from scratch up to a circulation of 446,000 during the six-year period between 1883 and 1889. Referring to the *Post, Printers' Ink,* the printing trade journal, commented that the *Ladies' Home Journal* was a "wonderful property" but that Curtis was "blowing his profits on an impossible venture" with the purchase of this latest magazine.[3]

Curtis was undaunted, for he felt that just as the *Journal* had become a success by dealing with what was most important to the American woman, her home, the *Post* would become a success by dealing with what was important to men, "their fight for livelihood in the business world."[4]

The Lorimer *Post:* 1899–1936

For the first year under Curtis, the *Post* was edited by William Jordan, but Curtis soon became dissatisfied, and the editorship passed to George Horace Lorimer. The son of a famous Boston minister, Lorimer was considered one of the best newspaper men in Boston.

Lorimer immediately proceeded to alter the *Post,* changing it from a weekly newspaper into a magazine, and cutting the price from ten cents to five, thus making it less expensive than any competitive periodical. He also instituted a new procedure in American publishing, that of paying authors at the time their material was accepted for publication rather than when it was actually published.

> Lorimer knew exactly what he wanted to make out of the *Post.* It was to be a magazine without class, clique, or sectional editing, but intended for every adult in America's seventy-five million population. He meant to edit it for the whole United States. He set out to interpret America to itself, always readably, but constructively.
>
> As he settled into the job of interpretation, Lorimer sensed accurately the mood of the country at the beginning of the new century. People were weary of reading about problems, politics, radicalism, war, and even uplift. They wanted to read historical novels and dwell in the past, and Lorimer gave them covers showing Ben Franklin, Washington, and Independence Hall in appropriate poses, while inside he displayed the romances of the Rev. Cyrus Townsend Brady and Robert W. Chambers.
>
> Always the accent was heaviest on business. Charles R. Flint praised the benefits of the business combination; the mayors of San Francisco and Baltimore wrote jointly on the need for better business methods in

---

[3] Goulden, *The Curtis Caper,* p. 22.
[4] Ibid., p. 22.

civic administration; and Harvard's director of physical culture advised the businessman on home gymnastics.[5]

Lorimer himself contributed several articles related to business, which appeared in the *Post* as an unsigned serial entitled "Letters from a Self-made Merchant to His Son." An immediate success, this series was later published in book form and translated into "a dozen" foreign languages.

Lorimer must have hit some chord in the heart of the country, for the *Post*'s circulation increased from 33,000 in 1898 to 97,000 in the following year, and then to 182,000 in the year after that. Circulation reached half a million in 1903, a million in 1909, two million in 1913, and three million in 1927.

A propitious environment. During the early 1900s fundamental changes were occurring in America. Mass production, transportation, and distribution were making America a nation rather than a collection of geographically contiguous regions. Curtis anticipated the need for a national magazine and adroitly applied the evolving principles of mass production and distribution to his publications.

Advertising revenue for the *Post* increased from $8,000 in 1898 to $160,000 in 1899 and then to more than $1 million in 1905, $3 million in 1909, and $5 million in 1910. By the end of the 1920s, advertising revenue was over $50 million and the *Post* collected almost 30 cents of every advertising dollar spent in magazines in the United States.

> The vehicle that the *Post* rode to tremendous financial success was the automobile. The *Post* carried its first auto ad, about a W. E. Roach horseless buggy, in an issue in March 1900. For the next two decades auto advertising expanded as rapidly as the industry; at one point it made up 25 per cent of the total volume.[6]

The zenith of this period of the *Post*'s history was the issue of December 1929, a virtual "paper monument" to Curtis and Lorimer.

> It contained 272 pages and weighed almost two pounds. Sixty forty-five ton presses rolled around the clock for three weeks to produce it, consuming 6,000,000 pounds of paper and 120,000 pounds of ink. The reading fare was enough to keep the average adult busy for more than 20 hours, *Post* editors estimated. And the issue—largest of any magazine in Curtis' history—put $1,512,000 from 214 national advertisers into Cyrus Curtis' money box. This grandiose effort was so mammoth in bulk that scrap dealers eagerly paid five cents to newstands for the paper alone.[7]

A series of blows. With the end of the prosperity of the 1920s, *Post* advertising revenues decreased substantially. By 1932, issues of only 60 pages, a quarter of them filled with advertising, were commonplace.

Cyrus Curtis died in 1933 at the age of 83, leaving his daughter and two grandsons effective control of the company with 32% of the stock. Lorimer, retaining his position as editor of the *Post*, assumed the presi-

---

[5] John Tebbel, *George Horace Lorimer and The Saturday Evening Post* (New York: Doubleday and Company, Inc., 1948), pp. 23–26.

[6] Goulden, *The Curtis Caper*, pp. 25–26.

[7] Ibid., p. 32.

dency. During the period between 1933 and 1936, the year of his retirement, Lorimer increased advertising revenue from an $18 million low in 1933 to $26 million in 1936 in spite of the severe economic conditions and increased competition from Henry Luce's *Time* and *Life*. During this same period, Lorimer placed the editorial power of the *Post* behind an attempt to defeat Franklin D. Roosevelt in his reelection bid in 1936.

> Lorimer called the New Deal "a discredited European ideology"; he railed against "undesirable and unassimilable aliens"; and the *Post* declared: "We might just as well say that the world failed as the American business leadership failed."[8]

The election landslide for Roosevelt and his New Deal in 1936 was a humiliating blow to Lorimer and indicated "a fundamental, distinct shift of the *Post*'s role in American life. It would be accepted as entertainment, but not as a guide to life."[9]

Hand-picked successors: 1936–1962

Following Lorimer's retirement in 1936, Walter D. Fuller, Lorimer's hand-picked successor, was named chief executive officer of Curtis. Fuller, a man more conservative politically than Lorimer, had worked his way up in the organization from the accounting department as successively controller, corporate secretary, first vice president, and president, all while under the guidance of Curtis and Lorimer.

Fuller became chairman of the board for 1950–1957, and his protégé, Robert MacNeal, took over the position of president and chief executive officer. MacNeal had first attracted management attention during the 1920s by designing a folding machine that enabled the *Post* to print more than 200 pages, the previous limit.

> Even when he became president he would go into the machine shops and, at the risk of soiled white cuffs, talk about and help solve mechanical problems. In his coat pocket was a little leatherbound black notebook crammed with facts and statistics about Curtis and its multitude of subsidiary companies. The information—even including the names and addresses of directors—was typed on a "miniature Gothic" typewriter so more characters would fit onto a page. Why the notebook? MacNeal's superior in the scheduling division had carried a similar book way back in the 1920s. "He was the fount of all knowledge, so we had to have one, too," MacNeal explained.[10]

Corporate strategy. The corporate strategy under the guidance of Fuller and MacNeal was to build Curtis into a fully integrated magazine publishing company which grew its own trees, made its own paper, printed every issue of every magazine, and distributed the magazines through a circulation subsidiary. This was an arrangement that other publishers looked upon unfavorably, inasmuch as it tended to accentuate corporate losses in periods of economic decline, served as a

---

[8] Friedrich, *Decline and Fall*, p. 10.
[9] Goulden, *The Curtis Caper*, p. 45.
[10] Ibid., pp. 71–72.

drain on funds available for diversification, and tended to increase the size and complexity of corporate management.

Otto Friedrich, in *Decline and Fall,* discussed the Fuller and Mac-Neal years as follows:

> Fuller's presidency began during the difficult days of the Depression, when Curtis and many other companies tottered near bankruptcy, and the value of ideas may well have seemed less obvious than it does today. And then, during World War II, the shortage of supplies convinced many an executive of the value of hoarding and stockpiling. Whatever his reasons, Fuller held to his empire-building philosophy with an exceptional singleness of purpose. He could have bought the entire Columbia Broadcasting System for $3 million, but he declined the offer; a few years later, he declined a similar opportunity to buy the American Broadcasting Corporation. Television, radio, the growth in book publishing, the so-called "paperback revolution," the rise of suburban newspapers, the increasing need for school texts—Walter Deane Fuller had not been blessed with a gift for prophesying such developments. Instead, just after World War II, he bought a 108-acre site on the outskirts of Philadelphia, shipped in twenty new printing presses, and constructed the gigantic Sharon Hill printing plant. It was, in its day, the largest and best-equipped printing plant in the world. And as late as 1950, when Fuller finally passed on the presidency to his protégé, Robert A. MacNeal, Curtis reaffirmed its dedication to machinery by investing $20 million to become full owner of a paper company in which it already held a controlling interest.[11]

By 1960, the number of individuals actually employed in creating the Curtis magazines was minuscule compared to the number engaged in its manufacture:

> The editorial staff of the *Post* numbered about 125 people; the employees in the printing division numbered 2,600; the employees of the whole corporation numbered about 11,000. And in surveying the corporate assets, Curtis executives liked to boast that the company owned not just a few magazines but a $40 million printing plant, three large paper mills, 262,000 acres of timberland, and a circulation company that distributed 50-odd magazines through 100,000 outlets.[12]

Editorial strategy. In 1936, Lorimer's successor as editor of the *Post* was Wesley W. Stout. Like Fuller and MacNeal, Stout was hand-picked by Lorimer and was a conservative politically:

> In editorial outlook, Stout was every bit as conservative as Lorimer; the popular support given the New Deal by voters in 1936 goaded the *Post* into increasingly vicious attacks on the Administration. President Roosevelt never answered directly, but he showed several visitors a large envelope containing what he termed the "dirtiest" attacks published against the government. The bulk of them were from the *Post.* The magazine's editorials were a cacophony of ridicule directed against organized labor, social reform programs, social security, the Tennessee

[11] Friedrich, *Decline and Fall,* p. 15.
[12] Ibid., p. 15.

Valley Administration—in sum, just about anything attempted by FDR.[13]

Advertising revenue dropped $4 million during Stout's first year as editor, and at a stockholders' meeting in 1941 minority stockholders "denounced management's isolationism and called for the opening of *Post* pages to opposing points of view."[14] Stout's editorship of the *Post* came to an end in 1942 with what has been called "the biggest misunderstanding in Curtis editorial history."[15] Stout had published a three-article series on the American Jew, the last article of which was entitled "The Case Against the Jew." A furor erupted with cancellations of subscriptions and advertising, threats of a boycott, and destruction of *Posts* at newsstands. In May of 1942, the *Post* ran an editorial apologizing for the article, saying that Stout had believed

> . . . "a frank airing of the whole question would serve to clear the atmosphere in this country and perhaps help prevent anti-Semitism from gaining a foothold here." The *Post* expressed regret that the article had been "misunderstood."[16]

Discord between Editor Stout and President Fuller had been rumored for some time, and the controversy over the article and the *Post's* operating loss for the first quarter of 1942 precipitated Stout's resignation. The editorship of the *Post* then went to Ben Hibbs, a native of Kansas, who had been the editor of another Curtis magazine, *Country Gentleman*. Hibbs immediately began making major changes in the *Post*. He found the *Post's* editorial content resting on the same "glamour of business" product that Lorimer had developed decades earlier. Feeling that this product was dated, Hibbs broadened the *Post* by stressing that he considered to be the more enduring part of America— namely, life in country towns. But Hibbs also looked beyond middle America and recognized the Second World War as "the greatest news story of our time. Things were happening more exciting than what fiction writers could dream up."

> Hibbs and his lanky young managing editor, Bob Fuoss, reduced the emphasis on fiction and set out to cover World War II. The *Post* then had only one war correspondent, who was home on leave in New York. Hibbs recruited MacKinlay Kantor, Samuel Lubell, Edgar Snow, Richard Tregaskis, Demaree Bess. C. S. Forester wrote about the sinking of the *Scharnhorst*, Ambassador Joseph E. Davies wrote from Moscow about the Russian front, and Norman Rockwell painted his version of Roosevelt's slogan, the Four Freedoms. In this silver age, the money came and went at an unprecedented rate. Hibbs spent $175,000, a record for extravagance at that time, for *My Three Years with Eisenhower*, by the general's naval aide, Captain Harry C. Butcher. He spent another $125,000 for the memoirs of Casey Stengel, and $100,000 for a biography of General Douglas MacArthur. The last of these, which had been commissioned without any safeguard as to its quality, was

---

[13] Goulden, *The Curtis Caper*, p. 48.

[14] Ibid., p. 49.

[15] Ibid., p. 51.

[16] Ibid.

never published, and Hibbs referred to it, in a private office memorandum, as "my worst mistake in twenty years." At the same time, Hibbs willingly led the *Post* into a circulation war against *Life* and *Look,* and the *Post* bought its way up from 3.3 million to more than 6.5 million during his twenty-year regime. Advertising revenue rose just as spectacularly, from $23 million to $104 million a year.[17]

Losing the postwar race with competition. Under the continued guidance of Fuller as chairman, MacNeal as president, and Hibbs as editor of the *Post,* the 1950s proved to be difficult years. Although *Post* advertising revenue increased over the decade, the number of advertising pages per issue decreased. The circulation battles of the late 1950s between the *Post, Life,* and *Look* were a mixed blessing for Curtis. A two-year subscription to the *Post* cost the subscriber $7.95 and represented a liability to the *Post* of $20, the production and delivery costs. The larger circulation figures led to increased advertising rates, but these made it impossible for many of the small manufacturers, on whom the *Post* had depended for a substantial amount of its advertising revenue, to continue advertising in the magazine. At the same time the *Post* was losing large corporation advertising to television, which in the years since World War II had built up advertising revenues twice those of magazines.

Market research studies continually eroded the effectiveness of the *Post* as an advertising medium. For example, *Life* underwrote a study which showed that each of its issues had a readership of 5.2 persons and that readership multiplied by circulation brought *Life* equal with radio and television in the numbers-game of media reach—a claim that the *Post* could not equal. *Life* then underwrote another study which indicated that the *Post* was a magazine bought for reading and not for looking; *Life* immediately turned this fact to its advantage by stressing to advertisers that the busy young housewife would not have time to read *Post* articles, so advertising in the *Post* would be less effective than in a magazine bought for looking, such as *Life.*

Madison Avenue wanted to cover the younger segment of the consumer market (base age of 35, with the extra dollars to give discretionary buying power). In the late fifties, *Life*'s circulation included twice as many families in this category as the *Post*'s. Madison Avenue began to feel that the *Post* was not reaching the market "where the action was."

Life was also active during the 1950s building a power base with merchants. *Life* persuaded merchants to tag goods "as advertised in *Life*," with the implication that *Life* put its editorial integrity behind the product.

> The retailers also received low-cost promotional material which a skilled young man would help convert into an attractive display, free of charge. The merchants, in turn, made their warm feelings toward *Life* felt all the way up the distribution line to top management at the manufacturer.[18]

---

[17] Friedrich, *Decline and Fall,* p. 12.
[18] Goulden, *The Curtis Caper,* p. 85.

The business recession of 1961 caused the number of advertising pages per *Post* issue to plummet even more. As the advertising pages decreased, the *Post* became thinner and thinner, and the professionals on Madison Avenue started placing even fewer ads in the *Post* as a result:

> "We're a bunch of sheep," David Ogilvy, of Ogilvy, Benson and Mather, said candidly. "One agency leaves a magazine, we all wonder why and follow. The magazine thins again, and more of us leave. Suddenly there's nothing left. No one wants his copy in a thin book."[19]

Curtis' profits declined during the 1950s from $6.2 million in 1950 to only $1.6 million in 1960. Although gross advertising revenue (including commissions) increased from $98.6 million to $151.8 million during the 10-year period, advertising pages decreased. Production and distribution expenses rose substantially over the same time, while selling and administrative expenses more than doubled, going from $27.7 million to $61.2 million.

The "new Post." Late in 1960, an administrative decision was made under President MacNeal that a "new *Post*" should be created with a "fashionable look" that would appeal to Madison Avenue, increase *Post* advertising revenue, and thus increase corporate profits. Editor Hibbs, on the other hand, felt that the *Post* was already hitting the American market:

> The *Post* was widely considered to be old and stodgy, edited by the old and stodgy to be read by the old and stodgy, and Ben Hibbs couldn't accept it. "The ad people were always hollering in my last year about the Norman Rockwell covers, that they were old-fashioned," he protested. "Heck, those were the *Post*'s most popular feature." And the books he kept buying kept becoming best sellers. "Dammit. We were hitting the American market," said Hibbs. "We had to be with that kind of record." And did someone say that *Post* fiction was unreal? "After all, the world is not entirely composed of hydrogen bombs, juvenile delinquency, race riots, mental institutions, heart disease and cancer," said Hibbs. "I can remember the time when people thought it was *fun to read*."[20]

The "new *Post*" was developed during 1961 and first appeared in September of that year. Six million dollars in advertising was sold for this issue, and its 148 pages created the thickest *Post* in years. Described as a "peculiar mixture of new and old,"[21] it featured a Norman Rockwell cover depicting the artist puzzling out a new *Post* cover; a new column entitled "Speaking Out," different print and layout styles; and articles ranging from the memoirs of Casey Stengel to an account of an American doctor in the jungles of Haiti. The response to the "new *Post*" was immediate.

> The look of the "new" *Post* infuriated its readers, and they wrote in to protest at a rate of ten thousand letters a week. "Idiotic . . . please

19 Ibid., p. 95.
20 Friedrich, *Decline and Fall*, p. 13.
21 Ibid., p. 17.

change it back . . . Cancel my subscription. . . . I have been betrayed—and many others with me." As for Madison Avenue, for which the "new *Post*" had been created, it responded as it usually does to such efforts—with a shrug. "The mistake was," in the words of one cynical old *Post* editor, "that you forced them to read the magazine." Basically, the *Post* had announced change and then attempted to counterfeit change, and the increased advertising didn't last a month. Over the whole year, in fact, advertising plummeted from $104 million to $86 million. The *Post* consequently went into the red by $3 million, and Curtis by $4 million.[22]

Challenge and change: 1962

On March 29, 1962, President MacNeal announced Curtis' $4 million loss for the previous fiscal year, the first corporate loss since the company's inception in 1891. Apparently the loss would have been nearly $9 million except for a tax credit of $1 million and a nonrecurring profit of $3.5 million from the sale of securities.

Ten days earlier, the *Gallagher Report*, a Madison Avenue newsletter, had suggested that a major shake-up in Curtis' corporate leadership might be in the cards:

> THE CURTIS CRISIS. Major changes in Curtis Publishing management and ownership expected shortly. Financier Peter G. Treves has been quietly buying Curtis stock for more than a year. Has acquired sizable holdings.[23]

Apparently Curtis was an attractive target for corporate raiders. For one thing, the corporate assets were understated: 250,000 acres of timberland, for example, were valued at between $10–$15 per acre, while they were carried on the books at $3 per acre. Moreover, the company's stock was underpriced by the market, with the two issues of Curtis preferred selling well below their liquidation values.

In 1962, when Treves was buying into the company, effective operating control was in the hands of Curtis' heirs. A trust, to continue through the life of Curtis' daughter and her two sons, controlled 17.3% of the outstanding stock, and the Curtis heirs themselves owned 14.6%. With 32% of the Curtis stock, the heirs over the years had placed family friends and management sympathetic to the wishes of the family on the board of directors.

True, a minor change had occurred in the late 1950s, when minority stockholders complained that common stock dividends were too low ($.00 for 1933–1950 and $.20 from 1951–1956), and threatened a stockholder suit. As a result, President MacNeal had increased the size of the board and had dropped from it those Curtis executives who held ex-officio seats. The newly opened board seats went to investment and insurance interests. At the same time, however, effective working control of the company became vested in a newly created executive committee which included the same editors and executives who had

---

[22] Ibid., pp. 17–18.

[23] Matthew Culligan, *The Curtis Culligan Story* (New York: Crown Publishers, Inc., 1970), p. 30.

been removed from the board. Moreover, the men filling the newly opened board seats were sympathetic to the wishes of the heirs and thus were considered "family members" of the board.

In April 1962, Treves and Co. and J. R. Williston and Beane, the firms which had been purchasing Curtis stock, sent an emissary to the Curtis Building. This was Milton Gould, a Philadelphia lawyer, who was to play a major role in Curtis' subsequent history. On this occasion, Gould requested an immediate appointment with MacNeal, and stated that the interests he represented wanted two seats on the Curtis board. Not knowing the extent of Treves' and Williston and Beane's ownership, the board agreed to enlarge the number of seats from 11 to 13, with the two new seats going to Gould and R. McLean Stewart, an investment banker. Asked why the directors did not fight the intrusion, Cary Bok, grandson of Cyrus Curtis and member of the board, replied as follows:

> "There are many reasons," Bok said one winter morning in 1964, during a rambling interview at his seaside home in Maine.
>
> "First of all, you never are assured of absolute control unless you have 51 per cent. We have only 32 per cent; we were unsure of what other people had.
>
> "Second, the Curtis board is elected with cumulative voting. The others could have pooled their votes and elected one director for sure; probably two, and possibly three."
>
> Third, Bok said, the company didn't relish the idea of a public proxy fight during a time of internal stress. First-quarter losses that year had already touched $4 million—more red ink than went on the books during all of 1961. Curtis management had more important things to do than scurry around the countryside soliciting proxies from widows and small-time investors. The Wall Street groups, on the other hand, specialized in just this type of scurrying. Had Curtis chosen to fight, there was at least a 50–50 chance that Curtis would have been licked. Management and the heirs feared this, because they didn't know any more about the investors' long-range intentions than they did of the investors' holdings.
>
> Additionally, Curtis by this time was so desperate for cash that it was ready to befriend anyone who came along and offered new ideas and fresh leadership. That spring it was forced to peddle two of its strongest sidelines to raise operating cash. Curtis sold part of its holdings in Bantam Books, Inc., and Treasure Books, Inc., to Grosset & Dunlap, Inc., for a $4.8 million profit. Both companies were returning a profit. But the need for immediate cash was overpowering and the book subsidiaries were something that could be conveniently cut from the empire.[24]

In an interview given shortly after he joined the Curtis board, Gould said that he had sought a directorship because the brokerage houses that had taken a substantial financial position in Curtis had become alarmed by the accelerated operating losses and by Curtis' inability to adapt to changing markets. "New and energetic management is

---

[24] Goulden, *The Curtis Caper*, pp. 123–124.

needed," he added.[25] (For a list of major changes in Curtis' direction during the 1960s, see Exhibit 2.)

"UNDER NEW MANAGEMENT": 1962–1969

In the early summer of 1962, MacNeal left for a trip to Europe, and during his absence, spurred by Gould, the board voted him out as president. Although it was decided to withhold the news from the press until his return, the news was leaked to *The Wall Street Journal* three hours after the meeting ended. An executive committee was formed to run the company until a new president could be found. Gould was named legal counsel to the executive committee.

The Culligan years: 1962–1968

Gould's personal choice for the presidency of Curtis was Matthew Culligan, an executive at Interpublic, an advertising conglomerate headed by Marion Harper. Previous to his employment at Interpublic, Culligan had been an executive vice president at NBC, where he had been credited with turning around the failing NBC Radio Network. Gould arranged a meeting between Culligan and the Curtis executive committee, which Culligan later described as follows:

> Gould conditioned the executive committee on my behalf, warning them that I was just about the final hope and softening them up for my salary demands and fringe benefits. He actually assigned one of his associates to write my contract for me![26]

Shortly after its meeting with Culligan, the executive committee named him president of Curtis. Culligan described his first week at the company as frantic. He raced between the editorial and sales offices in New York City and the corporate offices and the circulation, manufacturing, and paper companies in Pennsylvania. Marion Harper, Culligan's boss at Interpublic, got together the best "media brains" in his organization "to contribute the best cerebration and intuition to the problems at Curtis"[27] in order to help Culligan in his new position. Culligan described the resulting suggestions as follows:

> When the report was finished, Harper invited me to his office and gave me the benefit of the accumulated experience and judgment of a dozen of his best people. The report was fascinating. In essence, it said that Curtis could not survive in the form in which I had inherited it—with the same magazines, same circulations, same frequencies—under the economic conditions then prevailing at Curtis. The task force recommended that the *Post* go biweekly; that *Holiday* be sold to generate working capital; that *American Home* be folded into the *Ladies' Home Journal,* saving millions in subscription costs. The final recommendation was to get Curtis out of the paper and manufacturing business. I accepted the Harper report with overflowing gratitude and rushed back to Curtis as though I'd found the

---

25 Ibid., p. 125.
26 Culligan, *The Curtis Culligan Story,* p. 35.
27 Ibid., p. 60.

Holy Grail. Calling in my inherited key men—Bob Gibbon, secretary of the executive board; Ford Robinson, head of Operations; Leon Marks, head of Manufacturing; G. B. McCombs, number two man in Circulation—I discussed the report with them. My soaring spirits plummeted as each of the Harper recommendations was shot down in flames, not because the ideas were faulty, but because of artificial, legal, or financial strictures that appeared to block every turn.[28]

Immediate tasks.   After assuming the presidency of Curtis, Culligan was faced with several immediate tasks. Curtis owed $22 million to four creditor banks that were expressing concern over Curtis' financial position. Culligan promised an extensive cost-reduction program, and the banks agreed to a 12-month extension of the loan with a commitment for an additional $4 million in working capital. One additional stipulation added to the agreement was that Culligan would attempt to remove a debt restriction from the Curtis bylaws, which required a two-thirds vote of the preferred stockholders before management could pledge any collateral for loans. This provision protected the preferred stockholders in the case of liquidation, but it also barred long-term loans. Up to this point in time, all Curtis debt had been short-term at higher interest rates. Culligan proposed the removal of the restriction to the preferred stockholders, who eventually voted down the change.

During the period he was negotiating with the banks, Culligan also busied himself with two other major problems at Curtis: the need for cost reductions, and the increasing loss of advertising. In a move that was to have serious repercussions, Culligan called in a former colleague, J. M. Clifford, who was suffering from political infighting at NBC, and made him executive vice president of finance and operations. Clifford ordered an immediate 20% cut throughout the entire Curtis structure:

> By mid-1963 enough rank and file deadwood was chopped out of Curtis—3,500 jobs in all—to lower the annual payroll by $13 million. Printing operations were streamlined; workmen disassembled the huge mechanical innards of the Curtis building and packed the presses off to Sharon Hill. Fixed expenses dropped by $15 to $18 million annually, meaning the *Post* and the other magazines had a lower break-even per issue. According to Curtis annual reports, selling, general, and administrative expenses in 1961 were $62.6 million; this was down to $58.2 million in 1962 and $44.9 million in 1963. Production and delivery expenses dropped from $116.3 million to $106.5 and $103.2 million in the same stages.[29]

With the internal organization left to Clifford, Culligan set out to do what he knew best, selling.

> Curtis was bleeding to death. Too much unnecessary expense and not enough advertising income would bury Curtis by January 1963, unless . . . .
> I was the "unless"; no one else was in a position to deliver. This statement is not intended to be boastful—the burden was actually on

---

[28] Ibid., pp. 60–61.
[29] Friedrich, *Decline and Fall*, p. 64.

my shoulders. No amount of promotion, advertising, or sales calls by others would suffice. So I followed my instinct and decided on an unprecedented personal sales effort. I determined to do what no other executive in United States business had ever done—call personally on the heads of America's two hundred leading corporations within six months.[30]

Culligan, noted for his travels by helicopter, and described as a "rambunctious figure whose black eye patch had become a trade-mark,"[31] began selling the presidents of the nation's largest companies on the *Post:*

> The new president set out on an orgy of salesmanship, with press agents keeping track of every move. It was said that he traveled 3,500 miles a week to sell ads. It was said that he flew to Detroit and made presentations to General Motors, Chrysler, and Lincoln-Mercury all in one day. It was said that he signed $30 million in new ads within his first month. "From late fall of 1962 through the spring of 1963," said Culligan, "I ran Curtis almost entirely by telephone, memo and crash personal meetings at airports, in cars roaring along turnpikes, in the Curtis plane (a sturdy old twin Beech), and even a helicopter, which I leased, to cut down the time wasted getting from New York to Philadelphia." He expressed his philosophy by saying, "I had two choices. I could have stayed in Philadelphia and listened to everybody's problems, or I could go out and start selling, and let the problems take care of themselves."[32]

Despite Culligan's selling efforts, advertising revenue of the *Post* continued to decrease, from $86 million in 1961 to $66 million in 1962 to $60 million in 1963. Curtis' losses, which had been $4 million in 1961, soared to $18.9 million in 1962, then decreased to $3.4 million in 1963, the first year for which Culligan was fully responsible. But part of the improvement was of an accounting nature. At the time of Culligan's takeover, Price Waterhouse, attempting to get Curtis' business, had suggested that Curtis change its accounting policies and handle subscription liabilities in the same manner as most other publishing firms. Following this advice, Curtis spread its subscription liabilities over the life of the subscriptions and thus decreased its losses for 1963 from $10 million to $3.4 million.

By mid-1963, Culligan was again faced with the problem of the short-term bank loans coming due. Assistance came in the form of Serge Semenenko, vice president of the First National Bank of Boston. Russian-born Semenenko was considered one of the "mystery men" of U.S. finance. His loans from the First for the period 1920–1950 "practically supported the United States film industry,"[33] and his list of corporate "saves" included Fairbanks, Whitney; The International Paper Company; the Hearst publishing empire, and the Kindall Company.

By August 17, which was the deadline on the short-term loans to

[30] Culligan, *The Curtis Culligan Story,* pp. 78–79.

[31] Friedrich, *Decline and Fall,* p. 4.

[32] Ibid., p. 64.

[33] Goulden, *The Curtis Caper,* p. 157.

Curtis in 1963, Culligan and Semenenko had agreed on a $35 million loan from six banks.

Semenenko doesn't sign blank checks, however, and especially when they are for $35 million. From Curtis he elicited a pledge that all management decisions be "reasonably satisfactory" to him, as the designated agent of the banking syndicate. As a service fee Semenenko's bank got ¼ of one per cent of the loan ($87,500)—plus, of course, its interest, one per cent above the prime rate on its share of the total loan.

There is conflicting testimony on just how active a role Semenenko took for himself in the day-to-day conduct of Curtis' affairs. One former executive maintains that Culligan "wouldn't push the elevator button without calling Serge." This is disputed, however, by Cary W. Bok. "All he asks is that he be kept informed of what's going on," Bok said recently. "So long as he is given complete information on what management is doing, he's satisfied." Bok had unconcealed admiration for Semenenko.

"Were it not for Semenenko," he said, "Curtis would have been dead. . . . He is a quiet little genius who inspires confidence in everything he touches."[34]

Corporate infighting.   Although it appeared in early 1964, with the bank loans refinanced and a modest first-quarter profit for Curtis, that Culligan's major problems were over, internal problems were about to erupt that he had not anticipated. These problems were precipitated by Clay Blair, Jr., a Curtis executive who had aspired to Culligan's job, or, failing that, at least to the job which Culligan had given to Clifford.

Blair had come to Curtis in 1959 as assistant managing editor of the *Post* under managing editor Bill Sherrod, Blair's one-time supervisor at the Pentagon, when both had worked for *Time-Life*. When Fuoss, who had replaced Hibbs as editor in December 1961, resigned after four months, Sherrod became editor of the *Post*, with Blair moving up to managing editor. Back in 1962 Blair had been aware that Curtis was in financial trouble, that MacNeal would go, and that the result would be a void into which he might be able to move. In bidding for the presidency, Blair had hoped to gain some leverage from the fact that he was a personal friend of Admiral Lewis Strauss, formerly chairman of the Atomic Energy Commission, but currently a member of the New York brokerage firm which was providing the stimulus behind merger talks between Curtis and Doubleday & Company, book publishers. The Blair-Strauss friendship dated back to a time when Blair and his *Time-Life* colleague, James Shepley, had written a book praising Strauss' role in the development of the hydrogen bomb. What made the friendship relevant to Blair's ambitions was its implied ability to influence Doubleday.

At the same board meeting during which MacNeal had been fired, Blair had been elected vice president with unspecified responsibilities in the editorial offices of Curtis magazines. Asked by Gould what he

---
[34] Ibid., p. 163.

would do if elected president of Curtis, Blair had responded with a written report entitled "Tomorrow Morning Plan":

> Blair's recommendations were Draconian. For one, he recommended the liquidation of the *Ladies' Home Journal* and *American Home* which were losing several million dollars a year. He recommended selling the Curtis Building in Philadelphia, getting rid of the paper mills, tightening the Curtis Circulation Company, moving everything except printing and distribution to New York. For the *Post* he recommended a deliberate reduction in circulation from 6.5 to 5 million.[35]

Blair recounted that his "Tomorrow Morning Plan" had upset ex-president Fuller, who was still a power at Curtis as a member of the board and of its executive committee. Blair attributed his inability to attain the presidency of Curtis to Fuller's opposition:

> "Walter Fuller invited me privately to his office, a gloomy, oak-paneled room with a fireplace, on the fourth floor of the Curtis Building," Blair recalled. "It was Fuller who had integrated Curtis, bought the paper companies, built the Sharon Hill printing plant. Now he seemed disturbed that I wanted to divest them."[36]

After Culligan was chosen as president, Blair was placed in the newly created position of editorial director of all Curtis magazines, a position above that of his old boss and mentor, Sherrod. Blair related a conversation between Gould, Culligan, and himself on the day of Culligan's takeover:

> "Culligan," Gould said, "you're Mr. Outside." Then turning to me: "Blair," he said, "you're Mr. Inside." He paced the floor and puffed on a huge cigar. "Culligan, you bring in the advertising and straighten out the image of this company. Blair, you keep the books, fix the products, and deal with manufacturing and the rest of it." It was an eloquent proposition, and when he finished, Culligan and I took the deal, with Culligan pledging then that "no one will ever come between us." We shook hands all around.[37]

If Blair had believed that he would be "Mr. Inside," he was quickly disappointed, for Culligan in effect turned this position over to Clifford.

> The conflict between Clifford and Blair came quickly and inevitably. They fought over every one of the technical and financial problems that lie at the heart of corporate power. "During 1963, Clifford got a throttle hold on the company," Blair said later. "He took over circulation, manufacturing, and paper mills, then accounting, personnel, and legal. He brought in three obnoxious lieutenants: Maurice Poppei, controller; Gloria Swett, legal; Sidney Natkin, personnel. By summer, Clifford's control of money and people was so complete that nobody, including me, could hire or fire or give a raise or sign a check without his specific approval."[38]

[35] Friedrich, *Decline and Fall*, p. 32.
[36] Ibid., p. 33.
[37] Ibid., pp. 33–34.
[38] Ibid., p. 50.

By January 1964, Blair was refusing to permit any of Clifford's staff on the editorial floors of the Curtis Building in New York. Clifford retaliated by refusing any cooperation of the corporate operations and finance areas that he controlled. The conflict grew to include not only Blair, but most of the Curtis editors. Recognizing that action had to be taken, Culligan gave Clifford a $20,000 raise and removed him from his position as executive vice president of finance and operations. Culligan temporarily took over the duties of operations, which consisted mainly of manufacturing, and gave the financial responsibilities to Maurice Poppei, then treasurer.

Changing editorial policy.   At the same time he was fighting Clifford, Blair was also solidifying his control over the editorial pages of the Curtis magazines. Two months after becoming editorial director, Blair announced that he was taking over the editorship of the *Post* and that Sherrod would go to India to produce a story on Nehru with Norman Rockwell, the *Post* cover artist. Blair asserted his control over the other magazines by immediately firing the editor of the *Ladies' Home Journal* and three members of the *Journal*'s art department.

As editor of the *Post,* Blair set out to change the magazine:

> Blair really needed only a few weeks, all in all, to change the entire magazine—not just what it published, photographic covers, investigations and exposés, fiction by celebrities, and raucous editorials, but the way it operated. Instead of letting editors putter along in their departmental specialties, he insisted on getting everyone involved in the continuous uproar. And at the end of these first few weeks, in January of 1963, he sent us all a memorandum: ". . . You are putting out one hell of a fine magazine. The articles are timely, full of significance and exclusivity. The . . . visual aspects have improved tremendously. . . . [Fiction] could be one of the great breakthroughs in magazine publishing. The final yardstick: We have about six lawsuits pending, meaning we are hitting them where it hurts, with solid, meaningful journalism."[39]

One of the lawsuits was to cost the Curtis Publishing Company over $1 million. The *Post* had published an exposé of an alleged football fix between the coaches Butts of Georgia and Bryant of Alabama. Even though Georgia's Attorney General concluded that the evidence "indicates that vital and important information was given about the Georgia team, and that it could have affected the outcome of the game and the margin of points scored,"[40] Butts won his libel suit, and the *Post* settled with Bryant out of court.

Building coalitions against Culligan.   During the days of corporate infighting and changing editorial policy, Blair was busy building coalitions against Culligan. He formed an Editorial Board consisting of the editors of the major Curtis magazines, with the idea "that it might serve as a political tool to offset the tremendous corporate political drives of Culligan and Clifford."[41] Blair also formed an alliance with

---

[39] Ibid., p. 40.
[40] Ibid., p. 461.
[41] Ibid., p. 50.

Marvin Kantor, a former member of Williston and Beane, the brokerage firm that had helped to put Gould and Stewart on the Curtis board in 1962 (and, incidentally, a firm in which Culligan's father-in-law had once been a managing partner). Kantor had joined Curtis early in 1963 as a member of the board of directors and he had become chief executive assistant to Culligan in January 1964. Kantor stepped into the power vacuum created by the fight between Blair and Clifford:

> Within three months of his arrival at Curtis, Kantor had taken charge of editorial, advertising sales, manufacturing, and just about everything else that interested him. At this point, Culligan was doing his best to portray Curtis as a company that had been saved, a company that had already moved from paralyzing losses into a state of profit by the end of 1963. Once Kantor got access to the ledgers, however, he began expressing suspicions of Culligan's optimistic predictions. In March, Curtis neared the limits of its bank credit, and Kantor brought in some new cash by selling Curtis' one, halfhearted venture in book publishing, a one-third interest in Bantam Books, for $1.9 million. Culligan got the board to agree to new investments in Curtis' printing and paper plants, but Kantor, after looking into the plants, began arguing that they should be sold, just as Blair's group had said two years earlier. And when Kantor checked Culligan's advertising forecasts for the Post, he decided that they were going not up but down (in actual fact, Post ad revenues for the first six months of 1964 eventually proved to be 17 per cent lower than similar revenues for 1963). All in all, Kantor told Blair, Joe Culligan was leading Curtis not to salvation but to ruin. The company would again lose heavily during 1964, Kantor said—perhaps another $10 million. Blair was appalled.[42]

Blair and Kantor joined forces early in 1964 in an attempt to gain the presidency and control of Curtis. They presented findings of mismanagement to individual members of the board and rallied the editorial departments behind their bid. At one time, Blair and Kantor invited a dozen of the company's leading editors and publishing executives to Manero's steak house in Greenwich, Connecticut, to plot Culligan's overthrow. Largely at Kantor's insistence, Blair was elevated to the Curtis board in February 1964 replacing Stewart.

Culligan received a temporary reprieve from the Blair and Kantor onslaught in April 1964, when it was announced that Texas Gulf Sulphur had discovered major deposits of copper, zinc, and silver, valued at up to $2 billion, just 300 feet from 110,000 acres owned by a Canadian subsidiary of Curtis, the T. S. Woollings Company. Immediately Curtis stock rose from $6 to $19.25 per share.

Although the ore find promised a degree of financial solvency for Curtis, by Labor Day 1964 Curtis' losses for the year were predicted to be $7 million, and, in actuality, would reach $14 million. The company's working capital position was also dangerously close to the $27.5 million minimum level set by the banks. Given the discrepancy between Culligan's "turn around" predictions earlier in the year and the

---

[42] Ibid., p. 76.

company's actual financial position, Blair and Kantor made their move, armed with a proposal for saving the company and with a letter signed by most of the editors asking that Culligan be stripped of his executive power.

Confrontation—An "ancient tribunal." A confrontation took place between Blair, Kantor, and Culligan at an ensuing board meeting. Otto Friedrich, in *Decline and Fall*, discussed the composition of this tribunal at this time (Exhibit 3):

> Who, then, controlled the Curtis board of directors? Unlike many boards, which are acquiescent allies of the reigning management, the Curtis directors were divided into a number of factions, which not only were hostile to one another but scarcely even comprehended one another. The chairman was Joe Culligan, who counted on the support of his own appointees—Clifford and Poppei—but their loyalties were less than certain. Clifford, having been demoted from the Number Two position by Culligan, apparently believed that he himself would be a more efficient president than Culligan. Poppei's loyalties seemed to belong partly to Culligan, partly to Clifford, partly to the discipline of the accountant's profession. On the insurgent side, Blair spoke only for himself and the editors. Kantor had made himself an ally of Blair's but still had ties to the stock interests that had brought him to the board in the first place. The most ambiguous of all these new directors was Milton Gould, once the attorney for Kantor, once the discoverer of Culligan. Gould was also a partner in the law firm of Gallop, Climenko & Gould, and since the *Post* alone paid him more than $600,000 a year for legal expenses, Gould had a natural interest in this aspect of Curtis.
>
> Since none of the main antagonists could create a majority, their conflicts served as a kind of ballet staged for the amusement of the old board members, who represented a plurality of the stock, and who retained a veto over any attempts to save the corporation. Of these old board members, the basic group was known as "the family," which owned 32 per cent of all common stock and officially consisted of two people: Mary Louise Curtis Bok Zimbalist, then aged eighty-eight, the daughter of Cyrus H. K. Curtis, who occasionally was wheeled into critical board meetings by her Negro servants; and her son, Cary W. Bok, aged fifty-nine, who was in rather poor health but periodically came to Philadelphia, dressed in the old Khakis that he liked to wear at his country place in Maine. (There was another son, Curtis Bok, who might have helped to save the company, but that was not to be. Lorimer had denounced him a generation earlier as "that damned Bolshevik," and things were arranged so that Curtis Bok would never have a voice in the operation of the Curtis magazines. He went on to become a distinguished judge, and his son was recently made dean of the Harvard Law School.) As for Mrs. Zimbalist, let us remember her by a story told by a retired executive. Once a year, according to this chronicler, Mrs. Zimbalist would engage in exactly the same colloquy with Walter Deane Fuller, who was then president of the corporation. "She would very respectfully ask Mr. Fuller that her salary as a director be doubled. Very gravely he would reply that economic conditions were such that this could not be done. She would thank him and

sit down. Of course, her salary was only one dollar. But she and Mr. Fuller seemed to enjoy the byplay."

The rest of the old directors tended to support "the family," to the extent that they could determine what the family wanted, but Mrs. Zimbalist and her son rarely attended board meetings during these declining years—refusing either to sell the stocks they had held all their lives or to exercise the authority that these stocks gave them. The old directors were thus left to decide matters for themselves, and for this, they were of an age and distinction that would have done credit to the United States Senate. The most senior of them, of course, was Walter Deane Fuller, the tiny, bald gentleman of eighty-two, who had joined the accounting department of Curtis in 1908 and worked his way up to be president and board chairman for more than twenty-five years. Next came M. Albert Linton, seventy-seven, retired president of the Provident Life Insurance Company of Philadelphia and now chairman of the board's executive committee, assigned to deal with the accusations. Then there was Walter S. Franklin, aged eighty, retired president of the Pennsylvania Railroad; and Ellsworth Bunker, aged seventy, former president of the United Sugar Company, former U.S. Ambassador to India, former president of the American Red Cross; Moreau D. Brown, aged sixty-one, partner in the private banking firm of Brown Brothers, Harriman; Harry C. Mills, aged sixty-three, retired vice president of J. C. Penney; and Curtis Barkes, aged fifty-eight, executive vice president of United Air Lines.

Once the managerial civil war had broken out, it soon became apparent that this board, this ultimate court of appeals, knew relatively little about the Curtis Publishing Company and was quite bewildered by the problems that were being placed before it. More than half the directors were over sixty—"Why," someone asked Clemenceau, "are the presidents of France always octogenarians?" And Clemenceau replied: "Because we have run out of nonagenarians"—and most of them, except for the actual combatants, were weary of combat. Thus, when Blair and Culligan wanted to accuse each other of guilt for Curtis' condition, they had to carry their case before this ancient tribunal, which, in consenting to hear the arguments, denied that the ultimate guilt was its own.[43]

The result of the confrontation was the immediate dismissal of Blair and Kantor on October 30, 1964, and the eventual removal of Culligan from the presidency. Culligan's removal was announced after a meeting of several of the directors at Bok's apartment in Philadelphia. Culligan, not allowed to attend, found out a year later that Clifford and Poppei had threatened to resign if Culligan remained as president.

Rumors began to circulate as to who the next president of Curtis would be. Reportedly the job had been offered to Newton Minow, chairman of the FCC under Kennedy and to Ed Miller, publisher of *McCall's*, both of whom turned the position down. Miller commented on his reasons for rejecting the presidency of Curtis:

[43] Ibid., pp. 125–127. Reprinted from *Decline and Fall* by permission of Harper and Row. © 1969–1970 Otto Friedrich.

I came in ready to sign a contract that morning. The amount of money was almost embarrassing—$150,000 a year. But I had other conditions. One was that the banks guarantee a period of grace of twenty-four months, without anybody blowing the whistle, because no miracle would work in less than twenty-four months. Then the other element was John Kluge, the head of Metromedia. We talked to him about taking over the financial responsibilities, and Kluge loved the idea, but his bankers didn't see it in the same light. So that morning, I learned that neither of these conditions would be met, and I said, "To hell with it," and walked out.[44]

The Clifford presidency: 1964–1968

Apparently the board's difficulty in finding a new chief executive and the banks' increasing concern over Curtis' financial position created a situation into which Clifford could move. Clifford, supported by the second most senior board member, Linton, made a bid for the presidency and was accepted in December 1964.

Once in power, Clifford fired several editors, demanded that the magazines cut their budgets by 40%, appointed acting editor William Emerson editor of the *Post*, and changed the *Post* into a bi-weekly publication.

Worried about the $37.3 million that Curtis owed the banks, Clifford sold a paper mill in Pennsylvania for $10.3 million and used $8 million for debt reduction. He also negotiated $24 million in cash from Texas Gulf Sulphur for mining rights on Curtis' Canadian timberlands and utilized the money to pay off bank debts. During 1965, Curtis' assets decreased from $112.6 to $86.9 million with liabilities decreasing from $103 to $68.4 million. Curtis lost $3.4 million in 1965 and showed an operating profit of $347,000 in 1966, the first profit of the decade. Otto Friedrich described the method by which Clifford produced this profit:

> The technique was simple. The conscientious employees worked hard at their jobs, because that was their nature, and then the supreme command ordered everyone to cut costs until the year's activities came out even on the balance sheets. This was not simply a matter of operating expenses. It was a philosophy of life. It was a perfect example, however, of the cost accountants' system of doing business—to cut, shrink, tighten, until we reached the theoretical goal of not producing anything at all. Or, as Emerson put it, "It's like being nibbled to death by ducks."[45]

The nibbling apparently would not save Curtis. The company recorded a loss of $4.8 million for 1967, which Clifford blamed on an advertising decline "due primarily to softened national economic conditions and costly strikes in key industries."[46] The company's cash position during this period became dangerously low:

> As of the end of the year, current assets had declined by more than $6 million, liabilities had increased by more than $1 million, and

---

[44] Ibid., p. 172.

[45] Ibid., p. 270.

[46] Ibid., p. 307.

actual cash in hand had dropped from $10,102,000 at the start of 1967 to $425,000 at the start of 1968. Obviously, for a company that was operating on a budget of almost $130 million a year, a cash supply of $425,000 was virtually no cash at all.[47]

The low cash position necessitated a quick cash inflow. Clifford attempted to sell the old Curtis building in Philadelphia and offered CBS Curtis' magazines for $15 million provided CBS gave Curtis a printing and distribution contract. CBS reportedly was amazed, since they had just done a study on Curtis which indicated that the magazines alone would earn $10 million a year without the other Curtis overhead.

Ackerman takes over

Into this precarious financial position, with the banks reportedly pushing for a management change, stepped Martin Ackerman, who was quickly pressed into service as Curtis' next president. Aged 36, Ackerman, a former lawyer, was currently head of Perfect Film & Chemical Corporation, a conglomerate he had pushed from sales of $20 million in 1962 to $100 million in 1964 through a series of acquisitions.

Ackerman has related the origin of his interest in Curtis and also the events of a special meeting of the Curtis board in April 1968 that led to his entry into Curtis management:

> J. M. Clifford, then president of Curtis, reported a proposal which I had made under which Perfect Film & Chemical Corporation, which I headed, would arrange for a $5 million loan to Curtis. This loan was to be secured and guaranteed, and would give Perfect Film a chance to see whether the combinations of the activities of the two corporations made any sense. The proposal was discussed at length, along with a number of alternate proposals for obtaining the immediate capital needed by the company. Later in the afternoon, Milton Gould, a director, told the Board that I had informed him that the Perfect proposal was subject to withdrawal if not accepted then and there at the meeting. Accompanied by former governor Alfred Driscoll, another director, I was invited to attend the board meeting for about twenty minutes.
>
> After further discussion, my proposal was approved and I was elected a regular director, along with Eugene Mason, Perfect's attorney. Clifford was voted out of the presidency of Curtis and elected chairman of the Board of Directors. I was made president in his place.[48]

Ackerman began his presidency in April 1968 by arranging a two-month extension of all overdue bank loans and outlining a plan to save the *Post*. Ackerman announced that the *Post*'s circulation would be cut from 6.8 million to 3 million and that the *Post* would be promoted "as a magazine of class, not mass."[49]

In August 1968, Ackerman issued a report on the financial position at Curtis for the first half of 1968. A loss of $7 million on revenues of

---

[47] Ibid., pp. 307–308.

[48] Martin Ackerman, *The Curtis Affair* (Los Angeles: Nash Publishing, 1970), pp. 8–9.

[49] Friedrich, *Decline and Fall*, p. 328.

$58 million was reported, compared to a loss of $370,000 on revenues of $63 million for the first half of the previous year. He also disclosed that Curtis' bank loans of $13.2 million had been taken over by Perfect Film from the Semenenko group at an interest rate of one per cent above the prime rate with maturity on demand.

During his first six months at Curtis, while liquidating part of the Curtis empire, Ackerman also worked incessantly at the *Post* offices in New York, developing schemes to save the magazine, and attempting to write editorials and a column for it (much to the dismay of the editors). But with increased losses for 1968 becoming more evident, Ackerman moved out of the Curtis offices into a town house he had purchased. Friedrich describes the changes that ensued:

> An environment not only expresses a man's ambitions; it also changes his perspectives. The Ackerman who sat enthroned in the town house was not the same man who bustled in and out of offices on our editorial floor. Now, he received us only by appointment, negotiated through one of his two secretaries, and we appeared not as the managers of our own domain but as emissaries to his castle. And in the act of physical withdrawal from the Curtis building, he inevitably withdrew, to some extent, from his intense physical involvement in the day-to-day problems of the *Post*. This was quite understandable, too, for in six months of hard labor, his involvement had really accomplished relatively little. And so, as all executives like to fall back on the specialties that originally brought them their success, Ackerman in his town house began to revert to what he had been before he ever came to Curtis, a financier, a maneuverer of stocks and corporations, an expert at mergers and acquisitions, a banker and millionaire.[50]

As a financier and maneuverer of stocks and corporations, Ackerman reportedly was a master. For example, ostensibly to raise cash for Curtis, he sold the *Ladies' Home Journal* and *American Home* to Downe Communications, Inc., for 100,000 shares of Downe stock valued at $5.4 million, a price low enough to "evoke the image of a fire sale."[51] He later had Curtis turn the Downe stock over to Perfect Film for a $4.5 million reduction in the Curtis loans and then sold the stock privately through a Wall Street firm for $5 million.

> The same day that his sale of the Downe shares was disclosed, it was announced that Perfect Film was spending $9 million to buy from Gulf & Western two Desilu film studios in Culver City, California, the fourteen-acre Culver Studio and the twenty-nine-acre Culver Backlot, both of which were being used by Paramount and various television producers.[52]

But for all Ackerman's financial wizardry, by early 1969 he apparently had neither the ability nor the desire to save the *Post*. The predicted losses for the *Post* for 1969 were between $3.7 and $7 million, based on the trend of decreasing advertising revenue.

Utilizing this financial data as justification, Ackerman, who six

---

[50] Ibid., p. 416.
[51] Ibid., p. 417.
[52] Ibid.

months before had stated that as long as he was at Curtis "there would not be a last issue of the *Post*,"[53] announced the end:

> No other decision is possible in view of the sizable predicted losses which continued publication would have generated. Quite simply, this is an example of a new management which could not reduce expenses nor generate sales and income fast enough to halt mounting losses. . . . Having refinanced the Saturday Evening Post Company with $15 million in new capital, I assured directors and stockholders of the company that regardless of my own personal feelings, if we could not return a profit we would have to shut down the *Post*.[54]

The reaction from the stockholders was immediate. Philip Kalodner, a young Philadelphia lawyer and representative of minority stockholders, filed suit against Ackerman for alleged illegal, oppressive, and fraudulent action that had wasted and misapplied more than $45 million of Curtis assets. The trustees of the Cyrus Curtis estate also began an assault against Ackerman:

> They, too, accused Ackerman of dissipating the Curtis assets, and they publicly demanded that he resign from the presidency by noon on the coming Saturday, February 8. They also demanded the resignations of his closest allies on the board of directors. The trustees were vague in their accusations, citing only "conflict of interest," but Cary Bok told a reporter who telephoned his home in Camden, Maine: "That company is in such a damn mess that it's time we got into it—don't you think?"[55]

POSTSCRIPT

At the next board meeting (March 1969), Ackerman resigned as president in favor of G. B. McCombs, who had recently been promoted to senior vice president, after being with Curtis since 1930. Kalodner, who held only 100 shares of stock, was named vice president, director, and a member of the executive committee "in return for agreement not to press his lawsuit against the company."[56]

McCombs lasted five weeks as president; the position then went to Kalodner after some stormy meetings of the board:

> The board itself, depleted by the latest resignations of Ackerman, Gould, and McCombs, now consisted of only six members (one of whom was serving as U.S. Ambassador to Saigon). Three of these had been allies of the departed Milton Gould, and they all favored a petition of bankruptcy. "But I spoke up against them," Kalodner said. "In fact, I filibustered against them." The board meeting went on for five hours, and then ended inconclusively. And the day after the crisis, Kalodner simply decreed himself to be, if not the president of Curtis, then "chief executive officer." Once again, Curtis was without a president.
>
> The deadlock lasted through most of April, and then, on April 24,

---

53 *Newsweek*, May 20, 1968, p. 70.
54 Friedrich, *Decline and Fall*, p. 449.
55 Ibid., p. 466.
56 Ibid., p. 469.

it was broken long enough for Kalodner, like yet another Roman emperor, to become president. In that capacity, he offered repeated invitations to the unhappy trustees to "join" him in salvaging the wreckage of the company, but the trustees had no intention of collaborating in Kalodner's presidency. Kalodner alone, therefore, had the responsibility of announcing that the Curtis operating loss during the Ackerman year of 1968 had been $18.3 million. He also had to admit that the Curtis contract to print the *Ladies' Home Journal* and *American Home* for Downe Communications would run out at the end of June. "The contract," said *The Wall Street Journal*, "is practically the only ongoing venture Curtis has left."[57]

Kalodner and the trustees spent the early weeks of May 1969 mailing rival proxy statements to the stockholders in anticipation of the May 21 stockholders' meeting. At the meeting the trustees won nine seats on the board of directors, and a representative of the trustees, Arthur Murphy, past president of *McCall's*, took over as president and chairman of the board. A short time later, Murphy dropped the presidency, and W. J. MacIntosh, a lawyer for the board, took over as acting chief executive officer.

In May of 1970, the trustees sold the 700,000 shares of Curtis stock they had controlled since 1933 to Beurt SerVaas, a self-made millionaire from the Mid-West, who took over control as president and principal stockholder of Curtis. SerVaas related his initial actions as head of the company as follows:

> "I came into this company to preside over its death, but instead I decided I could save it," he said. "I'm the first person since Cyrus Curtis himself who's been both the chief executive and the chief stockholder, and so I've had the kind of authority you have to have in order to make vital decisions."
>
> Throughout the summer and fall Mr. SerVaas proceeded to make a series of "vital decisions." He sold all the manufacturing companies that Curtis owned, including a printing plant and a paper mill, decreased the over-all size of its staff from 9,000 people to 100, and "reduced its voluminous debts to zero."
>
> It was the burden of these financial responsibilities that prevented the company from reaping profits, Mr. SerVaas explained.
>
> "Now we're no longer in manufacturing and real estate," he added, "we're just a little publishing company that puts out magazines, and for the first time in years we're no longer in the red."[58]

SerVaas has decided that the *Post* will return to publication as a "200 page quarterly directed toward the 'middle American.' "

> "Toward the end the *Post* became worldly and sophisticated and hard-nosed in an attempt to rejuvenate itself," Mr. SerVaas said, "but it failed, and what we intend to do now should make everyone happy. We're not going to print any more exposés or muckraking articles; we're going to concentrate on writing about those institutions and mores in contemporary America that are good for America."[59]

---

[57] Ibid., pp. 472–473.
[58] *The New York Times*, November 6, 1970.
[59] Ibid.

Exhibit 1

FINANCIAL HIGHLIGHTS: 1960–1969
(dollars in millions)

Year	Operating revenues[a]	Operating profit[b]	Net profit	Stockholders' equity[c]	Current assets	Current liabilities	Total assets
1960	$192.8 (restated)	$ 3.5	$ 1.6	$ 49.7	$60.7	$23.3	$133.5
1961	178.4	(8.7)	(4.2)[d]	46.8[e]	56.7	24.5	135.5
1962	149.3	(21.0)	(18.9)[f]	27.9	55.6	41.9	127.8
1963	152.0	(1.4)	(3.4)	24.5	53.8	19.0	123.0
1964	139.4	(13.0)	(13.9)[g]	9.5	46.7	18.5	112.7
1965	122.7	(0.7)	(3.4)	20.5[h]	39.9	22.6	88.9
1966	128.8	2.0	0.3	21.5	44.4	24.6	94.6
1967	124.6	(3.2)	(4.8)	16.7	38.3	25.9	91.5
1968	98.7	(15.2)	(20.9)[i]	2.0[j]	16.7	19.8	43.6
1969	32.0	(10.7)	(19.4)[k]	(14.7)[l]	10.1	15.4	20.3

Note: Parentheses indicate deficit figures.

a Reflects advertising and circulation revenue (net of commissions), paper sales, and miscellaneous operations.
b After production and delivery expense, SGA, and depreciation, but before interest (ranging between $1.2 million and $2.7 million 1960–1968) and miscellaneous income and expenses.
c Includes prior preferred ($16.7 million), preferred ($2.4 million), common ($3.6 million), capital surplus (under $1 million) and undivided profits. As of December 31, 1969, arrears on preferred were $8.9 million.
d Reflects $3.5 million gain on sale of securities and $1.3 million tax credit.
e Reflects $1.7 million transferred to surplus from reserves.
f Reflects $3.8 million tax credit.
g Reflects $1.8 million profit on sale of securities.
h Reflects $14.3 million profit on sale of properties.
i Reflects $1.6 million loss on Saturday Evening Post, and $2.6 million net extraordinary charges (after $20 million provision for plant obsolescence and $1.5 million for future loss on home-office lease, partly offset by gains of $1.1 million on sale of property, $3.4 million on sale of circulation and subscription companies, $13.7 million on sale of Ladies' Home Journal and American Home, and $.7 million gain from reduction in Post circulation).
j Reflects $6.1 million recovery of pension plan funding.
k Reflects $8.3 million in net extraordinary charges associated with curtailment of operations.
l Reflects $2.7 million additional recovery of pension plan funding.
Sources: Curtis Publishing Company, Annual Reports, and Moody's Industrial Manual.

Exhibit 2
THE POWER STRUGGLE AT CURTIS—HOW THEY ROSE AND FELL

	1961	1962	1963	1964	1965	1966	1967	1968	1969
CHAIRMAN OF THE BOARD	Vacant since 1957			Mathew Culligan				Vacant	Thos Moses / Arthur Murphy
PRESIDENT	Robert MacNeal (since 1950)	Mathew Culligan						Martin Ackerman	Arthur Murphy
HEAD OF MAGAZINE DIVISION		Created in April 1963	John Veronis	Marvin Kantor		Vacant		G.B. McCombs	
POST EDITOR	Ben Hibbs (since 1942)	Robert Sherrod	Clay Blair		Vacant	William Emerson			DEATH OF THE POST
NO. 2 POST EDITOR	Robert Fuoss (since 1942)	Clay Vacant	Davis Thomas*	Don Schanche*	William Emerson	Otto Friedrich			
NO. 3 POST EDITOR	Robert Sherrod (since 1955)	Clay Vacant	Don Schanche*	William Emerson	Otto Friedrich	Don McKinney*			
TOP POST ADVERTISING EXECUTIVE	Peter Schruth* (since 1957)		C.L. MacNelly*		Vacant	Jess Ballew*		Stephen Kelly*	
MAIN EVENTS IN THE DECLINE AND FALL OF CURTIS	September 1961 Disastrous revamping of Post. December 1961 Curtis loses money for the first time.	July 1962 Blair hires new editors. September 1962 Post moves to New York.	March 1963 Butts article brings libel suits for $20 million. September 1963 Semenenko loans Curtis $35 million.	April 1964 Copper found under Curtis land. September 1964 Blair's rebels meet at Manero's. October 1964 Blair-Kantor dismissal.	January 1965 Post becomes a biweekly. October 1965 Clifford sells copper land for $24 million.	December 1966 Curtis manages a "mini-profit."	March 1967 Clifford purges Schanche. July 1967 Clifford purges Ballew.	April 1968 Ackerman arrives with $5 million.	January 1969 Ackerman kills Post. February 1969 Ackerman is sued. March 1969 Ackerman resigns.
FINANCIAL POSITION	LOSS $4 Million	LOSS $19 Million	LOSS $3.5 Million	LOSS $14 Million	LOSS $3.5 Million	PROFIT $347 Thousand	LOSS $5 Million	LOSS $18 Million	IN AUDIT

* Not mentioned in text.

Source: Otto Friedrich, *Decline and Fall* (New York, Harper & Row, Publishers, 1969), end papers.

Exhibit 3
THE CURTIS BOARD, 1964

(clockwise from Blair, nearest camera): John Clifford, Marvin Kantor, Walter Franklin, Harry Mills, M. Albert Linton, Mary Curtis Bok Zimbalist, Matthew Culligan, Gloria Swett, Cary Bok, Walter Fuller, Moreau Brown, Curtis Barkes, and Milton Gould.

The Rugby Portland Cement Company Limited (A)*

HISTORY, GROWTH, AND ORGANIZATION

THE RUGBY COMPANY began producing lime in the early 19th century at a works near Rugby, England. Cement manufacture under the company's "Crown Cement" trade-mark began at the works in the 1820s, and thereafter became its principal product. In 1925 the company, which hitherto had been a partnership, became a private limited company with a share capital of £100,000 owned by descendants of the previous partners. In 1929 Mr. (now Sir)[1] Halford Reddish, then a young chartered accountant with a consulting practice, joined the board, which previously had comprised only representatives of the two descendant branches of the original owners. Four years later, upon the death of the general manager, Sir Halford Reddish became managing director, and shortly afterwards, chairman.

At that time, the cement industry was in the middle of a deep depression. Prices were at a very unprofitable level. In spite of this crisis, Sir Halford decided to expand and modernize the company's production facilities. Contrary to previous industry tradition, he also decided to operate the plant 52 weeks per year, thus ensuring steady employment for the workers. Despite the depression and the difficulties of selling the increased output, a profit was realized at the end of the first year of the new management. A second manufacturing site was obtained when a nearby company went into receivership. Erection of a new factory at the second site, plus the modernization and expansion of the Rugby works, required substantial fresh capital. In 1935 the company became a public company with its shares quoted on The London Stock Exchange, and additional capital of £140,000 was introduced. Later, additional equity capital was raised by occasional "rights" issues.

---

* Copyright 1973 by L'Institut pour l'Etude des Méthodes de Direction de l'Entreprise (IMEDE), Lausanne, Switzerland. Reprinted by permission.
[1] In early 1958, Her Majesty Queen Elizabeth II knighted Mr. Halford Reddish for his public services.

Rugby also acquired substantial chalk-bearing lands near Dunstable (about 48 miles to the south of its Warwickshire plants) from which high calcium carbonate chalk was railed daily to its Warwickshire plants.

By the mid-1930s Rugby was already the second largest cement company in the United Kingdom. (For an operations flow chart, see Exhibit 1.)

In 1936 Rugby acquired a third site and erected its Rochester works. In 1939 another company was purchased and its facilities were combined with those at Rochester. In 1945 Rugby acquired still another company, and, although its production facilities were closed, Rugby used its brand name and distribution organization.

Many major additions were made to these three facilities in the period after World War II, and during the 1960s Rugby made three additional acquisitions that expanded its U.K. operations, not only in cement, but also in another industry serving the building materials field.

Thus, in 1962 Rugby acquired the entire share capital of Eastwoods Cement Limited (owning three cement plants in the United Kingdom) and in 1963 the entire share capital of Chinnor Industries Limited (owning one cement plant in the United Kingdom). In 1968 Rugby acquired the entire share capital of The Rom River Company Limited, designers, fabricators and fixing subcontractors of steel reinforcement.

During the immediate postwar years, export trade was very profitable, with unit margins several times those of the home-market sales. The proportion of Rugby's deliveries accounted for by exports reached a maximum in 1951 and 1952 at about 43%. In 1961, however, Sir Halford Reddish said that in recent years export sales had become almost marginal because of the increased competition (much of it subsidized) from non-British manufacturers and the growth of cement industries in areas formerly importing cement. Rugby had itself established overseas subsidiaries, and had built manufacturing plants in Trinidad and Western Australia. The former started production in 1954, the latter in 1955. Both units were able to underprice existing imports by a substantial margin, and these facilities made useful contributions to Rugby's consolidated profits.

With a rapidly developing local market plus export trade in the Eastern Caribbean, the Trinidad factory had to be extended within less than five years of starting its operation. In 1963 the capacity of the Australian plant had to be doubled. By 1971 its capacity had been raised to one million tons per annum.

In highlighting Rugby's growth, Sir Halford spoke as follows in 1971:

> In 1946 our total share and loan capital and reserves were £1,671,-551. By 1970 they had grown to £56,220,048, and if we substituted current values in place of the book values of the assets, they would amount to at least £25 million more.
>
> In 1946 our pretax profit was £135,664; in 1970, £7,111,867.
>
> For 1946 we paid out in dividends on the Ordinary shares £40,625. For 1970 dividends on the Ordinary and Participating (non-voting) shares amounted to £2,448,000.

We now have 27,942 shareholders compared with 2,877 twenty-five years ago.

Additional capital introduced from 1st January 1933 to 31st December 1971 amounted to £60,370,867. Here is how the money has been found:

Shareholders have subscribed for shares (including premiums and loan stock)	£28,982,500
Profits have been left in the company	28,836,245
Others have contributed (by minority interests, or loans to, subsidy companies)	1,863,285
From Investment Grants	688,837
Total	£60,370,867

Net profit before taxes rose from less than £4,000 in 1933 to over £9 million in 1971. Postwar growth produced 26 years of successively record group profits, 1946–1971 (see Exhibits 2–4). By 1972 the Stock Exchange value of the company's equity capital was approximately £120 million.

In 1971 the nine company works and their annual capacities in tons were as shown in Table 1.

Table 1

COMPANY WORKS AND CAPACITIES

United Kingdom		Overseas	
Southam	540,000	Trinidad	390,000
Rochester*	400,000	Western Australia	1,000,000
Rugby	600,000	Total	1,390,000
Barrington	500,000		
Ferriby*	350,000	Grand Total	4,140,000
Lewes	80,000		
Chinnor	280,000		
Total	2,750,000		

* The Rochester and Ferriby plants were in the process of being doubled in 1972.

The company also continued to work its extensive chalk quarries near Dunstable, some 48 miles from Rugby.

At the end of 1971, Rugby had about 3,900 employees in its seven U.K. factories and subsidiaries, its overseas operations, and its headquarters at Rugby, England. The head office was organized into nine departments: engineering, production, transportation, sales (home and export), finance and accounting, legal, secretarial, property management, and computer. Above these departments was a small control and coordination group, called the administration department. This group, consisting mostly of assistants to top management, directed and coordinated the activities of the functional departments and served as the intermediate link between subsidiary companies. The subsidiaries addressed all inquiries and reports to Sir Halford Reddish, who was the chairman of each, and to the headquarters staff departments.

The board of directors comprised eight members: four "outside" (non-executive) directors, and four full-time executive directors. For over 30 years Sir Halford Reddish, as chairman and managing director, had as his deputy Mr. R. L. Evans, who passed away in 1968. Sir Halford and Mr. Evans had worked closely with each other, attempting to attain an interchangeability of talents. Sir Halford played a leading role in all major policy decisions, and was particularly concerned with financial management and public relations. Mr. Evans' background was also in accounting; as second in command, he in effect had headed the administration department.

In 1972 the executive directors were Sir Halford Reddish, chairman and chief executive; Mr. Maurice Jenkins, managing director; Mr. R. J. Morgan, and Mr. R. H. Yeatman. The last three had been with the company for many years before appointed to the board. Mr. Jenkins had moved up from assistant managing director after Mr. Evans' death. Mr. Morgan, also a chartered accountant, was particularly concerned with accounting and taxation matters and with financial administration. Mr. Yeatman, for many years general sales manager, was still primarily concerned with sales.

Sir Halford, who served on the boards of five other corporations and on a number of semi-public councils, spent the greater part of each week in London. His days in Rugby included the weekend, and he normally met with the other executive directors on Sunday morning to discuss current operations and problems, and also to engage in planning for up to "two or three balance sheets ahead."

REASONS FOR GROWTH

Sir Halford believed that the company's growth and profitability were attributable to several interrelated factors. But overriding them all, he insisted, was the human element—good human relations. These he defined simply as a recognition of the essential human dignity of the individual:

> The efficiency, the good name, the prestige, the progress of any business depend in the final analysis, not on the magnificence of its plant, not on the splendor of its offices, but on the spirit of the human beings who are working together in that business and whose lives are bound up with its success.
>
> The most valuable asset in any company's balance sheet is one written in invisible ink. It reads something like this: "The loyalty, the efficiency, the capacity for work of all employed by the company, their pride in the job and in the company's achievements, and their joy in having a part in those achievements."

Besides good human relations, Sir Halford identified five other factors as critical to his company's success:

1. *Emphasis on operating efficiency* was considered one of the most

important of these factors. Sir Halford said that the key to lower unit costs when producing with expensive, continuous-process equipment was keeping the plant operating as close to full capacity as possible and minimizing every element of operating and overhead costs. Therefore, avoiding downtime, improving efficiency of men and machines, and achieving fuel and power economies were all-important. To accomplish these ends, Rugby employed an elaborate monthly cost-reporting system which facilitated pinpointing the items of excessive costs. The factory managers were held responsible for costs under their control, and the chief engineer and production manager and their staffs were continually watching fuel and power costs and working on means of increasing machine efficiency. Excess overtime, costly repairs, stores usage, and factory staff costs were other items which attracted the attention of the central cost control department. One manager said, "We continually work on the weakest point reflected by the cost analyses."

The company's research on improvement of its manufacturing process produced several cost savings. One major outcome of such research was the development of a "wetting" agent for the slurry. Without affecting the chemical properties of the finished product, this agent produced the same "liquidity" and thus the same mixing and handling properties in a slurry containing only 35% water contrasted with 41% previously required. The smaller amount of water to vaporize meant appreciable fuel savings.

Another recent development was the installation of a pipeline from the chalk quarries near Dunstable to the two Warwickshire plants, through which a chalk slurry was pumped a total distance of some 57 miles. This became a possibility when a Pipeline Act came into force in 1962. The Rugby company received the first authorization granted under this Act.

Worker efficiency was also a matter of continuous attention. Because of the expensive equipment and the need to operate without stoppages, misconduct on the job, unexcused absences, and excessive tardiness were considered grounds for release. Such strictness was necessary because, for example, a kiln burner[2] could, through 10 minutes' neglect, permit many thousands of pounds' worth of damage to the equipment. Sir Halford said that his insistence that all employees "play the game according to the rules of the organization" was not only necessary for efficiency but was also a matter of loyalty. "But," he added, "I hold firmly to the view that loyalty should be a two-way traffic. If the head of a business expects a man to be loyal to him, then I say that that man has every right to expect that same loyalty from the head of the business. And I am sure that without discipline there can be no real happiness or success in any organization."

Finally, emphasis was placed on clerical and procedural efficiency. Sir Halford said that greater use of mechanical accounting and invoicing, and continuous analysis and improvement of office procedures, had slightly reduced the head office staff in the past few years. Periodic

---

[2] The kiln burner was the worker in charge of operating one or more kilns.

evaluation of the forms and paper-work systems was conducted to eliminate the unnecessary. "We have even had our competitor friends," he said, "come to look over our reporting and accounting systems. They are amazed by the fact that we get our data faster than they do with a proportionately smaller clerical staff."

2. *An effective sales organization* was said to be the second contributing factor to growth and profits. Manufacturing savings effected by maintaining peak production were attainable only as long as the output could be sold. The general sales manager remarked, "Since the industry sells on a common price arrangement, you don't sell cement by selling cheaper than the next man. You sell on delivery service, good will, product quality, and on contact with the customer. We like to think that we rate very high on all these counts. Selling cement is very much of a team effort, and we have a fine organization here." Under the general sales manager were an export manager and five area sales managers. Depending upon the circumstances, each area manager controlled a number of salesmen, ranging from seven in the Midlands to three in the South West. There were in all 28 salesmen, all of whom worked from their homes. The greatest concentration of salesmen was in the London area where three were located. The salesmen were paid entirely by salary.

3. *Overseas manufacture and other subsidiary activities* were a third factor to which credit was given for much of the company's growth and its increased profits in the past few years. Rugby was continually conducting site investigations and negotiations in search of new overseas opportunities for expansion.

4. *"Efficient" transportation of the U.K. cement sales* was another reason given for Rugby's growth and profitability. Rugby's fleet had grown from 52 trucks in 1946 to 394 in 1971 (102 flat-bed trucks, 12 bulk tippers and 280 pressurized bulk wagons),[3] and extra trucks were hired in the peak construction season. Rugby was proud of the efficiency of its fleet, the operating costs of which remained below the transportation allowance in the delivered price. At one time the fleet averaged less than 7% delays for repairs, less than 10% nonoperating idleness, and 6% on-the-job delays. The requirements of the Transport Act of 1968 had, however, increased the delays for repairs. Company officials believed that their truck fleet was one of the most efficient in the industry. The major reason for this efficiency, the directors believed, was the highly centralized scheduling of truck dispatches. Each day the central transportation department, working with the sales department, prepared schedules of the following day's dispatches of all trucks from each of the works. Scheduling attempted to maximize the number of deliveries by each truck and to make as uniform as possible the work-load at the packing and loading plants.

5. *A company-wide philosophy of teamwork* was seen by Sir Halford and the other directors as the most important reason for the company's

---

[3] Flat-bed trucks carried cement in bags; pressurized bulk wagons carried loose cement in large tanks which were slightly pressurized to remove the cement at the delivery site; bulk tippers were fully enclosed dump trucks which carried loose cement.

success. Teamwork had been achieved, they believed, through the chairman's human relations philosophy and through the application of profit-sharing and employee-shareholding plans. Rugby had no "personnel" department; development of teamwork was the job of managers at all levels within the firm. The impersonal term "personnel" and the word "welfare," with its connotation of charity, were banned from the Rugby vocabulary.

During the course of his career, Sir Halford had developed a philosophy of business as a team effort. A concrete expression of this philosophy was his introduction at Rugby of employee-shareholding and profit-sharing plans. Commenting on the relationship between his philosophy and these plans, he said:

> I am convinced that no scheme of profit-sharing or employee-shareholding can succeed unless it is built on a firm foundation of confidence within the business and of real *esprit de corps*—a strong feeling on the part of all employees of pride in the company and its achievements. The good will of those working together in an industrial enterprise cannot be purchased for cash—of that I am sure. A scheme which is put in with the primary object of buying good will is almost certainly doomed to failure from the start. It may indeed not only do no good but may even do positive harm by creating suspicion, however ill-founded.[4]

Teamwork, seen as commendable in any organization, was held to be doubly important in the cement industry where production in large units of continuous-process plant made it impossible to associate individual effort with specific product output. Mutual confidence was felt to be the basic ingredient of teamwork: on the part of the board, this meant confidence that all employees would put forth a fair day's work, would operate and maintain the plant intelligently, and would follow the leadership of the company; on the part of the employees, it meant confidence in the capability and integrity of the directors and a conviction that discipline "which was as fair as it was firm" would be maintained.

Leadership, in Sir Halford's view, was primarily setting an example. "You lead from in front," he said, "not from behind. It is saying, 'Come on,' not 'Go on.' "

ESPRIT DE CORPS AND COMPANY POLICIES

The following paragraphs summarize the policies singled out by Sir Halford as making the most important contribution to the sense of *esprit de corps* within Rugby.

1. *Personal contact between top executives and operating people all over the world* was relatively frequent. Sir Halford visited the Trinidad and Australia plants at least once a year, and someone from the central headquarters staff visited them, on an average, every two or three months. At home, Sir Halford not only delivered his annual message to

---

[4] Quotation from "This Is Industrial Partnership," a pamphlet written by Sir Halford in 1955 to explain his philosophy and the profit-sharing and employee-shareholding schemes of Rugby.

his "fellow-workers," but he always personally made presentations which were given to men with 25 years' service and again after 50 years' service. Such presentations were made in the presence of the recipients' colleagues, and Sir Halford usually gave a brief review of the recent progress of the company.

2. *Annual messages from Sir Halford to his "fellow employees"* described recent developments within the company, and emphasized the cooperative roles played by employees and shareholders. On these occasions, Sir Halford frequently discussed the importance of profits. The following example is from his message on operations for 1951:

> I want now to say something about profits, because a lot of nonsense has been talked about profits in the last few years, often by politicians of all parties who have never been in industry and have no practical knowledge of industry.
>
> You and I know that profits are the reward and the measure of economy and efficiency, and are essential to the maintenance and expansion of a business. They are, in fact, the real and only bulwark behind our wages and salaries, for if this company ceases to make profits it can only be a comparatively short time before you and I are out.
>
> Let us recognize that it is up to every one of us in this team to go all-out all the time, to give of our best, to maintain and increase our production with economy and efficiency, and in turn, the profits of the company: first—and note that I put this first—because it is the job we are paid to do, and it is only common honesty to our shareholders to do it; and secondly in our own interest to safeguard our jobs for the future.

3. *A "Works Committee" at each plant* functioned as another instrument of teamwork. Composed of the works manager, the works engineer, the safety officer, and five representatives elected from the factory work force, the committee met without exception each month with a senior member of the headquarters staff in attendance. The committee discussed matters of particular interest to the works concerned, and considered suggestions for operational improvements. The head office staff took this opportunity to clarify and discuss newly announced changes in policy and other company developments, such as the annual financial statements.

Toward the end of 1961, an IMEDE[5] researcher had the opportunity to attend a Works Committee meeting at the Rochester Works. The late Mr. R. L. Evans was the head-office representative in attendance. The committee chiefly discussed matters of plant safety and amenities for the workers, such as a sink and hand towels for workers at a remote plant location. The Rochester Works manager said that this meeting was typical, especially insofar as it was primarily concerned with safety and working conditions. The researcher was impressed at the free and easy manner in which the workers entered into the discussions. Mr. Evans explained in great detail some minor points of company policy

---

[5] The *Institut pour l'Etude des Méthodes de Direction de l'Entreprise*, Lausanne, Switzerland.

on tardiness and vacation time. He commented that the worker representatives occasionally brought up very minor points in the committee. "I think," he added, "that some men do this just to show that they are on their toes and doing a good job for their fellow-workers. The result is that the committee functions very well, and in a very good spirit."

4. *Layoffs, and even decisions about layoffs,* were treated as a matter of top consideration. Thus, no one but Sir Halford had the authority to release people during slack periods. He had in fact never authorized a layoff. For instance, the rail strike in 1955 almost closed the Rochester factory as coal reserves ran low.[6] As the shutdown date approached, Sir Halford announced that no one would be laid off, but that (*a*) some men would have to take their vacations during the shutdown; and (*b*) everyone would have to agree to do any job given him (at his usual pay rate) during the shutdown.

5. *Low employee turnover* had long been the rule at Rugby. One executive commented on the fact that the turnover of weekly paid workers was low, as follows:

> If we set aside employees with less than two years of service, our average worker has been here about 13 years. We do find that some new employees, especially young men, are not prepared for the demanding work in a cement plant, and such men leave, usually within 12 months. Thus, new employees should not fairly be included in our average turnover figure.
>
> Incidentally, taking total annual wages and bonuses as an indicator, the cement industry ranks in the top half-dozen British industries in terms of earnings.

6. *Early and adequate communication* was regarded as important by Sir Halford, who summarized his views on this key policy as follows:

> If there is to be a lively interest and pride in the company and its doing, then it is necessary that all employees be kept informed as far as possible about what is going on.
>
> * * * * * *
>
> We try as far as we can to ensure that everyone has an opportunity of reading on the company's notice boards a few hours *before* it appears in the newspapers any release issued to the Press. We do not think it right that a man should learn from the newspapers something which he could quite properly have heard at first hand within the company.
>
> And all Press comments on the company are posted on all our notice boards as soon as they appear.[7]

Sir Halford held strongly to the view that, to be effective, leadership must embrace an adequate system of communication—and communication in the widest sense of the term. "Example," he said, "is in itself one facet of communication."

Besides all the above-listed means of building teamwork, other means

---

[6] Last-minute settlement of the rail strike saved Rugby Cement from its contemplated shutdown.

[7] Quotations from "This Is Industrial Partnership."

of interest to Sir Halford included well-designed profit-sharing or share-holding schemes. To be effective, Sir Halford believed these must have two necessary features. First, they must be tailored to suit the circumstances of the company and the outlook, philosophy, and intent of its leader. Second, the schemes must be simple.

THE PROFIT-SHARING SCHEME

Sir Halford said that the Rugby profit-sharing scheme, inaugurated in 1935, was designed to emphasize two things:

- *a)* that the efforts of the employees are the efforts of a team—that we are all working to one end; and
- *b)* the essential partnership which exists between the ordinary shareholders and the employees.[8]

In speeches to both shareholders and workers, Sir Halford referred to the partnership between capital and employees. He said that capital was nothing more than the "labor of yesterday—the production of yesterday which was surplus to the consumption of yesterday."

Fundamental to the partnership was the following bargain:

> . . . the labor of today is guaranteed payment for its services and the profit is calculated only after the remuneration of that labor has been paid. Capital, therefore, takes the risk and in return takes such profit (or loss) as arises after the labor of today has been paid in full.
>
> But to my mind this difference in the basis of their respective remuneration in no way destroys the conception of industrial enterprise as essentially a partnership between the labor of yesterday (capital) and the labor of today. Nor is it destroyed if the "bargain" is varied slightly by guaranteeing the greater part of labor's remuneration irrespective of profit or loss and by making an additional but smaller part of it dependent on the results of the enterprise as a whole.[9]

The Employees' Profit-Sharing scheme provided for an annual bonus in excess of industry-negotiated wages or contracted salary for all Rugby wage earners and staff. Basic points of the scheme are summarized below:[10]

1. To qualify for the profit-sharing bonus, an hourly or salaried employee must have completed, on December 31, 12 months' unbroken service to the satisfaction of the directors. An employee who joined the company after January 1 but not later than July 1 would for that year qualify for one-half of the bonus he would have received if he had completed one year of service.

2. For the purpose of calculating the bonus, each qualified employee was treated as if he held a certain number of Ordinary shares in the company. A staff employee's "notional shares" were related to his annual salary. An hourly worker's shares varied in proportion to his length of service up to 40 years.

---

[8] Ibid.

[9] Ibid.

[10] This explanation summarizes only the major aspects.

3. The bonus was calculated at the full rate per share of the gross dividend declared and paid to the Ordinary shareholders for the financial year in question, and was paid immediately after the annual general meeting. For example, in 1971 the Ordinary dividend declared was 3.75 pence per share. Thus a worker with five years' service holding 1,315 notional shares, would receive a bonus of (1,315 × 3.75p) or £49.31.

4. Certified sickness or compulsory National Service were ignored in calculating the number of years of unbroken service.

5. Any employee who left or was under notice to leave prior to the date of payment forfeited his bonus.

6. The scheme conferred no rights in respect of any capital distribution other than those declared as dividends on the Ordinary shares of the company out of profits.

7. The scheme was subject to modification or withdrawal at any time at the discretion of the directors.

Sir Halford emphasized that the bonus was not automatic. In a very small number of cases each year, bonuses were withheld completely or in part because service was not "to the satisfaction of the directors." If a man's record for the year was questionable, including several unexplained tardinesses, for instance, it was submitted, without name, to the Works Committee of the factory. In all cases, the directors had abided by the committee's recommendation. Sir Halford said that withholding the bonus was not so much a penalty to the slack worker as it was a necessary act of fairness to those who gave 100% service during the year. Summarizing, Sir Halford said:

> I believe that this is important: the bonus must be something that is earned—not something which becomes a right. I also feel that the link with the Ordinary shareholders' dividend is fundamental: if the dividend per share goes up, so does the bonus; if the dividend is reduced, the bonus falls too—which is as it should be.

THE "A" SHARE SCHEME[11]

After World War II, Sir Halford saw two factors that made the profit-sharing scheme inadequate for emphasizing the partnership between capital and labor. He felt that the twin virtues of hard work and thrift no longer assured a man of personal savings for his old age—*taxation* restricted savings and *inflation* devalued them. Unlike the Ordinary shareholder's income, which flowed from an asset whose market value reflected both the company's prosperity and inflationary pressures, the employee's profit-sharing bonus was not reflected in a realizable capital asset. Thus he did not have a "hedge" against inflation.

To supply this need, Sir Halford presented his "A" share plan, in late 1954, for approval by the Ordinary shareholders. He said that the scheme was designed to do three things:[12]

---

[11] In 1966 the "A" shares were re-named Participating (non-voting) shares.

[12] This explanation of the "A" share plan is summarized from "This Is Industrial Partnership."

To give practical form to the unity of interest which I have always held to exist between the Ordinary shareholders and the employees; to give a return to the Ordinary shareholders on profits "ploughed back" in the past; and to give to every full-time employee the opportunity to have in his hands a capital asset readily realizable on death or retirement. It was received enthusiastically by shareholders and employees alike.

One million "A" shares with a par value of one shilling each were created with the following conditions attached to them:

1. Starting with 1955, in any fiscal year for which (*a*) pretax net profits were not less than £900,000, and (*b*) the gross amount distributed as dividend to the Ordinary shareholders was not less than £300,000, the holders of the "A" shares would be entitled to an amount of £70,000 plus 20% of any excess of the said net profits over £900,000 (see Exhibit 5). However, (*i*) the amount attributable to the "A" shares would not exceed 12½% of the net profits; and (*ii*) in the event of the issue of additional Ordinary share capital by the company after 31st December 1954 (otherwise than by the way of a capitalization of reserves or undistributed profits), the said figure of £900,000 would be increased by a sum equal to 6% of the proceeds or other consideration received by the company.[13]

2. Any amount attributable to the "A" shares as ascertained under (1) above would be distributed as dividend or carried forward in the books of the company to the credit of the "A" shares for subsequent distribution, as the directors might decide.

3. The holders of "A" shares would have no voting rights.

4. In a winding-up, the "A" shares would participate only insofar as the amount of their paid-in capital value and the "A" share credit carried forward on the company books, but would have no further participation in assets.

5. No further "A" shares would be created without the sanction of an extraordinary resolution passed by the holders of the "A" shares.[14]

Half of the "A" shares were offered to the Ordinary shareholders at par and half to the employees.

"*All* full-time employees of the company were included: this was not a get-rich-quick exercise for the favored few," said Sir Halford.

Allocation to the employees was effected by dividing all employees into groups according to remuneration, responsibility, and status within the company; length of service was not a factor. Those in the first group (which included most factory production workers) were offered 250 shares; other groups were offered 500, 750, 1,000, 1,500, 2,000 shares, and so on. After some years, when these one shilling "A" shares were quoted at over £6 on the Stock Exchange, the allocation of shares to newcomers was proportionately reduced. Over 95% of Rugby's employees had exercised their option and purchased the "A" shares.

---

[13] Because additional equity was introduced after 1954, the "A" shares began participating at a net profit of £1,748,190 for 1972.

[14] After January 1964, the number of "A" shares was increased, however, by a "scrip" issue of five new shares for each one held. See "The 'A' Share Scrip Expansion," below.

Sir Halford was particularly concerned about two aspects of the scheme. About the first, he wrote as follows:

> I was anxious that there should be no element of a "gift" from one partner (the holders of the Ordinary shares) to the other (the employees), and that the equity owned by the Ordinary shares should be unimpaired. I was convinced that the holders of the Ordinary shares could have no legitimate cause for complaint if the profits were so substantially increased in the future and some comparatively small part of the increase went to the employees as a reward for their efforts.
>
> The "A" shares should be worth no more than was paid for them when issued, so that the employees could feel that whatever increased value accrued thereafter was due to their teamwork, with, I do not forget, nor do I allow them to forget, the capital provided by their partners in the enterprise.[15]

Both this reason and tax considerations [16] dictated that the minimum profit level at which the "A" shares would start participating (originally £900,000) should be well above the profit levels when the "A" shares were issued.

The second aspect of the scheme that was of concern to Sir Halford was that the main object would continue to be assuring employees a capital sum on death or retirement. Sir Halford foresaw that the "A" shares might have some speculative attraction to the general public, and he did not want the employees to be tempted into selling and thus depriving themselves of retirement or death benefits from the plan. He also felt that anyone leaving the firm should be required to sell his shares back at par, thus enabling newcomers to participate. To accomplish these ends, Sir Halford designated that the shares allocated to the employees were to be held on their behalf by an entity called Staff Nominees Limited. This would be accountable to the employees for dividends declared, and it would be authorized to act on their behalf in all matters relating to the "A" shares.

The following conditions applied:

1. Initially, whenever an employee moved upward to a new group, he would be given the opportunity to buy his allocation of shares at par. Failing to do so, he would not be given a subsequent opportunity.
2. "A" shares could be sold by the employee at any time at par to Staff Nominees Limited, and must be sold whenever he left the company.
3. An employee's shares could be sold at market value[17] *only* in the event of the employee's death while in the service of the company, or upon his reaching age 65 (55 for women).
4. Any dividend declared on the "A" shares would be paid immediately to the employee.

The "A" share scrip expansion. After the original "A" share distribution, 50,000 shares remained unallocated. These were held by RPC

---

[15] Quotation from "This Is Industrial Partnership."

[16] See "The Taxation Aspect," below.

[17] Market price was established by quotation on The London Stock Exchange of the "A" shares allotted originally at par to the Ordinary shareholders.

Benevolent Fund Ltd. (a company formed for the aim indicated by its title) pending their issue to newcomers. The directors felt that this block of shares, plus those which Staff Nominees Limited bought back at par from departing employees, would be sufficient to offer shares to new and promoted employees for the foreseeable future. Thus, no expansion in the number of "A" shares was originally contemplated.

In December 1963, however, the company's Articles of Association were amended, giving power to the "A" shareholders to capitalize from time to time any part of the profits allocated to the "A" shares in the past but remaining undistributed, and therefore to increase the number of "A" shares for this purpose. The "A" shareholders agreed to capitalize £250,000 of the net amount standing to the credit of the "A" shares by a scrip issue of five new shares for each one held. The effect was to amend the market price of the "A" shares, which had by then reached over £9, to around 30 shillings. By this action, the marketability of the shares was increased. In 1971 a second scrip expansion brought the par value of the "A" shares from £300,000 to £360,000.

The taxation aspect. For the company, the profit-sharing bonus was considered a wage bonus and therefore a before-tax expense. The "A" share dividends, however, were similar to Ordinary dividends, being paid out of after-tax profits.

For the employees, the profit-sharing bonus was taxed as ordinary wage or salary income. Taxation of the employees in connection with "A" share distribution was a most difficult problem and one on which Sir Halford spent many hours in consultation with the Board of Inland Revenue.

The law held that if, at the time of issue, the value of the shares was greater than the amount the employees paid for them, the difference was taxable as a "benefit" arising from employment. The Rugby "A" share sale to its employees, however, had two characteristics which affected any ruling under this law:

1. "A" shares were not quoted on the market until two months after issue; thus it was a matter of discussion whether at time of issue they were worth more than the par value paid for them.
2. Employees were not free to sell their shares at market price except on retirement or death.

Final agreement with the Inland Revenue was reached, putting the assessed value of the "A" shares at the time of issue slightly above par.

Tax assessment for shares issued subsequently to newcomers or to promoted employees required a different arrangement with the Inland Revenue, since by that time a market value had been established. Final agreement resulted in considering a variable fraction of the difference between current market value and par value as taxable income. The fraction varied inversely with the length of time between the recipient's age and the date when he would reach age 65, and be able to realize the market price of the "A" shares. For instance, a 25-year-old newcomer receiving 500 "A" shares would have to consider as income, for income tax purposes, only 10% of the difference between market value and the price

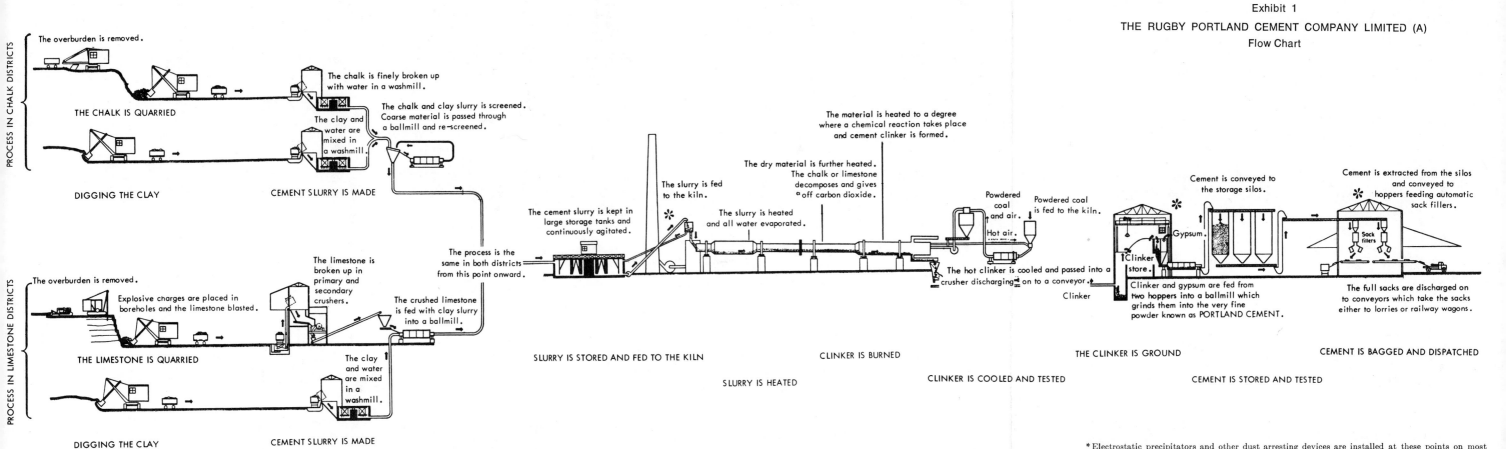

Exhibit 1

THE RUGBY PORTLAND CEMENT COMPANY LIMITED (A)

Flow Chart

PROCESS IN CHALK DISTRICTS

The overburden is removed.

THE CHALK IS QUARRIED

The chalk is finely broken up with water in a washmill.

The chalk and clay slurry is screened. Coarse material is passed through a ballmill and re-screened.

The clay and water are mixed in a washmill.

DIGGING THE CLAY

CEMENT SLURRY IS MADE

PROCESS IN LIMESTONE DISTRICTS

The overburden is removed.

Explosive charges are placed in boreholes and the limestone blasted.

The limestone is broken up in primary and secondary crushers.

THE LIMESTONE IS QUARRIED

The crushed limestone is fed with clay slurry into a ballmill.

The clay and water are mixed in a washmill.

DIGGING THE CLAY

CEMENT SLURRY IS MADE

The process is the same in both districts from this point onward.

The cement slurry is kept in large storage tanks and continuously agitated.

SLURRY IS STORED AND FED TO THE KILN

The slurry is fed to the kiln.

The slurry is heated and all water evaporated.

SLURRY IS HEATED

The dry material is further heated. The chalk or limestone decomposes and gives off carbon dioxide.

The material is heated to a degree where a chemical reaction takes place and cement clinker is formed.

CLINKER IS BURNED

Powdered coal and air.

Powdered coal is fed to the kiln.

Hot air.

The hot clinker is cooled and passed into a crusher discharging on to a conveyor.

Clinker

CLINKER IS COOLED AND TESTED

Clinker store.

Gypsum.

Clinker and gypsum are fed from two hoppers into a ballmill which grinds them into the very fine powder known as PORTLAND CEMENT.

THE CLINKER IS GROUND

Cement is conveyed to the storage silos.

Cement is extracted from the silos and conveyed to hoppers feeding automatic sack fillers.

Sack fillers

The full sacks are discharged on to conveyors which take the sacks either to lorries or railway wagons.

CEMENT IS BAGGED AND DISPATCHED

CEMENT IS STORED AND TESTED

* Electrostatic precipitators and other dust arresting devices are installed at these points on most cement works.

paid (one shilling per share), because he could not realize the market value for 40 years. On the other hand, a 50-year-old man receiving 500 "A" shares would have to consider 42½% of the difference as taxable income, because he was much closer to realizing the gain. (All dividends received by employees on their "A" shares up to retirement age were treated, for tax purposes, as "earned" income and therefore were subject to the earned income allowance.)

Results. In his message to his fellow-workers in the company following the 1958 operations, Sir Halford spoke about the "A" share plan as follows:

> . . . Quite often a man will say to me: "This 'A' share scheme of yours—tell me, has it increased production?" and I reply: "I haven't the slightest idea, but I shouldn't think so." So he says, "But surely that was the object. It's an incentive scheme, isn't it?" "On the contrary," I tell him, "I have always insisted that it should *not* be called an incentive scheme, because that to my mind would imply that we in Rugby Cement were not already doing our best, were not doing our duty in return for our wages and salaries. And that I will not have."
>
> What our "A" share scheme does is to give to the employees the opportunity to build up capital available on retirement or on earlier death, and to promote the feeling that we are all one team working on the same end in partnership with our shareholders. The value of the "A" shares depends in the long run on the success of our efforts in making profits. And don't overlook the fact that half the "A" shares were issued, also at par, to the holders of our Ordinary shares. They very rightly benefit too, as they have seen these one shilling shares change hands on the Stock Exchange at prices up to 42 shillings.[18]
>
> Apart from the capital aspect, the holding of "A" shares by the employees of the company, and also, of course, our "profit-sharing" schemes, give some reward for successful endeavor—which is surely right.

---

[18] In January 1964, prior to the scrip issue referred to above, the "A" shares were quoted on the Stock Exchange at up to the equivalent of 186 shillings per share.

Exhibit 2

THE RUGBY PORTLAND CEMENT COMPANY LIMITED (A)

Consolidated Balance Sheet Statements,
Selected Years, as of December 31
(in thousands of pounds)

	1946	1956	1961	1966	1967	1968	1969	1970	1971
ASSETS									
Current assets	576	4,521	8,226	14,581	17,560	22,875	27,592	30,550	31,592
Fixed assets (as valued, or at cost, less sales)	1,673	8,613	11,258	24,989	30,571	37,916	40,890	45,332	50,349
Less accumulated depreciation	436	1,969	3,930	7,589	8,876	10,328	13,119	15,064	17,129
Net fixed assets	1,237	6,644	7,328	17,400	21,695	27,588	27,771	30,268	33,217
Investment in subsidiary companies (nonconsolidated)	209	—	—	—	—	—	—	—	—
Premiums on acquisition of shares in subsidiary companies	—	—	—	4,226	4,226	7,424	7,424	7,424	7,424
Total assets	2,022	11,165	15,554	36,207	43,481	57887	62,787	68,242	72,233
LIABILITIES AND NET WORTH									
Current liabilities	367	1,759	1,328	4,138	5,134	5,898	6,073	7,945	10,410
Bank overdraft	—	—	—	2,126	4,382	961	2,490	3,085	1,343
Debt capital:									
4% debenture	420	—	—	—	—	—	—	—	—
Mortgage and unsecured loans	—	1,980	2,268	608	1,130	1,035	940	846	751
6% unsecured loan stock, 1993/98	—	—	—	—	—	12,000	12,000	12,000	12,000
7¾% unsecured loan stock, 1993/98	—	—	—	—	—	—	500	500	500
Total debt	420	1,980	2,268	608	1,130	13,035	13,440	13,346	13,251
Share capital:									
4% and 6% Preference shares*	325	825	825	1,000	1,000	1,000	—	—	—
Ordinary shares 5s. 0d. par	325	1,500	2,000	10,000	12,000	13,200	13,200	13,200	15,400
"A" shares 1s. 0d. par	—	50	50	300	300	300	300	300	360
Capital reserve	325	1,358	2,002	3,728	5,667	7,066	7,403	7,458	5,483

Revenue reserves:

General reserve‡	100	1,750	—	1,137	—	—	—	—	—
Taxation equalization account§	—	—	—	—	39	413	1,001	847	689
Investment Grants suspense account	—	—	—	—	—	—	—	—	—
Reserve for future taxation‖	—	320	1,373	380	594	790	1,140	1,163	1,023
Reserve for Ordinary and "A" share dividend payments¶	—	230	383	1,575	1,575	1,515	1,873	2,448	3,210
Undistributed profit	161	275	4,520	10,671	10,972	12,964	15,006	17,459	19,997
Total capital and reserves	1,236	6,308	11,153	28,791	32,147	37,248	39,923	42,875	46,117
Minority interests	—	1,117	805	544	688	745	861	991	1,112
Total liabilities and net worth	2,022	11,165	15,554	36,207	43,481	57,887	62,787	68,242	72,233
Net working capital	210	2,762	6,898	8,317	8,044	16,016	19,029	19,520	19,839
Equity debt ratio	2.9/1	3.2/1	4.9/1	47.4/1	28.4/1	2.9/1	3.0/1	3.2/1	3.5/1

Note: Some figures may fail to add because of rounding.
* Cancelled on December 31, 1969. Loan stock substituted.
† Name changed to Participating Non-Voting (PNV) shares in 1966.
‡ Merged with undistributed profit in 1958.
§ Transferred to undistributed profit in 1967.
‖ From 1966 onward, this reserve applied only to overseas taxes.
¶ Net in 1946–1961; gross for remaining years on the chart.
Source: Company records.

Exhibit 3

THE RUGBY PORTLAND CEMENT COMPANY LIMITED (A)

Consolidated Profit and Loss Account, Selected Years
(in thousands of pounds)

	1946	%	1955	%	1961	%	1966	%	1967	%	1968	%	1969	%	1970	%	1971	%
Consolidated trading profits	213		1,369		2,465		4,895		5,067		6,423		7,844		8,902		10,687	
Other income	—		65		105		103		170		157		241		284		402	
Less depreciation	79		340		550		1,070		1,276		1,415		2,166		2,074		2,083	
Net profit before taxes	134	100	1,093	100	2,020	100	3,928	100	4,561	100	5,165	100	5,919	100	7,112	100	9,006	100
Taxation—Profits tax/corporation tax	—		109		174		510		370		276		273		667		1,717	
Income tax/overseas tax*	39		255		602		393		733		912		1,170		1,305		1,247	
Total taxes	39	29	364	33	776	38	903	23	1,103	24	1,188	23	1,443	25	1,972	28	2,964	33
Net profit after taxes	95		729		1,244		3,025		3,458		3,977		4,476		5,140		6,042	
Minority interests	—		—		—		—		152	3	142	3	210	4	239	3	234	2
Preference dividends†	12	9	23	2	24	1	50	1	50	1	50	1	50	1	—		—	
Ordinary dividends†	22	16	194	18	306	15	1,200	31	1,200	26	1,380	27	1,650	28	1,848	26	2,310	26
"A" share dividends†	—		36	3	77	4	375	10	375	8	413	8	525	8	600	9	900	10
Retained in business	61	46	477	44	837	42	1,400	35	1,681	37	1,992	38	2,041	34	2,453	34	2,598	29
Ordinary dividend per share (gross)	7½d		1½d		⅓d		7.2d		6d		6.6d		7½d		8.4d		3.75p§	
Capital distribution per share (gross)	3d		—		—		—		—		—		—		—		—	
"A" share dividend per share (gross)	—		⅓d		⅓d		1s.3d		1s.3d		1s.4½d		1s.9d		2s.0d		12.50p	
Net profit before taxes as return on total capital and reserves	10.85%		17.30%		18.11%		13.64%		14.19%		13.87%		14.83%		16.66%		19.53%	
Gross Ordinary dividend as return on capital equity employed, i.e., Ordinary shares plus disclosed reserves (less reserves credited to "A" shares)	4.36%		6.36%		5.06%		4.47%		4.00%		3.95%		4.29%		4.49%		5.22%	

* Profits tax and corporation tax were the estimated liability for the year ending with the statement. Income tax was the estimated liability for the subsequent two-year period. This procedure gave rise to the reserve for future income tax in the balance sheet. The estimated income tax for the future period was put into this reserve, and at the end of each year, the actual tax liability for the year was withdrawn from the reserve and put into current liabilities, from which the actual remittance was made.

† Net 1946–1961; gross for remaining years on chart.

‡ Changed to Participating (Non-Voting) shares in 1966.

§ After Britain went on a metric monetary system, the number of pence per pound changed from 240d to 100p.

Source: Company records.

Exhibit 4

THE RUGBY PORTLAND CEMENT COMPANY LIMITED (A)
Indices of Deliveries, Profit, and Net Worth, Selected Years
(base: 1946 = 100)

Year	Deliveries*	Capital†	Profits
1946	100	100	100
1956	307	510	816
1961	388	902	1,507
1966	729	2,329	2.931
1967	766	2,601	3,404
1968	845	3,014	3,854
1969	851	3,230	4,417
1970	859	3,469	5,307
1971	946	3,731	6,723

* These are total group deliveries, in tons, and as an index basing point.

† "Capital" here equals total equity capital, including reserves.

From 1947 through 1971, the capital account was affected by the following transactions:

Year	Amount	Transaction
1947	£1,000,000	Sale of new Common shares (£500,000) and new preference shares (£500,000).
1953	500,000	Sale of new Common shares.
1954	1,050,000	Sale of new Common shares (£1,000,000) and of "A" shares (£50,000).
1959	1,075,000	Sale of new Common shares.
1962	n. a.	Rights issue of 2 million Ordinary shares, and payments of 2 million Ordinary and 175,000 preference shares to shareholders of the acquired Eastwoods Company.
1963	—	Ordinary shares split three for two; "A" shares split five for one.
1966	—	Ordinary shares split four for three.
1967	—	Ordinary shares split six for five.
1968	n. a.	Rights issue of 4,800,000 Ordinary shares on the basis of two new for twenty old.
1971	—	"A" shares split six for five.

Source: Company records.

Exhibit 5

THE RUGBY PORTLAND CEMENT COMPANY LIMITED (A)

Summary of Earnings and Gross Dividend Payments

Selected Years

(in thousands of pounds)

	1956	1961	1963	1964	1965	1966	1967	1968	1969	1970	1971
Profit before tax	1,093	2,020	2,656	3,311	3,664	3,928	4,561	5,165	5,919	7,112	9,006
Gross Ordinary dividend	338	500	938	1,125	1,125	1,200	1,200	1,380	1,650	1,848	2,310
Gross payable to "A" shares	109	252	287	414	458	491	540	613	696	836	1,074
Actual "A" share dividend	63	125	187	300	388	375	375	413	525	600	900
Difference carried forward as "A" share credit	46	127	100	114	120	116	165	200	171	236	174
Cumulative "A" share credit*	91	493	316†	430	550	666	831	1,031	1,202	1,438	1,514‡

* The "A" share (later PNV share) credit was contained in the undistributed profit account in the balance sheet. The directors considered this credit as a "dividend equalization reserve" to supply "A" dividends if they were not earned according to the formula (i.e., if pretax profits were below £1,568,190 from 1964 to 1967; £1,618,846 for 1968; and £1,748,190 from 1969 onwards).

† After deducting £408,163, the gross equivalent amount of the scrip issue of £250,000.

‡ After deducting £97,959, the gross equivalent of a scrip issue of £60,000.

Source: Company records.

The Rugby Portland Cement Company Limited (B)*

LATE IN 1961, an IMEDE research team decided to attempt to expand the Rugby Portland Cement case by adding information on the ways in which various employees of the company viewed their jobs. To this purpose, an IMEDE researcher toured each of the company's three cement works in England; he also conducted interviews with a number of hourly paid workers and with a substantial number of middle- and top-management executives. This case includes excerpts from some of these interviews, as well as some of the researcher's impressions of what he saw.

VIEWS OF SOME RUGBY WORKMEN

Rugby's management was very cooperative in helping the researcher to interview some of the workmen. Although, in theory, it would have been useful to interview a rather large number of workers selected at random, this was not practicable for certain reasons:

1. There were limitations on the research time available for these interviews.
2. There was a chance that some men, if chosen at random, might:
    a)   Not be able to articulate their views;
    b)   Be less than wholly frank;
    c)   Be unable to leave their work posts at the desired time.

Accordingly, Mr. R. L. Evans, deputy managing director, and Mr. Baker, works manager of the Rugby works, selected from the Rugby work force four workers who, they thought, would be articulate, honest, and as representative as possible of the general sentiments of the entire Rugby

* Copyright 1964 by l'Institut pour l'Etude des Méthodes de Direction de l'Entreprise (IMEDE), Lausanne, Switzerland. Reprinted by permission.

worker group. The researcher interviewed the four men separately, in an office at the Rugby plant; nobody else was present during the interviews. The names of the four men interviewed have been disguised.

Interview with Mr. Ryan

Mr. Evans and Mr. Baker, in arranging the interviews, mentioned that Mr. Ryan should provide a highly entertaining and useful interview, that he was outspoken and highly articulate. Mr. Ryan, who had been working for the company since 1956, was an Irishman; he appeared to be about 40 years old. He worked in the transport department of the company as a truck driver and had been a member of the Rugby works committee for some time. The researcher asked each of the four men only one question to begin: What did the man think about working for the company, what were the bad points and the good points? Mr. Ryan began:

> Well, I might tell you I'm an old union man, been a sort of union agitator all my working life. Before I came here I never held a job longer than eighteen months. I've been here almost six years now, and I can tell you this, I'm going to stay here the rest of my life. And, mind you, I got a lot less to gain by staying here than most of the men. I have no A-shares, because you know you only get one chance to buy them A-shares, and when I had to buy them, I didn't have the money because my wife just had to have an operation. So now for the rest of my life I got to work here knowing that I'll never have no A-shares, and I think this is unfair, and I keep fighting to get me shares, and maybe I will and maybe I won't, but I'll stay on here no matter what.
>
> And another thing is I'm a very bad timekeeper—sometimes it's my fault, and sometimes it was because I had to take my wife to the doctor and so I'd come in late, and so for three straight years I lost my profit-sharing bonus on account of being late so much. [Mr. Ryan had actually lost his bonus in two nonconsecutive years, management reported.] So you can see what I mean when I tell you that I got much less to gain by working here than the other men.
>
> But even though there's lots of little things could be done, this is a wonderful place to work, and that's the Lord's own truth. I'm not saying anything to you I wouldn't say right to the Chairman's face if he asked me—I'm not a man to say what he doesn't mean.
>
> You got to remember this: It's no good coming down to a cement works if you don't want to work hard. But they pay you good, and the main thing is, you always get treated fair. If you got a complaint, you can take it as high as you want, right up to the Chairman himself, but it's no good complaining unless you give 'em the facts. That's what they want to see: facts.
>
> Another thing you ought to write down is this: In this company, I'm just as good as anybody, as good as the Chairman or Mr. Evans—that's what you won't get anywhere else. We all know this here, and we know you've got to work as a team. And I'll tell you this, I know the Chairman would let me buy my A-shares if he could, but you see he's got to be fair to the other workers too. But I do think that you get punished awful hard for being late. [Mr. Ryan's profit-sharing bonus would have amounted, in those years when he lost it, to about £30. His weekly wages were about £15.]

Over in Coventry, you know [about 15 miles away], in the car and airplane factories a man can make £30 a week, while here he'll only make about £15, but we get the £15 for 52 weeks of the year, plus the profit-sharing, the A-shares, and lots of other benefits. The company buys up lots of clothes for us, so we can get them cheaper. I once compared what I earned in a year with a friend of mine who works in Coventry for £29 a week, and you know what? I came out £48 ahead of him for the year, because those fellows are always getting laid off.

And let me tell you this: You'd never get a better firm to work for, no matter where you went; there isn't another company like this, at least none I've ever heard about.

You know, when I tell you we work hard here, you've got to remember that the Chairman doesn't ask us to do anything he doesn't do himself. You know, he works 18 hours a day, and when he come down sick recently and had to have that operation, his doctors told him to take it easy, and so he did—he only worked ten hours a day.

[Mr. Ryan then gave the researcher a very detailed description of what was involved in his truck driving. He stressed that the equipment was the best obtainable, that the company paid much more attention to driver safety than to delivering a maximum daily tonnage of cement, that scrupulous care was taken, at great expense, to be certain that the customer received all the cement he had been billed for.]

You see my truck out there? That truck, it's brand new, and it cost £10,000, and they expect me to take care of it like if it was my own, and I do. [The truck in fact cost slightly over £3,500.] And I know I've got 42 hours a week guaranteed, and more hours on weekends if I want to make extra money, and that's a hell of a nice thing for a truck driver. And as soon as I've driven 11 hours in a single day, even if I didn't get home with the truck by the time my 11 hours was up, the company would send out another lorry with two drivers to drive me and my truck home, that's how careful they are about the 11-hour rule. And you see them fine overalls we drivers got, and them jackets? Mr. Reddish, I believe, bought them for us out of his own pocket. That's just the kind of man he is. [In fact he didn't; they are provided by the company.]

I told you I used to be a union man, but I tell you this, if a union came in here now, it would hurt the workers—they'd get less pay, they couldn't touch anything they weren't supposed to. That's the kind of a union man I am today.

In summing up, and this is God's own truth, I think Sir Halford Reddish ought to be England's Prime Minister, and Mr. Evans ought to be the Secretary for Foreign Affairs.

Interview with Mr. Mason

Mr. Mason was a foreman in the "raw plant," where the slurry was made. He had been working for the company about 14 years and appeared to be about 50. He began:

Well, wherever I went, I don't think I could better myself, that's what I'd say. The Chairman puts us in the picture about what's going on; he has more of a fatherly concern for us, I think. I've known the Chairman 30 years, and if he says a thing he means it. He's put in some wonderful plans for the men, he has. For example, when my father died, we got about £1,000 for his A-shares, and this was a big help, because I've got a sister who isn't very well, and this money pays for her. From the workman's point of view, if you want it, I find that they're very, very satisfied. I've got 30-odd men working for me, and I get all the points of view, so to speak, and I think I can say that they're all happy to be working here. Now, of course, there's some men as will always find something to complain about, you're going to have that anywhere, but in the main I think that the men like working here very much.

You're an American, so I'll put it in American: Damn it all, we're on to a good thing here and we know it.

I've got a brother, a son, and two brothers-in-law working here, and my father before he died. They all came to work here before I did. Now do you think they'd have come if this wasn't a good place to work?

I do believe honestly, and I'm not handing you any bull, that we couldn't better ourselves. And you've got to remember this: Sir Halford will give any of his men a proper hearing any time. And what's astonishing is that as the firm gets larger, the company seems to give us more attention, when you'd think it'd be the other way around.

Now you take your average Englishman, he's the biggest grumbler in the world, about anything at all. But you won't find much grumbling here. You'd have to kick them out to get the men here to leave.

Interview with Mr. Toot

Mr. Toot, who appeared to be about 50, had been with Rugby about seven years. The researcher received the distinct impression that Mr. Toot was temperamentally a sort of cynic who only grudgingly would admit that a workman's life could be decent, although this impression was formed on the basis of very little evidence. Mr. Toot began:

Taken all around, I should say that this is a very good place to work. A workman here knows that he can go as high as he likes, if he has the ability. You get fair treatment here. I suppose that work here is 80% satisfactory. For the other 20%, it's hard to say what the objections might be. But one thing is, when a man first came to work here, he didn't get enough participation in the bonus system [the profit-sharing scheme], but they've changed that now.

If a man's willing to do an honest day's work, he'll generally be satisfied here. I suppose I could say this: The longer a man's been here, the more he wants to stay.

Now, you get some fellows, especially young ones, come in and they can't stick the work; it's too heavy or too hard for them. They usually leave, if they're this type, in 12–18 months. If a man sticks it a year or a year and a half, he'll probably stay here until he's through working.

This is a long-term policy job, so to say. It's good if you're thinking about your old age, because the company really takes care of you after you retire. I don't suppose you know this, but all the company's pensioners [retired workers] get a ton of coal from the Chairman at Christmas. There's a Christmas party for the pensioners. And men like Mr. Evans and Mr. Baker visit the pensioners very regularly. The company doesn't just forget you when you've stopped working for them—they take care of you.

I suppose when I think of it, it's hard to say what kind of objections, you might say, a man could have to working here, if he's not just a casual laborer who doesn't care about doing an honest day's work, if he doesn't care about doing a good job. This is a good place to work.

Interview with Mr. Forster

Mr. Forster had been working for Rugby for 48 years, and he worked in the quarry. He talked rather little, much less than the previous three men.

> Well, I've been working here all my life, and that's a fact. It's hard work, and no doubt about it, but it's a wonderful company to work for I was here, you know, when Sir Halford took over, and it was wonderful when he did. He promised us steady work, and we've had it ever since. Some of your casual lads, now, who come here looking for an easy day's work and high pay, they don't stay; but a real man, a man who doesn't mind work, he'll be happier here than anywhere else I've ever heard of.

RANDOM IMPRESSIONS OF THE RESEARCHER

In the course of his tour of the three different works, the researcher spent a great deal of time with Mr. R. L. Evans, who toured each plant with him, and with the works managers. The researcher was especially struck by two facts. First, Mr. Evans and the works managers appeared to know a great deal about the background of every company employee. The researcher was, while walking through the plant, introduced to one worker who had been a chef in Wyoming some years ago. Another worker was pointed out as having been (he was now 72) a good rugby player in his youth. These and similar details were forthcoming quite frequently from Mr. Evans or the works managers. Second, the workers all said "Hello" to Mr. Evans as he passed through the plant, and Mr. Evans would chat with them about their families and how things were going.

Another impression, although a difficult one to justify with explicit evidence, was that the various managers were more than superficially concerned with their workers and their lives. Words and phrases which often recurred in the four days of conversation included: "fair treatment," "decent work for a man," "take care of our men," "expect them to work as part of a team." All individuals interviewed referred to themselves as being part of a single team; they did so either implicitly or explicitly.

The Real Paper, Inc. (A)

The Real Paper (*T.R.P.*) and its "give-away" school edition counterpart, the *Free Paper*, were organized in July of 1972 by a group of former staff members of the *Cambridge Phoenix* for the purpose of publishing "metropolitan Boston's weekly journal of news, opinion, and arts."

All of *T.R.P.*'s founders were former members of the Phoenix Employees Union. Their decision to form *The Real Paper* came after a bitter dispute with the ownership of the *Cambridge Phoenix*, which featured strikes, lockouts, picketing, fistfights, and legal action. Central to the organizing group's concept, *The Real Paper*'s operations and ownership were to be on a "community" basis. Staff members owned equal shares of T.R.P., Inc., and elected its board of directors. Paula Childs, a member of the editorial staff, described *The Real Paper* as "a staff-owned, capitalistic enterprise. It's a group of people who came together so that they could have control—complete control—over their own business and at the same time make money doing it."

Starting without facilities, operating funds, or an established circulation organization, *T.R.P.* achieved revenues of $462,000, profit before tax of $53,000, and a circulation of approximately 30,000 paid and 40,000 free in its first eight months of operations. Comparable data for fiscal 1974 were $998,000, $73,000, and approximately 40,000 paid and 50,000 free circulation.

Substantial achievements, however, had not left the staff of *The Real Paper* without uncertainties. Bob Rotner, publisher of *T.R.P.*, commented, "*The Real Paper* is making money, but we're still not out of the woods. We are subject to too many ups and downs." Jeff Albertson, associate publisher, noted "the personality of this paper is hard to talk about. It has been a problem, and we have had an identity crisis starting from day one. No one knows what 'it' is, and 'it' suffers from this lack of clearly defined purpose." And Paula Childs reflected:

418

The Real Paper was founded on the theory that most cooperatives are formed on—you know—everyone shares equally and things are fair, just, and good—and all that kind of stuff. But I think, and a lot of people who came to the paper since its founding with those same thoughts about it, have since been disillusioned. Within *The Real Paper* there's a definite hierarchy, there's a definite kind of bureaucracy. It's—it's a real—I mean it's—in some ways just like any other business.

THE MILIEU

Leaving the Harvard Business School with its carefully pruned plantings, manicured lawns, and freshly painted doorways, the researcher walked across the Larz Anderson bridge into Cambridge, past the Georgian-styled undergraduate living halls guarded by their high iron fences, and headed for the Lampoon Castle (home of Harvard's humor magazine). The Castle, itself a parody on Harvard's red brick and ivy style, served as a rough marker dividing University Cambridge from its more egalitarian neighborhood, Central Square.

Walking down Mt. Auburn Street, the researcher dodged plastic bags of refuse awaiting collection, as he passed a potpourri of small shops featuring services ranging from "Chinese Laundry" and "Tim's Lunch" to the "Mules Mirage" (a boutique) and "Bowl and Board" (an expensive furniture store). *The Real Paper* offices were located at 10–B Mt. Auburn on two floors of a yellow, wood-frame building nestled between the Cambridgeport Problem Center ("Free counseling, nonhassling assistance for legal, psychological, social, and family problems") and a row of triple-decker rooming houses. Ten–A housed a hairworks salon ("haircuts for men and women") and a school of dance whose students seemed to continue their lessons as they walked out of the building onto the sidewalk at the end of the class. Across the street other converted tripledeckers housed a number of research and professional offices.

The lamppost in front of *The Real Paper*'s office tolled a counterculture zeitgeist:

> Boycott Grapes: March! East–West Foundation Seminars in Spiritual Development. Meditations: Yin Meditations, Yang Meditations.—Meditations of Light, Nectar, Inner Sound, Love and Inner and Outer Infinity.—Declaration of Godhood; Basic techniques of Palm and Spiritual Healing; Stop Outrages in Psychiatry; Old Cambridge Common Pet Parade; Save the Cambridge Common Concerts; Filmmakers—workshops; Boycott Lettuce; Our rights we will defend with our lives if need be!

Mt. Auburn was a busy Cambridge street. Mixed with a heavy flow of commercial traffic were bicyclists, motorcyclists, and hordes of small foreign cars jousting with an infrequent standard size model as traffic inched its way forward to Central Square. Joggers were there too but in a minority position. And the pedestrian flow was heavy. Almost universally young, the passersby walked with a bounce that often sent long hair flying in the wind. Legs and faces tended to be unshaven. Clothing was simple: smocks or T-shirts, army surplus rucksacks, colorful headbands or hats of Humphrey Bogart fame, blue jeans, and sandals or hiking boots were the order of the day. The researcher was reminded that the metropolitan Boston area was a youth center heavily influenced by large numbers of young people who studied or worked there, or who merely drifted in and out.[1]

A loud exhaust backfire from a blue Porsche—a student with patched jeans of bright and varied hue—provided the last insight to the Mt. Auburn Street scene. "Porsche and Patches" mused the researcher as he turned and entered the door marked "The Real Paper." Coming into the ground-floor area, his first impression was that the area was too

Exhibit 1

THE REAL PAPER, INC.
Statement of Income for the Year
Ended April 26, 1974, and the Eight Months
Ended April 27, 1973

	1974	1973
Net sales	$995,793	$462,557
Other income	2,675	269
Total income	998,468	462,826
Costs and expenses:		
Cost of publication	618,802	273,468
Selling, general and administrative expenses	304,674	135,738
Interest expense	372	124
Total costs and expenses	923,848	409,330
Net income from operations, before provision for federal income tax	74,620	53,496
Provision for federal income tax	1,092	2,100
Net income	73,528	51,396
Retained earnings, beginning of period	51,396	—
Retained earnings, end of period	$124,924	$ 51,396
Net income per common share, based on the weighted average number of shares outstanding at the end of the year; which was 2,800 shares in 1974 and 3,300 shares in 1973	$ 26.26	$ 15.57

small for the 10 desks and numerous people working there. The main room was often a maelstrom of phone calls, shouts, advertising personnel walking back and forth, and a steady stream of visitors coming to place classified advertisements with Ellen Paul, the staff person in charge of that activity.

On one side of the main door a bicycle was stored; on the left wall

---

[1] At a later date, the researcher obtained some population data on two- and four-year colleges, degree-granting technical-trade institutes and universities located in the New England area. There were over 35 of these institutions in metropolitan Boston, with approximately 130,000 students; approximately 120 schools in Massachusetts, with approximately 320,000 students; and 250 in New England, with approximately 600,000 students (of which 2,262 were primarily students of religion). He was intrigued with the academic program for one of the schools: "The Institute of Anatomy, Sanitary Science and Embalming."

a bulletin board hosted a series of announcements: a lost cat, flea market sales, advertisements for the City Dance Theater, numerous plays, and The 100 Flowers Bookstore. Ellen's dog, Martha, padded around the room seeking attention, occasionally barking but never committing any grave social errors. To the left was the receptionist, Cyndi Robbins, wearing a flannel shirt, blue jeans, and sandals. Social pleasantries completed, she commented, "It is a hassling job with the phone and so many visitors, but I like it here—the people, the experience, and the atmosphere."

Looking to the back of the room, the researcher noticed a man (later identified as the comptroller, Howard Garsh) sweeping the floor and stacking telephone reminder slips in a cabinet. Cyndi's directions to the publisher's office sent the researcher to the back of the main room, where the publisher and the advertising sales director shared a small office furnished in the same spartan manner as the remainder of the office.

In a brief meeting the researcher explained his general interest in the alternative newspaper industry and his specific interest in *The Real Paper*. Both Rob Rotner and the researcher agreed there were opportunities for learning in the development of a case history on *The Real Paper*. Later, after consultation with other staff members, Bob welcomed the researcher to the group and agreed to collaborate on the project. (See Exhibits 1, 2, and 3.)

Exhibit 2

THE REAL PAPER, INC.
Balance Sheet
April 26, 1974, and April 27, 1973

Assets

Current assets	$161,812	$88,812
Fixed assets	6,220	2,223
Other assets	7,606	1,407
Total assets	$175,638	$92,442

Liabilities and stockholders' equity

Current liabilities	$ 48,507	$37,320
Stockholders' equity	127,131	55,122
Total liabilities and stockholders' equity	$175,638	$92,442

Exhibit 3

COST BREAKDOWN
(provided by Howard Garsh)

	Cost	Percent
Printing, composition, trucking, and circulation	$368,515	37%
Salaries—editorial, circulation, art, free-lance editorial (including bonus)	217,147	22
Salaries—sales, accounting, and clerical	125,613	12
Selling, general, and administrative expenses	212,001	21
Net profit before tax (note: bonus totaled 4%)	74,620	8

HISTORY OF *THE REAL PAPER* AND ITS COMPETITION

Early interviews with staff members highlighted the need to study the intertwined history of *The Real Paper* and its primary local competitor, the *Boston Phoenix.*

The story seemed to begin in September 1965, when *Boston After Dark* (*B.A.D.*) was born, in a spirit of entrepreneurialism, as a special centerfold supplement to the *Harbus,* the Harvard Business School student paper. *Boston After Dark* was meant to be a student's guide to Greater Boston's arts and entertainment world. As a "freebie" its distribution soon expanded to other Boston campus locations. In 1970, Stephen Mindich, a Boston University graduate and former art critic and advertising salesman for *B.A.D.,* purchased the paper. His early and major innovation was to add politically oriented news to *B.A.D.*'s coverage of arts and entertainment.

The second critical historical event was the founding, in October of 1969, of the *Cambridge Phoenix* by a 26-year-old Vietnam veteran as an "alternative" newspaper for the Boston area. The *Phoenix* statement of purpose indicated that it "was conceived with the discovery that Boston, the intellectual, artistic, and economic center of New England, was a journalistic vacuum." Within a year, the undercapitalized *Phoenix* was bought by Richard Missner, a 26-year-old M.B.A. Throughout 1970 and 1971, brisk competition developed between the *Phoenix* and *B.A.D. Fusion* magazine, commenting on the competitive situation noted:

> . . . local college students had a twin forum in which to see their revolutionary outrage expressed. . . . Horror stories of government murder and graft ran alongside reviews and advertisements for films and rock performances that created for viewers a fantasy world of glamorous sex and violence. . . . Needless to say, both writers and readers were college-educated, white and middle class, reveling in selfrighteousness as they defended people they rarely met, attacking the economic system while enjoying some of the most extravagant luxuries it could provide. Boston's weeklies provided access to the many valuable varieties of this lifestyle, as well as the impression that it was profound.

The *Phoenix,* however, soon began to develop major operating and financial problems. Its financial backer withdrew, and the staff of the *Phoenix* became increasingly disgruntled with Missner, his leadership style, and his vision of what the paper should be. Once, holding up a copy of *The Wall Street Journal,* Missner indicated editorial changes he wanted made.

On May 2, 1972, the *Phoenix* staff agreed to form a union in support of a popular, just-fired editor-in-chief, whom Missner had planned to replace with a former advertising executive. A strike, a series of confrontations, and negotiations ensued. By the end of the month, compromises were effected, and the union was officially recognized. Chuck Fager, one of the union leaders and a current member of *The Real Paper* staff commented on the strike and the effect it had:

> It was really a surprise that we unionized. Sort of WHAM! There it was. People in every department had gripes of their own. . . . So we went

out. As a result of the strike, we went through a proletarianization. For instance, we noticed the mailman. Well, he saw our picket signs and he refused to cross the line. Management had to go down to the post office to get their mail. We hadn't seen things from this perspective. . . . But once we were out, our jobs were on the line; we stood to lose everything. . . . But it was fun too. We were working together in a way that we had not worked before—making signs, picketing, and cooking food.

T.R.P. was "born" on July 31, 1972. The *Boston Globe*[2] reported this event as follows:

> On July 27, in a 2 P.M. memo, he [Missner] informs all Phoenix staffers to get out by 5 o'clock. The paper, it seems, has been sold to none other than *B.A.D.*'s Stephen Mindich for a figure Mindich claims to be $320,000. Outraged at Missner's move, they met outside their locked offices and decided to publish their own newspaper by working without pay. It hits the streets on July 31, and it is called *The Real Paper.* On the same day, the new *Boston Phoenix,* with a second section called *Boston After Dark,* appears.

Born into a field of competitive entrepreneurs, yet itself a creature of communal militance, *The Real Paper*'s trials were not yet over. For the first four weeks investors were sought, but to no avail. Chuck Fager said, "The most serious was the *New York* magazine, but they weren't certain as to how willing we would be to respond to management policy. They were quite right to question that."

Walter Harrison[3] recalled some of the sacrifices of that period:

> We worked virtually 24 hours a day. The financial sacrifices were great. We all started collecting unemployment compensation. People donated phones and office space. We had meetings virtually every night. For the first two weeks with donations and sales we just broke even.

Then by the fourth week, having found no backers but having established the viability of their new enterprise, Fager said, "A decision was reached. We had a meeting. Everyone wrote down on little cards what they had to have in order to keep going. Rotner presented a financial statement. And we found that we could cover salaries. Suddenly we had the option of independence, and almost everyone was willing to take it. Why have a backer if you don't need one?"

One hundred shares of stock were issued to each employee in lieu of back pay. Corporate and administrative positions were filled by elections. According to Fager, "We had the equivalent of $50,000 to $100,000 of capital in our momentum, i.e., free press coverage, willing advertisers, and hawker and reader willingness to buy."

The early months of the new association were rewarding, if not in a financial, certainly in a communal sense.

The biggest change, some of the staff members say, has been the new atmosphere. Paul Solman, *The Real Paper*'s editor, says: "Having our paper shot out from under us may have been the best thing that

---

[2] *Boston Globe—Globe Supplement,* June 9, 1974, p. 11.
[3] Assistant to the publisher.

ever happened. Coming over here and starting a new paper and running it ourselves, we've set a real precedent. Before this, 'democracy in the newsroom' has always had the clinker that one guy owns the paper, and you can't really tell the people what to do with their own money. But we've gotten rid of the clinker now."

Joe Klein, another writer, says that there is a greater feeling of participation at the paper by all of its staff. "I've never felt as close to the whole process of something I've worked on. I've never been so interested in the business side of the paper. . . . Everybody talks about how much like a family it is here."[4]

In the intervening year and one half, staff attention was turned to consolidating and expanding *T.R.P.*'s position. Advertisers and readers gained confidence in *The Real Paper* as evidenced by its substantial growth in revenues and circulation. And, as would be expected, operational policies and practices were modified and personnel came and left. In 1974, the *Real Paper* was a well-recognized Cambridge phenomenon.

THE ALTERNATIVE NEWSPAPER INDUSTRY

Various members of its staff characterized *The Real Paper* as an alternative newspaper. Local newspaper columnists had, on occasion, described *The Real Paper* and the *Boston Phoenix* as "underground press" or "counterculture" papers. Some news distributors interviewed referred to them as "radical sheets" or "sex papers for freaks."

With circulation in the tens of thousands and distribution via hundreds of news outlets, the term *underground* seemed inappropriate to the researcher. If *The Real Paper* and the *Boston Phoenix* were alternative papers, alternative to what? What were the key, current developments? A survey of literature available in libraries and observations by industry members provided some limited information and insight.

Although the alternative weekly was often referred to as "a paper," the genre suited more a magazine than a newspaper model. It assumed a readership that obtained its basic news from other sources, such as daily newspapers, radio, or television. The alternative press typically serviced one or two specialized segments of a larger reader market, for example, a politically liberal or youth subcommunity. Most of the large and thriving alternative papers were located in large cities or near large college campuses.

In 1972, the Underground Press Syndicate estimated that there were 300 regularly published "underground papers" in the United States, with a combined readership of 20 million. The UPS also estimated that one in three persons in the 15-to-30 age bracket were regularly exposed to underground publications.

The model for the alternative newspaper was judged by many observers to be the *Los Angeles Free Press*. That paper, founded in 1964, was described by the Underground Press Syndicate as:

---

[4] *Nation,* April 23, 1973, p. 531.

. . . in basic ways demonstrably different from all predecessors. First, the *Los Angeles Free Press* was specifically designed for a mass, though specialized, audience; second, it was in a format inexpensive to produce, simple to learn, yet with high readability, creativity, general appeal and possibilities for development and refinement; third, it was economically self-supporting and self-spreading—it was successful; fourth, it was both hip and radical (the same thing, as we now know); and fifth, it was part of a people's movement and remained a part because it was, in general, operated in a communistic style.

Paul Solman, editor of *T.R.P.*, commenting on the history of the industry and current trends noted:

. . . the rise of the underground press in the 1960s was concurrent with the rise of "The Movement" in this country. They were not so much businesses as they were political organizations. The relative inexpensiveness of offset printing enabled these organizations to turn to printed media. There was little stability and a great deal of manpower turnover within these organizations. Then as The Movement began to wane, these enterprises waned. The inheritor of these underground publications is the contemporary Alternative Press. It features the same format—offset tabloid—and many of the same people. But there was a dramatic transition in becoming a stable Alternative Press. This involved a commitment to becoming an ongoing business institution. It meant accepting responsibility, getting away from drug cartoons and sex stuff, avoiding the utter tripe we used to get, and making a transition from being purely political—and using language like "pig" and "Amerikka"—to doing something more than just indulging your political biases.

Change and evolution appeared to be very much a part not only of the alternative but also of the wider newspaper industry scene. That industry was the 10th largest American industry in terms of revenues ($5.5 billion in 1972) and the fifth largest employer (380,500 in 1972). Some 75 percent of that revenue came from advertising—local retail, classified, and national; the latter category appeared to be diminishing somewhat in terms of importance.

Economically the industry had to bear the cost of high capital investment characteristic of many manufacturing operations, as well as the relatively high labor cost of many service organizations. Efforts to improve profits, described as marginal by some investment houses, depended on the newspapers' abilities to deal with distribution problems, antiquated production facilities, and a continuing rise in the cost of newsprint. The latter item has habitually made up 25–30 percent of the revenue dollar. Cost of Canadian newsprint had gone up 20 percent in 1973, and further major increases, as well as shortages, were expected to occur in 1974. Some papers had adopted a strategy of diversification into related communication areas as a "solution" to these problems.

THE REAL PAPER AND THE FREE PAPER

The Real Paper "book," as it was referred to by its staff, was an unstapled and folded collection of newsprint pages, typically 50 to 60 in number, in tabloid format. The front page usually featured *T.R.P.*'s logo as well as a multicolored graphic design, which related to one of the feature articles in that issue. Titles or references to other stories were also highlighted on the front page.

In describing the paper's content, *T.R.P.*'s editorial department distinguished between "the front of the book" and "the back of the book," The front of the book section accounted for the first 20 to 25 pages. It typically included several long feature articles, human-interest articles—for example, an attempt by girls to enter the all-male Boston Little League baseball competition—and a number of shorter news or political items. In addition, there were four regular features: Letters to the Editor; "Short Takes," a news column; a political cartoon; and Burt Solomon's "Cambridge Report," a column covering the political and cultural life of Cambridge.

Paul Solman, the editor, indicated that two to three "compelling" front of the book feature articles were the key to his editorial composition of the paper. A random sampling of some of these articles, from the spring of 1974 issues, follows: "The Great Commuter Race. Bikes Beat Cars and MBTA by a Wheel"; "TV Guide to Impeachment"; "The Behavior Mod Squad. Clockwork Prisons: Brainwashing Saga Continues"; "A Shopper's Guide to Confession. What You Have to Know to Get the Best Deal on Penance"; "Have You Been Swindled? Nuclear Disaster Strikes Plymouth: A Shocking Scenario for the Future"; "The Death and Resurrection of the Black Panthers"; "The Strange CIA Past of Deputy Mayor Robert Kiley"; and "Prostitutes in Boston." It was evident, from a review of the titles listed on the front cover of these same editions, that feature and news articles ranged from local and national to international topics and touched on a variety of cultural and political topics.

Letters to the Editor made interesting reading in their own right and often created a dialogue between readers and staff that gave continuity to the weekly issues of *T.R.P.* The letters printed were usually only a fraction of those received. A random survey indicated letters from a variety of well-known personalities (Daniel Ellsberg) to unknown readers; from Boston College and MIT professors to AWOL American soldiers living in Sweden. Most of the letters printed appeared to be from students or the young in age or spirit living in the metropolitan Boston area. Correspondents' addresses, however, indicated readers in each of the New England states.

The second regular front of the book item, "Short Takes," in the words of its compiler Craig Unger, "tries to get six or seven news items which I think are most interesting, amusing, and politically significant that get the least media play. It has very broad limits ranging from local news to international news. About two thirds to three quarters are of a political nature, and the rest are amusing."

The back of the book section accounted for approximately 60 percent of *T.R.P.*'s pages. It featured a number of regular departments, such as commentary and reviews on theater, cinema, music, and art; and "Local Color" by Henry Armetta, a column about metropolitan Boston's entertainment field; plus a back page calendar for the upcoming week, which listed events of artistic interest in the Cambridge-Boston area. The staff of *T.R.P.* believes that its coverage of arts and entertainment, particularly the music field, was excellent, and customers interviewed by the researchers tended to support that conclusion.

A substantial section of the back of the book was devoted to listings and classified advertisements. The researcher's random sample of approximately 100 purchasers of *T.R.P.* indicated that the listings and classified sections were extremely popular. Listings provided an accurate and thorough calendar of well-known artistic events, as well as information on a host of lesser publicized activities, many of which were available at no or minimum cost. The film rating service gave staff evaluations of each film on a scale of worthless to masterpieces.

The classified pages' popularity was readily understandable to the researcher. They seemed to be an open-door communicating device among the many subgroup cultures in the community. This section had its own language system—the researcher was a WM–24–Stu (can you translate?). The advertisements or notices were a potpourri of every known youth interest or need. There were advertisements for jobs, apartments, and where to get advice about drugs, pregnancy, V.D., and low-blood-sugar problems; Personals—"Sarah from Newton—why did you walk out on me?"; leads on where to buy a wide range of products, inquiries for pen pals—often from prisoners; and a variety of travel and educational opportunities were presented (see Table 1).

And if the reader wanted new relationships, they came offered in group packages from "encounter" to "philosophic" discussion meetings. If one wanted individual companionship it came in a variety of formats: male-female, male-male, and female-female.

Bob Williams, *T.R.P.*'s advertising manager, commented on the importance of the listing and classified sections in an interview with a *Nation* writer.[5]

> The real reasons our paper or *B.A.D.* are essential to the lives of the people who read them are the classified ads and the listings. Around here, people move around a lot, a couple of times a year at least. Things change hands all the time. Apartments, stereos, TVs, cars, sex. There has to be a way for the things and the people to get together. Let's face it, Boston is one big party, with 350,000 kids looking for something to do. So the film listings, and the listings in general, are a big selling point. These things are the spine of the paper—the writers give it a competitive edge.

The *Free Paper* edition of *T.R.P.* was similar to *T.R.P.* in most respects. In any given week there were some differences in editorial content because of a post office ruling that price preferences given one reader over another must be accompanied by a minimum 20 percent content difference. The post office also required that a certain percentage of a paper's circulation must be paid to obtain second-class mailing privileges. Circulation of the *Free Paper,* since it was distributed to school living and dining halls, varied with the local student population, dropping during vacation periods.

---

[5] *Nation,* April 23, p. 533.

Table 1

REPRESENTATIVE CLASSIFIED ADVERTISEMENTS

WARM, sincere attractive WJM. Pisces, 29, dislikes dating bars and phony people, would like to meet warm, sincere, affectionate, cuddly slightly mesugah WJF 18–30, short and pretty, with long hair, for lasting relationship. White CF, PO Box _____Framingham, Mass. 01701

WHITE Male 25 Walpole Prisoner wants letters & visits from young women I'm 6′ tall weigh 160 blond hair blue eyes. Real Box 749

TALL dark and sane. Are you still out there? Sorry didn't get in touch. Please send phone number or suggest meetings. Let's get it together this time. Patricia Box 750

I'm a young woman planning to bring former hillside farm in Western Mass. to long lost fullness. Educated, intelligent, willful, crazy, occasionally impossible, but often spontaneous, loving, energetic, able, funny, practical. Smoke insanely and visions a joy to me. Physically attractive, but so what? Want to feel the isness of things but that takes time and living. Want to make a home for friends to visit when in need of love, slowness, wholeness, rest, healing. Box 728.

WM 27 grad student, warm, aware, seeks female to enjoy the intoxication of spring with. I like tennis, books, nature, hiking, beautiful sex, politics, playing guitar. Let's get together. Real Paper Box 752.

ONE well-adjusted woman wanted to share sunny spacious, furnished 2-bedroom apartment in North End for summer. $100/ month rent. Please call Joan at——

Supplements to *T.R.P.* and the *Free Paper* were added to the regular editions about once each month. Jeff Albertson, newly assigned supplements editor, felt that the frequency of supplements would increase in the fall of 1974. Supplements were similar to the regular book in format and design. However, each was typically organized around one theme, such as buying guides to high-fidelity equipment, camping equipment, etc. Articles on the theme were prepared, and advertisers with a particular interest in that field were sought.

The metropolitan Boston competitive situation

In addition to several dozen weekly suburban newspapers covering their local scenes, three standard daily and two major weekly alternative newspapers were published in Boston. The daily newspapers included the *Christian Science Monitor,* whose masthead declared it to be "An International Daily Newspaper," and whose principal circulation was outside of metropolitan Boston.

The second paper, the *Boston Herald-American,* owned by the Hearst Corporation, was a recent merger of the *Herald-Traveler,* which had circulation strength in the suburbs, and the *Record-American* with "blue collar" readership in Boston. An industry observer described it as an "independent, conservative, Republican paper. It's probably losing a lot of money. There is a rumor that Mr. Mindich is considering launching a major Boston daily, contingent upon future plans of the *Boston Herald-American*."

The *Boston Globe* was the largest of the three standard papers in circulation and was financially the most successful (net income of $3 million on $90 million in revenues in 1972). Local journalists conceded the *Globe*'s competitive aggressiveness, citing its use of specialists covering such topics as urban renewal, mental health, affairs of the elderly, and the women's movement. One observer described the *Globe* as a paper "which serves the liberal educational community well and the city of Boston with less enthusiasm. The *Globe* espouses its liberal causes stridently and rarely hesitates to show a bias in its reporting."

In attempting to gain information about the alternative newspaper competitive situation, the researcher visited a dozen newsstands in the Greater Boston area. Clearly the leaders in this race were *T.R.P.* and the *Boston Phoenix*. But the customer had a variety of papers from which to make a selection depending upon his or her particular mix of reading interests. Larger newsstands typically carried, as a minimum, three other nonlocal alternative papers: the *Village Voice*, the *Free Press*, and *Rolling Stone*. The *Village Voice* (weekly price 35 cents, 125 pages, over 150,000 circulation) was owned by *New York Magazine;* its masthead stated that it was "The Weekly Newspaper of New York." The *Voice* had an East Coast and national distribution pattern. Its content was focused on a wide range of local New York and national political issues and personalities; it had major, in-depth coverage of art, music, and the theater. As a member of the Audit Bureau of Circulation its advertisers included prominent local and national firms.

The *Los Angeles Free Press* (weekly, 35 cents, about 40 pages, circulation 150,000) also had achieved regional and national distribution. Its coverage included politics, the arts, and a 20-page classified "sex" insert—literally a cornucopia of erotica. In contrast to the more academic style of the *Voice* (an interview with three African female jurists and an analysis of Shakespearean theater), the *Freep*'s editorial style seemed to the researcher to be sensational, and its word system and headlines were strident in character.

The *Rolling Stone*'s (biweekly, 75 cents, over 100 pages, circulation 300,000) content was heavily built around popular music and the entertainment world, with some political coverage, e.g., an interview with Jane Fonda on her latest visit to North Vietnam. While both the *Voice* and *Rolling Stone* carried classified advertisements, these tended to downplay sex themes and products.

A Boston newsdealer mentioned the *Texas Monthly* as a prototype of recent entries in the field. *Newsweek* magazine reported that it sold for $1, "has taken provocative looks at the inner workings of the state's highway lobby, banks, law firms, and daily newspapers, dismissing the latter 'as strikingly weak and ineffectual.' The *Texas Monthly* received the prestigious 1974 National Magazine Award for Specialized Journalism."[6] "*Ramparts*, of course," the newsdealer said, "has been around a long time, and there are a batch of others of the same cast."

In metropolitan Boston, *T.R.P.*'s primary competitor was the *Boston Phoenix*. Both papers were similar in format and price, both were published weekly, both used the same distribution methods—although with different emphasis—and both had free school editions.

Differences were also apparent to the researcher. The *Phoenix* was a larger book—often over 80 pages compared with *T.R.P.*'s 50- to 60-page editions. The larger *Phoenix* was divided into two distinct subparts: the *Phoenix* and its insert, *Boston After Dark*—the arts and entertainment section. The *Phoenix* enjoyed a larger circulation; industry estimates ranged from 80,000 to 110,000, with approximately 40,000 being the free edition. The *Phoenix* appeared to the researcher to enjoy a wider range of local and national advertisers than did *T.R.P.* In terms of visual appearance, the *Phoenix* appeared to be more crowded and less willing to use open space to lead the reader's eye around a page than did *T.R.P.*

The researcher wanted to obtain data on why a customer purchased *T.R.P.* versus the *Phoenix* and what was the market for these two papers. A random survey of purchasers by the researcher obtained limited information. Most could not make explicit their preference for one paper over the other. *T.R.P.* customers often mentioned "better Cambridge coverage," "more liberal," "easier to read," while *Phoenix* purchasers stressed "red hot classifieds" and "*B.A.D.* is the best guide." (See Exhibit 4.)

In reviewing this competitive situation between *The Real Paper* and the *Phoenix*, a *Boston Globe* writer commented:[7]

> The two papers continue in the image of advocacy journalism planted firmly left of center and sprinkled with occasional muck-raking. But while in days past they overlapped on stories, they almost never do today. In fact, except for arts coverage—particularly music—you can browse through two issues of the same week and not see two pieces about the same thing. What you will find is that the *Phoenix*, reflecting its publisher's little-subdued dream to become a force in the community, concerns itself more with the news of the day, dealing with many of the same subjects and events as the city's dailies. "We've made a shift to respond to news happenings," says Miller. "We want to be topical." *The Real Paper*, on the other hand, seems to be moving more and more towards becoming a weekly magazine, opting for stylized features and columns rather than news reporting. Part of the reason for this is undoubtedly *The Real Paper's* constituency, which is more Cambridge-oriented than that of the *Phoenix*. . . .

What was the market for the two publications? Bob Williams, advertising manager for *T.R.P.*, gave one specific definition.

> In Boston you have 350,000 young people, under 30, within 2.5 square miles of space. You don't find a concentration like that anywhere in the

---

[6] *Newsweek*, June 17, 1974, p. 29.
[7] *Boston Globe—Sunday Supplement*, June 9, 1974, p. 7.

Exhibit 4

COMPARISON OF ARTICLE CONTENT OF *THE REAL PAPER* VERSUS
THE *BOSTON PHOENIX*

	The Real Paper		Boston Phoenix	
Category	Number of articles	Percent	Number of articles	Percent
International events or politics	2	1.7	5	2.8
Art, movies, books, TV, dance	32	26.7	59	33.0
Exposés	5	4.2	1	0.5
Rock music, other types of music, album review columns ...	15	12.5	32	17.9
Local events/politics	21	17.5	34	19.0
Counterculture, e.g., communes, drugs, etc.......................	1	0.8	2	1.1
National events/politics	9	7.5	20	11.2
Movements, including prison reform, women's, and gay	9	7.5	4	2.3
Sports............................	2	1.7	14	7.8
Miscellaneous, including food, "Local Color," travel, tax information	24	20.0	8	4.5
Totals	120	100.1	179	100.1

Source: These data were prepared by Kim Panushka of *T.R.P.* staff. She surveyed eight issues of each paper for the months of March and April 1974. The total number of major feature articles for *T.R.P.* was 120; for the *Boston Phoenix*, 179. Excluded were regular columns from staff writers.

country except Boston. It's a unique market. These kids spend around $40 million or $50 million a year.

As the researchers spoke with students of the "New Journalism," it became evident that these publications were not a new journalistic creation; protest publications had enjoyed a long and rich history in the United States. Rather, alternative newspapers had targeted a very specific audience—the young, white, relatively wealthy college student and the "hangers on" living around the typical college community. This audience, with its counterculture value system, had a strong need to see its antiestablishment point of view defended vigorously in print. They did not tolerate a questioning of these beliefs or their lifestyle. They expected the so-called alternative papers to defend them with the zeal of a "true believer."

Over a period of months, the researcher observed *T.R.P.*'s operations and interviewed a substantial number of its staff. Early in his research, he studied the production process, the financial and accounting systems, the circulation department, and the advertising sales activity. As the research progressed he then worked with the editorial area. A summary of this information follows.

Production

Getting the "book" out each week was a central activity at *T.R.P.* As in any daily or weekly publishing operation, this activity was characterized by speed, deadlines, coordination of a host of detail and people, and the ever-present last-minute changes.

The production of *T.R.P.* basically involved the laying out and printing of five types of copy within the time constraint of weekly publication, and the size constraint of how large a paper could be profitably published. This process could be summarized around six stages of production.

First, the various "copy traffic controllers" accumulated the five kinds of copy: editorial, advertising, art, classified, and listings. Each controller determined the space required for his or her copy and relayed that information to the layout editor.

Second, on Thursday, as the accumulation of copy was drawing to a close, the comptroller, managing editor, and advertising sales director met to determine the number of pages in the book. The comptroller would project the week's profit and loss statement under varying assumptions about advertising, density, and number of pages in the book.

Third, the layout editor was informed as to the number of pages to be published as well as about additions or deletions to copy. He then proceeded to allocate sections of each page of the book to various kinds of copy. This involved the use of a "paste-up board," a full-scale representation of a page.

Fourth, the paste-up boards were transferred to the composition shop. Here copy, which had been typed in even columns, was physically pasted onto the paste-up boards, which were photographed and the resulting negatives developed. These negatives, along with the negatives of copy photographs—called "halftones"—were combined by taping them together.

Fifth, the final negatives were taken to the printing plant where printing plates were made and the paper was printed on a web offset press. It took about three hours to print an edition of 50,000 papers.

Sixth, on Saturday morning the newsstand distributors picked up papers from the printing plant for distribution to newsstands on Sunday. The hawker edition was distributed at 5:30 A.M. Monday mornings to hawkers. Subscription copies were addressed and mailed on Saturday for delivery to the post office on Monday.

Production of the *Free Paper* followed on Monday, when editorial people altered the layout boards and changed the front page design to conform to the required 20 percent content difference regulation. The paper was printed that same day and delivered to college campuses on Tuesday.

Neither composition nor printing facilities were owned by *T.R.P.*, and that work was subcontracted to local, independent firms. "Both of those operations would require substantial capital investments in equipment," Howard Garsh explained.

Control

The comptroller's office consisted of two people, Howard Garsh, the comptroller, and Stanley Korytko, the bookkeeper.

One day, while walking into 10–B Mt. Auburn with the researcher,

Howard said, "I don't see how you can do this study without some reference to the figures. Let's talk for a few minutes?" The researcher and Garsh walked upstairs, through a small office and into a connecting closet that served as Garsh's "cubbyhole," as offices were referred to at *T.R.P.* Garsh proceeded to search for papers in his files and in the clutter on his desk.

A lot of what I do here deals with keeping track of the company's financial status, either projected or actual. Accordingly, there are several tools I use, the weekly P & L projection according to various book size assumptions, the monthly profit and loss statement, and the semiannual cash and operating budget projections. These budgets tend to be conservative, pessimistic, and possibly just a little extreme. That is, we overestimate expenses and underestimate income just so we don't get cocky and overextend ourselves.

Our auditor says he's never seen such beautiful papers. That's partly because we don't just make broad assumptions of percentage increases, but instead get down to the real arithmetic of it. For instance, the budget is based on Bob Williams' projection of revenue from display[8] advertising since that's the source of about 80 percent of our revenue. We ask for the most reasonable, honest estimate that doesn't pull the figures out of the air. He talks to the salesmen, looks at the economy, and maybe talks to some advertisers. And his estimate is usually conservative. As you can see from this. Remember, his projections were made one year ago.

April 5, 1974   Budgeted .... $12,000   April 19, 1974   Budgeted $12,000
             Billed 14,500   Billed 14,000
   (including a $2,000 ad insert)   (including a $2,000 ad insert)
April 12, 1974   Budgeted .... $12,000   April 26, 1974   Budgeted $12,000
             Billed 12,500   Billed 15,000

Our bread and butter is accounts receivable. We stay right on top of them. Our credit allowances are 30 days net. And we allocate 4 percent of revenue to bad debt although experience shows that 1 percent is sufficient.

And we virtually have no accounts payable. Other than salaries, our major expenses are printing, composition, subscriber service, mailing, trucking, and editorial free-lance payments. We've never been in a position to keep any of them waiting. Certainly every account is paid within 30 days. There are reasons for this: first, we want a top Dun & Bradstreet rating, a reputation of being a good company to do business with, a company that pays its bills. Right now our D&B rating is two. D&B told us that all it would take to get a number one is for us to be in business a little longer. Second, we have the money so why not pay it, so we try to help them out by paying on the spot.

The main reason why you'll find differences between actual and projected is in the economics of each week's book, that is, the number of pages and ad density. In order to consider those very issues in our weekly business planning, I project the weekly P&L based on assumptions about number of pages and ad density. We like to see about a $2,000 profit and not more

---

[8] Regular advertisements from commercial customers, as opposed to classified advertising, e.g., notices of apartments for rent.

than 55 percent ad density. Within those parameters we come to a decision about the number of pages in the book and transmit that decision to the layout editor, who plans the book accordingly.

The economics of our operation greatly affect our performance. For instance, profitability increases very rapidly with an increase in ad density. As past weekly projections have shown, most of our costs are fixed, e.g., mailing, trucking, sales expense, art expense. The only variable costs we have are composition, which really varies only slightly, editorial free-lance, which varies because nonstaff articles are used as editorial copy if we opt for a larger book. Printing costs, which increase by about $1,500 for every eight-page increase we make, and salesmen's commissions (10 percent of collections), which vary with billing but not by size of paper.

For instance, assuming a 56-page paper is average, we will probably spend a total of $20,000, most of which will be on fixed type costs. Typically we will get $2,800 from circulation revenue, and $3,000 from classified advertising, and that means we'd need about $14,000 from display advertising to break even. Usually the salesmen can bring in some last-minute advertising if we think we're running low. But there's a danger in thinking you can cram a lot of advertising into a book, because too much doesn't look good. So it can cause a problem: At what ad density do you decide you have to increase the size of the paper? And is increasing the size of the paper economically profitable? Anything over that $14,000 is gravy until we have to increase the book size. And increases come only in jumps of eight pages. Because each jump costs about $1,500, only one full page of ads (worth about $640) never justifies a book increase of eight pages. But what is the cutoff? I don't know.

The special supplements are pure gravy. The profit margin varies between 20 percent and 50 percent because the regular kinds of expenses are charged against the regular edition, and so that supplement must only cover its incidental printing, composition, editorial free-lance, artwork, and mailing expenses.

Garsh's responsibilities also included relationships with the First National Bank of Boston. That bank, since *T.R.P.*'s founding, had financed all major capital needs of the organization.

Circulation department

Kevin Dawkins, who had joined *T.R.P.* in January of 1973, had just been put in charge of circulation activities.

T.R.P. was distributed through four channels: newsstands, hawkers, subscription, and controlled circulation—i.e., free distribution. The percentage breakdown of distribution channels in 1974 was newsstands, 30 percent; hawkers, 14 percent; subscription, 4 percent; and controlled, 52 percent. In 1972, Kevin pointed out, the newsstand and hawker percentages had been reversed with hawkers selling over 30 percent and newsstands roughly 15 percent of *T.R.P.* circulation.

Controlled circulation of the *Free Paper* goes to "every conceivable college from here to Worcester, Massachusetts." A formula of one copy per four students was used, and never were more than 50,000 copies distributed. Dawkins commented, "It's gravy. It boosts our circulation which entitles us to boost our advertising rates. Besides, the audience is captive. This edition builds reading habits which can extend to higher newsstand sales. In college towns, though, if we miss delivery to the school for some reason, newsstand sales stay about the same. Sometimes I think the markets are separate."

As for newsstand circulation, two thirds occurred within Route 128 (metropolitan Boston), and one third beyond. *T.R.P.* worked through one distributor, Greater Boston Distributors, Inc., within the Route 128 area. Greater Boston Distributors had over 800 outlets including the Union News outlets in subways, railroad stations, and Logan Airport.

T.R.P. was sold at 75 percent of these newsstands. Money was paid only for copies sold. The price to the distributor was 12 cents; he sold it to the independent newsstand operators for 19 cents, and the newsstand price was 25 cents. Greater Boston Distributors handled between 1,500 and 2,000 titles, among which were the most profitable in the country. Dawkins felt that *T.R.P.* should be at more newsstands and be featured more prominently.

Newsstand relationships beyond Route 128 were handled through independent distributors. The newsstand circulation area extended as far to the west as Holyoke–Springfield, Massachusetts, as far east as Portland, Maine, and as far south as Providence, Rhode Island. The objective here was to penetrate outlying markets by first reaching college communities and communal areas.

Hawker relationships were one of Kevin's responsibilities. Hawkers were independent operators who bought a paper for 5 cents and sold it for 25 cents on busy street corners throughout Greater Boston.

> In 1970, 200 hawkers used to sell almost 40,000 copies of the *Old Cambridge Phoeniz;* now we have 100 hawkers selling 15,000 copies of *T.R.P.* We used to have 75 hawkers in Boston alone—now there are only 45. There is a very high turnover here, but we have a hard core of about 50 old-timers.
>
> The papers are trucked to a number of distribution points in Boston and Cambridge. The hawkers buy the papers for cash, but if someone is in a rough way we will front him or her for 10 or 20 copies. They can turn unsold copies in the next week for new papers. All hawkers sell both our paper and the *Phoenix.*
>
> The typical hawker is the kind of person you would see at a rock and roll concert: long hair, T-shirt, blue jeans, and sandals. They are street people, and they keep us anchored to that community.
>
> They do pretty well. Richie on the Boston University Bridge must make $80 from *T.R.P.* and the same from the *Phoenix* in a couple of days. Other hawkers can make $100 in two days, and some people living in a group setup can clear $25–$30 in two days and they can live on that.
>
> And they have their codes too: the oldest one in seniority gets to take the best corner, although the old-timers have the territory well staked out. We don't even know some of their real names. One of them calls himself King Kong. They don't want to have any tax records.
>
> I'm trying to push hawker sales. We are advertising in *T.R.P.,* and I'm preparing posters to put up around the city. Hawkers are great publicity for us, standing at each street corner and practically putting the paper through your car window. Everyone can see that front page, whereas on the newsstands we are buried. I'm trying to extend hawking to the suburbs by promoting hawking through guidance counselors.

They are street people—that community is important to us. And I don't think the *Phoenix* really wants to use them; they aren't sophisticated enough. The *Phoenix,* you know, has hired two former *Herald-American* pros for their circulation department.

3. Subscriptions had been an increasingly expensive channel of distribution to service. The paper was physically distributed by Hub Mail, Inc. The cost per paper per subscription was about 22 cents, making it the least economic of all channels. Since the mailing service refused to operate on weekends, a mailed paper arrives at its earliest on Tuesday, whereas *T.R.P.* was delivered to newsstands on Sundays. The one redeeming feature about subscription sales, Kevin noted, was that *T.R.P.* gets "the money up front." Kevin intended to eliminate the discount that subscribers get by subscribing (raising the price from $10 to $13 per year) in an attempt to cover cost increases, and he hoped to negotiate a new mailing agreement which would have the paper in the mail on Saturday and delivered by Monday.

Kevin had growth in *T.R.P.* circulation as one of his primary goals. He was assisted in this program by a "road man" who visited newsstand owners to "sell" them on the advantages of carrying *T.R.P.*

We are one of Greater Boston Distributors' top 10 best selling accounts. They formerly had sort of a monopoly and weren't aggressive. Terrible things happen to people when they have power. But they are getting competition now, and that helps us. We are considering selling papers via machines located in grocery stores.

Our toughest competition is the *Phoenix.* They are supposed to have 110,000 circulation, and their revenues are twice ours—they up their ad density and charge higher advertising rates than we do. But we will catch up with them! Within one year we will be bigger! I get excited about this! Walter Harrison (the former circulation director) has suggested to me that we experiment with a home delivery system.

In the spring of 1974 Bob Williams began to advocate broadcast media promotion as a means of building *T.R.P.*'s visibility and consumer demand. Except for development costs, it was anticipated that the program would operate largely through reciprocal advertising with commerical radio and television broadcasters.

Kevin concluded:

I want us to get recognition; we put out the best paper in the country, and I know because I am in touch with lots of them. Our problem is we just aren't taken as seriously as we should be. We want to be an important part of the Cambridge–Boston community in the near future. We want people to use *T.R.P.* as more than just reading material. We want to serve as "the reference" for what goes on here. We want it to be an important part of their lives.

Advertising sales department

The advertising sales department was concerned with selling display and classified advertising, and comprised five display salespeople, one classified salesperson, Linda Martin (the advertising traffic controller), and Bob Williams, the department director. Advertising sales accounted for approximately 80 percent of the revenue of *T.R.P.*

Talking about *T.R.P.*'s advertising market, Williams said:

> There are basically two levels of advertisers we're concerned with. The first group is people who have clubs, restaurants, concert tours, army-navy stores, clothing, bookstores, record stores—all the people who sell mainly to college students. These people came in right away. They really had to. They need papers like ours as much as we need them. The second level is the larger companies—GM, stereo companies, Jordan Marsh, and the other big clothing stores, which don't have an immediate relation between advertising money spent and dollars earned. With these people, it's only a matter of time.[9]

There was no formal system of account assignment, since Williams believed that a strict delineation of "turf" was not healthy. Nevertheless, each salesperson seemed to have specialized in one way or another. For example, one salesman, Steve Cummings, concentrated in cameras, symphony, sex, and religion; e.g., Boston Symphony Orchestra, adult bookstores, Indian gurus, and meditation movements. The four most important industries for advertising revenue were stereo components, liquor, phonograph records, and cameras.

The approach each salesman used was individualized. Price bargaining was allowed which "makes selling tougher," Bob commented. "Otherwise, it is just stating standard rates." A sense of flexibility, of tailoring to the advertiser's needs, seemed to the researcher to be a dominant theme in the advertising efforts of *T.R.P.* In two instances, the researcher observed that Williams was willing to bend contractual agreements or trade advertising for the specific products of the business. "It's those little guys we've got to help. They're where our future lies." *T.R.P.*'s advertisers were primarily Boston firms, but about 15 percent of display advertisements were placed by national firms.

It seemed to Bob Williams that the *T.R.P.* advertising staff sold access to a special kind of consumer—a youthful, liberal, student market. But "hard" and reliable data were limited. A 1974 company-financed survey of approximately 300 purchasers of *T.R.P.* (*Free Paper* customers were not canvassed) provided the following profile: Average age, 23.7; sex, 55 percent male and 45 percent female; 87 percent had some college education and 47 percent were college graduates; 24 percent were professional-technical personnel, 23 percent full-time students, 12 percent unemployed, 11 percent clerical, 10 percent blue collar, 5 percent sales, 4 percent managerial, 1 percent housewives, and 10 percent miscellaneous. Thirty-six percent of the papers were sold in Boston, 32 percent in Cambridge, 5 percent in Brookline, 3 percent in Newton, 3 percent in Somerville, and the remainder scattered in other Boston suburbs.

T.R.P.'s advertising charges were geared to its circulation rate base of 90,000 copies per week. Rates for display advertisements were $14 per column inch, or $1,120 for a full page. Discounts were given for

---

[9] *Nation*, April 23, 1973, p. 533.

discounts

continuity of placement: 13 weeks—10 percent, 26 weeks—15 percent, and 52 weeks—20 percent. Classified advertisements were $1.90 per line.

In terms of rates we want to get between $11.00 and $11.50 per thousand readers and stay about 50 cents per thousand under the *Phoenix*. The more specialized your market is, the higher you can charge. Publications get $2 to $3 per thousand for a very general audience, to $5 to $6 for a somewhat specialized audience, up to $30 to $40 for a very specialized group.

We don't cut our stated rates in the summer even though with school vacations, our free circulation drops, but we do make deals. Many of our advertisers are on yearly contract (a total of two thirds of *T.R.P.* advertisers were on some kind of contractual basis)—they get more power in the fall and winter than in the summer, but it balances out. In this business, one half your customers don't even know what your circulation is; they are only interested in how much response the advertisement gets, and we have a very loyal readership.

With free copies, we don't go above 52 percent at the top; Bob Rotner makes that decision. Free circulation is good, but it makes things a bit more fluffy—particularly for A.B.C.[10] counts. It makes it harder for you to really prove your circulation.

Some of the problems Williams noted were the business community's lack of respect for *T.R.P.* and the staff's prohibition of certain kinds of advertising. With regard to the former, Williams noted that some advertisers regularly abuse credit terms and said, "People don't respect us the first time around. They think we're just a weak underground paper. Meanwhile, the staff prohibits cigarette advertising because it felt that it was detrimental to the paper's image, but that means a loss of revenue."

As for the future, Williams doubted that *T.R.P.* should follow the *Phoenix* to pursue suburban advertisers. He noted that the *Phoenix* was his roughest competition.

But circulatn wants suburbs distrib. !

I don't think the future is necessarily there. There is a 50 percent bad-debt ratio on advertising beyond Route 128,[11] mostly motorcycle places, bars, and so on. The people who read *T.R.P.* and shop are here in town. We sell our circulation and a kind of readership. It would be foolish not to exploit it here. The *Phoenix* is entering the suburbs and doesn't have the circulation to back it up. That will hurt alternative weeklies in general. Furthermore, we're still thrashing around editorially. It would have been unwise to move until we get that straightened out. Finally, we are best sold to small and medium-sized businesses; and they are most concentrated here in town.

The trick is to get local advertisers to transfer ad money from radio to print and more particularly, *T.R.P.* There are about 50 stations in this area, and 10 of them program directly for the youth market. We do some reciprocal advertising with them now.

I love music and have a hi-fi set. The reality of Boston is that there is an important radio market here. If the company were interested, and it

---

[10] Audit Bureau of Circulation, an agency which attested to the circulation figures of newspapers and magazines.

[11] A belt highway, approximately 12 miles west of the central city. Route 128 tended to be a dividing line between the more-developed suburbs of Boston and the less-developed, higher-status suburbs of the city.

isn't, we could go into partnership with one of these stations. It would provide a great new combination for us. Bob Rotner once thought we should go into the newsstand distribution business.

By 1975–76, if my plans work out, we should be in a position to enter the suburbs. I am shooting for advertising sales this year of $1.5 million.

Editorial

Editorial offices were located on the second floor at 10–B Mt. Auburn Street. The physical layout consisted of a main room (about one fourth the size of the first floor) and two closet-size offices at the far end; one of the latter also served as a hallway to the back porch. Paul Solman (editor) and Tim Friedman (managing editor) were technically assigned this space, but all members of the department seemed to participate in its use. Jeff Albertson's (the associate publisher) desk was next to Tom's office.

The main room contained five desks, two tables, filing cabinets, and all of the usual paraphernalia of an editorial operation. A chair, with one of its casters off, occupied the center of the room. "We bought all of this equipment secondhand," Paula Childs noted. "We sure scrimp around here. Howard buys us discard, advertising promotion pencils but no pens. But we are getting more space in the basement here—that should help a lot."

The researcher agreed that space was needed. Even in a summer lull period, editorial personnel flowed in and out, and often there were not enough available desks and chairs. The room had a used and non-cleaned look with papers on the floor and boxes of editorial supplies stacked in every conceivable place. A number of bulletin boards seemed to be a part of the communication system, telling Peter to get a photo at 10:30 and noting that a free-lance writer wanted his check right away—"He is flat broke." Office decor consisted of wall-sized pictures of Katherine Hepburn, et al., and advertisements for concerts and artistic events; a somewhat tired and dehydrated plant provided the final touch.

The researcher sought to capture the office tone. Clearly busyness was the order of the day, with editorial personnel constantly using the multiple phones and the limited desk space. Friendliness was another factor. Martha, the receptionist, seemed unflappable despite the constant barrage of questions and calls with which she was confronted. There was an air of informality. Standard dress seemed to be T-shirts, shorts, and sandals; it made the first floor look almost "Establishment."

Editorial proved to be a complex part of *T.R.P.*'s scene to "paint" for the reader. After several abortive attempts, the researcher finally decided to look first at "who was in the area and what did they do," next at the "organization and leadership of the work," and finally at *T.R.P.*'s "editorial posture."

T.R.P.'s masthead (July) carried the names of 54 individuals, 32 of whom were listed under "Editorial." Of those names, Paul Solman commented, "14 are full-time personnel, 8 are part-time members who regularly contribute, and 10 are free-lance or irregular contributors to the book."

The editorial staff tended to specialize by function. On the "support" side, Paul and Tom were assisted by Jan Freeman (copy editor) and Paula Childs (listings and general editorial person), and general assistance to the entire group was given by Peter Southwick (photos) and recently "on board" Bruce Weinberg (production manager).

On the "creative" side the situation was more complicated since most staffers handled multiple assignments. The largest number worked primarily on "back of the book" material—the arts and entertainment section and, in addition, contributed regular columns used throughout the entire paper. The smallest number of full-time masthead personnel were involved with the development of feature stories. "When we came over from the *Phoenix* we had six full-time feature writers," Paul said. "Until recently we had four, but Joe Klein just left to go with *Rolling Stone* at twice what we could pay, and Ed Zuckerman is going back to journalism school. We need to hire another two writers; we're short-handed."

In addition to back of the book and feature writers, there were a number of individuals (often part-timers) who specialized in writing a political or news column or, as in the case of Omar White, created a political cartoon. In addition to masthead personnel, there was a pool of free-lance writers who, on occasion, submitted articles to *T.R.P.* Boston seemed to attract a large number of writers, many of whom could not find, or did not want, a regular organizational relationship.

The editorial group was responsible for the creation and processing of copy with copy coming from staff columnists, staff feature writers, solicited manuscripts from free-lancers, and unsolicited manuscripts. This editorial activity, Tom commented, was organized along the back and front of the book lines.

> Jim Miller is our music editor, and Stuart Byron is our film editor. They, along with Art Friedman, our regular theater columnist, and Kay Larson, our art columnist, hand me back of the book material each week. The back of the book tends to run itself, but Paul is looking for a back of the book editor. Both of us are front of the book oriented, and a good deal more of the budget goes into the front than the back of the book.

All staff members, with whom the researcher spoke, indicated that Paul was the central person in the process of generating or reviewing story concepts, interesting and assigning writers to develop those stories, and finally nurturing and reviewing the resultant manuscript as it evolved. It seemed to the researcher that this was an extremely personal and intuitive process, difficult for all involved to articulate and yet critical for *T.R.P.*'s success.

At a regular Friday morning meeting the editorial staffers gathered with Paul in an informal session to review the copy program. Story ideas were reviewed, modified, or discarded in a free-flowing meeting with staffers sitting on the floor and Paul, his chair tilted against the wall, leading the discussion.

Paul's primary operating pattern, however, seemed to be on an individual-to-individual basis. He often began the process of copy creation by talking with a writer about an idea. "At any given time I expect I

Exhibit 5

MASTHEAD—JULY 17, 1974

Real Paper

EDITORIAL
PAUL SOLMAN, EDITOR
TOM FRIEDMAN, MANAGING EDITOR
HENRY ARMETTA
HARPER BARNES
BO BURLINGHAM
STUART BYRON
PAULA CHILDS
STEPHEN DAVIS
CHUCK FAGER
JAN FREEMAN
ARTHUR FRIEDMAN
RUSSELL GERSTEN
ANITA HARRIS
JOE HUNT
JAMES ISAACS
JOE KLEIN, NEWS EDITOR
ANDREW KOPKIND
CHUCK KRAEMER
JON LANDAU
KAY LARSON
JON LIPSKY
DAVE MARSH
JIM MILLER
LILITH MOON
ARNIE REISMAN
LAURA SHAPIRO
BURT SOLOMON
PETER SOUTHWICK, PHOTOGRAPHER
CRAIG UNGER
BRUCE WEINBERG, PRODUCTION
DAVID OMAR WHITE
ED ZUCKERMAN

ADVERTISING
ROBERT WILLIAMS, DIRECTOR
JONATHAN BANNER
STEVE CUMMINGS
MIKE FORMAN
LINDA MARTIN
DONALD MONACK
ELLEN PAUL
RICHARD REITMAN
DICK YOUSOUFIAN

ART
RONN CAMPISI, DIRECTOR
DAVID BROWN
PAT MEARS
REBECCA WELZ

CIRCULATION
KEVIN DAWKINS, DIRECTOR
DON CUMMINGS
CYNDI ROBBINS
MIKE ZEGEL

BUSINESS
HOWARD GARSH, COMPTROLLER
STANLEY KORYTKO
WALTER HARRISON, ASST. TO THE
PUBLISHER
JEFF ALBERTSON, ASSOC. PUBLISHER
ROBERT ROTNER, PUBLISHER

Metropolitan Boston's Weekly Journal of News, Opinion and the
Arts. Address all correspondence to the Real Paper, 10B Mt.
Auburn St., Cambridge, Mass. 02138. Telephones: Editorial and
Art, 492-8101; Advertising, Circulation and Business, 492-1650.
Second-class postage paid at Boston, Mass. Published weekly by
The Real Paper, 10B Mt. Auburn St., Cambridge, Mass. 02138.
Copyright © 1974 by The Real Paper. All rights reserved.
Reproduction by any method whatsoever without permission of
staff is prohibited.
Unsolicited manuscripts should be addressed to Jan Freeman
and must be accompanied by stamped self-addressed envelope.
Photographs should be submitted to Jeff Albertson, Photo Editor.
Subscription rates: 1 year, $10.00; 2 years, $18.00.

Printing by Arlington Offset

JULY 17, 1974   Vol. 3, No. 29

am working on 50 story ideas of which 5 may actually come to print. I work at home two days a week because I can concentrate better there and handle the writers more effectively by telephone."

The researcher appreciated the latter comment since Paul's office routine could be described as frenetic. He was constantly on the phone, answering questions, reviewing edit problems with Tom, or working with a writer. Paul's informal style and personal warmth made it easy for all to approach him, and he seemed always to be "in conference" outside the office building, on the stairs, or even walking through the office. "When do you get time to reflect?" the researcher asked. Paul smiled, "It's tough."

With full-time, front of the book personnel, Paul's primary function seemed to be reviewing story ideas that they brought to him. With part-time and free-lance writers, Paul seemed to play a more active role in initiating concepts, but he also reviewed their suggestions and manuscripts. He had a wide acquaintanceship in the Boston community and seemed to the researcher to have knowledge about and interest in a wide range of topics and institutions.

> I handle all of the free-lance work. It is a shifting group of people. Some work for other outfits, some are teachers, some have a cause, most need money—it's hard to make a living free-lancing. We pay them $75 for a short 1,000-word story, $250 for a feature article or part thereof. Once in the judge and court system story, where a lot of research work was needed, we paid $600. But we negotiate with each; the budget puts on real limits.

Jan Freeman in commenting on copy development said:

> Paul's job is to think up ideas and then assign them to either regular or free-lance writers, although usually the regular staff generate their own ideas. It is a very difficult job, and I suspect the ratio of ideas to finished stories is about 15 to 1. The process depends a lot upon who is available and whether or not they are interested.
>
> A lot of what Paul wants to do this fall is to make the paper more useful. Tom would probably want more news stories of a political bent. Everyone's ideal would be to do more apartment rental agency stories. Did you read that? They are a real rip-off and take money under false circumstances. We did a lot of research on them. It was both an exposé and a news story.
>
> I want us to do more stories like that or the one in this week's issue on airline safety—more consumer-oriented pieces—but they take lots of time. We should do more local investigatives, like the article on the coroner's office in Boston's City Hall. We should do stories that make a real difference—a protest that demands a response.
>
> And we need more middle of the book material—material between the arts and listings and the political and news and feature stories at the front. We need think pieces, like the story in the *New York Times Magazine* section. A woman in an apartment house was robbed—bound and gagged. What was it like? What were her fears? Did she behave bravely enough? This was a special story, and a woman wrote it from a woman's point of view. We need more material on ideas and people. I suggested to Paul that we do an article on people living together—roommates or lovers—or whatever. It should be funny and yet factual. These aren't news stories—

Paul
wants

they are people and idea combinations. And we should do more on scientists and science articles—the article in the *New York Times* on "black holes" in space is a good example.

Tom, who had joined *T.R.P.* in November of 1973, had as his prime objective introducing more organization into the editorial process. He felt progress had been made in this area, and by July, lead feature articles had been planned and were in process for the next five months.

organization!!

It was in my own self-interest to get some planning going—things were frantic here when I first came. I wish we had more full-time feature writers; we need at least three now. It would make my job easier. You get to know the regulars and how to work with them; they have to produce. But it isn't as cost effective. People don't have story ideas regularly every week, and so there are bound to be slow times when we won't get stories.

Both Paul and Tom spoke highly of the caliber of *T.R.P.*'s editorial staff, and conversations with other Boston journalists confirmed that evaluation. Some staffers had achieved awards, national publicity, and peer recognition from the wider journalistic field.

In trying to pin down *T.R.P.*'s current editorial style and format, the researcher talked with various members of the staff. Tom Friedman reflected, "Partially it's form—longer paragraphs and in-depth analysis. Partially it's an emphasis on the human dimension. We just don't feed them information; we create an ambience whereby the reader can relate to the event. We give them more than historical background, we give them more than information—we get to the basic reasons."

Joe Klein, who had received several journalist awards, contrasted *T.R.P.*'s and the *Phoenix*'s editorial style.

Our style strives for both a sense of immediacy and perspective. Our copy is written more dramatically. We're also much more careful. We want to write the definite story on the subject. Paul and I talk it out and decide what the story should be; it has to have a larger focus than just what happened last week; we take specific incidents and show how they reflect on institutions. I don't see that happening with any other publication in town.

Paul Solman commented:

Our major articles, in contrast to the *Phoenix*, are long—we do in-depth reporting. Our feature article on selling the *Encyclopaedia Britannica* was a good example. The writer actually sold *Britannicas*. We want to be able to help people see why they behave as they do. Why does a blue collar making $14,000 spend 800 bucks on a set of encyclopaedias? Or our article on the hearing aid racket is another good example. We want to be at the cutting edge—what is really going on in that business. We want to answer questions. We want the truth. But the budget limits us; we are small and they are larger. We can't compete with them in terms of coverage.

He continued: The development of a pool of feature article ideas is fairly random. A lot depends on what I read or hear from friends. We get lots of suggestions from people outside the staff. And one of my critical inputs is to gather staff who can contribute ideas. I have a sense of balance for the make-up of the paper, but I don't have a specific formula for a certain amount of political, or human interest, or exposé material in any issue or any month.

intuitive

Chuck Fager, one of the original staffers, reflected, "We have an ephemeral editorial policy now. Writers just stream in and out. The *Phoenix* does a better job of covering Boston and the State House than we do. But any differences between the *Phoenix* and us now is more individual writer style than editorial strategy."

An evolving editorial posture

In the summer of 1974, the researcher noted, the topic of future editorial direction was the object of considerable discussion, not only within the editoral staff, but within the paper at large. Paula Childs commented:

> We're not covering events enough—issues that deal with people's daily lives. We're not covering what's happening with rent control, what's happening in the ecology movement, what's happening in the neighborhoods—that kind of stuff. Also, I think we're too Cambridge-oriented. Our strongest following is Cambridge. We cover Cambridge things to a much greater extent than Boston. And I think that that's one of the reasons why people on the other side of the river continue to pick up the *Phoenix* instead of *T.R.P.*

Howard Garsh believed "more hard investigative reporting should be our first priority now." Walter Harrison wanted more emphasis on quality editorial work. Tom Friedman commented feelingly, "I want to have more impact on people's lives. My basic attitude is deep distrust of the people who run our country and our businesses. Some staffers want more emphasis on entertainment; some just want more people to buy it. I want the people to get the information they wouldn't get otherwise. I want more investigations. I want to work on an investigative paper not just a successful operation. I'm trying to hold on to my sense of moral outrage."

to each his own !

Bob Rotner, from his perspective, saw two approaches to future editorial direction. "The edit people want witty headlines. The business people want headlines that sell. The edit people feel the paper ought to be political, serve the left. The business people see it as the ultimate guide to Boston, serving the consumer element. I want it to do more investigative reporting."

Paul Solman reflected not only on near-term and future editorial direction, but plans to get there, noting:

> We are planning some minor modifications for the fall. We will have two long feature stories and a larger number of shorter stories that will provide more information in readable form. And we will expand the number of vignettes from New York City and Washington events. One of the latter might be an interview with the aide of a congressman.
>
> And we're trying to figure out what we want the paper to be. The paper is essentially a reflection of the people here, and they are not homogeneous. But in the longer run, we're working toward a personality for this paper that is intelligent, political, which I mean to say politically progressive, interesting to people, compelling, and well written.
>
> We're not real close now, but we're making progress. Our effort now is oriented to four activities. First, we simply want to get more copy available for our use. Copy can always be edited and rewritten. So getting the

basic fund is important. This means asking more of our staff people, as well as really pursuing the free-lance sources. This also means we will have to pay higher rates than competitors, pay for research, and make appeals to the really good people based on prestige, personal ties, and even convenience.

2) Second, we want to tie down regular contributors—good writers who may not be on the staff but can be relied on for quality stuff. We want to create a circle of regular free-lancers.

3) Third, we have to fight the tendency to diffuse our efforts. Accordingly, we created the position of managing editor which will free me from the day-to-day operational problems.

4) Fourth, we want to run two or three solid articles per week in the front page of the book that are smart and fascinating.

Success for most people is to be big and powerful. I don't have a specific vision of *T.R.P.* and success, but I want it to be something that serves the people. I want us to be a wing of society—out there after the bad gals and guys. Yet I want it to be entertaining too, for literate people. And I want it to be instructive to the public.

LOOKING AHEAD

The former *Cambridge Phoenix* and *T.R.P.* had been organized and had their early operating years during a period of major societal and youth unrest. Campus stories headlined strikes, riots, and "take-overs," while on the wider scene, the counterculture movement was in full bloom.

Reporters of the mid-70s' youth movement indicated that much of the past turbulence seemed to have disappeared. While the president of Ohio University did resign in June of 1974, citing "the mindless destructive events of the past week," most college campuses seemed quiet, and the counterculture movement had, in many observers' judgments, "plateaued."

The transition from activism to a more restrained protest pattern was captured for the researcher in Sara Davidson's article on the Symbionese Liberation Army. She interviewed Dan Siegel, a well-known participant in the 1969 Berkeley disturbances, about his changing career and life style.

> Siegel is 28, an attractive, modest-looking young man in a sports shirt and slacks. In 1969, when he was student-body president at Berkeley, he gave a speech that sent thousands surging down Telegraph Avenue to reclaim People's Park. Bob Dylan was singing from speaker vans: "You can have your cake and eat it, too."
>
> Siegel says he no longer had "the illusion that revolution will be easy or that a few gallant people can do it. Winning the hearts and minds of tens of thousands of people—that's what making revolution is about." He walks toward the courthouse where he is preparing a test case in which the community is suing the district attorney, and he says that it's funny but in some ways, he feels old.[12]

---

[12] *New York Times Magazine,* June 2, 1974, p. 44.

Given these changes, as well as major developments in the wider environment, the researcher wondered what, if any, impact these forces would have on the future plans of *T.R.P.* He raised the question of future direction with Paula Childs. She commented:

> I'd like to see this paper eventually be able to own its own composition shop as well as its own printing company. I'd like to see this company own its own other media resources, like its own radio station. And I'd like to see the paper get to a large enough size that we can be covering the things we should be covering. You know. Right now we're in a tug-of-war between whether to be more like a magazine or whether to be more like a newspaper. Right now, we're much more like a magazine than a newspaper.

Joe Klein, a staff member, added:

> From here I'd like to see us grow in several ways. First, I want us to develop a broader base of readers and not be read by just street people and hippies. This would mean expanding into older neighborhoods and suburbs, as well as becoming more and more frequently read downtown. I want it to have impact. Furthermore, and I guess this is a second point, I want us to expand beyond Boston to a regional and even national scope. I want us to have as many readers outside of Boston as the *Village Voice* has outside New York. And third, I want us to become an alternative for top-notch daily journalists.

Bo Burlingham, another staff writer, asked:

> Have we reached the end of our growth with this format? It has worked so well. And the answer is so important because it affects so many things. Who do we hire? Young kids just out of college and ask them for a full-time commitment? Or do we hire older more experienced part-timers who can work here—and write the book they always really wanted to create?
> It raises questions as to who our audience is—is it Cambridge, Boston, New England, or ————? How we work with that influences Howard's financing plans and Bob Williams' advertising programs. And questions, too, need to be asked editorially. Should we go on primarily with feature stories about current causes or events or institutions? There are lots of reasons why we should. They take less resources and time and are less risky. Or do we become an investigative journal? That's really rough. It takes lots of money and time to do well and it's risky.

Jan Freeman reminisced:

> So much of what we are is what we were—a collection of people who grew up in the late 60s and who, by luck, got into an organization that we like and where we can do what we want.
> Our audience is like us—it's growing up! It's no longer the 60s. Our audience isn't clear any more—it is a mixture. Paul knows this. We know we can't just do what we do best. We never have been a doctrinaire leftist paper—we have sort of been, as I told you—a newspaper-magazine. But what's next?

A *Boston Globe* reporter, Nathan Cobb, raised the question of future direction with various members of *T.R.P.* and the *Phoenix* staff. He commented:

Times change. *T.R.P.*, having achieved financial success, wonders where to go. "It's much less clear now what we should be doing than it used to be," says Paul Solman. "It used to be automatic. You didn't have to think about what you did because there was a counterculture not being covered by anyone else. Now we're asking what kinds of things we can provide that no one else can."

*   *   *   *   *

One suspects, though, that the two papers really are still viewed as a legitimate journalistic alternative by the fading remnants of the "youth culture." But out in the great beyond, out in those suburbs where folks are easing into their 30s and 40s, each may indeed be viewed as just another newspaper. "The dailies are getting more like us and we're getting more like the dailies," says Joe Klein of *T.R.P.*, an experienced and professional newsperson. "And that's all right with me. I'd like to see *T.R.P.* on every doorstep."

Bob Rotner, publisher, in talking with the researcher about his job and responsibilities as publisher, noted:

But to plan the future of the paper, and to make sure that just because the paper is successful now, it doesn't mean that it's going to be successful in a year or two, and there are certain things happening in the city and the country which need to be understood. We're not making ourselves obsolete. . . . What I hope I can do now is to make the decisions about the future by going to the appropriate places and finding out what is going to happen in the future, and then to make sure that *T.R.P.* is going in the direction it needs to go, so that it doesn't have to worry about the future.

The company and its responsibilities to society: Relating corporate strategy to ethical values

WE COME at last to the fourth component of strategy formulation—the moral and social implications of what once was considered a purely economic choice. In our consideration of strategic alternatives, we have come from what strategists *might* and *can* do to what they *want* to do. We now move to what they *ought* to do—from the viewpoint of various leaders and segments of society and their standards of right and wrong.

Ethics, like preference, may be considered a product of values. To some the suggestion that an orderly and analytical process of strategy determination should include the discussion of highly controversial ethical issues, about which honest differences of opinion are common and self-deceiving rationalization endless, is repugnant. This body of opinion is led by an immovable and doughty band of economic isolationists, of which Milton Friedman is the leader. They argue that business should be required only to live up to its legal obligations and that consideration of strategic alternatives should be exclusively economic.[1] A larger group of business leaders remain silent, probably suspecting the rhetorical virtue in public statements of corporate intent. A host of small business people are too busy surviving adversity to dwell much on this subject.

THE MORAL COMPONENT OF CORPORATE STRATEGY

The emerging view in the liberal-professional leadership of our most prominent corporations is that determining future strategy must take into account—as part of its social environment—steadily rising moral and ethical standards. Reconciling the conflict in responsibility which occurs when maximum profit and social contribution appear on the

---

[1] The classic statement of this position, which is hardly subject to modernization, is still Milton Friedman, *Capitalism and Freedom* (Chicago: The University of Chicago Press, 1962).

same agenda adds to the complexity of strategy formulation and its already clear demands for creativity. Coming to terms with the morality of choice may be the most strenuous undertaking in strategic decision.

Attention is compelled to the noneconomic consequences of corporate power and activity by a combination of forces constituting the environment of business. Most dramatic is the decline in public confidence in public and private institutions accompanying the prosecution of the Vietnam War, Watergate, and the forced resignation of a vice president and president of the United States. Distrust of business flared with the revelation by the Watergate Special Prosecutor of illegal political contributions. The Securities and Exchange Commission's probe of other illegal and questionable payments has publicized the illegal or questionable behavior of scores of well-known companies. The deposition of the top leadership of such companies as the Gulf Oil Corporation and the Lockheed Aircraft Company was a blow to the supposition that our respected companies were abiding by the law and professional standards of ethical conduct. The quick confessions of other companies to avoid prosecution were given wide publicity.

The absence of disavowal by competitors of such practices left the impression with the public that this illegality was characteristic of all business. Successive Harris polls reported that 55 percent of the public in 1966 had felt great confidence in the chief executives of large corporations, that 21 percent felt that way in 1974, and only 15 percent in 1975. A Gallup poll in July 1975 showed big business scored lowest in confidence (34 percent) compared to organized labor (38 percent), Congress (40 percent), the Supreme Court (49 percent), the Executive branch (52 percent), the military (58 percent), education (67 percent), and organized religion (68 percent).[2]

Discussions of the responsibility of business have usually until now taken individual personal integrity for granted or have assumed that the courts were adequate discipline to ensure compliance with the law. The obvious necessity for explicit company policy now makes it necessary for decision to be made about at least how compliance with the law can be ensured. The first step is a stated policy that illegality will not be condoned and enforcement provisions will begin with corporate action rather than waiting for the law and the courts.

Since political contributions and bribery are neither illegal nor even unusual in other parts of the world, explicit policy must be made with respect to other marginal, technically legal, but in American eyes, improper kinds of payments. Once embarked on this path, companies are forced to include policy decisions about other corporate and personal ethical behavior in their strategies. Presumably, except possibly for such policy as proscribing political contributions where they are legally permitted, the economic isolationists would not object to the new necessity to articulate and enforce the unspoken strategic assumption that the company would pursue its economic objectives within the law.

---

[2] Leonard Silk and David Vogel, *Ethics and Profit: The Crisis of Confidence in American Business* (New York: Simon & Schuster, 1976), pp. 21–22.

As many a corporation that has regarded itself as socially responsible is finding out, specifying and securing ethical behavior is not easy in a company with responsibility delegated through many levels of authority and degrees of autonomy. The morality of personal behavior is not the only concern. Arguments for the active participation in public affairs and the exercise of concern for the impact of economic activity upon society are gaining ground for a number of reasons.

First, corporate executives of the caliber, integrity, intelligence, and humanity capable of coping with the problems of personal morality just cited are not happy to be tarred with the brush of bribery and corruption. They are not likely to turn their backs on other problems involving corporate behavior of the middle and late 70s. The mid-decade recession, the developing energy crisis, the growing sensitivity to environmental damage by industrial and community operations, the protection of the consumer from intended or unwitting exploitation or deception, the extension of social justice, as exemplified by the demands of minority populations and women for opportunity and recognition, the general concern for the limits of growth and the so-called quality of life—all these cannot be ignored. The need is widely acknowledged to respond as a matter of conscience as well as a matter of law.

Second, it is increasingly clear that government regulation is not a good substitute for knowledgeable self-restraint. As expectations for the protection and well-being of the environment, of customers, and of employees grow more insistent, it is clear that if corporate power is to be regulated more by public law than by private conscience, much of our national energy will have to be spent keeping watch over corporate behavior, ferreting out problems, designing and revising detailed laws to deal with them, and enforcing these laws even as they become obsolete.

Executives assuming top-management responsibility today may be more sensitive on the average than their predecessors to the upgrading of our goals as a society and more responsive to the opportunity to relate corporate and public purposes. But if not, they can be sure that new regulation will force this concern upon their strategic processes. Extending the reach of strategic decision to encompass public concerns is either a voluntary response permitting latitude in choice or acquiescence to law which may involve none. New forms of regulation or effective enforcement come late to the problem without regard for feasibility or cost. The strategist can consider much earlier whether the problem is susceptible to effective and economically satisfactory solution.

CATEGORIES OF CONCERN

If you elect to admit responsiveness to society's concern about corporate power and activities to your definition of strategy, you come face to face with two major questions. What is the range of corporate involvement available to a company? What considerations should guide its choice of opportunity?

The world. The problems affecting the quality of life in the society to which the company belongs may usefully be thought of as extending through a set of densely populated spheres from the firm itself to the world community. The multinational firm, to take world society first, would find (within its economic contribution to industrialization in the developing countries) the need to measure what it takes out before it could judge its participation responsible. The willingness to undertake joint ventures rather than insist on full ownership, to share management and profits in terms not immediately related to the actual contributions of other partners, to cooperate otherwise with governments looking for alternatives to capitalism, to train nationals for skilled jobs and management positions, to reconcile different codes of ethical practice in matters of taxes and bribery—all illustrate the opportunity for combining entrepreneurship with responsibility and the terms in which strategy might be expressed.

The nation.   Within the United States, for a firm of national scope, problems susceptible to constructive attention from business occur in virtually every walk of life. To narrow too wide a choice, a company would most naturally begin with the environmental consequences of its manufacturing processes or the impact of its products upon the public. Presumably a company would first put its own house in order or embark upon a long program to make it so. Then it might take interest in other problems, either through tax-deductible philanthropic contributions or through business ventures seeking economic opportunity in social need—for example, trash disposal or health care. Education, the arts, race relations, equal opportunity for women, or even such large issues as the impact upon society of technological change compete for attention. Our agenda of national problems is extensive. It is not hard to find opportunities. The question, as in product-market possibilities, is which ones to choose.

The local community.   Closer to home are the problems of the communities in which the company operates. These constitute the urban manifestations of the national problems already referred to—inadequate housing, unemployment in the poverty culture, substandard medical care, and the like. The city, special focus of national decay and vulnerable to fiscal and other mismanagement, is an attractive object of social strategy because of its nearness and compactness. The near community allows the development of mutually beneficial corporate projects such as vocational training. Business cannot remain healthy in a sick community.

Industry.   Moving from world to country to city takes us through the full range of social and political issues which engage the attention of corporate strategists who wish to factor social responsibility into their planning. Two other less obvious but even more relevant avenues of action would be considered—the industry or industries in which the company operates and the quality of life within the company itself. Every industry, like every profession, has problems which arise from a legacy of indifference, stresses of competition, the real or imagined impossibility of interfirm cooperation under the antitrust laws. Every industry has chronic problems of its own, such as safety, product quality, pricing, and pollution in which only cooperative action can effectively pick up where regulation leaves off or makes further regulation unnecessary.

The company. Within the firm itself, a company has open opportunity for satisfying its aspirations to responsibility. The quality of any company's present strategy, for example, is probably always subject to improvement, as new technology and higher aspirations work together. But besides such important tangible matters as the quality of goods and services being offered to the public and the maintenance and improvement of ordinary craftsmanship, there are three other areas which in the future will become much more important than they seem now. The first of these is the review process set up to estimate the quality of top-management decision. The second is the impact upon individuals of the control systems and other organization processes installed to secure results. The third is a recognition of the role of the individual in the corporation.

Review of management concerns for responsibility

The everyday pressures bearing on decisions about what to do and how to get it done make almost impossible the kind of detached self-criticism which is essential to the perpetuation of responsible freedom. The opportunity to provide for systematic review sessions becomes more explicit and self-conscious. At any rate, as a category of concern, how a management can maintain sufficient detachment to estimate without self-deception the quality of its management performance is as important as any other. The proper role of the board of directors in performing this function—long since lost sight of—requires revitalization.

The caliber and strategic usefulness of a board of directors will nonetheless remain the option of the chief executive who usually determines its function. How much he uses his board for the purposes of improving the quality of corporate strategy and planning turns, as usual, on the sincerity of his interest and his skill. Recent research has illuminated the irresponsibility of inaction in the face of problems requiring the perspective available only to properly constituted boards. This organization resource is available to general managers who recognize dormancy as waste and seek counsel in cases of conflicting responsibility. A number of large corporations, including General Motors, have established Public Responsibility Committees of the board to focus attention on social issues.

The effective provision by a board of responsible surveillance of the moral quality of a management's strategic decisions means that current stirrings of concern about conflicts of interest will soon result in the withdrawal from boards of bankers representing institutions performing services to the company, of lawyers (in some instances) representing a firm retained by the company, and other suppliers or customers, as well as more scrupulous attention to present regulations about interlocking interests. As much attention will soon be given to avoiding the possibility of imputing conflict of interest to a director as to avoiding the actual occurrence. Stronger restrictions on conflict of interest will also affect employees of the firm, including the involvement of individuals with social-action organizations attacking the firm.

Impact of control systems on ethical performance

Second, the ethical and economic quality of an organization's performance is vitally affected by its control system, which inevitably leads people, if it is effective at all, to do what will make them look good in the terms of the system rather than what their opportunities and problems, which the system may not take cognizance of, actually require. We will examine the unintended consequences of control and measurement systems when we come to the implementation of corporate strategy; in the meantime we should note that unanticipated pressures to act irresponsibly may be applied by top management who would deplore this consequence if they knew of it. The process of promotion by which persons are moved from place to place so fast that they do not develop concern for the problems of the community in which they live or effective relationships within which to accomplish anything unintentionally weakens the participation of executives in community affairs. The tendency to measure executives in divisionalized companies on this year's profits reduces sharply their motivation to invest in social action with returns over longer times. Lifelong habits of neutrality and noninvolvement eventually deprive the community, in a subtle weakening of its human resources, of executive experience and judgment. Executive cadres are in turn deprived of real-life experience with political and social systems which they ultimately much need.

The individual and the corporation

The actual quality of life in a business organization turns most crucially on how much freedom is accorded to the individual. Certainly most firms consider responsibility to their members a category of concern as important as external constituencies. It is as much a matter of enlightened self-interest as of responsibility to provide conditions encouraging the convergence of the individual's aspirations with those of the corporation, to provide conditions for effective productivity, and to reward employees for extraordinary performance.

With the entry of the corporation into controversial areas comes greater interest on the part of organization members to take part in public debate. It becomes possible for individuals to make comments on social problems that could be embarrassing to the corporation. It is at best difficult to balance the freedom of individuals and the consequences of their participation in public affairs against the interests of the corporation. The difficulty is increased if the attitudes of management, which are instinctively overprotective of the corporation, are harsh and restrictive. Short-run embarrassments and limited criticism from offended groups—even perhaps a threatened boycott—may be a small price to pay for the continued productivity within the corporation of people whose interests are deep and broad enough to cause them to take stands on public issues. The degree to which an organization is efficient, productive, creative, and capable of development is dependent in large part on the maintenance of a climate in which the individual does not feel suppressed, and in which a kind of freedom (analogous to that which the corporation enjoys in a free enterprise society) is permitted as a matter of course. Overregulation of the individual by corporate policy is no more appropriate internally than overregulation of the corporation by government. On the other hand, personal responsibility is as appropriate to individual liberty as corporate responsibility is to corporate freedom.

The range of concerns

What corporate strategists have to be concerned with, then, ranges from the most global of the problems of world society to the uses of freedom by a single person in the firm. The problems of their country, community, and industry lying between these extremes make opportunity for social contribution exactly coextensive with the range of economic opportunity before them. The problem of choice may be met in the area of responsibility in much the same way as in product-market combinations and in developing a program for growth and diversification.

The business firm, as an organic entity intricately affected by and affecting its environment, is as appropriately adaptive, our concept of corporate strategy suggests, to demands for responsible behavior as for economic service. Special satisfactions and prestige, if not economic rewards, are available for companies that are not merely adaptive but take the lead in shaping the moral and ethical environment within which their primary economic function is performed. Such firms are more persuasive than others, moreover, in convincing the public of the inherent impossibility of satisfying completely all the conflicting claims made upon business.

CHOICE OF STRATEGIC ALTERNATIVES FOR SOCIAL ACTION

The choice of avenues in which to participate will, of course, be influenced by the personal values of the managers making the decision. In the absence of powerful predispositions, the inner coherence of the corporate strategy would be extended by choosing issues most closely related to the economic strategy of the company, to the expansion of its markets, to the health of its immediate environment, and to its own industry and internal problems. The extent of appropriate involvement depends importantly on the resources available. Because the competence of the average corporation outside its economic functions is severely limited, it follows that a company should not venture into good works that are not strategically related to its present and prospective economic functions.

As in the case of personal values and individual idiosyncrasy, a company may be found making decisions erratically related to nonstrategic motives. However noble these may be, they are not made strategic and thus defensible and valid by good intentions alone. Rather than make large contributions to X University because its president is a graduate, it might better develop a pattern of educational support that blends the company's involvement in the whole educational system, its acknowledged debt for the contributions of technical or managerial education to the company, and its other contributions to its communities. What makes participation in public affairs strategic rather than improvisatory is (as we have seen in conceiving economic strategy) a definition of objectives taking all other objectives into account and a plan that reflects the company's definition of itself not only as a purveyor of goods and services but as a responsible institution in its society.

The strategically directed company then will have a strategy for support of community institutions as explicit as its economic stragegy and as its decisions about the kind of organization it intends to be and the kind of people it intends to attract to its membership. It is easy and proper, when margins allow it, to make full use of tax deductibility, through contributions, from which it expects no direct return. The choice of worthy causes, however, should relate to the company's concept of itself and thus directly to its economic mission. It should enter into new social service fields with the same questions about its resources and competence that new product-market combinations inspire. In good works as in new markets, opportunity without the competence to develop it is illusory. Deliberate concentration on limited objectives is preferable to scattered short-lived enthusiasm across a community's total need.

Policy for ethical and moral personal behavior, once the level of integrity has been decided, is not complicated by a wide range of choice. The nature of the company's operations defines the areas of vulnerability—purchasing, rebates, price fixing, fee splitting, customs facilitation, bribery, dubious agents' fees, conflict of interest, theft, or falsification of records. Where problems appear or danger is sensed specific rules can be issued. As in the case of government regulation of the firm, these should not be overdetailed or mechanical, for there is no hope of anticipating the ingenuity of the willful evader. Uncompromising penalties for violations of policy intent or the rarely specified rule will do more to clarify strategy in this area than thousands of words beforehand. The complexity of elevating individual behavior is thus a matter of implementation of strategy more properly discussed in the context of organization processes such as motivation and control.

DETERMINATION OF STRATEGY

We have now before us the major determinants of strategy. The cases studied so far have required consideration of what the strategy of the firm is and what, in your judgment, it ought to be. Concerned so far with the problem of formulating a proper strategy rather than implementing it, you have become familiar with the principal aspects of formulation—namely, (1) appraisal of present and foreseeable opportunity and risk in the company's environment, (2) assessment of the firm's unique combination of present and potential corporate resources or competences, (3) determination of the noneconomic personal and organizational preferences to be satisfied, and (4) identification and acceptance of the social responsibilities of the firm. The strategic decision is one that can be reached only after all these factors have been considered and the action implications of each assessed.

In your efforts to analyze the cases, you have experienced much more of the problem of the strategist than can be described on paper. When you have relinquished your original idea as to what a company's strategy should be in favor of a more imaginative one, you have seen that the formulation process has an essential creative aspect. In your effort to differentiate your thinking about an individual firm from the conventional thinking of its industry, you have looked for new opportunities and for new applications of corporate competence. You have learned how to define a product in terms of its present and potential functions rather than of its physical properties. You have probably learned a good deal about how to assess the special competence of a firm from its past accomplishments, and how to identify management's values and aspirations. You may have gained some ability to rank preferences in order of their strength—your own among others.

The problem implicit in striking a balance between the company's apparent opportunity and its evident competence and between your own personal values and concepts of responsibility and those of the company's actual management is not an easy one. The concepts we have been discussing should help you make a decision, but they will not determine your decision for you. Whenever choice is compounded of rational analysis which can have more than one outcome, of aspiration and desire which can run the whole range of human ambition, and a sense of responsibility which changes the appeal of alternatives, it cannot be reduced to quantitative approaches or to the exactness which management science can apply to narrower questions. Managers contemplating strategic decisions must be willing to make them without the guidance of decision rules, with confidence in their own judgment, which will have been seasoned by repeated analyses of similar questions. They must be aware that more than one decision is possible and that they are not seeking the single right answer. They can take encouragement from the fact that the manner in which an organization implements the chosen program can help to validate the original decision.

Some of the most difficult choices confronting a company are those which must be made among several alternatives that appear equally attractive and also equally desirable. Once the analysis of opportunity has produced an inconveniently large number of possibilities, any firm has difficulty in deciding what it wants to do and how the new activities will be related to the old.

In situations where opportunity is approximately equal and economic promise is offered by a wide range of activities, the problem of making a choice can be reduced by reference to the essential character of the company and to the kind of company the executives wish to run. The study of alternatives from this point of view will sooner or later reveal the greater attractiveness of some choices over others. Economic analysis and calculations of return on investment, though of course essential, may not crucially determine the outcome. Rather, the logjam of decision can only be broken by a frank exploration of executive aspirations regarding future development, including perhaps the president's own wishes with respect to the kind of institution he or she prefers to head, carried on as part of a free and untrammeled investigation of what human needs the organization would find satisfaction in serving. That return on investment alone will point the way ignores the values implicit in the calculations and the contribution which an enthusiastic commitment to new projects can make. The rational examination of alternatives and the determination of purpose are among the most important and most neglected of all human activities. The final decision, which should be made as deliberately as possible after a detailed consideration of the issues we have attempted to separate, is an act of will and desire as much as of intellect.

Xerox Corporation

On September 8, 1971, Mr. C. Peter McColough, then president and chief executive officer of the Xerox Corporation, announced an experimental Social Service Leave Program to begin in January 1972. The program provided an opportunity for approximately 20 Xerox employees in the United States to take up to a one-year leave of absence, with full pay and benefits, and devote the time to working with a social service organization of their choice. They were also guaranteed the same or an equivalent job with the same pay, responsibilities, status and opportunity for advancement upon return to the company.

In announcing the program to Xerox employees, Mr. McColough spoke of corporate and individual commitment and what the program represented for each:

> Xerox has always had a basic philosophy that we should be involved as a corporation in the problems of our society. We've encouraged our people to be involved. Social Service Leave is a logical extension of our commitment. We are determined to put something back into society.
>
> Many of our people share our commitment. But on a part-time basis, there is only so much they can do. A lot of them would like to really sink their teeth into a problem full time. We'll give them a chance to do this during the prime of their working careers, when they're best able to do it. They won't have to wait until they retire.
>
> Many of our best people would not be here today if Xerox stood only for profits.
>
> In the future, our conduct as corporate citizens will be even more important—if that's possible—as we try to recruit the best young people available. As a result of programs like the Social Service Leave, we think that the bright young people will be more apt to join us than some other big company.

By January, Mr. McColough and others in top management were beginning to evaluate the program to determine whether it ought to be continued and, if so, whether the scope, policies and procedures underlying it were appropriate. As far as they could determine, it had been favorably received both inside and outside the company. Several overseas affiliates had evidenced an interest in a program of their own, usually to be operated under somewhat different policies. Moreover, it had so far been implemented according to plan and without serious mishap. On the other hand, a number of unforeseen organizational problems had already been encountered and the difficult tasks of responding to the needs of the men and women on leave and replacing them in equivalent career opportunities remained ahead.

The evaluation was accompanied by a degree of urgency. There was a general feeling among those closely involved in planning the program that the best time from the employees' standpoint to begin a social leave was in September, which, if adopted, would advance the announcement of a 1972–73 program to April or May.

XEROX HISTORY

In 1971 Xerox had sales of $1.94 billion and profits of $212.6 million, placing it among the largest fifty-five industrial corporations in the *Fortune* 500. Growth had been spectacular since 1959 when sales were $33.3 million and profits $2.1 million. In fact, from 1960 to 1970, earnings per share increased at a compound rate of 47.3% per year, highest on the *Fortune* list.

The primary source of growth for Xerox had come through the commercial development of an electrostatic-photographic copying process later known as xerography. Formed in 1906 in Rochester, New York, as the Haloid Corporation by Joseph R. Wilson and three associates to process and sell sensitized photographic paper, the company had struggled through the depression and emerged from the war years with sales in 1946 of $6,750,000 and profits of $101,000. That year Joseph C. Wilson succeeded his father as president. Confronted by increasing competition and decreasing margins in traditional product lines, the younger Mr. Wilson was eager to develop new products but lacked the resources to support a significant research effort. At this time the Battelle Institute, a non-profit research organization, had been seeking industrial support for the development of a copying process patented by Chester Carlson in 1940 and since 1944 supported by the Institute. Although numerous corporations, including Kodak, IBM and RCA, had turned the invitation down, Mr. Wilson in 1947 agreed to acquire from Battelle certain licensing rights in return for future royalty payments and an annual contribution of $25,000. A short time later Xerox renegotiated the arrangement and became the sole licensing agency for all patents in the xerography field.

Xerox invested heavily in research during the next years, greatly expanding its patent position, and yielding a series of specialized applications for xerography which by the mid-1950s contributed over half of the company's revenues. From 1953 to 1960 over $70 million was poured into research, slightly more than half of it contributed by outside debt and equity financing. It was not, however, until 1960 and the introduction of the 914, the first fully automatic dry copier in the office equipment industry, that this investment really began to pay off.

On the strength of the 914, sales nearly tripled from 1960 to 1962 as Xerox became the leader in the copier field. The company sought to expand that position by aggressively broadening its product line to include desk top copiers and high-speed machines with expanded reproduction capabilities. As machine speeds increased and reproduction quality improved, the traditional distinction between the copying and duplicating fields became blurred. The pace of development and marketing efforts in office copiers and duplicators was intense as the partial list of product introductions below suggests:

Year	Product	Feature
1960	914	Basic console model (400 copies per hour)
1963	813	Desk top model (330 copies per hour)
1965	2400	Copier-duplicator (2,400 copies per hour)
1966	720	Expanded version of 914 (720 copies per hour)
1967	660	Expanded version of 813 (660 copies per hour)
1968	3600	Expanded version of 2400 (3,600 copies per hour)
1969	7000	Duplicator, expanded capabilities (3,600 copies per hour)
1971	4000	Small console, expanded capabilities (2,000 copies per hour)

By 1971, Xerox was estimated in the business press to have 65% to 80% of the office copier market in the United States. The company's record had encouraged competition from such large firms as Eastman Kodak, Minnesota Mining, Litton, Singer, and Sperry Rand and a variety of smaller ones. A recent entrant was IBM which in April 1970 introduced a machine having much in common with the Xerox model 720. *Financial World*,[1] noting that some 70% of commercial and government establishments already contained a copier, was among those predicting increasing competition in the future. Nevertheless, Xerox 1971 revenues from copiers and rentals in the United States increased 12% over the previous year, with steady improvement relative to 1970 throughout the year.

In 1956, Xerox formed a joint venture with the Rank organization of London to manufacture and sell xerographic products in world markets, a relationship which in 1961 also led to the formation of a second joint venture between Rank-Xerox and Fuji Photo Film Co., Fuji-Xerox, directed specifically at markets in the Far East. Revenues overseas also increased dramatically after the introduction of the 914. Then in 1969 Xerox purchased the 51st percent of Rank-Xerox and renegotiated certain royalty provisions in exchange for stock valued at $20 million.

During the 1970s, Xerox sought participation in several new fields. First, in 1963 Electro Optical Systems (EOS), an aerospace company involved in laser technology, solar power conversion and space reconnaissance, was acquired to gain entry into the high technology, government financed, R & D business. Then, beginning in 1964 and con-

---

[1] "Copiers: Competition Heating Up," *Financial World*, May 6, 1970, p. 6 ff.

cluding in 1968 with the acquisition of a prominent textbook publisher, Ginn & Co., Xerox assembled an education group producing a wide range of materials and information services. Finally, in 1969 in exchange for approximately $1 billion in stock, the company acquired Scientific Data Systems, a mainframe computer manufacturer with revenues of $100 million, about 70% of it derived from scientific and engineering applications.

These new ventures had not, as yet, produced a record approaching that in office copiers. Cutbacks and reallocations in government programs had seriously affected the aerospace business and dampened the growth in spending for education. The computer group, renamed Xerox Data Systems (XDS) had been subject to similar pressures and, in part due to more conservative accounting policies, had been operating at a loss. Revenues from computer products were off about 20% in 1971 and management indicated that losses were expected to continue through 1973.

A breakdown of revenues by product line was reported as follows:

	1969	1970	1971
Business products	56%	58%	56%
International operations	27	30	34
Computer products	8	5	3
Educational materials and information services	6	6	6
Government sponsored research and military products	3	1	1
	100%	100%	100%

Profits after taxes from international operations were $72 million in 1970 and $92 million in 1971 or 38% and 43%, respectively, of the corporate total. A financial summary is provided in Exhibit 1.

Xerox had a publicly stated goal of achieving continuing growth of 20% per year in earnings per share with a return on stockholder investment of 20%. This target was generally perceived in the organization to be a very demanding one. In 1971 Mr. McColough indicated that growth would be guided by two broad policies, the first directed toward industry leadership in the information industry and the second toward becoming a "great multinational company."

> We think that our field of interest is the business of supplying knowledge and information on a worldwide basis. It seems to me that this will be the fastest growing business in the world in the 1970s. The demand for knowledge and information in every country of the world is increasing geometrically each year. There seems to be no limit to where we can go in that field if we apply ourselves to it in the right way. . . . I think in the middle 70s, you will see us bring [computer and imaging capabilities] together in combination to offer new services that will be very important to our business worldwide.
>
> * * * * * *
>
> One of our major objectives for the 1970s clearly has to be to make Xerox a great multinational company. Multinational. Not inter-

national. In the 1960s, as we spread our wings from the United States into the rest of the world through various partnerships we became an international company in the sense that we operated in many parts of the world.

But in the 1970s we must become a multinational company. Among other things a multinational company must provide opportunities for all its people regardless of what country they come from. The young person who joins the company today—whether in Milan or Sao Paulo or New York City—should have an equal opportunity to take my job in the future.

* * * * *

We must also put great emphasis in the 1970s on having manufacturing operations in many locations. We have to realize that if we are going to be large in the major countries of the world, we are going to have to contribute to those countries. We can't simply go in with products manufactured somewhere else; we must put something back in.

ORGANIZATIONAL STRUCTURE

Managing the company's growth constituted a formidable challenge for the Xerox organization. The number of employees grew from 9,000 in 1960 to 63,000 in 1971, about 25,000 of them overseas. Moreover, by the late 1970s this total was expected to more than double again. The average employee in the United States was estimated to be less than 30 years old and about a third of them had been with the company less than three years. Xerox had entered the 1960s with a functional organization but over the next decade changes at all levels were frequent as the company moved toward a divisionalized structure. The consequences of growth for individual managers were described by one personnel executive in the Business Products Group (BPG), which alone had 33,000 employees:

> Xerox has the ability to make organization changes quickly. In BPG going from $100 million to $1.2 billion in ten years has meant that just by staying in the same job, a manager's responsibilities increase dramatically. One of the rewards of my work is seeing people literally grow. Of course, some don't and we have had to move them down or aside. We no longer have employment contracts with our top managers but instead give them a six-month turnaround time should we decide to part ways.

Rapid growth had also prompted the company to seek managers for high-level positions from outside the company. Mr. Archie McCardell (45), president, who joined Xerox in 1966 from Ford[2] where he had held various jobs in the finance and control area, commented:

> We have grown so fast that there has not been time for enough managers to come up through the ranks. We have brought in a num-

---

[2] Other senior executives coming to Xerox from other companies since 1967 included Dr. Jacob Goldman (Sr. V.P., R & D) and Mr. James O'Neill (Gr. V.P., BPG) from Ford, Mr. Joseph Flavin (Ex. V.P.) and Mr. William Glavin (Gr. V.P. XDS) from IBM, and Mr. Robert Haigh (Gr. V.P., Education Group) from Standard Oil (Ohio).

ber of outsiders at high levels and will probably continue to do so for another two or three years. With the pressures on our organization, getting sufficient attention devoted to management development has been a continuing source of concern for us.

In 1969, Xerox announced plans to relocate the corporate offices in Connecticut. On an interim basis, pending construction of a new office building in Greenwich, headquarters were moved to the neighboring town of Stamford, Connecticut.

In December 1971, a major rearrangement at the corporate level was announced to align the organization with the company's strategy for the 1970s. The announcement, although planned for some time, took place several weeks after the unexpected death of Mr. Wilson. Mr. McColough, who came to Xerox in 1954, rose through sales to executive vice president in 1962, president in 1966, and chief executive officer in 1968, became chairman. Mr. McCardell, executive vice president since 1968, became president and chief operating officer. All U.S. operations in computers, copying/duplicating, education and aerospace were assigned to Mr. Raymond Hay (43), who formerly was responsible for BPG and for a short time overseas activities as well. Mr. Joseph Flavin (43), formerly senior vice president for planning and finance and then briefly in charge of XDS, was made responsible for international operations. The new organization is shown in Exhibit 2.

CORPORATE RESPONSIBILITY

Xerox management believed that the company was a social as well as an economic institution and had responsibilities to society beyond economic performance. Mr. Wilson articulated this attitude in a 1964 speech:

> The corporation cannot refuse to take a stand on public issues of major concern; failure to act is to throw its weight on the side of the status quo, and the public interprets it that way.
>
> Inevitably the corporation is involved in economic, social and political dynamics whether it wills or not, and to ignore the noneconomic consequences of business decisions is to invite outside intervention. . . .

There was a general feeling in the company that Mr. McColough's commitment to this point of view was also very strong.

The company had been involved in a number of programs which related to this social concern. In 1968 Xerox participated with local community organizations in Rochester in the founding of FIGHTON, Inc., a manufacturing company owned and managed by Blacks in the inner city, and continued to be a major customer for its products and a consultant to its management. Investments and deposits had also been made in minority-owned banks. Internally Xerox had instituted a minority hiring and development program that had substantially increased the number of minority employees. A pollution abatement control committee had also been formed to monitor the company's activities in that area.

The company had been active in sharing sponsorship of TV events of educational or cultural significance, among the recent programs being the "Civilisation" series and Sesame Street. In addition, charitable contributions of about $5.0 million were made during 1971, up from $4.4 million in 1970 and $3.7 million in 1969. The majority of the funds went to educational institutions; other recipients included Community Chests and United Funds in locations having Xerox facilities and a wide variety of civic, legal, health and urban affairs organizations. Asked in 1969 whether contributions should be cut back, 90.2% of the stockholders, representing 96.9% of the shares, voted "no."

THE SOCIAL SERVICE LEAVE PROGRAM— CONCEPTION AND DESIGN

In August 1970, Mr. McCardell and Mr. James Wainger took the night flight from New York to Los Angeles. Mr. Wainger, who originally joined Xerox in 1960 but left the company from 1966 to 1969 to teach and write plays, had been made director of personnel two months earlier.[3] The conversation turned to how Xerox might be more responsive to social and employee needs in the 1970s. Mr. McCardell suggested that the company consider making some of its people available to work on problems of their choosing. By the time the wheels touched in Los Angeles, a leave program had been outlined in some detail.

Upon his return, Mr. Wainger discussed the idea briefly with Mr. Sanford Kaplan, his immediate superior at the time, and Mr. Mc-Colough, receiving in each case enthusiastic support. He then described the program in a memorandum sent to corporate executives (see Exhibit 3).

Mr. McColough suggested one modification almost immediately: that the evaluation committee be composed of lower level Xerox employees rather than a prestigious outside board. He commented:

> Xerox is a very young company. Our average age is less than 30 and we will be hiring tens of thousands of young people in the next few years. Large corporations inevitably tend to be dictatorial which runs counter to the needs of many young people. They would like to have a voice in policy and not have to wait until late in their careers. This committee is the first of a number of things that will involve our employees in either decision or advisory roles.
>
> I also believe that such a committee can do a better job of evaluating projects. Its members are probably more in tune with the needs that those applying for leave are hoping to satisfy. This procedure will erase any tinge that the committee is there to serve our [top management's] interests.

While the remainder of the top management group was positive about the leave program, there was some feeling that the fall of 1970 was not the appropriate time to initiate it. A soft economy in the latter

---

[3] Mr. Wainger recalled that his assignment had come as a surprise; "I told Peter [McColough] I had no experience in personnel, but he said what he was looking for was someone with a sense for the company in a society in evolution." He was elected vice president in 1971.

half of the year was putting pressure on operating budgets which in turn was forcing "modest" layoffs at headquarters and in Rochester. As one manager put it, "the psychology didn't set right—to be laying off and at the same time doing this." Mr. McColough decided to delay the announcement of the program.

Mr. Wainger began to reactivate the program the following spring. It was June, however, before the interview with Mr. McColough which was to appear in the brochure describing it could be arranged. Then with summer vacations approaching and the desire to "do the brochure right," the announcement date was put off until September.

In the meantime, Mr. Wainger set in motion a procedure for selecting members of the Evaluation Committee. He first contacted the top personnel executive in each division and asked them to identify people in their units who were relatively young, had some background in social service activities, possessed an "intellectual and emotional affinity for social issues," and were not members of top management. He then reviewed the list with Mr. Robert Schneider, assistant to the president and formerly manager of corporate contributions, and selected from it those that appeared most appropriate, keeping in mind the desire for a representative group in terms of operating unit, race, background and sex. The two men, individually, then visited these people in the field. Offers to join the committee were extended to and accepted on the spot by the first five interviewed. Messrs. Wainger and Schneider, as the two "old men," rounded out the committee shown in Exhibit 4.

The final ground rules for administering the program were also worked out for inclusion in the brochure. Xerox employees in the United States with three or more years of service were to be eligible for leave. No restrictions were to be placed on the type of projects acceptable except that they be legal, nonpartisan and under the sponsorship of an existing nonprofit organization of some kind. In addition to describing how they proposed to spend their time, applicants were to have the written acceptance of the sponsoring agency. It was Mr. McCardell's original idea that to help insure the commitment of applicants to projects, the company should play no part in matching people and opportunities.

Applications were to be submitted directly to the Evaluation Committee; employee names, however, were not to be available to the committee during their deliberations. Employees would not be asked to seek permission to apply nor were their superiors to be consulted at any time in the selection process. The brochure also noted that, "It's possible that in a rare case a person selected may be so essential in his work at Xerox that he cannot be released. If that should happen, the burden of proof will be on the manager and the final decision will be made by Peter McColough."

Mr. McColough commented on the reasons behind avoiding an "up the line" approval procedure:

> I do not want Social Service Leave to be looked upon in the organization as a reward for good performance. Nor do I want it, speaking pragmatically, to be a device for managers to get rid of people they

don't want. There are other ways of doing these things, and this program should not be used as a substitute. I also do not want managers to be able to block someone from seeking leave. I would say O.K. to a manager who is emphatic about not losing a subordinate, but I could not do it lightly. Finally, putting the decision in the hands of an independent committee removes the inference that we have our own pet projects. I am able to tell agencies who call me directly that the choice is not mine.

Mr. Wainger added some further thoughts on the organization of the program:

Having a multi-level approval process—God, doesn't that sound like jargon!—would dilute the corporate commitment to the project. This is *Xerox* doing something and not the units themselves, and the judgments should be those of the corporation. I favor functionalizing not decentralizing responsibility for an activity such as this.

A bottoms-up approach, I'm afraid, would introduce a lot of extraneous judgments in this case which would cut the heart out of the program. Worst of all, approval would be based on their [operation managers] view of the value of a project. That view could be influenced by administrative convenience—can't let a good subordinate go and so forth. That's especially serious when it comes to salesmen because so often those skills are what are most needed by social service agencies. We've gone to great lengths to involve on the committee the right people with right values to judge applications.

While the employees were on leave, their salaries, including a normal increase, were to be paid from a corporate account and not charged to the operating units. The aggregate cost was estimated at about $600,000.

ANNOUNCEMENT AND REACTION

On September 9, every Xerox employee in the United States was mailed a letter from Mr. McColough, the illustrated brochure and an application form (reproduced as Exhibit 5) which together described the program, the Evaluation Committee and the procedures for applying. Thus, everyone in the company, with the exception of those few corporate executives who had been directly involved, was apprised of the program at the same time. Although he did not like the idea of a press release, Mr. Wainger had one issued to avoid the confusion and conflicting stories that he felt might reach the media from such a large mailing.

The outside reaction was "overwhelming." Newspapers all over the country carried stories about the Social Service Leave, a television network inquired if a special feature might be made of it, and numerous radio stations and magazine reporters called for interviews. Mr. Wainger spoke for many in the corporation when he said:

I felt embarrassed about the attention this has received and did what I could to draw back from it. After all, the program is a very modest, experimental expression of our concern. Naturally, the publicity is good for our image, but that's not the reason we did it.

Several hundred social agencies have also called and we have had to send them a letter saying it's up to the employees, not us.

Within the organization, the response was described by one manager as that of "quiet admiration—a feeling that the company is really putting money and people behind its words."

From his vantage point, Mr. McColough said:

> The response I have had from the organization has all been favorable. In this case, that should not be surprising, of course, since it was clearly my decision and had already been done. I am sure, on the other hand, that had the expense gone into the operating budgets, there would have been some opposition.

There being no further policy matters to attend to, for the time being, Mr. Wainger's office settled down to wait until November 1, the deadline for applications.

APPLICATIONS

There was little conversation in the organization during September and October about social leave. Mr. Douglas Reid, manager of personnel operations at BPG, received a few phone calls from applicants in need of information which he referred to Mr. Wainger's office and on one occasion from a manager in support of a subordinate's project. However, the period was an active one for those assembling proposals. Mrs. Frayda Cooper, an editor at Ginn and eventually among those selected for leave, recalled her experience:

> I had lunch with Mr. Baker's[4] secretary on September 9 and she told me about the Social Leave Program. It perked my interest. For some time I have wanted to work with the aged. That night I talked about it with my son who encouraged me to try. When the brochure came a few days later I had mixed reactions; the committee didn't look very old—would they be interested in a program for the elderly? On the other hand, this field wasn't mentioned among the examples it provided —maybe if the committee tried to pick people in different areas, others wouldn't have thought of this one. Anyway, I decided to go ahead.
>
> I didn't talk about my plans in the company. The executive editor knew I was applying because I borrowed his brochure to write the proposal, having given mine away and being unable to find another one. Of course, out of courtesy, I had earlier told my immediate superior. I didn't have the sense that a lot of people around me were applying but with 25,000 people eligible, there were bound to be a lot.

In the next three weeks, Mrs. Cooper talked during lunch hours and Saturdays with a variety of people in government and social agencies and at Brandeis University about the problems of the elderly and her interests and background. These discussions resulted in a letter of support, including a budget of $17,000 for various expenses, and a four-page work plan from the Massachusetts Department of Community Affairs, which Mrs. Cooper appended to her handwritten application form. Since a manuscript had recently been accepted by Ginn con-

---

[4] Mr. Baker was president of Ginn.

ditional upon her availability to edit it, she advanced the starting date in the leave proposal to April 1972.

Another successful applicant was Mr. Irving Bell, a salesman with Xerox Graphic Services. Referring to these weeks he said:

> I found out about the program by reading the AP story in the newspaper. I was interested—said to myself, "Now that's a good idea!" I have a few rich friends and they never get a year to do their thing. I started to think about my background and where I'd fit; I wanted to contribute more than the ordinary person working at night.
>
> This was right after Attica.[5] I have some friends who talked with me about the prisons in Massachusetts and that got me thinking. A few years ago I had taught at a technical school, but unfortunately teaching was a luxury I couldn't afford then. Nevertheless, it was very gratifying. It seemed to me that someone who wanted to teach in penal institutions could give a little dignity and a pride of accomplishment to some people who really need it.
>
> It was a lonely time, but working on this was such a personal thing. I thought my program was pretty good—I used to dream about it. I brought my plans up a little at home, but never mentioned them to my boss. Maybe I was hedging my risk—in case I didn't get it. I figured there would be an application from everyone who was eligible.

A few applications were received in Mr. Wainger's office in the first two weeks, but then the flow virtually stopped. By mid-October only 30 were in hand. However, the number began to increase rapidly during the last week; the total rose to 96 by Friday, October 28 and to 197 by November 1, including all those postmarked before midnight. Another 20 or so were postmarked after the deadline and were regretfully disqualified. Each application was given a quick review by the legal department to assess whether the project and agency involved was politically nonpartisan and legal. None was eliminated.

EVALUATION AND SELECTION

On November 1 the Evaluation Committee was convened at Xerox headquarters in Stamford. Since, with the exception of the two corporate managers, the committee members did not know one another, Mr. Wainger invited them to his house for dinner the night before to help them become acquainted with one another. The next morning, the group met with Mr. McCardell who told them that the corporation was not going to give them instructions on who or what should be selected and that it was their responsibility to set standards to govern their choices.

The committee then read a dozen proposals and with this common background set about developing the evaluation process. After considerable discussion seven criteria evolved:

1. Social impact
2. Ability (of applicant to fulfill proposal)
3. Commitments (of both individual and agency)

---

[5] There had been a violent end to a prison revolt at Attica State Prison in New York State in September 1971.

4. Innovativeness
5. Multiplier effect
6. Continuity of program (after volunteer leaves)
7. Realism

An eighth one—favorable or unfavorable impact on the corporation—
was explicitly raised and set aside as not in the spirit of the Social
Leave Program. The committee then agreed that each member should
study each proposal and grade it high, medium, or low. After a batch
of 25 or 30 had been read, the committee would then stop and compare
notes before going on.

Mr. Wainger described the tenor of the ensuing deliberations in
these terms:

> The discussions were very democratic. There was surprisingly little
> ego involved. Although I acted as chairman to keep the book,[6] I con-
> sciously avoided dominating the discussion. In most cases there was
> a consensus on the low end. If there was wide disagreement, we
> would stop and talk it through, which often led to changes in opinions.
> As a result, some applications went quickly while others occupied us
> for two hours.
> After we had been through most of the proposals, it became clear
> that some of them were bubbling up as clear winners—seven in fact.
> We listed these by area of concern. Then someone said that they were
> all similar in that they exhibited a high intellectual content and were
> global in scope—proposals to set up programs or work on an institu-
> tional level. On the other hand, many of those we had given low
> evaluations to were one-on-one type projects. Someone else noted that
> all the pictures in the brochure showed people helping people in a very
> direct way. Was narrow bad? Was that what we had encouraged?
> The debate lasted a while and eventually resulted in a decision to go
> back and re-evaluate some of those we had rated poorly.

The committee labored with an increasing sense of cohesiveness
from 9:00 A.M. until dinnertime from Monday to Thursday and concluded in the midafternoon Friday. As the week progressed, the committee identified 38 proposals in 17 areas of social concern to be given
special attention. A conscious attempt was made to spread the final
choices across these areas of concern (15 were eventually included).
In addition, a less explicit effort was made to use the salary information
requested on the application to insure that a balanced cross-section of
levels in the organization was represented.

Ultimately 21 employees were selected, 2 of them requesting six-
month leaves. Included in the group were three women and eighteen
men. Their ages ranged from 26 to 60 and lengths of service at Xerox
from 3 to 10 years. Four had monthly salaries of less than $850 while
one had a monthly salary in excess of $4,000. Thirteen were employed
in BPG with the remainder spread among other line and staff groups.
People and projects are described in Exhibit 6. Another five employees
were named as alternates, with any substitutions to be made in the

---

[6] The only record of the meeting was kept on a flip chart; one page devoted to
criteria, two more to areas of social concern and employee proposals and two to an
analysis of those selected by age, salary level and operating unit.

same field if possible. The alternates were not to be notified and remained identified by number only.

Before the committee adjourned, Mr. McCardell met with them again. He asked the group, "If you had another 10 places, could you recommend individuals to fill them with equal enthusiasm?" The group said, "No." He then asked, "Are there five among the ones you have selected that you consider marginal?" Again the group said, "No."

That afternoon registered, special delivery letters of acceptance were sent to each of the winners. With the letter was a plane ticket and an invitation to attend a meeting at the Westchester Country Club near Stamford the following Friday and Saturday morning. The purposes of the meeting were to provide the participants with an opportunity to understand the policies to govern them while on leave, to share backgrounds to meet members of the Evaluation Committee and to receive some advance counseling on the stresses and frustrations many of them were likely to encounter as they left the structured life of a large corporation. They were told to keep their selection in confidence until after the meeting, though it was anticipated that they might have to tell their managers in order to explain their two-day absence.

All 21 attended the meeting. Mr. McColough and Mr. McCardell mingled with the group and addressed them briefly on Friday. In addition to a considerable amount of time for informal conversation, the schedule included group meetings in which each participant described his program, and others in which an industrial psychologist and a "down to earth" urban consultant discussed potential problems. Company public relations officials also discussed how to handle press inquiries.

Mr. Wainger commented later on the relationship between Xerox and those on leave that he had stressed with them.

> I could have thought of a long list of dos and don'ts but didn't want to get into that. Basically I told them that they were still Xerox employees and we wanted them back and that we would try to help them personally if they needed it. While they are away no reports will be required or evaluations made. Members of the Evaluation Committee will visit each person at least twice to see how the program is working and we have asked for a report from the volunteer at the end of the year.
>
> There are bound to be situations we haven't anticipated. For instance, what happens if one of our people gets into legal difficulties in the course of his work? It's the agency's responsibility to back him up, but we'll do all we can to help. Or the Massachusetts Correctional Agency asks our man teaching in their prisons if Xerox will interview inmates for jobs when they are released. In such cases I told them to call me. The relationship between Xerox and the agency is a corporate matter. My suspicion is that we won't start lots of little programs to suit agencies. We have several major on-going ones initiated from the corporate level and new ones will come in the same way.

By Saturday noon, the mood was described by one man as "euphoric." Another said, "It was beautiful—the most moving experience of my life." Still another remarked, "I could sense a sigh of relief from the committee after they had been with us for a little while. By the end, we had been transformed from a bunch of individuals into a group with common bonds and a sense of purpose."

SEPARATION

Prior to the meeting at the Westchester Country Club, Mr. Wainger reviewed the list for anyone he felt might be considered indispensable, Although Mr. John Teem, Director of the Technical Staff in R & D would be difficult to replace and Mr. William Gable was a senior executive at XDS, he anticipated no major problems securing their release. Then on November 18 he sent a letter to each manager having a subordinate chosen for leave, formally announcing the selection and forcefully reminding the manager of Mr. McColough's guarantee of the same or an equivalent job for the employee after the leave. One of these letters is reproduced in Exhibit 7.

The employees were greeted with applause and admiration, although as one account representative related, it was not always universal:

It's funny how people react. The first thing my boss said when I told him I was going to Stamford for two days was, "Who's going to look after your accounts?" Perhaps I'm expecting too much. After all, he has needs and losing his best producer won't help.

And the other night one of those who wasn't selected called me at 11 o'clock and said that he understood the Evaluation Committee had a tough job, but he couldn't see why they had picked my project rather than his. He had been with Xerox a lot longer than me and had really gone to a lot of work in putting his proposal together; it even included a letter from the governor.

But the response I've gotten from others, especially my clients, has more than made up for it. They have a lot of respect for Xerox. It makes me glad I'm working here.

While Mr. McColough received no petitions claiming indispensability, a number of situations were uncovered during the next several weeks which reflected the complexity of administering the Social Service Leave Program and foreshadowed the problems to be encountered reinstating those on leave in the organization.

In one instance, a manager was to have received a substantial increase in the scope of his job two days after he was notified of his selection by the Evaluation Committee. He had not known about the impending promotion prior to accepting the leave.

In another case, one of the people chosen was to have been laid off. He was a specialist, very well thought of in his division, for whom no work was available because of government spending cutbacks. The company had tried for some time to relocate him in some other unit but had been unsuccessful. In fact, while the Evaluation Committee was meeting, the lay-off request was waiting on Mr. Wainger's desk for his approval.[7] Along with the others, however, he had been guaranteed an equivalent career opportunity when he returned.

A more difficult variation of the above situation also arose. A rela-

---

[7] Xerox maintained the policy that before an employee with eight or more years of service could be released, permission had to be granted by either Mr. McColough or Mr. Wainger.

tively senior man selected for leave was in the process of being terminated because his performance did not measure up to the standards set by the manager of his department, and other departments were reluctant to pick him up. He had accepted this fact and informally agreed during the fall to use the next six months to relocate. The department manager indicated that he was not aware of the social leave application until about the time the news broke.

A final case was described by Mr. Reid:

> I got a call one day in December from a branch manager. That was unusual in itself since he was calling three or four levels up the line. He said one of his area sales managers had been selected for leave. He didn't have a replacement and regional management told him that with the budgets cut to the bone there wasn't $5,000 to cover the relocation costs associated with moving somene else in. They then suggested that he put the sales planning manager into the ASM slot. The branch manager said that meant he would end up covering for the sales planning manager.
>
> I didn't like the sound of it so I called the regional personnel manager. It finally came out that they were interested in getting the branch manager more involved in sales planning and saw this as a good way of doing it. I told him that wasn't in the spirit of the program and some way of getting a replacement had to be found.
>
> A later discussion with the branch manager revealed that there was a good salesman there who could be made ASM. The branch manager was reluctant to do this because it would mean demoting him when the old ASM returned. I suggested that he could be moved to an ASM job elsewhere, but apparently he can't move for personal reasons for two years.

Mr. Wainger indicated that he had been informed that non-budgeted relocation expense might be involved. Rather than providing the money from corporate funds, however, he decided to leave it as a proper operating unit responsibility.

CONSIDERATIONS FOR THE FUTURE

In addition to worrying through the problems of specific individuals, corporate executives were concerned about how to measure the success of the Social Service Leave Program. Mr. McCardell noted four conditions he felt were important:

1. The careers of people who have gone on leave do not suffer,
2. They have a sense of accomplishment in their year away,
3. They have a broadened perspective on the job and outside, and
4. The social agencies say their efforts have been useful.

Difficulties which he and others quickly acknowledged with such evaluation criteria were the lack of clear factual evidence and the long time span over which benefits were likely to occur.

Of more immediate concern were the number who returned to Xerox and the company's ability to reinstate them satisfactorily. A loss rate of 50% was generally viewed at corporate headquarters as "disappointing" and highly unlikely; 20% was thought by several to be "an acceptable price to pay" though again higher than expected. Mr. McCardell commented on reinstatement:

This is probably the biggest problem we face, but with only 20 we can take a personal interest. That's why Peter's name was on the letters to the employees' supervisors. Of course, letters have been written before which have gone unheeded. A chief executive can't rule by fiat. We'll have to wait and see.

Aside from evaluation, several policy questions were raised at various levels in the organization. The first involved accounting for the costs; should they be allocated to the operating units or retained in a corporate account similar to that for charitable contributions? If the former were chosen, how far down in the organization should charges be allocated? Some difference of opinion existed among corporate officers though an immediate choice was not deemed necessary. Mr. Wainger indicated, however, that if the program grew, as he hoped it would, pressure would mount for doing away with a large, easily identifiable corporate budget item.

The second question related to the selection procedure. A senior manager in BPG put it this way:

> Had I been doing this, I would have put in more feedback from the organization and made it less a corporate-individual deal. That way we could have ironed out a lot of the administrative problems beforehand. A study of who goes on leave might be useful too. Are we encouraging the right type of people to work here? Are the ones who do this marginal? At this level—only 21 people—it isn't so bad, but if it gets any larger, I think we'll have some problems.

While most corporate executives favored direct employee access to the Evaluation Committee in the United States, for the reasons noted earlier, the issue was not as clear overseas. Mr. McColough described his dilemma:

> Just after the Social Service Leave Program was announced, I was in Europe talking with our people there. They were enthusiastic about it but asked why they weren't included. Aside from saying it was experimental, I told them this is the way we get into trouble. If we limit it to the United States, it's favoritism and if we spread our program worldwide, it's applying United States solutions to foreign problems. I told them if you want it, you must *ask* for it.

Inquiries had been received from a number of overseas subsidiaries including those in Holland, New Zealand and Canada. In most instances the subsidiary leaned in the direction of an "up-the-line" selection and approval process. However, in January the nature and scope of overseas participation remained undefined.

As the month drew to a close, the management group considered again the direction of the Social Service Leave Program. Mr. McColough's original charge had been expressed in the following way:

> Granting twenty people a leave isn't much for a company as large as Xerox. There are certain to be problems which can't be anticipated with precision beforehand. However, if we dwell on the problems, we will end up doing nothing. So, let's be cautious, but let's do it.

He now shared the task of interpreting that charge in light of the events of the previous four months.

Exhibit 1

XEROX CORPORATION

Ten-Year Statistical Comparisons

	1971[1]	1970[1]	1969[1]
Yardsticks of Progress			
Net Income Per Common Share	$ 2.71	$ 2.40	$ 2.08
Dividends Declared Per Share	$ .80	$ .65	$ .58⅓
Operations (Dollars in thousands)			
Total Operating Revenues	$1,961,449	$1,718,587	$1,482,895
Rentals, Service and Royalties	1,563,805	1,343,252	1,094,794
Net Sales	397,644	375,335	388,101
Payroll (Excluding Benefits)	590,744	514,172	419,888
Depreciation of Rental Equipment	245,164	200,189	183,187
Depreciation of Buildings and Equipment	38,999	36,149	29,888
Amortization[3]	20,070	21,406	17,449
Expenditures for Research and Development	104,137	97,524	83,682
Income Before Income Taxes	471,081	432,938	389,722
Income Taxes	217,600	211,800	204,500
Outside Shareholders' Interests	40,871	33,447	23,854
Equity in Net Earnings of Rank Xerox Limited	—	—	—
Net Income	212,610	187,691	161,368
Dividends Declared	62;834	50,935	43,969
Financial Position (Dollars in thousands)			
Cash and Marketable Securities	$ 197,921	$ 148,982	$ 56,836
Net Trade Receivables	347,768	326,623	311,997
Inventories	226,597	222,001	172,747
Current Assets	916,731	825,416	649,011
Rental Equipment and Related Inventories at Cost	1,633,207	1,345,303	1,104,506
Accumulated Depreciation of Rental Equipment	872,283	714,833	577,832
Land, Buildings and Equipment at Cost	541,817	431,624	352,951
Accumulated Depreciation of Buildings and Equipment	172,383	144,339	116,056
Total Assets	2,156,094	1,857,325	1,531,271
Current Liabilities	532,806	457,571	391,257
Long-Term Debt (Including Current Portion)	482,731	429,690	319,407
Shareholders' Equity	1,051,767	892,500	738,455
Additions to Rental Equipment and Related Inventories[4]	382,792	312,580	279,519
Additions to Land, Buildings and Equipment[4]	121,498	88,869	75,890
General and Ratios			
Average Common Shares Outstanding During Year	78,533,533	78,315,911	77,445,464
Shareholders at Year End	143,554	146,534	129,944
Employees at Year End	66,728	59,862	54,882
Income Before Income Taxes to Total Operating Revenues	24.0%	25.2%	26.3%
Net Income to Average Shareholders' Equity	21.9%	23.0%	24.1%
Current Ratio	1.7	1.8	1.7
Long-Term Debt to Total Capitalization[5]	29.4%	30.5%	28.3%

1968[1]	1967[2]	1966[2]	1965[1]	1964	1963	1962
$ 1.68	$ 1.42	$ 1.20	$ .92	$ .68	$ .39	$ .24
$ .50	$ .40	$ .30¾	$ .20	$ .14¼	$ .08⅓	$ .04⅔
$1,224,352	$ 983,064	$752,508	$548,795	$317,840	$176,036	$115,220
896,673	673,548	477,954	327,814	184,157	114,077	65,847
327,679	309,516	274,554	220,981	133,683	61,959	49,373
336,602	289,009	223,855	160,725	93,921	55,112	36,653
175,692	135,975	97,221	69,110	37,295	20,236	12,454
26,747	23,779	18,519	12,637	7,243	4,338	3,267
12,304	8,437	6,026	5,439	3,695	3,070	1,570
59,888	50,806	53,329	38,170	24,050	14,609	8,547
309,096	226,500	182,113	138,872	86,800	50,423	30,779
164,020	108,576	86,490	68,199	44,598	27,850	16,801
16,126	11,540	8,923	4,984	—	—	—
—	—	—	—	1,523	428	(84)
128,950	106,384	86,700	65,689	43,725	23,001	13,894
34,363	28,555	21,996	14,698	10,788	4,895	2,688
$ 66,022	$ 70,670	$ 59,508	$ 26,289	$ 10,622	$ 6,933	$ 6,322
244,838	197,650	150,810	93,982	40,847	25,233	16,284
146,871	128,303	102,116	70,633	35,531	14,300	8,672
554,530	460,904	362,204	232,255	109,678	59,327	37,412
905,180	734,708	562,480	383,044	197,408	114,517	70,868
458,350	307,482	216,972	147,272	76,512	41,565	21,760
281,285	244,964	201,546	143,833	81,317	48,219	35,798
90,360	68,414	49,212	33,124	21,080	10,980	8,222
1,268,489	1,155,274	933,991	647,359	356,142	215,801	138,917
372,942	286,496	195,613	161,013	62,774	41,982	29,310
298,904	357,888	379,870	228,622	102,982	54,028	41,258
601,003	474,155	326,254	229,104	154,770	85,235	48,686
193,303	213,169	214,058	147,061	84,802	45,401	30,929
35,424	43,323	54,117	40,152	21,148	12,828	9,163
76,565,650	75,039,803	72,467,603	71,705,645	63,897,723	59,134,557	58,263,831
91,712	87,659	89,060	73,217	62,195	26,375	14,925
45,142	40,639	33,595	24,239	12,728	7,918	5,297
25.2%	23.0%	24.2%	25.3%	27.3%	28.6%	26.7%
24.0%	26.6%	31.2%	34.2%	36.4%	34.4%	33.4%
1.5	1.6	1.9	1.4	1.7	1.4	1.3
31.1%	40.8%	50.9%	47.4%	40.0%	38.8%	45.9%

[1] The data include the accounts of Xerox Data Systems and of Rank Xerox Limited for its fiscal year ended October 31.
[2] The data include the accounts of Xerox Data Systems and of Rank Xerox Limited for its fiscal year ended in June.
[3] Amortization of deferred research and development, patents, licenses and other intangible assets.
[4] Additions prior to 1969 shown net of disposals.
[5] Total capitalization defined as the sum of long-term debt (including current portion), outside shareholders' interests in net assets of subsidiaries, and shareholders' equity. Common share data adjusted to reflect change of each common share into five common shares effective December 17, 1963, and the distribution of two additional common shares for each common share held at May 16, 1969.

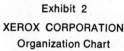

Exhibit 2

XEROX CORPORATION

Organization Chart

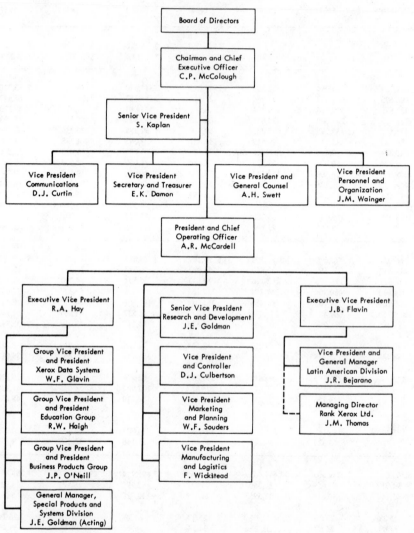

Board of Directors

Chairman and Chief Executive Officer
C.P. McColough

Senior Vice President
S. Kaplan

Vice President
Communications
D.J. Curtin

Vice President
Secretary and Treasurer
E.K. Damon

Vice President and
General Counsel
A.H. Swett

Vice President
Personnel and
Organization
J.M. Wainger

President and Chief Operating Officer
A.R. McCardell

Executive Vice President
R.A. Hay

Senior Vice President
Research and Development
J.E. Goldman

Executive Vice President
J.B. Flavin

Group Vice President
and President
Xerox Data Systems
W.F. Glavin

Vice President
and Controller
D.J. Culbertson

Vice President and
General Manager
Latin American Division
J.R. Bejarano

Group Vice President
and President
Education Group
R.W. Haigh

Vice President
Marketing
and Planning
W.F. Souders

Managing Director
Rank Xerox Ltd.
J.M. Thomas

Group Vice President
and President
Business Products Group
J.P. O'Neill

Vice President
Manufacturing
and Logistics
F. Wickstead

General Manager,
Special Products and
Systems Division
J.E. Goldman (Acting)

Exhibit 3

XEROX CORPORATION
Memorandum to Corporate Executives

To	See Distribution	Date	August 7, 1970
From	J. M. Wainger	Location	HR 2
Subject	Xerox Social Action	Organization	Corporate Personnel

We have decided to institute, as promptly as possible, a program for Xerox employees which we think will have substantial positive impact internally and externally, both now and for our future.

We will offer to twenty Xerox employees, regardless of level in the Corporation, (though excluding all of you) the opportunity to work for a year out of Xerox in some position that has high social value. As examples, the jobs might be with some community organization attacking urban problems, or some Federal Government agency, or a school, etc.

We plan to use the following approach. Through appropriate Xerox communications media, we will publicize the program and ask all those employees who are interested to submit a short description of the project they wish to work on and their reasons for choosing it. As part of their submission, they must include assurance that they have agreement from the prospective employer to take them on if they are freed up. We hope to receive many submissions.

All of these submissions will be screened by an impartial, outside board of prestigious men who will choose the twenty they consider to be most worthy according to the social criteria we've established.

The twenty selected employees will then be given a year to work at their chosen task. We assume they will return to Xerox at the end of that time, though no guarantee can be exacted. We will require that the projects they select be in or near their present communities. In other words, this program should not carry with it relocation subsidies for attractive long-range trips to such places as Los Angeles, Washington or Hawaii.

Xerox will maintain the employees' total compensation at the rate prevailing at the time they left Xerox by paying them the difference between whatever they receive from their outside job and their then Xerox salary.

We need to set up our outside screening board as soon as possible. I need your help. Would you please submit to me as soon as possible the names of one or more people you deem suitable to serve. The names you submit should be of people you feel fairly confident you can "deliver" if asked to contact them directly. I anticipate a board of perhaps five men, disparate in background but uniform quality.

I recognize that there are problems inherent in this program, and I'm sure you do too. However the results will more than justify taking the problems on. We will benefit and, by leading, we will influence.

You will, of course, be apprised of the details of the program as it is shaped up.

May I have your nominees for the selection board as soon as possible.

JMW/sd

Distribution:　D. J. Curtin　　　　A. R. McCardell
　　　　　　　　J. B. Flavin　　　　C. P. McColough
　　　　　　　　J. E. Goldman　　　J. W. Rutledge
　　　　　　　　S. Kaplan　　　　　J. C. Wilson

EUGENE R. ALLEN, director of international operations of the Xerox Education Group in Stamford, joined XEG in 1970 following three years as director of urban education at Litton Industries. Allen, 37, was born in Sacramento, Calif.

ROBERT M. FLEGAL, 29, is a scientist in the computer science laboratory at the Palo Alto Research Center. He served in the Peace Corps in Ghana for two years. He is a native of Salt Lake City, Utah. He joined Xerox in 1970.

ERROL L. FORKNER, 29, a commercial analyst in the product management department of Xerox Data Systems in El Segundo, is working for an MA in computer sciences at UCLA. He came to XDS in 1969 after three years with IBM.

JANET L. KNIGHTON is an educational and training specialist in the Business Products Group in Webster. Before joining Xerox in 1970, she had been assistant director of the adult department of the Rochester YWCA.

ROBERT M. SCHNEIDER, assistant to the president of Xerox in Stamford, was manager of corporate contributions for three years before assuming his present post in 1969. A native of Passaic, N.J., he is 40 years old.

ROLAND A. STENTA, 31, is national accounts manager of the Philadelphia branch of BPG, following work in personnel and sales. Born in Brooklyn, he joined Xerox in 1968, from the Office of Economic Opportunity in Washington.

JAMES M. WAINGER is corporate vice president, personnel and organization, in Stamford. He joined Xerox in 1960, but left from 1966 to 1969 to teach English in high school and write plays. He's 44, and a graduate of Harvard Law.

Exhibit 5

XEROX CORPORATION
Application

XEROX SOCIAL SERVICE LEAVE APPLICATION

To be returned to:

Evaluation Board,
Social Service Leave Program
Xerox Corporation
Stamford, Connecticut 06904

My name: _____

           (print)   first   middle   last

Home address: _____

Phone: _____

           home   Xerox

Xerox Group/Division: _____ Location: _____

Present Position: _____ Employee Number: _____ Date Hired: _____

don't write here | Application No :

- -

don't write here | Application No :

In one sentence, what I want to do is: _____

_____

Time desired: _____ Dates desired: _____

This is the organization I'll work with: _____

                                  name

    address   department   name & function of person I would report to

Phone: _____ Acceptance Letter attached ☐   Salary, if any, I'll receive from the organization: _____

These are the details of the program I want to work on: (goals, history, scope, program, people affected, other workers involved, nature of activities, budget — *very specific description, please,* that will help us understand the project; attach any literature or reports or clippings that will help)

_____

_____

_____

_____

_____

My specific work will be: (what skill, what function, what tasks, what aims — or programmed results, if these can be stated in advance)

_____

_____

_____

_____

_____

_____

_____

Exhibit 5—Continued

I am specially qualified to do this by: (cite specific experience, training, skills, prior involvement, personal history — or just gnawing desire)

_____

_____

This is why I want to work on this project and this is what I hope to accomplish:

_____

_____

_____

_____

_____

My present monthly salary is: $ _____

Circle Highest Grade Completed:

High School	College	Graduate
9 - 10 - 11 - 12	13 - 14 - 15 - 16	17 - 18 - 19 - 20 - 21 - 22

College or University Attended	Degree Awarded	Major Subject
_____	_____	_____
_____	_____	_____
_____	_____	_____
_____	_____	_____

Please use as many extra sheets as you need to answer the questions fully.

Exhibit 6

XEROX CORPORATION

1972 Recipients

Name & Xerox job	Age	Years with Xerox	Project	Agency
Joel N. Axelrod. Business Products Group Group Program Manager	39	5	Develop and implement techniques for evaluating training programs funded under the Drug Abuse Act	U.S. Office of Education
Oswaldo Aymat. Xerox Reproduction Center Quality Control Supervisor	35	11	Counsel and guide Puerto Rican college students with the objective of reducing the high dropout rate	Aspira of New York
James E. Bales. Business Products Group Technical Representative	35	10	Manage the development of a literacy program	Greater Little Rock Literacy Council
Irving C. Bell. Xerox Reproduction Center Sales Representative	43	4	Teach mathematics to inmates in two prisons and instruct them in building trade skills	Massachusetts Department of Correction
Robert P. Britton. Business Products Group Technical Representative	29	6	Set and teach an entry level course in electro-mechanical job skills for unskilled and unemployables	Opportunities Industrialization Center
Frank V. Cliff, Jr.. Business Products Group Account Executive	43	9	Work with minority businessmen	Economic Development Corporation of Greater Detroit
Mrs. Frayda F. Cooper. Ginn and Company Elementary Mathematics Editor	47	4	Organize an experimental program to provide services to the aged in a multi-town area where no such service is now available	Massachusetts Department of Community Affairs
Robert B. Cost. Business Products Group Account Representative	26	5	Teach and counsel in a drug rehabilitation center service high school age children from New York City	Pius XII School
Joe A. Duardo. Electro-Optical Systems Physicist	40	9	Counsel hard-core youth in a Mexican-American area	Abraham Lincoln High School
William Cable. Xerox Data Systems Vice President	43	3	Assist low-income families in black neighborhoods in achieving home ownership	Protestant Community Services
James P. Herget. Business Products Group A Regional Marketing Manager	27	4	As the agency's director of marketing, guide and assist minority-owned businesses in developing their marketing capability	Interracial Council for Business Opportunity of Greater Washington

Exhibit 6—Continued

Name & Xerox job	Age	Years with Xerox	Project	Agency
Robert S. Huddleston Business Products Group Technical Representative	44	9	Expand the work of an agency devoted to assisting former convicts in their return to life in their communities	The Seventh Step Foundation Topeka, Kansas
Paul S. Israel Business Products Group Area Sales Manager	38	8	Direct an effort to build a model classroom for teaching mentally retarded preschoolers	The Arizona Preschool for Retarded Children
Mrs. Esther E. Kapuschat Business Products Group Staff Nurse	60	7	Serve as director of nursing in an interdenominational crippled children's hospital	The Holy Land Christian Mission, Kansas City, Missouri
Kenneth R. Lane American Education Publications Special Education Department Editor	41	3	Establish an in-service training program leading to accreditation of house-parents in residential schools for the deaf	Conference of Executives of American Schools for the Deaf, White Plains, New York
Frederick Lightfoot Business Products Group Multiple Drill Operator	36	3	Work as a community organizer in central city area	Action for a Better Community Rochester, New York
Raymond E. Poehlein Business Products Group Development Engineering Manager	33	5	Help develop physical science curriculum and teach in a secondary school for Aglala Sioux Indians	Red Cloud Indian School
Lionel E. Reim Business Products Group A Regional Marketing Manager	28	3	Serve as business manager for an on-going coffeehouse and medical clinic for youth	General Conference of Seventh Day Adventists
Michael I. Slade Corporate Research Physicist	30	5	Provide research and develop information bulletins on ecology problems (transportation and water)	Rochester Committee for Scientific Information
John M. Teem Corporate Research and Development Director of Technical Staff	46	13	Develop and teach a science curriculum in an experimental "school without walls"	Alpha Learnings Community School
Mrs. Jean G. Williams Business Products Group Programmer	26	4	Tutor and counsel minority college and pre-college students to reduce dropout rate	Project Equal Opportunity University of Colorado

Exhibit 6—Concluded

Recapitulation

Division	
Business Products Group	13
Corporate Staff Group	2
Education Group	2
Xerox Reproduction Center	2
Electro-Optical Systems	1
Xerox Data Systems	1
	21

Salary per month	
850 or less	4
850–1,250	5
1,251–1,600	6
1,601–2,000	2
2,001–3,000	1
3,001–4,000	2
Over 4,000	1
	21

Exhibit 7

XEROX CORPORATION
Memorandum to Supervisors

November 18, 1971

Dr. J. E. Goldman
Xerox Corporation
Corporate Headquarters
Stamford, Connecticut 06904

Dear Jack:

John M. Teem, who is employed in your organization, has been selected to receive a Xerox Social Service Leave. Based on his application, he will be engaged full time away from the company for the next year on a voluntary social program of real value. Xerox is proud of the commitment of this employee, and I'm sure you share that pride.

As you know, Peter McColough has assured all employees that those who are chosen for Leaves are *guaranteed* that on their return they will return to their former job or one of equal pay, responsibility, status and opportunity for advancement. Peter and I will review each returning employee's job placement to make certain that this guarantee is fully honored.

Therefore, as you plan for the carrying on of John's work, I'm sure you'll want to keep in mind this essential provision of the Social Service Leave policy. If the job of the person going on leave is one of many jobs of the same type, I'd expect no special provisions need be made at this time.

If, however, the job is relatively unique, I suggest that you give consideration to designating any replacement as "acting." Certain jobs may even lend themselves to developmental use, permitting the rotation of several people in them during the period of the Social Service Leave.

I'm asking relevant Personnel Departments to monitor and approve the method used to fill each job vacated, and I'm requesting, too, that Personnel Departments inform me of the action taken to fill each job vacated by an employee going on Leave.

Sincerely,

James M. Wainger
Vice President
Personnel & Organization

JMW/sd
cc: C. P. McColough
    A. R. McCardell
    G. F. Wajda

Mead Corporation (A)

CEO – McSwiney
Pres + COOff. – Batts

MEAD CORPORATION was one of 35 U.S. companies with board-level committees dealing with questions of corporate social responsibility. Mead's corporate responsibility committee (CRC) was unique, however, in that it included company employees along with outside directors as regular members. The committee had been formed in 1972 at the recommendation of a special board committee and Mead's chairman and chief executive officer, James W. McSwiney. The hope was that by bringing together representatives of two groups—directors and employees—who seldom had an opportunity to share ideas, and by giving them the freedom to choose their own agenda, the flow of "unorthodox" and "unconventional" ideas could be encouraged and stimulated throughout the organization. McSwiney believed that this opening up of communication between the bottom of the organization and the top was essential to Mead's continued health in a society that was demanding that corporations be more responsive to social needs.

In April 1976 Warren Batts, Mead's president and chief operating officer—with the encouragement of McSwiney—was attempting to evaluate the effect of this four-year experiment and to determine whether, at this point, the company would benefit from having management establish more formal links with the committee. He had just received a paper prepared by an employee member of CRC recommending that Mead establish an ombudsman function with companywide responsibility. In formulating his response to the issues raised in the paper for the next CRC meeting, scheduled for May 27, 1976, Batts was considering whether operating management should become a more active participant in CRC's deliberations.

MEAD CORPORATION

The Mead Pulp & Paper Company was founded in Dayton, Ohio, in 1846 by Daniel E. Mead and several partners. Mead's grandson, George

H. Mead, became president of the corporation in 1910, served as chairman of the board from 1937 to 1948, and was honorary chairman until his death in 1963. Between 1910 and 1963, the Mead Corporation (renamed in 1930) added 37 plants and mills to its two original paper mills in Dayton and Chillicothe, Ohio. Mead's product line, originally limited to magazine paper, expanded under George Mead's leadership to include a wide variety of paper products.

In the 1960s the company determined to grow and broaden its base, and by 1976, largely as a result of acquisitions, it was producing such products as furniture, school and office products, rubber products, precision castings, and coal, as well as pulp and paper.[1] The company owned operating units in 30 states and 23 foreign countries and was one of the 10 largest paper manufacturers in the United States.[2] It owned or managed more than 1.5 million acres of timberland in North America. In 1976 forest products (paper, paperboard, packaging, containers, and pulp) accounted for 56 percent of Mead's sales; school, office, and home products, 28 percent; and industrial products (castings, coal, rubber parts, and piping), 13 percent.

Mead's sales reached the $1 billion mark for the first time in 1969, with record net earnings. (See Exhibit 1 for a financial history.) In 1970, however, net earnings dropped substantially because of national declines in the housing market, rising pulp costs, reduced demand for white papers, and strikes at a number of Mead plants. In 1971 earnings showed improvement, but this was followed by a sharp decline in 1972 when wildcat strikes closed plants in Atlanta, Georgia, and Anniston, Alabama.[3] These were the first major walkouts the company had experienced since the 1940s.[4]

Mead's sales and earnings reached record highs in 1974. But in the next year earnings were off because of the national recession and because more than 3,000 workers staged walkouts in Escanaba, Michigan (26 weeks), and Chillicothe, Ohio (11 weeks), in response to the company's determination to include social security offsets as part of its pension

---

[1] Between 1960 and 1974 Mead acquired 40 companies. The largest, in terms of sales volume, were the Woodward Corporation, manufacturers of castings and coal, rubber, and iron products; Chatfield & Woods, paper merchants; Westab, Inc., producers of educational and consumer products; and Stanley Furniture Company, Inc.

[2] Mead was usually compared with the following companies: Boise-Cascade, Champion, Crown Zellerbach, Georgia Pacific, Great Northern Nekoosa, Hammermill, International Paper, Kimberly Clark, Potlatch, Scott, St. Regis, Union Camp, Westvaro, and Weyerhaeuser.

[3] The following description of strike issues appeared in Mead's 1972 annual report: "Several hundred employees of Mead Packaging and Containers plants in Atlanta, in response to a local civil rights group that was attempting to organize a citywide minority union, staged a 55-day wildcat strike. Though illegal, it did focus attention on some real problems: minority promotional opportunities, a dust condition, blocked communications. The dust problem was soon dealt with, a representative council formed to surface employee feelings more directly, and a new presupervisory training program for blacks and females instituted. A 10-day wildcat strike in Anniston, Alabama, revealed several misunderstandings. New Anniston management has stepped up information sharing with employees; meetings to answer questions about pensions have proved especially helpful."

[4] Among Mead's 26,200 employees, 16,000 were represented by unions in 1976. The largest (in terms of number of Mead employees represented) were the United Paper Workers International, the Printing Specialists Union, and the United Steel Workers.

Exhibit 1

FINANCIAL HISTORY: 1970–1976

	1976	1975	1974	1973	1972	1971	1970
Net sales ($ millions) ...	1,599	1,245	1,526	1,299	1,129	1,056	1,038
Net earnings ($ millions) ...	89	53	82	49	18	23	20
Return on sales (percent)	5.6	4.2	5.4	3.8	2.3	2.2	2.0
Return on equity (percent)	14.9	9.9	16.2	10.9	5.9	5.2	4.5
Per common share ($):							
Net earnings (fully diluted)	2.94	1.78	2.72	1.59	0.57	0.91	0.70
Dividends	0.89	0.80	0.60	0.43	0.40	0.67	0.67
Book value	24.34	22.05	20.80	17.71	15.97	15.86	15.92
Capital expenditures ($ millions) ...	76	64	124	77	40	61	44
Total assets ($ millions) ...	1,227	1,091	1,057	941	862	865	861
Number of employees	26,200	24,000	27,000	32,000	32,000	34,000	34,200
Number of stockholders ..	29,525	31,197	31,372	32,164	30,119	30,555	30,924

benefits. In addition, Mead's affiliates in British Columbia were closed by industrywide unrest in Canada. The company recovered rapidly, however, and expected a 76 percent rise in profits for 1976.

MEAD ORGANIZATION

In 1976 the Mead Corporation was organized into six operating groups and a corporate staff headed by a group vice president on a peer level with the heads of the operating groups. (See Exhibit 2 for an organization chart.) Originally a paper company with centralized management, Mead began to move towards a decentralized structure during its acquisition program. In 1976 Mead's paper and paperboard groups were made up of the paper and paperboard mills that had previously been the cornerstone of the corporation, and the packaging and container plants that had been acquired and expanded. The four other groups consisted of all the remaining acquisitions.

The expansive phase of Mead's development had been engineered by James W. McSwiney, chairman of the board in 1976, who had joined Mead in 1934 at the age of 18. He had been president and chief executive officer between 1968 and 1971. When he became chairman in 1971, he retained his CEO position, and Paul Allemang (a group vice president since Mead acquired his company in 1966) became president and chief

Exhibit 2
ORGANIZATION CHART

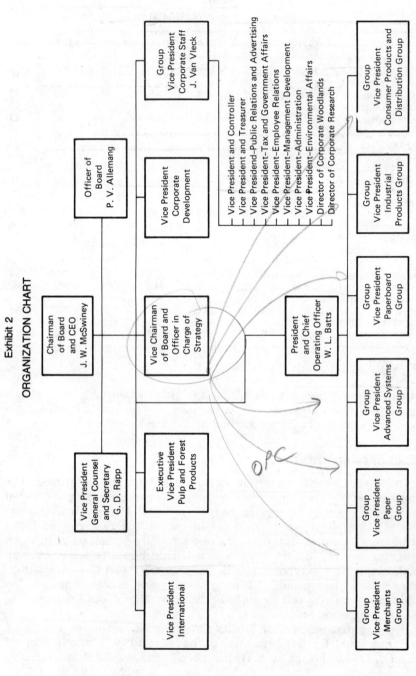

Source: Information supplied by the Mead Corporation.

operating officer. Allemang was succeeded in 1973 by Warren Batts, 42, who had joined Mead as a group vice president in 1971. (Before joining Mead, Batts had been co-founder, president, and CEO of a small handtool company.)

Despite its substantial diversity in business, until the late 1960s, Mead's management at the corporate level was made up largely of people with backgrounds in the paper industry. As new companies had been acquired, only one, the Stanley Furniture Company, had brought a "Mead man" into the ranks of its top management. Others, like the industrial products group (with the former Woodward Corporation as its core), were run exclusively by the acquired management. A senior executive commented:

> Relations became strained during the acquisition program, which brought on board a lot of new people and businesses. The corporate staff was strictly paper oriented and had real problems relating to foundries and coal mines.

A manager who had been with Mead since the 1950s described the paper industry as being high in capital investment, with slow growth and little chance for marketing innovation. "If you do everything right and your competitors do everything wrong," he said, "your market share might change a fraction of one percent." He went on:

> It is not unusual for the average paper manager to ride with his subordinates; he is willing to accept less than perfection. Personal relations always played a major role in the company. The old Mead Paper was almost as much a social organization as a business. When I came with the company, it seemed like a family.

When Batts became president in 1973, the company was examining the fruits of its acquisition phase and beginning to divest itself of 22 operations that did not fit into its long-range plans. In 1975 Batts began the process of integrating Mead's product groups while strengthening the decentralized management structure. He described Mead's previous structure and its current direction:

> It took time for McSwiney's philosophy of organization and planning to take on meaning. In some groups decentralization was taken to mean that a group vice president was a prince with a moat around his division and his people. You came across his drawbridge at his pleasure.
>
> Now, we have gotten to the point where decentralization means that the group vice presidents are totally responsible for choosing the right people to run their businesses, for seeing problems and opportunities, and for presenting alternatives. But the corporate officers make the final selection among alternatives. We share the responsibility with the group vice presidents for results.

Early in 1974 Batts established the operating policy committee (OPC), which he chaired and which included William Wommack (vice chairman of the board and officer in charge of strategy) and all the group vice presidents. He explained why:

> In order to maximize the results from a decentralized organization there had to be a vehicle for (1) building common beliefs and goals into the

company while recognizing critical differences among units, (2) establishing corporate policies, and (3) strengthening the position of the group vice presidents.

In the past, many people felt—and it was true in some instances—that if someone on the corporate staff had an idea, it was fired right down to the plant managers without the group vice presidents being consulted. Now the OPC serves as a buffer. Sometimes it takes 15 drafts to get an idea in shape. But by the time OPC signs off on it, each group vice president and his people are committed to getting it through the system.

In addition to developing better "top-down" communication, the OPC served as a vehicle for the divisions to exchange ideas. For example, in early 1976 the OPC was considering a program for improving internal communications that had been developed by the paper group. This program consisted of employee attitude surveys, management seminars, and management-employee councils. Batts intended that all the group vice presidents would eventually adopt a similar type of communications program as a result of OPC discussions. Still, he was aware that such adoption would best be voluntary: "Given our organizational philosophy, each group vice president should have final authority in operational matters. I would rather persuade than order them to establish a particular program for internal communications."

The change in the management structure was in some ways a function of the difference in style between McSwiney and Batts in the role of president and chief operating officer. A group vice president made this comparison:

> McSwiney is more likely to say something and then assume it will come out the way he wants it to. He is a powerful man, magnetic, very difficult to say no to, even when you know you should say no. I still have a tendency to think he can't do anything wrong. As CEO, he has the ability to see things that the rest of us, wrapped up in the day-to-day issues, don't think about. He never lets us get too satisfied with ourselves.
>
> When McSwiney was president, he knew all the details and had a compulsion to make all the decisions. Batts likes to know the sequence of steps involved, but he is more willing to give the group vice presidents independence. Still, he is very structured and wants to know how things are likely to turn out.

Since 1971, 5 of 6 group vice presidents and 19 of 24 division presidents had been changed—mostly replaced with people from within the company.

MEAD BOARD

During most of the Mead Corporation's history, many of its directors were members of the Mead family and officers of the corporation. As it acquired new businesses in the 1960s, Mead added top officers of the merged companies to the board. (Exhibit 3 lists the members of the board in 1976.)

In September 1970 James McSwiney became concerned about the board's composition. He was especially interested in achieving a better balance between inside and outside directors. (At that time, Mead's 22-member board included only 6 directors who were not associated with the Mead family or the company.) With the board's approval, McSwiney appointed a special committee consisting of four outside directors to study the board's functions, size, and composition. Alfred W. Jones, who

Exhibit 3

BOARD OF DIRECTORS
April 1976

Vernon R. Alden (1965)*
Chairman of the Board
The Boston Company, Inc.
Boston, Mass.
Common shares owned: 600

Ivan Allen, Jr. (1971)
Chairman of the Board
Ivan Allen Company
Atlanta, Georgia
Common shares owned: 200

Warren L. Batts (1973)
President and Chief Operating Officer
Mead Corporation
Common shares owned: 1,100

George B. Beitzel (1973)
Senior Vice President, International
Business Machines Corporation
Armonk, New York
Common shares owned: 200

William R. Bond (1968)
Chairman of the Board
Cement Asbestos Products Company
Birmingham, Alabama
Common shares owned: 7,500

Newton H. DeBardeleben (1968)
Vice Chairman of the Board
First National Bank
Birmingham, Alabama
Common shares owned: 720

James W. McSwiney (1963)
Chairman of the Board and Chief Executive Officer
Mead Corporation
Common shares owned: 102,801

H. Talbott Mead (1946)
President
Mead Investment Company
Dayton, Ohio
Common shares owned: 48,244

Nelson S. Mead (1959)
Vice President, International
Mead Corporation
Common shares owned: 28,408

Paul F. Miller, Jr. (1963)
Partner, Miller Anderson & Sherrerd
(Investment management firm)
Philadelphia, Pennsylvania
Common shares owned: 1,000

George H. Sheets (1963)
Executive Vice President
Mead Corporation
Common shares owned: 13,736

William M. Spencer III (1968)
Chairman of the Board
Motion Industries, Inc.
Birmingham, Alabama
Common shares owned: 26,648

Thomas B. Stanley, Jr. (1970)
Investor
Stanleytown, West Virginia
Common shares owned: 172,400

C. William Verity (1966)
Chairman of the Board and Chief Executive Officer
Armco Steel Corporation
Middletown, Ohio
Common shares owned: 2,232

John M. Walker, M.D. (1957)
Consultant
White Weld & Co., Inc.
New York, New York
Common shares owned: 5,715

William W. Wommack (1968)
Vice Chairman of the Board and Officer in Charge of Strategy
Mead Corporation
Common shares owned: 9,404

---

* Date of appointment to board.
Source: Mead Corporation.

would retire at the end of 1972 after 33 years as a Mead director, was named chairman of the committee. In its final report the Jones committee recommended that

> an effective number of directors for a company the size of Mead should be between 12 and 15, with inside directors not to exceed one third. . . . Outside directors should be chosen for breadth of experience and interest, and the balance they can bring to the board's deliberations.

The committee also described the type of person who should be considered for board membership in the future—namely, heads of companies similar to Mead in size; owners of large amounts of Mead stock; one or more people "oriented to minority, ethnic, or other social concerns"; and individuals with the ability to ask critical questions. Finally, the Jones committee analyzed the functions of existing board committees and recommended that the board establish a corporate responsibility committee, to provide the company with a "means of responding to salient social and environmental aspects of the world."

In keeping with the Jones committee's recommendations, the board began to meet six times each year, with meetings averaging three hours in length. In addition, the executive committee met with outside directors four times a year. Five other board committees—finance, compensation, audit, corporate responsibility, and corporate objectives (formed in 1975)—also met periodically throughout the year. In 1976 outside directors received compensation of $10,000 per year, plus $600 for each executive committee meeting and $400 for meetings of other board committees.

In 1974, at McSwiney's suggestion, Mead's board appointed another directors' task force, composed of outside directors and chaired by Vernon Alden, to reexamine the board and to bring the original Jones report up to date. (See Exhibit 4 for excerpts from this group's report.)

McSwiney often referred to the Mead Corporation's board as a "working board." The president of Mead, Warren Batts, offered his perception of the board:

> We have a core of outside directors who are truly tough-minded businessmen. They know that the job of a director is basically to protect the shareholder—first, foremost, and always. The board's role is to review and approve corporate objectives and to review management's actions but not to meddle in operations. Among our directors, however, there is a wide spectrum of opinion about the board's role in corporate responsibility. This is the most nebulous area for the board and one that we have to make more concrete.

INITIATION OF THE CORPORATE RESPONSIBILITY COMMITTEE

In March 1972 the full board of directors accepted the Jones committee's recommendation to form a corporate responsibility committee. McSwiney described his thinking:

> At the time there were several issues. Blacks were very vocal about the rights of minorities, and equal opportunity for women was also in the

spotlight. The term *corporate responsibility* was the new buzz word, and some people thought it was simply a fad. But I took the idea very seriously. I thought a corporate responsibility committee, with both directors and employees as members, could provide a way to send unfiltered information to the top of the organization.

I have a feeling that if you can't stand unfiltered information in an organization, or if you don't get it, you probably are going to make a lot of erroneous assumptions. I saw this committee as a mechanism for encouraging dialogue, and for breaking through the walls that surround managers at the top of the company.

Although he was instrumental in the formation of CRC, McSwiney felt very strongly that he himself should not be a member. He explained why:

I didn't feel the committee would make a real contribution if the chief executive meddled with it. The resolution of critical or sensitive issues, especially those that involve prestigious positions and talented people, can seldom be achieved by edict. Only when those people who are affected are involved in the process of working out their own solutions is the process likely to become an ongoing part of the system.

A CEO must not become so insecure that he blocks communications— sometimes accurate, sometimes inaccurate, but always believed by those in the system—from reaching the outside directors.

Consistent with this philosophy, McSwiney met with CRC only on two or three occasions after its initiation. However, he and the full board regularly received formal and informal reports from the committee's chairman and secretary on the work and functioning of CRC.

McSwiney chose Gerald D. Rapp, general counsel and vice president for human resources, to chair the committee and he asked three outside directors to serve as members. These four then took responsibility for recruiting three employee members. In their early discussion, the directors mentioned wide outside interests, college background, and youthful thinking as criteria for selection of employee members. One director argued that hourly workers should be represented; another felt that no one should be chosen simply to represent the union point of view. No definite criteria for employee membership emerged from these discussions.

Notices announcing openings for employee membership on CRC were posted at all Mead facilities in the United States. Rapp interviewed every candidate (nearly 100) and his or her supervisor. Next, 10 finalists, with their husbands and wives, were invited to meet with the CRC director members in July 1972. On the night they and their spouses arrived for scheduled interviews, finalists were asked to write essays on corporate responsibility and, at dinner, to speak informally about themselves and their goals. One of the finalists described the experience: "It was not enjoyable. You yank someone out of the bottom of the organization and bring him to the Plaza in New York City to meet the directors of the company and it produces some bizarre behavior." Three employees were finally chosen for CRC membership, and the committee was introduced to the company in a newsletter (Exhibit 5).

Exhibit 4

EXCERPTS FROM DIRECTORS' TASK FORCE REPORT, 1974

Board responsibilities and expectations of Mead directors

In the legal corporation framework the Mead board has ultimate *responsibility* for the management of the corporation. The board discharges this responsibility by delegating the executive function to management and by holding management accountable. In a broad sense, the board holds a *charter of trust* for the corporation. In this perspective, it stands between the Mead organization and the outside environment, including shareowners, customers, public, etc.

In operational terms, the board reviews and approves or rejects recommendations of Mead management on certain major decisions. . . . Final decisions on such matters as declaration of dividends, mergers, and disposition of principal assets constitute *reserved powers* and require formal action by the board. In addition to these formal actions, directors are expected to counsel management on decisions . . . of major importance . . . such as . . . the charting of business strategy with regard to particular products or markets and major employment fluctuations (growth or curtailment).

One way to sharpen the definition of what the board does might be to distinguish between the board's role and function and the role and function of Mead management. In the functioning of the board organization, directors should review, consider, contribute, formulate, and advise; operating and staff managers should propose, implement, operate, account for, and assist. . . .

Audit and accountability: The board agenda

In the discharge of its duties to audit the operation and to hold management accountable, the Mead board needs access to information. The board's effectiveness is based upon the capability of Mead directors to ask the right questions and their ability to receive prompt and responsive answers. The quality and efficiency of discussions and decisions at Mead board meetings is thus determined by the *quality of information* that the board members receive. It is the responsibility of the chairman of the board to ensure the adequacy of information services to Mead directors. In all cases, board members should have the opportunity (and should take the initiative) to seek information which they need, in addition to regular reports by management. . . .

Corporate responsibility

Corporate responsibility is an emergent but not well-defined function of corporate boards in their role as trustee, standing between the corporation and society. Corporations in general have not demonstrated a clear sense of how to articulate this function in operational terms (i.e., who in the board should do what, when). Fiscal accounting is precise and financial audits are feasible because measurement standards apply universally across divisional and corporate boundaries. No such universal means of measurement are available for corporate responsibility.

The Mead board has an opportunity to serve in this area, by virtue of the emphasis placed by the chief executive officer, by directors, and by the response throughout the corporation to the establishment and the work to date of the corporate responsibility committee of the board. *We believe and recommend that the board should continue to regard corporate responsibility as one of its major concerns.*

Exhibit 5

July 1972

THE CORPORATE RESPONSIBILITY COMMITTEE

These employees and outside directors will serve on the new Corporate Responsibility Committee

Randy Evans has just been promoted to manager of customer service for Mead Paperboard Products' Western Region. He has worked with Mead since 1968.

Annabel Clayton (Mead Packaging) sells convenience packaging to the industrial market in New York. She joined Mead in 1966.

Bobby Bullock started his Mead career in 1962 as an hourly worker at Durham and worked his way up to general foreman of Mead Containers' Spartanburg plant.

G. D. Rapp, Mead's assistant general counsel, has been appointed chairman of the new Corporate Responsibility Committee.

W. Walker Lewis, Jr. is general counsel for Mead. He serves as the Corporate Responsibility Committee's secretary.

Ivan Allen, Jr. is chairman of the board of the Ivan Allen Company in Atlanta, which merchandises office supplies and equipment. He served two terms as mayor of Atlanta from 1962 to 1969. He was elected to the Mead board in 1971.

Vernon R. Alden is chairman of the board at The Boston Company. He was President of Ohio University from 1962 to 1969, a period characterized by strong student unrest. He has been a Mead director since 1965.

N. H. DeBardeleben is president of the First National Bank of Birmingham. He joined the Mead Board of Directors in 1968.

Three employees chosen for directors' committee

A three-month search for three employees to fill out the Mead board of directors' new Corporate Responsibility Committee has resulted in the selection of a saleswoman, a general foreman, and a customer service manager to serve with three outside directors. The three were chosen from a panel of 10—narrowed down from a field of nearly 80 candidates from all parts of the company—for the contribution each can make to the committee's work.

The board created the committee to help Mead keep abreast of its changing responsibilities—toward the environment, the communities it operates in, its customers and employees—and to see that it is developing sound ways to deal with them. Chairman J. W. McSwiney says that it should "provide a means for unorthodox, unexpected, unconventional—perhaps unwelcome—ideas to emerge and find their way to top level attention."

A small task force is already accumulating fresh data on such topics as Mead woodlands policies, employment practices, and environmental quality programs. The committee expects to draw upon the ideas of all 80 original nominees and welcomes the input of any interested employee.

Here are the other finalists who vied for committee membership

Grady A. Roberts, Jr. came to Montag in Atlanta in 1971 to help with training for disadvantaged employees. He also works in the cost department.

Youns Kim, controller for Westab at Sunnyvale, Calif., came to the United States for an education and liked it so well he stayed. He joined Mead in 1971.

Ronald Sedenquist, an electrician at Mead Publishing Papers' Escanaba mill, takes an active role in his union. His service began in 1957.

Owen L. Gentry (Board Supply division) is superintendent of the Sylva, N.C. mill. He has been with Mead since 1960.

Mike Noonan, who joined Mead in 1968, is general sales manager for Mead Packaging division in Atlanta.

Howard Hughes is special projects manager with Murray Rubber in Houston, Texas. He came to Mead in 1968.

Lester (Bill) Reed is general manager of Woodward's Chattanooga Coke and Chemical division. He came to Mead in 1966.

early 83

Nine months later, a decision was made to recruit an hourly paid employee for the committee. Most of the applicants for committee membership were nominated by their supervisors. After employee members narrowed the list of applicants down to 10 finalists, all CRC members, in teams of 2, conducted interviews and chose 2 new members: Quepee Gates, a railroad conductor from a Mead facility in Woodward, Alabama; and Warden Seymour, a pipe fitter and union official from a paper mill in Chillicothe.

Early committee activities

In the summer of 1972, the corporate responsibility committee began to carry out the duties assigned by the full board—duties which represented the CRC's original charter:

- Examine and report on the attitudes of all levels of management toward social and environmental responsibilities and concerns.
- Examine and recommend specific issues for board and management consideration and determine their relative priority.
- Determine and recommend policy related to priority issues.
- Project potential new areas of social responsibility and involvement.
- Recommend where duties and responsibilities lie throughout the various levels of the company.

To help the committee select its priorities, Rapp, at the direction of the committee, formed a task force to study Mead's performance in pollution control, equal opportunity and land management, and to analyze the attitudes of outside groups (e.g., the National Council of Churches and the Environmental Protection Agency) toward industry. Research assistants to the task force were four recent college graduates who were about to enter graduate school. These researchers gave Mead managers their first inkling of what CRC might be up to. One recalled:

> Their three-month escapade certainly didn't help the credibility of the committee. CRC was brand new from the chairman of the board, so people knew it was important. The next thing they saw were these college kids— "Rapp's Raiders" as they came to be known—marching through their doors, telling them their EEO performance was lousy, their contributions budgets all wrong—and reporting to top management.
>
> One manager got fired. He should have been fired, but there was a direct link between the exposure these kids gave him and his dismissal. He happened to be a highly regarded—incompetent—guy. That he got fired scared a lot of people. Some people quietly let their stomachs churn. Others became outwardly hostile to the committee.

not helpful

At the conclusion of their studies, the students made several recommendations to CRC. The primary ones were that the company use incentives to reward and punish managers for pollution control and equal opportunity performance and that the company establish a multiple-use strategy for its forests. Within a year, corporate staff reported to CRC that Mead had begun a systematic expansion of hunting, fishing, and hiking rights in its forests, as part of a multiple-use program. By

April 1976, however, the company had not formally implemented the researchers' first recommendation.

Reaching the employees

The employee members of the CRC felt strongly in 1972 that contact with Mead employees was needed to communicate priorities to the committee. To help in this process, Rapp arranged to have Randy Evans released from his regular job and assigned to the human resources staff for three months to coordinate regional meetings. Under Evans's supervision, 140 employees were chosen, from names submitted by supervisors and general managers, to attend two-day conferences. The conferees included 56 hourly and 84 salaried workers from 48 operating units. Forty-six of the employees were members of minority groups; 38 were women. Evans described the employee meetings:

> Initially, a lot of people were uncertain about the purpose, but as things started unfolding on the first evening, they began to see that we were serious. By and large, a feeling of sincerity was communicated, and people said, "Well, if this is real, how can we make it worthwhile?"
> The interchange that began happening was just beautiful. One salesman said that salespeople have no job satisfaction. A black hourly worker said: "I'm not concerned with job satisfaction. I don't even know what you're talking about. I've got four children and I'm happy to have a job. And let me tell you what it's like to work in a foundry." This kind of exchange started going on.

Most of the employees who had spent two days discussing what was "right" and what was "wrong" with the Mead Corporation seemed to leave the meetings with good feelings. For many, the opportunity to share information and experiences, at meetings sponsored by the company itself, elicited a positive attitude toward management. One participant wrote to the organizer of a California meeting: "I think we all felt a little proud of Mead and the CRC for this opportunity. We may eventually let a little 'we' creep into our thinking, instead of the ominous 'they.' " In a report prepared for the directors, Evans wrote:

> Employees wanted the existing communications channels to work. They did not want the corporate responsibility committee to do an "end run" around management. Rather, they wanted the CRC to fix the system so that a mutual listening and trust relationship could be developed between the employee and his immediate supervisor.

CRC in 1973—reporting to management

Mead's group vice presidents had their first formal contact with CRC early in 1973 at a Hueston Woods, Ohio, retreat, where CRC employee members reported on the 1972 employee meetings. One group VP described the presentation:

> All of us were impressed with the eloquence of the people describing the problems they found in Mead. They were obviously words from the heart. We went down skeptical, but came away really impressed. The issues were pretty clear—better information sharing and communication and a need to make the system work more effectively.

After the Hueston Woods meeting, the employee members of CRC and a few employees who had attended the 1972 regional conferences met with managers throughout the company. Robert Richards (a manager chosen for CRC membership in 1975) recalled a story he had heard about a 1973 CRC plant visit:

> I heard about the visit from the plant manager. Some CRC people toured his place, a lovely old brick building surrounded by trees. He asked one CRC member how he liked the plant, expecting the usual praise. Instead, the CRC person said: "I don't see any blacks working here. Haven't you hired any?" The manager told him that no blacks lived in that area. In that case, the CRC member said, the manager should be recruiting blacks throughout the state. The manager told me that, in his opinion, CRC was out to manufacture issues where it couldn't find them.

After a year of management meetings, the employee members of CRC expected the organization to respond in some way. But nothing seemed to happen. A senior manager offered this explanation: "After the early meetings, there was an air of endorsement and enthusiasm among the operating managers, but it was not their role to pick up the responsibility for making things happen."

In addition to holding meetings for management and recruiting new committee members in 1973, CRC also heard reports from corporate staff on EEO performance, corporate contributions, programs for employees with drug and alcohol problems, and a placement effort for employees who were laid off when Mead closed a facility in Anniston, Alabama. Exhibits 6 and 7 are examples of the kinds of data the committee received in these reports.

In preparation for the last CRC meeting of 1973, Jerry Rapp, committee secretary, sent several recommendations for the next year's agenda to chairman Vernon Alden:

> Our basic task now is to see how Mead could institutionalize this process of employee communication. Next, we might consider new major projects that we should undertake ourselves or encourage other Mead people or groups to take on. From the employee meetings, we have identified problems falling into six clusters . . . equal employment opportunity; job satisfaction; communications; the external human environment; the external physical environment; and personal services for employees such as counseling for retirees, day-care centers, clean working conditions. . . .

New directors join CRC

In April 1974 two new director members were appointed. These were C. William Verity, chairman of the board of Armco Steel Company, and George B. Beitzel, senior vice president and director of IBM. (As a means of familiarizing directors with the company, the board rotated membership on CRC.) In the years that followed, members of CRC often referred to this April meeting as a turning point for the committee. It brought two issues into focus: the frustration and disappointment that employee members were experiencing after the intensity of CRC's start-up years, and the difference between director and employee members' perception of the role of CRC within the company.

Exhibit 6

EQUAL OPPORTUNITY PERCENTAGES 1974–1976

Category	April 1, 1976	April 1, 1975	April 1, 1974
Executives, officials, and managers	4.2/4.4	3.0/4.0	2.2/3.7
Professionals	15.3/3.6	12.0/3.4	9.9/3.5
Technicians	9.4/7.1	7.0/4.3	6.7/5.5
Sales workers	11.5/4.4	8.1/4.4	5.4/2.9
Office and clerical	75.9/9.8	72.1/9.4	71.0/8.7
Skilled crafts	1.1/12.3	0.9/11.8	1.4/11.6
Semiskilled operatives	14.7/27.7	12.7/26.6	11.8/27.1
Unskilled laborers	29.2/28.9	24.9/27.5	20.8/33.0
Service workers	9.9/37.9	9.6/32.4	8.9/31.1
Total work force	19.6/19.7	18.1/18.6	16.9/20.7

Key: All females percent/All minorities (male and female) percent.

Exhibit 7

CORPORATE GIFTS 1969–1975

Year	Net gifts ($000)	Gifts as percent of earnings before tax	
		Mead	All industry
1969	$624	1.07	1.24
1970	496	1.51	1.08
1971	408	1.06	1.03
1972	440	1.51	0.95
1973	453	0.90	0.86
1974	514	0.34	0.83
1975	492	0.96	n.a.

n.a. = Not available.

who's responsible?!

All the employee members were angry about the corporation's failure to deal with the problems discussed at the employee conferences in 1972 and reported to management in 1973. At the April meeting, they argued that if it did nothing else, CRC should at least respond to the most widespread complaint voiced at the employee meetings—dirty restroom facilities in plants and mills throughout the company. Both new director members expressed their surprise at the nature of the issue and the manner in which it had been uncovered. One recalled the meeting:

> It was hard to get a definition of what the committee was and what it should be doing. At my first meeting, somebody mentioned that the men's rooms were very dirty and said the committee ought to do something about that. I argued that it was not the committee's responsibility. If the company's policy was to keep the men's rooms clean, that was the responsibility of the plant managers.

I didn't think CRC should have been asking employees what was on their minds. That was management's job. I told them that the committee should not be a lightning rod for employee grievances. The only people CRC should be talking to is management, asking them questions about policy.

really ?!

The employees disagreed. One of the committee members described the April meeting as "the most intense we'd ever had." For all five employee members, it was a disheartening experience. One commented:

> Beitzel and Verity came on the committee and pretty much refuted the prior posture of the CRC as a committee that would go out and *do* things. They were most vocal in saying: "This is a committee of the board; you are to ask questions of management and let them respond." They felt actually going into the organization and holding employee meetings was something that management should do, not the members of CRC.
>
> You know, we had put our hearts and souls into this and there were these new members coming in and scaring the hell out of you just by sitting there, and then downgrading everything you'd been doing for the last year and a half.

As a result of this meeting, Jerry Rapp and consultant Constantine Simonides, an MIT vice president, worked together to fashion an agenda for CRC. They spoke with chief executive officers and other top management and staff people from companies all around the country with records of achievement in the area of corporate responsibility. In October 1974 they made a presentation to CRC. Their primary recommendation was that CRC should turn its attention to the world outside Mead and pass the responsibility for employee-oriented programs to management. Specifically, they recommended that Mead's president and group vice presidents take responsibility for improving communications between managers and employees, that corporate staff plan career development and personal service programs for employees and work more closely with supervisors on equal opportunity planning, and that CRC begin to assess the company's contributions policy and programs for involving Mead employees in the affairs of their communities. Rapp described the meeting: "Our recommendations fell on deaf ears. The employee members were just more interested in internal issues. Our discussion of what other companies were doing, what was going on in the outside world, made no impact at all."

A few weeks before Rapp made this presentation to CRC, employee member Warden Seymour had written a letter to Mead's chairman, expressing his concern about the committee's lack of activity:

> . . . From the time you informed me I had been selected for the committee, I have believed in the good it can do for all the employees and for the corporation. Recently though I have become very discouraged with the lack of activity by the committee. I feel the chairman of the board has a very deep sense of responsibility to all the employees but I feel people under you are reluctant to accept the changes recommended by this body. I feel the only way the committee can survive is with very strong support from you and Mr. Batts. . . .

McSwiney responded to Seymour early in November and emphasized his continued support of the committee:

> I also could be discouraged when I think of all the things that have not been accomplished. The existence of the corporate responsibility committee in some ways may aid in raising expectations beyond what can realistically be accomplished; but that is a risk I am willing to live with so long as we can have open dialogue throughout the company about the expectation level and the measures of performance (or lack of performance) about these expectations. . . .
>
> During 1975, I would urge you and other committee members to consider contact with fellow employees and others in the context of the committee's responsibility of monitoring progress within the company on the key corporate responsibility issues, with results to be reported to the board and corporate management. . . .

In November 1974 the employee members came together to discuss the issues they felt the whole committee should tackle in the coming year. They put together a list of 35 objectives to pursue in 1975 (Exhibit 8).

Exhibit 8

CRC PRIORITIES FOR 1975: RECOMMENDATIONS FROM EMPLOYEE MEMBERS

1. Examination by board of Mead's policy on involuntary separations, layoffs, terminations, and early retirements (equality of treatment with respect to notices and placement and committee audit).
2. Bring together board and employee members of committee.
3. Board examination of Mead's policy and performance regarding corporate contributions.
4. Board examination of Mead's policy regarding educational assistance including leave policy and family assistance.
5. Meetings:
   a. Full day.
   b. Operating locations.
   c. Outside contributors.
   d. Times other than board meetings.
   e. Six meetings per year.
   f. Workshop meetings.
   g. Annual meeting with board by full committee with report by employee members.
   h. Routine receipt of reports.
   i. Outsider take minutes.
6. Audit personal services effort.
7. Inquire, examine, or investigate policy or method of communications to employees, i.e., *Progress Report* (ask Mead people *and* outsiders to review for committee).
8. Board agenda to include CRC report and, perhaps, questions regarding employee concerns.
9. Board examine Mead's policy concerning handicapped people: ex-offenders, physically handicapped, Vietnam veterans, hard-core unemployed, etc.
10. Policy and performance at Mead regarding career planning.
11. Board examine Mead's policy concerning managerial rewards and punishments with respect to EEO performance.
12. Quarterly report to board by management of EEO performance.
13. Board require management to report routinely in advance on actions that impact Mead constituencies—employees, community, suppliers, customers.

Exhibit 8 *(concluded)*

14. Individual access to and control of information.
15. Recommend that Mead should have policy with respect to an individual nonunion employee appeals process.
16. Ask for policy on employee recognition.
17. Ask for policy concerning assistance to families of employee who dies.
18. Policy affecting contact with retired employees also disabled.
19. Ask for policy on age discrimination.
20. Ask what is company policy regarding minimum physical standards for Mead employee facilities.
21. Policy on CRC membership turnover.
22. Deal with personal problems of members due to CRC service.
23. Decision on staff support to committee.
24. Determine interest, policy, and posture regarding "external" concerns.
25. Decision regarding employee meetings—recommend to management.
26. Examine management efforts to place black males in *top* line positions— what are goals?
27. Company should address attention to determining concerns of middle managers.
28. Company policy regarding response to recent pension legislation.
29. What impact expected from "inflation management" concept and procedures.
30. What attempt and results of management efforts to improve quality of communication between supervisors and subordinates.
31. Connect 1975 CRC agenda with the past two years.
32. Examine the effect of attitude surveys and assessment mechanisms on employees.
33. Board emphasize performance measurement beyond financial results.
34. Ask for Mead's policy on the company's participation in the community.
35. Big external issues—work with other institutions:
    a. ZEG/ZPG impact on Mead.
    b. Cooperation versus competition with respect to unions, competitors, government communication.
    c. Conservation.
    d. How people relate to company and what are new ways of relating.
    e. Impact of future technology and discoveries on Mead and its constituencies.

Source: Mead Corporation.

New employees join CRC

In 1975 three employee members left the committee, and Rapp and Paul Allemang managed the recruitment process for replacements.[5] CRC discussed at great length the problems of recruiting new members because employee members believed that few in the company understood the committee's function. In response to a director's recommendation, Rapp and Allemang prepared a proposal for recruiting new members

[5] When Paul Allemang stepped down as president, chief operating officer, and director of Mead in 1973, he was appointed to the position of officer of the board. His main responsibility was to help coordinate CRC activities.

and discussed it with Warren Batts. They suggested that the group vice presidents select a panel of employees (managers, staff, and hourly workers) to screen candidates from groups other than their own. The candidates so chosen would then be interviewed by all the members of CRC. This would be an annual process.

Batts invited Allemang and Rapp to discuss the proposal at an April 1975 meeting of the group vice presidents. He described what happened at the meeting:

> I thought that Paul and Jerry's proposal for getting new members for CRC was sound since it got management involved. So they met with the group vice presidents to discuss the recruitment process. The response from the group vice presidents was not what I expected. They were upset. "We're closing down and selling plants and laying off many in the work force," they said, "and now we're going to have all this song and dance, at great expense." At their insistence, the process of selecting new members was toned down.

In July of 1975 Randy Evans (one of the retiring employee members) made a 10-day trip around the country to interview applicants for CRC, most of whom had been nominated by their supervisors and general managers. Evans chose 10 finalists, who were then interviewed by committee members. The four new employee members were Robert Richards, a marketing manager; Robi Love, coordinator for college employment; David Hubbard, a sales representative in California; and Ister Person, who worked in the order processing department of a paper merchant unit. All four had been nominated for CRC membership; only Person had been unaware of the committee's existence before receiving word of her nomination.

In August 1975 Jerry Rapp sent a memorandum to James McSwiney on the future of CRC. He made four recommendations:

1. Strengthen the leadership and active participation of director members.
2. Balance the employee membership by including middle management and clarify the selection process by involving local operating management.
3. Beef up the staff support to the committee in order to provide more information to members and to communicate the committee's concerns and activities to corporate staff and operating management.
4. Broaden the CRC agenda to include not only employee concerns but also the concerns of external groups such as customers, shareholders, government agencies, suppliers, and communities in which plants are located.

In October the new employee members attended an orientation meeting, and in December their first regular committee meeting. By their second meeting, in February 1976, they were expressing doubts about CRC's ability to get things done. One new member was especially concerned about the employee members' isolation from the directors, and the committee's isolation from the company:

What bothered me from the first was that all the employee members had suggestions for the agenda, issues we felt were important, but we didn't get a chance to discuss them with the directors. We rely on the directors for leadership, and without more direct communication with them, we probably won't have much of an impact on the company. What also bothered me was that we had no formal means of communicating with the organization. We seemed to be operating in a closet.

In a speech delivered at this time, McSwiney offered his views on the committee's progress:

After three years' experience with the Mead corporate responsibility committee, I have found the process in our company both rewarding and frustrating. Things that needed to be said to or about the organization have often been much more effectively stated without my direct participation . . . and this is, of course, a pleasant surprise! When a director, for instance, asks an officer, "Are you humane?" I assure you the penetration and subsequent attitudinal change is much different than if the same question were asked by the CEO. . . .

Gaining the understanding and support of middle managers is a crucial step in the effectiveness of a corporate responsibility effort. At Mead, we have not done as well as we would like in this area. We have learned, sometimes painfully, that we must take special care not to threaten middle managers by our anxiety to institute new programs and changes quickly. The understanding and cooperation of middle management is a vital part of making progress in this as well as in any other area that affects operations. We must not allow corporate responsibility to appear as the esoteric mental exercise of top management.

Plant-closing policy

At the same time that CRC was recruiting new members in 1975, it was giving its attention to a policy issue that both director and employee members agreed was of major importance to the corporation. This was the company's plant-closing policy and the question of management's responsibility to employees who lost their jobs when Mead closed or sold an operating unit. The issue gave the president of the company, Warren Batts, his first direct encounter with the committee.

Following the development and implementation of its strategic plan, between 1973 and 1976, Mead closed 22 of its operating facilities and dropped 8,500 employees from its payroll. The 1973 annual report explained;

We made a searching classification of all our businesses in 1971–72. Then we projected each ahead to 1977 and took a look at where they—and the corporation as a whole—would be. That indicated clearly which businesses we should cultivate and which we should move out of to give us the soundest portfolio for the long haul. . . .

We've been acting on the analysis, moving out of businesses no longer viable for us and zeroing in on opportunities of special promise. . . . To put it simply, we expect to fund businesses with strong growth potential aggressively and to withdraw from those that offer neither growth nor cash.

During CRC's early years, employee and director members occasionally discussed the need to learn whether Mead management had developed a formal companywide policy for dealing with employees affected by plant closings. In December 1974, they raised the issue with Robert Schuldt, vice president of employee development (who was present to report on EEO performance), after employee member Quepee Gates told the committee that he had lost his job in Mead's Woodward, Alabama, foundry that month. Gates was 60 years old and had worked at the foundry for 35 years. What especially troubled him, he said, was that management had notified him at 3 P.M., on what he thought was a normal working day, that the plant was closing at the end of the shift.

Two months later, in March 1975, Warren Batts attended a CRC meeting to discuss the company's plant-closing policy. Batts reported that a total of 1,825 employees had been laid off in 1974 as a result of 11 plant closings. In most cases, the employees had been notified of the closings from four days to three weeks ahead of time. One hundred fifty employees had chosen to retire, and Mead had helped another 500 to find jobs in other plants or with other companies. The balance chose to remain on unemployment compensation until their eligibility ran out. Batts explained that within the framework of Mead's policy of management decentralization, each division had its own closing policy. This accounted for the disparity in notification dates and severance pay. However, by edict each division followed a standard practice including help from a corporate task force in finding employment for those who wished to work. Progress was monitored by a regular reporting process, and managers were rewarded for finding jobs for displaced employees.

In January 1976 Batts reported that a policy statement on plant closings had been officially adopted. One outside director commented: "The one concrete thing CRC did was to get management to put together a policy on how we're going to handle people when we shut down a location. Had the committee not raised the question, we might still not have a policy." CRC members felt that the committee had at last been able to influence the company.

The ombudsman issue

In 1976 the employee members of CRC suggested that the committee begin to study Mead's grievance procedures for nonunion employees. Mead had no companywide procedures for handling such problems since the human resources staff in each group had this responsibility. Some divisions had set up employee councils that met several times a year to discuss problems directly with management. Others had letter-writing programs, with staff assigned to investigate employees' complaints. One employee member commented on the problem:

> I've worked at a number of locations and know the concerns of white-collar workers and middle managers. They're the unheard segment of the company. They perceive, rightly or wrongly, that the unions have a very effective grievance mechanism and that the top-management group takes care of itself but that nobody looks out for them.

Robert Richards, who felt strongly that Mead needed change in this area, volunteered to prepare a paper on an "ombuds function" as a basis for committee discussion at the CRC meeting scheduled for May 27, 1976.[6] In this paper, Richards wrote: "Without a mechanism whereby ideas, complaints, and suggestions are freely discussed, many white-collar workers will be functioning in an atmosphere of anxiety, apprehension, and fear." (Excerpts appear in the Appendix.)

The president's dilemma

Warren Batts had had no formal contact with the full CRC until attending the meeting in March 1975 to discuss plant-closing policy. In the years since becoming president, however, he had found that few people understood the reason for the committee's formation and he had heard numerous complaints about its activities:

> There was never any kind of message from the corporate level that explained why directors thought that Mead needed a CRC. Some managers inferred that either the board felt they were not acting in a responsible manner or else someone in the system was chasing the latest corporate fad at their expense.

An operating manager who had been with Mead for 30 years confirmed this view when he summed up his impressions of CRC:

> The general feeling has been that CRC was imposed from the top. It has little or no support or credibility with operating managers. It serves no genuinely constructive purpose. It's a corporate gimmick. The real job of transmitting information, handling two-way communications, and dealing with employee problems should be at the operating level, not the corporate level.
>
> I suppose the intent is to provide the top echelon with grassroots sentiments on what has to be done. But I question whether employee representatives can speak for anyone but themselves. Many things are important at the local level and should be handled locally, not escalated. CRC is kept in place because McSwiney wants it, with the endorsement of the board. But it doesn't enjoy prestige or status with the rest of the company.

A group vice president described his managers' reactions to the committee: "The basic problem is that CRC is seen as a complete bypass of management. Whenever employees can talk directly to directors there is bound to be trouble."

Mead's chairman was aware of the hostility to CRC, but he continued to support it in discussions with board members and management. He made these observations about the company's response to the committee:

> There were various types of management reaction to CRC: concern, fear, admiration, pride. But, in general, there was an avoidance of integrating the system into the company. The group vice presidents—their natural inclination reinforced by the negative attitude of some of their managers—constantly sent darts at the people who supported the committee. There

---

[6] An ombudsman is a person to whom aggrieved parties (e.g., consumers, hospitalized patients, employees) take their complaints. The ombudsman makes an investigation, prepares a report, and attempts to achieve a fair settlement. Traditionally, the ombudsman function was used to protect individuals from abuse by government agencies. The first U.S. corporations to appoint ombudsmen were Xerox Corporation in 1972 and General Electric Company and Boeing Vertel Company in 1973.

were two reasons for this. First, CRC did make some mistakes. It focused solely on employee issues, because this was what mattered to the employee members, as would be expected. But the board and the company had expected the committee to deal with external issues as well. Second, some senior managers wanted to test whether CRC could be eliminated if they criticized it long enough.

I realized from the first that if a new development were to be creative, it was likely to destroy something that already existed. That's the nature of creativity. And if something is destroyed, there is bound to be a certain amount of tension. The main thing is to keep the tension healthy, or at least contained within certain parameters. What has finally happened is that the president of the company has begun to realize that the issues being raised by CRC are real and that all of us are hearing things faster and more directly than we would through the usual channels. He is beginning to see that the full potential for CRC is not being realized because it is outside the system.

I've always believed in the validity of the premise on which CRC was founded, and the whole organization and the board saw that I wanted it to stay. Otherwise, it might have been eliminated. I still think the organization can absorb it. As we move forward, I think CRC will be helpful to Mead, no matter what form it ultimately takes. It could turn out to be a superb thing. The final decision is still out.

Batts, who had to formulate a response to Richards's paper for the next CRC meeting, had a number of questions about the committee and the proposal:

On the ombudsman question—it's true that there's always been a massive communications gap in companies from the division level down to the foreman level. Where we don't get good marks is with the nonexempt salaried people, the first- and second-level supervisors, and professional staff. But despite our problems, we've found from attitude surveys that Mead always scores higher than average as a good place to work. We have very little turnover at these levels. So we have to be careful about overreacting.

The fact that the CRC has become more and more of a concern to more and more of the operating people is what really bothers me. This is something that has to be wired into the organization; it has to be made into a positive force for the company instead of being a peripheral activity. One of my real questions is: will CRC be a directors' committee, like all other committees of the board, or will it be an employees' grievance committee?

The chairman thought there were two basic questions about the corporate responsibility committee:

First, how secure must an organization be in order to incorporate such a vehicle into its normal operations? Second, what other alternatives do we have to the "filtering out process" of the pyramid organization?

APPENDIX

EXCERPTS FROM RICHARDS'S BACKGROUND REPORT

Why the need at Mead for an ombuds-type function

Without exception, there is a feeling of frustration in all sectors of white-collar work force that they are squeezed between the unions and top management. They contend that there is no effective way to bring their complaints, concerns, or frustrations to the decision makers without the fear of possible disciplinary action. Some of the concerns I have heard are as follows:

1. There is no effective mechanism to protect an individual from unjustly being fired.

2. The company takes arbitrary decisions on work hours, retirement, and other fringe benefits without explaining why they made the change, how they arrived at the decision, etc.

3. Bitterness is arising over the differentials in wage/salary policy between union and unrepresented employees. I have had managers with titles such as director, comptroller, and general manager complain that the differentials, as they have existed over the past few years, have created an almost untenable labor environment. They ask, "Does Mead really believe they are treating our employees fairly? How much longer do they expect the nonrepresented employees to accept merit salary increases substantially below union settlements? We're headed for unionization faster than we think."

In the eyes of many nonrepresented white-collar employees, such problems are being managed through a philosophy of benign neglect. The frustrations being voiced are not from radicals, drug users, or trouble makers. They are from some of the outstanding, conservative, and loyal members of this company. Without a mechanism whereby ideas, complaints, and suggestions are freely discussed, many white-collar workers will be functioning in an atmosphere of anxiety, apprehension, and fear.

Possible options

While it is not the role of the corporate responsibility committee to develop solutions, I have taken the liberty to scope out some possible options which could be investigated by the directors.

1. *Personnel council.* This is a monthly forum where representatives of management and employees sit down to discuss mutual problems and opportunities. This is done on the sectional, departmental, and divisional level, with the main council serving as the top tribunal.

    It is a two-way communication. Employees voice their complaints and suggestions to their elected council representatives who bring

---

Source: Mead Corporation.

them to management's attention at the regular meetings. Management, at the same time, communicates its policies and ideas to employees. Some discussions bear on companywide matters of significance. Others cover irritations that, if allowed to fester, could cause unpleasant consequences.

2. *Corporate ombudsman.* This function could entail an individual or a number of individuals who serve as an intermediary between employees and the various departments that frequently make up the corporate staff such as the benefits department, salary administration, etc.

3. *Grievance committee.* It has been suggested that a formal grievance committee be set up. Its function would be a cross between a judge/jury system and an arbitrator. There are several concerns I have with this move. First, this step could lead to very legalistic approaches by some employees and could weaken management's ability to manage properly. Second, it could be too radical a step in solving potential problems that basically arise out of misunderstandings on both sides and therefore might not be as productive as desired.

4. *The inspector general.* The role of the inspector general within the military is well known by most of us and the use of this concept could have some decided merits. This office could function similar to the way our internal audit department works. It would work with the various divisions, departments, and managers to see that the corporate policies, benefits, and other services are properly explained and carried out. It would also function somewhat as an intermediary between the employees and the many aspects of the corporation which would affect the employee. This type of function should not impinge upon the managerial prerogatives of management, yet it should help to bring about positive results.

Summary

If the Mead Corporation were to establish a form of ombuds-type function, I believe the following benefits could arise:

1. It would serve as an early warning system (a DEW line) for top management, alerting them of potentially serious problems which might arise.

2. It could alert corporate officials to those areas or individuals whose human skills need improving.

3. Serve as a safety valve on issues that might otherwise create explosive situations.

4. It should help sharpen management to think out decisions affecting people without hindering their ability to manage. The old adage, "It's not what you say but how you say it," applies here.

5. This system should be a preferable alternative to unionization without being viewed as an antiunion movement.

Dayton Hudson Corporation

Few trends could so thoroughly undermine the very foundations
of our free society as the acceptance by corporate officials of a
social responsibility other than to make as much money for their
stockholders as possible. This is a fundamentally subversive
doctrine. . . . The claim that business should contribute to the
support of charitable activities . . . is an inappropriate use of
corporate funds in a free enterprise society.   *Milton Friedman**

I maintain that business must change its priorities. We are not in
business to make maximum profit for our shareholders. We are in
business for only one reason—to serve society. Profit is our reward
for doing it well. If business does not serve society, society will
not long tolerate our profits or even our existence.

Kenneth Dayton †

IN MARCH 1976 Wayne Thompson received an initial draft of the 1975
annual report for the Dayton Hudson Corporation. More than doubled
income before taxes seemed an unambiguous result, but Thompson's
position caused him to look at these numbers in a slightly different
light. As senior vice president of the environmental development department, Thompson had the responsibility for presenting management's
policy on charitable contributions, which for more than 30 years had
equaled 5 percent of taxable earnings.[1]

In a few days Thompson had to appear before a committee of the
board of directors with management's recommendations for the company's contributions activities for the year.[2] The numbers provided a starting point for his thoughts—for 1976 based on 1975 results, the 5 percent
came to $5 million, more than twice the largest amount ever before
available for charitable contributions. Final decisions had to be made
on how much should be spent as well as where and how the money
should be distributed.

---

* *Capitalism and Freedom* (Chicago, 1962), pp. 133, 135.

† Chairman, Dayton Hudson Corporation, "Seegal-Macy Lecture," delivered at the
University of Michigan, Ann Arbor, October 30, 1975.

[1] U.S. corporations are allowed to deduct a maximum of 5 percent of taxable earnings
as an expense in computing their federal tax liability.

[2] As will be discussed later in the case, contributions were given directly by the operating
units of Dayton Hudson Corporation as well as through the Dayton Hudson Foundation.
This was a separate nonprofit corporation qualified as a private foundation under the Internal
Revenue Code.

THE COMPANY: ITS ORGANIZATION AND LOCATION

Dayton's was originally a family-owned retailer established in 1902 in Minneapolis, Minnesota. In 1967 the company went public and in 1969 merged with Hudson's, a department store chain in Detroit, to become the Dayton Hudson Corporation. By fiscal 1975 consolidated revenues had reached $1.692 billion and the corporation's shares, which had reached a recent high of $34.75 in early 1976, were held by about 12,000 shareholders. (See Exhibit 1 for a financial history.) The annual report described the company:

> Dayton Hudson Corporation is a diversified retail company operating in 38 states through department stores, low-margin stores, and specialty stores. Through its real estate business, it also owns, develops, and manages regional shopping centers and commercial properties and office buildings.

The annual report went on to describe the philosophy behind "A Flexible Strategy for Profit Growth":

> We believe the primary advantage of our diversified approach lies in the ability of each of our companies to attune its merchandising to the particular environment in which it operates—to shape its business to fit the contours of its market with sensitivity and precision. It was this flexibility that gave our companies their competitive edge in 1975.

Dayton Hudson was organized into several autonomous divisions with corporate staff and headquarters located in the IDS Tower in Minneapolis. (See Exhibit 2 for organization chart.) The corporation's retail operating companies were reported in the annual report as shown in Table 1. In terms of profitability, the annual report indicated that Hudson's contributed the largest amount to the corporate total, followed by Target, Dayton's, B. Dalton, and Lechmere. Corporate sales were largely concentrated in the Midwest with Michigan and Minnesota each having approximately one third of 1975 sales according to estimates by the casewriter.

Throughout the corporation there existed a strong emphasis on growth and return on equity. A "Corporate Mission Statement" explained that the corporation's goal was "to grow and earn at a rate commensurate with the best in industry. Consistency of earnings growth and an optimum rate of current earnings are the primary criteria by which the corporation and its retail operating companies will be judged." In 1974 Dayton Hudson disclosed a specific goal of earning a 14 percent return on shareholders' equity—achieved for the first time in 1975. (See Exhibit 3 for a comparison of Dayton Hudson's performance with other retailers.)

The Mission Statement went on to outline the division of functions which would lead to the fulfillment of this goal, stressing the degree of independence enjoyed by the operating companies:

> The operating companies will be awarded the freedom and responsibility: to manage their own business within clear guidelines, to develop strategic plans and goals which optimize their growth, and to develop an organization which can assure consistency of results and optimum growth.

Exhibit 1

FINANCIAL RESULTS
($ millions, except per share data)

	1975	1974	1973	1972	1971	1970	1969	1968
Total revenues	$1,692	$1,504	$1,407	$1,297	$1,120	$971	$890	$813
Earnings before income taxes	107.0	50.1	53.3	53.9	45.7	37.6	48.1	51.0
Income taxes—federal, state, and local	55.7	24.9	26.0	26.4	21.0	18.6	24.4	26.4
Net earnings	51.3	25.2	27.3	27.5	24.7	19.0	23.7	24.6
Depreciation and amortization	29.9	27.6	25.3	24.4	22.6	19.7	16.2	14.0
Return on beginning shareholders' equity	14.4%	7.4	8.4	9.2	8.6	7.0	9.3	10.3
Per common share:								
Net earnings	3.22	1.57	1.70	1.70	1.52	1.16	1.49	1.54
Cash dividend	0.66	0.58½	0.54	0.52	0.50	0.50	0.50	0.40
Book value	24.62	22.09	21.10	19.88	18.70	17.69	16.84	15.94
Capital expenditures	39.8	58.1	55.8	36.9	33.3	56.8	92.8	52.9
Year-end financial position:								
Working capital	229.7	219.1	229.5	226.3	175.7	159.2	148.8	135.0
Property and equipment, net of depreciation	407.4	398.9	378.2	361.1	354.5	348.1	312.5	238.7
Long-term debt	241.2	263.8	268.8	259.0	227.2	222.6	193.7	118.8
Shareholders' equity	396.4	356.1	340.5	324.7	305.8	289.6	269.7	255.8
Average common shares outstanding (000)	15,850	15,850	15,890	16,017	16,017	16,020	15,814	15,850

Source: Dayton Hudson Corporation 1975 annual report.

Exhibit 2

ORGANIZATION: OCTOBER 1976

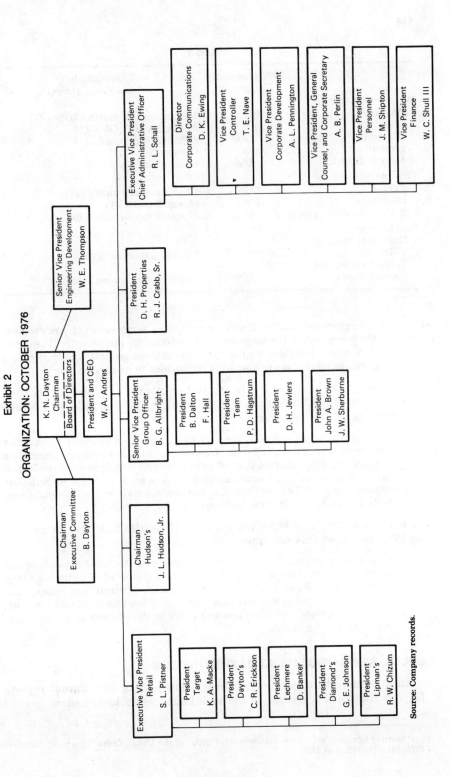

Source: Company records.

Table 1

	1975 revenues ($ millions)	Locations (number of stores)
Department stores:		
Dayton's	$256.6	Minnesota (7), North Dakota (1)
Hudson's	496.1	Michigan (12), Ohio (1)
Diamond's	68.6	Arizona (6), Nevada (1)
Lipman's	39.6	Oregon (7)
John A. Brown	27.8	Oklahoma (4)
Low-margin stores:		
Target	511.9	10 midwestern states (48)
Lechmere	104.2	Massachusetts (4)
B. Dalton, Bookseller	84.1	37 states nationwide (209)
Specialty stores:		
Dayton Hudson Jewelers	31.4	7 states nationwide (40)
Team (sound/audio equipment)	33.9	8 midwestern states (105)

The corporate staff will provide only those services which are essential to the protection of the corporation, are needed for the growth of the corporation, and are wanted by the operating companies and which provide a significant advantage to operating companies in quality or cost.

Minneapolis served as the headquarters not only for the corporation but also for Dayton's and Target. A January 1976 article in *Fortune* stressed the city's character:

In a magic sort of way, the city has taken on a cloak of glamour as the place where a lot of things are going right. . . . Corporate executives devote an astonishing amount of their time and money to good works and civic affairs. . . . Their business leaders have set a standard of corporate citizenship that, if widely copied, would profoundly alter the shape of American philanthropy, culture, and cities, all for the better.[3]

Bruce Dayton, in addressing a group of Seattle business executives in 1976, reflected this sentiment:

Business can take the initiative in addressing the priority needs of our society . . . it is clear to us in Minnesota that this kind of initiative, along with a high level of support of existing social, cultural, and educational institutions, is the primary reason that Minnesota and the Twin Cities always rank among the top states and cities in the country in all measurements of quality of life.

SOCIAL RESPONSIBILITY AT DAYTON HUDSON

In a section entitled "Corporate Citizenship" in the annual report, Dayton Hudson's activities in the social area were described:

---

[3] Gurney Breckenfeld, "How Minneapolis Fends Off the Urban Crisis," *Fortune,* January 1976, pp. 131, 132, and 182.

Exhibit 3

COMPARISON WITH OTHER RETAILERS

	Sales*	Net income*	Return on sales	Return on Assets†	Return on equity†	Price-earnings ratio‡
1. Dayton Hudson	$ 1,693	$ 51.3	3.0%	6.0%	14.4%	14
2. Federated Department Stores ...	3,713	157.4	4.2	9.7	16.4	18
3. May Department Stores	2,017	66.7	3.3	5.5	13.4	14
4. Associated Dry Goods	1,391	43.1	3.1	5.7	10.4	14
5. Carter Hawley Hale Stores	1,252	41.6	3.3	6.2	12.7	14
6. Sears, Roebuck	13,640	522.6	3.8	4.8	11.0	28
7. J. C. Penney	7,679	189.6	2.5	6.9	13.5	29
8. S. S. Kresge	6,798	200.8	3.0	10.6	19.8	36

Note: Comparability may not be exact because some companies used LIFO and some FIFO for inventory valuation.
* In millions for year ending January 31, 1976, for all companies.
† Return on beginning assets and equity.
‡ On March 1, 1976.
Sources: Independent research by casewriter from company annual reports and *The Wall Street Journal* of March 2, 1976.

Dayton Hudson Corporation and our operating companies have a commitment to corporate social responsibility that is expressed in four different ways:

1. Utilizing 5 percent of our federal taxable income to improve the quality of life in those communities in which the corporation and our operating companies are located. . . .
2. Contribution of executive time and talent through encouraging employees to be leaders in community service. . . .
3. Socially responsible business conduct of the highest level is expected of all Dayton Hudson operating companies. Our operating companies have formal programs in equal employment and advancement opportunity, consumerism, energy conservation, environmental impact, and community development.
4. Open and clear disclosure of the facts about our business. Dayton Hudson's 1974 annual report to shareholders received the *Financial World* award as the Best Annual Report of All Industry. We were recognized by *Business and Society Review* as one of 13 firms that have distinguished themselves in the area of corporate social responsibility, winning a specific award for disclosure of information on how we distribute our charitable contribution.

Through all of these practices, we have aimed at setting leadership standards for corporate citizenship. . . .

The corporation had a long history of concern for its community and active giving to charity. The roots of this practice went back to the Dayton family which, in 1976, still reportedly owned about 40 percent of the common stock. Kenneth Dayton commented:

Our current practices grew out of a private sense of social obligation that my grandfather had when he started this company. He was a very charitable man who made substantial contributions to the community.

In the early days, of course, the family and the business were closely related. When we were going public, we wanted to make sure that everything the company was doing was in the public interest. We made our first offering of common stock in 1967, but we prepared the way by publishing annual reports for two years before we went public. In fact, as a private company, we acted more publicly than many public companies.

One of the things we had to decide was whether these charitable instincts could be formalized as a business practice. We decided that they could, and the company continued the 5 percent policy. It was made clear in the original prospectus that we would do this.[4] While you can't divorce management from the giving pattern, there is no conflict between giving 5 percent in contributions and our long-term profit. In the long term, I feel that our contributions even strengthen our profitability because the contributions are investments in the quality of our communities.

The *Fortune* article on Minneapolis contained some observations on the family's current role in Minnesota philanthropy:

There's a regular route for raising money and it begins with the Daytons [says the admiring president of another firm]. Kenneth personally con-

---

[4] The 1967 Prospectus said, "The company has consistently contributed 5 percent of its annual income before taxes for charitable and civic purposes in the communities it serves and in which its employees and customers live and shop. The company plans to continue this program."

tributed $2.6 million to help build Minneapolis's new Orchestra Hall and Bruce led successful efforts to raise $26 million for the Institute of Arts.

To a question on the validity of this statement, Kenneth Dayton responded: "It may still be hard for this community to divorce the family, the store, and the corporation. In many people's minds they may be the same, yet the separation is real and perfectly clear within the corporation."

ORGANIZING FOR SOCIAL RESPONSIBILITY

The first organized effort in the social area was the establishment in 1917 of the Dayton Foundation (name changed to the Dayton Hudson Foundation after the 1969 merger), which was set up, according to an early brochure, to "aid in promoting the welfare of mankind everywhere in the world." The corporation continued to channel a substantial portion of its contributions through this body, which from 1969 onward published reports describing the company's and the foundation's donations. Four thousand copies of this report were distributed in 1975.

To handle a growing set of civic activities, in addition to charitable contributions, Wayne Thompson, former city manager of Oakland, California, was hired in 1965 to head the foundation and to be in charge of a new environmental development department. Thompson described his first day on the job: "Don Dayton, who was then chairman, drew a square on a sheet of paper. He said, 'Consider this square to represent the four walls of a store. Your job is to become involved with the well-being of everything outside of those four walls in our community. I am convinced that our profitability as a company is as much reliant, if not more reliant, on the quality of life which exists there than on our merchandising and management practices within the company.'"

In 1976 the department consisted of three professionals: Thompson, who had been called the "conscience" of the corporation by *The Washington Star,* and two staff members in the governmental affairs area.[5] According to Thompson, "Good government is a pivotal factor to the success of any community. These two people are devoted to the advancement and preservation of good government wherever the company operates or has interests." A full-time professional director of the foundation's charitable contributions program reported independently to Thompson in his capacity as president of the foundation.

The newest organizational innovation was the committee on social responsibility of the board of directors, formed in 1973. Bruce Dayton described this group in the 1973 contributions report:

> Chaired by Dr. Paul Ylvisaker, dean of the Graduate School of Education of Harvard University, the committee is a unique partnership between the board of directors and senior management, focusing attention of all operating units on the primary responsibilities of corporate citizenship. The committee provides direction to and monitors progress of the corporation in

---

[5] Ron Snider, "He's the Conscience of a Retailer," *The Washington Star,* Friday, March 5, 1976.

the areas of charitable contributions, consumerism, affirmative action, environmental development, and community development.

The committee required the heads of all the operating companies to report each year on their social responsibility programs. About 5 percent of the incentive compensation given to Dayton Hudson's operating management was determined by performance on social responsibility matters.

CORPORATE GIVING: NATIONAL NORMS

Conservative economists such as Milton Friedman and activist shareholders such as Evelyn Davis had attacked the notion of charitable contributions on the grounds that business had no right giving away shareholders' money.[6] Corporate charitable contributions were nonetheless an established part of American business practice. The concept of giving with only indirect business benefit was upheld as a legitimate corporate function by the New Jersey Supreme Court in the 1953 Smith case and had not been questioned seriously on legal grounds since.

However, a major study of private giving in America done in 1975 disclosed opposition of a different nature to corporate contributions:

> Ironically, in their doubts about or outright opposition to corporate giving, conservative skeptics are joined from the opposite end of the political spectrum by those who regard corporate giving as an instrument of corporate conservatism. ". . . it is especially inappropriate for business corporations to play any role in the philanthropic process," asserts an activist critique addressed to the Commission. ". . . the real problem posed by corporate 'philanthropic' activity is that corporations are the embodiment of concentrated wealth. As such, they can hardly be expected to underwrite the political needs of Americans who wish to redistribute and deconcentrate that wealth."[7]

This study concluded with a recommendation that all corporations set a goal of giving 2 percent of pretax net income by 1980 and argued that ". . . corporate giving remains the last major undeveloped frontier for private giving to philanthropic causes . . . and can be larger in light of the vast funds that flow through corporate treasuries."[8]

A dissent to the commission's basic recommendation was filed by one of its members: "Employing exhortation to increase corporate gifts to charity is a futile exercise. Most of the corporate members of the

---

[6] An anecdote about Davis was repeated in a *Fortune* article: "Don't make any charitable contributions, Mel," she once advised Melvin W. Allredge at a meeting of the great Atlantic and Pacific Tea Company. "Give us higher cash dividends, so we can make contributions to whoever we want." (Kurt Barnes, "Rethinking Corporate Charity," *Fortune,* October 1974, p. 164.) Dayton Hudson, however, had never had such a protest at an annual meeting and had received only one complaining letter, from a holder of 1,000 shares, who stated: "I take a dim view of people donating other people's money to various causes. It smacks of labor unions spending members' money to support all kinds of political candidates and causes with which members do not identify."

[7] *Giving in America: Toward a Stronger Voluntary Sector,* Report of the Commission on Private Philanthropy and Public Needs, 1975, p. 152 (known as the Filer Report).

[8] Ibid., p. 154.

Commission acknowledged in our meetings that mere talk had not and would not increase corporate contributions."[9] The author of this dissent called for a 2 percent needs tax on corporations which could be offset by charitable gifts.

In terms of actual practices, a number of major American corporations gave regularly, but they did not give much. Although the IRS allowed tax deductions of up to 5 percent of pretax income, most companies gave far less than this maximum. Corporate contributions averaged 0.85 percent in 1974, down from 0.94 percent in 1973, and the Filer Report claimed that only 6 percent of all corporate taxpayers made charitable contributions of $500 or more in 1974. Dayton Hudson and Cummins Engine were virtually alone among major companies in donating the 5 percent limit. According to Wayne Thompson, Dayton Hudson ranked 10th nationally in terms of the absolute size of its charitable giving and he knew of no other national retailer that gave more than 2 percent of its earnings in contributions.

THE DAYTON HUDSON 5 PERCENT POLICY

Dayton Hudson's 5 percent policy had existed for many years and was defended strongly by most members of corporate management. Kenneth Dayton, chairman of the board, was emphatic on the importance of this policy: "Business has to say to itself that a certain amount of its efforts, its energies, and its resources—meaning its profits—must be devoted to building better environments in this nation. If not, the free enterprise system has a limited life span."

Bill Andres, president, seconded this argument:

> This program is an important part of our strategy. The welfare of our business very much relates to the health of the communities to which we belong. Giving 5 percent in the community makes us a pacesetter which is where we want to be.
>
> From this standpoint of the shareholders, their concern is chiefly with the company's ability to sustain earnings growth over a period of time. For a corporation such as ours—one with heavy investment in regional retail franchises—the vitality of the community and our long-term investment prospects are inextricably tied together.

Dayton Hudson's areas of concentration for its giving program also differed from most companies. Nationally, according to the Filer Report, the greatest percentage of corporate contributions went to health and welfare organizations (38 percent), with education close behind (35 percent), and with only 7 percent going to cultural programs. Dayton Hudson and the foundation, on the other hand, gave almost exclusively to just two categories: social action and the arts. Examples of the contributions made in 1975 are listed in Exhibit 4.

The contributions report stated the rationale for social action projects:

> A community is an environment of many dimensions. Perhaps the most significant dimension is the state of its social health; thus, Dayton Hudson

---

[9] Ibid., p. 210.

Exhibit 4

CORPORATE AND FOUNDATION CONTRIBUTIONS TO MINNESOTA FOR 1975*

Boys' Club of Minneapolis
Support of activities for underprivileged boys.
$3,500.

Center for Community Action
Minneapolis
For riverfront environmental improvement program, financed by business, operated by college students, and providing summer employment for high school youths.
$2,000.

Citizens League
Minneapolis
For nonpartisan civic research and education programs.
$5,000.

Community Design Center
Minneapolis
To help provide low-cost design services to nonprofit organizations.
$1,000.

Congress for a Better Rochester, Inc.
Development of recreation facilities.
(Completes pledge of $20,000.)
$10,000.

Consumer Credit Counseling Service
Minneapolis and St. Paul
To provide money management assistance to troubled familes.
$1,000.

Freshwater Biological Research Foundation
Minneapolis
For establishment of an institute for research and education in freshwater ecology.
(Total pledge of $50,000.)
$10,000

Guthrie Theatre Foundation
Minneapolis
General support.
$20,000.

Junior Achievement
Minneapolis, St. Paul, and Rochester
Support of youth participation in their own business ventures.
$2,534.

Mayo Foundation
Rochester
For development of Mayo Medical School.
(Total pledge of $200,000.)
$50,000.

Metropolitan Cultural Arts Center
Minneapolis
Support of arts programs for inner city youth.
$1,000.

Metropolitan Economic Development Association
Minneapolis
To provide assistance and support for development of minority businesses.
(Total pledge of $75,000.)
$15,300.

Minneapolis Foundation
To enable prompt response to needs of the community's minorities and disadvantaged.
$7,500.

Minneapolis Society of Fine Arts
Capital program for new facilities for Art Institute, College of Art and Design, and Children's
Theatre. $100,000
(Total pledge of $1,250,000.)
General support .... $ 26,000

Minnesota Dance Theatre
Minneapolis
General support.
$2,500.

Minnesota Opera Company
Minneapolis
General support.
$5,000.

Minnesota Orchestral Association
Minneapolis
Capital program for new
Orchestra Hall $200,000
(Total pledge of $1,000,000.)
General support—1975 and
1976 .... $ 59,000

Exhibit 4—Continued

Minnesota Private College Fund
Minneapolis
Toward operating expenses of 15 private colleges.
$10,000.

Nature Conservancy
Minneapolis
Toward purchase of threatened Minnesota prairie that is the native habitat of the prairie chicken.
(Completes pledge of $10,000.)
$5,000.

Norwegian Sesquicentennial Celebration
Minneapolis
General support.
$1,450.

Public Affairs Leadership and Management Training Corporation
St. Paul
To help train public agency and non-profit managers in decision-making and organizational techniques.
(Completes pledge of $50,000.)
$26,000.

St. Mary's extended Care Center
Minneapolis
To improve home health-care services for the elderly.
$1,000.

St. Paul-Ramsey Council of Arts & Sciences
General support .... $ 20,000
Renovation of the Old Federal Courts Building into the Landmark Center for the Arts and
Sciences .... $ 10,000
(Total pledge of $100,000.)

St. Paul Urban Coalition
General support.
$4,000.

Spring Hill Conference Center
Wayzata
Toward capital costs.
$20,000.

State of Minnesota—Governor's Commission on the Arts
To examine the current and future financial needs of arts organizations in Minnesota.
$6,000.

United Funds
Duluth .... $ 4,500
Minneapolis 190,000
Olmsted County 3,000
St. Paul 40,000

University of Minnesota Foundation
Minneapolis
Regents Professorship Program.
$1,000.

Upper Midwest Council
Minneapolis
For research concerning area's future growth.
$2,500.

Urban Coalition of Minneapolis
General support.
$8,300.

Urban Council on Mobility
St. Paul
To encourage citizen participation in transportation planning.
$2,500.

Walker Art Center
Minneapolis
General support.
$10,000.

YMCA—Minneapolis
Capital program.
(Total pledge of $900,000.)
$160,000.

YWCA of Minneapolis
Construction of new downtown program center
(Total pledge of $350,000.)
$50,000.

Other contributions
$12,540.

---

* Total 1975 contributions were $1,837,495; total for Minnesota was $1,109,124.
Source: Contributions annual report.

places high priority on the support and development of programs that attack causes of social problems in the communities in which it operates. Special emphasis is placed on the most critical needs of youth and the disadvantaged.

The foundation's active giving to the arts was affirmed by a policy approved in 1972 which emphasized a need to be "the most dynamic supporter of the arts." By 1975 the stated goal of giving at least 40 percent of total contributions to the arts had almost been realized, and for 1976 initial plans called for the foundation to give 48 percent of its contributions in this area. The two most prominent examples of support of the arts were a pledge of $1.25 million made in 1971 to the Minneapolis Society of Fine Arts for new facilities for the Art Institute, and a total pledge of $1 million to the Minneapolis Orchestra Association for a new Orchestra Hall.

The rationale for the emphasis on the arts was found in the contributions report:

> Dayton Hudson supports cultural institutions because we believe a rich cultural environment helps to insure a high standard of living for the citizens of a community and that there is a direct relationship between a community's social health and the quality of its cultural institutions.

Yet giving to the arts was a subject of some concern among members of management. A senior manager in one of the operating companies offered this opinion:

> I have some question about a large amount of money being spent on institutions that don't represent the needs of great masses of people. If one believes, as I do, that we should be disseminating our dollars to organizations and charities that our employees can relate to, then our sizable contributions to the arts deter our ability to support these organizations and charities to the fullest.

THE MECHANICS OF GIVING AT DAYTON HUDSON CORPORATION

A complicated formula existed for computing and allocating the amount given to charitable contributions by Dayton Hudson. First, the previous year's taxable income was determined and 5 percent of this amount was computed and established as that year's giving goal. Taxable income before contributions could be computed as approximately $100 million for 1975. Thus the total amount allowable as a tax deduction would be about $5 million.

Some of this total was to be given directly by the operating companies within their local communities; these were their discretionary giving funds, based on a percentage formula of estimated current year pretax earnings. For 1976 these discretionary funds totaled $667,000. The Dayton Hudson Foundation allocated a similar amount of its resources for gifts outside of Minnesota. The initial proposals Thompson considered recommending were for disbursement as shown in Table 2.

Table 2

Operating company	Preliminary amounts designated for operating company discretionary giving ($000)	Maximum "matching" gift for area considered by foundation ($000)
Dayton's	$ 40	None
Hudson's	351	$351
Diamond's	40	40
Lipman's	22	22
John A. Brown	19	19
Target	100	100
Lechmere	47	47
B. Dalton	18	18
D-H Jewelers	12	12
Team	3	3
Real Estate	15	15
Contingency		100
	667	727

$1,394,000

Thus the total giving program could be summarized as follows:

Source:
Operating company decisions	$ 667	(23%)
Foundation decisions	4,555	(77)
	5,222	

Location:
Minnesota charities	3,828	(73)
Non-Minnesota charities	1,394	(27)
	5,222	

The amount designated for Minnesota was up from 47 percent of 1974 contributions and 60 percent of 1975 contributions. An executive in one of the operating companies commented on this concentration:

> The share of contributions dollars is not proportionate to individual operating company results, but we are trying to change this. From my previous experience in other companies, I know that emphasizing contributions programs in the headquarters community is often the case in business philanthropy.

OPERATING COMPANY INVOLVEMENT

The corporation was working toward more operating company involvement concerning charitable contributions. Wayne Thompson remarked:

We encourage all of the operating companies to develop formal programs for their giving. We want them to be leaders in their communities and to use their discretionary contributions funds to have an impact in a way which will benefit the community and which will help establish them as exemplary corporate citizens.

We assist the operating companies in devising effective programs which can achieve measurable results for the community. Without a formal program it is easy to be subjected to pressure groups and dissipate your money with nothing to show for it.

However, there were some difficulties in giving more of the contributions work to the operating companies. One constraint was the problem of expertise in the operating companies. Stephen Pistner, executive vice president-retail for the corporation and former chairman of Target, commented: "It's very difficult to know how to spend these dollars well. This may sound strange, but if you consider that Target is less than 15 years old and B. Dalton is only 10 years old—these companies have simply never had the experience."

Richard Schall, executive vice president and chief administrative officer, added his feelings:

We are encouraging the operating companies to do more. Still, we couldn't reduce our program to thousands of $100 gifts. Meaningful corporate giving requires that contributions be of sufficient size to impact the quality and effectiveness of the organizations you are supporting.

Pistner went on to warn of the dangers of trying to decentralize the giving too much, although he wished to make the dollars somewhat more representative:

At Target, for example, the problem is with 13,000 people, we cannot give to 13,000 organizations. Should we poll our employees to determine which organizations should be supported? I'm not sure. As I say, we're still a young company. As more and more of our employees become involved in social responsibility roles of their own within the community, they will certainly be more able to and more aggressive about offering an opinion as to which programs we should support and which we should not.

THE 1974 REVIEW OF THE 5 PERCENT POLICY

In 1974, when profits fell 7.7 percent to $25.2 million and the company's common stock reached a low of $6.50 a share, a major review of the contributions program and specifically of the 5 percent policy was undertaken. Wayne Thompson explained: "At a time of flat earnings and general economic uncertainty, top management and the board of directors wanted to take a fresh look at the cost of this policy and its value to the company. We studied all aspects of the charitable program and prepared a 30-page report."

This report culminated with two basic alternatives:

1. Continue the present 5 percent policy and centralized management of Twin Cities contributions within the foundation.

2. Discontinue the 5 percent policy and completely decentralize the charitable program outside Minnesota, so that each operating company has total financial and managerial responsibility for contributions in its community.

Some of the operating company executives were opposed to maintaining the policy. One commented:

> I believe our generosity is very little understood or appreciated where it counts the most for our business. Also, if the corporation realizes the long-range projected profit increase, a 5 percent policy would take a disproportionate amount of the charitable responsibility on our shoulders. I feel more of that should go to the shareholder.

Another operating company executive agreed with this perception:

> I'm not sure we should adhere without qualification to the 5 percent policy. When the going was tougher for Dayton Hudson, I felt that the policy should have been modified. At the present profit level it is probably the right thing, but I would not have maintained the 5 percent two years ago when we were putting constraints on our capital expansion and I couldn't do more to extend my business. And, given normal cycles, I'm sure we'll have such times again.

Others, however, supported the status quo. George Hite, senior vice president of Dayton Hudson Properties, commented:

> Among those corporations who are equally adept at the basics, it is often the intangibles that separate the great from the good. These intangibles include the perception a corporation holds about its role in society and the manner in which it chooses to implement that perception: The 5 percent charitable giving policy is testimony to Dayton Hudson Corporation's perception.

Dick Schall, executive vice president, agreed:

> I believe a good case can be made that a 5 percent policy, over time, if intelligently implemented, is in the best long-term interests of our shareholders, our employees, and the public as a whole. . . . If we reduce the level of our giving, there is a real danger that the business community will interpret it as a weakness or a lack of confidence in the future of those communities where we are doing business rather than merely a philosophical change. . . . I believe that many of our people would agree with me that one word which well describes the feelings that this policy gives to our employees is *CLASS*. . . . To me, that carries with it a connotation of integrity, pride, esprit de corps, leadership, of being a premier organization. Surely these are valuable assets.

In response to the environmental development department's analysis and presentation, the board of directors reaffirmed the 5 percent policy in the summer of 1974 and called for the maintenance of the company's "unique leadership posture on this subject."

THE 5 PERCENT CLUB

One of the ideas emphasized in this review was that Dayton Hudson's example might spur other companies to adopt similar policies. In 1976 the Minneapolis Chamber of Commerce formally established the "5 percent Club" with a recognition banquet chaired by the governor of Minnesota. Besides Dayton Hudson and a large bank, most of the members were small- and medium-sized firms headquartered in the Twin Cities. In his Seattle remarks, Bruce Dayton commented:

> In Minneapolis we have been far more fortunate than most communities. There is broad acceptance of corporate social responsibility and the 5 percent contribution philosophy is growing. There are now 23 companies in Minnesota who annually contribute 5 percent of their pretax profits. We like to think of the 5 percent program as the Minnesota standard. . . .
> Imagine the difference if all businesses chose to require themselves to stand up to their social responsibility opportunities. Not only would the benefits to society and to shareholders increase dramatically, but we could make extraordinary headway toward creating the climate of acceptance which business so desperately needs.

Wayne Thompson echoed this sentiment in remarking: "If every company today contributed its fully deductible 5 percent, as allowed by our tax laws, business could be providing up to $9 billion in resources toward improving our society, instead of less than the present $1 billion."

Most members of Dayton Hudson's management felt that "missionary work" in the contributions area was an important function. One operating company executive explained: "We are all encouraged to spread the 5 percent message in our professional contacts." Kenneth Dayton commented: "I'm convinced that one of the foundation's goals should be to do its job so well that it influences others to follow suit. The selling job is an important part of our social obligation." Wayne Thompson regarded missionary work as a key part of his job:

> The toughest thing is to get other firms to take the first step. We must lead by example and not by forcing or embarrassing others. We encourage them in ways such as sending out our annual contributions report.

Bill Andres described how he viewed the activity of convincing other firms:

> As an outside director on other boards I never lose an opportunity to "sell" the 5 percent message. I use subtle and sometimes not so subtle ways to publicize our own position and suggest it is a proper one for others. The constant encouragement for all of us has had increasing acceptance in our business community.

Kenneth Dayton summarized the difficulties faced in convincing some companies:

> The government has approved this practice and agrees with our philosophy. They've said we'll let you take up to 5 percent and, in effect, share costs on a 50–50 basis. You call the tune. But, the vast majority of businesses don't take advantage of this. Why not? I simply don't understand it, especially when so many business people complain about the ineffectiveness

of government. They have the option to do something themselves, and they don't do it.

THE TRANSACTION PROCESS

Although a few grants were continued automatically from year to year, the majority of grants were completely reviewed each year. Evaluating requests was done by the administrative director of the foundation. Requests were usually rejected if they were for a national organization such as the Heart Association, a religious group, or an individual. Organizations located in places where Dayton Hudson did not do business and specific colleges and universities were given lower priority than community social programs and the arts. These latter two areas received the majority of the foundation's grants.

In evaluating requests that fell within the established priorities of the foundation, an *Exemplary Giving Guide* was used. The guide stated that "the initial evaluation of a contribution request should be in terms of whether the grant would constitute the most effective use of our funds," and offered several criteria for determining this. A numerical rating system was devised and scores were given on six dimensions for every grant before approval or rejection (Exhibit 5).

These policies regarding areas where contributions were not made and the procedures for evaluating requests were followed closely by the foundation. The corporation expected the operating companies, with their discretionary funds, to do likewise although this was not always the case. An operating company executive commented:

> My primary criteria for a request for contributions is that the group or cause be supported by the United Fund or the Urban Coalition. In essence, I am using the evaluation skills of those agencies as opposed to our own evaluation. I'm sure that our gifts are going to organizations which would pass muster under the foundation's rating system—it's just that we don't use it consciously.

In making evaluations, the foundation used a number of contacts—direct visits, other company foundations, government agencies, community leaders, and operating company personnel. Occasionally a request was rejected because of a specific deficiency. Wayne Thompson described one case: "We turned down a request from a youth organization last year because it didn't serve disadvantaged youth which is one of our priority areas. They came back with a program for minorities and the foundation contributed $100,000."

As a final step in the process, large grants were formally approved by the trustees of the foundation—Messrs. Kenneth and Bruce Dayton, Andres, Erickson, Pistner, Schall, Hudson and Thompson.

Follow-up evaluations were also part of the contributions activities. The foundation encouraged recipients of funds to submit an annual report with an emphasis placed on plans for future funding. If no information was forthcoming, the foundation would go back to the organization within a year and request it. Formal evaluations often used the

Exhibit 5

RATING SYSTEM FOR CHARITABLE GRANTS

	1	2	3	4	5
Quality of leadership	Outstanding. (Top 2–3 percent in field and greatly respected in community.)	Very good. (Clearly competent. Totally dedicated, well qualified, respected in community. Top 3–15 percent in field.)	Satisfactory. (Qualified but undistinguished.)	Doubtful.	Unsatisfactory. (Incompetent in area of importance to success of grant; unreliable.)
Quality of management	Outstanding. (Excellent preparation of complex plans; farsighted consideration of details and contingencies; provision for evaluation; definite capability of achieving expected results and of identifying and overcoming problems.)	Very good. (Good consideration of major problems and tasks, but details incomplete; evaluation thought about but not concretely; should handle problems capably and can be reasonably expected to achieve results.)	Satisfactory. (Sufficient planning to indicate major direction and strategies but weak on details and follow-through; overall program will probably be handled satisfactorily but without distinction.)	Doubtful. (Highly uncertain that planning and management are sufficient to the task.)	Unsatisfactory.
Financial strength of institution	Outstanding. (Income sources stable and relatively assured, excellent expense control and management, clear plans to continue activity after this grant.)	Very good. (Income and expense in satisfactory balance and probably can remain so in near future. Strong intent to continue after this grant but exact means not clear.)	Satisfactory. (Financial management appears satisfactory but grantee subject to financial uncertainties for which there are no adequate solutions in sight.)	Doubtful. (Past history too brief to judge; budget seems unreasonable; inherently unstable financial picture; dubious quality of financial management.)	Unsatisfactory. (Demonstrates inability to control financial affairs, deal with income uncertainties or exercise realistic financial management.)

Potential favorable impact of grant in relation to its size	Outstanding. (Relatively large number of people are likely to benefit greatly. Side effects on grantee institutions or public should be extremely favorable. Activity commands highest social priority. If successful, major innovation or breakthrough, new pattern will be established.)	Very good. (Benefits appear sizable compared to dollars spent. Possibility exists for favorable side effects. Priority of activity high. Not a major innovation or breakthrough, however, if successful.)	Satisfactory. (Direct participants in grant activity will benefit from dollars spent, but not to high degree. Wider benefits unlikely. Purpose of grant is good, but not particularly innovative.)	Doubtful. (Nothing wrong with the prospective impact, but little commends it for special attention either. Outside DHF priorities.)	Unsatisfactory. (Probable impact of the grant seems neutral or more harm than good.)
Degree of risk	Virtually none. (Plans appear virtually certain to work out as proposed. Any uncertainties appear minor.)	Little. (Plans appear likely to work out as proposed. Uncertainties either are unlikely to damage the main purpose of the grant, or grantee seems able to deal with them satisfactorily.)	Moderate. (Range of possible outcomes is fairly broad. While the proposed favorable outcomes seem likely, there is some chance that the results may be inconclusive or even mildly unfavorable, or high degree of risk inherent in project is one of its attractions for DHF.)	Significant. (Possible outcome is good, but significant risk exists either that this outcome will not be achieved, or that unanticipated events may prove harmful to the project's stated purposes.)	Unacceptable. (Odds of favorable outcome seem small in relation to those of harmful results.)
Overall rating	Outstanding. (Rates with top 2–3 percent of DHF grants in recent years.)	Very good. (Clearly merits funding; within our priorities; should rank in top 10 percent of proposals we receive.)	Satisfactory. (Proposal within our priorities; good institution with good program, but not a definite must.)	Doubtful. (Adequate proposal on its own merits but not within our interests or distinguished in any way.)	Unsatisfactory. (Significant, controlling reasons why this grant should not be made.)

rating procedure designed for pregrant usage and were taken quite seriously by the foundation. For example, a postgrant evaluation conducted of a new youth facility in Minneapolis resulted in the reduction of a $10,000 grant because the club was not adequately serving the minority population of the area.

INNOVATIONS

Kenneth Dayton emphasized the need for Dayton Hudson and the foundation to lead by the "quality and the professionalism of its charitable programming," not just the size of its giving. One way the foundation was trying to be effective was by looking at community needs, as well as at the quality of the requesting organization. A formal mechanism for trying to match the giving with the needs, the Community Social Profile, was developed and carried out in 1975. This was a rating system

Exhibit 6

FORM USED FOR COMMUNITY SOCIAL PROFILE

(Community)   *(Date)*

This profile is intended to indicate how effectively a community is dealing with the problems of its disadvantaged citizens.

On the basis of interviews with knowledgeable community leaders, each of the five areas below is to be rated from 1 (worst) to 10 (best).

Rating

I. EDUCATION
Including (*a*) levels of achievement in basic skills and (*b*) quality and degree of implementation of integration plans. _____

II. EMPLOYMENT
Including (*a*) availability of entry level jobs to minorities, (*b*) availability of training and promotion on the job, and (*c*) numbers of minorities in managerial levels—in private industry and government. _____

III. HOUSING
Including (*a*) construction or rehabilitation of needed units of low and moderate income housing and (*b*) degree of commitment and progress to revitalizing deteriorating neighborhoods. _____

IV. JUSTICE
Including (*a*) sensitivity of law enforcement officials to needs of minorities, (*b*) fairness of prosecution, (*c*) promptness of arraignments and trials, (*d*) representative nature of juries, and (*e*) quality of corrections programs. _____

V. TRANSPORTATION
Including adequacy of public transit system to provide mobility for the disadvantaged. _____

Source: Dayton Hudson Foundation.

Exhibit 7

RESULTS OF COMMUNITY SOCIAL PROFILES*

	City A	City B	City C	City D	City E	City F	Total
Education	7	4	5	5	6	3	30
Employment	4	2	3	4	1	3	17
Housing	6	4	4	4	3	6	27
Justice	3	4	4	4	6	4	25
Transportation ...	3	4	4	6	3	4	24
	23	18	20	23	19	20	

* These scores were based on a rating system going from (1) worst to (10) best.
Source: Dayton Hudson Foundation.

for the cities where Dayton Hudson was most active, to ascertain their problems in the areas of education, employment, housing, justice, and transportation. Each city was rated on these key points after interviews with community leaders and operating company personnel. The results of this survey and a copy of the Community Social Profile are reproduced in Exhibits 6 and 7.

After the survey was completed in late 1975, a decision was made to focus attention on the justice issue which Thompson defined as the "sensitivity of law enforcement officials to needs of minorities, fairness of prosecution, promptness of arraignments and trials, representative nature of juries, and quality of corrections programs." In general, the goal of the project was to "improve the delivery of effective nondiscriminatory public safety and service programs within the community."

The specifics of this initially involved dealing with the Minneapolis police force. Thompson, who had reorganized police forces before as a city manager in Richmond and Oakland, described the project: "The results of our profile forced us to move into this area. The police have a problem and nobody else was taking the lead to help them. I'm working closely with the mayor, the police chief and a business group to get a police academy started and to have the police sponsor a program for minority youth."

A second major project of the foundation in early 1976 was the rehabilitation of the neighborhood around the Minneapolis Art Institute to which a major multiyear grant of $1.25 million had been made. The foundation had taken the lead in forming a steering committee of interested business leaders and neighborhood groups and had contributed $50,000 to pay for a redevelopment plan.

Beside these two projects, the environmental affairs department in 1976 was sponsoring numerous smaller projects—community development in Phoenix, beautification for the city of Cambridge, a downtown park in Portland, and a wilderness area in Minnesota.

THE BOARD PRESENTATION

In a few days Thompson was scheduled to appear before the board's corporate responsibility committee with management's final recommendations for the charitable activities for 1976. At a minimum he wanted to anticipate the questions and concerns about the program that the directors might raise. He also wondered if he should adhere to original recommendations on the amount to be given and the methods for allocating funds or if it was time to suggest a study of possible changes.

The Viking Air Compressor, Inc.

As HE LEFT the president's office, George Ames wondered what he ought to do.[1] His impulse was to resign, but he knew that could be a costly blot on his employment record. Moreover, there was the possibility that he was seeing things in a distorted way, that he might later regret leaving Viking before he really knew all the facts bearing on his position and its future. He decided to wait for another week before making up his mind, and in the meantime he made an appointment with Professor Farnsworth of the Amos Tuck School of Business Administration at Dartmouth College to get his advice. Mr. Ames had received his MBA degree from the Tuck School the previous June.[2]

The Viking Air Compressor company was founded in Bradley, Connecticut, in 1908 by Nels Larsen, an inventor and engineer who left the Westinghouse Electric Company to start his own organization. Mr. Larsen had both a successful design for a new type of air compressor and a talent for management. He led Viking to steadily increasing successes in the air compressor industry.

In 1971 Viking held a steady 25 percent of the air compressor business in the United States, with total annual sales of $180 million. Mr. John T. Larsen, grandson of the founder, was chairman of the board and chief executive officer. Three other descendants of the founder were officers of the company, and the rest of the management team had been developed from Viking employees who rose through the ranks. The ownership of Viking was substantially in the Larsen family hands.

In March 1971 Mr. Oscar Stewart, vice president for personnel administration of Viking, visited the Amos Tuck School to talk with MBA candidates interested in a new position to be created in the Viking structure

---

[1] Most of the names in this case have been disguised.

[2] Mr. Ames received his A.B. from the University of Michigan in June 1966. He spent three years as an army officer, concluding as a captain in Vietnam, before entering Tuck in September 1969. He was married in June 1971.

the following June. Mr. Stewart explained to Dean Robert Y. Kimball, Tuck's director of placement, that Viking had never hired MBAs directly from business schools, but wanted to experiment in 1971 with this method of bringing fresh ideas and new techniques into the firm.

The corporate officers had decided, according to Mr. Stewart, to begin to test the effectiveness of the recruitment of MBAs by hiring a business school graduate to become director of public affairs, with the assignment of coordinating the relationships between Viking and outside agencies seeking financial contributions from the company.

As Mr. Stewart described the job to the students he interviewed at Tuck in March 1971, it would contain such tasks as (a) proposing to the board of directors the best criteria to use in deciding how to make corporate gifts to charitable organizations of all kinds, (b) supplying the chief officers of the company with information about the participation of Viking employees in public service activities, (c) recommending future strategy for Viking in the employment of women and members of minority groups, and (d) serving as secretary to the newly formed committee on corporate responsibility which consisted of five members of the board of directors.

George Ames accepted the post of director of public affairs at Viking. He had been chosen by Vice President Stewart as the most promising of the five attractive Tuck applicants for the new position. After a short vacation, Mr. Ames reported for work on July 1, 1971, and immediately plunged into the difficult task of gathering information about his new assignment. It soon became clear that his primary task would be to work with the board committee on corporate responsibility, mainly to propose new policy guidelines to the board at its September 10 meeting. Mr. Stewart said there were two other areas of high priority: (1) the corporation's attitude toward public service of employees and (2) developing criteria for corporate philanthropic giving.

As Vice President Stewart explained to George in early July, the committee on corporate responsibility was created at the January meeting of the Viking board after unanimous endorsement of the suggestion made by Dr. Thomas A. Barr, pastor of the local Congregational Church and one of the four outside members of the 12-man board. Dr. Barr's major support for his recommendation was the observation that the General Motors Corporation had taken a similar step, under some pressure, and that corporate responsibility was an idea whose time had come on the American scene. In response to the question, what will such a committee do, Reverend Barr replied that there need be no hurry in defining the detailed responsibilities of the committee, but that furthermore there could not possibly be any harm or drawbacks from setting it up as soon as possible. He added that the public relations value of such a gesture should not be underestimated. In establishing the committee on corporate responsibility, the board voted to require the first progress report from the committee in September 1971.

The committee on corporate responsibility met following the February meeting of the board of directors and decided to delay any definite action until an executive secretary could be hired. Vice President Stewart was asked to keep this post in mind as he interviewed MBA graduates of several of the leading business schools, and so he did.

George Ames met with the chairman of the committee on corporate responsibility at a luncheon on July 21, 1971, arranged by Vice President Stewart. The committee chairman was Mr. Paul Merrow, one of the most respected lawyers in northern Connecticut and the son of one of the first board members of Viking when the company was incorporated in the 1920s. Mr. Merrow expressed his pleasure that George Ames was working on the corporate responsibility question and asked him to prepare a report that might be reviewed by the committee just prior to the September board meeting. What he wanted, he explained to Mr. Ames, was an analysis of the three or four possible approaches to corporate responsibility which the directors ought to consider. He asked for a listing of the pros and cons of these various approaches. He said that Mr. Ames should consider this very much like an assignment in a course at the Tuck School. He would be performing a task which none of the board members had the time or academic background to do, and thus he would substantially improve the decision making of the board of directors.

Mr. Merrow concluded the luncheon by saying that he would like Mr. Ames to proceed on his own during the summer, but that he would be glad to confer with him in early September. Mr. Merrow explained that he was leaving the next day for a legal conference in Europe and would be on an extended vacation until September 6. He said that he had "the proxies" of the other committee members and that they would prefer not to get involved in working on the committee tasks until after the September board meeting.

George Ames worked assiduously during August, reading all the articles and books he could find in the area of corporate responsibility, including the background of developments in the General Motors situation. He decided not to talk about this particular assignment with other officers of the company, primarily because of Mr. Merrow's injunction that the committee itself would prefer not to engage in substantive talk about the issues until the September board meeting. George feared he would do more harm than good by talking before he knew his subject well.

In early September John Larsen asked George to see him and the following conversation took place:

JOHN LARSEN: I've asked you to see me this morning and tell me what progress you have been making in developing background materials for the work of the committee on corporate responsibility. Mr. Merrow told me he had asked you to do some digging and that you would have a brief report to make at the September 10 meeting of the board. I know Mr. Merrow hoped he would be back from Europe in time to talk with you before the board meeting, but it now appears he will be lucky to make the meeting at all. He expects to arrive in town about noon on the 10th.

GEORGE AMES: Mr. Larsen, I appreciate the opportunity I have been given to help Viking by developing recommendations about possible strategies for the company to follow in the area of corporate responsibility. Mr. Merrow told me

I ought to develop alternative proposals for recommendations to the board and I have as recently as yesterday finally been able to narrow the field so that I can make four recommendations with confidence.

I realize the board may prefer to consider them one at a time, at different meetings, but I would like to tell you about all four so that you will know what my report will contain.

I have decided that the most important issue in the area of corporate responsibility is equal-opportunity hiring. I have been able to develop statistics from the personnel records which show that Viking is rather far behind most major national corporations in the percentage of blacks and women now employed, and although I am sure conscientious efforts have been made by all officers to remedy this, I cannot stress too strongly how much of a time bomb the present situation is. There will be wide ramifications if we do not improve our record.

The second item of priority which I see is the development of corporate sanctions for public service activities of employees. I believe the company should grant paid leaves of absence for employees who wish to accept public-service posts. At present we have done that only for two vice presidents who have been in charge of the Northern Connecticut United Fund. In each case the man was lent to the charitable organization for two full weeks. What I have in mind is a much wider program which would grant employees leaves of absence to work in poverty programs in urban ghettos, or in VISTA projects in Connecticut or neighboring states.

It seems to me a third priority is to develop a committee of consumers who will monitor the safety features and other quality items having to do with our products. If we do not do this we will have Ralph Nader breathing down our necks as has already happened in the automotive industry and some others.

Finally, I strongly recommend that we close our sales contact in Capetown, South Africa, and establish policies which will avoid our being embarrassed as a corporation by discriminatory or dictatorial policies of foreign governments which become critically important political and social issues here in this country.

I feel sure these are great issues of our times, and I hope the board will be willing to debate them at the September 10 meeting. I know I could learn a great deal in my position if such a debate could take place.

MR. LARSEN: Young man, I want to congratulate you on how articulately you have told me about some of the things you have learned in the MBA program at the Tuck School. I envy fellows of your generation who go through MBA programs because you get an opportunity to think about policy problems at a much earlier age than my generation ever did. Indeed my only complaint is that the business schools go too far to educate young men to think they know how to run a company long before they have enough real experience to be even a first-line supervisor.

Now I think you have your assignment all backwards as secretary to the committee on corporate responsibility and I will tell you why I think that. The committee hasn't even met yet and your remarks make it sound as if you have written the final report. Worse than that it sounds like the final report of the committee on corporate responsibility of the General Motors Company, not Viking. Everybody knows we've done as good a job as we can to hire blacks and women. There just aren't many such people in the work force in our part of Connecticut who could fit our talent standards, and we are going to follow our historical policy of nondiscrimination as we hire the best people to do Viking jobs. We owe it to our stockholders to make a profit, and if we don't do that we don't have the right to do anything else.

Your remarks on public-service activities for our employees are equally off target. The first obligation of our employees is to give a fair day's work for a fair day's pay. All public-service activities are extracurricular activities, and that's the way they must be. In order for us to sponsor public service on company time we would have to discriminate between good and bad activities and that would get us into partisan politics and preoccupy all of our executive time. How would the company have done if I had been a part-time chief executive officer in the last five years? That is a preposterous idea! At the same time, by working harder on my regular job I have been able to work some evenings and some weekends in fund-raising activities for the Boy Scouts, YMCA, and heaven knows how many other charitable organizations. I would expect every employee to do the same and not to expect the corporation to subsidize activities in their roles as private citizens. As far as public service is concerned, live and let live should be our corporate motto. If we encourage public-service activities and include them as part of our compensation and promotion system, we will be bogged down in a fantastic collection of information about private lives which will lead to chaos. Even the most superficial examination of this question should have led you to see the problems with the route your theory took you.

As far as the safety of our products and other demands consumers might make, that's all done through the marketplace, as you will come to understand. If our products were not safe or durable, they wouldn't sell. You could have found this out had you talked with our production and marketing people as you certainly should have done by now. It's our responsibility to decide after careful market research what the air compressor needs of America are and will be in the future. We don't need a special panel of bleeding hearts to lead us along paths where we are already expert.

As for our selling operations in South Africa, I'm afraid you just don't know what you are talking about. As long as there is no plank of American foreign policy or federal law which tells corporations where they can and where they can't sell their products, American businesses must depend on the free market system. President Nixon is talking about opening the trade doors to mainland China. Do you think for one moment the practices of the Chinese government are any less nefarious in some respects than the practices of the South African government? Of course not. And yet you would probably urge me in your liberal way to establish a selling office in Peking just to go along with the new liberal ideas of our President, and I call that kind of pragmatism ridiculous.

Come to think of it, how could you miss this opportunity to lecture the board on our responsibilities for pollution control and our obligations to get out of the military-industrial complex by cancelling all of our air compressor contracts with the federal government!

Young man, you have shown yourself to be a wooly-minded theoretician and I went to tell you that bluntly now so that you will not think me hypocritical at any later point. I will tell the committee on corporate responsibility that you have not had time to prepare your first briefing of the board of directors and then I want to have a meeting with you and the chairman of the corporate responsibility committee on Monday morning September 20.

That's all I have time for now, I'll see you later.

BOOK TWO

Implementing corporate strategy

The accomplishment of purpose: Strategy and organization

WE NOW TURN our attention to the concepts and skill essential to the implementation of strategy. The life of action requires more than analytical intelligence. It is not enough to have an idea and be able to evaluate its worth. Persons with responsibility for the achievement of goals, the accomplishment of results, and the solution of problems, finally know the worth of a strategy when its power is demonstrated. Furthermore, a unique corporate strategy determined in relation to a concrete situation is never complete, even as a formulation, until it is embodied in the organizational activities which reveal its soundness and begin to affect its nature. Even then it will continue to evolve.

INTERDEPENDENCE OF FORMULATION AND IMPLEMENTATION

It is convenient from the point of view of orderly study to divide a consideration of corporate strategy, as we have divided it, into aspects of formulation and implementation and to note, for example, the requirement of the former for analytical and conceptual ability and of the latter for administrative skill. But in real life the processes of formulation and implementation are intertwined. Feedback from operations gives notice of changing environmental factors to which strategy should be adjusted. The formulation of strategy is not finished when implementation begins. A business organization is always changing in response to its own makeup and past development. Similarly, it should be changing in response to changes in the larger systems in which it moves, and in response to its success or failure in affecting its environment. For the sake of orderly presentation, we have arranged the cases so that henceforth the data will require us to focus less on what the strategy should be than on ways to make it effective in action and to alter it as required. We are taking forward with us, however, all our previous interests. We shall continue to examine each firm's strategy against the criteria we have developed in order to practice the skills we have gained and to verify the decisions made by the executives of the company.

We have already seen that the determination of strategy has four continuous subactivities: the examination of the environment for opportunity and risk, the systematic assessment of corporate strengths and weaknesses, the identification and weighting of personal values, and the clarification of social responsibility. Implementation may also be thought of as having important subactivities. In very broad terms, these are the design of organizational structure and relationships for the execution and adaptation of strategy, and the effective administration of organizational processes affecting behavior. Finally the management of the strategic process itself, which we shall call strategic management for short, may be viewed as the essence of corporate governance. We come then to the strategic function of the board of directors. This body itself requires leadership, usually but not always, by the chief executive who presides over the formulation and implementation activities at other levels of the organization.

In deciding and confirming strategy, senior executives, (in our practitioner's theory) range over the whole vast territory of the technological, social, economic, ecological, and political systems which provide opportunity for their company or threaten its continued existence. When they turn their attention to carrying out the strategy tentatively determined, they are apparently required to address themselves, within the limitations of their knowledge, to all the techniques and skills of administration. To deal with so wide a range of activity, they need a simple and flexible approach to the aspects of organized activity which they must take into account. By considering the relationships between strategy and organizational structure, strategy and organizational processes, and reconceiving strategy itself as an organization process that can be managed, the student should be able to span a territory crowded with ideas without losing sight of the purpose sought in crossing it.

Each of the implementing subactivities constitutes in itself a special world in which many people are doing research, developing knowledge, and asserting the importance of their work over that of other specialists. Thus the nature of organization, about which every general manager must make some assumptions, is the subject of a richly entangled array of ideas upon which one could spend a lifetime. The design of information systems—particularly at a time when the speed and capacity of the computer continue to fascinate the processors of information—appears to require long study, an esoteric language, and even rearrangement of organizational activities for the sake of information processing. Similarly, performance appraisal, motivation and incentive systems, control systems, and systems of executive recruitment, development, and compensation all have their armies of theoretical and empirical proponents, each one fully equipped with manuals, code books, rules, and techniques.

It will, of course, be impossible for us to consider here in detail the knowledge and theory which have been developed during the course of a half century of researches in administration. It will be assumed that your own experience has introduced you to the major schools of thought contending in the developing administrative disciplines, and that where necessary, the knowledge you have will be supplemented by further study. Just as general managers must be able to draw upon the skills of special staffs in leading their organizations, so they must be able to draw upon these special studies in effecting their own combination of organizational design and organizational practices. The simple prescription we wish to add here is that *the corporate strategy must dominate the design of organizational structure and processes.* That is, the principal criteria for all decisions on organizational structure and behavior should be their relevance to the achievement of the organizational purpose, not their conformity to the dictates of special disciplines. A clear perception of strategy enables one to sort out and discard most of the prescriptions generated by a theoretical and abstract consideration or organization. It follows that seeking out a coherent strategic pattern of purpose and policy is more important than mastery of organization principles and theory.

Thus the theses we suggest for your consideration are first that conscious strategy can be consciously implemented through skills primarily administrative in nature. Second, the chief determinant of organizational structure and the processes by which tasks are assigned and performance motivated, rewarded, and controlled should be *the strategy of the firm,* not the history of the company, its position in its industry, the specialized background of its executives, the principles of organization as developed in textbooks, the recommendations of consultants, or the conviction that one form of organization is intrinsically better than another.

The successful implementation of strategy requires that executives shape to the peculiar needs of their strategy the formal structure of their organization, its informal relationships, and the processes of motivation and control which provide incentives and measure results. They try to bring about the commitment to organizational aims and policies of properly qualified individuals and groups to whom portions of the total task have been assigned. They must ensure not only that goals are clear and purposes are understood but also that individuals are developing in terms of compensation and personal satisfactions. Above all, they must do what they can to arrange that departmental interests, interdepartmental rivalries, and the machinery of measurement and evaluation do not deflect energy from organizational purpose into harmful or irrelevant activity.

To clarify our approach to the problem of adapting the concepts and findings of special disciplines to the requirements of policy, we summarize here some aspects of implementation they may serve as a convenient map of the territory to be traversed. It should be remembered that cases you will analyze have not been researched or written to prove these propositions. The list is designed only to make it possible for you to use your own specialized knowledge and adapt it, within limits imposed by your own characteristic attitudes toward risk and responsibility, to strategic requirements. It may help you attach significance to case data and shape your analysis of company situations.

1. Once strategy is tentatively or finally set, they key tasks to be performed and kinds of decisions required must be identified.

2. Once the size of operations exceeds the capacity of one person, responsibility for accomplishing key tasks and making decisions must be assigned to individuals or groups. The division of labor must permit efficient performance of subtasks and must be accompanied by some hierarchical allocation of authority to assure achievement.

3. Formal provisions for the coordination of activities thus separated must be made in various ways, for example, through a hierarchy of supervision, project and committee organizations, task forces, and other ad hoc units. The prescribed activities of these formally constituted bodies are not intended to preclude spontaneous voluntary coordination.

4. Information systems adequate for coordinating divided functions (i.e., for letting those performing part of the task know what they must know of the rest, and for letting those in supervisory positions know what is happening so that next steps may be taken) must be designed and installed.

5. The tasks to be performed should be arranged in a sequence comprising a program of action or a schedule of targets to be achieved at specified times. While long-range plans may be couched in relatively general terms, operating plans will often take the form of relatively detailed budgets. These can meet the need for the establishment of standards against which short-term performance can be judged.

6. Actual performance, as quantitatively reported in information systems and qualitatively estimated through observation by supervisors and judgment of customers, should be compared to budgeted performance and to standards in order to test achievement, budgeting processes, the adequacy of the standards, and the competence of individuals.

7. Individuals and groups of individuals must be recruited and assigned to essential tasks in accordance with the specialized or supervisory skills which they possess or can develop. At the same time, the assignment of tasks may well be adjusted to the nature of available skills.

8. Individual performance, evaluated both quantitatively and qualitatively, should be subjected to influences (constituting a pattern of incentives) which will help to make it effective in accomplishing organizational goals.

9. Since individual motives are complex and multiple, incentives for achievement should range from those that are universally appealing—such as adequate compensation and an organizational climate favorable to the simultaneous satisfaction of individual and organizational purposes—to specialized forms of recognition, financial or nonfinancial, designed to fit individual needs and unusual accomplishments.

10. In addition to financial and nonfinancial incentives and rewards to motivate individuals to voluntary achievement, a system of constraints, controls, and penalties must be devised to contain nonfunctional

activity and to enforce standards. Controls, like incentives, are both formal and informal. Effective control requires both quantitative and nonquantitative information which must always be used together.

11. Provision for the continuing development of requisite technical and managerial skills is a high-priority requirement. The development of individuals must take place chiefly within the milieu of their assigned responsibilities. This on-the-job development should be supplemented by intermittent formal instruction and study.

12. Energetic personal leadership is necessary for continued growth and improved achievement in any organization. Leadership may be expressed in many styles, but it must be expressed in some perceptible style. This style must be natural and also consistent with the requirements imposed upon the organization by its strategy and membership.

The general manager is principally concerned with determining and monitoring the adequacy of strategy, with adapting the firm to changes in its environment, and with securing and developing the people needed to carry out the strategy or to help with its constructive revision or evolution. Managers must also ensure that the processes which encourage and constrain individual performance and personal development are consistent with human and strategic needs. In large part, therefore, leadership consists of achieving commitments to strategy via clarification and dramatization of its requirements and value.

We shall return to each of these considerations, looking first at some general relationships between strategy and organizational structure. We shall look also at the need for specialization of tasks, coordination of divided responsibility, and the design of effective information systems.

STRATEGY AND ORGANIZATIONAL STRUCTURE

It is at once apparent that the accomplishment of strategic purpose requires organization. If a consciously formulated or coherently evolutionary strategy is to be effective, organizational development should be planned rather than left to evolve by itself. So long as a company is small enough for a single individual to direct both planning for the future and current operations, questions of organizational structure remain unimportant. Thus the one-man organization encounters no real organizational problem until the proprietor's quick walks through the plant, his wife's bookkeeping, and his sale agent's marketing activities are no longer adequate to growing volume. When the magnitude of operations increases, then departmentalization—usually into such clusters of activities as manufacturing, production, and finance—begins to appear. Most functional organizations ultimately encounter size problems again. With geographical dispersion, product complexity, and increased volume of sales, coordination must be accomplished somewhere else than at the top. We then find multiunit organizations with coordinating responsibility delegated to divisions, subsidiaries, profit centers, and the like. The difficulty of designing an organizational structure is directly proportionate to the diversity and size of the undertaking and to the clarity of its strategy.

The subject of organization is the most extensive and complex of all the subtopics of implementation. It has at various times attracted the interest of economists, sociologists, psychologists, political scientists, philosophers, and, in a curiously restricted way, of creative writers as well. These have contributed to the field a variety of theoretical formulations and empirical investigations. The policymaker will probably find himself unable to subscribe wholeheartedly to the precepts of any one school of thought or to the particulars of any one model of the firm. Indeed, established theories of the firm are inadequate for general management purposes. The impact of most organizational studies, from the point of view of the eclectic practitioner looking for counsel rather than confusion, has been to undermine confidence in other studies. The activities of present-day social science have in particular badly damaged the precepts of classical scientific management.

Regardless of disputes about theory among scholars, the executive in, say, a company that has reached some complexity, knows three things. The tasks essential to accomplishing purpose must in some way be subdivided; they must be assigned, if possible, to individuals whose skills are appropriately specialized; and tasks that have been subdivided must ultimately be reintegrated into a unified whole. The manager knows also that once performance is out of one pair of hands, and once no one in the organization is performing the total task, information about what one group is doing must be made available to the others. Otherwise problems and risks cannot be detected and dealt with.

SUBDIVISION OF TASK RESPONSIBILITY

In every industry conventional ways of dividing task by function have developed to the extent that the training of individuals skilled in these functions perpetuates organizational arrangements. But identification of the tasks *should* be made in terms of a company's distinctive purposes and unique strategy, not by following industry convention. True, the fact that every manufacturing firm procures and processes raw materials and sells and delivers finished products means that at least production and sales and probably procurement and distribution will always be critical functional areas which must be assigned to specialized organizational units. But these basic uniformities which cut across company and industry lines provide the individual firm with little useful guidance on the issues it finds so perplexing—namely, how much weight to assign to which function, or how to adapt nearly universal structural arrangements to its own particular needs.

A manufacturer who plans to perform services for the government under cost-plus-fixed-fee contracts, to cite a very limited example, feels less need for a fully developed cost control system and cost-related incentives than one whose contracts are governed by a fixed price. To illustrate more broadly the way in which strategic choice determines the relative importance of tasks, consider the manufacturer of a line of industrial products who decides to diversify in view of declining opportunity in the original field. Product improvement and the engineering organization responsible for it become less vital than the search for new products, either internally or through acquisition. But if the latter task is not recognized as crucial, then it is unlikely to be assigned to any individual or unit, but will rather be considered as an additional duty for many. Under the latter circumstances, little will get done.

Once the key tasks have been identified (or the identification customary in the industry has been ratified as proper for the individual firm), then responsibility for accomplishing these tasks must be assigned to individuals and groups. In addition to a rational principle for separating tasks from one another, the need will soon become apparent for some scale of relative importance among activities to be established.

Distribution of formal authority among those to whom tasks have been assigned is essential for the effective control of operations, the development of individual skills, the distribution of rewards, and for other organizational processes to which we shall soon give attention. The extent to which individuals, once assigned a task, need to be supervised and controlled is the subject of voluminous argument which, temporarily at least, must leave the general practitioner aware that too much control and too little are equally ineffective and that, as usual, the generalist is the person who must strike the balance.

The division of labor is thus accompanied by the specialization of task and the distribution of authority, with the relative importance of tasks as defined by strategy marked by status. The rational principle by which tasks are specialized and authority delegated may be separation by functions, by product or product lines, by geographical or regional subdivision, by customer and market, or by type of production equipment or processes. The intermixture of these principles in multiunit organizations has resulted in many hybrid types of formal structure which we need not investigate. The principal requirement is that the basis for division should be relatively consistent, easily understood, and conducive to the grouping of like activities. Above all, the formal pattern should have visible relationship to corporate purpose, should fix responsibility in such a way as not to preclude teamwork, and should provide for the solution of problems as close to the point of action as possible. In an organization governed by purpose, responsibility will often exceed authority (contrary to the classical doctrine of absolute equality); the resulting ambiguity provides opportunity for initiative and clarification in terms of shared objectives rather than separate fiefdoms. Structure should not be any more restrictive than necessary of the satisfaction of individual needs or of the inevitable emergence of informal organization. The design should also allow for more complex structure as the organization grows in size.

As you consider the need to create, build, and develop an organizational structure for the firms in the cases you will study shortly, you will wish to avoid choosing a pattern of organization on the grounds that it is "typical" or "generally sound." Any preference you may have for divisional versus functional organizations, for decentralized rather than centralized decision making, for a "flat" rather than a "steep" or many-stepped hierarchy, should be set aside until you have identified the activities made essential by the strategy, the skills available for their performance, and the needs and values of the individuals involved. The plan you devise should ignore neither the history of the company nor that of its industry, for in ongoing organizations formal structure may not be abruptly changed without great cost. Any new plan that you devise for gradual implementation should be as economical as is consistent with the requirements for technical skill, proper support for principal functions, and reserve capacity for further growth. The degree of centralization and decentralization that you prescribe should not turn on your personal preference, and certainly will vary from one activity to another. Strategic requirements as well as the abilities and experience of company executives should determine the extent to which responsibility for decisions should tend toward the center or toward the field. In a consumer credit company, for example, freedom to extend credit to doubtful risks can really be allowed only to relatively experienced branch managers though company strategy may prescribe it for all.

That so little need be said about the nature of the formal organization, and so much must be determined by the particulars of each individual situation, should not be taken as evidence that formal organization does not matter. On the contrary, progress in a growing organization is impossible without substrategies for organizational development. Restructuring the organization becomes a subgoal to be worked toward over a period of years—perhaps without the interim publication of the ultimate design.

But though it is impractical, except in cases of harsh emergency, to make sweeping organizational changes with little preparation and upon short notice, this is not to say that no major role is played by structure, by clear and logical subdivisions of task, or by an openly acknowledged hierarchy of authority, status, and prestige—all serving as the conscious embodiment of strategy and the harbinger of growth to come. As you check the relation between strategy and structure, whether in your study of cases or in your business experience, ask yourself always the policy questions: Is the strategy sound and clear? If goals are clear, have the tasks required been clearly identified and assessed for their relative importance? If key activities are know, have they been assigned to people with the requisite training, experience, and staff support they will need? If not are such people being sought? The answers to these questions do not carry one very far along the road toward successful strategy implementation, but they provide a convenient starting point.

COORDINATION OF DIVIDED RESPONSIBILITY

As soon as a task is divided, some formal provision must be made for coordination. In baseball, the park outside the diamond is subdivided into left, center, and right fields, and a player is assigned to each. But if there is no procedure for handling a ball hit halfway between any two areas, the formal division of labor will help only the team at bat and put colliding players on the injured list. Most important work in organizations requires cooperation among the departmental specialists to whom a portion of the total task has been allocated. Many forces are at work to make coordination so essential that it cannot be left to chance. For example, the flow of work from one station to another and from one administrative jurisdiction to another creates problems of scheduling and timing, of accommodating departmental needs, and of overall supervision lest departmental needs become more influential than organizational goals.

As soon as additional people join the first person in an organization, they bring with them their own goals, and these must be served, at least to a minimal degree, by the activity required of them in service to the organization. As soon as a group of such individuals, different in personal needs but similar in technical competence and point of view, is established to perform a given function, then departmental goals may attract more loyalty than the overall goals of the organization. To keep individual purposes and needs as well as departmental substrategies consistent with corporate strategy is, as we have said before, a considerable undertaking. It is a major top-management responsibility in all organizations, regardless of the degree of commitment and willingness to cooperate in the common cause.

The different needs of individuals and the distinctive goals of functional specialties mean that, at best, the organization's total strategy is understood differently and valued for different reasons by different parts of the organization. Some formal or informal means for resolving these differences is important. Where the climate is right, specialists will be aware of the relative validity of organizational and departmental needs and of the bias inevitable in any loyalty to expertise.

Formal organization provides for the coordination of divided responsibility through the hierarchy of supervision, through the establishment and use of committees, and through the project form of organization (which, like temporary task forces, can be superimposed upon a functional or divisional organization). The wider the sphere of any supervisor's jurisdiction, the more time is needed to bring into balance aspects of organized life which would otherwise influence performance toward the wrong goals. The true function of a committee—and were this role more widely understood and effectively played, committees would be less frequently maligned—is to bring to the exploration and solution of interdepartmental problems both the specialist and generalist abilities of its members. The need for formal committees would be largely obviated in an ideal organization, where all members were conscious of the impact of their own proposals, plans, and decisions upon the interests of others. To the extent that individual managers seek out advice and approval from those whose interests must be balanced with theirs, they perform in face-to-face encounters the essential coordination which is sometimes formalized in a committee structure.

Coordination can play a more creative role than merely composing differences. It is the quality of the way in which subdivided functions and interests are resynthesized that often distinguishes one organization from another in terms of results. The reintegration of the parts into the whole, when what is at stake is the execution of corporate strategy, is what creates a whole that is greater than the sum of its parts. Rivalry between competing subunits or individuals—if monitored to keep it *constructive* rivalry—can exhibit creative characteristics. It can be the source of a new solution to a problem, one that transcends earlier proposals that reflected only the rival units' parochial concerns. The ability to handle the coordinating function in a way that brings about a new synthesis among competing interests, a synthesis in harmony with the special competence of the total organization, is the administrator's most subtle and creative contribution to the successful functioning of an organization.

EFFECTIVE DESIGN OF INFORMATION SYSTEMS

If corporate strategy is to be effectively implemented, there must be organizational arrangements to provide members with the information they will need to perform their tasks and relate their work to that of others. Information flows inward from the environment to all organizational levels; within the company it should move both down and up. In view of the bulk of information moving upward, it must be reduced to manageable compass as it nears the top. This condensation can be accomplished only by having data synthesized at lower levels, so that part of what moves upward is interpretation rather than fact. To achieve synthesis without introducing distortion or bias or serious omission is a formidable problem to which management must remain alert. Well handled, the information system brings to the attention of those who have authority to act not the vast mass of routine data processed by the total system but the significant red-flag items that warn of outcomes contrary to expectations. A well-designed information system is thus the key to "management by exception." This in turn is one key to the prevailing problem of the overburdened executive.

In the gathering and transmitting of information, accounting and control departments play a major role. One obstacle to effective performance here is devotion to specialty and procedure for its own sake, as accountants look more to their forms than to larger purposes. The Internal Revenue Service, the Securities and Exchange Commission, the Census Bureau, the Environmental Protection Agency, and the Justice Department, all with requirements which must be met, impose uniformities on the ways in which information is collected and analyzed. But nothing in the conventions of accounting, the regulations of the government, or the rapidly advancing mathematical approaches to problem solving in any way prevents the generation and distribution within an organization of the kind of information management finds most useful.

Now, with the speed of the computer, data can be made available early enough to do some good. We shall have much more to say about the uses of information when we turn to the organizational processes that determine individual behavior. It is important to note that the generation of data is not an end in itself. Its function should be to permit individuals who necessarily perform only one of the many tasks required by the organizational mission to know what they need to know in order to perform their functions in balance with all others, and to gain that overview of total operations which will inform and guide the decisions they have discretion to make. To be useful it must be kept simple. Designing the flow of information is just as important as choosing a principle of subdivision in outlining organizational structure. Information is often the starting point in trying to determine how the organization should be changed. It is a way to monitor the continuing adequacy of strategy and to warn when change is necessary.

STRATEGY AS THE KEY TO SIMPLICITY

Strategy is conceived and implemented only in combinations of people to some degree "organized" or deployed in compatible task assignments. The strategy for each organization—in our conception of strategic management—will be in some ways unique because of distinctiveness of competence and pervasion of values. The uniqueness of a company's strategy, in turn, is the key element in organization design. It is strategy, we have said, that should determine structure and the nature of the processes going on throughout the structure. This essential element of our conception puts an early end to our generalizations about how to organize. Until we know the strategy we cannot begin to specify the appropriate structure. This exposition cannot advise you whether a functional or divisional organization is appropriate to the strategy you will be working as a manager to implement, although it is clear that in growing and diversifying organizations the functional form will ordinarily precede the divisional and follow along after as divisions are functionalized. Matrix management you can take or leave alone until you get to the case situation itself; all you need to know now is that the key competing considerations—geographical specialization versus worldwide product management, for example—must somehow be integrated in a working equilibrium with strategic importance specifying the weights in the balance.

The elements of thinking like a general manager that we have recommended to you are inert until they are applied to the cases of this book, the cases of your other courses, and ultimately the managerial circumstances in which you find yourself. The assignment of primacy to the application of an idea rather than its elegant theoretical development is anathema to orthodox theorists. It is inconvenient for students expecting to be equipped with the latest and best tools for the solution of management problems and a jargon with which to demonstrate their sophistication. But that the concept of strategy comes to full development only in the unique combination of circumstances in which any organization exists is a simplifying property of the idea that provides it much of its power in action.

If you acquire the ability to think strategically, you will be able to lay aside the burdens of management conceived of as a science which your education has laid upon you and tried to require you to remember. The more highly developed theories and propositions of most of the management sciences are either largely inapplicable or inappropriately applied, for they are usually presented by dedicated partisans as universally applicable. As a phenomenon of management, the uniqueness of situations properly takes primacy over the substance of the management disciplines. As we are unable to tell you in detail how to design an organization until we know the purposes you are organizing for and the resources available, we can say there is no one best way to organize. At the same time the quest for purpose prevents organization aimlessness or drifting.

A related paradox presents itself as we consider the unlikelihood that the strategy we have said should always govern will be clear and complete at any one time. Since purpose evolves ordinarily over time as the components of strategy (environmental change and internal resources, for example) develop, it can dictate no final answer in terms of organization structure and process even in the situational context. The structure and processes in place will in fact affect the strategy. If you have profit centers, divisions, or subsidiaries charged with medium- and long-term success, they are likely to develop strategically significant innovations simply because divisionalization produces commitment to division rather than to parent organization. If you send fur buyers to Alaska instructed under quotas only to buy skins, they may end up selling groceries and other necessities to the trappers and incrementally make your fur business into a worldwide trading company. Strategy follows structure in real life, just as it sometimes precedes it there.

What is important now is that in part structure is strategy. If, in short, the process of strategy formulation, as it must be, is distributed throughout an organization, the shape of that organization and the influences that motivate it will be reflected in the strategy it produces. The strategic decision must, of course, be made in the light of organization and human consequences. Furthermore, it must be arrived at recognizing the constraint of structure and systems derived from previous strategy which influence the generation of new alternatives. Context is both supportive and inhibiting. It may be necessary to change organization before certain strategic alternatives can be fully explored or experimentally attempted.

The subunits of an organization established to implement a given corporate purpose soon are developing divergent strategies to support their own growth and development, especially if responsibility for profit and growth has been assigned to those units. It is true, therefore, that the organization processes and measurement systems by which the functioning of the structure is evaluated will influence strategy. When an international company once tried to interest its Latin-American subsidiaries in profit rather than in the number of sewing machines sold, the country managers, inexperienced but responsive, began making ice cream, selling insurance, and manufacturing stove grates in unused plant space. These diversifications, all aimed at increasing profitability within one year, changed, at least for a time, the local strategy of this company. The structure—geographically discrete and relatively autonomous profit centers—and the incentive system—reward for short-run profitability—together could ultimately have changed the strategy of the entire company. As it happens it was the corporate intention that the company go through a transition emphasizing profitability while its future strategy, too difficult a question for anybody in a company unused to strategic planning to settle, became a problem which could be managed.

Worldwide, the result of similar experiments was a company that faltered between being an appliance and electronics firm, or an industrial and consumer products company without the resources or the organization form to make so wide a diversification work. The neglect of the sewing machine business, suffering under Japanese competition, and years of resulting losses led at long last, to the dismissal of the responsible executive. He had known his company needed to be profit conscious, but he could not institutionalize a way to deal continuously with the decision of what businesses to be in. His effective stimuli sent the strategic process galloping off in all directions.

The present management, incidentally, has written off most of the extraneous activities and appears to be concentrating on the historic capability that made the company the first great American multinational corporation. In this instance strategy was made chaotic by change in organization structure and compensation systems. The country managers, were neither provided nor required to develop a new strategy for their areas. A communicable corporate strategy was not generated at company headquarters to give coherent guidance to local initiatives.

Strategic management in the real world then contends with the alternatives generated by organization form and the administrative processes affecting the motivation of people. While the uncertainties of decision about new alternatives delay clear-cut major changes in direction, hundreds of minor decisions incrementally may change the nature of the business and affect the character of the organization.

The real-life development of strategy must be superimposed upon the natural tendency of persons to "satisfice" (if you have read Herbert Simon), or (if you have not) to settle on the first satisfactory, rather than the best solution to a problem. It envelopes and influences the direction of the incrementalism by which organizations devise ad hoc responses to new occurrences. It extends the bounds of rationality within which persons and groups react to challenge from the market and social environment. It disciplines the bargaining that can characterize the behavior of coalitions in organizations politicized by strategic uncertainty or dissatisfaction with the objectives and supporting policies in place.

The conclusion that attention to the conscious and deliberate choice of purpose can affect all aspects of an organization is in a sense a reassertion of the role in complex organizations of purposeful rationality. Strategy will evolve over time, no matter what. It will be affected by the consequences of its implementation. But the elucidation of goals can transcend incrementalism to make it a series of forays and experiments evaluated continuously against stated goals to result in the deliberate amendment of strategy or in the curtailment of strategic erosion. All organizations must be focused in purpose in order to avoid outstripping their resources or squandering their distinctive advantage.

The literature of organization theory is by itself, as we have said, of very little use in managing a live organization. What students and managers gain in discovering this fact is not that there is an advantage to being ignorant but that a powerful unitary idea can be developed in detail in a business situation which they and their associates can know better than anybody else. Selection from what is available to educated generalists and known by specialists concentrating in techniques applicable to classes of narrow problems becomes effective when the relation of specialized knowledge to key problems of organization is recognized as strategically relevant. Knowledge of the evolving situation is more important and practicable than mastering the whole corpus of management book learning. A rational procedure for comprehending the strategic posture of an organization, for seeing the intuitive purpose in its incremental development, and for assessing the extent to which its structure is effective in the performance of key tasks is much easier come by. It requires experience, judgment, and skill, rather than general knowledge as such for strategic management is and will remain more an art than a science. Artistic accomplishment depends heavily on the education, sensitivity, competence, and point of view of the artist. Simplicity is the essence of good art; a conception of strategy brings simplicity to complex organizations.

The Adams Corporation (A)

In January of 1972, the board of directors of The Adams Corporation simultaneously announced the highest sales in the company's history, the lowest after-tax profits (as a percentage of sales) of the World War II era, and the retirement (for personal reasons) of its long-tenure president and chief executive officer.

Founded in St. Louis in 1848, the Adams Brothers Company had long been identified as a family firm both in name and operating philosophy. Writing in a business history journal, a former family senior manager comments: "My grandfather wanted to lead a business organization with ethical standards. He wanted to produce a quality product and a quality working climate for both employees and managers. He thought the Holy Bible and the concept of family stewardship provided him with all the guidelines needed to lead his company. A belief in the fundamental goodness of mankind, in the power of fair play and in the importance of personal and corporate integrity were his trademarks. Those traditions exist today in the nineteen sixties."

In the early 1950s, two significant corporate events occurred. First, the name of the firm was changed to The Adams Corporation. Second, somewhat over 50 percent of the corporation shares were sold by various family groups to the wider public. In 1970, all branches of the family owned or "influenced" less than one fifth of the outstanding shares of Adams.

The Adams Corporation was widely known and respected as a manufacturer and distributor of quality, branded, and consumer products for the American, Canadian, and European (export) markets. Adams products were processed in four regional plants located near raw material sources,[1] were stored and distributed in a series of recently constructed

[1] No single plant processed the full line of Adams products, but each plant processed the main items in the line.

or renovated distribution centers located in key cities throughout North America, and were sold by a company sales force to thousands of retail outlets—primarily supermarkets.

In explaining the original long-term financial success of the company, a former officer commented: "Adams led the industry in the development of unique production processes that produced a quality product at a very low cost. The company has always been production-oriented and volume-oriented and it paid off for a long time. During those decades the Adams brand was all that was needed to sell our product; we didn't do anything but a little advertising. Competition was limited and our production efficiency and raw material sources enabled us to outspace the industry in sales and profit. Our strategy was to make a quality product, distribute it and sell it cheap.

"But that has all changed in the past 20 years," he continued. "Our three major competitors have outdistanced us in net profits and market aggressiveness. One of them—a first-class marketing group—has doubled sales and profits within the past five years. Our gross sales have increased to almost $250 million but our net profits have dropped continuously during that same period. While a consumer action group just designated us as 'best value,' we have fallen behind in marketing techniques, e.g., our packaging is just out of date."

Structurally, Adams was organized into eight major divisions. Seven of these were regional sales divisions, with responsibility for distribution and sales of the company's consumer products to retail stores in their area. Each regional sales division was further divided into organizational units at the state and county and/or trading area level. Each sales division was governed by a corporate price list in the selling of company products but had some leeway to meet the local competitive price developments. Each sales division was also assigned (by the home office) a quota of salesmen it could hire and was given the salary ranges within which these men could be employed. All salesmen were on straight salary and expense reimbursement salary plan, which resulted in compensation under industry averages.

A small central accounting office accumulated sales and expense information for each of the several sales divisions on a quarterly basis, and prepared the overall company financial statements. Each sales division received, without commentary, a quarterly statement showing the number of cases processed and sold for the overall division, sales revenue per case of the overall division, and local expenses per case for the overall division.

Somewhat similar information was obtained from the manufacturing division. Manufacturing division accounting was complicated by variations in the cost of obtaining and processing the basic materials used in Adams products. These variations—particularly in procurement—were largely beyond the control of that division. The accounting office did have, however, one rough external check on manufacturing division effectiveness. A crude market price for case lot goods, sold by smaller firms to some large national chains, did exist.

Once a quarter, the seven senior sales vice presidents met with general management in St. Louis. Typically, management discussion focused on divisional sales results and expense control. The company's objective of being "number one," the largest selling line in its field, directed group attention to sales versus budget. All knew that last year's sales targets had to be exceeded—"no matter what." The manufacturing division vice president sat in on these meetings to explain the product availability situation. Because of his St. Louis office location, he frequently talked with Mr. Jerome Adams about overall manufacturing operations and specifically about large procurement decisions.

The Adams Company, Mr. Millman knew, had a trade reputation for being very conservative with its compensation program. All officers were on a straight salary program. An officer might expect a modest salary increase every two or three years; these increases tended to be in the thousand dollar range regardless of divisional performance or company profit position. Salaries among the seven sales divisional vice presidents ranged from $32,000 to $42,000, with the higher amounts going to more senior officers. Mr. Jerome Adams's salary of $48,000 was the highest in the company. There was no corporate bonus plan. A very limited stock option program was in operation, but the depressed price of Adams stock meant that few officers exercised their options.

Of considerable pride to Mr. Jerome Adams had been the corporate climate at Adams. "We take care of our family" was his oft-repeated phrase at company banquets honoring long-service employees. "We are a team and it is a team spirit that has built Adams into its leading position in this industry." No member of first line, middle or senior management could be discharged (except in cases of moral crime or dishonesty) without a personal review of his case by Mr. Adams. In matter of fact, executive turnover at Adams was very low. Executives at all levels viewed their jobs as a lifetime career. There was no compulsory retirement plan and some managers were still active in their mid–70s.

The operational extension of this organization philosophy was quite evident to employees and managers. A private family trust, for over 75 years, provided emergency assistance to all members of the Adams organization. Adams led its industry in the granting of educational scholarships, in medical insurance for employees and managers, and in the encouragement of its "members" to give corporate and personal time and effort to community problems and organizations.

Mr. Adams noted two positive aspects of this organizational philosophy. "We have a high percentage of long-term employees—Joe Girly, a guard at East St. Louis, completes 55 years with us this year, and every one of his brothers and sisters has worked here. And it is not uncommon for a vice president to retire with a blue pin—that means 40 years of service. We have led this industry in manufacturing process innovation, quality control and value for low price for decades. I am proud of our accomplishments and this pride is shown by everyone—from janitors to directors." Industry sources noted that there was no question that Adams was "number one" in terms of manufacturing and logistic efficiency.

In December of 1971, the annual Adams management conference gathered over 80 of Adams's senior management in St. Louis. Most expected the usual formal routines—the announcement of 1971 results and 1972 budgets, the award of the "Gold Flag" to the top processing plant and sales division for exceeding targets, and the award of service pins to executives. All expected the usual social good times. It was an opportunity to meet and drink with "old buddies."

After a series of task force meetings, the managers gathered in a banquet room—good naturedly referred to as the "Rib Room" since a local singer "Eve" was to provide entertainment. At the front of the room, in the usual fashion, was a dais with a long, elaborately decorated head table. Sitting at the center of that table was Mr. Jerome Adams. Following tradition, Mr. Adams's vice presidents, in order of seniority with the company, sat on his right. On his left, sat major family shareholders, corporate staff, and—a newcomer—soon to be introduced.

After awarding service pins and the "Gold Flags" of achievement, Mr. Adams announced formally what had been a corporate "secret" for several months. First, a new investing group had assumed a "control" position on the board of Adams. Second, that Mr. Price Millman would take over as president and chief executive officer of Adams.

Introducing Mr. Millman, Adams pointed out the outstanding record of the firm's new president. "Price got his MBA in 1958, spent four years in control and marketing, and then was named as the youngest divisional president in the history of the Tenny Corporation. In the past years, he has made his division the most profitable in Tenny and the industry leader in its field. We are fortunate to have him with us. Please give him your complete support."

In a later informal meeting with the divisional vice presidents, Mr. Millman spoke about his respect for past Adams's accomplishments and the pressing need to infuse Adams with "fighting spirit" and "competitiveness." "My personal and organizational philosophy are the same— the name of the game is to fight and win. I almost drowned, but I won my first swimming race at 11 years of age! That philosophy of always winning is what enabled me to build the Ajax division into Tenny's most profitable operation. We are going to do this at Adams."

In conclusion, he commented, "The new owner group wants results. They have advised me to take some time to think through a new format for Adams's operations—to get a corporate design that will improve our effectiveness. Once we get that new format, gentlemen, I have but one goal—each month must be better than the past."

Exhibit 1
THE ADAMS CORPORATION (A)
Organization Chart

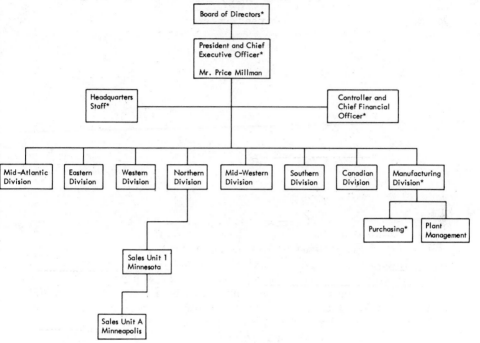

* Located in St. Louis.

Barclay, Inc. (A)

IN DECEMBER 1973, Mr. Robert Cannon became the new president and chief operating executive of Barclay, Inc., a firm operating in the electrical equipment field. In 1973, it was estimated, Barclay's sales were $100 million and the enterprise employed over 2,600 people.

Barclay, Inc., had recently been purchased by a group of wealthy investors. In view of their other varied business interests, the investing group planned to operate Barclay as a separate, independent company. Mr. Cannon was given complete responsibility for the direction of Barclay's affairs. He had achieved an excellent reputation among industrialists as a manager capable of dealing with difficult business problems, and the investors had agreed that he was to have a free hand to make whatever changes he thought necessary to improve the company's lackluster profit performance.

Barclay manufactured and sold electrical equipment for industrial and consumer use. Its industrial products included a wide variety of standard and specialty motors. The company had achieved an excellent reputation for engineering design work. Over the years its legal staff had built up an imposing number of patents protecting improvements created by company engineers. In the consumer products line, the firm manufactured and sold a line of small "traffic" household appliances for American markets.

In recent years company sales had increased substantially but profits had gradually declined to a point where only a very small profit was anticipated for 1973. While industrial products had been extremely profitable for many years, the competitive situation had changed substantially in the late 1960s. Consumer appliance operations varied from early losses to small profit contributions in 1970 through 1973. Barclay was encountering increasing competition for its appliances from full-line companies, e.g., Sunbeam. Despite this, Mr. Cannon believed that in the long run the consumer traffic appliance area would become the most important and profitable part of the firm's business. He hoped to add new appliance items as rapidly as production and marketing facilities permitted.

In the manufacture of these products, Barclay purchased substantial quantities of two raw materials (16 million, estimated in 1972). These raw materials were subject to substantial price fluctuations and it was important for Barclay to buy at "the right time and price."

The new owners of Barclay requested that Mr. Cannon prepare salary recommendations, for board consideration, in December 1973. His recommendations were to cover the top 20 executives in the company including himself. Knowing the backgrounds of the new owners, Mr. Cannon knew he would have to be able to defend his assignments of salary to specific jobs. He also knew that the owners had been critical of the "haphazard way" in which salary payments had been made by the former general manager.

To carry out this assignment, Mr. Cannon asked the member of the personnel department in charge of the executive payroll for the amount paid in salaries to the top 20 managers of the firm in the year 1973. This sum amounted to $860,000. He excluded individual bonus payments and incidental privileges, such as company furnished cars. Bonus payments for the Barclay management group had declined steadily during the past years and salary payments were now the important element in the firm's compensation program.

He then prepared to assign funds from this "common pool" to individual jobs in the organization. Mr. Cannon realized that, after he had determined an ideal salary structure, he would have to modify his assignments on the basis of historical precedent as well as other factors. But he believed that the process of allocating the total salary fund to individual jobs, without prejudice of past history, would help him in thinking through his problem.

Exhibit 1
BARCLAY, INC. (A)
Organization Chart

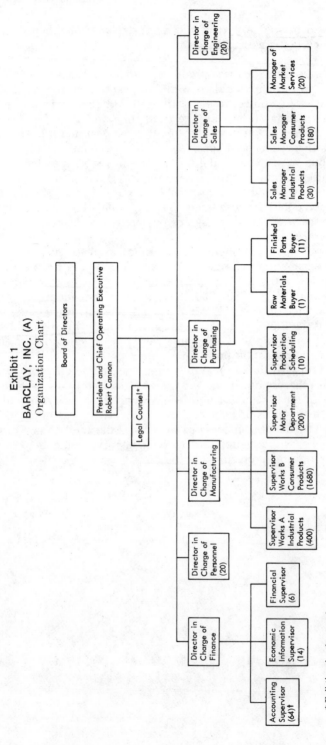

* Full-time legal counsel.
† Indicates number of staff/or employees, or both.

Mitek Corporation

ROBERT TWEED, president of the Mitek Corporation, knew that the company was at a critical point in its history. There was no question that the company was a success, more so than any of the three founders had allowed themselves to imagine a mere five years ago. But now was not the time to fall back on past laurels or reminisce about past challenges met and surpassed. Now was the time to decide the future direction of the company so as to continue the record of success. To begin this task, Tweed had written a major statement of policy to his managers, "Goals for the Future of Mitek Corporation." Now stacked in front of him was the pile of written responses he had received in return. To his surprise these responses had been frank, critical, and hardly supportive of his plans for the future. They betrayed a lack of cohesiveness and team spirit amongst his senior executives. Apparently, the camaraderie, excitement, and energy that had characterized the early building years of the company had disappeared. Without that energy and cohesiveness, Tweed knew any plans for the future growth of the company would be undermined. Indeed, one of the responses had ended with "I doubt if any goals can be achieved until the management discord and organizational deficiencies are resolved. The management team is talking to everyone but each other. The atmosphere exists today in which you are in serious jeopardy of losing every senior manager you have."

THE COMPANY AND INDUSTRY

The Mitek Corporation was a comparatively young, rapidly growing company in a high-growth, high-technology industry. In its five-year history, the company's revenues had grown steadily to $40 million. A healthy economy had made raising external capital relatively easy. Such a steady stream of external funding was needed to support the high R&D and manufacturing costs characteristic of a highly competitive industry with short product life cycles. Such life cycles were partly the logical outcome of readily obtained and widespread technical know-how needed to design and produce the products. Patent protection for new products was thus fairly ineffectual. Indeed, so long as outside capital was available, an engineer with an idea for a small improvement over an existing product could set up an independent shop and begin producing a "me-too" product with relative ease.

Learning curve pricing was a characteristic of the industry and led to competition on the basis of manufacturing cost structures. Success in the market was less a result of the product itself than of quick and timely product introduction, financial and quality control, and well-managed manufacturing operations. Further, companies in the industry suffered from a severe shortage of experienced general managers to coordinate and lead all of these activities. Lacking these abilities, many of the entrepreneurial companies were short lived, often being acquired by larger, better-managed companies.

THE FIRST FIVE YEARS

The Mitek Corporation's beginnings were similar in kind to others in the industry. The three founders all worked for the Ohmex Corporation, a large, multiproduct, multinational company and leader in several segments of the industry, with annual revenues in the $500 million range and manufacturing plants in several locations around the globe. The three men—Robert Tweed, assistant treasurer, and George Morrison and Harvey Knight, engineers from the technical R&D staff—were all in their late 30s or early 40s and had met each other socially outside of work. Their conversation revealed a similar dream to run a company of one's own. The group was more determined than most, and so these off-hour musings eventually evolved first into a serious search for a small, failing company to acquire and turn around, and finally to the idea of starting a company from scratch. It was felt that the technical know-how of the two engineers, coupled with the marketing and finance background of Tweed, would form a good management team.

Initially, three different ideas for possible product areas were suggested. Off-hour discussions about which of these ideas was most feasible were heated and progressed slowly. It was discovered that evening meetings were not sufficient to perform the analysis needed to make a timely decision on the definition of the business. Thus, all three quit Ohmex in order to devote full time to the project.

During the first month, Mitek was incorporated with each founder investing $6,000 in return for the same number of shares of stock. Bob Tweed was elected president since it was through his contacts in the financial world that future funding would be found. The major task of that first month was clearly deciding what the product line would be. After long discussions at the homes of one or the other of the group (money was not to be wasted on office space), the original favorite of the three ideas was rejected as technically possible but unmarketable. Instead, it was decided to try to make a go with the second product area, a failing line of the old Ohmex company. All three founders had experience with this product line while at Ohmex. Both Morrison and Knight had proposed improvement projects for this line, although these were rejected due to the low expected return on investment. Tweed had conducted several studies on how best to organize and run operations in the business. Conclusions from these studies had not been implemented, however, due to the cost of changing a large organization.

The engineers were convinced they could develop a much better product than currently available anywhere in the market. The Mitek product was based on a completely new technology and, for extra measure, used cheaper components. Although the new technology was the creation of Morrison and Knight, Mitek was now competing with the former employer of the principals. To avoid any suggestion of violating trade secret laws, the founders discussed their project with Ohmex, but the company was unconcerned inasmuch as it believed that no one could make money in the area anyway.

During the second and third month, the initial investment was used to rent an old warehouse, buy some used equipment, and begin to develop some prototype products. The burden of this task fell primarily on the shoulders of Morrison and his small team of technical people.

At the end of this period, sample products had been produced that could provide the basis for a prospectus of sufficient sophistication to present to investment bankers and other potential investors. Tweed then went to New York and Texas to raise capital. The market potential of Mitek's innovative product was immediately obvious to investors, who placed $2 million with the company.

For the next year and a half, Morrison and his research team pushed to bring the prototype products to a commercializable stage. Knight and Tweed meanwhile put their efforts to the construction and setting up of a manufacturing facility. After much search, a relatively inexpensive site for a plant was found in a small, rather unattractive town 30 miles away. The location had the benefit of a ready labor supply. The advantage of experience and knowledge of manufacturing operations now became significant. An expert in high-precision manufacturing processes, Knight designed all of the manufacturing and quality test equipment as well as the production process itself. The plant was then designed and built around this process. Even with all of this effort, it was found that it was relatively easy to produce prototypes of superior quality in the lab but extremely difficult to manufacture a large quantity on a continuously processed run of sufficiently consistent quality. Consequently, more time and money was being spent debugging and perfecting the processes than developing the product itself, an unforeseen situation. Delays reached a critical point in the middle of year 2 as the initial money ran out before a single successful manufacturing run had been completed.

Tweed, forced to return to the money markets, focused his efforts on venture capital firms. Fortunately he was able to secure another $2.5 million from one such firm in New York that represented a large wealthy family. Afterward, Tweed said of this period:

We had to bring forward the effort of getting that financing to an extent we hadn't contemplated. We had to get as much money as we could to build our facilities, to provide our working capital, to establish the business. It was the fallacy of our planning, that we originally planned that we could be in production for sale of a commercial product 9 months after we started. As it turned out it took 18 months—twice as long. The cost of the facilities and the equipment was twice as much, too.

We had capitalized the company with a contingency to take care of unforeseens; as it happened we used all of the contingency and still needed more. I was facing a situation where the technical people were saying, "We have this excellent product and we know we are going to be able to sell it, a lot of it. And the thing that's not permitting us to do that is the lack of capital. We've done our job right, now you do yours." Luckily for me and the company, I was able to find more capital.

With the infusion of new capital, the next few months saw the completion of the first successful manufacturing run and the hiring of a marketing vice president, Ted Rowman. The product was an instant success. Orders flowed in from an aggressive, efficiently organized field sales force faster than they could be filled. The emphasis on marketing with the early building of a direct sales force was seen later as a key to the company's rapid growth.

By the end of the second year, Mitek's new product had brought in over $800,000 in revenue, Significantly, in year 3 Mitek's bottom line was positive for the first time, with revenues of $8.2 million and net profits after tax of $1.1 million.

For the next couple of years the Mitek Corporation concentrated on the research and development, manufacturing, and marketing of this single line of products. Much effort was expended in developing improved manufacturing processes, extensive quality control, and the further expansion of the field sales force. Indeed, as the company quickly gained market share, a reputation was developed as the price quality leader. Growth continued with revenues of $8.2, $17.8 and $40 million in years, 3, 4, and 5 (Exhibit 1).

For Tweed, the pleasures of starting his own company certainly included monetary ones. Indeed, during year 5, the directors voted a stock split of 30 to 1. But it had always been Tweed's intention for Mitek to be a publicity owned company. Consequently, at the end of year 5, the company went public with the sale of 1 million shares of stock at $25 per share, which were soon listed on the New York Stock Exchange. The success of the stock particularly pleased the New York investors who found their reputations for picking future high flyers greatly enhanced.

THE PRESIDENT

One unique factor in the company's early growth and recognition was its president. On first acquaintance, Robert Tweed did not look the hard-hitting businessman and self-made millionaire that he was, but rather he had the abstracted air more common to a professor. Since

Exhibit 1

MITEK CORPORATION
Statement of Income
($000)

	Year 1	Year 2	Year 3	Year 4	Year 5
Net sales	—	$ 801	$8,212	$17,798	$39,453
Cost of sales	—	836	5,138	10,534	21,825
Gross profits (loss)	—	(35)	3,074	7,264	17,628
Operating expenses:					
Preproduction costs	$ 616	805	—	—	—
Research	—	168	678	1,015	2,350
Marketing and advertising	—	219	862	2,321	5,381
General and administrative	—	64	297	380	929
Total expenses	616	1,256	1,837	3,716	8,660
Operating income (loss)	(616)	(1,291)	1,237	3,548	8,968
Other expenses:					
Interest expense	12	81	174	178	596
Net income (loss) before taxes	(628)	(1,372)	1,063	3,370	8,372
Provision for taxes	—	—	556	1,562	3,970
Net income before loss carryforward	(628)	(1,372)	507	1,808	4,402
Reduction in taxes from loss carryforward	—	—	600	400	—
Net income (loss)	$(628)	$(1,372)	$1,107	$ 2,208	$ 4,402

his youth in the Midwest, however, a desire to excel and win at whatever he did motivated Tweed. He was driven to be "a success," which he understood as having money and a position of leadership. From a large, financially strapped family, he worked his way through the state university and law school by running several boarding houses for students. His college advisor remembered him as one of the most dogged workers he had ever counseled. At the end of law school, Tweed decided that the practice of law would not provide the kind of active role that he sought. He then went on to a well-known eastern business school where he received his MBA with an emphasis in finance. Like many of his colleagues, he left business school to join a prestigious firm on Wall Street. Early in his career he was transferred to Texas where he helped set up a new sales office. This proved to be a very exciting experience for Tweed. The uncertainty and early difficulties of a new operation, while intimidating to some, were an inspiration to Tweed. The New York home office had other ideas, however, and in recognition of the fast growth of the branch office, promoted Tweed to vice president and transferred him back to New York. This presented a problem for Tweed. If he went back to New York, he would become a prosperous investment banker. He knew that he would remain with the firm because the position would be an interesting one and the cost of leaving the firm would soon be too great. However, if he left the company now and started his own business, he foresaw two great disadvantages: no expertise in any particular business and inexperience in managing any type of manufacturing firm (no "line-type" experience). In the end, his desire to be his own boss and to be responsible for a large organization prevailed and he left investment banking. He decided to work for Ohmex first and gain some experience in a manufacturing company operating in a high-growth industry. He reasoned that working for such a company would make up for his deficiency in experience and would be a good training ground for starting his own company.

Tweed was a soft-spoken man but very articulate. He prided himself on his knowledge of up-to-date management practices and particularly enjoyed giving speeches both to outside groups and to his own managers on his ideas for management innovations and methods to stimulate cohesion, hard work, and quality for employees. Perhaps unfairly, such speechmaking led some managers to comment that the president did not listen to input from them and that corporate policy meetings of the president's advisory committee tended to be rather one-sided forums.[1] Tweed was generally viewed as very hard working, a believer in the Protestant work ethic. He believed that one's work and family should be strictly separated. Indeed, his wife and six children were rarely seen at the company, if at all. Consistent with these priorities, when asked about the risks encountered in starting a new venture like the Mitek Corporation, Tweed spoke primarily in terms of risks to his family and personal career:

---

[1] See Exhibit 2 for makeup of committee.

Exhibit 2
ORGANIZATION YEAR 5

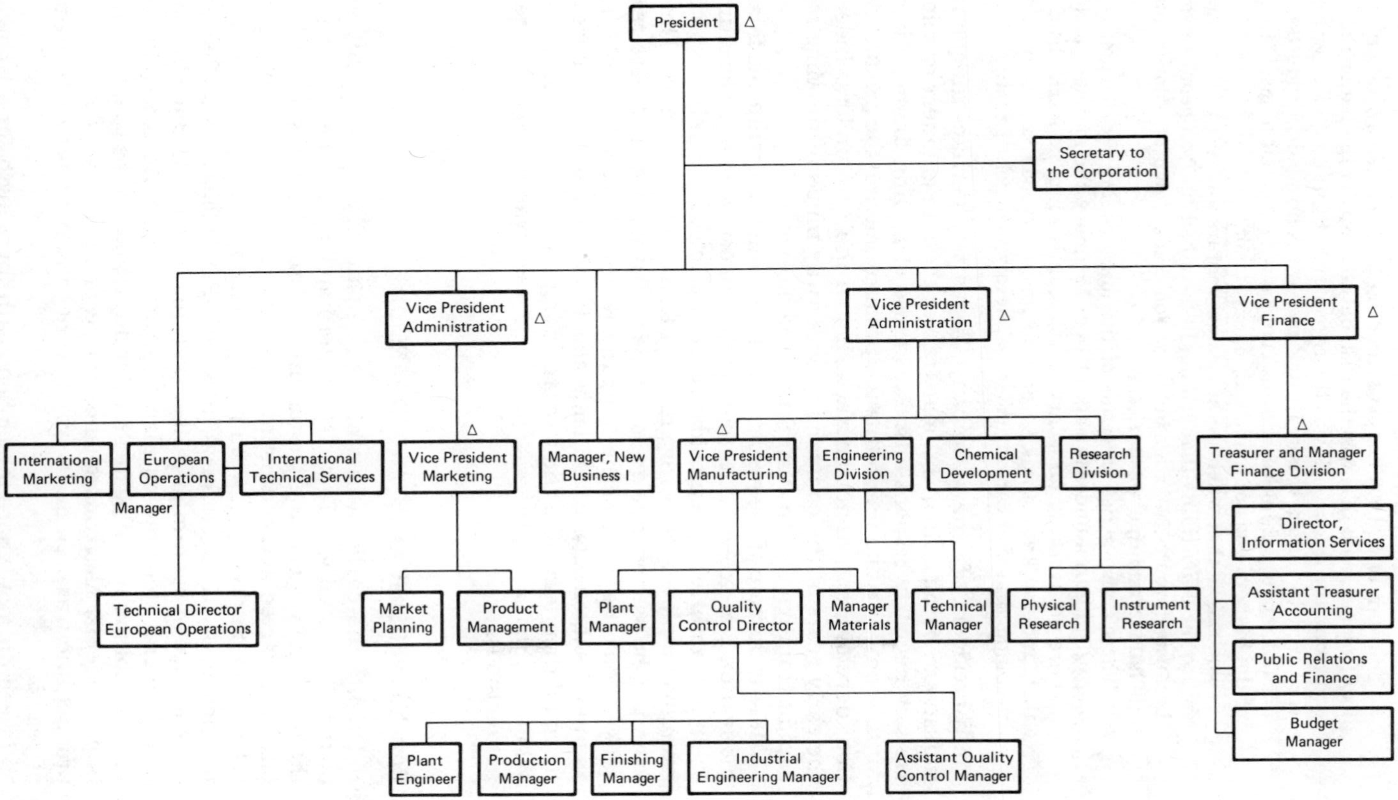

The sum of $18,000 doesn't sound like a lot of money. I didn't have a lot of money. And that was the risk, but that wasn't the major risk.

I think the major risk was the career risk. I think all of us were doing very well in industry, and I think had we continued in industry in the normal mode, I think most of us could have expected to graduate to one of the higher levels of industrial management.

The risk is that when you try a new venture and you fail, you not only forego the opportunity that you might have had but you penalize yourself because if you reenter an industry, you come down at a lower rung on the ladder, and that was a risk.

There's also a risk in terms of the families. My recollection is there were 20 children under the age of 14 or 15 among the founders, and when you are not working for salary there's a little bit of concern about doing that, and you know the kind of problems, everybody knows the kinds of problems that that can engender. So there was a risk of that.

For a president of a new company, Tweed was perhaps unique in the industry in being a financial man, rather than an engineer or scientist. He saw his early responsibilities as those of finding financial backing for the company and marketing the product, leaving the product definition, development, and manufacturing to the co-founders. Indeed, in the early years of the company he was away much of the time raising capital from friends on Wall Street and elsewhere.

He saw the role of the president as providing leadership and financial motivation for growth. He thought that most people underestimated their own abilities. The president's job was to call upon this extra effort from his employees and reward them for such performance. Thus, for example, he set revenue goals for the corporation which were realistically beyond the reach of the company. By hiring "good" people (defined as intelligent, energetic, and enthusiastic individuals), he believed that he could then leave the "how" of reaching these goals to the managers. Where his managers were concerned, Tweed was interested in results, not methods.

EARLY DIVERSIFICATION AND EXPANSION

Despite the early success of the company, Tweed was fully aware of the short product life cycles in the industry. By the end of year 4, the business was starting the mature, the initial success of the product having attracted new competitors. Hence, after the original product was released to marketing, Tweed hired a dynamic young scientist, recommended by a friend, to head up a new R&D department. Because of the shortage of such high-caliber personnel, Tweed had to offer to provide a liberal stock option plan to attract him. Fifteen percent of the revenue dollars was allocated for this department to be spent on product improvements. As a consequence, the second generation of the original product line was well on its way toward introduction by the beginning of year 5.

Tweed did not ignore the obvious path for growth for a young company: to increase market size and penetration. Through the first four years, marketing opened sales offices in 25 major cities across the country. Then, in year 5, Tweed was surprised by a visit from one of the early investors, a young man whom Tweed had known at Ohmex. John Hawley was now selling for Ohmex in Europe but seeing the quick acceptance of Mitek's products was eager to work for Tweed. Tweed was impressed with Hawley's energy and spirited attitude and decided that the company could benefit from Hawley's knowledge of the European market. With the advisory committee's assent, Tweed hired Hawley, with a very attractive incentive and bonus pay structure, to set up a European sales network. And indeed, in year 5, expansion continued with the opening of the first of several European offices. However, as orders from Europe began to be filled, the costs of transatlantic shipping proved to be quite high. To solve this problem, Tweed initiated planning for a European manufacturing plant. Tweed did not perceive Europe as a major growth area or a solution to the innovation problem, however. European sales branches were useful sources of income, but could not solve the longer term growth problem, since the same competitive forces were at work abroad. The European expansion was not without costs either, as both the domestic manufacturing and sales departments were aggravated by the organizational separation of these new operations from their American counterparts.

Tweed started to be concerned about the vulnerability inherent in his single-business firm. He recognized that continued high growth had to be supported by new product innovation. Therefore, toward the end of year 4, Mitek's top executives on the president's advisory committee met and decided to diversify through entry into a related product area, which promised much growth in the future.

A few weeks later, Tweed was taking one of his frequent trips to New York to meet with his investment bankers. On the way home, he happened to sit next to a young engineer from a competing company who not only was a known expert in Mitek's desired new product area but was looking for a way to leave his employer and head up his own operation. Tweed was impressed with the man's ability. Within the month, with the help of a substantial stock option plan, he was able to hire him. The new business was set up in a different location, with its manager reporting directly to Tweed.

While Tweed was actually quite excited about the new R&D developments, the European expansion and the new business, he was concerned with the way the moves had been made. Rather than the result of a controlled planning process, which had weighed the pros and cons of alternatives, the decisions had been made in a loose, ad hoc manner. Tweed was aware that the expansion and diversification moves had caused much bickering among the key executives, particularly by those who felt the decisions were made because of chance hiring of new key people. Tweed tended to ignore this bickering, expecting that any growth would cause some strain between executives.

PLANS FOR YEAR 6—THE PRESIDENT'S "GOALS FOR THE FUTURE"

Tweed's key concerns—how to sustain growth in the core business, where to expand after the European extension, and how and when to diversify—were very much on his mind as the company approached the regular annual budgetary process in the last quarter of year 5.

The budget process was a rather uncomplicated affair. In the first few years of the company's history, the primary goal had been one of survival. The management perspective was perforce extremely short term, and many planning activities were handled in an informal manner between senior executives. Within the perspective and scope of these informal discussions, top executives would create a budget during the third or fourth quarter of each year for both old and new projects. After the treasurer's office had consolidated them, the budgets would be submitted to Tweed, who reviewed and presented them to the board of directors. Given the expansion into Europe and the first diversification efforts during year 5, which had been constant topics of conversation in the company, Tweed expected that his executives would address the issue of growth and present plans for expansion in their budgets. Therefore, he was very disappointed as he began reviewing final budgets coming in from the various departments. While the numbers were all in place, the plans, when put together, did not make a cohesive whole. The plans did not address the diversification issue but were myopic, one-year extensions of year 5 activities. There was a distinct lack of analysis. The plans lacked an understanding of financial, market, and operating risks, a discussion of markets and market opportunities, and any strategies as to how to maintain growth.

Tweed realized that the output of the budget cycle was partially his own fault in not specifying his expectations. Given the increasing size of the company and its management staff, it was becoming necessary to instill a longer term perspective and more formal planning process and analysis into the company. Tweed was suspicious, on the other hand, that the lack of cohesion between the plans was due to the internal rivalries and bickering that had built up during the year. Tweed realized that the budgets had to be redone under his leadership. He had to set short- and long-term goals to guide managers in this process. He prepared a set of guidelines and policies entitled "Goals for the Future of the Mitek Corporation," a document which consisted of 25 pages plus exhibits (excerpts and summaries are in Exhibit 3). The "Goals" was sent to approximately 50 people, including the board of directors, all of the first- and second-line senior managers—vice presidents, division heads, the treasurer, and the secretary to the corporation—the key third-line managers, and a few fourth-line managers from the manufacturing division. The guidelines were also sent to McDougal Consulting Company. Recognizing that growth was putting strains on the management structure, Tweed had brought McDougal in to study and recommend changes in the organization design.[2]

The "Goals" document began by stating that its function was to provide a basis for dialogue concerning next year's budget and longer term plans. Written responses directed to the goals themselves were invited. Tweed then presented a corporate purpose and a long-term growth objec-

---

[2] See Exhibits 2 and 3 for organization chart of addresses and makeup of board of directors.

Exhibit 3

DESCRIPTION OF MEMBERS OF MITEK BOARD OF DIRECTORS

Member 1: Robert Tweed, president, Mitek.

Member 2: Harvey Knight, vice president administration, for research and development and manufacturing, Mitek.

Member 3: Vice president administration, for marketing, Mitek.

Member 4: Vice president, marketing, of a manufacturing firm in a related industry.

Member 5: Vice president of a major Wall Street investment banking house (had investments in Mitek).

Member 6: Vice president of a large research lab.

Member 7: Partner of a venture capital firm (which had placed the second $2.5 million in Mitek).

Member 8: Professor of engineering, from a prestigious engineering school.

Member 9: Chairman of the board of a manufacturing company.

---

tive. In the growth projections, Tweed even included the sales of a second new business venture to spur the development of new ideas by the managers. Finally, corporate policies on organization, employment, management philosophy, plans and controls, U.S. operations, R&D, marketing, European operations, and acquisitions were discussed.

REACTION TO "GOALS FOR THE FUTURE"

The presentation evoked written responses from more than half of the company's managers. These were primarily negative in tone. What surprised Tweed most, however, was not the reaction to the growth goals or other policies, which were by and large objective in nature. In fact he found them predictable. But the vehemence of the reaction to the management policy section in which Tweed had emphasized the need to decrease bickering and discord and increase teamwork and openness was a disturbing surprise. Excerpts from two of the typical responses are included in Exhibit 5 and 6: both of the authors were on the president's advisory committee, one being the vice president, marketing, Ted Rowman, and the other the vice president, administration (operations and R&D), Harvey Knight, one of the original founders.

Exhibit 4

GOALS FOR THE FUTURE

INTRODUCTION

In writing this statement of corporate goals, I am aware of a kind of pontification in establishing them. I sense the lack of "position papers" and the debating of alternatives, except with respect to the statements of organization policy and European operations which have been much discussed.

In connection with the objectives stated herein, as with other objectives in the past which have been benefited by the study and propositions of others, I solicit the ideas of every member of management. Cross-fertilization of each other's thinking can only produce superior results, and this process applied to this statement of objectives will evolve more definitive, solidly grounded, and well-reasoned goals for the company.

For the present, however, this statement of objectives represents the only basis for our planning and preparation of operating budgets for year 6. Undoubtedly in the review of submitted plans and budgets, the evolutionary process toward improvement of our objectives will begin.

Robert Tweed
President

CORPORATE PURPOSE

The purpose of Mitek is to operate an international business pursuant to policies and practices which represent the balanced best interests of customers, employees, and shareholders.

Because of the dynamic character and rapidly expanding opportunities of the company's field of interest, the ambitions and vitality of its people, and the capital gain profit motivation of its shareholders, the special emphasis of Mitek's operations is growth.

LONG-TERM GROWTH OBJECTIVES

Mitek Corporation's corporate objective for growth is to realize the potential which now exists within the existing operating units to achieve sales of $150 million four years from now (the target year).

This objective reflects a significant reduction in the past rate of growth of the company's core business in the United States and projected radical growth of International Operations (principally Europe), our current new business venture, and other new businesses yet to be defined. The sales objectives of each unit, which are set forth on the next page, have been proposed by the several managers who have the responsibility for achieving them and, hence, should be regarded as realistic targets.

Core business sales in the United States are targeted at $80 million in the target year, which reflects a compounded annual growth rate of 25 percent. This of course, compares to a growth rate of three or four times the projected figure during the past four years.

International sales are projected to increase to $20 million in the target year. After completion of the European manufacturing plant project, which will develop our capacity to transfer know-how overseas, it is likely that we shall undertake a Far East project.

Exhibit 4 (*continued*)

FOUR-YEAR SALES OBJECTIVES
($ millions)

	Core business			New business			
	United States	*Inter-national*	*Core sales subtotal*	*I*	*II*	*New business subtotal*	*Total Mitek sales*
Year 5..........	$33	$ 6	$ 39	—	—	—	$ 39
Year 6..........	45	12	57	$ 8	—	$ 8	65
Year 7..........	58	15	73	18	$ 8	26	99
Year 8..........	70	18	88	27	15	42	130
Year 9 (target year)	80	20	100	38	22	60	160

The current new business (I) objective is below its potential as a result of our increasing familiarity with the technology and market potential for the product. Sales can anticipate a sharply rising curve because the product will have the important advantages of our quality reputation and immediate international marketing efforts.

Other new business objectives are conjectural because other new products are only in the development stage and no consensus exists as to which direction expansion should take.

Net profits from these operations should be most satisfactory, if their respective technical, manufacturing, and marketing programs are successful. U.S. core business operations and European operations will face declining profit margins as the core business industry engenders the competitive conditions of a mature industry. Reduced profit margins may be countered periodically by new product improvements which do not represent technological breakthroughs, but these will not change the long-term results. Technical managers must calculate, in terms of market potentials and expected payoffs, the division of its resources between product improvement programs, programs which seek fundamental breakthroughs in core business technology, and other R&D programs which may be related to our existing technology but involve extension of our business into other fields.

During the coming year, an objective of top management of the company will be to prepare a definitive long-term corporate strategy and integrated operating and capital plans which will bring about consensus on the direction the company shall take to achieve maximum growth.

ORGANIZATION POLICY

The businesses of European operations, core business operations, and new business opportunities will be organized, under the "federal principle" of organization, into decentralized operating units.

Each unit will be a profit center, responsible to its own top management which enjoys full responsibility for success or failure.

In many, if not most, ways each unit will function in a manner similar to an independent business. It will function subject to a framework of policies, guides, and controls fixed by the president. These will differ from each operating unit. Two expected benefits are better decisions because decisions will be made as close to the operating level as possible, and better performance because manag-

Exhibit 4 (*continued*)

ers will perform best when objectives are set, resources provided, and operations are left unfettered.

MANAGEMENT

One of the company's principal objectives will be to improve our decision-making processes and to develop the kind of teamwork and achievement-oriented behavior that attract, motivate, and retain talented management people.

Unfortunately, Mitek's growth has been accompanied by increasing occurrences of management discord which are not in the company's best interests and for which we can no longer afford to make allowances. The indictment against our organization is long, but it should be repeated to emphasize the extent of the problem. Too often, problems that might have been approached from a more detached, factual base have been viewed as personal contests with all the attendant secretiveness, petty jealousies, exaggerations, and lack of common courtesy that are part of this unfortunate approach. Moreover, decisions, once made, have often not been followed, and in some instances have been deliberately ignored or undermined. Finally, accomplishments and difficulties have been exaggerated to make realistic performance appraisal impossible.

Elimination of these practices will not be easy because misconduct always has its roots in unclear causes. However, we must make every effort to identify these causes and improve our ability to work together. To the extent the causes lie within our management system, we shall improve the situation by:

1. Developing a better understanding of what is expected of each manager.
2. Improving communication channels to facilitate more open discussion of common problems.
3. Evaluating performance, in qualitative as well as quantitative terms, against responsibilities.
4. Rewarding teamwork with promotion and favorable compensation and imposing penalties, financial and otherwise, upon those who persist in misconduct.

Top management must set the example in this responsibility for proper business conduct. I am personally dedicated to this course in terms of my own practices. I shall also enjoin it upon other members of management through the rewards system. No amount of tangible accomplishment will excuse anyone's future misconduct, because without mutual respect and cooperative undertaking an effective management team cannot be welded together to achieve our programs.

PLANS AND CONTROLS

A principal objective of management will be to perform satisfactory planning and to develop a control system to verify the conformance of actions taken to the plans.

The corporate performance objectives which I have set forth herein will be fractionated by the vice presidents of administration, division managers, and department managers into subgoals, both qualitative and quantitative. Such subgoals, to be prepared in narrative and statistical form, will be the bases for division and department operating plans and their requests for year 6 budgets. This work shall be completed three weeks from this policy statement. When functional subgoals, plans, and budgets have been accepted by top management, individual

Exhibit 4 (*concluded*)

performance targets will be stipulated for each key manager to serve as a basis for performance appraisals and compensation adjustments.

A principal objective of top management, assisted by the finance division and by the management information systems group yet to be organized, will be to develop reports, standard costs, project costing, expense analyses, and other control measures. To this end, it is essential that a top caliber staff for the MIS function be recruited immediately.

In implementing improved controls, the purpose will be to present key information to management, highlight exceptions from planned operations, and direct attention to operating difficulties.

U.S. OPERATIONS

The plans from the manufacturing department do not place enough emphasis on cutting costs. Slowing the rate of capacity expansion, achieving economies of scale, better efficiencies, and cost cutting is required. The new target to decrease overhead expense will be 15 percent, as opposed to the 10 percent increase proposed by manufacturing.

Last year we set as our objective an increase in R&D activity of approximately 25 percent over that of the prior year. Our failure to achieve this objective is undoubtedly attributable to the effects of hiring the new director of R&D, which resulted in suspension of new programs and projects and reassignment of certain functions, the necessity to replace resigned personnel, and the difficulty of recruiting additional technical staff of high caliber.

Further, a new market research department will be established, and each researcher will be required to justify programs on the basis of market potential.

U.S. MARKETING OPERATIONS

Competition has increased. We can no longer skim the cream. A strong marketing effort is required. However, granting the necessity for a significant increase in unit marketing expenses, the submitted budgets from marketing for this year's expenses are untenable. From a three-year level of $1.50–$1.80 per unit sold, the budgets propose an increase to $2.28 per unit. Marketing management must review its programs upon which this projected increase has been based to determine where expenditures are beyond the point of diminishing returns. Lacking factual basis for alternatives, I shall fix the reasonable objective for year 6 to increase marketing expenses to no more than $2 per unit.

POLICY RELATED TO ACQUISITIONS

The company will not enter the acquisition game but will grow from within.

Only in the unlikely event of an acquisition opportunity which is possessed of good growth potential, demonstrated profit-making capability, and competent management, and which operates in an area similar or closely related to our current line of business, shall we consider diversification by acquiring another company. In short, our acquisition policy shall be one of disinterest and high opportunism.

Exhibit 5

COMMENTS ON TWEED'S "GOALS FOR THE FUTURE"
by
Ted Rowman, Vice President, Marketing

Corporate purpose

There can be no controversy over the statement of purpose. All of the loyal employees are indeed conscious of the emphasis placed on growth desires. The possibility of being outstripped by superior development by our competitors does indeed highlight the need for efficient operation of all divisions of the company.

Long-term growth objectives

None can quarrel with the burning desire of management to achieve sales of $150 million by the target year, and while there are many methods of achieving this figure, there will be little room for error. Our industry is no longer forgiving. When one considers the changes our industry has seen, the compounded annual growth rate of 25 percent per year in the face of the industry growth of approximately 15 percent per year, we should be able to continue increasing our market share which we all agree is mandatory (but it must be done profitably).

With regard to the international forecast of $20 million by the target year, it is imperative that no more time be wasted in getting our European facility on stream. My personal feeling is that we have delayed far too long and that the effects of our procrastination will be felt sooner than any of us would imagine.

Four-year sales objectives

It is my opinion that the new business venture must be carefully monitored by the corporation, and I feel the current method of monitoring is unsatisfactory. I am concerned that a small company cannot afford the expensive R&D necessary to develop innovative products as envisioned by new business I. We are best equipped to imitate the advances of other companies.

Organization policy

With regard to the organization of the "federal principle," I feel there is room for debate. In my opinion, the marketing division should be under one manager and a corporate marketing staff should be established to market our products worldwide. Hawley's operation in Europe should not be his autonomous barony.

Our principal competitor is currently operating under separate marketing organizations and is in the process of reorganizing their marketing division into a centralized marketing force with individual product managers. I feel this is the proper way to operate. The marketing strategies of our competitors overseas are becoming increasingly similar to the domestic marketing strategies.

With regard to the general organization of the company, it is very apparent that McDougal & Company will offer specific recommendations concerning our organization and while they report directly to the president, it is my feeling that the pros and cons of any suggested reorganization be discussed and carefully weighed by all officers of the company.

I will prepare proposed organization charts for consideration and will submit them at a later date.

I feel that our employment policies, in general, are good. However, I have the feeling that we are not aware of the problems at the lower echelon . . . the fact that we are cognizant of top-management problems is evident. I feel that we overrate the morale of our second- and third-line management. The gung ho spirit still seems to be here and I sincerely hope this is true, but with the tremendous growth Mitek has enjoyed, I cannot help but wonder if we truly

Exhibit 5 (*continued*)

have a handle on our employee policies. I feel there is the possibility that many of our employees will leave to start their own ventures.

Management

I feel that the management discord is undoubtedly the biggest problem facing us today. We will never reach the $150 million market without establishing a greater degree of harmony.

International, marketing, manufacturing and new business I, each operate as an independent company. This is an impossible situation. The comments made regarding personal contests, secretiveness, petty jealousies, and exaggerations are indeed factual. The comment regarding the lack of common courtesy is one of the most noticeable conditions prevalent at Mitek today and has been commented upon quite frequently.

Another serious situation exists when corporate decisions have been made and not followed or deliberately ignored. One can agree that independent thinkers are a necessity, but once the decision has been made, the book should be closed and every effort should be made to support the final decision. I personally find that old wounds are continually being reopened, but only to the benefit of our competitors. There is simply not enough energy available to fight our competitors and our associates too!

Your report listed a series of steps to be taken to improve the situation. None can quarrel with these proposals, but one can only pray that these suggestions are implemented.

You have stated that you are personally dedicated to this course of action in terms of your own practices. It is often said that an organization is the reflection of its leader. If this statement is true, then you are the one that has to change and lead the way.

Plans and controls

The three-week deadline placed on each division for subgoals both qualitative and quantitative do not permit sufficient time to adequately do the job. You ask for analysis but allocate no time or money to do it.

We have repeatedly stated that controls must be placed on our expenditures. In year 3 and 4, we were faced with the identical problems facing us today—overhead percentage outstripping profit margins. You vowed then that this would never happen again, and here we are at the end of year 5 with the very same problems. Why? We do not know, because we do not have the kind of management information to give us timely warning when things are going wrong, nor a way to systematically correct problems when they are discovered. Unfortunately, the sweet smell of success spoils us and permits us to don rose colored glasses.

U.S. operations

It would appear now that we have indeed reached the point whereby we will have to reduce profit margins to increase our share of the market. We have steadily felt that we wanted to skim the cream, but the cream is much thinner now. We cannot have our cake and eat it too. If we are to reach the $150 million figure as a corporation, we must adjust to economy of scale in all divisions, not just marketing.

U.S. marketing operations

While I understand the need to justify the increased marketing costs to $2.28 per unit, the arbitrary setting of the budget to $2 per unit is typical of the auto-

Exhibit 5 (*concluded*)

cratic methods you employ in this company. I do not accept this limitation and am preparing a justification for the budget submitted earlier.

Policy relating to acquisition

I feel the basic underlying statements concerning acquisitions is due to the lack of confidence in Mitek's ability to adequately manage and staff the acquired companies. I do not feel the door should be closed on this matter, and if indeed we can clear up our existing management problems, Mitek has sufficient talent to carry out a modest acquisition program and more rapidly achieve a position of a multiproduct company.

General policies

I agree basically with the general statement of policy. In fact, even greater emphasis could be placed on some of the statements made. It is a known fact that many people at Mitek have responsibility without authority . . . an impossible situation. The statement that no one person shall be given direction by more than one other person cannot be overemphasized. We have conditions whereby employees are giving orders to other employees that are not under their area of jurisdiction, unless our organizational charts are completely erroneous.

Summary

In summary, I should like to quote several excerpts from our facilities brochure written in year 2.

"Mitek enjoys the inherent selling advantages of a small company—no rigid procedures, no sacred cows, no ponderous decision making, no cross-purposes."

"It is ambitious to be responsive to the needs of its customers as only a small enterprise with singleness of purpose is able."

"The distinguishing mark of Mitek people, research scientists, engineers, sales force and accountants—is that we are user-oriented. We mean to prove it to you."

"Although intensely proud of our capabilities, we work by the rule that man's reach should exceed his grasp. In this sense, we shall never realize our ambitions."

I believe Mitek has drifted severely from this spirit.

Exhibit 6

To: Robert Tweed

From: H. Knight, vice president administration for manufacturing and R&D
Re: RT's "Goals for the Future"

Summary

These objectives, while in many ways the best and most comprehensive that you have produced, contain statements and implications, apparently directed toward several individuals, which I feel would be better discussed privately than to be included in a document distributed as widely as this one. Unsubstantiated charges such as "accomplishments and difficulties have been exaggerated" or "decisions . . . have been ignored or undermined" should be discussed forthrightly with the individuals being accused rather than be included in "Goals for the Future." It is quite true that management morale is very poor. It is also quite true that the morale of a ship is the reflection of the policies and practices of her officers and, to a very large extent, the captain. You have had it within your power to restore a high level of management morale and determination

Exhibit 6 (*continued*)

by removing several demotivating influences and situations, and by dealing forth-rightly with your people. Mitek, in my opinion, must have a leader who will work with and motivate his management, engender management commitment to carefully developed operating plans, and effectively delegate meaningful authority and responsibility to his management. Loyalty and commitment cannot be ordered, can only tenuously and ineffectively be bought, and must be created, nurtured, and won through just and forthright participative and empathetic intercourse with people.

It had been my understanding, or perhaps only my hope, that decisions relative to corporate organization and operating management would be deferred until the McDougal Company report was completed. I was therefore disappointed to find that certain decisions, which I cannot honestly support and which I feel strongly are not in the company's best interests, have apparently already been made. In particular I cannot agree with decisions regarding the European operation. Hawley has been given too much autonomy. With the addition of a plant, which apparently will be under his control, not under my manufacturing division, he will be even more difficult to control than he is now. This man is too young and unproven a manager to have such uncontrolled responsibilities. I feel that Mitek should be exploiting its new business opportunities at home to a much greater degree than it appears to be going to. However, the advisory committee has been excluded from forthright discussion on the domestic expansion and diversification as well.

I would like to see more specific goals as to acceptable return on investment, payout period, or other criteria by which discretionary projects in all areas of the company may be evaluated and ranked in order of priority, rather than the ad hoc opportunistic decisions that have been made by you recently.

Introduction

It was my understanding, shared by others, that you wished these proposed goals to stimulate some provocative thinking and that they would be discussed with and modified by members of management before being finalized. I am completely in agreement with you that you cannot have commitment to, nor whole-hearted support of, goals unless management participates in their formulation and is permitted an opportunity to freely discuss them. I personally feel the lack of factual and sincere objective discussions regarding certain of the goals and that if they are finalized as they now stand, they will seriously suffer from not having been arrived at by listing all of the pros and cons before arriving at the conclusion. You complain about the department plans being without analysis, but then you give us none either.

Long-term growth objectives

It is my personal feeling that $150 million sales goal in the target year is a relatively conservative figure. We have grown more than 40 percent per year in the past. However, as you have often pointed out, the real goal should not be sales but should be profitability. I believe it is important that, rather than talk about sales volume objectives for each unit, profit and return on investment objectives be discussed and established. The question of whether to enter new areas should be approached not from the concept of the size of market available but from the concept of realizable profit and return on investment.

There can be really no question but that core product profitability per unit will tend to decline in the forthcoming years and that substantial technical and managerial effort will be required to increase plant yields and efficiency, reduce

Exhibit 6 (*continued*)

working capital requirements, and improve return on capital invested. It is particularly important for these reasons that the new business venture succeeds. The separation of the old, core product R&D from the newer research efforts (in new business I for example) with more incentives given to the new groups, only hurts the cohesiveness of the company however. The critical importance of preparing early in year 6 a forthright, long-term corporate strategy and integrated operating and capital plans, corporate organization plans, corporate facilities plans, an objective evaluation of people and their capabilities and how they may be motivated cannot be overstressed.

Organization policy

While I cannot argue with the logic of profit centers, the concept is not being applied equitably. The core business division is conspicuous by its absence from consideration as a separate profit center with the same type of management incentive that has been provided for the new business venture and European operations. The stock options and incentive pay, offered to the new managers, are extremely generous and not available to the older, original group, which after all made Mitek what it is today.

If, as you say, managers perform best when objectives are set, resources provided, and operations are left unfettered in the new business areas, it would appear to me to be equally true in the core business area. I believe that whereas Mitek is striving to produce creative environments in its new businesses, it is in fact successfully striving to produce exactly the opposite in its parent corporation. It is obviously stifling the ambitions, aspirations and vitality of its core business people and encouraging and forcing them to consider possibilities other than long-term Mitek employment.

Management

I believe that in this area a much more specific discussion involving people and situations is in order. I do not believe that the causes of the management discord are unclear. I think they are quite clear. You have had it within your power to correct or remove these causes any time you so desired. The communications amongst the top-management people, and particularly between the president and his staff, are extremely poor and have been lacking in honesty, candor, and objectivity. In a list of ills stated, no one, including RT, is above reproach, and indeed in my opinion RT himself has been the biggest offender in viewing problems as personal contests and in failing to adhere to decisions once made. I am particularly concerned about performance evaluations in qualitative terms. Too high an emphasis on the qualitative leads only to nonfactual judgments and strongly emphasizes the personal contest viewpoints. In view of your request that the goals be viewed provocatively, I believe that the primary source of difficulty within the management group in the company lies within the president's office and in part because of his qualitative, nonfactual judgments of certain people, in some cases highly favorable, in some cases highly unfavorable, and in part because of his opportunistic nature and aversion to true planning. I do not believe that any successful management team can be developed until these matters are openly aired, the problems of secrecy, lack of forthrightness, lack of time, and apparent lack of interest in developing a truly participative performance-based management are resolved.

If unquestioning obedience is desired instead of tangible accomplishment, then initiative, creativity, and growth in Mitek will not persist. The statement

Exhibit 6 (*continued*)

"accomplishments and difficulties have been exaggerated" should not be made without reference to specific situations and the accused permitted a rebuttal. Actually, I suppose that there may even be those who feel that financing the company may not have been nearly as difficult as it has been made to appear.

Plans and controls

This section is contradictory within itself from the very start. Its initial paragraph states "To perform satisfactory planning . . ." and in the next paragraph it states that "subgoals to be prepared in narrative and statistical form . . . shall be completed in three weeks." This is a totally unrealistic date and it will result, as have such unrealistic dates in the past, in completely unsatisfactory planning and the preparation of unrealistic operating plans which cannot be adhered to, with the resulting management and operating confusion as to what is actually to be done.

Mitek has never been able to complete a satisfactory operating plan. It has never been able to grope through the last step of planning, of completing the loop and comparing what the technical capabilities are relative to the marketing requirements on the basis of economic evaluations and justifications, and to select an overall composite course of action for marketing-technical-manufacturing on the basis of need and profitability. Its top management has never been united in an understanding of the probability of achieving goals or the implication of its achieving or not achieving goals. A recent unsolicited sampling of junior managerial opinion relative to plans and controls and goals indicated that between 75 percent and 85 percent of the members of a particular meeting did not believe that any meaningful plans and goals would ever be prepared and that, even if they were, 90 percent felt there would be no follow-up on suggested changes in the plans or alterations indicated by the results of planning.

The company has tended to be highly opportunistic and unrealistic in its planning, has never appreciated the problems which it faced and the difficulties associated with their solution. Typically, all recent entry into new areas has been made in an ad hoc manner, following merely informal discussion and approval.

If today we were to spend substantial sums on a management information system, we must be prepared to implement and correct findings pointed out by the system.

U.S. operations

I cannot abide by the constant cost reductions demanded from manufacturing. While efficiency is always laudable, increasing the overhead reduction to 15 percent is not comprehensible, and most of the cost is passed on to us from finance. Indeed the finance department's projects (like the MIS system) are always approved without question, while many new technical and manufacturing projects are being passed over.

European operations

To attempt to establish Tweed's desired European empire in complete autonomy is in my opinion a most serious and erroneous technical judgment and one which has a high probability of failure. The probability of maintaining product uniformity and product interchangeability between autonomous plants operating in different hemispheres is quite low.

584

Exhibit 6 (*concluded*)

Policy relating to acquisitions

It is quite apparent from the whole tenor of the goals that the core business manufacturing personnel are to be confined to the original operation and are to be denied any growth potential. This is particularly evident in the policy relating to acquisitions.

With regard to the comment that "until Mitek has mastered its own basic problems of organization, planning, communications, and control," it must be remembered that the morale and effectiveness of an organization are a direct reflection of the effectiveness and human relations capability of the man leading that organization. The statement, "Our acquisition policy shall be one of disinterest and high opportunism" is precisely the type of planning which has characterized top-management organization with regard to all aspects of the business. One of the commodities which Mitek could export to one or two growing businesses would be experienced management which could take a company and put it into a sound growth situation. Unfortunately it is not recognized that this management capability exists here, and indeed there appears to be substantial effort directed toward driving it out of the company.

General policies

The goals are certainly desirable. Unfortunately RT is probably the most flagrant violator of all of these statements and until he corrects this and accepts the fact that the company reflects his image and that he must provide leadership and must devote sufficient time to the operations of the business, or seriously delegate authority to his subordinates, these general policies are ineffective. He frequently appears not to assume that the other person also wants to do a good job. RT has within his control the power to correct the management ills at Mitek if he truly desires to do so.

Texas Instruments, Incorporated (A) (Condensed)

On April 17, 1959, Texas Instruments Incorporated (TI) of Dallas, Texas, merged with the Metals and Controls Corporation (M & C) of Attleboro, Massachusetts. One of the fastest growing large corporations in the country, TI had achieved a compound annual growth from 1946 through 1958 of 38% in sales and 42% in net income. The president had publicly predicted that volume would more than double in 1959 to a sales level near $200 million. Almost half this growth, he added, might come through mergers, with M & C contributing $42 million to $45 million. To date TI's principal business had been in electronic and electromechanical equipment and systems, semiconductors and other components, and exploration services for oil, gas, and minerals.

So highly was TI regarded by the market that in May 1960 its common was selling at about 70 times the 1959 earnings of $3.59 a share.

M & C ACTIVITIES

Itself the product of a 1932 merger and a postwar diversification, M & C had three major groups of products: clad metals, control instruments, and nuclear fuel components and instrumented cores. The company had grown steadily, and in 1959 had plants in two U.S. locations and five foreign countries. Reflecting predecessor corporation names, the clad metal lines were known as General Plate (GP) products, and the control instrument lines were known as Spencer products. Included in the former were industrial, precious, and thermostat metals; fancy wire; and wire and tubing. Included in the latter were motor protectors, circuit breakers, thermostats, and precision switches. Among these Spencer lines there were some that utilized GP products as raw materials; i.e., GP thermostat bimetals and GP clad electrical contacts.

Apart from a portion of GP's precious metal products which went to the jewelry trade (where appearance and fast delivery from stock were key considerations), most GP and Spencer products had to be designed to specific customer requirements and produced to customer order. Thus engineering know-how and close coordination between the sales and production departments on delivery dates were important. Owing to the technical nature of the products and also to their fast-changing applications, a company sales force with a high degree of engineering competence was essential. To serve its several thousand customers, many of whom purchased both Spencer and GP products, the company maintained a force of 50 men in the field, divided into Spencer and GP units.

With Spencer products facing important competition from four other firms in the $10 million to $40 million annual sales bracket, tight control of costs was important for securing the large orders generally placed by the kinds of customers to whom these products were sold. Buyers included manufacturers of fractional horsepower motors, household appliances, air conditioning, and aircraft and missiles. In contrast, GP industrial metals met no direct competition, although clad metals for industrial uses met with competition from alloys.

M & C's PREMERGER ORGANIZATION

At the time TI took over M & C, a task force of four junior executives had just completed, at the acting president's request, a critical study of M & C's organizational structure. So far its nuclear activities had been conducted by an entirely separate subsidiary, and the GP and Spencer activities had been organized as shown on Exhibit 1.

Under the acting president at the top level came a tier of predominantly functional executives (the vice presidents for marketing, engineering, and finance, the treasurer, and the controller). At the third and fourth levels of command, the structure increasingly showed a breakdown by product lines. For example, at the fourth level in manufacturing there were four separate groups corresponding to the major Spencer lines, and six separate groups corresponding to the major GP lines. Approximately the same breakdown appeared among the fourth-level product specialists in marketing. Although there was no profit responsibility at this level, the controller had been sending marketing's product specialists a monthly P & L by product line, in the hope of encouraging informal meetings among the people in marketing, engineering, and production who were working on the same lines.

Even at the second level, the predominantly functional division of responsibilities was neither complete nor unalloyed. Thus the vice president for marketing was also the vice president of Spencer Products, and in this capacity he had reporting to him the Spencer engineers. As a result, the company's vice president of engineering was, in effect, the vice president only of GP engineering, although he also served in an other-than-functional role by acting as the vice president of M & C International. (In 1958 exports and other foreign sales totaled about $2 million.)

After confidential interviews with 140 people, members of the M & C

Exhibit 1

PREMERGER METALS AND CONTROLS ORGANIZATION

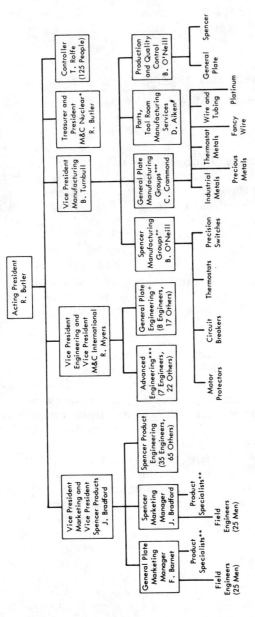

* Detail on M & C Nuclear not disclosed.

** Responsible for factory-customer coordination on specifications, prices, delivery, and new applications on different product lines (broken down about as shown in the manufacturing department).

⁺ Responsible for long-range product development for GP lines.

*** Worked on new applications and process designs for GP lines.

⁺⁺ Principal operations in Spencer production departments were parts-making and assembly.

⁺⁺⁺ Principal operations in GP industrial, precious, and thermostat metal departments were bonding and rolling; in GP wire and fancy wire departments, drawing; and in GP platinum department, melting and refining. Some GP facilities were shared, and roughly 5% of direct labor hours for each GP department were devoted to work for other departments.

Reporting to Aiken were units making two GP and three Spencer parts.

Source: Interviews and company records.

task force reportedly concluded that this organizational structure was causing or contributing to a number of company problems. Accordingly the task force recommended sweeping changes, first to the acting president by whom they had been appointed, then to his successor, Mr. Edward O. Vetter, a 39-year-old TI vice president brought in following the merger.

MR. VETTER'S REVIEW AND APPRAISAL

As soon as he arrived at M & C, Mr. Vetter spent most of four days in closed meetings with task force members. At the same time he scheduled public meetings with all executives; these sessions he devoted to general discussions of his aims for the organization and to reassurances that drastic changes would not be made.

From these discussions Vetter learned that a great many people at M & C felt that the three major functional departments were not cooperating well enough in the exploitation of new product opportunities based on existing markets and skills. Although in a few isolated instances, marketing, engineering, and production personnel concerned with a particular product had formed small informal groups to work on common problems, the three departments had not been seen as working together with maximum effectiveness, particularly in new product development. To blame, besides top management's inattention and the absence of a comprehensive plan, was a lack of clear-cut responsibility and authority.

Other problems, too, provided additional evidence of the failure of functional groups to work together harmoniously and effectively. Thus there was continued squabbling between process engineers and production supervisors, with neither group being willing to accept the other's suggestions for improvements in manufacturing methods. With both groups reporting to different vice presidents, conflicts too often came up for resolution at top levels. Here many times decisions were postponed and issues left unresolved.

Vetter was also told by many members of the organization that the personal influence of marketing's product specialists played too large a role in company' decisions. Formally assigned to coordinate certain aspects of factory-customer relations (see notes to Exhibit 1), these specialists were said to determine the amount of R&D time given to particular lines, with the result that some lines had grown quite strong while promising opportunities elsewhere were neglected. Similarly personal relationships between product specialists and production personnel largely determined scheduling priorities.

After becoming familiar with these problems, Mr. Vetter decided that M & C provided a golden opportunity for applying TI's philosophy of organization by what TI called "product-customer centered groups." Basically this plan involved putting a single manager in charge of sales, manufacturing, and engineering on a particular product line, and making this manager responsible for profits. This type of structure, Mr. Vetter noted, was what had been proposed by M & C's own task force on organization. According to TI's president, it offered advantages not only in managing existing lines but also in finding new opportunities for discerning and serving new customer needs.

As he was collecting information on M & C's organizational arrangements, Mr. Vetter had dictated the following set of notes for his own use:

It appears as if natural product groups already exist here. General Plate, Spencer and Nuclear have always been separate, and International sales are set apart under Richard Myers. Within these major groupings there is also a somewhat parallel division of the manufacturing and marketing facilities along product lines. There are ten production departments that are each organized to produce a particular product line, while there is an almost parallel organization of marketing product specialists under James Bradford.

Bringing together product managers and production supervisors for similar product lines would seem to be the logical implementation of TI's management philosophy. Of course, one problem would be the rearrangement of some of the production facilities in order to locate all the equipment under a product manager's control in one area. While we do have ten product-manufacturing departments, some of these share facilities and perform work for one another. In addition, the parts department performs fabrication operations for several production departments. In spite of this, there are no major pieces of equipment that would have to be physically relocated. We estimated that some duplicate equipment will have to be purchased if we go ahead with product-centered decentralization; in order to accomplish this about $1.5 million will have to be spent almost three years before it would otherwise have been committed.

I believe that the "inside" product specialist—the man at the factory who lives with both the manufacturing and the marketing problems for his line—is a key man. Our products are mainly engineered to customer order and, as such, require a great deal of coordination on delivery dates, specifications, and special applications. In addition to performing this liaison, the product managers could be the men who sense ideas for new product applications from their marketing contacts and then transmit these to the product engineering personnel at the factory.

These men would not be salesmen. A field sales force would still be needed to make regular calls on all of our clients and to cultivate the associations with our customers' engineering staffs. One significant question here is how to organize the sales force. These men are highly skilled and quite expensive to employ—each salesman should enter commitments of at least $1 million yearly in order to justify his expenses. Since our customers are spread all over the country, it would appear economical to assign field salesmen by geographical areas, each to sell all, or at least a number of, our products. Unfortunately, this system might take a good measure of the responsibility for the sales supervision. Our problem here is to leave sales responsibility at the product group level without having an undue duplication of field sales personnel.

The filtering down of responsibility and authority would mean that we would need more "management skill" in order for the product managers to be able to manage the little companies of which each would be in charge. The product manager must be capable of making sales, manufacturing, financial, and engineering decisions. He is no longer judged against a budget but becomes responsible for profits. We would need talented men to fill these positions—a shift in the organizational structure would undoubtedly force us to hire some new people. Nevertheless, there are tremendous benefits to be gained in terms of giving more people the chance to display their talents and in just plain better functioning of the M & C division.

The organization of engineering personnel brings up a whole hornets' nest of questions. First of all, there are two distinct engineering functions: product engineers, those concerned with current product designs and new applications for existing products; and advanced engineers, those who work on long-term product development. There is little doubt that the new applications sales effort would benefit from placing the product engineering personnel in close organizational contact with the marketers. This would mean splitting engineering up among all the product groups and would probably make for a less efficient overall operation. Decentralization of the advanced engineering groups is easily as ticklish a problem. Again, it would probably receive more marketing-oriented stimulus if it were placed under the supervision of the product manager. I wonder, however, if he might not be motivated to cut long-term development more drastically than top management normally would in times of business recession. Furthermore, I wonder if the economies of centralized advanced engineering and research in terms of combined effort and personnel selection are not so great as to make decentralization of this function an extremely poor choice. The basic question we have to answer here is to what degree should we sacrifice operating economy in order to give our engineering personnel a greater marketing orientation.

*   *   *   *   *

Scheduling has long been a bone of contention here wherever facilities are shared. Conflicts for priorities between product specialists are always occurring. If we decentralize, however, the amount of facilities that are shared will decrease substantially and this problem should be alleviated. Again we have the basic choice of retaining the centralized scheduling groups or splitting the function up among the various product groups.

In addition to the above issues, Mr. Vetter was considering the proper timing for an organizational change. He was debating whether a change should be made by gradual steps or whether the transfer in corporate ownership provided a convenient opportunity for making radical changes with a minimum of employee resentment. In general, the M & C personnel expressed some regrets because the family that had founded the company was no longer associated with it. They recognized, however, that the continual top management conflict of recent years necessitated a change and were pleased by the fact that a recognized leader in the industry had taken over the company.

Texas Instruments, Incorporated (B)

IN MAY 1960 Tom Pringle, the manager of the Industrial Metals product department at Texas Instruments' Metals & Controls division, was considering several courses of action in the face of his department's failure to meet forecasted sales and profits during the first four months of 1960. The rebuilding of inventories by M & C's customers, which had been expected as an aftermath of the settlement of the 1959 steel strike, had not materialized and shipments from Pringle's product department were running about 12% below forecast. Furthermore, incoming sales commitments during these four months were 15% below expectations. The product department's direct profit, according to preliminary statements, was 19% below plan.

In light of these adverse developments, Pringle was studying the advisability of three specific moves which would improve his profit performance: (1) eliminating his $30,000 advertising budget for the latter half of 1960, (2) postponing the addition of two engineers to his engineering group until 1961, and (3) reducing further purchases of raw materials in order to improve his department's return on assets ratio. Until now, Pringle had been reluctant to make any concessions in his department's scale of operations since there was a very strong accent on rapid growth throughout the Texas Instruments organization. This attitude toward expansion also appeared to prevail in the new top management group in the Metals & Controls division. The enthusiasm of the Texas Instruments' management had caught on at Metals & Controls with the formation of the product-centered decentralized organization.

THE 1959 REORGANIZATION

In June 1959, just three months after Metals & Controls Corporation had become a division of Texas Instruments, Incorporated, Mr. Edward

O. Vetter, the division vice president, instituted a product-centered organization. This decentralization was carried out in accordance with Texas Instruments' policy of placing ultimate responsibility for profitable operation at the product level. The framework that emerged was similar to that which existed elsewhere in the company.

Mr. Vetter organized four major product groups at Metals & Controls: General Plate, Spencer Controls, Nuclear Products, and International Operations. To augment these groups, six centralized staff units were organized at the division level: Research and Development, Legal, Industrial Engineering, Control, Marketing, and Personnel (Exhibit 1).

Exhibit 1

ORGANIZATION CHART, METALS & CONTROLS DIVISION

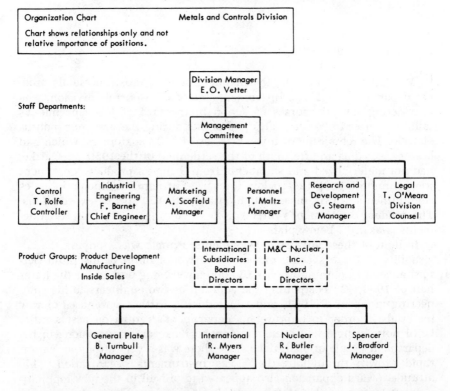

The four managers of the product groups and the six managers of these staff departments, along with Mr. Vetter, comprised the management committee for the Metals & Controls division. This committee was a sounding board for helping each responsible manager make the proper decision as required by his job responsibility. In the case of profit performance, the ultimate responsibility for the division was Vetter's.

Within each product group, several product departments were established. The General Plate products group, for example, included the Industrial Metals, Electrical Contacts, Industrial Wire, and Precious

Metals departments (Exhibit 2). The manager of each of these departments was responsible for its "profit performance." He was supported by staff units such as Industrial Engineering and Administration which reported directly to the group manager (Burt Turnbull for General Plate products). The expense of these staff units was charged to the individual product departments proportionally to the volume of activity in the various departments as measured by direct labor hours or by sales dollars less raw materials cost. The product departments were also charged with those expenses over which the manager and his supervisory group were able to exercise direct control, such as labor and materials.

Exhibit 2

ORGANIZATION CHART, GENERAL PLATE PRODUCTS GROUP

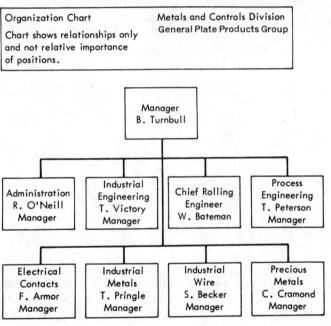

Organization Chart	Metals and Controls Division
Chart shows relationships only and not relative importance of positions.	General Plate Products Group

Manager
B. Turnbull

| Administration R. O'Neill Manager | Industrial Engineering T. Victory Manager | Chief Rolling Engineer W. Bateman | Process Engineering T. Peterson Manager |

| Electrical Contacts F. Armor Manager | Industrial Metals T. Pringle Manager | Industrial Wire S. Becker Manager | Precious Metals C. Cramond Manager |

The field sales force of 50 men was centralized under the manager for marketing, Al Scofield (Exhibit 1). These men were divided about evenly into two major selling groups: one for General Plate products, and the other for Spencer products. The 25 salesmen assigned to General Plate and the 25 salesmen assigned to Spencer were shared by the four General Plate and four Spencer product departments. Each individual product department also maintained "inside" marketing personnel who performed such functions as pricing, developing marketing strategy, order follow-up and providing the field sales engineers with information on new applications, designs, and product specifications for its particular line.

The Industrial Metals department

Tom Pringle was manager of the Industrial Metals department of the General Plate products group. Sales of this department in 1959 were approximately $4 million.[1] Pringle was responsible for the profitability of two product lines: (1) industrial metals and (2) thermostat metals. His department's sales were split about evenly between these lines, although industrial metals had the greater growth potential because of the almost infinite number of possible clad metals for which an ever increasing number of applications was being found. He was in charge of the marketing, engineering, and manufacturing activities for both these lines and had six key subordinates:

INDUSTRIAL METALS DEPARTMENT

Years of Service with the Metals and Controls Organization

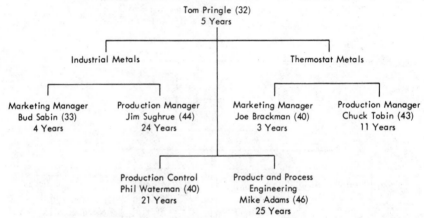

The function of the marketing managers in the Industrial Metals department (Bud Sabin and Joe Brackman) was to supervise the "inside selling units." These units were responsible for developing marketing strategy, pricing, contacting customers on special requests and factory problems, for promotional activities, and for coordinating product development and sales. In May 1960, in addition to its regular work, the Industrial Metals inside selling unit was developing a manual of special applications for its products which it hoped would improve the ability of the field sales force to envision new uses. The production managers had line responsibility for the efficient use of manufacturing facilities, for meeting delivery promises to customers, and for expenses incurred in producing the department's products. The product and process engineering group had responsibility for designing new products and devising new production processes. The production control manager formulated guidelines to aid the foremen in scheduling work through the

---

[1] All figures have been disguised.

plant, supervised the expediters and clerks who served as a clearing-house for information on delivery dates, and was responsible for ordering raw material and maintaining a balanced inventory.

In accordance with Texas Instruments' policy of placing ultimate responsibility for profitable operation at the product level, Tom Pringle's performance was measured, to a large extent, by the actual profits earned by the Industrial Metals department. The old M & C system of evaluating performance according to fixed and variable department budgets had been supplemented by the establishment of these "profit centers." Although the system passed actual profit responsibility to the product department manager level, the Texas Instruments' top management had always retained some control over the profit centers by requiring each manager to formulate a one-year plan which was subject to review by higher management. As a result, profit planning was instituted whereby each manager set forth a detailed plan for the year's operations under the direction of the management committee. His actual performance was continually being evaluated against the plan.

Formulation of the profit plan. In October 1959, Tom Pringle began to prepare his department's profit plan for 1960. This was part of a company-wide effort in which all department managers participated. The first step in the process was to prepare a detailed estimate of expected sales for the year. These estimates were gathered from two sources: the inside selling units and the field sales force. Management felt that one would serve as a good check on the other, and, furthermore, believed that widespread participation in preparing the plan was one way to insure its effectiveness. Bud Sabin and Joe Brackman, then, began to prepare estimates of 1960 sales by product lines with the help of the individual product specialists within the inside marketing group. Sabin and Brackman were also aided by the Texas Instruments central marketing group which prepared a report which estimated normal growth for their product lines. Pringle suggested that they prepare their estimates by subdividing the market into three parts: sales resulting from normal industry growth at current levels of market penetration; increased sales resulting from further penetration of the market with existing products; and increased sales from new products detailed by specific customers. At the same time, Herb Skinner, the manager of the General Plate field sales force, asked the field engineers to predict the volume of orders that each Industrial Metals customer would place in 1960, without referring to the reports being readied by the product marketing groups. In this way, the marketing managers made forecasts by product line and the field force made forecasts by customer.

The field selling force came up with estimated thermostat metal sales of $2,350,000 for 1960, and the inside group estimated sales of $2,420,000. Pringle felt that these two estimates were in reasonably good agreement. On the other hand, Bud Sabin, the Industrial Metals marketing manager, estimated sales of $3,050,000, while Skinner's group predicted only $2,500,000. Sabin predicted that 20% of the increase would come from normal growth, 50% from increased market penetration with existing products, and 30% from new products. Sales for Sabin's group had been $1,400,000 in 1958 and $2,100,000 in 1959. Pringle felt that the disparity between the two estimates was significant and he discussed the matter with both men. All three men finally decided that the sales force had submitted a conservative estimate and agreed that Sabin's figure was the most realistic goal.

Once the sales estimate of $5,470,000 was agreed upon by Pringle and his marketing managers, the process of estimating manufacturing costs began. The manufacturing superintendents, Chuck Tobin and Jim Sughrue, were furnished the thermostat and industrial metals sales estimates and were instructed to forecast direct labor costs, supervisory salaries, and overhead expenses. These forecasts were to be made for each manufacturing area, or cost center, under their supervision. Sughrue was responsible for five cost centers and Tobin for four, each of which was directly supervised by a foreman. These expenses were to be forecast monthly and were to be used as a yardstick by which the actual expense performance of the manufacturing personnel could later be measured.

Jim Sughrue had previously calculated the hourly labor cost and the output per hour for each of his cost centers for 1959. To estimate 1960 salaries and wages, he then increased 1959 expenses proportionately to the expected sales increase. He followed the same procedure in determining 1960 overhead expenses, such as expendable tools, travel, telephone, process supplies, and general supplies. Chuck Tobin's task was somewhat simpler since the sales projection for his cost centers required a level of output that exactly matched the current production level. For salaries and wages, he merely used as his 1960 estimate the actual cost experience that had been reported on the most recent monthly income statement he received. For overhead, he applied a historical percent-of-sales ratio and then reduced his estimate by 3% to account for increased efficiency. In discussing the overhead estimate with his foremen, Tobin informed them that he had allowed for an 8% efficiency increase.

Since this was the first time any attempt at such detailed planning had been made at M & C, and since the M & C accounting system had recently been changed to match Texas Instruments', very little historical information was available. For this reason, Pringle did not completely delegate the responsibility for the various marketing and manufacturing estimates to his subordinates. Instead he worked in conjunction with them to develop the forecasts. He hoped that his participation in this process would insure a more accurate forecast for the year. Furthermore, he hoped to develop the ability of his supervision to plan ahead.

Pringle estimated direct materials cost and consumption factors himself. Since it was impossible to predict what all the various strip metal prices would be, he calculated the ratio of materials expense to sales for 1959 and applied it to the 1960 sales projections for each of the product lines in his department.

The marketing, administration, and engineering groups that serviced Pringle's Industrial Metals group forecast their expenses by detailing their personnel requirements and then applying historical ratios of expenses to personnel to estimate their other expenses. From these dollar figures, Pringle was able to estimate what proportions of these amounts would be charged to his department.

With the various forecasts in hand, Pringle estimated a direct profit of $1,392,000 on a sales volume of $5,470,000. Once this plan had been drawn up, it was reviewed by the division management committee in relationship to the specific profit and sales goals which it has established for the division. In reviewing the plans for each product department in terms of the specific group goals, it became obvious that the combined plans of the General Plate product departments were not sufficient to meet the overall goal, and that based on market penetration, new product developments, and other factors, the planned sales volume for Industrial Metals should be revised upward to $6,050,000 and direct profit to $1,587,000 (Exhibit 3). This was discussed among Vetter, Turnbull, Scofield, and Pringle and they agreed that it was a difficult but achievable plan.

Exhibit 3

INDUSTRIAL METALS DEPARTMENT

Initial and Revised Profit Statements for 1960*

	Initial	Revised
Sales	$5,470,000	$6,050,000
Direct labor	435,000	480,000
Direct material	1,920,000	2,115,000
Overhead	875,000	968,000
Marketing	305,000	346,000
Administration	161,000	161,000
Engineering	382,000	393,000
Direct profit	1,392,000	1,587,000

* All figures have been disguised.

Actual performance, 1960. On May 10 Tom Pringle received a detailed statement comparing the actual performance of his department for January through April with his budget (Exhibit 4). Sales were 12% below plan, and direct profit was 19% below plan.

In addition to these figures, manufacturing expenses by cost centers were accumulated for Pringle. He passed these along to the production superintendents after he had made adjustments in the budgeted expense figures to allow for the sales decline. Pringle had devised a variable budget system whereby he applied factors to the forecast expenses to indicate what an acceptable expense performance was at sales levels other than the planned volume. Chuck Tobin and Jim Sughrue then analyzed the actual expenses and, one week later, held meetings with their foremen to discuss the causes of both favorable and unfavorable variances. The most common explanation of favorable manufacturing variances was either extremely efficient utilization of labor or close

Exhibit 4

COMPARISON OF ACTUAL AND
BUDGETED PERFORMANCE,
JANUARY–APRIL 1960*

	Budgeted	Actual
Sales	$2,020,000	$1,780,000
Direct labor	160,000	142,400
Direct material	704,000	593,000
Overhead	322,000	287,000
Marketing	100,000	116,400
Administration	54,000	55,800
Engineering	126,000	136,600
Direct profit	554,000	448,000

* All figures have been disguised.

control over overhead. Unfavorable variances most frequently resulted from machine delays which necessitated overtime labor payments.

Specific problems. Pringle was currently faced with three specific problems. In light of his department's poor performance these past months, he was considering the effects of eliminating his $30,000 advertising budget for the remainder of 1960, postponing the addition of two new engineers to his staff for six months, and reducing raw materials purchases in order to decrease inventory and thus improve his department's return on assets performance.

He had discussed the possibility of eliminating the advertising budget with Bud Sabin and Joe Brackman but had not yet reached a conclusion. Advertising expenditures had been budgeted at $30,000 for the final six months of 1960. The Industrial Metals department ads were generally placed in trade journals read by design engineers in the electrical, automobile, and appliance industries. Pringle did not know for certain how important an aid these advertisements were to his sales force. He did know that all of his major competitors allocated about the same proportion of sales revenue for advertising expenditures and that Industrial Metals ads were occasionally mentioned by customers.

In late 1959, Pringle had made plans to increase his engineering staff from eight men to ten men in mid-1960. He felt that the two men could begin functioning productively by early 1961 and could help to revise certain processes which were yielding excessive scrap, to develop new products, and to assist the field engineers in discovering new applications for existing products. Pringle estimated that postponing the hiring of these men for six months would save $20,000 in engineering salaries and supporting expenses.

Pringle also knew that one of the important indicators of his performance was the department's ratio of direct profit to assets used. This figure had been budgeted at 40% for 1961, but actual results to date were 31%. Pringle was considering reductions in raw materials purchases in order to decrease inventories and thus improve performance. He had discussed this possibility with Phil Waterman, the production control manager for Industrial Metals. Pringle knew that significant improvements in the overall ratio could be made in this way since raw materials inventories accounted for almost 20% of total assets and were at a level of ten months' usage at present consumption ratios. He recognized, however, that this course of action required accepting a greater risk of running out. This risk was important to assess since most customers required rapid delivery and Pringle's suppliers usually required four months' lead time to manufacture the nonstandard size metals in relatively small lots required for the Industrial Metals' cladding operation.

The purpose of the profit plan. The degree to which the plan was used as a method for evaluating performance and fixing compensation was not completely clear to Pringle. Everyone seemed to recognize that this first effort was imperfect and had errors built in because of inadequate historical data. He had never been explicitly informed of the extent to which top management desired product department decision making to be motivated by short-run effects on planned performance. Pringle stated that during the months immediately following the initiation of the plan he had concluded that short-term performance was much less significant than long-run growth and that he had preferred to concentrate on the longer run development of new products and markets.

Pringle knew that the Metals & Controls operating committee met every Monday to review the performance of each product department from preliminary reports. Customarily Burt Turnbull, the manager of the General Plate group, discussed both Pringle's incoming sales commitments and actual manufacturing expenses with him before each meeting. Pringle also knew that each manager was given a formal appraisal review every six months by his superior. It was common knowledge that the department's performance in relation to its plan was evaluated at both these sessions. Furthermore, Pringle was aware of the fact that Turnbull's performance as product group manager would be affected by his own performance with Industrial Metals. Over a period of months, Pringle had learned that the management committee utilized the comparison of actual and planned performance to pinpoint trouble spots. On occasion Vetter had called him in to explain any significant deviations from plan but normally he was represented at these meetings by Burt Turnbull. It was Pringle's impression that Vetter had been satisfied with the explanation he had given.

In their day-to-day decisions, Pringle's subordinates seemed to be influenced only in a very general way by the profit plan. They reviewed their monthly performance against plan with interest, but generally tended to bias their decisions in favor of long-run development at the expense of short-run deviations from the plan. More recently, however, Pringle realized that top management was not satisfied with his explanations of failure to meet plans. The message, though not stated explicitly, seemed to be that he was expected to take whatever remedial and alternate courses of action were needed in order to meet the one-year goals. He was certain that real pressure was building up for each department manager to meet his one-year plan.

In commenting on the use of planning at M & C, Mr. Vetter, the division vice president, stated four major purposes of the program:

> To set a par for the course. Vetter believed that performance was always improved if the manager proposed a realistic objective for his performance and was informed in advance of what was expected of him.
>
> To grow management ability. Vetter believed that the job of manager was to coordinate all the areas for which he was given responsibility. He saw the planning process as a tool for improving these managerial skills.
>
> To anticipate problems and look ahead. Vetter felt that the planning process gave the department managers a convenient tool for planning personnel requirements and sales strategy. It also set guideposts so that shifts in business conditions could be detected quickly and plans could be altered.
>
> To weld Texas Instruments into one unit. The basic goals for each division were formulated by Vetter in recognition of overall company goals as disseminated by Haggerty, the company president. These were passed down to the product department level by the product group manager at each Texas Instruments division. Profit planning was thus being carried out by the same process by every department manager in the corporation.

Vetter recognized, however, that many reasons could exist for performance being either better or worse than planned. He stated that in his experience extremely rigid profit plans often motivated managers to budget low in order to provide themselves with a safety cushion. In his view, this made the entire profit planning process worthless.

Introductory note to DAAG Europe

THIS NOTE provides a brief description of the elevator business in Western Europe as viewed by executives of the Deutsche Aufzugs A.G. European regional headquarters (DAAG Europe), located in Frankfurt, Germany. It pertains primarily to passenger elevators and relates to events only up to 1969.

THE PASSENGER ELEVATOR

With the arrival of the high-rise building, the passenger elevator passed from being a convenience to being a necessity. While usually an unobtrusive element of such large buildings, the elevators often occupied over 5 percent of the available volume in a building and accounted for about 3 percent to 7 percent of the total building cost.

The elevator system was made up of three major subsystems: (1) the electromechanical system, which guided and propelled the elevator; (2) the electrical/electronic system, which controlled the elevator movement in terms of acceleration, deceleration, and direction; and (3) the elevator cab itself with its moving doors. There were two basic lifting systems (the hydraulic type for low and slow applications, and the electric, cable-driven type for any applications) with many technical variations, a dozen or so basic circuits for the command controls, and countless configurations for the cab.

While the technology associated with each of these systems had remained fundamentally the same over the past 30 years, the product nonetheless called for relatively demanding technical content and expertise. First, since elevators transported people vertically and were exposed to the possibility of falling, they had to be absolutely safe and reliable. As one observer noted, "If your elevator ever should fall, it could ruin your whole day." Second, an elevator was a means of public transportation. As such, it was essential that it be "idiot proof" (that is, the mechanism should not be damaged or cause injury because of

601

an error by the operator) and also be vandal resistant. Third, for reasons of safety as well as of comfort, the elevator shaft and guide rails had to be straight within reasonably small tolerances and had to remain so. The difficulties in this regard were that the dimensions of buildings were far from exact and large buildings often sagged or were otherwise distorted over time. One of the most skillful jobs in the elevator business was trueing up the system when it had been installed. Fourth, accelerating and decelerating an elevator for comfortable riding posed difficult propulsion and braking problems for the larger and faster units. For example, in a high-rise office building an elevator might travel at speeds as high as 30 feet per second (the equivalent of about three stories). The system had to be capable of decelerating the cab weighing anywhere from one ton empty to almost three tons fully loaded from that speed to a dead stop within one-quarter inch of a given point in space, and do all this in such a way as to maintain passenger comfort.

Passenger elevators were generally classified as class A or class B units. Class A elevators were defined within the industry as the large and high-speed (over 300 feet per minute) units with relatively sophisticated electronic controls. These were typically employed in large office buidings, large hotels, and other high-rise buildings where pedestrian traffic was heavy. Class B elevators were defined as the small, slow-speed (around 200 feet per minute) units with manually operated swing doors found in small office buildings and apartments. In most cases, class B units did not have complex "memory" systems.

THE WESTERN EUROPEAN CUSTOMERS

The markets for class A and for class B elevators were distinct and had to be approached differently. In most cases, the customer for class B elevators was the general contractor. The contractor in smaller building projects in Europe was often responsible for the design, the costs, and the overall management of the building, including the elevator.

Government agencies were another major customer for class B elevators, especially for apartment buildings. In dealing with this market, a DAAG elevator salesman would call on the local housing authority, the project coordinator, and the general contractor. The general contractor was again considered to be the most important link in this highly price-oriented market.

In contrast to the class B market, there were usually several people involved in the purchase decision for class A elevators. These people typically included several high-ranking managers of the company owning or planning to use the building, the architect, and the general contractor. In the opinion of DAAG management, the architect was the person most influential in selecting an elevator.

Dr. Robert Pelz, managing director of DAAG Europe, described DAAG's approach to this market:

> Our salesmen learn about possible contracts in several different ways. For example, our marketing department monitors the future building activ-

ity in a given region and alerts the appropriate salesmen to upcoming projects. However, there are not many potential contracts which the salesmen learn about for the first time in this manner. Most of our contracts are brought to the salesmen's attention by the architects themselves. DAAG, after all, is well known throughout Europe.

It is our policy to have the DAAG salesman contact the architects in his region on a regular basis, whether or not they know of a definite contract possibility at the time of calling. After all, there are not all that many people who deal with larger building projects. The nature of the saleman's work brings him into contact with architects on a regular basis anyway as most of our salesmen already have contracts in progress. We estimate 80 percent of our sales in Europe are made to about 2,500 individual customers, who are constantly involved in the design of major buildings.

Another important source of information for DAAG salesmen was when architects called on the company to provide elevator engineering consultancy service for their building projects. To encourage this practice, it was company policy for salesmen to urge the architect to call for competitive bids. "In this way," noted the DAAG executive, "he can see for himself that DAAG can best supply his needs."

DAAG generally commanded a 10 percent premium in price over local competitors, as did the other major elevator manufacturers (Otis, Schindler, and Westinghouse). In selling elevators, DAAG salesmen stressed quality and service and played down price considerations. Although price was discussed in broad terms early in the contract negotiations, the actual price was not set until all specifications had been described. This delay of three to six months was enough time, according to DAAG management, to show why the extra cost was justified. Dr. Pelz described the advantages DAAG offered:

> You see, an elevator can cause an architect more trouble than most anything else in his building. If the president of a company who is housed in a particular building has trouble with an elevator—for example, if a door doesn't work properly—he will probably complain directly to the owner. The owner will, in turn, blame the architect. The architect not only wants to avoid such nuisances but he also has to guard his reputation for quality work.
>
> DAAG elevators can also save the architect and the building owner money in the long run. The installation of elevators is one of the last steps in the construction of a building. Any delays in installing elevators will therefore cause a similar delay in making the building serviceable, and this could be extremely costly. For example, we have a 15 million German mark contract to install 20 elevators in the Lorelei Tower in Frankfurt. This is a 46-story-high office building costing over 300 million marks. Now if the elevators were to cause a month's delay in opening the building, the additional cost just in terms of one month's extra interest charges on the full investment would run about 3 million marks. Even more impressive would be the rental income lost for that month which would come to about 5 million marks. These figures give you some idea how valuable our rapid and dependable installation can be for the architect and building owner.
>
> Finally, DAAG offers one of the finest maintenance services in the trade. Even though the price of our service contracts runs about 10 percent above our competitors' in many European countries, we service virtually all the

installed DAAG class A elevators and about 80 percent of the class B units. In many respects, we consider ourselves as primarily a service company. And while we sell our service contracts quite separately from elevators, the architect has it in mind when he selects an elevator.

Overall, I would say that an architect will usually make his decision on a DAAG elevator on the basis of past experience with the product and his relationship with a particular DAAG salesman.

With the exception of the largest high-rise buildings, the typical period of time for DAAG to be involved with a given class A elevator installation in Europe was about three years. A year would normally elapse between the initial proposal and the signing of the contract. The materials would be shipped from the factories roughly a year later, and finally installation would be completed after another year.

Because elevator sales often involved large sums of money and tended to be made at irregular intervals, DAAG salesmen were paid straight salaries. A well-qualified salesman for class A equipment earned about $14,000 per year. Salesmen for class B equipment and for maintenance service received about $7,000 to $8,000 per year.[1] Salesmen were also reimbursed for all out-of-pocket expenses. By way of comparison, the average DAAG factory worker earned about $3,000 per year.

MANUFACTURING OPERATIONS

An elevator system was made up of many individual parts, such as mechanical relays, motors, ropes (suspension cables), sheet metal, steel railing, and electronic circuitry. Most smaller firms purchased these parts for assembly and even subcontracted certain subassembly work. In contrast, the largest elevator firms had traditionally manufactured almost all of the required parts. According to one DAAG executive, this extensive backward integration was almost a matter of pride for these companies.

The variety of parts to be produced and handled was many times greater than that needed for current operations because of maintenance service requirements. DAAG, for example, serviced units which had been produced as much as 40 years earlier. In addition to its own units, DAAG typically provided parts for elevators which had been produced by the many companies it had acquired over the years. The resulting high number of different components required DAAG and the other major elevator manufacturers to carry large parts inventories.

Field operations were another salient characteristic of the elevator manufacturing business. The extent of field operations was indicated by the composition of DAAG employment in Europe. Out of a total force of 13,000 employees, 6,000 were manual workers in the field compared to about 3,700 factory workers. About half the field workers were responsible for elevator erection and the other half for maintenance service. Because of their deep involvement with building construction, elevator

---

[1] In Germany, DAAG employed five class A salesmen, about 40 class B salesmen, and 25 service salesmen. Total annual sales cost in 1969 amounted to almost 2 million German marks for sales of 130 million German marks.

manufacturers shared the building industry's special problems with respect to weather conditions, scattered sites, and sensitivity to economic conditions.

THE ELEVATOR MARKET AND INDUSTRY STRUCTURE IN EUROPE

The elevator business in Europe tended to be subdivided into national markets because of different building codes and in some cases because of tariff barriers. The codes generally defined the nature of the safety features which had to be employed. For example, car doors were not required for certain class B elevators in France. Such an elevator, called a flush hoistway, was prohibited in Germany.

The suppliers of these markets differed between class A and class B elevators. The class B sector was largely served by many small firms which competed in a local or national area. The class A sector in Europe was dominated by the multinational firms: Otis, Schindler, DAAG, and to some extent, Westinghouse. A number of strong local competitors also existed in many European countries. The size of each national market for all elevators in 1969 and DAAG's principal competitors for class A elevators are given in Exhibit 1. European expenditures for construction and for elevators are forecasted by country in Exhibit 2.

The Otis Elevator Company was the world's largest manufacturer of elevators. In addition to passenger and freight elevators, the company also produced escalators worldwide and a line of material handling equipment, automobile hydraulic lifts, and golf carts in the United States. Founded as a U.S. company in 1853, the company began a rapid extension of operations overseas at the turn of the century. By 1969 affiliated companies in 46 countries and sales representatives in 69 other countries generated almost half of the company's total sales of $536 million.

Schindler A. G. was a family-owned and -operated Swiss elevator firm with sales of approximately $170 million in 1969. It produced a line of high-quality products and was represented in all the European markets. Schindler held a 90 percent share of the Swiss elevator market (both class A and class B) and also held important positions in Germany and France. Most of Schindler's manufacturing facilities were in Switzerland, although it did have plants in several other European countries.

DAAG Europe was a subsidiary of the Pace Garner Corporation (referred to simply as Pace), a large, diversified U.S. firm with a major division which manufactured elevators, escalators, and conveyor equipment for the U.S., Canadian, and Latin American markets. Pace was represented in almost all major European countries by independent subsidiaries which, for management purposes, reported to DAAG Europe. With few exceptions, all these European subsidiaries, with combined sales in 1969 of about $160 million, produced class A and class B elevator equipment under the DAAG name.

Westinghouse Elevator (a subsidiary of the Westinghouse Company) had estimated worldwide elevator sales of about $150 million in 1969. Seventy percent of these sales were made in the United States. DAAG

Exhibit 1

ESTIMATED EUROPEAN ELEVATOR SALES IN 1969 AND DAAG'S MAJOR COMPETITORS
FOR CLASS A EQUIPMENT

	Sales (class A and class B)			
Country	Units (000)	Value ($ millions)	Average value ($000)	DAAG's major competitors
Austria	2.0	$ 23	$11.5	Wertheim, Sovitch, Otis
Belgium	1.4	21	14.9	Westinghouse, Schindler, Otis
Denmark	0.3	6	18.4	n.a.
France	11.4	102	9.0	Otis, Westinghouse, Schindler, Soretex
Germany (West)	11.0	165	15.0	R. Stahl, Schindler, Otis, Haushahn, Manessman
Italy	11.1	57	5.2	FIAM, Schindler, SABIEM, Otis
Netherlands	1.7	20	11.8	Schindler, Otis
Norway	0.4	5	13.2	Kone
Portugal	.2.1	10	4.6	Comportel, Esacec, Otis
Spain	10.1	52	5.1	Schindler, Zardoya
Sweden	1.2	14	12.1	Kone
Switzerland	3.4	38	11.2	Schindler, Schlieren
U.K.	5.2	87	16.8	General Electric (U.K.)
	61.3	600	9.8	

n.a. = Not available.
Sources: Official statistics and company data.

Exhibit 2

AVERAGE ANNUAL EUROPEAN BUILDING CONSTRUCTION AND ELEVATOR SALES FORECAST FOR 1970–1974

| | Construction ($ billions) | | | Elevator sales ($ millions) | | | Ratios (percent) | | |
	(A) Total	(B) Residential	(C) Nonresidential	(D) Total	(E) Residential	(F) Nonresidential	D/A	E/B	F/C
Austria	$ 2.1	$ 0.9	$ 1.2	$ 28	$ 11	$ 17	1.33	1.24	1.40
Belgium	4.1	1.3	2.8	27	11	16	0.11	0.83	0.58
Denmark	2.2	1.0	1.2	8	3	5	0.36	0.32	0.40
France	25.6	9.6	16.0	141	56	85	0.55	0.59	0.53
Germany (West)	29.4	10.4	19.0	194	78	116	0.66	0.74	0.61
Italy	14.8	6.5	8.3	69	28	41	0.46	0.42	0.50
Netherlands	5.8	2.5	3.3	24	10	14	0.41	0.38	0.44
Norway	1.9	0.7	1.2	7	3	4	0.37	0.40	0.35
Portugal	1.5	0.7	0.8	13	5	8	0.87	0.74	0.98
Spain	4.5	2.3	2.2	67	27	40	1.49	1.17	1.91
Sweden	4.6	1.5	3.1	18	7	11	0.39	0.48	0.35
Switzerland	1.5	0.6	0.9	48	19	29	3.20	3.20	3.20
U.K.	12.6	4.3	8.3	113	45	68	0.89	1.05	0.82
Total	111.6	42.6	69.0	758 (100%)	303 (40%)	455 (60%)	0.68	0.71	0.66

Source: Official statistics except Switzerland and Portugal, for which company estimates were used.

management did not consider Westinghouse as strong a competitor in Europe as Otis or Schindler.

While competition among the big four in Europe was keen, each knew the strengths and the limits of the others. Looming as unknown adversaries were the large Japanese companies, such as Mitsubishi, which had developed excellent class A elevator equipment and were beginning to compete for contracts abroad. As of 1969 the Japanese had not yet bid for elevator contracts in Europe, but European elevator manufacturers considered the Japanese first attempt as imminent.

The potential severity of the Japanese threat was yet to be gauged. Some European elevator people believed that the structural requirements of the business (namely the close relationships between salesmen and architects and the need to provide extensive maintenance service) would block or at least greatly curtail Japanese entry. Others disagreed, arguing that the Japanese had learned to provide quality service from their experience in selling automobiles and various industrial equipment in the United States and Europe. According to the latter, the Japanese could develop a strong position in the European elevator market in four or five years.

DAAG Europe (A)

DR. ROBERT PELZ, managing director of Deutsche Aufzugs A.G. European regional headquarters (DAAG Europe), faced a dilemma as he reviewed the preliminary financial statements for 1969. These showed a continuing deterioration of the company's current accounts. Accounts receivable and inventories had increased during 1969 by 42 percent and 48 percent respectively with a sales increase of only slightly more than 10 percent for the same period. Moreover, the company had failed to show profits on contracted sales of new elevators for the fourth consecutive year. Some action would have to be taken to improve DAAG's financial performance in Europe.

Yet, Dr. Pelz fully realized that these financial results were a direct consequence of the company's long-term strategy to develop low-cost operations through a European-wide rationalized manufacturing operation. This strategy had brought related changes to every aspect of doing business.[1] Dr. Pelz did not wish to jeopardize the major transformation still under way by any action he might take to remedy the immediate financial problems.

ORIGINS OF THE DAAG EUROPE STRATEGY

The changes in progress in 1969 with respect to organization, marketing, and manufacturing could be traced back to a series of moves initiated in the early 1960s by Dr. Pelz, the then managing director of the German operating company, DAAG. One of the early moves occurred in 1964 when he proposed to the U.S. corporate management (Pace Garner Corporation, located in Chicago, Illinois) that the company acquire the rival German firm, Rechtbau A.G. The most compelling reason for

---

[1] See *Introductory Note to DAAG Europe* for a description of the European elevator business.

this acquisition was that it would boost DAAG's share of the German market from 20 percent to a commanding 35 percent.

Rechtbau itself had been formed in 1960 through a merger of three German elevator companies. Dr. Wagner, managing director of Rechtbau, had engineered this merger in an effort to create a company which could compete with Otis, Westinghouse, DAAG, and Schindler. When Rechtbau was still unable to support the costly engineering and development work necessary to extend its operations from supplying elevators for small apartment and office buildings to the more profitable market for high-rise buildings, Dr. Wagner next attempted to form a multinational coalition with some of the larger independent elevator firms in other major European countries. Failing to interest these firms in joining forces with Rechtbau, Dr. Wagner decided to sell the company to one of the four dominant firms. Thus, if DAAG did not merge with Rechtbau, one of its key competitors would presumably pick up the German firm's 15 percent market share.

Dr. Pelz, who had been a member of the German Diplomatic Corps prior to joining DAAG, won his case. Mr. M. B. Bentley, president of Pace Garner, approved the acquisition on Pelz's terms. Dr. Wagner was appointed president of the new firm and Dr. Pelz, vice president. The two men were given three years to make the merger work without interference from Chicago. Aside from the requirement to reconcile its accounting system with that of Pace, the new German company was on its own. As an DAAG executive later remarked, "Pelz had put his neck on the line. He had to make the merger work."

In taking over Rechtbau A.G., DAAG acquired the largest manufacturer of class B elevators in Germany. While each of DAAG's major European affiliates manufactured and sold class B elevators, these efforts (almost always representing a continuation of business carried out by firms acquired in earlier years) were generally played down and assumed only secondary importance among DAAG's activities. This policy could be attributed to the generally low profitability associated with the class B elevator as well as the fragmented nature of the market. DAAG was organized to deal with the limited number of large and relatively sophisticated architectural and construction firms in Europe. The class B market, requiring contact with each of many small, local building contractors, had traditionally been served by small elevator manufacturers in their locality. The distinctly different requirements for selling and servicing class B elevators had long dissuaded DAAG from entering this market. Moreover, many DAAG executives were of the opinion that DAAG's image as a manufacturer of high-quality and highly sophisticated elevators might be tarnished were DAAG to enter the class B market in a major way.

Dr. Pelz believed that DAAG was wrong in neglecting this market segment, especially in Europe, where it accounted for about 50 percent of the industry's total elevator sales.[2] He argued that DAAG could not

---

[2] Pace headquarters management estimated class B elevators to represent less than 30 percent of total elevator sales in the United States. This estimate was only approximate because of the limited availability of market data.

afford to ignore one half of its potential market in Europe. He thus set out to launch an attack on this sector of the market from the enlarged base of Rechtbau's class B business and with some ideas on how a large, multinational firm might compete for these sales.

THE MOVE TO STANDARD MODELS

Elevators had always been custom designed for each building project. The elevator had to fit the space allotted—or "left over"—for this purpose. Elevator companies competed on the basis of their ability to meet these architectural specifications.

Around 1961, Dr. Pelz became attracted by the possibility of manufacturing and selling standardized elevator models. He knew as did others in the industry that elevators, although designed and manufactured to customers' individual specifications, were basically similar in design, engineering, and construction. This similarity was especially true for class B elevators. Dr. Pelz reasoned that if a line of elevator models similar to a line of automobile models could be developed, major savings would result from reduction in design costs and from economics associated with multiple production. Important savings would also accrue from the opportunity to standardize the technical and administrative processing of contracts. For example, the extensive engineering documentation required for an elevator system and its working parts had to be prepared for each custom unit. The original documentation would serve for repeat sales of a standard model.

The idea of standard models was not entirely novel to the elevator industry. One of DAAG's German competitors had attempted in 1952 to introduce standard models. This effort met with little success and was abandoned. Nonetheless, Dr. Pelz was convinced of the need to move in this direction and consequently initiated in 1962 the design of the first standard elevator model for the German apartment building market. This model, the MOD-S, was introduced in early 1963.

The new model met with some resistance from customers. It met with much more resistance from the DAAG organization and its sales force. Despite this lack of enthusiasm, the company managed to sell about 230 units the first year, and Dr. Pelz planned to build a factory at Mainz to produce the MOD-S. The acquisition of Rechtbau provided DAAG with a new factory at Köln which was well suited for producing the standard elevator model and also with a large clientele for class B elevators. Access to an operating factory represented a gain of two years for DAAG, and the Mainz project was consequently abandoned.

While the acquisition of Rechtbau admittedly gave impetus to DAAG's concept of standard models, Dr. Pelz firmly believed that the move to standard models was the only way DAAG could make the Rechtbau acquisition successful. He agreed with the general sentiment that a company like DAAG could not compete effectively against the small firm for class B elevator business under the present way of doing business. It would be necessary to change the nature of the class B elevator business so as to suit DAAG's strengths. In Dr. Pelz's opinion, the standard elevator model was the way to effect such a change.

His experience with the MOD-S convinced Pelz that standard class B elevator models would be successful only when manufacturing and installation costs could be reduced sufficiently to permit prices to be some 10–15 percent lower than current levels while still enabling the company to make a profit. Some of these cost savings would come from a reduction in parts inventories, special jigs and tools, and from a simplification of fabrication procedures. However, important additional savings could only be gained with an appreciably increased production volume compared to the volume handled by the individual DAAG companies in 1964.

The needed volume could be generated reasonably quickly, Pelz reasoned, if the other DAAG European subsidiaries were to join Germany in developing standard models for their own markets as well. Eventually, if the standard elevator model concept proved out, maximum advantage would be gained as models were extended to the class A part of the business, and as both class A and class B models could be standardized for all of Europe.

THE BEGINNINGS OF A EUROPEAN CONCEPT

Dr. Pelz had already begun to lay the groundwork for his idea of a European regional organization during his discussions in Chicago concerning the Rechtbau acquisition. Heretofore, each of Pace's foreign subsidiaries had reported directly to Pace Elevator divisional headquarters in Chicago. The large headquarters staff customarily became deeply involved with operations in each of the subsidiaries. Functional staff members at Chicago tended to work directly and closely with their functional counterparts in the field.

Dr. Pelz had found these relationships cumbersome and frustrating as he tried to manage his company in Germany. This centralized organizational arrangement would be even more dysfunctional were the European subsidiaries to try to coordinate their actions. Thus, Dr. Pelz argued for a European regional management on two grounds. First, the move to standard elevator models in Europe would require a great deal of coordinated effort best supervised on the spot. Related to this point was the rapid integration taking place in the European Common Market which undoubtedly would call for other forms of coordinated action on the European continent. Second, an increasingly important part of DAAG's business in Europe would come from class B elevators, and the Chicago staff was not particularly competent to advise the Europeans concerning this type of business.[3]

Although the newly formed German DAAG had yet to prove itself, Dr. Pelz had once again been sufficiently persuasive to gain his point. In late 1965 the general managers of Pace's European elevator companies were to report to Dr. Pelz as managing director of DAAG European

---

[3] Class A business accounted for almost 90 percent in value of all new elevator installations by Pace Elevator division in the United States.

regional headquarters. The subsidiaries remained legally independent entities owned by Pace.[4]

SHAPING THE NEW RELATIONSHIP

Dr. Pelz saw his first task as managing director of DAAG Europe to be that of convincing each subsidiary to offer a line of standard elevator models for the class B market segment. By 1966 the German DAAG had developed a product line of eight models for the German apartment building market. He acknowledged, however, that it might not be feasible to market German elevators in other European countries where tastes, the building codes, and market conditions were different. Moreover, while the subsidiaries had for years done little more than adapt the company's U.S. elevator designs to meet local needs, Dr. Pelz anticipated that country managers might tend to resist were he to try to relieve them of this engineering and design function. Consequently, in order to lessen resistance as well as to give the national companies an opportunity to gain experience with standard models, he decided as the first step to permit each subsidiary to develop its own national line of standard class B elevator models.

Dr. Pelz's persuasive powers were put to the test as he tried to sell the standard model concept to the national companies reporting to him. The general managers voiced doubt as to the applicability of German experience with elevator models to their national markets. Moreover, even in Germany the results were only preliminary and certainly not clear-cut.

The resistance voiced by each country manager no doubt reflected an opposition by his selling organization. The salesmen were proud of the DAAG reputation for being able to produce the highest quality equipment for whichever design the architect specified. The idea of selling standard, "off-the-shelf" elevators, even if only for the class B business, was somewhat repugnant to them. Furthermore, most salesmen doubted that standard models would catch on—at least rapidly enough to maintain sales performance.

These attitudes were too deeply ingrained, these men too important to his purpose, and their arguments too valid for Pelz to turn them aside. He knew that he had not only to sell the customer on the idea of standard models but, more important he had to sell each of the DAAG sales forces.

LOWERING PRICE

In 1965 Dr. Pelz moved to induce the DAAG salesmen in Germany to sell the MOD-S line of standard models by lowering prices by about 9 percent from an already artificially low base. (The price in 1963 had been set to reflect prospective cost savings.) He made this reduction in order to create the widest possible price spread between the standard

---

[4] With few exceptions, all these European subsidiaries, with combined sales in 1969 of about $160 million, produced class A and class B elevator equipment under the DAAG name.

and traditional elevator models. As a result of this move, annual MOD-S sales in Germany almost trebled in 1965 to a volume of 1,321 units.

Shortly after the price cut for MOD-S elevators, DAAG began to lower its prices on class A elevators as well. While Pelz wanted his salesmen to switch from selling traditional class B elevators to standard models, he did not want to divert their energies from selling class A elevators. The MOD-S price cut had that effect to some extent, and he believed it necessary to make a comparable price reduction for the class A equipment if a proper balance of sales effort were to be maintained between the two. Quite apart from this reasoning, as a DAAG executive later explained, the company's prices for class A elevators were lowered throughout Europe almost unconsciously at this time because of the general enthusiasm in DAAG for expansion and growth. By bringing its prices down, DAAG once again increased unit sales.

Competitors in both markets soon countered with price cuts of their own. Dr. Pelz knew the lower DAAG prices could only be justified and maintained when manufacturing costs had been fully driven down by means of large economies of scale.

THE EUROPEAN MODELS

These economies of scale could in Dr. Pelz's view be achieved by moving to the next major phase of his plan—standard European models. By 1968 the development of class B models had been successfully completed on a national basis. Germany, France, Italy, and the U.K. each had a line of between 10 and 15 models. The smaller DAAG companies—such as Austria, Belgium, and Holland—adopted variations of the models designed in larger neighboring companies. As a result, 80 standard models accounted for 90 percent of the DAAG total class B elevator sales on the European continent.[5]

The transition to standard models had been helped, as a DAAG executive pointed out, by increasing the company's class B elevator business through acquisitions. From 1965 through 1969 Pace had expanded the European elevator operations by establishing five additional subsidiaries in Sweden, Denmark, Switzerland, Portugal, and Austria. During this same period of time, the DAAG European region had also acquired through its existing subsidiary companies some 30 small, local elevator firms which manufactured or serviced class B elevators. Exhibit 1 shows the expansion of the DAAG European region from 1965 through 1969.

In 1968 DAAG management began working on the development of European models to replace the class B national models and the class A customized units. One of its major tasks for this purpose was to build up an engineering group in Europe which would be capable of developing the new designs. Because of the need to satisfy the half-dozen differ-

---

[5] While the differences in national building codes at the time limited the standardization of design in several important respects, management estimated that a line of 20 to 25 standard European-oriented models would have been sufficient to deal with most of the conflicting requirements.

Exhibit 1

COMPOSITION OF THE DAAG EUROPEAN REGION, 1965–1969

Creation of the
European region

	January 1965	1966	1967	1968	1969
Germany					
United Kingdom					
France					
Italy					
Belgium					
Netherlands					
Spain					
Sweden		Acquisition			
Austria			Acquisition		
Portugal			Created		
Switzerland			Created		
Denmark				Merger	

Source: Company document.

ent (and sometimes even conflicting) construction codes to be found on the European continent, the technical demands for designing a compatible model would exceed anything the DAAG engineers in Europe had formerly been called upon to do.

Early on, management decided to give the class A development program higher priority for several reasons. Class B national models were already beginning to produce some economies of scale. The incremental savings to be gained from further standardization of these elevators would therefore be much less than would be the case for the class A elevators. Moreover, the managers and salesmen for each subsidiary would probably object to any change from their national models so soon after bringing them to the market. Finally, the tangle of local building regulations for apartment buildings was proving to be much more difficult to deal with than was true for major high-rise building projects.

The DAAG line of European class A elevator models, the Europa, was scheduled to be introduced in 1970. This product line was to comprise 15 models. The different models would carry between 8 and 24 passengers and have several configurations with respect to such features as speed of travel, door widths, and maximum number of floor stops.

The introduction of a DAAG line of European class B models, to be known as the Continental, was projected for 1973. The development of this line was to take place in three stages. In the first stage, the 90 or so national models, including those in the U.K., would be replaced with 30 European models. The second stage would witness a reduction of European models to 20. The ultimate objective was to have 10 European models. This final objective was based on the fact that 5 to 7 models accounted for about 80 percent of class B sales in each major market. The actual timing for the second and third stages would depend in large measure on the rate at which building codes in the EEC could be harmonized.

PRODUCTION RATIONALIZATION AND DAAG EUROPE

The major payoff in a move to standard elevator models would come from the economies of scale associated with a rationalized production arrangement. As a DAAG executive noted:

> We do not know exactly what the increased savings through greater mass production will be, but common sense tells us it will be a lot. The largest selling German model has sales of about 1,500 units per year. We estimate the largest European model will have sales of between 3,000 and 4,000 per year.

Dr. Pelz's objective was to have each factory specialize in the production of standardized components which could then be sold to DAAG assembly plants within each market. Prior to 1965 each plant manufactured or purchased locally all the necessary components it needed to manufacture all the elevators sold in its market area. By 1969 DAAG had begun to implement the first phase of its plan to rationalize production, whereby the company's EEC factories (two in Germany, one in France, and one in Italy) were to specialize in producing and exchanging a number of basic components. These components were priced at full cost plus a 25 percent charge for intercompany transfers.

The second phase, to be completed around 1974, would also bring the factories in the U.K., Spain, and Austria into the arrangement. At that time, each factory would produce certain major elevator subunits (such as the motor, relays, and the control mechanism) to supply other plants. To ensure safety of supply, critical components were to be made in two plants.

A DETERIORATING FINANCIAL POSITION

As Dr. Pelz reviewed the situation in 1969, he was impressed with the progress that DAAG had shown in four short years in its attempt to move to standard models and to rationalize production facilities. Moreover, the company's strategy had led to a better than threefold increase in unit sales and to a more than doubling of DAAG's share of the European elevator market since its inception in 1963. Exhibit 2 graphically shows the decline of the average unit price during the period 1965 to 1969 and the corresponding increase in unit sales.[6]

---

[6] Since the price decline shown in Exhibit 2 resulted from a combination of actual price cuts and an increasing proportion of less costly class B business, price changes for a single unit (the MOD-S) are shown in Exhibit 3. The price changes for the MOD-S were said to be representative of most DAAG elevator units during this period.

Exhibit 2

DAAG WESTERN EUROPEAN REGION
ELEVATOR UNIT SALES AND AVERAGE PRICE PER UNIT

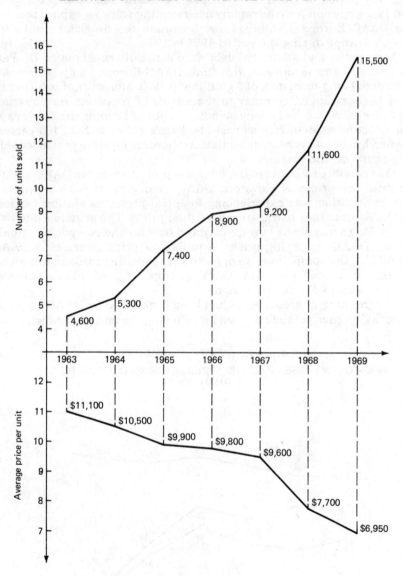

Profits, however, had suffered as a consequence of the failure to achieve cost savings sufficiently high to cover the decline in prices during this period of time. An even more pressing financial problem in Dr. Pelz's opinion was the rapidly deteriorating working capital position for DAAG Europe. Exhibits 4 and 5 contain the financial results for DAAG Europe during the period 1965 to 1969.

New equity and additional debt were generally ruled out by Dr. Pelz as viable financial moves at this time. DAAG Europe had just assumed additional long-term debt of $3 million in 1969. Moreover, this financing had been arranged contrary to the advice of corporate headquarters in Chicago, which had a long-standing policy of keeping the firm's capital structure as debt free as possible. Pace's policy to hold 100 percent ownership of its overseas subsidiaries wherever possible precluded selling equity on the market.

One possible response to the financial problem was for DAAG simply to raise the prices of elevators. DAAG management felt certain that the competition was experiencing financial pressures similar to those of DAAG since they had also dropped their prices. The principal question in Dr. Pelz's mind was how quickly and how far the competition would follow DAAG in raising prices. A unilateral price increase by DAAG could give the competitors an opportunity to make inroads in important markets at a time when DAAG was attempting to effect economies of scale through volume production.

A tightening of credit terms had been considered by DAAG management as another possible avenue for relieving the current financial bur-

Exhibit 3

INDEX OF AVERAGE PRICE AND MANUFACTURING COST OF THE MOD-S
GERMAN MODEL

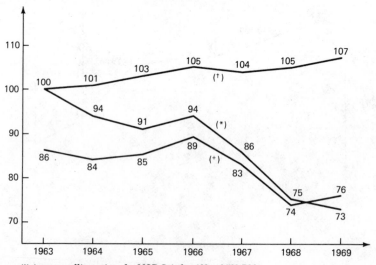

(*) Average selling price of a MOD-S; index 100 = 6,500 DM.
(†) Standard manufacturing cost of a MOD-S.
(‡) Index of price for industrial goods in Germany after 1967 including VAT.
Source: Company document.

Exhibit 4

DAAG EUROPE (A)
DAAG Europe Balance Sheets
For the Years Ending 1966–1969
($ millions)

	1966	1967	1968	1969
Assets				
Current assets:				
Cash and marketable securities	$ 1.1	$ 1.9	$ 1.4	$ 0.8
Net notes and accounts receivable	36.0	36.9	39.4	56.5
Associated companies receivables	6.1	7.1	11.3	15.0
Total receivables	42.1	44.0	50.7	71.5
Inventories	31.5	25.0	27.2	40.1
Cost of contracts in progress	64.2	65.8	74.1	88.1
Total inventories	95.7	90.8	101.3	128.2
Prepayments	0.7	0.6	0.5	0.8
Less billings on contracts in progress ..	(71.5)	(73.0)	(75.5)	(86.2)
Total current assets	68.2	64.4	78.4	115.2
Property, plant, equipment	38.8	40.7	41.3	50.7
Less: Depreciation	(14.7)	(17.0)	(18.4)	(21.1)
Net plant, equipment	24.1	23.7	22.8	29.6
Deferred charges	3.0	2.7	2.8	3.6
Total assets	$ 95.3	$ 90.9	$104.2	$148.5
Liabilities and Capital				
Current liabilities:				
Short-term loans	$ 23.2	$ 17.0	$ 23.0	$ 41.2
Notes and accounts payable	12.5	10.3	12.3	21.9
Associated company payables	4.7	5.6	7.6	7.7
Accrued liabilities	4.5	6.5	9.3	14.6
Income tax	2.5	2.5	2.1	2.5
Total current liabilities	46.7	42.2	54.4	88.1
Long-term notes and				
accounts payable	9.5	8.8	6.9	12.9
Total liabilities	57.1	51.1	61.5	100.9
Reserves for pensions and				
severance indemnities	—	4.2	4.2	4.6
All other reserves	7.3	3.5	9.4	11.0
Capital stock	17.0	17.0	17.2	19.3
Surplus	13.8	14.9	11.7	12.4
Net worth	38.1	39.8	42.6	47.5
Net worth exclusive of				
reserves for pensions	38.1	35.5	38.4	42.9
Total liabilities and capital	$ 95.3	$ 90.9	$104.2	$148.5

Note: Figures may not add due to rounding.
Source: Company records. The figures represent a consolidation of individual company accounts.

den on the company. Payments normally stretched out over a two- to three-year period with a major portion due after the completion of the job. Dr. Pelz had a proposal before him recommending that DAAG adhere to the industry's pro forma payment schedules, which for Germany

Exhibit 5

DAAG EUROPE PROFITS AND BOOKINGS FOR THE YEARS 1965–1969,
AND A FINANCIAL ANALYSIS OF THE STATEMENTS
($ millions)

	1965	1966	1967	1968	1969
Net profit before tax* ...	$ 3.6	$ 3.3	$ 3.7	$ 3.9	$ 4.0
New sales bookings	73	87	88	89	108
Service bookings	33	38	43	46	51
Total bookings	106	125	131	135	159

Analysis of the Financial Statements

	1966	1967	1968	1969
$\dfrac{\text{Current assets}}{\text{Current liabilities}}$	1.46	1.53	1.44	1.31
$\dfrac{\text{Cash plus receivables}}{\text{Current liabilities}}$	0.93	1.09	0.96	0.82
Collection period in days	121	121	135	162
Inventory/sales (excluding cost of contracts in progress)	0.25	0.19	0.20	0.25
Debt/net worth........................	0.25	0.22	0.16	0.27

* Net profit reflected the results of elevator contracts completed and service contracts performed during the year, as well as manufacturing variances for the year.
Source: Company records. The figures represent a consolidation of individual company accounts.

involved collecting a down payment of 30 percent at the time the contract was signed, an additional 30 percent when the elevator was delivered, 30 percent at the completion of the job, and the final 10 percent when the building received official approval (Exhibit 6). Actual payment schedules had long been more liberal than the announced formula. Moreover, as Dr. Pelz knew, his competitors had employed increasingly generous payment schedules to counter DAAG's aggressive pricing. For example, Westinghouse had reportedly required only 10 percent down payment and no further payment until completion of the project on certain occasions. In other instances, Westinghouse had not even required the customer to make a down payment.

Another possible step for DAAG was to reinstate a price escalation clause in new elevator sales contracts to protect against inflation. Customer pressure during the competitive battle of the middle 1960s had led DAAG and the other elevator manufacturers to accept fixed price contracts. Increasing inflation rates during the late 1960s led to losses for major projects which had been negotiated anywhere between two and five years earlier. In Dr. Pelz's opinion, for DAAG to tighten credit terms or to press for escalation clauses would have it run risks similar to those it would run in raising prices.

Exhibit 6

PRO FORMA PAYMENT SCHEDULES ON CLASS A
CONTRACTS IN GERMANY, FRANCE,
AND SWITZERLAND, 1969

	Percent
Germany:	
Signing of contract	30
Delivery to job site*	30
Completion†	30
Final acceptance‡	10
Switzerland:	
Signing of contract	30
Three months prior to delivery	30
During the course of erection	10
Completion	30
France:	
Signing of contract	30
Delivery to job site	30
Completion	40

* DAAG management estimated the time between booking a contract and delivery of the elevator to the job site ran an average of one year. The actual order usually did not arrive until six months after the closing of the contract. This one-year figure did not include the three to six months that normally elapsed between the time a bid was submitted and a contract was closed.

† Erection time (from delivery to completion) for class A elevator projects ranged between two months and two years with an average of one year. The Lorelei Tower, the tallest building in Germany, required about 2½ years for erecting elevators.

‡ Final acceptance was when both the owner and the building authorities approved the building. Final acceptance normally followed the completion of building construction by one to four months.

Source: Company document.

Air, Inc.*

In 1971, the board of directors of Air, Inc., Chicago, the oldest and one of the largest manufacturers of air filtration equipment in the world, nominated David Palma, 55, vice president as head of international operations. The International Division supervised about 50 companies throughout the world, which together generated a sales volume roughly equal to that of the U.S. operation.

David Palma, an Italian national, who had worked for Air, Inc., for 20 years, took on his new job at a moment when international operations were clearly in a bad way. During the preceding year they had netted only $50,000 profits on $300 million of sales; and although Air, Inc., was still the world leader in market share (with about 20 percent of the world market), its position was weakening.

David Palma noted the reasons for the situation to be the following:

1. Competition was cut-throat: as the industry was labor intensive, and as its products were old, without patent protection, and often custom-made, there seemed to be little advantage of size against hundreds of small local competitors.
2. Air, Inc., had made no thorough analysis of its competition, nor of the different markets it served.
3. There was no product policy; most products were developed in the United States and did not meet local needs nor local building code specifications; for lack of competitive products, Air Inc. found itself excluded from a series of growing markets; there was no product diversification.
4. Management at all levels was inadequate; it was complacent (in many cases, managers of local subsidiaries were not able to give even a gross figure on the financial performance of their unit). They

had not been asked for this information even when a company lost money for several years. There was almost no turnover in management, and no outside recruiting; there was no management development and training.

5. Controls were inadequate; there were no performance goals and standards, no job descriptions, no performance appraisal (nor rewards for outstanding work or punishment for poor performance).

6. Coordination between and control of the different local subsidiaries was almost nonexistent; as was any organization at division headquarters (where no one was specifically assigned to head Marketing, Production, Finance; adequate staff support was lacking in a situation where one had to turn to corporate staffs for the solution of almost every major functional problem).

David Palma, who immediately moved international headquarters to Milan, decided at once to turn the situation by taking dramatic action. He believed two major steps to be essential to realize a recovery and expansion: the introduction of a new product policy and a reorganization of structure and procedures.

As to products, one would revolutionize the industry, he believed, by trying to apply a new concept: Air, Inc. would build standardized models in a module system. This would allow for substantial economy through mass production of different standardized parts in different factories, it would allow for centralized R&D and, it would lead to better service performance. David Palma, himself an engineer, decided to focus all his attention on this strategic change in Air, Inc.'s traditional operations as well as on possibilities of diversification through mergers and acquisitions.

He decided, therefore, to leave the organizational and administrative problems to somebody else. He hired Joe Pfeffer as a director of human resources, and gave him "carte blanche" to implement these goals.

Joe Pfeffer, 38, was an American with a good record as a personnel administrator. He was the first manager to be hired from outside the company and only the third personnel administrator in the company's history. He described himself as a compulsive achiever who had struggled to advance in business ever since he was a young man. He had earned his MBA in evening courses and had written two books on management, between 10 P.M. and 3 A.M., as he said. When he moved to Milan, he left his wife and child in New York, so that he could concentrate all his energy on his new job. Work was his primary hobby. He considered business an exciting adventure and tough challenge.

He described how he approached the challenge at Air, Inc. International in the following way:

> My job was to turn this organization around from a paternalistic institution to a dynamic, successful, healthy, profitable, growing business.
>
> This meant, above all, to bring professionalism into the firm. Air, Inc. was at best 20, at worst 50 years behind in modern management techniques, with managers lacking discipline, drive, professional skills, the ability to work in teams.

Far-reaching changes were necessary. But you have to go slowly and not make mistakes. You have to establish a base from which to operate. You try to learn as much as possible. And as a human resources manager you must be as comfortable with a financial statement as a financial vice president; otherwise, nobody will listen to you.

The first thing I did, was to ask management at the operating companies controlled by Air, Inc. International to prepare action plans to improve their productivity and to reduce costs and expenses immediately. These plans were then discussed in Milan or, in the case of larger subsidiaries, at their local headquarters. If in these meetings someone came up with a watered-down budget, he was in trouble; we kicked the hell out of him. Note, however, that in a confrontation with a line man (especially one who is making money) the staff man always loses. So you have to know when to back off and wait until he makes a stupid mistake (they always do) and then sack him.

We set the objectives at headquarters—time was short; inertia had to be removed: we knew that South Africa was performing poorly and should have improved 200 percent; so we set a target of 100 percent. You have to be reasonable and practical. You can't let these people set their own goals; they'll set them too low.

I like to deal with people one by one. We had only 2 staff meetings in 3½ years. But we do have individually tailored management seminars which I conducted personally. These were really MBO sessions —very simple, basic, and completely authoritarian: We gave as an assignment to the participants to state their greatest problems at the present; we then selected from the problems mentioned a few which seemed most important and discussed possible solutions. We have come up with ideas which have saved the company millions, and I made sure that they were implemented. That is, I visited the companies frequently, giving them usually 2 months advance notice so they could shape up before my arrival.

We wanted the different companies to compete with each other. So we called, for instance, the Latin Americans together: the Mexicans were selling $11 million with 1,100 people; the Argentinians $35 million with 600—very embarrassing. . . . When I went to Australia for the first time, at 4:30 P.M. everybody was gone—no competitive spirit. Now, with my new man there, everybody works until 7:00 P.M.

As I met all these executives, I started to establish a worldwide manpower inventory. I interviewed systematically the 350 people in top positions. Interviews took typically about two hours. You give a guy the benefit of the doubt, but actually you know after 30 minutes what the man is like. In one case, I increased a man's salary by 20 percent on the spot (without even checking with his superior) and sometimes I started to look for a replacement the same day. Altogether we had to replace almost all of top management. Keeping them in their positions would really have been too costly. Either we kept them in an advisory function compatible with their technical expertise, or we just had to let them go. We hired only people from outside who had a good job; smart people . . . people who earned already $40,000, but were looking for better promotion prospects. The man on the top is decisive. I focus all the effort on him. If you have good top managers, you don't have to worry much more; they will not tolerate mediocrity down the line; you can leave them alone until they lack in performance. I have had no problems with them—I hired these guys. And none of them ever quit of his own desire.

I'll train the new men; then they'll report directly to me during the first year; and after that I maintain a heavy dotted-line relationship to them. Some may say that this is not my business—I answer that everything involving people is my business.

As to performance, I don't care what a man does (short of stealing from the company) as long as he gets results. That's why I like to hire locals as financial managers (while in many multinationals the finance men come from HQ). For they know the local conditions and how to circumvent the law, legally or illegally.

It's hard to measure the long-term impact of managers on an organization. I don't worry about the uncontrollable; there is enough of what is controllable to worry about—we measure performance; that's what counts. What happens in five years is an illusion, anyway.

After about two years, Joe Pfeffer started to (a) initiate a more formalized manpower planning system, (b) establish standard personnel policies (although he avoided having all policies down in writing—"often it is too dangerous to commit yourself"), and (c) reorganized Air, Inc. International's headquarters operations.

More specifically he developed position descriptions and performance standards for many key management positions; he introduced a uniform worldwide performance appraisal and review program (he established an incentive plan and formal annual salary reviews based on worldwide salary survey data); he encouraged on-the-job training of new managers away from their home country (while not supporting the attendance of training programs outside the company—"we can't afford to let our people go for two weeks training"); and he has made it an obligation for every manager to identify and develop high-potential young executives.

He also has worked on the (re)organization of the Milan headquarters. Operations were divided into four regional divisions: Europe, Far East, Latin America, and Other. Each of these new divisions had to be provided with sizable marketing, finance, and engineering staffs which were recruited either from the "cream" of what was available in the operating units or from outside the company. Joe Pfeffer did not create a large personal staff noting he did not have the budget to hire first-rate people and preferred to work alone rather than with second-rate people. The development of a strong group in Milan had the purpose of helping the International Division to gain more independence from Chicago (which he said lacked understanding of the international business) and at the same time of gaining control over the local operating units (which were believed to be drifting).

With all this, Air, Inc. International attained, in 1973, sales of $530 million and profits of $35 million, thus overtaking the North American operations, for the first time, both in sales volume and profitability. Employment was down 13 percent (since 1970) to 33,000.

Robert F. Kennedy High School

ON JULY 15, 1970, David King became principal of the Robert F. Kennedy High School, the newest of the six high schools in Great Ridge, Illinois. The school had opened in the fall of 1968 amid national acclaim for being one of the first schools in the country to be designed and constructed for the "house system" concept. Kennedy High's organization was broken down into four "houses" each of which contained 300 students, a faculty of 18, and a housemaster. The Kennedy complex was especially designed so that each house was in a separate building connected to the "core facilities" and other houses by an enclosed outside passageway.[1] Each house had its own entrance, classrooms, toilets, conference rooms, and housemaster's office. (See Exhibit 1 for the layout.)

King knew that Kennedy High was not intended to be an ordinary school when it was first conceived. It had been hailed as a major innovation in inner city education and a Chicago television station had made a documentary on it in 1968. Kennedy High had opened with a carefully selected staff of teachers, many of whom were chosen from other Great Ridge Schools and at least a dozen of whom had been especially recruited from out of state. Indeed, King knew his faculty included graduates from several elite East and West Coast schools such as Stanford, Yale, and Princeton, as well as several of the very best midwestern schools. Even the racial mix of students had been carefully balanced so that blacks, whites, and Puerto Ricans each comprised a third of the student body (although King also knew—perhaps better than its planners—that Kennedy's students were drawn from the toughest and poorest areas of town). The building itself was also widely admired for its beauty and functionality and had won several national architectural awards.

[1] The core facilities included the cafeteria, nurses's room, guidance offices, the boys' and girls' gyms, the offices, the shops, and auditorium.

Exhibit 1

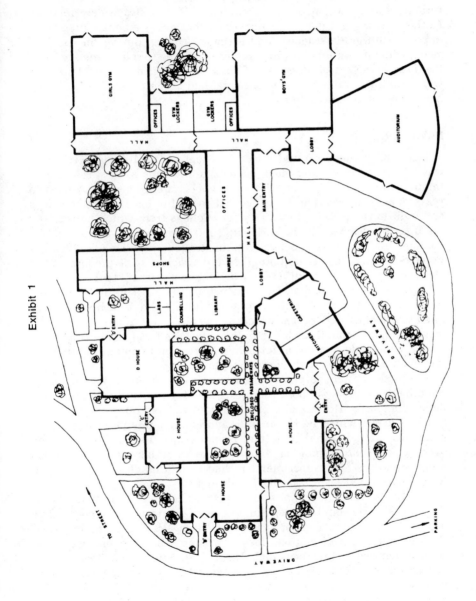

Despite these careful and elaborate preparations, Kennedy High School was in serious difficulty by July of 1970. It had been wracked by violence the preceding year, having been twice closed by student disturbances and once by a teacher walkout. It was also widely reported (although King did not know for sure), that achievement scores of its 9th and 10th grade students had actually declined during the last two years, while no significant improvement could be found in the scores of the 11th and 12th graders' tests. Thus, the Kennedy High School for which King was taking over as principal had fallen far short of its planners' hopes and expectations.

DAVID KING

David King was born and raised in Great Ridge, Illinois. His father was one of the city's first black principals and thus King was not only familiar with the city, but with its school system as well. After two years of military service, King decided to follow his father's footsteps and went to Great Ridge State Teachers College from which he received his B.Ed. in 1955 and his M.Ed. in 1960. King was certified in Elementary and Secondary School Administration, English and Physical Education. King had taught English and coached in a predominantly black middle school until 1960 when he was asked to become the school's assistant principal. He remained in that post until 1965 when he was asked to take over the George Thibeault Middle School, a large middle school of 900 pupils which at the time was reputed to be the most "difficult" middle school in the city. While at Thibeault, King gained a citywide reputation for being a gifted and popular administrator and was credited with changing Thibeault from the worst middle school in the system to one of the best. He had been very effective in building community support, recruiting new faculty, and in raising academic standards. He was also credited with turning out basketball and baseball teams which had won state and country middle school championships. King knew that he had been selected for the Kennedy job over several more senior candidates because of his ability to handle tough situations. The superintendent had made that clear when he told King why he had been selected for the job.

The superintendent had also told him that he would need every bit of skill and luck he could muster. King knew of the formidable credentials of Jack Weis, his predecessor at Kennedy High. Weis, a white, had been the superintendent of a small, local township school system before becoming Kennedy's first principal. He had also written a book on the "house system" concept, as well as a second book on inner city education. Weis had earned a Ph.D. from the University of Chicago and a divinity degree from Harvard. Yet, despite his impressive background and obvious ability, Weis had resigned in disillusionment, and was described by many as a "broken man." In fact, King remembered seeing the physical change which Weis had undergone over that two-year period. Weis' appearance had become progressively more fatigued and strained until he developed what appeared to be permanent black rings under his eyes and a perpetual stoop. King remembered how he had pitied the man and wondered how Weis could find the job worth the obvious personal toll it was taking on him.

HISTORY OF THE SCHOOL

1968–1969. The school's troubles began to manifest themselves in the school's first year of operation. Rumors of conflicts between the house-masters and the six subject area department heads were widespread throughout the system by the middle of the first year. The conflicts stemmed from differences in interpretations of curriculum policy on required learning and course content. In response to these conflicts, Dr. Weis had instituted a "free market" policy by which subject area department heads were supposed to convince headmasters of why they should offer certain courses, while headmasters were supposed to convince department heads of which teachers they wanted assigned to their houses and why they wanted those teachers. Many observers in the school system felt that this policy exacerbated the conflicts.

To add to this climate of conflict a teacher was assaulted in her classroom in February of 1969. The beating frightened many of the staff, particularly some of the older teachers. A delegation of eight teachers asked Weis to hire security guards a week after the assault. The request precipitated a debate within the faculty about the desirability of having guards in the school. One group felt that the guards would instill a sense of safety within the school, and thus promote a better learning climate, while the other group felt that the presence of guards in the school would be repressive and would destroy the sense of community and trust which was developing within the school. Dr. Weis refused the request for security guards because he believed that symbolically they would represent everything the school was trying to change. In April a second teacher was robbed and beaten in her classroom after school hours and the debate was rekindled, except that this time a group of Spanish-speaking parents threatened to boycott the school unless better security measures were instituted. Again Dr. Weis refused the request for security guards.

1969–1970. The second year of the school's existence was even more troubled than the first. Because of cutbacks ordered during the summer of 1969, Dr. Weis was not able to replace eight teachers who resigned during the summer and it was no longer possible for each house to staff all of its courses with its own faculty. Dr. Weis therefore instituted a "flexible staffing" policy whereby some teachers were asked to teach a course outside of their assigned house and students in the 11th and 12th grades were able to take some elective and required courses in other houses. During this period, Chauncey Carver, one of the house-masters, publicly attacked the move as a step toward destroying the house system. In a letter to the *Great Ridge Times*, he accused the Board of Education of trying to subvert the house concept by cutting back funds.

The debate over the flexible staffing policy was heightened when two of the other housemasters joined a group of faculty and department chairmen in opposing Chauncey Carver's criticisms. This group argued that the individual house faculties of 15 to 18 teachers could never offer their students the breadth of courses that a schoolwide faculty of 65 to 70 teachers could offer and that interhouse cross registration should be encouraged for that reason.

Further expansion of a cross registration or flexible staffing policy was halted, however, because of difficulties encountered in the scheduling of classes in the fall of 1969. Several errors were found in the master schedule which had been pre-planned during the preceding summer. Various schedule difficulties persisted until November of 1969 when the vice principal responsible for the scheduling of classes resigned. Mr. Burtram Perkins, a Kennedy housemaster who had formerly planned the schedule at Central High assumed the scheduling function in addition to his duties as housemaster. The scheduling activity took most of Perkins' time until February.

Security again became an issue when three sophomores were assaulted because they refused to give up their lunch money during a "shakedown." It was believed that the assailants were from outside of the school and were not students. Several teachers approached Dr. Weis and asked him to request security guards from the Board of Education. Again, Dr. Weis declined but he asked Bill Smith, a vice principal at the school, to secure all doors except for the entrances to each of the four houses, the main entrance to the school, and the cafeteria. This move appeared to reduce the number of outsiders in the school.

In May of 1970, a disturbance occurred in the cafeteria which appeared to grow out of a fight between two boys. The fight spread and resulted in considerable damage to the school including the breaking of classroom windows and desks. The disturbance was severe enough for Dr. Weis to close the school. A number of teachers and students reported that outsiders were involved in the fight and in damaging the classrooms. Several students were taken to the hospital for minor injuries but all were released. A similar disturbance occurred two weeks later and again the school was closed. The Board of Education then ordered a temporary detail of municipal police to the school despite Dr. Weis' advice to the contrary. In protest to the assignment of the police detail, 30 of Kennedy's 68 teachers staged a walkout which was joined by over half the student body. The police detail was removed from the school, and an agreement was worked out by an ad hoc subcommittee of the Board of Education with informal representatives of teachers who were for and against assigning a police detail. The compromise called for the temporary stationing of a police cruiser near the school.

KING'S FIRST WEEK AT KENNEDY HIGH

Mr. King arrived at Kennedy High on Monday, July 15th and spent most of his first week individually interviewing the school's key administrators (see Exhibit 2 for a listing of Kennedy's administrative staff as of July 15th). He also had a meeting with all of his adminis-

Exhibit 2

ROBERT F. KENNEDY HIGH SCHOOL
ADMINISTRATIVE ORGANIZATION

Principal:	David King, 42 (black)
	B.Ed.; M.Ed., Great Ridge State College
Vice principal:	William Smith, 44 (black)
	B.Ed., Breakwater State College
	M.Ed. (Counseling), Great Ridge State College
Vice principal:	Vacant—to be filled
Housemaster, A House:	Burtram Perkins, 47 (black)
	B.S.; M.Ed., University of Illinois
Housemaster, B House:	Frank Czepak, 36 (white)
	B.S. University of Illinois
	M.Ed. Great Ridge State College
Housemaster, C House:	Chauncey Carver, 32 (black)
	A.B. Wesleyan University
	B.F.A. Pratt Institute
	M.A.T. Yale University
Housemaster, D House:	John Bonavota, 26 (white)
	B.Ed. Great Ridge State College
	M.Ed. Ohio State University
Assistant to the principal:	Vacant—to be filled
Assistant to the principal: (for Community Affairs)	Vacant—to be filled

trators and department heads on Friday of that week. Mr. King's purpose in these meetings was to familiarize himself with the school, its problems, and its key people.

His first interview was with Bill Smith, who was one of his vice principals. Mr. Smith was black and had worked as a counselor and as a vice principal of a middle school prior to coming to Kennedy. King knew that Smith had a reputation for being a tough disciplinarian and was very much disliked among many of the younger faculty and students. However, King had also heard from several teachers, whose judgment he respected, that Smith had been instrumental in keeping the school from "blowing apart" the preceding year. It became clear early in the interview that Smith felt that more stringent steps were needed to keep outsiders from wandering the buildings. In particular Smith urged King to consider locking all of the school's 30 doors except for the front entrance so that everyone would enter and leave through one set of doors only. Smith also told him that many of the teachers and pupils had become fearful of living and working in the building and that "no learning will ever begin to take place until we make it so people don't have to be afraid anymore." At the end of the interview, Smith told King that he had been approached by a nearby school system to become its director of counselling but that he had not yet made up his mind. He said that he was committed enough to Kennedy High that he did not want to leave, but that his decision depended on how hopeful he felt about its future.

As King talked with others, he discovered that the "door question" was one of considerable controversy within the faculty and that feelings ran high, both in favor of the idea of locking all the doors as well as against it. Two of the housemasters in particular, Chauncey Carver, a black, and Frank Czepak, a white, were strongly against closing the house entrances. The two men felt that such an action would symbolically reduce house "autonomy" and the feeling of distinctness that was a central aspect of the house concept.

Chauncey Carver, master of "C" House, was particularly vehement on this issue as well as on the question of whether students of one house should be allowed to take classes in another house. Carver said that the flexible staffing program introduced the preceding year had nearly destroyed the house concept and that he, Carver, would resign if King intended to expand the cross-house enrollment of students. Carver also complained about what he described as "interference" from department heads in his teacher's autonomy.

Carver appeared to be an outstanding housemaster from everything that King had heard about him—even from his many enemies. Carver had an abrasive personality but seemed to have the best operating house in the school and was well liked by most of his teachers and pupils. His program also appeared to be the most innovative of all. However, it was also the program which was most frequently attacked by the department heads for lacking substance and not covering the requirements outlined in the system's curriculum guide. Even with these criticisms, King imagined how much easier it would be if he had four housemasters like Chauncey Carver.

During his interviews with the other three housemasters, King discovered that they all felt infringed upon by the department heads, but that only Carver and Czepak were strongly against "locking the doors" and that two other housemasters actively favored cross-house course enrollments. King's fourth interview was with Burtram Perkins who was also a housemaster. Perkins was a black in his late 40s who had been an assistant to the principal of Central High before coming to Kennedy. Perkins spent most of the interview discussing how schedule pressures could be relieved. Perkins was currently involved in developing the schedule for the 1970–71 school year until a vice principal was appointed to perform that job. (Kennedy High had allocations for two vice principals and two assistants in addition to the housemasters. See Exhibit 2.)

Two pieces of information concerning Perkins came to King's attention during his first week there. The first was that several teachers were circulating a letter requesting Perkins' removal as a housemaster because they felt he could not control the house or direct the faculty. This surprised King because he had heard that Perkins was widely respected within the faculty and had earned a reputation for supporting high academic standards and for working tirelessly with new teachers. However, as King inquired further he discovered that Perkins was greatly liked within the faculty but was also generally recognized as a poor housemaster. The second piece of information concerned how Perkins' house compared with the others. Although students had been randomly assigned to each house, Perkins' house had the largest absence rate and the greatest number of disciplinary problems in the school. Smith had also told him that Perkins' dropout rate for 1969–70 was three times that of any other house.

While King was in the process of interviewing his staff he was called on by Mr. David Crimmins, chairman of the History Department. Crimmins was a native of Great Ridge, white, and in his late 40s. Crimmins was scheduled for an appointment the following week, but asked King if he could see him immediately. Crimmins said he wanted to talk with King because he had heard that a letter was being circulated asking for Perkins' removal and that he wanted to present the other side of the argument. Crimmins became very emotional during the conversation, and said that Perkins was viewed by many of the teachers and department chairmen as the only housemaster who was making an effort to maintain high academic standards, and that his transfer would be seen as a blow to those concerned with quality education. He also described in detail Perkins' devotion and commitment to the school and the fact that Perkins was the only administrator with the ability to straighten out the schedule, and that he had done this in addition to all of his other duties. Crimmins departed by saying that if Perkins were transferred, that he, Crimmins, would personally write a letter to the regional accreditation council telling them how badly standards had sunk at Kennedy. King assured him that it would not be necessary to take such a drastic measure and that a cooperative resolution would be found. King was aware of the accreditation review that Kennedy High faced the following April and he did not wish to complicate the process unnecessarily in any way.

Within 20 minutes of Crimmins' departure, King was visited by a young white teacher named Tim Shea who said that he had heard that Crimmins had come in to see him. Shea said that he was one of the teachers who organized the movement to get rid of Perkins. Shea said that he liked and admired Perkins very much because of his devotion to the school but that Perkins' house was so disorganized and discipline so bad that it was nearly impossible to do any good teaching. Shea added that it was "a shame to lock the school up when stronger leadership is all that's needed."

King's impressions of his administrators generally matched what he had heard about them before arriving at the school. Carver seemed to be a very bright, innovative, and charismatic leader whose mere presence generated excitement. Czepak seemed to be a highly competent, though not very imaginative administrator, who had earned the respect of his faculty and students. Bonavota, who was only 26, seemed very bright and earnest but unseasoned and unsure of himself. King felt that with a little guidance and training Bonavota might have the greatest promise of all. At the moment, however, he appeared to be a very uncertain and somewhat confused person who had difficulty simply coping.

Perkins seemed to be a very sincere, and devoted person who had a good mind for administrative details but an almost total incapacity for leadership.

King knew that he would have the opportunity to make several administrative appointments because of the three vacancies which existed. Indeed, should Smith resign as vice principal, King would be in the position of filling both vice principalships. He knew that his recommendations for these positions would carry a great deal of weight with the central office. The only constraint that King felt in making these appointments was the need to achieve some kind of racial balance among the Kennedy administrative group. With his own appointment as principal, the number of black administrators exceeded the number of white administrators by a ratio of two to one, and as yet Kennedy did not have a single Puerto Rican administrator even though a third of its pupils had Spanish surnames.

THE FRIDAY AFTERNOON MEETING

In contrast to the individual interviews, King was surprised to find how quiet and conflict-free these same people were in the staff meeting that he called on Friday. He was amazed at how slow, polite, and friendly the conversation appeared to be among people who had so vehemently expressed negative opinions of each other in private. After about 45 minutes of discussion about the upcoming accreditation review, King broached the subject of housemaster-department head relations. The ensuing silence was finally broken by a joke which Czepak made about the uselessness of discussing that topic. King probed further by asking whether everyone was happy with the current practices. Crimmins suggested that this was a topic that might be better discussed in a smaller group. Everyone in the room seemed to agree with Crimmins except for Betsy Dula, a young white woman in her late 20s who was chairman of the English department. She said that one of the problems with the school was that no one was willing to tackle tough issues until they exploded. She said that relations between housemasters and department heads were terrible and it made her job very difficult. She then attacked Chauncey Carver for impeding her evaluation of a nontenured teacher in Carver's house. The two argued for several minutes about the teacher and the quality of the experimental Sophomore English course that the teacher was giving. Finally, Carver, who by now was quite angry, coldly warned Mrs. Dula that he would "break her neck" if she stepped into his house again. King intervened in an attempt to cool both their tempers and the meeting ended shortly thereafter.

The following morning, Mrs. Dula called King at home and told him that unless Chauncey Carver publicly apologized for his threat, she would file a grievance with the teachers' union and take it to court if necessary. King assured Mrs. Dula that he would talk with Carver on Monday. King then called Eleanor Debbs, one of the school's Math teachers whom he had known well for many years and whose judgment he respected. Mrs. Debbs was a close friend of both Carver and Mrs.

Dula and was also vice president of the city's teachers' union. He learned from her that both had been long-term adversaries but that she felt both were excellent professionals.

She also reported that Mrs. Dula would be a formidable opponent and could muster considerable support among the faculty. Mrs. Debbs, who was herself black, feared that a confrontation between Dula and Carver might create tensions along race lines within the school even though both Dula and Carver were generally quite popular with students of all races. Mrs. Debbs strongly urged King not to let the matter drop. Mrs. Debbs also told him that she had overheard Bill Smith, the vice principal, say at a party the preceding night that he felt that King didn't have either the stomach or the forcefulness necessary to survive at Kennedy. Smith further stated that the only reason he was staying was that he did not expect King to last the year. Should that prove to be the case, Smith felt that he would be appointed principal.

The accomplishment of purpose: Organizational processes and behavior

OUR STUDY of strategy has brought us to the prescription that organizational structure must follow strategy if implementation is to be effective. We have seen that structural design involves inevitably (1) a suitable specialization of task, (2) a parallel provision for coordination, and (3) information systems for meeting the requirement that specialists be well informed and their work coordinated. We have seen that a variety of structures may be suitable to a strategy so long as the performance influenced by structural characteristics is not diverted from strategic ends.

We turn now from structural considerations to other influences upon organizational behavior. A logical structure does not ensure effective organized effort any more than a high degree of technical skill in individual members ensures achievement of organizational purposes. We suggest the following proposition for testing in your analysis of cases: *Organizational performance is effective to the extent that (in an atmosphere deliberately created to encourage the development of required skills and to provide the satisfactions of personal progress) individual energy is successfully directed toward organizational goals.* Convergence of energy upon purpose is made effective by individual and group commitment to purpose.

Man-made and natural organizational *systems* and *processes* are available to influence individual development and performance. In any organization the system which relates specific influences upon behavior to each other (so as to constitute an ultimate impact upon behavior) is made up of some six elements: (1) standards, (2) measures, (3) incentives, (4) rewards, (5) penalties, and (6) controls. The distinguishing characteristic of a system, of course, is the interaction of its elements. This interdependence will vary from organization to organization and from situation to situation and cannot always be observed, controlled, or completely analyzed.

636

The familiar processes which bear on performance are (1) measurement, (2) evaluation, (3) motivation, (4) control, and (5) individual development. The most important aspects of a process are the speed and direction of its forward motion and the nature of its side effects. So far as the uniqueness of each company situation allows, we shall look at combinations of these organizational systems and processes in the following order:

1. The establishment of standards and measurement of performance.
2. The administration of motivation and incentive systems.
3. The operation of systems of restraint and control.
4. The recruitment and development of management.

These processes have been studied in detail by specialists of several kinds. We shall not attempt to extract all the wisdom or expose all the folly which, over the years, has accumulated in the study of human relations and organizational behavior. We are now concerned, as always, with the limited but important ways in which specialized bodies of knowledge can be put to use in the implementation of strategy. The idea of strategy will dominate our approach to the internal organizational systems which animate structure, just as it dominated our discussion of the factors that determine structure itself. It may be desirable to point out that our aim is not to coerce and manipulate unwilling individuals. It is instead to support and direct individuals who are at least assenting to or, more desirably, committed to organizational goals. Commitment to purpose remains in our scheme of things the overriding necessary condition of effective accomplishment.

ESTABLISHMENT OF STANDARDS AND MEASUREMENT OF PERFORMANCE

If progress toward goals is to be supervised at all, it will have to be observed and measured. If it is to be measured, whether quantitatively or qualitatively, there must be some idea of where an organization is compared to where it ought to be. To state where an organization ought to be is to set a standard. A standard takes shape as a projection of hoped-for or budgeted performance. As time passes, positive and negative variances between budgeted and actual performance are recorded. This comparison makes possible, although it does not necessarily justify, relating incentives and controls to performance as measured against standards. For example, managers in the Hilton Hotels group prepare detailed forecasts of their anticipated revenues, costs, and operating profits, all based on past records and future projections that take growth targets into account. The reward system recognizes not only good results but accuracy of forecasting.

It is virtually impossible to make meaningful generalizations about how proper standards might be set in particular companies. It can be said, however, that in any organization the overall strategy can be translated into more or less detailed future plans (the detail becoming less predictable as the time span grows longer), which permit comparison of actual with predicted performance. Whether standards are being set at exactly the proper level is less significant than the fact that an effort is being made to raise them steadily as organizational power and resources increase. External events may, however, invalidate predictions. It must be recognized that for good reasons as well as bad, standards are not always attainable. Hence the need for skill in variable budgeting.

By far the most important problem of measurement is that increased interest in the measurement of performance against standards brings increased danger that the executive evaluation program may encourage performance which detracts from rather than supports the overall strategy.

The temptation to use measurement primarily for the purpose of judging executive performance is acute. The desire to put management responsibility in the ablest hands leads to comparing managers in terms of results. Failure to meet a standard leads naturally to the assignment of blame to persons. The general manager's most urgent duty is to see that planned results are indeed accomplished. Such pressure, unfortunately, may lead to exaggerated respect for specific measures and for the short-run results they quantify, and thus to ultimate misevaluation of performance.

Fallacy of the single criterion

The problems of measurement cluster about the fallacy of the single criterion. When any single measure like return on investment, for example, is used to determine the compensation, promotion, or reassignment of a manager, the resultant behavior will often lead to unplanned and undesired outcomes. No single measure can encompass the total contribution of an individual either to immediate and longer term results or to the efforts of others. The sensitivity of individuals to evaluation leads them to produce the performance that will measure up in terms of the criterion rather than in terms of more important purposes. Since managers respond to the measures management actually takes to reward performance, mere verbal exhortations to behave in the manner required by long-range strategy carry no weight, and cannot be relied upon to preclude undesirable actions encouraged by a poorly designed measurement and reward system.

Faith in the efficacy of a standard measure like return on investment can reach extreme proportions, especially among managers to whom the idea of strategy is apparently unfamiliar. Instances in which performance is measured in terms of just one figure or ratio are so numerous as to suggest that the pursuit of quantification and measurement as such has overshadowed the real goal of management evaluation. If we return to our original hypothesis that profit and return on investment are terms that can be usefully employed to denote the results to be sought by business, but are too general to characterize its distinctive mission or purpose, then we must say that *short-term profitability is not by itself an adequate measure of managerial performance.* Return on investment, when used alone, is another dangerous criterion, since it can lead businessmen to postpone needed product research or the modernization of facilities in the interest of keeping down the investment on the basis of which their performance is measured. Certainly we must conclude that evaluation of performance must not be focused exclusively upon the criterion of short-run profitability or any other single standard which may cause managers to act contrary to the long-range interests of the company as a whole.

Need for multiple criteria

As you discuss the cases that follow, you will be concerned with developing more adequate criteria. Our concern for strategy naturally leads us to suggest that the management evaluation system which plays so great a part in influencing management performance must employ a number of criteria, some of which are subjective and thus difficult to quantify. It is easy to argue that subjective judgments are unfair. But use of a harmful or irrelevant criterion just because it lends itself to quantification is a poor exchange for alleged objectivity.

Against multiple criteria, it may be argued that they restrict the freedom of the profit-center manager to produce the results required through any means he elects. This may of course be true, but the manager who does not want his methods to be subject to scrutiny does not want to be judged. Accountants, sometimes indifferent to the imperfections of their figures and the artificiality of their conventions, do not always make clear the true meaning of an annual profit figure or the extent to which a sharp rise from one year to the next may reflect a decision not to make investments needed to sustain the future of a product line.

If multiple criteria are to be used, it is not enough for top management simply to announce that short-term profitability and return on investment are only two measures among many—including responsibility to society—by which executives are going to be judged. To give subordinates freedom to exercise judgment and simultaneously to demand profitability produces an enormous pressure which cannot be effectively controlled by endless talk about tying rewards to factors other than profit.

The tragic predicament of people who, though upright in other ways, engage in bribery, "questionable payments," price fixing, and subtler forms of corruption, and of their superiors who are often unaware of these practices, should dramatize one serious flaw of the profit center form of organization. Characteristically management expects this format to solve the problems of evaluation by decentralizing freedom of decision to subordinates so long as profit objectives are met. Decentralization seems sometimes to serve as a cloak for nonsupervision, except for the control implicit in the superficial measure of profitability. It would appear to preclude accurate evaluation, and the use of multiple criteria may indeed make a full measure of decentralization inappropriate.

Effective evaluation of performance

To delegate authority to profit centers and to base evaluation upon proper performance must not mean that the profit center's strategic decisions are left unsupervised. *Even under decentralization, top management must remain familiar with divisional substrategy, with the fortunes—good and bad—that attend implementation, and with the problems involved in attempting to achieve budgeted performance.* The true function of measurement is to increase perceptions of the problems limiting achievement. If an individual sees where he stands in meeting a schedule, he may be led to inquire why he is not somewhere else. If this kind of question is not asked, the answer is not proffered. An effective system of evaluation must include information which will allow top management to understand the problems faced by subordinates in achieving the results for which they are held responsible. And certainly if evaluation is to be comprehensive enough to avoid the distortions cited thus far, immediate results will not be the only object of evaluation. The effectiveness with which problems are handled along the way will be evaluated, even though this judgment, like most of the important decisions of management, must remain subjective.

The process of formulating and implementing strategy, which is supervised directly by the chief executive in a single-unit company, can be shared widely in a multiunit company. It can be the theme of the information exchanged between organization levels. Preoccupation with final results need not be so exclusive as to prevent top management from working with divisional management in establishing objectives and policies or in formulating plans to meet objectives. Such joint endeavor helps to ensure that divisional performance will not be evaluated without full knowledge of the problems encountered in implementation.

When the diversified company becomes so large that this process is impracticable, then new means must be devised. *Implicit in accurate evaluation is familiarity with performance on a basis other than through accounting figures.*

The division of corporate strategy into substrategies appropriate to each organization unit makes possible a meaningful "management by objectives" program. As superior and subordinate agree to the achievements which the subordinate will try to accomplish during the forthcoming year, priorities are dictated by strategy. The selection of objectives can be checked for the contribution they will make to the larger strategy of which they must be a part. The opportunity to discuss the relevance of a conventional objective to the total purpose of the effort undertaken can be invaluable in reconciling strategy and motivation. Quantitatively unmeasurable tasks, as well as budget items, can be included in the individual's own program of action. The concept of strategy encompassing the grand purposes of the entire firm can be brought down through each discussion to a limited strategy to guide and permit evaluation of individual effort.

A shared interest in the problems to be overcome in successfully implementing individual strategy makes possible a kind of communication, an accuracy of evaluation, and a constructive influence on behavior that cannot be approached by application of a single criterion. For one manager as for a whole company, the quality of objective and of subsequent attempts to overcome obstacles posed by circumstance and by competition is the most important aspect of a manager's performance to be evaluated.

MOTIVATION AND INCENTIVE SYSTEMS

The influences upon behavior in any organization are visible and invisible, planned and unplanned, formal and not formal. The intent to measure affects the performance which is the object of measurement; cause and effect obscure each other. The executive who refuses to leave the implementation of strategy to chance has available diverse means of encouraging behavior which advances strategy and deterring behavior which does not. The positive elements, always organized in patterns which make them influential in given situations, may be designated as motivation and incentive systems. The negative elements, similarly patterned, can be grouped as systems of restraint and control. Organization studies have led their authors variously to prefer positive or negative signals and to conclude that one or the other is preferable. The general manager will do well to conclude that each is indispensable.

Executive compensation

Whatever the necessity for and the difficulties of performance evaluation, the effort to encourage and reward takes precedence over the effort to deter and restrain. Thus, properly directed, incentives may have more positive effects than control. Certainly, general manager-strategists, whose own prior experiences are likely to have made them intensely interested in the subject of executive compensation, should welcome whatever guidance they can get from researchers or staff assistants working in the field of job evaluation and compensation. Unfortunately, here also the prevailing thinking is often oriented less toward the goals to be sought than toward the requirements of the systems adopted.

Executives, like workers, are influenced by nonmonetary as well as financial incentives. At the same time, financial rewards are very important, and much thought has been given to equitable compensation of executives.

Unfortunately for the analyst of executive performance, it is harder to describe for executives than for operators at the machine what they do and how they spend their time. The terminology of job descriptions is full of phrases like "has responsibility for," "maintains relationships with," and "supervises the operation of." The activities of planning, problem solving, and directing or administering are virtually invisible. And the activities of recruiting, training, and developing subordinates are hardly more concretely identifiable.

In any case, it is fallacious to assume that quality of performance is the only basis for the compensation of executives. Many other factors must be taken into account. The job itself has certain characteristics that help to determine the pay schedules. These include complexity of the work, the general education required, and the knowledge or technical training needed. Compensation also reflects the responsibility of job incumbents for people and property, the nature and number of decisions they must make, and the effect of their activities and decisions upon profits.

In addition to reflecting the quality of performance and the nature of the job, an executive's compensation must also have some logical relationship to rewards paid to others in the same organization. That is, the compensation system must reflect in some way a person's position in the hierarchy. On any one ladder there must be suitable steps between levels from top to bottom, if incentive is to be provided and increased scope recognized. At the same time, adjustments must be made to reflect the varying contributions that can be expected from individuals in the hierarchy of the staff versus that of the line.

Furthermore, in a compensation system, factors pertaining to the individual are almost as important as those pertaining to performance, the job, or the structure of the organization. People's age and length of service, the state of their health, some notion of their future potential, some idea of their material needs, and some insight into their views about all of these should influence either the amount of total pay or the distribution of total pay among base salary, bonuses, stock options, and other incentive measures.

Besides the many factors already listed, still another set of influences—this time coming from the environment—ordinarily affects the level of executive compensation. Included here are regional differences in the cost of living, the increments allowed for overseas assignment, the market price of given qualifications and experience, the level of local taxation, the desire for tax avoidance or delay, and the effect of high business salaries on other professions.

Just as multiple criteria are appropriate for the evaluation of performance, so many considerations must be taken into account in the compensation of executives. The company which says it pays only for results does not know what it is doing.[1]

Role of incentive pay

In addition to the problem of deciding what factors to reward, there is the equally complex issue of deciding what forms compensation should take. We would emphasize that financial rewards are especially important in business, and no matter how great the enthusiasm of people for their work, attention to the level of executive salary is an important ingredient in the achievement of strategy. Even after the desired standard of living is attained, money is still an effective incentive. Businessmen used to the struggle for profit find satisfaction in their own growing net worth.

There is no question about the desirability of paying high salaries for work of great value. Yet until recently, it was clearly social policy in the United States, as elsewhere, that executive take-home pay be kept at a modest ceiling. As a consequence, profit sharing, executive bonuses, stock options, performance shares, stock purchase plans, de-

---

[1] See Malcolm S. Salter and K. R. Srinivasa Murthy, "Should CEO Pay Be Linked to Results?" *Harvard Business Review,* May–June 1975, pp. 66–73.

ferred compensation contracts, pensions, insurance, savings plans, and other fringe benefits have multiplied enormously. They have been directed not so much toward providing incentive as toward enabling executives to avoid high taxes on current income. It is as incentives, however, that these various devices should be judged. Regarded as incentives to reward *individual* performance, many of these devices encounter two immediate objections, quite aside from the ethics of their tax-avoidance features. First, how compatible are the assumptions back of such rewards with the aspirations of the businessman to be viewed as a professional person? The student who begins to think of business as a profession will wonder what kind of executive will perform better with a profit-sharing bonus than with an equivalent salary. We may ask whether doctors should be paid according to the longevity of their patients and whether surgeons would try harder if given a bonus when their patients survived an operation. Second, how feasible is it to distinguish any one individual's contribution to the total accomplishment of the company? And even if contribution could be distinguished and correctly measured, what about the implications of the fact that the funds available for added incentive payments are a function of total rather than of individual performance? In view of these considerations, it can at least be argued that incentives for individual performance reflect dubious assumptions.

If, then, incentives are ruled out as an inappropriate or impractical means of rewarding individual effort, should they be cast out altogether? We believe not. There is certainly some merit in giving stock options or performance shares to the group of executives most responsible for strategy decisions, if the purpose is to assure reward for attention to the middle and longer run future.[2] There is some rationale for giving the same group current or even deferred bonuses, the amount of which is tied to annual profit, if the purpose is to motivate better cost control— something surprisingly difficult to do in a business environment marked by inflation, booming sales, and high income taxes. Certainly, too, incentive payments to the key executive group must be condoned where needed to attract and hold the scarce managerial talent without which any strategy will suffer.

In any case, as you examine the effort made by companies to provide adequate rewards, to stimulate effective executive performance, and to inspire commitment to organizational purposes, you will wish to look closely at the relation between the incentive offered and the kind of performance needed. This observation holds as true, of course, for nonmonetary as it does for financial rewards.

Nonmonetary incentives

The area of nonmonetary incentive systems is even more difficult to traverse quickly than that of financial objectives. Executives, as human as other employees, are as much affected as anyone else by pride

---

[2] G. H. Foote, "Performance Shares Revitalize Stock Plans," *Harvard Business Review,* November–December 1973, pp. 121–30.

in accomplishment, the climate for free expression, pleasure in able and honest associates, and satisfaction in work worth doing.

They are said to be moved also by status symbols like office carpets, thermos sets, or office location and size. The trappings of rank and small symbols of authority are too widely cultivated to be regarded as unimportant, but little is known of their real influence. If individual contribution to organized effort is abundantly clear, little attention is likely to be given to status symbols. For example, the R&D executive with the greatest contributions to the product line may favor the "reverse status symbol" of the lab technician's cotton jacket. This is not to say that symbols have no potentially useful role to play. Office decor, for example, can be used to symbolize strategy, as when a company introduces abstract art into its central office to help dramatize its break with the past.

Very little systematic work has been done to determine what incentives or company climate might be most conducive to executive creativity, executive commitment to forward planning, executive dedication to the training of subordinates, executive striving for personal development and growth, or commitment to high standards of personal and corporate integrity. All these are of utmost value, but their impact is longrun and in part intangible. It is well known, however, that the climate most commonly extolled by managers is one where they have freedom to experiment and apply their own ideas without unnecessary constraints. This type of positive incentive is particularly suited for use in combination with the "management-by-objectives" approach to the problem of executive evaluation. Given clear objectives and a broad consensus, then latitude can be safely granted to executives to choose their own course—so long as they do not conceal the problems they encounter. In other words, executives can be presumed to respond to the conditions likely to encourage the goal-oriented behavior expected of them.

We may not always know the influence exerted by evaluation, compensation, and advancement, but if we keep purpose clear and incentive systems simple, we may keep unintended distractions to a minimum. Above all, we should be able to see the relevance to desired outcomes of the rewards offered. The harder it is to relate achievement to motives, the more cautious we should be in proposing an incentives program.

SYSTEMS OF RESTRAINT AND CONTROL

Like the system of incentives, the system of restraints and controls should be designed with the requirements of strategy in mind, rather than the niceties of complex techniques and procedures. It is the function of penalties and controls to enforce rather than to encourage—to inhibit strategically undesirable behavior rather than to create new patterns. Motivation, as we have said, is a complex of both positive and negative influences. Working in conjunction, these induce desired performance and inhibit undesirable behavior.

The need for controls—even at the executive level—is rooted in the central facts of organization itself. The inevitable consequence of divided activity is the emergence of substrategies, which are at least slightly deflected from the true course by the needs of individuals and the concepts and procedures of specialized groups, each with its own quasi-professional precepts and ideals. We must have controls, therefore, even in healthy and competent organizations manned by people of goodwill who are aware of organization purpose.

Formal control

Like other aspects of organizational structure and processes, controls may be both formal and informal, that is, both prescribed and emergent. Both types are needed, and both are important. It is, however, in the nature of things that management is more likely to give explicit attention to the formal controls that it has itself prescribed than to the informal controls emergent within particular groups or subgroups.

Formal and informal controls differ in nature as well as in their genesis. The former have to do with data that are quantifiable, the latter with subjective values and behavior. Formal control derives from accounting; it reflects the conventions and assumptions of that discipline and implies the prior importance of what can be quantified over what cannot. Its influence arises from the responsiveness of individuals—if subject to supervision and appraisal—to information that reveals variances between what is recorded as being expected of them and what is recorded as being achieved. If the information depicts variances from strategically desirable behavior, then it tends to direct attention toward strategic goals and to support goal-oriented policy. But if, as is more often the case, the information simply focuses on those short-run results which the state of the art can measure, then it directs effort toward performance which, if not undesirable, is at least biased toward short-run objectives.

To emphasize the probable shortcomings of formal or quantifiable controls is not to assert that they have no value. Numbers do influence behavior—especially when pressures are applied to subordinates by superiors contemplating the same numbers. Numbers are essential in complex organizations, since personal acquaintance with what is being accomplished and personal surveillance over it by an owner-manager is no longer possible. As we have seen, the performance of individuals and subunits cannot be left to chance, even when acceptance and understanding of policy have been indicated and adequate competence and judgment are assured. Whether for surveillance from above or for self-control and self-guidance, numbers have a meaningful role to play, and well-selected numbers have a very meaningful role. We in no way mean to diminish the importance of figures, but only to emphasize that figures must be supplemented by informal or social controls.

Integrating formal and social control

Just as the idea of formal control is derived from accounting, the idea of informal control is derived from the inquiries of the behavioral sciences into the nature of organizational behavior. In all functioning groups, norms develop to which individuals are responsive if not obedient. These norms constitute the accepted way of doing things; they define the limits of proper behavior, and the type of action that will meet with approval from the group. In view of the way they operate, the control we have in mind is better described as *social* rather than *informal.* It is embedded in the activities, interactions, and sentiments characterizing group behavior. Sentiments take the form of likes and dislikes among people and evaluative judgments exercised upon each other. Negative sentiments, of great importance to their objects, may be activated by individual departure from a norm; such sentiments can either constitute a punishment in themselves, or can lead to some other form of punishment.

The shortcomings of formal control based on quantitative measurements of performance can be largely obviated by designing and implementing a system in which formal and social controls are integrated. For example, meetings of groups of managers to discuss control reports can facilitate inquiry into the significance of problems lying behind variances, can widen the range of solutions considered, and can bring pressure to bear from peers as well as from superiors. All these features can in turn contribute to finding a new course of action which addresses the problem rather than the figures.

Enforcing ethical standards

One of the most vexing problems in attempting to establish a functional system of formal and social controls lies in the area of ethical standards. In difficult competitive situations, the pressure for results can lead individuals into illegal and unethical practices. Instead of countering this tendency, group norms may encourage yielding to these pressures. For example, knowing that others were doing the same thing undoubtedly influenced foreign representatives of several aircraft companies to bribe government officials to secure contracts. Recurring violations of price-fixing regulations, in industries beset by overcapacity and aggressive competition, are sometimes responses to pressures to meet sales and profit expectations of a distant home office. On a lesser scale group norms can be supportive of suppliers making expensive gifts to purchasing agents, or to sales representatives offering extravagant entertainment to customers. The post-Watergate climate of the middle and late 1970s has modified sharply the general attitude toward long-established dubious practices. The environment is at least temporarily favorable to maintaining high ethical standards.

When top management refuses to condone pursuit of company goals by unethical methods, it must resort to penalties like dismissal that are severe enough to dramatize its opposition. If a division sales manager, who is caught having arranged call-girl attentions for an important customer, against both the standards of expected behavior and the policy of the company, is not penalized at all, or only mildly, because of the volume of his sales and the profit he generates, ethical standards will not long be of great importance. If he is fired, then his successor is likely to think twice about the means he employs to achieve the organizational purposes that are assigned to him. When, as happened in mid-

1977, a regional vice président of a large insurance firm was fired for misappropriating $250,000 of expense money, but was retained as a consultant because he controlled several millions of revenue, mixed signals are given which may confuse the communication but call attention to the dilemmas of enforcement. In due course the Internal Revenue Service may add an unambiguous comment on this transaction.

But there are limits to the effectiveness of punishment, in companies as well as in families and in society. If violations are not detected, the fear of punishment tends to weaken. A system of inspection is therefore implicit in formal control. But besides its expense and complexity, such policing of behavior has the drawback of adversely affecting the attitudes of people toward their organizations. Their commitment to creative accomplishment is likely to be shaken, especially if they are the kinds of persons who are not likely to cut corners in the performance of their duties. To undermine the motivation of the ethically inclined is a high price to pay for detection of the weak. It is the special task of the internal audit function and the audit committee of the corporate board of directors not only to make investigation more effective but to minimize its negative police-state connotations and distortions.

The student of general management is thus confronted by a dilemma: if an organization is sufficiently decentralized to permit individuals to develop new solutions to problems and new avenues to corporate achievement, then the opportunity for wrongdoing cannot be eliminated. This being so, a system of controls must be supplemented by a selective system of executive recruitment and training. No system of control, no program of rewards and penalties, no procedures of measuring and evaluating performance can take the place of the individual who has a clear idea of right and wrong, a consistent personal policy, and the strength to stand the gaff when results suffer because he or she stands firm. This kind of person is different from the human animal who grasps at every proffered reward and flinches at every punishment. His or her development is greatly assisted by the systems, standards, rewards, incentives, penalties, and controls which permit the application of qualitative criteria and avoid the oversimplification of numerical measures. It is always the way systems are administered that determines their ultimate usefulness and impact.

RECRUITMENT AND DEVELOPMENT OF MANAGEMENT

Organizational behavior, in the view we have just taken of it, is the product of interacting *systems* of measures, motives, standards, incentives, rewards, penalties, and controls. Put another way, behavior is the outcome of *processes* of measurement, evaluation, motivation, and control. These systems and processes affect and shape the development of all individuals, most crucially those in management positions. Management development is therefore an ongoing process in all organizations, whether planned or not. As you examine cases which permit a wide-angled view of organizational activities, it is appropriate to inquire into the need to plan this development, rather than to let it occur as it will.

In days gone by, before it was generally realized that relying on a consciously designated corporate strategy was far safer and more productive than simply trusting to good luck, a widely shared set of assumptions operated to inhibit the emergence of management development programs. These assumptions, which include the implication that managers are all male, have been described as follows:

1. Good management is instinct in action. A number of men are born with the qualities of energy, shrewdness of judgment, ambition, and capacity for responsibility. These men become the leaders of business.
2. A man prepares himself for advancement by performing well in his present job. The man who does best in competition with his fellows is best qualified to lead them.
3. If an organization does not happen to have adequate numbers of men with innate qualities of leadership who are equal to higher responsibilities, it may bring in such persons from other companies.
4. Men with the proper amount of ambition do not need to be "motivated" to demonstrate the personal qualities which qualify them for advancement.
5. Management cannot be taught formally—in school or anywhere else.[3]

The ideas that we have been examining here suggest that these assumptions are obsolete. People are, of course, born with different innate characteristics, but none of these precludes acquiring knowledge, attitudes, and skills which fill the gap between an identifiable personality trait and executive action. Good performance in lesser jobs is expected of persons considered for bigger jobs, but different and additional qualifications are required for higher responsibility. Thus the most scholarly professor, the most dexterous machine operator, and the most persuasive sales representative do not necessarily make a good college president, foreman, and sales manager. The abilities that make the difference can be learned from experience or to some extent from formal education. As a substitute for training and supplying the requisite experience internally, companies can import managers trained by competitors, but this approach, though sometimes unavoidable, is risky and expensive. The risk lies in the relative difficulty of appraising the quality of outsiders and estimating their ability to transfer their technical effectiveness to a new organization. The cost lies chiefly in the disruption of natural internal incentive systems.

The supply of men and women who, of their own volition, can or will arrange for their own development is smaller than required. Advances in technology, the internationalization of markets, and the progress of research on information processing and organizational behavior all make it absurd to suppose that persons can learn all they will need to know from what they are currently doing. In particular, the activities of the general manager differ so much in kind from those of other management that special preparation for the top job should be considered, unless it is demonstrably impossible.

The success of company-sponsored and university management train-

---

[3] K. R. Andrews, *The Effectiveness of University Management Development Programs* (Boston: Division of Research, Harvard Graduate School of Business Administration, 1966), p. 232.

ing programs is evidence that the old idea that managers are born not made has been displaced by the proposition that managers are born with capacities which can be developed. In the process of seeing to it that the company is adequately manned to implement its strategy, we can identify training requirements. In other words, strategy can be our guide to (1) the skills which will be required to perform the critical tasks; (2) the number of persons with specific skill, age, and experience characteristics who will be required in the light of planned growth and predicted attrition; and (3) the number of new individuals of requisite potential who must be recruited to ensure the availability, at the appropriate time, of skills that require years to develop.

Advanced recruitment

No matter what the outcome of these calculations, it can safely be said that every organization must actively recruit new talent if it aims to maintain its position and to grow. These recruits should have adequate ability not only for filling the junior positions to which they are initially called but also for learning the management skills needed to advance to higher positions. Like planning of all kinds, recruiting must be done well ahead of the actual need.

Men and women with the ultimate capacity to become general managers should be sought out in their 20s, for able people today in a society in which the level of education as well as economic means is rising rapidly are looking more for careers than jobs. Companies should recruit—not meeting the needs for specific skills alone but making an investment in the caliber of executives who in 25 years will be overseeing activities not even contemplated at the time of their joining the company.

One of the principal impediments to effective execution of plans is shortage of management manpower of the breadth required at the time required. This shortage is the result of faulty planning, not of a natural scarcity of good raw material. Consider the bank that wishes to open 50 branches overseas as part of its international expansion. It will not be able to export and replace 50 branch managers unless, years earlier, deliberate attention has been given to securing and to training banker-administrators. These are not technicians who know only credit, for example; they must know how to preside over an entire if small bank, learn and speak a foreign language, establish and maintain relationships with a foreign government, and provide banking services not for an exclusively American but for a different group of individual and corporate customers.

After successful recruitment of candidates with high potential, speeding the course of management development is usually the only way to keep manpower planning in phase with the requirements of strategy. Thus the recruit should be put to work at a job which uses the abilities he has and challenges him to acquire the knowledge he lacks about the company and industry:

> For [people] educated in this generation sweeping out the stockroom or carrying samples to the quality control laboratory are inappropriate unless these activities demand their level of education or will teach them

something besides humility. To introduce the school-trained men [and women] of high promise to everyday affairs may mean the devising of jobs which have not existed hitherto. Expansion of analytical sections and accounting and financial departments, projects in market research, rudimentary exploratory investigations in new products departments, process control or data processing projects are all work which will use school-taught techniques and yet require practical and essential exposure to the company and solutions to the problem of establishing working relationships with old hands.[4]

The labor force requirements imposed by commitment to a strategy of growth mean quite simply that men and women overqualified for conventional beginning assignments must be sought out and carefully cultivated thereafter. Individuals who respond well to the opportunities devised for them should be assigned to established organization positions and given responsibility as fast as capacity to absorb it is indicated. To promote rapidly is not the point so much as to maintain the initial momentum and to provide work to highly qualified individuals that is both essential and challenging.

Continuing education

The rise of professional business education and the development of advanced management programs make formal training available to men and women not only at the beginning of their careers but also at appropriate intervals thereafter. Short courses for executives are almost always stimulating and often of permanent value. But management development as such is predominantly an organizational process which must be supported, not thwarted, by the incentive and control systems to which we have already alluded. Distribution of rewards and penalties will effectively determine how much attention executives will give to the training of their subordinates. No amount of lip service will take the place of action in establishing effective management development as an important management activity. To evaluate managers in part on their effort and effectiveness in bringing along their juniors requires subjective measures and a time span longer than one fiscal year. These limitations do not seriously impede judgment, especially when both strategy and the urgency of its implications for manpower development are clearly known.

In designing on-the-job training, a focus on strategy makes possible a substantial economy of effort, in that management development and management evaluation can be carried on together. The evaluation of performance can be simultaneously administered as an instrument of development. For example, any manager could use a conference with his superiors not only to discuss variances from budgeted departmental performance but also to discover how far his or her suggested solutions are appropriate or inappropriate and why. In all such cases, discussion of objectives proposed, problems encountered, and results obtained pro-

---

[4] Ibid., pp. 240–41.

vide opportunities for inquiry, for instruction and counsel, for learning what needs to be done and at what level of effectiveness.

Besides providing an ideal opportunity for learning, concentration on objectives permits delegation to juniors of choice of means and other decision-making responsibilities otherwise hard to come by. Throughout the top levels of the corporation, if senior management is spending adequate time on the surveillance of the environment and on the study of strategic alternatives, then the responsibility for day-to-day operations must necessarily be delegated. Since juniors cannot learn how to bear responsibility without having it, this necessity is of itself conducive to learning. If, within limits, responsibility for the choice of means to obtain objectives is also delegated, opportunity is presented for innovation, experimentation, and creative approaches to problem solving. Where ends rather than means are the object of attention and agreement exists on what ends are and should be, means may be allowed to vary at the discretion of the developing junior manager. The clearer the company's goals, the smaller the emphasis that must be placed on uniformity, and the greater the opportunity for initiative. Freedom to make mistakes and achieve success is more productive in developing executive skills than practice in following detailed how-to-do-it instructions designed by superiors or staff specialists. Commitment to purpose rather than to procedures appears to energize initiative.

Management development and corporate purpose

A stress on purpose rather than on procedures suggests that organizational climate, though intangible, is more important to individual growth than the mechanisms of personnel administration. The development of each individual in the direction best suited both to his or her own powers and to organizational needs is most likely to take place in the company where everybody is encouraged to work at the height of his or her ability and is rewarded for doing so. Such a company must have a clear idea of what it is and what it intends to become. With this idea sufficiently institutionalized so that organization members grow committed to it, the effort required for achievement will be forthcoming without elaborate incentives and coercive controls. Purpose, especially if considered worth accomplishing, is the most powerful incentive to accomplishment. If goals are not set high enough, they must be reset—as high as developing creativity and accelerating momentum suggest.

In short, from the point of view of general management, management development is not a combination of staff activities and formal training designed to provide neophites with a common body of knowledge, or to produce a generalized good manager. Rather, development is inextricably linked to organizational purpose, which shapes to its own requirements the kind, rate, and amount of development which takes place. It is a process by which men and women are professionally equipped to be—as far as possible in advance of the need—what the evolving strategy of the firm requires them to be, at the required level of excellence.

Chief executives will have a special interest of their own in the process of management development. For standards of performance, measures for accurate evaluation, incentives, and controls will have a lower priority in their eyes than a committed organization, manned by people who know what they are supposed to do and committed to the overall ends to which their particular activities contribute. Senior managers are not blind to the needs of their subordinates to serve their own purposes as well as those of the organization. Wherever conflicting claims are made upon their attention, they require that reconciliation be found that does not obscure organizational objectives or slow down the action being taken to attain them.

* * * * *

In examining the cases that follow, try to identify the strategy of the company and the structure of relationships established to implement it. Note the standards that have been established for measurement purposes. Are they appropriate for measuring the progress of the organization toward its goals? Is the way performance is measured likely to assist or impede constructive behavior? What pattern of possible incentives encouraging appropriate behavior can be identified? Do they converge on desired outcomes? What restraints and controls discouraging inappropriate behavior are in force? What changes in measurement, incentive, and control systems would you recommend to facilitate achievement of goals? If your analysis of the company's situation suggests that strategy and structure should be changed, such recommendations should, of course, precede your suggested plans for effective implementation.

Basic Industries

In May 1966, Pete Adams, plant manager of Basic Industries' Chicago plant, was worried about the new facilities proposal for toranium. His division, metal products, was asking for $1 million to build facilities which would be at full capacity in less than a year and a half (if forecasted sales were realized). Yet the divisional vice president for production seemed more interested in where the new facility was to go than in how big it should be. Adams wondered how, as plant manager, his salary and performance review would look in 1968 with the new facility short of capacity.

BASIC INDUSTRIES, METAL PRODUCTS DIVISION

Basic Industries engaged in a number of activities ranging from shipbuilding to the manufacture of electronic components. The corporation was organized into five autonomous divisions (see Exhibit 1). In 1965 these divisions had sales totaling $500 million. Of the five, the metal products division was the most profitable. In 1965, this division realized an after-tax income of $16 million on sales of $110 million and an investment of $63.7 million.

This position of profit leadership within the company had not always been held by metal products. In fact, in the early 1950s, Basic's top management had considered dropping the division. At that time, the division's market share was declining owing to a lack of manufacturing facilities, high costs, and depressed prices.

A change in divisional management resulted in a marked improvement. Between 1960 and 1965, for example, the division's sales grew at 8% a year and profits at 20% a year. The division's ROI during this period rose from 12% in 1960 to 25% in 1965.

Ronald Brewer, president of metal products division since 1955, explained how this growth had been achieved:

Exhibit 1

ORGANIZATION CHART FOR BASIC INDUSTRIES

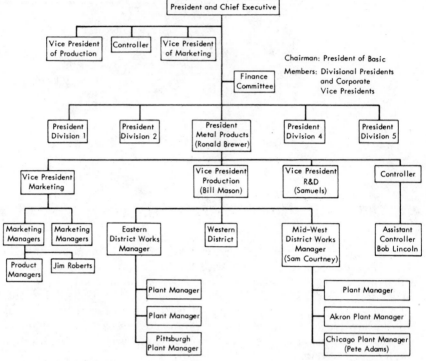

Source: Casewriter's notes.

Planning goes on in many places in the Metal Products Division, but we do go through a formal planning process to establish goals. We establish very specific goals for products and departments in every phase of the business. This formal and detailed planning is worked out on a yearly basis. We start at the end of the second quarter to begin to plan for the following year.

We plan on the basis of our expectations as to the market. If it's not there, we live a little harder. We cut back to assure ourselves of a good cash flow. Our record has been good, but it might not always be. Some of our products are 30 years old. We've just invested $5 million, which is a lot of money for our division, in expanding capacity for a 25-year-old product. But we're making money out of it and it's growing.

Along with detailed planning for the year to come, we ask for plans for years three and four. Our goal is to make sure that we can satisfy demand. Any time we approach 85% of capacity at one of our plants, our engineers get busy.

They will give the plant manager the information as to what he needs in the way of new equipment. The plant manager will then fit the engineer's recommendation into his expansion plans. The plant manager's plan then goes to our control manager. The marketing people then add their forecasts, and by that time we have built up the new facilities proposal. On the other hand, the marketing people may have spearheaded the project. Sometimes they alert the plant manager to a rapid growth in his product and he goes to the engineers. In this division, everyone is marketing minded.

*   *   *   *   *

We measure plants, and they measure their departments against plan. For example, we have a rule of thumb that a plant must meet its cost reduction goals. So if one idea doesn't work out, a plant must find another one to get costs to the planned level. We make damned sure that we make our goals as a division. Our objective is to have the best product in the market at the lowest cost. It's a simple concept, but the simpler the concept, the better it's understood.

Well, on the basis of his performance against plan, a man is looked at by his superior at least once a year, maybe more. We take a pretty hardnosed position with a guy. We tell him what we think his potential is, where he is going to go, what he is going to be able to do. We have run guys up *and* down the ladder. In this division, it's performance and fact that count. We have no formal incentive plan but we do recognize performance with salary increases and with promotions.

You know, we have divisions in this company which are volume happy. We here are profit conscious. We had to be to survive. What I'd like to see is interest allocated on a pro rata basis according to total investment. I grant you that this would hurt some of the other divisions more than us, but I think that treating interest as a corporate expense, as we do, changes your marketing philosophy and your pricing philosophy.

For example, most new facilities proposals are wrong with respect to their estimates of market size—volume attainable at a given price— and timing. You can second-guess a forecast though, in several ways, and hedge to protect yourself. There is a feeling at Basic Industries that there is a stigma attached to coming back for more money. That means that if you propose a project at the bare minimum requirement and then come back for more, some people feel that you've done something wrong. Generally, this leads to an overestimate of the amount of capital required. It turns out that if you have the money you do spend it, so that this stigma leads to overspending on capital projects. We at metal products are trying to correct this. First, we screen projects closely. We go over them with a fine tooth comb. Second, internally, we set a goal to spend less than we ask for where there is a contingency.

Also, when a project comes in at an estimated 50% return, we cut the estimate down. Everyone does. The figure might go out at 30%. But this practice works the other way too. For example, in 1958 Bill Mason [metal products' vice president of production] and I worked like hell to get a project through. Although it looked like 8% on paper, we knew that we could get the costs way down once it got going, so we put it through at 12%. We're making double that on it today. We haven't had a capital request rejected by the finance committee [see Exhibit 1] in 8 years.

Of course, every once in a while we shoot some craps, but not too often. We are committed to a specific growth rate in net income and ROI. Therefore, we are selective in what we do and how we spend our money. It's seldom that we spend $500,000 to develop something until we know it's got real market potential. You just don't send 100 samples out and then forecast a flood of orders. New products grow slowly. It takes six or seven years. And given that it takes this long, it doesn't take a lot of capital to develop and test our new ideas. Before you really invest, you've done your homework. Over the years we've done a good job in our new products, getting away from the aircraft industry. In 1945, 70% of our business was based on aircraft. Today it's 40%. The way we do things protects us. We have to have a very strong sense of the technical idea and the scope of the market before we invest heavily.

The metal products division's main business was producing a variety of basic and rare nonferrous metals and alloys such as nickel, nickel-beryllium, and titanium in a myriad of sizes and shapes for electrical, mechanical, and structural uses in industry. One of the division's major strengths was its leadership in high-performance material technology. Through patents and a great deal of proprietary experience, metal products had a substantial technological lead on its competitors.

TORANIUM

In the late 1950s metal products decided to follow its technological knowledge and proprietary production skills into the high-performance materials market. One of metal products' most promising new materials was toranium, for which Jim Roberts was product manager (see Exhibit 1).

Roberts was 33 years old and had a Ph.D. in chemical engineering. Prior to becoming a product manager, he had worked in one of metal products' research laboratories. Roberts explained some of toranium's history:

Developing toranium was a trial-and-error process. The lab knew that the properties of the class of high performance materials to which toranium belonged were unusually flexible, and, therefore, felt such materials had to be useful. So it was an act of faith that led R.&D. to experiment with different combinations of these materials. They had no particular application in mind.

In 1957 we developed the first usable toranium. Our next problem was finding applications for it. It cost $50 a pound. However, since a chemist in the lab thought we could make it for less, we began to look for applications.

In 1962, I entered the picture.

I discovered it was an aerospace business. When the characteristics of our material were announced to the aerospace people, they committed themselves to it. Our competitors were asleep. They weren't going to the customer. I went out and called on the customers and developed sales.

In 1963, we decided to shift the pilot plant from the lab and give it to the production people at Akron. We decided that we simply were not getting a good production-oriented consideration of the process problems. The people at Akron cut the costs by two-thirds and the price stayed the same.

In 1963, I also chose to shut off R.&D. on toranium because it couldn't help in the market place. We had to learn more in the market place before we could use and direct R.&D.

I ought to mention that under the management system used by Mr. Samuels [vice president of R.&D.], the product manager, along with R.&D. and production, shares in the responsibility for monitoring and directing an R.&D. program. This arrangement is part of an attempt to keep everyone market-oriented.

From 1962 to 1965, sales of toranium increased from $250,000 a year to $1 million a year just by seeking them, and in 1965 we put R.&D. back in.

This material can't miss. It has a great combination of properties: excellent machinability, thermal shock resistance and heat insulation. Moreover, it is an excellent electrical conductor.

We can sell all that we can produce. Customers are coming to us with their needs. They have found that toranium's properties and our technical capabilities are superior to anything or anyone in the market.

Moreover, pricing has not been a factor in the development of markets to date. In fact, sales have been generated by the introduction of improved grades of toranium at premium prices. Presently, General Electric represents our only competition, but we expect that Union Carbide will be in the market place with competitive materials during the next few years. However, I don't expect anyone to be significantly competitive before 1968. Anyway, competition might actually help a little bit in expanding the market and stimulating the customers as well as in educating our own R.&D.

Now, if one assumes that no other corporation will offer significant competition to toranium until 1968, the only real uncertainty in our forecasts for toranium is related to metal products' technical and marketing abilities. R.&D. must develop the applications it is currently working on, and production will have to make them efficiently.

This production area can be a real headache. For example, R.&D. developed a toranium part for one of our fighter bombers. However, two out of three castings cracked. On the other hand, we've got the best skills in the industry with respect to high pressure casting. If we can't do it, no one can.

The final uncertainty is new demand. I've got to bring in new applications, but that shouldn't be a problem. You know, I've placed toranium samples with over 17 major customers. Can you imagine what will happen if even two or three of them pay off? As far as I'm concerned, if the forecasts for toranium are inaccurate, they're underestimates of future sales.

NEW FACILITIES PROPOSAL

Sam Courtney, district works manager (to whom the plant managers of the Chicago, Akron, and Indianapolis plants reported) explained the origin of the new toranium facilities proposal:

The product manager makes a forecast once a year, and when it comes time to make major decisions, he makes long-range forecasts. In January 1965, we were at 35% of the toranium pilot-plant capacity. At that time we said, "We have to know beyond 1966, we need a long-range forecast. Volume is beginning to move up."

The production control manager usually collects the forecasts.

Each year it is his responsibility to see where we are approaching 85% or 90% of capacity. When that is the case in some product line, he warns the production vice president. However, in this instance, toranium was a transition product and Akron (where the pilot plant was located) picked up the problem and told the manager of product forecasting that we were in trouble.

The long-range forecast that Courtney requested arrived at his office about March 1, 1965, and clearly indicated a need for new capacity. Moreover, Roberts' 1966 regular forecast, which was sent to production in October 1965, was 28% higher than the March long-range projection. It called for additional capacity by October 1966.

Courtney's first response was to request a new long-range forecast. He also authorized the Akron plant to order certain equipment on which there would be a long lead time. The district works manager explained, "It is obvious we are going to need additional capacity in a hurry, and the unique properties of toranium require special, made-to-order, equipment. We can't afford to lose sales. Producing toranium is like coining money."

At the same time, Courtney began discussions on the problem with Bill Mason, vice president of production for metal products. They decided that the Akron plant was probably the wrong location in which to expand the toranium business. Courtney commented, "There are 20 products being produced in Akron, and that plant cannot possibly give toranium the kind of attention it deserves. The business is a new one, and it needs to be cared for like a young child. They won't do that in a plant with many important large-volume products. We have decided over a period of years that Akron is too complex, and this seems like a good time to do something about it."

The two locations proposed as new sites for the toranium facilities were Pittsburgh and Chicago. Each was a one-product plant which "could use product diversification." While Pittsburgh seemed to be favored initially, Mason and Courtney were concerned that the toranium would be contaminated if it came in contact with the rather dirty products produced at Pittsburgh. Therefore, Courtney asked engineering to make studies of both locations.

The results of these initial studies were inconclusive. The Pittsburgh plant felt that the problem of contamination was not severe, and the economic differential between the locations was not substantial.

After the initial studies were completed, Roberts' new long-range forecast arrived. The following table compares this forecast with Roberts' previous long-range forecasts:

ACTUAL AND PROJECTED SALES
(dollars in millions)

Date of forecast	1965	1966	1967	1968	1969	1970	1971
March 1964	1.08	1.30	...	...	2.20	...	...
March 1965	1.17	1.40	1.60	...	...	2.80	...
March 1966	...	1.80	2.50	3.40	...	...	5.60
Actual	1.00	...	...	...	...	...	...

In response to this accelerating market situation, Courtney and Mason asked Adams (plant manager at Chicago) to make a "full-fledged study of the three locations" (Akron, Pittsburgh, and Chicago). At the same time, Mason told Brewer (president of metal products), "We're now about 90% certain that Chicago will be the choice. Associated with the newness of the material is a rapidly changing technology. . . . The metal products R.&D. center at Evanston is only ten minutes away. . . . Another important factor is Adams. Titanium honeycomb at Chicago was in real trouble. We couldn't even cover our direct costs. Adams turned it around by giving it careful attention. That's the kind of job toranium needs."

Peter Adams was 35 years old. He had worked for Basic since he graduated from college with a B.S. in engineering. After spending a year in the corporate college training program, Adams was assigned to the metal products division. There he worked as an assistant to the midwestern district manager for production. Before becoming Chicago plant manager in 1963, Adams had been the assistant manager at the same plant for two years.

In working through the financial data on the toranium project, Adams chose to compare the three sites with respect to internal rates of return. He made this comparison for the case where capacity was expanded to meet forecasted sales for 1967 ($2.5 million), the case where capacity was expanded to meet forecasted sales for 1971 ($5.6 million) and the case where capacity was expanded from $2.5 to $5.6 million. The results of Adams' analysis are summarized in the following table:

		Chicago	Pittsburgh	Akron
			(dollars in thousands)	
1.	Incremental capital investment for capacity through 1967.....	$ 980	$1,092	$ 765
	Internal rate of return......	34%	37%	45%
2.	Incremental capital investment for capacity through 1971.....	$1,342	$1,412	$1,272
	Internal rate of return......	52%	54%	55%
3.	Incremental capital investment to raise capacity from $2.5 to $5.6 million................	$ 710	$ 735	$ 740
	Internal rate of return......	45%	47%	46%

While the economics favored Akron, Adams was aware that Mason favored Chicago. This feeling resulted from conversations with Courtney about the toranium project. Courtney pointed out the importance of quality, service to customers, liaison with R.&D., and production flexibility to a new product like toranium. Furthermore, Courtney expressed the view that Chicago looked good in these respects, despite its cost disadvantage. Courtney also suggested that a proposal which asked for enough capacity to meet 1967 forecasted demand would have the best prospects for divisional acceptance.

By the end of April 1966, Adams' work had progressed far enough to permit preparation of a draft of a new facilities proposal recommending a Chicago facility. Except for the marketing story which he obtained from Roberts, he had written the entire text. On May 3, Adams brought the completed draft to New York for a discussion with Mason and Courtney. The meeting, which was quite informal, began with Adams reading his draft proposal aloud to the group. Mason and Courtney commented on the draft as he went along. Some of the more substantial comments are included in the following excerpts from the meeting.

Meeting on the draft proposal

ADAMS: We expect that production inefficiencies and quality problems will be encountered upon start-up of the new facility in Chicago. In order to prevent these problems from interfering with the growth of ·toranium, the new facilities for producing toranium powder, pressing ingots, and casting finished products will be installed in Chicago and operated until normal production efficiency is attained. At that time, existing Akron equipment will be transferred to the Chicago location. Assuming early approval of the project, Chicago will be in production in the first quarter of 1967, and joint Akron and Chicago operations will continue through September 1967. The Akron equipment will be transferred in October and November 1967, and Chicago will be in full operation in December 1967.

MASON: Wait a minute! You're not in production until the first quarter of 1967, and the forecasts say we are going to be short in 1966!

ADAMS: There is a problem in machinery order lag.

MASON: Have you ordered a press?

ADAMS: Yes, and we'll be moving by October.

MASON: Well, then, say you'll be in business in the last quarter of 1966. Look, Pete, this document has to be approved by Brewer and then the finance committee. If Chicago's our choice, we've got to *sell* Chicago. Let's put our best foot forward! The problem is to make it clear that on economics alone we would go to Akron . . . but you have to bring out the flaw in the economics: that managing 20 product lines, especially when you've got fancy products, just isn't possible.

COURTNEY: And you have a better building.

MASON: All of this should be in a table in the text. It ought to cover incremental cost, incremental investment, incremental expense, incremental ROI, and the building space. And Sam's right. Akron is a poor building; it's a warehouse. Pittsburgh is better for something like high-pressure materials. But out in Chicago you've got a multi-story building with more than enough space that is perfect for this sort of project.

COURTNEY: Pete, are we getting this compact enough for you?

MASON: Hey, why don't we put some sexy looking graphs in the thing? I don't know, but maybe we could plot incremental investment vs. incremental return for each location. See what you can do, Pete.

COURTNEY: Yes, that's a good idea.

* * * * *

MASON: Now, Pete, one other thing. You'll have to include discounted cash flow on the other two locations. Some of those guys [division and corporate top management] are going to look at just the numbers. You'll show them they're not too different.

* * * * *

MASON: The biggest discussion will be, "Why the hell move to Chicago?"

COURTNEY: You know, Pete, you should discuss the labor content in the product.

MASON: Good. We have to weave in the idea that it's a product with a low labor content and explain that this means the high Chicago labor cost will not hurt us.

ADAMS: One last item: Shouldn't we be asking for more capacity? Two-and-one-half million dollars only carries us through 1967.

MASON: Pete, we certainly wouldn't do this for one of our established products. Where our main business is involved, we build capacity in five-and ten-year chunks. But we have to treat toranium a little differently. The problem here is to take a position in the market. Competition isn't going to clobber us if we don't have the capacity to satisfy everyone. If the market develops, we can move quickly.

After the meeting, Courtney explained that he and Mason had been disappointed with Adams' draft and were trying to help him improve it without really "clobbering" him. "Adams' draft was weak. His numbers were incomplete and his argument sloppy. I've asked him to meet with Bob Lincoln [assistant controller for metal products] to discuss the proposal."

The result of Adams' five meetings with Lincoln was three more drafts of the toranium proposal. The numerical exhibits were revised for greater clarity. The text was revised to lessen the number of technical terms.

Adams, however, was still very much concerned with the appropriate size of the new facility. "Mason is only interested in justifying the location of the new facility!" Adams exclaimed. "We plan to sell \$5.6 million worth of toranium in 1971. Yet we're asking for only \$2.5 million worth of capacity. It's crazy! But, you know, I think Mason doesn't really care what capacity we propose. He just wants 'sexy looking graphs.' That's O.K. for him, because I'm the one who's going to get it in the neck in 1968. So far as I can see, Brewer has built his reputation by bringing this division from chronic under-capacity to a full-capacity, high ROI position."

The next step in the toranium facilities proposal was a formal presentation to the top management of metal products on June 2, 1966. There were two capital projects on the agenda. Brewer began the meeting by announcing that its purpose was to "discuss the proposals and decide if they were any good." He turned the meeting over to Mason, who, in turn, asked Adams to "take over and direct the meeting."

Adams proceeded by reading the draft proposal, after first asking for comments. He got halfway down the first page before Brewer interrupted.

BREWER: Let me stop you right here. You have told them [the proposal was aimed at Basic Industries' finance committee] the name, and you have told them how much money you want, but you haven't told them what the name means, and you haven't told them what the products are.

At this point a discussion began as to what the name of the project was going to be. The meeting then continued with Adams reading and people occasionally making comments on his English and on the text.

BREWER: Look, let's get this straight. What we are doing in this proposal is trying to tell them what it is we are spending their money on. That's what they want to know. Tell me about the electronic applications in that table you have there. I have to be able to explain them to the finance committee. I understand "steel" and "aerospace" but I don't understand "electronic applications" and I don't understand "electronic industry." I need some more specific words.

SAMUELS: [vice president of R.&D.]: Let me ask you a question which someone in the finance committee might ask. It's a nasty one. You forecast here that the industry sales in 1971 are going to be about $7 million, or maybe a little less. You think we are going to have 75% or 85% of this business. You also think we are going to get competition from G.E. and others. Do you think companies of that stature are going to be satisfied with sharing $1.5 million of the business? Don't you think that we may lose some of our market share?

This question was answered by Roberts and pursued by a few others. Essentially Roberts argued that the proprietary technology of the metal products division was going to be strong enough to defend its market share.

BREWER: Let me tell you about an item which is much discussed in the finance committee. They are concerned, and basically this involves other divisions, with underestimating the cost of investment projects. I think, in fact, that there was a request for additional funds on a project recently which was as large as our entire annual capital budget.[1] Second of all, as a result of the capital expenditure cutback, there was a tendency, and again it has been in other divisions, to cut back on or delay facilities. Now it's not really just the capital expenditure cutback that is the reason for their behavior. If they had been doing their planning, they should have been thinking about these expenditures five or six years ago, not two years ago. But they didn't do the estimates, or their estimates weren't correct, and now they are sold out on a lot of items and are buying products from other people and reselling them and not making any money. It's affecting the corporate earnings, so the environment in the finance committee today is very much (1) "Tell us how much you want, and tell us *all* that you want," and (2) "Give us a damned good return." Now I don't want us to get *sloppy*, but, Bill, if you need something, ask for it. And then make Pete meet his numbers.

ADAMS: Well, on this one, as I think you know, the machinery is already on order and we are sure that our market estimates are correct.

BREWER: Yes, I know that. I just mean that if you want something, then plan it right and tell them what you are going to need so you don't come back asking for more money six months later.

* * * * *

BREWER: I am going to need some words on competition. I am also going to need some words on why we are ready so soon on this project. We are asking for money now, and we say we are going to be in operation in the fourth quarter.

SAMUELS: Foresight (*followed by general laughter*).

MASON: Well, it's really quite understandable. This began last October when we thought we were going to expand at Akron. At that time, it was obvious that we needed capacity so we ordered some machines. Then as the

---

[1] Metal products division's capital budget in 1965 was $7.9 million.

thing developed, it was clear that there would be some other things we needed, and because of the timing lag we had to order them.

BREWER: OK . . . now another thing. Numerical control is hot as a firecracker in the finance committee. I am not saying that we should have it on this project, but you should be aware that the corporation is thinking a lot about it.

* * * * *

BREWER: [Much later on in the discussion.] There are really three reasons for moving. Why not state them?

1. You want to free up some space at Akron which you need.
2. There are 20 products at Akron, and toranium can't get the attention it needs.
3. You can get operating efficiencies if you move.

If you set it out, you can cut out all of this crap. You know, it would do you people some good if you read a facilities proposal[2] on something you didn't know beforehand. You really have to think about the guy who doesn't know what you're talking about. I read a proposal yesterday that was absolutely ridiculous. It had pounds per hour and tons per year and tons per month and tons per day and—except for the simplest numbers, which were in a table—all the rest were spread out through the story.

* * * * *

Adams indicated that he was disappointed with the meeting. Brewer seemed to him to be preoccupied with "words," and the topic of additional capacity never really came up. The only encouraging sign was Brewer's statement, "Tell us all that you want." But it seemed that all Mason "wanted" was $2.5 million worth of capacity.

Adams saw three possibilities open to him. First, he could ask for additional capacity.

This alternative meant that Adams would have to speak with Courtney and Mason. The Chicago plant manager viewed the prospect of such a conversation with mixed feelings. In the past, his relations with Courtney and Mason had been excellent. He had been able to deal with these men on an informal and relaxed level. However, the experience of drafting the toranium proposal left Adams a little uneasy. Courtney and Mason had been quite critical of his draft and had made him meet with Bob Lincoln in order to revise it. What would their reaction be if he were to request a reconsideration of the proposal at this late date? Moreover, what new data or arguments could he offer in support of a request for additional capacity?

On the other hand, Adams saw a formal request for additional capacity as a way of getting his feelings on the record. Even if his superiors refused his request, he would be in a better position with respect to the 1968 performance review. However, Adams wondered how his performance review would go if he formally requested and received additional capacity and the market did not develop as forecasted.

As his second alternative, Adams believed he could ask that the new facilities proposal specify that metal products would be needing more money for toranium facilities in the future.

---

[2] The finance committee reviewed approximately 190 capital requests in 1965.

This alternative did not pose the same problems as the first with respect to Courtney and Mason. Adams felt that saying more funds might be needed would be acceptable to Courtney and Mason, whereas asking for more might not be. However, the alternative introduced a new problem. Brewer had been quite explicit in insisting that the division ask for all that was needed so that it would not have to come back and ask for more in six months. To admit a possible need for additional funds, therefore, might jeopardize the entire project.

In spite of this problem, Adams felt that this alternative was the best one available. It was a compromise between his point of view and Mason's. If top management felt that the future of toranium was too uncertain, then why not ask for contingent funds? This would get Adams off the hook and still not actually increase metal products' real investment.

As his third alternative, Adams decided he could drop the issue and hope to be transferred or promoted before 1968.

Industrial Products, Inc.

ON APRIL 5, 1967, the finance committee of Industrial Products, Inc. approved its Equipment Division's capital request for $5.8 million to build a new plant for FIREGUARD, a line of fire protection equipment. However, in October 1967 Mr. Robert Kendall, Manager of the Chemical Process Department (see Exhibit 1), the department in which FIRE-GUARD was produced, was considering the possibility of killing the expansion project. Divisional pressure for improved departmental earnings and FIREGUARD's continued record of substantial operating losses argued for not using the appropriated capital funds. On the other hand, Kendall was well aware that many people in his department were committed to growing the FIREGUARD business and would be quite upset if the project were killed. The context in which Kendall had to make his decision was the following.

EQUIPMENT DIVISION, INDUSTRIAL PRODUCTS, INC.

Industrial Products, Inc. was founded in 1949 as a producer of refrigeration equipment. Since that time, the company had diversified its activities into areas such as material handling systems, machine tools, heavy industrial equipment, and laboratory instruments. In 1966, the company's sales were in excess of $350 million.

The Equipment Division was the largest of Industrial's divisions measured in terms of sales revenue. In 1966, the Equipment Division's sales were $135.4 million and its net income before taxes was $31.2 million on an investment of $96.5 million. FIREGUARD, the division's new fire protection line, contributed sales of $2.2 million but produced a net loss before taxes of $1.1 million in 1966. However, with forecasted potential sales in excess of $30 million per year and forecasted net income before taxes in excess of $6.0 million per year, FIREGUARD was considered one of the most promising new products in the Equipment Division.

FIREGUARD

In its continuing work on refrigerants, the Equipment Division's Refrigeration Department had developed a number of new plastic materials that exhibited superior fire extinguishing properties. At the same time, the division already produced some of the kind of equipment needed to extinguish fires. Because both the equipment and materials required were readily available in existing businesses, experimental and then commercial sales soon followed. The brand name under which the division developed this business was FIREGUARD.

The division management was highly optimistic concerning FIRE-GUARD's commercial prospects. Whereas all automatic fire extinction equipment required extensive piping to create a system, FIREGUARD was able to operate with a number of physically independent modules. Thus the size of a FIREGUARD system depended principally on the number of module units in the area to be protected.

The source of FIREGUARD's advantage lay in the chemical process used to extinguish fires. The Equipment Division's scientists had discovered a relatively inexpensive chemical substance they called NO-OX that expanded with explosive speed when exposed to air, reacting with the oxygen to free a heavy inert gas. The fire extinction properties of the gas were immediately recognized as superb.

The attack on the fire protection and extinguishing market called for early sales of single module equipment to the "traditional" market for portable extinguishers (local governments, schools, fire departments, industrial plants, commercial offices). Sales of automatic fire protection systems to the same users would follow. Finally, the strategy called for expanding primary demand by eventually introducing automatic residential systems. Exhibit 2 shows sales of the portable units from 1961 to 1966. The automatic systems market was entered for the first time during 1966.

The FIREGUARD business was the responsibility of Mr. Robert Kendall, Manager of the Equipment Division's Chemical Process Department (see the organization chart, Exhibit 1). The department manufactured and sold equipment for chemical manufacturing processes. In 1960, the division's General Manager, Mr. Lon Fischer, had become concerned with the quality of performance in the manufacturing and construction of chemical process equipment while it was part of the general refrigeration area and had reorganized the activity in a new department—chemical processes—so that "the chemical phase of the business could get separate attention." Because FIREGUARD was a "chemical" business, it was moved into the Chemical Process Department at the time of its formation.[1]

The Equipment Division's assessment of the market was described by George Kramer, Product Manager for FIREGUARD.

When we went into FIREGUARD we thought we knew a great deal

---

[1] The NO-OX business remained in the Refrigeration Department. The Chemical Process Department "purchased" the chemical from the Refrigeration Department at a negotiated "market" price.

about the fire protection business. However, we discovered that we knew very little and our customers knew less. They couldn't have cared less about the product. They were protected because they had to be according to the law or the insurance company. So we have had to study the job for the customer. The result has been that we have had a big learning and education program.

Commenting on Mr. Kramer's description, Mr. Kendall observed:

We got into the FIREGUARD business because we knew how to build some equipment and we had superior extinguishing materials. In fact we know how to build the containers very well. We make them at our Akron, Ohio factory. But we're still learning how to put together the support equipment.

The difficulty in engineering has been to learn the requirements of different applications. We are marketing a system, not equipment, and not extinguishing material. Thus, most of our learning has to be in the field in a sequence of trial and error steps.

Out of the first 300 units, we had to take back 100 over time. Now it's 200 out of 3,000. The engineers are still worried: they can explain what happens after the fact but the problem of responding in a controlled way to undesired fires or explosions is still there.

The other aspect of FIREGUARD planning has been market definition. It has been going on for five or six years as we have tried to move from fire departments to industrial plants, to office building systems, to homeowners. Each area is a different problem in the field. Different costs can be cut, different customers have to be educated, and in some instances different parts of our division have to be educated.

For example, we have had an endless series of arguments with our automatic systems design group trying to define what fire protection was. When we finally got it settled, we found that we needed a larger container unit.

However, the decision to build a larger container posed an important facility problem for us. We knew we were going to have to expand because FIREGUARD was already using 250,000 out of 750,000 production man-hours available at Akron. By 1970, the forecasts indicated that FIREGUARD would require 650,000 man-hours. And our other lines were growing.

Add to this the problem of the large containers and it's clear we needed a new facility. We really weren't up to handle them in the existing facility. Therefore, I asked Steve Matthews, facilities planner for FIREGUARD, to study the Akron plant and make recommendations.

Steve Matthews' career at Industrial Products had begun at Akron. He left the company only to rejoin it later to work on a task force which introduced a new data processing system to the Cleveland facility. His performance on that job led to his assignment in February 1966, to head a team put together to study the organization and operation of the Equipment Division's activities at their Cleveland and Akron locations. This assignment was later expanded to cover a study in depth of the FIREGUARD facilities at Akron. Matthews commented on his approach to the study.

My problem was to get a feel for each of Akron's businesses out of marketing. I wanted a definition of the way we did business in each of these markets. It was not easy. For example, in FIREGUARD, George Kramer's forecast was the greatest problem. It was absurdly conservative. I needed to know everything about the business, the way it was going to grow, the role of the parts business, the nature of customer service, and exactly how the business was going to be run so we could design a facility that would meet these needs.

We started the study on the assumption that the business would expand at Akron (location) because it appeared economic to do so. It seemed that the question of relocation costs, the problem of building a new building, and the location of the market indicated that we stay at Akron.

So we were evaluating existing facilities in the light of the markets of 1970 and beyond. If our product managers didn't give us the forecast, we interpolated as best we could. We wanted to build a facility which would enable us to do business the right way in 1970.

Matthews had found the major elements of his problems to be (1) Akron was poorly run, the data available were poor and the manpower available to gather data not always adequate; (2) problems at Akron resulted from the way in which the relationship between engineering and production were organized, an issue outside the scope of the study; (3) many of the study group's findings reflected unfavorably on Akron management and therefore raised political problems; and (4) the group came to feel that the need was for a "mass production" type activity although Akron was typically "job shop" oriented. As a result, the facility being planned looked as if it would be a radical departure from existing facilities both in terms of physical design and the mode of operation.

In fact, by November 1966, when Matthews was to meet with Kendall for a final review of the FIREGUARD project, he had been ready to recommend a new plant in the Carolinas.[2] It was Matthews' judgment that it would be easier to implement the critical nonfacility[3] part of the FIREGUARD expansion project in the new location. He had explained to Kendall that "failure to undertake and effectively implement nonfacility programs would negate the effects of the proposed physical facility plan."

The last part of the meeting with Kendall held November 15 had concerned the size of the capital investment and its timing. An excerpt from that conversation is reproduced below:

MATTHEWS: . . . And, I may be wrapping it up too soon, but we strongly recommend going to South Carolina. The existing manufacturing facilities are theoretically adequate to meet the FIREGUARD market demands through 1969. But, practically, we believe that conditions demand the acceleration of this project. Expanded production to meet 1967 and 1968

---

[2] While Matthews formally reported to the Akron plant manager, he kept in close contact with Kendall throughout the FIREGUARD study. The Akron plant manager attended many of these meetings and was aware of Matthews' assessment of the Akron facility and its management. However, since the demand for Akron's other products was growing and their production caused less problems than FIREGUARD's, the Akron plant manager was not upset at the prospect of losing FIREGUARD.

[3] Accounting and information systems, inventory and production control systems, and material handling systems.

forecasts plus inventory build-up in anticipation of moving the production lines will be very difficult to achieve under the existing conditions. The new factory will be needed as soon as it can be constructed. We prefer to schedule the physical construction program to fit into the program for an orderly transfer of personnel, equipment and procedures. Systems and procedures are to be completely worked out before this move is made. Our schedule calls for completion of the plant in the late fall of 1968, assuming that authorization to proceed is obtained in the first quarter of 1967.

KENDALL: There is no way we can invest incrementally?

MATTHEWS: I don't really think so.

KENDALL: What are we going to do when they won't give us $5.8 million?

MATTHEWS: You either bet on a business or you don't. You either believe the forecasts or you don't.

KENDALL: What if you believe half a forecast?

MATTHEWS: You couldn't build half a plant. You save some, but not a lot. What's a half? What forecast are you going to hang your hat on?

KENDALL: Half: I'll commit myself for half but want to be able to make the whole thing. Can't you build one plant for 1971 and then another just like it for 1975? Or what about some added subcontracting? Why can't we do more subcontracting since our manufacturing process isn't that unique?

MATTHEWS: As for two plants, you put machines in for the product and you don't need more than one, even for peak volume. As for subcontracting, our make or buy analysis shows that if we realize forecasted sales, we can improve our return by manufacturing some parts that we now subcontract.

KENDALL: Well, yes, but if we really don't have a proprietary position in terms of knowledge and so on, why can't we subcontract our expansion in this area?

MATTHEWS: The trouble with subcontracting is that you never make your delivery promises. It's just impossible to get yourself organized so that you can produce the kind of customer service you need.

Bob, I know your problem. You're thinking about our original estimate of $1.9 million back in June. The original facility was just a factory. This is also a warehouse and a service center. And given the nonfacility expenditures for systems, the investment per unit of capacity is the same as the original proposal.

Kendall had accepted Matthews' argument and arranged to have the FIREGUARD project presented to a meeting of the Equipment Division's executive committee[4] on December 16. Matthews began that meeting by describing the basic strategic assumptions of the FIREGUARD business. He described it as "a business selling hardware at a profit, based on warehousing, service, and parts." He noted that at the rate the business was growing, by 1969, they would be handling five million parts. That meant, he argued, that FIREGUARD was a large-volume production-oriented operation rather than the traditional job shop kind of business typical of Akron.

Excerpts from the meeting included the exchange below:

BRIGGS (Gen Mgr.): The rumor mill had it that the new facility at

---

[4] The divisional executive committee consisted of the division's general manager, assistant general manager, department managers, and top functional managers.

Akron was going to cost only $2 million. Why is it that your proposal is so expensive?

KENDALL: The original facility the people were talking about was simply a plant for the large containers. This is a much larger operation with many more products.

MATTHEWS: Also, the original facility was just a factory. Not only are there more products but this is a warehouse and service center.

A substantial discussion of labor costs and related problems led to the question of systems.

HUGHES (Mgr. Eng.): What about systems, do you have any allowance for the cost of all these systems you are installing?

MATTHEWS: You have $175,000 project costs and $185,000 engineering and that ought to cover it.

HUGHES: That's not enough, how many programmers do you have?

MATTHEWS: Five, I think.

HUGHES: I think that is low. We had 10 programmers at East St. Louis [an earlier project] if I am not mistaken.

GOLDEN (Asst. Gen. Mgr.): How many accountants do you have?

Matthews looked the figure up in his back-up notebook. He explained that the nature of the FIREGUARD operation was such that it would produce for a full warehouse rather than on the basis of meeting customer demand. Therefore, the demand on accounting was different from traditional equipment businesses.

GOLDEN: I think traditionally we have had our overrun (spent more than budget) on systems and accounting.

MATTHEWS: I think I understand your point, Bill, and we will do our best to take care of it.

After this discussion, Matthews presented the project summary shown below.

	1967	1968	1969	1970	1975
			(millions of dollars)		
Sales..........................	$ 3.6	$ 9.0	$17.7	$24.5	$41.5
Net income before taxes..........	(1.1)*	(.4)*	.8*	3.9	7.5
ROI..........................	—	—	7.4	26.0	32.0
Fixed investment...............	1.0†	1.2†	4.3†	6.9†	8.0‡
Working capital................	2.5	4.7	6.5	8.1	15.5
Total investment...............	3.5	5.9	10.8	15.0	23.5

* Includes $1.1 million for noncapital items associated with the move: i.e., costs of transfers, lay-offs, training, equipment moving, and project management.

† Will provide space to satisfy forecasted sales through 1975 and equipment to satisfy forecasted sales through 1970.

‡ $1.1 million additional equipment will be needed to satisfy 1975 forecasted sales.

On April 5, 1967, Briggs presented the FIREGUARD project to the corporate finance committee. While questions of subcontracting, poor current performance, and future ROI were raised, the general feeling of the group was that the project was a good one and the business very promising. Therefore, after a short discussion, the project was approved.

SECOND THOUGHTS

However, Kendall was still uneasy about the FIREGUARD project. Matthews argued that the future market for FIREGUARD products was large and lucrative. Yet the earnings record of FIREGUARD since its inception in 1961 had been poor. Moreover, as sales for the product grew, so did the losses.

·Kendall's concern was intensified when the review of his department's 1968 Business Plan was conducted in October 1967.[5] Divisional executives had expressed concern with the department's recent earnings record (see Exhibit 4). Moreover, Kendall was well aware that the corporation had specifically asked about the FIREGUARD business the previous fall. Since corporate requests for detailed information on an individual business were quite unusual, Kendall knew that FIREGUARD was in the limelight and that most likely there was pressure on the division officers to see that the business' performance improved.

In an effort to secure some guidance in this matter, Kendall asked Mike Richards, Corporate Director of Planning, to discuss FIREGUARD with him. While Richards reflected corporate thinking he did not represent it. Therefore, the meeting between Kendall and Richards was in the nature of "informal advice" rather than "formal corporate review."

The October 27 meeting began with Kendall expressing his concerns to Richards.

KENDALL: Mike, Briggs is putting pressure on me to raise the department's profits. But if FIREGUARD goes ahead with the approved expansion, earnings are not going to get much better. On the other hand, Matthews has some convincing arguments for FIREGUARD's market potential. To tell the truth, I'm perplexed.

RICHARDS: Well, . . . from my point of view, FIREGUARD doesn't fit with the rest of our products. We make machine tools, material handling systems, and refrigeration equipment. We enjoy a close relationship with our customers so that we can understand and help solve their technical problems.

On the other hand, FIREGUARD is a mass-produced, standard design product. Moreover, compared to our existing product line, FIREGUARD is mass marketed. That means problems of distribution and service that we haven't faced before.

---

[5] The Equipment Division's Business Plan attempted to answer the questions "What will happen to our products next year and the year after that?" and "What do we plan to do about it?". Departmental Plans were reviewed each fall by the division. (Performance against current plan was reviewed quarterly.) This plan review was a formal meeting in which departmental managers made presentations of their Business Plan to divisional officers. Officers were free to make comments and often did.

Plans were typically concerned with market size, market share, product volume, product price, and profit. Return on investment was sometimes used as a tool to measure the quality of a "business," but the business plans did not include specific investment planning. At most, a crude forecast of "capital requirement" was included.

KENDALL: OK, but FIREGUARD's got a fantastic future potential. Its sales in 1975 could easily exceed the total department's sales today.

RICHARDS: Look, I'm not arguing that you drop FIREGUARD completely. I'm merely saying that you don't really know how to market or produce the product very well. If I were you, I would be inclined to concentrate on improving FIREGUARD's profits and then grow the business after you've learned how to run it profitably.

KENDALL: That's easier said than done. We've already asked for and received approval for a new plant. The division will not be too pleased if I now say that FIREGUARD should not be expanded for a while. Moreover, I'm sure Matthews will hit the roof.

RICHARDS: Mike, you asked for my opinion and I've given it to you. I think it's better to retrench now rather than sacrifice current earnings to a project that has yet to make a profit.

Following his conversation with Richards, Kendall decided to speak with Matthews about the FIREGUARD project. Kendall began the meeting by explaining his concern over FIREGUARD's past and current performance and expressing pessimism about its future performance. To support this view, Kendall used many of Richards' arguments. Matthews responded quickly.

MATTHEWS: First, it seems to me that the issue is closed since the corporation approved our request for capital funds. Moreover I think their decision was a wise one. It takes money to build the marketing and systems capabilities we need to take advantage of the FIREGUARD opportunity. If we don't spend money today, we'll surely fail in the years to come.

Anyway, we've carefully timed our expenditures for capital and noncapital items so that we can cut back if the assumed market doesn't develop. For example, by December we will have ordered about $1.1 million in equipment and spent about $160,000 on noncapital items. Yet since the penalty for cancelling the equipment order is only $290,000, our total exposure as of the beginning of 1968 will be $450,000. (Cancellation of equipment was not allowed after January 1, 1968.) Moreover, while the entire capital budget of $5.8 million will be irrevocably committed by the end of 1968, we will have spent only $650,000 of our $1.1 million noncapital budget by that time. In fact, we wouldn't spend our entire noncapital budget until September 1969.

Also, even if FIREGUARD doesn't make it, you've always got a new plant even though most of the machinery is specially designed for the FIREGUARD product line. (The plant represented 70% of the capital budget.)

But this isn't going to happen. FIREGUARD has an enormous business potential. Moreover, the division will make as much on the NO-OX as it does on the equipment. But we both know that FIREGUARD is a new kind of product for the Equipment Division. It depends on the sales and servicing of hardware. This coupled with distribution are major factors to cope with. It's just going to take time and money to develop the capabilities we need.

KENDALL: But we haven't done very well in the six years we've been trying to date.

MATTHEWS: That's because we've been producing at Akron. Our new plant in South Carolina will solve many of our problems. Bob, it takes time to develop a new business. The payoff doesn't come right away.

KENDALL: Steve, that all sounds very good but have you looked at

Kramer's monthly reports for the first seven months of this year (see Exhibit 5)? After six years it still sounds as if we just began.

MATTHEWS: Even a great business can do poorly if it's mismanaged. We haven't been coordinating design with production. We haven't had a production line suitable for high volume manufacturing. We haven't had adequate part standardization. We haven't put nearly enough money into developing the needed management and production control systems. Bob, I could go on like this for 10 minutes, but you know these problems as well as I do. How do you expect to make money given this situation? And you certainly can't blame Kramer for a manufacturing problem.

KENDALL: You've got a point, but then where the hell does Kramer get his forecasts? Doesn't he take the production constraint into consideration?

MATTHEWS: OK, you've got a point. However, I don't think that should influence your view of the future of FIREGUARD. A lot of people[6] here have spent a lot of time on this project. We have finally got it out from under Akron and have the resources to make it. I don't see how you can even consider changing it at this late date.

---

[6] While Matthews and about a dozen other men had spent over a year and half on the project, the possibility of moving the operation to South Carolina had been kept highly confidential because of its potential impact on the Akron work force. Thus, in addition to the people planning the facility, only the top division and corporate officers were aware of the decision to move the FIREGUARD production operation.

However, while the construction of the new plant had not begun by the time of the Matthews-Kendall meeting, some equipment had been ordered and options had been taken on a piece of land. The cost of cancelling the equipment order and the land option would be $105,000. Moreover, $114,500 had already been spent for non-capital items.

Exhibit 1

INDUSTRIAL PRODUCTS, INC.

Equipment Division
Partial Organization Chart as of March 1966

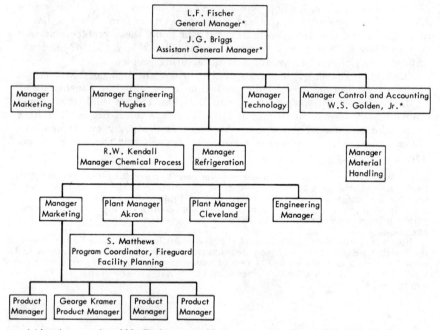

* After the promotion of Mr. Fischer to a position as a corporate officer, in July 1966, Mr. Briggs was made Division General Manager and Mr. Golden, Assistant General Manager.

Exhibit 2

INDUSTRIAL PRODUCTS, INC.

Sales of Portable FIREGUARD Units
1961–1966
(in number of units)

1961	400
1962	820
1963	1,450
1964	1,985
1965	3,775
1966	4,362

Exhibit 3

INDUSTRIAL PRODUCTS, INC.

Forecasted Sales for FIREGUARD

(millions of dollars)

Date of forecast	1964	1965	1966	1967	1968
September 1964................	$1.1	$2.5	$4.3		$13.3
July 1965....................		2.2	4.2	$8.1	
July 1966....................			3.4	4.8	9.2
April 1967...................				3.6	

Actual Sales and Earnings
for FIREGUARD
(millions of dollars)

Year	1961	1962	1963	1964	1965	1966
Sales.........................	$ .20	$ .41	$ .73	$ 1.0	$ 1.9	$ 2.2
Net income before taxes						
Actual.....................	(.05)	(.15)	(.38)	(.45)	(.8)	(1.1)
Plan					(.3)	.1

Exhibit 4

INDUSTRIAL PRODUCTS, INC.

Chemical Process Department Sales and Income
(millions of dollars)

	1960	1961	1962	1963	1964	1965	1966
Sales........................	$ 12.4	$13.4	$15.1	$16.2	$17.8	$20.4	$23.2
Net income before taxes........	(.50)	.04	.75	1.72	2.3	3.0	3.1

Exhibit 5

INDUSTRIAL PRODUCTS, INC.

Product Manager's Written Comments on the Monthly
Progress Reports for FIREGUARD

January 1967:   Equipment sales are 49% of plan because of large factory
backlog ($790,000 on 1/31/66 from $439,000 on 12/31/65).

February 1967:   Total equipment shipments are only 46% of plan. While
Akron backlog has risen $500,000 this year, part of this is the cus-
tomary seasonal build-up. It appears we may well be 20% below plan.

March 1967:   Total shipments continue to lag with year-to-date sales at
50% of plan, up only 4% from February. We continue to have new
equipment production difficulties as represented by a backlog of orders
at Akron $850,000. Backlog as a result of shipments withheld due to
production difficulties is $450,000 leaving sales to date substantially be-
low plan as reflected by the latest yearly forecast.

April 1967:   Sales continue to lag due to a continuing sales failure to
penetrate the commercial market. Automatic systems sales have been
delayed due to a lack of production of the new sensing device. Year-
to-date total sales have improved 7% from March due to heavy overseas shipments. This foreign business is accomplished at significantly
lower margins accounting for the continuing higher manufacturing cost
versus sales.

May 1967:   Sales continue to lag as reported in April with only slight improvement (0.4%). Equipment backlog is $725,000, about $300,000
above normal for sales to date. All costs to date are in line with the
latest forecast except for development where there will be an overrun
of $120,000 for 160% of plan due to automatic systems problems.

June 1967:   The above listed low sales have been reflected in our 1968
Business Plan. Our entry into the industrial systems market has been
set back at least one year for lack of satisfactory sensing equipment
and is reflected in our 1968 Business Plan by a 94% reduction in plan
sales in this area.

July 1967:   The high manufacturing costs were due to accounting errors
at Akron. One group of costs was cleared prior to sales clearing. Another group was cleared to cost of product when it should have been
transferred to an inventory account. When these are corrected in
August, the net effect will be to increase our August gross margin by
about $75,000.

General Health Company

In the summer of 1979, Carol London faced a dilemma. As department manager in charge of marketing for General Health Corporation's agricultural and veterinary products, she had succeeded in breathing life into an old line of products. But now she needed capital for the research and marketing programs she was planning. A new product search had borne fruit. There was an acquisition that looked like an attractive time-saving route to this new product market, but capital was allocated carefully by GHC's parent—International Diversified Corporation (IDC)—in relation to aggressive performance goals. In the context of the earnings and sales pressure these goals generated, Carol was seriously concerned about the future of her attractive but infant businesses. Could they survive the resource allocation wars? And if they could not, what was the implication for her future as a manager?

THE GENERAL HEALTH COMPANY BACKGROUND

Founded in 1914 in Chicago, the General Health Corporation was, in 1972, a $200 million producer of health products made of woven and nonwoven fiber products (see Exhibit 1 for data). Acquired in 1972 by the IDC for $400 million in stock, sales and net income had grown at a compound rate of about 10.5 percent and 15 percent per year between 1972 and 1978. Growth was even more impressive in the last four years. As GHC responded to the management systems introduced by IDC, the reshuffling of business units, and a series of acquisitions, sales had grown 40 percent and income had almost doubled. In 1978 GHC sales were $400 million, while aftertax net income was $17 million, a 1 percent point jump in return on sales over 1975.

Until 1971 GHC had been a highly decentralized organization. After the acquisition by IDC, General Health had been restructured into a more centralized firm with functional departments—manufacturing,

Exhibit 1

FINANCIAL SUMMARY
($ millions)

	1972	1973	1974	1975	1976	1977	1978
Sales	220	230	290	300	340	370	400
Gross profit	57	57	70	80	91	101	110
Operating expenses	42	44	53	59	64	70	75
Net profit	7.5	6.4	8.4	9.9	13.6	15.2	17.2
Return on sales	3.4%	2.8%	2.9%	3.3%	4.0%	4.1%	4.3%
Sales per product:							
Human health products ..	45	56	76	81	96	121	143
Miscellaneous products ...	41	41	53	54	60	63	68
Industrial applications	51	46	43	48	61	64	68
Consumer products	50	56	68	65	65	60	54
Sales per region:							
United States	187	199	240	248	285	308	333
International	33	31	50	52	58	62	67

Note: These figures have been disguised. They bear no systematic relationship to actual figures but are reflective of the administrative situation.

personnel, marketing services, administration services, and four sales and marketing divisions (Exhibit 2). The marketing divisions were autonomous from the operational point of view, but were constrained by shared use of the resources provided by the functional departments. Furthermore, the allocation of resources for investments and operations was strictly controlled by IDC's budgeting and finance organization.

In 1979 the resource allocation process was managed through the budget cycle. The cycle started in June and was to be finished before the end of August, the date at which the budget was sent up for review by the International Diversified head office. The budget represented a commitment to reach a certain objective and an instrument for the control of actual performance. These budgets, in turn, included capital and expense authorization.

Although there was no formal process for investment planning, current practice focused on incremental investments beyond cash generated. If a business, such as agriculture and veterinary products, generated profit in excess of what it had budgeted, these excess profits could be used for investment as a line item in the budget without special identification. But, if incremental funds were needed, a proposal had to be made. The proposals were screened successively by the division manager and by GHC's president's office. At each of these levels the process could be stopped either by rejection of the proposal or by reallocation of funds from the pool available to that level.[1] If the proposal was judged acceptable at both levels but no resources were available

---

[1] Where money in excess of the amount budgeted was generated by a business, it could be plowed back into the business to support its own growth if the growth plan was accepted at the divisional or the General Health Company level. Otherwise, it became available to the division or the company to support other more promising businesses.

Exhibit 2

GHC'S ORGANIZATIONAL CHART

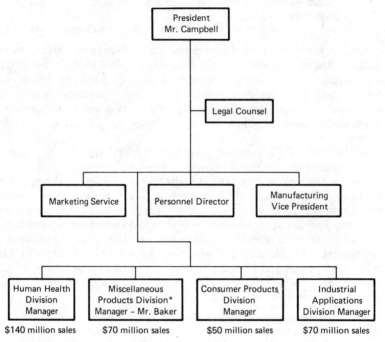

* See Exhibit 3.
Source: Casewriter understanding.

within the company, an individual request was made to the IDC head office. There was, in addition, an informal rule that to be acceptable a project should make money in the year it was introduced. Finally, as Mr. J. Baker, general manager for the miscellaneous products division noted,

> IDC wants only significant businesses. They say, "If you can't have $20 million to $40 million turnover, get the hell out of it."

Managers at General Health agreed that it was not easy to attract new investment money.

THE INTERNATIONAL DIVERSIFIED MANAGEMENT POLICY

During the later 1970s, International Diversified emphasis had consistently been on diversification through acquisition. As explained in a 1979 *Fortune* story:

> Garth (the retiring CEO) developed a program that called for maintaining IDC's lead abroad and end-running National Development Company

(NDC) at home by diversification into new businesses not competitive with the Chicago nemesis.

Garth had inherited a full treasury, and IDC's stock was selling at a high multiple. Given the nature of the resources, the obvious choice was to go on an acquisition binge rather than diversify internally.

This orientation also discouraged any attempt of existing operating units to divert resources to any project outside the main concern of the corporation. Resources were therefore allocated only to support the normal growth of basic businesses, if the latter were profitable enough. As a result management emphasis had been on cost reduction to increase profitability and to allow internal financing of existing businesses' growth.

In 1979 the IDC board of directors decided that it was time to stop the acquisitions and consolidate the existing businesses. For the future, growth was to come from the internal development of these businesses. To spread the message at General Health, a three-day seminar for managers was organized in the spring to determine what the company should become. The main conclusion was that the company should more than double its sales to about $1 billion before 1984. The implication of this conclusion was that all GHC's businesses were supposed to double their sales and profits in the next five years, or die. It was not at all clear what, if any, investment program would be associated with this growth. Mr. Baker commented:

> IDC management believes in stretching. They try to find your capability by pushing you ahead all the time. For example, I was general manager/ USA for miscellaneous products, now I am general manager/Europe as well, but without formal arrangements. . . . We are so damn busy that you don't have time to think. . . . It is a workaholic place but everybody likes it because we are allowing people to create.

These comments were not abstract reflections on a control and planning system. For Baker, his division's future was at stake.

The miscellaneous products division

In 1979 the miscellaneous products division was engaged in the manufacture and distribution of nonwoven products. GHC was the largest manufacturer of "dry-laid" technology nonwoven products.[2] The division was organized by product into four departments (Exhibit 3). Most of the $70 million sales of the division (see Exhibit 4 for financial data) was accounted for by the raw goods department ($45 million); each of the remaining departments contributed about $8 million. Since none of the latter had reached the critical size considered acceptable to the IDC policymakers, Baker and his department managers all faced the risk that their businesses might be abandoned (i.e., divested or phased out). In that case the viability of the division itself might also be ques-

---

[2] Other competitors used different technologies, but General Health was a major figure in the total field. The variety of approaches meant that product and process might have differing physical characteristics and economics.

Exhibit 3

MISCELLANEOUS PRODUCTS DIVISION ORGANIZATIONAL CHART

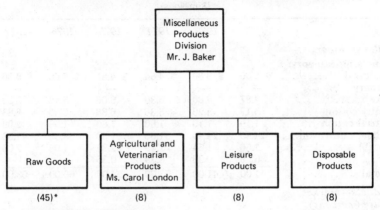

* Approximate size in $ millions.
Source: Casewriter understanding.

tioned. Not surprisingly, division management sought fast growth. Commenting on IDC's desire to double sales, Baker concluded:

> We have to deliver or leave. It's a requirement. To be able to deliver we need money, and all divisions fight like hell for the buck.

The competitive situation of the miscellaneous product division within GHC was not very strong. The division's major business, non-woven textiles, despite a strong market position (Exhibit 5), was at best a stagnating one. To boost revenues, new applications and new derived products had to be developed and marketed, and this meant higher expenses with important outcomes uncertain. Achieving this future growth while at the same time delivering current sales and net income growth was the "circle quadrature" of Baker's career. The problem was aggra-

Exhibit 4

MISCELLANEOUS PRODUCTS DIVISION, FINANCIAL SUMMARY
($ millions)

	1972	1973	1974	1975	1976	1977	1978
Sales............	$41.0	$41.0	$53.0	$54.0	$60.0	$63.0	$68.0
Marginal income*......	13.5	12.7	16.9	16.0	19.4	20.3	22.1
Media..........	0.45	0.35	0.30	0.25	0.35	0.40	0.50
Promotion......	0.40	0.35	0.38	0.32	0.45	0.35	0.40
Total advertising....	0.85	0.70	0.68	0.57	0.80	0.75	0.90
Profit before tax	4.0	3.1	3.2	2.0	3.9	4.0	4.2
Profit after tax..	2.0	1.5	1.6	1.0	1.9	2.0	2.1

Note: These figures have been disguised. They bear no systematic relationship with the actual data but are reflective of the administrative situation.
* Marginal income is income before tax, marketing, and nonvariable expenses.

Exhibit 5

MISCELLANEOUS PRODUCTS SALES/MARKET SHARE SUMMARY—TOTAL YEAR
($ millions)

	1972	1973	1974	1975	1976	1977	1978
Sales summary							
Merchandising category:							
Agricultural	$ 3.60	$ 3.60	$ 4.64	$ 4.81	$ 5.06	$ 5.30	$ 6.39
Veterinary	—	—	—	—	—	—	.87
Leisure	4.87	4.80	6.30	6.06	5.12	5.38	5.38
Specialty cotton	5.17	5.20	6.36	6.86	6.50	6.83	6.80
Industrial cotton	1.19	1.10	1.60	1.80	1.98	2.08	2.08
Industrial nonwoven ...	24.35	24.40	31.80	31.80	39.36	41.33	44.20
Disposables	1.56	1.54	1.19	2.32	1.98	2.08	2.28
Other	0.26	0.36	0.39	0.35	—	—	—
Total	41.00	41.00	53.00	54.00	60.00	63.00	68.00
Products—market share (percent)							
Merchandising category:							
Agricultural	60%	62%	60%	65%	64%	63%	65%
Leisure	55	56	60	55	54	56	57
Specialty	100	100	100	100	100	100	100
NDC*	44	45	47	46	47	46	47
Disposable	55	56	56	58	42	50	51

Note: These figures have been disguised. They bear no systematic relationship to actual figures but are reflective of the administrative situation.
* These are sales of raw fiber products to Procter & Gamble.

vated by the corporation's requirement that only sizable businesses be supported. The clear implication was that larger, more powerful divisions, such as the human health division, were preferred fields for investment. An internal strategy to deal with this problem had the division using internally generated funds to develop small promising businesses until they reached a size that justified request of independent funds for growth.

It was one of these ventures, agricultural and veterinary products, that Carol London was managing. The business was regarded as a small but impressive success.

Baker explained:

> My belief was that this company also belonged in the animal health business. I put Carol in charge of looking into it. She came up with the veterinarian business idea and made an exciting venture out of it. Nevertheless, it is really very difficult to start a new business in this corporation because it is too small and attracts little interest or support.

THE AGRICULTURAL-VETERINARY PRODUCTS DEPARTMENT

The agricultural-veterinary products department (A-V department) had developed from GHC's long-established milk filter business. It was this department that Carol London took over in 1978. For several years the A-V department had supplemented its milk filters with a line of over-the-counter (OTC) animal products which were sold through the same channels as the filters. In an effort to expand the business, Carol had begun searching out new product applications and new channels, and had identified two exciting new areas. The first was a new application for filters in the food industry. The second involved selling some of the company's health-care products to veterinarians.

The A-V department, as London perceived it in the future, could be envisioned as a portfolio of new and old product applications moving through new and old channels, as suggested by the following chart:

	Old products	New products
Old channels	Milk filter products	Over-the-counter animal products
New channels	Ethical veterinary products	Food filters (industrial/ commercial)

The organization of the A-V department reflected these relationships. Separate product managers managed the agricultural (milk filter), animal health (OTC), and veterinarian businesses. A part-time consultant had been retained to assist with much of the work on the food filters business. Exhibit 6 provides budget data describing the departments.

Agricultural products

In 1979 the basic business of the A-V department was the marketing of milk filters to farmers. General Health had entered the milk filter business in the early 60s when the aggressive general-purpose sales force for nonwovens saw the opportunity to penetrate a new field that was then largely in the hands of J&J. Pushing hard, and with skillful application of product development effort (an especially strong nonwoven was created to handle the milk processing pressures), General Health captured most of the market.

In 1979 milk filters were purchased by farmers off the shelf from retail farm supply stores, milk processing equipment dealers, and local milk processing plants. General Health sold directly to these outlets.

Milk filters was an aging business whose economics were getting worse every day. In describing it Carol London acknowledged that:

> In the milk filter business we have 65–70 percent market share. Our sales are now around $5 million, but I think it will go down and stabilize around $4 million. What explains the decrease is that the trend is toward less farmers, with larger cow herds per farm, thus the total number of farms is decreasing. Since a farm uses only one filter a milking this restructuring of the dairy farm business induces a total demand reduction.

The manufacturing of filters for A-V was carried out in old plants at Chicago; the labor content of the operations was high, and the resul-

Exhibit 6
FINANCIAL DATA ON AGRICULTURAL DEPARTMENT BUSINESS
($000)

	Agricultural products			Animal health			Veterinary		
	1977	1978	1979 budget	1977	1978	1979 budget	1977	1978	1979 budget
Sales	$3,489	$4,249	$4,879	$1,811	$2,141	$2,458	—	$870	$1,300
Marginal income	1,260	1,484	1,711	806	900	1,026	—	351	509
Marketing expenses	490	530	532	343	358	410	—	155	139
Nonvariable expenses	993	1,088	1,249	244	259	297	—	197	270
Profit before tax	–223	–134	–70	219	283	314	—	49	100

Note: These figures have been disguised. They bear no systematic relationship to actual figures but are reflective of the administrative situation.

tant cost of the filters was very high. The break-even sales level in 1979 was $6 million. According to London, if they bought the fabric and converted it, they would be able to do it with the same variable cost and save the fixed costs. The break-even sales level for vended items would then be only $2.5 million.

The milk filter business had lost money in 1979. London explained that she had forecasted the loss in the budget, but "no one would listen." It had been decided instead that she would raise her prices. Because demand was highly price elastic, a substantial volume of sales was lost and—though still high—market share deteriorated. The management of General Health had always been reluctant to close the Chicago facilities because this meant taking a loss of $1 million to $1.5 million, which they felt they could not afford for the time being. London suggested that the new management "seemed to be thinking about it"; she interpreted the reappointment of Chicago's general manager, without replacing him, as a signal in that direction.

Given IDC's policy, the negative trend in the agricultural products line was unacceptable. New uses seemed the only way out. In fact, London had been working hard to extend the business concept for milk filters. The most promising opportunity uncovered was in the *filtering of hot fats in the food industry.*

In the summer of 1978, a first-year MBA from Northwest Business School (NBS) had identified the use of the FDA-cleared milk filter fiber for industrial filtering of precooked foods such as french fries. When filtration was successfully demonstrated, for industrial use, a salesman was assigned to the product.

That salesman's efforts later revealed that restaurants were using sophisticated equipment to filter fats and, more interesting, that the equipment was costly, delicate, and difficult to maintain. Faced with the troublesome problems of filtering and reusing fat, restaurants tended to change their fat regularly. The salesman also discovered that a patent had been recently issued for a very simple process that could use General Health's filters. Furthermore, the patent holder expressed his interest in granting an exclusive license to GHC. As of August 1979, discussions were being held to determine the conditions for such a grant.

The hotel and restaurant chains contacted and informed about the solution were very enthusiastic and confirmed the attractiveness of such a market. On the basis of these discussions, new projections for both industrial and commercial business were used to develop the 1980 budget. (See forecasts in Exhibit 7.)

The animal health business

In 1963 General Health realized that the customers for milk filters purchased over-the-counter animal health products through the same channels used for milk filters. The farmer was a sophisticated owner of animals—in contrast to a typical urban pet owner—and carried out much of the animal husbandry required on his own, perhaps with the advice of a veterinarian in difficult cases.

As the human health division was already producing a full range

686

Exhibit 7

SALES PROJECTIONS FOR THE FOOD FILTRATION BUSINESS
($ millions)

	1979	1980	1981	1982	1983	1984	1985
Industrial segment	$0.50	$1.5	$1.6	$1.7	$1.8	$1.9	$ 2.0
Commercial segment ...	—	2.0	5.0	6.0	7.5	8.5	10.0

Note: These figures have been disguised. They bear no systematic relationship to actual figures but are reflective of the administrative situation.

of human health products, and as the farmer was used to using human health supplies, entering this market, with some repackaging and relabeling, seemed a natural way of using General Health capacity. The business took off but soon plateaued.

After taking responsibility for the business in 1978, London redirected the product line. "The key to future success was in going further in product adaptation designed for the vet—large sizes, for example, shaped to fit a horse's leg." The Chicago factory was able to accommodate the special items. Some "crummy commodities" were dropped and exclusivity of some sort was negotiated for the sourced products. New products were planned for new market niches in 1980. The business response to this new attention was an estimated sales increase in 1979 of almost $1 million over 1978 sales of $2 million, despite the unfavorable competitive situation detailed in Exhibit 8.

Exhibit 8

COMPETITIVE SITUATION IN THE ANIMAL HEALTH MARKET

Product	Competition	Share
Udder cream	Dairy Association	30%
	Dr. Naylor	29
	Kendall	14
	General Health	8
Calf scours	Pfizer	49
	Anchor	29
	General Health	10
	Kendall	9
Mastitis treatment.........	Upjohn/Tuco	45
	Pfizer	20
	Bristol	12
	Beecham	12
	General Health	6
Teat dip	West Agro	37
	Babson	20
	Monarch	12
	General Health	11
Fly spray..................	Hess & Clark	40
	Shell	30
	General Health	12
	Kendall	10

Note: These figures have been disguised. They bear no systematic relationship to actual figures but are reflective of the administrative situation.

Carol London's team entered the 1979 budget period taking a very aggressive stance. A $2 million increase was scheduled for 1980 (for a total of $5 million), and sales growth was forecasted to accelerate progressively leading to sales of $15 million in 1983. Profits were expected to grow even faster. The pro forma income statement (shown in Exhibit 9) called for 1983 profits almost 10 times those of 1979. The idea was to increase sales profitably by introducing new products directly related to the existing products. At the same time it was intended to build new market niches in the equine and swine areas. All these were to be combined with new distribution and delivery systems to increase convenience for the customer. In order to achieve these results, it was necessary to (a) develop a sales and marketing team, (b) be able to secure new different products essentially by using exclusivity contracts for products already developed by others, and (c) fund internal R&D to bring other new products to market.

The veterinary business

The veterinary business had been developed after London had taken over the A-V department. The origin of the business lay in a decision on London's part to seek R&D support for the animal health line as part of the nonwoven business. Two persons were finally allocated.

It was apparent that the GHC human health marketing force had been calling on veterinary customers in order to build sales. To get a better understanding of the market, London hired Duane Whitman, first-year Northwest Business School MBA for the summer of 1977. His analysis of the OTC business revealed that a line of ethical products to complement the OTC products would really be necessary for OTC success and growth. Sources of OTC products were really only interested in General if they had an ethical entry as well.

Veterinary ethical products were sold in much the same manner as prescription drugs for humans. Salesmen called on veterinary distribu-

Exhibit 9

Pro Forma Income Statement
Animal Health Products—1979–1983
($000)

	1979 estimate	1980	1981	1982	1983
Sales	$2,920	$5,000	$8,000	$13,000	15,000
Marginal income	1,020	1,960	2,980	4,660	5,590
Ad/promotion expenses	120	440	420	650	630
Marketing expenses (other)	350	500	700	840	950
R&D expenses	100	140	240	310	320
Fixed expenses	200	340	600	970	1,350
Profit after tax	126	270	512	949	1,170
Return on sales	4.3%	5.4%	6.4%	7.3%	7.8%

Note: These figures have been disguised. They bear no relationship to actual figures but are reflective of the administrative situation.

Exhibit 10

TOTAL PROJECTED INVESTMENT FOR THE VETERINARY
AND ANIMAL HEALTH PRODUCTS
($000)

	1980	1981	1982	1983
Veterinary	$ 900	$1,000	$1,500	$2,200
Animal health ...	1,200	2,000	2,200	3,500

Notes: GHC's definition of investment on which ROI is computed include investment in equipment, R&D, personnel, and working capital.

Figures have been disguised. They bear no relationship to actual figures but are reflective of the administrative situation.

tors, or the vets themselves who would either use the product or resell it to farmers.

From its 1977 creation, the veterinary business was an impressive success and widely recognized in the company. In fact, it had attracted praise from most executives, including the former GHC president, Mr. Campbell, now promoted to vice president for the IDC group, including the General Health Company. In a 1978 speech, Campbell used the veterinarian business as an example of entrepreneurship in a large organization.

In 1979 Whitman was the veterinary products manager. Sales were approximately $1.3 million and were growing rapidly. In London's mind it was time to obtain support and resources from the corporation to be able to make substantial progress in the field (Exhibit 10). Exhibit 11 is an excerpt from the 1979 budget statement. Baker agreed:

> Now we need additional money and the blessing of the corporation. I believe we have a strong case. We can convince the corporation to let us go.

To do that, Whitman's report had been updated for the 1980 budget. Excerpts from the latter are presented in Exhibit 12. The basic idea was to obtain commitment from the corporation to be able to grow both the veterinarian and the animal health businesses.[3] For the former, if the plan were adopted, sales were to grow steadily to reach $10.5 million in 1983 (see the pro forma income statement in Exhibit 13). The rationale for the plan was to expand into the equipment part of the market and mold a veterinary business around existing General Health resources. GHC was already a high-technology firm doing substantial amounts of applied R&D (mainly performed in the human health division). It was positioned in a small market segment of veterinary products where it could become a major force by using and adapting the human dressings and supplies (developed at the human health division) to the special

---

[3] The veterinary business, described in the section following, consists of the over-the-counter distribution of veterinary products. Thus, product development support for veterinarian business would help animal health.

Exhibit 11

1979 BUDGET STATEMENT—EXCERPTS

---

*Agricultural products**

In 1978 we stressed improvements in both volume and price. Because some of the increased volume came from insecticide products whose margins are slightly below average and because for competitive reasons we reformulated and repriced several filter products, the agricultural products marginal income percent slipped slightly in 1978. Nevertheless, marginal income did increase $0.32 million or 15 percent. This increase coupled with control of marketing expenses enabled agricultural products' profit after tax to improve from a break even in 1977 to $75,000 in 1978.

In 1978 we achieved more desirable volumes. In 1979 our plan is to put emphasis on price increases and promotion of new and old products which yield the highest margins. The majority of the 1979 11.5 percent volume increase is projected to come from two new products. Total 1979 sales of our new water-based mastitis treatment Wamast are budgeted to be $0.1 million. Sales of our new cow treatment are estimated to be $0.2 million. With this sales increase and the improvement in marginal income percent, the 1979 marginal income is budgeted to grow by $0.35 million or 15 percent. This improvement is largely offset by increases in nonvariable expenses. The largest increase is in fixed manufacturing. It increased 29 percent or $0.2 million; 32 percent or $0.07 million of this increase is attributable to a reallocation of overhead at the Chicago Plant. This reallocation was caused by the drop in budgeted volume of specialty cotton.

Veterinary products

This class of trade was new to miscellaneous products in 1978. In 1979 we are aggressively budgeting excellent growth with a dramatic 49 percent increase in sales to $1.3 million. With the help of a January 1, 1979, price increase, we project a $158,000 increase (45 percent) in marginal income. Marketing expenses have been reduced because we will not have to incur the start-up costs that were required in 1978. However, because this will be a regular class of trade in 1979, it is being allocated its full share of nonvariable expenses. In spite of this allocation, profits are budgeted to increase twofold to $0.1 million. The ROS will increase slightly to 7.7 percent.

Note: All figures have been disguised. They bear no systematic relationship to actual figures but are reflective of the administrative situation.

* The agricultural products are dairy filters and OTC animal health products.

needs of the veterinary market. This philosophy also stressed the need to avoid head-to-head confrontation with other major competitors unless the market niche chosen was secure. The major requirement for the plan to be achieved was thought to be the willingness of the company management to allocate funds for field trials, purchase of licenses, and product adaptation R&D, as well as for increase in sales and marketing personnel. The total investment needs were forecasted as shown in Exhibit 10.

The 1980 budget was believed to be decisive for the veterinary business. If the corporation failed to provide support, the business would stagnate for a while and then recede under competitive pressures. London and her subordinates invested heavily in preparing for the budget presentation scheduled for late August 1979.

Transfer to a new division

Carol London's concerns in the late spring and early summer turned on how she could best promote her new business opportunities. The context in which she had to present her plans concerned her as did the prospects for her business and her career if she were turned down. She had been attracted by the opportunity general health provided to apply basic analytic planning, and administrative skills to very traditionally run businesses. Unlike the marketing factories, such as P&G or Northwest, MBAs were relatively rare.

As she contemplated the prospects for A-V, London was aware that GHC was in somewhat of a turmoil. With Campbell's promotion to group vice president, an organization reshuffle was expected. It seemed that this would be an appropriate time to move to a new spot. Despite the prospects she had uncovered, there was a great uncertainty as to whether the A-V department would obtain the needed resources to grow. It was unclear whether the prepared plan would fit IDC's strategy or not.

She had come to GHC in the first place in order to have room to move quickly, but the pace of A-V's future seemed problematic. An English major from Yale with an MS in psychology, she had left social work for NBS in 1975. On graduation she joined MDC, the consulting firm, in the New York office. After 18 months she left for the "real world" of line management. Hired by Mr. Campbell as "new products manager," her assignment was to study the growth possibilities of the miscellaneous division for Baker.

Commenting on her work, Baker noted:

> Carol is best at doing marketing research, finding new directions to go. She is very good and did such a good job! I transferred her to the line because she wanted to.
>
> Carol is an unusual manager, one of the very few women who are willing to pay the price of a business career. She is both bright and smart. She understands very fast how much she can do, how she should do it. She also understands relationships at the top. And so she has obtained very good results. For example, she has built a new business—the veterinarian—which went in one year from $300K to $1M. At the same time she has developed a very good group with good morale and no turnover. But her weaknesses might be that she is in a hurry and is not really profit oriented. She is full of good ideas about new projects, and that's what I need but profit is not for 5–6 years, it is for next Friday. She might, along the same line, have the "consultant disease"—too much erudition, not enough delivery. . . .
>
> She is definitely among the very best in the division and the company. The only problem is that she's been here for too little time, and despite the pressures from the top to promote women we cannot do it too fast.

London knew that she was well regarded but sensed that there were limits to how fast she could move in A-V. To help her thinking, she discussed her concerns with GHC's personnel director. He was sympathetic and arranged in May for Carol to meet the manager of the human health division. But as of August 1979 nothing more had happened.

It was difficult to decide what action made sense. Riding with the A-V business without new money seemed like a potential trap. There was no way that profit and size could be jointly achieved without investment. And without growth she could lose the high morale and good performance that gave her pride and reputation. But a move to another part of the company did not seem imminent and the budget season was approaching.

Exhibit 12

VETERINARY PRODUCTS—STRATEGIC PLAN OVERVIEW

The market

The market for veterinary surgical supplies and equipment in 1979 is estimated at $42.6 million at the wholesale level. The market of interest to GHC initially was the surgical supply segment with sales of $15 million in 1979. Table 1 defines the veterinary market for surgical supplies and equipment.

The surgical supplies and equipment market for veterinarians has been growing at a rate of 8 percent a year. This healthy rate of growth can be explained by the increasing sophistication in veterinary operating techniques and procedures, resulting from several trends:

1. Greater concern for asepsis, sterility, and disposability from more modern, clinical training in the 22 U.S. schools of veterinary medicine.
2. A trend toward more specialization, i.e., surgery, orthopedics, preventive medicine, etc.
3. Increasing ethical standards from veterinarians who are attempting to develop a more professional self-image.
4. An increasing ability to pass on costs of higher quality supplies and equipment to clients.
5. Strong national, regional, and state organizations with regular educational seminars designed to help raise the surgical standards of veterinary medicine.
6. Greater legal and regulatory pressures for accountability.

Table 1

VETERINARY MARKET—SURGICAL SUPPLIES AND EQUIPMENT (1979)

Surgical supplies—$15 million	*Equipment—$28 million*
Adhesives	Instruments
Sponges	Hypo needles/syringes
Bandages	Catheters/endotracheal tubes
Cotton	Sutures
Other dressings (drapes, etc.)	X-ray equipment
Gloves and sleeves	Cleaners, soaps
Plaster bandages and splints	Other (catheters, masks, swabs, etc.)
Stockinette and wadding	

Exhibit 12 (*continued*)

The competition

The market leader in veterinary surgical supplies is Johnson & Johnson, marketing through their animal health division, Pitman-Moore. See Table 2 for current market share estimates. Pitman-Moore's lion's share of the total market for surgical supplies is explained by:

1. A large, well-managed direct sales force.
2. A well-recognized, respected name in the animal health business.
3. A full-line catalog of surgical products which enables one-order purchasing, a desired convenience.
4. A corporate commitment to growth in animal health.
5. Heavy advertising and promotion budget.
6. A $25 million animal health R&D facility built in 1978.

General Health's successful penetration in the surgical supply segment over the past two years has come at the expense of the other minor competitors, i.e., P-D, H-L, etc., those who are competing in the distributor channel of distribution. Further penetration of the market, i.e., at the expense of Pitman-Moore, will prove more difficult as the less competent distributor sales force begins to compete directly with the talented P-M sales force.

The $28 million equipment portion of the market is serviced by a fragmented, unaggressive array of companies, none of whom have a dollar share over 10 percent. These companies, for the most part, offer their products to the veterinarian as an add-on to their efforts in the human market. For competitive comparison purposes, it should be pointed out that major competitors in these surgical supply and equipment niches often have sales of less than $5 million annually.

Table 2

MARKET SHARE ANALYSIS FOR
VETERINARY SURGICAL SUPPLIES

	1977	1978
Pitman-Moore (J&J)	52%	52%
3M	11	10
Parke-Davis	8	3
GHC	6	16
Kendall	4	12
Haver-Lockhart	4	1

Distribution

The veterinarian is serviced by two distinct modes of distribution: direct by the manufacturer or indirect through local ethical distributors. Pharmaceuticals and biologicals are sold primarily (60 percent of all sales) direct, while supplies and equipment have traditionally gone primarily (63 percent) through local distributors.

Note: All figures have been disguised. They bear no systematic relationship to actual figures but are reflective of the administrative situation.

Exhibit 13

Pro Forma Income Statement
Veterinary Products 1979–1983
($000)

	1979 estimate	1980 budget	1981	1982	1983
Net sales	$1,910	$2,600	$5,000	$7,500	$10,500
Marginal income	560	990	1,820	2,820	3,870
Advertising expenses ..	70	140	290	390	440
Marketing expenses (other than ads)	80	110	190	280	300
R&D expenses	—	140	200	250	50
Fixed expenses	220	370	640	1,000	1,300
Profit after tax	96	115	250	450	777
Return on sales	5.0%	4.4%	5.0%	6.0%	7.4%

Note: These figures have been disguised. They bear no relationship to actual figures but are reflective of the administrative situation.

PC&D, Inc.

When we promoted you to the presidency five years ago, we expected that there would be changes, but we never expected you to diminish the importance of the old line businesses to the extent that you have. I think you have erred in doing so. . . .

The new entrepreneurial subs are certainly dynamic and have brought positive press to the company. But, by investing all new resources in them, you are jeopardizing the health of the company as a whole. . . .

My division's reputation has been built over the past 50 years on the superior quality of its products and sales force. But, as the leadership of our products begins to erode, my salesmen are beginning to leave. Without resources, I cannot stop this trend, and, as much as it saddens me to say so, I am losing my own motivation to stay with the company.

THESE WERE some excerpts from a letter that the senior vice president and head of the machinery division, George McElroy, 58, sent to John Martell, president of PC&D, Inc., in February 1976. McElroy was highly respected in both the company and the industry, a member of the board of directors, and a senior officer of the company for 20 years. Therefore, Martell knew that it was important to respond and resolve the issues with McElroy successfully. At the same time, Martell had no intention of giving up his own prerogatives to direct the company.

HISTORY OF PC&D, INC.

Payson & Clark Company

Payson & Clark, the forerunner of PC&D, Inc., was founded during the merger movement around the turn of the century. Four regional machinery companies merged to form a national industrial machinery manufacturing corporation named after the two largest enterprises in the merger, Payson and Clark. With the growth of industry across the

694

country at the time, the demand for heavy machinery took off. The new company benefited from economies of scale, both in production and distribution, and grew and prospered.

By 1965 Payson & Clark Company was an old, stable company, still producing machinery. With revenues of $300 million and net aftertax profits of $6 million, it was still the largest firm in the industry. (See Exhibits 1 and 2 for additional financial information.) The company offered the most complete line of heavy industrial equipment in the industry, the different available configurations of standard and custom models filling a large, encyclopedic sales manual. The consistently high quality and unusual breadth of the product line had made attracting high-caliber salesmen relatively easy. These people were highly knowledgeable in the applications of the product line and saw themselves as consultants to their industrial customers.

While Payson & Clark was the leader in quality and breadth of its product line, it was not the leader in innovations. It left expensive R&D to others, copying products after they were widely accepted. It could afford to follow others primarily because the industry itself was slow moving. In 1965 the business was essentially the same as when the company was founded. Its growth depended on the general growth of industry in the United States, efficiencies in purchasing raw materials, and the scale and automation of production. Indeed, the company's major innovation came in the early 50s with the introduction of plastics in some of the models.

The company was structured in 1965 as it had been in the 20s, with a standard functional organization and highly centralized chain of command. Its top executives were old-time managers, the average age being 55. Many had spent their entire careers with the firm and could remember the days when old Mr. Payson had kept tight reins on the company in the 30s and 40s. Harold C. Payson IV, aged 53 in 1965, was president of the company from the late 40s and president and chairman since 1955. Although the company was publicly held, the Payson family still owned a considerable amount of the stock.

In the early 1960s Harold Payson began to consider succession. He wanted to leave the company in good condition not only for his own personal pride but for the betterment of his heirs. From discussions with his investment bankers and friends in the business world, Mr. Payson had recognized that an association with a high-technology, high-growth industry would strengthen Payson & Clark's image. One way in which Mr. Payson sought to implement this suggestion was to use some of the excess capital thrown off by the machinery business to enter into joint ventures with young, new companies developing high-technology, innovative products. Several such investments were made in the early 1960s, including one with the Datronics Company in 1962.

Datronics Company

In 1965 the Datronics Company was 10 years old with revenues of $50 million. (See Exhibits 3 and 4 for additional financial information.) The company had started as an engineering firm subsisting on govern-

Exhibit 1

PAYSON & CLARK COMPANY
Income Statement, 1956–1965
($ millions)

	1956	1957	1958	1959	1960	1961	1962	1963	1964	1965
Sales	$177.6	$190.7	$205.0	$220.5	$237.2	$247.9	$259.1	$273.3	$288.1	$302.7
Cost of goods sold	136.1	145.8	157.6	171.0	184.4	192.4	202.1	218.7	230.8	243.6
Gross profit	41.5	44.9	47.4	49.5	52.8	55.5	57.0	54.6	57.3	59.1
Expenses:										
Depreciation	5.0	5.0	5.0	4.0	4.0	4.0	4.0	4.0	3.5	3.5
Marketing and G&A	18.2	19.7	20.5	22.2	25.6	27.5	28.4	28.0	30.0	33.3
Engineering and product development	8.1	8.6	9.9	10.1	10.6	11.0	11.4	8.8	9.2	7.1
Total expenses	31.3	33.3	35.4	36.3	40.2	42.5	43.8	40.8	42.7	43.9
Profit before interest and taxes	10.2	11.6	12.0	13.2	12.6	13.0	13.2	13.8	14.6	15.2
Interest	3.0	4.0	4.0	4.0	3.0	3.0	3.0	3.0	3.0	3.0
Profit before tax	7.2	7.6	8.0	9.2	9.6	10.0	10.2	10.8	11.6	12.2
Tax	3.6	3.8	4.0	4.6	4.8	5.0	5.1	5.4	5.8	6.1
Profit after tax	$ 3.6	$ 3.8	$ 4.0	$ 4.6	$ 4.8	$ 5.0	$ 5.1	$ 5.4	$ 5.8	$ 6.1
Earnings per share	$1.29	$1.36	$1.44	$1.65	$1.72	$1.80	$1.83	$1.94	$2.08	$2.19
Average stock price	$18	$22	$19	$30	$29	$29	$27	$31	$35	$33

Exhibit 2

PAYSON & CLARK COMPANY
Balance Sheet, 1956–1965
($ millions)

	1956	1957	1958	1959	1960	1961	1962	1963	1964	1965
Assets										
Current assets:										
Cash and securities	$ 6	$ 7	$ 3	$ 1	$ 2	$ 2	$ 2	$ 1	$ 1	$ 1
Accounts receivable	33	36	38	39	41	43	45	47	51	55
Inventories	56	61	64	66	69	74	78	82	88	91
Total current assets	95	103	105	106	112	119	125	130	140	147
Plant and equipment	65	60	60	61	63	67	65	65	64	65
Investments in joint ventures							5	10	11	14
Total assets	$160	$163	$165	$167	$175	$186	$195	$205	$215	$226
Liabilities and Net Worth										
Current liabilities:										
Accounts payable	$ 31	$ 33	$ 36	$ 38	$ 46	$ 54	$ 62	$ 65	$ 70	$ 75
Accrued liabilities	7	9	10	11	13	17	22	25	31	36
Long-term debt due	6	6	6	6	6	6	6	6	6	6
Total current liabilities	44	48	52	55	65	77	86	96	107	117
Long-term debt	52	47	41	35	29	23	18	12	6	—
Total liabilities	96	95	93	90	94	100	104	108	113	117
Common stock	27	27	27	27	27	27	27	27	27	27
Retained earnings	37	41	45	50	54	59	64	70	75	82
Total liabilities and net worth	$160	$163	$165	$167	$175	$186	$195	$205	$215	$226

Exhibit 3

DATRONICS COMPANY
Income Statement, 1956–1965
($ millions)

	1956	1957	1958	1959	1960	1961	1962	1963	1964	1965
Contracts	$ 1.2	$6.4	$8.2	$7.5	$ 8.0	$ 7.9	$ 6.0	$ 4.3	$ 3.4	$ 2.4
Sales			0.2	2.1	4.4	8.1	14.3	22.5	34.2	48.1
Revenues	1.2	6.4	8.4	9.6	12.4	16.0	20.3	26.8	37.6	50.5
Cost of goods sold	1.0	4.5	6.0	6.9	8.9	11.5	14.7	19.6	27.8	37.9
Gross profits	0.2	1.9	2.4	2.7	3.5	4.5	5.6	7.2	9.8	12.6
Expenses	0.5	0.6	0.7	0.7	0.7	0.7	0.9	0.9	1.0	1.1
R&D		0.7	0.8	1.0	1.2	1.5	2.2	3.0	4.0	5.1
Profit before tax	(0.3)	0.6	0.9	1.0	1.6	2.3	2.5	3.3	4.8	6.4
Tax	(0.15)	0.2	0.4	0.5	0.8	1.1	1.2	1.6	2.4	3.2
Net profit	(0.15)	0.4	0.5	0.5	0.8	1.2	1.3	1.7	2.4	3.2
Earnings per share	($1.50)	$4	$5	$5	$8	$12	$10.40	$13.60	$19.20	$25.60

Exhibit 4

DATRONICS COMPANY
Balance Sheet, 1956–1965
($ millions)

	1956	1957	1958	1959	1960	1961	1962	1963	1964	1965
Assets										
Current assets:										
Cash..................	$0.05	$0.10	$0.10	$0.40	$0.20	$ 0.60	$ 0.60	$ 0.65	$ 1.56	$ 0.70
Inventories...........	0.20	2.60	2.70	3.70	5.20	6.20	6.80	10.15	15.22	20.10
Accounts receivable...		0.30	0.50	1.00	2.00	2.20	3.00	4.00	5.12	6.00
Total current assets	0.25	3.00	3.30	5.10	7.30	9.00	10.40	14.85	21.90	26.80
Plant and equipment........	0.50	1.00	1.20	1.40	2.00	3.10	5.10	7.50	8.50	9.00
Total assets...............	$0.75	$4.00	$5.50	$6.50	$9.30	$12.10	$15.50	$22.35	$30.40	$35.80
Liabilities and Net Worth										
Liabilities:										
Accounts payable	$0.10	$2.15	$2.20	$2.60	$3.65	$ 4.75	$ 5.50	$ 8.78	$12.10	$14.25
Accrued liabilities	0.10	1.00	1.05	1.25	1.65	2.25	1.70	2.77	3.80	3.85
	0.20	3.15	3.25	3.85	5.30	7.00	7.20	11.55	15.90	18.10
Notes payable.............	0.60	0.50	1.40	1.30	1.85	1.75	2.50	2.20	3.50	3.50
Total liabilities.........	0.80	3.65	4.65	5.15	7.15	8.75	9.70	13.75	19.45	21.60
Additional paid-in capital..							1.125	2.225	2.225	2.225
Common stock ($1 par).....	0.10	0.10	0.10	0.10	0.10	0.10	0.125	0.125	0.125	0.125
Retained earnings..........	(0.15)	0.25	0.75	1.25	2.05	3.25	4.55	6.25	8.65	11.85
Total liabilities and net worth....	$0.75	$4.00	$5.50	$6.50	$9.30	$12.10	$15.50	$22.35	$30.40	$35.80

gov't work

ment research grants and contracts. As a by-product of the government projects, the company also developed several types of sophisticated electronic equipment with wide applications to industry. The company concentrated its efforts on R&D, however, and subcontracted the production and bought marketing services for its commercial products. The lack of control over marketing and production and the lost profits passed to the marketers and subcontractors displeased the company's young president, John Martell. In his opinion, the growth of the company was limited until the right product emerged to justify going to a full manufacturing and marketing company.

Following Payson & Clark's investment in 1962, Datronics' engineers developed an exciting new product toward the end of 1964 which promised to sell extremely well due to its increased capacity and lower cost. John Martell saw the promise of the new product as the waited-for opportunity to expand the company. It was clear, however, that a major influx of capital was needed to bring the product to the market, build a sales force, and begin volume production. Therefore, Martell began a search for external capital that included a presentation to the joint venture partner, Payson & Clark, which already owned 20 percent of Datronics's stock.

Meanwhile, Harold Payson had been following the activities at Datronics closely and was quite aware of the growth potential of the company before John Martell's visit. Further, he recognized that Datronics, once its manufacturing operations started, would have a continual need for new capital. If Payson & Clark invested once, it would not be long until another request for resources came from Datronics. With these factors in mind, Payson decided that the most beneficial arrangement for both parties would be for his company to acquire Datronics. Martell agreed to this offer, and negotiations for a friendly takeover were consummated. Payson & Clark acquired Datronics for $42 million in November 1965. John Martell himself received $8.4 million in cash, notes, and securities.

The acquisition provided an opportunity for the Payson & Clark Company to update its image. Patterning itself after other successful growth companies of the time, it changed its name to PC&D, Inc., to denote the beginning of a new era in the company.

review mismatch of approach !!   *copy !*

PC&D, INC., 1965–1970

After the acquisition, Harold Payson restructured the company with the help of consultants, setting up a divisional organization. The old Payson & Clark Company now became the machinery division, headed by George McElroy, formerly vice president, manufacturing. The Datronics Company became the electronics division, headed by John Martell.

The electronics division

At the time of the acquisition, the Datronics Company consisted of several scientific labs, some test equipment, 10 professional engineers, administrative staff, and John Martell.

unlike P+C

Martell, an electrical engineer by training, was a man in his mid-thirties. He was energetic and a risk taker by nature, and even as a child in Iowa could not imagine working for someone else all his life. After college at MIT, he worked for eight years at a large, scientific equipment company in the Boston area. Initially, he was hired for the research group, but he was more attracted to the management positions in the company. He transferred first to the corporate planning office and then became plant manager for one of the divisions. With his technical competence and management experience, it was not surprising that he was approached by several of the more innovative of the company's research engineers to invest in and head up a new, independent R&D company. Martell bought in for 25 percent of the founding stock, and thus began the Datronics Company. — *entrepreneurial venture*

During his term as president of Datronics, Martell was highly regarded by the small group of employees. While he had a respectable command of the technology, he left the research to the engineers, devoting his time to developing sources of challenging and lucrative contracts.

After the acquisition by the Payson & Clark Company, Martell retained full control of the operations of his old organization that was now the electronics division. He hired an experienced industrial marketer from a large technical firm to set up the marketing operations and a friend of his from his old employer to head up the production operations. As expected, the demand for the division's new product was very high. Five years later, by 1970, the division was a successful growing enterprise, having expanded into other electronics fields. It had 700 employees; marketing offices established or opening throughout the United States, Europe, and Japan; plants at three different sites; and revenues of over $160 million. The business press reported these activities very favorably, giving much credit to the leadership of Martell.

The machinery division

Meanwhile, the machinery division continued to be the stalwart of the industry it always had been, retaining its structure and activities of the earlier time. George McElroy, division manager and senior vice president, was considered the mainstay of the division. He had joined the company in the early 1950s and was primarily responsible for the plastics innovations of that time. Advisor and confidant of Payson, McElroy was thought by his subordinates to be the next in line for the presidency.

As for Harold Payson himself, he limited his involvement in the company's internal affairs to reviewing budgets and year-end results, and spent most of his time with community activities and lobbying in Washington. He felt justified in this hands-off policy because of the quality of both his division vice presidents, McElroy and Martell. PC&D's performance further supported Payson's approach. Revenues climbed to $530 million, and profits after tax to $14 million by 1970. The solid 26 multiple of its stock price reflected the confidence in PC&D's prospects (Exhibits 5 and 6).

The compensation schemes reflected the extent to which Harold Payson allowed the division managers to be autonomous. McElroy's compen-

but what is company's direction?

Exhibit 5

PC&D, INC.
Income Statement, 1966–1970
($ millions)

	1966	1967	1968	1969	1970
Sales:					
Machinery div..............	$315.1	$327.5	$340.2	$354.1	$368.2
Electronics div.	66.1	84.7	106.7	132.3	161.4
Total sales	381.2	412.2	446.9	486.4	529.6
Cost of goods sold:					
Machinery div..............	251.7	264.3	271.8	284.7	297.9
Electronics div.	49.6	63.0	79.6	96.8	118.5
Total cost of goods sold .	301.3	327.3	351.4	381.5	416.4
Gross margin	79.9	84.9	95.5	104.9	113.2
Expenses:					
Marketing G&A expense ...	46.1	48.3	50.3	51.6	53.1
Product development—					
machinery div............	4.9	4.6	4.7	4.1	4.5
R&D—electronics div.	4.2	5.3	10.3	17.8	27.3
Total expense	55.2	58.2	65.3	73.5	84.9
Profit before interest					
and taxes	24.7	26.7	30.2	31.4	28.3
Interest	3.0	3.0	0.2	0.2	0.2
Profit before tax	22.7	23.7	30.0	31.2	28.1
Taxes	10.8	11.8	15.0	15.6	14.0
Net profit	$ 10.9	$ 11.9	$ 15.0	$ 15.6	$ 14.1
Earnings per share...........	$3.63	$3.97	$5.00	$5.20	$4.70
Average stock price	$94	$111	$145	$146	$103

sation was 90 percent salary, with a 10 percent bonus based on ROI. Martell received two thirds of his pay as a bonus based on growth in revenues. Compensation policies within each division were entirely at the discretion of either Martell or McElroy. In general, Martell made much greater use of incentive compensation than McElroy.

1970 change at PC&D

Toward the end of 1970, Harold Payson decided that it was time to limit his involvement to that of chairman of the board, and to name a new president of PC&D. He, himself, supported the appointment of George McElroy as the next president. McElroy was the next senior officer in the company and, after years of working with Harold Payson, held many of the same views as to the traditional values of PC&D. However, Payson agreed with the school of thought that chief executives should not choose their own successors. He, therefore, established a search committee, consisting of three outside members of the board of directors. (See Exhibit 7 for a list of board members.) A thorough job was done. The committee interviewed several candidates within PC&D, including John Martell and George McElroy. Outside candidates were also considered. The committee utilized executive search firms and con-

Exhibit 6

PC&D, INC.
Balance Sheet, 1966–1970
($ millions)

	1966	1967	1968	1969	1970
Assets					
Current assets:					
Cash and securities...............	$ 2	$ 5	$ 9	$ 7	$ 11
Accounts receivable	67	71	77	87	101
Inventories	118	128	145	166	180
Total current assets	187	214	231	260	292
Plant and equipment	83	95	97	108	120
Investments in joint ventures	10	11	12	12	10
Goodwill	6	6	5	5	5
Total assets	$286	$320	$345	$385	$427
Liabilities and Net Worth					
Current liabilities:					
Accounts payable..................	$ 90	$ 96	$103	$111	$127
Accrued liabilities	31	33	31	32	35
Long-term debt due	1	1	1	2	3
Total current liabilities	122	130	135	145	165
Long-term debt.....................	16	30	35	49	57
Total liabilities	138	160	170	194	222
Common stock and paid-in capital...	55	55	55	55	55
Retained earnings..................	93	105	120	136	150
Total liabilities and net worth	$286	$320	$345	$385	$427

sultants to identify candidates and carefully compared external and internal prospects. The result was the nomination of John Martell. While his relative youth was a surprise to some, the search committee's report explained the thinking behind the choice that "during the past five years PC&D has experienced an exciting and profitable period of growth and diversification. But it is essential that the company not become complacent. One of our major criteria in choosing a new president was to find

Exhibit 7

MEMBERS, BOARD OF DIRECTORS, 1970

Harold Payson IV, president—PC&D
George McElroy, senior vice president—machinery division, PC&D
John Martell, vice president—electronics division, PC&D
Carl Northrup, treasurer—PC&D
David S. Curtis, partner—Barth & Gimbel, Wall Street brokerage firm
Elizabeth B. Payne, partner—Payne, Bartley & Springer, Washington law firm
Charles F. Sprague, president—Forrest Products, Inc. (large manufacturing firm)
Gardner L. Stacy III, Dean, Business School, State University
James Hoffman, vice president—Baltimore Analysts Association (international firm)

not McElroy!

a person with the energy and vision to continue PC&D's growth and expansion." The board unanimously approved the selection of John Martell as president and CEO.

Martell began his new position with the board's mandate in mind. He planned to continue the diversification of PS&D into high-growth industries. He expected to follow both an acquisition mode and a start-up mode, using the excess funds from the machinery division and PC&D's rising stock to finance the growth. For start-ups, Martell planned to use joint ventures supporting newer companies, much as the old Payson & Clark Company had supported his venture in its early days.

Martell brought to his position a very definite management style. He was a strong believer in the benefits accruing from an opportunistic, entrepreneurial spirit, and he wanted to inject PC&D with this kind of energy. However, he was concerned that the kind of people with this kind of spirit would not be attracted to work with PC&D because of the stigma, real or imagined, of being attached to a large company.

As Martell commented:

> It was my experience that there are two worlds of people, some of whom are very secure and comfortable and satisfied in their career pursuits in large institutionalized companies, and others of whom are, I think, wild ducks, and who are interested in perhaps greater challenges that small companies present in terms of the necessity to succeed or die.
>
> In many work environments, the constraints placed upon the individual by the nature of the institution are such as to sometimes make people uncomfortable.
>
> The decision-making process is long and involved, sometimes not known, in the sense that the people who act upon decisions are not in close proximity to those who benefit or suffer from the effects of those decisions.
>
> The formalization of the decision-making process is frequently an irritant, and for people who are unusually energetic and demanding, in the sense of desiring, themselves, to take action and to have their actions complemented by the actions of other people upon whom they are dependent, I would characterize these people as perhaps being wild ducks rather than tame ducks. In that sense, I wanted more "wild ducks" in our company.

Martell himself credited the success of the electronics division to Payson's willingness to turn the reins completely over to him. The secret, Martell thought, was in spotting the right person with both ability and integrity. Corporate headquarters' role should be to provide resources in terms of both money and expertise as needed, to set timetables, to provide measurement points and incentive, and then to keep hands off. While the board's directives were clear to Martell, the specifics for implementation were not. Not only were the larger questions of which way to diversify or how to encourage innovation unanswered, but how to plan and who to involve were also unclear. Martell was not given the luxury of time to resolve these issues. Within the first week in his new position, three professionals from the electronics division called on Martell. Bert Rogers and Elaine Patterson were key engineers from the research department, and Thomas Grennan was head of marketing, western region. They had been working on some ideas for a new product

plan!

(not competing with any PC&D current lines) and were ready to leave the company to start their own business to develop and market it. Indeed, they had already had a prospectus prepared for their new venture. They were hoping either Martell personally or PC&D, Inc., might be able to provide some venture capital. The president particularly liked these three and admired their willingness to take such personal risks with a product as yet unresearched as to market or design. Indeed, with his energy and "can do," aggressive style, Tom Grennan reminded Martell of himself just a few years ago when he left to start the Datronics Company.

Martell liked the product and saw the idea as a possible route for continuing the diversification and growth of PC&D. But there was a problem. It was clear from the presentation of the three that much of their motivation came from the desire to start their own company and, through their equity interest, to reap the high rewards of their efforts if successful. Martell did not fault this motivation, for it had been his as well. He could not expect PC&D's managers to take large personal risks if there was no potential for a large payoff. Further, a fair offer to the group, if in salary, required more than PC&D could afford or could justify to the older divisions. Martell told Rogers, Patterson, and Grennan that he was very interested and asked if he could review the prospectus overnight and get back to them the next day. That night, he devised a plan of which he was particularly proud. The major feature of the plan Martell called the "entrepreneurial subsidiary." Martell presented this proposal to Grennan, Rogers, and Patterson the next day. They readily accepted, and a pattern for most of PC&D's diversification over the next five years was begun.

THE ENTREPRENEURIAL SUBSIDIARY

Martell's plan was as follows:

When a proposal for a new product area was made to the PC&D corporate office, a new (entrepreneurial) subsidiary would be incorporated. The initiators of the idea would leave their old division or company and become officers and employees of the new subsidiary. In the current example, the new subsidiary was the Pro Instrument Corporation with Grennan as president and Rogers and Patterson as vice presidents.

The new subsidiary would issue stock in its name, $1 par value, 80 percent of which would be bought by PC&D, Inc., and 20 percent by the entrepreneurs involved—engineers and other key officers. This initial capitalization, plus sizable direct loans from PC&D, Inc., provided the funds for the research and development of the new product up to its commercialization. In the case of Pro Instruments, Patterson and Rogers hired 10 other researchers, while Grennan hired a market researcher and a finance/accounting person. These 15 people invested $50,000 together, and PC&D invested another $200,000.

Two kinds of agreements were signed between the two parties. The first was a research contract between the parent company and the subsidiary; setting time schedules for the research, defining requirements for a commercializable product, outlining budgets, and otherwise stipulating obligations on both sides. In general, the sub was responsible for the R&D and production and testing of a set number of prototypes of a new product, while the parent company would market and produce the product on an international scale. Pro Instruments's agreement stipulated two phases, one lasting 18 months to produce a prototype, and another lasting 6 months to test the product in the field and produce a marketing plan. Detailed budget and personnel needs were outlined, providing for a $900,000 working capital loan from PC&D during the first phase and $425,000 during the second.

While PC&D, Inc., had proprietary rights on the product and all revenues received from marketing it, the agreement often included an incentive kicker for the key engineers in the form of additional stock to be issued if the finished product produced certain specified amounts of revenue by given dates. Indeed, this was the case for Pro Instruments: 5,000 shares in year 1, to be issued if net profits were over $250,000; 20,000 shares in year 2 if profits were over $1 million; and 10,000 in year 3 if profits were over $3 million.

The second agreement specified the financial obligations and terms for merger. Once the terms of the research contract were met, PC&D, with board approval, had the option for a stated period of time (usually four years) to merge the subsidiary through a one-for-one exchange of PC&D stock for the stock of the subsidiary. The sub was then dissolved. To protect the interests of entrepreneurs, PC&D was required to vote on merger of the sub within 60 days if the sub met certain criteria. For Pro Instruments, the criteria were (1) the product earned cumulative profits of $500,000 and (2) if the earnings of PC&D and the sub were consolidated, dilution of PC&D's earnings per share would not have occurred over three consecutive quarters. If PC&D did not choose to merge during the 60 days, then the sub had a right to buy out PC&D's interest.

Since PC&D's stock was selling for $103 in 1970 and subsidiary stock was bought for $1 per share, the exchange of stock represented a tremendous potential return. Depending on the value of PC&D's stock at the time of merger, the net worth of the "entrepreneurs" who originally invested in the sub multiplied overnight. Indeed, as subs were merged in ensuing years, typical gains ranged from 100 to 200 times the original investments in the entrepreneurial sub. For example, PC&D exercised its option to merge Pro Instruments when its product was brought to market in 1972. Thomas Grennan, who had bought 6,000 shares of Pro Instruments stock, found his 6,000 shares of PC&D valued at $936,000 (PC&D common selling for $156 on the New York Stock Exchange at the time). By the end of 1974, Pro Instruments's new product had earned $50 million in revenue and $4.8 million in profits, thus qualifying the original entrepreneurs for stock bonuses. Grennan received another 4,200 shares valued at $684,600. Thus, in four years, he had earned about $1.6 million on a $6,000 investment.

By setting up entrepreneurial subs like Pro Instruments, Mr. Martell had several expectations. In the process of setting up a subsidiary with the dynamics of a small, independent group, Martell hoped to create the loyalty, cohesion, and informal structure conducive to successful research and development efforts. The sub would have a separate location and its own officers who decided structure and operating policies. Further, it provided the opportunity to buy into and reap the benefits of ownership in the equity of a company. In Mr. Martell's words:

> I think the concept of the entrepreneurial subsidiaries was the outgrowth of the insight that in many industrial corporations the system of rewards is perhaps inverted from what many people think it should be; that the hierarchy of the institution commends itself to those people who are capable of magaging other people's efforts, and those people at lower echelons who are unusually creative and who, as a result of their creativity and innovation and daring in the technical sense or perhaps in a marketing sense, are unusually responsible for the accomplishments of the business, are very frequently forgotten about in the larger rewards of the enterprise.
>
> I, on the other hand, recognized that such persons are frequently, perhaps by training, inclination or otherwise, not capable of marshaling the financial resources or organizing the manufacturing and marketing efforts required to exploit their creativity. Without the kind of assistance that PC&D was capable of lending to them—an assured marketing capability was often a key concern—they are wary of undertaking new ventures.

Further, it was Mr. Martell's opinion that the organizational and incentive structure of the entrepreneurial sub would attract the best engineers from older, more secure firms to PC&D—the so-called wild ducks. More important, Martell hoped to encourage the timely development of new products with minimal initial investment by PC&D. If Pro Instruments, for example, did not meet its timetable with the original money invested, its officers would have to approach PC&D for new money just as if they were an outside company. PC&D would then have multiple opportunities to review and consider the investment. If the entrepreneurial sub failed or could not get more money from the parent, PC&D was under no obligation to keep the company alive or to rehire its employees. If loans were involved, PC&D could act as any other creditor. As Martell observed,

> The benefit to PC&D shareholders was in the rapid expansion of PC&D's products, the size of the company, the ability of the company to compete in the marketplace in a way which PC&D, dependent upon only internal development projects, could never have achieved, or could have achieved only at much greater costs and over a longer period of years.

However, Martell felt the stock incentives would properly reward the genius of creative engineers for the service performed without having to pay high salaries over a long potentially unproductive period after the initial product was developed. Employees did not have to be rehired, nor were they obligated to continue employment, even if the sub was merged. Those that were rehired would be paid at the normal salary levels of comparable people at PC&D. The reasoning here was that:

> . . . there were two criteria for establishing an entrepreneurial subsidiary. The first criterion was that the R&D objectives of the subsidiary could

not be reached except under the aegis of the subsidiary, because it involved people who were not involved in PC&D's main lines of business.

The other criterion was that considerable career risk must exist for the people who would leave their established positions within the management structure of PC&D to undertake the entrepreneurial venture of the new subsidiary. Also, the people, in some part, had to be new talent who came from outside PC&D. When I refer to career risk, I mean for example that if a director of engineering at PC&D left his or her post to join an entrepreneurial subsidiary, a new director of engineering would be appointed, and given the lack of success of the entrepreneurial subsidiary, there would in effect be no position of director of engineering to which the person could return. Moreover, it is probable that we would not want the individual to return.

The stock incentive also motivated the engineers to produce without having to commit any resources of the parent company for the future, since the corporation was not required to merge the sub or to produce and market the new product. The incentive kicker, moreover, would ensure quality. A product that was rushed through development would be more likely to have problems and not reach revenue goals.

Another advantage of the entrepreneurial sub was its effect on decision making. Without the need to go through the entire corporate hierarchy, decisions would be made closer to the operating level. This would enhance the quality of decisions because managers performed best, according to Martell, when given objectives and resources from top managers but with operating decisions left unfettered.

Finally, Martell expected that the entrepreneurial sub would be the training and proving ground of PC&D's future top managers. By providing the means for these executives to gain great personal wealth, Martell expected to gain their loyalty and continued efforts for both himself and PC&D.

PC&D, INC., 1970–1975

During the first five years of Martell's presidency, PC&D's growth was quite impressive. With revenues topping the billion dollar mark in 1975, growth had averaged about 15 percent in revenues and 35 percent in profits after tax during the five years. (See Exhibits 8 and 9 for financials.) Such growth had been achieved, to a large extent, from new products developed in entrepreneurial subsidiaries. In 1975 sales of $179.2 million and profit before taxes and interest of $22.1 million came from these new products.[1] All together, 11 entrepreneurial subsidiaries had been organized during the 1970–75 time frame. Of these, four had successfully developed products and had been merged into PC&D—one in 1972, one in 1973, and two in 1974. The other seven were younger, and work was still in process. None had failed so far.

Most subsidiaries grew out of needs of the electronics division or

---

[1] Of PC&D total assets in 1975, approximately 40 percent were devoted to the machinery division, 35 percent to the traditional electronics division, and 25 percent to the entrepreneurial subsidiaries.

Exhibit 8

PC&D, INC.
Income Statement, 1971–1975
($ millions)

	1971	1972	1973	1974	1975
Sales:					
Machinery div.	$382.9	$397.8	$412.5	$426.9	$ 440.6
Electronics div.*	193.6	235.6	300.1	397.4	561.4
Total sales	576.5	633.4	712.6	824.3	1,002.0
Cost of goods sold:					
Machinery div.	311.3	322.6	338.2	350.9	359.1
Electronics div.	145.2	174.3	216.1	282.2	421.1
Total cost of goods sold	456.5	496.9	554.3	633.1	780.2
Gross margin	120.0	136.5	158.3	191.2	221.8
Expenses:					
Marketing G&A expense	54.7	56.3	59.1	63.3	67.7
Product development— machinery div.	5.0	5.1	5.2	5.2	5.3
R&D—electronics div.	28.4	29.5	30.7	31.9	33.5
Total expenses	88.1	90.9	95.0	100.4	106.5
Profit before interest and taxes	31.9	45.6	63.3	90.8	115.3
Interest	0.2	3.0	3.0	7.0	11.0
Profit before tax	31.7	42.6	60.3	83.8	104.3
Taxes	15.8	21.3	30.1	41.9	52.1
Net profit	15.9	21.3	30.2	41.9	52.2
Earnings per share	$5.30	$6.45†	$8.39	$10.47	$13.05
Average stock price	$106	$156	$158	$163	$238

* Sales figures for electronics include both sales by the original division plus sales of new subsidiaries after they are merged. Thus in 1975 the $561.4 million in sales for electronics includes $179.2 from products developed in subs. Profit before interest and taxes from new products was $22.1 million.

† Number of shares increased in 1972 by 0.3 million from the merger of Pro Instruments. They increased in 1973 by 0.3 million from merger of sub 2, and again by 0.4 million in 1974 from the merger of subs 3 and 4. Thus in 1974 there was a total of four million shares outstanding. In late 1973, there was a secondary offering of 1 million shares.

Pro Instruments. Competitors in the electronics equipment industry were beginning to integrate backward, lowering costs by producing their own semiconductors. The need to remain cost competitive caused PC&D to establish entrepreneurial subs to develop specialized components including semiconductors, assuming that these could be used both by PC&D and sold in outside markets. In the process of selling semiconductors to outside customers, ideas for new products using PC&D components were stimulated, and new subs were formed to develop these equipment products. The cost of merging the two types of subs, components or equipment, differed, however. Equipment subs were cheaper insofar as they could share the already existent sales force of the electronics division; many parts could be standard ones already utilized in other products; and the processes were similar to other electronics products.

Exhibit 9

PC&D, INC.
Balance Sheet, 1971–1975
($ millions)

	1971	1972	1973	1974	1975
Assets					
Current assets:					
Cash and securities	$ 10	$ 5	$ 2	$ 2	$ 3
Accounts receivable	117	131	155	171	213
Inventories	200	223	270	327	401
Total current assets	327	359	427	500	617
Plant and equipment	122	124	125	178	232
Investments in joint ventures	10	8	10	9	6
Investments in subsidiaries	5	10	21	16	25
Goodwill	4	4	3	3	2
Total assets	$468	$505	$586	$706	$882
Liabilities and Net Worth					
Current liabilities:					
Accounts payable	$151	$160	$179	$193	$243
Accrued liabilities	37	41	46	51	65
Long-term debt due	4	4	4	6	7
Total current liabilities	192	205	229	250	315
Long-term debt	55	58	84	138	193
Total liabilities	247	263	313	388	508
Common stock and paid-in capital	55	55	56	57	57
Retained earnings	166	187	217	261	317
Total liabilities and net worth	$468	$505	$586	$706	$882

But with semiconductors, new plant, new sales channels, new manufacturing processes, and new skills at all levels had to be built. While to Martell the move into semiconductors promised a large cash flow in the future in a booming industry, some in the company were concerned that the current cash drain was not the best use of scarce cash resources.

When Martell first became president, he made few changes in PC&D's organization structure. McElroy continued as vice president, machinery division, and retained control over that division's structure and policies. Martell himself retained his responsibilities as manager of the electronics division. This he did reluctantly and with all intentions of finding a new executive for the job; however, the unexpected nature of his promotion left Martell without a ready candidate.

As the subs began to be merged, beginning with Pro Instruments in 1972, questions of organization began to arise. In typical fashion, Martell wanted to pass involvement in these decisions down to the appropriate managers. There was also no question that Pro Instrument's president, Tom Grennan, had proven himself with the new subsidiary. So in 1972 Martell appointed Grennan to division vice president, electronics, based on Grennan's superlative performance. Further, because the products were complementary, all of the subs that were merged in this period were placed in the electronics division. Moreover, in recognition of the increased number of products, Grennan did reorganize the electronics division. He appointed his Pro Instruments colleague, Bert Rogers, to director of research which was organized by product area. Manufacturing, also organized by product, reflected the development by subsidiary as well. Marketing, on the other hand, was organized by region as it had been previously. Until they were merged, however, subsidiary presidents went directly to Mr. Martell for resolution of problems that arose. (See Exhibit 10 for an organization chart in 1975.)

By 1975 the electronics division's enlarged marketing and production departments employed 4,000 people with production plants in three different locations. Electronics now had sales of $561.4 million as compared to machinery's $440.6 million.

While successful development projects from subsidiaries had been largely responsible for the sales growth at PC&D, this result had not come without costs. First, the subsidiaries required funds—$60 million by the end of 1975. Some of these funds came from retained earnings, but much was new money raised in the form of long-term debt. Further, stock issued to capitalize subs and pay bonuses to "entrepreneurs" had a diluting effect on PC&D's shares. If all subsidiaries were merged and successful, the number of new shares could be significant. While raising such a sizable amount of new funds was not particularly difficult for a company as large as PC&D, the needs arising from the subsidiaries left little new money for the core businesses of PC&D. The machinery division, for example, had not had their development budget increased at all during the five years ending 1975.

Current concerns

Despite PC&D's recent successes, Mr. Martell was not without worries. Several problem areas had appeared in both the electronics and machinery divisions.

In electronics, personnel and products originating in subsidiaries now equaled or surpassed those from the original division. It had been part of the strategy of the entrepreneurial subsidiaries to use them as devices to attract talent from other firms. A key researcher hired from outside was encouraged to hire, in turn, the best of his or her former colleagues. Thus, the loyalty and friendships between key "entrepreneurs" and their staffs were often strong and of long standing. As the entrepreneurial subsidiaries were merged, their personnel tended to retain this loyalty to the president or key officers of the old sub rather than transferring it to PC&D. Thus, several warring spheres of influence were developing in the division, particularly in the research department and between research and other departments. Martell was concerned that such influences and warring would lead to poor decisions and much wasted energy in the division.

Turnover in electronics was also increasing. This was of particular concern to Martell for it was just those talented engineers that the entrepreneurial subsidiaries were meant to attract that were beginning to leave. For example, Elaine Patterson, formerly of Pro Instruments, left during 1975 to start her own company, taking 20 research engineers

Exhibit 10
ORGANIZATION CHART, 1975

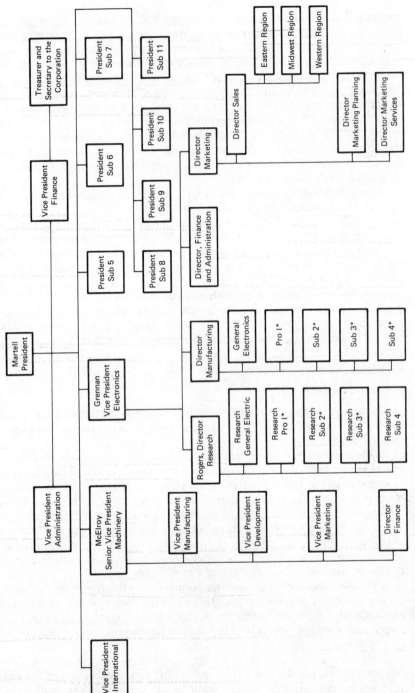

* Reference to subsidiaries indicates origin of personnel and product.

with her. The source of the turnover was unclear, but possible factors included distaste for the kind of warring atmosphere mentioned above and the inability to be a part of a large corporate R&D department with its demand for budgets and reports.

For many employees, however, the sudden absence of monetary incentives changed the climate drastically. This lack of incentive, coupled with the discovery that the most challenging projects were taken on by newly formed subsidiaries which favored hiring outside expertise, caused dissatisfaction. For Martell, such turnover was of greatest concern in the long run, for the inability to create a strong central R&D department in electronics created a continuing need for more entrepreneurial subs. These subsidiaries were still too new an idea for Martell to want to risk his entire future R&D program on their successes. Further, most of the new products were in highly competitive areas. Without continuing upgrades, these products would soon become obsolete. A strong central R&D department was needed for follow-up development of products started by subsidiaries.

Finally, Martell was concerned by recent indications of rather serious operating problems in the electronics division. This was particularly disturbing in that Martell had placed complete faith in Grennan's managerial ability. The most recent cost report, for example, indicated that marketing, G&A, and engineering expenses were way out of line in the division. Further, the marketing and production departments reported problems in several products originating in the subs. One product, with expected obsolescence of four years, now showed a six-year breakeven just to cover the engineering and production costs. Another product, completing its first year on the market, had been forecasted by the subsidiary to achieve $20 million in sales in its first two years. However, during the first six months, losses had been incurred because of customer returns. A report on the causes of the returns showed a predominance of product failures. The chances for breakeven on this product looked bleak. While none of these problems had affected operating results yet, Martell was especially concerned that these operating problems would have a negative impact on first quarter 1976 earnings.

Martell had not confronted Grennan with these operating problems as yet. He had wanted to see how the division itself was attacking these issues through its long-range plan. Martell had requested Grennan to prepare a long-range plan (five years) as well as the usual one-year operating plan. The product of this effort had only arrived recently (February 1976), and Martell had not had a chance to study it. (Table of contents is reproduced in Exhibit 11.) Its 100-page bulk loomed on Martell's desk. Quick perusal had indicated maybe four pages of prose scattered through the plan, and dozens of charts, graphs, and tables of numbers, every one of which manifested an upward trend.

In an attempt to get employee feedback on all of these problems, Martell had contracted an outside consulting firm to carry out confidential interviews with personnel in the electronics division. The interviews found middle managers quite concerned over the "confusion in the division" which was causing a loss of morale there. The consultant's report

Exhibit 11

ELECTRONICS DIVISION
1976 OPERATING PLAN
1977–1980 LONG-RANGE OUTLOOK

Table of Contents

Exhibit 11 (*continued*)

cited concrete problems, including lost equipment, missed billings, and confusion in the plant. Typical comments from lower level personnel included:

> Either upper management is not being informed of problems or they don't know how to solve them.
> Morale is very poor, job security is nil.
> There is little emphasis on production efficiencies.
> Scrap is unaccounted for.
> Market forecasts are grossly inaccurate.
> Production schedules have a definite saw-tooth pattern. There is very little good planning.
> There are no systematic controls.

These were not the sort of comments Martell expected from the division responsible for the major portion of PC&D's future growth. His concern, at this time, was not so much the problems themselves but what was being done about them. His preferred policy was obviously to stay out of day-to-day operating problems. He wondered how long it was prudent to allow such problems to continue without some intervention on his part.

Meanwhile, the machinery division had its own problems. The last major construction of new plant had been in the early 1950s. Since that time, McElroy had upgraded production methods, which succeeded in checking rising costs. However, since 1965, resources for such improvements had not been increased; and with inflation in the 1970s, less and less could be done on a marginal basis. McElroy was currently of the opinion that capacity was sufficient for the short term, but that it was impossible to remain state-of-the-art.[2] Indeed, the machinery division's products were beginning to fall behind the new developments of competitors. Further, the costs of the machinery division's products were beginning to inch up. As the production line aged, quality control reported an increasing percentage of defective goods. In contrast to the

---

[2] McElroy suspected that the machinery division would require an investment of $100 to $125 million over two to three years to revitalize the product line and plant and equipment. McElroy felt that in the long term the return on this investment would match the division's historic ROI.

situation in the machinery division, the rather extensive investment in new plant for the production of semiconductors did not sit too well with McElroy who was concerned with the lack of flexibility that could result from backward integrating and thought component needs should be farmed out to the cheapest bidder from the numerous small component firms. Martell was concerned how long he could keep McElroy satisfied without a major investment in the machinery division and how long he could count on the cash flow from the machinery division for other users.

Also, turnover, a problem never before experienced in the machinery division, had appeared. Here, however, it was the salespeople who were leaving. Martell worried over this trend, for the sales force was the strength of the division. According to the head of marketing the salespeople considered themselves the best in the industry, and they did not wish to sell products which were not the best. They saw the machinery division's products no longer as the best in quality or state-of-the-art. Further, they did not wish to work for a company where they felt unimportant. Whether true or not, the sales force certainly appeared less aggressive than in previous times.

Thus, Martell was not overly surprised to receive McElroy's letter nor was he certain that some of McElroy's anger concerning the electronics division was not justified. Martell knew he had to do something about McElroy, as well as Grennan and the electronics division. He also had to decide whether entrepreneurial subsidiaries should continue to be part of PC&D's research and development strategy. Finally, all of Martell's decisions concerning the divisions and subsidiaries needed to be consistent with a strategy that would continue PC&D's growth.

The Dexter Corporation

FOUNDED AT Windsor Locks, Connecticut, in 1767 as a sawmill, and subsequently a producer of paper products, the C. H. Dexter & Sons Company had by the 1950s become what David L. Coffin, chairman of The Dexter Corporation and a seventh generation descendant of the founding family, described as "a typical family-run New England company." When Mr. Coffin assumed the presidency of the company in 1958 at the age of 32, he had ambitions to expand the company. In order to achieve this he retained a consultant, and together they generated a five-year plan of growth through acquisition for Dexter. Over a period of years Mr. Coffin had changed the composition of the board of directors, instituted cost controls, and hired professional management.

One of the managers attracted to Dexter was Mr. Worth Loomis, who came to the company in 1970 as vice president finance from a career in manufacturing. Mr. Loomis became president of Dexter in 1973. Continuing the direction established by Mr. Coffin, Mr. Loomis guided the development of the company's long-range plan from a simple forecast to a document containing much more strategic information. Analytic approaches developed by The Boston Consulting Group and PIMS[1] facilitated this process. Since both these approaches required that all "businesses" within Dexter be identified and isolated for planning purposes, Dexter had divided its 5 divisions into 26 strategic business segments (SBSs).

Although Mr. Loomis was of the opinion that Dexter's approach to planning had contributed to the company's strong financial performance, he was undecided about some recent proposals to integrate Dexter's approach to planning with other administrative systems. One proposal called for monthly results, income statement and balance sheet,

---

[1] *Profit Impact of Market Strategies*, a model developed by the Strategic Planning Institute, Cambridge, Massachusetts.

to be reported by strategic business segment. Currently, divisional performance was reported monthly and SBS results annually. Although Mr. Loomis felt it made some sense to monitor SBS performance monthly, collecting the information presented problems of allocating shared manufacturing, selling, and R&D expenses. Another proposal called for a revamping of Dexter's incentive compensation system to pay bonuses based on SBS, rather than divisional performance. Although the details of this proposal had yet to be developed, the notions of changing monthly reporting and incentive compensation both had the virtues of focusing more attention on Dexter's strategic business segments. However, Mr. Loomis was aware that the definition of the business segments was by no means perfect and had involved considerable compromise. Indeed, limiting the company to 26 segments was somewhat arbitrary. He was also of the opinion that if the current operating format was working well, changes should not be made—"if it isn't broken, why fix it."

In dealing with the above issues, Mr. Loomis was most concerned whether any changes would help or hinder the performance of Dexter's businesses. An example that was of immediate concern was Dexter's Hysol division and particularly its semiconductor molding powder business. In two days, Mr. Loomis was scheduled to fly to California for the November 1978 review of Hysol's plans and performance with Mr. Lloyd Dixon, Hysol's president. A report prepared by The Boston Consulting Group in 1974 had concluded that Hysol had an opportunity in the next several years to establish a significant position in the rapidly growing semiconductor molding powder business. An aggressive growth strategy had been recommended and agreed upon. From 1974 to 1977 Hysol's sales of molding powder to the electronics industry had indeed grown considerably (17 percent compound growth per year), but it was not clear whether the division had established a strong competitive position. Hysol was still number two in this industry. Mr. Loomis wanted to discuss this situation with Mr. Dixon, but first he wanted to determine why Hysol had apparently been unable to improve its market position in semiconductor molding powders. Specifically, Mr. Loomis wondered if the lack of improvement was caused by competitive factors, or problems with Hysol's or Dexter's management practices.

The remainder of the case is divided into two parts. The first part describes the company and the corporate divisional relationships. The second part describes Mr. Loomis's understanding of the Hysol division, and particularly the situation in Hysol's molding powder business segment.

PART I—COMPANY BACKGROUND

CORPORATE PERFORMANCE AND OBJECTIVES

For 1967, the year Dexter went public, sales were $35.1 million, net income $2.2 million. Ten years later, in 1977, sales were $315.8 million; net income totaled $18.5 million. From 1973 to 1977 sales, including acquisitions, had grown at over 22 percent per annum, while net income

Exhibit 1

THE DEXTER CORPORATION
Five-Year Summary of Financial Data ($ millions)
(all years restated to take into account poolings)

	1977	1976	1975	1974	1973
Operating results:					
Net sales	$315.8	$255.1	$204.9	$199.7	$140.7
Cost of sales	198.4	158.6	126.3	128.4	83.5
Marketing and administrative	61.0	50.4	42.9	39.4	31.7
R&D expenditures.....	9.8	8.0	6.6	6.1	5.3
Income before interest, depreciation and foreign exchange	41.4	34.6	25.1	22.2	17.0
Net income (after interest, depreciation and taxes)	18.6	15.4	10.3	9.2*	7.6
Working capital	61.2	53.4	44.1	40.9	28.3
Total assets	185.5	176.9	n.a.	n.a.	n.a.
Other data:					
Debt to capital	16.0%	19.8%	21.5%	25.9%	19.7%
Earning on average stockholders' equity .	18.3%	17.3%	13.2%	13.0%	12.0%
Net income per share (in dollars)	2.04	1.70	1.15	1.01	.85
Dividend payout	29.4%	23.9%	22.1%	22.4%	20.9%
Price-earnings range ..	10–7	10–5	9–5	11–5	18–8

n.a. = Not available.
* Reduced $3.3 by a change from FIFO to LIFO.
Source: The Dexter Corporation 1977 annual report.

grew at almost 25 percent, and return on equity increased from 12 percent to 18 percent. Approximately two-thirds of Dexter's growth since 1967 was internally generated as opposed to acquired. Exhibit 1 presents a summary of financial performance.

Specific corporate objectives had originally been developed for the diversification program begun in 1958. The corporate objectives presently in place were formulated in 1970 and had been revised several times (Exhibit 2). Internal growth was expected to proceed at 12 percent per year. The expectation was for only one more major acquisition before 1985.

Although Mr. Coffin left the day-to-day operation of the company to Mr. Loomis, he was closely involved in any major acquisitions. In addition, each year he issued what had come to be known as the "DLC challenge" (*David L. Coffin*). The following were part of the 1978 challenge:

	Challenge for 1980	*Challenge for 1985*
Sales...................	$500 million	$1,000 million
Profits	$30 million	$60 million
Earnings per share....	$4	$4
Shares	7,400,000	15,000,000

Exhibit 2

POLICY STATEMENT

CORPORATE OBJECTIVES

The following objectives were developed by management:

1. To develop the corporation so that it can *achieve* and maintain over the 10-year period a *10–15 percent increase in net income per share each year.* This would come from a target 12 percent internal growth and the balance in acquisitions and special projects.
2. To carry out the above task while:
   a. Increasing dividends as profit increases but not necessarily by as large a percentage.
   b. Not yielding management control to an outside concentrated group of stockholders.
   c. Maintaining a strong financial position by:
      (1) Achieving an overall corporate return in total capital in excess of 12½ percent after taxes.
      (2) Limiting investment in nonproduction facilities to that which is necessary to the growth and maintenance of the business.
      (3) Utilizing the leverage of debt but not exceeding a debt-to-equity ratio of 40 percent.
3. To improve the qualitative nature of Dexter's earnings by *improving:*
   a. The company's participation in *recognized growth markets.*
   b. The company's dollar volume in *high-margin proprietary products.*
   c. Emphasis on marketing position.
   d. By limiting the company's dependence on a single product/single customer market to 10–15 percent of its sales volume.
4. At the same time to *maintain* the company's reputation for:
   a. *New product* introduction from *within.*
   b. Being a *leader* in its field of operation.
   c. Having a *low degree* of *vulnerability* to technoeconomic and governmental factors outside the corporation control.
   d. A *high level* of *management* expertise both at the corporate level and in divisions.
   e. Maintaining a *logical grouping* of its businesses.
   f. Maintaining a *sound financial* reputation.

To make such acquisitions as are necessary to carry out all the aforementioned objectives provided that such acquisitions are in related fields and will not damage the company's qualitative image.

Consistent with the above objectives, the corporation's *international* operation should represent not more than *30* percent of the total corporate *profits* either through export from the United States or growth in manufacturing overseas. The competitive nature of overseas markets requires emphasis on manufacturing abroad, in which case we prefer to own the equity, except in special situations.

Corporate development
long-range planning meeting
June 1970
1st Rev.—Oct. 16, 1970
2d Rev.—June 25, 1971
3d Rev.—Feb. 1972
4th Rev.—May 1972
5th Rev.—June 1978

emc
8/3/78

These challenges were intended more to stimulate thinking and discussion than as a "hard" objective for the company.

DIVERSIFICATION

The initial impetus for diversification had been to reduce the company's dependence on the highly capital-intensive nonwovens (paper) business. A listing of Dexter's acquisitions is given in Exhibit 3. All of these mergers and acquisitions were friendly, and Dexter often had long involvement (over five years in some instances) with a candidate prior to consummation of an acquisition. The nonwovens business characterized by such specialties as teabag paper (invented by Dexter) and surgical disposables remained a strong business growing as fast or faster than the acquisitions.

Dexter's major acquisitions and mergers were of Midland Industries, Hysol Corporation, Puritan Sanitation Chemical, Mogul Corporation, and Howe & Bainbridge. Midland was one of the earliest acquisitions and provided Dexter with a strong entry into the specialty coatings market. The Hysol Corporation produced epoxy (plastic) compounds used for coating and encapsulating electrical and electronic components. As a condition of the merger, Dexter went public in 1967. The acquisition of Puritan Chemical and the merger with Mogul Corporation gave Dexter a strong position in the sanitation and water treatment chemicals

Exhibit 3

ACQUISITION RECORD
($000)

	Acquisition	Date acquired	Sales in the 12 months preceding purchase	Pool or purchase	Division incorporated into (as of 1978)
1.	Chemical Coating	7/1/60	1,276	Purchase	Midland
2.	Lacquer Products	5/1/62	1,434	Purchase	Midland
3.	Midland Industries	10/31/63	4,841	Purchase	Midland
4.	Hysol	11/29/67	6,079	Pool	Hysol
5.	Magna	11/30/67	1,133	Purchase	Midland
6.	Shell Adhesives	10/1/69	2,531	Purchase	Hysol
7.	Wornow	6/30/70	988	Pool	Hysol
8.	Puritan	3/31/73	8,576	Purchase	Mogul
9.	Bouvet	4/1/73	10,745	Purchase	Midland
10.	Howe & Bainbridge	10/1/76	32,100	Purchase	C. H. Dexter
11.	Mogul*	5/9/77	66,555	Pool	Mogul Water treatment Gibco/Invenex Life sciences
12.	Adhesive Engineering	6/7/77	650	Purchase	Hysol

Note: Recently Dexter had made a number of small cash acquisitions—Micro-Tech Diagnostics, Tucson, Arizona (9/77); Hunter Chemical Company, Houston, Texas (5/78); De Beers Laboratories, Addison, Illinois (6/78); and Magnachem B.V. (Holland) and Magnachem GmbH (Germany) (9/78).

* From 1963 until being merged with Dexter, Mogul made 31 acquisitions of, or mergers with, companies with sales in excess of $200,000.

Source: Company internal records.

business. Finally, Howe & Bainbridge was a major developer and marketer of woven fabric, primarily for recreational uses, such as sailcloth or tents.

Although the acquired businesses were previously free-standing entities, not all of the acquisitions became separate divisions of Dexter. For example, Howe & Bainbridge had become part of Dexter's original core business, the C. H. Dexter division. Puritan and the water treatment part of the Mogul Corporation were combined to form the Mogul division of Dexter. The life science products of Mogul Corporation were made a separate division of Dexter called Gibco/Invenex. All of the smaller acquisitions listed in Exhibit 3 had become parts of existing Dexter divisions.

COMPOSITION OF DEXTER

As a result of its acquisitions, by 1978 Dexter competed in four major product groups:

1. *Coatings, encapsulant group* produced 35 percent of sales and included the Hysol and Midland divisions.
2. *Life science group* such as tissue cultures and related media were 17 percent of sales.
3. *Nonwovens group* accounted for 35 percent of sales and included the original Dexter nonwovens (specialty) paper business and Howe & Bainbridge's woven fabrics business.
4. *Water treatment group* accounted for 13 percent of sales.

More detailed financial information on each product group is presented in Exhibit 4.

COMMON ASPECTS OF DEXTER'S BUSINESSES

Although Dexter was composed of seemingly very different businesses, management felt there were several strong themes underlying Dexter's various businesses.

Throughout its 20 years of diversification and product development Dexter had always emphasized "specialty application" for its products. This evolved into management's conception of Dexter as a "specialty materials" company. The characteristics of a specialty materials business had been detailed in the 1978 long-range plan:

> Most of the products produced by Dexter are classified as specialty materials, rather than commodities, because they are formulated or designed to perform a specific, vital function in the manufacturing processes of Dexter customers or in their end products. These specialty materials are not sold in the high volumes normally associated with commodity businesses.
>
> Dexter specialty materials require a high degree of technical service on an individual customer basis. The value of these specialty materials stems not just from their raw materials composition, but from the results and performances they achieve in actual use.

Exhibit 4

PERFORMANCE BY PRODUCT GROUP
(restated to take into account acquisitions)
($ millions)

	Net sales							
	1977		1976		1975		1974	
Coatings, encapsulant group .	111.7	(35%)	100.0	(39%)	76.9	(38%)	77.0	(39%)
Life science group	52.8	(17%)	43.4	(17%)	39.6	(19%)	32.1	(16%)
Nonwovens group	111.3	(35%)	74.9	(29%)	56.4	(28%)	63.2	(32%)
Water treatment group	40.0	(13%)	36.6	(14%)	32.9	(16%)	27.3	(14%)
Total	315.8	(100%)	255.1	(100%)	204.9	(100%)	199.7	(100%)

	Operating income							
Coatings, encapsulant group .	15.9	(36%)	13.4	(37%)	9.5	(36%)	10.9	(46%)
Life science group	4.0	(9%)	3.3	(9%)	3.8	(15%)	3.2	(14%)
Nonwovens group	16.9	(38%)	12.7	(35%)	7.4	(28%)	6.2	(26%)
Water treatment group	7.4	(17%)	6.6	(18%)	5.4	(21%)	3.4	(14%)
Total	44.3	(100%)	36.0	(100%)	26.1		23.7	(100%)
Expenses:								
Interest	2.7		3.2		3.7		3.5	
Corporate expense	2.7		2.0		1.3		1.5	
Other expenses	0.8		(0.6)		(0.3)		(0.4)	
Income before taxes	38.8		31.5		21.4		18.7	

	Capital expenditures		Depreciation	
	1977	1976	1977	1976
Coatings, encapsulant group .	3.5	3.2	2.1	1.8
Life science group	3.2	2.2	1.5	1.4
Nonwovens group	3.7	2.9	2.3	2.0
Water treatment group	1.0	0.6	0.5	0.5
Total	11.4	8.9	6.4	5.7

	Assets at year-end			
	1977		1976	
Coatings, encapsulant group .	60.0	(32%)	58.4	(33%)
Life science group	42.2	(23%)	36.2	(20%)
Nonwovens group	67.5	(36%)	63.1	(36%)
Water treatment group	15.2	(8%)	14.4	(8%)
General corporate	2.6	(1%)	4.8	(3%)
Total	185.5	(100%)	176.9	(100%)

Note: Some figures may not add due to rounding.
Source: The Dexter Corporation 1977 annual report.

Being a major competitor in each of its markets was a second theme as Worth Loomis pointed out:

> For strategic planning purposes Dexter is divided into 26 stratetic business segments. . . . In 22 of these 26 units, we are number one or number two in market share. Sales in 1977 to markets in which we are number

one or number two totaled over 70 percent of our expected sales. Fundamentally, we regard this characteristic as our major strength.

Another attribute of most of Dexter's product lines was the highly specialized nature of the material and the fact that they were a generally small part of the customer's end-product cost. For example, a product such as the interior film coating of a beer can was important in protecting the taste of the end product, but the coating itself represented a very small part of the final cost of the product. This characteristic fostered customer loyalty and allowed price increases to be passed on to the customer relatively easily.

ORGANIZATION STRUCTURE

Corporate office

A total of 19 people worked at corporate headquarters, including the secretarial staff. In addition to the chairman and president the corporate office included Mr. Harold Fleming, vice president corporate development, and Mr. Bob Ottman, manager corporate development, who were responsible for all nonfinancial matters, primarily acquisition assessment and planning. The rest of the corporate staff were concerned with financial and budgetary matters and reported to Mr. Robert McGill, vice president finance.

Dexter's management prided itself on its small corporate office and its decentralized management structure. Mr. Loomis cited three advantages:

> (1) Decentralization naturally keeps corporate overhead to a minimum. . . . (2) It makes life a hell of a lot more interesting for people in the divisions because it allows them to run their own shows. (3) We think it produces better decisions because they are closer to the source of fact, particularly the marketplace.

Despite the small corporate office and the high degree of autonomy of the divisions, Mr. Coffin stressed that Dexter was not a holding company. The corporate management, through close and frequent contact with the division presidents, was well informed about divisional operations and concerns.

The divisions

As shown in Figure 1, Dexter had five operating divisions. The divisions tended to be formed after a large acquisition, with subsequent smaller acquisitions becoming part of an existing division. The merger with Mogul was somewhat unique in that it became two divisions; water treatment was combined with the former Puritan division to become the Mogul division, and the life sciences part of Mogul became the Gibco/Invenex division.

Dexter's divisions were traditionally the primary operating units in the company. Budgets, performance monitoring, and incentive compensation were all tied to a division's total activities. For major strategic

Figure 1

DIVISIONAL ORGANIZATION CHART
(1977 personnel employed in parentheses)

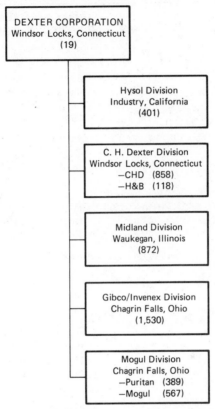

Source: Casewriter.

and operating decisions, it was the division president who almost always met and interacted with senior corporate management.

Summary measures of divisional performance are presented in Exhibit 5. Midland had been the fastest growing division in terms of both sales and profits; it also had the highest return on assets followed by C. H. Dexter and Hysol. All divisions except Mogul and Hysol were forecasting decreases in the rate of sales growth.

Strategic business segments

The identification of the component "businesses" that made up Dexter was not new. It had begun with a Boston Consulting Group (BCG) report on Dexter's portfolio of businesses done in 1973. Sixteen businesses had been identified. The increasing use of PIMS and other analytic techniques requiring careful business definitions had over time led to a re-

Exhibit 5

PERFORMANCE BY DIVISION
($ millions)

	C. H. Dexter*	Gibco/ Invenex	Mogul†	Hysol	Midland
Net sales:					
1973	$ 37	$26	$22	$20	$ 36
1975	56	40	32	19	58
1977	112	54	40	30	85
Budget 1978..............	124	66	46	34	93
Planned 1982‡					
(in 1977 $)	172	79	67	56	143
Operating profit (before tax):					
1973	4.6	2.9	2.3	3.1	4.4
1975	6.4	5.7	4.1	2.1	7.7
1977	17.5	7.3	5.0	4.5	11.7
Net assets§:					
1973	30	11	11.6	9.4	15.2
1975	41	19	13.9	10.0	19.9
1977	54	28	16.3	12.8	27.1
Cash flows (before interest and taxes) 1973–77:‖					
Used	25	6	5	7	20
Generated	35	4	7	12	29
Net	11	(1)	1	4	10
Return on investment (percent):					
1973	9%	13%	6%	17%	15%
1975	8	15	10	10	19
1977	16	14	13	17	21
Growth rate (internal): Sales:					
1972–77	22%	19%	12%	15%	30%
1978–82	8	8	10	14	11
Operating profit:					
1972–77	26%	23%	13%	17%	31%
1978–82	11	13	16	13	12

* From 1977, includes Howe & Bainbridge.
† All years include Puritan Sanitation Chemical and Mogul water treatment.
‡ Historical information is stated in actual dollars; planned or forecast amounts were supposed to be stated in constant 1977 dollars, but company officials acknowledged that some inflation still crept into these estimates. Figures as submitted, not as approved.
§ Operating profit after tax, divided by net property, plant, and equipment plus net working capital.
‖ Or from date of acquisition.
Source: The Dexter Corporation 1978 long-range plan.

finement of the definition of Dexter's businesses. However, the formal introduction of these still tentative business definitions as part of the planning and possibly the budgetary process was new. It had begun with the 1978 long-range plan, as Mr. Ottman observed:

This is a new thing this (past) year, previously we weren't so concerned about segments; we were more concerned about each of the divisions. We've always had segments, but the segments were, if you like, BCG-derived segments. One of the things Worth (Loomis) and the corporate development department decided upon when we were going to pick these segments was that we wanted no more than 30 business segments for the whole corporation—no more than 5 or 6 per division; otherwise we'd have just too many things to worry about. Next, we wanted the segments we picked to be something people could associate with, segments that people could identify and were familiar with. We wanted more background to avoid some of the traps we'd gotten into with BCG (defined segments). They weren't traps that we understood at the time but as we went along people became less and less interested because the segments were meaningless to them.

Exhibit 6 shows the 26 strategic business segments determined in 1977. The number per division varied from two for Mogul to seven for Gibco/Invenex. The largest single SBS—packaging—accounted for 9 percent of total corporate sales.

Not everyone was happy with the SBS definitions, as Mr. Ottman went on to point out:

> Some of the divisions contend that we didn't let them get involved in the definition of the segments, but in fact it was, and is, an interactive process. The Midland division, for instance, is unsatisfied with the ones we picked, so they're coming in in a few weeks and we're going to sit down and discuss what they think would be appropriate. I laid out the guidelines: give me something that is firm and rich enough so that I can write a description about it, define distinct competitors, come up with a market share on it, and put a growth rate on it. I want something I can put a handle on because we're going to use this for other purposes.
>
> We are willing to change the SBS definitions. We are willing to talk with them (the divisions) about it. The whole corporation may be going to go to a financial reporting package based upon the 26 segments. We're trying to find some mutual things that a division president can look at, the operating people can look at, and that we *all* can learn from.

The extent to which the SBS concept had been incorporated in the organization of the divisions varied considerably. A few of the SBSs had their own general manager, and some had established business teams for each SBS. However these were the exceptions; the divisions were primarily organized around the major functions.

Dexter's long-range plans had been prepared on an SBS basis since the first BCG study in 1973. Since then, the amount of strategic information contained in the plans had increased considerably and the definition of the SBSs had changed. Because the long-range plans included historic and projected income statements and balance sheets for each SBS, a rough allocation of joint expenses and shared assets were made. With the increasing use of the SBS concept, thought was being given to allocating expenses and assets on a more systematic and consistent basis and to report SBS performance, both profit and loss and balance sheet monthly. Mr. Robert McGill, vice president finance, estimated that it would cost around $100,000 to create such a system for producing SBS income statements and $300,000 for SBS balance sheets. Subsequent maintenance of these systems would cost $200,000 per year.

Exhibit 6

STRATEGIC BUSINESS SEGMENTS

No.	Business name	Growth performance 1978–82*
	C. H. Dexter division	
1.	Tea bag (paper)	0.7
2.	Fibrous casing	0.8
3.	Medical disposables—nonwovens	1.1
4.	Vacuum bag (paper)	0.9
	Other—nonwoven	0.9
5.	Sailcloth and hardware	0.7
6.	Recreational fabric	1.2
	Other woven	—
	Gibco/Invenex	
7.	Tissue culture	1.0
8.	Diagnostics	1.8
9.	Lab animals	0.3
10.	Medos	1.6
11.	International	0.9
	Other—Gibco	—
12.	Invenex	1.2
13.	Heun/Norwood	—
	Other—Invenex	—
	Mogul	
14.	Water treatment	1.2
15.	Puritan (sanitation chemicals)	0.9
	Hysol	
16.	Molding powder	2.1
17.	Coating powder	1.0
18.	Liquid coatings	0.95
19.	Wornow	1.4
20.	Adhesives	2.2
	Other—Hysol	1.1
	Midland	
21.	Packaging (coatings)	1.5
22.	Building—prefab (coatings)	1.6
23.	Recreational (coatings)	1.2
24.	Nonstick (coatings)	1.5
25.	Wood—Bouvet	0.6
26.	Bouvet—Other	0.2
	Other—Midland	1.2
		100%

* The figures are a ratio: $\dfrac{\text{Percent of planned corporate growth, 1978–82}}{\text{Percent of 1977 total corporate sales}}$.

Thus business segments with larger numbers are, relative to their 1977 sales, planning to contribute more to the internal growth of the company.

Source: Compiled from The Dexter Corporation 1978 long-range plan.

ADMINISTRATIVE SYSTEMS

Plans and planning

Since the late 1950s, Dexter had prepared five-year sales and profit plans, as well as plans for entering new markets. In the early 1970s, however, because Dexter faced a capital shortage, a new approach to planning was needed and The Boston Consulting Group was retained. The BCG study concluded that in previous years Dexter's investment policy had been "reasonably consistent with the portfolio management approach." But one important result of the study was that it served as a catalyst for efforts to identify which of Dexter's businesses might be supported and which should be harvested or divested. Even though Dexter's portfolio was displayed on various growth/share matrices, no attempt had been made to assign each business an explicit category such as "dog," "cow," or "star." One reason for this was that each of Dexter's divisions tended to have a balanced portfolio. As shown below, some growth opportunities had been identified in every division:

Growth business	Division
Surgical nonwovens	C. H. Dexter
Food nonwovens (overseas)	C. H. Dexter
Sailcloth	C. H. Dexter/Howe & Bainbridge
Electronic molding compounds	Hysol
Structural adhesives	Hysol
Water-based coatings	Midland
Sealing compounds container packaging	Midland
Water treatment chemicals	Mogul/Puritan
Diagnostic aids	Gibco/Invenex
Small volume parenteral solutions	Gibco/Invenex

Another important result of the BCG study was that it aroused corporate and divisional interest in business-by-business approaches to planning. This led to extensive usage of the PIMS model as one way of quantifying and comparing the performance of Dexter's business with the performance of the over 1,800 businesses in the PIMS data bank. Mr. Fleming, vice president corporate development, explained:

> From the beginning we have refined the planning approach more and more. BCG never talks about return on investment. They only talk about if you're number one you'll have the highest ROI and so on. We wanted to see all that quantified. The PIMS model enables us to tear into our businesses and take a look at a number of variables.

The long-range plans that were prepared as a result of these efforts presented a great deal of information on each SBS. As shown in Exhibit 7, a fact sheet on each SBS defined the served market and competitive structure, and quantified market size and growth. Some of the other information reported by SBS and included in the long-range plan was

Exhibit 7

EXAMPLES OF STRATEGIC BUSINESS SEGMENT

FACT SHEETS
HYSOL DIVISION

16. *Molding powder*
Definition of served market: Epoxy molding powder for encapsulation of electrical and electronic devices on a world-wide basis.

Competitive structure:

General purpose		Semiconductor	
Hysol	44%	Hysol	15%
Competitor A ..	15	Competitor A ..	49
Competitor C ..	20	Competitor B ..	14
Others	21	Others	22
	100%		100%

Hysol sales in 1977: 3.1 million + $4.7 million = 7.8
Size of total market: 7.0 million + $32.9 million = 39.0

Percent of total served market $\dfrac{7.8}{39.0} = 20$ percent

Projected real growth: 11 percent

Source: The Dexter Corporation 1978 long-range plan.

historical and projected five-year sales growth; next year's budgeted sales (in dollars and units); current, budgeted, and five-year planned gross and net profit margins; and planned capital expenditures over the next five years. Finally, Exhibit 8 shows an example of a PIMS report prepared using the actual and planned performance of each SBS. While Mr. Loomis thought analytic techniques, such as PIMS, were a useful tool and a convenient way to summarize information and highlight questions, he added that actions implied by such techniques must be treated with "a healthy skepticism."

Mr. Loomis thought it was particularly important for each SBS to present its plans in a variety of ways, using a range of analytic techniques. This prevented the rigid application of one approach and hopefully assured that all important issues were considered.

The long-range plans of each divisional SBS were compiled in the long-range planning manual. The long-range planning meeting, a three-day event held each June, was attended by the five division presidents, the corporate officers, and some key divisional and corporate staff employees. Typically 15 to 20 people attended.

Prior to 1978 the meetings had involved a presentation and critique of each of the divisions plans. In 1978 the long-range planning manual was still prepared, but in a shift of format the major part of the meeting involved discussion groups addressing corporatewide issues such as the availability of acquisition opportunities, whether some existing Dexter businesses fulfilled the specialty materials criteria and how large and fast Dexter should grow.

These questions dealt more with the company as a whole, rather than any division in particular. The conclusions of the discussion groups were described as reflecting a surprising degree of unanimity. Besides decid-

Exhibit 8

PIMS (LIM) ANALYSIS BY STRATEGIC BUSINESS SEGMENT, 1977, 1978, AND 1982
(SBS 16 only, presented as example)

The following information about molding powder was collected for 1977, estimated for 1978 and 1982, by the Hysol division for inclusion in the long-range plan. For example, market share was 20.0 percent in 1977 and expected to increase to 22.0 percent in 1978 and 33.0 percent by 1982.

Input Data

	Year	Molding powder 16		Year	Molding powder 16
Percent market	77	20.0	Percent invest-	77	72.1
share	78	22.0	ment/value	78	74.1
	82	33.0	added	82	83.5
Percent relative	77	30.5	Percent fixed capi-	77	37.2
market share	78	35.0	tal intensity	78	38.1
	82	60.0		82	35.3
Relative product	77	15.0	Percent vertical in-	77	58.4
quality	78	20.0	tegration	78	58.0
	82	20.0		82	52.8
Relative price	77	100.0	Value added/em-	77	40.3
	78	100.0	ployee ($1,000)	78	41.6
	82	103.0		82	46.8
Percent employees	77	–0–	Percent capacity	77	75
unionized	78	–0–	utilization	82	85
	82	–0–		82	95
Percent new prod-	77	20.0	Real market	77	11
ucts sales/sales	78	25.0	growth rate	78	11
	82	25.0		82	11
R&D expense/sales	77	7.0	Percent share of	77	77
	78	5.6	four largest firms	78	79
	82	4.5		82	85
Marketing ex-	77	13.8	Number of custom-	77	4
pense/sales	78	14.0	ers = 50 percent	78	3
	82	10.5	of sales	82	2
Investment/sales	77	42.7	Purchase amount—	77	6
	78	43.1	immediate cus-	78	6
	82	43.5	tomers	82	6

Using this information as input into the limited information model (LIM), an abbreviated version of the PIMS model, a PAR-ROI* was estimated and compared to the actual, or forecast, ROI. As shown below the LIM PAR estimate of ROI, using the above information, was 20.9 percent, actual ROI was 16.3 percent in 1977.

Exhibit 8 (*concluded*)

	Molding powder 16
1977 PIMS PAR-ROI	20.9
Actual ROI	16.3
Deviations from PAR	−4.6
1978 PIMS PAR-ROI	24.5
Budget ROI...........................	21.3
Deviations from PAR	−3.2
1982 PIMS PAR-ROI	33.9
Five-year plan ROI	28.4
Deviations from PAR	−5.5

Further, the model provided a more detailed explanation of the impact of different key factors upon PAR-ROI (relative to the PIMS mean ROI). For example, in 1977 the R&D expense/sales when compared to all PIMS businesses had the effect of reducing PAR-ROI by 4.4 percent.

1977
Key impacts
PIMS LIM model

Percent market share and relative market share	−0.4	Investment/sales and investment value added	4.0
Relative product quality	−1.2	Capital intensity	0.9
Percent R&D expense/sales ..	−4.4	Value added/employees	2.3
Percent marketing expense/ sales	−2.7	Capacity utilization	−0.7
Other	1.0	Total capital and production structure ...	6.6
Total competitive position and action	−7.7		
Total market environment	−0.1		
Total all impacts	−1.2		
+PIMS mean ROI	22.1		
Total PAR-ROI	20.9		

* PAR-ROI specified the return on investment that was "normal" for a business given the characteristics of its market, competition, technology, and cost structure.
Note: Figures may not add due to rounding.
Source: The Dexter Corporation 1978 long-range plan.

ing what businesses were likely, divestment candidates other important conclusions of the groups were:

> Spell out more clearly the 35 percent divisional ROI[2] concept, its gradations, its exceptions, and its relation to incentive compensation. What portfolios of strategic business segments need to average the 35 percent, if any, besides the corporate portfolio? What is the par ROI for each SBS?

> Organizationally we should continue our evolution toward group control of related portfolios of strategic business segments. Strategy should be developed and implemented at the SBS level. Such management concepts

---

[2] The 35 percent ROI was related to the division president's incentive compensation. See heading "Incentive compensation," in this section.

as product managers, business teams, and task forces should be encouraged as much as possible. The push toward product line financial statements should continue.

It was not clear what actions would result from these recommendations.

The emphasis on corporate issues at the planning meeting had left a gap in the formulation and review of division plans. In order to fill this need Bob Ottman was arranging meetings at the divisions in order to discuss their long-range plans.

Budgeting and resource allocation

In addition to the long-range plans, each division prepared detailed annual budgets. This process began in November with Mr. Loomis and each division president agreeing on a sales and profit goal for the total division. The divisions would then break these into product lines or businesses and arrive at a budgeted amount for each revenue and expense item. This would then be submitted to Robert McGill's office and subsequently reviewed; but by that time, as one division manager commented, "It's pretty well locked in." Major capital expenditures for the upcoming year were also included in this process.

The monthly performance of each division was scrutinized by Mr. Loomis as soon as the figures were available. Deviations from budget, particularly unanticipated deviations, would require an explanation from the division president, as Mr. Loomis explained:

> I am more concerned about surprises in the monthly figures than whether the budget was met. If I don't find out that something is wrong until it shows up in (monthly) performance then the company is not under (adequate) control.

Because division presidents had the opportunity to formally revise their expectation in a five-quarter rolling forecast, surprises were unusual. Performance was also reviewed at the monthly management committee meetings. The management committee was composed of the four corporate officers and the five division presidents who were also corporate vice presidents. Corporate financial performance, acquisitions, and current developments at divisions were typical topics of discussion. Each division hosted one session each year, and at that session that division's performance, past and present, was an additional agenda item.

Dexter had a standard capital appropriations procedure. Capital projects in excess of $200,000 were submitted by the divisions for board approval, after being reviewed by the management committee. Division presidents could approve projects up to $25,000. Mr. Loomis had authority to approve projects up to $200,000 provided the annual total did not exceed $700,000.

Capacity expansion and cost reduction projects were evaluated on a discounted cash flow basis, using a 15 percent hurdle rate. Mr. Loomis did not feel that the portfolio approach to planning mitigated the need for discounted cash flow analysis. Indeed, cross-subsidization between divisions was unusual.

We have not often faced the hard issues of funding some businesses and not others. When we have, we said that each division must be a "tub standing on its own bottom." Of course, we have applied some "english" to be sure that no high-potential businesses were shortchanged.

Explaining why this was so, Mr. Loomis went on:

Since every division has had both cash generating capability and growth opportunities, there has been no real need to move a lot of funds from one division to another. But even if this were not the case, we would be hesitant to do so because of the motivational and political problems of harvesting a whole division.

Incentive compensation

Dexter had a philosophy of profit sharing with *all* its employees, from those on the production floor to those in the corporate office. The corporate level promoted this policy at the divisions by the establishment of divisional profit-sharing pools. Annual contributions to the pool were 20 percent of divisional income before interest and tax, but after deducting 14 percent of divisional net assets.[3]

All bonus payments for divisional personnel came from the division's pool and could not exceed a specified percentage of base salary. For division presidents this limit was 60 percent. Funds not dispersed were returned to corporate. The division president's bonus was determined by the corporate office. For the presidents of the older divisions (C. H. Dexter, Hysol, Midland) it would typically be determined as follows:

10%	subjective by president and chairman
20	corporate performance
25	individual goals (meeting sales growth, cost reduction, reorganization, etc.)
45	division performance (explained below)
100%	(equal to 60 percent of base salary)

For that part of the division president's bonus related to division performance, increasing payments were made as return on net assets went from 14 percent to 35 percent.[4] It was felt that any pretax return in excess of 35 percent should be reinvested into R&D and marketing.

The division president determined on what criterion the pool was distributed to divisional personnel, but a profit-sharing plan would be submitted to the corporate office and Worth Loomis had to approve all disbursements to the division president and officers.

Management development

The selection and training of division personnel at all levels was the province of the division president. Even in the case of the position of division president, the outgoing president's recommendation for his replacement was sought and generally followed. The corporate office

---

[3] Net assets equals current assets minus current liabilities plus fixed net (tangible) assets.
[4] This scale (14–35 percent) was different for some of the presidents of newer acquisitions, but the intention was that eventually it would be uniform for all Dexter's divisions.

did hold corporate familiarization meetings for any new division managers. Worth Loomis and the division presidents reviewed second-level division people annually.

PART II—HYSOL DIVISION: A STRATEGY FOR MOLDING POWDER

The Hysol division was basically a manufacturer of compounds that were sold to the electrical/electronics and aerospace industries. Hysol became a part of Dexter in 1967 when it was sold by its founder, Mr. Donald Roon. At that time Mr. Roon expressed a desire to stay at Hysol for five more years, then retire, as he did in 1973. Mr. Lloyd Dixon assumed the presidency of the division at that time.

Mr. Dixon had graduated in chemistry from UCLA in 1949. Afterwards he had worked with Lockheed and Owens-Corning Fiberglas before being recruited by Mr. Roon in 1956. Mr. Dixon became Hysol's first direct salesman and was located on the West Coast. He stayed in sales/marketing until 1971 when he was made executive vice president for Hysol and eventually president in 1973.

Originally located at Olean in upstate New York, Hysol moved its headquarters to Industry, California, in 1973. This was a natural move because during the 1960s and early 1970s the West Coast electronics and aerospace industries, both of which required close customer support, became Hysol's largest customers.

Hysol's growth in the past five years had not been as large as most of Dexter's other divisions, but it was forecasting increased growth rates over the next five years. The Hysol division accounted for about 9 percent of Dexter's sales in 1977; the five-year plan indicated it would account for 14 percent of internally generated growth from 1978 to 1982. Certain business segments within Hysol were targeted for higher growth than others.

BUSINESS SEGMENTS

For corporate planning purposes Hysol was divided into the five strategic business segments given in Table 1, which also lists their performance data. In order to make the businesses more consistent with management's perception of the marketplace, the division had further divided the adhesives, liquid epoxy coating, and molding powder business segments. Hysol made extensive use of PIMS analysis, and this also fostered continuing refinement of business definitions.

The adhesives segment, located in Pittsburg, California, had been acquired in 1969. This business' products utilized the basic epoxy technology common to the rest of the division. These structural adhesives were used by aerospace manufacturers to bond metal to metal in high stress situations. Product integrity was crucial. Close customer contact was required, and it took a long lead time to become a qualified supplier. Adhesives had been further segmented based on the method of application. One segment was basic "pot and brush" applied adhesives; a second included those adhesives with a tape backing that allowed more pre-

Table 1

PERFORMANCE BY STRATEGIC BUSINESS SEGMENT—HYSOL DIVISION

			Five-year projections*	
SBS	Percent of 1977 division sales	Pretax ROI 1977	Real sales growth rate	Net cash flow†
16. Molding powder	26%	16%	18%	(0.2)
17. Coating powder	13	33	10	0
18. Liquid epoxy coating	24	52	9	2.1
19. Specialty inks (Wornow)	9	35	13	0.3
20. Adhesives	16	25	18	0.9
Other Hysol	12	48	10	0.5
Total Hysol	100%	35%	14%	3.6

* 1978 to 1982.
† Millions of dollars, before interest and taxes.
Source: Company internal records.

cisely controlled applications. The adhesives business was expected to experience high growth.

The remainder of the division's sales was to the electrical/electronics industry. The specialty inks and resists segment (Wornow) produced products used in marking electronic products and in the manufacture of printed circuit boards. The liquid epoxy coatings segment was made up of the first generation semiconductor encapsulation products. It was Hysol's first and largest product line. The product involved liquid epoxy resin and curing agents that were mixed and then dispensed in a liquid form that quickly hardened to encapsulate electronic devices (e.g., transistors). Although continued growth was expected and a high technology subsegment had been identified, the liquids business was generally recognized as mature. Hysol was the largest supplier in this business and continued to invest in order to maintain or marginally improve that position. The powdered coatings segment was the next generation beyond liquid coatings. This product was a fine epoxy powder which after being sprayed or blown onto a heated part would melt and coat it. Again Hysol was the largest supplier of this product to the electronics industry.[5]

Hysol's last SBS, molding powder, had during the 1972–77 period experienced real annual compounded growth of 17 percent. Similar sales growth was expected for the next five years. The powder business had been segmented into two separate businesses—electrical and semiconductor grades. The semiconductor subsegment, because of its rapid growth, accounted for the largest portion of this SBS's sales. This trend was expected to continue. (See Exhibit 7 for sales by subsegment.) Even though electrical and semiconductor grade molding powders could be

---

[5] A similar powder product was manufactured by the Midland division (and many other firms) and sold as a substitute for liquid coatings in many industrial requirements.

produced on the same equipment, the quality assurance standards were higher and the pace of production much slower for semiconductor grade molding powders. For reasons of history the production of both electrical and semiconductor molding powder was at Olean, New York.

Electrical molding powders were sold to firms like General Electric and Westinghouse. They were used to encapsulate bushings, transformers, and other conventional electrical components. This type of powder sold for about 90 cents per pound. The industry had grown at between 5 percent and 10 percent per year and was expected to continue to grow at the rate of the GNP or less. Hysol was the largest supplier of this product.

Semiconductor molding powders was the largest and most important of the electronic molding powder products.[6] It was used to make the plastic-like material that encapsulated integrated circuits (ICs) (Figure 2). Price was about $1.80 per pound. When the electronics industry devel-

Figure 2

SEMICONDUCTOR MOLDING POWDER APPLICATION

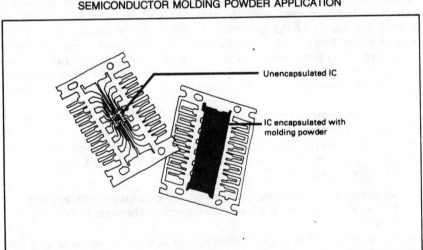

oped ICs, it needed a way to encapsulate them in order to protect the delicate IC chip. Initially, and as was still the case when a new integrated circuit was first developed, it would be put in a completely inert ceramic package at a cost of about $2 per package. At this stage the IC chip would usually cost $6 or more. But as production process and sales volume improved, the costs would fall to less than $2 per chip. At this point the incentive to develop a cheaper package was large. An epoxy package formed from molding powder could cost as little as 2–3 cents per unit.

---

[6] Compounds used in optoelectronics and other miscellaneous electronic applications were included in electronic molding powders but were not an important factor.

In the mid-1960s the semiconductor industry experimented with electrical grade molding powders as encapsulants and found this material unsuitable because the epoxy encapsulant affected the electrical performance of the semiconductor. Soon a molding powder with suitable electrical performance characteristics was developed. However, different types of semiconductors were subject to different electrical effects and therefore required new and improved molding powders. This fact, in addition to the pressure for the continual improvement of existing encapsulants, required close customer contact and an ongoing R&D effort by the manufacturers of these compounds. Price was not as important as quality since a bad batch of molding powder could have adverse effects on the performance of a very large number of ICs.

HYSOL'S POSITION—SEMICONDUCTOR MOLDING POWDER

When semiconductor manufacturers first started to use molding powders as encapsulants, Hysol, because of its experience in electrical grade molding powders, had a major position. Until the early 1970s, the semiconductor industry was quite fragmented and Hysol concentrated on serving the needs of the numerous smaller IC manufacturers rather than the few large firms. Hysol's emphasis on low-volume but high-margin molding powders gave the division the strong reputation as "the drugstore of the industry." However, during the 1970–71 recession most of the small manufacturers folded and four or five major manufacturers of ICs merged.

In 1974 the molding powder business was the subject of a BCG study.[7] This study, motivated by a desire to understand the business better, had resulted in a clearer idea of the differences between the electrical and semiconductor molding powder segments. With regard to the latter it was observed that:

1. Semiconductor molding powder was the high-growth segment of the molding powder business (20+ percent through 1978). (See Exhibit 9.)
2. Although Hysol was the largest manufacturer of molding powder, it was number two in the domestic semiconductor (but number one outside the United States) subsegment and had been losing share.
3. The battle for a viable long-term position in epoxy molding powders would be won or lost in the U.S. semiconductor segment.
4. A standard semiconductor molding powder would emerge during the next two to three years, after which market gains would be difficult.

Although the report had accurately predicted the growth of the market, it had incorrectly assumed that a standard semiconductor molding powder would evolve quickly. In fact, the development of new semiconductor technologies and applications, and the importance of improved

---

[7] This was the first Boston Consulting Group study done on an individual business at Dexter.

Exhibit 9

MOLDING POWDER MARKET

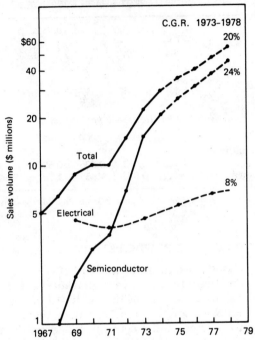

Source: BCG Report on molding powder; molding powder
business team.

molding powders to existing applications, had made new product developments important to continued product acceptance. According to estimates made in the study, Hysol's market share in the semiconductor
subsegment had declined (as shown in Table 2) even though sales had
increased.

Hysol's largest competitor had not produced molding powders until
the late 1960s when it acquired two small producers. Recognizing Hysol's
dominance in the general-purpose (electrical) segment, this firm chose
to concentrate on the semiconductor segment.

Mr. Dixon explained Hysol's position at that time:

> We were in a transition of management. I think that whenever you do
> have a major discontinuity in management and the goals of one manage-
> ment system change to the goals of another management system, then you
> have to be careful that you don't play it too close to the vest and too conserva-
> tive, which is essentially what happened in that transition period. We were
> doing very well but we were underinvesting in what turned out to be a
> very high-growth industry. We weren't putting in the marketing dollars
> and we weren't putting in the R&D dollars. More than anything else it
> was the company (i.e., the division) at the time, classically as I look back
> on it, it wasn't geared to taking that many risks at that particular time.

Table 2

MOLDING POWDER
WORLDWIDE MARKET SHARE ESTIMATES

	Hysol		*Competitor A*		*Competitor B*	
	1969	*1974*	*1969*	*1974*	*1969*	*1974*
Semiconductor	40%	18%	37%	42%	8%	21%
Electrical	36	39	28	21	6	6
Total	42%	29%	27%	32%	7%	16%

Sales ($ millions)—Hysol division

	1967	*1969*	*1971*	*1974*	*1976*	*1977*
Semiconductor molding powder	0.241	0.505	0.500	2.83	3.95	4.65
Total molding powder	0.983	1.85	1.78	5.24	6.11	7.74

Source: "Molding Powder Strategy," Boston Consulting Group, 1974, and company internal records.

SEMICONDUCTOR MOLDING POWDER STRATEGY—POST 1974

As a result of Hysol's own thinking and the BCG report, it was decided the division should attempt to improve its market share position in semiconductor molding powders. Actions had included increasing and focusing R&D, developing closer relationships with major customers, and the separation of electrical and electronic grade molding powder. The original objective of the division had been to be equal to its largest competitor by 1981–82; as of 1978, 1983–85 seemed a more realistic time frame for the achievement of this objective.

In Germany Hysol had set up a manufacturing facility and a sales force employing a total of 35 people to service the European market. A joint venture arrangement supplied Japan. Hysol had maintained the major position in both these markets. However, the U.S. semiconductor market accounted for roughly 60 percent of worldwide demand. Domestically, Hysol had continued to have a better sales effort and field support servicing the semiconductor industry than its major competitor. However, Hysol was at somewhat of a disadvantage in the area of R&D. It was difficult to overcome this problem because good technical people were not readily available.

According to Mr. Dixon some of the early problems with semiconductor molding powder had been organizational:

> Prior to 1973 we had an electronic sales manager and an electrical sales manager. This meant we had one man responsible for selling all of Hysol's products to the electrical industry and another who sold all of our products to the electronics industry. The fallacy with that was that they didn't have the commitment to promote semiconductor grade molding powders, or powder coatings, or liquids. Whatever came along was the product that they would sell.
>
> Immediately when I came on board we adopted a product sales manager approach for molding powders, coating powders, liquids, and general line.

Prior to and during that transition we kind of lost focus. We got out of touch with the dynamics of the growth of the semiconductor industry. The rest of our business had been growing at this 12–15 percent range; we were growing the semiconductor molding powders at close to 20 percent; however the semiconductor market was growing at 30 percent. So we were losing market share, and didn't know it. We weren't sophisticated enough at the time. We knew we were doing a good job on the earnings statement, but we weren't doing a good job on market share.

In the future the division hoped to improve its technical capabilities. The efforts were to be concentrated on refining the specifications and formulation of major products. Mr. Dixon described this as "bending a few molecules." Bringing the products out of the lab and up to production scale, reducing costs, and improving the consistency of the manufacturing process were secondary areas of emphasis. When these problems were solved, it would be the task of the sales force to communicate this to major customers. As shown in Table 1 and Exhibit 8, this was expected to result in an 18 percent growth rate, an increase in market share from 20 percent at present to 33 percent by 1982, and improvement in ROI for molding powder as a whole.

DIVISIONAL ORGANIZATION

Mr. Dixon had made a number of changes in Hysol's organization structure, but because of constraints imposed by the location of facilities and people and for reasons of history, such modifications came slowly. Hysol's organization structure (Figure 3) somewhat paralleled the strategic business segments. The adhesives business was relatively self-contained having its own manufacturing facilities, R&D, and marketing effort. The organizational arrangements were more complex for the rest of Hysol's businesses.

Insulating materials was composed of coating powders, liquid coatings, general line, and specialty inks. Each of these businesses had a product/sales manager but shared a common sales force and reported through a common superior to the division president. The semiconductor molding powder product/sales manager, Mr. Ron Benham, had a separate sales force and reported directly to the division president. He was also responsible for the semiconductor molding powder operations in Europe and Japan. Mr. Benham had been with Hysol for 15 years, initially in an R&D capacity. He was transferred to sales in 1973.

Manufacturing was done in three facilities; the largest was at Olean, New York. The plant managers reported to Mr. Dixon. Research and development was done at the manufacturing plants in Olean, New York, and Industry, California. Insulating materials (electrical molding powder, liquid coatings, etc.) and electronic molding powder used a similar epoxy technology and shared a common R&D resource. Although an R&D vice president monitored the overall research effort, people were assigned to head research groups for each of Hysol's businesses.

Mr. Dixon had organized "business teams" for each of the SBSs in his division. These teams were made up of a product sales manager,

Figure 3

HYSOL DIVISION ORGANIZATION CHART

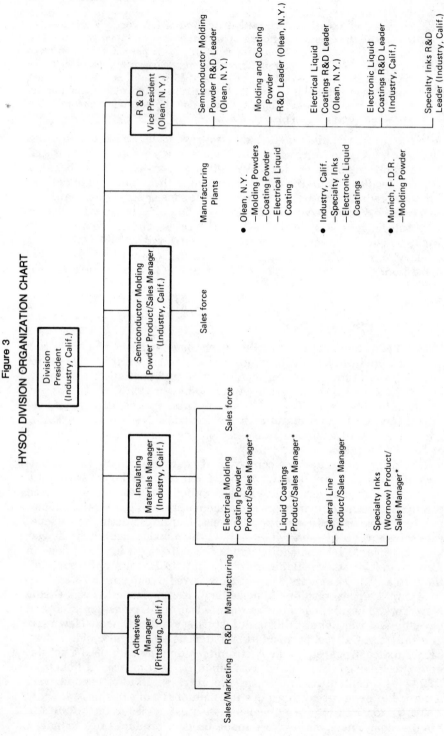

* Business team leader.
Source: Casewriter.

an R&D person, a manufacturing person, and a financial person. Mr. Dixon explained how they worked.

> Divisional product sales managers pick the accounts that we are going to concentrate on—the ones we'll fund. The product sales manager identifies the customers and is responsible for putting together the business team and programming the business team approach to the identified customers. The business team leader has P&L responsibility, and we do our best to evaluate these people on that basis.

This approach was considered very effective.

SEMICONDUCTOR MOLDING POWER—MR. DIXON'S VIEW

Trying to grow semiconductor molding powders aggressively was not without its problems. Even though Hysol had distributed sizable bonuses from its profit-sharing pool to divisional personnel for most of the years he had been division president, Mr. Dixon wondered whether Dexter's bonus system had provided the proper incentives for semiconductor molding powders:

> I would say going back one, two, or three years ago, that due to the constraints of the profit sharing and the incentive program for the divisions, we probably underinvested in our two growth businesses—semiconductor molding powder and adhesives—in order to keep a balanced portfolio within the division. Today, only because we're on a high-growth year, we are generating enough funds internally so that we can fund adhesives to the proper level. We are still underfunding semiconductors. Not intentionally, but we don't have the technical staff we need and that is a definite effect of not making the investment in the people two to three years ago.

Mr. Dixon noted that the problems of funding growth related mostly to expenses like marketing and R&D:

> R&D and marketing expenditures are pretty much up to us. We've told them (corporate) in our plans which they review, what our R&D as a percentage of sales will be, what we think is optimal, and what it will be by product line for the next five years. They don't criticize that if they say anything, they say we should be spending more; however, that comes off our profits. As an example they don't have the technical sensitivity to know whether R&D for tape adhesives should be 13 percent of sales or 15 percent of sales. So, they may say, "Spend more on R&D and marketing effort." But they don't say achieve less profit.

Although capital appropriations for growth had not generally been a problem, there was still some question in Mr. Dixon's mind as to how effectively funds moved between Dexter's different businesses, and especially across divisional boundaries:

> Dexter corporate says we (the division) should have our own balanced portfolio of businesses. Currently, we are supposed to have a net positive cash flow (before taxes, financial and corporate charges) and a divisional pretax ROI of 35 percent. BCG says that if we (the division) have the opportunity, we should be able to use cash generated from other Dexter businesses to grow some of our high opportunity businesses. I think there is

some reluctance in accepting the fact that Hysol as a division can grow product lines at greater than a 20 percent rate.

MR. LOOMIS'S VIEW

The above description, in Part II, summarizes Mr. Loomis's understanding of the Hysol division, particularly the situation in the molding powder business segment. In general, Mr. Loomis was satisfied with the performance of the Hysol division. However, in regard to the upcoming meeting with Mr. Dixon, Mr. Loomis still had two concerns:

> I still have two uncertainties. First, it is not clear (to corporate) that Hysol's semiconductor molding powder business will be so successful that we should divert still more cash to fund it. And this in spite of the fact that it is one of our most studied businesses. Second, I don't know that it is wise for me, or the corporate staff, to become deeply involved at the business level.

Hawaii Best Company (A)

GRADUALLY rising from his chair in his third-floor plush office overlooking Waikiki Beach in Honolulu, James Lind, president of Hawaii Best Company (HBC), greeted Charles Carson, vice president and general manager of the company's Islands Division, and invited him to take the seat across from his desk.

"Charlie, I am sure that something has gone wrong," he said as Carson remained standing. "You have many fine qualities—I was the one who recognized them when I promoted you to vice president—but I have been reviewing your progress these past few months and . . . and the results have not met our expectations."

Carson fidgeted at the window, watching the October morning across the harbor. His face reddened, his pulse quickened, and he waited for Lind to continue.

"The costs in your division are higher than budgeted, the morale is low, and your branch managers are unhappy with your stewardship," Lind said. "And your cooperation with Gil Harris has fallen short of satisfactory."

Carson grew angrier at the mention of Harris, a young aggressive man with a master's degree from a well-known eastern business school. Harris was a latecomer to HBC, but Carson knew that everyone was pleased with his performance.

"Charles, at the country club last week, I was speaking to one of our vendors. He intimated that your dealings with him had not been entirely clean. This is what hurts me the most.

"I know you are 49, that your son is only eight, that this is a difficult time for you and your family," Lind concluded as Carson stared out the window. "You have spent almost all your life in Hawaii; . . . it would be difficult for you to move to the mainland. It will be even harder for you to find a similar position in the Honolulu community. But I must

Exhibit 1

BOARD OF DIRECTORS—1972

Name	Age, place most of life spent	Background	Current activity	Previous association in years		Number of shares represented
				Industry	Company	
Choy, Eduardo	65, Hawaii	No academic degree; financial.	Entrepreneur; corporate chairman; banker.	0	15 as director	3,000
Donahue, John	70, Hawaii	Engineer; retired.	Retired corporate executive of the company; vice president of a property management company.	40 with company	8 as director	500
Eichi, Ishi	40, Hawaii	Legal; attorney.	Practicing attorney.	0	2 as director	0
Fields, J. B.*	54, Hawaii	M.B.A. (Harvard); finance.	Executive vice president of a very large multinational company headquartered in Honolulu.	0	15 as director	2,500 + 4% owned by his company.
Fong, Charles	40, Hawaii	M.B.A. (Harvard); Finance.	Executive vice president of a real estate development and investment firm.	0	2 as director	500
Hanley, Don*	70, Hawaii	Secretary.	Retired.	19	19 as director	10,000
Johnson, T.†	48, Hawaii	Accounting	Corporate treasurer of the company.	15	2 as director	1,000
Lind, James*†	53, Mainland U.S.A.	Engineer; alumnus of Columbia Business School.	Corporate president.	28	2 as president and director	4,000

Name	Age, residence	Occupation	Business affiliation			
North, Roy*	56, Mainland and 16 years in Hawaii	Engineer; financial analyst.	Executive vice president of a conglomerate headquartered in Honolulu.	16	10 as director	1,500
Rusk, Dean*	52, Hawaii	Accounting and finance insurance; alumnus of Harvard Business School.	Executive vice president of a local large company operating in insurance, sugar, real estate, and merchandising, business.	0	5 as director	0
Simon, A. F.*	65, Hawaii	Contractor; entrepreneur.	Corporate chairman and president; entrepreneur.	0	20 as director	30,000
Vogel, Lawrence	63, Hawaii	Finance; fiduciary.	Corporate president; fiduciary agent; represents a large local trust.	0	10 as director	0

* Member of the board's executive committee.
† HBC employee.

ask for your resignation, and I will do my best to help you find a more suitable opportunity."

"Jim, I can't believe it," Carson finally replied. "It's just all wrong." He turned slowly from the window, his face blood-red.

"I have been with this company for ten years. I built this division. Sure, this year's results are not quite what you expect but my division is still the largest contributor to corporate profits. I'll bet your friend Gil has been telling you about the vendor deals. Well, it's a damned lie, and I won't stand for it! That boy will stop at nothing to grab power."

There was a long silence as Lind and Carson stared at opposite corners of the large office. "I will not resign," Carson suddenly declared, and he left the president's office coughing, his face flushed and his heart pounding.

Lind stood motionless as he watched the door close. He was uncertain about what to do; it never had occurred to him that Carson might refuse to resign. He decided to proceed as he had planned, but with one modification.

"Janice, please take a memo," he said to his secretary, and he dictated a note to Charles Carson informing him that his employment with HBC was terminated as of that afternoon, October 10, 1972.

After sending out a general release memo informing all division heads that Carson had resigned and that Joseph Ward, a promising young executive, presently employed as the manager of planning in the Operations Division, would assume the position of acting general manager of the Islands Division, Lind hurriedly left the office. He had less than an hour to catch the 12:30 plane, intending to visit each of the seven branch heads on the outer islands, to tell them about the change and their new acting general manager.

While Lind was having his memos sent out, Carson was trying to contact his previous boss and old friend, Roy North, past president of HBC and presently an influential member of the company's board of directors and its powerful executive committee. Carson intended to have the matter taken to the board for deliberation.

BACKGROUND

Mr. North was one of five members of the board's executive committee, which customarily approved the appointments, promotions, stock options and salary adjustments of personnel earning over $10,000. This included department heads, division managers, and vice presidents. The committee held at least one meeting a month, and these, like the regular monthly meetings of all 12 board members, were well-attended. (Exhibit 1 shows selected data about the directors).

Several of the directors were descendants or close friends of the founders of the Hawaii Best Company, but only James Lind and Thomas Johnson were HBC employees. Board members held 5 percent of outstanding stock; the rest was widely owned by the people and business concerns in Hawaii. No one outside the board represented more than 1 percent of the HBC stock.

In 1971, with $30 million in sales and an e.p.s. of $1, the Hawaii Best Company was a manufacturer and marketer of a special formula. The company was listed on the Pacific Coast stock exchange with 1 million shares outstanding which yielded a stable dividend of $1 per share over the last five years. It sold its line of special formula X to industrial, commercial, and residential customers in the state of Hawaii. Its manufacturing facilities and three sales branches were strategically located in Honolulu, and seven other sales branches were spread over the outer islands. The company usually negotiated hard for its basic raw material K, used in the manufacture of special formula X, from its only locally available long-term supplier. Imports of the raw material were deemed uneconomical for HBC and a second source of local supply did not appear on the horizon.

The company also sold special formula Y, but only in the outer island branches and not in Honolulu. It was purchased in finished packaged form from several vendors within and outside the state of Hawaii, but the company was in no way involved in its manufacture.

Over the past five years the company's sales grew at an average annual rate of 4 percent, but its market share remained constant. Relative to the competition, HBC's profit performance had declined and, according to one competitor, "it was only through some 'creative' accounting that the company barely made its dividend in 1971."

HBC had two rivals in its industry: the larger company had annual sales of $60 million, the smaller sales of $15 million a year. It was a fiercely competitive industry, and special favors or discounts, although illegal, were sometimes granted to woo customers from another company. And customers were precious; just ten clients accounted for one-quarter of HBC sales.

HBC's ORGANIZATION STRUCTURE

Exhibit 2 shows HBC's skeletal organizational structure. The president, James Lind, was responsible to the board of directors. Thomas Johnson, vice president finance and secretary, and President James Lind regularly attended the monthly board meetings, and other vice presidents were also invited frequently to keep the board informed on matters of importance in the area of their specialty. According to Andrew Simon, chairman of the board of directors, "This practice gives us an opportunity to know what we have underneath the first layer."

In addition to managing five divisions and attending to the normal duties of the president, Lind took a special interest in the negotiations involving labor contracts and purchasing of raw material K and special formula Y. The specific responsibility for negotiating labor contracts rested with the vice president of industrial relations, John Wyle. Control of the purchase of raw material K lay with the senior vice president of operations. The vice president and general manager, Islands Division, was responsible for buying special formula Y.

In all these negotiations, however, it was not uncommon for Johnson to get involved as well.

Exhibit 2

ORGANIZATION STRUCTURE 1972

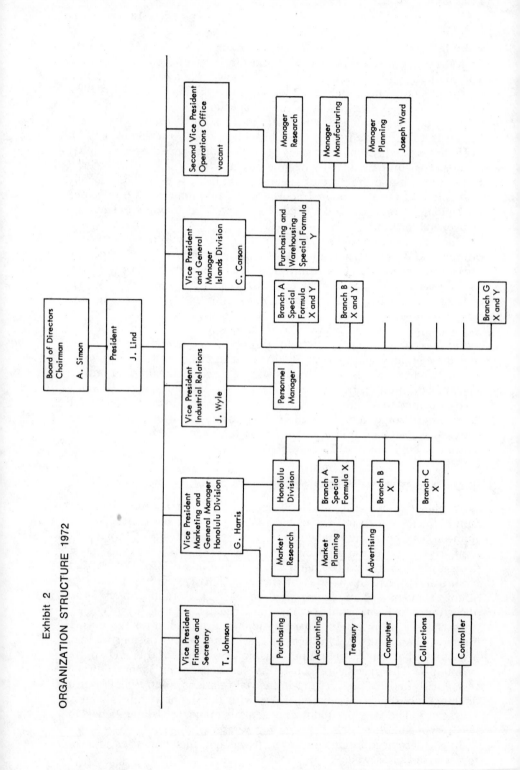

Among the corporate vice presidents in 1971, John Wyle, 51, had been the longest with the company. However, he had suffered two serious heart attacks since joining the company in 1945—one in ·1959 and the other in 1968. According to the former HBC president North, "Wyle is the best industrial relations man we can find and he is a good personal friend of ours [their wives played cards together] but, frankly, his health concerns me and several of the directors."

Since joining the company in 1947 as a clerk, Thomas Johnson had risen to the position of vice president finance by 1968. In 1970 at the age of 46, he was elected to the company's board of directors at the suggestion of President Lind. Johnson had been actively under consideration for the presidency when Roy North vacated the position in December, 1969. One member of the selection committee put it this way: "Johnson is quite happy in his present position. He is a little lazy. He never wanted the top job."

Gil Harris, 33, joined the company in March, 1970 as vice president for marketing and general manager of the Honolulu Division, responsible for the conduct and performance of the three Honolulu branches and for the companywide market research, market planning, and advertising campaigns.

As vice president and general manager of the Islands Division, Charles Carson had controlled the conduct and profit performance of all the branches in the state outside Honolulu. Carson also participated in the marketing decisions, such as advertising and promotions, and his division was charged a pro-rata share of expenses on the basis of divisional sales.

The Islands Division and the Honolulu Division were created by Lind in February 1970 after the sudden death of Vice President Sales Robert Gellerman, 46. Gellerman had been responsible for the companywide sales and advertising throughout the state. Prior to the establishment of the two divisions, Lind consulted Chairman Simon, former HBC President North, and other members of the executive committee, and received their unanimous support. Also included in the restructuring were the functions of market planning and market research, which were consolidated under the new vice president for marketing and general manager, Honolulu Division.

The position of senior vice president operations had been vacant since May 1970, when Lind asked for the resignation of the man who had held that office. The three managers within the division—manufacturing, planning, and research—had since been reporting directly to Lind. They constantly vied for the attentions of the president and the corporate vice presidents in the hope that one of them could assume the vice presidency. Three key members of the board were acquainted with Donald May, the research manager, but the other two were virtually unknown to the board.

Arrival of James Lind

On January 1, 1970, James Lind replaced Roy North as president of Hawaii Best Company when the latter left the company to become an executive vice president of a multinational conglomerate headquartered in Honolulu. North, under whose control HBC had prospered for seven years, recommended Lind for the presidency after an unfruitful search for a candidate within the company and the Hawaiian community. The board of directors accepted Lind, then a top executive in a trade association in New York, and he soon proved to be a man of integrity, dedication, and charm.

Although the business community in Hawaii, according to some observers, was tight-knit and nearly impervious to outsiders, Lind was readily admitted and liked. The morale at HBC soared during the early months of his presidency, because he was a man who was both extraordinarily hardworking—he put in up to 70 hours a week—and "human." He was one of the best fund raisers for community projects in Hawaii.

Financially, however, the company was not performing well under Lind's leadership. Rising labor and material costs, and the combination of the inflationary spiral and the fierce competition put pressure on the profit margins. Lind began to make changes in key personnel in an effort to offset the problem.

In February, he promoted Charles Carson, a man who had been with the company for over eight years, to vice president and general manager of the newly created Islands Division.

Three months later he asked for the resignation of Frank Adams, senior vice president for operations. Lind felt that Adams, after 27 years at HBC was "utterly lacking in an ability to negotiate for key raw materials," and brought his grievance to the board of directors. Before Adams was asked to resign, a severance package was worked out and approved by the board. Adams, then 53, was utterly shaken. He became an estimator for a local construction firm at one-quarter of his former salary. This was the first such severance in the history of the company and as one director put it: "The event was extremely painful; it left deep scars on us and our families."

Lind's final major organizational change was to bring in an old friend of his whom he hoped could develop new marketing strategies for the entire company. Gil Harris, from the Global Chemical Company of New York, was made vice president for marketing and general manager of the newly formed Honolulu Division.

Lunch at the club

"Jason, thank you for meeting me here, and for cancelling your other engagement to see me. I'm sorry, but I had to talk to you; something has happened that I think you should know about."

Charles Carson leaned heavily on the table in the restaurant of Honolulu's only country club. The man across from him curiously fingered the stem of his martini glass. Jason Fields, the executive vice president of the third largest international company based in Hawaii, was a busy and important man. An illustrious graduate of the Harvard Business School, Fields was one of the three most influential members of the company's board and its executive committee. Fields's employer controlled 4 percent of the HBC's outstanding stock. He did not have too much time to spend with Carson, his golf buddy and a VP of one of the two companies of which Fields was a director. (The other company was a major buyer from Carson's division at HBC.)

"I'll try to be brief," Carson said. "Jim called me to his office this morning and asked me to submit my resignation. I refused. But before he left for his bloodsucking trip, he terminated my association with the company as of this afternoon."

Fields raised his eyes briefly.

"I control the company's three largest customers, you know," Carson continued. "I can easily take them to the competition. But he still has the gall to accuse me of taking a kickback, with absolutely no proof! I think Harris has put him up to it. He's been charging a substantial proportion of his division's expenses to my division. I have been arguing with him about these expenses during the last several weeks, and he finally told me he'd have my head if I went to Lind about it."

"Not even a note of thanks. Not even a mention of it to the board," Carson murmured. "I wonder how long the board will allow Lind to destroy the very people who built this company."

"I don't know what to do."

"Neither do I, Charlie," Fields answered. "I'm truly sorry to hear about this. This is strange. I had no idea this was even being considered. The executive committee met this morning and Jim, of course, was there, but this was never mentioned. I'd like to help in any way I can, Charlie. . . . All I can say is wait and see what happens at the next board meeting. It's scheduled for October 17."

"Well," said Carson, "I just hope the board takes this chance to finally straighten up the organization. Its relationship to the company, the delegation of responsibility, the criteria for employee evaluation—there are a lot of things that have remained garbled and unclear ever since Frank Adams was asked to resign. The morale of the executive staff is low. Earnings are not improving. Everyone is concerned about his own skin. Who will be axed?"

Lind's turbulent ride

Lind was deeply shaken over Carson's refusal to resign, and on the plane to Maui he tried to analyze the situation. He realized that he had made a mistake in promoting Carson a year and a half ago, although the psychological tests that he had had administered to all executives at the time pointed strongly to Carson as the man for the job. Lind remembered, too, the annual physical checkup the company executives were required to undergo, and recalled sadly the high blood pressure and excessive cholesterol level that Carson's exams revealed.

"I must stick to my guns," Lind mused. "I refuse to be blackmailed by the three powerful customers Charlie has in his pocket. I cannot let my authority be challenged, especially by a man I believe has taken kickbacks."

After a sleepless night, Lind telephoned Andrew Simon to inform him of Carson's resignation.

"Yes, Jim, Jason Fields called me yesterday to tell me," Simon relayed. "He was quite upset. And I saw Roy North at a cocktail party last night. He, too, knew about the event, and he appeared visibly disturbed. This is a sad situation. I am a little more than concerned, but you are the boss. We'll try to handle the matter appropriately at the board meeting next week."

Simon returned the receiver to the cradle thoughtfully. For the first time in his 20 years as chairman of the board, he felt that there was a conflict between the management of company affairs and the way he thought they ought to be managed.

Approaching 65, Simon was still active and healthy, and never missed a board meeting. He was once the caretaker president of HBC for one year in 1956. His deep concern for the company was reflected in the way he usually helped in its decision-making process—carefully— after long consideration and debate. He had discussed the matter of Adams' resignation privately first with Lind, then with the executive committee, and then with the entire board before Simon had been fully convinced that Adams should go. Similarly, he had spent long hours deciding on Lind's appointment, consulted extensively with several members of the board individually. Both Mr. and Mrs. Lind were interviewed thoroughly before the board selected him for the presidency.

The Rose Company

MR. JAMES PIERCE had recently received word of his appointment as plant manager of Plant X, one of the older established units of the Rose Company. As such, Mr. Pierce was to be responsible for the management and administration at Plant X of all functions and personnel except sales.

Both top management and Mr. Pierce realized that there were several unique features about his new assignment. Mr. Pierce decided to assess his new situation and relationships before undertaking his assignment. He was personally acquainted with the home office executives, but had met few of the plant personnel. This case contains some of his reflections regarding the new assignment.

The Rose Company conducted marketing activities throughout the United States and in certain foreign countries. These activities were directed from the home office by a vice president in charge of sales.

Manufacturing operations and certain other departments were under the supervision and control of a senior vice president. These are shown in Exhibit 1. For many years the company had operated a highly centralized functional type of manufacturing organization. There was no general manager at any plant; each of the departments in a plant reported on a line basis to its functional counterpart at the home office. For instance, the industrial relations manager of a particular plant reported to the vice president in charge of industrial relations at the home office, the plant controller to the vice president and controller, and so on.

Mr. Pierce stated that in the opinion of the top management the record of Plant X had not been satisfactory for several years. The board had recently approved the erection of a new plant in a different part of the city and the use of new methods of production. Lower costs of processing and a reduced labor force requirement at the new plant were expected. Reduction of costs and improved quality of products were needed to maintain competitive leadership and gain some slight product

Exhibit 1

OLD ORGANIZATION

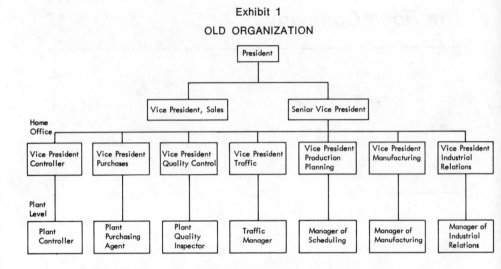

advantage. The proposed combination of methods of manufacturing and mixing materials had not been tried elsewhere in the company. Some features would be entirely new to employees.

According to Mr. Pierce the top management of the Rose Company was beginning to question the advisability of the central control of manufacturing operations. The officers decided to test the value of a decentralized operation in connection with Plant X. They apparently believed that a general management representative in Plant X was needed if the new equipment in manufacturing methods and the required rebuilding of the organization were to succeed.

Prior to the new assignment Mr. Pierce had been an accounting executive in the controller's department of the company. From independent sources the case writer learned that Mr. Pierce had demonstrated analytical ability and general administrative capacity. He was generally liked by people. From top management's point of view he had an essential toughness described as an ability to see anything important through. By some he was regarded as the company's efficiency expert. Others thought he was a perfectionist and aggressive in reaching the goals that had been set. Mr. Pierce was aware of these opinions about his personal behavior.

Mr. Pierce summarized his problem in part as follows: "I am going into a situation involving a large number of changes. I will have a new plant—new methods and processes—but most of all I will be dealing with a set of changed relationships. Heretofore all the heads of departments in the plant reported to their functional counterparts in the home office. Now they will report to me. I am a complete stranger and in addition this is my first assignment in a major 'line' job. The men will know this.

"When I was called into the senior vice president's office to be informed of my new assignment he asked me to talk with each of the functional members of his staff. The vice presidents in charge of production planning, manufacturing, and industrial relations said they were going to issue all headquarters instructions to me as plant manager and they were going to cut off their connections with their counterparts in my plant. The other home office executives admitted their functional counterparts would report to me in line capacity. They should obey my orders and I would be responsible for their pay and promotion. But these executives proposed to follow the common practice of many companies of maintaining a dotted line or functional relationship with these men. I realize that these two different patterns of home office—plant relationships will create real administrative problems for me."

Exhibit 2 shows the organization relationships as defined in these conferences.

Exhibit 2

NEW ORGANIZATION

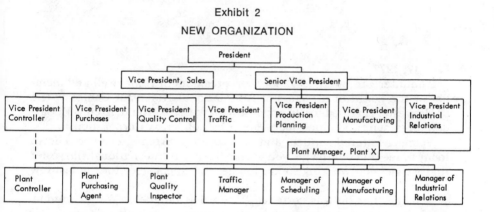

International Harvester (A)

MAY 17, 1977.

The intercom buzzed. Ed Spencer, president of Honeywell and member of the board of directors at International Harvester Company (IH or Harvester) arrived for an appointment with his friend, Archie McCardell, president and chief operating officer of Xerox Corporation.

Spencer entered, smiled, and opened with "Archie, I've come down today to see if I couldn't get you to take the job at International Harvester that we've been working so hard to get you to consider for the last few months."

Sensing that he was cornered, McCardell laughed, "Wait a minute, Ed, I thought we were going to talk computers. What's this about IH? I've already had at least three approaches from headhunters. One even discovered I was in New York at a meeting and I ended up at lunch with him. And another managed to get me to dinner with Brooks McCormick (CEO and chairman of IH) in Chicago. I've said no to all of them. I was in that industry when I was at Ford, and it's just a lousy business. I'll admit I don't know anything about International Harvester specifically but just take a look at the balance sheet and income statements—they speak for themselves—the company's in bad shape."

Spencer jumped in, "That's just the point. The challenge is a big one. If you could revitalize a company like Harvester, it would be a very real accomplishment. Besides, the compensation package will put you among the very highest paid executives in the country. And, while the initial appointment will be as president and COO, part of the deal will be to make you chief executive officer within the first year of your joining IH."

McCardell admittedly was intrigued. But before he could even begin to make a decision on such a major change, he needed to understand exactly what the challenges were at IH and what was going to be expected of him. He needed to have a better idea what people such as Ed Spencer and Brooks McCormick would expect, if the company had enough resources to meet the challenges, and what a reasonable plan of attack could be. After all, what could any one person do with a "venerable dinosaur" like International Harvester?

HISTORY OF THE COMPANY

International Harvester traced its antecedents back to 1831 when Cyrus Hall McCormick invented the reaper in Virginia, the first of many agricultural equipment inventions of those times. McCormick founded a company, moving the headquarters in 1846, when volume manufacturing was set up, to the "frontier" city of Chicago to serve the opening of the midwestern farmlands. McCormick farm equipment was distributed throughout the country and even to Canada and Europe from the 1850s onward. Despite this early presence in international markets and the strength such an image gave to the company, International Harvester retained its "American," indeed midwestern, tone—a tone audible even to this day. As a recent IH publication stated "International Harvester is a distinctly American enterprise. It has grown with the nation and helped the nation grow."

In 1902 the current company was incorporated through the merger of several agriculture equipment companies, with raw material resources and a steel mill completing the package. Cyrus McCormick's son became the first president. The purpose of the merger was to develop new products, diversify the product line, and develop foreign markets.

The initial Harvester products were all agricultural implements, the majority being used for harvesting (e.g., reapers). By the 1900s, however, a full line of equipment was offered. While the first motorized tractor dated back to the first decade of the century, World War I provided the real stimulus for the development of tractors. The first all-purpose tractor that might look familiar today appeared in 1922. IH was the recognized leader in agriculture equipment until the early 1960s.

IH produced a "truck" for farm use in 1907, but again it was the stimulus of World War I that saw the development of nonfarm trucks. Heavy-duty trucks became a separate product line in the early 1920s, and Harvester was the leading producer of a complete line of trucks by 1925. In 1977 the company was still the volume leader in certain segments of the truck industry.

Another outgrowth of agricultural equipment was construction and industrial equipment. Bulldozers, for example, could be configured by adding different attachments or crawlers to a standard farm tractor. The full line of construction equipment was not developed until the early 1950s, however.

After the basic engine technology (both gas and diesel) was established in the 20s and the development of pneumatic tires in the early 30s, the rate of technological change in all IH industries slowed and took on the familiar characteristics of a maturing industry—longer product life cycles and technological evolution rather than revolution. The trends that developed were toward lighter, bigger, and more powerful vehicles, whether in agriculture, trucking, or construction.

Throughout IH's history, sales have shown some volatility around an upward trend. The volatility was due not only to the dependence on the welfare of the farmer, which cannot be characterized as stable, but to the advent of war or depression. Harvester had always received a major boost in sales during wartime, not only from sales of its standard product line but also from the use of its plants for production of munitions. The readjustment to a civilian economy had similarly led to a decrease in sales.

By 1950 IH employed about 90,000 people. It had a reputation for quality, service, and good employee relations. Indeed, one executive who had joined the company around that time described Harvester as a "company with all these traditions. In 1950 people were still talking about the Depression, how everyone was so well treated. No one was ever fired. The company was as solid as the Rock of Gibraltar. Indeed, when I first joined the company and was in a management training program I was told by one of the group, a son of an executive, that I had already achieved the most important thing in my career and that was getting hired."

The tradition was to join the company as a young person and spend one's entire career there. Indeed, on its 50th anniversary, a dinner was given for 26 men who were still working at Harvester after those entire 50 years.

From postwar strength to 1970 hard times

From its Rock of Gibraltar position of strength after World War II, International Harvester deteriorated and lost its market leadership. Such declines are always complex, but several factors that contributed include its very size, its leadership, and several poor product-market decisions. (For historical sales and income data see Exhibit 1.)

Right after the war, Harvester was still essentially a farm implement company. A strategy of diversification was started with a major investment in the home appliance industry which was enjoying a huge postwar

Exhibit 1

HISTORICAL PERFORMANCE
($ millions)

	Sales	Net income	Return on sales	Equity	Return on equity
1910	$ 102.0	$16.1	15.8%	$ 156.1	10.3%
1920	225.0	16.7	7.4	218.4	7.6
1930	n.a.	25.7	—	316.6	8.1
1940	247.7*	23.2	8.4	337.9	6.9
1945	622.0*	24.5	3.9	396.6	6.2
1950	942.6	66.7	7.1	614.5	10.9
1955	1,165.8	55.5	4.8	761.3	7.3
1960	1,683.2	53.8	3.2	1,020.9	5.3
1965	2,336.7	97.7	4.2	1,088.7	9.0
1970	2,711.5	52.7	1.9	1,146.8	4.6

n.a. = Not available.
* $290 million of sales were war related.

boom. While on the product side, the move made some sense—Harvester had produced cooling equipment for dairy farms for many years—it was not experienced in the selling of refrigerators and similar appliances to consumers. Large capital investment was required, but sales never amounted to more than 5–6 percent of total sales and made little, if any, profit. The assets were sold to the Whirlpool-Seeger Corporation in 1956.

In the construction equipment line, Caterpillar Tractor Company and International Harvester had had an equal share of the market prior to World War II. But during the war, the U.S. government favored Caterpillar for military use throughout the world. Caterpillar thus gained a strong position for international distribution after the war with a developed and reliable product line that emphasized the largest sizes of construction equipment. In an attempt to catch up and regain its parity with Caterpillar, Harvester made large investments in their construction equipment line, particularly in more capital-intense, large machines. Unfortunately, less investment was placed in quality control and there were problems of reliability.

Other investments were made in new plant, in minor businesses (e.g., twine), and new plant or purchases of smaller companies in an effort to backward integrate (e.g., foundries or the Solar Turbine Company). While none of these investments was necessarily poor, taken one at a time, the end result was relative inattention to R&D in the core agriculture business. At the same time, major competitors, particularly Deere, had made large investments in product improvements of agriculture equipment.

By the mid-50s, the postwar shortages were gone, and the sellers' market became a competitive buyers' market. "Selling is our major challenge" claimed the annual reports of the era. But Harvester products no longer sold themselves, and competitors made major inroads into the company's market share. Perhaps the inevitable changes were masked in the early 50s because sales continued to grow. But the growth was the result of increasing Korean War–related contracts, the value of which reached 18 percent of revenues. Domestic sales meanwhile remained flat. When defense sales dried up in the mid-50s and the company was hit by several severe strikes (one for 10 weeks, another for 4 months), it was obvious that Harvester was falling behind. To top it all, Harvester geared up for a predicted boom in small tractor demand just as the over-100 horsepower tractor market was taking off. One executive described the situation, "We did more for Deere in the period than they did for themselves. As the ratios began to fall, panic set in, and a defensive management style started to appear. It was catch-up psychology from then on."

The problems of the 50s were compounded by the choice of leadership in the 60s. Harry O. Bercher became president in 1962. While he had been with the company for many years, most of his tenure had been in the Wisconsin steel division, the same steel capacity that had been part of the original 1902 merger. It produced steel solely for IH, and because of accounting practices, its profitability could not be determined exactly but was probably not very great. One executive commented, "We just misconstrued Bercher's experience. We thought he understood the Harvester business better than he apparently did." Whether he understood the business or not, large investments were made in capital improvements at the steel plant. Further, he managed by becoming very involved in day-to-day operations. One description portrayed him as "so involved in operations that it stifled us. He would have weekly meetings to go over the extreme details of operations. He even made hiring decisions down four levels into the divisions. There were no administrative systems, no planning, no position descriptions, no long-term view."

By the end of 1970 the company was "in the process of liquidation. Net income had dropped 52 percent from 1967–71 to $45 million, while sales had gone up 20 percent." Debt as a percentage of debt plus equity had increased from 19 percent to 28 percent. Or as another executive claimed, "We were heading down the path of the Penn Central."

The McCormick Era: 1971–1977

During 1971 Brooks McCormick, great-grandnephew of Cyrus H. McCormick, took over the presidency of International Harvester. Having joined the company in 1940, he was 54 when he gained the position of president. One executive surmised that this must have been "a traumatic experience for some executives. Brooks had been ignored for 30 years, and many executives found their career expectations cut short as the balance of power shifted." The situation could have created dissension in the leadership and stifled any attempts at change, particularly if McCormick lacked a power base. But he had the loyalty of the company. The many third- and fourth-generation employees felt a McCormick was properly the rightful heir to the presidency. "Brooks McCormick was Mr. Harvester," explained one older employee. On his side McCormick was "determined to save the company and rejuvenate it." It was a big task: the financial picture was weak, and the company's organization and management systems had remained the same since the 1940s.

Further, Brooks McCormick was a product of the very environment that he was trying to change, an environment described in an early consultants' report to him as "staid, old-fashioned, conservative, inbred, highly centralized, and nonentrepreneurial . . . an atmosphere of strict observance of protocol, status consciousness, and stuffiness." The same report characterized Harvester as having "little sense of direction," making "decisions from a short-term perspective rather than weighed against long-term goals," and having a "general focus on activities rather than results."

McCormick started with the basics. As one executive recalls, "It was a classic MBA situation—elementary textbook stuff: there were no business planning, strategic planning, or management systems to speak of." The core of McCormick's program centered around curing problems of people and planning, triggered by a series of consultants' studies.

Strategic planning. A consultant was brought in to help establish a corporate strategic planning process, a project that had been attempted several times by McCormick and his executive vice president, James

[Margin annotations: "steel got $", "near sighted", "no change", "not creative!", "must plan!", "no direction"]

Doyle. By 1975 the first strategic plans were made by the divisions. As one executive commented, "While this was certainly a step in the right direction, the company still lacked the infrastructure for proper planning. These first attempts tended to produce reams of paper with all the blanks filled out but planning was still not a part of management." McCormick also showed his willingness to bring outside talent to Harvester by hiring a corporate planning officer with strong academic and business credentials.

② Hay study. Hay Associates was hired to carry out a climate study and then to set up a system of individual accountability. Using the standard Hay methodology, position descriptions were written, positions were reevaluated, and a salary policy was established which would place Harvester's compensation in the top quarter compared to other companies. An incentive system for management was established that gave credit for individual achievements, a company first. Previously bonuses were based on overall corporate performance.

The changes in the incentive system created conflicts between individuals and the units they worked for. As one executive described it, "The incentive system raised questions for the first time about interdependencies between the divisions as manifested in such areas as transfer prices. Many people wanted to scrap the system, but McCormick realized that organization change was what was really needed."

③ Reorganization. Brooks McCormick asked Booz Allen to perform an organization study. One description of this study claimed that "the consultants came in and we started having all these meetings—a first at Harvester—I mean it was still all very paternalistic but we were included—and the consultants started by asking us what business we were in, what our goals were, what our strengths and weaknesses were. We all thought they were out of their tree . . . but we were really developing a common vocabulary for the first time."

In 1976 Booz Allen recommended a complete reorganization of the company. Included was a recommendation that Harvester needed a new president, preferably from outside of the company.

Brooks McCormick announced the reorganization to management in December 1976, following the year-long study of the company by Booz Allen. The plan to be implemented basically followed the consultants' recommendations.

The company was to be organized around five product groups. Four were end-product groups: trucks, agricultural equipment, construction equipment, and turbine engines. The fifth group, components, supplied the other groups. It was created from operations in agriculture, truck, and construction, and was responsible for the manufacture of engines and castings and the distribution of parts. Besides creating the components group, the major change in the reorganization was the dissolution of the overseas division. Foreign operations were divided by product area and profit responsibility placed in the worldwide product groups. In one sense, the biggest losers in the reorganization were the old country managing directors, who found their scope of responsibility much reduced.

The five group presidents were chosen by Brooks McCormick. They were all insiders but were not necessarily chosen from the product areas they were to manage. Thus Pat Kaine, formerly president of the agricultural/industrial equipment division, became president of the truck group; Ben Warren, formerly group vice president with corporatewide responsibilities, became president of the agricultural equipment group; Bob Musgjerd, the new president of construction equipment, was formerly president of the overseas division; Keith Mazurek as the president of the new components group switched from being president of the truck division; only Morris Seivert continued as president of the solar group.

only one staged

McCormick then asked each new president to recommend as starters three people for each of the jobs on the Booz Allen charts. They were told that they could staff their organizations with anyone they wanted from either inside or outside the company. In a sort of "players draft," McCormick and the group presidents got together with the corporate human resource executives and negotiated who would go where. The first three levels of the group organizations were determined in this manner. The reorganization was causing much turmoil in the spring of 1977, and shifts in jobs, facilities, and reporting were expected to continue through 1977 and 1978.

The Booz Allen plan essentially recognized Brooks McCormick's desire to decentralize, provide for truly autonomous operations, and assign accountability to the groups. Not only was the role of the corporate staff thereby much reduced but an entire tier of management was removed between the president and group presidents. Each group was allowed to organize as they saw fit, but with the guidelines set down by Booz Allen. Thus, the agriculture and truck groups were organized geographically, construction and solar were organized functionally, and components was organized by product line. (For pre- and post-1976 organization charts, see Exhibits 2 and 3.)

How much decentralization was really affected is another question. As one executive commented, "Brooks took over a company that was used to very autocratic systems . . . everything was centralized. So even though there was an attempt to decentralize, it can't be done overnight and is hard to do. The senior managers really didn't have any leeway." Another climate study was taken, and improvement was found, but there was still "a short-term perspective, and a management style that was hindering open communication and initiative."

While planning and human resources systems had now been instituted, there was the need to learn to use them judiciously, and to ask some critical strategic questions, questions often best asked by a newcomer. As one executive described it, "We were still following the mushroom theory of decision making—keep managers in the dark and requests for resources will pop up all over the place, at random and with no relation to each other. We had to think about the relations."

4. **Other changes.** Beyond the major programs in the planning and human resources areas, McCormick also hired a consultant in mid-1976 to conduct a study of plant-level manpower utilization. The purpose of the study was to pinpoint the sources of excess labor costs which

Exhibit 2

ORGANIZATION CHART, OCTOBER 31, 1974

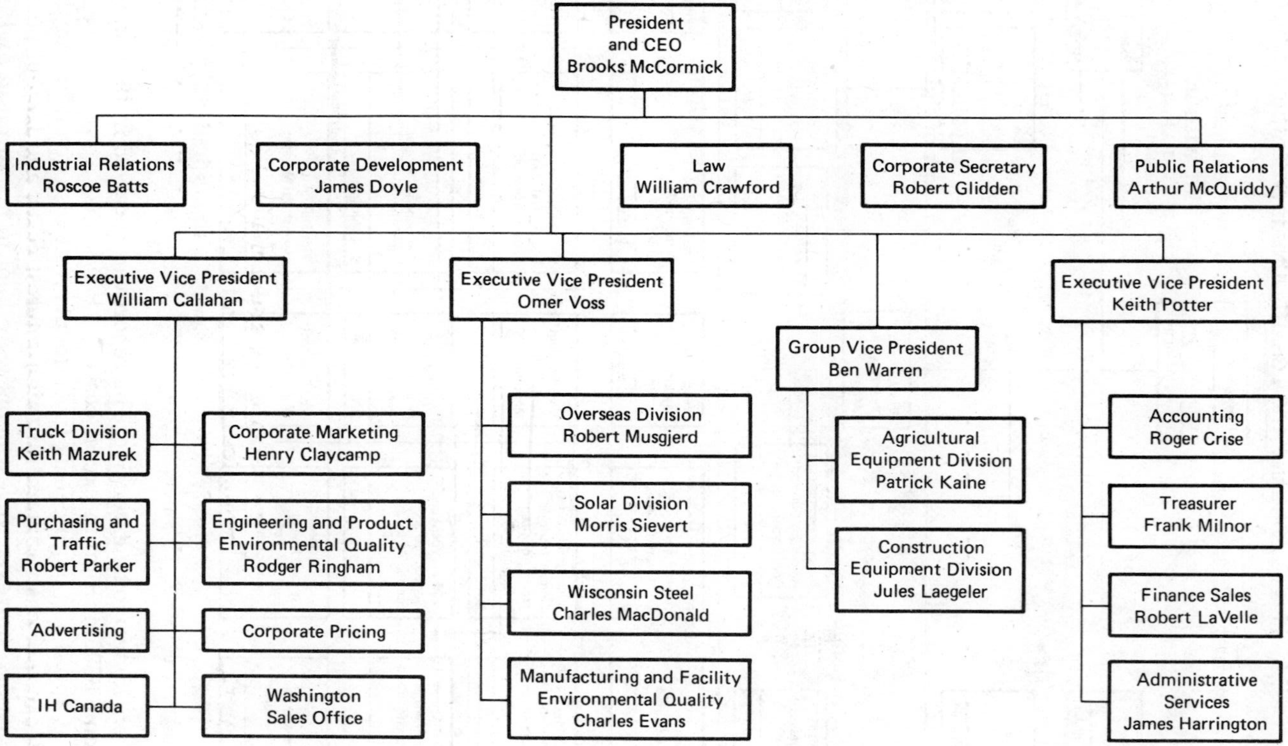

Exhibit 3

ORGANIZATION CHART, JUNE 1, 1977

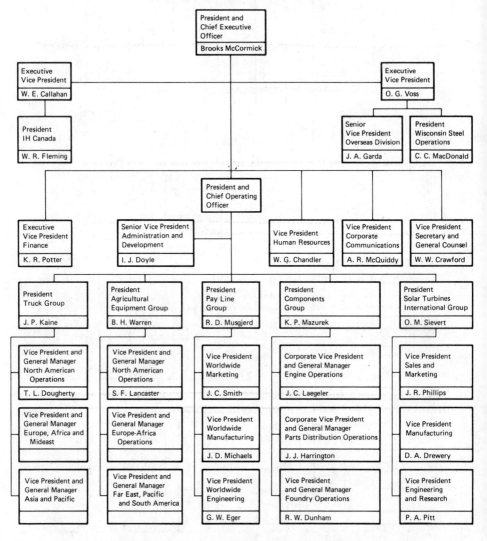

were known to be extensive. The report was received in 1977, indicating some $300 million in excess costs.

Capital and engineering investments were also given higher priority. Because of cash constraints, high interest costs, and lack of borrowing capacity, however, investments were kept to a minimum and emphasized end-product development rather than plant improvement, manufacturing process . . . innovation, or intermediate product research.

Finally, McCormick began to look for ways to divest some unprofitable operations. In 1975 it was decided to sell the Wisconsin steel division, but the sale was not consummated until 1977. IH received $15 million in cash and $50 million in notes, but the effect on net income was a loss of $37.6 million.

In the five years, 1971 to 1976, net income had grown from $45.2 million to $174.1 million, return on sales from 1.5 percent to 3.2 percent, and most impressively, return on equity from 3.9 percent to 12.1 percent. As one executive commented, "Brooks saved this company. He did a tremendous job of initiating change and getting the new programs going. His actions showed a lot of fortitude."

INTERNATIONAL HARVESTER IN 1977

In trying to assess the company in the spring of 1977, Archie McCardell had available to him the following kinds of information from public sources concerning the financial position of the company as a whole, the various industries in which it participated, and its internal resources.

In FY 1976 the company had sales of $5.5 billion and ranked 27th in sales in the *Fortune* 500, while net income was $174 million which ranked 51st, and return on equity ranked 340th. (For 1976 balance sheet, income statement, key statistics for 10 years, and comparative statistics, see Exhibits 4, 5, 6, and 7.) International Harvester's basic products were in three industries: heavy-duty trucks, agricultural equipment, and construction equipment. The company produced many of the components for these products. On a smaller scale, the company made medium-sized turbine engines mostly for the oil and gas industry. There was also a finance subsidiary to support sales.

Trucks

Trucks were usually segmented by their weight. There were eight different weight classes ranging from pickups and vans (class 1 or class 2) to long distance tractor trailers (class 8). Market growth had been 8–11 percent in the late 60s and early 70s. The growth rate was expected to slow to 3–6 percent in the United States due to several factors: higher prices for fuel and trucks, and the slowing of highway construction and population growth.

Table 1

U.S. TRUCK MARKET FACTORY SALES BY WEIGHT CLASS—1976
(trucks and buses; weight in pounds)

Class 1	Class 2	Class 3	Class 4	Class 5	Class 6	Class 7	Class 8
6,000	6,000–10,000	10,000–14,000	14,000–16,000	16,000–19,500	19,501–26,000	26,001–33,000	33,000+
			Unit sales				
1,248,034	1,389,707	22,444	1,129*	11,416	164,796	24,961	118,048

* 1975 figure.
Source: Motor Vehicle Manufacturers Association.

Exhibit 4

INTERNATIONAL HARVESTER (A)
Balance Sheet, 1976
($ millions)

Assets

Current assets:
Cash	$ 40.0
Marketable securities principally at cost	0.5
Net receivables	603.0
Inventories	1,584.4
Total current assets	2,227.9
Investments	495.8
Property	710.3
Wisconsin steel division	65.8
Other	75.0
Total assets	$3,574.8

Liabilities and Stockholders' Equity

Current liabilities:
Notes payable	$ 266.5
Accounts payable	282.4
Accrued liabilities	319.6
Current maturities of long-term debt	35.7
Total current liabilities	1,004.2
Long-term debt	922.9
Deferred income taxes	66.9

Stockholders' equity:
Preferred stock	50.0
Common stock, $20 par	576.9
Capital in excess of par value	4.0
Income retained	964.7
	1,595.6
Less 464,954 shares of common in treasury at cost	14.8
Total stockholders' equity	1,580.8
Total liabilities and stockholders' equity	$3,574.8

In the heavy-duty segment of the truck market (classes 6, 7, and 8), trucks were either straight trucks or tractor trucks. A straight truck consisted of a cab, frame, two or three axles, driveshaft, transmission, and engine. A body was added by another manufacturer. Typical straight trucks were dump, garbage, or construction trucks. A tractor truck was meant to pull trailers and had the same components as a straight truck but the frame was shorter. Trailers were bought elsewhere.

Cab design could either be conventional (engine in front) or cab-over engine (COE). Conventional models were generally cheaper to build, less complicated, simpler to maintain, smoother to ride and safer. The COE had better maneuverability, capacity for longer trailers, and higher visibility.

Within the heavy-duty segment, class 6 trucks were differentiated from class 7 and class 8 by use, mileage, and engine type. Class 6 trucks

Exhibit 5

INTERNATIONAL HARVESTER (A)
Income Statement, 1976
($ millions)

Sales and other revenues:	
Sales	$5,488.1
Interest and other income	49.1
Total revenues	5,537.2
Costs and expenses:	
Cost of sales	4,536.7
Marketing and administrative	547.3
Interest expenses	121.3
Other	110.5
Total costs and expenses	5,315.8
Income of consolidated group:	
Income before taxes	221.4
Taxes	95.6
Net income	125.8
Income of nonconsolidated companies:	
Income before taxes	93.6
Taxes	45.3
Net income	48.3
Total net income from continuing operations	174.1
Dividends	5.0
Earned on common stock	$ 169.1
Income per share of common stock	$6.02

were used for agriculture, wholesale, and retail trade (intracity delivery). Their annual mileage was lower, and they were more often gasoline powered. In 1976, 10 percent of class 6 trucks were diesel powered as compared to more than 95 percent for class 7 and class 8 trucks. But with gasoline prices on the rise, growth of diesel engines in class 6 trucks was predicted. Class 7 and class 8 trucks were found in intercity hauling, mining, construction, and lumbering. They had much greater annual mileage and were diesel powered.

The truck market could also be segmented by buyer. Heavy-duty truck buyers were either private owner-operators or fleet operators. The demarcation between the two was ownership of 10 or more trucks. Light-duty truck buyers were fleet operators (e.g., telephone repair trucks) or the consumer market (for pickup, recreational vehicles, or four-wheel drive vehicles).

American manufacturers were not a major factor in the European market in 1976 since their trucks were mostly too large for foreign roads. The European market was highly competitive, with many firms. Consolidation was predicted there, however. There was much opportunity for expansion, particularly in the Third World, but competition was stiff. European firms were threatening to enter the U.S. market with diesel trucks of the class 6 variety. Daimler Benz had started operations in

Exhibit 6

10-YEAR STATISTICAL DATA

	1967	1968	1969	1970	1971	1972	1973	1974	1975	1976
Sales by major product group (continuing operations):										
Trucks	$1,116.9	$1,145.0	$1,318.7	$1,335.6	$1,522.8	$1,780.4	$2,118.1	$2,282.9	$1,999.0	$2,310.4
Agricultural equipment	898.2	847.4	762.0	775.6	857.1	1,028.0	1,242.1	1,656.7	2,105.7	2,262.0
Construction and industrial equipment	386.7	383.0	408.8	426.5	447.6	497.3	627.2	751.9	886.8	668.4
Turbo machinery	72.8	84.4	85.1	97.3	102.4	107.2	104.4	172.0	254.5	247.3
Total	$2,474.6	$2,459.8	$2,574.6	$2,636.0	$2,929.9	$3,412.9	$4,091.8	$4,863.5	$5,246.0	$5,488.1
Sales by area of final sale (continuing operations):										
United States	$1,823.1	$1,823.4	$1,903.5	$1,955.8	$2,201.5	$2,551.2	$2,921.6	$3,375.0	$3,167.8	$3,457.6
Canada	182.4	158.7	172.2	150.9	199.6	269.1	338.8	407.9	422.1	486.8
Europe and Africa	253.3	249.8	263.9	285.1	301.3	358.5	536.1	651.0	1,097.5	1,057.2
Latin America	60.3	69.5	74.4	82.6	72.7	79.7	76.4	127.4	183.5	147.5
Pacific area	155.5	158.4	160.6	161.6	154.8	154.4	218.9	302.2	375.1	359.0
Total	$2,474.6	$2,459.8	$2,574.6	$2,636.0	$2,929.9	$3,412.9	$4,091.8	$4,863.5	$5,246.0	$5,488.1
Net income:										
Amount	$93.0	$75.4	$63.8	$52.4	$45.2	$86.6	$114.3	$124.1	$79.4	$174.1
Percent of sales	3.76%	3.07%	2.48%	1.99%	1.54%	2.54%	2.79%	2.55%	1.51%	3.17%
Return on stockholders' equity, beginning of year	8.52%	6.67%	5.54%	4.54%	3.94%	7.53%	9.54%	9.66%	5.82%	12.06%
Other statistical data:										
Working capital	$747.1	$768.7	$751.0	$766.4	$791.8	$845.3	$888.7	$947.3	$1,214.9	$1,223.8
Long-term debt	264.4	298.1	312.7	402.2	431.3	465.1	497.0	625.3	938.2	922.9
Total net assets	$1,130.0	$1,151.9	$1,155.2	$1,146.8	$1,149.5	$1,198.0	$1,284.6	$1,364.2	$1,443.9	$1,580.8
Capital expenditures	$93.5	$102.0	$97.0	$88.5	$62.7	$61.3	$106.5	$180.6	$173.2	$168.4
Per common share:										
Net income	3.31	2.69	2.30	3.92	1.65	3.17	4.13	4.46	2.77	6.02
Dividends paid	1.80	1.80	1.80	1.80	1.60	1.40	1.50	1.60	1.70	1.70
Book value, end of year	40.23	41.14	41.70	42.06	42.10	43.87	46.21	49.08	50.14	53.94
Market price range:										
High	41	38	38¾	29	33⅔	39	40¾	32¾	30¾	32½
Low	33%	30%	25	22	22⅔	23	26	16¾	18½	21½
Ratios:										
Current assets to current liabilities	2.8-1	2.7-1	2.4-1	2.2-1	2.2-1	2.0-1	1.9-1	1.7-1	2.1-1	2.2-1
Long-term debt as a percent of stockholders' equity plus long-term debt	19%	21%	21%	26%	27%	28%	28%	31%	39%	37%

Exhibit 7

1976—COMPARATIVE STATISTICS AND RANKING WITHIN THE *FORTUNE* 500

	IH		Deere		Caterpillar		Paccar	
	Amount	*Rank*	*Amount*	*Rank*	*Amount*	*Rank*	*Amount*	*Rank*
Sales*	$5,488.1	27	$3,133.8	66	$5,042.3	36	$1,001.4	227
Assets*	3,574.8	43	2,893.2	48	3,893.9	35	473.2	305
Sales/assets	1.5	n.a.	1.1	n.a.	1.3	n.a.	2.1	n.a.
Net income*	174.1	51	241.6	38	383.2	24	50.6	215
EBIT/interest expense	3.2	n.a.	9.0	n.a.	9.7	n.a.	32.3	n.a.
Equity*	1,580.8	40	1,378.8	48	2,027.3	34	271.9	277
Long-term debt/capital	35.9%	n.a.	26.1%	n.a.	33.7%	n.a.	7.6%	n.a.
Number of employees	97,550	22	55,242	52	77,793	31	10,747	336
Net income/sales	3.2%	360	7.7%	82	7.6%	87	5.1%	218
Net income/equity	11.0%	340	17.5%	79	18.9%	56	18.6%	59
Earnings per share	$ 6.02	—	$ 4.04	—	$ 4.45	—	$ 6.14	—
Ten-year growth rate of EPS	4.54%	318	11.42%	124	9.72%	168	10.91%	137
Total return to investors	55.10%	138	25.79%	295	27.88%	278	97.32%	33
Total return 10-year average	5.46%	294	10.19%	165	12.48%	109	n.a.	—
Sales per dollar of equity	$3.47		$2.27		$2.48		$3.68	
Sales per employee	$56,260		$56,728		$64,810		$93,180	
Assets per employee	$36,646		$52,372		$50,055		$44,032	

n.a. = Not available.
*In $ millions.

the United States and IVECO (Fiat, Magerius-Deutz) was to team up with Mack. Joint ventures also were allowing U.S. firms to enter the European market, for example, IH with DAF (Holland). (See Exhibits 8 and 9 for European market data.)

Exhibit 8

ESTIMATED SHARE OF MARKET—TRUCKS
OVER NINE TONS*
(as percent total)

	North America	Worldwide
Mercedes group	—	18%
GM	27%	17
Ford	28	15
IH	25	11
Iveco	—	8
Mack	6	3
Paccar	5	—
White	3	—

* Prior to the SAAB-Volvo merger.
Source: Wainwright Securities.

Exhibit 9

ESTIMATED PRODUCTION—OVER 15 TONS—1975
(units)

	Company	Units
1.	Daimler Benz	65,687
2.	Saab-Scandia & Volvo	40,181
3.	Iveco (Fiat, Magerius-Deutz)	38,760
4.	Mack (U.S.)	24,103
5.	Hino (Japan)	20,444
6.	International Harvester (U.S.)......	19,723
7.	Renault (Saviem, Berliet)	18,728
8.	Mitsubishi (Japan)	14,993
9.	General Motors (U.S.)	14,261
10.	Ford (U.S.)	14,045
11.	White (U.S.)	12,356
12.	Nissan (Japan)	12,350
13.	British Leyland	12,061

Source: Wainwright Securities.

Industry characteristics. Manufacturers of trucks were generally not backward integrated but merely assemblers of parts purchased elsewhere. For example, heavy-duty engines were purchased from Cummins, Detroit Diesel (GM), and Caterpillar. Manufacturers relied heavily on components suppliers not only for the parts but also for R&D of new engineering designs. Only Mack was fully backward integrated, making all its own components, specifically engines, transmissions, and axles, where there were higher profit margins. IH was also unusual in that it made some of its own components for trucks, primarily engines. IH still purchased 70 percent of its truck parts from outside sources, however.

Buyers of trucks were quite sophisticated. Owner-operators specified many of the parts to go into a truck, and fleet operators, who had their own engineering staff, sometimes even indicated how the truck should be designed and built. Hence, product differentiation between companies was based more on advertised image and reputation than substance. (See Exhibit 10 for an analysis of the structure of the truck industry.)

Competition. In 1976 International Harvester competed in the heavy-duty market with classes 6, 7, and 8 trucks and in the light-duty market with the four-wheel drive, class 2 vehicle, the Scout.

In the heavy-duty market, a shakeout of competitors occurred in the 50s. At that time there had been some 30 truck manufacturers in the United States, many of them operating only in one region of the country. By 1976 the market contained three giants—International Harvester, Ford, and General Motors; two or three smaller but profitable specialists—Paccar and Mack; and a handful of smaller companies clinging to specialized niches.

In class 7 and class 8 trucks, IH was the industry leader. Twenty-five percent of all class 8 trucks on the road were IH trucks. IH was strongest in the fleet-only segment. Major competitors were GM and Ford, and competition was on price. The rivalry was made stiffer since GM and Ford were lower cost producers and were backed by their parent companies.

Paccar was the leader in the owner-operator segment of the market. Paccar produced Kenworth and Peterbilt trucks which were considered the Rolls Royces of trucking. The company had lower market share than some competitors but the highest profitability in the industry. The lower market share was explained in part by the company's operations being concentrated in the western half of the country. Other analysts explained Paccar's performance as the result of remaining a pure assembler and very specialized. While higher margins were possible through component manufacture (Mack's strategy), a pure assembler retained maximal ability to respond to customer demands on product design. Other companies focusing on the owner-operator market were Mack, Freightliner, and White Motor. Competition in this segment was on service and features (customization) rather than price, and there was a significant degree of brand loyalty.

IH was uniquely positioned as the only major producer specializing in a full line of trucks as a major business. In a market where reputation was important, IH's reputation was as a manufacturer for fleet buyers. The company was known for an ability to produce a wide product range from standard components which lowered the cost and simplified maintenance. IH's strong sales and service dealerships and part distribution network were a major advantage with 800 dealerships versus GM or Ford's 300. However, IH could not match GM or Ford on price in the fleet market. In the owner-operator market, IH did price below competi-

Exhibit 10

STRUCTURAL ANALYSIS OF THE HEAVY-DUTY TRUCK INDUSTRY—DOMESTIC

ENTRY/MOBILITY BARRIERS ARE HIGH BUT DEPEND ON SEGMENT:
—Lower economies of scale/easier entry in owner-operator market, but higher costs for required service/dealer network.
—Higher economies of scale/tougher entry in fleet market, but dealer/service network not so important.
—High investment in capital equipment required to upgrade existing plant and build new plant.
—Some R&D necessary to keep up with government regulations and emission controls.

POWER OF SUPPLIERS IS MODERATE:
—Truck manufacturers differ in degree of backward integration.
—If backward integrated, manufacturers meet material shortages.
—If not backward integrated, suppliers are large but multiple sources exist.
—If manufacturer is active in other vehicle (e.g., autos), leverage over suppliers is increased by joint purchasing.

RIVALRY AMONG COMPETITORS IS STRONG BUT DIFFERS BY SEGMENT:
—Few firms in each segment, but more firms in the owner-operator market and fewer in the fleet and medium-heavy-duty markets. Some markets (C1.6) are being entered by foreign manufacturers.
—Growth is slow (1–2 percent per year) and cyclical.
—Physical product differentiation within segments is fairly low, high between segments.
—Some differentiation by brand name, image, and aftermarket services.

POWER OF BUYERS IS STRONG BUT VARIES BY SEGMENT:
—Owner-operators purchase small quantities, but are highly sophisticated, and together are a sizable market.
—Fleet buyers are large and buy large quantities.
—Fleet buyers tend to integrate backward into service, thus limiting the aftermarket.
—Price sensitivity varies but is higher for large fleet buyers and newer owner-operators.
—No threat of manufacturers integrating forward.

SUBSTITUTION THREAT IN NEAR TERM IS WEAK:
—Some intercity competition from rail and perhaps some air.
—All intracity and most intercity distribution dependent on trucks at least for next decade or two.
—Substitution pressure mostly from fuel shortages, but substitution of fossil fuels not in near future.

tion; but, as pointed out above, perceived reputation and product quality and customization were more important to owner-operators.

In class 6 trucks, Harvester, GM, and Ford were the only competitors. Market share estimates varied, but the following were representative:

Table 2

1976 MARKET SHARE ESTIMATES
(factory sales)

	Class 6	Classes 7 and 8
International Harvester	15%	26%
General Motors	45	12
Ford	36	19
White	—	12
Paccar	—	9
Mack	—	17

Source: Wainwright Securities.

IH was the major factor for some time in the utility/sport vehicle area, represented by the Scout. But GM and Ford entered that market aggressively in the early 70s and considerably weakened IH's position. In 1976 the Scout had about 14 percent of the market and volumes were not high enough to support efficient costs. Further, IH's dealerships for the Scout were weaker than that for the two automakers.

In 1976 International Harvester's most popular truck was the Transtar, a COE class 8 truck aimed at the fleet market. IH had introduced a premium COE, the Eagle, for the owner-operator. The S series of medium- and heavy-duty conventional models was to be introduced in 1977. The latter had many standardized components and provided the opportunity for the first serious U.S.-made entry into class 6 diesel-powered trucks. A line of construction trucks under the Paystart name finished out the product line.

IH's strengths were its dealer network and established market leadership. But capital spending had been low in the past, which had limited the ability for integration and modernization of plant and processes. Product proliferation had been somewhat high, increased by some rather random entries in various foreign countries. The S series promised to begin consolidation of the line. Sales in 1976 for the truck group were $2.3 billion, which represented 42 percent of total IH sales (the largest share). IH's operating margin (all groups combined) was 5.9 percent but only 1.4 percent (estimate) for trucks.

Agricultural equipment

The agricultural equipment industry included combines, tractors, and a wide range of attachments for crop production and harvesting, and hay and forage harvesting. Combines and tractors represented the largest share of sales. The worldwide market was relatively mature, with the major markets being North America, Europe, and certain Third

World countries. North American manufacturers were strongest in the large equipment end of the market, such as tractors with over 100 horsepower, which were largely inappropriate for foreign markets because of smaller field sizes.

Tractors represented 52 percent of industry sales and were used as a barometer of market trends. The size and growth potential of the major geographical segments of the tractor market are shown in Table 3.

Table 3

ESTIMATED WORLDWIDE TRACTOR MARKET, 1977

	Units	Average Horsepower	Total Horsepower	Long-term annual growth potential
United States and Canada	200,000	100	20 billion	0–2%
Europe	350,000	75	26 billion	5
Third World	280,000	40	11 billion	Mixed
Japan	200,000	40	8 billion	Closed to United States

Source: First Boston Research.

As Table 3 suggests, different geographical regions were more attractive than others in terms of growth. Other factors also affected the market risks. Over time, the market for agricultural equipment in North America was essentially flat, but it was also highly cyclical. In Europe, the size of the equipment used on farms had increased rapidly. Four percent of the tractors in Europe were over 70 horsepower in 1972, and 16 percent were by 1976. This trend benefited North American manufacturers. Also, Europe was not as cyclical as North America. The Third World seemed to offer strong opportunities. A problem there, however, was government's insistence on local production. Economies of scale required a plant to operate at 5,000 units per year at minimum. Few Third World countries offered a market of that size. In addition, the usual uncertainties caused by commodity prices, weather, and government regulation of farms made the Third World markets risky at best.

Industry characteristics. Farm equipment was sold on the characteristics and availability of the products and service. Thus competition centered on the strength of the dealer network. Agricultural equipment manufacturers were more integrated than truck assemblers. For example, IH made its own engines and purchased only 20 percent of its parts from outside sources.

As users of the equipment, buyers were fairly knowledgeable (though this varied by size of farm). Some training was provided by dealers, however.

The industry was cyclical. Sales of farm equipment were highly dependent on farm income. The ability to purchase new farm equipment was dependent in turn on a multitude of interconnected variables, including the weather, commodity prices, and government agricultural policies. Even in good times, purchases were financed and such financing was usually provided by the manufacturer.

The trend in agriculture was toward larger and larger farms which in turn supported larger and more powerful farm equipment. With the consequent increase in the economies of scale, these trends were adding pressure for an increase in the concentration of the industry. (See Exhibit 11 for a structural analysis of the agricultural equipment industry.)

Competition. For a slow-growth industry, the number of firms in the agricultural equipment industry was large and perhaps greater than the market could support at an efficient scale. The North American companies in order of sales were Deere & Company, International Harvester, Massey-Ferguson, Allis-Chalmers, J. I. Case, White Motor, and Ford. (For pertinent comparative data see Exhibit 12.)

The industry leader was Deere & Company. Prior to 1963, when Deere became number one, International Harvester had been the leader. IH had maintained a strong number two position since the early 60s. One estimate gave Deere about 36 percent and Harvester about 33 percent of the domestic market. The remaining five companies battled for the remaining 30 percent. With its long history of penetration in foreign markets, Harvester was the industry leader in Europe and was strong in several other countries particularly ex-Commonwealth countries. (Actually, Harvester sold a few units less than Massey-Ferguson in Europe in 1976, but sales of Massey, who had followed a strategy of trying to penetrate foreign markets, had trended steadily downward while Harvester's position had steadily improved.) Deere had begun a major and expensive effort to enter Europe, but was not as yet a strong presence in foreign markets. Competitive positions in mid-1977 were estimated as shown in Table 4.

Both International Harvester and Deere & Company had strong dealer networks unapproached by any others in the industry. Deere's dealerships were considered superior (see Table 5), but IH had been investing in dealer improvement particularly in its XL program, which included certified service through training, parts supports, audiovisual aids, formal planning, and computerized systems. Brand loyalty was particularly strong for IH and Deere, but was relatively absent for other equipment makers. One analyst estimated that 90 percent of first-time buyers of IH equipment returned to IH for future purchases of the same brand.

Deere was a formidable opponent. The company emphasized the high end of the product line (big 100+ horsepower tractors, for example) targeted at the 20 percent of the farmers who produced 75–80 percent of farm output. As one analyst put it, "Deere had the biggest share of the biggest machines with the biggest profitability." Deere was the low-cost producer but had chosen not to compete on price but to maintain high margins. They emphasized plant utilization. Indeed, one industry observer claimed that in the attempt to hold back overexpansion, Deere had become capacity constrained to the extent that it was limiting both its sales and market share below obvious potential.

IH produced a full line of such products for the farm market plus lawn and garden tractors for the consumer market. Sales for the agricul-

Exhibit 11

STRUCTURAL ANALYSIS OF THE AGRICULTURAL EQUIPMENT INDUSTRY—DOMESTIC

ENTRY/MOBILITY BARRIERS ARE HIGH:
—Capital costs are high.
—Production economies of scale are high; some economies from shared parts with other product lines.
—Minimum dealer network is large.
—Significant R&D required for manufacturing process as well as products.
—Brand name product differentiation is a factor.
—Ability to provide financing to buyers necessary.

POWER OF SUPPLIERS IS FAIRLY WEAK:
—Some degree of backward integration by manufacturers and economies from shared parts with other product lines.
—In general, there are multiple sources but some shortages are possible.

RIVALRY AMONG COMPETITORS IS RELATIVELY STRONG:
—Few firms; no new entrants threatening; but no clear industry leader and firms are closely balanced in size.
—Growth is slow and cyclical; most growth potential in foreign (but riskier) markets.
—High fixed capacity costs but high exit barriers retain financially shakier competitors.
—Some product differentiation based on dealer networks, service, and brand loyalty.

POWER OF BUYERS IS WEAK:
—Fragmented buyers made weaker by dependence on weather, government regulations, interest rates, and financing availability from sellers (the manufacturer).
—No threat of integrating backward by buyers.
—Agricultural equipment is the major capital cost item of buyers.

THREAT OF SUBSTITUTES IS WEAK:
—There are none, given current technology.

Exhibit 12

NORTH AMERICAN FARM EQUIPMENT PRODUCERS—1976

	North American farm equipment sales—1976(p)	Total farm equipment sales—1976	Pretax, pre-interest on net assets*	Ratio debt to capital	Capital expense 1975 and 1976 as percent 1976 gross plant	R&D as percent sales
Deere	$1,900	$2,523	26%	30%	32	3.5
International Harvester	1,295†	2,106	13	43	25	1.8
Massey-Ferguson	670	2,000	25	47	37	1.8
Allis-Chalmers	525	550	17	26	23	3.0
J. I. Case (division of Tenneco)	385	700	13‡	41	25‡	n.a.
White	332	332	12	60	30	1.0
Ford	270	960	21	24	11	3.2

n.a. = Not available.
* On prior years net assets (total assets less current liabilities).
† United States only.
‡ For J. I. Case only.
(p) Partially estimated.
Source: First Boston Research.

Table 4

ESTIMATED DOMESTIC FARM EQUIPMENT MARKET SHARE

	Deere	IH	Massey	Case	Chalmers	Other
Tractors (100 HP+)	37%	33%	9%	14%	5%	2%
Combines	37	20	18	—	15	10
Tillage plows	30	23	6	n.a.	n.a.	41
Cotton pickers	50	50	—	—	—	—
Balers	28	18	—	n.a.	n.a.	54

Source: Wainwright Securities and First Boston Research.

Table 5

COMPARATIVE DEALER STATISTICS, 1977

	Pretax return on sales		Return on net worth	
	All	Hi performers	All	Hi performers
Deere	3.9%	6.9%	25.6%	35.6%
International Harvester	2.5	5.5	20.7	38.6
Industry	1.3	5.7	18.6	37.6

Source: First Boston Research.

tural equipment group in 1976 were $2.26 billion or 41 percent of total sales. The group's operating margin was slightly above the company average (estimated at 6–8 percent). According to one financial analyst, agricultural equipment should have been IH's cash generator, but with the intensity of competition and the large investments needed for upgrading facilities and foreign expansion, this had not been possible.

Construction equipment

Products falling in the construction equipment category covered a broad range of end uses, power ranges, sizes, and size and needs of customers. Bulldozers, loaders, excavators, cranes, road-building and logging equipment, and forklift trucks were all included in the industry. Manufacturers varied in the breadth of their product line—some specializing in only one type, but none produced the entire range.

The construction equipment market was highly segmented, first by product line and then by weight, size, or capacity. For each of these products and within different geographic areas, a slightly different group of companies competed. The largest segment (about 25 percent) was crawler tractors (bulldozers) and loaders, another 15 percent went to wheel (or rubber-tired) loaders and loaders with a back hoe attachment, and finally excavators (hydraulic or cable) were 10 percent of the market. The other 50 percent was made up of many specialty products, like road scrapers, building construction cranes, off-highway trucks, logging or pipelaying equipment. By custom, industrial machinery such as forklift trucks was usually included in the construction equipment industry though the market followed different dynamics.

The market was also segmented by customer industry: residential building construction, highway construction, energy production (strip mining), and waste treatment. The relative size of these various markets is shown in Table 6.

Understanding the demand for construction equipment required understanding the dynamics of all of these very different markets. The end markets were changing in different ways: the end of the Interstate Highway program in the late 60s slowed the road construction market. Skyrocketing building costs and a problematic economy slowed the building construction industry (particularly the residential sector). Fuel shortages supported the resurgence of strip mining. With these factors added together, demand was predicted in the mid-70s to continue at a 6–8 percent growth rate domestically and at a 10–12 percent rate overseas.

The international market was a tough but lucrative one. Europe was a mature market and, because of the age and congestion of its cities, required different (mostly smaller) equipment than the United States. Most growth potential overseas was in developing and communist countries which required sizable capital to support the distribution and service networks required. Entry was made difficult in most countries, however, by the presence of strong, entrenched local manufacturers.

Industry characteristics. In the construction equipment industry, the customer was best viewed as not buying a piece of machinery alone but rather a package of a machine and service, or in industry parlance, so many machine hours per day. This was because construction equipment always experienced breakdowns. Such breakdowns were very costly for the customer. Thus, when purchasing construction equipment, a customer was not so much price sensitive as concerned with the speed and quality of repairs. Indeed, fully one third of industry sales were for attachments and parts. This aftermarket for parts and service was not only important to the customer but to the manufacturer who earned higher margins on these sales. (Parts support was another aspect of the difficulty of entering foreign markets.)

Customers for construction equipment varied considerably both within and among segments: governments were major procurers of

Table 6

ESTIMATED END MARKETS FOR CONSTRUCTION EQUIPMENT

	Relative size
Construction:	
Building	20–25%
Nonbuilding (highways)	20–30
Mining all types	20–35
Forestry.................................	5–10
Industrial	2–5
Government (includes waste treatment) ...	2–5

Source: First Boston Research.

equipment, but at the same time there were hundreds of small builders buying just a few pieces of equipment, particularly for the residential construction market. Key issues for the government buyer were price, parts availability, and dealer reputation; while for private customers, issues were parts availability, a personal dealer relationship, and production experience.

Excluding the aftermarket sales discussed above, profitability was higher on sales of larger equipment, but production for this equipment was also very capital intensive. There were segments within the industry which were not so capital intensive as evidenced by the multitude of smaller companies competing in them. Over 16 firms competed in the United States alone in the hydraulic excavator area, for example. Backward integration varied, but was an advantage. Caterpillar purchased only 10 percent of their parts outside while Harvester purchased from 50–70 percent outside parts. (See Exhibit 13 for a structural analysis of the construction equipment industry.)

Competition.   With the high degree of segmentation in the market, obtaining a clear picture of the competitive environment was difficult. One thing was clear—the worldwide market was dominated by Caterpillar Tractor Company (CAT). Depending on the market segment, CAT's share was anywhere from 35 percent to 65 percent. CAT maintained a price umbrella and followed a full product line strategy. Assuming the presence of the Justice Department would keep CAT in the range of 45–55 percent of the total market, the question was how and who would survive in the remaining half.

In 1977 there were seven other major contenders in the industry and a myriad of smaller, local specialists. The seven majors were J. I. Case (a division of Tenneco), John Deere, International Harvester, Komatsu (Japan), Clark Equipment, Allis-Chalmers, and Massey-Ferguson. In the worldwide market, consolidation in the industry was a recent phenomenon. In Europe, as equipment became larger and economies of scale caused export to become essential, major national firms, specializing in smaller equipment for the home market, merged with the weaker North American firms to fill out product lines. Negotiations were not one-sided by any means as the North American firms were gaining strong distribution systems abroad. The early 70s saw the merger of Allis-Chalmers and Fiat (Italy), Massey-Ferguson and Hannomag (Germany), J. I. Case and Poclaine (France). In a similar vein, IH had a joint venture with Komatsu to gain entry into the large Japanese market and Komatsu was expected to break into the U.S. market.

Obviously the strategic problem was how to coexist in a market dominated by CAT and still make a profit. Three strategies had succeeded in the industry thus far: (1) offer a full line of all types of products (CAT); (2) offer a full line of one type of product (Clark in loaders, or Terex (GM) in scrapers); or (3) offer one model of each type of product (Deere). Most companies followed a targeting strategy, finding niches CAT did not occupy. For example, competitors brought out either a larger or smaller version of a given product. How long these strategies would remain successful was questionable as a trend toward the expansion

Exhibit 13

STRUCTURAL ANALYSIS OF THE CONSTRUCTION EQUIPMENT INDUSTRY—DOMESTIC

ENTRY/MOBILITY BARRIERS ARE HIGH:
—High production economies of scale.
—Many opportunities for economies of shared parts with other product lines.
—Capital-intensive business requiring large capital expenditures.
—Continuing capital expenditures needed for upgrades of capacity.
—Some R&D required.
—Entry possible with a specialized product or limited region, but very difficult on full product line basis.

POWER OF BUYERS IS MODERATE BUT DEPENDS ON SEGMENT:
—Mining and large-scale construction or road building: buyers are large and buy large quantities.
—Buyers are sophisticated.
—Small-scale construction (housing): many small buyers who buy smaller quantities.
—Speed and quality of service more important than price.
—No threat of either backward integration by buyers or forward integration by sellers.

RIVALRY AMONG COMPETITORS IS MODERATE:
—Few firms: market dominated by Caterpillar; but strong rivalry for number 2 position among several closely matched firms.
—Growth is relatively slow and cyclical (6–8 percent average); 3 key segments (road, housing, and mining) vary in any given year.
—Product differentiation by brand name is low except for visibility of Cat.
—High fixed costs support pressure for volume and for international expansion where competition is stiff.
—Threat of foreign firms entering market is strong, particularly from Japan.

POWER OF SUPPLIERS IS FAIRLY WEAK:
—Companies vary as to the degree of backward integration and economies of shared parts with other product lines, but are more so than in the truck industry.
—Like the truck industry, material shortages may be a problem.
—Multiple suppliers usually exist.

THREAT OF SUBSTITUTES IS WEAK:
—There are none.

of company product lines was apparent, as shown in Exhibit 14. IH was considered in the strongest position productwise in head-to-head competition with CAT, IH having the second broadest product line.

Other essential ingredients for competitive success were a strong distribution system with excellent parts and after-sale services, strong manufacturing facilities for profitability and price competitiveness, and a strong balance sheet to support the necessary capital investment. CAT had 226 dealers with 950 outlets worldwide, and in the United States filled 99.6 percent of its parts orders within 48 hours. By comparison, IH, which was considered to have a good distribution system, had about 70 dealers with about 200 outlets worldwide. CAT was low-cost producer and was strong financially. While not an innovator, CAT spent a higher percentage of sales on R&D than the rest of the industry. Indeed, the company tended to let others take the market risks of product innovation and entered after a product was established in the marketplace with a slightly better version. With its reputation and superior distribution, CAT could then usurp the number one position. (Exhibits 15 and 16 give some idea of competitive positions in terms of financial indicators and market shares in certain product lines.)

Komatsu, the second largest company worldwide, was a fairly new entrant on the world scene, though it had long dominated Japan. It now threatened to enter the U.S. market.

IH was the number two domestic firm, primarily because it had a strong presence overseas in Asia and the Communist Bloc countries. IH had a decent distribution system and parts support. IH products in-

Exhibit 14

PRODUCT LINES OF MAJOR CONSTRUCTION MACHINERY MANUFACTURERS

1966 - 1976 ●

1966 ○

	IND TRACTOR	FORK-LIFTS	SKIDDER	WHEEL LOADERS	COMPAC-TORS	CRAWLER TRACTOR	CRAWLER LOADERS	EXCAVA-TORS	GRADERS	SCRAPERS	HAUL TRUCKS
CAT		○	○	●	○	●	●	○	●	●	●
KOMATSU		●		●	○	●	●	○	●	●	●
IH	●	○	●	○		●	●	○		●	●
CASE	●	●	○	○		●	●	○			
FIAT-ALLIS		●		●		●	●	○	●	●	
CLARK		●	●	●	○			○	○	○	
DEERE	●	●	○	○	○	●	●	○	○	○	
TEREX				○		●				○	○
MASSEY F	●	●	○	○	○	○	○	○			

Source: Wainwright Securities.

Exhibit 15

CONSTRUCTION EQUIPMENT INDUSTRY—1976
($ millions)

	Construction equipment sales[p]			Total sales	Pretax, pre-interest return on net assets	Total debt to capital	Capital spending 1975-76 as percent 1976 gross plant	R&D as percent sales
	U.S.	Foreign	Total					
Caterpillar Tractor	$1,840	$2,585	$4,425	$ 5,042	28%	34%	34%	3.7%
Komatsu[g]	90[b]	375[c]	945[d]	1,050	28	64	25[e]	n.a.
International Harvester	300	368	668	5,488	13	43	25	1.8
J. I. Case (Tenneco)	290[a]	357	647	6,423	13[h]	51	25[h]	n.a.
Fiat-Allis	175	381	556	556	2	37	22	2.0
Deere	302	105	452	3,134	26	30	32	3.5
Clark Equipment[f]	200	200	400	1,261	18	32	25	1.1
Massey-Ferguson	89[a]	291	380	2,772	25	47	37	1.8
Terex (GM)	175	200	375	47,181	38	11	12	2.7
Ford	90	170	260	28,840	21	24	11	3.2

n.a. = Not available.
[a] North America.
[b] North and South America (but excluding Brazilian and Mexican production).
[c] Outside Japan.
[d] Including Japan.
[e] Estimated.
[f] Excludes Melrose.
[g] At average exchange rate for the year.
[h] For J. I. Case division only.
[p] Partially estimated.
Source: Wainwright Securities.

Exhibit 16

ESTIMATED U.S. MARKET SHARE—SELECTED PRODUCTS

	Crawler tractors		Rubber-tired loaders		Conventional scrapers	
	Under 90 HP	Over 90 HP	Under 5 yards	Over 5 yards	7–18 yards (struck)	Over 18 yards (struck)
Caterpillar	0%	60%	35%	45%	45%	65%
International Harvester	20	10	10	20	15	—
Deere	40	—	15	—	—	—
Case	25	5	5	—	—	—
Fiat-Allis	—	10	—	—	—	—
Clark Equipment	—	—	—	—	—	—
Terex	—	5			35	30

Source: Wainwright Securities.

cluded crawler tractors, both rubber-tired and crawler loaders, tractors with hydraulic back-hoe attachments, excavators, scrapers, off-highway trucks and haulers, logging equipment, and industrial forklift trucks. As mentioned earlier, this was the broadest product line after CAT, although sales volume was only 15 percent of CAT's. IH's weaknesses stemmed from capital starvation in the past. As a consequence, its plant was old and generated high costs. Sales for the construction equipment group were $0.7 billion in 1976 (12 percent of IH total sales), but it had a history of volatile earnings: a $33.6 million profit in 1975, a $4.6 million loss in 1976, and an estimated $10–$12 million profit in 1977. The 1976 loss compared to CAT's average and steadier 14 percent return.

Components

When the components group became a separate entity in 1976, it followed the pattern of CAT and GM in the early 60s and Deere in the late 60s. Sales were almost entirely internal and lumped into the end-product groups for reporting purposes. Products included gas and diesel engines, foundry products (castings), other components (fasteners, bearings, and hydraulics, for example), and repair products. Parts distribution (as the sole cost center) was also part of the group's responsibility.

Turbine engines

The Solar Company, a California-based specialist in welding of exotic metals and turbine engine technology, was bought in the late 50s to develop turbine engines for other IH products. While this project never came to fruition, the division took off in the 60s, becoming the leading manufacturer of gas turbine engines. It sold its smaller engines primarily to the oil and gas industry on a worldwide basis, for pumping in gas pipelines or off-shore drilling rigs, for example.

A large (10,000 horsepower) turbine was under development in 1976–

profitable!

77 for use in power generation. Solar was its industry's leader. Further market growth potential was probably high—around 10 percent.

Solar's sales in 1976 were $0.25 billion or 3.5 percent of total IH sales. It was a highly profitable, if somewhat volatile, enterprise, having 1976 earnings of $20.7 million which compared to the $20.9 million for trucks.

IH Credit Company

Following industry custom, IH provided customer financing for their major product lines through the financing subsidiary, IH Credit Company. In 1977 IH Credit Company represented 13.3 percent of company assets and 29.1 percent of equity. In comparison, the numbers were 5.4 percent and 11.7 percent, respectively, for Deere. IH Credit had greater profitability than much of the manufacturing operation and provided a profit stabilizer for IH's financial position.

*　*　*　*　*

Archie McCardell interrupted Ed Spencer's latest monologue. "Well, Ed, all this information is certainly intriguing, indeed overwhelming. And I must say that I already have some ideas of what I might do. But ideas require capital to make them happen. So the question is, can I get the capital to do anything major or can Harvester only plod along—too big to go under, but not profitable enough to become a major factor in any market?"

Spencer replied, "That depends, of course, on how much you think you need. As you said yourself, the financials speak for themselves. The company is capital constrained. One thing to think about though, when looking at the financials, is the age of the company's plant. The average age of tooling, for example, is 23 years which is a lot older than the industry standard of 10 years. The company uses the average cost method for inventory valuation as opposed to the more conservative LIFO method used by the rest of the industry. The credit company should not be ignored either. It finances both retail and wholesale receivables. Realize that CAT doesn't have a credit subsidiary (its dealers are too strong to need one) and Deere only finances retail. You might consider this a $1.5 billion addition to short-term debt. Finally, there is about $900 million in unfunded pension-vested benefits that's a potential liability. For all these reasons and others, Harvester's rating was downgraded to BBB. And as I'm sure you're aware, IH common has been selling below book for years. (For data on capital expenditures, stock price history, profitability, and performance per employee see Exhibits 17, 18, 19, and 20.)

"But finances aside, the company may be in somewhat of a turmoil internally, as they are in the throes of a companywide reorganization.

"And as you can see, Archie, a lot has already started happening at Harvester, and a lot remains to be done. One person cannot turn around a company alone—but he can, with proper background and emphasis, speed the momentum that already exists."

Archie McCardell smiled slightly and added, "And I take it, you think I'm that person. We'll just have to wait and see."

Exhibit 17

SELECTED IH STOCK DATA, FISCAL 1967–1976

Year	Earnings per share	Dividend	Price range		P/E range		Book value per share*	Price as a percent of book value	
			High	Low	High	Low		High	Low
1967	$3.31	$1.80	41	34	12.4X	10.2X	$40.23	102%	84%
1968	2.69	1.80	38	30	14.1	11.3	41.14	92	74
1969	2.30	1.80	39	25	16.8	10.9	41.70	93	60
1970	1.92	1.80	29	22	15.1	11.5	42.06	69	52
1971	1.65	1.60	34	23	20.5	13.7	42.10	80	54
1972	3.17	1.40	39	23	12.3	7.3	43.87	88	52
1973	4.04	1.50	41	26	10.0	6.4	45.66	88	57
1974	4.41	1.60	32	17	7.3	3.8	48.47	66	35
1975	3.95	1.70	31	19	7.7	4.7	49.57	62	37
1976	5.98	1.70	33	22	5.4	3.6	53.34	61	40

* Year-end book value.
Source: Goldman Sachs.

Exhibit 18

SELECTED IH ASSET EFFICIENCY AND
PROFITABILITY RATIOS, FISCAL 1967–1976

Year	Asset turnover	As a percent of revenues		Capital expenditures as a percent of net plant	Return on average equity	Sustainable growth rate
		Working capital	Inventory			
1967	1.14	29.4	30.0	3.9	8.3%	4.7%
1968	1.10	30.3	31.0	4.0	6.6	3.8
1969	1.10	28.3	31.0	2.9	5.5	2.2
1970	1.07	28.3	34.0	2.5	4.6	2.0
1971	1.14	26.3	30.0	1.6	3.9	1.3
1972	1.24	24.2	32.0	1.5	7.4	2.9
1973	1.37	21.2	31.0	2.6	8.6	2.8
1974	1.46	19.1	30.0	3.7	8.9	2.7
1975	1.45	23.2	31.0	3.3	8.4	2.8
1976	1.52	22.3	29.0	2.9	11.6	8.3

Source: Goldman Sachs.

Exhibit 19

INTERNATIONAL HARVESTER'S CAPITAL SPENDING PROGRAM
($ millions)

Year	Capital spending	Gross plant	Capital spending as percent gross plant*	Capital spending as percent gross plant*	
				Deere	Caterpillar
1976	168.4	1,452.8	12.3	12.8	21.8
1975	173.2	1,373.4	12.1	27.4	19.7
1974	180.6	1,433.3	13.6	14.4	19.6
1973	106.5	1,329.1	8.4	8.9	20.2
1972	61.3	1,271.3	4.8	5.7	9.8
1971	62.7	1,275.1	5.0	4.6	9.9
1970	88.5	1,257.9	7.4	5.9	9.7
1969	99.2	1,200.4	8.7	7.2	10.2
1968	102.2	1,139.4	9.6	15.3	20.2
1967	93.5	1,063.1	9.0	12.3	31.1
1966	99.2	1,039.9	10.0	11.9	23.8
1965	120.4	989.4	13.2	17.6	18.6
1964	80.6	913.8	8.6	19.7	12.7
1963	76.1	934.0	8.5	10.7	10.3

* At previous year-end.
Source: Wainwright Securities.

Exhibit 20

VALUE ADDED AND GROSS MARGIN PER EMPLOYEE FOR INTERNATIONAL HARVESTER AND SELECTED
COMPANIES, 1968–1976*

Year	International Harvester		Deere & Company		Caterpillar		Paccar	
	Value added per employee	Gross profit margin	Value added per employee	Gross profit margin	Value added per employee	Gross profit margin	Value added per employee	Gross profit margin
1968	$ 4,836	20.2%	$ 6,377	26.1%	$ 7,595	26.6%	$ 4,987	12.2%
1969	4,688	18.4	6,295	24.9	8,767	28.0	8,743	12.2
1970	4,888	18.4	7,480	28.0	8,801	27.3	6,510	11.2
1971	5,106	16.7	8,708	27.7	8,994	25.9	8,516	13.2
1972	5,866	16.9	9,499	28.5	10,692	27.4	9,333	13.0
1973	6,658	17.1	11,222	28.1	10,556	24.7	10,884	13.5
1974	7,516	16.8	10,817	24.3	11,554	21.8	8,381	9.9
1975	8,888	17.6	13,670	24.9	15,882	25.4	10,462	12.1
1976	10,677	19.0	15,986	28.2	17,222	26.5	14,526	15.6
Average	7,141	18.0	10,714	26.9	11,987	26.0	10,303	12.9

* Gross profit margin excludes depreciation.
Source: Goldman Sachs.

Exhibit 21

ARCHIE R. McCARDELL

Archie R. McCardell was born on August 29, 1926, in Hazel Park, Michigan, and attended elementary and high schools there. Following service in the U.S. Air Force during World War II, he entered the University of Michigan where he graduated with a bachelor of business administration degree in 1948 and a master of business administration degree the next year.

Mr. McCardell began his business career with the Ford Motor Company in 1949 and served in a variety of financial positions with that organization until 1960 when he was appointed secretary-treasurer, Ford of Australia. Three years later, he became director of finance for Ford of Germany.

In 1966 he joined Xerox Corporation as group vice president for corporate service, and chief financial officer. Subsequently, he was elected executive vice president of Xerox and was named president of that organization in 1971.

Mr. McCardell currently serves on the boards of the American Express Company, American Express International Banking Corporation, and General Foods Corporation. He is also a member of the Business Council, the Conference Board, and the Advisory Council of the Stanford University Graduate School of Business. He previously served as chairman of the National Advisory Committee of the Blue Cross Association.

Mr. McCardell and his wife, Margaret, are the parents of three children.

International Harvester (B₂)

INTERNATIONAL HARVESTER'S contract with the United Auto Workers union expired October 1, 1979. The contract affected some 35,000 workers, essentially all direct labor in the truck, agriculture, construction, and components groups. The negotiations for the three-year renewal of the contract began on August 9, 1979, with the company presenting a list of seven demands and the union presenting a lengthy list of demands. The union was simultaneously negotiating with John Deere & Company and with Caterpillar Tractor Company. To understand the issues requires some sense of the history of union relations at Harvester.

THE UAW AND INTERNATIONAL HARVESTER, POST-WORLD WAR II

The UAW was not the first or only union to organize at International Harvester. It organized its first plant in 1941, and its first master contract was negotiated in 1950 when it represented about one half of IH's hourly employees. By the mid-50s the UAW was the major union at Harvester. Master contracts were negotiated with management every three years.

There were local supplemental agreements with each local union as well which covered only seniority. The locals could not negotiate any item covered in the master agreement.

Negotiations with the UAW have followed what was called "pattern bargaining."

While the union strategy evolved over a period of almost 20 years, a general description of the pattern follows: all the auto contracts ended on the same day, September 15. The union negotiated with one company first by picking a target company for possible strike, and made agreements on economics and any work rule changes. This settlement then became the minimum acceptable level for future agreements within the industry. All of the major agricultural equipment contracts expired on October 1. Again, the union picked a target company and began negotiations using the package just completed with the automobile companies as a starting position. Thus, negotiations began with a floor already established, and at issue was how much more the union would receive from the agriculture companies. The purpose of this procedure originally was to pull the agriculture companies up to the level of the automotive companies, a goal which was achieved by the mid-60s. Since that time the settlement within the agricultural equipment companies exceeded the agreement in the auto industry.

Harvester represented a bridge between the industries, and after parity was reached, it was usually chosen as the last contract to be settled. Thus, it would be faced with an established pattern and end up being the model for the next round of negotiations three years hence. While Harvester successfully negotiated within this pattern in order to keep its labor cost per hour worked very close to its major competitors, work rules covering things such as overtime and seniority created a competitive disadvantage on the utilization of labor, thus causing Harvester's union labor cost to be high relative to the industry.

With the limit on negotiations concerning the economic package, local negotiations centered on work rules: seniority, transfer rights, overtime, etc. Problems had arisen because many of the practices around work rule issues had grown out of customs and habits that were not negotiated in the first place and varied considerably from local to local and from company to company.

In the 1940s and 1950s, Harvester, with its paternalistic philosophy retained from the Depression and earlier, began very liberal policies on its own initiative concerning such things as voluntary overtime and transfer rights. With voluntary overtime, the company had to request workers to work overtime shifts when extra production was desired. But the individual worker could turn down the offer. Transfer rights allowed the worker to request transfer to another job—upward, laterally, or even downward—as new job opportunities opened up. These rights were not big issues at the time, and were not included in the master contracts. Significantly, they were not practices followed by competitors. Deere and Caterpillar, for example, maintained the power to assign overtime, to limit transfers, and to require temporary layoffs, among other powers.

As time passed, the cost implications of these customs and policies became apparent. Somewhere along the line, workers began using these policies as bargaining tools. The practice of the "Overtime Ban" began. If there was a grievance pending, for example, word would get around not to work daily overtime or on Saturday. The plant management would frequently back down on the grievance, in order to get people to work overtime. Essentially, the company was buying overtime. During the next negotiation these local agreements on grievances would get into the local supplements and in some instances into the main contract. Slowly, the ability to control operations in the plants had eroded.

By the 1970s a series of "horror stories" existed. For example, the contract now called for a complex system of scheduling overtime in which employees had to be contacted in order of least overtime worked and be offered the overtime opportunity. If for some reason an employee was missed in the process, that employee had to be paid even if the employee had not worked and historically had not worked. In another example, 201 employees, beginning at the top of the seniority list, were asked to show for overtime at the Melrose Park, Illinois, plant. Though 98 individuals agreed, on the day of overtime only 13 showed.

Also, the transfer rights, coupled with the bumping rights in the seniority system, meant that any given transfer created a long chain of job changes. Thus, if people changed jobs through transfer rights, the entire plant could be kept in a constant turmoil as employees all down the line changed positions. In one plant of 4,500 people there were 28,000 moves created by employee requests in one year.

Another type of problem arose from temporary layoffs, a contractual provision in other companies made more difficult because of the seniority bumping problems. In the event that a temporary layoff was needed for inventory adjustment, and would last longer than three days or the balance of a workweek, the contracts insisted that all remaining employees be transferred to reflect proper seniority order. Thus, if 1,000 employees were laid off, 5000–6,000 bumps often resulted.[1] The costs in training, quality reductions, and the like were huge.

These practices were not typical in the industry, but were at Harvester. One executive explained:

> The company claimed that they couldn't afford financially to be tough on the unions, but the problem had more to do with bad habits. The plant management was given the clear message from headquarters that they were being judged on quantity of production. "Supply the market" were the bywords. Plant management felt the pressure when they were on strike, but seldom if they had conceded another grievance or practice to get the plant back in production or keep it from going out. If margins went down the blame could be placed on the union contract. The plant managers' behavior was conditioned. The company was just giving away margins.

The company's history of (legal) strikes was relatively benign: there had not been a major strike in 20 years. The longest was in 1958 which lasted 9 weeks. Deere and Caterpillar began revising their seniority agreements during the 1967 negotiations. They gave the union more security in layoffs in return for simplifying the seniority system. Harvester tried to do the same thing. The union threatened to go out on strike, and the company "just gave up."

Through the 1960s, nothing of "major import" was achieved during labor negotiations. Grant Chandler, senior vice president, corporate relations, explained, "The problem was we never came in and said, 'We're serious.' The same issues were always put on the table at the beginning and then were dropped."

In 1973 the company decided to try again to obtain relief on the overtime issue. A 15-day strike resulted, but the union made a slight conces-

---

[1] These laid-off employees also received unemployment compensation and other benefits valued at 95 percent of aftertax pay.

sion by inserting in the contract that the union would "encourage" employees to work, if advance notice was received, for 14 Saturdays a year. The union also acknowledged that "concerted" overtime bans were illegal.

In 1976 Harvester did not take any demands to the bargaining table. Grant Chandler commented, "If we were not willing to take a strike to support demands, why bother bringing them." Instead, the company worked at getting a better deal on part of the economic package negotiated with the auto and agricultural and implement companies. The issue was attendance bonus. Under this system, for every week of full time worked, the employee accrued a specified amount of time. When eight weeks were accumulated, the employee could take a day off. The bonus system caused horrendous scheduling problems. Harvester successfully negotiated an alternative to the attendance bonus program which permitted better scheduling of time off.

The union had the legal right to go out on strike during a contract period for two reasons: changes of production standards and safety issues. But there was a grievance procedure that was to be utilized first. There had been four or five such strikes on production standards and a couple on safety standards in the entire history of UAW/Harvester relations. The history of wildcat (illegal) strikes was another matter, however. In the 10 years from 1968–78, there had been over 100 such strikes. Grant Chandler commented:

> They were often over very minor issues such as disciplining a person. This was a very unusual situation. I couldn't believe the (strike) situation here; but everyone was so used to it. People just said, "Another strike, happens all the time."

The incidence of wildcats, however, had been reduced considerably by a program instituted in 1978 by the company.

1979 NEGOTIATIONS

With this background, the 1979 negotiations opened in August. The UAW presented their wish list, but high in importance was a demand which they had achieved at General Motors, wherein GM agreed to remain neutral in any organization drives and to allow UAW employees to transfer to nonunionized plants. This was in anticipation of Harvester's increased capital spending program, that had already included one new plant in Oklahoma and promised others. Further, the union was sensitive to the cost-cutting programs and the procedure placed into effect to curb illegal strikers.

Management entered negotiations with a list of demands which would provide some relief from its historic problems but did not try to eliminate all of its competitive inequities by making too much of a change. It was, however, prepared to press for some improvement. This included the right to temporary layoffs without the resulting bumps throughout the plant, a procedure which would allow the scheduling of 14 Saturdays of overtime per year, and a limit on the number or frequency of employee-originated job transfers.

Toward the end of September, Harvester's contract with the UAW was extended to November 1. On October 1 the UAW went on strike against Deere. This strike was settled on October 20. On October 29 Caterpillar officially went on strike.

By the end of October 1979, negotiations between Harvester and the UAW were slowing. The union had been advised that the company would match the economic settlement negotiated earlier with GM after some solution to the other issues could be found. By late October a satisfactory settlement to the temporary layoff issue was negotiated, but the Saturday overtime, employee transfer, and the UAW's role at new plants issues remained unresolved when the union notified the company of the termination of the extension agreement on November 1.

For Archie McCardell and the management at Harvester, the issue was whether or not to stand tough and take a strike.

International Harvester (C)

EARLY in July 1980, Archie McCardell (chief executive officer and chairman of the board) was considering the agenda for the July 15 meeting of the corporate policy committee sent to him by Warren Hayford (president and chief operating officer).[1] Among agenda items for the July meeting was a request for approval of funds from the engine division to produce and market a 6.9 liter diesel engine. As part of its responsibilities, the policy committee routinely reviewed such proposals and approved funds for capital appropriations requested from the divisions.

The engine was a light/medium-duty diesel targeted primarily for use in class 2–6 trucks. Other markets also existed; for example, the engine could be used in recreational vehicles, vans, special cutaway trucks, pleasure craft (the marine market), irrigation pumps (the agriculture market), and the replacement of gasoline engines in existing light/medium-duty trucks (the repower market). The diesel engine project was conceived as a solution to low capacity utilization (16 percent) at IH's Indianapolis engine plant where medium-duty gasoline engines were currently produced. Demand for these gasoline engines had never materialized following their introduction in 1975 because of changes in IH's truck product line (Lightline trucks were dropped) and increasing customer concern for fuel economy. (See Exhibit 1 for an executive summary of the 6.9 liter engine project.)

For International Harvester, the 6.9 liter engine represented entry into a new market—light/medium-duty diesel engines—and was the culmination of several years of development work on a design to convert the currently produced gasoline engine into a diesel engine that would

---

[1] The corporate policy committee was the top decision-making committee for operations of the company. It was chaired by the president, Warren Hayford, and included as members the chief executive officer, the five group presidents, the senior VP, finance and planning, the senior VP, operations staff, the senior VP and chief technical officer, the senior VP, corporate relations, and the VP, general counsel & secretary.

Exhibit 1

6.9 LITER DIESEL ENGINE—APPROPRIATION APPROVAL REQUEST

The following summarizes this request:

Description of proposed product:

The 6.9 liter engine is a V-8 light/medium-duty diesel engine of 420 cubic inch displacement. The unit will be produced over refurbished MV-8 gasoline engine tooling currently in place at the Indianapolis plant. Financial results are based on production at Indianapolis, however, alternative sites, including a plant near South Bend, Indiana, and a new facility on the Mexican border, were evaluated.

Summary of project phases:

Consideration to convert MV gas to diesel	1974
Engineering feasibility study completed	11/77
C&F report approved	12/77
D&T approved by CPC	2/80

The 6.9 liter program is based on the following:

Increased dieselization rate of traditional gasoline engine markets in the 1980s.
Satisfies the need for a low-cost light/medium-duty truck diesel to replace in-house gasoline engines.
Provides competition to new low-cost diesels, both U.S. produced and imported.
Makes use of existing in-house technological strength.
Provides a means to increase divisional and company profitability.

Engineering data:

Maximum rating	170 HP. 3,300 RPM
Displacement........	6.9 liter (420 in³)
Weight	770 lbs. (w/o flywheel and housing)
	815 lbs. (w/o flywheel and housing)

Major design changes for diesel conversion:

Cylinder head
Injection pump drive
Piston cooling
New oil pump and drive
Structural changes in crankcase and crankshaft

Combustion system:

Indirect injection (50–85 percent better fuel economy than gasoline engines).

Will meet future noise and gaseous emissions legislation.

Market rationale:

The U.S. and Canadian market for factory sales of GVW 4–6 trucks currently has a 13 percent dieselization rate and is expected to be 85 percent dieselized by 1992. Light trucks requiring more than 100 HP are forecast at 900,000 units by 1992 with a dieselization rate of 50–60 percent.

The total target diesel market of 100–200 HP in North America available to the 6.9 is 495,000 units by 1990. The 6.9 is expected to capture 22 percent of this in 1990.

Competitors:

The current Oldsmobile 5.7 liter diesel is limited to cars and GVW I (up to 6,000 pounds) light trucks.

The D.D.A.D. 8.2 is $600 more expensive, 400 pounds heavier, and will not

Exhibit 1 (*continued*)

fit in light trucks. Ford has no plans to produce a comparable diesel and will purchase their heavy pickup truck diesel requirements.

Market evaluation:

The SRI study of 1978 confirmed the need for the 6.9 LD. Market research studies completed in the past year by Power Systems and Technology Consulting along with internal engine division and truck group forecasts reinforce the higher diesel forecasts in automotive markets. Industrial, marine, and repower of gasoline engines in medium trucks are identified as major target segments.

Forecast summary:

The total forecast for the 6.9 LD in 1990 is 117,000 units including service. IH Truck is estimated to need 32,000.

Volumes grow from 39,000 units in 1982 to 133,000 by 1992.

IH Truck, Minneapolis, KRI, Pioneer Boat, Seafarer Engine have already placed orders for pilot engines

Manufacturing data:

The 6.9 liter diesel will be the only engine produced on the converted MV gasoline tooling. A total of 204 machine tools will be utilized for machining, test, and assembly of the 6.9 liter diesel, of which 161 existing machine tools presently used on MV line will be converted to diesel production.

Production dates:

Limited production will start at approximately 10 units per day in August 1982. Full production will begin in December 1982 at 100 to 150 units per day.

Volume effect on manufacturing costs:

An analysis was performed on the cost effect of a plant at 100,000 unit capacity utilizing existing retooled equipment versus new. The results are:

	100,000 capacity	
	Indianapolis reworked tooling	*New tooling vacant plant*
Investment	$35MM	$149MM
Manpower	746	890
Material	$1,500	$1,500
Labor	$80	$80
Variable overhead	$250	$290
Fixed cost	$520	$630
Manufacturing cost	$2,350	$2,500

The lower manpower, variable overhead, and fixed costs in the first column are based on producing at Indianapolis where some manpower and facilities will be in place to support gasoline and 6.9 liter production.

Financial evaluation on a stand-alone basis:

Appropriation to convert tooling:

$33,179,000	Capital
2,160,000	Noncapital
$35,339,000	Total appropriation

Exhibit 1 (*concluded*)

Major capital items include machine tools for connecting rods, crankcase, cylinder heads, and camshafts.

Financial indexes for Indianapolis:

	(*Constant dollars*)
Capital investment	$33.2M
Internal rate of return	42.0%
Return on assets	
Simple payback from initial capital expenditure	5 yrs., 6 mos.
Typical billing price	$3,170
Total manufacturing cost	$2,350
Total cost	$2,680
Profit per unit	$480

Alternate manufacturing sites:

In addition to the manufacturing program at Indianapolis, an alternate site was evaluated for 6.9 LD production.

Mexican border:

Total investment (including building)	$71.1M
Total cost	$2,430
Profit per unit	$740
I.R.R.	41.3%
Payback	5 yrs., 3 mos.

Summary:

The 6.9 liter engine will be the lowest priced diesel in its target markets.

It will achieve a 22 percent share of a rapidly growing market and will sell up to 133,000 engines per year.

Pretax return on sales will range from 18 percent to 25 percent, with an internal return of 42 percent.

It will provide a product that offers our customers a substantial energy savings.

It will increase our productivity.

In order to maintain the program's momentum, it is urgent that we make tooling commitments as planned. Therefore, we are asking your approval for $35 million to proceed with the produce and market phase of this program.

Note: All data have been disguised. Key relationships have been preserved.

be economical, efficient, and meet expected government emission standards for the 80s. The engine also represented the initial implementation of a new strategy for the components group of which the engine division was a part. Whereas virtually all engines produced by the division were sold to other divisions of the company, the 6.9 was targeted for direct sales to outside customers. The product development work on the new engine had cost $4.1 million to date, and the current request for tools and equipment was for $35 million. The total cost, considering all related expenditures, would be $55 million.[2]

new

↳ only have $25 mm in cash !

---

[2] All data in the case have been disguised. Key relationships have been preserved.

Over the last two years, Archie McCardell had been aware that the development work for the project was underway. Not long after his arrival at Harvester, he had been apprised of the idea, among others, during strategy discussions with Keith Mazurek, president, components group. At that time, McCardell had been supportive of Mazurek's plans to point the new components group in the direction of the OEM markets,[3] in addition to continuing the support of internally generated demand for engines from the other groups (most engines were produced for the agriculture equipment group, but some also went to the construction equipment and truck groups).

McCardell was predisposed in favor of the project in that it fit with his own belief that the company needed to diversify eventually, and that engines could be a low risk beginning of such an effort. He had not, however, been involved directly with the project over the last year. His time had gone elsewhere, and he had delegated this issue (along with all operating problems) to Warren Hayford when the new COO had joined the company in the summer of 1979. McCardell was aware that Warren Hayford had not been impressed by the project when he first reviewed it in the fall of 1979. At that time, the level of analysis and the failure to consider alternatives or risks produced a proposal that Hayford found unconvincing. Hayford was concerned over many issues including the reliability of forecasts for sales and costs, plant location, and the implications of the OEM strategy given the lack of external marketing experience within the components group. But the key issue was not so much a question of forecasting. Rather, Hayford wondered if there were really any customers in the OEM market and would they materialize? While the shortcomings of the proposal itself had disappeared by July 1980, apparently Warren Hayford still had some misgivings.

McCardell was not concerned that there was divergence of opinion between himself and other officers of the company. Indeed, such disagreement was useful in getting all of the issues out in the open. He did need to decide, however, whether he should pursue the issue himself, and, if so, how. For example, should he have the 6.9 liter request taken off the agenda for the corporate policy committee? Should he meet with Hayford separately before the meeting? Or should he raise the issues directly during the policy committee meeting itself? Other options certainly existed as well. But first, Archie McCardell needed to consider the context of the project.

CONTEXT FOR THE 6.9 LITER ENGINE CAPITAL APPROPRIATION REQUEST

Organizational context

The components group was formed during the reorganization of 1976, in part as a way to resolve the inefficiencies in planning and operations

---

[3] OEM = Original equipment manufacturers.

that were created by many separate cost center operations spread out in plants across the country whose purpose was to supply whatever parts were demanded by the end-product groups. One of Keith Mazurek's first tasks as group president was to establish a charter for the new organization. Part of that charter was to reduce the vulnerability of the group's profits to volume and product decisions made by other groups. The components group had little, if any, input to these decisions. One solution was to build products for direct sale to outside customers.

Nowhere was the evidence stronger of this vulnerability to decisions made elsewhere than at the Indianapolis plant. Formerly, a foundry and engine assembly plant for the truck group, it was chosen in the early 1970s as the site for large capital improvement and expansion in order to build a line of medium-duty gasoline engines for installation in medium-duty trucks. The new facility was built with a 100,000 unit per year capacity and targeted to begin production of the new medium-duty gas engines in 1975. Great pride was taken in the modernity of the new plant, and even a promotional film was made about the facility. As a result of the first energy crisis, the plans for the Lightline trucks were dropped in 1974, and consequently internal demand for the new engine never rose above the 20,000 units per year produced by 1979. IH's 1976 reorganization gave the plant to the components group, which inherited the problem of turning around an extremely unprofitable and physically large plant or closing it down. The 6.9 diesel engine project was among the possible solutions offered for the Indianapolis engine problem. A study was initiated in 1974 but was put on hold in 1975.

Until he left to assume a position as president of another company in January 1980, Keith Mazurek worked to achieve independence and profitability for the components group. He rationalized and reduced the product line to those items that could be produced profitably. He had set prices on a competitive basis and tied the reward system to profitability. But most important, he had worked with the end-product groups to persuade them to establish production needs for components with enough lead time to support efficient production scheduling of components. One major project was setting up a centralized computerized production control system to support this effort. As Mazurek commented, "Someday in the not too distant future, with this computer system we have going, we're going to know what the groups need from us before they do!"

As of July 1980, the leadership position in components had not yet been filled. However, Don Lennox, senior vice president, operations staff, reporting directly to Hayford, was asked to be acting president, components group, in March 1980. Lennox had worked in high-level positions with and for McCardell for over 25 years at Ford Motor Company and Xerox Corporation and was officially in retirement.[4] Archie asked him to resume full-time work, and he joined IH in March 1980.

When the components group was initially organized, Jules Laegeler

---

[4] Executives officially retired at Xerox at the age of 60. Lennox had been consulting to IH on manufacturing problems since September 1979.

was appointed as VP and manager, engine division, one of four divisions within components. As part of his overall engine division strategy, Laegeler reactivated the 6.9 liter engine project in the fall of 1977. Laegeler was promoted by McCardell to vice president, facilities planning, a corporate staff position in 1978, and Vince Spedale was made vice president and general manager of the engine division. Vince, an engineer by training, had joined IH in 1971 after 17 years at Chrysler. He began his career at Harvester as VP, manufacturing, in the solar turbine division. Then in 1973, Mazurek, who had also been at Chrysler, convinced Spedale to work for him in the truck division. Spedale had worked for Mazurek ever since except for a brief hiatus as assistant to the president (Archie McCardell) during 1978 to work on the corporatewide cost-cutting effort.

Besides the Indianapolis plant, the engine division managed plants in Melrose Park, Illinois, and Neuss, Germany. The product line included small, medium, and large gasoline and diesel engines. These engines were all used in IH-produced trucks, agricultural, and construction equipment. The division had a small central staff in the corporate headquarters building in Chicago and was organized functionally. There were no permanent committees. Rather communications within the division were on an informal and open basis. But task forces were used extensively for specific projects. Product managers within the central staff were also appointed to coordinate specific products. (See Exhibits 2 and 3 for organization charts of the corporation and engine division.)

Capital budgeting procedures

Corporatewide procedures for capital appropriations had been formalized in 1974 (and revised in 1976 and 1977). For new products, the process called for reviews at three points in time or phases: the concept and feasibility phase, the design and test phase, and the produce and market phase. There was also a new product review committee at the corporate level, chaired by the senior vice president and chief technical officer, but this committee was abolished in November 1979. (See Exhibit 4 for a fuller explanation of corporate policies and procedures concerning new products.)

In many respects, the 6.9 liter diesel engine project followed the formal guidelines. In November 1977, the concept and feasibility request was approved by the division. A market analysis was carried out by the Stanford Research Institute in the summer of 1979, and on the basis of their report, a design and test proposal was completed and approved by the division in October 1979. The proposal was also reviewed and approved by the new product review committee in October 1979. However, the design and test proposal did not get on the agenda of the corporate policy committee until February 1980, where $8 million was approved to continue the engineering work. The produce and market request was ready for presentation and approval at the July 1980 meeting of the corporate policy committee, with an expected presentation to the board of directors during August 1980. However, since development of a new engine such as this one takes, on average, seven years to complete,

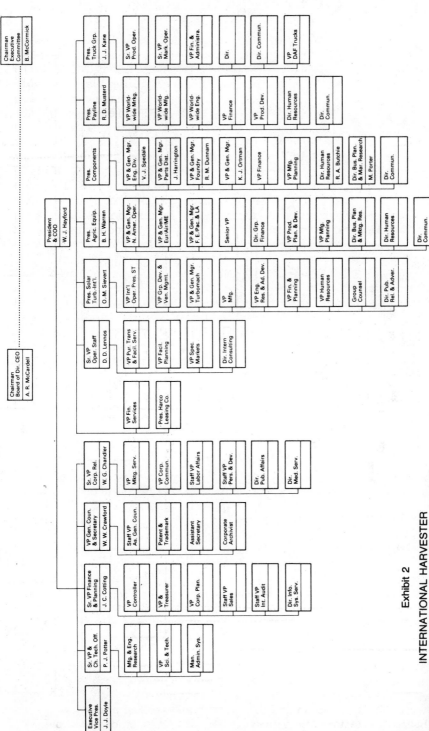

Exhibit 2

INTERNATIONAL HARVESTER
CORPORATE AND GROUP ORGANIZATION, MARCH 1980

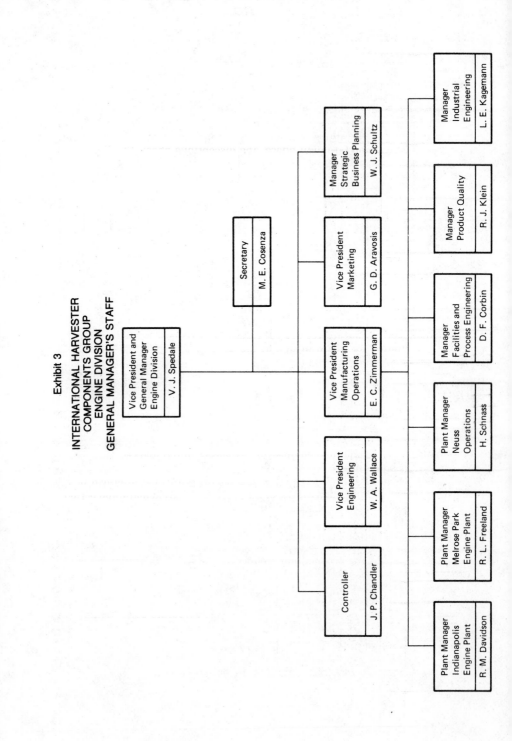

Exhibit 3

INTERNATIONAL HARVESTER
COMPONENTS GROUP
ENGINE DIVISION
GENERAL MANAGER'S STAFF

Vice President and General Manager Engine Division — V. J. Spedale

Secretary — M. E. Cosenza

Controller — J. P. Chandler

Vice President Engineering — W. A. Wallace

Vice President Manufacturing Operations — E. C. Zimmerman

Vice President Marketing — G. D. Aravosis

Manager Strategic Business Planning — W. J. Schultz

Plant Manager Indianapolis Engine Plant — R. M. Davidson

Plant Manager Melrose Park Engine Plant — R. L. Freeland

Plant Manager Neuss Operations — H. Schnass

Manager Facilities and Process Engineering — D. F. Corbin

Manager Product Quality — R. J. Klein

Manager Industrial Engineering — L. E. Kagemann

Exhibit 4

NEW PRODUCT PLANNING PROCEDURES

Corporatewide procedures for new product planning and capital appropriations were formalized and periodically updated in the *International Harvester Guidelines for Product Planning and Development.* For new products, six phases of product planning were recognized: initial screening phase, concept and feasibility study phase, develop and test phase, produce and market phase, performance monitoring and postaudit phase, and discontinue phase. Funding, as appropriate, was approved during reviews at each phase.

Initial screening phase. "This step determines broadly and at minimal cost whether the product idea has merit and whether the expenditure of additional resources to conduct a feasibility study can be justified." A request for concept and feasibility study is then initiated for approval at the division level only, and resulting funds are for initial engineering studies as to the technical feasibility of the product.

Concept and feasibility phase. "The product concept is analyzed to the extent necessary to determine if it can be produced and profitably marketed. The step also establishes whether the funds and time necessary to develop the product and construct and test prototypes can be fully justified. If during this phase the project is estimated to require engineering and capital investment levels exceeding $5 million, it will be designated a 'major project' and will be assigned to a project manager." A successful project results in a request to design and test, which is submitted for approval first at the division and group level and then to the corporate policy committee.

Design and test phase. "The product is designed, prototypes are constructed and tested, and all data relating to markets, costs, manufacturing procedures, and engineering considerations are reevaluated and the estimated profitability reassessed." A successful project leads to the production of a request to produce and market. Approval must be received from the division and group levels, the corporate policy committee, and the board of directors, and results in funding of all capital outlays and final engineering expenses, initial marketing expenses, and working capital needs.

Produce and market phase. "This phase begins with final approval of the request and continues through the life of the product. . . . Systematic and periodic reviews can lead to product improvement, modification programs, or discontinuance of the product."

Performance monitoring and postaudit phase. "This phase starts almost simultaneously with 'produce' above and monitors adherence to schedules and cost estimates of putting the product into production . . . and their continuing profitability." Corporate planning carried out this audit.

Product discontinuance phase. The division was responsible for monitoring and reevaluating product profitability throughout the life of the product and to submit a timely request for discontinuance to the corporate policy committee.

See the flowchart for a graphic depiction of the above process.

Exhibit 4 (*concluded*)

PRODUCT PLANNING AND DEVELOPMENT SYSTEM FLOWCHART

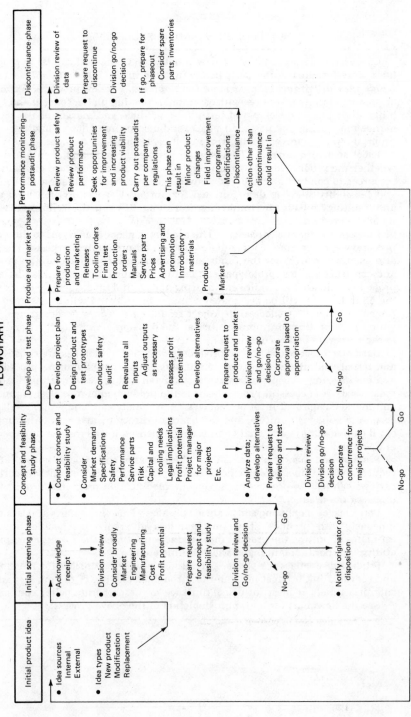

the history of the project was not as straightforward as the above account suggests.

Historical context

Due to several historical factors, the mid-1970s found the United States, for all practical purposes, without competitors in the light-medium diesel engine market. While small diesels (under 100 horsepower) were made for industrial use and there was quite a selection of big diesel engines for use in class 7 and class 8 trucks, construction, and agricultural equipment, there was a certain blindness to the market opportunity for light/medium-duty diesels. This was due in part to the fact that the market to some extent had to be created. But also there was the U.S. market's predilection for gas engines supported by the then-existent cheap fuel price. Further, diesel engines were more expensive and they were dirtier and noisier. Although diesels were less expensive to operate (better fuel economy), the trade-off required the kind of annual mileage of class 7 and class 8 tractor trailers before the diesel engines were worth purchasing. Moreover, a key factor to the producers was that their design and production expertise was in gasoline engine manufacture.

IH had also had some bad experience with diesels in the 1960s when the company had tried to convert a gas engine to a diesel and found that it was very difficult to produce a reliable product—"it just kept falling apart." Such experience made IH engineers shy of light/medium-duty diesel engines. With the oil crises of 1973, however, many predictions began appearing about changes that would occur in the market. One of these was that the class 4 to class 6 trucks, then fueled with gasoline, would increasingly be diesel powered. Indeed, from the level of 8.5 percent powered in 1977, over 60 percent of class 4 to class 6 trucks would be diesel powered by 1990. This so-called dieselization trend, offered a virgin market for whoever could produce a reliable, low-cost engine first.[5] It was also evident that the Europeans, who had years of experience producing high-quality diesel engines of just this size, were beginning to look at the U.S. market for their own expansion.

---

[5] Low cost was the key variable. If looked at in terms of horsepower or displacement, engines were available in every possible size. But those diesel engines most suitable for medium-duty trucks sold at a $4,000–$6,000 premium over the gasoline engine. In a study by the Stanford Research Institute, "first cost" (initial cost to the customer) was found to be "the most important single factor influencing purchase of a medium-duty truck." The 6.9 liter engine was targeted for a price that was at a $600–$1,000 premium over the gasoline engine. This study listed the reasons for lack of diesel penetration (in the domestic market only) as:

The high first cost of current diesel engines and vehicles is difficult for users to justify, particularly when they lack the knowledge about operating costs.

Poor experience of converted and medium-duty diesels in the early 1960s set back diesel penetration.

The lack of diesel mechanics and diesel fuel stations made the transition to diesel engines difficult.

The low cost of gasoline created little incentive to utilize more fuel-efficient engines.

Lack of knowledge of diesel engines created uncertainty in the decision to purchase one.

With the need to do something about the Indianapolis plant and the lack of near-term competition, in 1977 the engine division set March 1983 as a target "in production" date for a light/medium-duty diesel engine and pushed ahead on its own initiative to develop a design for such an engine. Thus, throughout 1977, work progressed on the design which would convert the MV446 gasoline engine to the 6.9 liter diesel engine.

The concept and feasibility request. The feasibility study was prepared by a task force composed of design engineers and production staff. The report included detailed engineering designs, production process and test facility designs, and capital outlay and manufacturing cost analysis. Throughout the report, cost and design comparisons were made with the gasoline engine (MV446) that the diesel engine was expected to replace. Essential planning parameters were: (1) use as much existing tooling at Indianapolis as possible, (2) use as many parts from the old gas engine as possible, and (3) produce a 170 horsepower engine that was the same physical size as the gas engine. The engine would cost about $600 more to produce than the gasoline engine (the technology was more complex) for a total cost of $2,100 per engine. The engineering expense was approximately $8.2 million and capital costs of $27 million were expected. No market analysis was made, but manufacturing costs were figured at both a 20,000 and 50,000 per year level.[6]

Given the amount of effort already expended on the project, the concept and feasibility request, which included the feasibility study discussed above, was a more extensive report than normally would have been the case. As Jack Reeves, product manager in January 1980, commented, "The concept and feasibility request is usually a very short form to receive approval for engineering expenditure money to make the *initial* studies. The C&F study here was voluminous. It looked more like a design and test proposal." It was approved by Jules Laegeler in December 1977.

The advanced state of the project at the time of the approval of the concept and feasibility request suggested that the design and test request could have been prepared for the policy committee early in 1978. But this did not occur and engineering expenditures were made beyond the normal amount for the concept and feasibility phase. Indeed, by September 1979, $2.1 million had been spent on what were clearly advanced engineering designs. Also, a market study was contracted for from the Stanford Research Institute and expensed by the engine division during the summer of 1978.

The Stanford Research Institute Study. This study, begun in February 1978 and completed in July of that year, was the first systematic consideration of market demand. It analyzed the entire IH engine product line and strategy, discussed the relevant technological factors and expectations through 1990, forecasted the size of the total diesel engine market, both domestic and international, and segmented the forecasted market in several ways. For each segment, the report looked at the level of

---

[6] Total plant capacity was for 97,000 engines.

demand, buyer characteristics, and competitive situation. The study assumed that IH would produce a product that was technically sound, have the appropriate sales and service backup for its product line, and have appropriate facility site and capacities to support the market opportunity. The major findings from the study concerning the 6.9 liter diesel engine can be summarized as follows: *1978 - July*

1. A major underlying demand for diesel engines existed that had not been satisfied. This demand did not represent growth in any particular application but rather the replacement of gas engines by diesels for these end uses.

2. Applications for the 6.9 liter diesel engine included medium-duty trucks, recreational vehicles, pleasure boats, generators, construction equipment, and irrigation pumps. Of these, the truck and marine uses were the major applications.

3. Consideration of any single variable (horsepower or displacement, for example) would lead to the conclusion that the market was completely covered, indeed overlapping. In other words, on first inspection, the 6.9 liter diesel engine was not unique. But when all relevant variables for diesel engine choice were weighed together, including torque range, size, displacement, power, durability, width, maintenance characteristics, and price, then the 6.9 liter engine was unique. One crude way of splitting diesel engines was between light, light-medium, medium, medium-heavy, and heavy applications. The 6.9 liter engine was then the low-priced entry in the light/medium-duty group. This was described by SRI as an entry into an unfilled niche.

4. Competitors currently did not exist in this niche. (The CAT 3208 and Harvester's own D (or 9 liter) series and DT466 diesel engines were close but were designed for medium-duty applications and were much higher priced.) Detroit Diesel (a subsidiary of General Motors) had scheduled an 8.2 liter diesel engine for introduction sometime in 1980–81. It was expected that this engine would be completely utilized by GM for their own products. As compared to the 6.9 liter engine, the 8.2 liter engine was higher priced ($400–$1,000 more), but possibly had advantages of longer life, technical superiority, better image because it was not a gasoline engine conversion, and included some noise reduction features. [Note: IH sources disagreed with SRI concerning these advantages and explained that the 8.2 liter engine was heavier, rated at 165–205 horsepower, and could be installed in vehicles where the 6.9 left off.]

5. The 6.9 liter engine had the following strengths:
    a. Low price in a very price-sensitive market.
    b. Along with the DT466 (a larger diesel engine in the IH product line), IH would have an entry in the market on either side of the 8.2 liter engine and thus could apply a competitive squeeze on that engine.
    c. IH had a reputation as a quality diesel engine producer.
    d. The horsepower/size/weight combination created an engine with low operating costs (high mileage per gallon).

e. It could replace gasoline engines up to 170 horsepower, and yet use the lower cost gas power train and suspension.

6. The 6.9 liter engine had the following weaknesses:

a. Maintenance problems developing early because of inappropriate use by consumers. This factor was tied to the lower duty cycle design of the engine (100,000 miles to overhaul as compared to the 8.2 liter's 150,000 miles to overhaul).

b. Gas conversion engine seen, by dealers at least, as causing maintenance problems.

c. Lack of sales force support in pushing the engine.

d. Lack of diesel maintenance/service network.

7. SRI projected sales for the 6.9 liter engine to be approximately 80,000 by 1992. Forty-nine thousand of these would be in the medium-duty truck area and another twenty-five thousand would be in the marine market. (See Exhibit 5 for detailed breakout of the market forecast.)

Exhibit 5

SRI FORECAST FOR 6.9 LITER

	1982	1988	1992
U.S.A.:			
Medium-duty truck and bus ...	3,500	25,800	49,700
RV	—	—	2,000
Marine	5,000	12,000	25,000
Generator sets	100	400	1,000
Portable compressor	—	—	—
Forklift truck	—	—	—
Construction equipment	—	—	300
Agriculture (irrigation)	200	400	600
	8,800	38,600	78,600
Europe:			
CV	—	100	200
Marine	200	500	1,000
Generator sets	200	500	1,000
Europe total	400	1,100	2,200
Grand total	9,200	39,700	80,800

The design and test proposal. As stated earlier, the design and test proposal was ready by October 1979. It went to the new product review committee first where it was supported unanimously. The only reservations that some members of the committee voiced were whether the division could keep the manufacturing cost low enough to retain the low price and still earn a high enough return, and whether the new marketing effort and development of a sales force could be accomplished.

Keith Mazurek then sent the proposal to Warren Hayford for inclusion on the November policy committee meeting agenda. The engine described in the proposal was a more refined, but essentially unchanged,

the SRI said 80,000 by 1992

product from the one described in the concept and feasibility request. But now financials and market forecasts were included. In the market forecast, sales were to the United States only, but were higher than forecasted by SRI (109,000 unit sales were projected for 1992, for example). The largest share of the sales (approximately 40 percent) were to OEM trucks. Another 30 percent was to the marine market, 20 percent to the IH truck group, and 5 percent each for recreational vehicles and industrial uses. The financial analysis indicated an internal rate of return of about 35 percent and discounted payback occurring in 5½ years. Engineering expense would total $12.2 million, manufacturing expense $3.7 million, and maximum cash exposure about $45 million. Capital appropriation was expected at $33 million.

Besides the financial and market forecasts, the design and test proposal included a discussion of two additional issues. Both of these involved the Minneapolis Truck Company.[7]

The Minneapolis connection. The first issue was whether Minneapolis would be a major customer and, if so, at what level. As discussed above, the market forecasts projected sales by major end use. These were not broken out by specific customer. From the text, however, it was clear that Minneapolis was the major customer within the OEM truck market. This expectation was based on verbal indications from Minneapolis that they were impressed enough by the 6.9 liter engine that they would use the engine in their pickups and vans as well as their new medium-duty trucks planned for introduction after 1982. The needs of this one customer could be as high as 75,000 units per year alone.

The second issue was whether to reschedule the introduction of the IH engine to fit the Minneapolis company's 1982 schedule. The components group thought this rescheduling was appropriate and, in the design and test proposal, moved the "in production" date up one year to March 1982. The effect of this new schedule was to move up the orders for long lead-time capital items (e.g., tooling) starting in February 1980. But approval of capital expenditures were supposed to be made for the produce and market phase. Therefore, the schedule in the design and test proposal indicated that a produce and market proposal would be presented for approval in March 1980, before the completion of the tests and final designs for the new engine. Indeed, although the design and test phase was well along already, technical success of the engine would not be guaranteed until the end of 1980 and by then much of the capital expenditure would already be committed.

By January, Minneapolis had pulled back from their earlier verbal offer to a position that they were considering use of the 6.9 among other engines (including their own DREMA[8] engine in development) for use in their new trucks. A letter of intent to this effect was received in January. Throughout the spring and summer, Minneapolis would continue to hold out promises but make no definite commitments. Several factors seemed to support an eventual order from them: Darrel Whitehead, a

---

[7] Disguised name.
[8] Disguised name.

Exhibit 6

PRINCIPAL CHARACTERS—6.9 LITER ENGINE PROJECT

Name	Title	Date with titel	Age	Date joined IH
Aravosis, George	VP, marketing, engine division	8/1/79	51	10/63
	Manager, product planning	10/1/78		
Chandler, John	Controller, engine division	10/29/79	37	10/79
Cotting, Jim	Senior VP, finance and planning	3/79	46	3/79
Hayford, Warren	President, chief operating officer	6/79	50	6/79
Horne, John	Manager, diesel engine engineering	9/1/77	42	10/66
Kaine, Pat	President, truck group	1/77	55	1949
Laegeler, Jules	VP, facilities planning	10/78	59	1951
	VP, general manager, engine division	1/77		
Lennox, Don	Senior VP, operations staff	3/80	61	3/80
Maat, George	Chief engineer, advanced design group	1/15/73	53	9/60
Mazurek, Keith	President, components group	1/77–1/80	56	1969–80
McCardell, Archie	President, COO	9/77	54	9/77
	CEO	1/78		
	CEO, chairman	6/79		
Mullen, Clark	Plant engineer (Indianapolis)	8/79	39	1/72
	Leader, 6.9 liter engine task force			
Musjerd, Bob	President, pay line group	1/77	56	1947
Palaoro, Hans	Business research and forecasting manager, engine division	10/1/79	35	1/68
	Marketing and forecasting manager, engine division	8/15/77		
Potter, Bob	Senior VP, chief technical officer	12/78	48	12/78
Reeves, Jack	Business manager, heavy-duty diesel and gasoline engines, engine division	8/15/79	53	8/53
	Manager, product planning, engine division	8/77		
Sievert, Morris	President, solar turbines group	1/77	58	1960
Spedale, Vince	VP, general manager, engine division	10/78	50	1971
	Assistant to president	11/77–10/78		
Warren, Ben	President, agriculture equipment group	1/77	55	1950

nothing more than talk ?

supporter of the 6.9 liter engine within Minneapolis, became the new president in March 1980; the DREMA engine, which had been a pet project of the former president, was dropped; orders were received for several 6.9 liter prototype engines; and conversations during visits by Vince Spedale, Don Lennox and other engine division staff continued to be enthusiastic.

Returning to the earlier discussion of the history of the design and test proposal, despite the first favorable signs from Minneapolis, Warren Hayford did not allow the proposal to go on the agenda of the policy committee in November, December, and again in January. Instead, a number of questions were directed to Mazurek and the engine division staff. Examples of Hayford's questions were:

How does the 6.9 liter compare with the 8.2 liter (Detroit diesel) . . . in price, cost, weight, fuel efficiency, horsepower range, annual projected mileage per engine, annual production volume?

Who are the major OEM customers targeted for the 6.9 liter? How many are planned for Ford, GM, Chrysler, etc., as we reach out into the late 1980s and early 1990s?

How did we get the 6.9 liter contribution margin up to 38 percent when our best other engines are much lower in the 25–27 percent range?

How do we show a profit in 1983 operating at only about 23 percent of the five-day utilization capacity of this line?

How will our proposed 6.9 liter engine meet our least cost manufacturing aspirations?

Vince Spedale explained how he reacted to Hayford's queries:

It was not so much that our proposal was being rejected. We were pulling it out ourselves. Rather it took us a while to understand Warren's style, to realize that Warren liked alternatives. Before this, we, as a division, weighed alternatives and figured out the "one best way" to do something. When we had convinced ourselves of the most likely level of market demand or the best technical configuration, etc., we presented that one best estimate. Our approach to corporate was to present our best effort, and then take the responsibility for the result. That's what I'm being paid to do: to take responsibility for any risks we take. The buck stopped at the division.

Hayford wants to see the alternatives we considered. He wants a worst case, most likely case, and a best case analysis of the market and financials. In the end, he wants to have an influence on the choices we make.

As Jack Reeves, program manager on the 6.9 liter project, commented:

The only problem with all these alternatives, is the timing issue. As you can see we are under a time crunch to get this project going and get to the market on time and before any competitors. It's an issue of supply and demand. If we spend too much time worrying about alternatives, by the time we're supplying the market, the demand won't be there anymore.

The proposal for the design and test phase was placed on the February 12, 1980, agenda of the policy committee.

The February 12, 1980 meeting of the corporate policy committee. The policy committee meeting was an all-day affair. Vince Spedale arrived to make the 6.9 liter engine presentation about 3 in the afternoon. Copies of the proposal had been sent to members of the committee beforehand. Vince read a prepared talk accompanied by slides (a few members of the engine division staff were in the projection room operating the slide projector and listening to the proceedings). Most of the members of the committee were present, but most obviously missing was Pat Kaine, president, truck group. During the presentation, various members interrupted to ask questions concerning engineering features, market demand (the likelihood of Minneapolis coming through with an order, for example), and financials. A typical interchange follows:

ARCHIE MCCARDELL:[9] What price did you give Minneapolis?

VINCE SPEDALE:[10] $2,900.

MCCARDELL: And that gives a 12 percent return? (to Cotting) That's not the guideline is it?

JIM COTTING:[11] No, we should get 15 percent.

MCCARDELL: Would that blow the deal out of the water? (i.e., raising the price to Minneapolis to get a 15 percent return)[12]

SPEDALE: We just have to be priced under the 8.2, that's the only key.

COTTING: A five-year break-even isn't enough, we would just have two years left to make a profit.

MCCARDELL: We need, Jim, some standard margins as we get into OEM markets. We need a formula for large OEM customers. We need something to get these people before they put these presentations together.

COTTING: Looking at ROI and other measures, you've taken the numbers for just one part of the Indianapolis plant, but what if you fit these numbers into the Indy plant as a whole, looked at all the overhead costs, etc.? Does this one project carry this plant or is the plant still operating at a loss? We have to consider this project in light of the plant as a whole, if it doesn't break even we still may not want the plant at all.

SPEDALE: We looked at that, and it makes the plant profitable.

COTTING: Let me look separately at this with you. Whether it really is a break-even project.

MCCARDELL: It's only a partial solution. We still have to figure out what to do with the other 600,000 square feet.

At the end of the formal presentation McCardell asked each group president what they thought about the project proposal. All were generally favorable. The following is a part of the final discussion.

BOB MUSJERD:[13] I have a few questions about what the trade-offs would be—the initial costs against getting a better than 100,000 mile engine. What are the trade-offs between gas and diesel? What are the real fuel savings? We need to have some answers before we really bring this to market.

SPEDALE: . . . The customer can pay back the diesel price premium in one to two years.

MCCARDELL: Is the diesel efficient as compared to GM's 8.2 liter engine?

---

[9] Chief executive officer.

[10] Vice president and general manager, engine division.

[11] Senior vice president, finance and planning.

[12] Disguised numbers.

[13] President, payline group (construction and industrial equipment).

SPEDALE: It's 15 percent worse than theirs. . . . The 8.2 liter engine is a 150–175,000 mile engine.

MUSJERD: . . . . It's a throwaway versus the 150,000 mile engine, what's the trade-off?

BEN WARREN:[14]   I'm concerned that no one can sell a 50,000 or even a 100,000 mile engine.

McCARDELL: There's a lot of questions to answer.

MORRIS SIEVERT:[15]   In California, and not to sound like a kook, but there's a lot of publicity about the carcinogenic effects of these engines. We have to consider the impact of the environmentalists. Are we?

WARREN: Well the Riccardo system is cleaner, so that's one leg up.

BOB POTTER:[16]   When this proposal came to the product review committee, these and a lot of other questions were raised. It's whether you accept dieselization as the coming thing or not. It's an OEM opportunity. The problem is that this program is out of phase. The produce and market proposal is just around the corner, however, and will answer a lot of this.

SPEDALE: Slow down a bit. We originally thought we'd do both at once (the design and test and the produce and market), but we want to look at the numbers closer.

POTTER: What will you learn that you don't know now?

SPEDALE: What the key markets look like. What will happen to Indianapolis as a going concern.

WARREN HAYFORD: Could you identify for us, Vince, the three options that you're discussing with Minneapolis?

McCARDELL: In the spirit of looking for the right decision, of course.

SPEDALE: Yes, we are looking at whether to have a conventional supplier/customer relation, whether to go into a joint venture with them, or whether to sell them both the product and the plant as is or as a turnkey. We also are looking into going to Mexico, Spain, or even Ireland and building a new plant for production of the 6.9 engine.

The presentation was then over and Vince left. Nothing was said as to approval, but Vince reacted that a positive outcome had been achieved. Indeed, approval for $8 million engineering expense came from the corporate planning department several days later.

Preparation for the produce and market request.   Preparation for the produce and market proposal began immediately after the design and test presentation. At least 40 people were involved in the proposal presentation. A task force had been formed at the Indianapolis plant. Chaired by Clark Mullen, production engineer, the task force included members from production, quality control, purchasing, accounting, and process engineering departments. This task force developed all of the cost data, process designs, quality control procedures, financial analysis, and other manufacturing data. All of this was expected to be coordinated with the product design team. Marketing plans and forecasts were handled at division headquarters (George Aravosis, then VP, marketing), product engineering and testing continued at Melrose Park, Illinois (under George Maat and John Horne), financial forecasts were coordinated from

---

[14] President, agriculture and equipment group.
[15] President, solar turbines international group.
[16] Senior vice president and chief technical officer.

818

headquarters (John Chandler, controller), and the whole proposal was coordinated and written by Hans Palaoro, program manager.

Vince Spedale (and others from headquarters staff) met with the Indianapolis task force shortly after the February design and test meeting in what would become approximately monthly meetings. These were primarily informational meetings for both groups.

In the first meeting, it became evident that keeping production costs in line was going to be a major problem. With inflationary pressure, each month that passed without commitments on orders to suppliers caused costs to rise. In this February meeting, expected capital expenditures had increased to $43.8 million. But more important, manufacturing costs had risen $300 and the price by about $500. It was one thing to see a decrease in ROI, but another to see the erosion of the major competitive advantage provided by a low price.

Over the next few months, these problems were attacked vigorously. Purchasing was induced to apply more pressure on suppliers to obtain lower bids. Pressure was placed on engineering to keep the product design within the cost parameters: not to build a state of the art engine but a good-quality engine that could be built efficiently and would sell. This meant much more coordination between production at Indianapolis and engineering at Melrose Park than was customary on these projects. Neither of these were easy tasks. But, eventually both capital and manufacturing costs were brought back into the range that was presented in the original design and test proposal. Of course, each passing month increased the difficulty of holding to these price and cost levels.

The strike by the UAW was also affecting the project. Obviously, the Indianapolis plant was not in production at this time. One of the issues was what would be done about the so-called All Time Run of the MV446 gasoline engine. It will be recalled that the 6.9 liter engine production lines would replace the gasoline engine production lines. Therefore, it was necessary to build inventories for all future expected needs of the gasoline engine (including spare parts for servicing existing engines). This All Time Run had to occur first before the new production lines could be set up. Each month that the strike continued pushed back the beginning of the All Time Run and squeezed the March 1982 "in production" date for the 6.9 liter engine.

Meanwhile, marketing was hunting for potential customers. A possibility surfaced with KRI, who was bidding for a large truck contract with the U.S. Army. Two of several marine companies seemed serious and ordered a prototype engine for testing. But, the IH truck group did not show much interest. Their projected needs remained at the relatively low 20,000 units per year level.

Finally, Don Lennox's arrival on the scene in March affected the proposal's progress. As a member of the engine division saw it:

First, we had to educate Archie; then we brought Bob Potter up to speed; then we had to do it again with Warren Hayford; and now we have to go through the whole process again to educate a fourth newcomer from corporate. This project's great, so let's get on with it and quit talking.

total strategy

Don Lennox, however, was concerned with more than just this project. Granted, he needed time to understand the quality of the proposal's content itself; but, he was more interested in how the 6.9 liter engine fit into the total engine division and components group strategy. He was concerned that many proposals were reviewed at the corporate level out of context, one after the other and, since each looked good on a stand-alone basis, were approved. Lennox was also aware of the endemic components group problem: positioned so as to be dependent on the decisions of the other groups. He saw the 6.9 liter engine proposal as one of those that offered an opportunity to change the decision-making process at corporate level. Part of his approach was to get corporate to understand and approve the entire components group strategy first, so that any given proposal could be reviewed within the strategic context. Prior to Lennox's arrival, Hayford had requested Spedale to prepare a review of the engine division overall strategy. That presentation was made to the policy committee in March 1980, highlighting all outstanding issues and providing a long-term action plan. But it was unclear if the strategy was "approved" in its parts by top management.

To resolve these issues, Lennox set up a series of task forces in April. The task forces worked on issues which included the overall engine division strategy, and specific product strategies. Lennox included the relevant components group personnel in each task force; but he also asked someone from each of the three major groups (agriculture, truck, and construction) and from corporate staff (finance or facilities planning) to be a member. In one view, these mirrored the corporate policy committee structure. Lennox commented:

> I'm not usually a management-by-committee person, but in this case we had to get input and agreement from the groups before we got to the corporate level in a formal way. The task force members were expected to keep the group presidents informed. If I decided to send a project through to the policy committee, I wanted no one to be surprised.

One of these task forces had, as part of its charter, to review and decide on the 6.9 liter engine project. Lennox appointed the member from the truck group (vice president, medium-duty truck SBU) to chair that committee. By May the task force had fully endorsed the 6.9 liter project and supported sending the produce and market proposal to the policy committee. One of the benefits or by-products of the task force, was that it encouraged the truck group to come on board. They became enthusiastic about the potential of the new engine and increased their expected needs to 36,000 units per year. This meant that it was possible to reach break-even on the 6.9 liter engine on internal sales alone. A disadvantage of the task force was that it took time. As one member commented, "The two key issues are costs and timing. And every day that passes we're spending money and not making any."

As soon as the strike was over, toward the end of April, the All Time Run on the gasoline engine was begun. And given the pressure of time a request was sent to Lennox for $1.3 million to begin ordering advanced tooling. One comment was heard, "Here we go again, spending the produce and market money before it is approved." Lennox, however, did not sign this request until the task force had made its decision to support the project. Lennox signed and sent the advanced appropriation request to Hayford in June.

Lennox, now fully in support of the 6.9 liter project, decided the appropriate course was to hold meetings with Warren Hayford and Jim Cotting separately to make a presentation concerning the new engine. Any real objections could be hashed out before the policy committee. These were held in June and Lennox then sent the proposal to produce and market to Hayford for inclusion on the July meeting agenda of the corporate policy committee. The proposal was included on the agenda.

All of this would have been straightforward, but for one "new" issue that came to the fore during discussion with Hayford. The location at Indianapolis was questioned, and the option of building a new plant located on the Mexican border was argued. While the cost of building an entirely new plant was considerably higher (at least an additional $36 million in capital expenditures alone), the tax breaks that the Mexican government offered along with the lower manufacturing costs provided a total cost saving of $500. Hayford requested an analysis of the trade-off between Indianapolis and Mexico for inclusion in the policy committee presentation. (See Exhibit 1 for the summary of the analysis.)

* * * * *

It was in the above context then, that Archie McCardell was considering the 6.9 liter engine agenda item for the July 15 policy committee. As he pondered the issues, Don Lennox knocked on the door and came in and said, "I see you have the 6.9 liter engine proposal on your desk. I was just talking to Warren and, if I understand him correctly, he is not ready to go forward on this project yet."

Archie responded, "Yes, I know . . ." and considered his next remark.

Strategy revisited or strategy with a grain of salt

PRESIDENT: Waiter, that takes care of the drinks; we'll wait a while before ordering dinner.

Now, look, professor, you have been working on us all day, and I think we at least begin to understand what you are talking about when you ask us about strategy. I think it is time we turned the tables a bit. I will be frank and say that I think the whole idea is just one big fat platitude. You guys at Harvard always think things to death. Aren't there any tough, hungry doers left? Look, we have got a guy in our industrial division who never got past high school and probably couldn't even read Andrews on corporate strategy—which I have, incidentally—and I don't think I'd want him to. He may not have a lot of smooth reasons for why he does what he does, but I do know he's got a lot of crust and a lot of gall which he uses to get in to see people that would not otherwise see him, and he sells a terrific lot of salt for us. Our problem is the same as everyone else has, and it shows up particularly when we deal with your graduates, if I may say so. That is, how do we get people off their dime and out doing something instead of sitting around worrying all the problems to death?

Another problem I have is that I think committing myself and the company to any such idea would completely tie my hands when it came to responding to new opportunities that are always coming up. Again, in our industrial division, we have got some specialists in salt dispensing. It's kind of a complicated history, but we have found ourselves as a result of this activity owning a patent on a new solenoid principle. Now when we got that patent, we began to be swamped with inquiries from all kinds of industries, because if the thing performed the way it is supposed to it would solve problems that a whole lot of people seem to have. Now, it seems to me that if I was wedded to some notion of strategy or image, we'd throw that opportunity away. It sure isn't "our business," whatever that means.

TREASURER: Let me take a couple of whacks too, because that solenoid example brings to mind a more general problem. We have been investigating quite intensively different capital budgeting systems. Of course, if we do anything with the solenoid, we have to make an appropriation, but of course it gets thrown into the hopper with all the other appropriations we might make. Now, as it is, we are a national and international company; we mine salt, we evaporate salt, and we sell it as a food product to consumers and to processors—canners, bakers, and the like—and we sell it on contract to chemical companies where it is the raw input in chlorine manufacture which in turn is the basic process for a major segment of the chemical industry, and we sell it on a bid basis to government agencies for ice control. The chemical business involves not only a real tough competitive situation, but the sales are negotiated on a long-term relationship basis, frequently involving the top officers of the companies. Of course, we are also selling to farmers and to a lot of other users. In short, we're already in about every kind of market you can think of.

Now, what I want to know is why we can't solve these so-called strategic problems simply by a good capital budgeting procedure. What does the idea offer that adds anything to a good hard look, project by project, at the different uses we might put our capital to?

ASSISTANT TO THE PRESIDENT: Well, why confine it to capital budgeting? There are a lot of other things going on which meet the same kind of purpose. This consensus-on-what-we're-trying-to-do and consistency-in-the-way-we-go-about-it idea seems to ignore a lot of things that have been happening. Take as one example the possibilities for information and control that a good size computer offers. I have been very interested in the hordes of articles about computers in the *Harvard Business Review*. Those authors say that with the computer you can simulate all the operations of a business, see all the interdependence of actions and decisions, get all the feedback you need, and keep everything going on a really integrated and efficient basis. Why couldn't you tie something like that in with a good capital budgeting procedure and solve most of your problems of consistent operating implementation of what you are trying to do?

Or, for that matter, there's been a lot of work in management science, and I am particularly interested in these sequential decision models where you plan a course of action which makes a series of small moves that gain information and then use the information in making the next move. Why isn't it better to recognize that you don't know what the future holds, that you can't really predict with accuracy, and work out a program like that? It seems to me that your strategy concept involves making a terrific commitment on pretty shaky information.

ADMINISTRATIVE VICE PRESIDENT: Well, believe it or not, I read those journals, too, but mathematics, computers, and that stuff I leave to these fellows. I do, however, pay quite a bit of attention to these management philosophers and that stuff which comes from the behavioral sciences, whatever they are. While you are answering these fellows who think that numbers and scientific method can do everything, I am going to be listening from that side.

It seems to me that our history indicates that this thing you call strategy only can come from the intuitive judgment of a strong leader. Don, here, [indicating the president], has had the imagination and foresight which has enabled us to go from a small company, specializing in consumer salt, strong only in one region and possessing only one mine, to where we are today. He did it, I think he will agree, by constant needling and pushing to get the rest of the organization to move. There wasn't any particular "we" stuff, and I will be frank to say that if there had been, it would have been one of these pretty stagnant committee-type operations. So I guess I come back to what he said about that fellow in our sales force, only I would apply it to him. It was his insight and imagination, plus twenty years of constant needling, that got us where we are.

So, I guess my questions are these: How would a company that did not have such a concept develop and apply one? Also, what beneficial results would you expect to follow from a program to develop and implement a strategy, and finally, why do you think they would follow and what evidence have you got that they would be so beneficial? I guess that about sums up all our questions.

PROFESSOR: Waiter, another round please, and make mine a double!

Conclusion

In retrospect:
Strategic management and
corporate governance

MANY OF THE cases in this book have given you an opportunity to observe the range, unity, and interrelation of the concepts and subconcepts essential to the conscious formulation and implementation of a strategy governing the planned development of a total organization. The idea and its components have now been quite carefully and separately explored. It becomes appropriate at this point, as you reflect on the cases you have studied, to return to the view of corporate strategy not as a concept complete and still but as an organizational process forever in motion, never ending. The merger of the process and substantive content of the concept of strategy takes us to the principal problems of corporate governance and the responsibilities of the board of directors.

STRATEGY AS A PROCESS

For the purposes of analysis, as you have already noted, we have presented strategy formulation as being reasonably complete before implementation begins, as if it made sense to know where we are going before we start. Yet we know that we often move without knowing where we will end; the determination of purpose is in reality in dynamic interrelation with implementation. Implementation is itself a complex process including many subprocesses of thought and organization which introduce into prior resolution tentativeness and doubt and lead us to change direction.

That strategy formulation is itself a *process of organization*, rather than the masterly conception of a single mind, must finally become clear. We tried to introduce you to it when we were considering organization design. Many facts of life conspire to complicate the simple notion that persons or organizations should decide what they can, want, and should do and then do it. The sheer difficulty of recognizing and reconciling uncertain environmental opportunity, unclear corporate capabilities and limited resources, submerged personal values, and emerging aspirations to social responsibility suggests that at least in complicated organizations strategy must be an organizational achievement and may often be unfinished. Important as leadership is, the range of strategic alternatives which must be considered in a decentralized or diversified company exceeds what one person can conceive of. As technology develops, chief executives cannot usually maintain their own technical knowledge at the level necessary for accurate personal critical discriminations. As a firm extends its activities internationally, the senior person in the company cannot himself learn in detail the cultural and geographical conditions which require local adaptation of both ends and means.

As in all administrative processes, managing the process becomes a function distinct from performing it. The principal strategists of technically or otherwise complex organizations therefore manage a strategic decision-making process rather than make strategic decisions. When they "make" a decision approving proposals originating from appraisals of need and opportunity made by others, they are ratifying decisions emerging from lower echelons in which the earliest and most junior participants may have played importantly decisive roles.[1] The structure of the organization, as observed earlier, may predetermine the nature of subsequent changes in strategy. In this sense strategy formulation is an activity widely shared in the hierarchy of management, rather than being concentrated at its highest levels.

Participation in strategy formulation may begin with the market manager who sees a new product opportunity or the analyst who first arranges the assumptions that make possible a 30 percent return on investment in a new venture. (A return-on-investment hurdle may in itself contribute to a distortion of strategy by becoming illusory goal rather than achieved result.) Because of the response to reward and punishment systems considered earlier, the strategic alternatives generated in autonomous corporate units may be the product of competition for limited resources or of divisional empire building.

The strategy process, with its evolutionary, structural, analytical, and emotional components, encounters then the real-life challenges for which conscious professional management has been devised. Opportunism remains the principal counterforce; it need not be put down, for it can be turned to use. In the course of an established strategy, changing only imperceptibly in response to changing capabilities and changing market environments, sudden opportunity or major tactical decision may intrude to distract attention from distant goals to immediate gain. Thus the opportunity for a computer firm to merge with a large finance company may seem too good to pass up, but the strategy of the company will change with the acquisition or its ability to implement its strategy will be affected. A strategy may suddenly be rationalized to mean something very different from what was originally intended because of the opportunism which at the beginning of this book we declared the concep-

---

[1] See Joseph L. Bower, *Managing the Resource Allocation Process* (Boston: Division of Research, Harvard Business School, 1970).

tual enemy of strategy. The necessity to accommodate unexpected opportunity in the course of continuous strategic decision is a crucial aspect of process. Accepting or refusing specific opportunity will strengthen or weaken the capability of an organization and thus alter what is probably the most crucial determinant of strategy in an organization with already developed market power.

MANAGING THE PROCESS

It is clear then that the strategic process should not be left untended. Study of the cases and ideas of this book usually leads to acceptance of the need for a continuous process of strategic decision as the basis for management action. This process extends from the origin of a discrete decision to its successful completion and incorporation into subsequent decisions. With this need established in an organization, the next step is to initiate the process and secure the participation first of those in senior management positions and then of those in intermediate and junior positions. The simplest way for the chief executive of a company to begin is to put corporate objectives on the agenda of appropriate meetings of functional staff, management, or directors.

Consider, for example, a large, long-established, diversified, and increasingly unprofitable company. Its principal division was fully integrated from ownership of sources of raw materials to delivery of manufactured products to the consumer. Its president, after a day's discussion of the concept of strategy, asked his seven vice presidents, who had worked together for years, to submit to him a one-page statement expressing each officer's concept of the company's business, a summary statement of its strategy. He had in mind to go on from there, as users of this book have done in handling these cases. After identifying the strategy deducible from the company's established operations and taking advantage of their participation in resource allocation decisions, the vice presidents would be asked to evaluate apparent current strategy and make suggestions for its change and improvement. This first effort to establish a conscious process of strategic decision came to a sudden halt when the president found that it took weeks to get the statements submitted and that, once collected, they read like descriptions of seven different companies.

When discussion of current strategy resumed, a number of key issues emerged from a study of a central question—why so successful a company was seeing its margins shrink and its profits decline. The communication of similar issues to those assigned responsibility to deal with the function they affect was an obvious next step. The soundness of the company's recent diversification was assigned as a question to the division managers concerned. They found themselves asked to present a strategy for a scheduled achievement of adequate return or of orderly divestment. The alternative uses of the company's enormous resources of raw material were examined for the first time. The record of the research and development department, venerable in the industry for former achievements, was suddenly seen to be of little consequence in the competition that had grown up to take away market share. Decisions long since postponed or ignored began to seem urgent. Two divisions were discontinued, and expectations of improved performance began to alert the attention of division and functional managers throughout the organization to strategic issues.

Getting people who know the business to identify issues needing resolution, communicating these issues to all the managers affected, and programming action leading to resolution usually leads to the articulation of a strategy to which annual operating plans—otherwise merely numerical extrapolations of hope applied to past experience—can be successively related. It is not our purpose here, however, to present a master design for formal planning systems. This is a specialty of its own, which like all such other specialties, needs to be related to corporate strategy but not allowed to smother or substitute for it.

When formal plans are prepared and submitted as the program to which performance is compared as a basis for evaluation, managers in intermediate position are necessarily involved in initiating projects within a concept of strategy rather than proceeding ad hoc from situation to situation. Senior managers can be guided in their approval of investment decisions by a pattern more rational than their hunches, their instinct for risk, and their faith in the track record of those making proposals, important as all these are. They have a key question to ask: what impact upon present and projected strategy will this decision make?

Sustaining the strategic process requires monitoring resource allocation with awareness of its strategic—as well as operational—consequences and its social, political, as well as financial, characteristics. Seeing to it that the process works right means that the roles of the middle-level general manager be known and appropriately supported.

As Hugo Uyterhoeven has pointed out, middle-level general managers occupy a role quite different from that of the senior general manager, relevant as is their experience as preparation for later advancement.[2] With strategic language and summary corporate goals coming to them from their superiors and the language and problems of everyday operations coming to them from their subordinates, they have the responsibility of translating the operational proposals, improvisations, and piecemeal solutions of their subordinates into the strategic pattern suggested to them by their superiors.

Faced with the need to make reconciliation between short-term and long-term considerations, they must examine proposals and supervise operations with an eye to their effect on long-term development. As they transform general strategic directions into operating plans and programs, they are required to practice the overview of the general manager under the usual circumstance that their responsibility for balanced attention to short- and long-term needs and for bringing diverse everyday activities within the stream of evolving strategy far outruns their author-

---

[2] See Hugo E. R. Uyterhoeven, "General Managers in the Middle," *Harvard Business Review*, March–April 1972, pp. 75–85.

ity to require either change in strategy or to alter radically the product line of their division.

General managers at middle level, certainly in a crucial position to implement strategy in such a way as to advance it rather than depart from it, need to be protected against such distractions as performance evaluation systems overemphasizing short-term performance and to be supported continually in their duty of securing results which run beyond their authority to order certain outcomes. They need to learn how to interpret the signals they get as proposals they submit for top-management approval are accepted or turned down. Their superiors will be dependent upon their judgment as their proposals for new investment come in and will often be guided more by past performance or the desire to give them greater responsibility than by the detailed content of their proposals. Their seniors will do well then to realize the complexity of their juniors' positions and the necessity of the juniors being equal to the exigencies of making tactical reality subject to strategic guidance and to directing observation of operations toward appropriate amendment of strategy.

Developing the accuracy of strategic decision in a multiproduct, technically complex company requires ultimately direct attention to organization climate and individual development. The judgment required is to conduct operations against a demanding operating plan and to plan simultaneously for a changing future, to negotiate with superiors and subordinates the level of expected performance and to see, in short, the strategic implications of what is happening in the company and in its environment. The capacity of the general manager, outlined early in this book, must be consciously cultivated as part of the process of managing the strategy process, if the firm is to mature in its capacity to conduct its business and be able to recognize in time the changes in strategy it must effect.

Executive development, viewed from the perspective of the general manager, is essentially the nurturing of the generalist capabilities referred to throughout the text portions of this book. The management of the process of strategic decision must be concerned principally with continuous surveillance of the environment and development of the internal capabilities and distinctive competence of the company. The breadth of vision and the quality of judgment brought to the application of corporate capability to environmental opportunity are crucial. The senior managers who keep their organization involved continuously in appraising its performance against its goals, appraising its goals against the company's concept of its place in its industry and in society, and debating openly and often the continued validity of its strategy will find corporate attention to strategic questions gradually proving effective in letting the organization know what it is, what its activities are about, where it is going, and why its existence and growth are worth the best contributions of its members.

The chief executive of a company has as his or her highest function the management of a continuous process of strategic decision in which a succession of corporate objectives of ever-increasing appropriateness provides the means of economic contribution, the necessary commensurate return, and the opportunity for the men and women of the organization to live and develop through productive and rewarding careers.

THE STRATEGIC FUNCTION OF THE BOARD OF DIRECTORS

If the highest function of the chief executive is the management of the future-oriented purposeful development of the enterprise, then it is necessarily the responsibility of the board of directors to see that this job is adequately done. Although in the common conception of corporate governance the board is ultimately responsible, its outside directors cannot themselves customarily originate the strategy they must approve. The chief recourse of directors ratifying strategy in highly complex situations is not to substitute their judgment for that of management but to see that the proposals presented to them have been properly prepared and can be defended as strategically consistent and superior to available alternatives. If they are flawed they are usually withdrawn for revision by management. Although the board is usually unable to originate strategy, its detachment from operations equips it to analyze developing strategic decisions with fresh objectivity and breadth of experience. It can be free of the management myopia sometimes produced by operations, in places where keeping things going obscures the direction they are taking.

The cases concluding this book gave you opportunity to examine the role and function of the board. Under pressure from the public, the Securities and Exchange Commission, and indirectly by the U.S. Senate's Subcommittee on Shareholders' Rights, the board of directors is undergoing revitalization as the only available source of legitimacy for corporate power and assurance of corporate responsibility, given the archaism of corporation law and the dispersed ownership of the large public corporation.

The consensus developing in the current revival of board effectiveness is that working boards will not only actively support, advise, and assist management but also will monitor and evaluate management's performance in the attainment of planned objectives. Boards nowadays are expected to exhibit in decision behavior their responsibility (while representing the economic interest of the shareholders) for the legality, integrity, and ethical quality of the corporation's activities and financial reporting and their sensitivity to the interests of segments of society legitimately concerned about corporate performance.

For our purposes here the central function of a working board is to review the management's formulation and implementation of strategy and to exercise final authority in ratifying with good reason management's adherence to established objectives and policy or in contributing constructively to management's recommendation for change.

It is now widely recognized that boards should be diversely composed, should consist largely of outside directors, and should structure themselves to make their monitoring functions practicable. All firms registered on the New York Stock Exchange, for example, must have audit committees as a condition of membership. Their functions are to recommend to the board and then to shareholders the choice of external auditors, to ensure to the extent possible that the company's control personnel are generating and reporting accurate and complete data fairly representing the financial performance of the company and to ascertain that internal auditors are examining in detail those situations in which the company is vulnerable to fraud or improper behavior.

Despite the assumptions of some regulatory agency personnel, it is of course not possible for outside directors to detect fraud or identify questionable payments with their own eyes when well-intentioned and competent management auditors have not been able to do so. Their contribution is to inquire into the quality of intention, competence, process, to observe the capability and command of information of those reporting to the committee, and to raise questions prompted by experience not available in the company. When necessary they recommend to the board replacement of controllers or change of auditors.

Executive compensation committees are expected to oversee the incentive salary programs of the companies and to set the compensation of the most senior managers, evaluating their performance in the course of that activity. A trend is developing toward the establishment of nominating committees to consider executive succession, board composition and performance, and to make recommendations to the board of new members. The flow of information to these committees is supposed to economize the time and inform the judgment of the independent directors and to enable them to appraise the caliber of the company's management. The possibility of overwhelming outsiders with information is always imminent. Information useable by the board cannot usually be siphoned off the management information systems. Organization and selection to serve the special functions of the board are required.

In view of the difficulty entailed in enabling independent directors to pass judgment on strategic decisions, it is interesting to note that among the development of other committees (like public responsibility and legal affairs) strategy committees of the board, whatever they might be called, have not come into wide use. It appears likely that as boards become aware of the need to relate approval of specific investment decisions to the purposes of the company, they may wish to focus the attention of some of the directors upon strategic questions now presented without prior detailed consideration to the full board.

Like members of the audit and compensation committees, board members assigned to give additional time to the evaluation of total strategy could in theory become familiar not necessarily with the detailed debates shaping specific strategic alternatives but with how the strategic process is managed in the company. You may wish to consider the extent to which familiarity with the strategy of the company and the ability to relate financial performance to it would affect the evaluation by the board of the chief executive officer's performance and to what extent it is available otherwise.

In most boards at the moment it is assumed that the independent directors will support the chief executive until it is necessary to remove him. Removal ordinarily comes late after disaster has struck or after early strategic mistakes have produced repeated irretrievable losses. The go/no-go dilemma, which does not apply in any other superior-subordinate relationship in the corporation, could presumably be replaced by discussion and debate at board level of strategic questions presented to the board by the chief executive officer. When interim remediable dissatisfaction with the quality of this discussion appeared, advice to the chief executive officer could be offered in time for it to do some good. The chief executive's longevity is extended in some situations by his securing the participation of the board in crucial strategic decisions. When one of these fails after such participation, responsibility is shared by the board and the chief executive rather than borne by the latter alone. Routine ratification, without real discussion, does not secure the commitment of directors to any major decision. The attainment of this easy generalization is sometimes complicated by insecurity, unwillingness to share power, and lack of skill in board management on the part of chief executive officers.

The problem of securing competent outside director preparation and participation is compounded by the relationship resulting from the simple fact that independent directors have ordinarily owed their board membership to the chairman or chief executive officer they are supposed to evaluate. It is possible that the active participation of nominating committees will increase the independence of boards, especially if the chief executive officers participating in the selection process want such a result.

The management of effective boards of directors is a proper research topic in Business Policy and is indeed being studied. The power of strategy as a simplifying concept enabling independent directors to *know* the business (in a sense) without being *in* the business will one day be more widely tested at board level. If strategic management can be made less intuitive and more explicit, it will be possible for management directors and chief executive officers to identify existing strategy, evaluate it against the criteria we suggested at the beginning of this book, consider alternatives for improvement in the presence of the board, and make recommendations to a board equipped to make an intelligent critical response in strategic terms—i.e., relating specific proposals to corporate strategy. It is the hope of the authors of this book that your practice in identification, evaluation, and recommendation of strategy in analysis of these cases has introduced you to the possibilities of effectiveness in your own future participation in strategic management at whatever level. The ability to sense the pattern of progress in the welter of operations is essential not only as an economizing analytical concept for outside directors but to junior executives who do not want to get lost among the trees and thickets in which they move.

Strategic management comes to its culmination in the chairmanship of effective boards. For the moment, the Securities and Exchange Commission, the Department of Justice, and the Federal Trade Commission appear to prefer the restructured and revitalized board of directors as the route to a kind of corporate governance sufficiently responsible to meet current concerns about autonomous management power. Most defenders of our mixed economic system prefer this approach to the introduction of new regulation. Voluntary adaptation to public expectations allows the special circumstances of each industry and company situation to be taken into account; regulation does not. On the other hand, doing nothing remains a possible response to the call for voluntary action.

The mastery of the concept of strategy makes easier the kind of discussion in board rooms that helps managements make better decisions. It performs this function by reducing the world of detail to be considered to those central aspects of external environment and internal resources that affect the company and bear on the definition of its business. The special skill involved in perceiving and communicating the strategic significance of a business decision may be of the highest importance in engaging independent directors in the exercise of their assumed responsibility and in establishing active and effective boards as normal adjuncts to competent professional management. Such a development may reduce the likelihood that corporate governance be judged sufficiently irresponsible that radical legislative checks are imposed upon corporate freedom and initiative.

Index of cases

This book has been set in 9 point Primer, leaded 2 points. The book sections and text titles are in 16 point Spectra Bold. The case titles are in 16 pt Spectra Bold italic. The size of the type page is 27 picas by 46½ picas.